The Gower Handbook
of
Management

THE
GOWER
HANDBOOK
OF
MANAGEMENT

Edited by
Dennis Lock and Nigel Farrow

Published by
Gower Publishing Company Limited
Aldershot, Hants, England

Reprinted 1985

British Library Cataloguing in Publication Data
The Gower handbook of management.
  1. Management
  I. Lock, Dennis   II. Farrow, Nigel

ISBN 0-566-02333-4

Printed and bound in Great Britain
at The Bath Press, Avon

Contents

PART 9 HUMAN RESOURCE MANAGEMENT

to be Posted — Checklist of Notices to be Sent to Factory Inspector or Other Authority — Checklist of Registers to be Kept — Advice and Further Information — Further Reading

PART 10   THE SKILLS OF MANAGEMENT

Illustrations

Figures

Notes on Contributors

Bryan Atkin (Pricing) is Director of the Office Products Division of Industrial Market Research Ltd. He joined the company as a graduate trainee, after studying at the London School of Economics, and was made a director in 1973. Mr Atkin created IMR's Travel Research Unit and more recently designed and launched a major syndicated survey programme on office equipment in Great Britain. In 1978 he was seconded to the Price Commission as Assistant Secretary which gave him a keen insight into the theory and practice of pricing. He is joint author, with R N Skinner, of *How British Industry Prices* (IMR, 1975).

Stephen Badger (Sources of Finance) is a Director of Morgan Grenfell & Co. Limited, where he advises companies on mergers, raising long-term capital and general financial problems. He joined Morgan Grenfell after leaving Oxford where he read Greats. Mr Badger is an Associate of the Institute of Chartered Secretaries and Administrators.

Peter Baily (Procurement Policy *and* Purchasing Procedures) is a Lecturer in Business Studies at the Polytechnic of Wales. He started off as a telecommunications mechanic and later worked in machine tool manufacturing and textile industries as buyer, materials controller, chief buyer and assistant to company secretary. Mr Baily has worked with the Business Education Council for several years as Board member, moderator and member of the Validating Committee and of several working parties. He is a member of the Education and Training Committee of the Institute of Purchasing and Supply. Author of several books and numerous articles, he has addressed conferences and contributed to courses in the USA, Ireland, Holland, Italy, Switzerland and the UK. He is co-author of *Materials Management Handbook* (Gower, 1982).

Gordon Bell (Effective Communication), a lapsed scientist, has been Senior Partner of Gordon Bell and Partners since its foundation in 1955. Based in south-west London, the firm runs courses in communications skills in many parts of the world. Mr Bell has written and appeared in television programmes since the pioneer days at Alexandra Palace. His work in the theatre and practical work in industry have fitted him to help people improve their communications skills. He is an occasional contributor to several journals.

Ted Bennett (Managing the Electronic Office) is Data Processing Manager of Saudi Oger Services (UK) Ltd. He entered data processing in 1967 and has worked in various capacities in environments as diverse as retailing and process engineering. Most of his time as a consultant was spent working on office automation applications and projects for clients in both the public and private sectors. Mr Bennett has an MA in Systems Engineering. In 1970–71 he was Research Fellow in Management Information Systems at Sussex University.

G A Bloxam (Patents and Trade-Marks), now retired, is a former Head of the Patent Department of Albright & Wilson Limited, the chemical manufacturing group. On graduating from Cambridge in chemistry and physics he entered the patent profession in private practice and became a Fellow of the Chartered Institute of Patent Agents. Before joining Albright & Wilson he was Patents Manager of the National Research Development Corporation.

Denis Boyle (The Strategic Planning Process) is Managing Director of Service Management International Ltd. He was formerly Director of the Scandinavian Institutes for Administrative Research in London and Milan. Mr Boyle has also acted as a senior adviser to the Institute for Industrial Reconstruction in Rome and has been a consultant to a wide range of major corporations in several countries. He lectures widely in Europe and the United States and is a visiting professor at the University of Bocconi in Milan. Mr Boyle is an Industrial Fellow of the English Electric Company. His publications include numerous articles on strategic management and he is co-author of *The Challenge of Change* (Gower, 1981).

Ron H Bradnam (Corporate Strategies for the 1980s) works in private practice as a consultant in technology management with special interests in working with scientists, engineers and technologists in various management fields. After his military service he worked for EMI, Mullard and Plessey where he was responsible for the engineering design and management of research and development projects for commercial and military applications. While with EASAMS he planned and managed several important innovation projects before moving to Urwick Technology Management where his assignments were concerned with improvements to the management of technical and business functions. Mr Bradnam has had a varied academic career, acting as a visiting lecturer and course leader at various academic institutions. His present appointments include visiting lectureships at the University of Southampton and Cranfield School of Management.

A Brearley (Design Management) first worked as a design engineer after an engineering degree and military service. He became Production Manager of the Talbot Stead Tube Company and then a Works Engineer with ICI. He then worked for five years as a management consultant with PA Ltd before becoming Managing Director of the heavy engineering company Adamson and Hatchett. His next appointment was as Managing Director of Don International, a major manufacturer of automotive friction materials and components. Dr Brearly is currently Director of Management Development Programmes at Bradford University Management Centre. He also works as chairman and a director of a number of public companies and advises a range of major multinational companies on management development. He holds an MSc in Management Sciences and a Doctorate in Management and Administration. His publications include *Management of Drawing and Design* (Gower, 1975) and *The Control of Staff Related Overheads* (Macmillan, 1976).

J E Broyles (Capital Project Planning) lectures in finance at the London Business School. He is the author of two books and numerous articles on financial management, consultant to major companies, banks and H M Treasury and a former Planning Manager at Ludlow Corporation. Dr Broyles is a member of the Board of Editors of the *Journal of Business Finance and Accounting* and is co-editor of *Financial Management Handbook* (Gower, 2nd edition, 1983).

Tom Carew (Redundancy and Redeployment) retired from the army as a Lieutenant-Colonel in the 1950s. He then became a boat builder and ran a yacht yard until the demand for wooden-hulled boats fell. In his mid-forties he discovered his hitherto unrecognised talent for selling management consultancy. In 1970 he bought Percy Coutts and Co Ltd before it was widely recognised that executives needed help in marketing themselves. The company survived early financial struggles and, with increasing awareness of the need for the marketing of executives, became the thriving concern of which Tom Carew is now Chairman.

E S M Chadwick (Manpower Planning) has had a varied experience in industrial and personnel management and management consultancy at home and abroad. While working as Manager of Manpower Research and Planning for the BP Group he was one of the pioneers of the development of manpower planning in companies. Mr Chadwick is a Fellow of the Chartered Institute of Secretaries and the British Institute of Management. He has published a number of articles and books on manpower planning including a chapter of the *Engineer's Handbook of Management Techniques* (Gower, 1973) and *Integrating Enterprise Manpower Planning with External Manpower Planning and Programmes,* (OECD, 1970).

Garfield Collins (Managing the Electronic Office) is a company director whose early career was spent in developing advanced electronic micro-circuit production methods and industrial process control. He then worked on communications and real time systems for a computer manufacturer before becoming a consultant in information processing, covering a variety of fields at levels from broad strategy to detailed implementation. In his present post Mr Collins' main activities are in the fields of office automation and telecommunications. He has published numerous articles and monographs as well as *Real Time System Design* (McGraw-Hill, 1977), *Database Techniques* (On-line, 1980) and *Structured System Development Techniques* (Pitman, 1982).

J L Cookson (Employee Relations) is Principal Lecturer in Labour Law in the Department of Management at Manchester Polytechnic. After graduating in Law from Cambridge University, he spent four years in private legal practice followed by three years in corporate planning overseas. His particular academic interest is in labour law and its impact on industrial relations at organisational level, on which subject he has lectured extensively in both the public and private sectors of industry. Publications include *Handbook of Industrial Relations* (Gower, 1972) and *Encyclopaedia of Personnel Management* (Gower, 1974).

Ian Cooper (Capital Project Planning) is Baring Brothers Research Fellow at the London Business School, where he is Director of the Corporate Finance Programme. He previously taught corporate finance at the University of North Carolina and is a consultant to several large companies, to banks and to the US National Science Foundation. Dr Cooper is the author of a number of articles on financial management and is co-editor of *Financial Management Handbook* (Gower, 2nd edition, 1983); he is an Associate Editor of the *Journal of Business Finance and Accounting* and is also on the Executive Committee of the European Finance Association.

J C Craig (Taxation) is a taxation partner at Thomson McLintock & Co KMG where he deals with both personal and company taxation. He is a Member of the Institute of Chartered Accountants of Scotland and a former convener of its taxation committee.

Michael Day (Management Development) is Manager of the Employee Relations Division of BP Oil Ltd. Most of his career has been within the BP Group where he has held a number of posts including those of training officer, personnel manager and internal organisation consultant. While with BP Oil he has previously managed the personnel resources and personnel policies division. Mr Day is a visiting lecturer at the University of Manchester Institute of Science and Technology. He is co-author of several papers and contributed two chapters to *Administration of Personnel Policies* edited by Naylor and Torrington (Gower, 1974).

David Desmond (Quality Control) started his career as a research engineer with Joseph Lucas Ltd in Birmingham and then became a Research Fellow in the Department of Engineering Production of the University of Birmingham where he worked on the application of quality control and statistical methods to work study and other management techniques. He was then appointed as a quality control expert by the United Nations Industrial Development Organisation and worked in India, the Philippines and Indonesia. Until his retirement in 1975, Mr Desmond worked as a management consultant specialising in quality control and interpretation of technical data. He holds three degrees from King's College London and was a fellow of several professional institutes, including the British Institute of Management, until his retirement. His publications include the *Quality Control Workbook* (Gower, 1971).

R Dick-Larkam (Energy Management) retired from BOC Ltd in 1977 where he had held various appointments culminating in Internal Consultancy and Energy Manager for the UK Group of Companies. Mr Dick-Larkam started his career at the National Physical Laboratory and spent the war years as an Engineer Officer in the RAFVR. He worked on engineering development in various companies before joining BOC in 1954. He has lectured on productivity and energy management both within BOC and to many other companies including the Management Centre Europe. His publications include *Profit Improvement Techniques* (Gower, 1973) and *Cutting Energy Costs* (Gower, 1978). Mr Dick-Larkam is a Freeman of the City of London.

Ken Firth (Warehouse Operation and Management) started his career in the depot stock control department of a Unilever organisation and, apart from National Service and a period of full-time management studies, has spent the rest of his career in posts associated with storage, handling and distribution. Mr Firth joined the National Materials Handling Centre at Cranfield Institute of Technology in 1971 and combined consultancy work with the setting-up of short in-career courses. He became Assistant Director of the centre in 1975 and is now fully occupied with the in-career educational programme. He has worked on various official committees associated with warehousing and wrote the report on which the HMSO Publication *Materials Handling Costs – A New Look at Manufacture* is based.

J C Gentles (The Total Cost Approach to Distribution) is a Principal in the London office of Booz, Allen and Hamilton. Since joining this company he has completed assignments all over the world in such industries as domestic consumer products, automotive supply, aerospace and medical supplies. Previously he was employed by Burroughs Machines Ltd as Senior Production Control Systems Specialist. Prior to this he worked on manufacturing systems for aircraft production for Hawker Siddeley Aviation Ltd.

Patricia George (Working Conditions) was Senior Adviser of the Industrial Society's Information and Personnel Advisory Services Department. Miss George is an Associate Member of the Institute of Personnel Management, and is now a Principal Personnel Officer working for Surrey County Council.

Norman Hart (Corporate Relations) is Director of the CAM Education Foundation Ltd. His previous career, with several companies, has been mostly in marketing. He is a regular international speaker on marketing, advertising, public relations and education and has written, or contributed to, numerous books on these subjects including *Marketing Handbook* (Gower, 2nd edition, 1981), *Industrial Advertising and Publicity* (ABP, 1978) and *Careers in Marketing, Advertising and Communications* (Heinemann, 1980). Mr Hart is a Fellow of the Institute of Public Relations and has an MSc from the University of Bradford. He also holds several educational appointments.

R S Henderson (Office Services) is Managing Director of Space Planning Services Ltd, an office planning and design consultancy. After graduating from Cambridge he commenced his career as a civil engineer in Nigeria. On returning to the UK he became director of a property development company for a number of years. Since joining SPS in 1969 he has gained wide experience in the office planning field through many major projects. From 1973 to 1977 he was Chairman of the Office Design Division of the Institute of Administrative Management which runs the 'Office of the Year Award' scheme. He has written several articles on office planning for the national and business press.

John Hobson, CBE (Advertising) Honorary President of the advertising agency Ted Bates Limited, is a former President of the Institute of Practitioners in Advertising, a former Chairman of the Advertising Association and a former President of the European Association of Advertising Agencies. He formed his own agency, John Hobson & Partners, in 1955 and merged it in 1959 with Ted Bates New York to form Hobson, Bates & Partners.

R C Horsley (International Trade) is a manager at the centre for Physical Distribution Management in London. He has previously worked for ICI Ltd, the Rank Organisation and Fisher Price in posts associated with distribution. Mr Horsley is a Fellow of the British Institute of Management, the Chartered Institute of Transport and the Institute of Physical Distribution Management.

P T Humphrey (Recruitment and Selection) is Managing Director of Ashton Containers (Southern) Ltd and was previously Personnel Director with the same organisation. He holds several academic appointments and is a Companion of the Institute of Personnel Management and a Fellow of the British Institute of Management. He is a contributor to *Administration of Personnel Policies* edited by Torrington and Naylor (Gower, 1974) and author of *How to be Your Own Personnel Manager* (Institute of Personnel Management, 1981).

Irene Innes (Salary Management *and* Wage Management) has spent some twenty years within personnel management. She has an unusually wide background, having worked for organisations such as Wiggins Teape Ltd, the Industrial Society and Reed International. Having reached the top of the personnel tree, she then set up business as an independent industrial relations consultant specialising in pay policies and job evaluation and works from her home in Wimborne, Dorset. She is also a member of the Central Arbitration Committee as well as being on the ACAS list of single arbitrators and mediators.

Peter Jackson (Production Control) is a Senior Lecturer and Consultant at the Coventry Management Training Centre. He has previously worked for GEC Telecommunications and PA Management Consultants.

Alan R Leaper (Budgetary Control) was Financial Controller of Hoover Worldwide Eastern Region Headquarters for ten years in which capacity he was responsible for review and control of the budgets of thirteen overseas subsidiaries. His previous experience includes three years in Canada on cost and general accounting assignments and eleven years with the Frigidaire Division of General Motors Ltd in various factory accounting positions. Mr Leaper is now managing his own retail and wholesale business. He is a member of the Advisory Committee to the Management Division of Management Centre Europe where he frequently chairs various seminars and Round Table meetings.

Colin McDonald (Market Research) has twenty years' experience of market research on a wide scale in both commercial and social contexts. During this time he has written numerous articles on various aspects of the subject. He is an Oxford graduate and has worked for Reckitt & Sons Ltd and Distillers Co Ltd. Mr McDonald is now Senior Associate Director of the British Market Research Bureau Ltd.

J Mapes (Planning for Production) lectures on the quantitative aspects of management at Cranfield School of Management. Earlier in his career he worked for ICI in Productivity Services before taking up a lectureship in the Department of Management at Middlesex Polytechnic. Prior to his present appointment he worked as an internal consultant for Clayton Dewandre Ltd. Mr Mapes holds degrees from Cambridge and Brunel and is joint author of *Model Building Techniques for Managers* (Gower, 1976).

John Muir (Employee Benefits) is Associate Consultant with Cockman, Copeman & Partners Limited, Remuneration and Benefits Consultants. He was for some years a full-time official with a white collar trade union before assuming senior industrial relations posts with London Transport and the P & O Shipping Group. He has a Bachelor of Commerce degree from the London School of Economics and is a Fellow of the Institute of Personnel Management. He lectures on employment law and teaches negotiating skills. Mr Muir is the author of *Industrial Relations Procedures and Agreements* (Gower, 1981).

Peter Mumford (Redundancy and Redeployment) organises residential and in-company supervisory and management development courses at Brighton Polytechnic. He developed the Leadership and Group Development training programme and acts as a consultant to a number of organisations. His interest in redundancy and personnel policies started when he was in industry.

C C New (Planning for Production) is Professor of Operations Management at Cranfield School of Management. Professor New, who has a degree from Cambridge, worked in the aero engine division of Rolls Royce Ltd for seven years before joining the London Business School in 1971. While at the London Business School he obtained an MSc and wrote three books, including *Requirements Planning* (Gower, 1975), and many papers.

John Parfitt (Administration of Commercial Property) is in multi-disciplinary practice, as an architect, surveyor and project manager, in central London. Before the war he worked in the estate office of a well known London estate. After the war Mr Parfitt, already a Chartered Surveyor, studied town planning and architecture and worked for the Ministry of Town and Country Planning before setting up in private practice, as an architect and surveyor, in the City of London.

Sydney Paulden (Marketing Overseas) is Finance Editor of *Export Times* and a Consultant to the UNCTAD/GATT International Trade Centre. He was previously Consultant Editor of *Export Direction* and Director of Envoy Journals Ltd. Mr Paulden has a degree from Cambridge and was Winston Churchill Fellow in Marketing in 1969. He has written several books on export marketing including *Export Agents* (Gower, 1974) and *How to Deliver on Time* (Gower, 1977).

A W Pearson (Managing Research and Development) is Senior Lecturer in Decision Analysis and Director of the R & D Research Unit in the Manchester Business School. He graduated from the University of London and was employed by Pilkington Brothers and Simon Engineering Ltd as a scientist before joining the University of Manchester in the Faculty of Economics and Social Studies. Subsequently appointed to a lectureship in Operational Research at Manchester Business School, and in 1967 to the directorship of the R & D Research Unit, which is an interdisciplinary unit looking at problems of managing R & D, Mr Pearson has directed courses in this field for both industrial and government organisations. He is editor of the journal *R & D Management*, a member of the advisory board of IEEE *Transactions on Engineering Management*, member of the board of COLRAD (College of R & D of the Institute of Management Science) and member of the Research Committee of the Shirley Institute.

Christian Petersen (Sales Promotion) was the youngest-ever member of the Institute of Practitioners in Advertising and of the Advertising Association, and a founder member of the SPEA (now the Institute of Sales Promotion). He is Managing Director of Kingsland Lloyd Petersen Ltd, Britain's largest sales promotion consultancy. He lectures in Britain and abroad, and is a regular contributor to the marketing press. He was Chief Editor of *The Handbook of*

Consumer Sales Promotion (1976–77) and is the author of *Sales Promotion in Action* (Associated Business Press, 1979).

W P Ridley (The Annual Accounts) is a Partner in Wood Mackenzie and Company, a firm of stockbrokers he joined in 1973 after five years as a financial consultant with Merrett Cyriax Associates. He read law at Oxford and became an Associate of the Institute of Chartered Accountants in 1961. He taught in Uganda and at Hendon Technical College before joining the Economic and Investment Research Department of the Bank of London and South America. Between 1965 and 1968, Mr Ridley worked for the Commonwealth Development Corporation.

R W Rooke (Insurance of Company Operations) is Insurance Manager of British Gas Corporation. After graduating from Nottingham University, he taught mathematics before joining Atlas Assurance. He then became Insurance Manager of Berk Limited and Thomas De La Rue International Limited. Mr. Rooke is an Associate of the Chartered Insurance Institute, a member of the Association of Insurance and Risk Managers in Industry and Commerce, and a Professional Associate of the Institution of Gas Engineers. He was chairman of the Association's research group which in 1968 investigated the status and techniques of insurance managers.

F W Rose (Company Law *and* Contracts between Companies) is Principal Lecturer in Law at the City of Birmingham Polytechnic and Course Director for the Solicitors' Final Course. Mr Rose has an LIB from Birmingham University and an LIM from King's College, London. He served as Assistant to the Secretary of Associated Iliffe Press Limited before spending a year at the Institute of Actuaries in a similar function. Mr Rose is an Associate of the Chartered Institute of Secretaries and he was called to the bar at Gray's Inn. He is author of *Personnel Management Law* (Gower, 1975) and has had several articles published in the *Legal Executive*.

Don Rushton (Solution Engineering) is a Principal with Ingersoll Engineers. He has over 35 years' experience in manufacturing industry, including the planning and execution of capital investment programmes, factory management and operations and working in 'new technology' areas. After graduating Mr Rushton completed a post-graduate apprenticeship with English Electric, while studying production engineering externally. Before joining Ingersoll Engineers he had wide career experience in various fields of engineering. He is a Fellow of the Institutes of Mechanical and Production Engineers.

Tessa V Ryder Runton (Capital Project Planning) started her career as a patent examiner and then had a spell overseas working as a secretary for the Tea Estates Agency in Sri Lanka. She then spent six years employed as a Financial Analyst by the Rio-Tinto Zinc Corporation. Mrs Ryder Runton, who was educated at Cheltenham Ladies College, Newnham College Cambridge and the London School of Economics, occasionally lectures on financial analysis at business schools, including Ashridge Management College and the London Business School.

Philip Sadler (Principles of Management) is the Principal of Ashridge Management College. He started his career in advertising after graduating from the London School of Economics. He then joined the Civil Service where he worked for ten years before moving to the National Economic Development Office. In 1964 he was appointed Director of Research at Ashridge and held this post for four years before becoming Principal. Mr Sadler has published numerous journal articles on management topics and is co-author of *Organisation Development: Case Studies in the Printing Industry* (Longmans, 1970). He is a Companion of the British Institute of Management and President of its Luton Branch and is also on the Executive Committee of the Society for Long Range Planning.

George S Sanders (Corporate Strategies for the 1980s) is currently self-employed as a freelance Management Consultant and holds part-time posts as Chairman of Millstream Conferences Ltd and Technical Education and Training Enterprises Ltd. Having qualified as a Chartered Engineer he worked for ten years with ICI as a mechanical engineer before moving to Solartron Electronic Group Ltd where he spent four years as their Production Director. Mr Sanders then joined Urwick Orr and Partners Ltd where he worked for 28 years as Senior Partner and Director. He has written many articles on both general and research management themes. He was a contributor to *Improving the Performance of the Experienced Manager* edited by John Humble (McGraw-Hill, 1973) and author of *Urwick Orr on Management*, in collaboration with F W Latham (Heinemann, 1980). Mr Sanders is a Fellow of the Institute of Management Consultants and of the British Institute of Management.

Bill Scott (Negotiating) is an independent consultant working internationally and specialising in communication. His background comprises a rare mixture of industrial and academic achievement. He conducted business research from the University of Keele and later became Project Director of the Centre for Business Research and eventually Assistant Director of Manchester Business School. His experience in industry includes six years as Group Training Manager with Wiggins Teape and six directing management development in the 22,000-strong Carrington and Dewhurst Group. Mr Scott has lectured for Management Centre Europe, the ILO and numerous other organisations, and runs seminars regularly, in the UK and overseas, on communication and negotiation skills. He is the author of *The Skills of Negotiating* (Gower, 1981).

Leon Simons (Managing Working Capital) has wide experience of finance and accountancy acquired in industry, the City and the profession. He was formerly a Senior Lecturer with Glacier Institute of Management. Currently Mr Simons works as an independent Management Consultant and lectures on finance. He has made contributions to numerous books and journals and is the author of *Basic Arts of Financial Management* (2nd edition, Business Books, 1978).

John Stapleton (Marketing Planning) is founder and Chief Executive of the Marketing Tuition Centre for Businessmen and Executives, and Senior Lecturer at the College for the Distributive Trades. Mr Stapleton began his marketing career with the Inveresk Paper Group becoming, at 27, field sales manager of the merchanting division where he introduced planned selling techniques and devised profit planning procedures. In 1967 he joined the Private Communications Division of STC, where he supervised marketing studies into the applications of, and demand for, communication equipment. In 1972 he won a scholarship award from the University of Aston in Birmingham to undertake an advanced management course. Mr Stapleton acts as a consultant to export award winners Ayala Sales Limited and other organisations. He is well known as a writer on marketing: he has contributed many magazine articles and is the author of *Teach Yourself Marketing, How to Prepare a Marketing Plan* (3rd edition, Gower, 1982) and co-author of *Glossary of Marketing Terms*.

Derek Torrington (Industrial Training *and* Employee Relations) is Senior Lecturer in Personnel Management at the University of Manchester Institute of Science and Technology. Previously he spent fifteen years in the engineering industry and five years at Manchester Polytechnic. Publications include *Successful Personnel Management* (Staples Press, 1969), *Face to Face* (Gower, 1972), *Handbook of Industrial Relations* (Gower, 1972), *Handbook of Management Development*, with D F Sutton (Gower, 1973), *Administration of Personnel Policies*, with R Naylor (Gower, 1974), *Encyclopaedia of Personnel Management* (Gower, 1974), and *Comparative Industrial Relations in Europe* (Associated Business Press, 1978). He is a Companion of the Institute of Personnel Management.

Brian Walley (Plant Layout) is Director and General Manager Operational Planning of Ferodo Ltd. He has considerable industrial experience gained during his career with Metal Box, Turner and Newall, GE Co and J Bibby. His publications include *Efficiency Auditing* (Macmillan, 1974), *Management Services Handbook* (Business Books, 1973), *Profit Planning Handbook* (Business Books, 1978) and *Production Management Handbook* (Gower, 1980).

A N Welsh (Personal Organisation) is Management Adviser to the Welsh Development Agency in Carmarthen and lectures on 'Be your own Boss' courses run by the Manpower Services Commission with the WDA. A graduate of Oxford University, his varied career has given him considerable industrial experience. He has been Director and Secretary of the Three Hands Evan Williams Group, manufacturers of household products and toiletries, Director of Training for the international management consultants W D Scott & Co and Managing Director of the Haverfordwest firm of agricultural engineers and builders merchants S & F Green Ltd. He is the author of *The Skills of Management* (Gower, 1980).

Jack Wheatley (Distribution Channels) is Managing Director of Moore's Modern Methods Ltd. His previous appointments include Managing Director of Kolor Ltd, Area Sales Manager for James Keiler Ltd and Deputy (London) General Manager of Spicer Cowan Ltd. He has held the posts of Chairman and National Treasurer of the Institute of Marketing and is a past President of the Junior Chamber of Commerce of London.

E N White (Maintenance) is a Director and Consultant with M & E White Consultants Ltd. He has held a number of management posts in quality control, product support, customer service and engineering maintenance, and was Managing Director of a technical services company for ten years. He has published many papers and is a frequent lecturer on maintenance management topics in the UK and overseas. He also manages a number of training programmes. His book *Maintenance Planning, Control and Documentation* (Gower, 1974) has become a standard reference work for engineering training.

Dennis Whitmore (Industrial Engineering) is Director of Research and Development at Harrow College of Higher Education and also works as a management consultant. Previously he was Senior Production Manager with Mullards and a Senior Consultant with Philips. Dr Whitmore was educated at London, Brunel and Surrey Universities and is a Fellow of the British Institute of Management. He has written numerous books including *Work Study and Related Management Services* (Heinemann, 1976), *Work Measurement* (Institute of Management Services, 1976) and *Management of Motivation and Remuneration* (Business Books, 1977).

R E Wiggins (Managing Information) graduated with an honours degree in metallurgy from Nottingham University and subsequently gained post-graduate qualifications in the areas of information science, systems management and computerised information systems. He started his information science career in private industry in the early 1960s , moving thereafter to the British Gas Corporation. He is now responsible for a computer-based information retrieval system in a major British oil company.

Michael Williams (Management Self-development *and* Career Planning) is Senior Partner of Michael Williams and Partners and Director of Applied Skills for Management. He held posts in organisation development and management development in BL Cars following experience in personnel, marketing and production in a variety of major UK companies. In 1980 he set up his own consultancy specialising in organisation development, team building and individual development. Mr Williams has lectured extensively in the UK and Europe on various management topics – especially leadership and management style. His publications include *Human Relations* (Longmans, 1967), *Supervisory Management in the Office* (Heinemann, 1969) and *Performance Appraisal in Management* (Heinemann, 1972).

John Wilson (Security) is a security adviser and writer, recently retired from his position of Company Security Officer for the IMI Yorkshire Imperial Group where he held an omnibus remit for advising on all aspects of security policy. A former Detective Chief Inspector and Deputy Head of CID in the Leeds City Police, he is a Fellow and past governor of the Institute of Industrial Security, former National Chairman of the International Professional Security Association and its representative on the Home Office Standing Committee for Crime Prevention from 1975 to 1981. He has been visiting lecturer on security in industry to the Home Office Crime Prevention School at Stafford for the last decade and to management seminars in the UK and abroad. He is co-author of the textbooks for the Institute examinations and a security chapter contributor to other textbooks dealing with management, distribution, administration and computers. With Eric Oliver, Mr Wilson wrote *Practical Security in Commerce and Industry* (Gower, 3rd edition, 1978).

M T Wilson (Managing a Sales Force) is Managing Director of Marketing Improvements Limited and President of MI Europe SA, the leading European marketing consultancy and training group. Operating out of offices in London and Brussels, MI covers all major European markets and languages, as well as spanning the Americas, Asia and Africa on behalf of its numerous clients in the consumer, industrial and service sectors. Marketing Improvements was formed in 1964 by Mike Wilson following experience in the Institute of Marketing and Ford Motor Company, which he joined on graduating from Manchester University. Mike Wilson is widely known for the hundreds of seminars and courses on all aspects of marketing which he has run in all five continents. He is perhaps even better known within industry for the highly creative consultancy advice given to companies through Europe, including multinationals. He is the author of *Managing a Sales Force* (Gower, 2nd edition 1983) and *The Management of Marketing* (Gower, 1981).

R M S Wilson (Cost Accounting) is a Senior Lecturer in accounting and financial management at the University of Sheffield, a Director of Minworth Ltd and a Consultant to Harbridge House (Europe). He gained his commercial experience in a variety of industries covering consumer goods, industrial goods and services. Mr Wilson is a former faculty member of the University of Bradford Management Centre and has held visiting appointments at universities in Australia, Kenya and South Africa. He also spent a year seconded to the Committee of Vice-Chancellors to carry out an assignment on costing for resource allocation and control within British universities. Mr Wilson holds degrees in economics, management and sociology/technology and is a Fellow of both the Institute of Cost and Management Accountants and the Association of Certified Accountants. He is a regular contributor to several journals and is the author of eight books including *Cost Control Handbook* (Gower, 2nd edition, 1983), *The Marketing of Financial Services* (MCB, 1980) and *Financial Dimensions of Marketing* (edited for Macmillan, 1981).

F H Woodward (Managing Transport Services) is Managing Director of SPE (Vehicle Services) Limited, a company forming part of The Plessey Group of

Companies. SPE (Vehicle Services) Limited provides all transport services to the Companies within the Group as well as distributing all Plessey products by all modes. Frank Woodward is a Member of the Institute of Transport, and Fellow of the Chartered Institute of Secretaries and Administrators, and a Fellow of the Royal Society of Arts. He is a well known speaker at vehicle management conferences and an author of books on transport services management including *Managing the Transport Services Function* (Gower, 1978). He is also a regular contributor to transport publications, having over thirty years' practical experience in managing all functions within the area of vehicle management.

John Woolhouse (Organisation Development) is a Director of Atkins Planning, a member company of the WS Atkins Group, and Head of the Human Resources Development Department. This department specialises in manpower resourcing, training and the transfer of technology, and organisation development. Mr Woolhouse is a Fellow of the British Institute of Management, an Honorary Fellow of the Institution of Works Managers and a Member of the European Foundation for Management Development. He has been involved in education and training for 23 years since becoming a divisional training manager in the Rolls-Royce group in 1959. In 1968 he became Company Education and Training Officer for the Rolls-Royce Group and was responsible for one of the largest industrial training programmes in Europe. He spent six years as Assistant Director of a British polytechnic and Director of a Regional Management Centre. He has served on a number of government and public committees concerned with education, training and management development, and in the last three years has travelled widely in the course of his work with the WS Atkins Group.

Avison Wormald (International Trade) is Executive Vice-President of Lansberg, Wormald Humble y Asociados C.A., Management Consultants, Caracas, Venezuela, Professor of International Trade at the Universidad Metropolitana, Caracas and author of *International Business*, published by Pan Books. He was Director and Managing Director of Fisons Limited, London from 1950 to 1962, Chairman Grace Bros. Limited (W. R. Grace and Co.) and a director of many companies in six countries. He graduated from London University with first class honours and is a Fellow of the British Institute of Management.

David Wragg (Promotional Public Relations) is Group Public Relations Manager with Twinlock Ltd. He entered public relations in 1974, joining the P & O Group, where he eventually became Manager of Public Relations Services before leaving in 1979. He subsequently handled a number of short-term PR projects, including one for the Chartered Institute of Transport, before joining Twinlock in 1981. Mr Wragg is the author of *Publicity and Customer Relations in Transport Management* (Gower, 1982) and has written seven books on aeronautical history. He is also a contributor to the Inter-Company Comparisons and Keynotes range of industry reports.

The once and future manager

Nigel Farrow

Merlin, wizard and medieval management consultant, is sitting in his study. He is wrestling with one of his most difficult assignments: the tuition of the young King Arthur in the arts of management.

The course is full of practical work. Using his magical powers and the experience of already having lived in the future, Merlin often projects himself and King Arthur into the twentieth century in order to work on real business problems. Together they have designed a small car for British Leyland, which has taken 60 per cent of the Japanese domestic market. They have negotiated one-man-one-job agreements in the British newspaper industry and modernised French agriculture. They have found an uncontested site for the third London airport, re-financed Poland and raised the Titanic. In 1933 they bought IBM and in 1965 they sold Rolls Royce. Merlin believes in the case study method.

But Arthur notices that whenever a particularly difficult issue arises, Merlin consults a big book which lies on his desk, along with his portable crucible, philosopher's stone, and bottled bat's blood.

Arthur   *Merlin, please tell me what's in that great tome you keep referring to? Is it a book of spells?*

Merlin   No, it's *The Gower Handbook of Management*, which I acquired on a trip to 1983. . . . There's no wizardry in it, just sound advice on almost every aspect of management.

Arthur   *But was it written by a wizard?*

Merlin   Not by a wizard, but by many experts. Over 60 of them.

Arthur   *(after some thought) – Merlin, there's something that's been troubling me. If there are going to be so many management experts in those days-*

yet-to-come and so much written and published on management and so many people tutored in the arts of management, why will they have so much trouble with their businesses?

Merlin Because they will attempt so much. It will be an heroic age. Ordinary managers, without the weapons of social privilege or personal wealth, will be required to ride out as champions of the whole kingdom to defeat poverty, ignorance and sloth.

Arthur *You make these managers sound like a new order of chivalry. I thought that they would be arriving as bag-men and the servants of bag-men. People who will be out to line their own pockets.*

Merlin It may well start like that, but it will have become something very different by the time *The Gower Handbook of Management* is written. I see that a little yet-to-be-history lesson is required.

First, I will let you into a secret about the system of free business enterprise, which by some will be called 'capitalism'. Contrary to reports, mostly put about by its own practitioners, it will be a tremendous success. By the twentieth century, it will provide the material means of feeding, housing and clothing huge populations. It will sustain individuals and groups of individuals regardless of their origins and promote their fortunes largely on the basis of their usefulness to society. It will transmit wealth and knowledge around the world. It will finance science and encourage the arts. In fact, it will be far too successful for its own good.

Arthur *What do you mean?*

Merlin Because of its success, governments and individuals will link their hopes and programmes for social development to its economic performance. By the middle of the twentieth century, business will be the main source of income in work and in retirement for most men and many women. Through taxation, business will contribute massively to the welfare services of the community, as well as developing many health, educational and housing schemes of its own. Through legislation, business will be obliged to advance racial and sexual equality, protect the natural world and train the young. Not content with the controls of taxation and legislation, governments will force themselves into partnership with business so as to be able to direct its resources to the achievement of their social goals.

Arthur *But will this be a bad thing? If, as you tell me, the Age of Chivalry cannot last forever, then the Age of Business Enterprise sounds as though it will provide a better life for most people than many of the ages that will come between now and then.*

Merlin   Indeed it will. And that's the point. Having – as another old wizard will say – never had it so good, people and their popularly elected governments will seek to extract from business enterprise ever better conditions of living. You only have to look at the contents of this book (*he taps The Gower Handbook of Management*) to see that by the late twentieth century the manager will have taken over many of the functions performed in previous ages by the feudal lord, the priest, the teacher, the money-lender, the physician, the lawyer, the watchman and even (*he glances with suspicion at the section on corporate planning*) the astrologer.

Arthur   *Are you saying that the decline of some businesses in the late twentieth century is therefore not the responsibility of the managers but the fault of society?*

Merlin   Not entirely, of course not. Management incompetence, fraud and idleness will contribute their share of failures, as in all other occupations. But the feeling of weakness that you have observed in some areas of business and government during our visits to the mid-to-late twentieth century is in large part a reflection of managers' frustration with their social roles and people's disappointment at the failure to fulfil their expectations. Indeed, some businesses will fail just because the original purposes and skills of business management – buying, making, selling – will be lost in a mass of unproductive administration. For a while, this trend will be encouraged by the very people who should stand out against it – the Business Schoolmen. They will be teaching high finance to those who need low cunning; planning to those who should be doing; organisational theory to those who need personal skills. It will take a great recession in business to bring some of them back to teaching the basic arts.

Arthur   *Merlin, you said that the system of free business enterprise will be a success. And that to cope with this success and the expectations that it will create, the arts of business management will be developed. However, in spite of this development, the managers will not always be able to deliver all the benefits that the people expect. Does that mean that in the end management and managers will be rejected as the means of controlling business? On our study tours, we have never been beyond 1982. What happens after that?*

Merlin   Ah . . . I'm not going to tell you the answers before you have done the practical research. You will have to wait and see. But you should have already observed that towards the end of the 1970s there will be significant changes in the context of management.

Small businesses, whether owned by their managers or by large corporations, will come back into favour. Governments will notice that small businesses employ the majority of people. Large corporations will realise that smaller operating units have smaller costs of administration. The costs of basic resources – manpower, energy, materials – will all rise dramatically as the owners of these resources realise that they can fix a market price for them – and that society is no longer prepared to risk wars or revolutions in order to hold down the cost of such resources. More people and nations will acquire the means of production and the skills of management, so that competition will increase faster than custom. As a function, management will be invaded by machines, which will take over the task of assembling and analysing information, and by working people, who will seek to participate in the process of decision making.

Arthur   *So, what will this mean for the manager?*

Merlin   That he needs to go back to the basics of business – and with the consent and encouragement of a society which has a better appreciation of the true role of business. Increased competition will mean getting closer to the customer and involving the whole workforce in the satisfaction of his needs. The scarcity and expense of resources will mean developing better ways of making things and generating less waste. With more machine-produced information and analysis, there will be a greater need for human judgement. Smaller business units employing better educated people will require more effective styles of leadership.

These are all reasons why *The Gower Handbook of Management* will be such a good guide for businesses in the 1980s. It is concerned with the basic practicalities of managing a business and it also contains a section on personal skills, such as negotiation, communication, and self-development.

Arthur   *If it is so full of wisdom and if management is so important to the future, I think I should have the copy of this Handbook. After all, I am the once and future king.*

Merlin contemplates this suggestion. For Arthur to study the Handbook himself would save a lot of time in tutorials. Time in which he could be earning fees from other consultancy assignments – like the Round Table Project, a plan to start a quality circle for knights. But Merlin considers that to let *The Gower Handbook of Management* out of his possession could be dangerous for his own business. It is the Middle Ages: wizards are two a penny, but good management consultants are few and far between. Better not risk spoiling the market.

Merlin   No, thank you, Arthur. I think it would be most appropriate if I kept the Handbook – just for the next few hundred years.

With apologies to T. H. White, author of *The Sword in the Stone.*

PART ONE

PRINCIPLES, POLICY AND ORGANISATION

1 Principles of management

Philip Sadler

When practising managers are faced with difficult and complex problems – for example, designing an organisation structure for a new manufacturing plant, or attempting to motivate a workforce characterised by apathy and low productivity – they quite naturally feel the need for a set of principles to turn to, in order to help them reach the right decisions.

This is sensible when it involves a willingness to learn from the experience of others as opposed to a stubborn determination to learn only from one's own mistakes. There is also the risk that so called 'principles' which carry all the authority of tablets of stone, but which are frequently based on limited experience, may be accepted uncritically as if they were eternal truths and used by managers as substitutes for their own thought processes.

The principles of management are, of course, quite unlike the principles of mathematics or the laws of the natural sciences. In the management field there is no universal agreement as to what the principles are, nor can it be said that the principles of management are valid for all situations. (There is little point in adding the qualification 'other things being equal' since in the human context in which management is set the 'other things' are rarely if ever 'equal'.)

It would, perhaps, be better not to use the term 'principles' at all, but to refer instead to 'guidelines'. They are, quite simply, sets of potentially useful generalisations about the factors which make for success in management. People have been making such general statements for thousands of years, usually as a result of thinking deeply about their own experiences in organisations. In modern times the wide-ranging types of experience gained by successful management consultants has been a particularly fertile source of such ideas.

In this chapter the historical development of management principles will be traced briefly in order to set the scene for a more detailed examination of some of the more recent and contemporary writings on the subject. The chapter will conclude with a statement of some management principles which have emerged from experience and research in recent years.

THE BEGINNINGS OF MANAGEMENT THOUGHT

The search for 'principles of management' – rules or 'laws' which, if observed, will result in effective managerial performance in all situations – has been going on for thousands of years (George, 1968). Early Egyptian writings show that the builders of the pyramids recognised certain basic principles such as authority, responsibility and specialisation. The Babylonian Code of Hammurabi set out principles of control and responsibility and Moses developed principles of organisation when leading the tribes of Israel on the flight from Egypt. Mencius, writing in China in 500 BC emphasised the importance of the systematic application of principles of management: 'Whoever pursues a business in this world must have a system. A business which has attained success without a system does not exist.' Plato, in the *Republic*, argued the merits of the principle of specialisation, and Socrates stressed the universal nature of management: 'I say that over whatever a man may preside he will, if he knows what he needs, and is able to provide it, be a good president, whether he have the direction of a chorus, a family, a city or an army.'

Many instances of early management thought come from the writings of great military strategists, for example, the staff principle, probably first used during the reign of Alexander the Great (336–323 BC). Machiavelli, in the sixteenth century, developed four principles – reliance on mass consent; cohesiveness; leadership; and the will to survive. Although he was writing about government in his time, the same principles might be applied to the management of companies today.

Modern industrial management theory dates from the introduction of the factory system. Techniques for financial control, incentive payment schemes, planning systems and investment appraisal methods were rapidly developed and applied. A rational approach to management was developed in the nineteenth century, and became known as 'scientific management'. Typical of pioneering work of this kind was the development of techniques such as product forecasting, production planning and work study at the Boulton, Watt Co. Engineering Works in England in the early years of the century. At the same time, in the United States, Eli Whitney was developing cost accounting, quality control and the concept of interchangeable parts. In Scotland, Robert Owen laid the foundations of modern personnel management at the New Lanark Mill, demonstrating that concern for employee welfare and the provision of good working conditions were compatible with a profitable and thriving business.

In 1881 the first business school (the Wharton School at the University of Pennsylvania) was established – some eighty or more years before the decision to establish business schools in London and Manchester.

Thirty years later Frederick Winslow Taylor published the work which has possibly had more influence on management practice than anything published since, his famous *Principles of Scientific Management* (Taylor, 1911). He advocated that managers should gather together all the traditional knowledge possessed by workmen and then classify it and reduce it to laws, rules and formulae. They should then develop a 'science' for each element of a man's work to replace old rule-of-thumb methods and 'scientifically' select and train workmen in the new methods. Finally, managers should take over certain tasks, such as planning and scheduling of work, which were previously left to the workmen to cope with as well as they could.

THE PRE-WAR MANAGEMENT WRITERS

Taylor's work had a profound and far-reaching influence on works management and much workshop practice today still reflects this. In the field of general management, however, a number of writers, in the years up to the Second World War, exercised a similarly powerful influence – most notably Henri Fayol, a French mining engineer; Elton Mayo, a Harvard professor; Mary Parker Follett, an American educationalist trained in philosophy, law and political science; Chester Barnard, president of the New Jersey Bell Telephone Company; and Lyndall F. Urwick, a British army officer who became a management consultant.

Fayol's work was first published in France in 1916 under the title *Administration Industrielle et Générale* and failed to be noticed in Britain and North America until translated and published by Pitman in 1949 as *General and Industrial Management* (Fayol, 1949). He analysed management activity into five elements – planning, organising, commanding (or directing), co-ordinating and controlling – an analytical framework which has been borrowed and built upon by countless writers since. He also argued that, to be effective, management should be founded upon fourteen principles as follows:

1 Division of work and specialisation
2 Authority must match responsibility
3 Discipline
4 Unity of command (one man, one boss)
5 Unity of direction
6 Subordination of individual interest to the general interest
7 Remuneration must be fair in relation to effort
8 Centralisation
9 The scalar or hierarchical principle of line authority
10 The principle of order (a place for everyone and everyone in his place)
11 Equity
12 Stability of tenure of personnel
13 Importance of initiative
14 Importance of *esprit de corps*.

This represented the first attempt at a complete theory of management. The fact that it received widespread recognition and acclaim when published in the English language more than thirty years after it was originally written is an indication of the extent to which Fayol was regarded as an authority on management matters.

Elton Mayo's distinction lies in the fact that his contribution was based on

5

research rather than on direct personal experience, and in the way he shifted attention away from the more mechanistic issues of structure and control on to the human factors affecting industrial performance. The now famous studies he conducted at the Hawthorne Works of the Western Electric Company (Mayo, 1933) led to the conclusion that questions of human motivation and the emotional response elicited by the work situation were more important than logical and rational arrangements in determining output. Mayo also held that social relationships in working groups were the most important factor influencing the satisfaction the workers derived from their work.

Mary Parker Follett (Follett, 1949), reached similar conclusions, but on philosophical grounds rather than as a result of applied research. She emphasised the importance of group processes in decision making and had much to say that is relevant today on the question of resolving conflict.

Chester Barnard was a practising manager, but his analysis of the managerial role and the nature of organisations in *The Functions of the Executive* (Barnard, 1937), constitutes an important part of our sociological literature. His analysis linked together hitherto unrelated ideas about the factors affecting individual performance, the nature of organisations and the role of the manager.

The final figure in this group of people writing in the 1930s and '40s is Lyndall F. Urwick, whose most influential work was *The Elements of Administration* (Urwick, 1949). He produced a new synthesis based on the work of such people as Taylor, Fayol and Follett.

The principles which Urwick gathered together in this way have come to be known as the 'classical' principles of management. They are based on a combination of experience and philosophy rather than rigorous research and have been widely criticised for this. They have attracted criticism on other grounds also. First, the underlying assumption of their work – that there exists a common set of principles applicable to management in all types of situation – has been frequently challenged. Second, their work is criticised (perhaps unfairly) on the grounds that the world in which they had their experience no longer exists and that the principles they derived from that experience have little or no validity for the contemporary organisation operating in the modern business environment. (An example of the way ideas have changed in recent years in the widespread loss of confidence in the so-called economies of scale; another is the extent to which the principle of specialisation has been challenged as a result both of new ideas and much research and experimentation in the field of job design.)

Thus, changes in our ideas about management have conspired with the march of events to destroy the credibility of the classical management principles. The main changes which have affected the managerial role and altered it beyond recognition in the last quarter of a century include:

1 The impact of the computer, and more recently the microprocessor, on information processing tasks in production and administration
2 The increase in the pace of technological change generally, with consequences for the speed with which manufacturing processes and products themselves become obsolete

3   The growth of international trade and the associated intensification of competition, together with the growth of the multinational corporation and the impact on business of unstable exchange rates

4   The much greater impact of legislation on business activity – in such fields as employment protection, consumer protection, environmental care, health and safety, etc.

5   Changes in social climate leading to demands for employee participation in decision making

6   High rates of inflation

These and other factors have brought about a geometric increase in the complexity of the management task such that decisions can not easily be taken in the light of a few clearly formulated principles or guidelines of the classical kind.

MANAGEMENT THEORY IN THE POST-WAR ERA

The post-war era has seen great expansion in the volume of literature on management. The range and variety of approaches is so great as to defy any simple grouping or system of classification into schools of thought, but some commonalities can be detected.

First, the tradition of the consultant or practitioner theorising on the basis of his experience has continued, primarily because this approach genuinely meets the needs of many practising managers seeking to bring a greater degree of system and order into their own thinking. Often the most successful writers in this category have been those who can most clearly communicate, and elaborate into a system of thought, what practising managers already believe to be the case on the basis of their own experience. The best-known writers in this category in the English language have been such eminently successful consultants as Brech, Louis Allen and, above all, Peter Drucker.

Drucker in particular has taken account of changes in the nature of business environment and the managerial task, and has been successful precisely because he speaks to the contemporary manager and deals with the issues that currently concern him (Drucker, 1971).

Second, and closely related to the first group, is a smaller number of highly influential writers who have illuminated management thought with shafts of humour or satire. The most outstanding in this respect are C. Northcote Parkinson's *Parkinson's Law* (Parkinson, 1957); Robert Townsend's *Up the Organisation* (Townsend, 1970) and Antony Jay's *Management and Machiavelli* (Jay, 1967).

The ideas of these writers are well known outside management circles and indeed Parkinson's work has a place of its own in the literature of post-war society.

Third, there are the propounders of functional principles or of principles concerned with part rather than the whole of the management task. We have already seen that the classical principles of management were developed by people such as Fayol and Urwick on the basis of earlier work in production management by Taylor and others. In the post-war period we have seen considerable elaboration of theory in such areas as principles of marketing (Levitt, 1969, and Kotler, 1976), principles of personnel management (Pigors and Myers, 1969) and corporate strategy and planning (Ansoff, 1965).

This third group differs from the previous two in that it is dominated by academics as distinct from practitioners or consultants, reflecting the growth of management studies as an academic subject in the universities and the growing influence of the business school – initially in the US but more recently in Britain and other European countries. This group, in consequence, overlaps to some extent with the fourth and perhaps most important group – the management researchers. Primarily industrial psychologists and sociologists, their work builds on the tradition pioneered by Elton Mayo of detached, empirical and comparative studies of behaviour in industrial organisations. In turn they can be subdivided according to the main focus of their research. Looked at in this way the field breaks down quite logically into studies of the individual industrial worker and his motivation; studies of the behaviour of industrial work groups; studies of the factors influencing organisation effectiveness and researches into managerial and leadership behaviour.

Under the first heading three American psychologists, Herzberg, McClelland and Maslow, have had a strong and enduring influence on management theory and practice.

Herzberg is best known for his distinction between 'motivators' such as the work itself, achievement, responsibility and recognition, and what he describes as 'hygiene' factors, which do not provide motivation but merely act so as to prevent workers from being dissatisfied. These factors include pay, working conditions and relations with supervisors. Herzberg's work has led to important experiments in job enrichment as well as casting doubt on the effectiveness of many financial incentive schemes (Herzberg, 1959).

McClelland's researches emphasised the importance of the motivation to achieve in relation to the performance of work (McClelland, 1969), while Maslow's most important contribution was to draw attention to the way in which human needs are ordered into a hierarchical system, with basic needs such as survival and security as the foundation of motivation but with higher-order needs such as belonging, esteem, achievement and self-actualisation acting as the more important day-to-day motivators in advanced societies where survival and security can reasonably be taken for granted (Maslow, 1954).

Insight into the behaviour of industrial work groups has been provided by researchers on both sides of the Atlantic. Outstanding examples include Gouldner's study of gypsum mineworkers (Gouldner, 1954), and Walker and Guest's work on assembly line workers in the US (Walker and Guest, 1952), while in Britain there have been equally illuminating studies such as Lupton's participant observation of shop floor behaviour (Lupton, 1963).

The functioning of whole organisations and relationships between different forms of organisation structure and effectiveness have been the focus of a great deal of research on both sides of the Atlantic. This work in particular has had a powerful influence both in demolishing the credibility of the simple classical principles and in establishing new but more complex guidelines for management decisions.

In Britain, the work of members of the Tavistock Institute of Relations has demonstrated the importance of taking account both of the constraints imposed by technology and the needs of human beings for satisfying social relationships when designing organisation structures. From their work emerged the principles of 'joint optimisation of the social and technical systems', which stresses the need to search for forms of organisation in which technical requirements and human aspirations are simultaneously fulfilled (Rice, 1963, and Trist *et al*, 1963).

Joan Woodward (in her studies of organisation structures and levels of technology) conclusively showed that there is no one best way to organise a business and that the form of organisation advocated in the classical principles, with its emphasis on unity of command, hierarchy and clarity of structure, was far from universally adopted by successful firms (Woodward, 1965).

In a similar vein Burns and Stalker were able to demonstrate that the classical principles worked well in firms with highly stable technologies and markets but failed to be associated with successful performance in firms faced with the need for rapid adjustment to changing conditions (Burns and Stalker, 1961).

Organisation studies in the US that have contributed to the theory and practice of management include the work of Rensis Likert and in particular his concept of the organisation as a series of interlocking groups (Likert, 1961). These US studies also include the analysis by Lawrence and Lorsch of the problems faced by firms which need on the one hand to differentiate their activities to be able to relate to different markets, but which must simultaneously integrate these activities into a coherent and cohesive organisation for purposes of control and co-ordination (Lawrence & Lorsch, 1967).

Among the many studies of managerial behaviour, those of Mintzberg in the US (Mintzberg, 1973), and Rosemary Stewart in Britain (Stewart, 1967) have thrown much needed light on what managers actually do, and how the job content of managers with different roles in the organisation varies. The relationship between leadership style and management effectiveness has also proved to be a fruitful area of research, with outstanding contributions to our knowledge of leadership processes emerging from the work of Bass (Bass, 1960), and Fiedler (Fiedler, 1971) in the US.

The fourth and final group of contributors to modern management theory can be traced in its origins to two main sources: first, the application of scientific methods and mathematical problem-solving techniques to the solution of operational problems in wartime and second, to the subsequent development of computers and related mathematical approaches to solving complex problems. This fourth group is variously known as operational research or management scientists. It has included a number of eminent thinkers who have moved beyond the development and application of techniques to develop whole theories of management and organisation based on concepts derived from systems theory or information theory. In the US the outstanding personalities are March and Simon of the Massachusetts Institute of Technology (March and Simon, 1958); Diebold, the 'father of automation' (Diebold, 1965) and Norbert Weiner (Weiner, 1948), the man who first developed ideas in the field of cybernetics and related them to management.

In Britain, Stafford Beer clearly falls into this category. Beer exemplifies the approach of this group of writers in several ways. He is enthusiastic about prospects of management becoming more 'scientific'. He regards the computer as a potential tool for revolutionary changes in the practice of management. He conceptualises management as an information-processing activity and management's task as primarily one of *control*. Given that cybernetics is the science of control systems, it follows that the principles of cybernetics are also the key principles of management (Beer, 1972).

The management world described by Beer and others writing in the same vein is one with a strange language of its own – familiar perhaps to specialists in control engineering or to consultant neurologists, but foreign to generalists, and marketing and personnel specialists to whom terms such as 'heuristic', 'negentropy' and 'reticulum' convey little or nothing. At the same time it is a world in which problems of labour relations, emotions, attitudes, irrational conflicts and organisational politics have no place.

The main influence of this school of writers has been in the design, development and application of mathematically based operational research techniques to the solution of certain types of business problem.

MODERN MANAGEMENT PRINCIPLES

To what extent is it possible to draw from these various approaches a body of knowledge which, when summarised and distilled down to its essentials, could be said to represent the principles of modern management as distinct from the 'classical' ones? The task is a daunting one, not only because of the sheer volume of literature that now exists, but also because the principle trends have been towards divergence of theory, specialisation of topic and fragmentation of knowledge rather than reflecting convergence, integration and synthesis.

It is possible, however, to identify a number of recurring ideas or themes which, albeit given different treatment by different authorities and accorded differing degrees of importance in different conceptual schemes, would, nevertheless, command widespread acceptance. What follows is an attempt to state these.

The main propositions, 'principles' or guidelines about management which command widespread agreement today are:

The organisation as a complex system

The achievement of the purposes of a human organisation will involve a wide range of activities which are interconnected so as to form a system, such that changes to the pattern of activities in one part of the system will trigger related changes in other parts of it.

The technical and social sub-systems

The organisation as a system is made up of two princpal sub-systems – the technical and the social. The former is made up of such elements as the plant and machinery in use, the work flow between the different production stations and the system of production adopted (batch, mass production, continuous flow, etc.). The social system consists of the pattern of relations between the people who work in the organisation. In designing organisations regard must be given both to the need to adapt the structure to the technical system and to provide a structure which makes for a satisfying pattern of human relationships.

The organisation as an open system

The existence of any organisation depends on some process of exchange of goods or services with other organisations, social units or individuals in its environment. From this it follows that in the long run, organisations cannot survive if they are managed exclusively in ways which meet the needs of their members. Management is, therefore, partly the process of achieving a delicate balance between the expectations and needs of such internal 'stakeholders' as shareholders, managers, employees and pensioners on the one hand, and the demands and constraints imposed upon the organisation by its markets, its customers, its suppliers, trades unions, government departments, pressure groups of various kinds and, not least, by the strategies and tactics of competitors. To create and preserve such a balance calls for the continuous monitoring of the organisation's environment and the will to bring about appropriate responses on the part of the organisation.

The key resource of the modern business organisation in advanced industrial societies is knowledge

The key workers are the 'knowledge workers'; management, therefore, is more to do with the profitable exploitation of knowledge than with the productivity of labour or the utilisation of physical capacity. 'Knowledge' in this context may mean product knowledge, process 'know-how' or knowledge of the market. It is the task of management to ensure that the organisation's level of investment in the acquisition of new knowledge is sufficient to give it the competitive strength it requires to achieve profitable growth.

Management's key task is to secure the future survival of the organisation by means of appropriate and timely innovation

The classical principles of management tend to conjure up a vision of some mythical factory for producing 'widgets' which has always produced widgets and always will, using the same technology for the purpose and selling them in a stable market to loyal customers and without any Japanese competition! In the modern organisation, by contrast, successful innovation in both products and processes is indispensable to survival. Effective management, therefore, involves the ability to develop an innovative, creative climate, to establish an efficient system of market intelligence so as to discover needs for new products and to generate the funds needed for R & D and investment in new plant and equipment.

Management is the process of getting things done by other people

From this proposition it follows that the achievements of an organisation will reflect the degree of motivation and commitment of employees. Motivation is an extremely complex aspect of human behaviour about which we still have much to learn. We have, however, advanced beyond the naïve belief that it is a simple response to reward (in the form of financial incentives, for example) or punishment (fear of 'the sack'). Other factors such as job satisfaction, leadership and recognition clearly play an important part.

Management as an activity is universal but does not take the same form in all situations

Managers in all organisations and at all levels have to get things done by others, have to ensure that decisions are taken and cannot escape the need to exercise leadership. At the same time the qualities and skills required in the chief executive of a large organisation are very different from those required in a first-line manager, while the qualities needed to be effective as manager of a building site differ from those required in the successful manager of an R & D group in the electronics industry.

There is no one best way to organise a business

The most successful systems of organisation differ markedly from one kind of business to another. Any one business must continuously adapt its organisation to meet the demands of changing circumstances.

Small is beautiful

Entrepreneurial drive, creativity, adaptability and innovation alike are stifled by the bureaucratic systems of administration and control which characterise large, monolithic organisations. Effective management structures therefore involve autonomous profit centres, served rather than directed by small head-office teams.

Management is a process involving a mix of rational, logical decision-making and problem solving activities and intuitive, judgemental activities

In this sense it is both science and art. An important skill is to be able to recognise which problems and decisions fall into which category and to treat them accordingly.

None of the foregoing statements, whether they are described as generalisations, precepts, principles, or guidelines, has necessarily any enduring validity. There is no point in smashing one set of tablets of stone in order to create another. Given the high level of uncertainty and, indeed, turbulence in today's business environment, coupled with the values system of our modern society, and the stage of development of our economic institutions, these statements provide some indication of the likely paths to success. Should further radical changes take place in the nature of the environment, new guiding principles will inevitably be needed.

FURTHER READING

Ansoff, H.I., *Corporate Strategy*, McGraw-Hill, New York, 1965

Barnard, C., *The Functions of the Executive*, Harvard University Press, Cambridge, Mass, 1938

Bass, B., *Leadership, Psychology and Organisational Behaviour*, Harper, New York, 1960

Beer, S., *Brain of the Firm*, Allen Lane, The Penguin Press, London, 1972

Burns, T. and Stalker, G. M., *The Management of Innovation*, Tavistock, London, 1961

Diebold, J., *Focus on Automation*, British Institute of Management, London, 1965

Drucker, P., *Drucker on Management*, Management Publications Ltd, for the British Institute of Management, London, 1971

Fayol, H. *General and Industrial Administration*, Pitman, London, 1949

Fiedler, F., *Leadership*, General Learning Press, New York, 1971

Follett, Mary P., *Freedom and Coordination*, Management Publications Trust, London, 1949

George, C.S., *The History of Management Thought*, Prentice-Hall, Englewood Cliffs, NJ, 1968

Gouldner, A. W., *Patterns of Industrial Bureaucracy*, The Free Press, Glencoe, Ill, 1954

Herzberg, F. J., *The Motivation to Work*, Wiley, New York, 1959

Jay, A., *Management and Machiavelli*, Hodder & Stoughton, London, 1967

Kotler, P., *Marketing Mangement*, Prentice-Hall, Englewood Cliffs, NJ, 1976

Lawrence, P. R. and Lorsch, J. W., *Organisation and Environment*, Harvard Business School, Cambridge, Mass, 1967

Levitt, T., *The Marketing Mode*, McGraw Hill, New York, 1969

Likert, R., *New Patterns of Management*, McGraw Hill, New York, 1961

Lupton, T., *On the Shop Floor*, Pergamon Press, Oxford, 1963

McClelland, D. C. and Winter, D. G., *Motivating Economic Achievement*, Free Press, New York, 1969

March, J. G. and Simon, H. A., *Organisations*, Wiley, New York, 1958

Maslow, A., *Motivation and Personality*, Harper & Row, New York, 1954

Mayo, G. E., *The Human Problems of an Industrial Civilization*, Harvard

Business School, Boston, Mass, 1933

Mintzberg, H., *The Nature of Managerial Work*, Harper & Row, New York, 1973

Parkinson, C. Northcote, *Parkinson's Law*, John Murray, London, 1957

Pigors, P. and Myers, C. A., *Personnel Administration*, McGraw-Hill, New York, 1969

Rice, A. K., *The Enterprise and its Environment*, Tavistock, London, 1963

Stewart, R., *Managers and their Jobs*, Macmillan, London, 1967

Taylor, F. W., *Principles of Scientific Management*, Harper and Brothers, New York, 1911

Townsend, R., *Up The Organisation*, Michael Joseph, London, 1970

Trist, E. L., Higgin, G. W., Murray, H. and Pollock, A. B., *Organisational Choice*, Tavistock, London, 1963

Urwick, L., *The Elements of Administration*, Harper & Brothers, New York, 1944

Walker, C. R. and Guest, R. H., *The Man on The Assembly Line*, Harvard University Press, Cambridge, Mass, 1952

Weiner, N., *Cybernetics*, Wiley, New York, 1948

Woodward, J., *Industrial Organisation: Theory and Practice*, Oxford University Press, Oxford, 1965

2 Corporate strategies for the 1980s

George S Sanders and Ron H Bradnam

Corporate strategy cannot exist in isolation from the world in which the customer lives, in which the business must exhibit acceptable behaviour and from which the business draws its resources. Hence this chapter contains some speculation concerning possible developments in the 1980s in the hope that it may help businesses to adopt strategies that are compatible with the opportunities and threats they may face. No attempt has been made to forecast quantitatively – partly because of the inherent uncertainty in the process but more importantly because each business must research its own input data in accordance with its unique markets, technologies and resources.

Strategy must take into account:

- future social attitudes
- future legal structures

and must be considered in relation to:

- future markets
- future resources
- future technologies
- future organisation and management style.

Each of these factors will now be examined in broad outline, with particular emphasis on those that are liable to affect the enterprise at strategic level.

FUTURE SOCIAL ATTITUDES

There is a growing feeling among leaders in industrialised nations that the assertion 'everyone has the right to work' (Universal Declaration of Human Rights) may have to change to 'everyone has the right to an income'. Europe and the US appear to be entering an age where:

1   If work is defined as toil in exchange for money, then providing work for all is becoming increasingly difficult

2   If work is so defined, an ever-increasing amount of creative work is enjoyed and undertaken for no monetary return – including 'do it yourself', home food growing and preparation, charitable work and arts and crafts. In some advanced countries this has been estimated as accounting for over 50 per cent of the gross national product (GNP)

3   More people are finding satisfaction from working on their own or in small groups earning money (or engaging in barter) from efforts that may well have started as hobbies.

Work has traditionally provided people with their means of livelihood, status in the community and an outlet for contributing. Unless an alternative can be found of providing these three, work remains the essential vehicle. It is the responsibility therefore of management to find ways of creating suitable work opportunities for all people for reasonable periods of their lives. The greatest problems (or, more correctly, opportunities to influence this situation) currently lie in the lower age range. There are particular problems with school leavers whose lack of experience means that they have less to offer an employer. However a strength of their situation is to be found (with the right motivations) in their willingness to learn and adapt to circumstances. This motivation can be developed by the creation of closer bonds with the establishments that provide the workforce (i.e. schools, colleges and universities) in order to foster a better understanding of industry, commerce and government. All companies, if they have not already started, should be encouraging the concept of continuing education throughout the careers of their staff. Training and public relations consume time and resources but the consequence of ignoring the needs of the present and future employee cannot be underestimated. In addition, once the work has been provided, there is an increasing demand for the work to be more satisfying and 'owned' by the worker, while at the same time the employer is endeavouring to improve the competitiveness of the operation.

One outcome of this trend may well be that employment, as it has been known, will no longer be for life but may last for less than half life. New opportunities must therefore be sought to provide for continuing employment, which may include the acceptance of other forms of work. The implications reach beyond the usual scope of most corporate plans, but if we accept that the organisation must respond to the environment in which it operates, there is an urgent need for management to get out into that environment and learn from it. Businesses will have to meet the expectations of the community by creating opportunities to discuss the activities of the business and perhaps also to participate (if only by visits, etc.) in operations being undertaken. Improvements in the relationship with the community include the need to create closer links with, and awareness by, policy makers in government and the financial institutions. Planners can sometimes get quite skilled at 'sorting out the wood from the trees' but often they have no idea of what view they wish to see when emerging from the forest at the far side! These changes will become unacceptable in companies practising a more open management style. Ronald Ellis, managing director of the Truck and Bus Division of British Leyland, has observed that there are six stages to 'managing to survive':

1   entrepreneurial stage
2   survival stage
3   stabilisation
4   reputation and pride
5   uniqueness and adaptability
6   contribution – to society, industry, profession.

He suggested that companies tend to grow through these stages but can, all too easily, slip back to an earlier stage if anything goes wrong. He considered that far too few companies reached the last stage – that of social responsibility – and found it relatively difficult to remain at that stage for long periods. Yet that is increasingly what is expected of the organisation.

These changes in social attitudes could affect the strategy of the medium-sized and the large companies in the following ways:

1   Companies may be forced to employ more people on shorter working weeks (shift work) and part timers, despite the difficulties in training, change overs, continuity and planning, etc. and the adverse effect on costs
2   Since the result of work which appears as GNP is only part of the picture, market forecasting will have to be reassessed to take into account this changing social practice
3   A move towards work sharing, once dismissed by all European governments as 'an impractical method of reducing unemployment', is being officially promoted in the Netherlands with the aim of reaching a target of 25 per cent of the working population by the end of the decade.

Each of these issues arouses different responses. In the Netherlands experiment, the Government subsidised both the company and the employee to buffer the effects of lower wages and increased indirect costs. However a prominent industrialist has suggested, quite independently, in a private communication, a way in which the costs of work sharing may not be so prohibitive as at first thought, and the administrative burden kept small by implementing adjustment at the company level before the company pays its dues to the Government.

Another factor that will undoubtedly affect corporate strategy in the years ahead is the growing public concern over the potential dangers in high technology. Harmful side effects of drugs, factory explosions with or without noxious emissions, fear of nuclear energy – all these and others have illustrated the need for extreme caution in launching new products and commissioning new processes. And yet the paradox is that, given a choice, the buying public do not seem willing to pay the premium for more safety, more testing and more precautions (lead-free petrol marketed in the US at a few cents per gallon above normal pump prices just didn't sell).

There is also public concern at the more obvious results of heavy industry and the throw-away society. Pollution by noise, fumes, throw-away packaging or ugly buildings, tips and pylons will be increasingly resisted; and the possibility exists of stronger legislation in this area.

A study published in 1979 for the UK Department of Energy set out six prerequisites for full employment in an environment of technological change:

1 An adaptable and better educated workforce
2 More trained manpower in electronics and software skills and traditional skills
3 An expanded retraining effort
4 Less hierarchical industrial structures
5 Greater willingness by management to consult
6 Positive attitude to opportunities in new technology.

These prerequisites assume that, with the increase of technological choice, effective planning and policy making is essential. Important steps have already been taken to aid effective planning, but with industry moving towards basic technologies and modules requiring systems of management based on project rather than on functional structures. The development of appropriate strategies, methodologies and auditing techniques must proceed.

These and other issues are now explored, with the aim of ensuring that human and material resources are responsibly used.

FUTURE LEGAL STRUCTURES

Ever since the earliest Companies Acts (notably incorporation in 1844 and limited liability in 1855), company law reform has continued on the basis of a commission every 20 years or so. Succeeding Acts made small changes based upon problems that cropped up as business activities developed. In recent years, however, and largely in responce to EEC directives, changes have been coming faster. To the harassed small business man these changes seem too fast, whereas to others they seem pitifully inadequate. One commentator has remarked, 'If we have a mess in 1981, we ought to expect chaos by 1984. What kind of company law will we have in 2001? If neither the politicians nor the administrators ask this question, then those who will be most affected must do so for themselves. The initiative must be taken by commerce, industry and the professions, on the American pattern. There is little enough time.' (Sealey).

As well as company law reforms and EEC harmonisation, there are various voluntary codes and guidelines that should also be acknowledged as having an impact on corporate strategy. For OECD member countries, there are guidelines on international investment and multinational enterprises amongst other matters; from various pressure groups there is a bewildering array of codes concerning product liability and environmental impact. Even in 1976, a certain chemical plant under construction in the US required 26 permits from 13 separate government agencies.

The corporate strategist must be aware of current and impending legislation that could affect his company's plans. Admittedly a large amount of legislation will have only minor effects on tactical plans but some laws can have major impact: some companies have already been forced to abandon products that cannot be brought into line; in some processes excessive investment is needed to meet new safety requirements; other companies have had to invest huge sums in R & D to meet future standards (car exhaust emissions for example).

These problems due to legislation are all in addition to fiscal changes in respect of which Sir David Steel has said '...I must repeat my frequently expressed concern at the growing tendency of governments, not least in the UK, to alter the terms on which business is conducted' (BP Annual Report, 1980).

Consider just four areas where changes in legislation will probably have increasing influence on corporate strategy:

1 directors' responsibility
2 employee rights
3 product liability
4 environmental impact.

For each of these areas, points that may need consideration in relation to planning are briefly discussed.

Director's responsibilities have long been catalogued but in response to public disquiet and to EEC directives, changes are imminent. Already the UK Companies Act of 1980 requires directors to have regard to the interests of their employees. Many will assert that they always have had such regard, which anyway is the long term interests of shareholders, so only time and case law will give clear interpretation.

Attempts to force more responsible attitudes take broadly two forms; firstly a demand for more disclosure and secondly for more nonexecutive directors (including employee representatives) on company boards.

Disclosure is already dramatically different from what was considered acceptable 25 or 30 years ago when most business men saw no need to disclose anything more than was required by law and often no more than a couple of sheets of typescript was issued to shareholders. Now glossy multicoloured annual reports are commonplace, perhaps reflecting the company's need to woo the shareholder but also containing much social reporting (community activities, waste recycling, pollotion control, employment practices, etc.). If all the other current codes were followed (for example intragroup trading practices, third world technology investment, etc.) the present day 40 page annual report would double or treble in size.

The pressure for more nonexecutive directors has already led to two-tier boards in West Germany and a wide range of consultative devices in other countries. In the UK there will probably be legislation merely requiring management and trade unions to agree arrangements for participation. The problems of ensuring joint regulation of strategic planning will no doubt be fiercely debated. It would be a disaster, however, if fear on either side of industry were allowed to stop progress towards consultation. Still far too few companies hold regular meetings between the board and employee representatives.

In parallel to these statutory approaches, City of London institutions, alarmed at the effect of more dramatic revelations of director behaviour, have appointed a bureau to promote the appointment of nonexecutive directors. The theory, presumably, is that directors who do not depend on the company for their livelihood will probably be willing to challenge proposals that are morally dubious. Of course, in theory, the shareholders are supposed to watch over the behaviour of those they have elected as directors; but many directors have grown up in the period when shareholder power was minimal, when private investors (often referred to as absentee landlords) were interested only in short term capital gain. Growth in the power of the institutional investor is fairly recent and there are now a number of cases of pension fund trustees and the like becoming openly critical over company revelations (take overs, gratuitous payments, etc.). It will be interesting to see how the City's take-over code (published in February 1981) works out in practice. In the past, the City has been able to enforce the spirit as well as the letter of its codes.

Enormous changes in the laws governing employee rights in the UK took place in the 1970s. Equal pay, discrimination, health and safety, redundancy compensation were all the subject of legislation. Trade Union immunity was strengthened and the closed shop protected (though this is now being modified). Minority groups are also being increasingly safeguarded. Since 1980, every directors' report must include a statement on company policy over employment of the disabled (companies with over 250 employees only). There is no doubt that pressure from other minority groups for similar consideration will follow.

As far as product liability is concerned, the current laws tend to be based upon proven negligence. It seems probable that strict liability will become the determining factor. The need for harmonisation in product liability laws is important. Without it, the country with lenient legislation risks becoming a dumping ground for products of foreign manufacturers who cannot meet the high standards elsewhere. Similarly their own manufacturers would have difficulty in exporting products that meet only domestic lower level requirements. It is also of interest to note that in the USA, in the event of a take over, the principal corporation must accept liability for product damages caused previously by the taken-over company. In addition, putting a guilty subsidiary into liquidation, whilst not affecting the rest of the group, is a procedure which will probably not be accepted much longer. Future corporate strategy may require closer control of product quality by headquarters than has hitherto been customary.

Environmental impact is an immensely wide subject. Opencast mining, the laying of underground pipes, the effect of throw-away packaging, non-degradable plastic rubbish as well as noise and air pollution – all these affect almost every company directly or indirectly. Corporate sensitivity is already manifest in many advertising campaigns claiming responsible behaviour. Those companies who intend to introduce some new product or process in the future will have to think deeply about its environmental impact and take steps to alleviate any adverse effects or spend time and money to change public attitude.

FUTURE MARKETS

During the 1960s and 1970s financial management skills dominated strategic thinking. This was a period when thriving businesses based their success on growth. In the 1980s, slow growth and intense competition mean that strategic thinking must be dominated by marketing skills. Indeed marketing will probably be the critical management function in strategic terms. However, marketing will not be able to slide easily into the driving seat; rather it must earn its position through greatly improved productivity. With sales and distribution costs rising rapidly and advertising getting keener, innovative thinking will be necessary. The new thinking will have to include more effective promotional methods (the information revolution is supposed to be imminent and promotion is, after all a form of communication) and will have to:

- cover novel distribution methods (congested city centres will not much longer tolerate heavy goods traffic)
- experiment with breaking bulk and assembling locally, and
- computerise all the routine operations of stock control; regularise reordering, delivery and invoice documentation (and could extend to computer-to-computer links).

Let us consider three separate types of business and their market future:

1 Bespoke goods, major capital equipment and all such specials which, in general, are not made until a customer is found and has ordered. In this situation, marketing is followed by selling and then by manufacture
2 Standard goods, consumer durables and consumables where marketing is followed by manufacture and then by selling
3 Service industries selling financial skills, techonolgy, consultancy licences, software franchises, etc. where marketing and operating are so closely linked as to be inseparable.

In the first case, marketing and selling are closely linked and will probably continue so. The larger the unit sale, the more the marketing/selling process becomes prolonged and often political. Under such circumstances the problem of keeping a manufacturing or operating unit occupied becomes of secondary importance. Peaks and troughs of activity are difficult to avoid and with world politics in a turbulent state continuous production is not going to get easier to achieve. Strategically it would seem wise to maintain a lean operating unit capable of handling the work load in the troughs and to subcontract the peaks.

In the second case, manufacture of consumer and industrial goods, the skills of forecasting and careful control of unsold stock will be paramount. In this type of business, the marketing man has traditionally thought in terms of volume and market share and has used these measures as his main objectives and controls. In future broader thinking will become necessary and the marketing man of the 1980s must start thinking of contribution and return on investment. His goals must be set in these terms which will take account of stocks and productive capacity left idle through unequal loading. For many marketing men, the idea that it will be his duty to load the factory to capacity will come as a shock.

There will also be a greater need for marketing to give better guidance to product R & D with clearer indication of customer needs and attractive product features.

In the third category, service and sales of know-how, opportunities in the export field will dominate. For more than a century, countries rich in raw materials have sold them to developed countries who have had the skills of conversion. Now many of the developing countries are rapidly acquiring their own skills of conversion, so developed countries have moved towards the provision of capital goods for the factories, power stations and general infrastructures of the developing world. Following this will be a thriving market in the provision of technical, management and training skills. Countries which have moved in one generation from a nomadic or agrarian culture require an immense amount of help in adopting a manufacturing and commercial culture. This must however be provided with sensitivity and due regard for underlying cultural mores. The company that can so provide should reap a rich harvest.

Important to those who trade in know-how, is the protection of their wares. The patent system of the world although complex is reasonably effective. The same cannot always be said for trade marks and copyright. Whether tapes contain music or computer programs, they are easily and widely copied. The development of security systems protecting intellectual property is long overdue.

In summary marketing competence is at a critical stage and must be greatly improved to face the slow-growth highly competitive markets of the next decade. It is not surprising that some will adopt the strategy of diversification into the sale of their know-how via service contracts or franchise operations to overseas markets keen to become self sufficient and hungry for help to achieve this.

FUTURE RESOURCES

Corporate manpower, apart from the obvious impact of technology, will probably change in method of employment. For the shorter working week to become practical, for instance, much greater versatility will be necessary. Since the first industrial revolution, specialisation has been the goal as mechanical tools were developed and special skills were needed to operate them. Now the trend could well reverse, leading to general machine minding and maintenance skills in both manufacturing industry and information-dominated commercial and administrative offices. The implications for training, trade union organisation and social attitudes are considerable and such changes are expected to be slow.

As has already been mentioned, an increase in numbers of small specialist companies and even sole practitioners and self-employed craftsmen is to be expected. Some businessmen have already taken advantage of this trend by establishing business format franchise operations. Carl-Henry Wingwist, the Secretary General of the International Chamber of Commerce said recently, 'the need to rekindle the entrepreneurial spirit is urgent in all our countries. A restoration of confidence and a rise in the world's standard of living depends on this vital point' ('Tomorrow the World', *Vision*, November 1981).

As far as the larger business is concerned, corporate strategy will probably include the greater use of subcontractors, consultants, software houses, and so on, leaving the principal leaner, more flexible and with clearer corporate goals associated with the kernel of the business.

As a result the problems to be solved will become more complex, also the art of managing people will require further development if the workforce is to help freely in the problem-solving process. Indeed a 'no threat' environment is going to be required in most enterprises, if the decision takers are to be expected to perform in an effective way. The advent of the cheap microcomputer, and its associated software make the possibility of 'what if?' modelling a practical option for even the smallest company. Given a degree of competence in the specialised requirements of the business and a certain general business experience and understanding of the economy, the possible consequences of decisions will be easily computed before major investments are made.

A major change experienced in the last decade has been the increase in worldwide trade and co-operation. The procurement of resources is no exception. As examples:

1   manpower, the ready international exchange of staff
2   materials, procured in a world market
3   machines and facilities, bought, hired, leased
4   finance, available in all the money markets
5   time, intercontinental sharing of computer systems
6   management, exchange of know-how, experience and information.

A further complication for the strategist is to be found in the potential 'problem resources', that is those whose availability is limited and may become scarce by the year 2000; these include: aluminium, copper, gold, lead, mercury, natural gas, petroleum, tin, silver, tungsten and zinc. Any user of these materials needs to model the implications of future supply, as the necessary data becomes available.

In the 1980s the main change will probably be the ease with which information on such resources can be obtained, processed and reviewed by the judicious and careful use of the technologies developed in the 1970s. With more reliable inputs, decisions will be quicker and themselves more reliable. Additionally, it will become easier to test the sensitivities of decisions before they are taken, and so enable a greater degree of realism to be built into the modelling. A demand will arise for more flexibility than currently exists in many organisations, if advantage is to be taken of this new capability. The workforce will have to be prepared and protected in the transition period.

With increased flexibility will come a need for improved specification of what is to be achieved and the resource procurement function will become a more professional activity; by the end of the decade, the existing make/buy and inventory management decision, is expected to be replaced by decisions in the field of employment strategies and business policy (for example, should company X purchase finished sub-assemblies or design, develop and manufacture the item itself). To be able to contribute effectively to such decisions will require a keen awareness of what the practicalities of any particular situation may be, and how external changes in the environment may influence the performance of the enterprise. The contributor will therefore have to extend his vision from the relatively narrow functional approach to a more system oriented approach. The real aim is to map out the possibilities and to make the optimum selection, a very much more attractive prospect.

FUTURE TECHNOLOGIES

All too often, new technology is seen as a threat. Corporate strategy in the 1980s must be founded on technology as an opportunity.

The ability to forecast future growth technologies has been the dream of strategists for at least 20 years. In the late 1960s technological forecasting was popular. Now with the benefit of hindsight, many of the forecasts of those days can be seen to be unimpressive.

It has been said that anything is possible in a technical field given enough money. Although an exaggerated statement, there is more than a grain of truth in it. The technological advances coming from the conquest of space happened only because two great powers decided to fund space exploration, mainly for political reasons. Novel techniques and equipment that have been developed enabling oil majors to explore deep sea concessions and drill at ever increasing depths would never have been developed if oil were still traded at $2 per barrel. The need and the finance must precede the research and development; on the other hand, the Swiss watch industry was transformed almost overnight by the advent of quartz as a time piece. The mistake in the 'technological forecasting' era was to forecast from a starting point of scientific feasibility rather than the starting point of need; science push instead of needs pull. Jantsch (1967) made a valiant effort to redress the balance with his review of frameworks, techniques and organisation of the technological forecasting function. Of course both viewpoints – science push and market pull – are necessary but each must be given its proper weight.

As far as strategy in the 1980s is concerned, we are looking at relatively short term developments in the pure science timescale and so new ideas for exploitation within ten years are already born. The question is more which will die in infancy and which will reach maturity.

There are some obvious candidates that are already mature and, to continue the analogy, are themselves ready for selective breeding. Such is the general area known variously as the information explosion, informatics, telematics, etc. mostly dependent upon microcomputer technology. Predictions on how this will affect our lives are legion, ranging from programmable domestic hardware to the total disappearance of paper as the medium for information storage and transmission. Forecast spin off effects include the absence of commuter traffic assuming everyone will work at home (somewhat neglecting the social aspects of work) and the evanescence of transport and stocks and spares and component parts; local manufacture will be possible using computer controlled machines receiving instructions, by satellite if necessary, from a remote head office.

We are concerned in this chapter with shorter term technologies of the type that have already been born and are now adolescent.

In the food industry it has been estimated that 50 per cent of the world's food is wasted before reaching the point of consumption, and this may become the spearhead to action. With large areas of the world still at starvation level, any developments which could satisfy this need are likely candidates for investment in the short term. Among these are marine farming, enzyme technology and hydroponics. In the packaging and distribution of food, retort packaging will go a long way to replacing cans and frozen foods.

In the medical field, improved methods of diagnosis are expected to have a marked effect on health and life expectancy.

Mechanical equipment of all kinds will probably become more durable. Increased durability will be achieved by greater use of adhesives to replace rivets and welds, by the introduction of ceramic unlubricated bearings and by the adoption of design lives of 20 to 30 years instead of the present 3 or 4 years. A motor car, for example, consumes more energy in its construction than in its propulsion in a 10-year life. Doubling its life will save more energy than making marginal improvements to its fuel consumption. This appreciation must inevitably lead to the adoption of 'whole life cost' concepts (already used in the defence and space technologies) in everyday industry, commerce and consumer affairs.

In the field of metal manufacture, means of conserving and recylcing are likely to see rapid development. In assembly, robotics should of course make further progress.

Rising crime rates and terrorist activity could lead to the development of security systems capable of recognising individuals, with probable spin offs into the management of money and financial transactions.

Lasers have been with us for almost 20 years but many hold the view that their development is only just starting. The fields of information processing, telecommunications, metal forming and medical work are still open to considerable development.

Free thinking speculation can be a valuable technique for the strategist but positive and negative feedback must be taken into account. The authors of *The Limits to Growth* used system dynamics as developed by Professor Jay Forrester at the Massachusetts Institute of Technology to explore the effects of such feedback. The questions posed when considering any new development were:

1 What will be the side effects, both physical and social, if this development is introduced on a large scale?
2 What social changes will be necessary before this development can be implemented properly, and how long will it take to achieve them?
3 If the development is fully successful and removes some natural limit to growth, what limit will the growing system meet next? Will society prefer its pressures to be the ones this development is designed to remove?

The third industrial revolution is about to begin! The question that arises is 'where do we join in?' Ansoff and Stewart (1967) suggested four categories of participation:

- first to market
- follow the leader
- application
- me too!

What management has to decide is where their particular organisation should be, and the probable answer for most is a blend of all four, so that risks may be balanced and opportunities adequately exploited.

When a new product or process is developed the company has to decide if it should patent, publish or keep the idea secret until exploitation. Sometimes secrecy is the best policy because the rate of innovation is so great that the product is out of date by the time it is available in the market place; but in other cases, awareness of the risk must be based upon knowledge of competitors capability. One multinational has reported that a particular competitor needs only about six months to produce a competing product from scratch – and that with no evidence of commercial espionage. Patents provide some safety in such situations, but it is worth considering whether the cost of international protection is worthwhile; using the same funds to reduce the selling price and so making it more difficult for competition to take the market, might be an alternative worth considering.

It is worth considering also, that there is ample scope for useful exploitation of intermediate technologies – particularly in the developing countries.

FUTURE ORGANISATION

The organisation of most present day businesses and public institutions is based upon the principle of delegation and orderly specialisation. This pattern has changed little from the day when a few knowledgeable managers administered a largely manual labour force. Indeed it is still a relevant pattern where such a situation still exists, as in agriculture, high volume manufacture or assembly of a single product (or product family) as well as in routine clerical industry. Such a pattern is becoming less and less relevant in the growing knowledge-based businesses where multifunctional decisions must be made by those who have the knowledge and local perspective.

Traditional organisation based mainly on fuctional specialisation has dominated management thinking for almost a century. This thinking has penetrated deeply and has spawned job descriptions, definitions of authority and responsibility, functional procedures, training programmes and the whole structure of rewards and promotions. Under such a system, there is a risk that functional and parochial objectives will dominate and obscure overall business objectives. The popularity of long range planning and management by objectives was due in part to this dichotomy. In addition the demand for in-house management development courses to focus on interfunctional interdependence indicates a recognition of the deficiences of traditional organisation.

In response to the needs of the more knowledge-based and innovative business, two trends have evolved in recent years and are expected to accelerate in the 1980s.

The first trend is towards small self-sufficient units. It has been argued that '...there is every reason why a business unit should grow to an optimum size and no good reason for growing beyond it. This, of course, looks like a self-justifying statement that makes sense when "optimum" is defined – which will never be easy. . . . A whole business might still grow but on the biological principle of the dividing cell.' (Latham and Saunders, 1980). Professor A. Piatier (1981) argues similarly pointing out that up to a certain size the economies of scale enhance the results but thereafter the diseconomies of scale take over. These economic arguments are supported by many writers from the behavioural viewpoint. Dr Sheane forecasts the era of self management within power distributed federations. That remarkable prophet Dr Schumacher said '. . . we must learn to think in terms of an articulated structure that can cope with a multiplicity of small scale units'.

The second trend is towards the superimposition of project teams, task forces, new venture teams – call them what you will – operating within the hierarchical structure. The leaders of more enterprising businesses have discovered that if they want entrepreneurial or innovative management then they must delegate those responsibilities with a broadly defined strategy to small multidisciplinary teams of knowledge workers. Project management has grown in popularity, in practice, in publications, and in management training by leaps and bounds. Teams which can be given one single clear objective are usually highly motivated and are an ultimate manifestation of management by objectives. In the construction and civil engineering industries, project teams assigned to the dam, the hospital, the motorway or the factory building are the only logical way of organising. Aerospace and many other high technology businesses do likewise. It is in the more traditional industries where functional organisation has thrived that project teams have found that cohabiting is uncomfortable; yet it is in these industries more than any that change and innovation are long overdue.

As for top management and its responsibility for overall strategy, it is vital that these three organisational systems – hierarchy, small units and transient project teams – are not seen as alternatives or as mutually exclusive. As Peter Drucker has pointed our (1973) '. . . just as statesmen learned long ago that both good laws and good rulers are needed, so organisation builders (and even organisation theorists) will have to learn that sound organisation structure needs both a hierarchical structure of authority and decision making, and the capacity to organise task forces, teams and individuals for work both on a permanent and temporary basis'.

The role of top management must increasingly move towards the identification of overall strategy within which small teams can turn social and market needs into possible opportunities. Thereafter, top management must provide support coupled with reward systems that identify contribution to overall goals rather than functional and parochial objectives. The top manager of the 1980s will be a spokesman and representative of the business to the outside world in general and to the external stakeholders in particular. The top managers and indeed all managers will see their role as a service to the wealth generating units – a service of helping, facilitating, supporting and training. The top manager will talk and think less about 'subordinates' and more about 'colleagues', 'teams' and 'juniors'. He will set high standards but will never underestimate the contribution of others.

Perhaps the most important strategic role of the future manager in an organisational context is the provision of strategic continuity. The average middle manager or project team leader is unlikely to be in his post more than three years (if he is any good) and yet major strategic decisions can take ten years to implement. It follows that middle managers, team leaders and small unit executives are unlikely to be motivated to give care and consideration to ten-year decisions; the top management team must provide that input. To do so effectively will need a new skill and much time spent in listening, travelling, reading and debating and will (to quote Drucker again) '. . . require thinking and understanding in at least three areas – the functional or operating; the moral; and the political' (1968).

FURTHER READING

Ansoff and Stewart, 'Strategies for technology-based businesses', *Harvard Business Review*, November/December, 1967

Drucker, P. F., *The Age of Discontinuity*, Heinemann, London, 1968

Drucker, P. F., *Management: Tasks, Responsibilities, Practices*, Heinemann, London, 1973

Halley, J. C. G., *Management Issues of the '80s – Topic Papers*, BIM, London, 1980

Jantsch, E., *Technological forecasting in Perspective*, OECD, 1967

Latham, F. W. and Sanders, G. S., *Urwick Orr on Management*, Heinemann, London, 1980

Meadows, Meadows, Randers and Behrens, *The Limits to Growth*, Earth Island, London, 1972

Piater, A., 'Innovation, information and long-term growth', *Futures*, October, 1981

Schumacher, E. F., *Small is Beautiful*, Blond and Briggs, London, 1973

Sealey, L. 'A company law for tomorrow's world', *The Company Lawyer*, vol. 2, no. 5

Sheane, D., 'Beyond Bureaucracy', *Management Research*, 1976

3 The strategic planning process

Denis Boyle

The objectives of a company's planning process, as reflected in its strategic management and control system, are to:

1 Improve strategic problem-solving within a business and communication between corporate management and business management
2 Build a bridge between strategic thinking and functional operational action
3 Clarify objectives, strategies and action plans throughout different levels of the organisation
4 Mobilise potential corporate synergy so that the power of the firm is fully exploited and its resources deployed to optimum advantage in meeting its strategic goals, ultimately expressed in the growth of earnings per share
5 Provide a framework within which managers are motivated to action by having participated in the goal-setting process as well as the formulation of specific strategies and action plans. This provides the basis of a psychological contract and the means for highlighting performance so that desired behaviour can be rewarded and consistent under-achievement eliminated
6 Create a mechanism for providing early warning of fundamental environmental changes as well as the tools for developing and implementing appropriate kinds of business and organisational responses.

In order to achieve these goals management at all levels in the organisation must share a common strategic language for analysing and interpreting problems as well as developing appropriate actions. It is essential for the planning process to operate as an integral part of the company's management process.

Rather than a rigid, standardised approach, which often runs the risk of becoming a bureaucratic and expensive time-waster, the planning process should have a built-in flexibility which is 'strategic problem oriented'. This means that within a multibusiness corporation a distinction is made between 'in' and 'out' of strategic control situations.

Businesses said to be 'in' strategic control are those which have an established, effective strategy and (by definition) a management team and resources giving the capability to resolve issues necessary for the achievement of agreed goals.

'Out' of control situations represent businesses which for several years have failed to achieve planned results. Typically these will be suffering from major industrial changes which have made their traditional strategy obsolete. In the worst instances they will be locked into a vicious circle of decline which can only be broken by direct intervention from corporate management. Depending on the strategic situation of a particular division or business unit the planning process takes on the character of dialogue, discussion and monitoring, or of intervention and restructuring. This is shown diagrammatically in Figure 3.1.

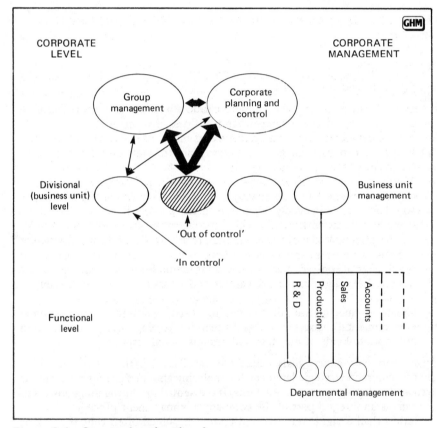

Figure 3.1 Structuring the planning process

The character of the planning process varies according to the level in the organisation at which it takes place. For example, in a multi business group the concern is not only with overseeing the planning activities of individual divisions or business units but also generating a group plan. This will focus on optimising performance by fully exploiting interdependencies, preventing inefficient duplications and ensuring that cash generated and funds raised are disposed so as to achieve corporate objectives at an acceptable risk.

Corporate management specifies the roles and financial targets to be achieved by divisional and business unit managers. Within these constraints the planning process is one of developing an appropriate strategy and the action plans by which it can be implemented. This means that planning has to be pushed down into every functional area. As a consequence, for a company's planning process to be effective it is necessary that individuals at all levels understand the goals of the corporation as a whole. This enables each individual to focus on his own particular activity within the general strategic framework.

MAKING THE PLANNING PROCESS FIT THE COMPANY'S REALITY

Since the planning process is one of an organisation's key management mechanisms then naturally it must be fitted to the unique situation in which it has to operate. Certain common principles apply generally, but the creation of standardised approaches can lead to bureaucracy which hinders rather than helps the achievement of business goals.

Ideally, the planning process should represent the systematic formulation of techniques which the company has itself found successful over the years. A key role of the planning staff is helping management at several levels to make these established principles or rules of thumb explicit.

A classic example is the extremely complex and detailed OST (objectives, strategies, tactics) system of Texas Instruments, one of the most successful electronics corporations in the world. The reasons for its success lie not in the use of computers, cost experience curve models and the like, but rather in the way in which it was designed by the president Patrick Haggar who built the business and then designed the planning process to institutionalise the way in which they had been historically sucessful.

For any company an appropriate planning process will depend on its history, the characteristics of its management team and the particular industries in which it operates.

PROVISION OF SHORT-RUN CONTROL WITHIN A STRATEGIC FRAMEWORK

The planning process determines the strategic framework in which daily action occurs. As shown diagrammatically in Figure 3.2 the strategic plan is updated annually to provide a rolling perspective for immediate action. The first year of the plan forms the operating plan, which is then broken down to create an operating budget.

The 'time horizon' of a strategic plan will vary from business to business, although a period of three or five years is often selected to ease the problem of consolidation at group level. However, in capital-intensive industries plans may need to look further ahead, for example because of construction lead times. In a rapidly changing industrial situation short-range planning covering one or two years may be combined with a scenario of likely events in the coming decade, together with an assessment of possible roles that the company could play. Whatever form it takes, whether five-year plan or general scenario, the strategic framework so provided is the basis for immediate action. Hence, although the planning process considers the future, it does so only to provide a context in which to initiate daily action.

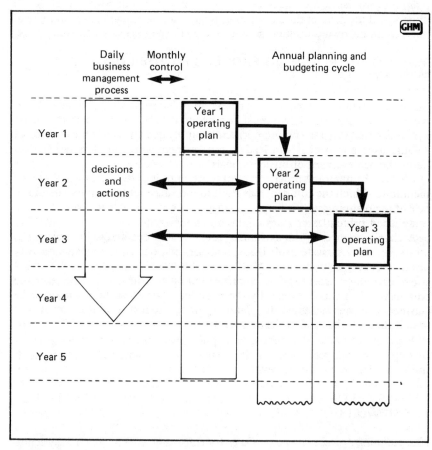

Figure 3.2   The strategic plan framework and annual operating plan

Actions may be aimed at defending and improving existing profitability, for example by increasing productivity. However, the pursuit of a sound strategy may sometimes necessitate an activity which shows up as 'red' figures. Investment in research and development is a common example. Retaliating against a competitor by selling at a loss may sometimes be just as critical for ensuring long-term success (to give another example).

In the development of strategic plans it is therefore helpful to distinguish among the following:

1 The profit/productivity improvement plan. This focuses mainly on refining the traditional business concept and divesting of those products or activities which are no longer viable
2 Normal business growth plan. This is the kind of development which takes place as a result of natural driving forces, such as maintaining a position within an expanding market
3 New strategic development projects, aimed at repositioning the company as a response to long-term industrial trends: for example, developing an electronic version of a previously mechanical product.

The strategic plan must integrate all of these sub-plans in order to provide the framework for different kinds of daily decisions.

A TYPICAL MULTIBUSINESS PLANNING CYCLE

The creation of a viable strategy is more the result of experience over a number of years, rather than a 'one off' analytical exercise. It is crucial to regard planning as a systematic 'learning by doing' process, which builds on the results of practical experience.

Figure 3.3 shows a typical planning cycle in a multibusiness company. The cycle begins with group management working closely with its planning staff, providing individual divisions or business units with planned guidelines and financial goals. Every individual unit then undertakes an analysis of its strategic situation and decides if and by what strategy and action plans it can reach its targeted goals. At this stage there may well be discussion and negotiation about constraints and preconditions.

Once agreement has been reached then each unit prepares its strategic plan which specifies the strategy, action plans and investment requirements necessary for its achievement, the first year of the strategic plan representing the operating plan. The different purposes of these two types of plan are reflected not only in the planning horizontal but in the levels of detail and management focus.

The strategic plan integrates the various product and functional strategies of a particular business unit and presents the projected financial results over the planned period.

Though flexibility is to be encouraged, so that plans fit the unique reality of an individual business, a typical strategic plan would cover the following areas:

1 The main problems and strategic direction of the business
2 Historical and current year financial performance
3 Sales forecast and marketing strategy
4 Production strategy, new capacity, improved technology

Figure 3.3   The strategic plan development

5   Research and development, product improvement and new product programmes
6   Summary of capital investments
7   Personnel resources, costs and development programmes for key individuals
8   Significant changes to be made in the organisation structure and the control systems
9   Specific analyses of major problems.

This kind of qualitative description and analysis is summarised in financial terms as shown in a simplified form in Figure 3.4.

This plan (and its strategies) is submitted to corporate management by the operating unit executives. Plans are typically reviewed by corporate staff prior to a corporate management review. Their assessments are forwarded both to

	line	Year 0 1981 Actual	%	Year 1 1982 Budget	%	Year 2 1983 Plan	%	Year 3 1984 Plan	%	Year 4 1985 Plan	%	Year 5 1986 Plan	%
Sales & Profit													
Net sales	1												
Gross profit on sales	2												
Total overheads	3												
Trading profit	4												
Net interest	5												
Net profit	6												
Operating Assets													
Stocks	7												
Debtors	8												
Creditors	9												
Total working capital	10												
Total fixed assets	11												
Total operating assets	12												
Borrowing													
Total borrowing	13												
Operational Cash Flow													
Tax (paid)	14												
Dividend (paid)	15												
Capital expenditure	16												
Fixed assets disposals	17												
Working capital (increase)	18												
Depreciation	19												
Operational cash flow	20												
Financing Plan													
Increase (decrease) share capital	21												
Increase (decrease) long term loans	22												
Increase (decrease) short term loans	23												
Total financing	24												
Key Ratios													
Trading profit/sales %	25												
Net profit/sales %	26												
Sales/operating assets	27												
Trading profit/operating assets	28												

Figure 3.4   Example of simplified financial quantification of a plan 1982

corporate management and business unit management. Among the bases for these assessments are:

1 Consistency with the proved strategic direction and the role of a particular business in the group portfolio
2 Balance between objective sought and resources required to make sure that in pursuing 'glamour projects' more traditional but high-profit opportunities have not been ignored
3 Relationships to plans of other operating units so as to avoid duplication of effort or non-constructive competition
4 Excellence in each functional area as measured by indicators relative to competition.

Typically, the corporate staff will write short critiques of the strengths, weaknesses or risks associated with individual plans. On the basis of these, staff inputs and the operating unit's own presentation, corporate management approves the unit's proposed business strategy, resolves any inconsistencies and re-evaluates its own targets. The outcome of this negotiation and dialogue is a commitment by business unit management to a specific strategy and clear financial results.

The consolidation of business unit plans forms an input to the creation of the group strategic and operating plan. In developing this, the total portfolio is reconsidered and, for example, group strategy will determine:

1 Which businesses have high growth potential and should receive heavy cash inputs for, for example, capacity build-up
2 Which companies have a strong position which must be maintained and whose role is to provide cash for disposal elsewhere
3 Which businesses are undergoing an intensive turn-around operation.

The process of plan implementation is then undertaken by the managers responsible.

'In control' strategic situations are generally monitored by corporate management on the basis of financial control data and key check points, possibly every three months.

'Out of control' situations require a more direct intervention from corporate management. This is typically achieved by appointing a task force team to work at the business level while corporate management actively supports the process by providing necessary resources and changing key constraints.

During the year, as operational plans are implemented, unforeseen events may occasionally occur and necessitate unplanned activities, though in most instances these will have been previously considered during the strategic review session. A detailed analysis of actual performance is undertaken annually as a prelude to the next cycle. This ensures that the company as a whole learns from experience and consistently refines its strategic thinking and behaviour. Practical experience shows that when a strategy must be developed anew because of fundamental external changes the process of business and organisational development involved will generally take three years to accomplish.

In an increasingly uncertain world corporate management commonly requests contingency analyses to test the effect of more pessimistic or optimistic assumptions on business unit plans. To facilitate both planning and operational management, computer models are widely used at many levels, though naturally these are complementary to, not a substitute for, a sound business judgement.

SUMMARY

A planning and control system for an organisation reflects the history and culture of the organisation, the style and philosophy of its management and the characteristics of the industry in which it operates. The planning process rests on a few principles which have in recent years gained wide acceptance:

1 The 'doer' is the planner. Operating unit management is responsible for developing and implementing its plans. Within any unit, planning is further decentralised to the various functional departments
2 Given this decentralisation, there must be widespread understanding at all levels of management as to individual roles and responsibilities in the planning and control processes
3 Top management must maintain a continuing focus both on the strategic plan of the individual business units and the commitment to, and control against, the operating plan
4 The plan for a multibusiness group as a whole must exploit ways of using natural interdependencies between business units and their different strategic positions to create positive group synergy
5 The degree of corporate management involvement in a particular business unit is selective, depending on whether it is 'in' or 'out of' strategic control. The annual strategic review should ensure that early warning of the need for fundamental strategy and structure changes is forthcoming early on. The longer an 'out of strategic control' situation is left, the more difficult it becomes to resolve.

FURTHER READING

Ansoff, H. I., *et al* (eds.), *From Strategic Planning to Strategic Management*, Wiley, New York, 1975
Argenti, John, *Practical Corporate Planning*, Allen and Unwin, London, 1980
Hussey, David E., *Corporate Planning: theory and practice*, Pergamon, Oxford, 1974
Jones, Harry, *Preparing Company Plans: a workbook for effective corporate planning*, Gower, Aldershot, 1974
Taylor, Bernard, and Sparkes, John R. (eds.), *Corporate Strategy and Planning*, Heinemann, London, 1977

4 Organisation development

John Woolhouse

Managing an organisation in a constantly changing environment, often against formidable national or international competition, is a task that calls for exceptional skill, judgement and resourcefulness. The purpose of this chapter is to explore some aspects of this task and to describe some of the ways in which a manager can plan and implement those changes that are essential to the proper functioning of the organisation for which he or she is responsible.

The term 'organisation development' is used in this chapter to describe a planned programme of organisational change designed to help an organisation to achieve the strategic purposes and objectives for which it was created. The concepts discussed do not apply only to the problems of changing existing organisations; they apply equally to the creation of new institutions or enterprises. In many parts of the world the creation and rapid growth of new industry, commerce, government departments and public services present serious organisational problems. There is a need, as yet too rarely understood, to apply to the design, formation and development of new organisations, the disciplines of systematic planning that are common practice in the design, construction and commissioning of buildings, plant and other physical facilities.

In discussing the relationship between strategy and organisation, Professor K. R. Andrews of the Harvard Business School sums up the theme to be developed in this chapter, as follows: 'It is at once apparent that the accomplishment of strategic purpose requires organisation. If a consciously formulated strategy is to be effective, organisational development should be planned rather than left to evolve by itself'.

Organisation development concerns not only structure, procedures or systems, but also such intangible factors as the styles of leadership, teamwork, collaboration between functions or departments, the motivation of staff, and the problems of power and influence, of co-ordination and conflict that arise in the working life of an organisation.

39

THE NEED FOR PLANNED ORGANISATION DEVELOPMENT

The need for a planned programme of organisational development will arise in many situations. Perhaps the most common are:

1 The creation of new institutions or enterprises in industry, commerce, government or the public services
2 Enabling existing organisations to adapt more readily to changes in their external environment (for example in markets, in products or services, or in the range, scale or location of their operations)
3 Where the organisation is failing to accomplish its objectives in terms of output, quality or profitability, and where the nature of the organisation is itself limiting the performance of those who work in it
4 Where the adoption of new technology, systems or methods requires corresponding changes in the organisation for their proper implementation.

Organisations vary in purpose, in constitution, in the methods and technologies which they use to achieve their purpose, and in the scope, size and location of their operations and markets. Furthermore, they exist in different economic, political and social environments, and in different cultures and subcultures.

Organisations are not merely a product of a particular technology: they are designed and directed by individuals with different values, experience and perceptions, and are, to some extent a reflection of the personality of those who direct and shape them. Each organisation is, in a sense, a social experiment which is constantly evolving and adapting in response to changes in the environment.

The structure and style of any particular organisation, at any given time in its history, are the products of a complex mixture of technology, culture, environment and personal styles, so that there is no single solution to the problem of what constitutes the best organisation in a given situation.

The management of organisational change is complex because it involves an understanding, first of organisational purpose, secondly of organisational structure, procedures and systems and thirdly of what may be described as the 'dynamics' of organisation; that is, the relationships between people and between groups, the role of leadership and teamwork, and the significance of learning and motivation in creating an understanding of the need for change, and in generating commitment to action.

The unique character of each organisation indicates that the objectives and content of any programme of organisational change will vary with the situation for which it is designed, but the theme common to all programmes is that the development of an organisation can be systematically planned and managed.

STRUCTURE, PROCESS AND STYLE

What exactly is an organisation, and how does it work?

In the space of this chapter, it is not possible to examine this extremely complex subject in depth, but it is appropriate to identify some of the elements involved.

Industrial organisations are socio-technical systems which incorporate three main subsystems:

1 The 'executive system' by which the organisation is directed and controlled
2 The 'operating system' by which it carries out work
3 A 'representative system' through which consultation and negotiation with members of the organisation is conducted.

What an organisation *is* can be described in terms of structure, procedures and systems. What it *does* can be defined as 'processes'. The *manner* in which it conducts those processes is usually called the 'style' of the organisation.

The structure of any organisation is a product of many inter-related factors including the culture of the society in which it was created, and the idiosyncracies of those who direct it. Among the factors on which the design of a new organisation should be based, or an existing organisation assessed, are:

1 The strategy or purpose which the organisation is designed to achieve
2 Legal status, accountability and sources of financing
3 The methods or technology by which the strategy is to be implemented
4 The information process and procedures for making decisions, for planning and control and for operating and resourcing
5 The geographical distribution of resources and of markets or clients
6 The scale and range of the activities and resources to be controlled.

The variety of structures that have developed, particularly in large industrial, government and military organisations is so great that it has become a subject in its own right. Simple line, staff, and functional structures have been superseded by the creation of profit centres and cost centres within organisations; by project, programme and product management groups; by various forms of matrix organisation for managing multi-skill or multi-discipline resources; by the extensive use of 'temporary' structures such as project teams, task forces and working parties.

What forms of both 'permanent' and 'temporary' structures are appropriate to any particular organisation at any particular stage in its evolution is a question requiring detailed and thorough examination of each unique situation.

The chief executive is the architect of the organisation. It is his vision of what the organisation should and could become that will generate the need for change; it is his judgement as to when change is needed and what form that change should take. He must, above all, be aware that old structures are rarely an effective way of implementing new strategies.

Organisational 'processes' are the interactions, communications, and 'transactions' between people. This 'dynamic' aspect of organisation is of special significance for all those involved in organisational change. Every organisation is in essence an interlocking set of contracts between people. These contracts determine what people will do, and how they conduct the thousands of 'transactions' such as giving and receiving information, or authorising the acquisition, deployment or disposal of resources. In effect all the members of an organisation enter into a complex set of contracts by which they relate to other members. The majority of these contracts are not legal contracts; they are informal 'psychological contracts'. They are not written down; they are frequently changed; they are determined partly by logical factors, and partly by subjective and emotional factors.

By looking at the day-to-day activities of an organisation in terms of 'contracts' regulating action and behaviour, and of 'transactions' between individuals and groups who are collaborating and communicating with each other, it is possible to gain a much clearer idea of what happens when changes are made in structure, technology, procedures or systems; the result of all such changes is that informal 'contracts' between people have to be renegotiated, not necessarily in a legal sense, but certainly in a psychological sense. Any change such as the introduction of a new piece of equipment, or of a new management information system, requires the renegotiation of the contracts which regulate what a member of the organisation does and how he or she does it.

The *manner* in which relationships and transactions between people, and between groups, between managers and subordinates, between departments, divisions and functions are conducted, is usually referred to as the 'style' of the organisation. A considerable amount of research has been conducted into organisation and leadership 'styles', and into the psychological factors which determine or influence behaviour. Some of this research is summarised in Chapter 1 under the heading 'Management theory in the post-war era', and the subject of leadership is discussed briefly later in this chapter.

THE ROLE OF THE CHIEF EXECUTIVE

With this perspective, it is possible to examine more closely the responsibility of the chief executive or general manager for organisation development, and to do so in the knowledge that it is the will to achieve, the will to survive, the will to manage and the will to work that are the sources of the energy which drive an organisation.

The chief executive and those of his colleagues who share his responsibility for the direction of an enterprise perform four basic functions. They must:

1 Define strategy
2 Specify the methods, technology and resources by which that strategy is to be achieved
3 Prepare plans and programmes
4 Create and manage an organisation through which those plans and programmes will be implemented.

Andrews describes the role of the general manager in the following terms: 'The successful implementation of strategy requires that the general manager shape to the peculiar needs of his strategy the formal structure of his organisation, its informal relationships, and the processes of motivation and control which provide incentives and measure results. He must bring about the commitment to organisational aims and policies of properly qualified individuals and groups to whom portions of the total task have been assigned. He must ensure not only that goals are clear and purposes are understood, but also that individuals are developing in terms of capacity and achievement and are reaping proper rewards in terms of compensation and personal satisfactions. Above all, he must do what he can to ensure that departmental interests, inter-departmental rivalries, and the machinery of measurement and evaluation do not deflect from organisational purpose into harmful and irrelevant activity'.

Translating these issues into specific activities is the task of the chief executive who must ensure that:

1 Key tasks and decisions are identified and defined
2 The responsibility for carrying out tasks and making decisions is assigned to individuals or groups; the authority for acquiring and allocating resources is defined
3 Procedures are established for planning, co-ordinating and controlling the activities or work programmes to be undertaken by each work group
4 Information systems for obtaining, storing, analysing and retrieving the data needed both for management and operational purposes are designed and installed
5 Activities are arranged in a programme to be completed within defined time and resource limits
6 Individuals or groups are made accountable for the achievement of objectives and their performance is evaluated against time, quality and resource standards
7 Actual performance is monitored quantitatively against programmes, estimates or budgets, and qualitatively by the judgement of managers and supervisors, or by feedback from users, customers or clients
8 Procedures for internal consultation and communications are established so that information can be transmitted and feedback obtained on any given activity and on problems encountered in carrying it out
9 Individual staff are selected, recruited, trained and assigned to particular roles, and roles are adapted to make optimum use of the skills which are available or which can be acquired
10 A system of rewards and constraints is established, and procedures are developed for negotiating change with members of the organisation or with their representatives
11 Arrangements are made to facilitate and encourage the acquisition and development of individual technical, professional and managerial skills, and for the improvement and adaptation of methods, systems and procedures.

These tasks and procedures are part of the agenda that will be considered in planning the content of any programme.

PLANNING A PROGRAMME OF ORGANISATION DEVELOPMENT

The purpose of an organisation development programme may be to create a new organisation, or to adapt an existing organisation in ways that will enable it to achieve the purposes for which it was established. In most cases the institution will seek to achieve those purposes with the minimum consumption of time, energy and resources.

Because each institution or enterprise is unique it must define *for itself* the criteria that will guide the development of its organisation. Because all institutions are subject to change these criteria will need to be redefined at intervals in response to changes in strategy, environment or technology.

Figure 4.1 illustrates some criteria that can be used in analysing the extent to which existing or proposed organisational arrangements help or hinder the achievement of purpose, and in identifying priorities for change. In practice attention and effort must be focused on a limited selection of factors which are critical to successful performance, and which the institution itself has the capacity to change. If the programme is too narrowly based it will be ineffective; if it is too ambitious it will be impossible to implement. The structure and content of each programme will vary according to the needs of the organisation concerned, but most programmes will include four main stages (see Figure 4.2).

The first stage is concerned primarily with defining, diagnosing and understanding the task to be performed or the problems to be resolved. A useful starting point for Stage 1 is a discussion in which senior managers define the present state of the organisation by seeking answers to the following questions:

1   Where are we now?
2   Where do we want to get to?
3   What are the forces helping or preventing us from getting there?
4   What do we have to change to enable us to get there?

While these questions are an apparent over-simplification, it is common experience among those engaged in organisation development that the process of analysing and questioning the 'status quo' is an essential first step in the planning of a programme.

Feedback on what is happening within the organisation may be obtained by informal discussion or by a systematic survey depending on the nature and complexity of the problem. What is important is that those aspects of the organisation which are under review – whether they be matters of procedure, relationships, attitudes to work, or to new plans or to new technology – are tested against reactions and responses of those directly involved.

Issues arising from this examination will often become a subject for much more detailed analysis of specific problems of roles, relationships or procedures, and for action planning in the second phase. This phase is usually conducted by one or more internal management teams who will often be given training in the use of appropriate analytical and planning techniques.

In the implementation phase, which may last for many months in cases of major changes in the organisation or its procedures, it is very important to obtain feedback on problems experienced in practice, and to include arrangements for making any modifications necessary to the success of the programme. Every programme is an experiment in managing change, and the implications of that statement must be understood and acted upon by everyone involved.

Figure 4.1 *Criteria for organisation development*

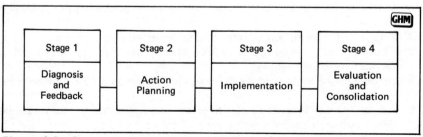

Figure 4.2 *Stages in an organisation development programme*

Evaluation should be made against realistic criteria agreed at the outset of the programme. There are several difficulties in evaluation which must be acknowledged: organisational changes may take a long time to become effective and a proper evaluation can be made only after a reasonable period of operation of new structures or procedures. Some of the most important benefits of a programme, particularly those concerned with management styles, with co-operation between teams, or with job satisfaction cannot be quantitifed and can only be assessed by collecting and analysing responses from managers and staff who have taken part.

At the end of the programme it is vital to consolidate and reinforce those changes that prove effective in practice. It is only too easy to lose the advantages of a programme by failing to ensure that successful procedures and processes become a permanent part of the organisation's ways of working.

Diagnostic methods

Because organisations exist to accomplish strategy, any organisational design or analysis must begin with a definition of strategy, and an examination of the extent to which existing structure, systems and procedures consistute a logical and effective means of implementing that strategy. It is relatively easy to conceive new ideas and new strategies. Because the time and effort needed to implement change is considerable, particularly in large organisations, there is a tendency for organisation structure and systems to 'lag' so that the enterprise is trying to tackle today's or even tomorrow's problem with yesterday's organisation. The time-lag problem can also be serious when major structural or procedural changes have been introduced because, in the absence of any action to accelerate the 'natural' rate of change, members of the organisation can (if not helped to make the adjustment) take a long time to absorb the implications of change and to modify their actions accordingly.

In a comprehensive programme a variety of analytical or diagnostic methods will need to be employed. These methods may, for example, include:

1 Examination of work roles and of co-ordination between individuals, or between departments and functions
2 Evaluation of procedures for planning, co-ordinating, allocating resources, setting performance standards, monitoring performance, output quality or cost
3 Analysis of information systems and information flows
4 Collecting and analysing feedback on operational problems, on attitudes, morale or job satisfaction
5 Assessment of leadership styles, or of the relationships within or between work groups
6 Review of rewards and incentives and of opportunities for personal development or career progression
7 Investigating internal procedures for negotiating terms and conditions of employment, or for resolving conflicts and disputes.

In programmes involving a study of work organisation it may also be necessary to use such techniques as process analysis, task analysis, activity analysis, method study or operational research to analyse work flows or procedures for planning and controlling operations in the allocation of resources. Studies of this type are best carried out by small multi-discipline teams which inlclude members with expertise in appropriate technology, in operational research and in organisation development. In specialist industries and services, teams of this type can make a powerful contribution to the development of structures, systems and procedures which are properly matched to the technological requirements of the enterprise.

Underlying all structural and procedural issues there is, in every organisation, a 'culture', and 'atmosphere', a set of values which is partly a reflection of the style of leadership within the institution itself, and partly of the society within which the institution operates. Technology is a major factor in determining structure and systems, but social and cultural factors are the main determinant of organisational style.

The most important and intangible of these factors are concerned with leadership, with motivation and with team work. All organisation development programmes centre on the role of leadership, on the use of teams as the agents of change, and on the use of learning and feedback.

STYLES OF LEADERSHIP

There is no single 'best' style of leadership, just as there is no 'test' type of organisation structure. Different situations call for different styles of leadership. One of the problems in developing an effective organisation is to develop a style that is appropriate to that organisation.

The effect of leadership style on individual performance, team work and morale can be studied by analysing feedback from people in the organisation. Feedback can be collected and analysed in many different ways ranging from informal interviews with individuals or groups to highly structured diagnostic procedures. Two of the best known diagnostic methods are the 'Managerial Grid' developed by Blake and Mouton and Rensis Likert's 'System 4'. In his work at the Michigan Institute for Social Research, Likert found evidence to suggest that the prevailing management style of an organisation could be depicted on a continuum from 'System 1' (a very authoritarian style) to 'System 4' (a style based on team work, trust and confidence). In most of the companies studied, those closest to 'System 4' were more likely to have a continuous record of high productivity. The extent to which such instruments are useful in any particular situation is a matter for judgement, but the following summary by Hersey and Blanchard of Likert's four systems illustrates some of the issues which need to be explored in a study of the leadership style.

System 1

Management is seen as having no confidence or trust in subordinates, since they are seldom involved in any aspect of the decision-making process. The bulk of the decisions and the goal setting of the organisation are made at the top and issued down the chain of command. Subordinates are forced to work with fear, threats, punishment and occasional rewards and need satisfaction at the physiological and safety levels. The little superior-subordinate interaction that does take place is usually with fear and mistrust. Although the control process is highly concentrated in top management, an informal organisation generally develops, which opposes the goals of the formal organisation.

System 2

Management is seen as having condescending confidence and trust in subordinates, such as master has toward servant. The bulk of the decisions and goal setting of the organisation are made at the top, but many decisions are made within a predescribed framework at lower levels. Rewards and some actual or potential punishment are used to motivate workers. Any superior-subordinate interaction takes place with some condescension by superiors and fear and caution by subordinates. Although the control process is still concentrated in top management, some is delegated to middle and lower levels. An informal organisation usually develops, but it does not always resist formal organisational goals.

System 3

Management is seen as having substantial but not complete confidence and trust in subordinates. Broad policy and general decisions are kept at the top, but subordinates are permitted to make more specific decisions at lower levels. Communications flow both up and down the hierarchy. Rewards, occasional punishment, and some involvement are used to motivate workers. There is a moderate amount of superior-subordinate interaction, often with a fair amount of confidence and trust. Significant aspects of the control process are delegated downward with a feeling of responsibility at both higher and lower levels. An informal organisation may develop, but it may either support or partially resist goals of the organisation.

System 4

Management is seen as having complete confidence and trust in subordinates. Decision-making is widely dispersed throughout the organisation, although well integrated. Communications flow not only up and down the hierarchy but among peers. Workers are motivated by participation and involvement in developing economic rewards, setting goals, improving methods, and appraising progress towards goals. There is extensive, friendly, superior-subordinate interaction with a high degree of confidence and trust. There is widespread responsibility for the control process, with the lower units fully involved. The informal and formal organisations are often one and the same. Thus, all social forces support efforts to achieve stated organisational goals.

TEAMS AND TEAM BUILDING

Teams are the building blocks from which organisations are constructed, the cells from which the various organs of the corporate body are assembled. An organisation development programme is a planned programme of learning and action, carried out over a considerable period of time, in which *teams*, rather than individuals, are the agents of change. In recent years valuable research has been carried out into the dynamics of group behaviour, for example at the National Training Institute in the US and at the Tavistock Institute in the UK.

Work has been carried out by these Institutes both on individual relationships within a group, described as *intra-group* relations, and on the relationships between groups, known as *inter-group* relations. The results of this research, and of experience in large industrial and military organisations, are of great practical value to managers because they provide the foundation for team building programmes which form a central part of all organisation development programmes. Advice and assistance in team building is now available from many sources and the skills needed are within the capability of most competent managers.

Team building sessions (in which diagnosis and feedback of problems at several levels in an organisation are linked together as part of an integrated programme of problem identification, feedback, analysis, planning and implementation) are a major component of all programmes designed to accelerate the development of new organisations, to facilitate the transfer of an introduction of new technology, and to improve the performance of existing organisation. They also provide one of the main instruments for coping with conflict between levels or functions within an organisation or between the organisation and external groups such as suppliers and distributors.

The methods used in any particular circumstances will differ with the objectives of the programme but all processes depend on providing the group as a whole, and its individual members, with feedback or situations with which they have to cope. The intelligent and sensitive use of feedback is fundamental to any process of organisation development. It is the experience of most researchers into organisational problems, first, that a significant proportion of problems whose causes are either not known, or are attributed to individual deficiences, are the result of organisational defects; and secondly that many of these defects can be identified by feedback from individuals and by methodical examination of the logic underlying the definition of responsibilities, procedures and information flows. The key to all change in behaviour is learning. Not theoretical learning, but learning about the facts, the myths and the conditions which are present in every human and social situation.

This type of learning process is one in which the 'agenda' is not a syllabus but a real problem: it draws on the combined knowledge and experience of members of a group, incorporates any 'external' advice that may be appropriate; and its purpose is to take action and not solely to acquire knowledge or skill. The result is that the approach makes a real contribution to the difficult task of changing perceptions, attitudes and behaviour in organisations. Different enterprises use different terms to define this process: action-learning, group-learning, achievement learning, joint development programmes, and quality circles, which have attracted so much attention in recent years, are all attempts to tap the latent energy of groups and individuals by creating opportunities for learning related to the need for action and the need for change. The management of change is a complex process; but collaborative or 'synergistic' learning is a powerful catalyst of change.

A full-scale organisation development programme is appropriate only where major organisational change needs to be managed. Team building programmes can be started, with proper preparation and instruction, by any departmental manager or project manager who wants to improve the performance of his team. A day or two spent in the early stages of team formation, given wise selection of team members, can yield rich returns in collaboration, cooperation and personal development features essential to successful project work.

CHARACTERISTICS OF A SUCCESSFUL PROGRAMME

Richard Beckhard of the Massachusetts Institute of Technology in his essay on organisation development lists eight characteristics of a successful programme:

1 It is a planned programme which involves the whole of an organisation, or of a relatively autonomous unit within an organisation
2 It is not a programme to improve managerial effectiveness in the abstract. It is designed to create organisational conditions that will directly help the institution to accomplish a specific strategy
3 The senior management of the organisation are personally committed to the goals of the programme
4 It is a long term effort, because two or three years are usually required for any significant organisational change to be planned, implemented, and its benefits realised and rewarded
5 The programme is action-oriented. In this respect an organisational development programme differs from a training programme in which the individual is left to transfer any knowledge or skill acquired, because the programme is designed from the outside to generate action by those involved
6 Particular emphasis is placed on changing perceptions, attitudes and behaviour, and not solely on structural or procedural change
7 It relies on some form of experience-based learning through which participants can examine the present situation, define new goals, and explore new ways of achieving them
8 The basis of all programmes are the groups or teams from which the organisation is constructed

CONCLUSIONS

No discussion of organisation or of organisation development can be concluded without reference to the character and quality of the people who work in it. The selection, training and development of individual managers and staff is discussed elsewhere in this book. It is sufficient here to observe that while the relationship between individual competence and organisational success is widely understood, the extent to which organisation structure and style encourages or inhibits individual growth and development is not always so clearly perceived. People create organisations; successful organisations develop capable people: capable people help to keep organisations flexible and responsive to changing needs and goals.

FURTHER READING

Beckhard, R., *Organisational Development: Strategies and Models*, Addison-Wesley, Reading, Mass, 1969

Bennis, E. G., *Organisation Development: Its Nature, Origins and Prospects*, Addison-Wesley, Reading, Mass, 1969

Blake, R. R. and Mouton, J. S., *Building a Dynamic Corporation through Grid Organisation Development*. Reading, Mass: Addison-Wesley, 1969

Bower, M., *The Will to Manage*, McGraw-Hill, New York, 1966

Burns, J. and Stalker, G. M., *The Management of Innovation*, Tavistock Publications, London, 1961

Hersey, P. and Blanchard, K. H., *Management of Organisational Behaviour*, Prentice-Hall, Englewood Cliffs, NJ, 3rd edition, 1977

Jaques, E., *Work, Creativity and Social Justice*, Heinemann, London, 1970

Katz, D. and Kahn, R. I., *The Social Psychology of Organisations*, Wiley, New York, 1965

Lawrence, P. R. and Lorsch, J. W., *Developing Organisations: Diagnosis and Action*, Addison-Wesley, Reading, Mass, 1969

Learned, E. P., Christensen, C. R., Andrews, K. R. and Guth, W. D., *Business Policy*, Irwin, Homewood, 1969

Mant, A., *The Experienced Manager: A Major Resource*, British Institute of Management, London, 1969

Parker, H., Bower, M., Smith, E. E. and Morrison, J. R., *Effective Boardroom Management*, McKinsey & Co. Inc., and British Institute of Management, London, 1971

Schein, E. H., *Process Consultation: Its Role in Organisation Development*, Addison-Wesley, Reading, Mass, 1969

Sofer, C., *The Organisation from Within*, Tavistock Publication, London, 1961

Sutermeister, R. A., *People and Productivity*, McGraw-Hill, New York, 1969

Tannehill, R. E., 'The Management of Technological Change', *Manufacturing Engineering and Management*, 1971

Tannehill, R. E., *Motivation and Management Development*, Butterworth, London, 1970

Walton, R. E., *Interpersonal Peacemaking: Confrontations and Third-party Consultation*, Addison-Wesley, Reading, Mass, 1969

5 Corporate relations

Norman Hart

The need for a planned programme of corporate relations stems not from some new management concept but from the fact that organisations are realising sometimes to their dismay, the need for a formalised corporate strategy. This has been dealt with earlier in the book but, simply stated, it is no longer good enough to take random actions for long-term effects: rather it is necessary to give mature consideration to future objectives and the means of achieving them. Such objectives will incorporate financial investment, labour force and staffing, marketing aspects, production, research and development and of course profit. This is no more than a move from past practices, in which future events were just allowed to take their natural course, to a position in which a company sets out deliberately to move to a predetermined position. The weakness of any attempt at corporate planning is that unforeseeable events are bound to cause the objectives to be changed, but this is no reason for not taking action to influence the course of events so as to hit the desired target as closely as possible. Corporate relations is but one of the management functions which can be used to help achieve this goal.

The need for corporate goals and for a strategy to achieve them stems from a growing number of influences, external and internal, which if ignored may well undermine the profitable development of a company and indeed threaten its very existence. The increasing tendency by governments to impose controls is a major factor as are international regulations at one extreme and a vigorous consumerist movement at the other. Thus trade barriers and constraints, scarcity of raw materials, inflation and high taxation are factors which now play a larger part in the development of business. Equally the growing interest by employees and trade unions with their sometimes massive influence must be taken into consideration in any future planning.

This chapter will examine corporate relations from the point of view of *what* they are, *why* they are necessary, to *whom* they should be addressed, *when,* and *how.* Finally, it will consider the all important question of the results that might reasonably be expected of such an activity.

First, *what*. Corporate relations is a term used to signify the deliberate attempt by an organisation to maintain the best possible relations with each and every identifiable group of people whose interests and activities might be supposed to have an effect, for good or ill, on the prosperity and progress of the business. Such an operation is linked with communications in both directions since without communications of some kind it is difficult to see how any change or impact can be achieved. It is important at the outset to realise two things. First, that no matter how efficient any corporate communications system may be, it will be of no avail unless the object of the communication is sound. In just the same way no amount of advertising will ever sell an unsatisfactory product. The second point to be made is that every single source of communications must be considered for possible use, not just the classical PR media such as press releases, factory visits, booklets and special events.

What then are corporate communications? A good example was given in a report by *The Financial Times*, as summarised in Figure 5.1. The list is not, and was not intended to be, comprehensive. It misses for instance the communications element of the product, its packaging and branding, as well as the place from which it is distributed. It does not touch on the vital role of

Public	Example of communication GHM
Consumer	media advertising
	press release
Supplier	trade exhibitions
Employees	house journal
Trades Unions	statement of company policy
Competitors	public lectures
Local residents	local radio information
Trade association	journal article
Technical groups	technical journal articles
Shareholders	annual reports
Financial community	financial press release
Government	co-operation with CSO
Distributors	promotion literature
Universities	scientific information
Other pressure groups	local community action

Figure 5.1   The company public and an example of a typical outward communication for each component of that public (The Financial Times)

employees, from people answering the phone and writing letters, to salesmen meeting customers. Then there is the appearance of the factory, the livery, the letterheading: the list is endless. Corporate relations then is the building-up of a good *reputation* with a company's many and varied publics. An old-fashioned term sums it up very well – *goodwill*.

Clearly the kind of activity being described is going to cost money. Hence the need to ask *why*? The fact is that all companies have an image whether they like it or not, or even if they are totally unaware of it. A company is perceived by people in a variety of ways, depending upon the messages, conscious or unconscious, they have received about it. And the perception varies from one public to another. Customers may view a supplier as a thoroughly reliable and trustworthy organisation with which to do business, whereas its employees may take the very opposite view. The reason why corporate relations is important then is that it is only when relationships are positive and sound that the most effective and efficient business can be conducted. For example, is it reasonable to expect the best possible applicants for a job with a company which has a very poor reputation as an employer? It may be argued that in such a case the solution is to change the conditions of employment so that they are really attractive, but this is overlooking the essential ingredient of corporate communications for if people are unaware of a situation they cannot react to it. And if, as often happens, they are misinformed about it the opposite result to what was intended may be the outcome. The reason why corporate communications, for it people are unaware of a situation they cannot react to it. messages about itself from all the interested publics, and on the other hand it is sending out messages to those same people to ensure that they are fully informed, that they understand and that they are convinced. The reason why, then, is in order to establish and maintain a series of relationships in which business can be conducted most efficiently.

To *whom* is corporate relations meant to apply? Once again a simplified diagram taken from *The Financial Times* shows the answer (Figure 5.2). In addition, of course, each individual company will have a number of specialist groups whose goodwill it is vital to maintain. These might be termed 'special interest groups' such as Women's Institutes, teachers, consumerists, youth movements and even, say, cycling clubs, bird-watchers and farmers.

The *when* of corporate relations can be dealt with simply. A reputation is with a company all its life. It is no use having a corporate relations function and a corporate communication programme for a couple of years and then closing it down. People's memories and attitudes are dynamic and will change over time. A company must decide whether or not it is really serious in the matter of building its reputation. If it is, and it wishes to maintain it, this can be achieved in one way only, and that is by a continuous programme of activities. It is as well also to bear in mind that achieving any major change may take years rather than months, so advance planning is required as well as continuity.

Turning now to *how* corporate relations is to be implemented. First, it is necessary to draw up plans, both strategic and tactical, to set objectives, to measure results, to co-ordinate all related and parallel activities, and to ensure than an adequate administration and professional facility exists to ensure proper execution.

STRATEGIC PLANNING

The key to successful strategic planning for good corporate relations is in the

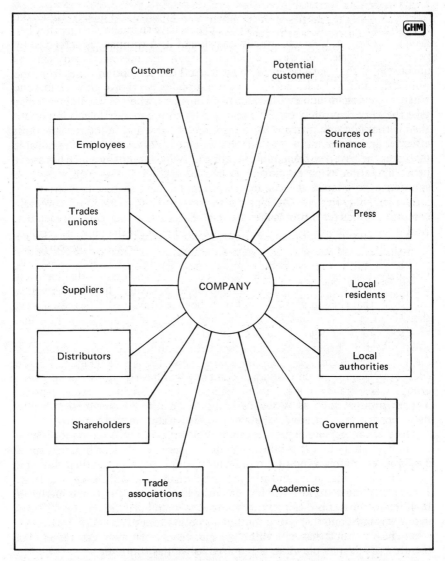

Figure 5.2 **The company as a corporate citizen and its communication links**
(The Financial Times)

setting of comprehensive objectives. Two examples have been chosen to illustrate this point. First, a major multinational corporation which listed five aims:

1 To increase the share of people's minds available to the company

2 To engender favourable attention and acceptability from its diverse publics
3 To explain the realities of the company's social and economic contributions to the countries where it does business
4 To state the case for business in general and for multinational corporations in particular
5 To correct some of the myths and refute irresponsible allegations.

The programme which evolved consisted of a package of five interdependent activities, each mutually supporting, making its own unique contribution, but working to the same plan and objectives. The elements of the package were an advertising campaign, a public information brochure, an external house magazine, a press relations programme and the establishment of a speaker's panel. The complete programme was based on a publicly stated philosophy of openness, frankness and fact.

The second example is that of a well-known company in the high technology business. The programme had five objectives:

1 To extend the company's corporate identity and to enhance/improve attitudes held towards the company among the defined target audiences
2 To establish and promote the company as a leader and innovator in advanced technology
3 To promote the company's capabilities and achievements in selected areas of advanced technology
4 To create high level awareness and knowledge among target groups in prospective market areas for the technological excellence of its products
5 To create a favourable attitude among target groups so that divisional marketing activities for particular products or systems could be carried out more effectively.

The main thrust of the campaign to achieve these aims was a very adventurous press campaign of large advertisments in the colour supplements, backed by supportive advertising in 'management newspapers' and the specialist press.

TACTICAL PLANNING

It is not sufficient to produce one big homogeneous campaign and leave it at that; it is also necessary to examine each and every other sector of communications with its own specialised objectives, audiences, messages and media in order to ensure that these also contribute to the common objective of the company's reputation. In this way marketing communications, employee communications, a safety campaign, city and financial news, and all the rest add together to make up a synergistic whole. It can be seen that organisationally there is a need for the provision of top management direction to ensure the proper orchestration of all the many parts which are being conducted on a day-to-day basis.

The second part of tactical operations relates to what might be termed 'reactive activities'. This is the response to events which, if not handled properly, can work against the corporate objectives, or alternatively fail to give the potential support which might otherwise be achieved. Examples might be an industrial dispute where bad handling can undo much of the goodwill which may have been built up over a period of years. Equally, but in the opposite direction, failure to exploit fully the securing of a major overseas contract is a loss in terms of the very favourable light in which such an achievement can be shown to the target groups which together make up the corporate public.

Such contingencies cannot by their very nature be incorporated in any plan, but the organisation must be sufficiently flexible to be able to react quickly to each of them and to have in mind not just the event itself and how to deal with or exploit it, but also the overall objectives.

CORPORATE RESEARCH

Early in the growth of the marketing concept and of corporate planning, communications activities were characterised by 'prestige advertising' and by a narrow form of public relations which relied mainly on what was loosely termed 'press relations'. It was unusual to have specific goals, and large sums of money were spent in putting out almost self-congratulatory messages about the company without much regard to the interest of the audiences or indeed what the effect on them might be. Companies indulging in these activities became sceptical of their value and as economic conditions became tougher interest in buying prestige declined.

The growth of corporate affairs as a function, and corporate relations as an activity has been accompanied by the precise setting of objectives in quantified form, and by a programme of research to ensure that any investment was achieving results. Businessmen have begun to demand that expenditure in this area should be accountable and the effects measurable.

The starting point of any properly constructed programme of corporate communications is to make benchmark measurements against which progress can be compared as the campaign proceeds. It is no use making such measurements at the end of a campaign as by that time it is too late to take any corrective action. A company might decide that it wishes to increase the level of awareness amongst certain discrete publics and at the same time gain an improved attitude towards itself and its products. Sample groups from each segment must be chosen and an assessment made of their current level of awareness and the nature of their attitudes. Only with this information can an effective plan be drawn up. From this a budget is set with the task of moving from a perceived level A to a targeted level B in a given period of time. Using the same audience segments, methods of sampling and questioning techniques, research must be planned at intermediate stages to find out whether the results are on schedule, in advance of it or behind it. Variations can be made at this stage to bring the campaign back on course; changes may be in the direction of the campaign, or it may be necessary to increase expenditure, or for that matter cut it back. So the operation breaks down into four stages – set objectives, quantify, research, verify.

ORGANISING FOR CORPORATE RELATIONS

If corporate relations is not recognised as a top management function it stands little chance of success. If there is not to be a corporate affairs director, at least the executive responsible must have direct access to the chief executive and the top-level strategic thinking which is going on at that level. The person concerned needs professional communications expertise across all channels of persuasion and information, but more than that he must have the perspective of an all-round business man equally at home with financial matters as with technical, personnel and marketing.

Depending on the size of the company he may require a small staff, but increasingly there is a reluctance to add what almost amounts to a fixed overhead, and the alternative of outside services is looked upon with greater favour. It is said that outside consultants find it difficult to relate closely to the company and its inside and outside complexities. This may be so and is one of the reasons for having at least one really good staff man. On the other hand, the body of knowledge and expertise in corporate activities, particularly in effective communications, is limited and in all probability will not be found among more than a handful of consultants. The position is further complicated by the fact that many corporate campaigns have been devised and executed by advertising agencies, and so the acquired cumulative experience is shared between two professional groups of practitioners. There are signs that a new breed of total communications agencies will emerge which will set out to provide counselling at a corporate level and then follow on with a full range of services on an *à la carte* basis so that a client company can select which executive activities he will take upon himself, and which he will leave in the hands of the outside service. This combination, all under one strategic plan, facilitates the use of the respective strengths of both the consultant and the client, is highly flexible, professionally more effective, and arguably cheaper.

BENEFITS

A well constructed and properly funded corporate relations programme can lead to many benefits of which the following are but a few of the more obvious examples.

1 Increased market reputation and market share
2 Happier and more satisfied employees
3 Rise in share price
4 Greater productivity
5 Favourable government support
6 Better quality applicants for jobs
7 Improved treatment from suppliers
8 Better understanding by, and less criticism from, outside pressure groups.

While benefits will accrue to any company as a result of a planned corporate relations effort the chances are that the larger the organisation, the greater the need for a formalised corporate policy. This applies to an even greater extent where the products concerned fall into the category known as 'undifferentiated'. With little to choose between one brand and another (for example with petrol, oil, banks, cigarettes, detergents) what are the real determinants of a purchasing decision? There is a good deal of evidence to suggest that the customer will prefer the brand or name he knows best and for which he has the greatest regard. Where products are intrinsically the same, the most important factor must become that undefinable property which lies behind the product – its reputation.

THE FUTURE

There can be little doubt that corporate relations as a new management function is here to stay. Increasingly corporations are having to accept a social responsibility and, what is more important, to be seen to accept it. Customers, employees, shareholders and all the other interested public groups wish to be better informed and to feel comfortable in the knowledge that they are not being unfairly exploited by faceless, impersonal organisations whose sole purpose is to make as much profit as they can, regardless of the feelings or sensitivites of others.

One portent of future growth is to be found by looking at the United States where there are many indicators of the firm foundation and significant benefits of corporate relations. Other industrialised countries have a long way to go in comparison, but it would be surprising if corporate relations did not become a way of business in most of them during the next decade.

FURTHER READING

Markham, Vic, *Planning the Corporate Reputation*, Allen & Unwin, London, 1972

Moore, G. S., *Managing Corporate Relations: a practical guide to business survival*, Gower, Aldershot, 1980

Olins, W., *The Corporate Personality: an inquiry into the nature of corporate identity*, Design Council, London, 1978

Watts, R., *Public Relations for Top Management*, Croner Publications, New Malden, Surrey, 1977

PART TWO

FINANCIAL MANAGEMENT

6 Sources of finance

Stephen Badger

In theory three sources of wealth are available to a company – land, labour and capital. These are not wholly interchangeable, but to some extent the balance in any given company can be changed by the entrepreneur; land can be turned into capital by sale and leaseback (see Long-term facilities, below) or a given process can be made more capital-intensive and so generally require less labour (or vice versa). These decisions are within the scope of management, one of whose functions is to optimise the balance between the different factors of production. The first step before raising capital is therefore to ensure that it is really financial capital that is required.

WHY CAPITAL MAY BE REQUIRED

Capital is required to finance the conduct of the business. When a manufacturing business is first established, for instance, factory and office premises will be needed and plant and machinery and transport vehicles. These can either be bought outright or hired; in the first case the expenditure represents capital permanently invested in the business (for the second, see Medium-term facilities, below). In addition funds will be required to finance production from the initial purchase of raw materials until the sale of the finished product to an external purchaser, to pay wages and to meet overheads: these funds are known as working or revolving capital. As the business expands, fresh injections of both permanent and working capital will be required. If on the contrary it contracts (or is merely run more efficiently) capital will be freed for alternative uses. When the original fixed assets need replacing, more expenditure will be needed. This should have been adequately provided out of profits by depreciation provisions over the life of the assets, but in times of inflation there may well be a shortfall which will need an injection of new capital.

Capital may also be required for acquisitions.

TYPE OF CAPITAL REQUIRED

Capital is conventionally described as short-term, medium-term or long-term. The distinctions are not rigid, but short-term capital may be regarded as any liability repayable within one year; medium-term as being repayable between one and ten years in the future; and everything else as being long-term capital (this covers both the proprietors' ordinary risk capital, or equity, and long-term borrowings, or debt capital). In general, working capital requirements should be financed by short-term capital and capital permanently invested in the business should be long-term. Medium-term capital is useful to give added flexibility and balance to the overall financial structure: if a project is expected to generate sufficient cash flow to repay the initial investment within, say, seven years, medium-term financing may be appropriate.

This chapter deals primarily with sources of long-term finance (both debt and equity) but sources of short- and medium-term finance are considered in outline.

SOURCES OF LONG-TERM FINANCE FOR UNLISTED COMPANIES

The types of finance availabe to a company that is not listed on a stock exchange are much the same as those for one that is. The difference in the two situations is that the unlisted company is restricted to a much narrower range of sources, since many potential lenders or shareholders will be unwilling to put up funds if their investment is unlisted and so not marketable. In addition, if the company is private in the legal sense it is not permitted to make any invitation to the public to subscribe for shares or debentures.

In the first place an unlisted company will rely on the permanent capital put up by its promoter and his friends and relations, supplemented by bank borrowings. But in due course, if the company expands faster than retained earnings by themselves allow, there will come a time when these individuals are unable to find all the funds required; or they may wish to realise part of their investment. If the company has not yet reached a stage where a public flotation is appropriate, it should be possible to find one or more institutions to put up more capital (consisting either of ordinary shares or a mixture of ordinary and loan capital) on the basis that a flotation will take place within a few years so that the institutions will then be able to realise their investment if they wish. This type of investment is referred to as venture capital and there are a number of specialist institutions providing this kind of finance, such as Industrial and Commerical Finance Corporation, a subsidiary of Finance for Industry which is owned by the Bank of England and the clearing banks. The merchant banks are also active in this field, and insurance companies, pension funds and investment trusts may participate in a placing if the company is large enough.

In recent years considerable attention has been focused on the financial needs of the smaller company and this has led to the proliferation of bodies prepared to make money available. These include a number of consortia specially set up by banks and investment institutions. There has also been increasing interest in arrangements to effect greater marketability without a formal listing, such as the over-the-counter market sponsored by M. J. H. Nightingale and the Unlisted Securities Market instituted by the Stock Exchange.

GOING PUBLIC

Obtaining a listing on the Stock Exchange is a most important step in any company's development. But at the end of 1979 there were a total of more than 677 000 companies registered in the UK of which about 660 000 were private companies (in the legal sense) and only 3000 were listed on the Stock Exchange, including nearly 400 overseas companies. Many companies will therefore never reach a stage at which a listing is appropriate, or their proprietors may for various reasons not wish to seek a listing; taking in new shareholders provides an additional source of capital but at the same time involves added responsibilities towards those shareholders typified by the Stock Exchange's requirements on disclosure. The interests of 'outside' shareholders may at times differ from those of 'family' shareholders and the future management of the company must reflect the new spread of interests represented.

The reasons for going public are usually among the following:

1 To make the shares marketable and hence more valuable
2 To diversify the family investment and so to reduce the degree of risk
3 To provide funds to meet capital transfer tax liabilities when necessary
4 To make acquisitions of other companies for shares practicable
5 To raise new funds once the resources of the existing shareholders cease to be adequate.

This chapter is concerned with the last of these, but it is important to realise that going public does not necessarily involve raising money for the company – the shares sold to the public are often existing shares being sold on behalf of existing shareholders.

Where money is being raised for the company the procedure is normally to use an offer for sale made by a merchant bank or a firm of issuing brokers. The offer will be underwritten so that the money will be available even if sufficient public subscriptions are not forthcoming. But it is most important for the company's future capital-raising ability that the issue should be successful, which means that it should be fully subscribed, that the shares should open at a premium and that a free after-market should be maintained. To achieve this it is essential that the company should have the continuity of good management and attractive prospects and that large shareholders should not continue selling frequent blocks of shares once the offer for sale is complete. The amount of money that can be raised initially will depend primarily on the present and future profit levels of the company and hence on its ability to pay reasonable dividends on the increased capital. The Stock Exchange will not grant a listing unless the company as a whole is expected to have a market value of at least £500 000 (which probably involves after-tax profits of at least £75 000), but in practice it is probably not worth a company going public until it is several times this size since the amount of money raised will otherwise be relatively small, the proportion of it consumed by the expenses of the issue will be unduly high and an adequate after-market is unlikely to result. To cater for companies which want marketability for their shares without a full listing, the Stock Exchange has recently instituted the United Securities Market.

SOURCES OF LONG-TERM FINANCE FOR LISTED COMPANIES

Once a company has taken the important step of going public it can seek to raise funds from the whole range of investors, both private and institutional, without restriction.

In recent years private investors have tended to an increasing extent to channel their saving through life assurance policies, pension schemes and unit trust purchases rather than making direct investments in securities themselves. Figure 6.1 illustrates this by showing, for recent years, selected uses of funds by the personal sector and by financial institutions (other than the banking sector). This shows that there has been a steady net divestment of corporate securities by individuals, whereas financial institutions have been substantial net purchasers. They have also increased their rate of investment in property significantly. Any company wishing to raise funds therefore has to try to issue the sort of security that will appeal to this type of investor – primarily insurance companies, pension funds and unit and investment trusts.

Figure 6.2 shows some of the ways in which companies have in fact raised finance over the same period. It can be seen from this that bank lending plays a very important role, since banks are the first (and often the cheapest) source of finance to which all companies turn. Even more important in the overall picture are internally generated funds: the figures in Figure 6.2 must be viewed in the perspective of a total figure for undistributed income (before providing for depreciation or stock appreciation) of £14 824 million in 1980.

Types of security

The types of security usually issued are the following:

1   Ordinary shares
2   Preference shares
3   Debentures, secured either by a floating charge or a specific mortgage
4   Unsecured loan stocks
5   Unsecured loan stocks with conversion rights or warrant attached
6   Foreign-currency bonds

Ordinary shares

Ordinary shares represent the equity or risk capital in a business. They entitle their holders to a share of the profits by way of dividend only to the extent that the directors think fit. Thus if the business prospers its ordinary shares may become very valuable but if it declines they may become valueless. Ordinary

YEAR	PERSONAL USES OF FUND		USES OF FUNDS BY FINANCIAL INSTITUTIONS		
	Investment in company securities	Life assurance and super-annuation funds	Corporate loan capital	Ordinary shares	Land, property and ground rents
1971	-1213	2004	214	937	333
1972	- 997	2455	237	1843	323
1973	-1872	3354	111	544	664
1974	-1041	3493	-10	-283	788
1975	- 897	4450	57	1552	817
1976	-1511	5568	7	1135	1111
1977	-1817	6138	-117	1815	1084
1978	-1152	7333	-33	1430	1313
1979	-2105	9320	-68	1825	1328
1980	-2026	10688	-31	2017	1909

Figure 6.1 Uses of funds by individuals and institutions (CSO Financial Statistics)

YEAR	BANK BORROWING	OTHER LOANS AND MORTGAGES	UK CORPORATE ISSUES		ISSUES OVERSEAS
			Ordinary Shares	Fixed Interest (net)	
1971	732	286	152	215	75
1972	2988	139	317	289	119
1973	4504	875	143	51	113
1974	4411	245	126	-56	20
1975	482	491	1003	202	-9
1976	2398	439	785	42	6
1977	2966	38	730	-67	102
1978	2890	386	829	-71	-32
1979	4903	616	906	-22	-15
1980	6640	667	897	423	5

Figure 6.2   Selected sources of capital funds for industrial and commercial companies (CSO Financial Statistics)

shareholders are also usually entitled to control the company's activities by voting at general meetings.

Preference shares

Preference shares carry the right to receive a fixed dividend in every year that the company makes a sufficient profit, but to no further participation unless they are specifically participating preference shares. They may in some cases be redeemable at a fixed future time or at the company's option and they can also be issued on the basis that they are convertible in a specified ratio into ordinary shares of the company, but they will normally only carry full voting rights in special circumstances. Preference shares became relatively unpopular after the tax changes introduced by the Finance Act 1965 but more recently they have been used as a way of increasing the capital base without diluting the interests of ordinary shareholders.

Debentures and loan stocks

The other types of capital are generically referred to as loan capital, which may be either secured or unsecured. It can be seen from Figure 6.2 that the use of these instruments has declined substantially in recent years.

A debenture, according to s455 of the Companies Act 1948, includes debenture stock, bonds and any other securities of a company whether constituting a charge on the assets of the company or not; but in stock exchange parlance the expression debenture normally means a secured stock while unsecured loan stock is used to refer to a stock which is not secured. This is the terminology used here.

Unlike shareholders, holders of a debenture or unsecured loan stock are not members of a company, simply its creditors. They are therefore entitled merely to receive the agreed rate of interest (which is normally paid semi-annually) and to receive repayment of capital on final maturity. Their rights will be incorporated in the trust deed constituting the stock which will be made between the company and (usually) a trustee on behalf of the stockholders. It is a requirement of the Stock Exchange that there must be such a trustee if the stock is to be listed; the trustee will normally be one of the insurance companies or investment trusts which specialise in this type of work.

Investors in fixed-interest stocks have historically required a long life to final maturity. In fact most stocks issued in the London market have a term of twenty to twenty-five years, although some medium-term issues have been seen. There is usually a period of five years before final maturity when the company can repay the stock without penalty and the average life of the stock may be reduced by the operation of a sinking fund. Since the creditworthiness of a company, and even the nature of its business, can change materially over an interval of this length the trust deed constituting the stock will impose certain restrictions on the company. These will vary from case to case, but they may include limitations on such things as disposing of more than a certain proportion of the business, changing the nature of the business and giving security. An unsecured loan stock deed will also probably contain a permanent limit on the overall borrowings of the company and its subsidiaries and a separate limit on secured borrowings and the borrowings of UK subsidiaries. A debenture deed will not impose a continuing limit but will require the presence of a certain level of cover in terms both of income and of assets before any further issue of another tranche of the stock can be made. In general, debenture stock holders, since their claims are supported by security, will require rather less in terms of restrictions than the holders of an unsecured loan stock who merely rank alongside trade and other unsecured creditors. But in either case the trustee will have the power to declare the stock immediately repayable if interest is not paid or if the company defaults on certain other obligations.

Convertible and warrant stocks

These are a compromise between borrowing and equity. A convertible is an unsecured loan stock which initially merely carried a fixed rate of interest but which, on specified dates or within a specified period, may be converted, at the option of the holder, into ordinary shares of the company at a fixed ratio. Warrant stocks are stocks which are not convertible but which are issued together with warrants which entitle the holder to subscribe for ordinary shares of the company at specified times and at a specified price. Convertible stocks have been popular for a long time, but warrant stocks have never really become familiar in the UK.

The advantage to a company of issuing convertible stock is that for the initial period it can service the stock at a lower rate of interest than would be necessary for a stock that was not convertible, that when it is finally converted the effective price of issuing the resultant shares will be higher than it could have been initially, and that in the interval the interest payments (unlike ordinary dividends) will have been an allowable expense for tax purposes. A warrant stock gives the company a long-term borrowing (at a lower rate of interest than a simple borrowing), and when the warrants are exercised there is a further inflow of cash into the company. Both kinds of stock will impose the same sort of restriction on the company as an ordinary unsecured loan stock with additional provisions to protect the holders' rights to convert or exercise their warrant rights.

Foreign-currency bond

Only the very largest companies will want long-term loans in foreign currencies. In the great majority of cases, the UK market will be amply sufficient as a source of capital and in general it is unwise to incur a foreign-currency liability unless one has corresponding assets in that currency. Moreover only the largest companies would be well enough known to attract the interest of foreign lenders. However, in the 1960s a substantial international capital market developed in eurodollars (US dollars deposited outside the USA, but not necessarily in Europe, and so not subject to any national restrictions on capital flows). A large number of US, and a smaller number of European companies have taken advantage of this to raise the quoted eurodollar loans (both fixed interest and convertible) and there have also been issues in Deutschemarks, French and Swiss francs, eurosterling and artificial units such as the European unit of account. Unlike domestic issues, eurobond issues usually have a life to final maturity of not more than fifteen – and in some cases as little as five – years. With the abolition of exchange control in the UK the dividing line between the domestic and Euro issues in sterling has become blurred.

METHODS OF ISSUE WITH A LISTING

The four chief methods of making an issue for cash on the Stock Exchange are:

1 Offer for sale
2 Rights issue
3 Open offer
4 Placing

Offer for sale

In this case all members of the public are invited to subscribe for the issue by advertisments inserted in the press. The offer is usually made at a fixed price. Sometimes an offer for sale by tender is used where only a minimum price is fixed and applicants themselves decide how much they are willing to pay; a striking price is then fixed at a level at which the issues will be fully subscribed and the shares fixed at that price to all applicants who applied at that price or above. In either case, only a fixed number of shares are available for issue and, if a greater number of applications are received, each applicant is scaled down proportionately. Priority is sometimes given to existing shareholders or employees who are sent special application forms.

An offer for sale is normally used when a company goes public for the first time, as described earlier. It may also be used in an issue of loan capital where the amount of capital required is very large or where it is necessary to appeal to a particularly wide circle of investors for some other reason. In most cases, however, a placing is preferred because of its speed and simplicity (see overleaf). By comparison an offer for sale involves significantly larger advertising and administrative costs.

Rights issue

In a rights issue new ordinary shares or other securities are offered to existing shareholders of the company *pro rata* to their holdings. Shareholders can then choose between taking up their entitlement (their rights) by subscribing the set amount per share, or they can sell some or all of their rights in the market if these are quoted at a premium. If they choose to sell they of course receive money rather than paying it out, but their percentage holding in the company is reduced so that in theory the effect is the same as if they had sold some of their existing shares. From the company's point of view the subscription money will still be received from the purchaser of the rights.

It is a requirement of a listing on the Stock Exchange that new equity shares (or other securities involving an element of equity) should only be issued for cash to existing shareholders of the company in proportion to their holdings (unless they consent otherwise in general meeting), and this has now been given wider application by the Companies Act 1980. As a result, issues of ordinary shares or convertible stocks are normally made by way of rights so that shareholders have the opportunity of maintaining their proportionate stake in the company.

Open offer

An open offer is an offer of loan capital restricted to shareholders (and possibly the holders of loan capital) of the company making the issue. However, the offer is not made *pro rata* to their holdings. Each shareholder can apply for as much stock as he wishes or for none; if more applications are received than stock is being issued, each application will be scaled down proportionately. This method of issue is relatively infrequent, but it may be used if it is thought that the stock being issued may attract a large premium and the benefit of this should accrue to shareholders. It is appropriate only where the company has a large number of shareholders, but in that case the effect is very similar to an offer for sale but without the attendant advertising costs.

Placing

In a placing, stock is offered direct to a relatively small number of large institutional investors who are the principle holders of fixed interest stock; it is therefore a quick and effective method of issue which allows the most precise pricing. Placing for an unlisted company was considered under Sources of Long-term Finance. Stock Exchange permission must be obtained for a placing with a listing and it is a condition of such permission that a proportion of the stock should be available publicly in the market. As already noted, a placing of new equity issued for cash is only possible with shareholders' consent but, because of its simplicity, placing has become the most usual method of raising loan capital for UK companies.

Underwriting and expenses of an issue

Once a company has decided that it needs money, it will clearly wish to be assured of that money as soon as possible, come what may. Rather than making an issue itself it will therefore go to a merchant bank or issuing broker who, in addition to advising on the documentation and terms of the issue, will arrange for it to be underwritten; that is, the issuing house will undertake to subscribe or find subscribers for the issue on the terms fixed in so far as it is not fully subscribed by the public or shareholders as the case may be. In return for accepting this risk and for its overall co-ordinating work on the issue, the issuing house normally charges a total commission of 2 per cent, $1\frac{1}{4}$ per cent of which is passed on to the subunderwriters, that is the institutions who agree to take up different amounts of the issue *pro rata* to the extent that it is not fully subscribed. In the case of a placing, however, the stock is placed directly with a number of the same institutions. Accordingly, no subunderwriting commission is required and only a placing commission of perhaps ¾ per cent (varying with the size of the issue) is payable; however, the issue terms will be slightly worse so that the net proceeds receivable by the company will be much the same. The other major expense of an issue of share capital duty levied at a rate of 1 per cent on the value of the shares being issued. Duty is no longer payable on the issue of loan capital but, in the case of a convertible stock, capital duty arises on conversion. By comparison the administrative costs of an issue, especially in a placing, are small.

OTHER METHODS OF SUPPLEMENTING CASH FLOW

The main methods of raising long-term capital with a listing have now been outlined. It remains to consider briefly the various other possible methods of supplementing cash flow, which are of course open to quoted and unquoted companies alike. Some of these can provide relatively long-term finance, but the majority are short-term.

Long-term facilities

These include mortgages, sale and leaseback transactions and public authority and specialist institution lending. The main sources of mortgage and sale and leaseback finance are the insurance companies and pension funds. In the case of a mortgage loan, a single lender will advance up to two-thirds of the value of a building for a specified term on the specific security of that building – the borrower retains the ownership of the building but his rights are subject to a mortgage charge for the term of the loan. In a sale and leaseback transaction he will actually sell the building (and so forfeit any appreciation in value) in return for a capital sum and at the same time lease the building back for his own use from the purchasing institution for a long period at a specified rent. Other sources of relatively long-term facilities include the Department of Industry (for specified purposes in development areas and in accordance with such schemes as may be in effect from time to time), local authorities where employment is being created in their areas, and various specialist semi-official organisations such as Finance for Industry, Agricultural Mortgage Corporation, Commonwealth Development Finance Company and National Research Development Corporation, all of which exist to lend for certain purposes. Similarly, Equity Capital for Industry has been formed as a vehicle through which insurance companies and other institutions can subscribe new share capital in certain circumstances.

Medium-term facilities

These include leasing, hire-purchase, project finance and term loans.

Leasing and hire-purchase are most appropriate for items such as vehicles, plant, machinery and office equipment. In leasing, the ownership of the item remains with the lessor, but the lessee is entitled to the use of it for a specified term in return for regular payments under the lease. This is not strictly a borrowing at all and it is often referred to as off-balance-sheet finance since it need not as yet be shown on the face of the company's balance sheet. A tax-based lease may also be particularly attractive to a company with no immediate liability to taxation. In a hire-purchase transaction the purchase price of the item and interest thereon is paid in instalments over a set period, at the end of which ownership of the item does pass to the hirer. There are a large number of finance houses which specialise in these activities.

Similarly, merchant and other banks may undertake to arrange finance for a specific project. This will involve tapping a number of different sources of finance in accordance with the cash flow requirements of the individual project and is a particularly flexible form of financing.

Finally, banks sometimes engage in term lending for periods up to five or even ten years. A term loan could come from a single bank or it might be syndicated among a number of different banks. It might be at a fixed rate of interest but it will more usually be on a roll-over basis; that is, with interest fixed periodically at the prevailing rate. In the latter case it is also possible to arrange for drawings to be made in different currencies at different times.

Export finance

Particularly to assist exporters in financing their contracts with overseas buyers the UK Government, in common with other major industrialised countries, runs an export credit programme which has two purposes; firstly, to provide UK exporters with insurance against political, transfer and commercial risks in respect of export contracts; and secondly, to assist in the provision of attractive credit to overseas buyers of UK capital goods and related services. The UK export credit authority is the Export Credits Guarantee Department (ECGD), which operates as an autonomous unit within the overall responsibility of the Secretary of State for Trade.

With the support of ECGD, finance can be made available in several different forms. For short-term transactions, the supplier can insure his receivables with ECGD and assign the insurance policy to the bank, thereby obtaining commercial finance from his bank on more attractive terms than may otherwise be available to him; alternatively, the supplier can secure from the buyer bills of exchange or promissory notes and discount or sell them to his bank at commercial rates, again using his ECGD insurance policy as security. In such cases the transaction can be done without recourse to the supplier.

For transactions with a credit period of more than two years, the available export finance is not on a commercial basis, but has a fixed and subsidised rate of interest. The applicable fixed rate is established with reference to the total term of the credit, to the credit rating of the borrower's country in the eyes of the ECGD, and to the general consensus on export credit terms arrived at by OECD member countries. Broadly speaking the fixed interest rates vary between 7.5 per cent for the poorest countries through to 8.75 per cent for the richest countries.

For smaller supply of goods transactions the most appropriate finance structure is a supplier credit. Under such a structure the supplier receives bills or notes from the buyer and insures those receivables with ECGD. The supplier then sells those bills or notes to his bank who is guaranteed as to 100 per cent by ECGD under a Specific Bank Guarantee. Legally, the ECGD then has rights of recourse against the supplier for 100 per cent of any amount paid out to the bank, but this is set off against the supplier's insurance cover which is normally for 90 per cent of commercial risk and 95 per cent for political risk in respect of contract receivables. It will be seen, therefore, that under a supplier credit the supplier carries a continuing financial risk on the buyer throughout the credit period. The second appropriate credit structure for medium-term transactions is a buyer credit, under which the supplier essentially enters into a cash contract. He does take out specific insurance cover in respect of such a contract, but instead is paid a loan made available by a bank explicitly and solely to the foreign buyer. Advances by the bank are guaranteed by ECGD as to 100 per cent of principal and interest at the appropriate fixed rate of interest. ECGD is entitled to take recourse on the supplier in the event of a claim by the bank on ECGD only in the circumstances where the UK supplier is in default under his contract. There is thus no continuing financial risk throughout the credit period on the UK supplier, and it is worth noting that ECGD has never to date exercised its right of recourse against a supplier under a buyer credit. Buyer credits are more normally used for major or turnkey contracts.

Because the rate of interest payable under a medium-term contract is on the above mentioned fixed rates, ECGD agrees with the banks who provide the funds that they will receive make-up to give them a commercial return on their lending. The cost of this subsidy to the UK government is causing concern to the UK authorities – in the fiscal year 1980-81 it amounted to over £500 million. The greatest providers of export credit finance are the UK clearing banks. A large proportion of the major projects are, however, arranged by the UK merchant banks with the clearing banks and certain active non-UK banks (for example the large American banks) providing a substantial proportion of the funding. If finance for an export order is required it is advisable to contact ECGD or a merchant/clearing bank sooner rather than later, since ECGD is not allowed by Act of Parliament to support export orders which have already been secured.

Short-term facilities

These include bank overdrafts and loans, bank acceptance credits, bills of exchange, trade credit, invoice discounting and factoring. Of these, bank overdrafts and loans are the most common and are used universally by companies, as Figure 6.2 shows. They may be supplemented by acceptance credits, where a bank undertakes to accept approved bills of exchange up to a certain limit so that the bills can be discounted at the finest rates. Alternatively, bills of exchange can be used as a form of trade credit, whether or not discounted with a bank or discount house, or various arrangements may be made between buyers and suppliers as to the length of credit given in payment for goods. Finally, invoice discounting and factoring are undertaken by various specialist institutions. Invoice discounting means financing the collection of specific invoices (at the risk of the selling company). Factoring involves making immediate payment against invoiced debts which are then normally collected at the factor's own risk for an appropriate charge. All these methods have in common the fact that they finance relatively small revolving trade transactions, but in aggregate they provide the finance of a vast amount of business on a continuing basis.

Current trends

The willingness of lenders to lend for long periods will depend on their being able to foresee a reasonable rate of return in real terms. In times of high inflation there is therefore a reluctance to tie up funds in this way except at rates so high as to be unacceptable to many borrowers. Equally, companies may prefer to borrow for relatively short periods in the hope of being able to refinance their obligations later at a lower rate. For these reasons, there has been a considerable shift in recent years away from long-term issues to more flexible short-term borrowing. This has been encouraged by the greater availability of bank credit following the new monetary policy adopted by the Bank of England from 1971 onwards in its new approach to competition and credit control.

LOOKING AT THE OVERALL CAPITAL STRUCTURE

We have outlined the chief avenues open to a company wishing to raise new capital. Before raising any new capital a company should consider what the capital is needed for, whether it is permanent or likely to be repaid out of cash flow within a period and what rate of return it is likely to earn. One can then go on to decide how it can best be supplied. For instance in the case of an investment with a high degree of risk the best source of finance is likely to be equity (or risk) capital; but, if it is a relatively risk-free long-term investment, loan capital may be more appropriate. If it is a specific project of medium-term duration, project finance should be considered, while if it is a working capital requirement, bank overdraft facilities are likely to be the answer. In all cases the various methods of supplementing cash flow in other ways must be borne in mind so as to minimise the amount of new capital actually required. Finally, the rate of return must be set against the cost of capital to ensure than an adequate margin exists to justify the investment.

One of the most important considerations is to preserve a proper balance between debt and equity in the company's financial structure. This relationship is described as the company's financial gearing; if the company's source of income is reasonably stable and assured (such as the rental income of a property company) it is safe for it to be highly geared, but if it is operating in a cyclical industry (such as machine tools) it is prudent to keep the gearing (that is, the element of borrowing) at a low level, for interest on borrowings has to be paid in adverse as well as favourable times and if a temporary set-back combined with high interest charges results in the company making a loss, its overall status will suffer. The degree of gearing will depend both on the absolute amount of borrowing and the extent to which any of this borrowing is at fluctuating interest rates which may rise faster than the company's income. In inflationary times, borrowing at a fixed cost can be most advantageous to a company. But the closer the company gets to what is thought to be an unduly high level of borrowings, the more reluctant lenders will be to provide new funds and the more the equity interest of existing shareholders will be endangered.

The object of company financial management should be to see that the company has adequate funds at the lowest cost consonant with all these factors and so to seek to maximise its earnings for ordinary shareholders.

FURTHER READING

Admission of Securities to Listing, Stock Exchange, London, revised 1973, with subsequent amendments

Brearley, R. A., and Pyle, C., *Bibliography of Finance and Investment*, Elek Books, London, 1973

'Competition and Credit Control', Bank of England, reprinted in *Bank of England Quarterly Bulletin*, June 1971

Leach, J. H. C., 'The Role of the Institutions in the UK Ordinary Share Market', *Investment Analyst, December, 1971*

Leach, J. H. C., 'The Weight of New Money – Once Again', *Investment Analyst*, September, 1975

Merrett, Howe and Newbould, *Equity Issues and the London Capital Market*, Longmans, London, 1967

'New Capital Issues Statistics', *Midland Bank Review*,, commentary published annually in Spring edition

Royal Commission on the Distribution of Income and Wealth (Diamond Report), Report No. 2 (Cmnd. 6172), HMSO, London, July, 1975

'The UK Corporate Bond Market', *Bank of England Quarterly Bulletin*, March, 1981

The various volumes of evidence given to the Committee to Review the Functioning of Financial Institutions (the Wilson Committee) and published by HMSO may also be of interest.

7 Capital project planning

Tessa V Ryder Runton, Jack Broyles and Ian Cooper

Capital project planning is the process by which companies allocate funds to various investment projects designed to ensure profitability and growth. Evaluation of such projects involves estimating their future benefits to the company and comparing these with their costs. Such analysis is appropriate not only to the purchase of long-lived physical assets, but to any decision which has impacts extending into the future. Thus capital project planning can encompass, for example, long-term contracts for goods and services, marketing expenditures, disinvestment by sale, mergers and plant closures. While capital project planning is a process that takes place in an organisational context over extended periods of time, certain elements of this process are essential to good project planning. These are:

1 Access to the appropriate information
2 Knowledge of the company's required financial return
3 Realistic evaluation of the prospective cash flow and profit impacts of projects
4 Analysis of the costs and benefits of projects with attention to the timing of their occurrence
5 Evaluation by senior management of the strategic implications of large projects
6 A well-defined approval process
7 Consistency with strategic planning and budgeting procedures
8 A review procedure.

THE GOALS OF CAPITAL PROJECT PLANNING

Businesses have responsibilities to various interested groups including employees, customers, suppliers, bankers and shareholders. Most companies claim that their financial goal is to satisfy their shareholder. This goal is met by maximising the total market value of the company's shares. The capital market values shares at the present value of current and future cash flows attributable to shareholders. If the company maximises the net present value of all the operations that make up its business, the sum will be the maximisation of the value of the company. This value, net of debt, belongs to shareholders. Companies pursuing other objectives whether social or technological must primarily be profitable. Should shareholders, corporate members or financiers become dissatisfied with the company's operations, they may withdraw their support, causing such awkward problems as loss of morale and personnel, shortage of funds, a fall in the company's share price if it is publicly quoted, or stormy annual general meetings. Any of these can lead to undesirable vulnerability and result in a takeover, close-down or governmental interference.

REQUIRED RATE OF RETURN STANDARDS AND THE COST OF CAPITAL

Cost of capital is a major standard of comparison used in financial analysis and is a vital company statistic needing careful calculation. The return on capital resources must equal or exceed the cost of that capital. Although zero or negative returns are acceptable in special cases, the necessary subsidies may lead to costs in another form.

The realities of commercial life have caused the cost of capital to be a very complex subject. Any comparisons must be made between like numbers. A percentage profit before tax made on a hotel in Bermuda bears no relationship to the same figure made after tax on a farm in Scotland. A profit expressed as a percentage of capital employed should not be compared with a discounted cash flow internal rate of return. Many measures of company performance can be devised but these are valuable only to those who are completely familiar with the definitions involved. The appraisal of projected cash flow discounted at a rate equal to a carefully estimated required rate of return leads to fewer pitfalls. In particular, the time-value of money is taken into account, all the financial effects are assessed, and tax and inflation are taken into account in the calculation of the cash flow and the estimation of the cost of capital.

Capital investment analysis aims to discover the financial truth about the plan under investigation. If it does not meet the survival standard of the organisation, that fact should be stated clearly before the discussion as to its desirability begins. In practice many apparently unprofitable processes go on in any business because they enhance the profitable activities which, of course, should outnumber them. Obvious examples are the provision of catering and other services for the workforce, advertising, research and so on. It used to be thought that discounted cash flow analysis led to categorical 'yes' or 'no' judgements on any plan; in fact, all it does is marshal the financial facts for the guidance of the decision-takers. In addition, it can point to the least unprofitable way of tackling a loss-making but necessary job.

The cost of capital to the firm

Most companies raise funds from many sources – retained earnings, new equity, grants and many forms of loans. The overall cost of capital to the firm is the return it must earn on its assets to meet the requirement of all those providing it with financing. Lenders require interest payments and shareholders expect to receive dividends and see capital growth.

In the past, UK shareholders have expected to earn a real net return of about 8 per cent after tax on average risk shares. To obtain this required net return in money terms, the expected inflation rate must be added. If this expected inflation rate is 10 per cent, the required return on the company's present and equity and retained earnings is 18 per cent. The cost of new equity raised by means of 'rights' is a little more than this to allow for the costs of the issue. Other forms of new equity issues incur further costs of about 2 per cent.

Although the average real expected return on shares is about 8 per cent, companies in risky industries or with high gearing (borrowing relative to equity funds) will have more vulnerable shares than average. The real return required by their shareholders will be commensurately higher. This means that borrowing is not necessarily a cheap way of raising funds. Although the interest rate on borrowing may be lower than the return expected by shareholders, increased gearing will raise the risk of shares and not change the overall cost of funds to the company. (For a more detailed discussion see Franks and Broyles, 1979.)

If a company maintains a proportion of debt capital agreed with its lenders, it can compute a *weighted average cost of capital*. For example, if the interest rate on debt is 10 per cent, and the company has 25 per cent debt and 75 per cent equity, the weighted average cost of capital in money terms including 10 per cent average inflation is $(0.25 \times 10$ per cent$) + (0.75 \times 18$ per cent$) = 16$ per cent. This cost does not allow for the tax savings from interest payments. This benefit is added separately.

In deciding the appropriate standards for an organisation, the marginal cost of capital is a vital guide. In a growing company, new capital will be needed and, therefore, the return on a project of normal risk should be judged against a standard of the weighted average cost of new capital. Companies making investment decisions continuously should use this marginal cost of capital as the standard for all projects with risks normal to the company's business. If a project cannot pass this test, it will diminish the company's value.

Required rates of return on projects

Obviously projects involve differing risks. Some, such as cost-saving investments and lease or buy decisions, are of low risk; others, such as research projects, involve greater than average levels of risk. A company should classify its risk categories for projects and set required returns for each. A large project of risk significantly different from normal can alter the overall character of a company, its cost of capital, its accepted gearing and the returns expected by financiers.

The required rate of return for a project can be significantly different from the weighted average cost of capital for the company. High-risk projects are characterised by high fixed-operating expenditure and high revenue variability. These should be expected to earn high rates of return. The exact return required will depend upon a judgement about the level of risk in the project compared with the average risk of the company. In the case shown above, where the weighted average cost of capital in real terms is 6 per cent, the real required return on a project twice as risky as the market should be 12 per cent. With 10 per cent expected inflation the money required return should be 22 per cent.

The use of a separate required rate of return for each individual project is most important when the projects are large relative to the company and/or when the projects being considered have long lives. A typical classification scheme, in increasing order of risk is: cost reduction, replacement, scale expansion, new products. The risks of these different types of investment differ, and so should their required returns.

By evaluating different projects at different required rates of return, the company is seeking to protect its shareholders. Shareholders require high rates of return for higher levels of risk, and receive compensation for high risk in the capital markets. Companies undertaking high-risk investment decisions must seek to achieve higher returns than their shareholders can earn for that level of risk in the capital markets.

Effect of debt finance on required returns

Unless there are non-financial incentives, a project is acceptable only if it stands on its own feet – that is, its cash flow should at least meet the company's return criterion for whatever risks are involved. With the possibility of debt financing is the position changed? A typical case arises where new assets simply increase the total assets on a proportion of which debt is available. Some people argue that, even apart from tax advantages, debt is cheap since the interest rate is lower than the cost of equity funds. This argument ignores the hidden cost of debt: the increased vulnerability of the equity as more borrowing is undertaken. The total operating risk of the company remains constant as more debt financing is used, so it is unrealistic to believe that the overall cost of funds can be reduced in this way.

One advantage that borrowing does confer is the reduction in taxes caused by the deductibility of interest payments. The impact on cash flows of this tax saving is simply the future stream of tax payments that are saved by the interest payments on the debt. The value of these tax savings can be added to the value of the operating cash flows from the project to get an overall value including the benefits of debt financing. This is preferable to using a weighted average cost of capital including the cost of debt at an after-tax rate. Use of the latter assumes that the debt available for a project will be very long term and will be the same proportion of the project financing as it is for the company. Both these assumptions can be very erroneous when projects have short-maturity debt or very high or low gearing.

Care needs to be taken when a project merits special loans. Usually these are projects of significant size for which government incentives are available, or for which special working capital loans can be raised, or involving mortgageable property. If the result is a new company finance structure, then cost of capital and risk classifications must be reassessed. Some large capital investments, such as in mining, involve parent companies in special financial guarantees and these need special attention. Other capital investments, such as in research, do not result in increased total assets which can be partly debt financed.

TRADITIONAL TECHNIQUES FOR TESTING VIABILITY

The natural question: 'When do I get my money back?' has often been answered by the traditional technique of adding up the forecast net cash inflow (sometimes the sum of the profit before depreciation from the forecast profit and loss account) year by year until the amount of the original capital investment is reached, thereby giving the years to payback. Such a calculation is inconclusive because standards vary, definitions of the original capital vary, tax is not always deducted and most of the benefits of tax allowances are obscured. The method ignores the *time-value of money*, cannot cope with inflation and takes no account of the later profits, if any. Whether, in fact, any profit is made on the investment is not measured at all. Payback calculations give some guidance in matters of liquidity in which case the cash inflow should be carefully defined and be free of any 'accounting numbers' such as 'tax provision' instead of 'tax payable'. A better payback calculation is the discounted payback, which is computed using the present values of the future cash inflows.

Another traditional technique involves the use of balance sheet ratios for current and proposed operations. These include the ratios of profit to capital employed, of profit to sales, and many others concerning the stock, current assets and liabilities, and working capital. These ratios are useful for regulating smooth operations but are unhelpful for judging profitability owing to definition problems and the choice of standards, but mostly because the time-value of money is not included.

One ratio used is the return on capital known as 'the accountant's return' or the 'book rate of return'. An average profit, before or after tax is calculated for a number of years of the proposed project and this is expressed as a percentage of the capital employed. The latter is often defined as the initial investment or the average capital employed over the years, thereby allowing for further investment and depreciation. This procedure suffers from the same snags as the techniques mentioned above and, in addition, smooths out the effect of irregular annual profits. Clearly, quick profits are preferable to a slow build-up, but advantages or disadvantages are obscured.

MODERN TECHNIQUES FOR TESTING VIABILITY

The traditional techniques take no account of the time-value of money. But money received today is much more valuable than the same money received later. Present inflationary conditions magnify the difference. This is the principal fact which modern analysis techniques have incorporated to improve on past procedures. Analysis concentrates on the incremental cash flow of a project. The cash flow is discounted at the project's discount rate to the present time, giving a present value. The work involved has increased, but once an analysis discipline has been set up, decision-takers can expect that the realities of the given data for some plan will be clearly identified. They can then concentrate on the non-financial problems involved, judge whether the data is sufficient to work with and act accordingly.

The concepts of moving money in time using the relevant discount rate is not new. Today's quoted price for benefits to be received in the future can be judged by netting the price, or capital cost, from the present value of the future cash flow. A positive resultant net present value (NPV), if properly calculated, shows that the transaction is financially worth while. The value of the transaction can also be assessed by judging its internal rate of return (IRR).

CASH FLOW DISCIPLINE IN CAPITAL PROJECT ANALYSIS

The discounted cash flow techniques use as their raw material the incremental cash flow resulting from some plan. Profit flow study is necessary for proper annual accounting as required by shareholders, but it is the cash flow that should be studied to identify the return forecast and the finance that is required. Provisions for depreciation are excluded, but expenditures on working capital and capital expenditures are included. The cash flow of a project is a forecast of the total monetary effects computed periodically (usually annually or monthly) over the whole life of the project, including scrap values. Such items as tax savings achieved on other profits of the organisation because of allowances due to the new project or any other cash effects which would not occur without the new project–for example, the cost of head office extensions or replacing an executive who would be transferred–should be included. Interest payments are often wrongly deducted from the cash flow, but they are not operating flows, being part of the cost of funds included in the cost of capital. A project can be defined as any procedure which alters the organisation's cash flow. Projects, therefore, include opportunities for cost savings and productivity improvements, where capital cost is not necessarily involved. What, therefore, is analysed is the total cash flow effect of an opportunity, that is, the net incremental cash flow which is the difference between the cash flow in the company if the project is undertaken and the cash flow if it is not.

This analysis must be in real terms or in money terms with respect to inflations and, if necessary, alterations must be made so that real terms cash flows are judged by a real terms required return standard and money cash flows are judged by a money terms required return standard. Tax allowances and loan-servicing schedules are always in money terms but sales and cost figures are usually forecast in real terms. It is usual for the marketing and production departments to project schedules showing changes in sales percentages or production costs without allowing for external price changes. However, the estimation of taxable profits and taxes requires that these data be converted to money terms. In cases of high inflation forecasts, or different effects on prices and costs, and for lengthy projects, some estimate must be made of the inflation pattern over the life of the project. This estimate could differ for use on prices, on costs and on the overall situation including the cost of capital. All figures must be converted to money terms so that expected tax payments can then be estimated.

It should go without saying that cash flows are forecast after the effects of company taxes when paid. Because tax allowances are normally in money terms, consistent cash flows almost certainly have to be forecast in money terms, unless real terms tax allowances can be calculated. Sometimes it is necessary to consider any likely future changes in tax structure. In this, as in treating inflation and in all problems of data uncertainties, it is important not to be over-meticulous, particularly at the outset. Analysis of the most roughly prepared cash flow will show whether it is worth spending any further time attending to the details. The first question to answer is: "What is the profitability of the given set of data (warts included)?' If the answer looks promising it is then sensible to take the time to examine the given data, prepare a detailed net incremental cash flow in money terms and look at possible outcomes of the project as opposed to one set of data. The analysis should then examine sensitivities, risks and probabilities and the effect of the project on the organisation as a whole. Decision-takers prefer consistent analysis disciplines so that they can use consistent standards of judgement and comparison.

NET PRESENT VALUE (NPV) AND INTERNAL RATE OF RETURN (IRR) IN MORE DETAIL

The use of the concept of net present value (NPV)

The net present value (NPV) of a project is the net present value of the net incremental cash flow discounted at the project's required rate of return. A zero NPV shows that the project repays the capital invested plus the minimum acceptable return on the invested capital throughout the project's life. The minimum acceptable return is equal to the opportunity cost of that capital including a return required for the risk taken by investing in that operation for that period. NPVs show that the minimum return is achieved plus extra value.

Given a discount rate of 11 per cent for a project, the NPV is found as shown in Figure 7.1. Other things being equal, this project looks financially acceptable. One could pay up to £199 more for the opportunity and still not lose. NPV represents the analyst's estimate of the net increase in the value of the company which would accrue from the project. If the discount rate used is the capital market's capitalisation rate for the risk of the project, the NPV represents an estimate of the incremental market value of the firm due to the project. The NPV technique thus gives a simple assessment tool, but is inaccurate if there is doubt or dispute as to the correct discount rate.

GHM

Time in years from today	Cash flow (£)	11% Discount factor	Present value (£)
0	(1500)	1.00	(1500)
1	100	0.901	90
2	1000	0.812	812
3	1000	0.731	731
4	100	0.659	66

The NPV, the sum of the present values of the cash flow = +£199

Figure 7.1   Calculation of net present value (NPV)

The use of the concept of internal rate of return (IRR)

The internal rate of return (IRR) is also known as the discounted cash flow yield (DCF), the DCF return or the actuarial return. IRR is defined as the break-even financing rate for the project. This is not to say that the capital released by the project earns such a return. Reinvestments, whether wise or not, should be kept separate from the analysis of a project on its own merits. The IRR of a project is judged against the cost of capital standard or the minimum required return.

The mathematical definition of the IRR is that it is the discount rate which, when used to discount the net incremental cash flow, gives a zero net present value for the project. The NPV (which is calculated at the project's required rate of return discount rate) should not be confused with the many net present values which can be calculated using other rates.

The calculation of the NPV consists in setting out the cash flow, discounting it to the present time and adding up the net total. DCF or IRR calculations necessitate trial and error. If, however, the graph shown in Figure 7.2 is borne in mind, the process need not be lengthy.

Most practitioners find it convenient to calculate the NPV first. If this shows, for example by being positive, that it is worth doing more sums, a guess must be made of the next trial rate. A positive NPV indicates that the DCF/IRR will be greater than the cost of capital rate, how much greater can sometimes be guessed by the size of the NPV. Trial rate A per cent is used and will give a net present value VA. Consideration of this result might lead to trial rate B per cent and VB. Having thus both over- and under-estimated the answer, the true IRR can be found by mathematical interpolation, or by drawing a similar graph (always provided that the trial rates are not more than

Figure 7.2   The use of trial rates to calculate the internal rate of return (IRR)

one or two percentage points apart–if they are, the curve that represents the relationship will give too inaccurate a result, which should be checked by the another trial and interpolation or extrapolation).

An example will show how this procedure applies. Suppose that the cost of capital is 11 per cent, and an investment is being considered which costs £1500, lasts four years, and has no terminal value. All calculations are tabulated in Figure 7.3. By interpolation between the net present value calculated at 16 per cent and 17 per cent the IRR is found to be:

$$16 + \frac{25}{31} = 16.8 \text{ per cent}$$

The same result is obtained extrapolating from the 17 per cent and 20 per cent:

$$\text{IRR} = 17 - \frac{3 \times 6}{90} = 16.8 \text{ per cent}$$

GHM

Time in years from today	Cash flow (£)	Cash flow discounted at:							
		11 per cent		20 per cent		17 per cent		16 per cent	
		Discount factor	value	factor	value	factor	value	factor	value
0	(1500)	1.000	(1500)	1.000	(1500)	1.000	(1500)	1.000	(1500)
1	100	0.901	90	0.833	83	0.855	86	0.862	86
2	1000	0.812	812	0.694	694	0.731	731	0.743	743
3	1000	0.731	731	0.579	579	0.624	624	0.641	641
4	100	0.659	66	0.482	48	0.534	53	0.522	55
Net present values			199 this is the NPV		(96)		(6)		25

Figure 7.3 Tabulation using actual and trial rates, leading to calculation of IRR
(The calculation process is described in the text)

Interpolation between the 11 per cent and 20 per cent figures, however, gives the answer:

$$11 + \frac{9 \times 199}{295} = 17.1 \text{ per cent}$$

which may be too inaccurate, although in this case the return would probably be quoted at 17 per cent. These figures could also be found graphically.

The use of present value: mid-year discounting

Discount tables are available for all periods–weeks, quarters, years–and to various numbers of places of decimals. It is not normally helpful to calculate the cash flow in too small periods or to discount it using more than four-figure tables. It is more important to notice that the tables usually refer to points of time and the cash flows represent a total for a period. A fitting asumption is needed. It is easy if the majority of receipts and payments occur at the beginning or at the end of the periods. For flows which are continuous and irregular over the periods, the total cash flow is often assumed to arise mid-year. The calculation should therefore be refined. If only annual discount tables are available, the half-year discount factor at r per cent can be calculated from the equation:

$$\text{Discount factor} = \frac{1}{\text{Square root of } (1+r \text{ expressed as a decimal})}$$

Example A

Suppose the investment is bought today and the operation is immediate and continuous. The NPV calculation becomes:

Time from today	Cash flow ($£$)	Present value at 11 per cent Discount factor	Present value
0	(1500)	1.000	(1500)
$\frac{1}{2}$	100	0.949	95
$1\frac{1}{2}$	1000	0.901×0.949	855
$2\frac{1}{2}$	1000	0.812×0.949	770
$3\frac{1}{2}$	100	0.731×0.949	69
			NPV = 289

The IRR now needs to be recalculated to take account of the refined timing. The IRR is now $21\frac{1}{2}$ per cent because of the earlier cash flow.

Example B

Suppose again that the operation were to be built up and paid for over one construction year. In this case the £1500 cash flow is similarly assumed to be mid year and the other cash flows occur six months later than before. The NPV can then be obtained from the first calculation, which has so far given a present value six months from today, by discounting the result by six months. NPV today equals

$$199 \times 0.949 = £189$$

The IRR is 17 per cent in this case, as at first, because it is mathematically true that the same yield is given wherever period zero is assumed to occur if the succeeding time periods bear the same relationship to period zero.

In some cases, such as natural resource projects, which involve large negative cash flows at the end of the project, a special problem arises in using IRR. Projects of this sort can have more than one IRR, some of which may be above the required return and some below. Complex techniques have been developed to salvage the IRR method in these circumstances. These adjustments usually involve procedures similar to the present value approach, and fewer problems will be encountered by the use of the NPV rule in these circumstances.

The use of present value–optimisation of mutually exclusive alternatives

Financial analysts are constantly being asked to advise as to which of two viable alternatives is financially preferable. Such choices include large long-life machinery versus cheaper short-life machinery, labour versus automation, the choice of site, speed of construction, shaft versus open-pit mining, air versus sea transport, and so on; in each case choice of one excludes the possibility of choosing the other alternative. Use of the net present value calculation is the easiest approach. Suppose that in a company with a cost of capital of 11 per cent the choice is between:

Method A (which is capital intensive) showing a NPV of +£1500 and
Method B (with a lower capital cost) showing a NPV of +£1300

If the analyst calculates NPVs using the minimum acceptable return discount rate for the risk of the project, different discount rates might be appropriate to A and B. For example, one method might involve installing a possibly risky unproven technological improvement, whereas the other method would re-equip as before.

The actual question to be answered, since both methods are financially desirable, is whether the expenditure of the extra capital involved on Method A is worth while. The incremental investment, which is represented by the difference between the cash flows of the two alternatives (cash flow A and cash flow B, for each period), shows a NPV of +£200 (NPV A – NPV B). It is therefore worth spending the extra money. Where the patterns of the alternative cash flows are very different, the incremental approach avoids problems in comparing projects with different levels of capital expenditure. Indeed, different cash flows can arise from the same total capital invested but the incremental cash flow analysis still gives the financially preferable operational plan.

Use of the DCF/IRR approach is also straightforward but contains a snare for the unwary. The question of whether the incremental investment would be desirable is answered by finding the DCF/IRR on the incremental cash flow (cash flow A minus cash flow B, for each period). If the incremental IRR is greater than the company's minimum acceptable return, then alternative A is financially preferable. When setting out the results, however, an apparent problem frequently arises. For example:

Method		11 per cent NPV	IRR
A	Expensive	+£1500	14 per cent
B	Cheaper	+£1300	16 per cent
A–B	Incremental investment	+ £200	13 per cent

It looks as though one should choose method B because the IRR is better than that in A. This is an illusion because the capital on which the yield is earned is different in each case. The analysis of the incremental investment points to the same answer whichever method is used. It is often argued that, perhaps, the incremental capital should be spent on some other investment which might show a better return than the 13 per cent here. This could be the case in conditions of severe capital rationing when investments yielding 13 per cent cannot be financed. In other conditions there is no conflict and both investments are desirable. Of course, more than two projects might be available, in which case, several incremental investment choices would be necessary. It is easier simply to compare the NPVs–the most preferable choice has the highest NPV.

Some practitioners approve the calculation of the NPV but find the answer, which is of necessity expressed in currency, difficult to use. The *profitability index* is therefore sometimes used, particularly when projects need to be ranked because budgets are limited. The index is calculated by dividing the present value of the net cash returns by the present value of the net cash investments. In the example shown in Figure 7.3 the profitability index is 1699/1500 = 1.13 which means that every unit of investment earns 1.13 units of present value in the project. Care must be taken not to confuse this with the IRR which is 17 per cent. In practice many analysts report the profitability of a project both in terms of NPV in currency and of IRR as a percentage to assist understanding.

When mutually exclusive opportunities are being analysed, equal project lives should be compared. This is often difficult, but a three-year life machine can be compared with a five-year machine by assuming that the longer-life machine will be sold at the end of the third year. Alternatively a fifteen-year period can be taken with five three-year machines compared with three five-year machines. The most sensible assumption will be obvious.

Present value and expected value–decision trees

Much of capital investment planning involves arranging a continuous series of actions which may be altered in the light of future events or future actual patterns of marketing. It is possible to set out likely outcomes in a map known as a decision tree – it grows as it is extended further into the future. NPVs of each likely chain of events can be prepared and this could help the decision that must be taken later. Very often decision-tree calculations are of the expected value of the outcome. To calculate expected values the probabilities of likely intermediate events of outcomes are incorporated. Decision trees have been described extensively. A decision tree is shown in Figure 7.4.

Faced with the need to decide whether to install a computer, the possibilities or likely events might appear as shown. The decision taken would depend, financially, on the relative NPVs or expected values of the three good

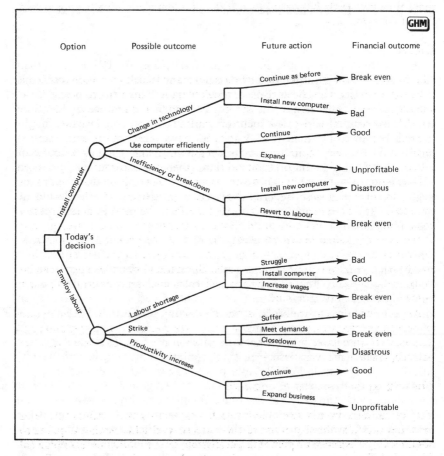

Figure 7.4   Example of a decision tree

possibilities. Expected values are weighted by the relevant probability; for example, if there is a 60 per cent chance of an NPV of £100 and a 40 per cent chance of an NPV of zero, the expected value is £60.

COMPUTATIONAL RESOURCES

Although computers, big and small, are invaluable as calculating aids for complex problems they should not be used indiscriminately because the cost, and the time taken to eliminate errors, can become disproportionate to the problem being analysed. Time-sharing on computer terminals using borrowed working programs can be invaluable. Modern analytical methods can generally be employed for problems, using everyday hand calculators.

Calculation short-cuts and standard procedures for all problems are often sought in this field. If, however, they are used without understanding or without necessary adaption to the different circumstances of each case, much more time can easily be wasted than if the problem were initially approached from first principles.

DATA

The collection and sifting of project data normally leads to far more problems than the analysis. This is no reason for allowing less than rigorous analytical techniques. If a quick look at the first set of data indicates a promising idea, it is sensible to re-examine the data before extending the analysis. Data are given, begged, borrowed or stolen, but in spite of (or because of) the uncertainties involved the best way to obtain good understanding leading to better decisions is to establish good communications with the project initiators as a top priority.

Discussions should be held 'on site' as early as possible so that there is no suggestion of ivory tower thinking. Diplomatic approaches to the hard-worked estimators who have to grapple with difficult forecasting problems can lead to a good understanding, not only of the best realistic guess at some figure, but also of the possible range in which it may lie and of the probabilities involved. Conversation with outsiders often helps clarification. Much the best hunches are those agreed by two or more experts. Special and outside experts can be called in to advise on variables found by sensitivity analysis to be critical enough to merit the cost of the advice.

A special problem to be tackled is that of inflation, particularly when costs are subject to special pressures leading to price rises greater than the general rate. The analyst will have to take a view as to when it is safe to assume that, on balance, costs and revenues will be similarly inflated.

Missing data – reverse economics

Very often, data are not available for such vital factors as the achievable price for a new product, the size of the reserves in a new oilfield, the time required to obtain safety clearance or planning permission, or the market or technological life period. Reverse economics is the formal technique whereby it is possible to define the achievable or viable range for the missing data. If a graph is drawn of the profitability (NPV or IRR/DCF) of the project against invented values of the missing data, it is possible to find the value that gives the minimum acceptable result. If that value is very unrealistic, it may be possible to conclude that the new product will not be profitable, or that the oilfield cannot be economically exploited in present circumstances. A decision might then be taken to stop any further expenditure on the promotion of the idea. If a project must be killed off or frozen it is far better halted early before reputations become involved.

This technique is also useful when considering the merger, takeover or sale of a company, or its flotation on the public market. An attempt is made to forecast the foreseeable cash flow of the company – possibly including benefits caused by savings in the new managerial context. The difference between the present value of the forecast cash flow and the debt divided by the number of issued shares will give a measure of the acceptability of a quoted or offered price, or will indicate what price to set at the beginning of negotiations. In a takeover situation the buyer should use the incremental required return for the project, that is the required rate of return for the risk of the company being taken over. If the company is quoted, the value of its equity share capital is given in the market-place, unless there are undisclosed facts such as technological advance, or unless the market has anticipated a possible merger. The premium paid should be less than the NPV of the merger benefits.

Uncertain and erroneous data

A good approach to uncertain data is to attempt to identify the range in which the answer may lie. This is sometimes done by adding to the best guess two more guesses, one of which is the most pessimistic and the other the most optimistic. In this way it may be possible to exclude too much subjectivity on the part of the estimator, who might previously have thought that his future depended on the success of his estimates and who therefore, understandably, introduced too much conservatism. In large organisations a chain of conservatism may be introduced. In such cases the analyst must try to assess the realities, and it is helpful if the motivations of the personnel are adjusted so as not to interfere. Overestimating can be as wrong as underestimating and can easily lead to raising too much finance or premature expansion.

Often data are manipulated, either innocently or deliberately, to achieve the desired result – perhaps acceptance of a scheme by head office or of a contract in a tendering competition. The results can lead to public embarrassment, if not disaster. A good review discipline can help to avoid or to sort out such problems.

Once the range in which critical data lie is found, sensitivity analysis can be carried out. Alternatively, a calculation of the likely profit or loss, should everything turn out for the worst, can help in a discussion. If the organisation simply cannot survive such a loss and the chances of it are significant, then the project may well have to be forgone.

Sensitivity analysis

This technique can highlight the facts and problems caused by the risks and uncertainties of the plan under discussion. It has limitations but can be carried out with a minimum of calculating aids if necessary. The aim of this analysis is to discover the value of an uncertain variable at which the project is just profitable. Two or three calculations will give the necessary sensitivity curve.

Example of sensitivity analysis

A project is showing a negative net present value at the company's cost of capital rate. What would need to be done to make it profitable? The sensitivity graph is drawn (Figure 7.5) and shows that the operating profit would need to be raised by 10 per cent to give a zero NPV of the net incremental cash flow for the project. All other things are assumed at first to remain constant (capital cost, speed of coming into operation, life of the project, tax, inflation etc.).
Data which give the desired result:

	Original estimate	Acceptable estimates					
Price per unit (£)	20	21	20	20	20	20	20.3
Volume/number sold	10	10	10.5	10	10	10	10.15
Labour Cost (£)	40	40	40	30	40	40	38
Materials cost (£)	50	50	50	50	40	50	47.5
Overhead cost (£)	10	10	10	10	10	0	9.5
Operating Profit	100	110	110	110	110	110	111.045

It is thus possible to say that the project would be acceptable if either the price could be raised by 5 per cent, or the volume sold increased by 5 per cent, or if the labour cost could be lowered by 25 per cent, or the materials cost by 20 per cent or the overhead cost by 100 per cent. Another possibility to explore would be if (as shown in the final column) both the price and volume sold could be raised by 1½ per cent at the same time as all costs are reduced by 5 per cent. However, one should try to ensure that joint changes in variables are not contradictory and fit a plausible and consistent scenario. The graph could have been plotted using IRR and the company's required rate of return as the cut-off line but this involves more sums.

One more uncertainty can be explored to extend the analysis. Suppose, for example, that the market for the product is thought to last ten years but could be hit by competition in eight to twelve years time; further calculations give the graph shown in Figure 7.6. Annual operating profit is thought likely to lie between 95 and 120. Assuming the variables examined to be the most critical, the profitability 'envelope' is shown by the two outer curves and the dotted

Figure 7.5 *Graph of project viability's sensitivity to profit variation*

Figure 7.6 *Two variable sensitivity analysis graph*

connecting lines. This envelope is divided into two parts by the cut-off line of zero net present value. By inspection of the two areas it is possible to conclude that the project has roughly only a 40 per cent chance of being viable. The worst likely outcome is also shown. The decision may then be taken more easily.

Should the whole envelope be above the cut-off line it would be possible to conclude that the project is profitable in spite of the uncertainty in the variables considered, which are then defined as uncritical. Further effort could then be concentrated on other variables. This technique is limited to two dimensions. It is, however, of great value, even without calculating aids, because of its simplicity in demonstrating the effect of apparently daunting uncertainties.

PROBABILITY ANALYSIS

This is the ideal towards which sensitivity analysis is the first step, but the calculation usually requires the help of a computer. Great efforts are being made by large organisations and consultants to prepare flexible computer programs to conduct probability analyses on a wide variety of projects.

The data required are further examined to discover a range of probabilities for every variable which may lie in each part of the likely range. Subjectivity is not avoided by this, but the further discussion can sometimes help clarify the situation. The results could be shown for each variable in a histogram, which is a practical approach to the underlying mathematical curve. An example is shown in Figure 7.7. Mathematical sampling using such data for each significant variable results in the type of profitability/probability graph shown in Figure 7.8. The peak of the curve in Figure 7.8 shows the most likely outcome, but there is a significant chance that the yield might be negative or that the original investment would not be recovered. The area under the curve being taken as unity, the area to the left of the cost of capital or required rate of return cut-off line, if measured, gives the probability of unprofitability. The use of

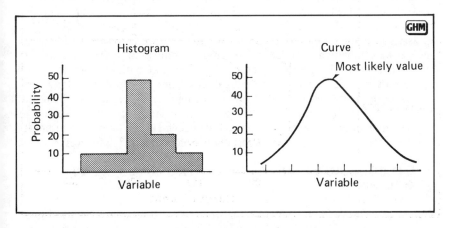

Figure 7.7   Examples of probability distributions

sensitivity and probability analyses does not remove uncertainty and subjectivity of data; it helps decision-takers to judge the likelihood of profit or loss in projects.

Figure 7.8   Example of a profitability/probability graph

RISK

Uncertainty of data is not the only unknown bedevilling projects. There are also many possible events which could have a highly significant effect. Such events include acts of God (earthquake, flood), of governments (tariffs, nationalisation), of competitors, of technological improvement. Some risks can be insured against. In every case it is helpful to define the risk and assess its possible effect ('what happens if. . .?') and in particular when such an effect might occur. If the likely loss caused by the risky circumstances were to be disastrous to the company, then perhaps the venture is too risky. There are several ways in which organisations of different kinds can proceed to minimise the effect of risk. Obvious examples are diversification, both geographically and in the nature of the business, the tying of customers or suppliers to long-term contracts, and the cautious introduction of new or different scale business. Other risks can be eliminated through markets in which risk is traded. A surprising variety of risks can be insured against and others, such as commodity price variation and exchange rate variations, can be hedged in futures markets.

THE DISCUSSION FORUM FOR CAPITAL INVESTMENT PROBLEMS

Good decision-taking depends more than anything else on good communication. The decision-takers (at the level appropriate to the size of the proposal) do well to arrange a free debate between the project sponsors, the experts, the analysts and themselves. Documentation of the proposal, the analysis, the decision and any argument or discussion are of great value to all concerned in future planning, as well as to interrelated projects in the context of the organisation's future as a whole. The techniques described in this chapter contribute only by assembling such facts as can be established and highlighting the likely probabilities. This, however, is of great value in releasing management effort for the interpretation of the problems.

Most private organisations are to some extent limited as to the amount of capital available, particularly for unspectacular investments. It would be convenient if all projects turned up simultaneously and could be ranked in order of profitability and then accepted in turn until available funds were used up. (Such a procedure is to a certain extent available to the public sector at budget time.) In most companies, however, capital investment or operational optimisation opportunities turn up irregularly. It is therefore highly desirable to establish and monitor a clearly understood set of criteria and discount rates, reflecting the company's required rates of return for different risks, against which each scheme can be measured as it arises and progresses. With the aid of the right criteria there is some chance that a good source of investments will have been chosen so that, at the minimum, returns can exceed costs; and the company's value can be increased, leading to a healthy financial context for future development.

Tactics

When analysis precedes or accompanies negotiations with governments, financiers, associates or opponents, it is usually helpful to make calculations in order that one can understand the opposite point of view, which might be based on different methods or criteria.

Few organisations can avoid differences of opinion which lead to apparent or very real conflicts. The experienced decision-taker and his advisers can normally recognise the behavioural signs. Avoidance of discussion is not always for good reasons, such as a real emergency. Emergencies can be contrived by skilful delays and, perhaps, decisions can be precipitated by prompted outside pressures. Decisions taken in real emergencies should be appraised and documented as soon as possible. If a decision-taker is known to be susceptible to private discussions, then project sponsors will be quick to arrange suitable lobbying. Such a situation has obvious dangers.

A very real problem can arise in planning investments which can or should be phased. The purchase of options or expenditure on pilot plants, which lead either to subsequent large investment or to embarrassment if the second stage is deemed unacceptable, should not be appraised in isolation. Appraisal of the first stage should be accompanied by a best guess of the likely subsequent history, and the project should be discussed at the level relevant to the whole operation, in which case the decision will be taken after consideration of the future commitments. The decision-tree technique examined earlier can help.

When a superficially attractive proposal is financially marginal, special care must be taken. At this time criticism may be made of the company's criteria which were otherwise accepted when the proposals were better than marginal. Such criticism at this time may not always be valid. In this situation excessive subjectivity may be introduced into uncertain data; in fact, some estimators claim to be able to produce estimates which pass company tests. Wide discussions of parameters, perhaps calling in outside advice, as well as the discipline contained in carrying out sensitivity and probability analysis, go some way to reduce this risk. Afterwards a well-established routine of project monitoring reappraisal, review or *ex post* evaluation, or whatever the subsequent comparison of forecast with actual results is called, may be especially appropriate.

REAPPRAISAL: *EX POST* EVALUATION AND CAPITAL EXPENDITURE REVIEWS

It has been said that, without subsequent re-examination, formal planning appraisal techniques are largely counter-productive. *Ex-ante* evaluation – the prior preparation of forecast results – is very necessary when raising finance for a project, either internally or externally, and obtaining the desired go-ahead. There is, however, no certainty that the combined estimates and skills which resulted in the forecasts have been optimised unless a subsequent view is taken.

There are well-established commercial routines whereby periodic (weekly, monthly, quarterly, annual) accounts are compiled of both financial and physical resources used and benefits achieved, and reports are made to relevant technical and financial monitors. Usually the results are compared with annual and three- or five-year plans for the project of the organisation as a whole. Variations are studied and adjustments are made.

Projects which were initially appraised using cash flow disciplines should be reviewed using the same disciplines. If the conclusions drawn differ, speedy action may be desirable or, if it is not, it would be nice to know that it is not.

It is unfortunately necessary to take a cynical look at projects built for less than the forecast cost, sales that noticeably exceed budget, and other such successes. If the planners' faults were not in their stars but in themselves they should remain as underlings. People have gone as far as saying that it is useless to plan at all unless one also reviews the results. But, as always, too much is as bad as too little.

It is not always clear who should conduct reappraisal reviews. Conflicts may be avoided if the project operators undertake the review in the normal course of their duties. It is highly desirable also to include some sort of outside view to ensure a balanced opinion as to why the resulting return differs from that first forecast. The review should, of course, cover all the unquantifiable as well as the measurable aspects. If the organisation sets up a separate reviewing team, its members may need great powers of diplomacy as well as of detection and endurance.

Reviews are discussed preferably at the same forum as are capital expenditure proposals, or, at least, the decision-takers should check that re-evaluation has taken place. Very often the lessons do not need to be driven home but have been learnt in the course of the operation.

The introduction of this routine is often problematical. As usual, opposition may be a cover. Other avoidance tactics can include radical changes of scope of a project leading, among other things, to a delay in the review date. Significant changes of scope should be appraised as rigorously as new projects.

FURTHER READING

Franks, J. R., and Broyles, J. E., *Modern Managerial Finance*, Wiley, New York, 1979

Merrett, A. J. and Sykes, A., *The Finance and Analysis of Capital Projects*, 2nd edition, Longmans, London, 1973

Merrett, A. J., and Sykes, A., *Capital Budgeting and Company Finance*, 2nd edition, Longmans, London, 1973

Thomas, Howard, *Decision Theory and the Manager*, Pitman, London, 1972

8 The annual accounts

W P Ridley

Anyone interested in the management of a company, whether taking an active part or merely investing capital, needs to have financial information of two kinds concerning the company:

1 Where the capital is invested (shown in the balance sheet)
2 The return earned from the investment (shown in the profit and loss account).

Those in active management can call for financial reports and accounts to be designed according to their own requirements. But, for investors and others, forms of balance sheet and profit and loss account have been laid down by Acts of Parliament. This chapter starts by describing the formal requirements, and then proceeds to discuss other aspects of the accounts, including the interpretation of accounts in order to judge a company's financial performance.

ACCOUNTING REQUIREMENTS OF THE COMPANIES ACTS

The form of the published accounts and the directors' report is set by the Companies Act 1981, but this Act must be read in conjunction with the previous major Acts on the subject dated 1948, 1967, 1973, 1976 and 1980. These documents must be sent to each member of the company, debenture holder and certain other interested parties at prescribed intervals.

The final accounts in the prescribed form, together with the directors' report, must also be filed with the Registrar of Companies.

Note that filing of accounts does not imply an inspection of such accounts by the Registrar or the Department of Trade. It means exactly what it says–the documents are filed. Such filing, however, involves laying the documents open to public inspection at Companies House. A search fee is payable before the accounts and report can be inspected. These accounts, however, are likely to be markedly different from management accounts, particularly the profit and loss account. The contrast between typical management accounts and accounts prescribed for shareholders is shown in Figures 8.1 and 8.2.

GHM	£'000	£'000
SALES		5000
less		
Purchases of raw materials	2000	
Manufacturing wages	1500	
Foremen's wages	50	
Factory expenses	150	
Depreciation of plant and machinery	60	3760
GROSS PROFIT ON SALES		1240
add		
Investment income from:		
quoted investments	10	
unquoted investments	45	
Rents	300	
		355
		1595
less		
Distribution costs	80	
Directors' fees	10	
Directors' remuneration	80	
Salaries	600	
Rent	10	
Rates	12	
Insurance	20	
Property repairs	100	
Provision for renewal of office building	5	
Depreciation of office equipment	2	
Telephone and postage	6	
Provision for doubtful debts	11	
Bad debts	25	
Interest on bank loans	6	
Interest on debentures	8	
Plant hire	2	
Auditors' remuneration	1	
		978
NET PROFIT BEFORE TAXATION		617

Figure 8.1   *Profit and loss account of a limited company as presented to its management*

	£'000	£'000	£'000
			GHM
TURNOVER			5000
Cost of sales			3760
Gross profit			1240
Distribution costs		80	
Administrative costs		884	964
			276
Rents receivable (net)			300
			576
Income from shares in companies outside the group		55	
less interest payable outside the group		14	41
NET PROFIT BEFORE TAXATION			617

Note depreciation in fixed assets of £62,000 charged in above figures

Figure 8.2   The accounts shown in Figure 8.1 in the form to be filed with the Registrar

The Companies Acts do not limit the information to be presented, but they set out what must be included in the final accounts and directors' report, including any notes which may be required for clarification. Such information is termed the minimum legal requirements. In fact, the Companies Acts select the information that needs to be filed. The full final accounts must therefore be adapted to meet the needs of the Acts. The balance sheet and profit and loss account of a company based on this selected information are termed the statutory accounts.

Growth of information required

The information required for the statutory accounts has grown enormously during the past sixty years, owing to pressure from investors, the government and the general public. The pressure from investors for more information has grown with their increasing separation from management in industry and commerce. This separation has led to a need of investors to learn as much as possible of the state of the companies, in order to assess the security of their investment. The general public, which in this connection includes creditors and potential investors, are concerned to know how companies are being managed, and whether they are financially sound. (This demand for information becomes especially apparent when public confidence in company administration has been shaken by a well-publicised fraud.) Successive governments have responded to these two pressures in their legislation.

The government itself may wish to have more information made public if it feels that this will have a beneficial effect upon industry or commerce as a whole. Thus the publication of export figures by each company, for example, can have the effect of increasing emphasis on overseas sales and thereby stimulating trade. As a result, the successive Companies Acts tend to set increasingly stringent requirements for company disclosure while accounting standards are continually being tightened to achieve uniformity in reporting.

STANDARD PRESENTATION

Figures 8.1 and 8.2 highlighted typical differences between management and shareholder information. However, the accounts shown were not comprehensive since they took company information only to the stage of profit before taxation and did not cover all the possible items that can be included. After this point there is no difference between the information required by the Companies Acts and that normally presented to the management. The balance sheet designed for management is also broadly similar (in most cases) to that which is required by the Companies Acts to be presented to the investors and filed with the Registrar.

Full details of a stand profit and loss account are given in Figure 8.3 indicating information that has to be published, if not in the face of the accounts by way of note.

Directors' emoluments

In addition to the information shown in Figure 8.3, certain information concerning directors' emoluments must be given, either in the accounts or in a statement attached to the accounts. All directors' remuneration and past directors' pensions, paid by the company or by any other person, either for their services as directors or for services in other capacities, must be shown. Likewise the statements or accounts must show any compensation paid by the company or any other person to past or present directors for loss of office. In addition the statement must show the number of directors who have waived their rights to emoluments and the aggregate amount that has been waived. The chairman's emoluments must be shown, and also those of the highest paid director if these are in excess of the chairman's emoluments.

The number of directors must be shown, broken down into income groups; that is, the number of directors whose emoluments do not exceed £2500; the number whose emoluments exceed £2500 but do not exceed £5000; and so on for each successive integral multiple of £2500. For each of these items, the term

GHM	1982 £m.	1981 £m.
Sales outside the group (directors' report to give split by major activities and show exports)	=	=
Trading profit (cost of items inset in Figure 8.2 to be noted)	+	+
Interest paid less dividends and interest receivable (The amount of interest payable on overdraft bank loans and loans repayable within five years to be distinguished from other interest payable; and income from investments listed on a recognised stock exchange to be distinguished from income on unlisted companies)	+	+
Profit before tax	+	+
Taxation (see below)	+	+
Minority interests	+	+
Profit after tax and minority interest	+	+
Extraordinary items (to be noted separately)	+	+
Profits after extraordinary items	+	+
Dividends (cost of dividends net of tax to be shown split between amounts paid and amounts proposed to be paid)	+	+
Retained profits for the year		
Profit & loss brought forward		
Profit and loss A/c at end of year		
Earnings per share (based on profit after tax and minority interest and average shares issued during year)		

Figure 8.3 Format of the statutory profit and loss account

'emoluments' does not include contributions paid by the company for the benefit of directors under any pension scheme.

Taxation items

The more detailed requirements about disclosure of taxation items are covered by the layout shown in Figure 8.4.

Taxation based on profits for the year:		GHM
Corporation tax at 52% (including £xx (previous year £) transferred to deferred taxation) on profits excluding those of associates	x	x
Less relief for overseas taxation	x	x
	x	x
Overseas taxation	x	x
Prior-year adjustments	x	x
Tax on share of profits of associates	x	x
Total tax charge		

Note: Taxation charged against profit for the year has been reduced by £xx due to deferment of tax liabilities for which provision has not been made.

Figure 8.4   Presentation of taxation details

The balance sheet

Figure 8.5 provides a format for a company's balance sheet, together with the notes which relate to the corresponding figures shown in the table. The principles of valuation are also set out.

1   Fixed assets: the amount to be included in respect of a firm's fixed assets is the amount of its purchase price or production cost less provisions for depreciation. Similar principles shall be applied where goodwill or development costs (only rarely to be treated as an asset) are given balance sheet values.

For fixed assets shown at valuations, the year in which the valuations were made must be disclosed. For fixed assets valued during the last financial year, the names or qualifications of the valuers and the bases of valuation they used must be given.

Freehold land must be shown separately from leasehold land, and land held on a long lease (one having not less than fifty years to run) must be distinguished from that held on a short lease (having less than fifty years to run).

There must also be shown (i) the aggregate amount of fixed assets acquired during the year; and (ii) the book value at the date of the last balance sheet of fixed assets disposed of during the year.

If the detail to be disclosed is considerable it might best be given on a statement attached to the accounts, reference thereto being made in the balance sheet.

2 As with other fixed assets, for long-term investments it is necessary to show the cost of valuation and the aggregate amount written off, except in the case of:
(*a*)   Shares in subsidiaries which may be shown as a single figure – but it is necessary to state the basis on which the amount was arrived at, as illustrated in the balance sheet;
(*b*) Quoted investments and unquoted investments, provided the value as estimated by the directors is shown either as the amount of the investment or by way of note.

For any investments in the form of unquoted equity shares in respect of

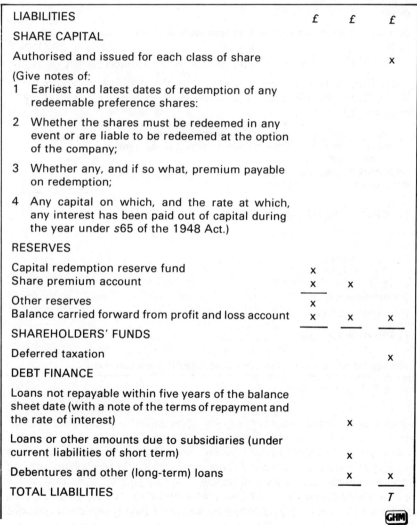

LIABILITIES	£	£	£
SHARE CAPITAL			
Authorised and issued for each class of share			x
(Give notes of:			
1 Earliest and latest dates of redemption of any redeemable preference shares:			
2 Whether the shares must be redeemed in any event or are liable to be redeemed at the option of the company;			
3 Whether any, and if so what, premium payable on redemption;			
4 Any capital on which, and the rate at which, any interest has been paid out of capital during the year under *s*65 of the 1948 Act.)			
RESERVES			
Capital redemption reserve fund	x		
Share premium account	x	x	
Other reserves	x		
Balance carried forward from profit and loss account	x	x	x
SHAREHOLDERS' FUNDS			
Deferred taxation			x
DEBT FINANCE			
Loans not repayable within five years of the balance sheet date (with a note of the terms of repayment and the rate of interest)		x	
Loans or other amounts due to subsidiaries (under current liabilities of short term)		x	
Debentures and other (long-term) loans		x	x
TOTAL LIABILITIES			T

GHM

Figure 8.5   Format of the statutory balance sheet

ASSETS					GHM

FIXED ASSETS (Other than investment) **(1)**

	AT COST	AT VALUATION	DEPRECIATION	£	£	£
	£	£	£			
Freehold land and buildings					x	
Leasehold property:						
long lease					x	
short lease					x	
Plant and machinery					x	
Other					x	x
Goodwill, patents and trade-marks; at cost less amounts written off					x	x

INVESTMENTS (any short-term items should be shown under current assets) **(2)**

Quoted investments	x	
Unquoted investments	x	x

CURRENT ASSETS **(3)**

Stocks and work in progress (if the amount is material a note must be given of the manner in which these items were computed)	x	
Debtors (after deducting any provision)	x	
Balances at bank, and cash	x	x

less
CURRENT LIABILITIES AND PROVISIONS

	£	£	£
Bank loans	x		
Bank overdrafts	x		
Taxation currently due	x		
Creditors	x		
Dividends proposed	x	x	
WORKING CAPITAL		x	x
TOTAL ASSETS			T

The figures in parentheses refer to the notes in the main text.

Figure 8.5   (continued)

which the estimated value is not given, there must be disclosed:

(*a*) The year's gross income from those investments;

(*b*) The company's share of the profits (or losses) both before and after taxation, for the last accounting period of the bodies in which the investments are held;

(*c*) The company's share of the undistributed profits (or losses) accumulated by those bodies since the investments were acquired;

(*d*) The manner in which any losses incurred by those bodies have been dealt within the company's accounts.

3   Current assets shall normally be valued at production costs or purchase price (which may be calculated on a last in first out or first in first out price or average weighted price). However, where the net realisable value is estimated to be lower than this cost, this lower value will be substituted.

Items requiring disclosure

Other matters to be disclosed in the published accounts (by notes if not otherwise shown) include:

(a)   The corresponding figures for the preceding year:

(b)   The nature and amount, or estimated amount, of any contingent liabilities not provided for;

(c)   The amount or estimated amount of any contracts for capital expenditure, so far as not provided for, and of any capital expenditure authorised by the directors but not yet contracted for;

(d)   The bases on which foreign currencies have been converted into sterling;

(e)   Any special circumstances affecting the company's taxation liability for the current or succeeding financial years;

(f)   The number of employees (other than directors of the company) whose emoluments for the year (from the company, its subsidiaries or any other person in respect of services to the company or its subsidiaries):

> exceeded £10 000 but did not exceed £12 500
> exceeded £12 500 but did not exceed £15 000
> exceeded £15 000 but did not exceed £17 500

and so on in successive integral multiples of £2500;

(g)   The information required by s3 of the 1976 Act concerning each of the company's subsidiaries;

(h)   The information required by s4 of the 1967 Act:

(i) where the company holds equity shares in another company (other than a subsidiary) exceeding one-tenth of the nominal value of the issued equity of that other company, or

(ii) where the company holds shares in another company (other than a subsidiary) which, in the investing company's balance sheet, are shown at an amount exceeding one-tenth of the investing company's assets (as stated in its balance sheet).

(j)   Under s5, a subsidiary has to give the name and country of incorporation of its ultimate holding company.

THE DIRECTORS' REPORT

The directors' report must accompany the balance sheet and profit and loss account filed with the Registrar of Companies, and must be sent to all members of the company, debenture holders and other interested parties.

The report, which is presented by the board of directors, contains much relevant information concerning a company's activities, and its minimum contents, summarised below, were considerably extended by the Companies Act 1967. It should be especially noted that these minimum contents are required by legislation and are not subject to directors' choice any more than the information contained in the statutory account.

Minimum contents of directors' report

Review

A review of the company's affairs during the period covered by the accounts: particulars of important events that have occurred since the year end; likely future developments; an indication of research and development activities.

Dividends

The amount(s) recommended to be paid by way of dividend.

Reserves

The amount(s) proposed to be transferred to reserves.

Activities

The principal activities of the company and significant changes in these activities.

Directors

The names of all directors who acted in such a capacity at any time during the period under review.

Changes in fixed assets

Significant changes in the company's fixed assets. If the market value of land is substantially different from the value shown in the balance sheet, an indication of the difference in value.

Share and debenture issue

The reason(s) for making any issue of shares or debentures during the period under review, and details of classes issued and amounts received in each class. Particulars of dealings by a company in its own shares.

Contracts

Contracts with the company (except service contracts) in which a director of the company has an interest; the parties to the contract, the director involved, the nature of the contract and the nature of the director's interest must be specified.

Arrangements between company and directors

Any arrangement whereby the directors are able to obtain benefits by the acquisition of shares or debentures in the company or any other body corporate.

Directors' interests

Directors' interests (at the beginning and end of each year) in shares or debentures of the company. This requirement is extended to include the directors' spouses and infant children (the directors' 'family interests').

Matters showing the state of the company's affairs

Particulars of any matter required for an appreciation by its members of the state of the company's affairs, so long as in the opinion of the directors the publication of such information would not be harmful to the company.

Relative profitability of different activities

Turnover and profit or loss of each class of business carried on by the company, if such classes differ substantially.

Persons employed

The average number of persons employed in the UK by the company (on a weekly basis) during the year, and the aggregate remuneration paid or payable to such persons in respect of that year. This information is not required where a company has fewer than one hundred employees.

Political and charitable contributions

The amount of contributions, if exceeding £50, given for political or charitable purposes, and the identity of the political party concerned.

Exports

The turnover from exports when the value exceeds £50 000, and a note where no goods are exported.

Previous year

The corresponding amounts in each section for the immediately preceding year.

ORGANISATION OF INFORMATION

It is clear that the company's book-keeping systems must be designed to ensure that this statutory information can be easily obtained. This requires an analysis for each category of data that has to be published under the relevant Acts of Parliament. Careful organisation on these lines can avoid a great deal of end-of-year panic, which so often delays preparation of final accounts. It will also give the directors of the company a better opportunity of reviewing their progress, thus facilitating a more meaningful review of their activities and management of the funds under their control.

JUDGING A COMPANY FROM ITS ACCOUNTS

Reports by a company to its shareholders are regulated in detail by law. As a result, outside assessments of the financial standing of a company are almost inevitably based on the information given in these reports (normally issued annually) rather than on other publications of the company or on its trade reputation. Increasingly it is being realised that this outside assessment is important to the company – in raising finance, whether by loan or equity, in merger discussions with other companies, or in trading negotiations. It is therefore advisable for senior company executives to consider in detail the standards against which their company's financial performance – as set out in the fully audited report to shareholders – will be judged.

PROFIT AND LOSS ACCOUNT FOR PANGLOSS PLC

This chapter takes the abridged accounts of a company called Pangloss PLC to highlight information on which a financial examination is based (see Figure 8.6).

In the year to 31 March 1981, Pangloss earned £1.4m, before a charge of £0.4m for depreciation; depreciation is singled out because it does not represent a direct cash outflow but an accounting adjustment to the value of fixed assets – some of which are likely to have been bought many years before. Therefore when considering the cash resources available to the company both the level of depreciation and retained profits will be taken into account. The trading surplus net of depreciation gives pre-interest profits – an important indicator of company trading performance – of £1.0m (see Figure 8.8).

YEAR TO 31 MARCH 1982	GHM
	£m
Trading surplus (before depreciation)	1.4
Less: Depreciation	0.4
Pre-interest profits	1.0
Less: Interest	0.3
Pre-tax profits	0.7
Less: Tax	0.3
Available to shareholders	0.4

Figure 8.6   Abbreviated profit and loss account of Pangloss PLC

Interest charge

The interest charge depends on the amount of loans and overdrafts outstanding, which is an integral part of the financing of the company's assets, rather than of current trading. It is therefore of prime significance to those providing finance, whether as lenders or investors. From the point of view of a potential lender, the relation of the interest charge to the level of pre-interest profits give some indication of the security for loans; in this case with interest at £0.3m he is likely to be deterred by the relatively high ratio of 30 per cent of pre-interest profits (of £1m) already absorbed by interest. From the point of view of the equity investor, this ratio represents the gearing given to the amounts available to ordinary shareholders. Thus if pre-interest profits increase by 70 per cent to £1.7m with interest remaining at £0.3m, pre-tax profits will double to £1.4m, while if they fall by 70 per cent pre-tax profits will be reduced to nil. So the element of gearing offers both opportunity for increasing the return to shareholders where the company is successful and additional risk if trading returns fall. The degree of gearing that investors are prepared to accept varies according to the industrial risk and this must be borne in mind by the company executive when negotiating loans, overdraft facilities or equity finance.

Tax charge

The tax charge depends not only on the rates of tax ruling in the countries where profits are earned, but also on any special allowances or grants offered. Where the charge appears abnormal it will be analysed to ascertain whether this is due to temporary or permanent factors. The tax charge shown for Pangloss, however, of £0.3m on £0.7m represents a tax rate of 43 per cent which is unexceptional. This leaves £0.4m available for distribution to shareholders which will be evaluated by investors with reference to the number of shares issued.

RETURN TO SHAREHOLDERS

Earnings of £0.4m on 2 million shares (see Figure 8.7) are equivalent to 20p per share in Pangloss. The value of the share is normally directly related to this figure; thus, if the share price is £2, an investor will consider whether it is reasonable to buy or sell the share, given that £2 is equivalent to ten times the earnings attributable to that share (that is a p/e ratio of 5). The dividend must also be considered – for long term investors, this represents the direct return. At a price of £2, the dividend of £0.1 per share represents a 5 per cent net return on the investment; because tax is already deducted, the dividend is free of tax up to the standard rate in the hands of the recipient. The 5 per cent return is therefore worth 7.5 per cent in gross terms to the standard taxpayer at current rates of tax. Better returns are offered by an investment in gilts. The investor has therefore to judge whether the trading prospects of Pangloss offer scope for this dividend to be steadily increased.

YEAR ENDED 31 MARCH 1982 [GHM]

Earning for the year to 31.3.82	= £0.4m or 20p per share*
Recommended dividend	= £0.2m or 10p per share*
Retained profits	= £0.2m

*Issued capital 2 million ordinary shares of £1

Figure 8.7   Earnings, dividends and retentions of Pangloss PLC

TRADING PROSPECTS

The record of Pangloss will first be examined to assess the management's abilities to secure satisfactory returns. Figure 8.8 shows the ratios normally applied to the results published in the accounts to judge the management's ability in running the trading of the business.

INDUSTRIAL AVERAGE		YEAR ENDED 31 MARCH		GHM
		1980	1981	1982
	Pre-interest profit (£m) a	0.8	0.9	1.0
	Turnover (£m) b	8.0	8.0	9.0
11%	Margin on sales a/b	10%	11%	11%
	Capital employed (£m) c	10.0	11.0	11.0
11%	Return on capital a/c	8%	8%	9%

Figure 8.8   Performance ratios for Pangloss PLC

Performance

Figure 8.8 shows Pangloss's performance measured against sales and capital employed. These criteria are used as a guide to management efficiency, as they allow comparison with other companies in the same industry, as well as to the underlying viability of the company. In this table, pre-interest profit (taken because it excludes interest which depends on the method of funding of the capital employed) has advanced by a quarter from £0.8m in 1980 to £1.0m in 1982; with turnover (up from £8m to £9m) and capital employed (up from £10m to £11m) both rising less fast, margins on sales and returns on capital have increased over the period. Margins at 11 per cent in 1982 are the same as for the industry as a whole, which therefore indicates normal trading returns and one without volatile fluctuations; return on capital, however, at 9 per cent, is well below the industry level of 11 per cent indicating that the amount of capital employed is high compared with other companies in the industry. Moreover, since the return of 9 per cent falls below the general level of interest rates, it is insufficient to justify the use of new capital in the business; indeed disposal of the existing assets or a change of management – whether through merger or staff recruitment – could be justified in these conditions. For the business cannot justify to its shareholders the employment of funds which could be better invested elsewhere. Thus return on capital forms a key element in the financial assessment of a company; capital in this context however has to be carefully defined and this is considered in detail with reference to the Pangloss balance sheet.

BALANCE SHEET FOR PANGLOSS PLC

Pangloss's balance sheet is given in abbreviated form in Figure 8.9.

GHM		£M
Sources of Finance		
Share capital 2 million ordinary shares of £1		2
Retained profits		4
Shareholders' funds		6
Debt finance		
4% Debenture 1982	3	
Bank overdraft	2	5
Total funds		11
Assets Employed		
Fixed assets		
Property	5	
Machinery	1	
Vehicles	1	7
Net current assets		4
Total assets		11

Figure 8.9   Abbreviated 1982 balance sheet for Pangloss PLC

Values of shares

The first point of interest raised by the balance sheet is the book value of the shares. Of the £11m capital employed in Pangloss at the end of the 1981-2 year, £6 m is shown to be financed by shareholders' funds giving a book value of £3 each for the 2 m shares. (This allows for the assets of the company fetching the £11 m shown and thus providing £6 m surplus after paying off the debt finance of £5m.)

Scope for raising funds

Secondly the balance sheet gives an indication of the scope for raising further finance. In this case with borrowing at £5 m against £11 m capital employed, it is unlikely that lenders would be interested in advancing further funds to Pangloss. In addition to checking the company's ability to service the interest charge out of current profits, lenders are concerned with the asset backing for loans. It is rare for a company to obtain half its funds from borrowing. Within the £5 m debt the £3 m 4 per cent debenture explains the relatively low interest charge given in the profit and loss account. However, since it falls to be redeemed in 1982 it can be considered, with the bank overdraft, as short-term finance; the refinancing of the debenture could well be at a rate of interest of 15 per cent instead of 4 per cent, increasing the interest charge by £420 000 from £120 000 to £540 000. Thus the funding problems of the Pangloss Company are clearly likely to discourage investors, for shareholders will expect to be asked to contribute further equity finance.

Assets employed

However, close attention must also be paid to the assets shown in the balance sheet, for the value attributed to these assets is critical to measuring the efficiency of the company through the rate of return on capital and the potential debt finance that they can secure. In particular the value given to the property must be considered; for if the book figure represents cost or an out-of-date valuation, the current value may be considerably higher provided the property is freehold or on a long lease. The annual report must therefore be examined for details of the basis of valuation of the property; if the up-to-date value of the Pangloss property was, for instance, £8m against £5m shown, the total assets employed come to £14m; and with pre-interest profits of £1m, return on capital is little over 7 per cent, indicating that higher rewards could be gained by investing the money in gilt-edged stocks. (This assumes that the machinery, vehicles and current assets, which include stocks and debtors net of creditors, raise their book value of £6 m.) On the other hand the prospect of raising debt finance is clearly less forbidding; not only does property tend to appreciate but legal rights to it can be granted to lenders. As a result up to two-thirds of the value of the property can commonly be raised by debt finance and, provided it is invested at a rate of return that exceeds the interest charge, this offers opportunities for expansion. Property may make Pangloss attractive as a takeover prospect whether on a break-up basis or on the prospect of improving the present returns.

Assets other than land have to be treated more cautiously; the value of the plant may be minimal on a break-up basis, while current assets, such as debtors and stock, may not fully realise their book values – particularly if the company does not impose sufficient financial control. The trend of these assets to turnover will therefore be examined closely to see whether normal business standards are being achieved. On a forced realisation, these assets may recover much less than their book value if standards have not been maintained.

Other information

There is much other information that can be taken from the report, for instance on the extent of capital commitments, or the subsidiaries and associated companies of the group. These do not affect the key standards applied to the balance sheet and profit and loss account that have been examined here. These standards are used for assessing the company from several standpoints. For the shareholder the attraction of the company may be measured by the trend in earnings per share. Potential lenders will look at the cover for the interest charge, the proportion of capital funded by loans and the type of security offered. Management will be gauged by the margin on sales and return on capital secured. The significance of the information given in the annual report is therefore of fundamentl importance to a company in any assessment of its financial standing and the efficiency of its management.

INFLATION ACCOUNTING

As inflation is becoming more and more an accepted part of the economic environment, considerable attention has been paid to adjust company results to take this factor into account. A simple approach is to charge to the profit and loss account with the amount that is required to maintain the real value of the equity base.

However, after much debate the official approach adopted is to apply adjustments to the profit and loss account that reflect the rate of change of prices experienced by each company in its existing business, rather than the general rate of inflation – as represented, for instance, in the changes in the retail price index. The purpose of this approach is to check the success of the company in maintaining its interests rather than providing for the equity base to be maintained.

From 1 January, 1981, quoted companies with few exceptions (such as property companies, investment trusts, and insurance companies) were required to include current cost statements in their annual reports.

To judge the company's effectiveness in coping with inflation the following adjustments are made to conventional profits:

1   A cost of sales adjustment
2   An adjustment to the depreciation provision to take account of replacement value (rather than historic value) of fixed assets
3   An adjustment to allow for the consequential change in the net working capital required
4   The impact of gearing.

The impact of these adjustments is shown in Figure 8.10, and the amended profit and loss account would normally be as illustrated in Figure 8.11

The figures can be carried down to show current cost earnings per share; current cost retentions and reserves which take account of supluses on assets valued on a current cost basis, and an amended balance sheet reconciling the liabilities (as amended by the current cost reserve) with assets on a current value basis. The major advantage of current cost accounts (CCA) is that they concentrate attention on the impact of inflation on the cash flow of a business. While accounts provided on an historical cost convention still provide the prime analysis of a company's past performance, CCA figures indicate the ability of a company to finance its operations in the future.

Depreciation	To adjust the depreciation charge to take account of the current value of fixed assets rather than historical cost.
Gearing	Offsets the impact of the previous adjustments by taking into account the proportion of funding secured by borrowings (partly reflected in the profit and loss account through the interest charge.)

GHM

Assuming:
(a) depreciation charge of 10% – on fixed assets.
(b) the current value of fixed assets is £1,000 but the book value is £600.

A further charge of 10% on £400 (£1,000 less £600) would be made against profits.

Borrowings typically comprise

loan capital (say)	£800
deferred tax	£300
other current liabilities	£200
	£1300

Net operating assets include:

fixed assets	1,000
stocks	4,000
monetary working capital	200
	5,200

The gearing adjustment is there-fore 1300 or 25%
5200

Adjustment	Effect	Example
Cost of Sales	To charge against profits the current cost of stocks. This ensures profits made from holding stocks are excluded since they do not form part of operating profits.	Assuming: (a) opening stocks were valued at £100 per ton. (b) all opening stocks (say 20 tons) were used during the year. (c) the value of stocks doubled to £200 per ton during the year. (d) profits would be reduced by the difference between the replacement value of opening stocks and the opening value – i.e. £100 × 20 tons = £2,000.

Monetary Working Capital	To take account of the change in working capital required to finance the net creditor/debtor position.	Assuming:
		
		           1 Jan 31 Dec
		creditors £300 £400
		debtors £500 £700
		net increase £200 £300
		  in funding
		
		On the basis that the net increase in funding is entirely due to inflation within the business, a charge of £100 (£300 less £200) would be made against profits.

Figure 8.10 *The impact of current cost accounting adjustments*

	Comment GHM
Operating profit on the historical cost basis (after depreciation but before interest).	£4,000
Current cost adjustments (see note 1)	£2,140
Current cost operating profit	£1,860
Gearing adjustment	465 25% of £1860
	£1,395
Interest	395 as in 'historical accounts'
Pre-tax profits on current cost basis	£1,000

Note 1
The current cost adjustments comprise:

Cost of sales adjustment	£2000
Monetary working capital	100
Depreciation adjustment	40
	£2140

Figure 8.11   Profit and loss account after current cost adjustments
This relates to the examples in Figure 8.10

FURTHER READING

How to Read a Balance Sheet, ILO, Geneva, 1975

Merrett, A. J. and Sykes, A., *Finance and Analysis of Capital Projects*, Longman, London, 1973.

Reid, W., and Myddelton, D. R., *The Meaning of Company Accounts*, Gower, 3rd edition, 1982

Rockley, L. E., *The Meaning of Balance Sheets and Company Reports*, Business Books, London, 1975

9 Budgetary control

Alan R Leaper

All businesses have some form of budgetary control in existence whether or not they recognise it or call it by that name. Someone in the organisation co-ordinates the resources of the business in some degree to achieve some sort of plan, but whether they examine alternative plans, ideal criterion and harmony of objectives is possibly another question.

There are many benefits to be derived from the introduction of a formalised budgetary control system among which are:

1   It defines the objectives of an organisation as a whole and in financial terms
2   It provides yardsticks by which to measure efficiency for various parts of the organisation
3   It reveals the extent by which actual results have varied from the defined objective
4   It provides a guide for corrective action
5   It facilitates centralised control with delegated responsibility.

The disadvantages of a formalised procedure are by no means so readily identifiable; in general terms they usually concern the following:

1   The additional costs/personnel necessary to perform the function
2   The suspicions aroused by its introduction that it is merely another vehicle to implement cost reduction programmes
3   The complacency of paper work becoming routine with the eventual possibility that little notice or action is taken.

Immediate benefits should not be expected from the introduction of a budget procedure. It may take a year or two to educate those concerned in the proper compilation of the data required and in the proper application of the data subsequently made available.

WHAT IS A BUDGET?

A budget, in business planning, is the expression in financial (and rather summarised) terms of a comprehensive short-term operational plan for a business entity. The financial numbers relate to specific action programmes, which give rise to asset acquisitions and disposals, the earning of revenues and the incurring of expenditure. A budget in which these financial numbers have been 'pulled out of the air' is worse than useless.

Many alternative plans may be considered before the final one showing the most practical profit is chosen. Executives and other responsible officials from all functions of the company must contribute towards the plan. Data in the unit terms of each of the functions concerned must be collected and translated into monetary terms. For example, the sales manager is primarily concerned with units of the finished article or service and he would therefore contribute the volume and models to be included in the plan. The production manager talks in standard hours and efficiencies. The personnel manager will be responsible for the levels of wage rates, absenteeism factors, welfare schemes, etc. The chief executive must be fully convinced of the benefits to be derived from the plan and really believe in it.

Budgetary control is the process of managing these facets – planning and co-ordinating all functions so that they work in harmony and control performances and costs. It establishes the responsibility, throughout the corporate structure, of all managers for achieving the company's budgeted objectives. It entails measuring at suitable intervals how the plan is actually progressing and, if divergencies are occurring, taking the necessary corrective action to ensure that the company gets back on course again.

By having a budget built up in this manner it is possible to fix responsibility at every level of the organisation – and this is important.

Most managements have found that it is not sufficient to face the problems of a business on a day-to-day basis or even on a year-to-year basis; medium-term operational (or programme) planning is therefore carried out over a time-horizon of three to five years ahead. Generally, such planning involves a projection of the total market for the company's products and an assessment of what the company's share of that market should be, based on historical per-formance and management objectives. Obviously the degree of accuracy of the projections and plans varies with the period covered. As a matter of fact, in view of the many uncertainties involved in projecting activities over, say, a three-year period, the usual procedure is to prepare plans for the first year in considerable detail, i.e., the Budget, and then to resort to summary projections for the remaining two years. As each year's plan is done, refinements are made on the basis of recent experience and a new third year is added.

BUDGET CENTRES

Efficient control requires acceptance that costs are best controlled at the point where they are incurred. The transport manager should therefore control the transport department's cost. But the control span of any one person should not be unduly large. The area controlled by an individual is known as a *budget centre*, defined by the Institute of Cost and Management Accountants as 'A section of the organisation of the undertaking defined for the purposes of budgetary control.'

Budgets prepared at a given level of budget centre are then consolidated at the next level up (profit centre, division or company, as the case may be). A substantial business organisation will generally comprise a number of operating units, each with primary responsibility for its own profits and cash flow (profit centres) as well, perhaps, as its own capital investment (investment centres).

Thus a business may include several profit centres which, in larger organisations, may be grouped into investment centres or divisions. Every division will normally have its own financial controller, responsible for preparing the divisional master budget (see the following section of this chapter). Larger profit centres may also employ their own management accountants, who prepare draft profit and loss and cash budgets. Within each budget centre there may be other smaller areas to which costs are attributable: for example, it may be desirable to identify and control groups of trucks in a transport department. Such a smaller area of control is defined as a *cost centre*, which the Institute of Cost and Management Accountants describes as 'A location, person or item of equipment, or a group of these, in or connected with an undertaking in relation to which costs may be ascertained and used for purposes of cost control.'

Within each budget centre, only one person should be responsible for incurring costs. Ultimate responsibility for budgetary control lies with the chief executive.

COMPILING A BUDGET

There is really no established order in which budgets should be prepared provided all parts are geared into a common factor. This is generally the principal limiting or bottlneck factor which varies for each individual company.

Most companies tend to establish a sales target determined on market potential and their share of the market as the basis of their budgets. Many others prefer to establish their production capacity and plan a budget to ensure the full utilisation of available equipment. The ideal, of course, is to achieve a harmony of both of these important items. However, there are many other factors which may determine the level of activity to be budgeted, amongst which are insufficient cash to finance expansion, a scarce raw material, and, possibly, the non-availability of skilled labour.

Having established the basis for compiling the budget all known external factors which could have a bearing on its fulfilment must be examined – national wage awards, sales taxes, credit squeezes, the movement of purchase prices, etc.

In larger organisations a budget committee is usually formed to review these items and determine, as best it can, the likely effect they will have on business during the period to be used in the budget. Having determined these external factors, the budget accountant/committee would advise functional and departmental managers of their effects and provide guidelines for the compilation of the subsidiary departmental budgets, the main examples of which are considered below.

Sales budget

The sales budget should show total sales, expressed both by value and quantity. It may be further analysed by product, by area, by customer and, of course, by seasonal pattern of expected sales. The main problems arise in determining quantities and in the calculation of standard prices. Constraints such as competitive activity have to be borne in mind (new products and aggressive pricing policies).

The budget should be compiled by the sales manager. He will seek the opinions of his salesmen and use any statistical forecasting techniques arising from market research. Other considerations include general business and economic conditions, company advertising policy, new products, supplies, product demand and plant capacity. A special pricing study is usually helpful at this stage, and this should show the complete product range, the relevant market sector, competitive models or products (taking into account both the pricing and the features available), introduction dates, discount structures and advertising strategy. In some cases, when jobbing production is involved, budgets must be made in terms of the expected sales value only.

Production budget

The production budget is a statement of the output by product, and is generally expressed in standard hours. It should take into consideration the sales budget, plant capacity, whether stocks are to be increased or decreased and outside purchases. The form the production budget would take depends on circumstances. Usually, the quantities are shown for each department (budget centres) and information is taken from machine loading charts, material specifications, time schedules and other production or time-study records.

When computing labour cost, the average labour rate used depends on the wage plan in effect. For hourly rated employees not on incentive bonuses, an overall plant rate may be sufficient. In other cases, departmental or labour grade rates may be used. When a straight piece rate plan is in force, the labour cost is the amount paid per unit produced. When other incentive plans are used, labour rates have to be computed to include estimated amounts for bonus payments. In companies using standard costs, cost accounting records can be very useful in determining budget requirements for non-productive direct labour. Many cost accounting systems are sophisticated enough to indicate the breakdown of non-productive direct labour into down time, waiting time, changeover or set-up time and so on.

The plant manager will prepare the production budget in close collaboration with accountants, production engineers, work study engineers and other key personnel. Adequate lead times for the delivery of new equipment and the development of new processes must be considered.

At this stage, the sales and production budgets should be compared to ensure maximum utilisation of capacity aligned to satisfactory sales growth. If the sales budget exceeds production capacity, then decisions on capital expenditure and new plant may be required before proceeding further. If, on the other hand, significant under-utilisation of capacity is denoted, decisions on how best to use this spare capacity must be taken (to determine, for example, if sub-contract work would be profitable, if a revised pricing structure could increase the volume of sales, or if plant should be declared surplus and sold off or scrapped, etc.).

Production costs budget

This supplementary budget should determine the 'cost of sales' allied to the required production.

Generally, by far the largest element in cost terms is direct material. This part should be compiled by the chief buyer in conjunction with the production manager. Using the sales and production budgets, it will determine the requirements of raw material and piece-parts, period by period, to meet the output, and will be evaluated in cash cost terms. Considerations should take into account bulk buying, delivery periods, stock holding, suppliers credit terms and trade discounts, as well as recognising any changes in material specifications, new model introductions, etc. In timing the purchase of raw materials, piece-parts etc., consideration must be given to the necessity to keep inventory levels to the very minimum and thereby not tie up valuable capital. Special competitive pricing exercises should be undertaken from potential suppliers to ensure that costs are strictly controlled and keen.

Direct labour is another most important element of production costs. The work study department should be called upon to establish standard times for individual units. These may then be evaluated by the required volumes and converted into direct labour requirements. The degree of labour efficiency must be determined, as must the type of employee necessary, that is, male/female; skilled/semi-skilled/unskilled.

Direct expense budgets covering warehousing, transportation, warranty and special tools should be determined by the appropriate managers responsible for incurring or approving the respective expenses.

Factory overhead costs (burden) should be established by departmental foremen and consolidated by the production manager. Expenses of all types should be considered and some assistance may be necessary from the finance department in determining depreciation, insurance and other expenses possibly beyond the control of the local foremen.

Personnel budget

This is a headcount schedule of the total labour requirements necessary to carry out the sales and production budgets and, in fact, run the whole business from managing director to office boy and production worker to office cleaner. It should be prepared by the personnel department in conjunction with all other functional departmental heads.

The schedule will show the number of personnel required, the hours to be worked, wage rates, salaries etc., and should be built up by departments. The respective costs should, of course, be incorporated in the applicable departmental budgets. The recruitment and training policies of the company will be incorporated in the budget and cognisance should be taken of all labour-related costs – for example, national insurance, and pension schemes.

Operating and service department budgets

The type of department falling into this category may be administration, finance, selling, advertising and service, and might also include warehousing and shipping. The departmental head of each of these functions will be responsible for compiling his individual budget. The data included will cover personnel requirements by number and grade and be cost-determined in conjunction with the personnel manager; and departmental running costs detailed by account, namely utilities, operating expenses, depreciation, insurance, rates, etc.

Special note should be taken of competitors' activity in determining the size and use of the advertising budget.

If raw material or bulk purchases are necessary, the usage and cost of these will be planned with the purchasing agent or chief buyer.

The basis of determining costs included in these budgets invariably depends on the actual trend in previous years adjusted, of course, for known changes. It should also be remembered that historical costs will include inefficiencies and these must be identified and determined if likely to continue. The considered effects of volume and activity should also be borne in mind.

Capital expenditure budget

This supplementary budget is usually compiled by senior management in conjunction with engineering and technical services.

The budget will show details of the capital expenditure proposals in the period of the master budget and will probably be prepared for a number of years because of its longer-term implications. Items included will be distinguished by the various types of asset – land, buildings, equipment, furniture, etc., and should also state the reasons for proposals – replacement, new methods, capacity, etc.

Back-up data should also accompany the proposals to justify the expenditures, and will take the usual forms of capital evaluations, such as return on investment and discounted cash flow analysis. The strain on cash resources should also be considered when compiling this budget.

Profit and loss account

The first component of the master budget is the budgeted profit and loss account. This budget will summarise the effects of all the relevant data contained in the supplementary operating and service budgets, sales, purchasing, personnel and capital expenditure (depreciation, salvage receipts) budgets. It will be prepared in months or other chosen periods and be compiled by the financial controller. A sample profit and loss statement incorporating provisions for budget and standards is shown in Figure 9.1.

Cash budget

The second component of the master budget is the cash budget, which is critical in view of the possible constraints that an unsatisfactory cash availability position may have on the required expansion of a business and hence on the acceptability of the master budget as a whole.

The financial controller, with the assistance of all other management, should determine the timing by period, usually monthly, of production, sales, fixed asset purchases etc., and then prepare the effects on the cash balance. The reason for this budget is to determine by period where additional cash may be required or where surplus cash may be available for short-term investments.

The income side is built up from the sales and debtors budget plus any other miscellaneous receipts, such as loans, new capital, sale of assets, grants, interest, etc. On the expenditure side will be the incurred expenses of the production and service department budgets, purchasing and capital expenditure budgets plus other payments relating to the distribution of profits, such as dividends and income taxes.

Balance sheet

The third component of the master budget is the projected balance sheet which will show the net effect of the budgets on the financial position of the company. Again, being compiled by the financial controller, it will consider information contained in the budgeted profit and loss account, capital expenditures and cash and the related movement of the working capital and financing.

Management must examine these results of the profit and loss, cash and balance sheet master budgets that result from the consolidation of the subsidiary budgets and determine if they are acceptable. Do they show the most practical overall profit to be accepted as a plan for the ensuing year or period to be budgeted? If the answer is negative then the problem areas should be determined and the departments concerned advised specifically of their shortcomings. As all the budgets are mainly interrelated, such a change generally means the re-submission of all the subsidiary budgets. Whilst this exercise may appear to be rather long-winded and even time-wasting, it is one of the real values of preparing budgets in this manner in that the consideration, discussion and communication of the short-term profit objective of the company is involving all levels of management in its achievement, and by this process is most likely to reveal the maximum practical profit objective for the company.

In practice, a lot of companies tend to take either sales or production in

	Budget	%	Standard	%	Actual	%	Variance
Current Month							
Gross Sales							
Less: Deductions from sales							
Total Net Sales							
Manufacturing Standard Costs							
Material							
Labour							
Burden							
Direct expense							
Total Standard Costs							
Standard Manufacturing Gross Profit							
Budget and Volume Variances							
Actual Manufacturing Gross Profit							
Expenses							
Selling							
Advertising							
Administrative							
Engineering							
Total Expenses							
Operating Profit							
Net Profit Before Taxes							
Income Tax Provision							
Net Profit							

Figure 9.1 Example of a profit and loss statement with provision for budgets and standards

isolation and agree independently what the level of activity should be in these fields; once decided on, they proceed to build all the other budgets around them. If the resultant profit is in excess of the outlook for the current year, they are happy to leave it as such. However, assuming that the job is to be tackled properly, it is at this stage of review that any attempts at over-budgeting or, worse still, conservative budgeting, should be weeded out. The level of responsibility for performance of the plan from each manager should be agreed upon, so that he fully commits himself to its attainment.

When the master budgets have been finally agreed upon and accepted, they should be adopted formally by management as its policy and plan for the forth-coming year or period and thereby provide a budget against which performance or achievement will be measured.

CONTROLLING THE PLAN

As indicated, budgets are built up by responsibility. It follows, therefore, that operating statements will be prepared for each budget centre involved. These operating statements should form part of the management information system used to control actual performance against the budget plan.

Good budgetary control follows the theory of 'management by exception'. Whilst management is provided with full details of expenditure, sales, production, etc., under its functional control, reports and information should be focused on matters that are adverse, or that show an unusual favourable variance, so that its energy is concentrated in the right direction and its effort is not being diluted with a lot of information which merely indicates that things are going as planned.

There are differing schools of thought on the amount of detail that should be provided to management. Some management accountants prefer to provide only data over which managers have some degree of control. For instance, if depreciation policy is decided by the board, there is no point in giving an operational manager a depreciation charge for say, the machine shop. He has no control over what that charge will be; according to this theory, this information is unnecessary and does not help him to perform his part of the plan under normal conditions. This theory does not give management the full picture and lacks the important benefit of enabling management to see the overall effect and contribution of its department to the business as a whole. The statement may be broken down into two sections labelled 'controllable' and 'uncontrollable'. Just what is controllable or uncontrollable can be surprising. For example, a shop foreman shown a list of fixed assets in his area on which there is a depreciation charge may well indicate items of equipment which are surplus to his require-ments but for which he has not bothered to raise a disposal request. These items can then be removed from the department, sold with good salvage values being obtained, valuable floor space being released, routine maintenance checks ceasing and administration time and effort being saved in searching for and identifying equipment at physical inventory time.

Timing of feedback

Timing is of great importance. When should the measurement of control be effected, and over what period? Having decided what period the budget is to cover (usually annual) the budget itself will be divided into sub-periods: possibly months and quarters, or perhaps into thirteen four-weekly intervals, depending on the type of business. In addition to the detailed annual budget, most companies have some form of long-range planning for a number of years ahead covering, for instance, the profit and loss account, balance sheet, cash flow and capital expenditure.

This longer-term planning concerns itself primarily with determining whether or not the internal fund flow of the business will cover its commitments and capital expenditure programme, etc., but of course the longer-term plans will not be prepared in anything like the same detail as the yearly short-term operating budget. It is a matter of individual company requirements to determine which data is best controlled on a quarterly, monthly, weekly or even daily basis.

An organisation must generally have a fairly sophisticated accounting system to generate and disseminate information on a daily basis and this type of data is generally confined to production data. Standard hours produced, finished units, efficiencies, absenteeism, etc., all lend themselves to daily control. Billings in terms of unit sales and value would best be reviewed on a weekly basis, although for local consumption this, again, may be preferred on a rough daily basis.

All other profit and loss and cash flow data would be embodied in monthly financial statements. A balance sheet could be prepared on a quarterly basis.

Whatever is right for a business must be determined by the constraints within which it works and what is needed to control the situation. Normally, data of a daily and weekly nature are restricted to middle management to facilitate operational control and are not fed through the pyramid of top management unless a special situation demands such close control. As a general rule, the lower down the management line one goes, the sooner information should be in management's hands. The foreman should have his output in standard hours measured against budget and his material usage for his batch of machines during the following morning so that he can take the necessary corrective action to correct any deviation from his target.

Thus it has been said that this first-line information is the life blood of the business, and the accounting results which follow at the end of the month confirm and quantify an already known situation.

FLEXIBLE BUDGETS

One criticism sometimes levelled at budgetary control is its rigidity. In practice, actual results may be the outcome of circumstances which have changed from those existing when the budget was first prepared. Budgets, when set and agreed upon, can only be based on one set of circumstances. As actual conditions seldom equate with budgeted conditions, the difference between actual costs and budgeted costs must be demonstrated. Information should therefore be available to suggest the appropriate level of expenses, generally known as budget standards, which fluctuate at varying levels of production activity or sales volume.

Flexible budgetary control (as opposed to fixed budgeting) was introduced to control this situation. Flexible budgeting is applied in businesses where it is impossible to make a firm forecast of future conditions. Although fixed budgeting should be satisfactory for the more stable industries, these are very few and far between. Flexible budgeting is more widely applicable.

Flexible budgeting is designed to provide a more realistic picture of the variance between actual expenses and budgeted expenses. One expects to be able to distinguish that part of the variance which is due to volume and for which a manager will not have control, and that part of the variance over which the manager should have control. To achieve this, one must be in a position to calculate budget standards at varying levels of activity.

The application of this calculation is demonstrated below by considering first a report on the basis of fixed budgeting and then showing a similar report calculated on a flexible budgeting basis. Before looking at these reports, it must be clear that costs are classified for flexible budgeting purposes. This in itself is a most difficult task and one that may be tackled in many ways which cannot be amplified in this chapter. However, for the purpose of this exercise, the following broad categories are used:

1 Fixed costs – costs which do not vary in the short term with volume
2 Variable costs – costs which do so vary
3 Semi-variable costs – costs which will vary with volume but not in direct relationship.

The later chapter on cost accounting gives more details of these types of costs: of course, if standard costing is already applied in the company, the setting of a flexible budget is rendered considerably easier. If standard costs are not available, the technique of marginal costing will need to be applied in dealing with individual costs to determine the degree of variability. Scatter graphs or

Expense type	Budget (£)	Actual (£)	Variance (£)
Material	10 000	12 500	+ 2500
Labour	5 000	5 900	+ 900
Rent	3 000	3 000	—
Salaries	1 000	1 100	+ 100
GHM	19 000	22 500	+3500

Figure 9.2   Example of fixed budgeting

the regression theory may be used. Figure 9.2 is based on fixed budgeting and demonstrates how much the actual is off target. This type of measurement is an improvement on, say, measuring against last year's performance when circumstances may have been different. The report provides some conception of the amount by which actual experience varies from budgeted plans.

However, if one is to adhere to one of the basic principles of budgetary control, that people should only be responsible for cost over which they have control, this report may not provide the solution.

Figure 9.3 applies similar information but is calculated on the basis of flexible budgeting. Thus, clearly, the advantages of flexible budgeting are demonstrated by the second report. It shows in reality that instead of the manager being responsible for an adverse variance of £3500 as he was in the first report, he is, in fact, only responsible for the adverse variance of £500, the

GHM		Budget			Actual	Variance Analysis	
	Standard per unit	Fixed budget	Flexed budget			Control-able	Volume
Output in units		10 000	12 000	12 000		—	+ 2 000
% of original budget		100%	120%	120%		—	+ 20%
		£	£	£		£	£
Variable Costs							
Material	£1.00	10 000	12 000	12 500		+ 500	+ 2 000
Labour	£0.50	5 000	6 000	5 900		– 100	+ 1 000
Fixed Costs							
Rent		3 000	3 000	3 000		—	—
Salaries		1 000	1 000	1 100		+ 100	—
TOTAL		19 000	22 000	22 500		+ 500	+ 3 000

Figure 9.3   Example of flexible budgeting

remaining £3000 being due to increased volume in production which may be the result of conservative sales forecasting, or some other factor which must be taken up with some other department in the organisation.

Flexible budgeting is thus extremely useful for getting behind the causes of variances, particularly if quantities, as well as costs, have been budgeted. With sales variances, for example, one can determine whether the variance is due to prices, volume, outlet mixture, product mixture, or a combination of these.

USE OF COMPUTERS

Generally, manual methods of making the planning computations are time-consuming, with the result that only a few alternative plans of operation can be fully evaluated when setting a budget and analysis of variances may be limited by time constraints. Computerised financial models have been developed to assist in simulating what the results would be under many different assumptions as to volume, products and plans of operation. Most steps in budgeting usually involve some alternative assumptions or decisions, and the final outcome of the budget process can vary greatly in terms of the profits and resources which will result from each assumption or decision. As a practical matter, the burden of making the planning and budgeting computations, under even one set of assumptions, is generally considered to be all that a company can expect its people to carry in addition to their current operating responsibilities. Very often the work is such that deadlines are missed and budgets for the new year are not available on time. The computerised financial model takes the drudgery out of the computations, once the computer programs are prepared, by applying the given relationships to different sets of assumptions and conditions. This process of simulating different methods of operations is a big help in exploring the alternatives available in the planning process.

ZERO-BASE BUDGETING

Zero-base budgeting is a technique for short-term operational planning, whereby existing levels of expenditure on ongoing activities are systematically questioned. This is in contrast to the more common 'incremental' approach. In incremental budgeting, the benchmark tends to be the level of activity and expenditure in the immediate past, budget proposals being related to this in terms of 'more' or 'less'. In zero-base budgeting, the benchmark is the 'minimum survival' level of activity and expenditure as seen by the manager of the activity in question. If the budget proposal is only to maintain the existing level of activity, assuming this to be above the 'minimum survival' level, the proposal must explain why the additional expenditure involved over and above the 'minimum survival' level is justified. A manager in charge of several activities will be required to state which level of expenditure on each of these activities he would choose if he could only spend, say, 80 per cent of his budget. The point of this approach is to squeeze out 'budget slack' at the lower levels of decision-making and to allow the senior levels to decide how, if at all, the balance of the budget will be spent.

INSTALLING THE SYSTEM

The organisational chart should be examined with a view to determining where the responsibility for sales, costs and profits really lies. Revisions where appropriate, may be considered at this time. The organisation structure should be so developed as to fix responsibility right down the line. There must be an organisation chart which clearly defines the levels of responsibility and the chain of command, setting out who is responsible for what and to whom. It is desirable to support each functional position with a job description defining the function, duty and responsibility. Tradition must be ignored, responsibility and control being given to those who are responsible for taking the decisions, but care must be taken to preserve the 'business flair' of an organisation, and those given the responsibility should be placed where their individual resources can be best used.

The key factors should then be determined before designing the system most suitable to the company's needs. The system design should cover flow diagrams of the information generated, collection data necessary for budget preparation and control reports to be subsequently prepared. During this period consideration should be given to the level of sophistication of the existing information system, whether the proposed system will provide an improvement and also the level of human resources with which one has to work the new system.

Having obtained a positive reaction to these considerations, the next step is to test the initial design with various personnel at all levels in order to determine its suitability to meet their requirements for management information.

Once initial design is finalised, the next step is to prepare a series of seminars and teach-ins to explain the thinking behind the purpose and operation of the system. Questions, constructive criticisms and improvements should be invited so that all are involved and communicate at all levels.

A timetable for installation of the programme should be established. A critical path analysis is the ideal basis for identifying the order in which the budget data should be collected and which information is to be cross-referred to two or more departments.

Now is the time for the collection of information for the 'first budget'. Considerable time, assistance and guidance should be made available to staff at this stage, and perseverance on behalf of those taking responsibility for the installation of the system will be required. It is vital that all levels of management go through the discipline of thinking through and preparing their portion of the budgets. Miracles should not be expected from the first results. It is not unusual for a company to take two or three years to get a control system of this nature fully operational. However, at each stage one should expect to produce some results which are usable even in the first year. What these results will be may differ from company to company but initially they usually provide a good insight to sales and cash flow data. An important by-product is management eduction and awareness of what the business is all about.

Budget period

There is no general rule governing the selection of a period of time for a budget. This will be decided by the particular circumstances of the business. For instance the fashion industry must, of necessity, have a very short budget period, sometimes of three or four months duration, whereas in the shipbuilding industry a budget may range over three or four years. For most businesses, however, the calendar year is normally the accepted period: it is broken down into twelve monthly periods and the information is complementary to the published accounts.

However, if there is a strong seasonal influence affecting sales, it is sometimes prudent to have a 'model year' upon which to base the budget and this usually starts just ahead of the main selling period. Businesses which rely mainly on the summer or Christmas trade may well justify a model year. Model years, as the name implies, usually commence with the introduction of new models. A car manufacturer, for example, may run its model year from September to the following August in order to have a good start to the year following the autumn motor shows and new year car registrations. The motive behind this is that if business has not gone as well as expected there is still sufficient time before the end of the model year to curtail activity, restrict costs and reconsider expansion programmes or introduce special promotions in order to keep profits in line with, or better than, budget.

Budget manual

It is helpful to have such a document available within the company so that there is no ambiguity about what is required of each individual in relation to budgets. The type of information one might expect the budget manual to contain is a brief explanation of the purposes of budgetary control as practiced within the company and organisation charts and job descriptions showing quite specifically the budget responsibilities for each function; routing of budgetary control forms for collection and control documentation; timetables or programmes for completion of budgets and control data feedback; budget periods; samples of reports and statements to be employed and accounts classification and coding data.

Budget committees

The question of who should control the preparation of budgets and who should review these controls is one that each organisation arrives at during some stage of the budget preparation.

It is desirable that top and middle management contribute to and agree levels of activity to be budgeted, although it must be recognised that the human factor involved makes this difficult to achieve. A keen manager, anxious to please at a budget review meeting, will possibly incorporate a stretch element to his plan. Another manager setting his own targets against which his performance is to be measured may be inclined to be over cautious (particularly if an achievement bonus is paid). Investigations have been made in this area and the results carry important lessons for the business man interested in making the most of his budget system. One conclusion is that the budgets studied were used as pressure devices for constantly increasing efficiency, but because of the effects on people, the budgets tended to generate a long-run result of decreased efficiency. Naturally enough, this is attributed to the lack of participation in the budget preparation phase by those being budgeted and to the lack of sales ability on the part of accounting personnel. Another study concludes that successful budgeting is more concerned with human relationships than with accounting techniques and that if good principles of human relationships are applied, successful budget practices become inevitable. Yet another appraisal of current business budgeting indicates that important weaknesses in practice are the result of superficial appreciation of budget concepts by management, inadequate techniques, and the absence of a disciplined environment in many organisations. Upon reflection, it becomes apparent that the requirements for a successful budget operation are not restricted to accounting or finance planning techniques but that successful managers are those who keep such considerations in mind while executing the more mechanical aspects of the budget process.

There are various views held on this point. If operating managements are made responsible for profits, then one of the objectives of budgetary control, that is, the proper co-ordination of the organisation, is achieved.

The same processes should be involved as with the control aspect. What an organisation should attempt to achieve is the total commitment of all levels of management to the plan. Each level of management should review its plans and performances through the usual management committees, be they formal or informal groupings, right up to the chief executive, and the overall objective should be clear and unambiguous at each stage.

However, one person will be responsible for pulling together the various parts of the master budget. This job usually falls on the chief accountant or financial controller or his department. Larger companies employ a budget manager and, of course, this co-ordinating exercise naturally falls into his lap. He may be called upon to undertake a number of exercises to determine what the various results thrown up mean within the overall company objectives, but it must be emphasised that his role is one of support. The responsibility is fixed upon the persons committing and accepting stewardship over resources.

The budget organisation can be regarded as analogous to a telephone company operating an important communications system; it is responsible for the speed, accuracy and clarity with which the messages flow through the system, but not for the content of the messages themselves.

Information codes

Budgetary control has extended control information beyond the more traditional accounting information to broader aspects of control, setting out data in terms of hours worked, output of production in standard hours, information on market share, quality of product, etc. This is all necessary for the achievement of the plan. However, looking at the pure accounting contribution to budgetary control, a suitable system of accounts coding should be designed so that the information is collected and analysed within the budget and cost centres.

The accounting code should be what is commonly called a subjective/objective system. The subjective part of the code should qualify information into its primary or traditional classification, that is, the nature of the expenses, for example, wages, fuel, rent, etc. The objective part of the code will be used to analyse the expenditure to the cost and burden centres, that is machine X in the machine shop.

It is important to give considerable thought to the design of the coding system, as it should not only be able to cope with existing needs for information, but also have the flexibility to be expanded to meet future demands. A system of this sort should enable a company, using the subjective code, to produce information necessary for the preparation of the traditional statutory accounts. And by going through the objective section of the code, the information required for budgetary control and management accounting can be produced which should be made available to those drawing up the budgets as appropriate.

CONCLUSIONS

Budgetary control often strikes apprehension or fear into non-financial people. People tend to be sceptical or untrusting of having their performances measured against a standard. This is a human and understandable response. Most people, at some time during their careers, have had budgetary control used against them as a cost reduction tool.

It is up to finance managers to clarify and emphasise that budget flexing and control is an essential and deliverate need of modern-day management. It is a management tool designed as a *fair* basis upon which to measure performance against a predetermined plan, and conduct business in the most efficient manner possible, thereby improving profitability.

FURTHER READING

Cave, S. R., *Budgetary Control and Standard Costing*, 3rd edition, Gee, London, 1973

Willsmore, A. W., *Business Budgets in Practice*, 5th edition, Pitman, London, 1973

10 Managing working capital

Leon Simons

LIQUIDITY

Working capital is normally taken to mean the excess of current assets over current liabilities, this amount being the net current assets. If the balance sheet for ABC PLC is examined (Figure 10.1) the working capital for that company is seen to be £3 065 539 minus £2 505 132, which amounts to £560 407.

The working capital indicates the liquidity of the company, and there are two commonly used ratios to express the degree of liquidity. One is the current ratio which is simply the current assets divided by the current liabilities. ABC's current ratio is $\frac{3065}{2505}$ = approximately 1.2.

Some accountants consider that it is more useful to ignore inventories when looking at liquidity, since they could take considerably longer to turn into cash than debtors or creditors. They feel that it is more pertinent to compare the quick assets (current assets minus inventories) with the current liabilities. This is known as the quick ratio or acid test ratio and is

$\frac{\text{quick assets}}{\text{current liabilities}}$ which in ABC's case is $\frac{2190}{2505}$ or 0.88.

There is no generally ideal current ratio since companies differ so greatly from each other. 1.2 may be appropriate for a light engineering company like ABC PLC with a short production cycle. The same ratio, however, may be too low for a company with a longer cycle and a proportionately bigger stock investment. On the other hand, a supermarket with no work in progress (because it does not manufacturer) and no debtors (because its business is purely cash) would very likely have a current ratio of less than 1; that is, an excess of current liabilities over current assets.

One should try neither to maximise nor minimise the liquidity ratios; one should try to optimise them in relation to the objective, which in the case of a commercial company is probably the maximisation of profit on capital employed. The lower the liquidity ratios are, the more vulnerable the company is to pressure from creditors which it is unable to meet. The higher the liquidity ratios, the more the capital which is not being fully exploited in terms of the return earned on it. Therefore, one should seek to have as little working capital as is consistent with not being unduly vulnerable to pressure from creditors. This ideal level of liquidity would not only vary from company to company but would vary through time in one company as conditions changed.

Stock

Excess stockholding has an adverse effect on liquidity. The ratio normally used for assessing stock level is the stock/turnover ratio. ABC's ratio is

$$\frac{875}{6364} = 13\tfrac{3}{4}\%,$$ which expressed as a percentage of a year is about 7 weeks.

(The denominator is the turnover stated in Figure 10.2.)

This figure on its own has little absolute significance but, like most other management ratios, can be used to monitor changes through time. We do not know if 7 weeks' average stock is too high or too low or how great a deviation there is around the average. Like liquidity, stockholding has to be balanced; it should be neither maximised nor minimised but optimised in terms of profit. Too much stock means that there is money tied up in it which is costing more than it is contributing. Too little stock means that the cost of lost sales due to being out of stock exceeds the savings made in not holding the additional stock.

However, there are other factors to be considered in deciding the optimum stock level: for example, whether there are additional costs in holding increased stock rather than just the interest on the capital. If the stock level were to be reduced by a given amount, would the company be able to vacate a warehouse with consequent savings in rates, rent, insurance, heating etc? How many storemen could be dismissed or redeployed?

Stock appreciation should also be brought into account. If the company uses volatile commodities, it might save a great deal of money in holding more than its immediate requirements of a material whose market price is expected to rise during the period covered by the holding: this saving may far outweigh the extra stocking costs and throw in as a bonus freedom from the danger of being caught out of stock.

The stock ratio is not ideal in a number of respects. Firstly, the turnover is at selling prices, while the stock is at cost. Secondly, the turnover covers a period, while the stock is at a point of time which may not be typical of the period. Thirdly, the cost of the stock is not factual but is a function of the company's costing system which includes arbitrary assumptions and subjective judgements.

Debtors

Apart from inventories, a major development of working capital is in the credit

ABC PLC · GHM

BALANCE SHEET

as at 28 February 1982

Share capital and reserves		1982		1981
	£	£	£	£
Share capital				
5 500 000 ordinary				
shares of 10p each				
(authorised 7 400 000)		550 000		550 000
Reserves				
Share premium	182 727			
Other reserves	734 412			
Ordinary shareholders'		917 139		814 543
funds		1467 139		1364 543
Minority shareholders'				
interest		154 620		82 050
Secured loans		360 957		—
Current liabilities				
Creditors	938 009		545 552	
Taxation	394 246	356 311	356 311	
Bank overdraft (secured)	936 927		634 619	
Proposed dividends	235 950		206 250	
		2 505 132		1 742 732
		4 487 848		3 189 325

Fixed assets	Cost or valuation	Aggregate Depreciation	Written down value		Written down value
Freehold land					
and buildings	585 818	7 044	578 774		400 346
Plant and motor					
vehicles	1 191 729	348 194	843 535		453 603
	1 777 547	355 238	1 422 309		853 949
Interest in subsidiary not					
consolidated			—		88 765
Current Assets					
Stocks and work-in-					
progress		875 196		594 628	
Debtors		1 906 981		1 621 063	
Cash at bank and in hand		283 362		30 920	
			3 065 539		2 246 611
			4 487 848		3 189 325

Figure 10.1 Group balance sheet for ABC PLC
Group balance sheet of a manufacturing light engineering company and its
subsidiaries as at 28 February 1982 with the corresponding figures (as required
by law) as at 28 February 1981

	1982	1981
ABC PLC [GHM]		
PROFIT AND LOSS ACCOUNT		
For the year ended 28 February 1982		
	1982	1981
	£	£
Turnover	6 364 014	5 088 579
Profit before taxation (see note 1)	613 883	922 022
Deduct: taxation	262 108	370 691
	351 775	551 331
Deduct: exceptional item	—	12 500
Profit after taxation	351 775	538 831
Add: proportion of losses attributable to minority shareholders	6 648	2 500
	358 423	541 331
Dividends	235 950	288 750
Balance retained and added to reserves	122 473	252 581
Earnings per 10p ordinary share	6.5p	9.8p
Note 1		
After deducting:		
Depreciation	133 808	90 780
Emoluments of directors	61 573	42 480
Auditors' remuneration	12 723	9 500
Interest on bank overdraft	32 330	14 772
Interest on secured loans	25 573	—
Hire of equipment	10 321	5 004

Figure 10.2   Profit and loss account for ABC PLC
The profit and loss account summarises receipts and costs of a company over a given period. This example covers the year ended 28 February 1982 and complements the balance sheet for ABC PLC shown in Figure 10.1.

taken by customers. This does not of course apply to those retailers and others who do not conduct a credit trade. The debtors/sales ratio is the measure, and this again is usually expressed in weeks. ABC's ratio is

$\dfrac{1907}{6364}$ = 30% or about 15½ weeks. This ratio has the same disadvantage as that

mentioned concerning the stock ratio, namely that the point of time at which the debtors are taken may not be typical of the period to which the turnover relates. Alternatively, there may be a strong seasonal bias within the year's total sales figure. For example, if two-thirds of the year's turnover was sold in the second six months, then the ratio is $\dfrac{1907}{4242} \times 26$ weeks, which is just under 12 weeks. However, this is a problem for the external readers of the balance sheet, since managers with access to the management accounts could take the seasonal bias into consideration in calculating the ratio.

Creditors

These are the opposite side of the coin to the debtors. They are a source of funds to the company, and the more capital the company can borrow from this source, the less it requires from others, or alternatively the more it can deploy in various assets and build up the activity (and possibly the return) on the same net capital.

The creditors, being money owing in respect of purchases, will be compared with the purchases in the recent period and expressed in weeks. The purchases are not a figure which is required to be shown separately in the published accounts, but once again it will be available to managers. They should use it in the same way as the debtors' ratio by allowing for the seasonal bias.

Readers of the published accounts can make the assumption that purchases are roughly the same proportion of sales in the recent year as they were in the previous year. Then they can compare the movement of creditors with that of debtors, ABC's debtors increased from £1 621 063 to £1 906 981 by 17½ per cent. The creditors rose from £545 552 to £938 009 which is over 73 per cent and a considerable relative improvement. Indeed, in absolute terms the increase in creditors exceeds the increase in debtors, so that the net cost of credit to the company may have fallen despite the increase in turnover.

However, the average length of credit taken by the company from its suppliers is still not known. Suppose for the sake of argument that the £938 000 represents two months credit, that is, average monthly purchases have been running at half that level. Then, an increase of one month to three months will, other things being equal, raise borrowing from this source by about £469 000 and at the same time reduce the bank overdraft by the same amount. The total current liabilities will remain the same but the company will have substituted additional borrowing from suppliers for part of what it previously borrowed from the bank. The effect on profit of the change, assuming overdraft interest at, say, 15 per cent pa, is a gain of about £70 000 pa. This is not a once and for all gain but will continue at that rate for as long as the additional credit is taken. This assumes that (a) purchases continue at the current level, (b) interest rates continue at 15 per cent pa and (c) relations with suppliers remain unaltered.

If there are changes in either (a) or (b) the effects can be easily ascertained, but assumption (c) requires careful consideration. If we take more credit from a supplier, will that supplier react and if so how will his reaction affect us?

There are a number of things the supplier can do, from writing a letter (which costs the customer nothing) to withholding supplies (which may cost the customer a great deal). Between these extremes, he may reduce quality, increase prices, cut down deliveries and so on. However, there is doubt about the validity of these intermediate reactions.

He may reduce the quality of the product or the frequency of delivery or after-sales service, but this may not be acceptable to the customer who may then withdraw his custom. Before taking any of these steps, the supplier would have to be prepared for this eventuality, the effect of which would be the same as if he himself withheld supplies.

Similarly, if the supplier increases his prices, the higher prices may or may not be acceptable to the customer. If they are, why did the supplier not increase them previously? If they are not, he once again risks losing the business. Therefore, the question facing the supplier is whether or not he can risk losing the business.

From the customer's point of view, he must decide whether he can tolerate loss of supplies from this source because, even though it may not be in the supplier's best interest to stop supplies, he may act irrationally and the customer must be prepared for this. The summary of this discussion is that the customer's ability to take longer credit from a particular supplier depends on the balance of power between them.

Since this varies with different suppliers it follows that an individual credit policy with at least the major suppliers is necessary if optimum credit is to be taken. If a blanket credit policy is adopted to cover all suppliers, this assumes that they are all equally powerful, which is most unlikely to be the case. The consequence of this would be to take from some less credit than one could take with impunity, and to take from others more than is wise.

These arguments apply with equal force to debtor control, and since sales exceed purchases tight debtor control is even more important.

It is often suggested that if a company takes longer credit from its suppliers, its own customers will in turn extend their credit and the move will be self-defeating. This is woolly thinking.

Customers cannot know how a company behaves to its suppliers, save in the exceptional case where customer and supplier are the same and a two-way trade is conducted. In the normal case, the customer will take whatever credit he thinks he can get away with – with impunity. This consideration is based on the same assessment of relative power as already discussed concerning creditors.

However, many companies recognise the importance of intelligent debtor control and designate is as a specific management function, whilst attention is paid to prompt invoicing and follow-up procedures. It is the treatment of credit obtainable from suppliers that is relatively neglected.

Cash discount

So far we have not considered the effect on one's credit policy if one is offered a discount for prompt payment. For example, a supplier may offer a discount of $2\frac{1}{2}$ per cent on invoice for payment within 30 days.

If one pays two months from date of invoice and forgoes the discount, one has in fact borrowed for one extra month (since the first 30 days would be taken in any event) at a cost of $2\frac{1}{2}$ per cent which is equivalent to a straight annual cost of $12 \times 2\frac{1}{2}$ per cent = 30 per cent. The discounted annual rate would be even higher than this. Since one is borrowing at say 15 per cent from the bank, 30 per cent is far too dear to contemplate. Break-even point would occur with 3 months' credit; ie 2 extra months at a cost of $2\frac{1}{2}$ per cent = $\dfrac{12 \times 2\frac{1}{2} \text{ per cent}}{2}$ or 15 per cent pa. Therefore, it is only worthwhile losing the discount if one can take at least 3 months' credit. However, if bank facilities are scarce it will pay to borrow at more than 15 per cent from suppliers if the benefit derived from the utilisation of the extra credit exceeds the cost.

So far in this chapter the various factors concerning liquidity have been discussed. We have seen that suboptimal utilisation of working capital is expensive. At least, if costs the interest on the unnecessary money used, but it also prevents that money from being properly employed in the company and could inhibit the company's growth through lack of cash.

Cash flow

Liquidity is the life-blood of the company and lack of cash is the only thing which could force the company out of business. Cash flows into the company by direct cash sales and the collection of debts from customers, and also, though less regularly, from the sale of assets. Cash flows out in direct purchases and payments to creditors, in payment of wages and other costs, and in the purchase of capital equipment. It also flows out in payment of taxes and interest on borrowed money and dividends to shareholders.

These flows have to be predicted and controlled. This is done by forecasting and budgeting (see Chapter 9). Cash has always to be available to meet committed expenditure. If not, the company can be forced into liquidation by its creditors even though it has an overall excess of assets over liabilities. The company can also obtain additional transfusions of cash from time to time by means of additional bank facilities, which are likely to be relatively short-term, by raising fresh loans which are likely to be long-term and by rights issues of further ordinary shares which are permanent funds.

PROFITABILITY

We shall assume, since there is not the space here to argue it, that the objective of a public commercial company is the maximisation of profit on capital employed. This objective covers the total future and, of course, does not apply to any single year. Almost every company could make a bigger profit this year if in so doing it was prepared to jeopardise the future. The cessation of advertising and research, for example, would often increase this year's profit but might cripple the business in the following year.

Profit on capital employed, on its own, does not mean very much. Are we talking about profit before tax or profit after tax, shareholders' capital or total capital, for example? In fact, different definitions of profit are appropriate at different levels in a company because of varying degrees of authority to control resources and made decisions.

At parent company board level, the directors are directly accountable to ordinary shareholders, and therefore the capital for which the directors are accountable is the ordinary shareholders' funds (OSF) which consists of the ordinary share capital plus reserves. Similarly, the profit which the directors are seeking to maximise is the profit attributable to the ordinary shareholders. This profit is often referred to as the company's earnings, and the earnings divided by the number of ordinary shares in issue is the earnings per share (EPS). The earnings are the trading profit less all interest charges, taxation, minority shareholders' interest and preference dividend, since these are all the deductions which must be made before the ordinary shareholders are entitled to the remainder.

Thus the profitability ratio relevant in assessing the performace of the directors is $\dfrac{\text{earnings}}{\text{OSF}}$ which, in the case of ABC PLC, is $\dfrac{358\ 423}{1\ 467\ 139}$, ie about 24½ per cent. Notice that the earnings figure is struck before deducting ordinary dividends. The earnings can be used by the directors either in paying a divident to the ordinary shareholders or by being retained in the company as an addition to the OSF. How the directors dispose of the earnings is entirely within their discretion.

Let us now look at the position of the chief executive. He is directly accountable to the board of directors and is sometimes called the managing director (if he also sits on the board) or the general manager (if he does not). The chief executive is accountable for profit since he controls both sides of the profit equation – income and expenditure. However, he does not control dividends, since he does not raise capital, and for the same reason he does not control loan interest. On the other hand, he does control the level of bank borrowing by his credit policies, etc, and so he is accountable for bank interest.

Taxation is affected within the company by board decisions, particularly those regarding capital expenditure and the raising of capital. Capital expenditure gives rise to government capital allowances. New capital may be raised by a rights issue of shares (on which dividends are paid) or by the issue of loan stock (on which interest is paid). However, interest (being a cost) is allowable for corporation tax. Dividends, which are distributions of profit, are paid after corporation tax has been charged, but are paid net of income tax. with corporation tax at 52 per cent and the basic rate of income tax at 30 per cent, every £1 of gross interest actually costs the company 48p and a £1 of gross equivalent dividend costs 70p.

Minority interests are no concern of the chief executive since the decision of whether to own subsidiaries partly or wholly is a board decision. The chief executive is therefore accountable for $\dfrac{\text{trading profit}}{\text{total investment}}$. Trading profit is defined as profit after bank interest but before deducting loan interest, taxation, minority interests and dividens. Total investment is the total long-term capital made available by the board to the chief executive. It consists of the ordinary shareholders' funds, plus preference capital, plus loan capital, plus minority interests.

$$\frac{\text{ABC PLC's trading profit}}{\text{total investment}} \quad \text{is} \quad \frac{639456^{\star}}{1521759} \quad \text{or about 32 per cent.}$$

* The 639456 comprises the profit before tax (613883) plus the interest on secured loans (25573).

The chief executive's ratio is different from the board's, but contributes towards it: the better the trading profit, the better the earnings (other things being equal). The chief executive's profitability is almost always higher than the board's because his is before tax and theirs is after.

These profitability ratios have little absolute significance, since both profit and capital employed are worked out in an arbitrary manner, and within a given factual context there is a wide range of possibilities for both.

The elements which make annual profit arbitrary are depreciation, stock valuation and the capitalising or writing off of expenditure. Capital employed is arbitrary because assets are often included at cost, or at cost less depreciation, or at valuation. It is not uncommon to find a balance sheet with some assets at cost less depreciation, some assets at 1965 valuation, and other assets at 1982 valuation all added together as if they were the same currency.

The main use of ratios is in monitoring trends. It might be thought that a given ratio at one time can be compared with the equivalent ratio at another time if, although they have certain arbitrary elements, they are calculated consistently.

This would only be partly true. Suppose, for example, that assets are entered in the balance sheet at cost, or at cost less depreciation, and not at value. At a time of inflation, profit will reflect the effects as prices and costs rise, except for depreciation which is usually based on historical cost instead of replacement cost. However, capital employed, in being consistently 'valued' at cost, will depart more and more from reality and so, therefore, will return on capital employed. The ratio will tend to rise, simply because the conventions used are holding back the denominator to a far greater extent than the numerator.

Furthermore, the ratios are determined by judgements as well as by conventions. Whilst the same conventions can be used in the calculation of ratios through time, there will inevitably be changes caused by different judgements being used, even by the same people. Thus, ratios can be no more than broad indicators.

Whereas the shareholders have to accept the accounts as they are published, and make the best of what is too often a bad job, fortunately more can be done by management, in this case the board of directors. They can ensure that the accounts (at least the management accounts if not the published ones) are prepared with maximum reality in order that they can provide a basis for management decision-making.

In the calculation of profit, stocks should be based on net realisable value instead of cost which is irrelevant. Depreciation should be the reduction in the market value of the assets between the beginning and end of the year plus the increase in the replacement cost of these assets during the year.

The reduction in the market value of the assets should be deducted from the asset value in the balance sheet at the end of the previous year to arrive at the balance sheet value at the end of the current year. In this way the assets will always be included at market value, which is the only treatment of relevance to the readers of the balance sheet.

The increase in the replacement cost of the asset will not be deducted from the balance sheet value as this could eventually cause a negative value of the asset which is of course impossible. Instead, it is taken to an asset replacement provision on the sources side of the balance sheet. Thus when as asset is sold, a figure similar to the balance-sheet value should be obtained, in addition to which depreciation has been provided between the historical cost and realisable value of the asset, and between the replacement cost and the historical cost, so that the company will have provided sufficient funds for the replacement of the asset. Conventional historical cost depreciation does not achieve this, as a result of which profit is overstated, non-existent profit may be distributed as a dividend, and the company may leave itself short of the capital necessary to continue the business at the same level as before.

Gearing

The principle of gearing is a very important one in any decision to raise new capital and it is also one of the differences between the board's profitability ratio of $\frac{\text{earnings}}{\text{OSF}}$ and the chief executive's ratio of $\frac{\text{trading profit}}{\text{total investment}}$. The measure of gearing is the gearing ratio, which is $\frac{\text{total investment}}{\text{OSF}}$. Total investment has already been described as the total long-term capital, including OSF, preference and loan capital. OSF (ordinary shareholders' funds) is the ordinary share capital and reserves. ABC PLC (Figure 10.1) has no long-term capital other than OSF and is, therefore, ungeared. The ratio of an ungeared company is 1.

Now suppose that an ungeared company has OSF of £10m and makes a trading profit of £2m. The profitability ratios can be set out thus:

Trading profit	£2.0m	Chief executive's ratio =
Loan interest	nil	
Profit before tax	2.0m	$\frac{\text{trading profit}}{\text{total investment}} = \frac{2m}{10m} = 20 \text{ per cent}$
total investment	10m	
		Board's ratio = $\frac{0.8m}{1.2m}$ $\frac{\text{earnings}}{\text{OSF}}$
Corporation tax		
(at 40%)		$= \frac{1.2m}{10m} = 12 \text{ per cent}$
Earnings		

Now suppose that the chief executive makes an application to the board for £4m additional capital, the additional funds being required for a long-term project on which the chief executive is confident of making his present 20 per cent return. The board, after examining his proposals, and comparing them with alternatives, decide to go ahead with the project and raise the necessary capital. Basically, the choice facing them is a rights issue to increase the equity (owners' capital or OSF) or an issue of 10 per cent loan stock. We shall look at both possibilities on the assumption that the chief executive (CE) meets his forecast of 20 per cent return. Here are the figures:

	Case 1 (rights issue)	*Case 2 (loan stock issue)*
OSF	£14m	£10m
10% loan capital	nil	4m
Total investment	14m	14m
Trading profit	2.8m (CE's ratio = 20%)	2.8m (CE's ratio = 20%)
Loan interest	nil	0.4m
Profit before tax	2.8m	2.4m
Corporation tax at 40%	1.12m	0.96m
Earnings	1.68m (board's ratio = 12%)	1.44m (board's ratio = 14.4%)

In case 1, the board's ratio is $\dfrac{1.68\text{m}}{14\text{m (OSF)}}$ and in case 2 it is $\dfrac{1.44\text{m}}{10\text{m (OSF)}}$

Case 2 is preferable because money has been borrowed at 10 per cent pre-tax, and invested at 20 per cent pre-tax, the difference going to the benefit of the ordinary shareholders with no further investment on their part. The gearing ratio in case 1 is 1 and in case 2 is 1.4.

Gearing, however, is a two-edged weapon. It will magnify the effect of a change in trading profit on the earnings. Suppose that in the following year (year 2) trading profit doubles and in year 3 it falls to half of the year 1 level. Then, assuming the capital structure in case 2, the positions would be as follows:

	Year 2	Year 3
Trading profit	£5.6m (CE's ratio = 40%)	£1.4m (CE's ratio = 10%)
Loan interest	0.4m	0.4m
Pre-tax profit	5.2m	1.0m
Corporation tax at 40%	2.08m	0.4m
Earnings	3.12m (board's ratio = 31.2%)	0.6m (board's ratio = 6%)

Notice that in the year 2 the $\dfrac{\text{earnings}}{\text{OSF}}$ has more than doubled from 14.4 per cent to 31.2 per cent and from year 1 to year 3 it has more than halved from 14.4 per cent to 6 per cent.

A simple and dramatic example of the effect of gearing is to be seen in the case of the private house. A man buys a house in 1964 for £5000 and finances it by a deposit of £1000 and a 25-year endowment-linked building society mortgage of £4000. In 1974 he sells the house for £15 000 and repays the mortgage. The gearing ratio is $\dfrac{\text{total investment}}{\text{OSF}}$ which is $\dfrac{5000}{1000} = 5$.

		1964		1974
Deposit	(equity)	£1 000	+1 000%	£11 000
Mortgage	(loan capital)	4 000		4 000
House	(total investment)	5 000	+200%	15 000

Although the house has appreciated by only 200 per cent, the owner's equity has increased by five times that proportion (since the gearing ratio is 5), namely, 1000 per cent. Equally, of course, if the house had fallen in value by £1000, which is 20%, the fall in the equity would have been 5 × 20 per cent = 100 per cent. In other words, the owner would have lost his entire capital since the remaining £4000 in the value of the house would have been just sufficient to repay the mortgage.

There is no generally ideal gearing ratio. It can be seen that gearing adds a speculative element to a company in the method of financing it, but the degree of speculation tolerated in the financial structure of the company depends on how basically speculative the company is. A nice steady company which is relatively unaffected by seasonal and cyclical variations in profit can stand a considerable degree of gearing whereas a company whose profit fluctuates a great deal is perhaps better left ungeared.

SOLVENCY

Finally, we come to the concept of solvency. Just as liquidity is concerned with a company's ability to meet its current liabilities out of its current assets, solvency is concerned with the ability of the company to meet its total liabilities out of its total assets. The solvency ratio is $\dfrac{\text{OSF}}{\text{total assets}} \times 100$ per cent which in ABC's case is $\dfrac{1467}{4488} \times 100$ per cent which is approximately 32.7 per cent.

This means that 32.7 per cent of all ABC's assets are financed by the owners and therefore borrowed money is the source of the remaining 67.3 per cent of the assets. In other words, even if 32.7 per of the assets are lost, the company is still solvent since there is enough value remaining just to repay all the borrowing and no more.

Once again, optimum solvency is a question of balance. A company financing too high a proportion of its total assets by equity is not maximising its profitability (since the denominator of the profitability ratio is unneccesarily high) even though it is extremely safe. The art is in judging how much external financing an individual company can stand.

The true degree of solvency, like the true degree of liquidity and gearing, can only be ascertained if the values of the assets in the balance sheet are realistic.

Book values based on cost are of little help in making these assessments.

FURTHER READING

Simons, L., *The Basic Arts of Financial Management*, 2nd edition, London, Business Books, 1978

11 Cost accounting

R M S Wilson

Cost accounting has traditionally been associated with product costing. This is concerned with determining the amount of cost to be assigned to each unit of output as a basis for valuing stocks of goods (as shown in a balance sheet) and as a basis for computing the cost of goods sold (which is deducted from sales revenue to show profit). Apart from aiding in these ways in inventory valuation and income determination, product costing is employed in the cost-plus approach to product pricing (e.g., in the contracting and printing industries).

THE NATURE OF COST ACCOUNTING

Cost is synonymous with sacrifice, but its precise definition must depend on the situation in which a measure of sacrifice is required. Different cost concepts apply to different sets of circumstances. There are only three elements of cost:

1 Materials
2 Labour
3 Expenses

Any of these can be directly related to a cost unit (*direct cost*) or indirectly related (*indirect cost*). Costs that change in accordance with the level of activity or output are termed *variable costs* and have a different behaviour pattern from *fixed costs,* which only vary with the passage of time. Some costs are partly fixed and partly variable, but it is possible to separate the two types by statistical means. Break-even analysis and other techniques relevant in cost control are based on these important distinctions between variable costs and fixed costs, and between direct costs and indirect costs.

The approach to product costing is generally to assign to each unit of output a 'fair share' of the total cost of operations. This is quite straightforward in a single product (or single service) company, but complexity tends to increase in proportion to the number of product lines manufactured and/or marketed. In a single product company all costs can be seen to be incurred to support that product (e.g., an output of 1 000 000 units at a cost of £5 000 000 gives a unit cost of £5.00). If there are two product lines – or 2000 product lines – the problem is much more difficult and the cost of any one item from a multiproduct line is impossible to measure accurately.

In addition to product costing, cost accounting is also concerned with deriving costs for other units of activity. The products produced by a company are not the only cost units; one can be interested in the cost of operating particular departments; in the cost of operating in certain sales territories; in the cost of serving various industries and customer groups; in the cost of using different channels of distribution; in the cost of servicing orders below a given value; in the cost of hiring new salesmen; and so forth.

Whatever cost unit (i.e., product, department, etc.) is selected as the focus of attention, some costs will be direct (e.g., direct labour and direct materials for a unit of manufactured output, a salesman's salary and expenses for a sales territory) while the other costs will be indirect (i.e., overheads). Much of this chapter will be concerned with the treatment accorded by cost analysts to overheads.

Overhead costs are those that cannot be traced directly to units of output. An increasing proportion of costs are of this indirect nature for various reasons (mainly relating to technological developments). While the classification of overhead costs according to their behaviour patterns (with time in the case of fixed costs, against the level of activity in the case of variable costs, and in relation to both time and activity in the case of mixed costs) is of fundamental significance, another important way of categorising these costs is under natural and functional headings. A *natural expense* is an outlay that is classified by its nature (e.g., salary, rent, etc.) rather than by the purpose for which it was incurred. On the other hand a *functional expense* is one incurred either within a particular section (or function) of an organisation – such as the marketing or manufacturing function – or to carry out a specific function (e.g., typing a letter). In a cost control context the latter category (functional classification) is more useful than the former (natural classification).

By definition, overhead costs cannot be traced directly to cost units, so any procedure whereby overheads are assigned to cost units means that the resulting *absorbed cost* is inaccurate to an unknown degree. The assigning of a fair share of cost (made up of direct costs plus a portion of overhead costs the magnitude of which depends upon the costing techniques used) to cost units is at the heart of product costing, but cost accounting exists for other reasons. In particular these are:

1　Control purposes, the aim of which is to assign controllable costs to responsibility centres
2　Planning purposes, the aim being to collect cost information that can help to indicate the cost implications of alternative courses of action. These decision-making purposes require cost information to answer such questions as:
　　(a)　What would be the effect on the company's net profit of discontinuing

product A and re-allocating the resources to product B?

(b) If an order/contract is accepted at a given price, will that price be sufficient to enable the company to earn a profit on the job?

(c) Why was last year's profit low despite a major increase in output?

(d) What will be the effect of a given wage increase on product costs and hence on profits?

(e) What effect will replacing specified equipment have on costs?

In some discussions cost accounting is defined to include management accounting, budgeting, investment appraisal, and other areas, but it is seen in the present context as being narrower in scope than this and complementary to, for instance, budgeting. Cost accounting, therefore, is seen to be an essential part of a company's total accounting and control system, but not synonymous with that system.

The orthodox financial accounting system found in every company has a major objective of recording all income and expenditure to permit a measure of profit to be derived which can then be reconciled with the increase or decrease in net worth as shown in the company's balance sheet. Income determination (i.e., the measurement of profit) is certainly the central problem of financial accounting, but the scope of financial accounting extends beyond purely recording financial transactions to include the summarising, analysing, and reporting of financial information. Its purposes can then be seen to include:

1 The provision of a working basis for the annual distribution of profits to shareholders, along with details of retained earnings, contributed capital, and other measures relating to net worth

2 The classifying of liabilities on the basis of, for example, maturity, with other information on security, and the division and grouping of assets according to significant characteristics

3 The provision of a basis on which tax assessments can be made

4 An indication to shareholders and creditors of the future prospects of the company, and of the relative success of the directors and the effectiveness of broad managerial policies and stewardship

5 To indicate to shareholders the remuneration that has been enjoyed by the directors.

The first, third and fourth purposes relate directly to the income measurement problem, illustrating how pervasive this problem is. Nevertheless, solutions must be found within the conventions on which financial accounts are drawn up. Apart from the conventional accounting principles that are prescribed by the professional authorities, the content of financial accounts is prescribed to a large extent by law. This permits the satisfying of shareholders and tax authorities, and good practice in this sphere is largely a matter of learning and applying the relevant law. An outcome of this restriction, from a management control viewpoint, is that financial accounting deals with financial flows classified by natural expense headings, whereas other types of accounting consider functional flows. This accords with the financial accounting imperative to record and interpret financial facts in as objective a manner as possible, but it does not aid in controlling costs or the activities that give rise to costs. Accounting is an expensive activity that in itself has no value: its value is derived from the importance of its objectives and its success in attaining these objectives. In so far as financial accounting has managerial objectives, these can be thought of as the provision of data to enable management to plan and control operations, but it has been shown that financial accounting is not successful in this endeavour.

The effectiveness of traditional financial accounting lies in its authoritative character rather than in the nature of the information that it produces. The existence of internal controls relating to the financial accounting system acts in a disciplining way on employees and enables the company's financial structure to be depicted in a simple and crude, but overall model that constitutes a huge barrier to chaos. But it can go further.

The intelligent presentation and classification of financial accounts; the provision of comparative figures, percentages and notes; the accompanying of the accounts with tables, graphs, diagrams, and other interpretative devices; and the supplying of supplementary information, such as funds statements and trend tables, enables the financial accountant to make his statements more informative to those who must study and use them. In this way it is possible for financial accounts to be of some limited value in cost control by giving a wide view of events in the recent past, but their value in controlling day-to-day operations is even less, and their relevance to the future is almost nil. Generally, financial accounts are too incomplete, compiled too infrequently, and too late to be of prime value in cost control.

In contrast to the reliance of financial accounting on standard accounting conventions and legal requirements, cost accounting is governed by the particular characteristics (in the form of products, structure, personalities, processes, policies, etc.) of the organisation within which is operates. Furthermore, cost accounting is concerned with internal matters whereas financial accounting is largely concerned with dealings between the company and third parties (such as creditors, shareholders, inland revenue, customers, etc.)

Needless to say, the distinguishing feature between cost accounting and financial accounting is not just that the former deals with costs. Cost accounting is concerned with the composition and control of costs, whereas financial accounting deals mainly with income determination. Once financial accountants have (in what purports to be and objective manner) ascertained income, cost accountants (in what they admit to being a subjective approach) proceed to analyse it. The analysis performed by cost accountants enables them to show not only whether a profit has been made on the working of the business as a whole, but whether a profit has been made for each process, job, product, or whatever. Such an analysis aids management in determining the output level and products that should lead to the most desirable level of operations.

The cost accounting function is therefore concerned with:

1 Cost findings (from measurement and estimation)
2 Cost analysis (covering relationships and behaviour)

3   Cost recording (including classification)
4   Reporting.

In overall terms cost accounting's objective is related to the company's profit goals, but accounting (as a service function) is a charge against profits. In relation to its contribution to managerial cost control, therefore, the cost of financial accounting should be minimised and the overhead constituted by cost accounting should be rendered as efficient as possible.

Although the cost accountant must be familiar with managerial problems if he is to perform his duties adequately, he must always be aware of the fact that the actual controlling of costs is a management function rather than an accounting one (i.e., line rather than staff). Control requires both data and action, with the accountant endeavouring to supply the former and with management providing the latter if the control process is to be effective.

COLLECTION OF COST DATA

The type of data that are to be gathered together for costing purposes will depend on the type of costing system in force and this will tend to depend on the nature of the type of production being undertaken by the company. Essentially there are three types of production. These are:

1   Job production.   This involves the manufacturing of a single complete unit. The building of bridges and ships are good examples of the one-off nature of job production. 'Jobbing' is a term used to describe work carried out against a customer's order rather than for stock.
2   Batch production.   This is employed when the number of units to be manufactured of a given production increases. It involves the work being divided into operations, and each operation will be carried out on the whole batch before the next operation is undertaken. Batch production permits the specialisation of labour, although the organisation and planning required to ensure freedom from idle time are considerable.
    In principle there is little difference between job and batch production.
3   Flow production.   Since the various operations in batch production will inevitably take up different amounts of time, programming the work flow to avoid wasted time is almost impossible. As the scale of operations increases it often becomes possible to establish continuous flow production where there is no wasted time between operations. Such an arrangement requires balancing the times of every operation (including inspection) so that bottlenecks or surplus capacity do not render the line inefficient. Clearly a fault at any stage will have effects on all other stages of the production line.

The distinction between process costing and job/batch costing is that the former deals with broad averages and large numbers of like units whilst the latter attempts to apply costs to specific jobs.

Attention can now be turned to considering the costing treatment of overheads.

ABSORPTION COSTING

Both process costing and job costing can be carried out in accordance with overhead absorption principles. The aim of overhead aborption is to ultimately spread the total cost of the company's operations over the jobs, batches, contracts, units, etc., that pass through the company's manufacturing facilities. Dangers abound in attempting to do this: overhead is applied as an average to products that are not average, and this is only partly resolved by subdividing the factory into cost centres.

The basic procedure for applying overhead to manufactured throughput involves developing overhead rates along the following lines:

1 Analyse and classify all costs into their direct and indirect categories. (This can be done as a retrospective exercise using actual costs, or as a predictive exercise using estimated costs.)
2 Relate direct costs to the particular jobs, processes, etc., for which they were/are to be specifically incurred.
3 Of the indirect costs, some will relate to particular production departments through which products pass in the course of the manufacturing cycle, and others will relate (on a responsibility basis) to service or ancillary departments (i.e., non-production departments such as maintenance, production control, stores, costing, etc.). The cost of these service departments is then apportioned to the production departments on some 'fair' basis relating to the benefits enjoyed by different production departments.

The whole question of apportioning service department costs to production departments is complicated by the fact that some service departments render services in a reciprocal manner to each other – the boiler-house supplies heating to the stores which in turn supply stores to the boiler-house, and the canteen supplies meals for personnel department employees who in turn help in administering the canteen. This problem can be dealt with in various ways:

(a) It may be thought best to disregard the cost of any service rendered by one service department to another, and to apportion the total expenses of each service department directly to the manufacturing departments
(b) It may be felt to be most appropriate to first apportion the expenses of that service department that renders services to the greatest number of other service departments but which receives in return the least service from these other departments. The expenses of the next most important provider of services can then be apportioned over the remaining service departments, and so on until all the expenses have been distributed to manufacturing departments
(c) Perhaps the most accurate – and also the most complex – method is to proceed as in item (b) above, but with the difference that when the expenses of the second service department are apportioned, some of these expenses may be carried back to the first department, provided that it has benefited from the services rendered by the second depart-

ment. The whole cycle of apportioning service department expenses in this way will have to be repeated on account of the re-apportionments until the remaining balances are so small that they can be charged directly to manufacturing

4   An overhead rate can be established for each production department or cost centre, determined by the formula

$$\frac{\text{departmental overhead + apportioned service overheads}}{\text{level of activity}}$$

and applied to each job, process, or whatever. This is termed the *recovery of overheads*. (A simpler alternative of obvious applicability in a single product company, but also applicable in other circumstances, is to have a single company-wide overhead rate. However, even in the single product company it will often be desirable to know the cost of each operation through which the work passes, and also to know the cumulative cost of the product as it passes through the various stages of manufacture.)

Overhead rates in practice are generally determined once a year – and preferably in advance rather than retrospectively, but in changing circumstances it will be advisable to revise them as necessary. The level of activity at which a department is expected to operate is of crucial importance and whenever overhead rates are determined in advance very careful attention must be paid to estimating this dimension.

Items 3 and 4 in the above list will now be considered in a little more detail.

APPORTIONMENT OF OVERHEADS

Initially, management must specify the cost centres that are to be used – the company itself as one all-embracing cost centre; major service and production departments; sub-departments; responsibility centres; or some variation of these.

Overhead costs that are directly attributable to the selected centres should be allocated to them. Once this has been done, the objective is to apportion service centre costs to production cost centres on a 'reasonable' basis, which means some basis that seems to reflect the benefits received by each production centre (and service centre if the approach suggested in item 3 (c) above is adopted), or which is seen to represent a 'fair share' of service centre costs.

It will be seen, of course, that this procedure contradicts the criterion of responsibility (that is, a responsible individual – such as a departmental manager – cannot control apportioned costs, and there is a strong argument against apportionments of overhead costs for this reason. However, a certain amount of influence may be brought to bear on such apportioned costs as heating, cleaning, and so forth). It follows, therefore, that the methods generally employed for apportioning and reapportioning overhead costs among departments for product costing purposes do not give rise to meaningful data for cost control purposes: an individual cannot be made accountable for cost apportionments from a cost centre over which he has no control. A clear distinction must always be made between cost control (be responsibility accounting for instance) and product costing (by overhead apportionment and absorption).

Possible bases for apportioning service department costs are generally related to physical identification (e.g., in items 9, 10 and 11 below), facilities provided (e.g., in items 4, 5 and 6 below), or the ease of apportionment itself (e.g., in item 3 below). Before apportioning costs it will usually be necessary to make a survey of the factory to ascertain the floor space per department, the number of employees and their distribution throughout the organisation, the investment in plant and equipment per department, the horse-power hours worked by each department, and similar matters. Suggested bases of apportionment for service department costs are:

1 Direct wages paid to production employees
2 Direct material costs incurred by production departments
3 Number of employees per department. (This is especially useful for personnel, canteen, welfare, supervision, and costing overheads. But its efficacy is affected by differences in the skilled/unskilled ratio, the rate of labour turnover, the variations in attention given by different services to different production departments irrespective of the number of employees – as when the people using a subsidised factory canteen do not represent a proportional cross section of employees.)
4 Floor area occupied (in square metres). (This is frequently used for apportioning rents, rates, building costs, insurances, and depreciation. However, it presupposes that each square metre of space is of equal value to the organisation, and it is complicated by having to find ways of dealing with corridors, stairways, washrooms, etc.)
5 Cubic space occupied. (This modification of 4 can be used for the same purposes, but is more useful for heating overheads.)
6 Capital employed. (Maintenance, depreciation, rates, and insurance costs can all be apportioned on this basis. Care must be taken in deciding on the values to be put on capital assets: replacement value may be more appropriate than written-down book value.)
7 Direct labour hours worked. (As a measure of productive activity this can be useful for apportioning personnel, medical and production planning/control overheads.)
8 Machine hours worked. (As with 7, this can be a good basis for production planning and similar costs, and it is particularly suitable for dealing with maintenance overheads.)
9 Actual measurement/technical estimates. (Electricity, gas, water, oil, compressed air and steam can either be metered so that the actual consumption per department will be given, or technical estimates can be made with reasonable accuracy.)
10 Units of output. (Materials handling, production control, stores, maintenance, depreciation, etc., can be spread on the basis of physical output.)
11 Number of requisitions received. (Purchasing, stores, tool-room activity

revolves around the processing of requisitions which make the number of requisitions processed a sensible basis for making apportionments. However, it must be borne in mind that differing degrees of attention must be paid to different requisitions – some materials are easy to obtain whilst suppliers must be sought for others, some items can be issued simply from stores whilst others must be cut before being issued.)

The most important criterion in selecting a base is to relate the overhead cost to its most causal factor: machines require maintenance, space involves paying rates, outputs require inputs. Nevertheless, the whole methodology of apportioning service department costs is plagued by the necessity of having to rely on some arbitrary rules (i.e., relating to 'benefit' or 'fair share') that have been developed in order that service departments costs might be rationally spread over production departments. Such apportionments are carried out solely for product costing purposes: the control of individual overhead costs will not be achieved by cost apportionments, and nor will the method of cost apportionment influence cost control.

ABSORPTION OF OVERHEADS

The absorption of recovery of overheads entails computing and applying overhead rates for each production department to products passing through those departments. The absorbed cost of each job or process can be derived by adding the overhead element (calculated on the basis of one of the methods shown below) to the prime cost of the job or process. (Prime cost is the aggregate of direct material cost, direct labour cost and direct expenses.) A more accurate absorbed cost will tend to result from overhead rates developed for each cost centre through which a product passes as opposed to the absorbed cost that results from one company-wide overhead rate. The essential rationale is to consider why one unit of product or particular job should bear more overhead cost than another, and then to select a suitable basis from the seven given below to reflect the answer. The bases on which production overheads (including apportioned service department costs) may be absorbed are:

1   As a percentage of prime cost. This is given by:

$$\frac{\text{Expected overheads}}{\text{Estimated prime cost}} \times 100$$

Its major failing is in not considering the time factor since overheads tend to be incurred over time. Unless a standard product is being manufactured that requires constant material and labour inputs per unit the absorbed cost computed on this basis will be inaccurate (see items 2 and 3 below).

2   As a percentage of direct labour cost, given by the formula:

$$\frac{\text{Expected overheads}}{\text{Estimated direct labour cost}} \times 100$$

This basis gives some consideration to the factor of time since, for a given grade of labour, the higher the cost the greater the time spent. It has the advantage of simplicity and is economical in that it can be developed directly from payroll data, but it fails to allow for different mixes of labour or for overtime or for payment by results.

3 As a percentage of direct material cost, given by:

$$\frac{\text{Expected overheads}}{\text{Estimated direct material cost}} \times 100$$

Only when output is uniform (i.e., when only one kind of product is manufactured, involving a constant material input for each unit of output) is this method fair. Fluctuations in material prices render it unstable, and because an expensive material may be used on one product in a multi-product company, this does not mean that that product should be expected to recover a proportionally higher amount of overhead.

Items 1–3 will only be acceptable if overheads vary in proportion to the cost base selected – prime cost, direct labour cost, or direct material cost. Any variations in wage rates or material prices will require a change in the overhead rate.

4 As a rate per unit of productive output. This method is appropriate for flow production (i.e., process costing) and separate rates can be developed for each process. The rate is derived by applying the formula:

$$\frac{\text{Expected overheads}}{\text{Estimated output (in units)}}$$

and is only suitable when the units being produced are homogeneous and recieve identical (or nearly identical) attention.

5 As a rate per direct labour hour, computed as:

$$\frac{\text{Expected overheads}}{\text{Estimated direct labour hours}}$$

The base depends for its accuracy on proper records being kept of the direct labour time being spent on each activity. It is best suited to labour-intensive operations and may not give very satisfactory results when one group of operatives use machines and another group do not.

6 As a rate per machine hour, given by:

$$\frac{\text{Expected overheads}}{\text{Estimated machine hours}}$$

7 This complements 5 above in being suitable for capital intensive situations. As a rate per production hour for situations which are neither suitable for method 5 nor for method 6. The formula is:

$$\frac{\text{Expected overheads}}{\text{Estimated production hours}}$$

Since fixed overhead costs are related in time it is often suggested that time (i.e., methods 5, 6 and 7) is the most important dimension for overhead absorption. There seems to be a very general acceptance that rates based on time or output (i.e., methods 4–7 above) are to be preferred to those based on value (i.e., methods 1–3 above). But whether they are developed in relation to time or output, overhead absorption rates should be based on a consideration of such factors as:

(a) The nature of the manufacturing processes – manual versus mechanical
(b) The nature of the materials used
(c) The constancy (or otherwise) of material prices and quality
(d) The differentials in pay rates
(e) The seasonality (if any) of production
(f) The extent to which available capacity is utilised.

There should be some cause-and-effect link between an overhead cost and the basis of absorption (e.g., if supervisory labour is apportioned to productive cost centres on the basis of direct labour cost, then it should be absorbed into product costs in accordance with direct labour costs).

It is not always necessary to distribute each overhead cost separately: some fixed costs – such as depreciation, rates, insurance premiums and rent – can be spread collectively on the basis of, say, machine hours (since this factor represents the time during which a product 'rents' the machinery and premises).

Other costs – such as maintenance, certain utilities, operating supplies, and so forth, may be distributed on the basis of units of output. However, those costs that are proportional to direct labour (such as indirect labour, supervision, holiday accurals, overtime premiums, welfare services, peronnel department, etc.) can be distributed on the basis of labour cost, man-hours, or the number of people employed – whichever seems most appropriate.

Diagrammatically, Figure 11.1 summarises the apportionment/absorption routine. The first step is to separate service centre costs from production department overheads. The service department overheads are then apportioned over the production departments. Finally, the resulting departmentalised overheads are absorbed into units of production.

It should again be emphasised that when a company produces a heterogeneous range of jobs/products, with each receiving an unequal amount of attention as it moves from one cost centre to another, it is essential to develop and apply departmental overhead rates (rather than one total company-wide overhead rate) to each job if the resulting product cost is to bear and relation to the true (but unknown) full product cost.

OVER AND UNDER RECOVERY

The actual overhead costs of a particular period will only be equal to the applied overheads of that period (i.e., predetermined overhead rate × number of units produced) by chance (unless, of course, the period's costs and activities were all rigidly determined in advance, or the forecaster was in the improbable position of having a perfect view of the future).

If more overheads are applied to units of output than are actually incurred, then overheads are said to be over-absorbed (or over-applied or over-

165

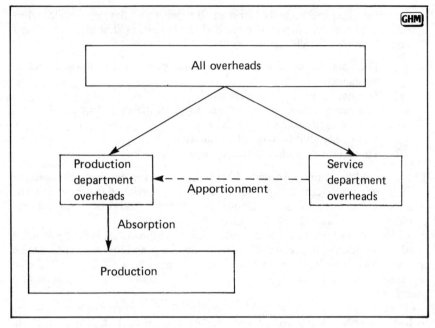

Figure 11.1   Overhead apportionment and absorption

recovered). Conversely, if too little overhead is applied to units of output, then overheads are said to be under-absorbed (under-applied, under-recovered). The degree to which overhead costs are over- or under-absorbed is a useful piece of management information. A record should be kept of the extent to which the overheads of each cost centre are over- or under-absorbed, and this can be a guide that indicates when overhead recovery rates require adjustment. (Because over- and under-absorbed overhead costs are charged directly to the profit and loss account, they are not reflected at all in any product cost. Clearly this is unsatisfactory in an absorption costing system that exists purely for product costing reasons.)

An over- or under-absorption of overheads may arise because the actual level of overhead costs has varied from the amount anticipated, or because the level of activity actually experienced during a period has differed from the level predicted. Either of these causes – or the two of them acting together – can render the predetermined overhead recovery rate inappropriate. (It is also possible for these two causes to act together in such a way that the overhead rate remains appropriate: thus an expected level of activity of 10 000 direct labour hours in conjunction with a predicted level of overhead costs of £20 000 gives an overhead rate per direct labour hour of £2.00. If costs actually amount to £25 000 and the level of activity was 12 500 direct labour hours, the effective overhead recovery rate remains £2.00 per direct labour hour.)

The explanations behind the major causes of over- and under-recovery are price rises, an expanding level of general economic activity, poor marketing, and so on. If plant capacity along with materials are available but sales volume is so low as to create an under-recovery of overheads, then this may be considered to be a marketing responsibility. However, if there is a backlog of orders and under-absorbed overhead costs result from the ineffective use of manufacturing facilities, then it becomes a manufacturing responsibility.

Normalised overhead rates save having to make minor changes every month in attempting to recover precisely 100 per cent of overhead costs during a year. For example, if overhead costs are expected to be £60 000 for a forthcoming year in which a company is expected to produce 120 000 units of output at an uneven rate, then a monthly over- or under-recovery is bound to occur if a normalised rate of $\frac{£60\,000}{120\,000}$ = £0.50 per cent unit is chosen. However, over the full year it should even out.

Figure 11.2 illustrates this more fully, with cumulative figures for over- and under-recovered overheads balancing out over the whole period of twelve months. The effect of different monthly production levels of a more extreme nature is shown in Figure 11.3. If a normalised rate (of £3.715) is used, the overhead per unit of product will vary from £51.00 at one extreme to £2.00 at the other, depending on the month in which the product was made (August or April). These extremes are unacceptable because they are not representative of the typical, or normalised, production circumstances which have a horizon beyond the end of the current month.

Apart from highlighting the need to use normalised overhead recovery rates for seasonal products, these examples further illustrate the point that the product costing imperative to absorb all overheads is of no value in controlling costs since cost control cannot operate under a regime that is confined to apportionments and absorption.

FIXED AND VARIABLE OVERHEAD RATES

So far the discussion has focused exclusively on deriving overhead rates that do no distinguish fixed from variable costs, but an important refinement of absorption costing it to derive different rates for both variable overheads and for fixed overheads.

Consider, for instance, a labour-intensive cost centre having estimated fixed overheads of £40 000 for a period, and estimated variable overheads of £30 000 for the same period, with an expectation of working 20 000 direct labour hours. A fixed overhead recovery rate of $\frac{£40\,000}{20\,000}$ = £2.00 per direct labour hour, and a variable overhead recovery rate of $\frac{£30\,000}{20\,000}$ = £1.50 per direct labour hour can be readily derived. If the actual figures for the period in question are:

Fixed overheads	£41 500
Variable overheads	£31 500
Direct labour hours	19 500

then the fixed overhead will be under-applied by £1000 [i.e., £40 000 – (19 500

Month	Production units	Annual overhead rate (£)	Monthly applied overhead (£)	Monthly actual overhead (£)	Over-applied overhead (£)	Under-applied overhead (£)	Cumulative balance over (under) (£)
January	6 000	0.5	3 000	4 200	—	1 200	(1 200)
February	5 500	0.5	2 750	4 100	—	1 350	(2 500)
March	8 000	0.5	4 000	4 600	—	600	(3 150)
April	11 000	0.5	5 500	5 200	300	—	(2 850)
May	16 000	0.5	8 000	6 200	1 800	—	(1 050)
June	19 000	0.5	9 500	6 800	2 700	—	1 650
July	11 000	0.5	5 500	5 200	300	—	1 950
August	8 000	0.5	4 000	4 600	—	600	1 350
September	10 500	0.5	5 250	5 100	150	—	1 500
October	13 000	0.5	6 500	5 600	900	—	2 400
November	7 000	0.5	3 500	4 400	—	900	1 500
December	5 000	0.5	2 500	4 000	—	1 500	—
Total	120 000	0.5	60 000	60 000	6 150	6 150	0

GHM

Figure 11.2 *Over- and under-recovered overheads*

Month	Total budgeted overhead (£)	Units to be produced	Monthly rate per unit (£)	Annual rate per unit (£)
January	70 000	20 000	3.50	3.715
February	80 000	30 000	2.67	3.715
March	90 000	40 000	2.25	3.715
April	100 000	50 000	2.00	3.715
May	65 000	15 000	4.33	3.715
June	60 000	10 000	6.00	3.715
July	55 000	5 000	11.00	3 715
August	51 000	1 000	51.00	3.715
September	55 000	5 000	11.00	3.715
October	60 000	10 000	6.00	3.715
November	65 000	15 000	4.33	3.715
December	70 000	20 000	3.50	3.715
	821 000	221 000		3.715

Figure 11.3   Monthly and annual overhead rates

× £2.00)] whilst fixed overhead prices have risen by £2500 [i.e., £41 500 – (19 500 × £2.00)]. Variable overheads to the extent of £29 250 (i.e., 19 500 × £1.50) will have been absorbed, but the actual variable overheads incurred (£31 500) is made up of price changes and inefficiencies of £2 250 (i.e., £31 500 – £29 250).

To take a slightly more involved example, Figure 11.4 shows a flexible budget for a machining department of a company for anticipated monthly levels of activity. (A flexible budget is one that recognises the differences in behaviour patterns of fixed and variable costs, and which is designed to change in relation to the level of activity actually attained during a period.) This budget gives a variable overhead rate of £1.70 per direct labour hour. If variable overhead costs have been properly analysed and classified, and if the estimates forming the basis of the flexible budget are accurate, then this rate should be valid over the relevant range.

Fixed overheads cannot be absorbed on the basis of this type of flexible budget, but must be absorbed on the basis of some predetermined estimate of capacity utilisation – such as normal capacity. (Normal capacity is defined as that level of activity – or productive output – that can be expected to be attained over a future period of time covering the ups and down of the business cycle.)

Suppose that normal capacity is 10 000 direct labour hours, and that the combined flexible budget is as shown in Figure 11.5. At normal capacity of

10 000 direct labour hours, the fixed overhead recovery rate is given by $\frac{£10\ 000}{10\ 000}$ = £1.00 per direct labour hour.

Standard direct labour hours	8 000	9 000	10 000	11 000
Variable factory overhead:				
Material handling	£8 000	£9 000	£10 000	£11 000
Idle time	800	900	1 000	1 100
Rework	800	900	1 000	1 100
Overtime premium	400	450	500	550
Supplies	3 600	4 050	4 500	4 950
Total	£13 600	£15 300	£17 000	£18 700
Variable overhead rate = £1.70 per direct labour hour				GHM

Figure 11.4   Flexible overhead budget

			Normal capacity GHM	
Standard direct labour hours	8 000	9 000	10 000	11 000
Variable factory overhead:				
Material handling	£8 000	£9 000	£10 000	£11 000
Idle time	800	900	1 000	1 000
Rework	800	900	1 000	1 100
Overtime premium	400	450	500	550
Supplies	3 600	4 050	4 500	4 950
Total	£13 600	£15 300	£17 000	£18 700
Variable overhead rate = £1.70 per direct labour hour				
Fixed factory overhead:				
Supervision	1 700	1 700	1 700	1 700
Depreciation – plant	2 000	2 000	2 000	2 000
Depreciation – equipment	5 000	5 000	5 000	5 000
Rates	1 000	1 000	1 000	1 000
Insurance	300	300	300	300
Total	£10 000	£10 000	£10 000	£10 000
Fixed overhead rate for normal capacity = £1.00 per direct labour hour				

Figure 11.5   Combined flexible overhead budget

The combined overhead rate (at normal level of output of 10 000 direct labour hours) is thus a variable rate of £1.70 per direct labour hour and a fixed rate of £1.00 per direct labour hour, amounting to £2.70 per direct labour hour.

WHY ABSORB OVERHEADS?

The simple answer to this question is 'product costing'. Overheads are applied to products because management needs to have some idea of the fully absorbed cost of each product as a guide, perhaps, for pricing decisions, as a basis for inventory valuation, and hence as a prerequisition to income measurement (i.e., the determination of profit). *But* flexible budgets require the predetermining of overhead rates also, and the purpose of flexible budgets is to control costs.

If a company has estimated the level of sales for the next operating period, and if the planned overhead costs have been spread over the planned output along with the expected prime costs, then management may tend to feel that as long as the company sells the budgeted level of output of each product at a price that is at least equivalent to the sum of prime cost plus overhead element plus required profit margin, the company will achieve at least its planned level of profit. This way of thinking focuses attention on 'full' cost, but since different expenses are aggregated in overhead recovery rates, it is difficult to see what is implied in a unit overhead cost figure, and hence in a unit 'full' cost figure. The very fact that any one of several bases may be used for both apportioning and absorbing overhead costs, with the resulting full cost differing under each method, demonstrates the lack of accuracy and meaning that may be exhibited. However, when a company must base its prices on cost plus a desired profit margin (as in contracting) then overheads must be allocated to jobs. Yet pricing on the basis of full costs in other circumstances can be distinctly damaging. For instance, the higher the level of activity, the lower will be the unit full cost. That is, direct material cost per unit, direct labour cost per unit, and variable overhead cost per unit are all assumed to be constant within the relevant range (the range of activity within which the company is expected to be operating during a given period of time) but fixed overhead costs are lower per unit the more units over which they are spread.) This means that a company using full cost as its basis for pricing will tend to have lower prices the higher level of activity and higher prices the lower the level of activity. Let us assume that a company bases its prices on full cost plus 25 per cent, that fixed overhead costs are £10 000 per period, and that the level of sales may vary from 100 000 units (giving a unit fixed overhead element of £0.10) to 50 000 units (giving a unit fixed overhead element of £0.20).

Assume that direct material cost is £0.25 per unit, direct labour cost is £0.30 per unit and variable overhead cost is £0.15 per unit. Then the price per unit can be calculated as in Figure 11.6.

The outcome of cost-plus pricing may be to depress sales when it is desired to encourage sales because prices rise as demand falls. Cost-plus pricing is unable to respond to market conditions, and for this reason - along with a general dissatisfaction with overhead allocations - marginal costing has been more and more widely adopted in recent years. Whilst absorption costing aims to ascertain the 'full' cost of jobs and processes, marginal costing aims to deal with the effects of changes in either the volume or type of output.

MARGINAL COSTING

Marginal - or direct - costing is concerned with differences in aggregate cost (i.e., direct labour + direct material + direct expense + variable overhead) caused by producing one unit more or one unit less (where a 'unit' will usually – but not always – refer to a unit of manufactured output).

GHM	High sales 100 000	Low sales 50 000 units
Direct material cost	0.25	0.25
Direct labour cost	0.30	0.30
Variable overhead cost	0.15	0.15
Fixed overhead cost	0.10	0.20
Full cost	0.80	0.90
Profit @ 25 per cent	0.20	0.225
Selling price per unit	£1.00	£1.125

Figure 11.6 Cost-plus pricing

Marginal costing is essentially short-run in nature and is concerned with variable costs. In contrast, differential costing (also known as incremental costing or relevant costing) is concerned with longer-run questions (e.g., adding or dropping a product line, make-or-buy decisions, lease-versus-own decisions, etc.), and since these questions involve a consideration of the costs of following one course of action rather than another, fixed costs are important.

In direct costing systems, fixed overheads are viewed as being *period costs* and are changed directly to the profit and loss account as costs of a period of time instead of being spread over processes and units of output as product costs. Fixed costs are thus treated as costs of being in business rather than as operating costs related to manufacturing given product lines. This approach facilitates the analysis of the effects of changes in the volume and type of output by means of the cost-volume-profit (or break-even) technique. The fundamental distinction between variable costs and fixed costs is here seen to be of great significance again in controlling costs – for flexible budgets, in cost-volume-profit analysis, and in marginal costing.

The highlight of marginal costing is the contribution margin (i.e., the excess of sales revenue over variable cost). This margin represents the contribution that the item in question makes to fixed costs and profit. In Figure 11.7 it is the distance between the variable cost curve and the revenue curve.

In simple equation form:

Contribution = sales revenue – variable costs
Since: sales revenue = fixed costs + variable costs + profit
By substitution: contribution = fixed costs + profit

A contribution margin per unit can be easily worked out. If the selling price of a product is £1.00 and its variable cost amounts to £0.60 then the contribution margin will be £0.40. The immediate implication of this is that for every increase in sales, 40 per cent of that increase for this product is the contribution

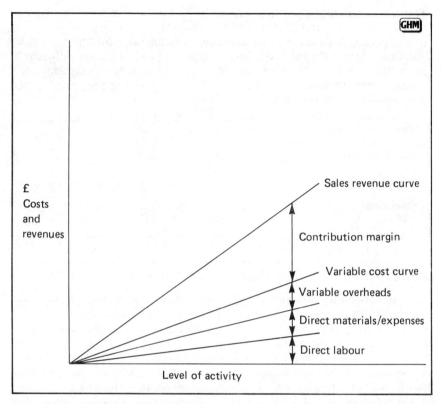

Figure 11.7 Contributed margin

towards fixed costs and profit. If the level of fixed costs is £100 000 and it is sought to make a profit of £50 000, how many units should be sold? The answer can be readily determined by substituting known variables into the basic equation:

$$\text{Sales revenue} = \text{fixed costs} + \text{variable costs} + \text{profit}$$

Let R = desired sales revenue, and as it is already known that FC = £100 000, P = £50 000, and VC = $0.60R$

Then $\quad\quad\quad R \quad = \quad 100\,000 + 0.60R + 50\,000$

Therefore $\quad 0.40\,R \quad = \quad 150\,000$
Therefore $\quad\quad\quad R \quad = \quad 375\,000$ at £1.00 .... = £375 000
Or more simply $\quad\dfrac{\text{Fixed costs} + \text{profit}}{\text{Contribution margin}} = \dfrac{150\,000}{0.40} \quad = \quad 375\,000$

Determining total contribution

It is important to determine how much contribution exists for a given product line, and whether the total contribution from all product lines is sufficient to cover fixed costs and leave a satisfactory profit. Let us take the example of a company producing three products – A, B and C – with aggregate cost, profit and sales figures as shown in Figure 11.8.

GHM	Product A (£)	Product B (£)	Product C (£)	Total (£)
Direct materials	20 400	35 600	16 000	72 000
Direct labour	6 000	12 200	1 800	20 000
Overheads	6 600	13 500	1 900	22 000
Total cost	33 000	61 300	19 700	114 000
Profit	2 000	3 700	300	6 000
Sales Revenue	35 000	65 000	20 000	120 000

Figure 11.8   Cost, profit and sales revenue summary

It would seem from Figure 11.8 that product A is making a profit of £2000, and if product A is deleted from the range it may be thought that total profit would fall to £4000 from its current level of £6000. But the allocation of overheads (of £6600) to product A includes various fixed overhead costs amounting to, say, £5500 that would still need to be paid even though product A was no longer in the range. Let us suppose that £5275 of this amount is transferred (i.e., re-allocated) to product B and the balance of £225 is re-allocated to product C. The outcome of deleting product A and transferring the fixed charges is given in Figure 11.9.

GHM	Product B (£)	Product C (£)	Total (£)
Direct material	35 600	16 000	51 600
Direct labour	12 200	1 800	14 000
Overheads	18 775	2 125	20 900
Total cost	66 575	19 925	86 500
Profit or (loss)	(1575)	75	(1 500)
Sales Revenue	65 000	20 000	85 000

Figure 11.9   Revised cost, profit and revenue summary - 1

Figure 11.9 shows that the deletion of product A causes a reduction in profit of £7500 (i.e., from a profit of £6000 to a loss of £1500). To think that the fall in profit would only be £2000 is clearly erroneous because it ignores the fixed costs that must be re-allocated once A is deleted. Mistaken assumptions can be avoided if fixed overheads are separated from variable overheads (in accordance with Figure 11.10) in such a way that the contribution that each product makes to common fixed overheads and profit is evident. The contribution approach is highlighted in Figure 11.11.

If a product is not covering its marginal cost (i.e., it is making a negative contribution), it would be essential to ensure that its selling price is not too low (given its quality in relation to competitive products) and that the production methods and materials are appropriate. In cases where a product's sales revenue is below its marginal cost but prices cannot be increased and production methods cannot be improved, careful consideration should be given before it is deleted lest the picture of Figure 11.8 is found.

GHM	Product A (£)	Product B (£)	Product C (£)	Total (£)
Direct materials	20 400	35 600	16 000	72 000
Direct labour	6 000	12 200	1 800	20 000
Variable overheads	1 100	6 600	1 625	9 325
Marginal cost	27 500	54 400	19 425	101 325
Fixed overheads	5 500	6 900	275	12 675
Total cost	33 000	61 300	19 700	114 000

Figure 11.10 Revised cost, profit and sales revenue summary - 2

GHM	Product A (£)	Product B (£)	Product C (£)	Total (£)
Sales	35 000	65 000	20 000	120 000
Marginal cost	27 500	54 400	19 425	101 325
Contribution	7 500	10 600	575	18 675
Total fixed costs				12 675
Profit				6 000

Figure 11.11 Contribution margin statement

Margin of safety

Within the context of marginal costing and cost-volume-profit analysis, a useful concept is that of the *margin of safety*. This refers to the amount by which sales revenue can fall before a loss is incurred. For instance, if a company can break even at 50 per cent of expected sales, then it has a margin of safety of 50 per cent. The expected sales level may be 1000 units, and the break-even volume may be sales of 500 units, so sales can fall by 500 units or 50 per cent before a loss will be made and the margin of safety is given by the formula:

$$\frac{\text{Actual sales} - \text{break-even sales}}{\text{Actual sales}}$$

$$\text{Margin of safety} = \frac{1000-500}{1000} = 0.5 = 50 \text{ per cent}$$

Summary of the value of marginal costing

The following points summarise the value of the contribution approach of cost-volume-profit analysis and marginal costing to management planning and control:

1 A change in either the selling price of a product or its variable cost rate will alter the break-even point and the contribution margin ratio (i.e., the proportion of sales revenue that is left when variable cost is deducted)
2 When sales are above the break-even point, a high contribution margin ratio will result in greater profits than will a small contribution margin ratio
3 A low contribution margin ratio will require a large increase in sales volume to create a significant increase in profit
4 If other factors stay constant, a change in total fixed costs will alter the break-even point by the same percentage and the net profit will vary by the same amount as the change in total fixed costs
5 A large margin of safety will mean that a major fall in sales can occur before losses are incurred.

ABSORPTION COSTING VERSUS DIRECT COSTING

There are various advantages of using marginal costing, amongst the most important of which are the following:

1 Marginal costing systems are simpler to operate than are absorption costing systems because they do not involve the problems of overhead apportionments and recovery. This makes costs easier to identify and accumulate, and it does not confuse product costing with cost control
2 Marginal costing avoids the difficulties of having to explain the purpose and basis of overhead absorption to management that accompany absorption costing. Fluctuations in profit are easier to explain because they result from cost-volume interactions and not from changes in inventory. In absorption costing systems a varying element of fixed overhead will be contained in the cost of inventories, and fluctuations in inventory levels can affect profit due to the fixed cost element. However, marginal costing introduces a direct relationship between sales volume and marginal income (i.e., the contribution)
3 It is easier to make decisions on the basis of marginal cost presentations. For example, marginal costing shows which products are making a contribution and which are failing to cover their avoidable (i.e., variable) costs. Under absorption costing the relevant information is difficult to gather, and there is the added danger that management may be misled by reliance on unit costs that contain an element of irrelevant fixed costs.

However, on the other side of the coin are various disadvantages of using marginal costing. For example:

1 Economic selling prices over the long run cannot be set without some attention being paid to fixed costs. Each product line/job must not just

cover its marginal costs, but collectively the contributions of all jobs must cover at least all costs if a profit is to be made

2   The importance of time tends to be overlooked in marginal costing: two jobs may have the same marginal cost, but one may take twice as long to complete as the other and hence its 'true' cost will be more. This aspect of capacity-utilisation is not brought out in marginal costing

3   The difficulties and dangers of spreading fixed overhead costs do not mean that they should be ignored: they are just as vital as are direct wage costs, etc. In fact, as production becomes more automated and greater in volume, more costs will tend to be fixed, and hence they should not be overlooked.

The choice between using absorption costing and marginal costing will be determined by such factors as:

1   The system of financial control in use (e.g., responsibility accounting is in-consistent with absorption costing)

2   The production methods in use (e.g., marginal costing is favoured in simple processing situations in which all products receive similar attention; but when different products receive widely differing amounts of attention, then absorption costing may be more realistic)

3   The significance of the prevailing level of fixed overhead costs.

How a cost system is to be used is more important than its form, since a technique *per se* does not achieve anything. From the point of view of cost control, a costing system should be able to show promptly costs that are running out of control, guide corrective action, indicate the effects of alterna-tive decisions, and focus on helping to secure control rather than being the perfect systems design.

STANDARD COSTING

A logical step onwards from either absorption costing or marginal costing, especially in view of the fact that both approaches already involve a consider-able amount of future cost level prediction, is to institute a system of standard costs. The principle is to develop a complete specification of all expenditure levels from which standards are derived.

A predetermined standard can be established for each element of cost at each stage of production. For direct materials, the standard cost would indicate the estimated amount of each kind of material and the cost per kilo (or other unit). For labour, the standard would show the number of hours in each department or cost centre; the hourly rate; and the total cost in each department.

The standard cost for overheads in each department would indicate the number of hours of machine time, direct labour hours, or whatever; the standard overhead recovery rate; and the total expense (i.e., hours × rate). When all the cost elements (direct materials, direct labour, direct expenses, fixed and variable overheads) have been accumulated, the standard should indicate the desired cost of all elements of a unit of productive output.

The standard cost of materials shows what the cost *should be* if the correct types of material are used in the right quantities with the minimum of waste. Similarly, the standard labour cost shows what labour *should cost* if the job is performed at a specified level of efficiency by properly trained operatives of the appropriate grade working for agreed rates of pay. The standard overhead cost for a unit of output will be based upon standard fixed overhead rates and standard variable overhead rates developed in relation to particular assumed circumstances.

Standard costing differs from conventional absorption costing because the latter aims to charge units of output with a 'fair' share of the *actual* costs (either predictively or retrospectively) of making the product. In contrast, standard costing is based (either wholly or in part) on the principle that the costs to be charged to units of output are the costs that *should* have been incurred.

Direct or marginal costing systems can be developed along standard costing lines, in which event fixed overhead costs are not standardised but all direct costs, along with variable overheads, are standardised.

When a standard costing system is in operation, it can be operated in an integrated manner with the budgeting system, since both are concerned with what costs ought to be, what they actually are, and the reasons for the differences that arise. In other words, both standard costing and budgeting are concerned with cost control.

CHECKLIST ON COST ACCOUNTING

1 Is the company's costing system tailored to the company's needs?
2 Have cost centres been clearly defined?
3 Are the benefits of the system commensurate with its costs?
4 Are all costs classified into their direct and indirect, fixed and variable, controllable and uncontrollable, and separable and joint categories?
5 Is the behaviour of different costs understood in relation to changes in the level of activity?
6 Are cost reports made available promptly? How often? How quickly?
7 Could statements be presented earlier if more estimates were used? (Are estimating procedures reliable?)
8 Are figures rounded so that results are more easily understood?
9 Can any figures of small value (as shown on the chart of accounts) be grouped?
10 Are the descriptions of reported items clear?
11 Are unusual items adequately explained?
12 Will further (or less) mechanisation affect the overhead of cost accounting?
13 Can the effectiveness of cost accounting procedures be improved?
14 Has sufficient thought been given to the type of costing system to use? (That is, standard costing, absorption costing, or marginal costing.)
15 Has the purpose for which costing is being performed been fully considered? (For example, pricing, product costing, cost control.)
16 Is the costing system adequate in determining the relative efficiencies and profitability of divisions, processes, product lines, jobs, etc?

17 Is the costing system adequate for the needs of EDP and operations research analysts?

18 Are ratios, graphs, etc., used to supplement the figures produced by the costing system?

19 Is a satisfactory procedure being operated to price material issues from stores?

20 Are all withdrawals of stock and ordering of goods from outside suppliers duly authorised by requisitions?

21 Are job allocation numbers recorded against labour time, material usage, etc., in all cases?

22 Do employees understand the importance of recording the allocation of time to jobs? How are they encouraged to do this accurately?

23 What is the basis for the apportionment of each service department's costs? Is the most suitable basis selected in every case?

24 How are overheads absorbed into productive output? Is the most suitable basis used?

25 What action is taken on the basis of over- or under-recovery of overheads?

26 Are normalised overhead recovery rates used? if not, why not? For example, is the level of activity stable from month to month?

27 Have separate overhead rates been developed for fixed overhead costs and variable overhead costs?

28 Why are overheads absorbed (if they are absorbed)?

29 Is the contribution margin concept understood within the company?

30 Is cost-volume-profit analysis undertaken?

31 Is marginal costing undertaken?

32 Has the company's margin of safety ever been worked out?

33 Are the comparative advantages and disadvantages of marginal costing versus absorption costing fully appreciated?

34 Is the costing system closely geared to the type of production processes operated?

35 What role does cost accounting play in relation to special decision-making?

SUMMARY

Cost accounting is principally concerned with product costing (for pricing, inventory valuation, and income determination purposes), and only concerned in a secondary manner with cost control.

Data for product costing (and cost control) is derived from many sources, such as labour summaries, weekly time sheets, job cards, material requisitions, stock cards, and expense summaries. The pricing of material issues from stores is a particularly difficult topic in times of rising prices.

The type of costing system – and hence the nature and source of much costing data – will be determined by the structure of the organisation and its methods of production. Job costing and process costing have been developed to deal with job/batch production and flow production respectively.

Conventional absorption cost accounting requires that all overheads be spread in some way over the productive output of the company. This is achieved by apportioning service department overheads to production departments, and then absorbing these accumulated production + service overheads over units of output. Many different bases exist for both apportioning and absorbing overheads, and the most suitable will be that which characterises a cause-and-effect relationship between the activities and the outputs.

Overhead rates can be developed for fixed and variable overheads, but when the actual level of activity differs from the estimated level, there will be an over- or an under-recovery of overheads. This may signal the need to revise overhead recovery rates.

For various reasons the apportioning/absorbing of overheads is dangerous (or at least gives misleading results) and marginal costing has developed to overcome these problems. Attention centres around the contribution margin, and the interrelationships of cost-volume-profit are a focal point for decision-making. Whilst marginal costing is a short-run function, relevant (or differential) costing is more suited to longer-run decisions in which fixed costs may vary in addition to changes in variable costs.

Standard costing is a normative refinement of either absorption or marginal costing that can be usefully integrated with budgeting in attempting to control costs.

FURTHER READING

Anton, H. R., Firmin, P. A. and Grove, H. D. (eds.), *Contemporary Issues in Cost & Managerial Accounting*, 3rd edition, Houghton Mifflin, Boston, Mass, 1978. A comprehensive selection of articles on aspects of cost and management accounting, with suggestions as to further reading on specialist topics

Benston, G. J. (ed.), *Contemporary Cost Accounting and Control*, 2nd edition, Dickenson, Encino, Calif., 1977. Another valuable collection of articles but less comprehensive than Anton, et al.

Hart, H., *Overhead Costs: Analysis and Control*, Heinemann, London, 1973. This short book looks at the how's and why's of overhead apportionment, etc., with a strong emphasis on linking UK company practices to an evaluative framework.

Hongren, C. T., *Cost Accounting*, 4th edition, Prentice-Hall, Englewood Cliffs, NJ, 1977. This is the standard international textbook on cost accounting.

Shillinglaw, G., *Managerial Cost Accounting*, 4th edition, Irwin, Homewood, Illi., 1977. Another standard textbook that is even more comprehensive than that by Horngren.

Sizer, J., *An Insight into Management Accounting*, 2nd edn., Penguin Books, Harmondsworth, 1979. The most widely used British introductory book: very readable and lucid.

Solomons, D., (Ed.), *Studies in Cost Analysis*, 2nd edition, Associated Business Publishers, London, 1968. An advanced collection of key articles on aspects of cost analysis.

Thomas, W. E., (ed.), *Readings in Cost Accounting, Budgeting & Control*, 5th edition, South-Western, Cincinnati, Ohio, 1978. The longest established compilation of articles in the field – but regularly revised – and one which probably has greatest appeal to the non-specialist.

12 Taxation

J C Craig

Tax law is mainly based on the Income and Corporation Taxes Act 1970, the Taxes Management Act 1970, the Capital Allowances Act 1968, the Capital Gains Tax Act 1979 and annual Finance Acts. The first of these Acts brought together the combined effects of the Income Tax 1952 and subsequent Finance Acts to 1969 with the principal exception of personal capital gains tax; this is now governed by the Capital Gains Tax Act 1979 which consolidated the law on capital gains tax up to 5 April 1979.

Each year (sometimes more frequently) following the budget speech, a Finance Act is introduced, so it is always necessary to look at the accumulated effect of amendments when examining a tax problem.

Interpretation of the law follows the standard pattern of court decisions, and there are now more than two thousand references to decided cases, each of which is normally binding on everyone in similar circumstances, unless reversed by a subsequent enactment or by a decision in a superior court. (Very occasionally the House of Lords will overturn a previous decision of the same Court.)

RETURNS AND ASSESSMENTS

Every person who receives income of any kind is under statutory obligation to complete a return of income each year; the senior partner deals with the form for a partnership, and the officers for a limited company. Personal responsibility for making correct returns cannot be avoided even if an agent is employed to complete the return form.

Tax assessment

Assessments for tax are made by local Inspectors of Taxes in accordance with the return of income and supplementary figures supplied by the taxpayers, including a copy of the annual accounts of a business. Where necessary, an assessment may be altered within six years of the end of the accounting period to which it relates, for example if a mistake is discovered by either the Revenue or the taxpayer. However, there is no time-limit to the correction of assessments which were wrong because of the fraud, wilful default or neglect of the taxpayer. A case heard in 1970 (Rose v. Humbles) referred to assessments stretching back to 1942.

Appeals against assessment

Where the taxpayer does not agree with the Inspector's assessment, he may appeal in writing within thirty days. Usually the appeal is settled by correspondence or at a meeting with the Inspector, with or without professional advice. If agreement cannot be reached the taxpayer may have the appeal heard by either:

1 General Commissioners, who are leading local citizens, unpaid, not civil servants and not specialists in tax, but hear each case on its merits and aim to give a fair decision according to the facts; or
2 Special Commissioners, who are civil servants concentrating wholly on the complexities of tax and therefore better able to unravel an argument of a complex nature.

It tends to be more costly to ask for the appeal to be heard by the Special Commissioners because, though no charge is made, it may be necessary to travel some distance with professional advisers for the appeal to be heard, and it is usually advisable to brief Counsel to put the case.

A decision of the Commissioners is binding on both Revenue and taxpayer unless it can be shown that the query is based on an interpretation of the law, when permission may be asked to appeal to the High Court in England or the Court of Session in Scotland.

Further appeals may go beyond the High Court to the Court of Appeal and then to the House of Lords, or in Scotland from the Court of Session to the House of Lords, if it can be shown there is still doubt as to whether the law has been interpreted correctly. Occasionally in England an appeal may be taken direct from the High Court to the House of Lords.

Appeals are an expensive, troublesome activity. A good working relationship between the company's management, its auditors who commonly handle the tax returns, and the local Inspector of Taxes, with the management taking a close personal interest in the tax computations, is recommended as the most practical approach to tax.

Interest on tax assessments

If tax is not paid on its due date, or if unpaid tax is held over for too long pending an appeal, interest will be payable at 12 per cent – not allowable for tax purposes. In practice it is preferable to avoid this charge by paying tax not in dispute and buying a certificate of tax deposit for the balance. If after negotiations the amount of tax in dispute is payable the certificate can be surrendered in satisfaction of the tax and there will be no interest charges. If the tax is not payable the certificate can be encashed or used to pay other tax and interest will be received.

ADJUSTMENT OF PROFIT AND COMPUTATION OF AMOUNT LIABLE TO TAX

The normal pattern for an industrial or commercial business is to measure and adjust the income from all sources, to arrive at the total on which corporation tax is payable as shown in Figure 12.1.

In making the adjustment of profit to arrive at the amount liable to tax, the starting point is the profit shown in the ordinary profit and loss account. Expenses not allowable must be added back; income which is either not taxable or taxable under a different Case or Schedule must be deducted, to arrive at the adjusted trading profit assessable under Schedule D Case I (or Case II).

Apart from advance corporation tax paid to the Collector of Taxes following the payment of dividends (dealt with later), the balance of the liability to corporation tax (the 'mainstream' liability) is due for payment nine months after the end of the accounting period except in the case of companies which carry on the same trade as they did prior to 1965. Such companies may have a longer interval; normally they pay their mainstream liability on 1 January in the fiscal year following that in which the accounting period ends, unless there has been a change of accounting date.

Rate of tax

The rate of corporation tax is announced for each 'financial year', which runs from 1 April to the following 31 March, in the Chancellor's end-of-year budget. For the financial year 1981, which ended on 31 March 1982, a rate of 52 per cent was announced in the budget on 11 March 1982. For 'small' companies the rate of corporation tax on income was fixed at 40 per cent. For this purpose a company is small if profits do not exceed £90 000 (unless the company has associated companies, in which case a lower level applies); a sliding scale applies to profits between £90 000 and £225 000. These limits are revised periodically.

Accounting year

If the company's accounting year spans two financial years in which the percentage differs, the profits are apportioned on a time basis. In, for example, the accounting year ended 31 December 1981, three-twelfths of the profit (for January, February, March 1981) is taxed at the rate announced in 1981, and the remaining nine-twelfths at the rate announced in 1982.

ALLOWABLE EXPENSES

For any expense to be allowable, it must have been incurred 'wholly and exclusively' for purposes of the business. Certain forms of expenditure are disallowed, either by definite statements in the Acts, or as a result of cases

(a)		GHM
Income		
Gross trading profit		300 000
Rent from industrial premises let to tenants		20 000
Interest from bank deposit account		6 000
Dividends from shares held		10 000
Interest from debentures held (gross)		4 000
		340 000
Expenditure		
Depreciation	26 000	
Salaries, wages, employer's contributions to national insurance and graduated pensions	60 000	
Directors' salaries and fees	10 000	
Bad debts	300	
Specific provision for the bad debt of a named customer	100	
General provision for bad debts	800	
Legal expenses	200	
Rent, rates and insurance	3 000	
Superannuation (company's contribution to an approved scheme)	2 000	
Heating and lighting	1 000	
Travelling expenses	2 000	
Entertainment expenses	600	
Distribution costs	20 000	
Sundry expenses	3 000	
Loss on sale of machinery	1 000	
		130 000
Net profit		210 000

Figure 12.1   Example of a Corporation Tax computation
Shows the profit and loss account (a), adjustment for corporation tax purposes (b) and the calculation of corporation tax (c)

(b)

Net profit show in the accounts		210 000
Add back items not allowable		
Depreciation	26 000	
General provision for bad debts	800	
Entertainment expenses	600	
Loss on sale of machinery	1 000	
		28 400
		238 400
Deduct items, either not taxable or taxable under different headings		
Rent	20 000	
Interest income	6 000	
Dividends	10 000	
Interest	4 000	
		40 000
		198 400
Less		
Capital allowances (in lieu of depreciation)		28 400
Case I Income		170 000

(c)

Case I income – business profits adjusted	170 000
Case III income – untaxed income from bank deposit interest	6 000
Schedule A income – rent	20 000
Income received subject to deduction of income tax at source – debenture interest but not dividends	4 000
	200 000
Corporation tax at 52% on £200 000	104 000
	96 000
Dividend income, not liable to corporation tax, is not part of the computation	10 000
Remainder, which may be retained or paid out as dividend	106 000

Fig. 12.1 (continued)

decided by the Courts. It would be impossible to give an exhaustive list here, particularly as many of them concern only a restricted range of industries, but a selection of the more common ones is given below.

General advice is: when in doubt, check with the detailed tax textbooks; if these do not settle the doubt, claim the expense is allowable and see the Inspector's reaction. There is no penalty for this approach provided the true nature of the expense is stated openly and honestly.

Salaries and wages

Salaries and wages of employees and directors are normally allowable in full. Excessive payments to part-time directors are liable to be restricted if the Inspector is not satisfied that the amount is reasonable considering the services rendered. This does not prevent large fees from being paid, or from being taxed as earned income in the hands of the directors, but simply means they are added back in the corporation tax computation.

Entertaining

Entertainment expenses are not allowable, except for entertaining overseas customers, and even in this case the amount must be reasonable considering the potential business arising. A UK resident agent of a foreign customer is not an overseas customer for this purpose.

'Entertainment' includes gifts of food, drink and tobacco – for example, as Christmas presents.

When a senior employee is reimbursed for the cost of entertaining UK customers, the amount is not treated as part of his personal income, but if he is given an allowance to cover entertaining, among other expenses, it becomes part of his earned income from which he cannot deduct any part of the cost of the entertaining.

Bad debts

A general reserve for bad debts is not allowable, but actual bad debts and a specific provision for the bad debts of a named customer are allowable.

Depreciation

Depreciation is not allowable, but capital allowances are given in appropriate cases instead.

Capital expenditure

No kind of capital expenditure is allowable other than by way of capital allowances. Capital profit or loss on the sale of an asset is excluded from the computation of business profit, but may be subject to a separate calculation for capital gains tax.

Legal expenses

Some legal expenses are and some are not allowable, the distinction being broadly that they are allowable if they relate to a transaction of a revenue nature but not if they are of a capital nature. For example, legal expenses for the preparation of a service agreement for a manager, or the collection of debts, or the renewal of an existing short lease are revenue and allowable, but legal expenses in connection with the purchase of freehold premises or a long lease are capital and are not allowable.

Retirement benefits

Retirement benefits for employees are allowable whether they are direct pensions or contributions to a superannuation scheme approved by the Inland Revenue. A moderate lump sum to an employee on his retirement would be allowable, but an exceptional lump to a superannuation fund would be spread forward over future years.

RELIEF FOR INCREASE IN STOCK VALUE

History

In a time of inflation, an increasing amount of cash becomes tied up in trading stock, causing cash flow problems. To alleviate these difficulties, stock relief has been introduced. Relief was first granted as a deferment of tax by the Finance Act 1975, and was extended by Finance (No 2) Act 1975. A more permanent relief was provided for in the Finance Act 1976: broadly, the taxable profit for an accounting period was reduced by the increase in the value of stock held less a percentage of the Case I or II profit which would otherwise be liable to tax. In any period in which there was a decrease in the value of stock held, then taxable profit was increased by the amount of the fall or the amount of unrecovered past stock relief, whichever is smaller.

Because a large potential charge to tax existed in many companies should their stock levels fall, the Finance (No 2) Act 1979 provided that certain stock relief granted be excluded from the amount of unrecovered past stock relief and thus effectively be written off.

Present system

On 14 November 1980 a new system came into effect under which relief is given by reference to an 'all stocks' index published monthly by the Department of Industry. The movement in the 'all stocks' index over the period of account is applied to the closing stock of the previous period less a *de minimis* amount of £2000. If there is a reduction or no movement in the index no relief is granted and no addition is made to taxable profits. There is no clawback of relief unless trade ceases or the scale of activities in the company becomes small in relation to past levels.

Unused relief under the new system may only be carried forward for six years. If it is unused by that time the relief is lost. There are rules for determining the order of set-off of reliefs available in each year. Unused relief under the old systems may be carried forward without time limit.

THE NECESSARY BOOK-KEEPING

Adjustment of profit and computation of tax payable are made outside the double-entry book-keeping system, but settlement of the tax requires three ledger accounts:

1 Corporation tax account (including advance corporation tax and tax credits)
2 Income tax account for unfranked investment income
3 Income tax account for PAYE deducted from employees' income

The foundation for accounts 1 and 2 is that a company suffers corporation tax but not income tax on its own income. Income tax which has been deducted at source from investment income received by the company may be offset against income tax deducted from payments made out by the company, and if a net balance is due by the company it is payable to the Collector of Taxes. If a balance is due to the company it will be treated as a payment to account of any corporation tax due for the period. It is important to keep franked items separate from unfranked, and PAYE separate from both.

The necessary entries are summarised in Figure 12.2.

CAPITAL ALLOWANCES

Capital allowances exist on seven main types of fixed assets used wholly and exclusively for purposes of the business:

1 Industrial buildings
2 Plant and machinery
3 Agricultural land and buildings
4 Mines and oil-wells
5 Capital expenditure on scientific research
6 Patents
7 Know-how.

Only the first two types will be considered in detail here.

When any asset which qualifies for allowances is purchased, the year's allowances are given in full for the company's accounting period no matter how late in the period the asset was obtained. This rule may need to be modified where the accounting period is shorter than twelve months.

It is important to consider the overall position before deciding whether or not, or to what extent capital allowances should be claimed.

Corporation tax account	with double entry in: GHM
Debit:	
(a) adjustment for overprovision of last year's liability	Profit and loss (appropriation) a/c
(b) Excess tax suffered on unfranked investment income tax	Unfranked investment income a/c
Credit:	
(a) Estimated rax on the profits for the year now ending	Profit and loss (appropriation) a/c
(b) Adjustment for under provision for last year's liability	Profit and loss (appropriation) a/c

Tax on unfranked investment income account

Debit:	
Income tax suffered at source on unfranked investment income received	Unfranked investment income a/c
Credit:	
Tax retained when paying out debenture interest and other annual interest payments	Accounts for debenture, etc interest paid
Where credit is greater than debit, the difference is settled by paying tax to the Collector	Bank a/c
Where debit is greater than credit, the difference is settled by transfer to corporation tax a/c	Corporation tax a/c

Advance corporation tax

Debit:	
Tax credit accompanying franked investment income received	Memorandum only – not passed through books of account
Credit:	
ACT paid when paying out dividends	

Figure 12.2 Entries to make in the tax accounts

Industrial buildings

The nature of the business must be industrial as distinct from commercial, retailing or wholesaling, or professional. Even for an industrial company the allowance is not given for offices and showrooms, except where these form an integral part of a factory and account for less than 10 per cent of its whole cost.

The allowances to the first owner are now:

1 Initial allowance which has been 75 per cent since March 1981 (previously 50 per cent since November 1974)
2 Writing-down allowance of 4 per cent of the cost price (or 2 per cent if the building was erected before November 1962).

In the year of disposal, instead of the writing-down allowance there is a balancing allowance or balancing charge to bring total allowances into line with net cost.

Where the building is sold for more than it cost, the balancing charge cannot exceed the total of allowances already received. (There may, however, be a taxable capital gain in addition to the balancing charge.)

On sale of a factory built before November 1962 there is no balancing adjustment if it is sold after it is fifty years old, and for factories built since November 1962 none after they are twenty-five years old.

Cost price includes: the building, plus the architect's fees, plus cost of tunnelling, levelling and preparing the land; installing main services, fences, perimeter walls and roadways on the site.

It does not include: the cost of land, legal and estate agency fees; preparation of a lease; purchase price of a lease; demolition of a former building.

When a building is demolished, the cost of demolition is added to the original cost before working out the balancing adjustment.

For the second and subsequent owners, the allowances are equal to the residue of cost spread over the remainder of twenty-five or fifty years. An example is given in Figure 12.3. The importance of distinguishing between

Original cost to first owner, 1971		£10 000
Initial allowance in first year 30%	£3 000	
Writing-down allowance 4% a year for 10 years	4 000	7 000
Written-down value in 1980 (end of year)		3 000
Sell on 1 January 1981 for		7 350
Balancing charge on first owner		£ 4 350

Second owner: residue of cost is £7 350
  balance of 25 years is 15 years
  so annual allowance is £490 a year		

Check: £490 × 15 = £7 350		GHM

Figure 12.3 **Example of allowances for expenditure on industrial buildings**

land and buildings is vital, with seller and buyer having opposing interests.

From 12 April 1978 industrial buildings allowances have been extended to apply also to hotels but the rate of initial allowance is 20 per cent against 75 per cent for other industrial buildings.

Expenditure incurred between 26 March 1980 and 27 March 1983 on small workshops of up to 2500 square feet will qualify for an initial allowance of 100 per cent.

Any industrial or commercial structure or qualifying hotel in an Enterprise Zone (an area designated as such by the Government) will also qualify for 100 per cent initial allowance.

Plant and machinery

Allowances may be claimed by any type of business assessed as trading income under Case I or Case II of Schedule D, or against Schedule A assessments on income from real property, or in respect of assets owned by an employee and used by the employee for his employer's business, or against profits of a trade assessed under Schedule D Case V.

The definition of 'plant and machinery' spreads remarkably widely to include office and canteen equipment, furniture, dry docks and virtually every type of fixed tangible asset which is not 'building'.

The allowances available for plant are now:

(a) In the year of purchase a first-year allowance, the balance of the cost being carried forward to the next year.

(b) In each subsequent year the brought-forward balance of cost for all the different assets is combined and there is a single writing-down allowance of 25 per cent on their total ('the pool').

(c) When an asset is sold or scrapped, its disposal price is deducted from the total figure on which writing-down allowances are being calculated.

The first-year allowance began at 60 per cent but was increased to 80 per cent for machinery bought between 20 July 1971 and 21 March 1972. For assets bought after 21 March 1972, the first-year allowance was increased to 100 per cent. It is given in full no matter how late in the accounting year the machine may have been bought.

It is possible for the company to take any smaller amount of first-year allowance and so take a correspondingly larger writing-down allowance in subsequent years. The allowance applies equally to new or secondhand assets unless a secondhand machine is bought from a connected company or transactions are entered into mainly with a view to obtaining a larger allowance, in which case the first-year allowance is restricted.

There is no first-year allowance on private cars, unless they are hired on a short-term basis in the course of a trade and no capital allowances will be given on assets bought for purposes of business entertainment. Details of cars should be shown in a separate 'pool'.

Private cars costing over £8000 (£5000 prior to 12 June 1979) are kept separate from other assets and qualify only for a writing-down allowance at 25 per cent of the writing-down value but restricted to a maximum of £2000 per year, starting in the year of purchase and with a balancing adjustment for the year of sale.

For assets acquired on hire-purchase, allowances are given on the equivalent of the cash price, and the hire charge is treated as an allowable revenue expense in the years in which it is paid. For assets on straight hire, contract hire or lease, there are no capital allowances but the rental is allowed as a revenue expense in the years in which it is paid.

The lessor will be eligible for capital allowances like any other trader but subject to certain conditions. These are that the asset is used for short-term hire in the UK or the asset is used for the 'requisite' period, of four years (or shorter if the asset is sold within four years) by a trader who would have been granted first-year allowance had he purchased the asset himself. If the lessee does not fall into one of these categories the lessor will be entitled to 25 per cent of writing-down allowance on the cost of the asset.

Where private cars costing over £8000 are hired a proportion of the rental charge payable by the lessee is disallowable.

Expenditure incurred on the provision of a new ship is eligible for 'free' depreciation in that any part of the 100 per cent first-year allowance not claimed for the year of purchase may be claimed at the discretion of the taxpayer in any subsequent year. This contrasts with other plant where allowances not claimed merely augment the balance eligible for 25 per cent writing-down allowance.

LOSSES

Setting losses against profits

A trading loss in one accounting period may be set against:

1 Other sources of profit in the same accounting period in which the loss is suffered
2 The trading profit of the immediately preceding accounting period provided that the company was then carrying on the trade
3 Other sources of profit in that preceding accounting period.

To the extent that a trading loss has been created by first-year allowances it may be set against profits in the three years preceding the year of the loss (again provided that the trade was then being carried on).

Claims for relief in this way are optional. If they are not made, or if they leave a balance of loss still unrelieved, the remaining loss may be set against the first available future profits from the same trade, but not against future profits from other sources.

The right to carry forward any losses is ended when a majority of the shares changes hands and there is a major change in the nature or conduct of the trade being carried on. The effect of this restriction has been virtually to end the sale of tax-loss companies.

An example of a normal loss claim is given in Figure 12.4.

PQ Ltd – Accounting period to 31 December annually: **GHM**

Trading results – 1978 profit	£20 000
1979 loss	60 000
1980 profit	8 000
Unfranked investment income – 1978	5 000
1979	7 000
1980	6 000
Set off of loss	
1 Other income in 1979	7 000
2 Profits in 1978 (£20 000 + £5 000)	25 000
3 Trading profit in 1980	8 000
4 Carry forward against future trading profits	20 000
	£60 000

Losses carried forward may only be set against future profits from the same trades and not other income hence unfranked investment income in 1980 is taxable. Corporation tax payable for the year to 31 December 1978 would be cancelled, or if already paid it will be refunded.

Note the cash flow advantage of submitting promptly the figures for 1979 and the claim for loss relief.

Corporation tax will be payable on the 1980 investment income, while the remaining £20 000 of 1979 loss is being carried forward to 1981.

Figure 12.4   Example of normal loss relief

Terminal loss relief

A loss suffered during the final twelve months up to the time a trade is discontinued may be carried backwards and set against the trading profits of the three preceding years. An example is given in Figure 12.5.

Note particularly that to make a terminal loss claim it is sufficient that the trade has been permanently discontinued. This is not necessarily the same as winding up the company, as a company may have more than one activity and its existence may continue without the discontinued trade, or a fresh trade of a different nature may be started after the loss-making enterprise has been discontinued.

Directors' remuneration as it affects loss

It will be seen that skill is needed in arranging a company's affairs in the way to take the best advantage of the many variations of the loss relief rules. For example, even in a small private company it may be sound policy to pay the directors at least a portion of their customary remuneration, even though this makes the loss larger. Otherwise the directors might be without income from which to offset their personal tax reliefs.

	RS Ltd	**TU Ltd**
Profit for year to		
31 December 1976	£40 000	£40 000
31 December 1977	15 000	15 000
31 December 1978	10 000	10 000
31 December 1979 (Loss)	(80 000)	(80 000)
RS closed trade at 31 December 1979		
31 December 1980		5 000
TU closed trade at 31 December 1980		

RS Ltd will have a terminal loss claim of £80 000 which will successfully be offset to the extent of £65 000 against the profits of 1976, 1977 and 1978. TU Ltd has no terminal loss because the loss was not made in the final twelve months and so will only be able to use normal loss claims against 1978 (£10 000) and 1980 (£5000).

Figure 12.5   Example of terminal loss relief

Example:

Williams is sole director and principal shareholder of WL Ltd. He customarily draws £5000 a year from the company as director's remuneration and leaves the company with no profit to suffer corporation tax. In 1980/81 trade is poor and before paying himself any remuneration there is trading loss of £1000. If Williams forgoes remuneration his personal reliefs will be wasted, so he declares himself £2300 and leaves the company showing £3300 loss.

His personal income then is		£2300
from which he deducts:		
Personal allowance	£2145	
Dependent relative relief	100	
		2245
		£ 55

Income tax payable by Williams will be only:
£44 at 30 per cent = £16.50

The company's trading loss will go forward to set against future trading profits if Williams is confident he can restore the profit-making basis of the trade. His personal reliefs would have been wasted had he not taken any remuneration, as they cannot be carried forward.

ADVANCE CORPORATION TAX

On the occasion when a company pays a dividend (or other distribution to members), it is required to make a payment of advance corporation tax (ACT) to the Inland Revenue. The rate of ACT is fixed annually and applied to the actual or net dividend but is equivalent to income tax at the basic rate on the gross of the dividend plus the ACT. Payment of ACT is due quarterly and must be made fourteen days after the end of the quarter in which the dividend is paid. When the dividend is paid, the member is given a tax credit for the ACT in respect of the dividend.

Treatment of shareholders

Every individual in the UK who receives a dividend and tax credit can treat the tax credit as if it were a voucher for income tax paid. If he is liable at the basic rate of income tax, no further liability will arise; if he is liable at more than the basic rate, he will be required to pay only at the excess of his higher rate over the basic rate. If his income is so small that he pays no income tax, he will recover the tax credit.

Where a company receives a dividend with a tax credit the sum of the two will be treated as 'franked investment income', i.e., income which has already borne corporation tax and therefore income upon which no further tax is payable. The company may set the amount of the tax credit against an obligation to pay ACT in respect of its own dividends, and pay only the balance to the Inland Revenue.

Treatment of ACT by company paying dividends

In respect of dividends paid during an accounting period, ACT is treated as a payment to account of the corporation tax liability for that accounting period and only the balance (or mainstream liability) is payable nine months after the balance date (or later in respect of certain companies – see Adjustment of profit, above). The ACT must, however, be set against corporation tax on income – it must not be set against tax on capital gains – and the maximum which may be set off is the ACT on a distribution such that the sum of the two is equal to the income charged on corporation tax.

Any ACT not relieved in this way may be carried back for two years and any balance still not relieved may be carried forward. An example is given in Figure 12.6. During the year to 31 March 1981, when the rate of corporation tax was 52 per cent and of ACT three-sevenths, Z Ltd had the taxable profits shown in Figure 12.6.

GROUPS OF COMPANIES

There are special concessions in the taxation of groups of companies, their main effect being to reduce or cut out the tax on inter-company transactions within the group. It requires considerable skill to arrange group affairs to take the best advantage of these arrangements, and the administrator should either make a specialised study or else form a regular practice of consulting the group's professional advisers before making transfers of assets or dividends within the group.

For example, for some purposes a 'subsidiary' is one in which the parent company owns more than half the ordinary shares, for others the minimum is

	[GHM]
Trading profit, Schedule D Case I, year to 31 March 1981	£220 000
Unfranked investment income	£ 20 000
Capital gains £52 000 less excluded £22 000	
(see section on capital gains tax, below)	£ 30 000
In May 1980, Z Ltd paid a dividend of £171 500 on which ACT amounted to £73 500.	
The mainstream liability is computed:	
Taxable profits – Income £220 000 + £20 000	£240 000
– Capital	30 000
	£270 000
Corporation tax at 52 per cent	£140 400
ACT for set off – £73 500	
Restricted to tax on gross dividend of £240 000, i.e., to	72 000
(Since £168 000 + ACT thereon of £72 000 = £240 000)	
Mainstream liability	£ 68 400

Figure 12.6   Example of set-off of Advanced Corporation Tax (ACT)

75 per cent of the ordinary shares, and for yet others 75 per cent of the whole equity capital including certain non-commercial loans. The main advantages of group taxation are:

1 *Subsidiaries*
   A subsidiary may pay dividends to its parent company with or without paying ACT thereon. It may be valuable to pay the dividend without ACT when the parent company is not making distributions to its own share-holders, or when it has other sources of franked investment income receivable net and no trading income of its own
2 *Loss on one company against profit in others*
   When one company has suffered a trading loss, this may be set off against the profits of any one or more members of the group. It should be noted that this concession does not extend to capital losses, so where possible any assets likely to show a capital loss on disposal should be transferred to a company which will be showing a capital gain on other transactions, before selling them outside the group
3 *Transfers of capital assets*
   No chargeable gain arises when capital assets are transferred between members of a group. Care is required however when a company which has received an asset leaves the group within six years of the transfer.

CAPITAL GAINS TAX

Companies pay corporation tax on chargeable gains as well as on income but a proportion of the capital gain is excluded from the assessment at the full rate of corporation tax to bring the effective rate of corporation tax on capital gains down to 30 per cent – the normal rate for individuals. All forms of property are included as assets for capital gains tax purposes but certain of them are exempt from charge. These include:

1   Wasting assets with a predictable life of less than fifty years, if they are chattels (tangible moveable objects) but excluding assets which have qualified for capital allowances
2   Gains on certain government securities
3   Winnings from betting or lotteries
4   Gains on discharge of liabilities (e.g. the repayment of debentures at less than their issue price).

If assets were acquired before April 1965 any part of the gain arising before that date is not taxable.

The list is not exhaustive and does not include assets such as dwelling houses for which the gain may be exempt if made by an individual. When a capital gain made by a company has suffered tax and the balance is paid out to shareholders, a further round of tax is deducted. For example, if it sells its premises and goes into liquidation the position is as shown in Figure 12.7. This example has been

Purchase price of asset, £400 000, is absorbed into his own business as a fixed asset, or:

Sell the assets and then go into liquidation:		Alternatively sell the company's shares	
Selling price 1981	£400 000	for	£400 000
Cost price 1965	300 000	Cost price 1965	300 000
Capital gain	£100 000		£100 000
Tax at effective rate of 30%	30 000		
Balance distributed to shareholders	£ 70 000		£100 000
Less: Personal capital gains tax 30%	21 000		30 000
Net remainder in hands of shareholders	£ 49 000		£ 70 000

If the shares are purchased, the asset will thence be treated as a subsidiary of the buying company. It may subsequently be sold to the parent company which may declare a dividend to dispose of its capital gain without suffering any tax; alternatively, the proceeds may simply be lent to the parent company.   GHM

Figure 12.7   Simplified example to show that sale as a going concern is better than liquidation where assets have appreciated

simplified to illustrate the principle, which in an actual company would be clouded but not overthrown by the existence of other assets.

Underlying capital gains

A company with an underlying capital gain in its assets is always better sold as a going concern than put into liquidation, and to the purchaser it may be a matter of indifference whether he obtains ownership of the valuable assets in the one way or the other. He is not obliged to run the company as a trading concern when he has acquired its shares. The directors of a private company should give thought to the chances of 'retirement exemption' before disposing of their shares. The first £50 000 of gain will be exempt if they are aged over sixty-five and have been full-time directors for not less than ten years and hold either:

1 Not less than 25 per cent of the voting share capital in own right, or
2 Not less than 5 per cent in own right, and members of immediate family own sufficient to bring the total of family holding up to 51 per cent.

A proportionate amount of relief is available if the shares have been owned for less than ten years (but more than one year). The exemption is restricted to the underlying chargeable business assets; it is not available in respect of portfolio investments held by the company.

Replacement of assets

Deferment of tax on capital gains may be claimed where the asset has been used only for trading purposes and is replaced by fresh assets (not necessarily of a similar nature, or even serving the same function) if they are of one of the following classes:

1 Land, building, fixed plant and machinery
2 Ships
3 Aircraft
4 Goodwill
5 Hovercraft.

It is important that the replacement is bought within twelve months before or three years after the sale of the previous asset. These time limits may be extended at the discretion of the Inland Revenue. Deferment continues indefinitely if the replacement asset is permanent, but if a 'depreciating asset' is bought it will continue only for ten years. If the depreciating asset is sold within ten years and replaced by a fresh permanent asset, the permanence of the deferment is established, but if it is replaced by a fresh depreciating asset the deferment ends immediately.

Depreciating assets for this purpose are assets with an expected life of less than sixty years, i.e., they are wasting assets, or items which will become wasting assets within ten years. The most common example is fixed plant. Full deferment is given only where it is requested and where the whole proceeds from sale of the previous asset are used for the purchase of the replacement. Where only a portion of the sale proceeds are used, the amount on which deferment can be claimed is restricted.

THE COMPANY AS A TAX COLLECTOR

Although the company does not itself pay any income tax, it is obliged to serve as an unpaid collector by withholding income tax when making payment of:

1 Wages and salaries, for the PAYE system
2 Annual interest, the most common example being debenture interest

The amount of PAYE deducted in a month has to be passed to the Collector of Taxes on the nineteenth of the month next following. For example, month from 6 April to 5 May; tax to be paid on 19 May. Income tax on annual interest is payable quarterly, fourteen days after the end of the quarter.

Extension for close companies: When a close company does not pay a sufficient dividend, part of its income may be treated as if it had been distributed by the company and income tax thereon at the higher rates applicable to its members may be recovered from the company.

CLOSE COMPANY DISABILITIES

1 If money is lent to a 'participator' an amount equal to tax at the basic rate on the grossed up amount of the loan is payable by the company
2 Where a close company fails to make an adequate distribution out of income, tax may be payable as if such a distribution had in fact been made. The amount of the shortfall in distribution is apportioned to members and the appropriate income tax is computed; this income tax may be paid by the members or by the company. A trading company may retain the whole of its trading income and 50 per cent of its estate income.

For apportionment purposes, the trading and estate income is disregarded if it is below £25 000; or if it is between £25 000 and £75 000 it is abated by one-half of the amount by which the income falls short of £75 000. (These limits apply to accounting periods ending after October 1977.)

It is always open to a trading company to justify a smaller distribution, on the grounds that the company needs to retain more of the profit to meet the requirements of its business – to finance improvements, modernisation or expansion and to repay short-term loans; cash required to finance a wholly new trade will be treated as a business expense for this purpose.

Negotiations with a view to ensuring there will be no apportionment of income should be opened by an approach to the Inspector backed by a clear statement of intentions such as the forecast of sources and application of funds which forms part of the management accounting routine of most companies.

CONTRAST BETWEEN LIMITED COMPANY AND PARTNERSHIP

Partners pay income tax at graduating rates on the whole of their profit, which is regarded as earned income in their hands, except in the case of a limited (or 'sleeping') partner whose share is normally treated as investment income for tax purposes.

In a limited company, whether private or public, corporation tax is payable on the profit after deducting remuneration of its directors, who are classed as employees. Profit remaining in the company after paying corporation tax is not subject to further tax but if it is withdrawn as dividend this may be liable to income tax at the higher rates as personal investment income of the shareholder.

In a small business where a few individuals share both management and ownership, there is no important difference in the overall effect of tax between limited company and partnership, unless profit is appreciably higher than £22 250 a year per individual. Where the profit is larger, the limited company has the advantage so long as profits retained in the business are needed to finance expansion. However, where there are shareholders who are not concerned in managing or working for the company, there may be tax drawbacks in paying them a return on their capital.

There are many powerful legal advantages for running a limited company and these often far outweigh the importance of tax differences. The larger the business and the more involved its ownership, the more important it becomes to operate it as a limited company. Also a company pension scheme for the directors can provide better benefits than a self-employed retirement annuity scheme. On the other hand certain undertakings, such as most of the professions, are not allowed to operate through limited companies.

CHANGES IN PERSONAL AND CORPORATION TAX

From 1973/74, income tax and surtax were replaced by a single unified tax, but the change was one of administration. It did not alter the total tax liability, the only real difference to the taxpayer being that the new high rates of tax on large incomes are payable more promptly than the surtax they replaced (but now only marginally so: surtax was due nine months after the year end, higher rates of the new unified tax were originally due three months after the year end but this was extended to eight months in 1980).

Changes in the corporation tax system were effected from 1 April 1973 when the system was changed from a 'classical' one (corporation tax on profits, with income tax deducted from dividends) to an 'imputation' one (corporation tax on profits, part of the tax being passed on as a credit to the recipients of dividends). The object of the change was to make the corporation tax on retained profits as heavy as the combined tax on distributed profits. This reduces the incentive to retain profits for reinvestment in expansion of the company's business, the plan being strangely at odds with the then government's supposed encouragement to increased industrial investment.

DEFINITIONS OF SOME PHRASES USED IN THE CORPORATION TAX RULES

Accounting date

The date to which a company makes up its accounts.

Accounting period

The period for which corporation tax is charged: this will normally be a period for which a company makes up its accounts but it may be a shorter period and must not exceed a year.

Close company

A UK resident company under the control of five or fewer participators, or any number of participators who are directors, or if more than half of the company's income could be apportioned for tax purposes among five or fewer participators or among any number of participators who are directors. However, any company in which shares carrying at least 35 per cent of the voting power are held by the public is excluded from the definition provided such shares have been dealt in and officially listed on a recognised stock exchange within the preceding twelve months.

Participator in a close company

Primarily a person who is a shareholder or has an interest in the capital or income of the company.

Distribution

Any dividend paid by a company, including a capital dividend. It also includes any other distribution out of the assets of a company, whether in cash or otherwise, except for a repayment of capital on liquidation or any amount for which new consideration has been given.

Franked investment income

Income from a source which has already suffered corporation tax and is consequently not liable to further corporation tax in the hands of the receiving company. Dividends from British companies are the most common example.

Unfranked investment income

Income from a source which has not suffered corporation tax and is therefore to be included in this company's total income for corporation tax purposes. Debenture interest from other companies is a common example.

VALUE ADDED TAX

The scope of the tax

The tax is chargeable on the supply of goods and services in the UK and on the importation of goods and certain services into the UK. The tax will be charged only where the supply is a taxable supply and where the goods are supplied by a taxable person in the course of a business which he is carrying on. The tax is normally payable by the person supplying the goods or services. Tax is chargeable on the importation of goods whether for business purposes or not and the tax is payable whether or not the importer is carrying on a business. In cases where imported goods may be used for private purposes the tax cannot be the subject of a VAT input deduction but a separate claim to the Commissioners for repayment. Where goods are imported by a registered taxable person who imports goods in the course of his trade, payment of the tax can be deferred. New rules apply from 1 January 1978 where certain overseas services are imported. In such instances the taxable person in the UK has to account for the tax as if he had supplied the services to himself. Also with effect from 1 January 1978 the supply of services includes the letting of goods on hire and the making of certain gifts or loans of goods.

The arithmetic of the tax

Strictly speaking, value added tax is not a tax on value added in the true economic sense. Rather it is a tax on consumption, collected at each stage in the economy, on the difference (broadly) between the purchase price of goods and services acquired to make the product and the sale price of that product. Purchases are called inputs, and the tax which a business pays on buying those inputs is called input tax; sales are called outputs, and the tax which a business charges on its customers is called output tax. The excess of output tax over input tax is payable by the business to Customs and Excise, who are responsible for administering the tax, but if the input tax exceeds the output tax the difference is repayable by Customs and Excise to the business. Assuming then that a business is wholly within the VAT system, the business bears no VAT itself but recovers all the tax it pays on its inputs either by way of deduction from its output tax or by way of repayment from Customs and Excise.

Rates of tax

There are three classifications of goods and services. Exempt, zero-rated and standard-rate goods. Standard rate of VAT has been 15 per cent since 18 June 1979.

Zero rating

References should be made to the Finance Act 1972, Schedule 4 (as amended) for a list of zero-rated items. These are principally food, books, newspapers, periodicals, news services and advertisements, fuel and power, transport and certain drugs and medicines. In addition, the export of all goods and most services is zero rated. This ensures that no VAT enters into the price of any export.

Exemption

Exemption is of two kinds:

1 Finance Act 1972, Schedule 5 (as amended) gives exemption to a list of items of which the most important are land, insurance, postal services, certain financial services (mainly banking), education and health
2 Small traders whose turnover of taxable supplies does not exceed £15 000 per annum are exempt but they may elect to come within the system if it is to their advantage to do so.

The difference between zero rating and exemption is that a business dealing in zero-rated supplies charges VAT at the rate of zero per cent but is nevertheless fully within the system; thus it can recover from Customs and Excist any input tax which it has paid on its purchases. Exemption on the other hand is generally a less favourable status in that, whereas the business cannot charge VAT on its supplies, it cannot recover the VAT on its purchases; thus the exempt business must either bear any input tax itself, or if it can, pass it on in the form of higher prices.

Many businesses are taxable on some part of their sales (whether at the standard rate or zero rate) and exempt on another part. In these cases an apportionment of the input tax is made, and only that part considered to be referable to taxable sales is deductible.

Time of supply

In order to determine which VAT accounting period a transaction falls into, the time of supply has to be ascertained. Broadly the time of supply is as follows:

Goods

1 If the goods are to be removed the basic tax point is the time when they are removed
2 If the goods are not to be removed the basic tax point is the time when they are made available to the person to whom they are being supplied
3 There are special rules for sale or return and for certain other transactions. A hire-purchase transaction is deemed to be a sale. The construction industry is subject to special rules
4 Where a tax invoice is issued within fourteen days after the basic tax point, the invoice date becomes the tax point unless the taxpayer elects to use the basic tax point instead. The fourteen-day period may be extended by agreement with Customs and Excise
5 If a tax invoice is rendered before the date of the basic tax point or if payment is received in respect of a supply before the basic tax point, the earlier of the invoice date and the payment date becomes the tax point. The taxpayer in this case has no option to elect for the tax point in 1 or 2 above.

Services

1 The basic tax point in the case of the supply of services is when those services are performed.
2 If a tax invoice is issued within fourteen days after the basic tax point (extendable by negotiation with Customs and Excise), the invoice date is the tax point unless the taxpayer elects to the contrary.
3 In other cases, the tax point is the earlier of the tax invoice date and the date on which payment is made for the services.

Businesses should ensure that where an option is open they choose the best tax point for their accounting and administrative systems.

Place of supply

Broadly, if goods are supplied within the UK for use in the UK, the supply is a taxable supply. If goods are supplied in the UK and exported, the goods are still a taxable supply but at the time of export are zero rated. Goods supplied outside the UK but imported into the UK are liable to VAT at the time of importation. There are special accounting rules for VAT purposes which are designed to each the cash flow problems of importers. A supply of goods made outside the UK but not imported into the UK is outside the VAT net altogether; this applies whether or not the goods are ordered from the UK.

The rules regarding the place of supply of services initially only applied to a supply rendered and enjoyed within the UK and services rendered in the UK for the benefit of someone outside the UK. The implementation of the EEC Sixth Directive on VAT has extended the scope of the tax in the UK to include the importation of certain services. Where a taxable person receives, from a person who does not belong in the UK, any of the services listed in Schedule 2A to the Finance Act 1972 (except services which would be exempt if supplied in the UK) he is required to account for tax as if he had supplied the services himself.

The tax invoice

No special form of tax invoice is laid down but certain minimum requirements have to be met. In particular every tax invoice must show an identifying number, the date of the supply, the name and address and VAT registration number of the supplier, the name and address of the person to whom the supply is made, the type of supply (i.e., sale, lease, etc.), a description of the supply, the price for each supply before the addition of VAT, any discount offered and the rate and amount of tax chargeable. An abbreviated form of tax invoice may be used in some cases; these are generally small transactions at retail level.

It is not necessary, unless requested, for a retailer to issue a tax invoice. Tax invoices need not be rendered where the transaction is zero rated. In the case of exempt transactions it is not legally possible to issue a tax invoice.

Discounts

Where a discount is offered for prompt or immediate payment, VAT should be shown on the tax invoice as though the discount had been earned by the person to whom the goods or services are being supplied. If in the event the discount is not earned no recalculation of the VAT should be made. Where a trade discount is offered, VAT should similarly be calculated on the discounted price. Where on the other hand a contingent discount is offered which will be available, for example, when a certain level of purchases have been achieved by the customer, the VAT should be calculated on the assumption that the volume target will not be reached.

Retrospective adjustments

Where a downwards adjustment to the price charged for a supply is made, the VAT on the original invoice will be overstated. This may be corrected by showing VAT on a credit note issued to the customer; the VAT must be at the same rate as that originally charged by the supplier. Retrospective adjustments of any kind can be made by the use of the credit note mechanism.

Bad debts

In line with the EEC Sixth Directive the Finance Act 1978 introduced relief for VAT on bad debts. However, relief is restricted in that a taxable person is not entitled to relief unless he has proved the insolvency and the amount for which he has proved is the outstanding amount of the consideration less the amount of his claim. The relief applies where the person liable to pay the outstanding amount of the consideration becomes insolvent after 1 October 1978.

Secondhand goods

In principle secondhand goods are treated in the same way as new goods. There are, however, special schemes for secondhand works of art, antiques, precious stones, postage stamps, scientific collections, cars, motor cycles and caravans. The effect of these schemes is to make liable to VAT only the dealer's margin rather than the full sale price.

Capital goods

In principle, capital goods are treated in the same way as any other items and there is no question of spreading the input tax over the life of the asset or indeed in any other way. Thus, heavy purchases of plant within a short period may put a business into a temporary repayment position. The effect on cash flow ought to be studied before engaging in large-scale plant acquisitions.

Disallowances of VAT

Powers are given to Customs and Excise to disallow certain amounts of input tax even though the expenditure is for the purposes of a taxable business. The two main disallowances at the present time are for business entertaining (other than of overseas customers) and business cars.

Apportionments

Reference has been made above to the part-exempt business. A business whose outputs are part taxable and part exempt may have a disallowance of some part of its input tax.

Special apportionment schemes are prescribed for retailers. These are somewhat complicated and Public Note No 727 (as amended) should be consulted.

Groups

Provision is made so that groups of commonly controlled companies can be treated as one single VAT paying entity. Transactions within companies in such a group are then ignored for VAT purposes and a single return is made by the 'representative member' of the group to Customs and Excise. Not all members of a Companies Act group need be grouped for VAT purposes, and the cash flow of a Companies Act group can be improved if the correct selection of companies is made.

Divisions

A company organised in divisions may request to have each division treated separately for VAT.

Accounting period

The basic VAT accounting period is three months but a company which is in a habitual repayment position may elect for a one-month period. This minimises the delay between the payment of input tax by a business and its recovery from Customs and Excise.

Accounting records

The quarterly VAT return (form VAT 100), which has to be submitted to Customs and Excise, requires information to be extracted from the accounting records of the registered person in such a way that the trader can make his own assessment.

For VAT recording purposes, the accounts will have to provide the following figures:

1   VAT – output tax
2   VAT – tax on imports
3   VAT – deductible input tax
4   Total outputs (sales etc.)
5   Total inputs (purchases, etc., excluding wages and salaries).

It is very important therefore to ensure that the accounting records are maintained in such a form that the tax return can be completed with the minimum of additional work.

Although accounting for VAT is a burden on most businesses the quarterly return imposes a discipline on the accounting function and should be used as a method of providing up-to-date information for the trader, and thus result in increased efficiency.

Retention of records

Invoices both in and out should be retained for a minimum period of three years to enable Customs and Excise to perform their periodical audit of the business's VAT position. By agreement with Customs and Excise, invoices may be kept in microfilm or any other form. Invoices should be stored and recorded in such a way that the periodical VAT return can be completed without difficulty. The amount of record keeping which has to be done is likely to be far greater than many businesses are used to.

Cash flows

The combination of the rules on the tax point and the date on which tax is payable to Customs and Excise gives rise to cash flow advantages or disadvantages. Thus a business which secures a long period of credit on its purchases will very likely not have to pay the VAT on the purchase price until after it has received credit for the tax on the purchase. On the other hand a business which allows long periods of credit on its sales may find that it has to pay the appropriate output tax to Customs before receiving payment of that tax from the customer. The rule must therefore be that the maximum credit should be obtained from one's supplies but the minimum credit should be given to one's customers. This is not at variance with normal financial strategy.

Appeal procedures

Large numbers of disputes have arisen between businesses and Customs and Excise. If agreement cannot be reached with the local VAT office, it is usually prudent to seek a ruling from Customs and Excise head office in London. If agreement is still not possible, an appeal may be lodged to a VAT tribunal. These are presided over by lawyers, and meet in various parts of the country. Their proceedings are sometimes publicised and sometimes not; in so far as they are not, Customs clearly have an advantage over the taxpayer. A determination by a tribunal on a question of fact is final but on a question of law there is a right to appeal first to the High Court (in England), then to the Court of Appeal and (with permission) to the House of Lords, or Court of Session (in Scotland) and (with permission) to the House of Lords.

Professional advice

It is evident, in an area of taxation which is a mixture of law and administrative practice, that the taxpayer is at a disadvantage in dealing with Customs and Excise. It is important, therefore, to take professional advice not merely in negotiations with Customs and Excise but also in the handling of appeals.

FURTHER READING

The aim in this chapter has been to highlight those aspects of a company taxation which appear to be of most consequence to administrators. All the rules are hedged around with ifs and buts which make it imperative to check details before making major decisions.

Useful explanatory booklets may be obtained free from the Revenue; these include Corporation Tax; Capital Gains Tax; Directors' Benefits and Expenses; Capital Allowances on Plant and Machinery; and from Customs and Excise.

The taxation of banks, insurance companies, building societies and other financial organisations, and of agricultural concerns, is outside the scope of this work.

The following books may prove useful:

Carmichael, K. S., *Corporation Tax*, 3rd edition, HFL Publishers, London, 1980

Cretton, Colin, *Capital Gains Tax*, Guild Press, St Helier, Jersey, 1980

Gammie, Malcolm, *Tax Strategy for Companies*, Oyez, London, 1981

Harris, David R., *Tolley's Capital Gains Tax*, Tolley, Croydon, Surrey, annually, latest edn., Oct., 1981

Harris, David R. and Sutcliffe, John W., *Tolley's Corporation Tax*, Tolley, Croydon, Surrey, annually

Harvey, Eric L., *Tolley's Income Tax*, Tolley, Croydon, Surrey, annually

Ritchie, K. J. M., *Tax Forms Manual*, Oyez, London, 1981

Wheatcroft, G. S. A. and Avery Jones, J. F., *Encyclopaedia of Value Added Tax*, Sweet & Maxwell, London, 1973 (updated annually)

Whiteman and Wheatcroft, G. S. A., *Income Tax*, 2nd edition, Sweet & Maxwell, London, 1976 (with supplements)

PART THREE

MARKETING

13 Marketing planning

John Stapleton

Every marketing activity is an investment in time, energy and money. Few companies would spend thousands of pounds on, say, a purchase of capital equipment without a full investigation into its justification, the alternatives available, and the expected return on expenditure. Yet every year the vast majority of companies allocate a substantial part of their revenue to marketing actions without fully assessing the value or likely return on that investment. By introducing the disciplines arising from marketing planning a company should be able to ensure that the costs of marketing show an equitable return and are subject to measurement in the same way as all other business investments.

Many executives believe that the costs of marketing form an additional expense that has to be borne in order to sell their goods. Whilst it is true that many companies use certain tools of marketing for this purpose, it is true also that the most successful companies accept marketing as an essential and integral part of the company's total commercial operation, for it is an essential cost in just the same way as production or finance.

Companies often avoid marketing planning procedures because of the effort needed to express their forward policy in a written form. Executives commonly consider that their time is too valuable to spend on anything other than pressing operational problems; those that face them from day to day. In fact, the manager who devotes his time to dealing with current administrative detail is almost certain to have ignored proper planning in the past. For if properly prepared the marketing plan will contain sufficient details of the company's policy and operational strategy for the implementation to be undertaken by an assistant. As the many alternative courses of action are programmed it is merely necessary for the assistant to activate the appropriate remedy or decision. Only unusual situations need be dealt with by the manager.

The first step in preparing a marketing plan is that of producing the information necessary for decision making. Usually, a company will have within its own administration and control system the raw material necessary for the plan's foundations. In addition, there is an abundance of published information which is made available by government departments, para-governmental bodies, institutions, associations, and the national, trade, and technical press.

Marketing research is an activity which has yet to be fully exploited by the majority of companies. It has so far only been used by companies that have recognised that their existing information sources are inadequate. Because of the scale of operations that now confront the typical businessman it is essential that investment decisions are based upon relevant information, so reducing the number of variables and, hence, business risk.

STANDARDS FOR MEASURING PERFORMANCE

For a marketing-oriented activity to produce lasting results the entire operation has to be systematically planned. By producing basic information in written form and establishing goals and aims for the future the company is creating standards against which actual performance can be measured. Documentation of detailed policy actions then provide the basis for monitoring and controlling the company's operation. Future trends may be predicted through the investigation of all factors that are likely to influence company results.

It is, however, unusual for future opportunities to be easily isolated or even defined. The possibilities are infinite, but it is essential that the most promising are fully investigated and the potential assessed. It is particularly important that the man responsible for planning be a senior executive, for the full appraisal of market opportunities will enable that executive to gain far more intimate knowledge of the workings and the environment of the business operation than could be achieved from a lifetime of working within the close confines of the limited philosophy and procedure of one company. The executive will be able to learn about the interactive forces that affect the company, the industry and, more important, its markets.

In studying the company's future market the businessman will try to discover basic needs for which there is no satisfaction or possibly where there is an inadequate match. It is by discovering the peculiar needs of each existing and potential customer that the enlightened company starts its marketing-orientation. It is upon such special needs that the foundations are laid. Looking at the market and listing the operational needs of each industry, then measuring the extent of each need and then the value that the market places on overcoming the problem gives an indication of the potential – in volume and in profit opportunity.

THE NEW PRODUCT DEVELOPMENT PROGRAMME

From this stage the company will embark on a new product development programme in an effort to resolve the problems that face the market. Once a satisfactory product has been produced the basis for a promotional campaign is already apparent, as the original market assessment will have shown the prospects either by size, industry of location, and the product feasibility studies will have indicated the most appealing stimulus to demand for advertising and field selling purposes.

It must be apparent from these observations that success in marketing cannot be achieved overnight except by coincidence or good fortune. Often a minimum of three years will be required before the first hopeful signs become apparent. Successful use of certain marketing activities alone does not automatically mean a company is marketing-oriented. This situation frequently presents management with an almost insoluble problem. As the whole company has to become involved with marketing principles for success to be possible, it is unlikely that a new recruit hired for his expertise will be able to win sufficient confidence from colleagues by results in the time span that is normally allowed a new manager.

There is usually only one man in a company who can inspire the confidence and support that is necessary and who will automatically have the authority to implement the total changes that may be justified, and he is the chief executive. Introducing satisfactory marketing-orientation is more likely to be successful if the present chief executive delegates most of his daily activities to an assistant or to senior line managers and devotes his entire energies to planning, than if a manager is appointed with such responsibilities.

DETERMINING COMPANY OBJECTIVES

Few company executives have ever formally determined their company's business activity. If they have it is often specified in terms of the means by which the business activity is achieved, e.g. printing rather than communications; or the end-product, e.g. aero-engines rather than propulsion; or by convention, e.g. insurance rather than security. The only sure means of defining the business activity is by thinking in terms of applications for a product, for whilst products, no matter how successful they are now, are heading for eventual decline, the need will usually remain – to be satisfied by the latest innovation.

Determining the appropriate business activity is the first essential step in the marketing plan. In this first step the executive will establish the parameters within which his efforts should be confined initially, but will also rely upon the know-how, expertise, market reputation, and resources the company has accumulated during its history.

At the preliminary planning stage the company will need to decide upon the course that it wishes to take and the stages that have to be reached during each step in the journey. These objectives have to be achievable and yet sufficiently challenging to enable executives and staff to take pride in their fulfilment. The aims and goals of each company have to be expressed in the marketing plan in a way that is beyond dispute while being capable of measurement and comparison. The only medium that achieves these standards is money – the means by which company prosperity is valued. The prime requirement for the survival and development of any business is profit. Too many managers still regard profit as the amount of money that is left over after all the operating expenses have been met. This view almost has connotations with a death wish, for profit is the prerequisite of all business activity and as such must be the first cost to the business.

PROFIT IS THE FIRST OPERATING EXPENSE

By writing in the profit required as its first operating expense the company recognises its major priority and then gears all its other objectives to ensure the acquisition of that profit. The sales volume needed, the orders to be won, the tenders or quotations to be sent out, the inquiries to be solicited, and all the means by which they are obtained are secondary objectives to be achieved before the prime objective becomes possible – in practice.

Any objectives of this sort must be based upon certain assumptions. It may have to be assumed that raw materials will continue to be available or that the government will not cause a market to dry up following an Act of Parliament. Whatever the objectives they will depend for their satisfaction on certain events happening or not happening. These assumptions are incorporated in the plan with a cross-reference to the strategies that will have to be implemented or the tactics employed should the assumptions become invalid. The strategies a company adopts are the means by which the company approaches its market opportunities and by which it adjusts its resources to exploit those opportunities. Its tactics are the methods it uses to meet short-term situations or more frequently the steps it takes when in immediate contact with customers.

In documenting the preliminary marketing plan it is also necessary to list all the major problems that have faced the company during its immediate history, as well as those that are expected to confront the company in the future. At the same time it is prudent to list all opportunities that have been under consideration with the expected profit return, when they are to be achieved and under what circumstances. Both problems and opportunities are then subjected to the same appraisal as the objectives and assumptions when the company strategies are built into the plan.

Every company struggles to improve its profit performance and any attempts planned for the period of the marketing plan, in detail for one year and in outline for five years, should be included. It is possible that improved productivity at the plant will make it possible for the company to improve its profitability through increased sales volume. Sales may be improved either by additional expenditure on marketing actions or by reducing price in an effort to expand the total market. It is by marketing planning that a company can be sure that whatever action it chooses will be based upon facts and information obtained from the marketplace.

Every action and every decision taken by the company executives will have an effect somewhere in the business. It may be favourable, it might be unfavourable. In formulating a marketing plan the company will be formalising its actions, weighing its alternatives, and deciding the most appropriate route open to it. Unless each marketing decision is made with the full and detailed consideration of the known, likely and possible effects upon the business, the investment that marketing actions require will be unmonitored and the management will have lost effective control of a major asset and the benefits that should accrue from that asset.

DEVELOPING THE MARKET PLAN

Preparing a sales forecast, the basis of the total marketing plan, is not just a matter of looking at past sales and trying to establish trends, but a conscious effort to look into the future and assess potential sales opportunity.

A company has started to be objective about its future when it attempts to evaluate the future and forecast what the market will require in the way of new or improved products. Most companies, in making long-range sales forecasts, choose a period varying between five and twenty years, while more detailed sales targets are usually prepared for the financial year immediately ahead. Many products which will be available in five years' time are already on the market and firmly established in the product range. It is often possible to use such historical sales performance as the basis for projections into the future, but only as the basis, for such projections are dependent upon future events being similar to events which have happened in the past. Allowance must be made for changes due to economic circumstances and changes in competitive forces within the industry under investigation.

Comparison of movements, either short-term fluctuations or medium- to long-term trends, can often be achieved using the published economic data. Sometimes, acceptable degrees of correlation can be traced and these tied indicators will be useful parameters in forecasting.

The sales forecast can be as sophisticated or as simple as is justified by the business. The small- to medium-sized business is usually better placed than its larger competitors for maintaining close contact with its markets and can use elementary methods of forecasting which often produce better results than the methods employed by larger firms, where customer contact has become more remote because of larger lines of communication.

While the larger company will normally handle the research necessary to prepare a sales forecast by using its own personnel, the smaller concern cannot justify the expense of recruiting and retaining specialist staff. Where such forecasts are prepared, outside agencies are usually brought in for the task and, in recent years, multi-client projects have been evolved to cater for this demand. As the cost of research is spread over several sponsors, the research organisation can afford to employ highly skilled staff and carry out projects in some depth across a wide front. In addition, the research organisation is often able to prepare a report confidential to each client concerned.

BIAS TOWARDS ONE'S OWN COMPANY

Any sales forecast is subject to numerous influential factors, each of which must be isolated and measured. Some factors will have more effect than others and the forecaster must attempt to isolate and grade those factors according to their significance in such a way that weightings can be applied and an acceptable forecast determined within tolerable limits. In forecasting there is inevitably some bias towards the forecaster's own company and this must be avoided otherwise operating budgets, based on the forecasts, will be over-estimated, adversely affecting profitability.

It is also necessary to predict trends in related industries which provide indirect competition to the company's own products and which could have a bearing on the growth rate of the industry concerned. It is here that the forecaster can discover opportunities for product innovation or new product development. Since new products are the lifeblood of a company their discovery, development and subsequent production programming are necessary parts of the sales forecasting procedure.

To maintain a constant growth rate it is essential that every company estimates the life cycle of each of its products and introduces new products at the apex, or earlier, of an established product's life cycle in order to continue company growth. New products should not be introduced in a haphazard manner, but properly planned to fit the firm's expansion programme.

Price cutting, the most often observed tactical device in the struggles against competition, is a negative approach unless done from a position of strength with the company anticipating growth in the market and increased consumption achieved as a result of the price stimulus.

New markets are occasionally created following new legislation by government. Such changes can also be the cause of a substantial growth or decline in established markets and are often put forward as attempts to improve the social and/or economic life of the nation. Sudden changes in taste or fashion can cause sudden shifts in demand. Climatic changes can seriously affect sales of products which rely on extremes of temperature for their sales volume. Economic recessions, strikes of industrial disputes often bring in their train changes in purchasing habits.

CONTINGENCY PLANNING

Fortunately, many of these factors are predictable. There will certainly be any amount of published comment indicating possibilities. Research into future events is sometimes sponsored by trade and professional bodies; many thousands of words are produced by numerous authoritative writers in scores of newspapers, magazines, and trade and professional publications. These reports can be very valuable to businessmen seeking an insight into the future.

While one cannot forecast accurately what is going to happen, plans can be laid to cover any eventuality in advance of the event, at different levels of effectiveness. If the consequences of events are quantified in purely monetary terms, the businessman will be able to equate consequences with sales volume and, thus, profitability. Where necessary, contingency plans can be brought into operation.

It is true to say that many manufacturers take their products for granted and rarely investigate the uses to which they are put by customers, or how relevant they are to the customer's applications. Research can establish whether new features introduced by the manufacturer in good faith in the belief that they provide a plus for the buyer are not really required and not used, although paid for by the customer in the original selling price. It is possible, of course, that customers may not have realised the significance or relevance at the time of purchase.

In assessing product performance the businessman needs to relate application to product characteristics. Several companies have developed their share of the market as a direct result of providing a superior finish or excellent design. Buyers are often impressed by tales of long life for some mechanical item and sometimes make buying decisions in favour of such devices because the cost can be amortised over several years' operational life.

In arriving at the final assessment based on established standards relating each factor to every other factor, the researcher can compare the total significance of these in terms of market share and will be able to relate the performance of individual companies according to factors on which they concentrate. Comparison of results is the only certain way of monitoring company performance in a competitive commercial environment. The standards established in the appraisal of competitor profiles provide the foundations for a full analysis of market shares. Companies desiring to break into a completely new market will need to examine the extent to which policies adopted by those already serving this market have been successful.

Having obtained full information on total market size it is necessary to assess the extent to which the market can be penetrated either by winning a share of the existing market or by concentrating on growth and winning the business which would otherwise have gone to present suppliers. Once this work has been done the company can make a full and realistic evaluation of the marketing budget necessary to achieve its objectives.

It may be easier in some industries to take business from established suppliers than to expand the total market. In other projects it may be more feasible to opt for developing the growth market potential than to get involved in a battle with those already active in the market. Only when the business activity of the company has been decided should any attempt be made to measure the total market and to prepare a reasoned definition of the market.

DEFINITION OF THE TOTAL MARKET

Many people are confused about the total market for a particular product. It is the total amount of money spent in satisfying a need, irrespective of the products which satisfy that need. This means that all types of food are in competition with one another, the various forms of transport are competitors, and all aids to business efficiency are locked in combat for the purchaser's money.

The market situation for any given company or industry is continually changing and violent fluctuations can occur in market shares from day to day. Over a period shifts in the pattern of demand will become evident and it is imperative that a check be kept on such trends. Steadily rising sales turnover is not, in itself, a true indicator that a company is making the best use of its potential. It is quite possible for a company to achieve reasonable increases in sales year by year yet find that it has a rapidly diminishing share of the market. It will be losing sales opportunities unless sales volume is rising at least as rapidly as that of the industry as a whole.

A company also needs to keep track of its competitors' market shares and be able to explain any change that becomes apparent. There must be a reason why a competitor is expanding his market share faster than anyone else. If, on the other hand, a competitor with a strong marketing team is seen to be losing out on a market share, it could be that he has decided to diversify because of a forecast over capacity or a decreasing growth rate. It is for these reasons that it is vital to carry out constant analyses of market share at frequent intervals, even if in a simple form, rather than rely on occasional extensive research projects, no matter how sophisticated.

Confusion sometimes arises when referring to marketing research and market research. The former is the activity which examines all the elements which make up marketing practice, including markets, products, channels of distribution, pricing behaviour and opinions. Market research is only one element of marketing research, albeit the most widely known and practised.

When it comes to getting the goods to the customer, different companies use different channels of distribution. While some use stockists or distributors, others deliver direct to the retailer or even direct to the ultimate consumer. Different channels of distribution achieve different levels of success in selling their suppliers' products, and their effectiveness can be critical to the sales volume achieved by any one company. Channels of distribution in the consumer field have undergone considerable change in recent years. The development of supermarkets and self-service stores has progressed very rapidly in some areas of retailing, more slowly in others. Some companies have achieved considerable growth through the provision of mail order facilities, while others have built their share of the market through new selling methods such as party plan or vending machines or through selling direct to the household.

In the industrial field there have not yet been such fundamental changes in the pattern of distribution, although some changes have become apparent, for example leasing of factories and capital equipment, and the use of time sharing for data processing equipment.

CONTROL OF DISTRIBUTION

It is not generally realised that the cost to industry of distributing a product may range between 5 and 60 per cent of the final selling price, depending upon the nature of the product and the method of distribution selected. Active control of distribution can reduce these expenses and allow a substantial increase in profitability. Many related activities could be improved following an improvement in actual distribution.

The marketing executive must endeavour to reconcile the needs of the customer for a full service with his company's requirements for the provision of an economic level of service. If he decides that the most appropriate way to win sales from a competitor is by providing a superior distribution service, then that is a deliberate expense incurred in the marketing budget as an alternative to other marketing activities and expenditure.

Because of the forces of competition, demand for any one product from one source can vary considerably. It is the distributive function to provide a contingency against wide fluctuations in demand, and the businessman's responsibility to develop a distributive pattern to cater for those deviations from the norm. Some are more predictable than others and the product mix from the factory must be adjusted to cope with the demand.

Properly controlled, the distributive system can protect a company against giving customer dissatisfaction and will enable it to achieve a high level of productivity by ensuring economical production runs according to pre-determined planning.

MONITORING THE MARKET PLAN

No matter how carefully a management may plan, some objectives will always be more difficult to achieve than others. Marketing planning is not a panacea for all commercial and industrial problems.

Ideally the marketing plan will include any action which may have to be taken to avoid diminution of profits. Even if actual performance exceeds all expectations there should be built-in provisions for the favourable conditions which have become apparent. If proper care has been taken to structure the marketing plan the contingency section should be straightforward, being no more than the detailed consideration of alternative courses of action. The contingency plan should include action which may need to be taken in the short term to minimise or maximise the possible consequences of deviation from the schedule as well as the medium- to long-term action necessary to exploit a changed environment.

To ensure that the right action is taken at the right time – to ensure best results – it is essential that a barometer of company and industry performance be developed. Steps must be taken to monitor actual results against forecast company sales and forecast market shares.

There are several specialist organisations which provide, at reasonable cost, performance comparisons within an industry. If one of these organisations is used, the company needs to develop only an internal early warning system. This can be done by plotting orders received by major product groups against the purchasing industry by standard industrial classification.

In the shorter term, signals can be provided by relating actual inquiries, quotations, orders received, and sales by major product groups against the forecast. Then if the average timelag between inquiry and order is, say, six weeks, and between order and delivery is four to six weeks, the company will have, automatically, nearly three months' notice of an imminent fall-off in sales. Care must be taken to ensure that conversion ratios between each stage do not vary, or that if they do adjustment be made accordingly.

Whilst it would not be wise to institute remedial action as a result of one deviation from plan – for occasional fluctuations *do* happen – once a trend becomes apparent, the cause should be established and appropriate action taken. In addition to showing industrial performance as a whole, some specialist comparison organisations quote the detailed performance of unspecified companies against which the performance of one's own firm can be measured.

Here, the company should be able to judge the extent to which it will be able to exert influence on the market. If the entire industry is suffering the same deteriorating position, it is probably wise to curtail any plans for expansion unless there is a clear indication that the present circumstances can be favourably exploited. The timing and extent of any cutback in this area should be provided for in the contingency plan, which should show detailed profit and loss statements for 70, 80, 90, 110 and 120 per cent actual performance against forecast. Each of the detailed accounts should include the appropriate departmental budgets and head counts. The major driving principles must be to preserve net profit and indemnify future profits. These considerations often prove incompatible in practice and a working compromise may be necessary. Sometimes, profit comes from the last 15 to 20 per cent of sales, after overheads have been covered, and when costs become marginal. Under such circumstances a reduction of 20 per cent in sales volume will warrant, perhaps, a cut of 30 per cent in expenditure in order to maintain net profit at par value.

A company can sometimes avoid the disaster of a temporarily poor market position by acquiring another company. A study of competitive profiles in the marketing plan, followed by detailed investigation of suitable partners, may disclose a competitor which could supplement, or ideally complement, the company's own operations.

Although the possibility of making a takeover bid will almost always be considered first, realistic management must not discount the advantages of soliciting a bid for one's own company, as this may be more prudent.

Detailed consideration of both rationalisation and diversification policies should form a logical part of any contingency plan. There is nearly always conflict between the sales department, anxious to meet individual customer requirements, and the production department needing long production runs and the elimination of time-consuming 'specials'. Some firms reconcile these differences by adopting a market segmentation policy, producing 'specials' for each industry group. They then become so well-established within these industries that they achieve long production runs of these so-called specials. While these firms concentrate their efforts on the part of the market for which they are best suited, others have diversified into other activities in order to absorb their surplus production capacity.

Where there is a possibility that an imminent scientific breakthrough will bring product obsolescence, companies affected should attempt to concentrate future plans on less vulnerable fields of operation. A side-step into a related industry or technology is a natural and logical move for most companies as their technology and management expertise can then be put to profitable use.

INVESTMENT IN COMPANY RESOURCES

Although the need for improved efficiency and productivity has long been accepted by manufacturing processes in industry, and a similar need recognised for some time in the marketing function, it has never been satisfactorily resolved in the latter because of the difficulties of reconciling accounting principles with a business function which is considered part art and part science. While many marketing activities operate under disciplines not widely appreciated – let alone understood – by management, the practice of marketing is still an investment in company resources. If control is to be maintained marketing will be subject to the same accounting appraisal as any other form of investment.

The cost of handling orders of varying sizes must be ascertained if stock levels are to be controlled with great accuracy. It may be found more profitable to refuse orders selling below a price-level considered to be uneconomic. Such selective selling often increases profitability. Location of warehouses, planning of sales territories and routes of salesmen can be organised, using accurate cost statistics rather than intuition. Improving direction and supervision of salesmen through the setting of performance and activity targets can result in increased selling and operating efficiency.

Management in many companies is not always able to recognise that its products or services are mediocre or even inferior to others on the market. Where such blindness exists the company is unlikely to introduce new methods or procedures to assist in rectifying or overcoming the problem. In the same way the firm is unlikely to experiment with new ideas or make a fresh approach in an attempt to improve its future prospects. In these circumstances the only avenue left for that firm is to continue in its own fashion no matter how much the position may deteriorate.

Because of the pace of technological change, a greater demand is manifesting itself for information to be employed in decision making. Investment decisions become more and more complex as businesses grow. The businessman must endeavour to forecast growth potential, and the factors likely to influence his company's penetration of that potential, in an attempt to reduce the risk of facing every business enterprise.

Companies should be able to identify the influences on their major activities and show how they are being controlled to the benefit of the entire organisation. The extent to which the information provided is relevant to the company's needs should be assessed. Executives need to eliminate unused material being prepared and to discover additional information previously unknown. Such research into the marketing effort will help to ensure that an economic level of expenditure is being maintained. Appropriate marketing policies should ensure that all products are developed according to the needs of the market and resources are not wasted on products which the market shows are unsatisfactory.

COMMUNICATING PROFIT RESPONSIBILITY

One of the important developments in marketing consumer goods is the change in emphasis to impersonal selling techniques such as advertising and point-of-sale display. Personal selling still has the most important role in industrial marketing. Improvement in the function and performance of industrial sales forces justifies more attention than is now perhaps necessary in consumer goods selling efforts. These salesmen cannot be expected to sell the ideal product mix without guidance and direction nor differentiate between the profitability of various products.

In any organisation the level of profit responsibility must not only be decided but also widely communicated to ensure the satisfactory implementation of the most critical of business activities.

The marketing plan and all its ancillary documents must be used by executives as a day to day control and development manual. The planning process must not be treated as an annual political exercise suffered by busy executives concerned with other tasks. Planning, organisation, direction and control are basic management jobs and, in a successful marketing-oriented company, will fill the management's working days. Each manager needs to understand the interactive nature of the individual tasks which have to be completed during each period of the marketing plan.

The timing of each step, at all levels, and in each function, is critical if the total plan is to be satisfactorily co-ordinated and the anticipated results achieved. A flexible attitude to planning principles needs to be adopted so that management recognises the need for contingencies and their control within corporate strategy.

Unforeseen events create a different scale of priorities, and flexibility in policy interpretation as allowed for in the plan must be recognised if the company's interests are to be best served. The results of monitoring actual performance against forecasts have a definite value in personnel development and in operating efficiency, as does the preparation of forecasts itself.

The chief executive of any marketing-oriented company retains the final responsibility for marketing policies. The marketing manager gives advice in the field of marketing and may well carry a line responsibility. If the marketing concept is to be adopted the entire company and, in particular, the management team must be oriented towards customer satisfaction. And this is the essence of planning in marketing. For the end result – the marketing plan – is not so important as the benefits gained from the input. The effort, study, appraisal, and evaluation of the business environment provides the major bonuses from the preparation of the plan and it all starts from considering customer needs.

In the foreseeable future most companies will become increasingly involved in computerisation. Even if not directly concerned as users, companies will become involved by the extent to which suppliers, competitors and customers become geared to electronic data processing. Every businessman must appreciate how the computer can be applied to marketing problems. He needs some appreciation of the effects of computers on present-day and future marketing decisions. Future growth potential of computer-linked terminals making computerisation possible and economic for many smaller firms will certainly assist in the scientific application of marketing. The day is not far off when a company's entire planning process will be subject to computer storage and processing.

FURTHER READING

Allen, Peter, *Marketing Techniques for Analysis and Control*, Macdonald and Evans, Plymouth, 1977

Kotler, Philip, *Marketing Management: analysis, planning, and control*, 4th edition, Prentice-Hall International, London, 1981

Stapleton, John, *How to Prepare a Marketing Plan*, 3rd edition, Gower, Aldershot, 1982

Wilson, Richard M.S., *Management Controls and Marketing Planning*, Heinemann on behalf of the Institute of Marketing and the CAM Foundation, London, 1979

14 Market research

Colin McDonald

It is a favourite military adage that 'time spent in reconnaissance is seldom wasted'. Market research is the way in which industry does reconnaissance. It seeks to provide knowledge of customers, how they behave and to what they respond and, the current and expected state of the market. Without this knowledge it would be very much more difficult and less safe to plan marketing, to decide between options and to evaluate the effect of decisions.

Market research is by no means all the information a marketer needs, but it is a quite specific sector of it. The military analogy is useful here. 'Reconnaissance' is a survey of the ground before a battle, knowledge of the enemy and how his troops are disposed. It cannot itself determine military objectives; other information (for example, about the resources available on one's own side and their state of readiness) is necessary for this. Nor can it decide the political objectives of the war. But it can modify the general's appreciation of his objectives and suggest the best ways of achieving them (provided of course that it is good reconnaissance; misleading information is worse than none, as Napolean doubtless felt after Moscow). In the same way, well-conducted market research provides systematic and accurate knowledge of the market 'out there', the people we are trying to sell to; it can correct false impressions and aid understanding of their needs and responses. It cannot *by itself* determine marketing objectives but, allied to a proper appreciation of the product it helps the resources of a business to be deployed effectively.

Market research does not guarantee success. Even the best-conducted intelligence service may be misinterpreted or misused; Napolean did not fail at Moscow through lack of information, but because he refused to pay attention to the information he had available. Market research costs money, and there are often strong pressures to skimp on it or to think of it too late, instead of integrating it into the marketing plan. Market research provides an important part of the basis for better, more cost-effective marketing, but only if it is well designed and well thought out in accordance with marketing objectives, and if the results are taken seriously and understood.

THE GROWTH OF MARKET RESEARCH

Although the beginnings of market research can be said to date back to the turn of the century, when advertising agencies such as the J. Walter Thompson Company in America began to build successful businesses on the basis that they understood the market, its growth into a substantial industry is entirely post-war. In Britain a few advertising agencies had established market research subsidiaries before the war, and one or two successful entrepreneurs (A. C. Nielsen, Gallup, Mass Observation, for example) had set up their own specialised services. Government work for the Ministry of Food and other departments kept these bodies in operation during the war, but when the Market Research Society was formed in 1947 there were only a dozen market research agencies in the country, six of which still operate today: British Market Research Bureau (the oldest *ad hoc* agency in Britain), Bureau of Commercial Research, Mass Observation, Nielsen, Research Services and Gallup.

Today the market for research in Britian is estimated to be worth over £80 million. During the 1970s the increase in real terms, adjusted for inflation, was more than two-thirds. Some 4000 persons are thought to be employed in market research, three-quarters of whom are members of the Market Research Society, and there are nearly 200 supplying agencies.

It is still the case that the industry depends heavily on consumer goods clients, especially in food and drink. Advertising agencies, the original founders of most market research suppliers, now directly commission less than 10 per cent; the post-war years have seen the development of in-house research departments, staffed by professionals, with an established place in the marketing organisation of their companies, and the decline of the full-service agency. In 1979 the following distribution of research revenue was estimated (based on the returns of members of AMSO, the Association of Market Survey Organisations, adjusted for non-members):

1	Food, drink and tobacco	35
2	Other manufacturing companies	15
3	Advertising agencies and media	15
4	Public sector	10
5	Service traders	5
6	Overseas	5
7	Miscellaneous	15
		100 per cent

It is now generally felt by commentators that the very rapid growth in the industry during the 1960s and 1970s has probably reached its peak, and that it will settle down to follow more closely the national rate of economic growth.

THE OCCASIONS FOR MARKET RESEARCH

The variety of problems presented for treatment by market research methods, and of sources from which they come, is so great these days that no classification can give its full flavour. However, some sort of intelligible grouping is needed to break up the subject. Let us consider first the occasions when, and the purposes for which, market research is used. Since this book is intended for managers, we shall concentrate on market research for industrial and commercial clients making consumer goods; but much of what follows will apply in the different context of work for government departments, local authorities, nationalised and non-consumer industries or university research projects. All of these use the same tools of the trade in differing degrees.

As a first step, one might distinguish three aspects of business where market research is naturally involved:

1 *Description* of the market
2 *Monitoring* how the market changes
3 *Action* taken by the company, both at the state of *initiation* (choosing which action to take) and *evaluation* of the results of action taken.

Each of these three can be applied at two levels of distribution: the level of the *retailer*, and the level of the eventual *consumer*. Thus we can think of the field divided into a sixfold framework:

	Retailer level	Consumer level
Description		
Monitoring		
Action (initiation and evaluation)		

The way in which research methods fit into the cells of this framework will be discussed later, but first these three aspects of business will be described:

Description

The primary purpose for which research is required. The need is obvious for a company coming new to a market. To work out the overall strategy, to formulate the product correctly and to decide how to market and promote it, it is clearly necessary to learn whatever relevant information is not already known about the brands (if any) already in the market, how they are distributed, their share of market, who the users are, how frequently and how they use the brands, whether they are single- or multiple-brand users, and the reasons why they make their choices. A new entrant would *have* to learn these things but it is equally important, if less obvious, for an established brand that those who market it should keep up to date with the context in which their product is bought.

Yankelovitch, in a paper in 1966, tells the story of the runaway success of Timex watches in the United States, and attributes it to their correct appreciation of the actual demand in their market. The Swiss manufacturers, against whom Timex were competing, discovered (from a survey which they misunderstood) that low-cost Timex watches were being purchased not merely by low-income groups but by high-income groups also. They failed to appreciate that as many as two-thirds of the watch-buying population either

229

wanted a low-cost watch which they could replace if it wore out, or a reliable watch (paying extra for the quality); in both cases a *practical* purchase. They continued to address all their promotion to the remaining third of the market, which saw a watch solely as a gift for a special occasion with an emotional content. The quality watch companies stressed the symbolic aspect in their advertising and concentrated it all around Christmas and graduation day, leaving the rest of the year uncovered. Timex exploited the gap with brilliant effect. It is unusual to find so clear a case history, but there have been other examples quoted publicly, by managers responsible for brands of acknowledged success and prestige, which have stressed the importance they attach to keeping up to date their knowledge of the 'health' of the brand, and the place this takes in their marketing strategy.

Monitoring

By this is meant period checking for *changes*, in the brand's share or distribution, usage or image. There are obvious dangers in formulating plans on out-of-date information when significant changes have occurred since the original picture was taken.

A typical research strategy might involve periodic studies of a market in some depth, taking a cross-section at a certain point in time, linking these together by continuous measurement of a limited number of key variables which are expected to be liable to change.

Action

Whereas 'description' and 'monitoring' refer to obtaining information about the market 'out there', the 'action' heading would include all the ways in which market research can help a company to operate within that situation, both in initiating and deciding between options, and in evaluating action taken. It can include the following areas of activity:

1   New product launches and development
2   Alteration to existing products (i.e., testing for acceptability)
3   Developing and evaluating advertising campaigns, in matching creative treatment and media to target markets
4   Developing and evaluating promotions, sampling drops, mailing shots etc.
5   Promoting the company's image.

Another area of research which really deserves a separate heading, although it is not included in the 'management' scheme above, is *media*. Information on the audiences for different media is needed on a continuous basis to provide the currency in which agency buyers can deal with media sellers. Television viewing, radio listening and newspaper and magazine readership are all regularly measured in surveys paid for by media owners and controlled by joint industry committees representing media, agencies and advertisers. Apart from these, a number of specific surveys are carried out to establish the coverage or effectiveness of particular media.

WHY RESEARCH AT ALL?

As already stated, market research is not the whole of the information needed for marketing, but a special kind of information, obtained by survey methods from the population of potential consumers or from the distribution system. Before moving on to consider how the different purposes outlined above are satisfied by different research methods, it is pertinent to ask why we need market research at all. After all, it costs money to collect and process research data, and it is not so long ago that there was no market research at all. Didn't people manage then, and are there not firms who seem successful enough today without it?

It is tempting, especially in times of financial stringency, to believe that a company's own knowledge of its product and contacts with the trade should be adequate. Nor would it be right to decry the know-how of (for example) a good sales force. But there are several problems in relying solely on reports from salesmen or other departments. One is lack of the coverage we need: salemen's contacts with the trade are not likely to tell us enough about *customers'* attitudes. Second, what salesmen are able to discover is limited by the contacts they make among retailers and will not represent them all. Third, information gathering is not their principal job, and their selection and interpretation of what seems important will inevitably be affected by their primary interest in selling. Although information from salesmen or other sources may have considerable qualitative value, we need to be sure that the information on which decisions are based is as far as possible complete and representative in coverage, and objective.

To ensure representativeness and objectivity, market research makes extensive use of *sampling.*

Sampling in market research

Sampling is not, of course, exclusive to market research; it is a familiar concept in quality control. It is the only practical way of measuring the composition (taking a sounding) of a very large population which it would be impossible, or prohibitively expensive, to measure in a complete census (a 'population', by the way, in statistics means any defined group of people or things which is to be sampled).

If a sample is selected by correct methods, every member of the population will have an equal probability of being selected (or, if not equal, a known and deliberately weighted probability). There is thus no bias in the selection, so that the results remain unknown and uncalculated.

Central to the theory of sampling is the concept of standard error. From a very large population there is a very large number of ways, almost an infinity of ways, of selecting samples. Suppose a very large number of different samples of a given size were selected. What would we expect the variation to be in any estimate derived from samples? To make it concrete, let us suppose we want to find out the proportion of all adults who are men. We happen to know it should be about half, but the same principle applies to any other unknown proportion we want to estimate. The different samples will not give exactly the same estimate, but we would expect *most* of them to give *roughly* the right estimate; otherwise sampling would be of little value. In fact, we know from sampling theory that the estimates given by a very large number of samples fit into a standard pattern, called the *normal distribution*, a bell-shaped curve in which most of the sample estimates bunch together around the centre while some tail off in either direction, above and below the central estimate. It is possible to calculate how sample estimates form themselves into a normal distribution, by calculating the standard error; two-thirds of all the estimates would be within plus or minus one standard error of the average (central) estimate, 95 per cent within two and 99 per cent within three standard erros. Thus we know, by calculation based on sampling theory, the probability that the true proportion for the population (or the average estimate from a number of samples, which approaches closer to the true proportion as the number of samples approach infinity) lies within a certain range of the estimate given by our *one* sample.

A very important point here, and one often not understood by laymen, is that the error probability we can calculate for a sample depends only on the size of the sample itself and *not at all* on the proportion of the population sampled. People are often surprised at the idea that one can estimate a quantity for a population of many millions from 'only' 500 or 1000 people. But if it is a properly selected sample, the error calculation depends only on the sample size and the fact that the sample is only a tiny proportion of the population is irrelevant. If from a sample of 1000 people we estimate that 45 per cent of the population of the country is male we know that there is a 95 per cent chance that the true figure will lie between plus or minus 3 per cent (in other words, there is only one chance in twenty that any similar sample would have produced an estimate lower than 42 per cent or higher than 48 per cent). If the sample size were increased to 4000, the range of error would be reduced to plus or minus 1.5, i.e., between 43.5 per cent and 46.5 per cent. The general rule is that to *halve* the standard error you have to increase the sample size by four times.

The above explains why sampling theory provides a safe and economical a procedure for accurate estimation of large populations. In practice, in market research, the pure theory just described nearly always has to be modified. This is because we sample people, and people living all over a country are expensive to contact and interview; a simple equal probability sample of the population of Britain would involve a great deal of expensive travelling by interviewers to contact isolated individuals.

Basic sampling theory has been developed in many ways so as to combine statistical validity with practical cost-effective interviewing. The two most important modifications are *clustering* and *stratification*. By clustering is meant that, instead of sampling across the board, we sample in *stages*, selecting first a sample of geographical areas (e.g. wards, polling districts or census enumeration districts) and taking the sample of people within those districts. Clustering slightly increases the standard error of a sample, but this is calculable and is normally a small price to pay for the benefit of cost-effective interviewing, since interviewers can be given assignments with contacts all living reasonably close together and can then achieve a higher rate per day's work. Stratification means that before selecting the geographical areas (normally called sampling points) within which we are to sample, they are arranged in an order which makes sure that we include in correct proportions all relevant local characteristics: north and south, urban and rural areas and so on. There are now in existence very sophisticated methods for classifying geographical areas, based on information from the census, and computer programmes for picking stratified sampling points.

There are many possible ways of sampling individuals but they group essentially into two: random and non-random. In random, or probability, sampling, the interviewer has no choice: he has to try to contact a specific individual pointed out to him. Most samples in the UK are picked from the electoral register, and there are systems for picking either households or individuals from the register and for sampling adults with the correct probability from selected households even if they are themselves not registered. With a probability sample one knows what proportion of the selected sample could not be contacted and therefore has a chance to estimate any bias in the results; the statistical calculations of standard error, etc., all apply. Probability samples are usually demanded for government surveys and for others which are required to be publicly accountable. There is however a cost penalty, since it is more expensive to require interviewers to contact specific individuals, calling a number of times if necessary, than to allow them some latitude in their selection of persons to interview. For this reason, many market research projects use a form of non-random, or quota sampling, in which interviewers are required to deliver certain numbers of interviews with specified types of people whom they must find themselves. Quotas can be set in line with what is known of the population. Strictly, quota sampling does not have the statistical theoretical base of random sampling, although empirical tests of the consistency (stability) of non-random samples are possible. In much sampling practice quota samples are selected multi-stage, with the primary sample of areas (wards etc.) being chosen by strict probability methods after stratification. The interviewers are issued with lists of street numbers and given strict instructions to obtain their interviews within those streets. The only quota controls which then remain necessary are those relating to the probability of someone being at home: typically, interviewers have to find a certain proportion of working women or women with children, and must interview men in the evening so as not to find only unemployed or shift workers. Most of the major research agencies operate a system of this general kind.

The above account of sampling applies (obviously) to consumer research. But the variety of problems which can arise often calls for ingenuity in devising new ways of sampling, often in cases where there does not exist a 'universe' from which the sample can be drawn: industrial firms, people in professions, people with certain minority characteristics, users of certain products etc.

RESEARCH METHODS

We can now consider in broad terms the research approaches which are appropriate for the different levels of information required, classified above as description, monitoring and action. It should not be thought that these are hard-and-fast distinctions. Good research is always designed to fit a specific problem and there are cases, for example, where retailers or manufacturers are properly researched by sample survey (certainly where we are involved in measuring their opinions). Much detail is omitted from the table in Figure 14.1. Nevertheless, it is a convenient way of breaking up the subject so that we can *start* thinking about it.

GHM	For retailers	For consumers
Description of market	Retail audit	Sample surveys
Monitoring changes and trends	Retail audit	Panels or sequential surveys
Action: 　Initiation 　Evaluation	Test market Area evaluation	Experimental tests Product tests etc.
The media	Not applicable	Sample surveys or panels

Figure 14.1　Market research appropriate to different purposes

Retail audits

The retail audit is one of the earliest known types of research, pioneered by Nielsen in the United States. It stemmed from the realisation that relying on measurements of sales ex-factory was not fast enough or accurate enough to identify areas of weakness in distribution or adverse trends that would need correction. A falling demand could be concealed by stock build-up at the wholesalers; conversely, retailers might be content to tolerate shortages of stock in areas where a little activity could stimulate a healthy demand, etc. It was necessary to go to the front line, so to speak, and observe directly what consumers were taking off the shelves.

Retail audits work in the following way. A panel of stores is recruited to represent the universe (grocery outlets, chemists, off-licences or whatever the definition is) being stratified so that different turnover levels and types of organisation (multiple, independent, voluntary group, cash and carry etc.) are represented. The audits are carried out at regular intervals, usually bi-monthly. At each audit, an interviewer counts the stock of the audited items on display on the shelves and in the storeroom, and all goods invoiced since the previous check. Movement off the shelf between two checks is then calculated by the simple formula:

(Stock at check 1) + (Goods invoice since check 1) – (Stock at check 2)

The key data normally reported for audited product fields are sales brand shares and volume trends, purchase brand shares and volume trends, and distribution. These are broken down by relevant classifications such as area of the country, type of shop or turnover level, and all shown both in unit volume and sterling value terms: where relevant, pack sizes within brands are also broken out separately. Advertising expenditure is usually monitored and fluctuations in this can be set alongside sales and purchase movements, although it may be dangerous to draw simple conclusions about relationships between them. Most retail audit companies will, for a lower charge, supply a distribution check which merely tells one what proportion of stores have the brand in stock and on display. Merchandising material and display advertising can also be monitored.

Setting up a retail audit panel and the facilities to process the data is an expensive investment, and it is crucial to this kind of operation that it should be *syndicable* (that is; sold to a number of clients). Syndication is economically possible because, once the initial investment of recruiting and visiting the panel is made, it is relatively inexpensive to collect the data for a large number of product fields. Following the pattern pioneered and still operated by Nielsen, clients pay agreed subscriptions for packages of selected brands within a defined product field, reported and presented so that the information is tailored to their needs.

Although most retail audit work is thought of in connection with grocery and chemist products, audits are run in hardware stores, tobacconists, garages, off-licences, travel agents, record shops and other specialist outlets. Prescription auditing, in which either chemists' invoices or doctors' prescriptions (from duplicate pads) are counted, is also an established service.

In buying an audit, of course, one always has to be aware of the proportion of trade that passes through outlets *other* than the particular group being measured by the audit.

It is widely expected that the spread of new technology, especially electronic data capture at the checkout, will eventually change the face of auditing. Through scanners, retailers can acquire instant, accurate and continuous knowledge and therefore control to assist them in their day-to-day management. They may not wish to make this information available to competitors; alternatively, they may agree amongst themselves upon the extent to which information for the whole trade (or the few companies responsible for 80 per cent of it) is to be disseminated and shared. The detail available from scanners will make traditional auditing seem very slow and old fashioned; on the other hand part of the market (the smaller outlets) will be relatively slow to adopt scanners. In America (where some 4000 stores now have scanners) there are already a number of research firms who have set up consumer panels in association with scanner stores, so that these people's purchases can be logged automatically over time (without trouble to the respondent) and related to their opportunities for seeing advertising, etc. It will be a few years yet before new-look audit facilities are in being but eventually (we may be confident) scanner-based data will win on cheapness as well as quality and new types of service will compete for the business.

Consumer sample surveys

These are what most people automatically think of as 'market research': the interviewer with a clipboard, the structured questionnaire, the so-called opinion poll. Indeed, these methods are still the backbone of market research, and are likely to remain so. To stop short at the level of the retailer's counter is not enough; marketers must know what consumers do with their products, how they buy them, what they like or dislike, what needs are unsatisfied. New products could not otherwise be optimally designed and launched; existing ones could not be promoted to best effect.

The personal interview, with the interviewer knocking at the door or stopping people in the street, is the popular picture of consumer surveying but not the whole story. Occasionally the necessary data are collected by *observation*. Often *self-completion* questionnaires are used, either in the course of a personal interview, or left with informants to return by post or to be collected later. Self-completion is used for the Target Group Index (a syndicated survey of 25 000 people covering usage of over 2000 brands and services and media). It is also a good procedure for certain kinds of scaled attitude data. Finally, there are the alternatives of *postal* and *telephone* interviewing.

Personal interviewing is the most costly alternative, and this trend is likely to continue. The reason is obvious: it is a highly labour-intensive method. Interviewers are paid some £10–£20 for a roughly six-hour day, depending on their quality and experience. Pay is increased for unsocial hours (evenings or weekends) which are necessary in most surveys these days even when only housewives are being interviewed, since so many of them are out at work during the day. In addition, interviewers have to be paid for their time in travelling to the place where the work has to be carried out, which may be some distance from their home, and their mileage expenses, which must increase in line with petrol prices. The days of interviewing as a relatively low-cost part-time job are over. More importantly, a large section of the time paid for is 'dead' time, travelling to and between contacts, and this lowers the effective daily interviewing rate, which is the principal variable determining the cost of a survey.

Nevertheless, for many survey purposes personal face-to-face interviewing is considered necessary. A good interviewer forms a rapport with respondents which can lead them to focus their minds in a relaxed and concentrated way on the subject under discussion. The interaction between two people plays a part in improving the quality of the response. Stimuli can be shown, ranging from words on a card through photographs to actual products. Also, a questionnaire can be taken in a designed order, with respondents not being alerted to questions due to come later and which could affect the earlier response.

A device commonly used to offset the high cost of face-to-face surveys where the method is judged necessary is *syndication*, in which the data collection costs of the survey are shared between a number of subscribers. The commonest form of such syndication is what has come to be known as the 'omnibus' survey. In this a regular sample is interviewed weekly (so many housewives or adults) and subscribers buy questions on the survey at a standardised fee per question and sample size. Many regularly repeated surveys, advertising tracking studies and so on, have been successfully and economically run on omnibus survey vehicles. The only serious limitation is the length of the interview. No individual can tolerate being interviewed for too long, however fascinating the subject matter, and if a number of topic areas for different subscribers have to be fitted into an interview the amount of time which can be allowed for any one of them is clearly much less than would be the case if the whole interview could be given over to that topic. For this reason, if a subject has to be explored in some depth by a large number of questions, an omnibus is unlikely to be suitable and a tailor-made survey will probably be required. The same is true if there is some special requirement in the sample which cannot be fulfilled by the general purpose sample used for the omnibus. But if only one or two things are required to be known and if a representative sample of the total population will do, an omnibus can offer significant savings. A special advantage of an omnibus is that because relatively large samples are interviewed weekly it can be an excellent way of finding minority samples quickly; for example where questions are to be asked of users of a product which is known to be used by only 2 per cent (say) of the population. With a tailor-made survey the cost of contacting the other 98 per cent to find out that they are not eligible for our survey is considerable, but on the omnibus that cost is almost entirely shared between the other subscribers.

Postal and *telephone surveys* are ways of interviewing which do not incur the cost penalties of sending interviewers out to people's homes to make their contacts.

The postal survey is perhaps neglected a little unfairly in the UK except where a special sample assumed to be highly interested in the subject matter is involved (for example, the members of an organisation being asked their opinions about that organisation). There is an obvious incentive to use postal surveys where we have a population to sample for whom it is easy to obtain names and addresses and where the sample is so scattered as to make the cost of face-to-face interviewing prohibitive (the same applies, of course, to telephone interviewing). There are two main potential disadvantages with postal interviewing. The first is that a respondent can scan the whole questionnaire before he answers it (there is no possibility of leading the respondent through one stage at a time) and he can take as long over answering it as he likes; postal surveys are therefore suitable for 'considered opinions' but not for 'instant reactions'. The second and more serious disadvantage is that it is so easy for people not to reply at all. The normal procedure is to send out the questionnaires with reply-paid return envelopes, to send a reminder (with a spare questionnaire) after (say) ten days, and a second reminder some ten days after the first.

Even so, it is common to get not more than 40–50 per cent of the sample responding, and it has been known to be as low as 20 per cent. There is no simple answer to this difficulty, the important question being whether the non-respondents are *biased* in some way which would affect our interpretation of the survey results. However, this is certainly not a reason for avoiding postal surveys altogether. Postal surveys are suitable for an *interested* population, and much can be done to encourage people to respond by good design, good layout and (occasionally) incentive payment; non-response bias can be checked by telephone calls on a sub-sample.

Telephone interviewing is, in Britain and other industrialised countries, the most likely main development for the future. In the United States, where 95 per cent of the population have telephones, it is now a major data collection method. In the UK the proportion with a telephone at home has passed the 70 per cent mark, which is about the point at which telephone interviewing began to take off in the US. At these levels the question of what bias there may be among non-telephone households assumes less and less importance for most marketing interests.

Telephone interviewing preserves the interviewer–respondent interaction but in a rather different form: the interviewers' *voice* becomes crucial, other aspects of the interviewer's personality much less so. It is acknowledged that telephone interviewing is a different type of operation with its own require-ments of questionnaire design and the kind of person suitable to be an inter-viewer. It can achieve much greater productivity than face-to-face interviewing because it can be centrally organised. No costs are incurred in travel to locate respondents and many more calls (both contact calls and successful interview calls) can be made in a day. Moreover, there is a facility for instant supervision and correction of interviewer error which is lacking in a face-to-face survey. As technology improves, telephone interviewing will make possible the automated questionnaires and immediate data capture and processing by computer which are already in operation to a limited extent in the United States.

There are some obvious limitations. One cannot show stimulus material over the telephone (although it is possible to mail stimulus material to people already recruited to a sample with instructions not to look at it until the interview). There are worries also about the psychological reaction of respondents to the telephone: will they be nervous of a disembodied voice or resentful at the intrusion into their privacy that the telephone may seem to represent? American experience does not suggest that these are serious problems, but only time will tell whether in other countries there is an anti-telephone feeling. That any such problem can be overcome with time and good design, there is little doubt.

Although telephones are not yet used widely in general consumer surveys in Britain, they are extensively used for surveys among respondents at the executive level who can, of course, most easily be contacted by telephone. Frequently, such respondents are recruited by telephone for face-to-face interviews in greater depth.

Panels

If you wish to measure *change* in attitudes or behaviour, an obvious approach is to interview the same set of people twice. Any change observed is subject to the standard error of the one sample only, whereas, if two separate samples are used, there are two standard errors to take into account. One can get a more direct, more accurate picture of change within people, and perhaps that can be related to a stimulus such as a new advertising campaign. The drawback, of course, is that one must be careful not to alert people by questions which in themselves could lead them to notice things or to modify their behaviour and thus distort their answers the second time round.

Any repeat interviewing of the same people could be called a panel. Normally, in research parlance, a panel has a more restricted meaning than that. *Either* it is a sample which agrees, on recruitment, to be available for contact on all sorts of subjects (some firms run telephone panels on this basis) *or* (more commonly in the UK) a panel is recruited to provide *continuous* information over a period, typically information which needs to be recorded day by day otherwise it would not be remembered. Such panels may be run either as continuous syndicated services (requiring an investment too great for a single company to underwrite) or for specific *ad hoc* projects. Examples of operations suitable for panel treatment include:

1 *Retail audits*, where the data are provided from panels of shops
2 *Consumer audits*, where panel members keep records of purchases and interviewers periodically call and check stocks (one method is the so-called 'dustbin check', where special containers are provided for used cans or cartons of the product being measured)
3 *Media*; the television audience measurement required for the industry is provided by a panel of homes with meters showing when the set is switched on and to which channel; diaries record who was watching. The radio audience measurement is based on diary panels
4 *New product launches*; there are well-established techniques for covering the launch period of a new brand with a panel record of purchases and, forecasting from that, the eventual development of penetration and repeat purchasing.

Panels on any scale are expensive to operate. If the panel is continuous, new members have to be continuously recruited to replace those who drop out or have to be dropped because they grow stale or too 'professional'. With diaries or similar records the task is heavier than with a single interview, and panel members may need much more in the way of 'nursing' by frequent calls from interviewers (if not more practical incentives) to make certain they keep at it. And panels generate very large amounts of data, which are seldom analysed in enough detail to get full advantage from the panel's unique capacity to trace changes over time within individuals; better analysis of panel data may be expected to be one of the major benefits of new technology in the next few years.

Experimental design

Hitherto we have been thinking mainly of strategic research, with population descriptions and monitoring of change. But much market research is concerned directly with marketing action, not only planning but evaluating it. Which option to take? What happens if we do that? What has happened as a result of action already taken, and how should it be modified in future?

The key to such questions is *comparison*, and the problem is to control for other possible sources of variation than the one we are trying to measure. Suppose we want to try out, or learn the effect of, a new advertisement. A typical approach would be (assuming the advertisement had not yet appeared on the air) to show the advertisement to a group of people and then ask questions about the brand, their attitudes to it and what the advertisement conveyed to them. The trouble is that from just this one sample it would be difficult to be sure just how far their answers were being determined, not by the new advertisement at all, but by previous experience of the brand, other advertising seen, and other influences triggered off by our questioning. To deal with this difficulty we could take another sample, like the first in all relevant respects (such as social grade, age groups, usage of the brand) and ask them the same questions but *without* showing the advertisement. Comparing the two sets of answers gives one a much better basis for believing that the *differences* between them are due to the advertisement, since that is the only relevant factor we have allowed to vary.

Many research users do not distinguish clearly enough between *survey* and *experiment* in market research, or appreciate the important part that well-designed experiments could play in their decisions.

A survey has description as its main purpose and may range widely in its coverage, but it must be based on a sample which represents the population properly. Experiments may be (and usually are) based on representative samples, but the point is less crucial for them; much more important is the matching of samples to control for extraneous sources of variation. An experiment is set up with a specific objective, usually to establish the relation between two specific variables (for example, seeing advertising and changing one's state of awareness or attitudes) and it achieves that objective by ensuring as far as possible that other sources of the effect are accounted for. The objective of an experiment determines how it is designed and how the results are to be looked at, and as a rule it is not possible to follow more than one such objective at a time.

One of the commonest types of experimental research is *product testing*. When a new version is developed (for example, a new flavour) it needs to be tested out on consumers in natural conditions to establish whether it is a good investment. Alternatively, opportunity of economy may arise by a change in the ingredients, but this must be tested on the consumers to assess whether they notice or object to any difference. There are many approaches to product testing. Members of the sample can compare two or more versions directly, test them one at a time, or the comparison can be made between samples testing one product each. The versions can be tested blind, or in their full dress concept; it may be the package or the label which is to be tested, etc. The correct design should be chosen to obtain, as economically as possible, what is needed for decision: for example, a blind paired comparison would often be appropriate if one was trying to check that a minor alteration in ingredients would remain unnoticed whereas, if two clearly different versions were being tested for overall preference, a good approach would be to take two matched samples and test each version blind on one of the sample against a 'control': since the control is common to both samples, the two sets of differences between test product and control can be compared. Sample sizes should be chosen on the basis of the degree of difference required for decision; for instance, if it is decided that a new ingredient should be adopted *unless* the old one is preferred by a difference of 10 per cent or more, the sample would be set so that a 10 per cent difference would be unlikely to occur in the sample by chance.

In real life, in the market-place, it is usually impossible to set up perfect laboratory-style experiments. Human beings and their environments are so complex that the influences which *could* affect relevant attitudes or behaviour cannot all be controlled. This does not invalidate the experimental approach; it merely means one has to keep one's head. *Advertising evaluation*, for example, is often done by a 'before and after' approach: a survey is done before the new campaign and another done after it has finished (with perhaps others at stages during it) and the differences between them measured. There can often be a problem with timing: the precise point at which the second measurement is taken could affect the result according to how long it is after the end of the campaign. It may therefore be advisable, even if a little more expensive, to run a continuous tracking measurement or, alternatively, to obtain some measure of probable exposure to the advertisement so that one can compare *within* the sample those likely and unlikely to have seen it. There are no general rules; the right tactics have to be worked out according to the case. But common sense and intelligent thought about the research design and the required outcome *before* embarking upon it pay dividends.

Test marketing for new brands, and *area tests* of advertising weights and treatments, are normal management practice for most major consumer goods companies. The reason is that however careful one may be to test the effect of product or promotional variations on a small scale, there are so many influences on consumer behaviour in the market-place which cannot be controlled that the only secure way of predicting what will happen after a major launch decision is to try it out in real life. The basis of all such work is implied experimental comparison, involving an estimate of what sales *would have been* in the test area without the action taken (taking account of all other known special features of the test area which make it different from other areas) and a comparison of that prediction with sales actually achieved.

There are many difficulties with test marketing. Suitable areas for test are difficult to select and isolate in a small country like Britain. Some operators believe that the domination of the retail trade by a few large multiples has now made test marketing in a restricted area much less practical, since they are often unwilling to negotiate the special deals required. Nevertheless, provided the maximum care is taken to understand all the factors which could affect a test, it is usually thought better to subject a plan to the discipline of an area evaluation, depending on the marketing circumstances. Time can be a problem; practitioners of test marketing usually stress the importance of allowing the test market to continue for long enough to allow the product to settle down in a normal sales pattern. With an advertising test, since advertising interacts with many other variables to induce sales, one should beware of generalising too readily that a relationship found in a test would always be reproduced.

Qualitative research

It would be wrong to conclude this brief review of market research methodology without a mention of qualitative research. Qualitative research is a form of research in which small groups of people, not sufficient for *statistical* analysis or for quoting as numbers representing the population, are interviewed in much greater depth and a more free-ranging manner than is possible with a quantitative survey. Typically this is done through group discussions, or by single taped, in-depth interviews; the interviewers or group leaders follow through points raised from a discussion brief, instead of asking fixed-format questions from a questionnaire precoded for instant analysis.

The distribution between qualitative and quantitative is often presented as a rather sterile conflict between opposing research schools. It should not be so. Each method has its benefits, its limitations and its place. Qualitative methods may provide deeper insight into a situation, and are often a necessary preliminary for the selection and correct wording of questions in a quantitative survey which, in turn, is needed to provide sound numerical estimates. The two approaches are thus complementary. Danger can come from ignoring either aspect. Questionnaire design is the most difficult part of research, and a base of qualitative understanding may enable one to avoid stupid mistakes through, for example, not realising the way in which people talk about a subject naturally. On the other hand, reliance on qualitative work only, because it is cheaper, can lead to unwarranted assumptions about what the population believes. This does not mean that qualitative work ignores the need to be representative. Frequently, great care is taken to set quotas, and in major projects as many as thirty or forty groups may be recruited from different strata of society and areas of the country. But the inference that the results represent the population remains an inference, not based on statistical theory.

ANALYSIS, INTERPRETATION AND USE

Even a modest research project may produce very large amounts of data, in the form of cross-tabulations and combinations of variables. The management of this information can pose problems. The development of data handling by computer has made it very easy to produce pages of tabulation; it has not made it easier to draw relevant and useful information from the data in a form which management can appreciate and use. The expensive research report gathering dust on the library shelf is, unfortunately, very often a reality.

The key to the problem is integration. Research will be effective if it is planned as part of a marketing process into which the information produced fits in its proper place. It follows that before going to the expense of collecting information one must have a clear picture of where that information is to fit in the scheme of things, how it is to be used and the actions or consequences which are to follow from different anticipated results. Indiscriminate, undirected information is an expensive luxury. It follows that thought must be given in advance not merely to the content of the information but also to its dissemination: the right people must have it presented to them in a form which they can use.

These considerations should be effective not merely at the analysis and reporting stage of a research project but at the beginning, when it is being planned and designed. This is not to say that there will be no scope for creative ideas once the survey has gone out into the field. It usually happens that the process of analysis itself suggests new ways of looking at the subject which are worth following through. But this does not absolve a researcher from recognising in advance the limitations of any research proposed and designing the project to take advantage of those limitations. If the marketers who commission work are to get full value from their investment, they need themselves to be aware that the research will only answer the questions it is designed to do, and to realise the importance of being clear about their objectives so as to ensure that the design will meet them.

Normally a research project begins with a written brief from a client to one or more agencies. It is sadly true that most briefs from commercial sources are very badly written indeed. It is often impossible for the reader to draw from the brief a clear idea what the research is intended to do or how it will be used: if it is to be descriptive, what measures are relevant; if experimental, what are the criteria for action.

The best results nearly always require that the research designer be taken into his client's confidence. His speciality is to map out the route from A to B, but to do that effectively he must know where B is. Interaction between a researcher and his marketing client can be very fruitful. Research designers do not seek to have everything cut and dried in a brief, but they must obtain somehow a clear, agreed view of the objectives; from this, the design, the choice of methods and the analysis often fall naturally into place. It is relatively easy to choose the best route and means of travel, once one knows where one has to go and how quickly. Research can never be an alternative to clear thinking on the part of the management which commissions it.

The objectives determine the design and the main thrust of the analysis in one go. Analysis in quantitative survey or experimental work is rarely exploratory: it confirms or tests ideas rather than searches for them. Computers have made possible an increasing sophistication in analysis, but it is a mistake on the part of the researcher or his client if this is allowed to get out of control and confuse the reader. It is very tempting to think that, since it is easy to obtain certain tabular breakdowns in the same computer run, we 'might as well have it' because 'it may show something', even if there is no purpose in mind. This temptation has to be resisted firmly. Unnecessary tables adding to thick volumes increase the probability that none of the tables, including the most useful ones, will be read at all.

It is important to pay attention to the way in which results are presented. It is common practice to prepare research reports at least at two levels:

1 A detailed commentary with technical appendices. This gives the specialists a clear account of the basis from which conclusions are drawn
2 A summary of the main findings, with their conclusions and implications. This part of the report is for the benefit of senior management, who need such information as a basis for decisions, but who do not have the time or inclination to absorb all the detail. This summary can be reinforced by visual presentation in person, which gives the opportunity for questions and discussion. The executors of the research should not be too shy to make recommendations where the results justify them.

New technology is making it increasingly possible to access data banks in a flexible way. Random access storage of information on disks and the use of on-line terminals enable a client to buy not merely a set of tabulations on paper but also the right to run off tabulations of his own, piecemeal, at relatively little expense. As these facilities spread, especially with continuous research services, the habits of users will change and they will become accustomed to *interacting* with a data source, asking questions of it to order, and linking data banks together. With the development of on-line data sources, the dusty books on the shelf should become an anachronism.

FURTHER READING

Davies, Anthony H., *The Practice of Marketing Research*, Heinemann, London, 1973

Green, Paul E., and Tull, Donald S., *Research for Marketing Decisions*, Prentice-Hall, Englewood Cliffs, NJ, 1975

Harris, E. Edward, *Marketing Research*, 2nd edition, McGraw-Hill, New York, 1978

Rawnsley, Alan (ed.), *Manual of Industrial Marketing Research*, Wiley, Chichester, 1978

Stacey, N. A. H., and Wilson, A., *Industrial Marketing Research*, Hutchinson, London, 1963

Stapleton, John, *How to Prepare a Marketing Plan*, 3rd edition, Gower, 1982

Wentz, Walter B., *Marketing Research: management and methods*, Harper & Row, New York, 1972

15 Advertising

John Hobson

In a modern industrialised society virtually the whole population has some discretionary spending power, i.e. money to spend on goods which are not necessities, like basic foods, shelter and clothing. It has the capacity to buy improved utilities, extra amenities and modest luxuries. Industry responds by making goods and offering services to suit a wide variety of tastes. No one could want or afford them all. People have to choose.

In order to choose, the consumer needs suggestions and information about what is available, what might suit his personal preferences, what could be new and interesting experiences. Before buying goods or services, he wants to hear about the performance or satisfaction which those goods and services will give him. He may see the products on display in shops or supermarkets; the satisfactions he can be informed about through advertising. If one were to say that the totality of advertising as it appears in print, or on television, or by radio is a kind of supermarket of satisfactions, it would not be an unfair definition of the place of advertising in modern society.

Although advertising owes its existence in this way to the service it gives the consumer, it becomes a vital service also to the producer. To him advertising offers the lowest-cost channel of communication for his messages offering the goods or services he has for sale. As a result of low-cost communication to millions of people with considerable frequency, he can achieve economies of scale which enable him to reduce prices. He can influence demand in such a way as to maintain a steady flow, which in turn enables him to maintain a steady flow of production. He can modify seasonal influences on demand with the same advantage, and can assure himself of the rapid pay-off of investment in new production lines and machinery and in research and development. Although advertising is only one element – the communication element – in the marketing mix, it very often can be the critical factor in a marketing decision because it can control the speed at which vital costs can be reimbursed, and new products or improvements to existing products launched.

As a result, advertising has a vital role to play in the economy of the consumer societies of the West. It is one of the most vital tools of competition and innovation which maintain the dynamics and the initiative of industry. It provides the outlet for the results of sound research and development, without which an industrial nation must go into a decline. Advertising helps to maintain employment and the uses of all resources, at a steady pace, without undue swings in supply or demand. It increases the aspirations of the public so that the desires to work harder and earn more money are increased. It improves the quality of material life for the mass of the public. It may be objected that it puts too much emphasis on material aspiration and well-being, but advertising is only responding to social trends, encouraged by the redistribution of wealth over the last century. Advertising does not govern the shape of society, it only reflects the shape that exists.

Advertising is basically communication. There are many kinds of advertising other than in the marketing context: government propaganda, advertising for churches and charities, financial news, advertising to fill jobs and get jobs, and so on. In the rest of this chapter, the word 'advertising' is used in the context of the commercial functions of advertising.

ADVERTISING AS A MARKETING ACTIVITY

The impression the public has of advertising might be that a vast amount of money and effort is being spent on a lot of bright ideas or momentary inspirations. It is a misunderstanding for which even the less well-informed social observers could be pardoned, but it is curiously prevalent also among many people concerned wth industry even in the consumer goods fields.

In fact, good advertising is the result of careful planning and research, which lead in almost every case to each advertisement being given its particular content or form, and its direction to a selected audience of potentially interested consumers. The serious sponsors of advertising have no money to waste; for them it is not an art form, or a display of ego or personal interests. When industry spends nearly £2 000 million a year on consumer goods advertising it not only expects to get, but actually does get, what it regards as a proper return for its outlay.

The basic purpose of advertising, then, is to offer goods and services for sale. Each particular advertising campaign for a particular product at a particular time is part of what one may term a deliberate marketing intention on the part of the sponsors, who base their carefully considered strategy and tactics in the first instance on the properties and utilities, shape, packaging and colour of the product, and calculate the latest trends of public behaviour, recreation or outlook, new factors in retail distribution and effect of competition. The marketing intention takes in the method of transport, trade margins, price merchandising, wholesaling and retailing decisions, the role of the sales force, the after-sales service facilities, and a number of similar considerations. It will comprise a careful identification of the best potential market in terms of people, geography, seasons and spending power; and will duly arrive at the advertising message, and the deployment of budget best calculated to carry it. The choice of advertising is virtually the last element to be decided in the marketing complex, and, although it may represent a very large part of the financial outlay and may in the result determine the success or failure of the whole marketing plan, it is in itself very largely governed by the other elements in the plan. Because the advertisements are the main, and certainly most obvious, outward and visible signs of the plan, many people get the impression that the advertising is the only really important element, that it *is* the plan in its own right.

Next, it is worth remarking that virtually no two marketing plans, or their consequent advertising programmes, have identical intentions. There are, of course, certain broad groups of similar circumstances which call for fairly similar treatments; but with each tactical situation, on which each plan is based, there are differing weights of contributory factors which make every case different from any other. It is not feasible to lay down a kind of blueprint that will fit the needs of a number of marketing or advertising intentions.

ADVERTISING OBJECTIVES AND TECHNIQUES

The two most crucial stages in developing an advertising campaign are (*a*) the strategic decision on objectives and (*b*) the choice of creative treatment. The former is bound up in the total marketing intention; the latter is a matter of advertising techniques.

The considerations leading to decisions of strategy are as wide and various as the field of commerce itself. Nevertheless, it is possible to list five main types of consideration which normally affect the advertising objectives:

1 The range, type and intensity of consumer wants comprising the market for our product, together with estimates of the trends of public outlook or trade development, which may affect those wants in the future
2 The efficacy of the product itself
3 The strength of the sponsor's resources for promoting it
4 The existing disposition of competitor's strength
5 The type of purchasing occasion arising from the character of distribution for this type of product.

One talks of 'the market' for a type of product, but this apparently straight-forward concept of the market conceals a wide variety of types and degrees of want varying by age, geography, outlook, habit, price, occasion of usage, availability and so on. By means of a painstaking assembly of facts through market research, retail contacts, and all other methods of fact finding, the size of the potential sale for our product, associated with each degree of necessity can be calculated, thus setting-up a choice of differing objectives for the advertising. It is axiomatic that no product is ever equally perfect for all sectors of the market.

The first consideration in choosing an objective will probably be the special qualities or performance of a product. The addition or adjustment of qualities would be considered in order to create a better advertising proposition. The decision will also be affected by the areas of strength or weakness of the competition. It is no good tackling an objective head-on where strong competition is entrenched.

A vital factor is the resources which our sponsor can put behind his campaign. Only too often, ambitious sponsors with slender resources attempt an objective too big for them.

The strategic advertising decision will also be greatly influenced by the type of purchasing occasion, e.g. an impulse market, a carefully considered purchase, a product limited by distributive conditions to tied outlets, a cut-price supermarket situation etc.

Finally, one must look forward from the market, the competition and the distribution, as they now exist, to possible developments foreseen as a result of trends in public spending, outlook and living patterns, and position of the product in its market accordingly.

An illustration of the strategic advertising decision might be given in the case of the breakfast cereal market. Here are five products which have been deliberately aimed at five sectors of the market. The market leader uses his dominant resources to promote a broad sense of pleasure and wholesomeness, which can apply to everyone. Another brand with a more rugged product and a lower budget concentrates on youngsters through their sporting interests. A third attacks a limited but specific health area. A fourth goes for the children's market with the appeal of a sense of fantasy and fun, while a fifth tackles the same market with the appeal of premium gifts.

It is probable that this strategic decision overrides even the creative decision of importance. The most sparkling and competent creative execution will be wasted if the policy objectives are not correctly chosen. It happens only too often. At the same time, within the right strategic decision there is wide scope for success or failure, brilliance or dullness, competence or incompetence, in the creative execution.

There are three main considerations likely to influence the approach to the creative decision, (a) the tactical objective of the particular phase of advertising (b) the choice of main and secondary selling arguments, and (c) the manner or atmosphere of the presentation of those selling arguments.

TACTICS

There are an infinite variety of tactical situations. To name a few – we may be launching a new product with new utilities which need proclaiming and explaining. A dramatic piece of news like a price reduction or a new model may be announced, or the memory of an estabished brand name may be merely sustained with a fresh rendering of its well-known claim. The virtues and the responsibility of a serious industrial concern may be expounded to an audience of managers, or the objective may be to give a company in the popular consumer goods field a favourable image against which its goods will sell automatically. A race for our brand against a very similar brand of some other firm to gain a larger share of the market may occupy much of out time, or it may be that greater concern is felt for widening the total market for a class of goods because, if the market widens, our brand must automatically gain the lion's share.

There are probably three main elements in the tactical case of advertising – to penetrate, remind and create favourable associations. The relative importance of each element in the plan of the particular campaign will tend to determine which type of media or campaign approach will be used. For example, television and large spaces in the press and magazines are ideal outlets for telling a story in depth, while posters and smaller spaces in the press and short television flashes (little more than moving posters) are good for repetition which, as Dr Kelvin points out in *Advertising and the Human Memory*, not only prevents us forgetting but serves as the means of progressive assimilation of the advertising message.

Then the question of the selling arguments arises. It might seem as if the choice were obvious, determined simply by the properties of the product. This, however, is unlikely to be so in the majority of cases. It will be true at the moment when a product has clear and simply expressed product advantages over its competitors; but this situation will not hold good for long because it will only be a matter of time before the competition is forced to include those same advantages. Look around the whole field of consumer goods and you will find very few markets in which there is not a handful of equally good competitive brands. If one has edged ahead in product quality, the others have caught up. Indeed, this continuous competitive improvement is one of the great merits of the system of which advertising is a part. In this situation advertising has to find some aspect of a brand on which to focus, an aspect on which the competition has not focused. Nor is this limitation of the scope of the product claim to a single aspect a disadvantage; indeed quite the reverse. The consumer finds it far easier to identify, and therefore to remember at time of purchase, a product which has one single claim associated with it. So, however many good points a product may have, it is wise for the purposes of advertising to focus on one only, and allow the other values to emerge in course of use. Naturally, that one point must be an important one capable of influencing a sizeable part of the market.

ADVERTISING AND MARKET RESEARCH

What are the techniques for assessing the best choice of product claim? First, there is the obvious selection of an objective built-in utility superior to that of competition, but this is usually a short-lived advantage. Next, there is the historic flair and inspiration of the salesman for judging what the public wants most in the area of this product, and for concentrating on this aspect of the brand's properties. This competence, whether rational or intuitive, is one of the chief qualities of a great industrialist or a great salesman.

But in the intensive competition of today, and where the stakes are high and the penalties great, the hit-or-miss risks of intuition are not always acceptable. Market research, and especially depth research, are employed more and more to help in defining those areas to which the product's copy claims can best be directed. Market research covers all types of consumer investigation, but is generally associated with research designed to establish a pattern of behaviour. From the patterns of behaviour by people of various descriptions the motives of that behaviour are deduced. Depth research, or motivation study as it is called, consists of interviews directly designed to establish attitudes, motives and feelings about products and their usage, without the risks of deducing them

249

from behaviour patterns.

A lot has been written and spoken about 'hidden persuaders' since Vance Packard's book of that title was written. Certainly, the book overdramatised what is a very natural and sensible process. Let us be clear that in buying, as in many aspects of life, the number of decisions that can be taken on strictly rational grounds is very few; not only because it is seldom possible to assemble all the facts, but also because rational decisions involve a painful and complicated mental process which only a few people are either capable of or willing to undertake. Therefore, the majority of decisions are made out of feelings, habits, instincts and impulses. It is commonsense, therefore, to try to chart those feelings, habits and impulses which surround the purchase of goods being sold.

The purpose of any such research, as indeed of the alternative – flair and intuition – is to establish that aspect of the product's claims which interests a large enough market, which has been neglected by competitors, and with which therefore this particular brand can become associated with major selling effect. Sometimes, of course, the need for being different leads to an exaggerated or partly untenable vision of a claim, even among well-intentioned salesmen. The public's safeguard in this case is that, since the success of any product depends on repeat purchases, not merely on a single purchase, and since nothing makes the public react against a product more than disappointment in an advertised claim, it is bad commercial policy as well as undesirable ethically to fall into the trap of exaggerated or dishonest claims.

DEVELOPING IMAGE AND SUBJECTIVE VALUES

The third main area of consideration in the approach to the creative decision is the associations with which the advertising can endow the product. This is something quite apart from the substance of the claims one makes for the product, yet it is of very real significance in the selling situation. It is the same subjective element which, when applied to corporations, is sometimes called the 'image'. It arises from the fact that when people make a purchase, they do not only buy something having objective values, but they buy satisfaction which includes subjective values also. The most obvious case is a woman buying a hat. She does not only buy a head-covering or a piece of coloured felt, she buys a satisfaction that includes such subjective values as fashionableness, a feeling of style, a sense of daring or renewed youth or whatever. But while this is an obvious case, the same principle applies just as readily to purchases of everyday things. With petrol you buy a sense of power or the feeling of a wise bargain. With beer you may buy a sense of manliness, or a sense of fun or a sense of healthfulness. With chocolate biscuits you may buy a feeling of gaiety, and with a car you certainly do not only buy a means of transport, but also a feel of dashingness, of luxury, of importance, of smartness, or whatever attribute has been added to the machinery by the advertising, the line of the bonnet, or the number of marginal gadgets.

There is plenty of evidence to show that these subjective values represent a very real increase of satisfaction in the purchase and use of the product; and the improved product commands a definite preference, and often a higher price, from the buyer than the same product not so improved. In the advertising aspect of their creation (and it is one of the most potent effects of advertising) the method is usually that of building up certain deliberate associations by the type of verbal or visual treatment, the use of colour and the associated pictures or personalities. It is as if a pattern of subjective associations is integrated with the substance of the product and becomes a real part of it. In an economy where the public could afford to pay for nothing except objective values this situation could hardly arise, but in an affluent society where almost everyone has a spending power in excess of physical needs, scope is widening for following one's whims into the area of subjective satisfactions.

Techniques of advertising presentation are a subject of endless fascination. They embrace all the most intricate aspects of perception, communication and persuasiveness. They cover everything in verbal and visual techniques from journalism to poetry, from realism to impressionism, from the *News of the World* to *Vogue*. One can only hope to touch on a few of the main points.

The first is to recognise the different audiences to whom the advertising must be addressed: top management or the housewife in the Durham back streets; children or the fashion-conscious women of society; bank managers or miners. The tone, the contents and the treatment will vary according to the audience. But certain factors will remain reasonably constant.

The first need for any advertisement is to gain attention. By and large, people do not aim to read advertisements – though in fact the advertisement section of a woman's magazine has a high readership in its own right. However, even here one is wise to start with the assumption that people will not want to read a particular advertisement. In the newspapers advertisements have to capture attention. On television there is much talk of a captive audience, but this can be misleading. The audience may be captive, but its attention is not necessarily so; it may be talking or knitting or reading.

TECHNIQUES OF ADVERTISING

Here is a first axiom for getting attention: that it is the interest of the message that attracts attention – not the size, visual impact or its violence. The eye and mind work so fast that they shrug off instinctively a first impact of size or surprise or violence in an advertisement, before they have even assimilated what it is about, unless subconsciously there is an awakening of genuine interest. Clearly, interest in a product message is not universal; it will always limit itself to some section of the total public. For example, even a little advertisement headed 'Indigestion' will be noticed by the 3 or 4 per cent of people who at that moment are conscious of having a problem of indigestion. One of the reasons why advertising gets a bad name for being excessive or boring is that far more people every year are being exposed to far more messages than can be of interest to them personally. Men particulary become irritated with all the household advertisements which have no interest for them. In newspapers one can select those advertisements on which, because they say something of personal interest, one wants to focus, and ignore the rest. On television it is not so easy to ignore those of no personal interest, and this is why television tends to get a worse name in the context of intrusion that the press does.

Since the attention of an advertisement is gained by the first awakening of interest, it is vital that the attention-getting element should signal the sector of interest the advertisement aims to attract. Otherwise, one may only attract interest that cannot lead to sales. Humour, so beloved of many superficial observers of advertising, is a dangerous weapon for this reason, because (although it can add a certain cheerfulness to the image of the product) it too often attracts the attention of masses of people who are not potential buyers, and it may obscure or even damage the serious appeal to those who are.

The second key factor is the essential need to offer a benefit to those forming the potential market. People neither buy, nor want to think about buying, something that does not promise them a benefit for their money. It may sound a self-evident truth, but it is surprising how often it gets overlooked in the intricate and elaborate process of advertisement creation. Ideally, the benefit should be clearly conveyed in the attention-getting element in the advertisement. Sometimes the sponsors of advertisements, or their creators, are so shy about their whole function of selling they will go to great lengths to avoid seeming to intrude anything so blatant as a selling-point in the advertisement. But really the function of advertising is not to amuse, not to educate; not to decorate the hoardings or enliven the newspapers, but to sell; and only when an assured commitment emerges can it afford to do the other things as well.

The third element worthy of focus as important is that of giving a 'reason why', i.e. the reason why the product can offer such and such a benefit. More is often achieved through an appeal to the emotions than to the mind (because people are lazy about using their minds); but people are both mind and emotion, and their emotions react more easily if they are offered some concession to their logical process as well. It is wiser therefore to say 'X is better because . . . ' than just 'X is better'.

The final element in a good advertisement is a bold display of the brand name. Once again this may seem obvious. After all, the function of an advertisement is to get the public to ask for a product or at least to recall its name in the shops. But there are some people who believe that a prominent display of a brand name will make people pass on from your advertisement because they believe they know what you are going to say about that product. This is a risk which must be taken, and be counteracted by the other elements in your advertisement. There are advertisers who believe that their advertisements are so well-liked and recognised that it is a good idea to leave the name out altogether. This is treating advertising as some kind of parlour game, not the expensive, productive and important process it really is.

THE UNIQUE SELLING PROPOSITION

Ideally the benefit should be one which the product alone can offer: it may be desirable to go back to the product formula and build-in some unique added benefit that its competitors do not comprise. It may only be possible to seek a unique way to express the benefit, or a unique aspect of the benefit to stress.

Most products can offer a whole spectrum of benefits ranging from solid factors such as the price and performance, to elaborate subjective benefits derived from the manner of presenting either the product or the advertising. Somewhere at some point of this spectrum the advertising can be coloured with a unique shade, giving it a separate identity from its competitors. It is vital to end up by leaving in the public's mind a clear identity for your product – a uniqueness in an important selling area; what has been termed by one great American expert, Rosser Reeves, a Unique Selling Proposition.

This positive proposition of a benefit can then be enhanced by any one of a wide range of subjective associations which, providing they are relevant to the purchase of the product, can add to its total attraction. Such associations may be gay or fanciful or fashionable; they may offer a sense of a bargain, youthfulness, or keeping up with the Joneses. These are well-tried examples; there are many others. From these elements the total advertising presentation is built up to do its job of making a potential market interested in trying this product through the promise of a satisfaction which is part objective and part subjective.

THE ADVERTISING CAMPAIGN

A campaign concerns the total effect and sequence of the advertisements for a product. This technique was crystallised by Sir William Crawford, one of the great advertising technicians of the early days, in the three-word precept, 'concentration, domination, repetition'. It is still, and must always be, the clearest reflection of the processes which go to make up mass selling.

Concentration

This is the selection of one shade in the spectrum of possible appeals for the product and the avoidance of diversity of appeal and dispersal of resources. It implies, of course, the careful selection of the appeal best calculated to gain a response from a sector of the market, which in turn is calculated to offer the best sales potential, having regard to the particular attributes of the product, the state of competitive activity and the resources available for promotion. It would be useless to select an area of product appeal which brought head-on collision with a competitor of much greater resources or to comprise a sector of wants to which the available budget was insufficient to do justice. It implies also the virtues of simplicity and single-mindedness in execution.

Domination

Domination is the gathering of the available forces of money and presentation techniques in such a way as to create a dominant impact on the minds of the chosen public. It will comprise an element of size at the initial stages of the campaign so as to gain attention and outweigh competitive claims. It will ensure that in the selected area of consumer needs, the name of the product will come out top of the alternatives in the memory of the potential customers. Given a budget insufficient to cover all areas, classes or segments of the public,

253

domination will necessitate a concentration of effort in terms of geography or choice of media or some other means so that in that area of concentration the product can outweigh all rivals.

Repetition

Repetition is an essential part of the techniques of all advertising. With most consumer goods it is the repeated purchase that makes the selling investment pay off. The product drops only too easily out of mind and memory, and is supplanted by some lively newcomer unless the satisfied customers are reminded. Then it must be remembered that virtually no first impact of advertising reaches everybody; what appears to be repetition is very often merely a continuation of first impact on groups of customers not previously reached with the message. Every week of every year a new group of potential customers grows into the market. The advertising campaign therefore needs to be continued over a period of time, and a disposition of available resources must be made accordingly.

THE STRATEGIC FRAMEWORK OF ADVERTISING

The above are the salient factors which go to the strategic framework of an advertising campaign. There are executive processes which have then to be considered.

First and foremost comes the creative execution. To some people the creative element appears to be the most important, and certainly it is usually the most noticeable. A campaign tends to be judged superficially on its creative impact; in fact, unless the marketing conception is right, the creative impact can increase and intensify the misdirection of the expenditure and effort. Creative execution can only be considered after the strategic conception. It is usually a wise plan to present the strategy as a document for agreement by all concerned before going to the next stage of writing or visualising the actual advertisements.

Clearly, there must be vitality, craftsmanship, humanity and hopefully, a touch of creative inspiration, to turn a campaign plan into warm, sparkling communication. The agreed campaign message can be given vividness and brilliance, but it is wise to remember that vividness and brilliance have their own glamour and can divert the critical instinct from the fact that the basic message may be the wrong one. Both in the creative process and in the initial selection of the creative executive, those concerned must keep their eyes firmly on the ball.

It is of little value to try to define the right ingredients for creative quality. Too many experts would give different answers. Tastes change from year to year. Different media require different treatment. If an advertisement is to be as helpful as possible to the consumer in making a choice, it needs to portray a realistic situation with which that consumer, usually a woman, can identify. In that situation her need is defined, and the usefulness of the product or service in satisfying that need realistically presented. The creative quality will emerge in the vividness, the impression, the humanity, in which the need and its satisfaction are pictured. Television is of course an ideal medium for this kind of treatment, because realism and demonstration are a natural part of it. The essence of creative ability then becomes the capacity to stand in the very shoes of the people you are appealing to, understand their needs, sensitivities and feelings, so that the process of identification comes most cogently to them.

A good deal of advertising creativity concerns itself wrongly with over-emphasis on technique, and the intrusion of the creator's own ego and feelings. A typical case is the use of sex interest or symbols into irrelevant contexts, simply because the creator is interested in these symbols. Many advertisements appealing to women portray sex interests which are clearly male because the creator is a man. A certain amount of advertising also betrays the creator's desire for applause for his own cleverness among his own confrères, rather like the centre forward who has just scored a goal, lifting up his arms and waiting to be embraced by his colleagues. And other advertising betrays a misuse of techniques admired and copied from more relevant contexts, which in a wrong context become just plain silly.

The right creative execution is a vital part of the marketing concept of the campaign because clearly the more effectively and cogently the advertisement can communicate with the maximum number of potential buyers, the quicker the budget cost of the advertising will pay off, to the profit and success of the advertiser.

MEDIA PLANNING

The next step in the executive process will be the choice of media. Indeed, it may need to be considered at an early stage because it may govern both the economics and the creative execution of the whole campaign. The choice of media is a whole subject in its own right. Suffice it to say here that the essence of the choice is to reach the maximum number of the clearly defined target audience, in the right atmosphere for the particular message, at the lowest cost. Since target audiences for a particular product seldom identify themselves, in the consumer goods area, exactly with media readership, the problem very often comes down to choosing the media with the minimum wastage. Again, however, television which may involve maximum wastage may nevertheless be the best choice simply because it offers the best medium for the message. The available media statistics, whether sifted by computer or other techniques can offer extensive guidance to relate coverage of a particular audience to cost, but there still remains an imponderable element of choosing the best media to suit the character of the product or the particular type of message.

The only other aspect of running an advertising campaign that this chapter will cover is the function of the advertising agency in this context. The basic contribution of the agency must be its expertise in particular services – top creative ability, experienced media men for selecting and buying media, good technicians in the printing and blockmaking and other mechanical processes, and competent coordination, at executive level, of all the many details of a campaign. It is possible for an advertiser to buy many of these services from specialists outside the service agency, but, in this country at least, there is no real sign that advertisers prefer to take on the job of coordinating such outside services themselves. The agency package is still the most convenient method.

THE AGENCY RELATIONSHIP

There is, however, one other great value in the agency arrangement. The manufacturer tends to look at his marketing proposition from the boardroom downwards. He relates it to his manufacturing, profits, raw materials, distribution and the like. It is, to many manufacturers, an enormous advantage to have the compensating service of people who look at the same proposition from the market upwards. This is the special competence of the good agency. The manufacturer's personnel, even if they have the ability and training to take a consumer's view may, in certain circumstances, not have the independence to prevail on the board to make essential changes. The agency is an independent body and will be listened to more readily by the board. Finally the manufacturer, being concerned with his own type of business and immersed in it, may not have had the useful experience of outside industries, of successes and failures in other related or unrelated fields, which an agency with many clients can gather together. The manufacturer values someone competent to trade ideas with as a means of measuring his own interests against outside criticism.

ETHICS

Much has been written about the ethics of advertising. Essentially, since advertising is a communication process, the ethics of advertising are the ethics of those who utter the communication. The advertising of bad products or services is bad ethics. Sometimes, also the urgent search for additional sales may lead an advertiser into promoting his product for purposes outside its normal range, for which it is of dubious value. But good marketing, which is offering products which clearly have a true and well calculated market, does not need 'sell at all costs' advertising.

Within the limits of advertising itself there are two aspects of ethics which may be considered. The first is the honesty and truthfulness of the satisfactions offered and the information given. In the UK this requirement is controlled by the combination of the Advertising Standards Authority (operating through the Code of Advertising Practice Committee) in relation to print and other non-broadcast media, and the control committee of the Independent Broadcasting Authority, in relation to television and radio. And the International Chamber of Commerce operates a Code of Advertising Practice that applies throughout the world.

The second is a much more subjective area of advertising, what may be called the helpfulness of the advertisement to the consumer in making his or her choice. Questions of relevance, good taste, sufficient information, and other factors which cannot be controlled by a rule-of-thumb system as easily as truth and honesty can be, are inevitably left to the good sense and sensitivity of those, whether advertisers or agencies, who are practising advertising. At the same time, self-interest works to encourage the advertiser to make his advertisements helpful, because they will improve the long-term goodwill of his business, and the confidence of the public in his advertising. Social sense and business expediency combine, and in the long run the factor of consumer acceptance will be paramount.

FURTHER READING

Jefkins, F., *Advertising Made Simple*, W.H. Allen, London, 1973.

Nicholl, D., *Advertising: its purpose, principles and practice*, Macdonald & Evans, 1973.

White, R., *Advertising: what it is and how to do it*, McGraw-Hill, Maidenhead, 1980.

16 Sales promotion

Christian Petersen

Sales promotion is important. Every day, sales promotion reaches out to the consumer, salesman, and retailer. Promotion techniques are used to market a vast variety of goods and services. In many markets, expenditure on sales promotion equals or exceeds expenditure on advertising.

This importance is recent. Although the techniques involved have been in use for decades, and often for centuries, the spectacular growth of promotion dates only from the mid 1960s. In many markets sales promotion expenditure (discounting inflation) has grown *five times or more* in the last twenty years.

Such dynamism reflects a change in western economies. There has been a change from 'pull' purchasing to 'push' selling. In the 1950s and the 1960s, the growth of consumer spending power, accelerated by easily available credit, meant that people were keen to purchase whatever could be manufactured and retailed.

With the slowing and then flattening of the demand trend, the primary effort has switched to 'push' selling, in order to maintain, as far as possible, the momentum of manufacturing and retailing.

As more inducement is now necessary to get people to purchase, sales promotion techniques have come into full play.

WHAT IS SALES PROMOTION?

Sales promotion covers just about everything you can do to give people a *tangible* incentive to purchase. Everything, that is, on top of the basic sales message.

The variety of promotional techniques is as extensive as our ingenuity can devise, and as disciplined as the laws of different countries allow. New developments and refinements of technique happen every year. And because sales promotion is part of the total marketing mix, and usually co-exists with other forms of marketing, it is often difficult to decide what sales promotion is, and what it is not.

259

No one has yet produced a wholly satisfactory definition of sales promotion. A definition that attempts to be thorough and precise is usually too limiting for so dynamic a function. Such definitions, if accepted, cut out creative opportunism. Loose definitions hardly help either, since they give no firm idea of promotion, and often could be defining marketing as a whole. Also, the practical dimensions of sales promotion vary from country to country, so definitions adopted from other markets can be misleading and even legally dangerous.

The reader may like to experiment with his own definition of sales promotion. Any valid definition is likely to include the following elements:

1 There must be a *featured offer* (something done as a normal part of trade and not featured in any special way does not count as sales promotion)
2 The offer must be of *tangible* advantage. A message alone is intangible
3 The offer must be designed *to achieve marketing objectives*, which will usually, but not necessarily, mean sales.

These are, of course, rather abstract terms. An easier, though less objective, way of recognising sales promotion is to look for any of these *four key propositions:*

SAVE!
FREE!
WIN!
GIVE!

Just about every known form of sales promotion will include one or more of those propositions.

Save!

People have always loved a bargain. And keen pricing is central to 'push'-selling.

The promotional use of bargains, where featured offers of a price saving are made, can be classified under the following headings:

1 A retailer's price cut
2 A manufacturer's price cut
3 Coupons
4 Rebate schemes
5 Self-liquidating offers

1 A retailer's price cut

The format is usually simple: the retailer cuts the price of a product or service and features the promotional price on store material and perhaps in his advertising.

Many retailers now consistently cut the price of the goods they stock, so that the prices they offer are no longer specially featured bargains of a promotional nature, but an integral, and often *the main*, aspect of their business.

2 A manufacturer's price cut

Again, usually a simple format. The manufacturer cuts the price of his product and features the promotional price on his pack, or on display material, or in advertising.

Most promotions of this kind are straightforward and regular aspects of a brand's existence. Sometimes, however, a price cut can be exploited in spectacular fashion.

For example, the British motorist has become aware that a car costs more to buy in the UK than the identical car bought in most parts of Europe. In March 1982 the Ford Motor Company announced substantial cuts in the UK prices of many of its more expensive models, presenting this as the company's single-handed effort to bring UK prices into line with Europe.

Ford's competitors rushed into print to say that the savings were not all that exceptional, but Ford had scored a major victory in putting its proposition into the front of the consumer's mind, in a believable way.

3 Coupons

A coupon is a promissory note entitling the consumer to a saving on a product or service.

Some coupons are printed on or inserted in a pack, entitling the consumer to money off his or her *next* purchase.

Coupons are a popular method of offering savings, and can be more precisely targeted than price cuts. An audience can be selected by placing a coupon in a newspaper with a particular kind of readership, or an area can be selected by delivering coupons door-to-door there. Increasingly, promoters select a retailer and make a coupon redeemable only in his stores. A development of the technique in the United States is that the manufacturer issues a coupon for, say, 3 cents off his product, and an individual retailer offers to double the value of the coupon if it is redeemed in his stores.

4 Rebate schemes

The rebate scheme offers either cash or a coupon by return if the consumer *mails in* a stated number of proofs of purchase.

An advantage of the rebate technique over coupons is that the promoter receives proof of purchase, whereas ordinary coupons can be wrongly used for other purchases (the two categories of wrong redemption are *malredemption*, where the wrong use is deliberate, and *misredemption*, where the wrong use is accidental. Because coupons are, effectively, currency, malredemption and misredemption are serious dangers).

Rebate schemes are frequently used to retain the loyalty of customers. Effectively, the loyal customer is receiving a volume discount. The proofs of purchase required can be carefully calculated against the regular user's repeat purchase pattern, and the rate can be speeded up (e.g. five packs purchased over the time usually taken to purchase four packs).

A variant of the technique is the *step-sum rebate* where each proof of purchase qualifies for a rebate amount, say 20p per proof of purchase. This variant can be used to attract the occasional purchaser or the non-purchaser sampling for the first time. And, of course, once a customer starts on the scheme, there is an incentive to go on collecting proofs of purchase in order to qualify for more and more money.

5 Self-liquidating offers

The first four 'save' techniques relate to savings on the price of the promoted product. The self-liquidating technique involves the offer of a bargain price on another item, which the consumer usually applies for by mail.

The price the consumer pays for the offer item covers all the costs of making the offer – hence the term 'self-liquidating'. Essentially, the promoter is acting as a direct marketer, buying the item in bulk and cutting out profit margins.

In a class of merchandise where regular retail prices and margins are high, significant success can be achieved with a dramatic bargain offer. But consumers can be suspicious, expecting the offer item to be of inferior quality. Therefore it is usual to seek items which carry well-known brand names and are of that manufacturer's regular quality, or to offer the item on approval.

Of course, as mass retailing spreads to cover most classes of merchandise, and prices and margins fall, it becomes difficult to find known, branded items, which can be liquidated at a price below retail, especially when the increasing costs of postage have to be offset.

There are two ways round that problem. One is to regard the self-liquidating offer as a nil-cost opportunity to develop the character of a brand. A coffee manufacturer, for example, might offer a coffee mug imprinted with the brand name – an item unique to the product. This is a simple and frequent use of the self-liquidating technique.

A more ambitious way of communicating brand values is shown by the case of the Ovaltineys LP. Ovaltine (Ovomaltine in Europe) is a food beverage; its TV campaign recalls the brand's advertising of the 1930s, when it was known to everyone via a Radio Luxembourg show featuring the 'Ovaltineys of the Air': children who sang songs and made jokes. So, in 1980 an LP record was made of the Ovaltineys singing many of their famous songs. This was offered to Ovaltine's customers at a self-liquidating price. But the LP was also put on sale in leading record stores throughout the country (at a price £1 higher than the bargain price available to Ovaltine purchasers), and copies of the record were given to radio disc jockeys for airplay. Also a short television film of the singing Ovaltineys was made and offered to producers of suitable TV shows for inclusion in their programmes.

The overall effect was to create increased awareness of the brand, not only through on-pack promotion but also via free radio and television exposure (the value of this exposure, if it had been purchased at ratecard cost, was around £750 000).

Another creative use of the self-liquidating technique was developed for Marlboro cigarettes: the mail-in element was eliminated. Marlboro retailers were offered cigarette lighters carrying the Marlboro name for resale to their customers at a price of 89p if the customer did not also purchase Marlboro cigarettes, or 69p if he or she did. This simple mechanism produced very big business – Marlboro became the biggest selling brand of cigarette lighter, and the effect on Marlboro cigarette sales was very beneficial too.

Free!

'Free' is a very powerful word. Most people are irresistibly drawn to the prospect of something for nothing.

Of course, for a free offer to be of commercial value, the something will usually be for something. And the power of the promotion will depend on whether the value offered is as good as it appears to be at first sight. It is possible to lose customers by misleading them with the word 'free', and it is also possible to attract the attention of the regulatory authorities.

There are two main types of free offer – the free product and the free item.

1 Free product

Here the promoter gives away some of his product. For example, a *free sample*, distributed door-to-door, or included in a magazine, or handed out in-store, or banded to another product. Or *extra product free*, where, for example, a product usually sold in a 100g size will be sold in, say, a 120g size at the same price. Free product promotions are often an excellent way to get occasional purchasers or trialists to buy your brand. Where the offer is being made on-pack, a devastatingly effective 'sales appearance' is achieved.

2 Free item

Here the promoter gives away an item with his product. It can be fixed on or packed inside the product; or the product can be packed in it – for example, a free storage jar containing coffee.

The free item can be handed out to the customer, and sometimes purchase is not required; the item serves as an advertising device. Such giveaways were legion in the nineteenth century. For example, that great promoter, H J Heinz, drew massive crowds to his stand at the World's Columbian Exposition in Chicago in 1893 by advertising a free badge to all asking for it. The badge showed a pickle with the name Heinz enamelled on it. The crowd was so dense that the floor sagged under their weight. And the pickle badge became the trademark of the Company.

Or the free item can be available by mail. An attractive free item allows the promoter (where permitted by law) to 'charge' a large number of proofs of purchase.

A remarkable free offer was mounted for Chivers Jelly in the UK in the early 1970s. The marketing objective was to persuade consumers to buy the Chivers brand loyally (and to take the opportunity to try out the various flavours). In return for *eighteen* proofs of purchase mailed in, the consumer was offered a free family of goldfish! Five live goldfish were delivered to the consumer's house (in an aerated water-filled container); there was also a self-liquidating offer of a fish tank if the consumer didn't already have one. Considerable planning and management went into the organisation of that promotion, which was a huge success.

The free item offer gave rise to two forms which are almost techniques in their own right. The *free picture card*, inserted in or printed on a pack, was originally developed in the cigarette industry. When cigarettes were sold in paper packets, a piece of card was put in to stiffen the pack. In Canada, in 1879, someone had the idea of printing something on the card and this developed into the 'cigarette card'. Cigarette cards were issued in series, and each series had a theme – famous actors, flowers, warships – to encourage collection (and therefore loyal brand purchasing). Though cards disappeared from cigarettes a long time ago, the picture card is still a widely used free in-pack offer.

The other major development of the free item offer is the *trading stamp promotion*. A retailer issues trading stamps in proportion to the amount you spend in his store; you save the stamps and then redeem them against a wide range of gifts published in a catalogue. The same mechanism applies if you substitute a 'voucher' for a stamp: vouchers related to free gifts in a catalogue have been widely used to motivate retailers and salesmen.

Win!

Promoters did not invent the idea of winning a prize. Gambling and prize contests and games of skill have been part of life in most civilisations. In the UK in 1978, for example, gamblers laid out £7 000 000 000 on stakes (though £6 000 000 000 was returned in the form of prize money). Apart from horse-race betting, we trade fortunes in casinos and bingo halls, on dogs and in amusement machines, doing the football pools, and a host of other activities. Games of skill – crosswords, Monopoly, and now video games – provide hours, even weeks, of amusement.

All this would continue if there were no sales promotion. But sales promotion can harness the appeal of winning to marketing, and can do so very effectively.

The most important quality of a prize promotion is, or should be , *excitement*. This is often ignored. One attraction of a prize promotion is that the value of the prizes, and therefore the main cost of the promotion, is usually fixed. This appeals to promoters who want to mount activity which won't overrun budget. With such pedestrian ambition, these promoters run contests as routine and often poorly executed activities. They attract few entrants, and those few contain a proportion of *professional* contest entrants.

Lose excitement and you have lost the basic value of a prize promotion.

The main types of prize promotion are:

1 *A contest*, in which success depends to a substantial degree upon the exercise of mental or physical skill
2 *A free draw* (also known as a sweepstake), in which success depends on your name being drawn at random
3 *A game*, where you compete but your success does not depend primarily upon skill
4 *A lottery*, where you purchase (or make a contribution of some kind to get) a ticket which entitles you to entry into a prize draw of some kind.

It must be stressed that the laws relating to prize promotions are individual to different countries and are usually vigorously policed. Expert advice is needed when planning a prize promotion.

Some examples of prize promotions

One of the most effective prize promotions ever run in the UK is *free bingo*, tied to the sale of daily newspapers. The promotion format was pioneered by *The Daily Star*, immediately taken up by *The Sun*, and soon copied or adapted by every popular national daily and Sunday newspaper. Taking advantage of highly sophisticated random printing techniques, the promoters deliver cards with assortments of numbers to every home in the UK; you check your numbers against those published in the newspapers and, when you have matched all the numbers on your card, you can claim a large cash prize.

The mechanics of the game are the same as in the traditional game of bingo played in halls and social clubs for generations: the excitement comes from the scale of the exercise and the size of the prizes.

The drawback to the promoters is that since *every* popular newspaper is running its own variant of the scheme, the high expense is not being matched by additional circulation. Only a truce, or fresh creative thinking, can free the promoters from a costly battle.

A quite different kind of excitement was achieved by a British Airways contest. Everyone buying a British Airways ticket to any destination became eligible to enter; the prize was a place on a British Airways' Concorde aircraft making a special flight to the 1982 World Cup venue, Madrid. The beauty of this scheme is that it associates the excitement of the World Cup with British Airways' most exciting product – and the prize is unique. The idea justified British Airways in heavily advertising the scheme.

What is sales promotion and what is not? A remarkable kind of prize contest, demanding extraordinary skill, was the core idea of a book, *Masquerade*; the book contained a series of highly cryptic clues, woven into the storyline; if a reader correctly solved the clues he or she would find a jewel, buried somewhere in England. Finally, after phenomenal world sales of the book, someone did find the jewel. It is very rare indeed for a book to have this kind of built-in *real* dimension.

The use of prize promotions is heavily regulated in many European countries; for example, in France entry to a contest must be open to purchaser and non-purchaser alike. This discipline should make the promoter aim for fresh ideas which create news and interest around his product. One example: a vermouth manufacturer staged an angling contest – an enjoyable day's fishing of the normal kind – but with the added bonus that some of the fish in the river had been specially marked with indelible ink. If you hooked one of the marked fish you won an angling holiday for two in Norway!

Give!

Sales promotion's 'big three' – Save! Free! Win! – have recently been joined by a fourth – Give!

Promotions linked to charitable causes appeared only rarely until the early

1970s. Now charity promotions form a very large and visible part of promotional activity in the United States and in the UK – less so, as yet, in Europe.

The basic charity promotion asks the consumer to collect the promoting brand's proofs of purchase, and then hand them in or mail them to the promoter, who will donate to the chosen charity a specified amount per proof of purchase.

Frequently the charitable aspect is coupled with a free offer, especially where children may be involved. Badges and wallcharts relating to the charity's sphere of action can be very popular.

The Olympic Games gave the first serious impetus to charitable collections – to raise funds to train a country's athletes. Rothman's cigarettes were linked to a major appeal for 1972, and many promoters have since followed the Olympic theme. Association with sporting endeavour, and the achievements of the national team, can be a very effective form of publicity.

The H J Heinz Co has chosen a charitable theme for several of its annual, block-busting, multi-brand promotions. Heinz twice ran an appeal to raise funds to build a new children's home. In 1980 they pursued the charitable theme into a wholly new area – the public were asked to collect labels, against which Heinz would make a donation, to provide the things needed by schools that had registered with the scheme – sports equipment, for example. Since such material had traditionally been financed out of public funds, the promotion raised some eyebrows. And you did have to collect a lot of labels to get anything worthwhile!

The *Sunday Express* commented: 'Three thousand five hundred cans of baked beans for a football? Isn't it a mercy for hundreds of little tummies, not to mention the Clean Air Society, that they hadn't set their sights on a swimming pool?'.

In 1980/81, Golden Wonder, makers of crisps, snacks and nuts, linked with the World Wildlife Fund to celebrate that fund's twentieth anniversary. Against the proofs of purchase received, Golden Wonder financed the cost of six specially equipped Landrovers for use by the WWF in protecting the game parks of East Africa; the scheme was coupled with the offer of a free set of badges showing the various endangered animals helped by the WWF. Thirty million proofs of purchase were sent in to Golden Wonder.

SALES PROMOTION MEDIA

Sales promotion is a combination of content – the various techniques – and *media* – the channels via which the promoter reaches the market. All forms of advertising can be used, and frequently are used, as sales promotion media.

In addition, there are certain media specially associated with sales promotion:

1 The pack
2 Point-of-sale material
3 Field personnel

4 Direct mail
5 The telephone
6 Presentation material

1 The pack

The pack in which a product travels is a fine communication medium. Admittedly, it does not have moving pictures, nor does it talk, but it is umbilically bound to the product; it is there at the point of sale at the time of sale; it goes into the home; often a pack offers space, the advantages of colour printing, and the facility of a proof of purchase. And since the pack is required in any case, the extra cost of having it carry a sales promotion message is minimal.

2 Point-of-sale material

A promotion should not exist in limbo: it should be an integral part of the marketing mix, and in many cases the most significant integration will be between the promotion and the *total effect* created at the point of sale.

The pack is an item of point-of-sale material. So too are window bills, showcards, shelf-strips and many other vehicles for point-of-sale advertising. The trend to mass-retailing through supermarkets and superstores has created many disciplines for, and often against, point-of-sale material of the conventional kind. Such material can be messy, and, in fairness, it has to be admitted that much material was produced with no idea of the real situation in-store. So many retailers have banned display material. The resulting drabness has been fashionable for some time, but is likely to give way to revived point-of-sale advertising if that material is designed with awareness and flair.

3 Field personnel

Field personnel – salespeople, demonstrators, and merchandisers – augment the regular sales teams of their clients. They can be used in many ways – to offer samples, or coupons, to show how a product works, to give information and answer questions, or just to ask people if they'd like to buy the product. And specially hired personnel are often used to sell goods into the trade, reinforcing the regular sales people.

4 Direct mail

Though direct mail can succeed simply through the use of words, most direct mail solicitations include a promotional offer of some kind.

Heavy direct mail promoters, such as magazine publishers, usually offer a price cut to a new subscriber, or a free gift such as an atlas or set of cutlery.

The key to effective direct mail is the quality of the mailing list. Thorough up-dating of the names on a list is vital, especially if the message is to be personally addressed. Changes of status must be meticulously monitored.

Don't send a message 'Dear Mr Smith, You as a captain of industry . . .' to a man who has just been made redundant.

A great amount of thought has gone into the writing and designing of direct mail messages, and into the development and use of successful incentives. Because most direct mail asks the recipient to respond in some way, the responses can be counted and carefully analysed: every ingredient can be thoroughly tested. So direct mail can be an exceptionally accurate promotional medium.

5 The telephone

Few people today write letters as a matter of personal choice. Most people use the telephone. And since many promotional techniques require the public to respond in some way, it is natural to choose the means of response that they normally prefer.

Consumers can be asked to telephone to claim a voucher; or to enter a prize promotion; or to hear further details of an offer. Complications are that the cost of a telephone call varies by distance, and a customer may be loath to call long-distance; a list of local telephone numbers can be presented, but some administration is needed to set that up. And it is difficult to obtain proof of purchase via the telephone.

But the telephone offers considerable scope for immediacy, and creativity in promotion.

6 Presentation material

A manufacturer mounting a promotion will want to tell his salesforce and retailers about it. So printed and audio-visual media are used to communicate the message. Generally speaking, these presentations are accorded low priority by marketing departments and are often poorly executed. This is thoroughly bad business practice: improved presentation must be a major objective for promoters in the 1980s.

SPECIAL TARGETS

Most of this chapter is about consumer promotion. But all the techniques can be used for *industrial promotion*, both to reach new customers (frequently via personal selling, exhibitions, and direct mail), and to maintain business with existing customers. There are many factors specially relevant to industrial promotion which cannot be covered in this chapter. A useful guide to these will be found in *Sales Promotion – Its Place in Marketing Strategy* by Peter Spillard.

Promoting to retailers is an important aspect of manufacturer's marketing, with techniques ranging from special discounts to free gifts to competitions. Such activity is governed by law in many countries, and there can be a fine dividing line between legitimate promotion and bribery.

And, of course, most companies will seek to motivate their own sales teams with incentives ranging from cash bonuses to holiday prizes to free items. If it is true that a salesman loves being sold to, then sales motivation must be particularly effective.

INTERNATIONAL SALES PROMOTION

The opportunity to mount international marketing campaigns will be substantially increased by the development of satellite television. It is therefore possible to conceive of a sales promotion campaign operating simultaneously in many countries.

But different countries have different laws. Even the individual states of the USA have different laws affecting certain kinds of sales promotion.

There has been much talk of a 'harmonisation' of the laws of EEC countries which affect sales promotion. This task, which would make Europe-wide promotion an attractive possibility, has proved to be difficult, if not impossible, to progress. Harmonisation, if it comes at all, is likely to be a long way off in the future.

RESEARCHING AND EVALUATING SALES PROMOTION

Most kinds of sales promotion activity can be easily evaluated; sales perform-ance can be measured, and redemptions and applications can be counted, and compared with track record.

Promotions are rarely researched in advance, largely because the activity is likely to be of short duration, with few strategic implications. There is an important trend, however, towards *strategic sales promotion*, where one technique, or one 'strategy platform' is intended to apply for many years. In this case, researching the technique or platform is as valuable and essential as researching a long-term advertising strategy.

SUMMING UP

A short chapter in a wide-ranging book can touch on only the most important aspects of sales promotion. More comprehensive information is available in the books listed below. And the reader must look carefully at the nature and practice of sales promotion in his or her own market, because the differences are not only interesting, but of crucial practical importance – differences of law, for example.

Moreover, sales promotion is dynamic, and what applies today can have changed dramatically in many respects within a few years.

This very dynamism makes sales promotion a key marketing tool. It is especially relevant to 'push'-selling market conditions, but in tough or prosperous economies modern sales promotion has a major role to play.

FURTHER READING

Petersen, C., *Sales Promotion in Action*, Associated Business Press, London, 1979

Piper, J., (ed.), *Managing Sales Promotion,* Gower, 1980

Spillard, P., *Sales Promotion – Its Place in Marketing Strategy,* Business Books, London, 2nd edition, 1975

Toop, A., *Choosing the Right Sales Promotion,* The Sales Machine, London, revised (paperback) 1978

Toop, A., *'Only £3.95?!' – The Creative Element in Sales Promotion,* The Sales Machine, London, 1978

17 Pricing

Bryan Atkin

Setting and maintaining the right prices for its products is perhaps the most delicate and important of all the problems facing a company. Whatever other things impinge on sales volume and on profitability, the pricing executive can be sure that the consequence of *his* decisions will be reflected in his firm's financial performance. However successful a firm may appear, poor pricing will inevitably result in sacrificed profit either through loss of sales or loss of margin or both. The importance of the pricing decision is, moreover, not diminished by limitations faced by the individual firm in its degree of flexibility in setting prices – even relatively small differences or changes in price can have a dramatic effect on the profitability of a product or service.

It is, however, a reality of business life that there is probably no area of business activity in which practice differs so widely from theory as the area of pricing. The simple – and well attested – truth is that in a great many firms, prices are set in a way which is disorganised, inconsistent and often illogical. The reasons for this are not hard to find. Pricing decisions, even under the best of conditions, are difficult to make and frequently have to be taken against what can often seem overwhelming odds – inadequate information; time pressures; corporate demands; changing and sometimes unpredictable competitive situations; higher than budgeted R and D and other overhead costs; inflationary pressures on labour, material and other production costs. Added to this, those responsible for pricing in the firm are often managing directors, sales or marketing managers or financial managers who face a great many other demands on their time.

The purpose of this chapter is to provide a framework within which the reader can evaluate the opportunities for greater profitability available to his own firm through the development of a more rational pricing policy and implement practical procedures leading to the shaping, introduction and control of this policy.

ECONOMIC THEORY AND THE PRACTICAL BUSINESSMAN

There is a substantial body of economic theory dealing with price and pricing. The practical businessman can, however, expect little direct help from the academic in applying economic theory to the solution of everyday pricing problems. Certainly, theories of price are effective in describing *in general* the way markets behave: demand and to some extent supply volumes do respond to price approximately as predicted by theory and markets do vary in the degree of responsiveness to price changes as provided for by the concept of price elasticity. Technically, price elasticity is measured by dividing the percentage increase or decrease in the volume of demand (or sales) resulting from a change in price by the percentage change in price. 'Elastic' markets are those where the change in demand is more than a proportionate price change. Conversely, 'inelastic' markets are those in which a change in price is greater, proportionately, than the effective change in demand.

The problem is that the theory breaks down when applied in particular cases largely because the assumptions on which theoretical calculations are based turn out to be inappropriate in real life. For one thing firms rarely possess the empirical data required to construct actual demand or revenue curves for their products and are often unable to distinguish costs sufficiently clearly to construct cost curves. Second, the goals which businessmen set themselves and the constraints which surround their achievement are usually far different – and less rational – than the idealised principles and responses of the theoretical firm. Third, markets do not in practice display the assumed characteristics of perfect competition and rational purchasing behaviour on which theory is based.

Nevertheless, since it has long enjoyed a certain popularity, an adaptation of economic theory worth mentioning at this point is the concept of 'breakeven'. The concept, in its simplest form, purports to show the minimum quantity of its product(s) a firm has to sell simply to cover its costs. Figure 17.1 shows the classic breakeven chart in its most widely reproduced form.

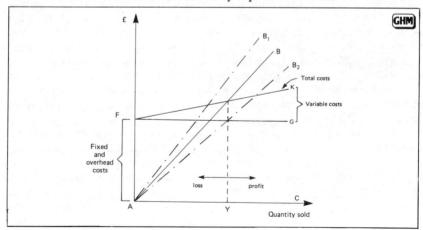

Figure 17.1   Simple breakeven chart

In the chart, the line AB represents gross revenue from unit sales at a specified price, and the line FK denotes the total costs of making those units. These total costs are made up of fixed costs (incurred whether or not the product is made and sold at all) and variable costs (which vary according to the number of units produced). The intersection of lines AB and FK represents breakeven – the point at which gross sales income is exactly equal to the costs involved in producing those units (Y) for sales. At the price set, the firm makes increasing losses with every unit as sales fall short of Y and an increasing profit with every unit in excess of Y. The chart can be developed to show alternative breakeven points at assumed different selling prices (represented by lines AB_1 and AB_2 in Figure 17.1).

The attractiveness of the 'breakeven' idea – which in principle can be applied both to individual products and to the firm as a whole – is obvious in the context of a chart on the managing director's wall dramatising what the firm has to do to stay in business *once selling price has been determined*, by indicating the volume of sales to be achieved to reach breakeven. However, the concept is of little help in actually setting prices because of the crude and unrealistic assumptions which the theory assumes about the level of, and relationship between, price, demand and costs. Thus:

1   The sales income line (AB) takes no account of the price elasticity of demand. The breakeven quantity (Y) is a 'formula' calculation – not a fore-cast of the actual sales, which would still need to be made to determine the profits likely to be generated at a particular price (or indeed whether break-even were achievable at all at that price)

2   The assumptions that variable costs increase proportionately with unit output (as represented in line FK) and that fixed costs remain the same irrespective of the level of output are poor representations of business reality.

In Gabor (1977), a more sophisticated variant of the concept is described. This takes account of the relationship between price and quantity in drawing the curve of gross sales returns, but goes on to observe that its practical value is similarly diminished by the lack of information on costs and demand elasticity available to the average firm.

One of the problems in applying the concept of elasticity is that the theory assumes a constant relationship between demand volume and price, when in fact research has shown that consumers (and industrial buyers) respond differently to the *size* of price changes – particularly when these are measured in a competitive (one brand versus another) rather than a global (total market change) context. Depending on the circumstances therefore a market can be both elastic and inelastic in terms of response to the pricing activities of the individual firm – a paradoxical situation requiring sound judgement and market knowledge.

At best the 'breakeven' concept – which is closely associated with cost-based pricing formulae described later – is mostly of value as a simple 'rule of thumb' method for evaluating pricing options in the context of other market-oriented information on (potential) demand and competition.

PRICING POLICY, STRATEGY AND TACTICS

Before looking in more detail at pricing decisions and the way they are arrived at, it is useful to draw a distinction between three terms often used rather interchangeably by businessmen – insofar as they are used at all! These terms are *pricing policy, pricing strategy* and *pricing tactics.*

Pricing policy refers to the framework of rules and constraints within which pricing decisions are taken. The nature and scope of this framework can vary widely from one firm to another, even within the same industry or between firms with apparently similar pricing problems. At one extreme pricing policy can be little more than a rationalisation of rule of thumb judgements or historical practice. At the other end of the scale can be policies devised and spelled out in considerable detail. An example is the policy operated by the Metal Box Company (1978) described by the Price Commission as comprising the following elements:

1 An immediate objective of raising return on capital to 17 per cent
2 Through the discount structure to pass on to large customers the cost savings commensurate with the scale, continuity and stability of their demand
3 For non-standard containers to price these at a level related to the operating costs of the lines while producing these containers
4 To ensure that customers share with the company the benefits arising from productivity improvements and reductions in specification
5 In the case of new business, selling prices are to be set on the basis of (achieving) 70 per cent capacity usage of (production) equipment. (If demand fails to reach target volume, a decision has to be taken whether to increase selling price or to eliminate the product.)
6 To obtain high export prices wherever possible but retain flexibility to use marginal cost techniques for opportunistic business
7 Regular review of standard margins to ensure equity across the range.

Simply having a pricing policy, however formal, does not imply that it is either logical or sensible in the broader arena of the market place. Nor does the existence of a policy guarantee that it will be observed in practice – policies are often more honoured in the breach than the observance. Indeed it is entirely feasible for a firm to trade without a pricing policy at all or for decisions to be justified by reference to a policy which is to all intents and purposes a *post hoc* rationalisation. This is often the case with small companies where pricing, like many other decisions, is in the hands of one forceful personality – a situation in which whim, prejudice and ignorance can easily play a powerful role.

Whereas *pricing policy* is the outcome of largely internalised objective of a financial or other corporate nature, or statements of pricing principles, *pricing strategy* reflects the (longer-term) market-oriented (or externalised) objectives of a firm. In effect *pricing strategy* involves the systematic manipulation or planning of pricing decisions and policies over a period of time in the context of achieving the broader objectives contained in corporate and marketing plans. It implies recognition of the role of price as an active, and important, component of the overall marketing 'mix' rather than a largely intractable obstacle which marketing has to overcome in order to compete successfully. Insofar as pricing policies and strategies are the expression of needs and objectives over different time periods and on different planes it is not unusual for firms to have a pricing *policy* but no pricing *strategy*.

Whereas pricing strategy is concerned with the projection over the long term, without regard to short term fluctuations in market conditions, pricing tactics are concerned with the manipulation of prices themselves, and the way in which prices are presented to achieve optimum response from a targeted customer group against competition. Pricing tactics take as much from interpreting the psychology of the buyer as from more rational 'economic' judgements. Tactics are, by their nature, often short-term. They may be changed several times during the life of the strategy of which they form a part. Such changes are the practical means of responding on a more day-to-day basis to changing market conditions. There are a great many variations of pricing tactics, some of which are described later in this chapter, and in practice they are often mistakenly elevated to the level of pricing strategy.

Oxenfeldt (1960) sees the pricing process involving a series of decisions taken over a period of time, rather than as a single all-embracing solution. The six steps he proposes are:

1　Identification of target markets
2　Choosing an appropriate image
3　Constructing the marketing mix
4　Selecting a pricing policy
5　Determining price strategy (and tactics)
6　Definition of a specific price.

This multi-stage approach has a particular relevance to new product development but can be recycled wholly or in part as a means of reappraising existing products. The approach is particularly interesting in the emphasis it gives to broader issues of market segmentation and planning the marketing mix as the essential framework for pricing decisions.

PRICING POLICIES AND TECHNIQUES

In Wilson (1972), pricing is described as 'an exercise which must be undertaken on two dimensions. First it is necessary to think in terms of establishing the right price and second of using the correct methodology for arriving at it.' In a way this observation neatly encapsulates the practical dilemma facing most firms. At one level the pricing process takes place within a framework which is the product of many influences, inside and outside the firm. These factors, which provide the basis for defining pricing policy, strategy and tactics, include:

Internal	*External*
Corporate objectives and business goals – both generalised and specific	The nature, strength and pricing behaviour of competition (direct and indirect; existing and potential)

Cost structures – direct and indirect	The role and importance of distributors and their attitudes and needs
Existing prices (e.g. of other products in the same or other product lines)	relating to price (including need to create/maintain acceptable margins)
Historical practice and precedent in price setting within the firm	(Pressure from) suppliers of raw materials, components etc. used in the product
Degree of market knowledge (or ignorance) of key executives	The size, structure and perceived price sensitivity of demand
Pressures from feedback of other individuals within the firm, e.g. salesmen	The purchasing procedures and motivations of (potential) customers
Levels of R and D and pace of new product development	Existing and anticipated government policies
	General conditions prevailing in different markets (especially where export markets are concerned).

At the second level pricing should involve a sensible and coherent procedure for actually determining the final price at which the product will sell. That this procedure or methodology needs to be conceived and operated within a broader framework of attitudes and subjective judgements which may not always be logical (and may even be in conflict) is simply a fact of commercial life.

However, pricing policies and strategies do not necessarily define, or even imply, a particular methodology for arriving at the selling price itself. In many cases this is set as much by guesswork, trial and error, historical analogy and simple entrepreneurial judgement as it is by some more formal procedure.

There is no single 'correct' methodology or golden rule for arriving at the right price. For example, the pricing decision process and the degree of flexibility available are heavily conditioned by whether prices are *declared* or *negotiated* (the pricing system). At one extreme the executive responsible for setting catalogue or list prices is in theory at least creating a structure of 'ruling' prices for his products which will remain in force for all or a substantial proportion of sales until a change is notified; at the other extreme the executive involved in contract or tender pricing is faced with a new pricing decision with each new order or customer. The apparent coherence and stability of published prices have to be seen, however, in the context of the discounts, concessions, rebates, differentials and other devices employed by firms to manipulate the prices actually paid by customers. In a substantial number of firms list prices can be said to exist mainly as a basis for discounting with the bulk of turnover being generated from sales at discounted and negotiated prices (see Atkin, 1975). An apparently logical framework of declared prices can, therefore, be rendered meaningless and misleading by the reality of a haphazard system of discounts and/or individual negotiations with strong customers. (See Discounts and discounting later in this chapter).

The 'right' price is not necessarily what theorists would call the 'best selling price' in the sense that it maximises profit for a given product considered by itself. In any meaningful sense what is 'right' can only be assessed in the context of what the firm identifies as its general strategic or operational goals. Because these differ according to the size, product range, historical development, future ambitions, geographical trading pattern, financial resources and management philosophy of individual companies, so the concept of 'right' price will vary.

The precise combination and weighting of factors will depend on the product, the market and other circumstances. The following paragraphs look in more detail at five categories of factor which both shape pricing policy and contribute to the process of actual price setting. To the extent that one of these categories may carry the greatest weight it is possible to talk about pricing which is profit, cost, competition, demand- (customer) or distribution system-oriented.

Profit targets and other corporate objectives

Perhaps the most widely quoted of all business aphorisms is that it is the objective of every firm to maximise its profits. The most cursory examination of this proposition in practice, however, shows it to be one which should not be taken too literally. Firms rarely set out even with the *theoretical* objective of maximising profits (or return on capital employed) and often introduce criteria into pricing strategies and policies the deliberate effect of which is to contain profits at a level below that which otherwise might be achievable.

Few would deny that, in a free market economy, a firm exists to make a profit and, indeed, needs to make a profit to exist. More fundamentally, perhaps, the profits generated by the firm have to be sufficient to satisfy the providers of the capital – shareholders, bankers, etc. – on whom the firm's existence and future ultimately depend. Simply making a profit does not itself guarantee the continued flow of funds required to renew current plant and invest in facilities for producing new products. Equally, given the scarcity and cost of capital, it is nonsense to suggest that a firm would be able, even if it wished, to continue to pour capital into the production of a product until the last drop of profit has been extracted from the market.

Profit is therefore a less meaningful criterion for judging performance in the longer term than return on capital employed or 'return on investment'. Thus the Price Commission commented, with respect to UG Glass Containers Ltd (1978), that 'for (the company's) profit to be adequate it must be sufficient after paying for the cost of capital to fund all expenditure on fixed and working capital necessary to maintain the fabric of the business and to make a contribution towards capital required for expansion'. The Commission went on to state that the company's corporate strategy provided specific targets relating to pre-tax profit and return on investment to be 'achieved and maintained'.

The question of time dimension also needs to be considered. A quick glance at the city pages of any national newspaper shows that profits achieved by even the largest firms fluctuate from year to year for reasons, often connected with the general economic, environmental and trading conditions, over which the firm has no control. Financial objectives can therefore be expressed both as long-term and immediate.

Longer-term financial objectives tend to be set in the context of achieving a targeted average level of return on investment or profit for the whole of the company which is considered to be 'reasonable' taken over a period of years (and across all products). Judgement of what is reasonable is in this context largely a pragmatic affair, owing more to general perceptions within society of what might be considered as 'fair trading profit' or to historical experience or analogy, than to the projection of a mechanistic formula. In the short term, different targets may be set either for return on capital for profit or for margins or contributions (difference between selling price and *direct* costs usually expressed as a percentage) which reflect prevailing economic and market conditions in individual years or even short planning periods.

As indicated earlier, however, financial objectives are not the only determinants of corporate policy and are therefore by no means the only factor underlying pricing decision. Other considerations include:

1 *(Market) growth aspirations.* Targets relating to achievement of an annual percentage rate of growth in revenue and/or volume terms or of an overall target for a period of time (for example, a five-year plan)
2 *Market share* Targets relating to achievement either of some specific share of total industry sales (or consumer uptake) of some or all of the company's products or of some more vaguely defined objective such as 'market leadership'
3 *Corporate stability/expansion.* Development of products and businesses to achieve more broadly conceived goals concerning the longer-term stability and growth of the firm as a whole with implications for balancing investment decisions, R and D expenditure and other aspects. Decisions which appear unattractive from a purely financial standpoint in the short term may have important longer-term implications for the firm's financial health either individually or as part of a framework of such decisions
4 *Corporate image.* Pursuit or rejection of a course of action in the light of judgements – objective and subjective – about the way the company wishes to be seen in the market place. This may be related to protection of an existing image, for example where a manufacturer of a range of products with a reputation for quality rejects the chance of selling a range of popularly priced goods (however profitable potentially) because of the risk of tarnishing a carefully fostered image. Or it may be related to development of a targeted image (e.g. for product reliability, speed of after-sales response, innovative design) which has attendant implications for costs and prices
5 *R and D.* This can be both the lifeblood to and a leech on corporate profit-

ability depending on the extent to which it is controlled and goal-oriented. Where R and D, especially in fast-moving high-technology industries, becomes tied up with the image and reputation of a company it is possible to generate sunk costs which for reasons of competition or strength of demand are difficult to recover through the prices the company is able to command in the market place

6 *Costs and efficiency.* Corporate plans often contain cost reduction and efficiency objectives linked to opportunities that provide for keen competitive pricing and/or greater margins

7 *Customer/public opinion.* Winning and retaining the regard of customers and perhaps of a broader public through performance or specific design, e.g. safety aspects of equipment for which profit may be a secondary consideration, or by being seen to be trading 'responsibly'

8 *Competitive arena.* Implementation of strategies for pre-empting, containing or meeting competition

9 *Capacity.* Gearing of pricing and marketing strategies to achieve acceptable level of use of production capacity.

An example of the way in which various strands of corporate policy combine to affect prices was demonstrated in the Price Commission report on BOC Ltd (1979) which stated:

> The company's central thinking is based on the need to manage a portfolio of businesses. Essentially, this is to invest for market growth and to increase market share on the assumption that scale benefits on costs will be obtained. This gives the investor market dominance based on competitively low cost which in turn provides the power further to secure market position by keen pricing. When the growth slackens off the rate of investment can be reduced to yield a positive cash flow which may be reinvested in another growth market. . .

The role of costs in pricing

It has often been claimed that the pricing of industrial products is based on costs and very little else – a process which Wilson has derided as 'faith, hope and fifty per cent'. The argument runs that the cost accountant and the engineer have dominated the pricing process and that neat formulae based on cost are most easily comprehended by these types of executive whose knowledge of, and exposure to, the market place itself is limited. Research into pricing behaviour has tended to support this view of the pricing process: when asked directly about the pricing of their products firms will indeed claim that they arrive at their prices largely by the application of some formula related to costs.

How rigidly companies stand by such formulae or, indeed, whether they actually have a formula at all, is very much open to doubt. Gabor claims that 'pricing is not in fact carried out by the alleged mechanistic application of cost-based formulae' and goes on to quote Edwards: 'the manufacturer has a "hunch" as to the price at which his article can be sold and makes use of "costing" or "estimating" to justify that price'. In other words a price 'derived from cost' can often be in effect the reverse procedure, with margins and contributions justified *post hoc* by reference to costs when in fact they are subsumed from price. Nevertheless if prices are rarely based exclusively on cost, it is equally rare for costs not in some way to form the starting point either for calculating prices or for evaluating the profit consequences of various prices indicated or set by reference to other factors. Indeed, insofar as goods ultimately have to be sold at a profit for the firm to survive, it is inevitable that costs will enter into the pricing equation in some form.

In order to use costs at all in pricing it is obviously necessary for the firm to have a clear idea of what its costs are and how these should be allocated to individual products. This is all very well for the firm producing only one product since all costs are, by definition, attributable to that product. Where more than one product is concerned, as it is for most firms, cost allocation can be exceedingly complex and the solutions at best arbitrary. The costs of producing and selling a range of products can be classified broadly into three main components:

1 *Variable (including direct) costs* – costs which vary in relation to output, e.g. materials and components, labour, advertising
2 *Fixed costs* – costs which do not vary in relation to output except in the longer term, e.g. buildings, machines, vehicles
3 *Overhead costs* – costs attributable to management.

The problem of allocating management overheads will be obvious but what of variable and fixed costs? *Shared costs* are a common feature with respect, say, to vehicles and buildings but can also occur with respect to materials and labour. Consider, for example, the furniture factory which uses the same labour force, the same machinery and to some extent the same materials to make beds, wardrobes and dining room tables. Add to this a constantly changing balance of production volume between these different product lines – and within each product line between different model ranges – and the problems of allocation assume daunting proportions. The cost accountant might be able to devise an acceptable formula for allocation if each product was always produced in the same proportions but the formula becomes increasingly unworkable and arbitrary where these are constantly changing. Basing a formula on historical experience is equally undesirable as it makes pricing for the future dependent on past and possibly greatly outdated sales levels. The scale of difficulty increases still further where several products are produced by the same process (as in oil refining or dairy processes) and therefore incur, not so much shared costs as *joint costs*, or where a marketable product is a by-product of the production process for another good.

The problems outlined above become highly relevant when costs are used as a means of calculating price. There are two main concepts or procedures for cost-based pricing – *absorption or full cost pricing* and *variable cost or incremental cost pricing*.

Absorption cost pricing, to put it simply, involves the principle of adding a pre-determined mark-up to total unit costs derived from the formula

$$\frac{\text{total of fixed and variable costs attributable to the product}}{\text{total units produced}}$$

By this procedure, sometimes known as 'cost-plus', each product produced by the firm is made, in theory, to cover all of its costs and make a known profit on each unit of sale or order.

Variable cost pricing is based on the principle of relating prices not to total costs but to variable costs only with the mark-up on costs (or the price less variable costs if the price is set by a procedure independent of costs) making a *contribution* to fixed costs and to profit, the scale of which depends on sales objectives being achieved. Gabor distinguishes two variants of variable cost pricing: one is based on average variable costs (for a predicted level of output) and the other, which he calls incremental cost pricing, is based on the incremental or additional cost of producing a particular batch of the product which may be different from the variable costs of total production when considered in unit terms. Incremental cost pricing is a concept particularly appropriate to pricing individual orders, in cases where demand is made up of discrete orders or batches, or in evaluating the relative contribution of alternative possible orders where the price available is fixed by some other means perhaps beyond the firm's direct control.

Absorption cost pricing is a method which has had particular appeal to the firm with a substantial proportion of its total costs in the form of fixed costs and overheads, since it places all products, in theory, on a sound profit footing and eliminates cross-subsidisation and below-cost trading. It is particularly useful in tender or contract pricing as a reference basis for pricing where there are no other useful indicators and in setting some practical limits to prices of new products with no relevant competitors. However, absorption costing has a number of major drawbacks as the basis for pricing. The arguments can be summarised as follows:

1   It is not always easy to isolate the total costs attributable to a particular product where there are several product lines and ranges. Depending on the conventions and assumptions used to apportion costs, the outcome of absorption cost pricing could be sustantially varying price levels for individual products

2   There is, anyway, no compelling reason why any particular segment of the business, individual product, or specific order *should* be made to bear its proportionate or 'fair' share of overheads even where these can be calculated. Looked at in an overall corporate sense, the ability to offer a full product range, stability of production, attraction or retention of a major customer, response to a change in the competitive environment and many other factors may in individual cases and pricing decisions be considered to carry greater weight

3   Absorption costing takes no account of demand. The fact that a price can be computed by this method does not guarantee that consumers will buy the item at that price or at the predicted volumes. Nor are firms willing in reality to implement one of the apparent implications of the method which

is to *raise* prices when demand falls short of expectations or declines from a previous level (since total costs will be spread over a smaller volume of output). The inclination of most firms in this situation would be to *reduce* prices

4 Absorption costing takes no account of competition. No firm can guarantee that its competitors will play by the same rules either by adopting the same method of costing or by allocating its overhead and fixed costs to particular products on the same basis. The firm rigidly applying absorption cost pricing would find its products highly vulnerable to a competitor using direct or incremental cost methods or simply pricing irrationally.

The proponents of incremental cost pricing tend to use arguments which are the obverse of their criticisms of absorption cost pricing emphasising the flexibility of the method as a means of responding to changing demand and competitive conditions. Thus is is pointed out, for example, that since market conditions vary between different industry segments of a given national market and even more, perhaps, between different national markets it is logical to seek (or accept) prices which reflect those conditions. Using a direct or an incremental cost approach enables the firm to operate at different prices in different markets while maintaining overall control over the aggregated contribution derived from sales and provides a means of assigning supply priorities between them in the event of demand outstripping capacity. Similarly the method enables the firm to consider and respond to individual orders in a way appropriate to specific circumstances. Thus, at times of high demand a means is provided of selecting orders or pieces of business which yield the greatest contribution and at times of low demand of indicating how far the firm might reduce its prices before an order ceases to make any contribution at all.

Despite its apparent pragmatism, variable or incremental costing is not without its dangers. In the first place, it has been said with some truth that all costs become variable if the firm is to survive – that is, in the end, the firm depends on making sufficient revenue from its sales to cover all costs incurred whether variable, fixed or overhead. Incremental cost pricing cannot therefore be pursued unchecked. It must be conducted within some framework of required contribution based on profit targets or targets for return on capital invested.

Second, firms using incremental cost pricing to justify accepting an order at reduced contribution may find they have made a rod for their own backs in subsequent dealings with the same customer. However logical the concept of variable pricing might be to the seller, the buyer is given a weapon to use in subsequent negotiations, when general demand conditions have improved and the firm has been able to command higher prices. If the seller gets to the point of refusing an order offered at too low a price there is a danger that the buyer may simply eliminate him from future consideration or allow a competitor to gain entry.

Third, there is always a risk of provoking price retaliation from competitors resulting in reduced margins all round and a steep hill to climb back to acceptable profitability in a market environment which can become accustomed with remarkable rapidity to low prices.

Finally, it must be appreciated that it is not always easy to determine clearly either the variable costs attributable to a particular product or the incremental costs associated with a particular batch or order. Some so-called variable costs are not, in fact, more than marginally variable, at least in the shorter term. Few firms are able or willing, for example, to manipulate the size of their labour forces constantly to reflect changes in the level of orders. Unionisation and a natural desire on the part of firms to keep a trained and effective work force together play an important role here. It is easy for firms to delude themselves therefore as to what the incremental or marginal unit cost of a product actually is. Similarly, taking on an additional order in certain circumstances may have its own 'hidden' incremental costs in the form of overtime working, loss of efficiency in output in machines pushed closer to maximum capacity, extra 'blocks' of production space requiring heating, lighting and maintenance and many other items.

Pricing is not only difficult in practice to base entirely on costs but it renders the firm vulnerable in other respects. In a strictly competitive sense it hardly matters a jot how reasonable a profit mark-up or contribution target a firm sets in relation to its own costs if these costs are higher than those of competitors. Indeed the costs which ultimately matter are those of the lowest-cost producer. Of course, most markets support producers who vary in efficiency, but the greater the disparity in efficiency, the greater is the pressure exerted on the least efficient producers.

More broadly, cost-based pricing formulae often provide little encouragement to company management to consider improving margins by reducing costs as distinct from raising prices. Firms rarely explore as rigorously as they might the various ways in which costs might be cut, from better materials purchasing to tighter control of office costs. This is not, however, the only way costs can be cut and here we return again to the need to be alive to *market* needs and conditions. Research has consistently shown over the years that products and services can quite simply be 'over-engineered' – that is contain features to which the user attaches little economic significance or which are designed to a quality standard which exceeds customer needs. By eliminating these features from the product the firm may well be able to make considerable savings in costs without reducing prices, at least to anything like the same extent.

Competition and pricing

There are few products or services indeed for which there is no effective competition. Even when a firm has no direct competitors – as in the case of an innovative product – it usually has to take into account products capable of acting as alternatives or substitutes in some way, or the prospect of competition developing.

Long-term monopolies are therefore rare outside the realms of state enterprises but it is possible for short-term monopolies to develop on the basis of new products, particularly where high technology is involved. Firms may be able to protect themselves for a time from direct competition by taking out patents, as Xerox Corporation did with plain paper copiers and Polaroid Corporation with instant photography. But in the end competition will come, either through expiry of patents or through a competitor finding a means of entry which does not infringe the patents (as Kodak did with instant photography). The short-term monopolist needs to consider pricing in the context of the breathing space he has to establish himself in the market place before competition develops, rather than in terms of the apparent freedom of action of the true monopolist.

At the most fundamental level, the product competes on the basis of its usefulness or value to the buyer compared with the many other items on which income or resources can be expended.

Price acts as an element in competition therefore at up to three levels: it can help determine whether or not a product is bought at all (or whether the decision to purchase is taken now or at a later date); it can help determine in which of a number of alternative ways a particular need is satisfied; and it can help determine which supplier's product is selected.

It is not surprising then that in most cases prices are set and maintained with some reference to the general level and range of competitive prices. In a more specific sense, however, pricing against competition can become in itself a technique of pricing. This can work in one of two main ways:

1   By establishing the prices being charged by all (or a selected cross-section) of the competitive suppliers active in the market and positioning one's own price to occupy a certain position in the range. This may reflect either 'safety' pricing (pricing in the middle of the range) or 'aggressive' pricing (pricing at either extreme). In the latter case particularly, given that price variations reflect product differentiation, the adoption of competition pricing also tends to imply judgements about demand response and price segmentation in the market (see below)

2   By gearing prices to those charged by a specific competitor on the basis of achieving parity with them or of achieving a designated discount or premium. This approach is often used where one company has achieved a position of such pre-eminence in the market place that both sellers and customers accept its prices as a reference level. An example is the market for open-top containers in relation to which the Price Commission commented that 'where prices are negotiated by individual contract they are set by reference to Metal Box levels'.

In so far as competitors' prices are declared or easily established, competition-orientated pricing is relatively straightforward and has the advantage of placing prices within the known parameters of the market place. The price structure of markets is not, however, always easy to establish. Published price lists often give a highly misleading guide to actual price levels which may be arrived at largely by discounting or special negotiation. Further, buyers are frequently reluctant to indicate even to independent researchers, let alone company salesmen, the terms of a bargain struck with a competitor. There is always a danger therefore that prices may be set on the basis of a competitive price structure which is different in reality from that assumed.

The extent to which firms are willing and able to take a competitively independent line in setting and maintaining prices is partly a reflection of factors such as market share, established reputation, financial strength, distinctiveness of product and relative costs of production, and partly a reflection of competitive psychology. Many writers on pricing have drawn attention to the fact that price competition often tends to be of a muted and controlled nature in which a few (perhaps only one or two) dominant suppliers (price leaders) both set the price levels and pricing systems around which competition is fought, and determine the timing and scale of price changes. Other firms (price followers) are essentially content to respond – raising and lowering prices in line with the price leaders. Markets operating on this basis can become highly conservative and regulated structures in which price competition is to all intents and purposes eliminated. In certain industries, typified by large commodity-type businesses such as cement, animal feeds and tyres, the institutionalisation of competition among a small number of large companies has resulted in prices fixed and maintained at very similar levels with price rises taking place in rounds under the 'leadership' of one company – a situation to all intents analogous to the outlawed price ring'.

In theory, price leaders 'undertake' to behave in a responsible manner with respect to price setting and act as 'policemen' for any firm threatening to take a more aggressive and independent pricing line. However, in practice the *status quo* is protected more by mutual compliance than any genuinely effective sanction which the price leaders can bring to bear. As Japanese companies have demonstrated repeatedly in European markets, complacent and conservative competitive environments – which in turn lead to reduced interest in increasing efficiency and cost savings – are highly vulnerable to a bold and determined aggressor.

The attitudes and motivations of the buyer

Price is rarely, if ever, the only factor entering into the purchasing decision and is sometimes only secondary. The success of pricing decisions is therefore highly dependent on the ability of the firm to comprehend and respond to the purchasing environment into which its products are sold. Many ineffective, even disastrous, pricing policies can be traced back to misconceptions about the attitude of buyers to price and the role of price in the purchase decision. These misconceptions are often rooted in a popular industry folklore the credibility of which has been reinforced by constant repetition to a point at which the desire or willingness of firms to go against this conventional wisdom has been almost totally sapped. The philosophy of price cutting as the only effective means of competition which pervades some industries is often due more to uncritical acceptance of this folklore than to a sober analysis of marketing options.

Distinguishing fact from fiction in the market place is therefore the first task of the would-be rational pricing executive. Some of the elements bearing on the role of price in the purchase decision will now be considered. The most important of these is the concept of 'product differentiation'. This relates to the differences in functions, performance, design and other product-related or physical attributes which a manufacturer can introduce to distinguish his products from those of his competitors. The greater the differentiation, it is argued, the more invidious direct price comparisons by the buyer become, thus giving the firm greater flexibility in turn to gear its prices to the value it believes, or can persuade buyers to believe, attaches to the features or benefits it is offering. In many industrial markets this is characterised by the weighting attached by buyers to factors such as 'technical specification' and 'quality'. The range of price competition in such markets reflects the fact that buyers vary in the value they attach to different product features. The principle of segmentation – designing and pricing products to cater to a particular target group of customers within the market as a whole – derives from the concept of differentiation.

Economists usually assume, in theorising on purchasing behaviour, that the buyer, being rational and efficient, will tend to purchase at the lowest price prevailing in the market place, for the product which best fits his needs and requirements. Where there is little or no product differentiation, such as in the case of electrical cable or industrial fasteners, he might be expected to look for the lowest price *per se*. Where there is substantial differentiation, such as in an industrial engine or a conveying system, then the buyer will weigh up all the economic aspects of the alternatives to arrive at the product which offers him the highest cost benefit. As consumer goods companies and advertising agencies have long appreciated, the domestic consumer is neither rational nor efficient but there is a widely held belief that the industrial buyer, being a 'professional', cannot be deceived as easily and will go unerringly to the 'bottom line'. Research into the buying decision has consistently shown this simply not to be true when considered in any detail.

In the first place, economic factors are not the only criteria employed in the purchase decision. Even in the case of non-differentiated products, many other factors can intrude to justify purchases at other than the lowest price available. These include:

1   Delivery (firms are often prepared to pay more for fast delivery or guaranteed delivery or for a delivery particularly convenient to the purchaser)
2   After-sales service/availability of spare parts
3   Previous good experience of the product or other things produced by the same manufacturer
4   Proximity of supplier to the purchaser
5   Security of supply/risk spreading (e.g. by dividing requirements between two or more suppliers)
6   General reputation of supplier/advice and recommendation of own staff and other firms in buyer's industry
7   The volume of other goods purchased from the same supplier
8   Good personal relationship with salesman, technical staff and other aspects of the supplier's organisation.

Second, economic considerations can go far beyond the 'price' of the product. In the case of a capital product such as a commercial vehicle, a forklift truck or a machine tool, the purchase price of the product is only one of several cost-related considerations such as running costs (in terms of fuel and power, cost of spare parts); 'whole life' cost (the estimated total cost of the machine or vehicle over the whole of its expected operational life, reliability in service, running costs and disposal value); facilities for financing the purchase (are credit or deferred payment terms available? Is a leasing or rental facility available as an alternative to purchase?).

Third, industrial buyers are perfectly capable of being irrationally influenced by factors such as a persuasive salesman; clever advertising; cosmetic product features such as design; fashion trends within the industry and simple prejudice. A manufacturer of circular knitting machines for whom the author once carried out a research project found it hard to accept that many customers rejected his technically well-engineered but old-fashioned looking product in favour of a streamlined, push-button import with, by objective standards, an inferior price/performance relationship. Various writers have drawn attention to cases where new products have been unsuccessful initially because they were priced too cheaply, thus creating buyer suspicion, and became successful when the price was brought more into line with what the buyers expected to pay! Differentiation is therefore feasible at a level well short of genuine product differences.

Finally buyers rarely have perfect knowledge of the markets for all the products they have to buy. Thus the buyer for a fabrications firm may have an extensive and systematically compiled knowledge of the suppliers and prices for the steel products which make up a substantial proportion of his firm's costs but has neither time nor the inclination to develop the same knowledge for less significant items he may also be responsible for such as paper clips and toilet rolls.

It has rightly been said that the price the final buyer is prepared to pay for a product is, in the end, the best guide to optimum pricing. Because it is the best guide, however, it is inevitably the most difficult concept to employ as a practical technique in pricing. The attraction of cost-based pricing formulae and using competitors' prices as a yardstick for price setting can be attributed at least in part to the fact that they are simple to understand and employ information which, in theory at least, is readily to hand or easily generated. By contrast it is often exceedingly difficult to establish in a direct way how much customers for a product are prepared to pay for it, or put another way, how many customers would be won at different alternative prices, given the variety of factors which affect the purchase decision of individual buyers. Nevertheless it is within the capacity and resources of most firms to develop sufficient information from their own knowledge and experience of trading in particular market places or by talking to some potential customers, or by some experimentation or by extrapolating the results of market research surveys. Then they can make broad assumptions about the size and structure of demand for a product and responsiveness to price in a competitive context which can be used to narrow the limits within which price should be set and define the strategy and tactics which best fit market conditions.

Distribution structure

Where a product is sold direct from manufacturer to end user, as many industrial products are, the pricing executive has only to consider pricing at a single level. The situation becomes more complex when distributive inter-mediaries – agents, wholesalers and retailers – are involved, as he then has to consider not just the price at which the product is sold to his immediate customer, say a wholesaler, but also the price at which it ultimately sells to the final consumer after it has passed through one, two or even three sets of hands each of which have added their own mark-up. Wholesalers and retailers tend to price by adding a designated percentage mark-up to the price they buy-in the product in order to cover overhead and sales costs and yield a profit. It is, however, relatively unusual for a single fixed percentage to be applied to all products. Rather the percentage mark-up is manipulated between products according to circumstances or design around some overall average (which may itself reflect long-standing practice or folklore in a particular industry rather than any independent judgement on the part of the distributor).

Since the ending of resale price maintenance the manufacturer is unable to dictate the ultimate selling price of his products (and therefore in effect distributors' margins). Distributors may therefore manipulate margins in a way which favours or disfavours the products of the individual manufacturer and thereby impacts on ultimate sales. Pricing to the *distributor* but with an eye to reselling prices is therefore a special component of the art of pricing.

It should also be recognised that the effect of passing on, say, a reduction (or an increase) in the cost of materials or components is heavily affected by the length of the distribution chain. Not only might the change be much smaller proportionately in respect of the final selling price than it is to the ex-factory price but distributors can choose to pass on the change across a spectrum of options ranging from no price adjustement at all to one in excess of that made by the manufacturer.

AIDS TO PRICING

Models and computer simulations

In the main, however practical or logical the basic technique adopted, pricing decisions tend to involve a great deal of individual judgement by the pricing executive. Because the individual has to apply precise weightings to the many influences bearing in practice or in theory on this decision, the final outcome is at best an approximation of the best selling price and is as good, or as bad, as the quality of judgement applied to it. Various attempts have been made to construct 'models' of a more formal nature designed to help the firm fix the optimum price of its products under actual competitive conditions. These models differ widely in their nature, purpose and origin, but most frequently relate to the pricing of goods for retail sale (particularly fast-moving goods such as baked beans and washing powder) and pricing in a competitive bid or tender situation.

All models work by simulating, in terms of mathematical relationships, the interaction of the variables – company-, competition- and demand-related – which govern the pricing decision. They share therefore inevitable problems in defining and assigning a value to each variable. Their success depends on the quality of research or of the market knowledge or insight the firm is able to feed into the model, and on the manipulation of the variables which normally requires access to a computer. The cost and complexity of model building has tended to make it the preserve of the largest firms only at present, although it is possible with the development of modestly priced small computing systems and more effective pricing research techniques that some elements of modelling may come within the compass of a great many more firms in the future.

Market research

Whether or not a pricing model is being developed, firms still require information on customers and competitors to help them reach sensible pricing decisions. This information is rarely readily available 'off the shelf' and some level of active information gathering is therefore predicated. The most widely employed source of intelligence is the salesman. The reasons for collecting information via the salesman are, naturally, seductive; the salesman is already employed by the firm 'on the road' and he is in constant contact with customers, In theory he ought to be particularly alive both to competitors' prices and to the price sensitivity and purchasing considerations of the buyer. In practice, however, salesmen are a highly unreliable source of pricing intelligence and tactical judgement. Research into the pricing of industrial products has suggested that it is not unusual for salesmen to convince themselves that they have lost orders on the basis of price when in fact other factors were of greater or equal importance in the purchase decision and it seems likely that many buyers use price as an excuse for not placing an order with a particular firm rather than give the real, possibly more contentious, reason.

While it is not suggested that firms should give up monitoring price through feedback from salesmen, it would seem prudent that where key pricing decisions are concerned, such as pricing a new product or a change in pricing strategy, information should be generated where required by means of more systematic market research conducted by a reputable and competent consultancy with experience in asking and interpreting questions about price and setting these in the context of other data on market structure and the purchasing process. Market research can make a valuable contribution to the analysis of pricing situations and the selection of appropriate strategies and tactics, although in view of the difficulties in collecting detailed information on prices actually paid and in measuring likely response to hypothetical price levels, it is not usually a tool for setting actual selling prices.

DEVISING PRICING STRATEGY AND TACTICS

Entry strategies

The concept of pricing strategy as a means of using price as an element in the achievement of specific marketing goals was mentioned earlier. This involves the co-ordination of pricing decisions in the context of their longer-term impact and implications rather than their short-term or tactical benefits and requires the firm to take an extended view of such factors as probable product life; volume and price sensitivity of potential demand; opportunities for segmentation of demand by price and the optimum phasing of segmentation; pace of likely consumer acceptance taking into account competitive, alternative and substitute products; build-up of production capacity and the opportunity for scale economies in unit costs; timescale for recovery of R and D costs.

The most sensitive, and probably the most important, time for strategy formulation is before the launch of a new product – whether or not the product concerned is an innovative or unique one with no direct competitors or is a new brand entrant on an established market place. It is frequently stated that at the stage of market entry the firm has a choice between two basic strategy options known as *skimming* and *penetration*.

Skimming strategies involve the deliberate setting of an initial price which is high in relation to anticipated long-term price levels towards which the price will be progressively lowered as competition and demand conditions change. The benefits of this strategy derive from the high gross margins achieved at the outset against which R and D and other 'sunk' costs and often heavy initial promotional costs can be set and from the flexibility afforded for using subsequent price changes as a means of controlling market expansion (since, setting aside inflation the direction of price changes will be downward) and meeting merging competition by aggressive pricing. Skimming enables the firm to cream off that component of demand prepared to buy the product at its highest price before attacking the broader potential market which may exist for the product at a lower price. In so far as the progressive effective price reductions can be implemented on a 'step-wise' basis, the market may be, in effect, creamed off at different (and progressively larger) levels. The firm employing a skimming entry strategy also gives itself the option of approaching the anticipated longer-term downward adjustment in price by introducing variations of its original product or even a different brand rather than by simple price reduction, thus enabling it to maintain a premium price on its original product. This strategy might be termed progressive segmentation. A further advantage of skimming which should not be overlooked is that it conforms to the well attested dictum that it is easier to correct a pricing mistake in a downward direction than in an upward one.

Penetration strategies are intended to generate the highest possible volume of sales from the outset by keen (low margin) pricing. In practice they can be divided into two categories – demand-oriented and competition-oriented strategies (see Figure 17.2). Demand-oriented penetration strategies are based in the main on a combination of an expected high level of price sensitivity

Skimming	Penetration: demand-oriented	Penetration: competition-oriented
Anticipated short product life (technological changes, fashion)	Anticipated long product life	Anticipated need to tempt users to try new product rather than continue with existing functional alternatives (gain foothold especially where differentiation not immediately clear to, or valued by, consumers)
Slow initial consumer acceptance (new applications, new technology)	Belief in rapid consumer acceptance/high price elasticity	
Uncertainty over ultimate scale and elasticity of demand	Economies of scale in output – threshold sales level before economies can be achieved	Pre-emption of competition – exclude prospective competitors by raising entry costs/establishing entrenched position
Market segmentation – 'cream' those prepared to pay high price before moving to mass market (perhaps with lower priced variants)	Expectation of rapid competitive response – establish sound market position/market leadership before competition can develop	Displacement of entrenched competition by aggressive pricing in directly competitive market (market launch of similar or identical product)
Inelastic production costs/capacity constraints	Exploitation of established reputation/sales, marketing, distribution strengths	
Recovery of high R and D costs	Create platform for continued sale of related products e.g. labelling machines and labels	
Generation of funds for mass marketing		
Competition slow to develop due to patent protection, research lead time, high production entry costs		
Exploitation of established reputation/differentiation aspects of product		

Figure 17.2 Evaluation of entry price strategy

among potential buyers and a need for a high volume of demand to justify plant investment or achieve projected economies of scale in production (i.e. some products have to be produced in volume or not at all). Competitively they have the advantage of potentially creating a strong market position or an image as market leaders before competition emerges (although this will depend on the speed and strength of the competitive response).

One specific variant of demand-orientated penetration strategies is worth mentioning – this might be called the 'razor and razor blades' strategy. Basically it involves pricing a unit of hardware (e.g. razor, labelling gun, copier, abrading machine) at a level which achieves the maximum market penetration or placement so that profits can be achieved on repeated sales of related consumables. If the consumable can be made unique in some way to the hardware, at least initially, a curious combination strategy of penetration for the hardware and what amounts to skimming on the consumable presents itself.

Demand-oriented penetration strategies usually assume a slight under-lying downward trend in prices under the impetus of further economies of scale and competitive pressure. This assumption is not necessarily true of competition-orientated penetration strategies. Penetration pricing in the broadest sense can be regarded as a means of deterring potential competitors by pressuring the margins which can be achieved to offset the costs of entry implicit in product development, investment in production facilities and marketing/promotional efforts. To this extent bold penetration pricing might be employed to pre-empt the (immediate) risk of competition. Even so the strategy may still call for prices to be kept, in relative terms, around the launch level or even drifting lower to keep up the deterrent.

Two situations exist, however, where the strategy may be one of low entry price and an underlying plan for either a sharp or gradual increase in price. First, where a new product is being launched in a market where the competition comprises substitute or alternative products, price has been used as a means of persuading potential users to try the product (about which they may have, for example, technical doubts) on the assumption that when it has proved itself they would be prepared to pay a price equal to, or higher than, the existing alternatives. The second example concerns the use of a low entry price as a means of displacing or forcing out entrenched competition from an established market place or of gaining a substantial market share on the basis of which prices can subsequently be increased to a more profitable level. This highly aggressive strategy is one which has been successfully employed by Japanese companies in European markets for a wide variety of products. An example is marine engines. 'The prime target for the Japanese . . . was the European market and the view in the trade was that their strategy would follow the familiar pattern of gaining a large initial market share at cut prices, forcing the opposition out and then raising prices' (*Marketing*, 1979, Oct., p. 32).

The temptation to use price as an entry wedge becomes increasingly great the more difficult it is for the firm entering a well established existing market to differentiate its product sufficiently clearly from those already available to ensure achievement of a satisfactory foothold on other competitive grounds. It can, however, be a high-risk strategy: if competitors have the resources to fight a rear-guard battle or even to step up the price war or if customers do not respond to the entry price as expected, the firm employing this strategy might find itself blocked, forced even to lower prices with consequent loss of profit margins all round or even faced with a situation in which serious resistance is encountered to the subsequent price rises implied by the strategy.

In general terms the more innovative the product the more the firm is likely to incline towards a skimming rather than a penetration strategy, particularly if R and D costs have been high and production capacity is limited, at least in the short term. However, the right strategy will depend on the firm, the product and the market.

Reviewing strategy after entry

Although pricing strategies are conceived as operating over a period of time, ignoring short-term fluctuations or pressures which may demand a tactical response, this does not mean that the strategy does not need to be kept under regular review. Nor that it is not necessary for strategies to be changed if conditions in the market place become sufficiently different from those that prompted the original plan.

The firm which has adopted a skimming strategy is faced with the need to decide when to implement the price cuts envisaged by the strategy and how large these should be on each occasion. There can be no hard and fast rules to guide these decisions. Depending on the pace at which competition develops – and this may be slowed down by patent protection, high entry costs and other factors – a high initial price might be retained for some considerable time before it needs to be reduced. On the other hand it can be advantageous to make the first cut well ahead of competition as a pre-emptive measure. Equally the timing and size of the cut may be best related to taking advantage of the demand interest opened up by initial entry to boost sales by a substantial cut in price justified by reference to cost savings from increased scale of production and greater efficiency. Similar considerations apply to subsequent cuts.

The firm which has implemented a penetration strategy has less room to manoeuvre in terms of price adjustments in the face of developing competition. The major problem facing pricing executives is maintaining a long-term view of price developments when competitive pressures appear to be forcing the firm into a growing number of reactive or short-term tactical decisions most probably associated with price cuts. In order to maintain its strategic grip the firm must be able to retain a broader view of the development of demand, its sensitivity to price changes and its susceptibility to non-price differentials.

It is probable that for many products, pricing decisions shade from the strategic to the tactical in the longer term whichever entry strategy is adopted as competition develops, as product differentiation becomes increasingly difficult to sustain and as sales approach saturation. Even so it would pay the firm to be alive to the opportunities which exist for using a deliberate change in strategy to revitalise its position in the market place or improve profits. The variations of strategy option are legion but include:

1　Switching from a skimming strategy to a penetration strategy to exploit mass market potential of a product initially pioneered at a high price – perhaps by introducing a simplified and cheaper version rather than by cutting the price of the original product

2　Introduction of replacement or second generation products which can be differentiated sufficiently to command a premium price (return to skimming strategy)

3　'Re-packaging' of products in a way which takes them out of the competitive arena. A good example is the development of 'electronic office' concepts linking more conventional pieces of equipment in a unique total way (return to skimming strategy)

4　Concentration of attention on more profitable market segments even at the cost of volume – diversion of released production resources into other products

5　Improve margins by concentration on cost savings through more efficient production rather than by increasing prices (although the ability of the firm to use this strategy is limited by the long-term tendency of all production methods to ape the most efficient).

Tactical considerations

In theory, strategy precedes tactics in the pricing process, the latter providing the short-term dimension to the implementation of strategy which governs the actual prices charged and the way these are expressed to the customer. In practice it is not always easy to separate the two. Tactics can be considered at two levels. First there are tactical decisions which relate to gearing actual price levels, and the form they take, to what might be termed the 'psychology' of the customer and the nature of the purchasing process. Such tactical considerations, insofar as they hold true over a period of time, in effect form part of strategy.

The semantics of such pricing tactics tend to be those of the consumer market and retail pricing. However, many have a more universal relevance whatever the product or service being sold. Probably the most widespread tactical device is discounting and this is considered in more detail below. However, mention might also be made of such tactics (based on Wilson, 1972) as:

1　Offset – low basic price, 'lost' margin recouped on extras, replacement parts or consumables

2　Diversionary – low basic price on some products (in range or line) developing overall image of low cost

3　Discrete – tailoring of price to bring product within the purchasing competence of a given seniority of buyer (relevant where the location of purchase decision is determined by corporate price ceilings)

4　Price lining – price kept constant but quality of product or extent of service adjusted to reflect changes in costs

5　Financing – alternative options to purchase such as leasing and rental (can be used as a specific means of extracting greater profit by changing the bases on which 'price' is assessed by the customer); might be coupled with special credit terms, trade-in allowances and special offers.

The above tactics are basically concerned with price. However, these need to be considered alongside what might be termed non-price differentials – ways of competing with command customer loyalty outside the framework of direct price competition, such as delivery services, after-sales support, technical back-up and advice and advertising and promotion effort.

In addition to these 'tactics of strategy' there are tactical questions of a more practical day-to-day level: what is the best way to pass on a price increase forced by rises in costs? Should ways be sought of keeping prices stable by modifying the product? Is it better to make price changes at regular and infrequent intervals (as until recently was mainly the case) or often in line with cost changes (as inflation is increasingly forcing on firms)? Should prices be changed to take into account positions of short-term strengths or weaknesses in the market place? How should the firm react to changes in competitors' pricing – is it necessary to react at all? By how much?

The combination and application of tactics require, if they are to have the desired effect, a detailed knowledge of the customer groups to which they are applied and the way these take purchasing decisions as well as a good appreciation of the likely response from competitors and the tactics which they are using themselves.

DISCOUNTS AND DISCOUNTING

The principle of discounting, whether formal or discretionary, is entrenched in most sectors of manufacturing industry where list prices of some kind or other are employed. The variations in discounting practice in everyday use are numerous. Four main types of discount: quantity discounts, trade discounts, cash discounts and seasonal/load shedding discounts are summarised in Figure 17.3. Other types of discount include those based on geographical factors (e.g. zonal pricing based on delivery distance); delivery method (e.g. discounts for customer collection); trade-in allowances on old equipment; 'free' supply of related consumables (e.g. labels used in price marking equipment). There are various ways also in which discounts are actually effected: they can be based on physical volume or money sales; be a percentage discount or a cash difference from a 'list' price; be shown as a flat sum rebate or a net price; be made 'on-invoice' or 'off invoice'. Finally discount structures can be formal (with details published for customer use) or discretionary (in the form of guidelines within which sales managers can negotiate) or a combination of the two.

Special contract or 'net price' arrangements with key customers are, in effect, an extension of the discounting principle but with the essential difference that the terms of the sales agreement are usually the result of direct negotiation between buyer and seller rather than a development of the existing discount formula. Prices are inevitably keen but how much so will depend in individual cases on the bargaining strength of buyer and seller at the time and can be obscured by the introduction of product modifications, non-standard delivery

	Method of operation	Reasons for use
Quantity or rebates	1 Single order – discount based on physical volume purchased at one particular time	1 Respond to individual purchasing power of customer in a competitive environment
	2 Cumulative – discount based on physical volume purchased over a fixed period of time usually one year)	2 Pass on cost savings involved in servicing larger orders (economies in packaging, transportation, sales, administration)
	3 Guaranteed offtake – version of cumulative discount involving commitment by the buyer to take up either a fixed minimum quantity over the period as a whole or in specified amounts at fixed intervals (e.g. monthly) or both. Sometimes penalties in the form of sur-charges are made for exceeding a contract offtake as well as for falling short. In other cases bonuses can be paid for exceeding contract minimum	3 Encourage customers to purchase in larger quantities than they might otherwise do
		4 Discourage small orders which are expensive to process or unprofitable
		5 Promote repeat purchasing
		6 Create stability in demand and foster greater regularity and consistency in supply (benefits in stock-holding, organisation of transportation, operation of product lines, etc.)

Trade discounts	Usually percentage discount from a specified 'list' price, designed to represent the distributors' operating expenses and profit. Alternatively may be represented as net trade prices available only to recognised 'trade' customers. Where more than one level exists in the distribution chain, discounts may discriminate between levels (e.g. between wholesalers and retailers) Trade discounts may be characterised as a flat rate trade concession (e.g. 25 per cent to trade, list to other buyers) or combined with a quantity discount	1 Aid in controlling or guiding final selling price (subject to legislation) 2 Means of discriminating between different types of distributor, e.g. wholesaler and retailer; general distributor and special distributor who may offer additional or enhanced service 3 Simplicity – easily understood by distributors 4 Economy – reduce need to keep changing catalogues (since discounts, not 'list' prices can be manipulated 5 Protection of distributor against direct buyers
Cash discounts	Deductions offered by the seller if payment of an invoice is made within a specified time period	Encourage immediate or early payment thus saving costs involved in the extension of credit and management of overdue accounts
Seasonal discounts/ load shedding	Differential prices according to season, day of week or time of day, where demand has a cyclical pattern and supply is fixed or intractable – most appropriate in consumer markets	Encourage spreading of demand, diversion of peak loading, boosting of demand at low periods Examples – electricity, coal, hotels, cross channel ferries, public transport, cinemas

Figure 17.3 Types of discount

arrangements and other special conditions. Special terms can come to dominate sales, for example, approximately 80 per cent of the sales of the Metal Box Company (open-top group) in 1977 were covered by special arrangements.

Of course in theory and in practice there are excellent reasons for operating a discount policy, some of which are indicated in Figure 17.3. Carefully operated and controlled, discounting provides firms with a flexible facility for fine-tuning response to (changing) demand and competitive conditions while retaining the overall integrity of catalogue and list price structures. The danger of discounting as general practice is that it can lead to inconsistency and lack of control. Special terms to important customers can individually be defended on the basis of pragmatism and expediency but add up in total to a jungle of prices which inevitably becomes perpetuated in successive deals with the same customers.

Discounts and special details in effect represent the reality of pricing while formal price lists and formulas represent the theory. The greater the flexibility or informality of the discounting procedure, and the more discretion which is granted to individual sales executives in negotiating actual prices, then the more the difficulty the company faces in maintaining a firm grip over the effects of its pricing activities. Anticipating revenues and profit is a basic component of financial budgeting and control. However, the ability to make realistic fore-casts and impose meaningful controls is directly related to an appreciation of the way prices are actually arrived at, the extent and 'mix' of sales at discounted prices and the relationship these prices have with formal price structures.

The firm operating discounts should keep asking itself:

1 *Do we need to discount at all?* Tradition and convention often play a major role in the operation of formal discount policies and structures. Yet firms have successfully fought the weight of conventional practice. For example, one major US-owned manufacturer of office furnishing systems has successfully operated a list price only policy for sales of whatever size in a market where discounting is notoriously widespread

2 *What types of discount should we offer?* The types and scales of discount appropriate in individual cases cannot be embodied within a general set of rules. These will depend on the markets concerned, on the cost structures faced by the firm, perceived customer sensitivity to price changes, on the competitive situation and many other factors. What is important is that discounting procedures are subjected to rational evaluation of all the factors involved and kept consistent with changes in cost, sales structure and the market environment. Discount structures have a habit of becoming entrenched so that they remain in force long after they have ceased to be relevant to the firm's business. A manufacturer who has switched from selling through distributors to mainly direct sales does not, for example, need to offer trade discounts pitched at a level which encourages heavy stocking

3 *What proportion of sales will be made at discounted prices?* Company manage-ment should be aware of the sensitivity of revenue and profit to the extent and level of discounting. This should include a particular appreciation of

the role of special terms negotiated with large customers and the impact of a wide flexibility or discretion in fixing discount prices.

PRICING AND NEW PRODUCT PLANNING

It can be said that the only time a firm genuinely has complete discretion in pricing is before it has committed itself to developing and marketing a new product at all! Once resources start to be committed to R and D, and even more once production facilities have been invested in, the pricing options available to the firm become progressively narrowed by practical considerations: the costs 'sunk' in bringing the product to market; the fixed costs represented by the scale of plant laid down to produce it; the direct costs of production consequent on choice of production process and scale of production; the constraints imposed by demand and competitive conditions and by the pricing of existing product lines with which the new product might be expected to interact.

New product development has always been a high-risk activity – various studies in the USA have shown failure rates among those actually launched running as high as 60 per cent. Many others are abandoned before they reach the production stage after large sums have been spent on R and D. The risks are moreover tending to become greater as the pace of technological change and competitive pressures force up development costs. The more greedy on resources new product development is, the more careful the firm needs to be that the products selected for development are those standing the best chance of achieving a good rate of return on investment when the product finally goes into production. Many writers on new product planning have emphasised the need for establishing clear frameworks of controls, systems and guidelines for appraising the relative merits of new product ideas so that management time and resources are channelled to those products offering the most attractive investment opportunity.

The process of new product appraisal is one which involves a large number of corporate and marketing considerations. However, anticipation of the price ranges at which the product is likely to sell and the market conditions or assumptions underlying those ranges is something which should normally take place at the earliest stages of product planning and be held under review throughout the development process. In effect it is argued that firms should think far more concretely about gearing new product development to a broad target selling price derived in turn from a realistic valuation of potential demand and the nature of competition than they do at present. This would have several major benefits:

1 It would contain the tendency in R and D to 'over-engineer' products (since the price target will also imply production cost targets which would have to be met if satisfactory profits are to be made)
2 It would prevent the development of products based on unrealistic assumptions about likely sales volumes (which often result from the use of cost plus formulas to project price, at the planning stage)
3 It would provide a framework for 'fine-tuning' the product during the later

stages of development to maximise competitive success within the selected price range.

Admittedly this approach is not easy to apply to the product which is itself a dramatic technological breakthrough or creative innovation for which existing price indications in the market place are inadequate and hypothetical testing of consumer responses at best unreliable. However, the great majority of new products do not fall into this category but relate in some reasonably direct way to established applications and existing products against which price targets can reasonably be set.

PRICING AND PRODUCT LINES

A great many pricing decisions take place in the context of product lines or ranges rather than as entirely independent exercises. Product lines or ranges comprise individual products linked together in some identifiable way – by a common function, by a common design or structure, by a common production process, by a common user group or application area. An office equipment manufacturer may, for example, offer a range of copiers of different print speeds or output capacities; within each model type a choice of features, e.g. automatic or manual operation; ranges of other office products, e.g. type-writers, word processors and facsimile transceivers.

The basis for product-line policies and the justification for offering different models, lines and ranges is a subject in itself. It is sufficient to note here that the existence of product lines raises particularly complex issues of pricing because of the way demand for each individual product interacts. Product lines as a whole may be mutually supportive but individual products within the line can easily be competitive with each other, particularly if encouraged by lack of care in pricing. Simply applying a common mark-up to each individual product is clearly unsatisfactory since it is probable that each product will vary in its production and marketing cost profile and in the opportunities and constraints implied by demand and the competitor environment it is selling into. This argues for a pricing policy which provides for each product in a line to be individually priced according to costs and market conditions subject to certain broad principles of consistency to minimise the risk of anomalies leading to the firm competing with itself.

Even so the firm faces sensitive issues each time a product line is extended, supplemented or modified by introduction of revised models or when a new product line is introduced. An example of the dangers faced, in the author's own experience, is provided by a building board company which tried to launch a new and superior grade of board at a premium price in a market which turned out to place much less value on the higher quality offered by the new product than the company expected. The result was that as the price of the new product was forced down to a level close to that of the firm's existing range of building board, buyers of the original range simply switched allegiance to the new product forcing the price of the original range still lower in order to maintain sales. What started off as an exercise in market segmentation turned out to cause disastrous loss of profit all round.

SUMMARY

This chapter has sought to demonstrate why pricing is perhaps the most complex and demanding – and least clearly understood – of all tasks facing company management. Some conclusions are now drawn which might help the financial executive, in particular, contribute more effectively to pricing policy formulation and price setting.

1   *Pricing is much more of an art than a science.* There is no universal formula or golden rule for arriving at the right price. Those responsible for price setting have to balance and allow for a variety of factors and influences both internal to and external to the firm itself which, far from the ordered and rational world of the theoretical economist, may not always be logical and may even be in conflict. Nevertheless, profitability can significantly be enhanced by injecting greater coherence into the rules and principles, whatever these may be, which govern the way prices are fixed and maintained. The financial executive has an important part to play in the preparation and implementation of pricing policy

2   *Successful pricing decisions cannot be based on costs alone.* Prices are far less often arrived at by the mechanistic application of cost-based formulae than is widely believed. Even so, costs and cost-related profit targets remain a major obsession of many firms in pricing, particularly in the case of industrial products. Financial executives have tended on the whole to encourage and reinforce this essentially inward-looking approach. The success of pricing decisions is, however, highly dependent on the ability of the firm to comprehend and respond to *market* needs and conditions. The contribution of the financial executive to pricing decisions would be substantially enhanced by greater recognition of the role of such factors as competition, buyer attitudes and motivations and the impact of distributive systems in optimum pricing

3   *Price is a much neglected and potentially powerful element in the marketing mix.* Price is widely treated more as a handicap which has to be borne rather than as a positive tool for achieving designated marketing goals. This chapter has looked at the ways pricing can contribute to overall marketing plans both in the longer term (pricing strategy) and in the short term (pricing tactics). The financial executive should be prepared to be 'sufficiently flexible in his own advice and policies not to inhibit sales and marketing personnel from manipulation of price as a marketing weapon

4   *Pricing considerations are a key element in product planning.* Anticipation of price ranges and market conditions are an essential precondition to effective investment and product planning. The financial executive should seek to ensure that pricing factors are introduced at the beginning and not at the end of the planning cycle for new products.

REFERENCES AND FURTHER READING

Atkin, B. and Skinner, R., *How British Industry Prices*, IMR, 1975.

Price Commission, *Compressed Permanent Gases and Dissolved Acetylene Sold in Cylinders, Cylinder Rentals and Fixed Charges* (BOC Ltd), HC 223, 1979.

Gabor, A., *Pricing, Principles and Practices*, Heinemann, London, 1977.

Price Commission, *Open Top Food and Beverage Cans and Aerosol Cans* (Metal Box Ltd), HC 135, 1978.

Oxenfeldt, A. R., 'Multi-Stage Approach to Pricing', *Harvard Business Review*, July/August 1960.

Price Commission, *Report for the period 1st February to 30th April 1980*.

Price Commission, *Prices of Glass Containers* (UG Glass Containers Ltd) HC 170, 1978.

Wilson, A., *The Marketing of Professional Services*, McGraw-Hill, 1972.

18 Distribution channels

Jack Wheatley

The process of distribution is not merely concerned with physically getting goods from a manufacturer to his eventual customer. Distribution strategy covers the following basic activities: the choice of available channels, whether or not to confine distribution to one channel or several; whether to go direct to the customer or deal through intermediaries; how much expenditure to allocate for distribution and whether to take a complete or partial financial interest in the available channels.

What might seem the best or only channels available at the start of a marketing campaign may prove to be inadequate or too restrictive for subsequent development of sales, so a manufacturer who opts to distribute entirely through wholesalers may regret his lack of contact with retail outlets when he needs extra sales or when he realises that his wholesaler is also promoting a competitor's output, perhaps to the exclusion of his products.

The choice of distribution channels is therefore one requiring careful thought and a full consideration of the available alternatives.

PLANNING FOR DISTRIBUTION

In arriving at a final decision on which channel or combination of channels should be used many points have to be taken into account. The choice depends not only on costs in relation to funds available, but also on the location of the consumer, the places where he is most likely to see the product and the extent to which it is desirable and/or necessary to maintain direct contact with the consumer. It also depends on the bulkiness of the product, anticipated average order value, credit risks involved in the alternative methods available and the risks entailed in placing all distributions in the hands of an outside and independent agent or wholesaler.

With a new product, and particularly if the market is a new one to the manufacturer, it still takes great courage to try and by-pass traditional channels. The patterns of distribution and demand are now changing, however, as the ranges of choice open to consumers widen.

Not so long ago, nobody would have considered garages as an outlet for confectionery and soft drinks, newsagents for pop records, chemists for wines and spirits or food supermarkets for clothing and furniture, but all these changes have taken place to the advantage of the retailing outlets and the manufacturers.

Distribution itself cannot be considered in isolation from other aspects of the marketing plan because it is usually up to the manufacturer to promote his products to the eventual consumer and to stimulate demand that will materialise into a decision to buy at the chosen point of distribution.

New methods of large-scale distribution such as hypermarkets and cash and carries are attractive in that they facilitate bulk distribution to a limited number of outlets but, in opting for this method as a sole means of distribution, the manufacturer is vulnerable in the sense that changes in the buying policies of one or two of the outlets can have a significantly adverse impact on his sales volume. The ultimate decision on which distributive channels to use must depend on the costs involved and the estimated net profit contribution available within the various alternatives.

What might seem the best short-term solutions are not necessarily in the long-term interests of the manufacturer and therefore extreme care must be taken before placing all distribution in the hands of an outside body be it a wholesaler, agent or merchant.

The ideal is to have full control over all aspects of distribution, but this may well involve the manufacturer in direct selling costs that the product could not carry in the light of the anticipated sales forecast.

THE WHOLESALER

Traditionally the wholesaler has been one of the oldest links in the distribution chain but, while still popular, this method is losing some of its appeal with manufacturers beginning to develop their own images to their consumers. Even so, the wholesaler still offers the cheapest form of distribution as he takes responsibility for storing in bulk and delivering in small quantities to the consumer. This relieves the manufacturer of the major part of delivery costs for he is only concerned with making the more economical bulk deliveries to the wholesaler's warehouses. The wholesaler takes all the small credit risks and absorbs direct selling costs, but very rarely will he avoid selling a competitive product.

Because of the nature of their business, wholesalers carry wide brand ranges and their salesmen become initially 'order takers' with no specific selling emphasis on any particular brand. They tend, therefore, to reflect consumer demand rather than create it.

Although wholesalers can handle all distribution it is advisable for a manufacturer to employ at least a small sales force calling on ultimate outlets to persuade them to place orders for his products from the designated local wholesaler. Orders can be taken and passed to the wholesaler as a gesture of good faith but also as a positive encouragement to stock the manufacturer's product.

Some companies have set up their own wholesaling operations. The speedy, prompt, delivery (SPD) organisation set up by Unilever is an example, and in this case the wholesaling/distribution company stores and distributes for other organisations on a proper commercial basis. In the main, it is better to regard wholesaling as a specialist function and to set up an in-company operation only if it can be done properly and expertly. Few organisations have the required range to do that.

A combination of direct distribution and wholesaling is preferable as the sales contacts that the wholesalers have built up over the years are very useful, but if wholesaling is used it is important to remember that the eventual consumer will need to be exposed to product promotion from the manufacturer. The wholesaler cannot be expected to create the demand, for he has too many competing interests.

To avoid conflict with a wholesaler's selling policy a manufacturer can give a different brand name to his product sold through the wholesaler. This technique is used successfully with such products as stationery, clothing and certain foodstuffs.

THE RETAIL TRADES

The structure of the retail trades has altered considerably since Napoleon referred to Britain as 'a nation of shopkeepers'. Many smaller shops have been forced out of business but many that have changed their style of management to compete with the larger, and often impersonal multiples and supermarkets, have survived. Often location has proved to be the prime factor.

Independent retailers

Independent retailers provide an efficient local service at higher prices than the larger chains and multiples and they often provide extended credit and/or free delivery for their customers. As outlets, they tend to sell the products for which there is an established demand, but are often very responsive to good sales promotion of new products and can be more easily persuaded to try new lines than wholesalers.

Voluntary groups

To combat the threat posed by multiple chains and supermarkets, independent retailers have banded together into voluntary groups which started as central buying groups but have now developed into highly efficient retail outlets following common policies extending to product ranges, stock control, accounting, store layout and store promotions. Examples are VG and Mace. Other groups have been formed by large wholesalers to guarantee outlets for the lines they sell and this, in turn, has led wholesalers to develop their own label brands for distribution via the retailers in their group.

Multiple stores

The advantage of using this channel of distribution is that the buying points can be covered by a very small sales force as most items are bought centrally from head office. Store managers work to central promotional and stocking policies and, provided a manufacturer can persuade the central buyer to stock his product, he is assured that the necessary efforts will be made at store level. Because of the need to achieve fast turnover on what are often narrow margins, multiple stores will not persist with slow moving lines and so the manufacturer needs to back up the stores with adequate promotion to consumers. Multiples have developed from being the outlets set up by food manufacturers who wished to extend vertically into retailing, but some have taken the opposite path backwards into manufacturing; this is what has stimulated the growth of 'own label' brands.

Alternatively, some multiples have arranged own label production by outside manufacturers. This is useful to the independent producer as a channel of distribution but he has to be assured of long-term contracts if he uses this channel as a sole outlet for distribution.

Retail chains

Again, store managers follow centrally laid-down policies but there is usually more flexibility allowed according to local conditions. Stores often trade under different names, but the manufacturer is usually offered multiple outlet distribution and, consequently, a wider coverage.

Local chain store managers are usually very responsive to store promotions backed up by press and television advertising. The combination of a television spot naming a particular retail chain as a stockist of a product and a display of that product with a card saying, 'As seen on television' is very successful.

Department stores

Department stores carry a wide variety of merchandise under one roof with specific departments under their own separate buying and selling management. Each department is organised to sell particular product ranges.

The standard of personal service is often very high. Some of the larger stores have almost become institutions to the criterion of good service and are respected as such all over the world. Buyers are usually very skilled professionals who anticipate fashion trends and buy accordingly. Manufacturers using this channel can obtain extremely useful market research information by maintaining contact with store buyers. This channel is also used by companies setting up their own boutiques or 'shops within shops', a method particularly suitable for such products as jewellery, cosmetics and clothing. Exporters would find this a useful means of getting established in a new overseas market. Travel agencies are another example.

Co-operative societies

These are becoming combinations of multiples, department stores and super-markets with the apparent aim of selling their own manufactured products. This is the complete evolutionary cycle, for the first co-operative societies in the middle of the last century were manufacturers setting up as manufacturers and retailers.

Private brands, however, still account for a significant proportion of total turnover and the use of this channel offers the possibilities of large-scale distribution from a limited number of outlets.

Supermarkets

These are a natural development of multiples and self-service outlets and now account for a significant proportion of total retail trade. Product ranges have extended from food into a wide variety of non-food items operating under very tight control and measuring efficiency in terms of profit per square foot of floor space instead of as a percentage of sales.

Because of their vast buying power, supermarkets are able to extract hard bargains from manufacturers and lay down very strict conditions of delivery times, quantities, packaging, etc. Manufacturers are offered economic distribution in that delivery points are far fewer than for indepedent retailers; buying, however, is in the hands of an equally small number of head offices. A manufacturer who opts for supermarkets as his only outlets is subject to sudden changes of buying policy.

Supermarkets are becoming increasingly concerned with multiple product ranges to such an extent that specialist supermarkets dealing solely in product ranges, such as carpets, radio and television, are appearing to attract the customers who are becoming somewhat disenchanted with the lack of choice in the non-food departments of supermarkets.

Hypermarkets

Regarded as the ultimate in retailing, this type of outlet is now well established in the UK. The principle is to provide 'one-stop shopping' for a wide variety of products in an out-of-town location where space is available at lower rents than in town centres. These outlets are very attractive to manufacturers as access and egress is usually easier because of geographical location.

Cash and carry

These outlets have been developed by wholesalers and voluntary groups whereby retailers select the goods they are going to sell from the wide range displayed and collect, pay and transport them back to the shops. This method tends to be used by the smaller retailers, for example, restaurants, canteens and newsagents. The cash and carry outlets usually maintain regular promotional mailing to their retail customers and run special offer campaigns, but otherwise provide a minimum of service.

As a channel of distribution the manufacturer can make good use of cash and carry outlets to deal with the problems of small deliveries provided he can create a demand by promotion to the eventual outlet and consumer. However, as cash and carries are retailers' supermarkets, good packaging and presentation can be very helpful in persuading retailers to pick products off the shelves and to try selling them in their own stores.

Discount stores

A comparatively recent innovation to the retail scene is the discount store which provides cut-price products with the minimum customer service. This channel is particularly useful for sales of consumer durables and toiletries. Chemists' lines are being increasingly distributed in this manner. Discount trading became increasingly evident following the banning of resale price maintenance.

Mobile retailers

To strengthen the personal service there has been a growth in the number of retailers taking their products direct to the housewife. Grocers, greengrocers, bakers and butchers are using this method and yet dairies who, by tradition have made deliveries of milk direct to the consumer, are trying to cut down on the number of deliveries to reduce costs. Prices charged do not reflect the service provided. Dairies are adding soft drinks and confectionary to the range carried by their milk floats in order to increase sales per journey.

Ready-cooked foods like fish and chips, hamburgers, meat pies and chickens are now sold from mobiles as well as the normal tea, coffee and light refreshments.

Van selling

Van selling is used by manufacturers of perishable foods, particularly bread and meat products, and allows complete control of the distribution operation. Cost per order can be high, particularly in large items where so much time can be lost in finding a suitable parking place or waiting in traffic jams, but total distribution costs can be lower than would be incurred with a separate delivery fleet and a sales force.

Door-to-door selling

This is a very expensive method of distribution. Apart from a few highly successful exceptions, door-to-door selling is not widely practised. Government legislation was formulated to prevent the worst excesses of this type of selling whereby housewives were persuaded by unscrupulous salesmen to buy products that would not work or that they did not need or could not afford. It is often used in combination with a national or local advertising campaign. The regular wider promotion gives an air of respectability to the sales staff who follow up and call from door to door.

Considerable success has been achieved by companies selling cosmetics, but to be effective the use of this channel for such products requires a very large sales force as the average unit of sale is very low in value. Double glazing, central heating and encyclopedias are more applicable to this type of distribution as the average unit of sale tends to be much higher than with the smaller products.

Garages

Apart from selling petrol and oil, garages are now retailing wide ranges of motor accessories and food lines. The appeal is largely geared to impulse buying because consumers do not normally go to garages just to buy ancillary items. As channels of distribution, however, garages are becoming increasingly important.

THE COMMODITY MARKET

Perishables are usually distributed through the commodity markets in the UK, but many of them have become so heavily congested that producers are tending to fix up long-term contracts with outlets and deliver direct. Such contracts can be beneficial to the producer in so far as his selling prices are stabilised, but they have to be fixed in the light of a very accurate assessment of future supply and demand which the commodity markets reflect on a daily basis. Other commodities such as rubber, copper, tin, tea and gold are still bought and sold through the traditional markets in London.

Franchising

This is a method of distribution used mainly to further the sales of an idea or a process rather than a product itself. Successful exploitation of this method has been achieved with a wide variety of products including fried chickens, hamburgers, instant printing, drain cleaning, tyre and exhaust fitting, ice-cream, steaks and Chinese food. Financial assistance is provided to the franchisee to set up his business, with the manufacturer taking a share of the resulting profits and providing training in business management. Common standards and common forms of presentation are very important and are enshrined in agreements between the franchisor and franchisee.

Party plan selling

Under this method a manufacturer appoints agents – usually women – who hold sponsored parties in their homes and invite their friends to see the products. Orders are taken and more agents are recruited and so the operation develops. This channel is useful for selling kitchen and other domestic ware, clothing, jewellery and cosmetics but is difficult to use in conjunction with distribution through traditional retail outlets for these do not take kindly to this type of sponsored competition from their suppliers.

Mail order

This has become a popular channel for a very wide range of products and services. Large department stores and mail order houses are investing large sums in postage, printing and distribution of catalogues direct to the public. At the other end of the scale, rare books, classical records and even collections of specially minted coins and medals are promoted and distributed via direct mail to a specialist public. The big attraction of this method is the direct promotion to the consumer to the complete exclusion of any intermediaries. But perhaps the most spectacular growth in recent years has been direct selling through couponed advertisements in newspapers and magazines – through the Sunday supplements in particular. The method has also spread to television.

Direct selling costs are negligible, but advertising costs are extremely high; however, companies successful in this field continue to use this channel and are clearly satisfied with the returns obtained. Some distributors have extended their operation by setting up their own stores selling nothing but the products advertised by their direct mailing, thus relieving them of small distribution costs. This combination of previously separate channels is typical of what often happens as a marketing operation develops.

AGENTS, BROKERS AND MERCHANTS

The advantage of all of these channels is the personal contact and knowledge they have of a particular market. Agencies are established on an exclusive and semi-exclusive basis and can be very helpful to the supplier entering a completely new market or to one who does not want to employ his own sales force. The agent should act as a member of the manufacturer's sales team as distinct from the wholesaler who is more concerned with the burden of the physical distribution.

Clearly, the granting of a sole agency is a step not to be taken lightly because, if the wrong agent is appointed, considerable harm can be done to the principal's image and development plans before such an agent can be replaced.

Brokers act as intermediaries working on very fine profit margins but, as with agents, they often have very useful contacts. A danger with the broker is that he can depress the market price by selling at cut rates sufficient for him to earn a minimal margin, particularly on volume sales.

Merchants generally operate as a mixture of agents and wholesalers and usually have a good standing in the market place. Care has to be taken in passing them sole selling rights because they tend to carry a wide range of lines and are sometimes unable to put significant emphasis behind any one product.

EXPORTING

Selection of the proper channels of distribution for overseas markets is even more important than in the UK markets where the lines of communication are shorter and mistakes can be more speedily rectified. It is essential that proper account be taken of local customs and practices, attitudes and patterns of demand. For entry into an overseas market the best method of distribution is probably through an export agent. Selection of the agent is clearly very important and the Chamber of Commerce, the Department of Trade and Industry and trade associations can all offer good advice on where to find agents.

Direct representation in large department stores is another successfully used method of distribution because, as in the UK, leading stores are barometers of current demand and can usually place sizeable orders offering economies of scale to distributors.

With some countries, particularly those of the eastern bloc, the distribution has to be through large buying offices in the UK and often there is no direct contact between the manufactuer and his ultimate consumer.

INDUSTRIAL DISTRIBUTION

Techniques of good marketing are being applied increasingly in the industrial field. As far as channels of distribution are concerned the choice is almost as wide as that available for consumer goods.

Industrial products tend to be of a more technical nature so consideration has to be given to after-sales service irrespective of the chosen channel of distribution. Very often a manufacturer will deal with his customer via an agent on all matters of sale and supply, but will deal direct on servicing and maintenance.

Package deals involving products from within a large group of companies can be offered to one common outlet; similarly, a manufacturer may well find many captive outlets within his own group. This opportunity is often missed or just not pursued.

Licensing is a method often used in the engineering industry, for example, with motor cars and aero-engines. Under these arrangements, the licensee undertakes to produce and sell goods to the licensee's specification for a consideration of the resultant profits. This method enables the manufacturer to expand his revenue without a corresponding increase in investment.

Heavy engineering industries make use of consortia to distribute their products. This applies to such projects as off-shore drilling equipment, building and civil engineering contracts, power station supplies, shipbuilding, etc.

CONCLUSION

Inevitably, the final decision on which channels to use must be a compromise, but it is the purpose of this chapter to provide an outline of the range of possibilities, and even if no more than a stimulation of more detailed and rational thinking on this vital aspect of marketing occurs it will have served its purpose.

FURTHER READING

Butcher, M.E., *Elements of Distribution*, Heinemann, London, 1980.
Flipjer, M.T., *Distribution for Exporters*, BIM, 1977.
Guirdham, M., *Management of Distribution Channels*, Pergamon, Oxford, 1972.
Mallen, B., *Principles of Marketing Channel Techniques*, Lexington Books, Lexington, Mass., 1977.

19 Overseas marketing

Sydney Paulden

There are many companies that derive the major part of their business from overseas markets. There are others that export a smaller part of their production but generate a higher rate of profit on exported goods than on goods sold in the domestic market. However, the factor that is common to all companies that export successfully is the commitment that they make to their overseas markets. Failures, and they can be costly, occur when export markets are only turned to in times of emergency, when overseas buyers suddenly appear to be lifesavers during severe recessions on the home market. Export marketing requires a long-term commitment. It requires the support of senior management. It must be allocated the resources, in management, manpower and investment, commensurate with the volume of business that a company regards as feasible. This means, therefore, that the overseas markets have to be approached on similar lines to those described in earlier chapters for the domestic scene. Business from foreign buyers should be part of the corporate strategy, targets must be defined as the result of research, and resources must be allocated in order to achieve the targets. There must also be the same lead time as for the opening of any type of domestic market, or possibly a longer lead time. Disappointments often occur in overseas markets simply because senior management despatches a salesman on an overseas sales trip and judges the potential or the performance by the orders brought back in the salesman's briefcase. Yet this approach would hardly be regarded as adequate for the testing of a brand new market at home, unless it was the launch of a miracle product.

Overseas marketing, therefore, is usually best left to a time when a company has established itself on the home market when there is less likelihood of a shortage of management time or of capital. The export 'pipeline' is longer than that for domestic transactions. It can take longer to become established, longer to deliver goods and to receive payments. Communications are more stretched, after-sales service more critical, so that it is all the more vital for possible teething troubles with a new company or a new product to have been overcome before launching into overseas territories.

MARKET SELECTION

Once a company knows that it has a product suitable for export and once it has checked that it has sufficient capacity for growth into export markets on a long term basis, then the moment has come for selection of priority markets overseas. It is rare for a launch to be successfully carried out into many foreign markets simulataneously. Resources have to be focused on those areas that are likely to yield the most immediate returns.

It is stressed again and again in export marketing literature that it is essential for exporters to travel in person to their overseas markets. That is undeniably true, but it is also true that an enormous amount of effort and money can be wasted by hurrying to foreign territories without sufficient advance preparation. The first essential is to carry out so-called 'desk research' at home in order to identify the initial target markets, picking, from the 150 or more potential new territories, those that stand the best chance of being profitable.

Desk research

This encompasses any relevant published material that can help to create a picture of market conditions and opportunities; and also includes visits within the home market to any organisations that can provide an insight into trading overseas. There are usually scores of possible sources of data and assistance. They include government export service bodies, clearing banks, merchant banks, branches of banks from the overseas markets, specialist libraries, trade associations, general chambers of commerce, as well as those chambers relating to particular foreign territories.

The data can take the form of market surveys, bulletins, reports from trade missions that have visited the territories, statistics on exports to the overseas territories, statistics on the overseas territories' imports from the world at large. (Some suppliers from second and third markets might be supplying your type of goods, even if there is little export from your own country.) It is also frequently possible to obtain catalogues of competitive product lines that are available on the foreign markets through the services of the trade commissioners at overseas embassies, enabling the would-be exporter to compare quality, design and even price.

Newspaper articles and surveys should not be forgotten. The national press and trade papers frequently review prospects in different overseas markets, giving a broad or a specialist analysis of a country's economy, imports and future plans.

A fascinating exercise is to pinpoint some easily obtainable statistic that can give a valuable guide to the potential market for your product range. A company selling graphite, for example, was able to relate the use of sulphuric acid to the need for its products. Although there were virtually no statistics available on the purchase of graphite products, figures could fairly easily be obtained for consumption of sulphuric acid by industry worldwide, broken down by country, and this led directly to the largest potential markets. A leather shoe manufacturer was also able to obtain details of the sale of shoe polish in a country and this gave an immediate guide to the volume of shoe sales and the shoe colours that were popular.

In desk research the trick is not only to identify markets that have been using your products in volume, but also, and even better, to spot those that are about to embark on a much greater use of them. It might then be possible to move into a new market before competitors have become too strongly established there. In today's world, markets can change very rapidly and even the veteran exporters might be missing an opportunity that the newcomer can spot. Features in the press recently, for example, have indicated that Trinidad is now a rich country with over 50 separate development budgets that have accumulated oil funds to be used for specific expansion projects in many fields. Other reports have shown that the Philippines is embarking on a massive 10-year plan to diversify its energy production into coal mining, alcohol-gas production, geothermal plants and even genetic engineering. Do these leads suggest potential new markets?

Cost-saving

The point about desk research is that it is less costly to dig for data at the home market end than in the overseas territory; especially when the exporter might be making a bee-line for the wrong territory, anyway. First select the target markets, then check every possible aspect before travelling there; and make sure that every trip is well prepared, with introductions to useful contacts prior to flying from home. Hotel bills, food, local travel and entertainment expenses can be very high, even in the apparently poorer areas of the world. In fact, often the poorer countries cost more *per diem*, because the traveller simply cannot risk living cheaply. It is essential to stay at the best hotels and eat in the best restaurants, whereas a seasoned traveller might well know his way to using more modest facilities in a market such as the US, say, or Germany, where the range of suitable accommodation is much wider.

It should also be remembered that a wasted trip not only costs money and time, it might also cause such disappointment that the whole approach to export marketing can wind down as a result, losing a company all the potential that could exist in the right markets.

PREPARATION OF A SALES/RESEARCH TOUR

It is usually cost-effective to plan a sales-cum-research trip to a group of markets rather than to a single market. However, it is also wise to guard against taking in too many new territories on one tour. A businessman can tire after a given time away from home and from then on there is less and less value to be gained from each successive market visited. A rough survey of a number of different exporters suggests that five weeks is probably the limit to a foreign tour, that three weeks is probably optimum for distant markets (over 8 hours flight, say), whilst one working week of five or six days is not a bad idea for markets closer to hand (3 to 8 hours flight). One or two days are frequently allocated to a visit to a market no more than 2 hours away. It is a trade-off between making use of the money spent on the longer flights and keeping alert and enthusiastic whilst away. Also, it has to be remembered that a trip is not ended when the businessman arrives home. The real finish only comes when all the leads have been followed up; when the information requested by people met on the trip has been collected and despatched; when letters and telexes have been sent to confirm arrangements; when people back at head office or at the factory have been briefed on what they have to do to meet orders, prepare prototypes or set up a marketing channel for the new markets.

One common failing in preparing a foreign sales tour is to neglect to allocate sufficient time for tying up all these ends at the finish of the actual travelling. There is always a huge pile of accumulated work on the desk awaiting the returning traveller and then the true value of the trip can be lost due to neglect of the follow-up.

Once the main target markets have been defined for a visit, an agenda for the trip should be drawn up. A possible checklist of such an agenda might be:

1   Identify current and future size of market for product range
2   Identify methods of distribution to major buyers
3   Shortlist suitable agents or distributors
4   Appoint or interview potential agent
5   Check competitive prices, trade credit terms and product quality
6   Check best method of carriage of goods (air, sea, road)
7   Double check any technical or import tariff complications
8   Meet major buyers in person

To achieve these objectives, within a reasonable time to be spent in the field, a lot of groundwork must be done before departure. The businessman should have arranged appointments with, say, the trade officials at his embassy, with officers of the relevant chamber of commerce, with local banks, trade associations and so on. It is often a good idea to fill the first two or three days with pre-arranged appointments, leaving plenty of spare time in a market to follow up the leads that arise on the spot. Markets and opportunities always look very different once one is there, compared with the view that might be created from afar. This is the whole point of making the trip in person.

OVERSEAS SALES AGENTS

Much more than half the world's international trade is conducted through agents of one kind or another. The selection and management of agents in overseas markets is the key to success. A common failing is for a would-be exporter to appoint the first agent who approaches him and then to leave the market in the hands of the agent, complaining later if the market does not live up to its potential.

The prime objective of most first visits to overseas markets is to find and appoint the best possible form of representation. To do this, the exporter must first have a detailed picture of the market, so that he can devise the best strategy and then home in on an agent that fits it. The following factors will greatly influence the choice of a representative in a market.

Geography

It is seldom wise to give an agent in one country the rights to business in another country, even though this might appear to be a very convenient arrangement. It is rare, for example, for Finns to welcome US or British goods sold to them through an agency in Sweden, or for Thais to feel easy about buying through Malaysia.

Nor can it be assumed that a single agent is capable of representing an exporter's interests in the whole of the agent's own country. There can frequently be problems relating to local geography or traditional distribution channels, or even ethnic and language barriers. The USA and West Germany, for example, are very fragmented markets, being federal countries with a lot of trade focused on the different commercial centres in each separate state or *Land*. Very few agents would have the necessary contacts in each part of the country where the exporter might have a big potential market. New York salesmen can rarely cover the rich markets of California. A Hamburg firm is not likely to spend a lot of time selling in Munich or Nuremberg. Similarly, there could be problems in even a tiny country such as Belgium, where there are linguistic and commercial differences arising from the divide between Flemish and French-speaking buyers.

On the other hand, there are often areas that are regarded regionally as centres of trade, where representatives can cover a wider field. Hong Kong and Singapore, for example, are seen in the East as professional trading centres and, being very small territories, have developed traders who are often capable of tackling other neighbouring markets on behalf of principals. Singapore-based agencies often take on the rights for Malaysia and Indonesia. However, it is vital for an exporter to check how acceptable this arrangement might be – not with the agent, but with the potential customers. How do they view it? And has the agency the resources to cover more than one territory?

Customer contacts

Is the market for the product range segmented? If so, can a single agent tap each segment effectively? Some products or services might have applications in industry and at the same time find outlets through retail trade stores (hand tools for example); or a product might have two very distinct market segments, such as the construction industry and the vehicle repair industry, or the original equipment industry and the spares and replacement trade. The distribution channels feeding these industries and trade might differ from one market to another. Can one importer cope or should there be two?

Size of representation

Exporters very often face the agony of decision between a potential agent who is well established but who handles scores of different product lines, and the new firm that is hungry for business. One has the age-old contacts and reputation, but may not give a new line very much attention. The other will have to spend time building up contacts and might also have problems in financing his expansion. There is no rule-of-thumb guide to this problem. It is the exporter's decision, but it is well to be aware that the problem exists and give it thought. Often, the newcomer to an overseas market does not have the choice, as the older agencies already have competitive lines on their books. More and more, however, in the rapidly developing territories, young capable staff are leaving the older agencies and setting up on their own, and these go-getters welcome the chance to prove themselves with a new principal. Again, these people can rarely be identified from afar in the home market. It takes a personal visit to the territory to track them down.

Service facilities

Service is often a function of size of representation. If a product requires substantial technical back-up or personal attention, the exporter has to be satisfied that the representation appointed in a market has the capability to provide the service *in all the corners of the market that are allocated as his territory*. Does the agent cover these remoter areas effectively? Can the potential customers be expected to communicate with the agent's headquarters?

FINANCIAL CONSIDERATIONS

Export finance is covered in Chapter 6 of this handbook but it is very necessary to look at finance as part of the export marketing strategy. There are two important aspects to be considered. First, there is the question of financing export business, seen from the exporter's own point of view. Secondly, there is the financing of exports seen from the point of view of the buyer. How attractive are the financial terms to him, compared with offers from other exporters or from domestic suppliers within his own territory?

Financing exports

The problem is that exporting has a lengthy pipeline and there can be a long period between production of the goods and receipt of final payment. The situation can be aggravated by one of the rosier aspects of exporting – the average size of order from overseas is frequently much bigger than that from the home market. Importers often place orders for a whole territory, whereas home orders are for tiny pieces of a market. It is usually economic for foreign buyers to purchase in larger units, because of transport costs. Long credit terms are also the fashion in exporting, due to the fierce competition between the exporting nations of the world. A foreign importer might expect 120 days, whereas a home market transaction might assume 30 or 60 days.

Export finance facilities exist that can transform the credit sale into a cash sale. Naturally, they imply a discount and so the exporter must investigate these facilities prior to quoting a final price to the foreign buyer, as the cost of finance may have to be built into the price to be paid by the overseas importer. It is a common complaint in financial circles that exporters too often land an order and only then run to the financial experts for help in handling the credit – to find that they cannot afford services that would otherwise have been ideal.

There is a whole host of export finance services and this is obviously a critical topic that must be studied carefully in relation to the type of business on hand. Exporters should call on the services of financial specialists. However, it is possible to provide a very brief review of some of the possibilities, so that the exporter can appreciate how important it is to study the topic further and also how the financial side can affect the pricing of export orders and even the approach to a market.

Credit insurance

Export credit can be insured through an exporter's official bodies, such as Export Credits Guarantee Department in the UK (ECGD). In the UK, this form of insurance not only provides cover against possible default by the foreign buyer after he has received the goods and against political risks (the foreign government stopping all foreign payments, for example) but can often be used to raise money at favourable rates of interest. Invoices for exported goods covered by credit insurance can often be used as collateral to support an overdraft at the bank.

Factoring

There is a growing range of export factoring services. These mainly apply to companies that have a large number of export deliveries to a wide range of overseas buyers on open account, with up to, say, a maximum of 90 or 120 days credit. The factoring company, often the subsidiary of a major bank, can provide two distinct services. One is the management of the export sales ledger, sending reminders to the foreign buyers and taking responsibility for insurance of the debt and for collection of the payments, permitting the exporter to concentrate on sales and production. The second service is the provision of working capital, by remitting a given monthly sum to the exporter that is an average of what can be expected back from foreign payments. This enables the exporter to plan his cash flow programme, ironing out the unpredictable nature of foreign receipts.

Forfeiting

This is a service whereby a finance house buys the debt from an exporter at a discount immediately on shipment of the goods. The exporter has his money in the bank just as with a cash transaction. Payment is in the home currency, no matter which hard currency has been used for the invoice. The exporter then has no exposure to currency exchange risks during the period of credit. This technique is valuable for one-off transactions for capital goods of some substantial value.

Confirming

A confirming house can greatly assist an exporter in setting up a financial package for a foreign buyer that provides the buyer with good credit terms and the exporter with immediate cash for his consignments. The confirming house can *contract with the buyer* to provide a loan to purchase the goods in the buyer's own currency with a favourable term of credit. This loan is then used to pay the exporter on shipment in his own currency. The exporter is relieved of the exchange risk, of the risk of default and of the problem of financing the term of credit.

Marketing tool

These services can be used by the exporter as a marketing tool, because nowadays the financial package that accompanies the offer of goods can rank in importance with quality, delivery and price. In the developing countries, particularly, buyers aim to finance the purchase of foreign goods or equipment from the profits made with the goods during the period of credit. The financial services available to the exporter can enable him to tailor a package to suit the needs of the buyer and his own need for funds.

One warning should be sounded, however. Export finance almost always relates exclusively to the financing of post-shipment credit and does not make life easier for the exporter who needs funds to expand his production in order to produce the goods for export. This kind of pre-shipment finance is only available in connection with huge capital plant contracts, where foreign buyers might be expected to agree to stage payments during manufacture.

Instruments of payment

Documentation for shipment and for payment is an area of exporting that requires careful attention. Again, it needs study with the assistance of financial experts from a bank or consultancy to ascertain the best means of payment and of raising the documents. Strangely enough, the most common form of transaction is open account exporting, just as in domestic marketing. The supplier sends an invoice and expects payment within an agreed time limit of 30, 60 or so days. The exporter must, however, be sure that the buyer is creditworthy and reliable and should carry out checks through specialist agencies and banks.

However, there are still very large numbers of export transactions that require special payment documentation, particularly on sales to the non-industrialised countries. Documentation has to cover insurance (of carriage and of credit), customs regulations, transportation requirements, and methods of payment.

It is an appalling truth that over 50 per cent of claims on insurance and over 25 per cent of documents lodged for payment with banks have errors or omissions that seriously delay handling of the transactions. These delays add to the cost of exporting and can erode profit margins, so it is essential for exporters to set up systems that ensure accuracy and expertise in producing documentation. Help is available through the banks and also through the government services that provide advice for exporters. There are specially devised 'aligned documentation systems' that ensure that once a basic document has been prepared with all the relevant data, then there are no errors in transcribing that information to the various different forms that have to be produced from it.

Letters of credit

Letters of credit (l/c's) are a common form of payment arrangement in exporting that are often misunderstood or misused. A letter of credit is a document that is signed by the importer or buyer, giving a bank instructions to pay the exporter when the exporter has performed to the terms of the sales contract. The exporter proves his performance with the presentation of documents that are enumerated in the letter of credit. They are likely to be bills of lading, certificates of origin, and so on, to show that the right kind of product has been dispatched by the agreed form of transport by the due date.

A letter of credit is given by the importer to his local bank. The bank then guarantees that the funds are available to pay on performance. This then makes the l/c an irrevocable letter of credit, as the bank has the importer's funds available to pay the exporter as soon as the right documents have been presented. The buyer cannot revoke payment provided that the exporter carries out the correct procedure.

The local bank can pass the l/c to a bank in the country of the exporter. This bank can then *confirm* that it will pay the exporter on sight of the correct documents, or within an agreed period of credit after receipt of the completed documents. This then makes the l/c a *confirmed* irrevocable letter of credit – in other words, the exporter's bank will pay even if the buyer's bank goes bust. It is a very safe way of ensuring payment according to contract, but only if the exporter's documents are in good shape. If even one tiny discrepancy arises, the banks in the middle will not be authorised to pay on behalf of the buyer and the exporter is then vulnerable – the goods may have been despatched and there is no certainty of payment.

CONCLUSION

Export marketing brings in its wake an obvious spread of complications in relation to transport, communications, pricing, credit, financing and cash collection. That is precisely why it is advisable to enter the field in a planned and gradual way, so that the international scene is opened up steadily, market by market. This gives the chance to a company's management to digest the market, exploit it effectively and iron out problems on the way. The best way to learn is to get the maximum amount of advice to avoid obvious pitfalls and then gain personal experience. Expertise can readily be accumulated.

A steady, regulated approach to export marketing does not mean an inordinately slow entry. The words 'steady and regulated' are relative. They can suggest a new market every two years to a company whose marketing cycle is lengthy, or a new territory every three months to one that has an easily shipped product with no service or back-up complications. It is still vital, however, to get pricing right, to get the right representation locally and to ensure reliable receipt of payments. No export contract is complete until payment is in the bank, providing a profit on the transaction.

The steady entry into overseas markets demands an allied development of management facilities. There are those companies that have a brisk early success but whose export performance falls off as they fail to relieve the salesman of the administration that builds up as a consequence of his very success. In-house administration and documentation facilities have to be provided, or outside services hired, to ensure that the successful export salesman is kept free of encumbrance. It is a surprising and illogical fact that the average export salesman is expected to produce a turnover about ten times greater than his home market equivalent and that he normally has less than half the back-up of the domestic salesman. Cinderella treatment eventually leads to declining success.

A salesman might be allocated the task of identifying and opening a string of new markets. Then it might be necessary to appoint area or regional salesmen to specialise in groups of markets, supporting and monitoring agents in several territories; for example, in the five markets of ASEAN, or the four agents located in the USA and Mexico, or the three or four markets of Scandinavia or possibly there might be one man supervising sales for the whole of West Europe.

The product quality, price and the reliable performance of the exporting company are vital ingredients in export success, but there is no denying the enormous impact of the personality of the export salesman, the relationships he creates with agents and buyers and his dedication to his territories. Personal relationships seem more vital to success in overseas marketing because a market is linked to the company very much more through the single contact of the regular salesman. On the home market, a buyer is exposed to a large number of contacts with a supplier. He is likely to see more salesmen, to see management more often, to read of a company in the local press, see its advertising and so on. Links between supplier and overseas market are much more restricted as a general rule, putting all the more responsibility for success on the performance of the salesman. And his performance will be influenced by the kind of support he receives from the company at home.

FURTHER READING

Branch, A.E., *The Elements of Export Practice*, Chapman and Hall, London, 1979

Day, A., *Exporting for Profit: a practical handbook for improving export sales*, Graham and Trotman, London 1976

Horten, H.E., *Export-import Correspondence in Four Languages: English, French, German and Spanish*, Gower, 1970

Livingstone, J.M., *International Marketing Management*, Macmillan, London, 1976

McMillan, C., and Paulden, S., *Export Agents: a complete guide to their selection and control*, 2nd edition, Gower, 1974

Paulden, S., *How to Deliver on Time*, Gower, 1977

20 Managing a sales force

M T Wilson

The strategy of marketing is concerned with arranging the resources of the company so that the needs of customers can be satisfied by presenting to them a product/price offering which when purchased provides a profit to the firm. This strategy is implemented through a number of tactical tools, some concerned with finding out what the needs are (marketing research), some with ensuring the product/price offering is correct (product development and testing), and some with presenting the offering to the customer. The sales function is a major tactic in this last area, while having a role to play in the first two.

The importance of the sales function cannot be overemphasised in those companies where the bulk of the presentational effort is carried by the sales force. This covers most industrial and speciality markets and many consumer goods industries. In fact, it is not exaggerating far to say that in some markets – for example, office equipment and life insurance – the main difference between competing companies lies in the quality of their sales forces.

Moreover, the sales force can make valuable contributions in the definition of market segments and customer needs, and product development and rationalisation. This is particularly true in industrial markets, where formal market research is less used. Obviously, since salesmen are not usually trained researchers, the information they collect has to be treated with care.

As sales management is a function (often the most important) within the marketing strategy, it is essential for the sales manager at least to be aware of the other tactics of marketing so that he can contribute to and benefit from them. These include:

1 New product development
2 Distribution
3 Sales forecasting
4 Pricing
5 Advertising and sales promotion

6 Public relations
7 Marketing planning and control (particularly the financial aspects).

In some companies the sales manager will directly control some of these; in others, they will be looked after by marketing staff. In every firm, the sales manager must integrate his activities with the rest of the marketing effort if the maximum value is to be gained from marketing expenditure.

The sales manager is the key man in developing a successful sales operation. He must do this by managing his team – not by doing their jobs for them. As a manager he is responsible for working through others to achieve economic objectives, but this process is hindered by the difficulties of dealing with geographically spread subordinates who spend most of their time with people other than their colleagues.

To do his job successfully, the sales manager must possess knowledge and skill in four major areas; selling, management, sales management and marketing. Only then can he claim to be a fully productive member of the executive team.

Sales management comprises five key elements – planning, organisation, training, motivation and control. It is on these that this chapter concentrates.

HOW TO PLAN THE SALES OPERATION

The planning process is only one part of the basic and repetitive management activity necessary in any company seeking to grow. The firm must continuously answer three questions:

1 Where are we going? This is the objective-setting process
2 How shall we get there? This is the planning process
3 How shall we know if we are getting there? This is the control process.

These questions first appear at top management level and the answers constitute the corporate objectives, corporate plans and policies, and corporate control mechanisms. Typically they will result in a statement of the profit objectives of the company (usually expressed in terms of return on capital employed), a description of the business the company is in and its desired position in that industry, its plans and policies for each function of the company, and specific goals and targets to be met within set time-periods.

The whole process will then be repeated for each function of the company. Thus marketing, production, R & D, finance and so on, will each formulate its objectives, plans and controls. Within the marketing framework, the sales manager must specify his answers to the three questions in order to produce a format for his staff to work to. Each salesman may well be required to repeat the process with individual customers.

The sales manager's role in the continuum is obviously critical. If he fails to set clear objectives that are compatible within the hierarchy and does not initiate the appropriate action, the whole firm must suffer.

Setting sales objectives

The sales manager will commence by considering the marketing objectives, policies and strategies and control criteria. He will probably have a forecast of sales by revenue and volume, a forecast of gross profit required, perhaps an expense budget, a description of the product range available with additions and deletions, price structure, promotional support, etc.

Forecasting sales

In many firms the sales manager will be involved as a member of the marketing team in the definition of these items. The process will normally start with forecasting sales for the next period. This is the most critical prediction in the company as it will determine the production schedule, raw materials and finished stocks, promotional expenditure, etc. It is best to approach the forecast in two stages. First, what will sales be, assuming all variables in the situation are the same in the future as they have been in the past? Second, which variables will change and what will the impact be? Some of the variables will be internal factors which management decides to change, others will be external factors which are uncontrollable by the company but whose effect must be predicted.

Developing the sales plan

Having set the sales forecast and targets, the manager must now consider how they can be achieved. Obviously some thought will already have been given to the plan in formulating the objectives. After the plan is written it might well be necessary to reconsider the goals that were previously identified.

The sales manager has to consider five basic questions:

1 What is to be sold?
2 To whom?
3 At what price?
4 By what methods?
5 At what costs?

In some of these areas, notably the product range and pricing structure, he may well have limited influence; they are often controlled by the marketing planning department, through a brand or product management structure. In respect of all five he will certainly have to consider the inputs of other parts of the business. What stocks will be available from production, what money is available from finance, what advertising and sales promotion support is planned, etc.?

Deciding what is to be sold

In determining what the product range should be the sales manager can at least advise his marketing planning colleagues on the saleability of the various items in the range as well as new product requirements.

From a sales management viewpoint he will have to decide whether the full range should be sold to everybody. In some capital equipment markets, for example, where the distributor has to make a heavy investment in stock, it may not be in the interests of the company to supply dealers whose resources may not be adequate to finance the more costly products. Likewise, companies who have to make after-sales service arrangements may well decide not to sell products to customers who are geographically isolated.

To whom are the products to be sold

Next, the sales manager must consider the customers and prospects for his products. First, he will study the existing markets and decide whether business with them is likely to increase, decrease or remain static. This judgement will be based on a study of previous buying records.

By analysing customers in terms of their potential and actual purchasing of the various products he has to offer, he can identify the areas to be attacked. Prospective customers can be analysed in the same way.

Choosing the methods

Having identified from the product/market analysis the segments to be attacked, the sales manager can now consider the methods most likely to achieve the objectives set.

The first question to be answered is – what sort of service should the sales force provide in order to influence the buyer? For example, a crop-protection firm pondering how to increase sales to agricultural merchants will have to consider how the merchant will market the product to farmers. Perhaps the job of the sales force in this case will be to help the merchant develop his skills.

Such an analysis of the kind of sales effort needed will lead to identification of the appropriate sales methods. The complexity of seller/buyer relationships becomes rapidly obvious. It is only by such definition that the sales manager can develop the presentational approach that will enable him to succeed in the face of product/price parity.

Having identified the nature of the sales method he can then consider the scale of effort required. He must calculate how many customers and prospects should be called on how often.

The customers are relatively easy to specify because obviously they are known by name to the company. The level of prospecting is more difficult to calculate, as in many companies potential customers cannot be identified by name. At least, however, the sales manager can indicate the characteristics of likely prospects. Such a profile can then be used by the sales force to select prospects to be called upon. Alternatively, the sales manager can plan simply to allow a certain percentage of time or calls for seeking new business, giving the salesmen the responsibility of using the time or calls wisely.

How often calls should be made is always difficult to assess. Obviously different categories of accounts will require different call frequencies. In some trades where there is an established buying pattern, usually little is gained by calling at a different frequency.

The support of the field force will also be covered by the sales manager's study of the methods required to achieve his objectives. Parts of the supplier/buyer relationship can often be more economically handled by techniques other than personal visiting by representatives. Telephone selling is one method that is successfully used to handle routine ordering, thus freeing the salesmen's costly time for more creative work.

Evaluating the costs of selling

The best approach is to look at the cost-effectiveness of the methods used and particularly to try to analyse the values gained for the costs incurred. For example, if the manager were concerned with the cost of generating prospects he could compare the cost per prospect from advertising, direct mail and cold canvassing. If he were analysing sales force activity, he might question what value was gained from 'courtesy calling' (i.e., routine visiting to check that the customer is satisfied with the products and service supplied). In such a case the manager might experiment by eliminating such calls in a test area and evaluating what, if anything, happened to the sales.

HOW TO ORGANISE THE SALES FORCE

Many sales organisations have developed without objective analysis of their purpose or structure. Today they are out of date and unable to fulfil the purposes for which they were originally designed. This is because the traditional hierarchical structure is based upon conditions which no longer hold true in a great number of firms. Such organisations assume that there is a large number of relatively small, geographically separate and independent buying-points all with similar requirements, and that these can be serviced by a large number of geographically separated salesmen who can perform similar tasks and who represent the major promotional activity of the company.

Changes in buyer/seller relationships

The foregoing suppositions have been made obsolete by two fundamental changes in the buyer/seller relationship.

First, the buying power in many industries is no longer evenly distributed. In a large number of markets, a few big firms control the majority of the purchasing decisions. These oligopolies, developed largely through the processes of merger and acquisition, have resulted in a dramatic reduction in the numbers of independent outlets in the trades concerned. Thus, whilst sales organisations' structures have in many cases changed little, the number and type of customers with whom they deal have altered dramatically.

Second, the development of new marketing techniques has meant that some tasks traditionally performed by the sales force can be more economically or efficiently handled by other methods. The development of advertising and sales promotion in general, as well as the growing use of specific techniques such as telephone selling and contract ordering, have all had an impact on the nature and scale of the sales effort required. Furthermore, the reduction in sales force sizes and improvements in communications have in some cases obviated the need for regionally based management.

The prime objective of all salesmen is to gain business. From an organisational point of view, however, how they are to achieve their goals must be defined in order to identify what kind and quality of skills are required.

Matching the sales effort to customer requirements

Organising the sales effort so that it matches the reality of the market-place can alleviate such problems. First, the level and quantity of customer service must be defined and the personnel concerned identified.

Such an analysis will also begin to identify the work-loads of each level and suggest ways of grouping the various elements so that they can be better managed.

The sales force structure should also be scrutinised. A geographical split may be the most economical in that travel time is minimised. It may not, however, be the most effective. In one glass-container company it was seen that the prime service to be provided to the buyer was a technical knowledge of bottling as applied to the customer's particular industry. Thus the sales force was regrouped on an industry basis, changing the organisation structure. Obviously there was some increase in travel costs because each industry group worked nationally but this was more than offset by the increase in sales.

At sales force level common groupings other than geographical are by industry, by customer size category, by buyer type (for example, purchasers and specifiers), or by service to be provided (for example, order taking and merchandising).

By conducting a customer service requirements analysis the sales manager can identify which organisational approach is appropriate.

The number of salesmen needed

The aim of building an organisation is to give the appropriate level of service to each customer and the appropriate amount of work to each man. The only factor common to all salesmen is the number of working hours and this should be the starting point for a work-load analysis, which is the only really logical way of constructing a sales force. The amount of work per salesman can then be calculated by assessing the elements and the time taken on each. Typically, they include: prospecting, travelling, waiting, selling and report-writing. If the number of actual and potential accounts to be visited and the frequency of visiting can be assessed, it is possible to calculate the number of salesmen needed as follows:

$$\frac{\text{Number of actual and potential customers} \times \text{Call frequency}}{\text{Average daily call rate} \times \text{Number of working days per year}}$$

TRAINING THE SALES TEAM

The art of selling is the presentation of product benefits in such a way that the buyer is persuaded that his needs will be satisfied. If the salesman is to be successful he must not only be knowledgeable about his product and his customer but also skilful in the presentation of this knowledge.

Induction training

When a new salesman joins a company he should be given some form of training. Too often, even when training is given, the whole time is devoted to company and product knowledge in the hope (usually unfulfilled) that the salesman will somehow pick up sales techniques in the field.

This initial training can be critical to the ultimate success of the new man as it will affect both his ability and morale. It must therefore be very carefully planned and skilfully executed.

The programme material will obviously vary from firm to firm, particularly in terms of the company and product knowledge to be taught.

There are, however, some basic areas of the sales job that should be included in most initial training courses, although with specific biases being given by different companies. Ten major elements should be covered.

1   *The marketing concept and the role of the sales force.* The salesman must understand fully the part he plays in the total effort of the company. Otherwise, he will find it difficult to integrate his work with that of other departments

2   *The nature of salesmanship.* It is essential that the salesman has a clear definition of what selling is, its role in society and the basic requirements of the sales job

3   *Communications.* As selling depends on persuasive communication, the salesman must understand the inherent difficulties of interpersonal relationships and be given techniques for overcoming these problems. He must be skilled in other forms of communication, such as reporting and talking on the telephone

4   *Preparation for selling.* This is normally a very weak area of sales skill and yet if a coherent, logical approach to the customer is to be adopted, it has to be structured in advance, and the technique for doing this has to be taught

5   *Prospecting.* Every business depends to some extent on gaining new customers. This is probably the most difficult part of selling and the salesman should be taught a systematic approach to the finding of potential buyers. Having learnt how to look for new business, he will also be better motivated and less likely to avoid prospecting, as so often happens

6   *Opening the sales.* Obtaining interviews with buyers and making the right impression in the early stages of the presentation are areas where skill is required. A casual approach will lead to failure to pass the receptionist or even when that is achieved to curtailed, unsuccessful interviews

7   *Making sales presentations.* To be effective as a persuader, the salesman must

be skilled in oral presentation, visual aid handling and product demonstration. There is a body of techniques that can be learnt which will help the salesman to communicate convincingly

8 *Handling objections.* Every sales interview is likely to produce customer objections on such topics as price, delivery, etc. Some of these can be prevented, others overcome. Certainly most objections can be predicted and the salesman trained in the answers to be given and the methods of expressing them

9 *Closing the sale.* Again, this is normally a very weak area because the salesman fears rejection. He therefore tends to avoid it by never asking for the order. If he never asks the buyer to buy, the buyer never has to refuse. Obviously the whole point of selling is to gain sales and the salesman can be encouraged to request orders more often and more persuasively by thorough training in proven closing techniques

10 *Work organisation.* The main emphasis of initial training is on improving the quality of the salesman's skill. Due regard should also be paid to the quantity of selling so that the man knows how to utilise his very limited time to the maximum. He should be taught techniques of journey planning and day planning.

Concept of customer orientation

Throughout the initial training programme certain themes will have to be constantly emphasised as some of the basic concepts are hard to instil. One of the most fundamental of these is the philosophy of customer orientation. Without this approach, the salesman will find it hard to succeed and yet it is difficult to ensure that it will be practised.

Every salesman must recognise that buyers buy to satisfy needs, both rational and emotional. These needs are fulfilled by benefits of the product and these benefits are derived from product features.

Because of the difficulty of reversing the viewpoint in this way, successful training in this concept can be hard to achieve. It is helped if a product analysis is demonstrated and this technique is inculcated so that the salesmen analyse the needs, benefits and features of a situation before they commence selling.

Field training

The objective of field training is to ensure a continuous improvement in the salesman's performance. To achieve this goal there are five tasks that must be carried out by the manager:

1 Field performance must be assessed systematically against known standards.
2 Deficiencies must be identified and agreed and coaching given in the knowledge and skills necessary to correct the identified faults.
3 Guidance must be given on the self-training that is expected from the salesman.

4   Information should be collected about common faults that can be more economically or effectively corrected on a collective basis.
5   The effectiveness of the initial training should be assessed so that it can be improved in the future.

Sales meetings

The regular gatherings of the sales team create the other major opportunity for developing sales force performance. In all but the smallest sales forces, these are held at local level, where the regional, area or district manager meets with his salesmen. Where there are no intermediate supervisory levels between the national sales manager and the sales force these gatherings have to be held on a national basis. The objectives of such meetings should be:

1   To administer corporate training and development
2   To inform and get feedback from the sales force
3   To stimulate and if necessary rekindle the salesmen's enthusiasm and motivation
4   To provide a meeting place and forum for all the salesmen.

HOW TO MOTIVATE THE SALES FORCE

The motivation of salesmen is probably the most common topic of conversation whenever sales managers meet. Every manager has his own pet theories on how to get the best out of his team. The reason why it is such a popular discussion point is because salesmen can be directly supervised only intermittently. It is therefore vital to success that they are deeply motivated to work on their own. Moreover, the sales job inevitably involves loneliness and certain customer contacts which can depress the morale of any but the most enthusiastic salesmen.

The nature of motivation

Because of the geographical separation and the wearing aspects of the job, it is vital for success that the sales manager possesses or develops the ability to motivate his men. In order to do so he needs a clear understanding of why people work and what they wish to gain from their work. Only then can he create an environment which will cause his men to apply their full abilities to their jobs.

Incentives and disincentives

The basis of motivation is the provision of incentives which encourage salesmen to give of their best and the removal of disincentives which prevent them from devoting their whole energies to their work. Unfortunately, far too often, motivation is equated with incentives only, although it is common to find that the elimination of disincentives – for example, unfair treatment – is the more powerful influence.

It must also be recognised that virtually every incentive brings with it a disincentive, either for the same person or for his colleagues. For example, a competition may be a strong motivation for the winners; but it can be demoralising for the losers, particularly if they believe that because of the poor construction of the contest they never had a real chance of winning.

The task of the manager is therefore to consider the needs of his team, both individually and as a group, and to arrange a balance of motivational influences that will encourage them to achieve the company's objectives. In essence, this is best done by ensuring that the individual's own goals in life are consistent with the aims of the firm. For example, there is little point recruiting people who are highly money-motivated into a company which offers security as its major satisfaction.

Although recognising that everyone has his own individual need pattern, there are five motivational influences that the sales manager must fully understand. These are:

1 Remuneration
2 Direct incentives
3 Job satisfaction
4 Security
5 Status.

Remuneration

First, management should define the salary grades appropriate to the job level. This grade will represent the market value of the position as well as the worth of the job to the company. The bottom of the category will represent the remuneration of a man entering the position exhibiting minimum standards of performance, the upper limit being paid to a man who can achieve completely all the criteria of the job.

Second, the position of any individual within his grade should be determined by his performance against the job standards. An average performer would therefore be paid at the mid-point of the grade. Thus, the salary philosophy will reflect the two main elements of a logical payment structure: the degree of responsibility carried by the position, and the effectiveness with which the man discharges it.

Payment by results system

Such an approach to job grading and appraisal presupposes that the salesman will be remunerated at least in part by salary. Many sales forces are of course paid in addition, to some degree or another, according to results. In a relatively small number of companies the salesmen are paid entirely on commission. The choice of remuneration system – salary only, salary plus some form of commission, or commission only – will depend upon the desired mix of security and incentive.

Direct incentives

This term is used to cover the many systems of payment in cash or in kind other than basic remuneration. It includes fringe benefits, merchandise awards, points schemes and competitions. Apart from fringe benefits, such schemes do not usually make a significant difference to total earnings and their basic intention is motivational. Merchandise awards and competitive schemes are best used to focus short-term attention on particular aspects of the business. They are a tactical rather than a strategic motivational weapon. When employed in this way, they can be very effective to concentrate sales force attention on, for example, gaining new accounts, increasing sales of lower volume products, or even submitting call reports on time!

Job satisfaction

Direct incentives in either cash or kind are important elements in any motivational scheme. The so-called 'psychic wages' of the job however must be given at least equivalent priority. Salesmen spend more than half their waking life working. It is not surprising therefore that they seek fulfilment in the job as well as rewards for the job. It is an essential function of any manager to ensure that such satisfaction can be gained by the sales force from their work.

Security

The need for security is a very common, although seldom admitted, motive. The nature of the remuneration system and the relative importance of salary and commission will obviously affect job security and must be considered from this aspect.

However, the less obvious facets of security should not escape the sales manager's attention. In companies where insecurity is a constant feature of the environment morale tends to be low and, although there is often an appearance of frenetic action, achievement is usually very limited.

Status

The sales manager can help to improve the status of selling within the company and the market by ensuring that the job titles given carry as much prestige as possible. He should ensure, too, that the rest of the company realises the importance of the function so that when a customer telephones and asks for one of the field force by name, the switchboard operator does not reply that as Mr Smith is 'only one of our salesmen (or worse still, "travellers"), he is not in the office'. Likewise when the caller is eventually put through to the sales department, he should be greeted by a girl who says she is Mr Smith's secretary. She can, of course, be 'secretary' to a number of other salesmen as well.

The salesman should be provided with the best possible equipment for his job. Well-printed visiting cards with his name in the middle, a well-made briefcase or sample case and good literature all contribute to his status in the eyes of his customers. His car is perhaps the most significant symbol of all, not only to his buyers but also to his family and friends.

HOW TO CONTROL THE SALES OPERATION

In order to control any activity, there must first be an objective and a plan. Unless it is known what is to be achieved and how, whether it is being achieved cannot be assessed. Conversely, there is little point in setting goals and defining actions unless there is an evaluation procedure.

For example, in one business equipment firm, the sales manager developed a system whereby he could analyse the monthly performance of every salesman under eighteen different categories of activity. Thus he could identify how many hours each man had spent on each facet of his job. He could ascertain for instance that salesman X spent seven and a half hours on prospecting, salesman Y eight hours on report-writing. He obviously believed that control was constituted by the collection of detailed information. Such attitudes are common among sales management and part of the impact of computerisation is that data suddenly becomes available in vast quantities, thus apparently giving even more minute control.

The concept of control

It must be realised that the collection of information, however accurate, up to date and detailed, in itself in no way constitutes control. This is for the very basic reason that there is little point in knowing what *has* happened unless there is a clear conception of what *should* have happened. Control can then be exercised by comparing actual performance with planned performance and deriving variances. It is on these variances that corrective action should be based. Control can be summarised therefore as:

$$A - S = \pm V$$

where A is the actual performance, S is the pre-set standard and V is the variance between the two.

To know that salesman X spent seven and a half hours prospecting is meaningless by itself. However, if the standard for this activity is ten hours then there is a minus variance of two and a half hours and it is this figure which should cause the manager to take corrective action. If, however, the standard were seven and a half hours, as the actual performance is equivalent to the desired standard no managerial action is required. Only by adopting such a concept can management time be economically utilised.

Setting standards of field sales performance

To identify appropriate standards for control, the manager should ask two questions:

1 What constitutes success?
2 What affects the achievement of success?

Descriptive standards

In a sales operation success can usually be defined as the achievement of the sales targets. These serve as the prime standards of control. By themselves, however, they are insufficient. The achievement or otherwise of the annual sales target constitutes a descriptive standard. It measures what has happened but it is then usually far too late to redress the balance. Moreover, it does not indicate *why* the performance has been poor.

Diagnostic standards

Diagnostic standards, which help to identify why performance is varying from target, are defined by asking the second question: 'What affects the achievement of success?'

The manager must consider in the case of a particular salesman failing to achieve target what actions by the salesman himself should lead to the goals being met. Surprisingly, there are only four and these can be identified by the following questions:

1 What kind of people does he call upon?
2 How many does he call upon?
3 How often does he call?
4 What does he do while he is there?

How to set standards

One of the aims of setting standards is to control the sales activity at an early stage to prevent failure to achieve orders. This aspect of control can be further refined by evaluating planned performance against standard before the activity takes place. In fact it is only by assessing the intended action of the sales force that the sales manager can directly prevent failure. Obviously he must check his own plans to ensure that, if achieved, they reach the desired objectives. He can go further by assessing each salesman's activity plans before they are put into action. This is normally done by the submission of weekly calling plans on which each man identifies whom he is intending to visit, for what reason and when he last saw this customer (if applicable).

Variance production and analysis

Variances are produced by comparing actual results against the pre-set standards. However, this simple method may need refining as high variances can result which reflect the forecast error of the standards. For example, if the average daily call rate is set at eight, there is probably no cause for alarm if this varies between six and ten. Because so many of the standards are produced by averaging past performance it may well be necessary to process the actual results before comparing them against standard.

When the actual results are compared with the standards, variances will become apparent. These discrepancies may need more careful analysis before corrective action is taken. For example, in one firm it was known from past experience that most of the selling depended upon seeing the senior management of the customers, which could only be done by appointment. The results of some salesmen, however, were disappointing despite the fact that the percentage of calls by appointment was well up to the pre-set standard. But when performance against other standards was examined it was noted that their call rate was below par. Thus although the appointment to total call ratio was high, this was due to a smaller number of other calls rather than to an over-achievement of appointments. Furthermore, it was discovered that as they increased their number of appointments, their overall call rates decreased markedly.

What in fact was happening was that these men, in their enthusiasm to gain appointments, had not controlled the timing of such meetings. They had placed them in the middle of the mornings and afternoons, thereby limiting their ability to make other calls. The more experienced men systematically made appointments early in the morning, immediately before lunch, immediately after lunch or late afternoon, leaving mid-morning and mid-afternoon free to make cold calls which, although not as important, resulted in enough business to make their results superior. It would have been very easy to jump to the conclusion that the disappointing results of the less experienced men were due to a lack of sales skill. It was only by careful variance analysis that the real problem of appointment timing was identified.

Taking corrective action

Having identified the true nature of the variance, the sales manager has to decide whether it results from faulty standard setting or inadequate salesman performance. If the former, the standards will have to be modified. If the latter, the performance of the man will have to be improved, usually by some form of training or instruction. If the man is to improve he must be given specific targets to achieve within specific time periods, otherwise little or no change will result.

FURTHER READING

Lidstone, J.L., *Motivating Your Sales Force*, Gower, 1978
Lidstone, J.L., *Training Salesmen on the Job*, Gower, 1975
Wilson, M.T., *Managing a Sales Force*, 2nd edition, Gower, 1983

21 Promotional public relations

David Wragg

If one ignores the jargon, public relations is concerned simply with the relation-ship between an organisation and the community as a whole. Occasionally, there is some confusion between public relations and press or media relations, which are important parts of PR, and this is because these different means of mass communications are important to the whole of public relations. A PR man can never forget the media: he has to think like a journalist when advising his employers or clients, and he has to think like a manager when dealing with the media, whether they be press, television or radio. The media are one of the main avenues for communication and it is important to realise their value in influencing attitudes or bringing a message to the notice of the greatest number of people in the shortest time.

PUBLIC RELATIONS WITHIN THE ORGANISATION

Most large organisations have their own public relations staff, and sometimes they will break the activity of the PR department down into those handling PR and those handling press relations, as the simpler and more junior task. This is seldom a wise move, not only because it tends to devalue press relations, but also because it can lead to duplication of effort, and press relations must be seen as a part of a wider picture.

Many organisations use consultants. PR consultants, unlike advertising agencies, seldom have any major item of expenditure on which their fees can be based. This is why the term 'consultant' is used, implying that payment is for their advice, while advertising agencies are agents who place advertising, although they also do other things. This is a simplification in both cases, for in the case of the public relations consultant, it implies that they do little more, when in fact most draft and distribute press material, arrange interviews and facilities for journalists, organise photography and even, sometimes, prepare brochures and mailing shots, help in the preparations for an exhibition or a conference, or produce a house newspaper for the client. Consultants are sometimes paid an agreed fee for a specific project, but normally they are appointed for a year at a time and the fee is based on the amount of executive time required, paid quarterly in advance plus the costs incurred, sometimes with special inclusive charges for such items as press releases to account for the cost of paper and postage, and for the clerical or secretarial time involved in despatch.

Hybrid consultant and in-house arrangements are quite common. Sometimes the consultancy will do the donkey work, despatching releases and so on, but it is not unknown for the in-house PR person to be relatively junior and working under the wing of an experienced consultant. More usually, the consultancy will handle a specific project or a certain area of activity. Some managements keep a consultant on a retainer, which grants them the right simply to telephone and consult; anything further is charged for as an extra. Others will use a consultant for corporate or financial relations, or to ease the pressure of work in the in-house public relations department, especially when a certain promotional task creates a short-term workload.

It is sometimes worth while employing a locally based consultant when a company moves away from its normal home base, and where local knowledge and language can be useful.

A number of companies believe that their managers ought to act as communicators, usually with guidance and co-ordination from a central PR staff. This can be an excellent approach, but only if the guidelines are understood by all concerned, and for that there must be a sound management communications programme which keeps all members of management fully in the picture. The advantages are that this system enhances the status of the local manager, giving him a broader view of his company and his industry, and also pleases the local media who would far rather deal with him than with a distant press office.

MEDIA RELATIONS

The prime rule to remember when using the media to gain attention for a company's products or services, is that the media are not working for the company, but for their own readers, viewers, listeners or subscribers. Even though a manager in a company which is a substantial advertiser may feel that he is entitled to preferential treatment, it is important to remember the ethical requirement for impartiality on the part of the journalists, and the fact that without the provision of an adequate service to readers, listeners or viewers, there could be no medium in which to advertise.

A frequent plea from many managers is that they have not received coverage in the media for a considerable period. Sometimes, this is allied to a complaint that their competitors are receiving more attention. However, the media do not allocate space on the basis of fair shares, although they would not like any one company to appear to monopolise their output. To them the main question is whether or not the story would interest the reader, listener or viewer; does the company have something worth saying? Of course, good media contact will ensure a flow of potentially useful material for the media, to the benefit of the company or organisation.

The media need news, pictures and features. Some complain that only bad news is ever printed, but this is not really true and the object of a successful promotional public relations campaign is to ensure that the good news, the new products or services, or improvements to existing products and services, appears in print or is broadcast. New products and services do receive attention, but the object of the exercise in the view of the media is not to help the producer to sell, but to advise their readers, listeners or viewers. This means that a substantial proportion of the readership has to be interested, in the view of the editorial staff, before space can be provided, and the significance of a new product, for example, has to be considerable before national or regional coverage can be provided. There are limits on both time and space, and strong competition from major national and international developments. These pressures vary, so that a story which one day might be given some prominence can, just a few days later, be given low rating and little space on an inside page. Time is most at a premium on broadcast news bulletins.

One picture remains worth a thousand words, if not more, in terms of publicity. A good picture provided by an organisation seeking to draw attention to itself or its products will be used if the subject is newsworthy enough, or if it appeals to a certain slot, such as a gardening or travel page, or is an appealing gimmick (although really good gimmicks are extremely rare). The national press has a strong preference for using the work of its own photographers or those of the major press agencies, and some object to anything which displays a company name too strongly. As a rule, the local press and specialised media are far less demanding.

Of course, one buys a newspaper, listens to the radio or even watches television for far more than just the news. All types of media seek to entertain as well as to inform, and this means that there is usually a demand for good features material as well. Features vary, from those giving the background to the news to those which entertain, including travel, motoring, gardening, hobbies, new products and womens' columns. Even when a company has nothing interesting to say, there are occasions when its products or services may find a slot on the features pages. Trade or specialised publications are sometimes anxious to find companies on whose products and management they can write a background article.

Into the news

Obtaining news coverage is a highly disciplined procedure, rather than luck or influence. A number of steps must be taken before news coverage can be expected, and ideally one should start by asking the following questions:

1 Is it newsworthy? If so, to whom?
2 Which media will be most interested? National, regional, local, special interest or trade? Are there any contacts who might be interested?
3 When should the news be released? Avoid weekends, but will it be worth while offering it to the periodicals early, so that they do not miss it because

of their longer production and distribution periods?

4   Does any statement give the salient points simply, without raising fresh questions or misunderstandings? Remember:

(a)   Never say 'announces'; the fact that it is a press statement is sufficient.

(b)   The essence of the news must be in the headline.

(c)   The first paragraph should contain the most important points, so that it can be used on its own if necessary, if the journalist should be too lazy or busy to go any further.

5   Would a photograph help, and if so which of the media would use it?

6   Is any follow-up action necessary? Are there arrangements for handling press enquiries?

One important outlet for any British company is the Central Office of Information, which will translate and release British news stories of sufficient importance to the media abroad. This can be invaluable for companies with an interest in reaching export markets, or hoping to find agents or to license overseas manufacturers to produce the goods.

Sometimes, it can help to release news stories early, protected by an *embargo* to prevent early publication. This gives journalists the time to research the story accurately and fully, and the embargo will usually be observed for fear of being denied future news. However, it might not necessarily keep the news from your competitors, who may be telephoned for comment by the media.

Onto the feature pages

Many organisations rely heavily on the features pages for public attention, whether it be gaining the interest of holidaymakers, or perhaps those interested in different types of sporting or cultural events, including the theatre, or those who might attend a county show or agricultural fair, as well as those who might look at the new products pages, the beauty and fashion pages, the books, gardening, hobbies, motoring or home interest pages of the daily and weekly press. Also of considerable importance are the specialised and technical press, helping to reach either particular segments of the market, or wholesalers and distributors and their staff, or even retailers. Good press coverage even in specialised publications can be a cost-effective alternative to additional visits from members of the sales team.

Some aspects of features work require the product or service being publicised to be relatively newsworthy. Take, for example, a new play or film that will need to be publicised while it is still new, and not after it has been running for several months. The same can be said about sporting events, which often justify news coverage pure and simple. Motoring correspondents have been known to react bitterly, and in print, to manufacturers who have offered foreign journalists an earlier opportunity of testing a new car than they themselves have enjoyed; and boating journalists have been known to take a similar attitude. Fashions must be promoted while they are still fashionable. Others tend to be relatively timeless, such as a handy gadget or compound for use in the garden, or for servicing the car, and others are seasonal, insulating material for example, which can sometimes hope for press coverage every autumn!

Holidays and holiday travel facilities can sometimes prove to be unusual in that they have to be promoted indirectly. A ferry company might only obtain the features coverage in the travel pages that is necessary if it indulges in promotion of the destination, for example, and joins with a tourist authority to do this. This is because few people travel for the sake of it. A manufacturer of home improvements products may, on the other hand, find that his best chance of features publicity arises when a journalist is writing on the subject generally, mentioning many of the products available, and so the manufacturer finds his goods mentioned along with those of competitors and those which are suitable for other jobs around the home. However, on the assumption that the reader is interested in getting on with the job, this type of publicity, even if it is merely a passing reference, can be extremely valuable.

The means of attracting the attention of features writers vary. Publishers, record manufacturers, and many others, send samples of their wares, sometimes with a covering press release, a handout article of their own, or a brochure. In many cases, photographs will be offered. A motor vehicle manufacturer will invite specialised motoring writers to sample the new cars, following this up later with the opportunity of an extended trial. This concept of testing the product tends to be essential, whether journalists do so *en masse*, so that a new product can be launched, or as individuals, so that an existing product, a holiday, a boat or a car, can be written about at some length, providing valuable follow-up publicity. Clearly, it is pointless to waste time and effort, not to mention money, on journalists who will not be interested, neither is it worth while considering those who are more interested in a free gift or a free ride, and this is where good knowledge of the requirements of the media can prove so useful.

In many cases, parties of journalists can be organised. If the product or service on show is not new, the best way to ensure coverage of a holiday destination, for example, is to keep journalists from rival publications away from the same party, allowing them some scope for exclusivity, with perhaps a typical mix including a national daily, a regional newspaper, an up-market magazine and a general woman's interest magazine, with perhaps a trade journalist. Freelance journalists can be very valuable, often writing for several outlets.

Facing the media

For many managers, facing the media is not a question of 'if' but of 'when'. Media contact should not always be regarded as a good thing. After all, what does the journalist want to know? Is a particular manager ideal, or should someone else be found? It is as well to know a little beforehand, to avoid wasting everyone's time.

Contact with the press, radio or television, apart from that over the telephone, can take the form of an interview or a press conference, with a press reception being a further possibility. One should usually leave it to the journalist to request an interview, although it can sometimes be offered. Press

343

conferences should be reserved for important developments, such as heavy capital investment programmes, significant acquisitions, or clarifying a matter of urgent general interest (perhaps if a subsidiary company has collapsed, or there has been criticism of a product). Press receptions can be useful for minor announcements and also for a more generalised 'getting to know' contact with specialised journalists, maintaining or establishing a relationship.

Many press conferences and receptions will require a speech, possibly drafted by the public relations adviser. Leaving aside the obvious recommendation that these should be 'short and sweet', it is important to provide copies of the speech for journalists, and to ask them, and a member of the PR staff, to check the speech against delivery, so that changes are noted.

In facing the media the following points should be borne in mind:

1 Interviews and telephone conversations are always liable to be quoted and attributed to the interviewee unless understood to be
  (a) *off the record* and for background briefing only, or
  (b) *non attributable*, in which case they can be quoted, but without reference to the source
2 Journalists will seldom allow their copy to be vetted, but if they do, alterations must be restricted to points of accuracy
3 No confidences, no hints! Never try to be too clever
4 Avoid using jargon
5 Never forget to provide additional information or photographs when requested
6 Always accept the journalist's deadline
7 Keep the PR adviser at the interview, partly to brief him and partly so that he can deal with any follow-up work, and of course he will be a witness if anything is subsequently misquoted
8 Particularly at conferences, it is a good idea to ask the PR adviser to draw up a list of possible questions beforehand, getting the management to prepare answers, which can be circulated within the organisation as a management briefing exercise.

Obviously, every media contact must be put to good use. While long questions are in order, long answers can be misunderstood, and even catch the interviewee himself off-guard. Too short an answer is rather rude, and misses the opportunity to expand a little.

It is easy to ensure that good black-and-white photographs are available and can be offered to the press, showing equipment, new products, even premises and staff, and all pictures have to be captioned. Background articles and illustrations, especially useful for the trade press, must be up-dated at intervals.

Always remember that if a customer or a distributor is involved in any PR effort, he must be consulted and the story cleared with his management first.

EXHIBITIONS

Exhibitions are a form of promotional public relations which offers direct contact with customers, distributors, wholesalers and retailers, as well as the benefit of media coverage in publications, and even broadcast programmes, covering the event and those taking part. The media coverage varies widely, and it is obviously best for those exhibitions with a wide appeal, such as the London Boat Show, the Ideal Home Exhibition and the National Motor Show, although even very specialised exhibitions can attract national media coverage if the subject is newsworthy and there is felt to be some novelty about the exhibits.

Whether or not an exhibition is viewed as an avenue for sales will depend on the nature of the business. Cars and boats are sold at exhibitions, aircraft seldom are. In many cases, even though orders may be timed to be announced during an exhibition, exhibitions are also offering a chance of informal contact with customers and prospective customers, developing a relationship which may ultimately lead to business, or perhaps discussing a problem with an existing customer. Ideas can be floated, and the sales staff do not have to feel that they are wasting a customer's time since the customer for his part has ventured into this particular market-place, and is obviously interested in what may be on offer.

Unfortunately, exhibitions are relatively costly, and the space occupied by the stand is but a small part of the total expense. One must add staff time, the cost of travel, subsistence and accommodation, the preparation of the stand and special sales literature. It is worth while ensuring a good position for the stand; the cost of the stand space, even if it is in a prime spot, is such a small proportion of the total cost that any saving by moving to a cheaper and less prominent position can never match the loss of opportunity. Do it properly, or not at all!

When considering participation in an exhibition, the following questions should be asked:

1 What is the aim of the exhibition? Will it reach the right customers?
2 Are the timing and the location suitable?
3 Is the layout suitable, allowing space where the organisation will want it, with an adequate flow of visitors past the stand?
4 Can sufficient staff be made available? Remember that staffing must be adequate and must allow for staff to be absent from the stand on occasion.
5 Does the company have anything worth showing? There can be times when this question might not seem so silly!

It is a fortunate man who can put a house, a lorry or a boat on his stand to fill the space and provide a focal point. However, even such a stand needs some thought as to its presentation. Good exhibition stands need not be difficult, and if planned wisely, they can be used again and again, with any illustrations suitably up-dated. It is usually a mistake to insist on a purpose-built stand; instead it is wiser to use standardised components from one of the several ranges available, and which can be adapted to different stand sizes and layouts, since these will vary from exhibition to exhibition. Ideally, the standardised components will break down easily and be reasonably light, so that they can be carried in an estate car or even a good hatchback. It should be possible to assemble or dismantle such a stand in two or three hours.

Naturally, a good stand will not be too crowded, and will have room for visitors to circulate. It should not be too bare. It should convey a message and leave visitors in no doubt as to its purpose. Some literature should be available for visitors, but it can make sense to display only a cheap general-purpose leaflet leaving the more elaborate and expensive brochures out of reach of casual visitors. If any serious discussion is to take place, there should be a secluded area with seating in which customers can relax and talk with the sales team.

DEALER COMMUNICATIONS

Sales literature and point-of-sale material will usually be provided as an extension of the work of the advertising agency and the marketing department. However, public relations techniques are frequently of assistance in maintaining and developing contact with dealers and even customers.

There is frequently a need for a newsletter, possibly monthly or bi-monthly, or even quarterly, providing up-to-the-minute information on new products, changes to existing products, management changes, alterations to distribution patterns, and so on. A flow of regular information in this way enhances the contact which dealers or customers may have with the company. Some companies elevate the enterprise above this fairly simple and direct level, and provide a newspaper or magazine for their dealers, and large industrial customers, basing this on a house newspaper format, with rather more than just the basic company and product news. One pharmaceutical manufacturer has provided a tabloid (i.e. *Daily Mirror* format) newspaper for general practitioners, including articles on hobbies, such as angling, and the problems of general practice, as well as information on new products. The newspaper format was enhanced by including advertisements, in fact the manufacturer's current advertising. This type of approach is ambitious and needs to be done well. That said, it can be as least as aceptable as many trade publications (notably those controlled circulation 'free sheets' which rely entirely on advertising for their revenue, and to a great extent on editorial copy supplied by company PR departments whose style is dreary and where the sales pitch is barely concealed). Obviously, if the major customer, dealer or retailer accepts such a publication, and even becomes accustomed to looking out for it at a certain time each month, it is doing much to improve contact and to create additional goodwill.

SPONSORSHIP

Sponsorship is one of the oldest activities of followers of the arts and of sport, and today it is one of the fastest-growing areas of publicity. The privilege of sponsorship has passed from the monarchy and the nobility, and from wealthy individuals, to the company. This is partly because of the effects of inflation and taxation but also because, for certain types of business, sponsorship is a way of furthering their publicity plans, and for some the only way. The prime example is the sponsorship of sporting events by the tobacco industry, as a way around the ban on television advertising of their products.

Sponsorship takes many forms, but can generally be considered as the funding by business of otherwise uneconomic activity. It can be sport or the arts, or it may be an entertainment or even some feat of endurance. Not only does the activity to be sponsored vary enormously, but the way in which sponsorship can be applied also varies. The only common element should be that it earns its keep for the sponsor, and is not a waste of money or time, remembering always that ill-used management time is a waste which any organisation can never recover.

The main ways in which sponsorship works are that it either publicises an organisation and its products directly, or it benefits the customers. One company might sponsor an orchestra, and in doing so will meet a proportion of their costs which it is agreed between the orchestra and the sponsor are unlikely to be covered by box office receipts. If the orchestra does better than expected, its funds benefit, but if it fails, the sponsor has safeguarded himself by limiting his support. In such a scheme with an agreed level of sponsorship, the sponsor will be able to obtain a considerable initial publicity benefit from having committed a certain sum, and will of course still expect to have either the company or one of its products credited with the sponsorship in programme and publicity material.

An alternative method would be to agree to cover the shortfall between receipts and costs, provided that seats are sold at normal rates. However, this can take on the form of an open-ended commitment, and worse, there is some reduction in the publicity benefit simply because the media love to be able to put a firm price tag on any sponsorship. On the other hand, if all goes well, costs could be much lower than anticipated. This type of sponsorship is really for the gambler, rather than for the professional manager.

A sponsor should expect the organisers of any event which is benefiting from the sponsorship to have some idea of the demand for tickets. This is important, not only because of the cost of sponsorship, but also because those tickets which are unlikely to be sold can be used by the sponsor as part of the agreement to be used as gifts to customers or agents, or even as an incentive to members of the sales staff. There is no reason why the sponsor should not ask for a certain number of tickets for every performance or match, but if attendance or audience is likely to vary, it is sound financial sense to confine this to the poorly attended events.

To some extent, sporting sponsorship is more limited. Not all sports, for example, permit the sponsor's name on players' clothing. There can also be difficulty over changing the name of a horse to one acceptable to a sponsor, but this apart, it is possible to sponsor a horse, a yacht or even a motor racing team. Alternatively, a particular event can be sponsored, for example a race, a race meeting, or perhaps a series of competitions leading eventually to a trophy and prizes offered by the sponsor. Not every sport requires the sponsor to cover all costs, but some do! Any company contemplating sponsoring sporting or artistic events would do well to seek the professional advice which is available from certain specialists.

Of course, it is also open to a company to sponsor its own brass band (which can also do much for staff morale), provide a scholarship for gifted children to continue their studies, or even award a prize for students of a relevant

347

professional body (which is reasonably inexpensive but can associate the organisation with the aims of a profession). The smallest firm can afford to take a page or two in the programme for a charity event or sponsor local people on a charity walk, gaining purely local publicity and goodwill, but which can still be of value if the business is confined to a certain area.

Which is the ideal form of sponsorship? Some cynics say that firms sponsor their chairman's favourite activity and there is some truth in this, partly because the support of the chairman is sometimes essential to overcome management opposition. Many managers are still very cynical about sponsorship, and sometimes with justification, since there have been instances of companies being misled by those whom they have sponsored. In any case, companies must be clear whether or not they are seeking publicity as a result of sponsorship, or indulging in philanthropy (although this can sometimes also show publicity benefits).

On the positive side, the chairman's involvement is sometimes beneficial because he often knows his customers, and he and they have something in common. On this basis, one insurance broker has sponsored a particular rugby football match every year because many of his clients support one or other of the two teams. An insurance company sponsored a series of cricket matches and found that, with its name displayed liberally around the pitch, market awareness of the company had risen sevenfold (the snag was that the increased awareness was among male television viewers and cricket fans!).

To be truly effective, sponsorship must be directed at an audience interested in both the event being sponsored and in the product or service provided by the sponsor. It would be silly for a fishing-rod manufacturer to sponsor motor racing, but it could make good sense for ferry operators, motor manufacturers, or oil companies, amongst others. Point-to-point racing or gymkhanas are ideal if the market lies amongst country people, possibly making sense for a tractor manufacturer. A firm sponsoring classical music performances would have a fairly up-market clientele, suitable for an insurance company or a bank for example.

Novelty in sponsorship can be a good thing, and it can be cheaper than other established forms of sponsorship, but of course the risk of failure is that much higher.

It is seldom a good idea to sponsor a beauty contest. All too often the winner receives a number of prizes but few of the sponsors receive a worthwhile mention; terms such as 'car' or 'holiday' are used, bringing little benefit to the sponsor. Prizes in charity draws can be more effective, although often the potential market which hears of these is rather limited.

The management of a potential sponsor should consider the following:

1 Do our competitors sponsor?
2 If not, then why not?
3 What interests the customer?
4 Where are the customers located?
5 Would they hear of the event, or is it likely to be broadcast?
6 What are the snags in this form of sponsorship?

7   What will the costs be – at the outside?
8   Have the budgets been properly prepared?
9   What will the organisers provide in turn? For example:
    (*a*)   mention in their publicity
    (*b*)   first refusal of advertising opportunities
    (*c*)   change of name of the event, if practicable
    (*d*)   co-operation in the sponsor's publicity, if necessary
    (*e*)   good planning and costing
    (*f*)   public appearances on behalf of the sponsor
    (*g*)   a reasonable chance of a favourable press reception to the play, etc.
    (*h*)   reliability.

The list may be daunting, and constructive scepticism is called for. However, if done well, sponsorship can produce a highly cost-effective success for the firm or its products. Since much of the funding for sponsorship comes from publicity or advertising budgets, and quite rightly, bear in mind too that the advertising agency is likely to be hostile to the idea.

The constituent parts of a public relations programme can only be effective if managed well, and if occasional opportunities for publicity are not ignored. It is this flexibility, and the ability to react quickly, which is amongst the strengths of public relations. The scope of PR activity is wide. Promotional work is but a part of the whole, with sound corporate work often doing much to enhance the image of a company and its products, with far-reaching benefits.

FURTHER READING

Bland, M., *Be Your Own PR Man*, Kogan Page, London, 1981

Jefkins, F., *Public Relations*, Macdonald & Evans, Plymouth, 1980

Lloyd, H., *Teach Yourself Public Relations*, 3rd edition, Hodder & Stoughton, Sevenoaks, 1980

Wragg, D. W., *Publicity and Customer Relations in Transport Management*, Gower, 1981

You're On Next, Kogan Page, London, 1979.

PART FOUR

RESEARCH AND DEVELOPMENT

22 Solution Engineering

Dennis Lock and Don Rushton

Consider a company which has a need to establish a new, complex machining plant. Starting from a knowledge of product design and the volume of output required, it would be usual for the company to approach at least two potential suppliers to obtain competitive proposals for providing the machinery. Except in the very simplest case, it can be taken for granted that the number of machining arrangements proposed will be at least as great as the number of bidders. At one extreme a supplier may be able to suggest a range of equipment taken from his standard catalogue, offering a solution which requires no development costs but which may have to be a compromise, not exactly tailored to manufacturing needs. At the other end of the scale is the bidder who offers to design purpose-built, fully automated equipment – very expensive in terms of initial investment but capable (theoretically) of superb performance and low manufacturing costs.

In arriving at a final solution with any potential supplier a dialogue takes place between the customer and the supplier's sales engineers. During this process the supplier has to learn the customer's problems and work with him to develop a mutually acceptable working solution. In the course of these discussions, manufacturing methods, work practices and even the design of the product itself could be changed to facilitate the establishment of an efficient manufacturing system. The supplier has to arrive at a solution which will satisfy the customer's needs for volume of output, product quality, plant life and reliability and total manufacturing cost; however, the equipment must not be *too* superior, driving its cost up beyond economic limits (there is no point in designing plant with an expected life of twenty years for a product that will become obsolete in five). The bidder who gets this balance right deserves to win the order. The whole process, from first contact to the signing of a sales contract, is known as 'solution engineering'.

Capital investment in manufacturing plant is only one example of a sales negotiation involving solution engineering. Any contract for the construction of a building, supply of a computer system or any other complex project with no obvious single solution is bound to involve lengthy discussion and development before a final solution is reached. A contractor's solution engineering capability is bound to be a major factor in his chance of winning orders against competition. Solution engineering is in any case an essential procedure for ensuring that:

1 A customer's order accurately specifies his requirements
2 The contractor's internal sales specification and manufacturing or construction plans generate the equipment or buildings which the customer *thinks* he ordered
3 The final costs to the customer and to the contractor are in line with the estimates, so that the customer is satisfied and the contractor makes an equitable profit.

THE NATURE AND SCOPE OF SOLUTION ENGINEERING

Generally speaking, the provision of a solution to any industrial problem which can be solved through investment in new plant or buildings can be regarded as solution engineering. For simplicity, the discussion in this chapter will centre upon an organisation which supplies and installs manufacturing plant. Although the arguments are based on a solution embodied in a sales proposal, it should also be recognised that a similar logical approach is involved when an engineering consultant is engaged. The difference here is that the consultant is less likely to have any vested interest in recommending a particular machine type or make.

Objectives

From the contractor's point of view the objectives of solution engineering must be to produce a scheme which satisfies the customer's requirements, results in a profitable deal and enhances the contractor's own reputation in the market place. This is a summary definition of a complex process. It is obvious that there will be many cases where these objectives simply cannot be met, and where the contractor should decline to commit his solution engineering team to a quest for a non-existent solution to an impossible problem.

Organisation and people involved

Since solution engineering takes place before a contract is signed, it is usually regarded as part of the marketing process. It therefore falls within the scope of the marketing director. It is desirable that the potential customer should only have to deal with one point of contact in the contractor's organisation from the start, in order to keep communications simple and to avoid later expensive contractual contradictions. The wise contractor will ensure that only one of his most competent, professional engineers is allowed to spearhead such an operation. Although many others may become involved, the identification of one co-ordinating individual throughout the formative stages ensures continuity. This individual, although under the control of the marketing department during solution engineering, need not be a marketing man himself. He could be one of the engineering staff. An excellent practice, when planning and workload allow, is to arrange for the person who heads the solution engineering phase to become the project manager (or project engineer) in the event of a contract being signed.

Solution engineering for any but the very smallest company will involve several departments outside the sales and marketing organisation. In order to prove a possible solution it is often necessary to set up a small team comprising engineers and designers, draughtsmen, planners, cost estimators, buyers and production management representatives. This is necessary to ensure that the eventual solution is practicable, and properly assessed for its costs and effects on company workload. At this stage the managers of all contributing departments are really committing themselves to the solution. These managers must afterwards be held responsible if work actually goes ahead. But, although many individuals may come together from a number of departments during solution engineering, the process remains a marketing function and control should be vested in the marketing manager or his senior delegate.

Just as it is sensible for the contractor to nominate one individual to act as a contact for the customer, it also makes sense for the customer to reciprocate (if he can) by appointing his own representative.

Functions necessary

Quite obviously, engineering at the highest possible professional level is necessary to arrive at the best solution, and to assure a potential customer of the expertise and credibility of the contractor. While solution engineering centres on this engineering design function, it is useful here to list some of the other functions needed to achieve a total solution.

It may be that the engineer appointed to the task is brilliant at his job, but is not a skilled communicator and has little sales ability. Such shortcomings must be recognised by the controlling marketing person, and the necessary guidance and support given to assist in face to face meetings with the customer. In other words, salesmanship (of a high order) is one of the contributing functions.

Where manufacturing forms part of the work plan, production management and production engineers may need to be consulted. In any case the production management will need to consider the effect on workload. Early discussions between production engineers and the solution engineers can often lead to discovery of cost saving methods, thus allowing a relatively low price to be given in the final quotation.

Although setting the selling price is not part of the solution engineer's job, the data which he assembles is obviously essential to the price setting process. Here, the company's estimating engineers have a vital role to play, and their estimates usually require augmenting with quotations from all subcontractors and outside suppliers of large components likely to be involved. Such requests for quotations may have to be channelled through the purchasing department.

In addition to price, the customer is also going to ask when he can expect completion of his order – the date when he can take up occupation of a new building, the date when he can first cut metal on his new machining installation, or a date when he can change over from clerical control to a proven new computerised system. Such predictions have to be made realistically. Too much optimism at the order stage may be good for winning one order, but broken delivery promises are a very good way of achieving a terrible market reputation. Delivery dates must, therefore, be estimated with care, and those responsible for day-to-day planning and workload should be consulted during the process.

Solution engineering is, then, a team effort. With the number of people needed, performing all the functions just mentioned, it is clear that solution engineering is also expensive. If an order is not obtained, substantial costs may have to be written off.

STAGES OF SOLUTION ENGINEERING

Initial screening

The first stage of solution engineering is deciding whether or not to commit expensive company resources to a customer's enquiry. Further attention to an enquiry must depend upon the likely success of any proposal. The enquiry will be rejected (politely) if such success seems remote, if the contractor does not want the business, or if it is suspected that the customer is not in earnest or is not a desirable partner for a contract. An alternative to outright rejection is to allow a limited amount of preliminary study in order to evaluate the enquiry and its possibilities, but such limited work must have clearly defined upper expenditure cut-off for obvious reasons. Screening decisions have to be made at top level and are not part of the solution engineer's responsibility. They are particularly relevant here, however, since they authorise the solution engineering process and (usually) set a limit to the amount of expenditure that can take place before a further review.

It is prudent to set up regular, formalised screening committee meetings. Such assemblies would include the marketing director, senior sales engineers involved in customer contracts, the engineering director (or his delegate) and senior representation from the manufacturing organisation. Each customer enquiry would be presented by the sales engineer responsible, and considered on its merits. If the committee decided that the enquiry showed promise, the committee would decide upon a course of action directed towards the preparation of a sales proposal. In order that the committee's decisions receive due attention, without ambiguity, it is important that an *action plan* is drawn up at this stage. Action plans list every significant stage of the solution engineering process authorised, with required completion dates alongside each item, the names of those responsible for carrying out the actions and the budget allowed. A very promising enquiry may be given a full go-ahead, while more doubtful projects would typically be given partial clearance, to be reviewed more critically as each intermediate stage is reached.

Problem definition

The first step is to learn the cusomter's requirements and define his problem. He may not even know himself where the problem lies. Solution engineering has to start, therefore, from the customer's declaration of his own long term objectives. The contractor's job then is to ensure that the objectives are sufficiently clear, and supported by quantities where necessary.

For example, if the problem is to design a new building to house a commercial organisation, the fundamental details needed are the numbers of people to be housed, standards for office accommodation according to grades of people employed, common service requirements such as conference rooms, catering, air conditioning, ventilation, lighting standards, and so on and so on. Coupled with a knowledge of communications between different departments of the customer's organisation, the solution engineers (architects and their supporters in this case) can proceed to plan the building layout and suggest construction methods.

Even in cases where the client specifies building layout and office sizes, a potential contractor's design staff must still establish many details of the customer's needs before producing a fully costed solution.

Similar complexities arise in defining solutions for manufacturing organisations. The introduction of robotics has added a new dimension to automated production systems, and this increases the possible number of solutions to some production problems. Here is a case where the solution seeker must try to establish with the customer the expected life of the production requirement. If the product is expected to continue in high volume production for a number of years, flexibility may not be necessary in the plant. If, on the other hand, the customer is uncertain about the life of his product, the use of standard machines, or of re-programmable robots, may provide the more flexible approach appropriate to this situation.

An example of the task definition sequence for a manufacturing system is shown in Figure 22.1. Such a logic diagram, prepared at the start of a project:

1 Helps the engineers to thread their way systematically through a mass of information
2 Can be discussed with the client to give him confidence that a realistic approach is to be followed
3 Highlights all essential input data about the client's existing production practices – a necessary starting point and essential as a basis for comparing potential advantages offered by new solution proposals
4 Can be used to monitor progress
5 Shows that the heart of good problem definition is the work of gathering realistic workload data
6 Maximises the opportunity of building shop experience into the problem definition and gives people in the customer's workshops the feeling that they have made a contribution.

From the morass of data collected and sifted during this phase the problem summary will be prepared. This identifies those things which a good solution must eliminate or overcome.

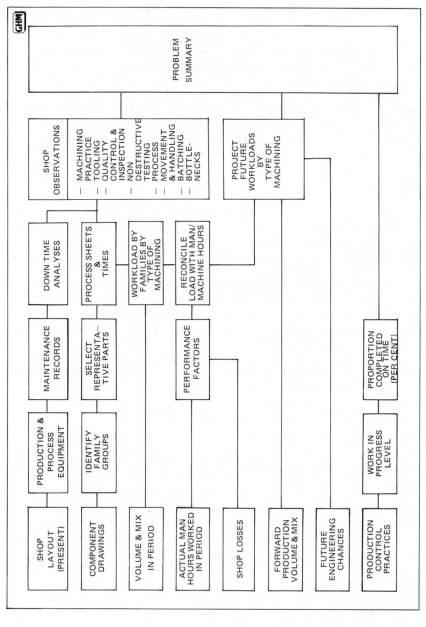

Figure 22.1   An example of problem definition sequence (for a component manufacturing system)

Problem definition review

For complex problems it is essential that the contractor reviews his problem definition with the customer. This would certainly be necessary in the manufacturing system example quoted above, when a working session would have to be organised at which key client personnel would be given a formal presentation of the facts as understood by the contractor. Review meetings of this nature carry sufficient importance to ask that priority is given to attendance, and the use of visual aids in the presentation is fully justified and recommended.

The review meeting with client's staff is, of course, far more important than a one-way presentation. Those attending will be asked to contribute any additional data or experience considered relevant, to confirm the data presented, and to point out any anomalies or areas which may have been missed. In effect, the review meeting completes and ratifies the problem definition. From this base solution engineering can proceed, and the guidelines for future work form the last item on the review meeting agenda.

Solution development

In developing the solution, the process and details cannot be generalised here because they are too dependent upon the technology involved. It is not part of the purpose of this book to instruct professional engineers in their own disciplines. However, an example (again from the manufacturing system case) is given later in this chapter.

Developing alternative solutions

As a continuation of the solution development phase, alternative schemes have to be developed and evaluated.

Review and recommendation

When the solution (or preferably two or more alternative solutions) has been arrived at and evaluated, it has to be presented to the customer for consideration. This review should take the form of a meeting with users and managers to examine the technical and the economic aspects of each proposal. Obviously the quality of presentation is important, with technical facts and financial statements properly set out in clear charts, drawings and any other appropriate visual aids. Assuming that the customer remains interested, and has not rejected the contractor already in favour of a competitor, it is from this meeting that the final technical and cost specification must emerge to be built into the formal sales proposal document.

Sales specification

Once a clear agreement has been reached with the customer on the preferred solution, a formal sales proposal is prepared. Vital among the contents of this proposal must be the *sales specification* which sets out the scope of supply, and accurately defines the technical aspects of the project. This statement crystallises all the work done during the solution engineering phases, and provides the unambiguous basis from which detailed design and production follow on. Obviously, the sales proposal contains much more information, notably the commercial and contractual terms of the proposed deal, but it is the sales specification element which is particularly concerned with the solution description.

The sales specification must define the equipment or other items to be supplied in clear terms, by reference to statements of performance and dimensions, and with adequate back-up drawings and schedules. It is usual for such specifications to undergo several revisions during discussions with the customer, and such revisions *must* be properly accounted for and documented. When any significant change is made, the specification has to be updated and reissued accordingly. Changes in the text should be highlighted by writing the revision number alongside the affected paragraph (an alternative method is to draw a set of parallel vertical lines in the margin, with the number of lines corresponding to the revision number). The correct revision numbers of all associated drawings and schedules must also be given – it is safer to avoid stating any revision numbers for such complementary documents in the text (where they could easily be missed during revisions) but to list them instead in a schedule of 'documents which are to be read with and form part of this specification'.

Subsequent stages

Remaining stages follow only if a contract is concluded. They are outside the role of solution engineering, although the original solution engineering team will have a continuing involvement in the progress. The follow-on stages are; setting up planning, work scheduling and cost control, preparation of detailed drawings and manufacturing instructions, procurement of bought-out items and materials, actual production, work on the customer's site, commissioning and final hand over.

Summary of solution engineering stages

Although the sequence given is not rigid, with overlaps and reruns to be expected, the established logic outlined above has been found to be the most rewarding in handling solution searching. The summary is:

1　*Screening* – decide whether or not to bid against a customer's enquiry and, if appropriate, produce an action plan with dates and expenditure limits
2　*Task definition* – find out, in depth, exactly what the customer's requirements are
3　*Task definition review* – go back to the customer and review the interpretation of his problems with the users and managers to ensure that the task has been correctly defined

4   *Solution development* – which involves the development of a solution, plus alternatives if possible, all of which have to be analysed and evaluated for their technical and economic merit

5   *Solution review and recommendation* – present the alternative solutions to the customer and work with his users and managers to arrive at a preferred solution

6   *Specification* – write up the solution in a detailed sales specification to ensure that the project proceeds into production and fulfilment exactly as the customer intended.

EXAMPLE OF SOLUTION ENGINEERING – 1

In this example a system for machining large automotive engine crankcases was studied. Six variations of the crankcase were to be produced, and a detailed analysis and comparison of all six designs was made to determine which features were common and those which needed special treatment.

Where a greater number of variants is to be machined, the logical approach is to classify them into 'families' based on manufacturing criteria and the commonality of design features, with a representative part being chosen for each family. Detailed study of representative parts has proved to be satisfactory for planning purposes in many projects, provided that a capability check for all parts is not omitted, covering size envelope ranges and all specific features.

Design of the manufacturing system in this example commenced with consideration of the amount of cast iron stock to be removed. Foundry and pattern making practices and problems were questioned to establish the minimum stock removal that could be anticipated repeatedly. Next the method of location and qualifying was decided, and some changes were introduced to permit automatic location to optimise metal removal before clamping for the first operation: to mill location pads used as datum for all subsequent operations.

The machining process

The major job of deciding the optimum machining sequence and selection of appropriate machine tools was a complex task. It was subdivided into three sections, by type of machining:

– flat surface
– boring
– drilling and tapping

Each of these areas was considered in turn, commencing with an understanding of the present practices adopted in the factory and the reasons for them. Special attention was paid to the causes of quality problems in each machining area. Alternative approaches and machine combinations were identified and compared, and the best available selected for each area. The logical sequence in which this project was approached is illustrated diagrammatically in Figure 22.2.

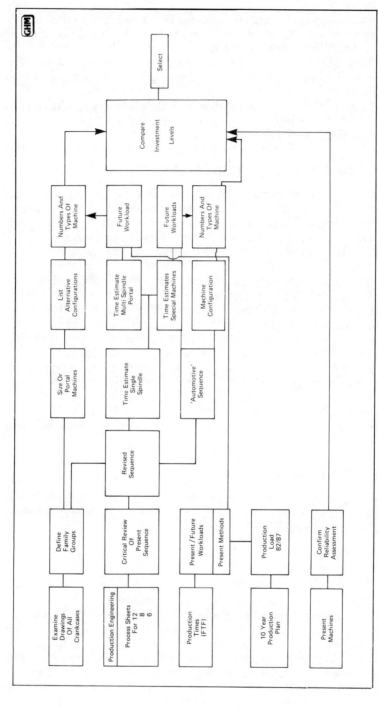

Figure 22.2 Example of a solution engineering sequence in the selection of short-term investment for the manufacture of crankcases (Ingersoll Engineers Inc)

Among factors taken into consideration were:

- The choice between general purpose and special purpose machines in each case
- The flow path for the part down the line
- Grouping of similar operations (for example, surfaces to be flat milled, common to all types of crankcases in the range)
- Part location and fixtures for holding the part during machining
- Cutting speeds and feed rates
- Response to design changes – flexibility
- The amount of operator attention required
- Accumulation of work in progress
- Capital investment needed.

The total system

From the foregoing, the best overall system was put together, involving a total of 15 machines. The next consideration was the handling and movement of this family of large crankcases. In order to obtain total control of the movement of the crankcases in the shop, a computer controlled inter-operation storage system was required with discreet identification of location of each individual crankcase, and identification within the computer of the exact state of manufacturing progress which it had reached. Further, to accommodate the imbalance between operation times within the sequence for one crankcase routing, differences between the different part numbers in the family, and at the same time to maximise utilisation of machine tools, it was concluded that a total flexible capability was required which would permit any crankcase to be routed to any machine in any desired sequence.

To meet this specification a random access inter-operation storage area was provided using pallet racking down the centre of the shop. Access to pallets was obtained by a controlled stacker for each side of the machining line (the arrangement is shown in Figure 22.3). The stacker was under computer control, and capable of delivering any specific crankcase to a required machine tool location. After machining, the crankcases could be collected and returned to store by the stacker. The solution included the provision of separate local transfer mechanisms and reorientation devices at some workstations so that the crankcases were presented into the machining positions in the correct orientation.

Solution justification

The benefits available to the customer from implementing the recommendations of the above study are best stated by comparing them with the alternative option of linear expansion using 'traditional' methods. Although some 15 per cent more initial capital investment was needed, the incremental investment was recoverable in three years. On a cash flow analysis at current costs, the break-even point would be reached in four years, compared with the seven

Figure 22.3 Crankcase handling arrangement (Ingersoll Engineers Inc)

years needed for a linear expansion.

The performance figures were substantially improved using the results of the study. Manufacturing lead times were reduced from ten weeks to only two, coupled with a 57 per cent reduction in work-in-progress. These results were obtainable for a 60 per cent increase in output, and the whole plant occupied considerably less factory floor space.

EXAMPLE OF SOLUTION ENGINEERING - 2

Planning an engine factory

In a comparative evaluation of alternative sites for a new generation engine factory, advantage was taken to maximise the benefits from recent developments:

1. It was to produce a new family of engines which had been 'rationalised' during the design phase
2. Maximum advantage had been taken of improving the 'productibility' of the components
3. Subassemblies were to be tested and 'quality approved' before reaching the assembly line
4. Only 'quality assured' parts were to be supplied to assembly
5. 'Cold testing' devices were to be included in the assembly line to ensure correctness before proceeding to the next station
6. Finally, computerised engine testing in fully automated test cells, but on relatively short cycles, would ensure correct performance before despatch, and provide a birth certificate for each engine.

These requirements together with the other relevant data about production volumes, mix, and manning policy statements, were collected into a descriptive document (the task definition). This document was reissued several times during the course of the project, additional facts being added as they became available so that all members of the team could be kept up to date.

The level of integration was the first major factor to be established. Parts requiring dedicated high-volume transfer machinery were identified for in-house manufacture (cylinder blocks, cylinder heads and connecting rods). So were other parts specific to the engine design but which could be manufactured on dedicated lines of standalone machines (gear housings, manifolds, flywheels, flywheel housings, being some of the principal items). Forgings and some other items requiring heavy capital investment were selected for purchase from appropriate vendors.

For all those parts considered as possible for in-house manufacture, machining lines were planned and detailed estimates made for the manning, space and capital requirements. 'Make or buy' decisions were made later on the basis of unit cost for each item. The best assembly sequence for the family of engines was determined from assembly logic diagrams, and maximum use of subassemblies was made. The engine test cycle and procedures stipulated by the designers were met in concepts using the latest available computer control of test cycles.

Resulting from this work, a plant layout was developed (the best being selected from several alternatives) and the area of the building determined. Specifications for building services together with the factory layout enabled preliminary capital estimates for the factory building to be made. As a forward looking plan, low energy concepts were used for the building construction.

A radical approach to manning levels was adopted. Equipment was selected to minimise the number of direct operators required to perform an operation on each engine or component before it could proceed. Indirect tasks were screened for elimination, but necessary supporting tasks were carefully defined, and manpower allocations developed so as to complete the assessment of true product unit cost.

Significant reductions were achieved against the numbers employed in traditional plants by vigorously adhering to strict planning guidelines. For example all parts were contracted to be delivered packed in a manner to be determined by the user. Strict limits were determined for the number of days of stock to be held ahead of the line, depending on whether the item was sources from UK, Europe, or transocean. Automatic counting and recording were used wherever possible to eliminate clerical work and direct links were specified between the production control computer and each operating line, thus eliminating many traditional 'office' personnel.

The planned productivity levels which this study revealed could be achieved on a practical basis represented a very significant gain over the performances currently achieved in existing plants. Also the true cost difference of operating at each of the different sites was identified, so that in the final decision-making process management was able to assess these differences against the significant commercial or political considerations favouring one or other site locations: for example, the existence of a workforce with relevant skills, the availability of grants to assist in capital investment or the need to redevelop an existing site and utilise its assets more effectively.

CONCLUSION

The two foregoing examples illustrate the benefits available to the end user after successful solution engineering carried out by a contractor or consultant. There was obviously a large element of high-level production engineering involved in achieving the benefits quoted, but this only describes a part of the total function of solution engineering. Complementing the benefits experienced by the plant user are those enjoyed by the project contractor who, as a result of the clear specification and cost estimates provided by the solution engineering team, has been able to carry out the work with clear objectives and within a well-defined and documented design and cost budget framework – vital as a basis for profitable project fulfilment.

Although manufacturing examples have been used in this chapter, proficient solution engineering is the essential forefunner of any industrial project. As technology advances and international competition grows still keener, the company with the best solution engineering capability has a head start over its competitors in the winning and profitable execution of engineering contracts.

FURTHER READING

Leech, D. J., *Management of Engineering Design,* Wiley, London, 1972

Lock, D., *Project Management*, 2nd edition, Gower, 1977

Topalian, A., *The Management of Design Projects,* Associated Business Press, London, 1979

23 Managing research and development

A W Pearson

Investment in research and development must be looked at in the same way as any other investment in the business – the benefits it produces must exceed the costs. However, it is by no means easy to ensure that the practice lines up with the theory. The available evidence from a wide range of companies suggests that the costs incurred in the R and D phase of well-managed projects can be reasonably controlled, but that the time to completion is often significantly underestimated. Problems are also frequently encountered in the implementation phase and this causes further delays. Lengthening of the timescale to completion can have adverse effects upon the benefits stream which may not only be delayed but may be significantly altered due to external influences; for example, competitive activity and changes in economic, social, political and environmental factors.

Financial planning of R and D expenditures must recognise these uncertainties, particularly with respect to longer-term work, and any monitoring or control procedure must be capable of recognising significant changes and indicating corrective action as early as possible.

In examining ways and means by which this might be done, it is useful to approach the problem from two directions: first, to consider the overall allocation of funds to R and D based on identified organisational needs, and second, to consider the planning and monitoring of individual projects. The evidence is that attention to the former has a significant influence upon the success of the latter, allowing individual initiatives to be encouraged and managed within an agreed overall framework. The two approaches are complementary and in most organisations both will be used as starting points, with links becoming apparent at a very early stage, as the next two sections aim to show.

TOP-DOWN PLANNING

In the late 1960s the word 'relevance' was frequently heard in discussions about the allocation of funds to R and D. Very simply this was meant to direct attention to the need to support R and D work which if successful would be put

369

to effective use by the organisation. In the late 1970s the phrase 'top-down planning' was used very frequently. This refers to an approach which systematically questions where the organisation is going, and examines the structure of the organisation in terms of its size, the nature of the component parts, their growth and profitability and their strengths and weaknesses in relation to competitive and other environmental forces. The purpose of this exercise is to identify where the organisation is likely to end up if it continues in the way it has done in the past, and where it may need to change in order to improve its viability in the future.

Such an analysis will usually be undertaken by individuals or groups of people who are responsible for, and knowledgeable about, a specific area of activity and will often follow organisational lines, for example, focused on products or areas of like characteristics. Within the analysis a 'technological audit' should be undertaken and this will reveal both the level and type of R and D activity which can be directly related to the support of specific areas of the organisation. Such information then forms the necessary background to detailed discussion about the relationship (or 'relevance') of the R and D expenditures to the needs of the organisation, with emphasis being placed on the longer- as well as the short-term needs.

The time orientation of the people involved in such discussions may be different, with R and D tending to look further ahead than, say, production or marketing people. This must be accepted. The purpose of top-down planning is to focus attention on the organisation needs and each function should have an opportunity to make its view clear about these needs, bearing in mind the specialist knowledge it can contribute to the discussion. Differences of opinion are best brought out into the open at this stage, and it must be accepted that there is no certainty about the future. All opinions must be listened to. Where wide differences arise more information may need to be collected, and more views canvassed. However, it may well be that such differences still persist, and in this case it may be necessary to consider the variation of views as being a good representation of the actual situation, i.e. to accept that a high level of uncertainty exists about the future. In this case a decision may have to be taken to authorise a programme of work which will cover the different views and hence allow flexibility. This will almost certainly require the allocation of more resources to the area, with a consequent reduction in the risk. If this is the accepted strategy efforts must be focused on identifying those features of the situation which can be monitored to indicate at the earliest possible time where most needs to be done.

Top-down planning is therefore a way of focusing senior management attention on the needs of the organisation. It forces people to ask questions about the relationship between the expenditures on the different functional areas and the alternative futures which the organisation may encounter. In this process the R and D people should have every opportunity to put their own views forward and to make a significant contribution in respect of, for example, potential new technologies which may be seen as threats or opportunities. A thorough discussion of all these issues will reveal areas for attention and will generate commitment to a project, by the organisation and by the project leader and the team. Such a commitment is a necessary condition for success.

It is not, however, also a sufficient condition, as many champions of 'non-successful' projects know to their disappointment. Many other factors need to be taken into account and as some of these change over time, for example legislation, it is important to have a planning and monitoring procedure which will provide useful information to all parties. Such a procedure can form an important part of the 'bottom-up' form of planning.

BOTTOM-UP PLANNING

This approach implies that individual activities or projects are the starting point for analysis. In many areas this is indeed the case. Ideas arise in a variety of ways: from discussions, casual meetings, problems, etc., and they often form the basis for a request for funds to develop the idea into a proposal backing a request for a larger allocation of resources. Requests for small amounts of funds for developing ideas should always be encouraged and seriously considered. In general such ideas will lie within areas which will be of potential relevance, simply because they will utilise the skills of people who have been recruited in line with the organisation's needs. The major cost of encouraging such requests is in fact the 'opportunity' one of not applying the same resources to other ongoing or preselected projects. However, the positive side of this is the increased motivation which can be generated by allowing some freedom for individuals to pursue their own ideas, and to convert them into projects which they can 'champion'. In most organisations the decision as to how much of this type of activity to encourage, and in which direction, is left to the R and D director, whose responsibility it is to develop and maintain an exciting and creative environment which will be a positive asset to the organisation. Many R and D directors report a lack of initiative on the part of their scientists and technologists in bringing forward new ideas, rather than any excessive demand. In some organisations this is partly due to pressure from projects of a more immediate concern to the organisation's needs, which itself can be due to lack of an adequate planning and monitoring system.

The important point about the bottom-up planning approach is that it focuses attention on the level of resources which will be required to service all the projects which have been accepted into the R and D portfolio. If these projects are to be progressed well they cannot command in total more resources than are available, at any one time. This may sound an obvious statement, but the evidence is that many organisations consistently fail to complete projects on time due to the pressure on resources. If this is the case, corrective action must be taken either to reduce the number of projects which are being progressed simultaneously, or to bring in assistance from outside agencies, for example contract research organisations. Both of these are essentially short-term measures. In the long term serious consideration needs to be given either to reducing the number of projects which are accepted into the portfolio or to increasing the level of in-house resources in particular areas subject to delays. If the first of these alternatives is chosen it will be necessary to examine carefully all the projects and to assess their relative importance to the organisation, so that any trimming down can be done in areas which are likely to have less significant effects. This can only be done after due consideration of the plans produced by the approach discussed in the previous section, and hence the top-down and bottom-up approach will come together when questions of direction and priority are raised. An important point to note is that unless this trimming down is well managed there will be a continuing scramble for resources which will lead to the not uncommon situation in which progress meetings end up as being primarily concerned with establishing priorities. The inevitable consequence is a lowering of motivation of the people involved in low-priority projects and a reduction in financial return when compared with that planned.

PLANNING AND MONITORING

The success of the approaches outlined in the previous two sections will depend upon the degree to which the performance on individual projects matches up to the expectations. The purpose of a good planning and monitoring procedure is to ensure that any differences can be quickly identified and appropriate action taken. Those which have been found to be successful in practice are designed to monitor future expectations as well as past achievements. A number of methods is available for doing this, and the choice should be made in the light of the organisation's needs, with one point being emphasised – the simplest and most flexible approach should be adopted. Many people still consider that the intro-duction of formal planning and control procedures into R and D will stifle creativity and initiative. Most attempts to impose standardised systems seem to have met with little success. It is comparatively easy for an individual or group to get around a system they do not see as useful and which takes up time they feel could be better allocated to their scientific and technical activities.

Planning and monitoring must be seen as a positive aid to the individual, the project group and the organisation. It must place emphasis on obtaining and presenting information in a form which is useful for management purposes. This leads to a variety of methods being used for the planning of individual projects, the choice depending upon the type of work and the management style of the project leader. However, there is a need for a reporting and monitoring procedure which will provide common information across the whole of an R and D establishment. These two are not incompatible, and approaches which have been found useful in practice are discussed in the following sections.

Project planning

Several methods have been described in the literature and further information can be obtained from the articles listed in the bibliography. Briefly they fall into the following categories.

The bar chart

This is probably the oldest and yet still the most used method in many R and D establishments. The chart is really a calendar planner on which individual activities are identified and the time over which they are expected to be progressed indicated by a bar. The degree to which a particular activity has been completed if often indicated by a dotted line under the main bar. The advantages of this approach are its simplicity and its visual impact. It is not, however, always easy to update it, and not so easy to show dependencies between activities. Although both these disadvantages can be overcome, more complicated projects are often planned using a form of network diagram.

The network diagram

This can take a variety of forms. Until recently the most commonly met was the simple form of PERT or activity on arrow diagram. Standard computer programs are available which allow easy presentation and analysis of such networks and also easy updating. In most cases the same programmes allow for the printing out of a standard bar chart for any section or all of the network. They also include facilities for multi-project scheduling and for resource levelling. These can be very useful. Networks of this type are most commonly encountered in larger projects of a more development type and particularly where external inputs are required, and external deadlines have to be met. They are used also where standard practices must be followed to satisfy, for example, government and legislative requirements.

Alternative forms of network diagrams are available, notably the activity on node, or activity in box method sometimes referred to as the metra potential method (MPM). As the name implies, the activities are written inside the boxes or nodes and these are linked by arrows which show the dependencies. This variation is claimed to provide more flexibility at the initial project design stage and is more closely related to the engineering flow diagrams with which many scientists and technologists are already familiar.

Arguments against the use of networks have, however, been put forward by many people who believe they are too structured and inflexible and not capable of handling the uncertainties associated with R and D projects. Some of these arguments have been countered by the further development of the methods, for example, to allow alternative outcomes to be considered at any node or activity completion point. At such points allowance can also be made for recycling by incorporating feedback loops into the diagram.

Research planning diagrams (RPDs)

A further development of the network diagram, essentially following on from the activity in box approach, specifically calls for the incorporation of decision nodes. This is a very valuable addition in an area like R and D and the approach has been generally found most useful. Another point in its favour is the similarity to the commonly accepted logic or flow diagram which is used in other areas of business activity.

The milestone chart

This is perhaps the simplest of all approaches and is generally used to provide a summary of the information which has been spelled out in more detail using one or more of the previously outlined methods. As will be seen later, it can form the basis of a very effective reporting and monitoring system. The basic characteristic of the approach is the identification of milestones, or key events, which can be readily identified in advance and recognised when they occur in time. In the case of R and D projects these may be defined in terms of, for example, technical specifications which have to be met, tests which must be completed, pilot plants built, production facilities designed, or specific market research information gathered, etc. The dates by which these activities should be completed then become the milestones. These will often be associated with specific review meetings.

The milestone chart is used in many organisations and expanded versions often include a breakdown of the activities by function or by individual, so that the responsibility for actions can be clearly identified. For this reason the name 'activity matrix' has been used to describe this form of presentation.

Monitoring

The purpose of outlining some of the approaches to planning individual projects was to illustrate the variety. As stated earlier, the preference for a particular method will depend upon the type of project, and the management style of the team leader. Any method must be seen as an aid to, and not as a substitute for, management. The project leader is responsible for planning, or agreeing the plans, and for progressing the project. However, it must be accepted that many things can change during the course of the work, and corrective action may need to be taken during the life of a project. The first person to recognise this is likely to be the project leader, and in general it is he who will be responsible for taking the necessary initiatives. The purpose of a good monitoring procedure is to record progress and to report actions which have been taken which were not originally planned and which might have consequences for the organisation. In addition it should highlight, if necessary, where actions are not being taken at the correct time.

The monitoring procedure should be essentially a communication system which adds to, but does not replace, the direct contact which is always necessary between the various parties interested in a particular project. It will almost certainly provide some historical information, but its value will be significantly increased if it also focuses attention on future expectations.

Historical analysis

Most organisations require all people involved in project work to record on a standard form information about the allocation of their time on different activities. Such forms are usually completed weekly and relate to the actual expenditure of time over the immediately preceding time period. Breakdown of time may be in half-hour intervals, half or whole days. This is converted into cost information by the use of simple factors based on the salaries of different categories of individuals with overheads being added in many cases. Sometimes the accumulated costs form the basis for direct charging to customers or departments within the organisation. In most cases they are presented so as to show the actual expenditure on the project alongside that originally agreed. Such information may be given in the form of a cumulative expenditure chart, but it is obvious that such information is of little value unless one can be clear about how much progress has actually been made on the scientific and technical work. That is why it is essential to have some form of plan, along the lines discussed earlier, set out in such a way that the actual work progress can be assessed at regular intervals against identifiable and agreed criteria.

An important point to note is that it is the exception rather than the rule for individuals to be working on only one project at any given time. If this is the case, it must be accepted that information about time, and hence cost, allocation to individual projects cannot be accurately assessed. Experience therefore suggests that although it is usually thought necessary to collect historical information on project costs it is not of very great practical use for management purposes. Clearly it can be used as an indicator of how much effort is being applied to a project, but its value is diminished if it cannot be directly related to the expected technical progress as set out in the original plan. One way of doing this is through the milestone chart. As defined earlier, a milestone is a point at which agreed and recognisable criteria have to be met. The actual cost of reaching a given milestone can therefore be compared with the original estimate and a simple chart can be used to illustrate progress (see Figure 23.1).

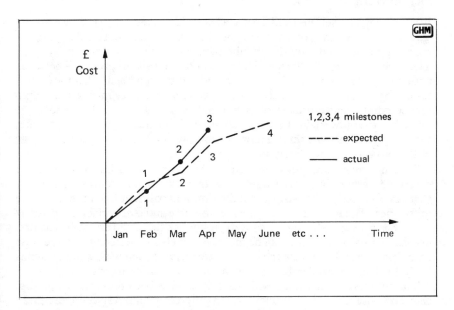

Figure 23.1   Progress illustrated by a milestone chart

This figure shows that milestone 1 was reached on time, but at lower cost, 2 on time but at higher cost, and 3 again on time, but with cost exceeding expectation. Delays in time to reach any given milestone would be shown on such a chart as movement of the numbers to the right of the vertical line through the original estimates. However, such a chart only indicates actual achievement against milestones and information about progress between these key points cannot be easily gained without a more detailed breakdown of the project into smaller activities. It is possible to do this and at the extreme every activity can be individually monitored and progress of cost and time against expectation almost continuously assessed. In this case computer analysis of network-based plan is useful, but in general the amount of information required and generated becomes too much to handle effectively, and it often leads to an anti-reaction from scientists and technologists who think too much of their time is taken up in what they see as unnecessary administration. This is particularly so in projects with a relatively high degree of uncertainty, where they feel they may require to take initiatives which were not specifically planned but which will ultimately be of advantage in steering the project to a successful conclusion. Such initiatives should be encouraged in R and D and it has been found possible to allow a reasonable degree of flexibility by staying with the broad milestone approach but calling for information about future expectations as well as accounting for past expenditures as outlined in the following section.

Progress charts

When a project is selected and a project leader identified a plan is drawn up and agreed. This plan may be based on one of the approaches outlined earlier, but the key point is that it should highlight important decision points or milestones. The number of these will depend upon the type and size of project. They need not be very close together, but they should not be so far apart that the opportunity for taking corrective action is delayed too long. They may coincide with review points, and estimates of both time and cost to reach them should be made however uncertain these may appear to be at the outset. Such estimates can be updated as more information becomes available and as such the learning of the project is more clearly indicated.

This information could be added to the simple historical analysis chart described earlier, but this would very quickly become confusing if many changes occurred in the estimates of the time and cost required to reach future milestones. An alternative is to consider the time and cost variables separately and it has proved to be most useful to emphasise the time variable in the first instance partly because this can be more accurately monitored but also because time delays usually indicate the need for corrective action which if not taken is likely to reduce considerably the financial return on a project.

The simplest of the time-based charts in use has been referred to as a 'slip' chart, because it very clearly shows when progress is slipping (see Figure 23.2).

The numbers refer to key stages or milestones in the project, and the chart acts as a historical record of how the estimates of the time required to reach a particular stage have changed as the project is progressed. In this respect it provides future-oriented information which is extremely valuable for planning purposes. Anticipated slippage is clearly shown as a movement to the right in the number associated with the milestone, and commands the attention of all interested parties. The chart therefore acts as an extremely powerful

				Calendar time				
		Jan	Feb	Mar	Apr	May	June	etc.
	Jan	1	2	3	4	5		6
	Feb	1	2	3	4	5		
Review	Mar	1	2		3	4		5
time	Apr	1	2		3	4		
	May	1	2		3			4
	Jun							
	etc.							

GHM

Figure 23.2   Example of a slip chart

communication device. The information contained in the graphical presentation can quite easily be put on to a computer. Print-outs can then be obtained as required of the progress of any individual project or of groups of projects associated, for example, with one area of activity or under a single management, or relevant to and perhaps supported by a particular client.

Other forms of presentation can also be of value. For example, progress against expectations for an individual project can be portrayed graphically (see Figure 23.3).

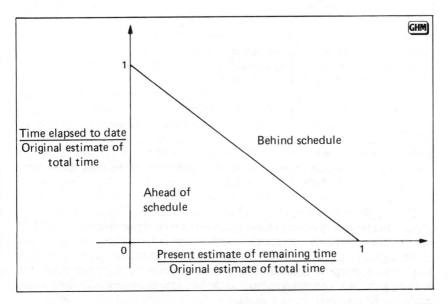

Figure 23.3   Progress against expectations for an individual project using time dimensions

A plot of the progress of a project on these two dimensions will show up deviations from plans as overruns above the line and ahead of schedule below the line. Both these methods are simple to use and are visually very easy to understand. They clearly indicate deviations from plan, not only those that have occurred, but also any that are expected in future periods. This is most important if corrective action is to be taken.

The reason for choosing time as the major variable on which to focus was discussed earlier. Overruns on time are more frequent and often much larger in many projects.

The effects of such overryns on the financial return can be very large. However, this does not mean that cost can be ignored. Historical methods of accounting were discussed earlier, and these can be extended to include future projections in a number of ways. Using the same format as one of the progress charts described earlier leads to the presentation in Figure 23.4.

Figure 23.4   Progress against expectations for an individual project using cost dimensions

An organisation may choose to emphasise time or cost reporting as its needs dictate. However, it is obvious that both can provide useful information and taken together will often provide additional information. For example, keeping time and cost progress charts side-by-side will enable slippage in either or both of these parameters to be considered at the same time. Some conclusions which might then be drawn are as follows:

1   Time overruns but not cost overruns suggest a lack of effort on the project

2 Cost overruns but not time overruns suggest problems are being encountered but extra effort is being allocated which looks like overcoming them

3 Cost overruns and time overruns suggest there are problems which are proving more difficult to handle.

These three will require different types of management action and the value of the reporting system is the simple indication which is given of the possible area for attention.

PORTFOLIO ANALYSIS

The approaches described above are essentially designed for assisting in the management of individual projects. The project leader and his team are the people who supply the information and as such are the first people to identify deviations from the plan. They are therefore able to take corrective action if this is within their terms of reference, or to suggest alternative courses of action if they require additional resources and/or support from other key people in the organisation. The value of the approaches must therefore be that they do not take away the responsibility for managing a project from those most closely concerned with its progress. Essentially what they do is recognise the uncertainty associated with research and development and encourage project leaders to provide regular position reports in the light of the progress made.

The individual planning methods focus attention on key decision points, milestones or review points. At these times the project leader will be expected to make a more detailed report on the project. Such review points will normally be agreed in advance. The progress chart, by its very nature, provides much more up-to-date information about the state of a project but without requiring this information in a detailed form. If milestones are not going to be met then the sooner this is recognised the better. In some cases this can lead to more rapid corrective action being taken; in others it may lead to an earlier decision to terminate a project which would otherwise become a cash drain with little prospect of providing an adequate financial return.

An important point about the progress chart approach is that it is clearly first and foremost an information system, with the project leader at the centre of the information network and primarily responsible for any necessary actions. It is possible to go further than this and provide some information to management on a more general basis. This can be done by presenting the information from the progress charts in an alternative form. Simple ratios can be calculated from the basic information already provided for the progress charts in a number of ways. For example:

$$\frac{1 - \dfrac{\text{Cost to date}}{\text{Original estimate of total cost}}}{\dfrac{\text{Present estimate of remaining cost}}{\text{Original estimate of total cost}}}$$

which becomes

$$\frac{\text{Original estimate of total cost} - \text{cost to date}}{\text{Present estimate of remaining cost}}$$

where

a ratio of one indicates a project on schedule for cost (but not necessarily time) and a ratio which is less than one indicates a project on which over-spending is likely.

They can be used in conjunction with other information, e.g. expenditure to date, but they must be treated with some caution. They can clearly form part of a management by exception system but here there is a danger that they will take away the main feature of the progress chart which is its value as a communication device. Management by exception systems can too easily become the tools of people who know little about either the technical side of the work or the needs of the organisation in respect of the output. Some projects may need urgent attention when only very small exceptions are reported; others can tolerate much larger variations without causing undue alarm. The people who should be most concerned are those closely concerned with the project and outside interference should only be required if they are not taking the necessary actions. The use of ratios must therefore be seen essentially as a back-up mechanism, used mostly for senior management to monitor key projects. Their value will be diminished if an attempt is made to use them as the main control mechanism.

However, it is useful to consider whether additional information of a more general nature might be obtained about the overall performance of an R and D establishment which could be put to good use. There are two particular approaches which should be given serious consideration. The first focuses on the factors which cause delays to projects and the second on the outputs from projects in relation to the expectations. Obviously these two are interrelated, but can be usefully examined separately.

Constraints on individual projects

The progress chart is built up from information supplied by the project leader. Deviations from the original plan will be due to a variety of causes. A simple request for information about the nature of factors causing delays can be very illuminating. In practice these usually fall into a few categories, for example lack of resources, external factors, technical problems.

An analysis of all the projects in the R and D establishment may also reveal a significant number of delays due to the same factor. If so, corrective action should be taken, which will reinforce the value of the planning and monitoring system, as people will see that the information they are providing is being used to their advantage. For example, if lack of resources is a common constraint then action to increase the level of resources or to reduce the number of projects will be much appreciated. It will also be of considerable motivational value to project leaders who will have to spend less of their time fighting for priority and working with inadequate support facilities. The advantage of the progress chart is that it focuses attention on any likely changes in future resource requirements on individual projects due to changes in expectations about the achievement of particular milestones. Taken over the R and D establishment as a whole this information is of great value from the resource allocation point of view.

Output assessment

At the beginning of the chapter the potential value of top-down planning was discussed. The actual value of this approach will be partly determined by the ability of the R and D establishment to complete the projects which are agreed to be relevant to the different needs of the organisation. A coding system can be developed which shows the relationship of an individual project to a particular need, e.g. business area, short or long term, product or process development, etc. Projects can then be identified readily and at appropriate intervals, say quarterly or annually; all projects related to a given need can be examined and their progress noted. This analysis may well reveal areas for concern, for example, that short-term projects are being progressed more effectively than long-term ones, etc. From the financial planning point of view, it will provide a simple breakdown of the expenditures and the progress which has been made against the expectation in each area. Deviations between these two can then be examined to see whether corrective action needs to be taken.

It must also be remembered that an R and D establishment will have activities which cover a wide range of uncertainties. The proportion of low to high probability of success projects will depend upon the needs of the organisation at a particular point in time as well as the attitudes to risk of the key decision makers. This balance must be reviewed at regular intervals and the monitoring procedure should highlight those projects in which the uncertainty is not decreasing over time at the expected rate. Again, the project leader will be the first to recognise the lack of uncertainty reduction, but this will also be highlighted through the lack of progress towards meeting defined milestones within the agreed timescales and cost. Decisions on whether to continue with such projects are not easy to make, as many major innovations have come about after sustained effort over many years with success always looking possible but always appearing to be just out of reach. In such cases the size of the potential benefits will usually be the deciding factor in obtaining further backing, but this must be balanced against the potential losses of not being successful, or of being beaten by competitive activity. There are many examples of organisations falling into difficulties through backing innovations requiring excessively large cash outflows with benefits appearing very far in the future.

CONCLUSIONS

A financial planning and control system is just as necessary in research and development as in any other area. However, it must take into account the uncertainty surrounding the activity. It must be flexible and it does not need to be complicated. It must be motivational rather than penalising and the responsibility for management has to remain at the level at which the work is being done.

There is considerable evidence that the internal evaluation of projects is very compatible with external evaluations where the goals are agreed and accepted. The aim therefore is to provide the right environment in which the project leader and his team are motivated to be honest with themselves and with the organisation in the reporting of progress. The monitoring system can then be oriented towards signalling deviations about which other people might express different concerns than those most closely connected with the work. Such signals will encourage communication and agreement on actions which will be of benefit to all interested parties. The emphasis is on the positive aspects of monitoring which are too often hidden by disagreements about the reasons for deviations and the implied blame which often leads to the adoption of defensive positions by the different parties.

Planning methods can be allowed to vary within the organisation, although there may be some advantage in agreeing the type of approach which is likely to be most suitable for different types of projects. Monitoring is more useful if there is a high degree of standardisation, so that comparative analysis can be done and attention paid to those factors which will improve the overall management of the R and D establishment.

In looking at possible approaches more emphasis is placed on forward than on historical analysis, with time being considered of prime importance. It must be remembered that the largest part of the cost of an R and D establishment is in the people, and unless significant amounts of outside work can be rapidly commissioned it is not easy to overspend significantly on the overall budget. The evidence is that many organisations fail to live up to their expectations in respect of completed projects in any given time period. It must therefore be more sensible to develop a monitoring system which focuses on outputs and the approaches outlined in the previous sections are of assistance in this respect.

The basic characteristics of the suggested approaches should be carefully examined before any new system is considered, as experience suggests that the imposition of formal planning and control systems on R and D has not met with a great deal of success. Any system which is likely to be accepted and effectively used will be one which can be seen to be helpful to all parties. In this respect a monitoring of the system itself is also necessary, so that adaptations can be made in the light of experience, to ensure that the maximum use continues to be made of the information generated.

REFERENCES AND FURTHER READING

Beastall, H., 'The relevance tree in Post Office R & D', *R & D Management*, vol. 1, no. 2, February 1971.

Bergen, S. A., 'The new product matrix', *R & D Management*, vol. 5, no. 2, February 1975.

Brooke, D. G., 'The use of slip charts to review research projects', *R & D Management*, vol. 4, no. 1, October 1973.

Davies, D. G. S., 'Research planning diagrams', *R & D Management*, vol. 1, no. 1, October 1970.

Fishlock, D., *The Business of Science*, Associated Business Programmes, London, 1975.

Hardingham, R. P., 'A simple model approach to multi-project monitoring', *R & D Management*, vol. 1, no. 1, October 1970.

Longbottom, D. A. and Hay, S. J. D., 'Experience in the use of research planning diagrams in a synthetic fibres R & D unit', *R & D Management*, vol. 7, no. 3, June 1977.

Parker, R. C. and Sabberwal, A. J. P., 'Controlling R & D projects by networks', *R & D Management*, vol. 1, no. 3, June 1971.

24 Design management

A Brearley

This chapter considers issues relevant to the design and drawing activity. It examines arrangements for investigating and analysing design and drawing office work, for improving output quality, for improving productivity and for reducing cost. The technical aspects of design are not discussed.

A very concise definition of design describes it as a creative process by which product innovations and ideas are reduced to an economically viable arrangement, this arrangement being set down on paper as a proper scheme. The concept of economic viability can be expanded to include:

1 The economic objective
2 A product to meet that objective
3 How effectively the product meets the economic objective
4 How well the product works
5 How the product can be made
6 Hence, how much the product will cost to make
7 What the product will cost to maintain.

To these can be added consideration of how the product will look, quite apart from effects on appearance resulting from the above criteria alone, without concern for attractiveness. This is the area of design commonly known as styling. Apart from the general desirability of elegance, styling is of fundamental importance in many products such as fabrics or motor cars. It is of less significance, even unimportant, in such products as aero engines.

It follows that design management involves the initiation, organisation and control of all those matters to enable effective results to be obtained. This involves design staff, a design organisation and a design process, the whole interaction taking place within design and drawing offices of various kinds.

It might seem self-evident that design does actually require to be managed. However, wide-ranging experience of investigating design matters does lead to the conclusion that in what is a creative activity there is very often a failure to appreciate the need for the process to be managed carefully and skilfully. Also common is a tendency to give inadequate attention to design costs, which in themselves then form a part of product cost. These issues are considered later in this chapter.

COMMON ISSUES

Some key issues relevant to the management of design and drawing can be summarised:

General

In all developed countries the numbers employed in design and drawing offices are high; the training periods for such employees are lengthy and the retraining needs are extensive; salaries paid are also high.

Management control

Senior management often takes the view that it has inadequate information and skills to enable it to control design and drawing office work and to bring it within a reasonable framework of sound management. This attitude does not seem to depend particularly on whether senior management is itself technically qualified and experienced or not. As a result, productivity and cost figures and controls for the drawing office are often inadequate. It is also often found even in an integrated design-to-manufacture business that the design and drawing office organisation is not readily recognised as part of the production or construction facilities of the business.

Staff attitudes

Technical staff traditionally have little interest in administration and organisation. Its members consider themselves as creative (which is obviously true to some extent) but there sometimes they take the view that since they are creative they are not suitable for normal managerial control. There is often little appreciation of the importance of improved productivity and of reduced unit costs.

These issues are important for designers and draughtsmen; they are considerably more important when the same attitudes are found among design and drawing office managers, supervisors and higher management. There is not infrequently a reluctance to accept the managerial disciplines which would be regarded as normal in other parts of a business enterprise.

Ineffective use of staff

Because of inadequate attention to management organisation and control, highly qualified design staff often spend too much of their time in work that does not involve the exercise of their particular skills. The resulting inefficiency is obvious, and will be discussed later. At the same time resentment is felt by qualified design staff at the high proportion of their time spent on tasks which they quite reasonably regard as beneath them, but which nevertheless have to be carried out.

Inadequate standardisation

It is not unusual to find insufficient attention being given to the standardisation of materials, components and finished products. The general attitude to productivity and cost within the drawing office as mentioned above encourages this and may well show itself in the design and detailing of the product. The lack of management and accounting expertise means there is often an insufficient attempt (if any) to evaluate the total cost of meeting the design requirements.

Unreliable completion and priority information

Inadequate information for calculating design completion dates means that design completion estimates may be unreliable, and the consequent extended through-put times cause expensive and damaging pressures on the provisioning and manufacturing or construction processes. At the same time drawing office priorities become subject to changes as a result of inadequate planning and (since the effects of those changes are difficult to evaluate in advance) the time given to developing ideas is frequently inadequate. Again, time pressures often result in inadequate consideration being given to alternative materials, processes and designs, and design modifications or errors result in expensive production or construction interruptions.

Inadequate definition of responsibilities

Insufficient attention to managerial control often leads to overlapping and confusion in the various departments of the business responsible for design and spceification; sales departments, product development engineers, sales engineers and others who have an influence on design do not work to clear understandings of how their influence is to be applied and how broad it is to be. When coupled with inadequate attention to the definition and limitation of the authority to create modifications to existing or to new products, the scope for expensive confusion is considerable.

TYPES OF DESIGN AND DRAWING OFFICE

There is a very wide range of design and drawing office types. Attempts to separate them into exclusive categories are of little real value. The best approach in classification is to consider where any particular design or drawing office lies between a number of possible extremes:

1 The office designing and drawing custom-built products at one extreme.
   The office designing and drawing standard products at the other extreme
2 The production detailing office with negligible design work at one extreme.

Offices where the design content is higher, usually meaning that output in terms of finished drawings is not closely related to the number of hours worked, at the other extreme

3   Offices with a very high level of creativity, usually found where the design content is high, at one extreme. Offices with a very low level of creativity, which is still possible when the design content is high, at the other extreme.

The production of designs and drawings is obviously not an end in itself. The objective is to give clear instructions to the user (in other words to the production or the construction department) on the configuration and methods of manufacture or construction of the final product. The medium for doing this will usually be some combination of drawings and written instructions but, as will be discussed later, many variations are possible.

The unit of output from a design and drawing office, however defined, will have a relationship to the amount of work carried out which will vary considerably in different types of office. In general, offices with a high design content or high creativity levels will have instruction outputs bearing a less direct relationship to the input of design and drawing effort. Offices with a lower creativity level and a greater element of detailed drawing rather than design will have much closer correlation.

As would be expected, the more creative the work the more difficult it is to supervise it, control it and measure it. Figure 24.1 shows the variability involved. In cases of higher creative levels, however, the scope for improving the value of the product and for reducing its manufacturing or construction costs through better design is greater. If the aim is to improve effectiveness, the greatest scope will lie in improving the product rather than in reducing the unit cost of creating the instructions.

Figure 24.1   Work measurement in the design and drawing process

Some attempts have been made to classify design offices in relation to the annual production or construction costs controlled by the work carried out in that office. The costs of operating a design office are often a small proportion of the costs controlled or influenced by that design office. In those circumstances when considering any programme of reorganisation or improvement we again need to give priority to improving the product rather than to improving the efficiency of the office as measured by the output of instructions related to the expenditure of design and drawing effort.

DESIGN AND DEVELOPMENT

In some industries design is an easily identifiable function, moving from a broad specification to the production of detailed drawings, whilst throughout the process striking agreements and compromises with relevant interests so that finally a product can be made or constructed. Various frameworks for the design process are considered later in this chapter.

In many fields, particularly in engineering, the additional function of development may have to be incorporated in some way into the scheme. The whole design process is an iterative one as is emphasised below. In many cases development (involving the manufacture and testing of prototypes so that the design assumptions can be tested and the results fed back into the design process) becomes a major part of that design process.

Obviously the significance of development varies greatly with the end product and the investment structure of the particular industry. A business making heavy capital equipment must give priority to getting the initial design correct because prototypes usually cannot be constructed and the cost of failure is very high indeed. In such cases the whole bias of design is naturally towards conservatism in most aspects.

Again, small mass-produced products for static applications, such as containers, components for incorporation into domestic products and similar items, do not involve development to a major extent. The initial design need not necessarily be conservative but is then likely to remain unchanged for long periods.

At another extreme, products which are of relatively low value and made in large quantities often for dynamic applications involve large investment in the production facilities. In such cases large amounts of development work are likely to be necessary and designers are probably much less conservative in techniques and materials. There is a continuous spectrum of the relative importance of development between these alternatives.

Extreme examples of high involvement of development have been mentioned by Perkins (1974) as being in the aerospace and automotive industries. Both cases involve complex assemblies of parts, each part rigorously developed and tested; the whole assembly is then further developed and tested in programmes intended to evaluate the interaction of each part's performance with overall performance. In these industries it is not possible accurately to quantify the parameters affecting performance of either the individual components or the completed assembly. Emphasising the importance of development as an integral part of the design process is the only feasible solution.

The actual organisation of the design function will obviously vary to take these differences into account and this question is considered later.

CREATIVITY IN DESIGN

Clearly design is a creative process although the depth and sophistication of the creative element varies greatly in different industries and with different products. The actual periods of creative activity are often comparatively short and are overshadowed by longer periods of calculation, technical administration and drawing.

Figure 24.2 shows a broad view of the scope for creative inputs as the design process proceeds. This shows a factor which is of considerable importance, namely, that the greatest scope for creative inputs is in the earlier stages of the design. It can also be seen that, since the cost of making important changes in

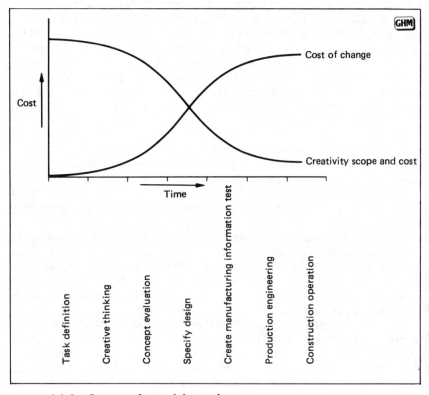

Figure 24.2   Curves of creativity and cost

design increases as the process proceeds, it is highly desirable to ensure that as far as possible a major creative effort is encouraged in the earlier stages (though obviously not excluded from any stage).

There are a number of conceptual frameworks which encourage creative thinking. Most of these are well summarised in Twiss (1974). This chapter is not the place to set them out in detail; all stem from the distinction between analytical or convergent methods (in which we move towards an answer by logical deduction from known facts) and creative or divergent methods (in which we stimulate imagination in situations where the facts do not encourage or permit logical deduction and a range of possible answers can be created). There appear to be many barriers to creative thinking imposed by conformity, by lack of willingness to challenge obvious conclusions, by self-imposed idea limitations, by a belief in one 'best' answer or by a reluctance to be thought a fool for introducing ideas which look improbable.

Among techniques for assisting creativity the following should be considered:

Analytical techniques

Attribute analysis (Twiss, 1980); morphological analysis (Twiss, 1980); and needs research (Haines, 1968).

Non-analytical techniques

Brainstorming (Rickard, 1973; De Bono, 1969); synectics (Gordon, 1961); and lateral thinking (De Bono, 1969 and 1971).

DESIGN FRAMEWORKS

The first and crucial point to make about any design framework is that design is an iterative process; it does not occur in a simple sequential manner. There is constant feedback of information and adjustment of objectives and concepts throughout the process.

The second point is that design is also a hierarchical process. If we take a motor car as an example, the entire design is at the highest level of the hierarchy. The task is then composed of a range of divisions and subdivisions, with the design taks being progressively delegated down the design structure as the scale of each task decreases. At each level there is scope for all the functions in a design scheme including creativity. There is, however, in addition a continuous and iterative exchange between the various levels if success is to be achieved.

The third point is that the design process very largely decides not only the effectiveness of the end product but also its cost. The National Economic Development Office (London, 1974) calculated that in mechanical engineering 80 per cent of the cost of a product may be determined in the design office and that it is the organisation and quality of design which produces cost-effective results quite apart from those revolutionary design advances which are sometimes possible.

There are considerable organisational problems involved. Also there is a real risk that a product is designed as a set of components with much less interaction than is desirable. These points are mentioned again later.

Many writers have discussed the processes involved in design, an interesting early example being Marples (1960), a later one Allen (1965). It is useful to set out a simple conceptual framework for the design process. This enables us to clarify our minds about that process whilst reminding ourselves of the risk to oversimplification and of the obvious need to avoid any simple framework becoming dogmatic. One suitable framework is as follows:

Definition of the task

It is first necessary to set out the task in specific and qualitative terms. A specification is needed in a form which will describe both the functions to be carried out and the performance tolerances. A suitable specification provides a guide to continued design activity and enables us to judge both the final design and the various ideas raised as the design progresses.

Application of creative thinking

It now becomes necessary to formulate a concept which may meet the defined task, and it is now that we draw on the designer's experience and knowledge. The creative process can also be helped by group discussion and a conscious use of various aids to creativity mentioned later in this chapter. A range of possible concepts will probably emerge, all of them ill-defined in the early stages. As the process advances and the definition improves it should be possible to arrive at one or more primary concepts to meet the specification.

Evaluation of the concept

In formulating the concept clearly it is neither possible nor desirable to eliminate an informal evaluation of it as the idea develops nor would we wish to. It can, however, be inhibiting if that evaluation is carried too far at the earlier stage. It is now that the concept or range of concepts should be considered, evaluating them by later quantitative analysis and by qualitative judgement. It should then be possible to arrive at an evaluated concept which seems likely best to satisfy requirements. The specification of the solution is then largely complete.

Specification of the solution

The solution can now be more formally specified, although possibly still retaining one or more alternatives. Clearly, if a single choice is not made, the cost in time and resources of the next stages will be greatly increased.

Creation of the manufacturing information

Detailed manufacturing information is now created following detailed design work. This information can be in a range of forms, written instructions, detailed drawings, sketches, photographs, physical models and others. By this stage the investment in time and resources is very considerable.

Building of prototypes and testing

This stage may not always exist, particularly in the case of large capital projects. More typically it does exist and the implications of it for the relationship between design and development have already been mentioned. It is at this stage that the iterative nature of the process becomes particularly clear.

Development of production methods

Detailed production or construction methods can be defined; the implications and problems are outlined later in this chapter.

Production, building and operation

The obvious last stage in the process but still very much part of the iterative scheme. Aircraft and motor cars are clear cases where this part of the scheme frequently results in considerable feedback. This is also true in many large capital projects such as process plant.

Figure 24.2 showed an approximate picture of the curve of cost of design changes as the work proceeds. This is also referred to later in considering the role and timing of creative inputs.

SYSTEMISED DESIGN

A number of design methods have been developed in an attempt to ensure that design is approached in a systematic and logical way so as to make certain that vital issues are not missed. Most of these involve systematically asking a series of questions. Obviously there is a risk that designers will give the stock answer to schemes of this kind in many areas of management, namely, that they already do all that but without the paperwork. It is also obvious that asking questions of itself creates nothing unless answers of depth, breadth and originality are forthcoming.

No system should ever be allowed to become a rigid, dogmatic structure. Systemised approaches must, therefore, be approached with caution. The particular approaches mentioned are themselves subject to change and the three examples are given so that the use of systems of this kind, suitably amended for specific circumstances, can be considered.

Fundamental design method

Fundamental design method (FDM) was developed by Matchett. The method is devised to increase the designer's awareness of his thought process. It is really an application of method study thinking to design, intended to ensure that the

393

designer analyses problems in a controlled and disciplined way.

Problem analysis by logical approach (PABLA)

Problem analysis by logical approach (PABLA) was developed by the United Kingdom Atomic Energy Authority (UKAEA), Aldermaston, for design work involving new processes and unfamiliar environmental conditions. The approach can be regarded as an extension of FDM. A set of charts covering four main areas of design are shown below.

Chart 1: operational and environmental aspects

This chart (Figure 24.3) is used as a first step. It provides a storage space for the factors affecting a job; the limitations, the resources, operational requirements, experience, etc., are all recorded.

The titles on each box are in effect labels on pigeon holes in which information can be filed; however, the titles are also intended as questions to ensure that all factors are considered. These titles are interpreted in their widest possible meaning. For example, 'Test and install' means how do we move the job from A to B, who does it, will it go through the doors, will we need specialised labour, is the lift big enough, who will test it, to what specification, before or after installation, do we need test equipment, test points on the job and can we test it?

Operational and environmental aspects		GHM
Usage	**Influences**	**Existing resources**
Occasion 1	Environment 2	Previous designs 3
Duration 4	Safety 5	Existing equipment 6
Frequency 7	Policies 8	Services available 9
Sequence 10	Test and install 11	Experience 12
Operators 13	Time scale 14	15
Maintenance 16	Finance 17	18
Personnel acceptability 19	Manufacture 20	

Figure 24.3 Pabla chart 1: operational and environmental aspects

And so on. The titles are used as a prompt for systematic scanning over a broad area rather than as a question requiring a single answer.

This chart then is a word picture of the whole environment of the job; any conceivable factor that can influence a decision is shown. It is axiomatic that, unless all the parameters have been determined, it is unlikely that a correct decision will be made.

Chart 2: engineering design specification

On this chart (Figure 24.4) the true objective of the problem is defined, together with the performance expected of the solution. The assumptions made in determining the objective are also listed.

Engineering design specification			GHM
Objective	Performance	Assumptions	This specification to be read in conjunction with chart nos.
			Effect on environment
			Limitations

Figure 24.4 Pabla chart 2: engineering and design specification

Chart 3: principles of systems

The primary thinking about possible solutions is recorded on this chart, which is shown in Figure 24.5 and is used as follows:

All possible means of meeting the objective are listed in the first column; no attention must be paid to whether they are practical or not – this can come later. It is essential at this stage to cast off inhibition and just to put down anything that could do the job. The aim should be to get a long list of ideas, no matter how practical or otherwise. These ideas should only be rough ones. If 'layout' type ideas come to mind one is thinking in too much detail.

Expand the ideas to cover the ground needed before they can become usable. First, is the theory of this idea known? If not, why not? What are the practical problems in using this idea? Is it an unusual size, etc.?

It is a quicker process to expand the ideas into theory and practice as a first

395

step. Then check with charts 1 and 2 to see what it is that stops them being used. This can be noted in the 'Conflicts with' column. Having eliminated some of the ideas the remainder can be expanded further and eventually either only one will be left or the different problems associated with a number of solutions will be exposed. The choice of the best line of attack can then be made.

Principles of systems											
Methods of fulfilling requirement	conflicts with	Considerations									
		Theoretical	conflicts with	Practical	conflicts with	Size and material	conflicts with	Production aspects incl. manufacture test, install, transportation	conflicts with	Probable cost, research needed	conflicts with

Figure 24.5   Pabla chart 3: principles of systems

Chart 4: requirements of system features

Chart 4 is shown as Figure 24.6. Having selected our proposed design we break

Requirements of system features									
Feature									
Function and method of functioning									
Characteristics	Decided								
	Undecided								
Decision by	Customer								
	Project engineer								
	Design engineer								
Source of supply	Stores								
	Purchase								
	Design								
	Existing								

Figure 24.6   Pabla chart 4: requirements of system features

down the complex system into discrete units and note the performance required for each one, the feature we know, the questions needed to be answered and, more important still, who has to answer them. This is an essential part of the process for only by considering the constituent units side by side can one see their effect on each other. Each feature is listed at the top of the column whilst beneath it is a short description of its function and method of functioning. Beneath that again is shown what is known it has to do, whilst further down is shown the unknown areas concerning this item. This enables anyone reading the chart to see what is needed before the design can be completed.

Information flow

The information flow system for the PABLA method is summarised in Figure 24.7.

Integrated component approach

Middleton and Martin (1974 and 1975) describe an approach intended to ensure that the interaction of various components in a design assembly is carefully considered using a suitable mathematical model.

The approach starts from the assumption that, in many design situations, after consideration of the design effort required the work is then frequently divided among several people or groups, each with separate design responsibility. As a result, it is suggested, many products are designed as sets of independent components with each designer or group tending to proceed with little reference to the design effects of that work in other areas of the design. In the result, although the design of each component may be optimised, the final product may be less than adequate.

This approach to design is sometimes assumed to be the only practicable way to proceed if the design is to be completed in a reasonable time. Arguably, however, it leads to the rapid production of information and manufacturing instructions without necessarily resulting in the design of the most suitable product.

A procedure developed by Middleton and Martin includes the systematic examination of component interactions. Design begins with an examination of the requirements and constraints of the whole system and development of qualitative information on the static and dynamic interaction between components. A model of the system – mathematical, analogue or scale model – is then developed with concentration on a mathematical model as being quickest and cheapest. The construction of this theoretical model involves identification of all the basic physical phenomena controlling the behaviour of the product. Analysis of the model is devised to relate to the real thing, and wherever possible the behaviour of the model is checked against the known behaviour of an existing system before design starts.

The accuracy of the correlations may well depend on the assumptions made to simplify analysis, and in applying the results to a particular problem it is

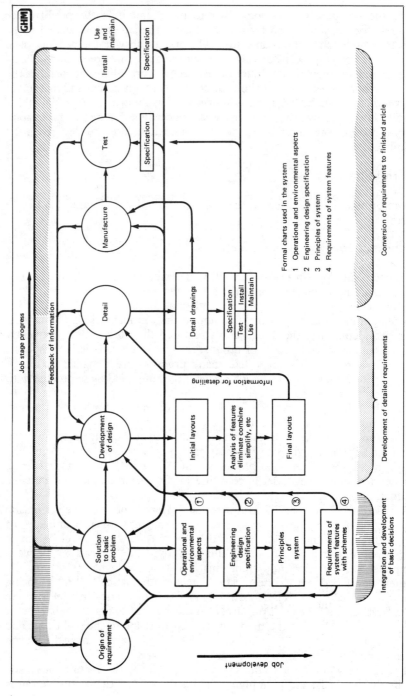

Figure 24.7   Pabla information flow chart

often necessary to change both the model and the assumptions as the design proceeds. The model is first examined with its operating parameters set for nominal values, thus providing an indication of behaviour under normal running conditions. It is then advisable to move away from the design values so that a complete range of conditions is examined. The calculations frequently justify the use of a computer although in simpler cases a tabular method is used. Middleton and Martin give an example of the successful design of a mass-produced hand-drill using this system; outline drawings of the tool and two of the design models are given as Figure 24.8.

DESIGN FOR PRODUCTION

As shown in Figure 24.2 the cost penalty of design changes rapidly increases as the stages in the design process evolve. At the stage of detailed drawing preparation and transmission to the production or construction department the cost of changes is very high. It is essential that by this stage the problems of production or construction and the limitations of the production and construction processes have been fed back into the design chain.

This is often done in a haphazard way, relying on the informal production or construction knowledge of designers or on a hurried examination of the drawings by a production or construction planning department before issue. It is preferable to ensure that an organised approach to the feedback of this information is devised either by suitable administrative procedures or by organisational arrangements – possibly including consideration by joint teams of designers with production and construction people. This is crucial in applications where product economies may justify expensive rearrangements to overcome the present limitations of the production or construction techniques and facilities.

There seems little doubt that the interaction of the techniques of value engineering (VE) and value analysis (VA) with all their associated disciplines can be of great value in such matters. These techniques are briefly described in Gage (1967 and 1970) and Miles (1961).

THE COMPUTER IN DESIGN

This chapter is not the place to examine in any great detail the use of the computer in design. It is necessary only to set the scene and to comment on the effects of the computer on the design function. Cooley gave a good concise guide to the computer in design as matters stood in 1972 and particularly emphasised the effects on staff.

Until recently the computer was used only for very complex calculations, mainly in the larger companies. Now it is common to find computer terminals and mini- or micro-computers in design and drawing offices. This results from the development of time sharing and multi-programming systems in recent years and from the later development of mini- and micro-computers.

The extent of computer use varies enormously with the sophistication of the

Figure 24.8 Integrated component design: (a) proposed power tool; (b) power balance model; (c) cooling air conditions; (d) section

particular design process, and there are many design areas in which the computer is never likely to play a major part. The computer's main advantages are the reliable performance of functions which need large data storage, rapid retrieval and an ability to make computations and logical decisions at very high speed. Clearly the computer can only do this if the sequence can be predetermined in great detail.

On the other hand, the design engineer brings to his problems a large, ill-defined store of knowledge about his environment, about the world in general, about his own design situation and about his personal experience of products, events and relationships. He can form qualitative judgements, and only he can introduce the innovative and creative elements into the design situation. He is also capable of making intuitive judgements at various stages of the design at which inadequate information is available, then of checking and possibly of changing those judgements at later stages.

The problem throughout is to use the design engineer for the work which only he can do but also to give him the appropriate computer-based facilities to enable there to be a continuous interaction between the designer and the computer throughout all the iterations of the design process. there are thus at present two broad areas where computers are used in design.

Computing and analysis

Hand calculators are now available in increasingly sophisticated versions at comparatively modest prices and are of course widely used. Design calculations however, range from simple arithmetic up to highly sophisticated multi-factor problems, and it is at the more sophisticated level that computers have increased their use in recent years.

The manipulation of large quantities of data and the solution of equations are tasks frequently given to the computer. Also the more difficult tasks of analysis, when the design concept is sufficiently developed to enable a conceptual model to be constructed, can often be performed and the limited example given by Middleton and Martin (1974) points to the sort of work involved although a very wide range of more complicated examples exists. Many programmes have been developed in the high-technology industries, such as the aerospace and automotive industries, and also in structural applications.

Computer graphics

The application of computer graphics began with the offline transmission of graphic information to the computer, and a wide range of equipment is available for this purpose. The arrangements have particular value in the preparation of drawings in a range of scales and projections and sometimes for the direct preparation of manufacturing templates. In some systems the computer can interact with the designer to prepare three dimensional mock-ups while the designer relates other factors. In the container industry designs have been used to prepare and optimise material and structural requirements.

Later developments sometimes described as 'active' computer graphics allow the design to input directly to the video display unit or to a 'graphics pad'. These facilities allow rapid design changes and have reduced the complexity of the machine interface considerably. One application of such a system using a microcomputer allows civil engineers to calculate areas or volumes of various alternative designs on an immediate and interactive basis.

Again the applications are still mainly restricted to the more sophisticated industries. The important point is that a stage has now been reached where active graphics systems can finally provide the design engineer with the capability he needs. There is communication in the designer's natural medium; there is the facility for continuous interaction between the designer and the machine; and the designer can work at his own pace with the machine carrying out the time-consuming analyses, whilst maintaining a continuous record of the current stage of the design. The machine can also be used to integrate various sections of a design, to display the result and to convert internally stored designs to copies when needed.

In recent years there has been further rapid development of computer-aided design. As at 1981 there were 290 manufacturers of computer graphics and CAD products in the world, 220 of them having UK bases or a UK presence. All these are scheduled and analysed in Computer Graphics CAD and CAD/CAM Product Guide and Suppliers' Directory 1981.

The UK Department of Industry's Computer Aided Design Centre has played a leading role in the development of computer-aided design techniques and facilities. The work of the CADCENTRE is well illustrated in three papers; Davies and Clarke (1979); Simkins (1980) and Gibbs (1980). These describe three separate projects in the use of computers in design.

ORGANISATION OF DESIGN AND DRAWING

Organisation patterns

There is a very wide range of alternatives in the organisation of companies and hence of the position of the drawing office within the company. There is also a wide range of variation in the internal organisation of drawing offices. In those circumstances any attempt to specify the 'best' type of organisation in particular circumstances will inevitably fail. What is important is to familiarise oneself with the objectives and plans of the business and with the organisational patterns used in various businesses, so that the appropriate pattern for the particular circumstances can be kept under constant review.

Wearne (1973) gives an excellent survey of the principles of engineering organisation which should be read when considering the present pattern in any business and the possibility of changes to that pattern. In any one business at any one time it is necessary to take a clear view of the most appropriate patterns of organisation for the time being and the various possibilities are briefly examined below.

Company structure

Company structure and the relative importance of the design and drawing office functions vary greatly between industries and between organisations of differing capital and cost structures. Wearne (1970–71) gives a number of specific examples from manufacturing, consulting engineering and contracting and capital project promotion; there are many others.

Also to be considered are the various broad categories for the grouping of people in business. The general structure of design decisions was discussed earlier and the structure adopted has significant implications for the grouping of people in the business as a whole. There are a number of broad alternatives and the choice will depend on the decision structure adopted. Among the possible choices are the following:

Grouping by phase

In this system people are grouped according to the phases of the project, one group carrying out feasibility studies, the next group doing overall design of each project and so on.

Grouping by experience levels

In this grouping the authority to make decisions is formulated in a hierarchy based on the experience and technological ability of the people concerned. This method has clear affinities with grouping by phase.

Grouping by functional subject

In this system people are grouped by technological specialism such as electrical, fluid flow, etc., or by component type specialism.

Grouping by project

In this system the teams needed for one particular project are grouped together. This is obviously used in 'one time' organisations, but can be used in organisations carrying out projects of various sizes and complexity at different times.

Matrix organisation

A final interesting variant is the matrix organisation in which the various responsibilities and alternatives, both project and specialist, are combined in a matrix permitting wide variability. In the formal sense this type of organisation is very rare. In the informal sense, however, almost any organisation, however structured, takes on some limited aspects of the matrix system. This should particularly be borne in mind when considering changes in the organisation. The apparent formal organisation may in fact operate rather differently than appears and it is possible that the matrix element of the organisation, even though it is not obvious, is making a major contribution to its actual operation.

IMPORTANT ORGANISATIONAL FACTORS

A number of general points can be made.

Geography

The organisation pattern decided will be used to settle the geographical dispersion of the people concerned. That is inevitable but immediately raises problems of communication and problems of rigidity.

Definition

Even though an organisation may frequently change, it is of importance that the position of the drawing office in the organisation is defined in writing if reasonable managerial control is to be effective. The relationship with other functions, with customers and in particular with the manufacturing or construction function requires clear definition. The responsibility and authority for giving executive instructions, such as firm commitments to purchase materials and components and to manufacture, needs clear definition.

Drawing office management

Equally important is a clear definition of the responsibility and authority of drawing office management. It is frequently necessary to clarify the drawing office managers' responsibility for managing the drawing office in its full sense as opposed to the technical supervision of the office. Surprisingly, it is still often found that drawing office management is reluctant to accept full responsibility for matters other than technical areas; in particular the responsibility for employee relations and for meeting completion and cost targets will need definition. If the executive in charge of the drawing office is not already called the drawing office manager a change to that title may well be effective in emphasising the role.

Integral organisation

The remarks made above about the organisation also apply to the internal organisation of the drawing office. The range of possible groupings by phase, by experience level, by function or by project are all relevant and possible methods of organisation. Again almost any system will in practice have some of the characteristics of a matrix.

In the small drawing office the drawing office manager will himself deal with the pre-drawing problems and will issue work to the individual draughtsmen; he will supervise the details and will note the progress of the work. This organisation is necessarily modifed when the drawing office is larger and more complex. When the drawing office is larger a number of changes are possible, among these are the following:

Section heads

Section heads may be appointed. These are responsible for a specific part of the work of the office divided on functional, experience level or component lines and they act as subordinate managers directly responsible to the drawing office manager. They should preferably supervise administration and discipline in their sections as well as technical matters. This not only relieves the drawing office manager of a sizeable load but also ensures that section heads do not stand aside when administration and disciplinary problems are at issue. Their duties should be defined in writing.

Separate drawing offices

In the larger company separate drawing offices may be set up for different aspects of the work. Each drawing office then has its own manager and subordinate section heads. The basis for separation may be any of the variants mentioned above for a geographically integrated drawing office. This approach is sound but, as the work load on different offices may be difficult to balance, a procedure for easy transfer of staff is vital.

Contract engineers

Contract engineers may also be appointed. Their main job is usually to deal with customer liaison on technical matters and to relieve the drawing office manager and section heads of this work. They will be of senior status, usually senior to section heads. Contract engineering is a functional responsibility and does not normally affect the line management relationship between the drawing office manager and section heads. The presence of a number of contract engineers, each calling on the same resources, emphasises the need for a proper loading, planning and progressing procedure within the drawing office.

Project engineers or leaders

Project engineers or leaders may be appointed for the duration of projects. This type of arrangement may be formalised as a matrix organisation as already discussed. Project teams can encourage efficient use of manpower by good communications within the groups and by breaking down the sometimes artificial boundaries. It should be remembered that externally imposed delays may leave a project team under-employed unless it has a reservoir of other work or can readily transfer men to other teams.

Production methods engineers

In the NEDO Report (1974) the view was expressed that 80 per cent of product costs in engineering can be determined in the design and drawing office. If this is accepted then clearly the infusion of detailed knowledge of production engineering methods into the drawing office is vital. It is not necessary to repeat the points already made about the VA and VE techniques. The point here is that production methods engineers are often appointed as members of the drawing office staff to provide the necessary knowledge.

Work control

The question of production control within the drawing office is discussed later. The type of work control methods clearly affects organisation and vice versa. Figure 24.9 shows a conventional drawing office organisation with the section heads holding responsibility for parts of the organisation split in one of the ways mentioned earlier. The various subsections or individual staff members may be combined in one of the various ways mentioned above. Any section head may have subordinates of one functional specialism or in a combination suitable to the organisation actually in being.

There is an obvious problem with this organisation as it stands. The only managerial link between the various section heads is the drawing office manager himself. In practice this problem can be overcome in a variety of informal ways. It may, however, be very desirable particularly in the more complex drawing office to introduce some form of central planning unit reporting to the drawing office manager with responsibility for planning, scheduling, controlling and progressing the work throughout the office. This arrangement can be used to introduce a greater flexibility in the arrangement of capacity or it can simply be used for the routine functions with an additional responsibility for drawing attention to areas and periods when work loads are, or will be, out of balance.

Feiner (1969) gives an example of two methods of organisation used to introduce maximum flexibility and these are illustrated in Figure 24.9. Figure 24.10 shows the change in work distribution seen as a result of introducing this method of operation into a sample group of drawing office situations, although the sample is not necessarily a fully representative one.

Checking work for errors

It is often still the custom for all drawing and calculations to be checked by a draughtsman other than the one originating the work. This procedure can be wasteful and inefficient; the extra work involved can amount to between 20 and 30 per cent. Even if the checker spends as long on the job as the originating draughtsman he can miss unfamiliar details. Checking by another draughtsman can induce a slacker attitude in the originating draughtsman, and the final effect is a reduced sense of responsibility for his own work. The section head and the drawing office manager should both feel a responsibility for work quality and style; although they cannot check all details, they should make an overall inspection; checking by another draughtsman tends to reduce their sense of responsibility also. A random check can sometimes be used if necessary but even this is open to doubt.

Any errors or omissions on drawings will usually be quickly discovered in the manufacturing or construction function. Reporting them immediately should

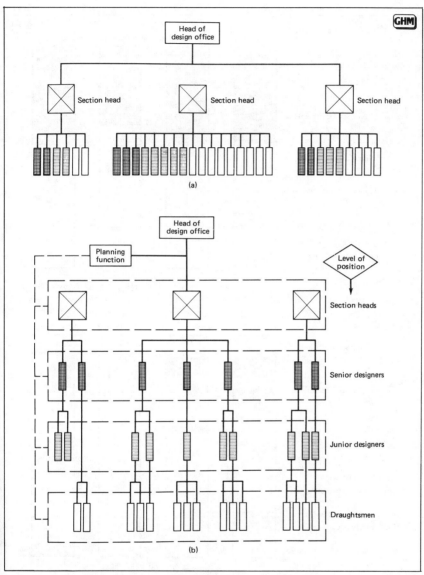

Figure 24.9   Organisation patterns: (a) organisation chart for conventional design office; (b) organisation with planning function

be encouraged and immediate action should be taken to correct them. Obvious exceptions to this philosophy on checking are design areas where safety is of crucial importance and where errors are unlikely to be discovered until it is too late or too expensive; for example, the stress calculations in civil engineering structures.

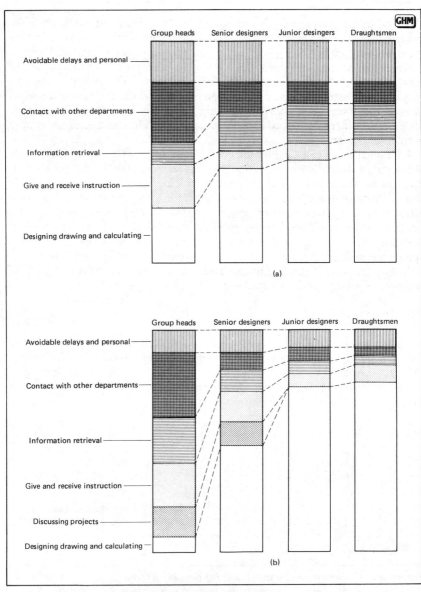

Figure 24.10 *Design drawing office work distribution (a) work distribution in a conventional engineering design office; (b) work distribution in an engineering design office with planning function*

Other functions

Drawing office productivity is a crucial issue. In industry generally since the industrial revolution, massive productivity increases have been achieved with a considerable contribution made by the concept of division of labour. There is, however, an obvious dilemma which has been discussed since that industrial revolution began. If the division of labour is increased, efficiency increases but very often job satisfaction and motivation decrease. If the decrease in job satisfaction and motivation goes far enough, there may be a drop in efficiency offsetting the increases hoped for from the division. The question of motivation is thus fundamental.

In drawing offices, where the staff are intelligent professional people although at widely differing levels of education and skills, the problem of division of labour is particularly important. No simple rules are possible. It should be particularly borne in mind when considering the division of drawing office work that job satisfaction and motivation are very easily impaired, particularly where the work has a significant creative element. It is very often desirable to avoid the elimination of some of the activities which may apparently reduce productivity but which may be vital to job satisfaction. The following groups of work often carried out in drawing offices should be considered with these issues in mind.

Development

In the larger companies (as already discussed) development may be a separate function but in smaller companies it will often be mixed with design and drawing. If the design and drawing office organisation includes project teams or has a matrix structure, it will be possible to treat a development project in much the same way as any other project.

Sales estimating

Sales estimating is not generally regarded as drawing office work but in many companies will be found there. The attitudes required by a sales estimator are different from those required by a draghtsman. The estimator should be more ready to approximate, and commercial acumen is required in addition to technical knowledge. If this work is done in the drawing office it is desirable to have specialist staff doing it. In many cases there is also scope for improving the mechanics of estimating; better synthetics, multiple regression using commonly recurring parameters in the types of work undertaken, improved data retrieval and other methods are all often appropriate.

Specifications

Specifications other than initial design specifications may be written for sales purposes or for use in other departments. It is possible in large companies for this work to be done by specially trained staff. Writing specifications is difficult; they require economical language but will often be based by people with less technical knowledge than the writer, and technical staff frequently do not have an adequate command of the appropriate skills.

Parts lists

Parts lists vary from simple lists of parts referred to on drawings up to lengthy descriptions of parts listed. They are frequently contained on drawings but are best prepared as separate documents. It is often desirable to have a parts list prepared by a different number of staff from the one originating the relevant drawing, as this ensures adequate checks, and results in better detailed lists. Parts explosions are sometimes produced by computer.

Parts lists should be recorded and filed in a similar way to drawings and they require cross-reference to the drawings involved.

Materials lists

In some offices materials lists may be more important than parts lists, and the same considerations apply.

External relations

The following are among the important external relations of the drawing office.

Relations with manufacturing or construction

It is necessary to clarify in writing the channels of communication with production or construction departments on such matters as drawing errors and proposed shop-floor modifications. The relationship between the drawing office work control function and the overall production control function of the business must be defined – usually involving close co-ordination. Already mentioned are the effects of VA and VE techniques on relations with manufacturing or construction departments and the possible appointment of production methods engineers which also affects the relationship.

Relations with customers

There should be clear definition of the aspects of customer relations to be dealt with by the drawing office manager, contract engineers, project engineers, section heads and draughtsmen, respectively. If contract engineers are employed it is often preferable for most of these contacts to be made by them and, if so, possible overlap with sales functions must be carefully controlled.

Relations with other business functions

The important issue again is a clear definition of the channels and of where authority and responsibility lies in the matters dealt with by those channels.

Technical information service

Any drawing office, however small, should maintain a library of essential publications and technical information, and in large companies a fully comprehensive library service may be desirable. A sound working relationship may also be established with the local lending and reference library; the free assistance thus available is considerable. Contact is best maintained by one person, who can acquire familiarity with sources and avoid individual draughtsmen wasting time. Collecting technical information is a specialist job.

Standard practice

The main code of practice for drawing offices in the UK is BS 308 (British Standards Institution, 1972). This will be found useful in standardising actual drawing methods. Even where offices have already standardised on this specification, however, the fact will sometimes not have been stated in writing, and individual draughtsmen may be deviating from it. This can result in dificulty in reading drawings, in customers being given a bad impression and in wide variations in work content for similar drawings made by different draughtsmen. The question of functional draughting is discussed later and, as will be seen, company standards for drawings may permit a far greater degree of simpliciation than indicated in BS 308. For general standards reference there should be an up-to-date copy of the *BSI Yearbook*.

Since standard practices are of crucial importance to the usefulness of drawings and to the efficiency with which they are produced it is necessary for the responsibility for issuing and maintaining the standard practices approved for use in the company to be very clearly defined. A comprehensive schedule of the standards to be used is essential and a system for disseminating the information thoroughly is needed.

WORK SCHEDULING AND OFFICE CONTROL

The design and drawing office as a production department

In an organisation of any size and complexity the design and drawing office is itself a major production department. In some cases the drawing office can be of such size and complexity that the work scheduling and control problems are as difficult and important as the production control problems of many factories.

It seems clear that four basic steps are involved in achieving effective control in any managerial situation:

1 Plan what should be achieved
2 Record at regular intervals what is being achieved
3 Compare actual achievement with planned achievement
4 Take action to correct any deviation from the plan.

It is also possible to see each of these steps in four distinct but interdependent aspects of control, namely, work scheduling, managerial control, manpower budgeting and supervision or work control. These are considered below.

411

Time estimates

Without some form of time estimates satisfactory control is not possible. Even in the least sophisticated systems some estimates are made, even though they may be informal and not set down in writing at all. For methods of work measurement and time estimating in offices see Brearley (1975 and 1975). In this chapter it is assumed that some form of time estimates are created for use in the control system.

If the design and creative content of the work is low, the problem is fairly simple and output figures for satisfactory control can readily be defined. If the design content is high, a varying number of solutions to each design problem may have to be tried and evaluated before an acceptable solution is found and then suitable control measures are more difficult to define. Possible control parameters are numbers and values of products for which design solutions are found; alternatively the estimated value increase or cost reduction between the various alternative solutions and the one finally adopted. Always a key control is the conformance with scheduled delivery dates for drawings and designs.

Even so it is essential to have time estimates prepared in advance for the work content of designs and drawings to be used for planning forward loads, for setting clear control targets and for advanced pricing for tenders where necessary.

When making time estimates the following points should be borne in mind:

1 *Validity* – care must be taken to avoid unknowingly including time spent on extraneous activities when accepting staff time recording as a basis for analysis. This requires a good knowledge of the work.
2 *Improvement* – the target times for planning will not remain static, but will reduce as methods, skill and experience are improved (often referred to as the 'learning curve' effect).
3 *Adjustment* – time targets set for planning will be continually adjusted as made necessary by changes in organisation and methods.

Unless these points are acted upon the time estimates will become fixed, so that over a period a distorting (and possibly slackening) effect on efficiency will result.

Work scheduling

A scheduling system is necessary in the drawing office for a wide range of reasons:

1 Providing accurate completion dates for projects
2 Providing accurate completion dates for drawings for parts of projects as work proceeds, so as to give targets for staff motivation
3 Providing sound sequencing of parts or projects so that external require-ments such as materials orders can be dealt with
4 Providing a means of checking in advance the need to change the capacity of the drawing office or of a part of the project

5   Providing a means of balancing load against capacity in order to achieve acceptable delivery times at economic target levels.

The broad needs of such a scheduling system are as follows:

1   *Information provision.* A system for collating the results of all preliminary information such as initial investigations, feasbility studies and overall design parameters
2   *Forward load.* A medium- to long-term forward load picture which shows the forward load and indicates the smoothing necessary to maintain adequate control, and the extention of load shedding to other sources of help if that is appropriate
3   *Work planning.* A system of planning the work in the shorter term, allowing for the work alrady in progress and waiting to start, and then balanced to the total capacity available or planned. If the drawing office is closely linked to production or construction facilities where major unpredicted changes of plan may be created, then this system will need to be very flexible. This short-term plan is also a major factor in productivity and cost control and these aspects are dealt with later in the chapter
4   *Work issue.* A system intended to ensure that the requirements of the work schedule are communicated in adequate detail to the management and staff responsible for doing the work and to ensure that acceptance of that work is clear
5   *Progress.* A system to check the progress of all work in the drawing office, revealing delays and potential delays so that information can readily be obtained to ensure corrections to the arrangements. This also enables information on any really unavoidable delays to be fed back into the forward load and work planning systems.

Work scheduling techniques

A wide range of techniques at various levels of sophistication are available for carrying out this work. The most likely techniques are as follows, the likely usage depending on the complexity and character of the work.

1   Project critical path networks, possibly scheduled by computer
2   Load simulation using mathematical techniques
3   Aggregation of loads within control periods for a range of projects, possibly by computer
4   Job sequencing to groups or to individuals, probably by the use of visual bar charts in one form or another.

Managerial control

Managerial control is necessary to fulfil two objectives.

First, it provides a system of access by senior management in the drawing office and outside it to the scheduling systems mentioned earlier so that decisions on changes in priorities, acceptance of urgent demands and the possible build-up of drawing office delivery problems can be made with adequate information to hand. It also provides rapid access to accurate progress information on particular projects and gives summary information on such matters as achievement of the programme and of delivery promises.

Second, it provides senior management in the drawing office and outside it with information enabling them to take a broader, long-term view and to set budgets for the main features of the drawing office activity, such as staffing levels, productivity and cost. It also provides management with a means of comparing actual results with budgeted results so that action can be taken to maintain high levels of productivity and the lowerst possible levels of drawing office cost.

The object of any management control system is to provide each manager with key information on the activities under his control in a clear quantified way, thus promoting action by management. It needs to be prompt, frequent, directly relevant, sufficiently accurate, and stimulating in that it contrasts actual results with standard results in a clear manner. All this information can only be available if some form of measurement has been applied as discussed earlier. The information necessary for management control is discussed in Brearley (1975).

Manpower budgeting

The importance of medium-term manpower budgets, in other words determining the staff requirements to deal with the required workload – has already been mentioned. This process can sometimes be carried out for a twelve-month period, although sometimes a shorter period is necessary. In considering the calculation of staff levels on the basis of the future twelve months (whilst remembering the possibility of other periods being more suitable) appropriate stages in the procedure are as follows:

1 Determine the workload for the next twelve months
2 Calculate the effective staff requirement
3 Modify the staff figures to make provision for holidays and other absences
4 Review the figures to see whether fluctuations in staff requirements can be levelled
5 Consider the effect of short-term work cycles.

Determination of workload

Clearly in a reasonably stable situation the workload can be based on figures for the previous twelve months amended for any expected changes over the next twelve months. There will be some stability in the drawing office situation, overlaid with information from forward visualisation. The required workload in units of output is reached by multiplying the work unit value by the number of output units. Work unit values would be in the time units of any of the various work measurement systems. Where the mix of work changes very little, this calculation may be speeded by choosing the predominant unit and by calculating an equivalent time for the remaining units. The workload is calculated for each month or accounting period and the workloads then tabulated by months or by accounting periods.

Determination of effective staff requirements

Effective staff requirements can be defined as the equivalent number of full-time staff working a complete week. The requirement for the forecast volume is determined by two factors: the length of the working week allowing for meal breaks, and the expected performance of staff taking into account their motivation and the type of work they perform.

In the absence of direct monetary incentives, but with good control procedures it is reasonable to expect performances around 70 per cent effective use of time, though a judgement is necessary for each office. In this way the effective staff requirement can readily be calculated and again tabulated by month or by accounting period.

Holidays and other absence

The effective staff figure makes no allowance for time lost through holidays and absence and therefore needs to be adjusted. A suitable procedure is to determine the percentage incidence of holidays and sickness from an analysis of past records; these figures should then be adjusted to allow for management policy, such as any changes in holiday entitlement or the retirement or dismissal of those frequently absent through illness. This adjusted percentage must then be converted to the equivalent number of staff lost. Finally, the total staff required is calculated by the addition of the effective staff required and the effective staff lost through holidays and sickness.

Levelling staff requirements

Staff requirements often show variations from month to month. To achieve optimum manpower usage some means of dealing with these variations is necessary. Possible solutions are as follows:

1 *Change the work flow pattern* by changing requirements which can be shown to be the cause of peak work loads. Examine the possibility of adjusting the seasonal characteristics of the work if such characteristics exist
2 *Employ temporary staff.* If peak requirements are essentially seasonal this is often a solution. It is, however, one which is overused and uncontrolled in many businesses and is not welcomed by drawing office staff
3 *Transfer staff internally* or combine departments. A system of easy temporary transfers can be set up. In some cases compatible departments can be combined, making the interchange of staff easier and enabling peaks and troughs to be balanced.

Short-term levelling

A procedure of the kind already mentioned allows for monthly fluctuations throughout the year. It is also necessary to consider fluctuations in workload over much shorter periods and to answer the fundamental question of what work delay is acceptable; in many cases a preplanned reasonable work delay can be tolerated and, if so, work patterns should take this into account.

Where requirements exist for dealing with peaks as they occur, possible solutions are borrowing staff from other sections, employing part-time staff and using controlled overtime. Clearly a considerable degree of extra-staff flexibility will be essential and this can present a major training problem for staff and also for managers in setting up adequate control systems.

WORK SUPERVISION OR CONTROL

By work supervision or control is meant close day-to-day control of the work of a group or section by the supervisor. The manager immediately supervising design and drawing office staff is the key figure in improving and maintaining the performance of the section. Depending on adequate time estimates or work measurement standards for control, work supervision is essentially day-to-day and hour-to-hour control; the objectives are to increase productivity by eliminating non-productive time, and to improve service by reducing work backlogs and delays. The fundamental aspects of work control needed to meet these objectives are clear:

1　Determine the time required to complete each job
2　Schedule the work to staff in manageable units, so as to maintain an even work flow
3　Maintain records from which the supervisor can see the work in progress and take action to reduce delays
4　Report results especially exceptions to management at suitable regular intervals.

These fundamentals can only be fully achieved if realistic work standards are available to the supervisor. The standards can then be presented to supervisors so that they are both easy to understand and quick and effective to use. The precise manner in which results are presented to supervisors will vary considerably but would normally be either tables or work values or variable manning tables. Detailed methods are summarised in Brearley (1975).

IMPROVING DRAWING OFFICE PERFORMANCE

There is clear evidence of considerable scope for improvement in design and drawing office performance. Such improvements can be classified broadly into three areas:

1　*Improved output quality* – improving the end result of the instructions. In other words improving the design of the product functionally or in its cheapness of production.

2 *Changing the output* – changing the balance of instructions to more effective means by reconsidering the proportion of drawings, sketches, written instructions, photographs or models.
3 *Improving productivity* – increasing the output of instructions from the drawing office for every unit of design and drawing input effort.

As in productivity investigations in most other areas of management the balance between these three aspects needs to be very carefully considered. It would clearly be pointless to concentrate on internal productivity improvements in a drawing office if those improvements were to be gained at the expense of a deterioration in the effectiveness of the output instructions produced.

A recommended comprehensive scheme for investigating and improving the operation of design and drawing offices is set out in Brearley (1975). This chapter is not the place for a detailed treatment of the subject, but some aspects are dealt with below.

Change of output

The output can be changed in the following way:

1 Reduce unnecessarily high grade drawing. (The concept of functional draughting is outlined below in this context.)
2 Increase the use of sketches and written instructions using the simple cost information which is often made available as a result of measurement and control to decide which methods are in fact the most effective.

Functional draughting

A particular important potential area of change is that of functional or simplified draughting. The objective of producing a drawing is to communicate information; this information is intended to depict the shape and to give details of dimensions and tolerances. The first approach to functional draughting is to consider whether the information is being communicated in the best way. In many cases it is found that much of the information can be communicated by technical notes or sketches, and detailed drawings either are unnecessary or can be produced for only part of the communication need.

It is not necessary to summarise the detailed procedures examining drawing specification; these are summarised in Brearley (1975). Reference to Figure 24.11 shows the type of simplification possible even in an unsophisticated example. It is immediately clear from this figure the enormous scope that is found in most drawing and design offices for the simplification of drawings. The important point to be made in this chapter is that early realisation of the possibilities before the investigation gets under way will greatly simplify the evaluation of those possibilities at this stage.

Figure 24.11   Functional draughting results

Improving drawing office productivity

Drawing office costs can be reduced, and the effectiveness of the output instructions increased by:

1   Increasing the output from each draughtsman by drawing simplification
2   Possibly, increasing the output effort made by draughtsmen
3   Eliminating delays and the inefficient use of time
4   Using effective work scheduling with realistic dates; but avoiding being over ambitious in raising productivity so that schedule dates become too optimistic

5 Saving office space and creating functional layouts for optimum super-vision and communications
6 Increasing productivity through improved general office and working conditions (e.g., lighting)
7 Reducing the incidence of drawing mistakes, therefore reducing time needed to make corrections – and reducing the risk of production scrap later
8 Encouraging the application of VA and VE techniques
9 Providing for better liaison between drawing office and production departments, and to customers where appropriate, so as to provide a good service on technical queries and attendance to complaints
9 Improving supervision and management control.

Improvement of management control

The following measures contribute to more effective management of the drawing office:

1 Clarifying the position of the drawing office within the company management structure and reducing any confusion of objectives
2 Improving administrative procedures within the drawing office and en-suring that these are compatible with procedures in the remainder of the organisation
3 Providing internal productivity information which can form a basis for establishing drawing office performance standards
4 Providing overall control information on drawing office performance for use by management
5 If necessary, reducing the difficulties of recruitment and staff training.

Improvement of morale and employee relations

This improvement can be achieved in the following manner:

1 General working conditions and equipment must be adequate, and should be improved if necessary
2 Costing and control information can be used as a foundation for the payment of adequate and sensibly graded salaries
3 A more equitable work distribution can be created
4 Improved control information can provide management with additional opportunity for assessing drawing office managers, supervisors and other staff. This information can frequently be used for formal management and staff appraisal, and it can sometimes be used as part of an improved salary review procedure
5 The availability of better information for setting detailed objectives and for providing better means for controlling and motivating staff can, if properly used, contribute to the development of managers, supervisors and other staff

6   Obviously no internal improvement can counteract external effects on workload, a decrease in which could lead to redundancies. It should, however, be possible to reduce the risk of redundancies by the use of sound manpower planning and workload balancing techniques.

Use of time: increasing productivity

Many consultants and executives carrying out productivity investigations emphasise that their programmes do not involve staff in 'working harder'. This contention is rather difficult to sustain and the thinking behind the comment requires further investigation. In most cases it is found that the major proportion of any productivity increase in the drawing office does not come from increased effort in the work study sense – i.e., it does not come from individuals achieving higher ratings whilst actually working. The improvement comes in the main from a significant reduction in delay time of all kinds. The survey of possible productivity gains given later shows this. A particularly important issue is to ensure that studies are capable of isolating delay time of all kinds so that the amount can possibly later be reduced by sensible control and motivation.

Of even greater significance is that in discussions with staff during all the consultation and participation processes of any reorganisation work it is specious and undesirable to talk about staff not being asked to 'work harder'. It is vastly better to put all the relevant issues to the staff concerned and, if the end result desired is a reduction in delay time and ineffective time, then this should be openly discussed to see if active co-operation is possible, which it frequently will be.

The scale of possible performance improvements

It is possible to evaluate improvements under any of the foregoing headings in financial terms, although it is obvious that this must sometimes be extremely difficult. There is a considerable body of evidence that the general effectiveness of white collar workers in offices without adequate control is around 50 per cent. This figure is well substantiated by reference to a wide range of design and drawing office reorganisation studies; substantial improvements in productivity are clearly obtainable theoretically.

Improvements in direct productivity vary considerably, as might be expected. The sort of average figures found to be available are set out below, with the average figure for overall increase in output for a draughtsman being 35 per cent.

Reductions in actual drawing work after the application of functional draughting techniques average 30 per cent, ranging from 10 to 80 per cent. Allowing that, before any improvement, the average effectiveness was 50 per cent, then this 30 per cent reduction of effort is equivalent to an improvement of 15 per cent in productivity. Productivity improvements from the elimination of unnecessary tasks could add another 5 per cent, with better planning yielding 15 per cent. Obviously these figures are given only as averages, and they are taken from a wide range of actual figures.

If part of the increase in productivity is applied to the value engineering aspects, the indirect benefits can be considerably larger than the direct benefits quoted above. Better products, more sales and higher prices through improved quality are probable. Reduction in manufacturing costs are also probable, with multi-component products being most likely to benefit.

THE DESIGN AUDIT

However much care and attention is given to the management issues relevant to design, problems may still arise in manufacture or use. It has therefore become widely accepted that some further assurance is required that new designs do not have features which lead to manufacturing or service failures. An overview technique is therefore desirable. A particularly useful one is *design audit*, an outline of which is given in Jeffries and Westgarth (1981) which describes the work developed by the Design Audit Group of British Steel. The technique has been developed for use on high-cost capital plant, but it has obvious possibilities of development for other applications.

The design audit is a multi-disciplinary activity conducted by a team of managers and investment analysts to examine the design of new plant to ensure that it is built to the optimum specification with a minimum of design deficiencies. The technique is a development of review procedures used by NASA in the space programme. The audit can typically be operated at two distinct levels: total systems level or component level.

Total system audit

The total system audit studies the overall process and engineering route. It identifies the capital, operational and maintenance costs associated with each functional unit within that system. It then optimises these costs to attain minimum life-cycle cost comparable with reliability and easy maintenance. Basic design features of the plant are studied using systems engineering and reliability modelling techniques to appraise and modify the plant layout.

Component audit

This is design auditing of individual components as an integrity assessment. At this level it is directed at the individual plant items to ensure their fitness for purpose under working conditions within the total plant design. The analysis is carried out in detail and takes account of such requirements as:

Component capacity
Reliability
Maintainability
Stress tolerances
Environmental compatibility, etc.

Components may, when required, be subject to detailed examination and testing to ascertain their performance under specific plant operating conditions. Consideration is given to basic design, the effect of environmental conditions, accessibility for maintenance, component wear rate, compatibility of parts, and the ways in which these interact to influence component reliability. The timing of the audit function is obviously critical to derive the best value from design trade-offs, and should preferably occur prior to the finalisation of plant or equipment design.

The audit programme

While the course of any individual design audit depends upon customer plant and equipment reqirements, as does composition of the audit team, there is a common logical format for most circumstances:

Stage 1: familiarisation

Following initial customer discussions, a specific design audit team is formed. This team then acquaints itself with plant operation, examines relevant documentation and establishes with the customer the availability of the necessary customer, plant and contractor's data, drawings and design parameters. It is essential at this stage that clear and regular lines of communication between customer, contractor and audit team are set up and maintained throughout the audit study.

Stage 2: criticality study

Further to the preparatory work of stage 1, a detailed examination and evaluation of the plant and equipment design is conducted in the light of the proposed layout, process considerations and the in-service environment. Critical items of plant, particularly interfaces with other plant and equipment, are identified and examined in detail, through reliability studies. In conjunction with this engineering and design evaluation, an economic assessment is conducted to establish and quantify the proposed trade-offs between plant design, reliability requirements and the total

Stage 3: finalisation and recommendation

This is the most necessary element and, as common practice, the independent audit team has detailed discussions with customer and contractor to ensure complete understanding of the design analysis and reliability assessments to reach tripartite agreement.

The final report encompasses all the design analyses conducted on the plant and is presented in a simple, readable layout.

There seems no doubt that design auditing is a valuable technique to facilitate the efficient operation of high-cost capital plant by minimising construction, maintenance and replacement costs. The technique has proved itself to be cost-effective in those circumstances and it will inevitably be extended to other applications.

FURTHER READING

Allen, T.J., *Problem Solving Strategies in Parallel Research and Development*, Working paper 125–65, Sloan School of Management, MIT, Mass., 1965.

Brearley, A., *The Management of Drawing and Design*, Gower, 1975

Brearley, A., *The Control of Staff Related Overheads*, Macmillan, London, 1976

British Standards Institution, *Engineering Drawing Practice*, BS 308, British Standards Institution, London, 1972

Conway, H., 'Design and Produce – The 1977 George Bray Memorial Lecture', *The Production Engineer*, London, May 1977.

Computer Graphics CAD and CAD/CAM Product Guide and Computer Suppliers Directory 1981, Interco Business Consultants, Richmond, Surrey, 1981

Davies, R.S., and Clarke, A., 'A Surface Modeller for the Turbine Blade Industry', *Chartered Mechanical Engineer*, London, Dec. 1979

De Bono, E., *Mechanism of the Mind*, Cape, London, 1969

De Bono, E., *Practical Thinking*, Cape, London, 1971

Feiner, P., 'Engineering Design Office Efficiency', *Work Study and Management Services Magazine, Nov. 1969*

Gage, W.L., *Value Analysis*, McGraw-Hill, Maidenhead, 1967

Gage, W.L., *Outline of Value Analysis*, DATA, Richmond, Surrey, 1970

Gibbs, P.J., 'Computer Aided Integrated Systems', *Chartered Mechanical Engineer*, London, Feb. 1980

Gordon, W.T.T., *Synectics*, Harper & Row, London, 1961

Haines, W.R.R., *The Company View – Needs Research Conference Proceedings Managing Technological Innovation*, University of Bradford, 1968

Jeffries, B., and Westgarth, D., 'The Design Audit – A Management Tool for the 1980s, *Chartered Mechanical Engineer*, London, March 1981

Marples, D.L., *The Decisions of Engineering Design*, Institution of Engineering Designers, London, 1960

Middleton, J., and Martin, P., 'Design Rationalisation, the Key to Cost Reduction, *Chartered Mechanical Engineer*, London, Jan. 1975

Middleton, J., and Martin, P., 'A Design is more than the sum of its parts', *Chartered Mechanical Engineer*, London, July 1974

Miles, L.D., *Techniques of Value Analysis and Engineering*, McGraw-Hill, New York, 1961

National Board for Prices and Incomes, *Agreement made between certain engineering firms and DATA*, Report No. 68, Command 3632, HMSO, London

National Economic Development Office, *Mechanical Engineering Review to 1974*, NEDO, London, 1974

Perkins, C.A., 'Development, its Influence on Design', *Chartered Mechanical Engineer*, London, Nov. 1974

Richards, T., 'Brainstorming in an R&D environment', *R and D Management*, No. 3, June 1973

Simkins, P., *The Computer as a Production Tool*, CAD Centre, Cambridge, 1980

Twiss, B.C., *Managing Technological Innovation*, 2nd edition, Longman, London, 1980

Wearne, S.H., 'Systems of Engineering Organisation' *Proceedings of the Institution of Mechanical Engineers, 185, No. 3, 1970*–71
Wearne, S.H., *Principles of Engineering Organisation*, Arnold, London, 1973

25 Patents and trade-marks

G A Bloxam

Letters patent for inventions ('patents' in present parlance) have a long lineage in England. They were being granted by the Crown, along with other monopoly rights, in pre-Tudor times, but the first legislative enactment was the Statute of Monopolies of 1623, which made all monopolies void except (under s6) those granted for fourteen years (now twenty) in respect of 'any manner of new manufacture'.

The latest in a long series of enactments is the Patents Act 1977 (referred to in this chapter as 'the New Act') which came into force on 1 June 1978. Before this date, the current act was the Patents Act 1949 (referred to here as 'the Old Act'). Another major change is the coming into force (also on 1 June 1978) of the European Patent Convention (EPC), with the opening of the European Patent Office (EPO) in Munich. A further development is the Community Patent Convention (CPC), which has been signed by the EEC members, but will not come into force for a considerable time because the Danish Parliament has refused to ratify it.

The EPC provides a system whereby a single application at the EPO designating a number of member countries (which will include all the Western European countries when all the signatories have ratified the Convention) selected by the applicant will be examined by the EPO and, if accepted, will result in the grant of a bundle of identical patents in the designated countries. The CPC goes further, in that an application at the EPO designating the EEC will (if successful) result in the granting of a single 'Community Patent'. Thus, there will be three kinds of patents in the UK:

1 National Patents, granted by the UK Patent Office (UKPO) and effective only in the UK
2 European Patents (UK), granted by the EPO and effective only in the UK (although identical patents in the bundle will be effective in the other designated countries)
3 Community patents, granted by the EPO and effective as a single entity throughout the EEC.

One object of the New Act is to provide a system of law and procedure which can be applied equally to these three kinds of patents and yet will be workable in the UK Courts. Since the two European conventions achieve a far lower standard of precision than is required by the British legal system, this was an extremely difficult task, and it must be said that the New Act presents many problems of interpretation. In grappling with these, the courts and the UKPO are likely, where two interpretations are possible, to choose the one which conforms with the concepts of patent law which have developed over the years from successive UK patents acts and case law. But there can be no certainty until a new body of case law has been built up, and the best that can be done in the present Chapter is to indicate the points of doubt and give a view as to how they are likely to be resolved. Bearing in mind that the going rate for fighting a patent action in the Court of first instance is well up to the five-figure bracket, it will be many years before the system reaches the degree of certainty it had under the Old Act and even that, unfortunately, was not particularly high.

INVENTION

An adequate guide to the meaning of 'invention' for present purposes is that an invention is a new article or substance, or a new machine, or a new method or process of carrying out an industrial operation – the word 'industrial' including agriculture and horticulture. Computer programming is not included, but the Whitford Committee on Copyright has recommended (Cmnd 6732) that new computer programmes should have a form of copyright protection, as is now the case in the USA.

Further types of activity may, with the advance of technology, become suitable for patenting in the future, and the New Act provides that such new developments can be included within its scope by Statutory Instrument, without the need for legislation.

Not all inventions can be *validly* patented; certain attributes are necessary to make an invention 'patentable'. Before considering these, we need to know more about the nature of patents.

PATENT SPECIFICATION

The grant of a patent can be regarded in a sense as a contract between the State and the patentee under which the State grants the patentee a twenty-year monopoly in making or using the invention in return for a disclosure to the public of the invention and how to put it into practice. The vehicle for this disclosure is the patent specification, a document printed and published by the Patent Office as a prerequisite to every granted patent.

The claim

Besides disclosing the invention, the specification has another essential function: the definition of the area of monopoly to which the patentee claims to be entitled, this being contained in the *claim* of the specification.

It has long been recognized that to confine the patentee's monopoly exactly to his invention would stultify the whole system, since a competitor could evade the monopoly simply by making an inconsequential variation. The patentee is therefore allowed to include in this monopoly a range of constructions or processes centred on the original invention but in return he must delineate by exact wording the total range to which he claims to be entitled. This wording is the claim of specification.

A simple example will help to clarify this rather difficult concept. Suppose the invention is a ball-cock for a cistern. It is a piece of mechanism which includes a float in the form of a hollow sphere. If the patent monopoly were confined to the exact mechanism as conceived by the inventor, a competitor might be able to evade it quite easily by replacing the sphere by an egg-shaped float or even perhaps a rectangular one. So the patentee does not refer in his claim to a 'hollow spherical float' but to a 'hollow body serving as a float' or perhaps just to a 'float'.

The extent to which the inventor can extrapolate from his original invention is dealt with in the New Act by the provision that the claim must be supported by the matter disclosed in the specification $(s14(5)(c))$, but this can in the last analysis only be a subjective judgment by the tribunal considering the matter.

Explaining the nature and function of patent claims is not made easier by the fact that the word 'invention' is used not only as above to mean the concrete article or process devised by the inventor but also in the quite different sense of 'the invention claimed' – that is the area of the monopoly. Although these two meanings are hallowed in the legal phraseology of patents and by time-honoured usage generally, the word will in this chapter be used only in the first of the above senses, thus removing at least one semantic obstacle from the reader's path.

WHAT A PATENT IS

We can now consider what sort of thing a patent is. A simple analogy may be helpful. A patent can be likened to a fence erected round an area of technology and bearing the sign 'trespassers will be prosecuted'. The area of technology will be recognizable as the claim discussed above, while somewhere near the middle of the area is the 'invention'.

By way of illustration, let us vary the theme from a ball-cock to a chemical process – say a process for making sulphuric acid by passing sulphur dioxide over a catalyst at a temperature of $x°C$. The patentee will probably have been allowed to include in his claim a range of catalysts and a range of temperatures on either side of x. The fence delimits these ranges.

It will be observed that the fence in itself does not prevent anyone from trespassing on the forbidden area, or *infringing* the patent as it is called. But once the fence is crossed the patentee has a cause of action in the High Court claiming damages and (usually much more significant) an injunction to stop the infringer from doing it again. A patent thus belongs to the species of property known in law as a close-in-action but it has one peculiar feature: although it is a right granted by the State after due administrative process, the validity of the grant is not only open to challenge in the courts but such challenge is quite likely to succeed.

VALIDITY OF PATENTS

The validity of a granted patent can be the subject of proceedings in the Patent Office acting in a judicial capacity, or the Patents Court, which is a branch of the High Court. If the patent is held to be invalid, it is revoked.

The grounds of revocation under the New Act are of three types:

1 That the invention is not patentable
2 That the patent was granted to somebody who was not the inventor(s) or a person deriving title from him or them
3 That the specification does not adequately tell the expert how to put the invention into effect.

Oddly enough the objection that the claim extrapolates too far from the actual invention ($s14(5)(c)$ – see above) is not a ground of revocation and it is left to the UKPO examiner to enforce the requirement. This follows the EPC, which omits the objection from the grounds of revocation in spite of strong British representations to have it included.

Patentability

This question is dealt with differently under the Old and New Acts. Both systems need to be considered, because that of the Old Act still applies to 'existing patents', i.e. those granted before 1 June 1978, some of which will last until the 1990s. The Old Act adopted a negative approach, giving a number of 'grounds of revocation'. The New Act sets out positively what makes an invention patentable. To simplify matters, we shall ignore this technical difference and set out the two sets of requirements side by side in the New Act style, i.e. as positive requirements for validity.

The state of the art

The fundamental requirements of patentability in both Acts are concerned with the relationship of the invention to the 'State of the Art'. This phrase means the sum total of the knowledge available to the public in the relevant 'art' (i.e. technology) at the 'priority date' (see p. 435) of the patent. The knowledge can be documentary, e.g. in the technical journals or above all in prior patent specifications (usually referred to for short, but inaccurately, as 'prior patents'), or it can be prior use of the technology, provided the nature of the use was known to the public, e.g. as a product available on the market.

Under the Old Act the knowledge had to exist in the UK to be effective, but under the New Act it can be anywhere in the world. This will not make as much difference as might be thought, because most technical publications, including patent specifications, become available here shortly after publication.

Novelty

The first requirement for patentability is that the invention shall be new. This means that if a comparison is made between the alleged invention and the state of the art, there must be some genuine difference between them. In making the comparison, account must be taken not only of the express wording of the relevant documents, but also any clear implications. The approach is to ask the relevant expert what, on a fair reading, the document actually means to him.

There is no difference between the Old and New Acts so far as the concept of novelty is concerned.

Obviousness

The commonest ground of invalidity is probably that the invention is 'obvious and does not involve any inventive step' having regard to the state of the art. This means that while there is some difference between the invention and the prior art, so that it can properly be described as new, the difference is such as would have been obvious to the 'man skilled in the art' such as, for instance, a 'mere workshop variant'. To justify a monopoly the inventor must have taken an 'inventive step'. This need not be of breakthrough proportions; quite the contrary. In one case it was held that a 'mere scintilla of invention' will suffice. What is certain is that there is no definition of what it consists of. As in the case of the phrase 'supported by' the description in the specification as referred to above, it is a matter of the subjective judgment of the tribunal considering the case. It is possible by a study of the decided cases to arrive at various generalisations to assist in judging particular cases but such a study would not be appropriate here.

There is, however, one criterion which is worth discussing as it enters in one form or other into most arguments on obviousness. Let us take as an example, the mixing of two well-known fungicides. One's first reaction is likely to be that this cannot be inventive, especially as it is generally well known that biocidal agents can be mixed in order to enlarge their 'spectrum' of activity. If, however, the inventor shows that the fungicides have a marked synergistic effect on each other, so that the mixture is more effective than the sum of the components, it is very difficult to say that it was obvious to make the mixture. The incentive was there, but nobody before the inventor thought of doing it. That the invention produces an unexpected advantage is thus often decisive in justifying a finding of inventiveness, although it must be emphasised that it is not an indispensable condition.

What it amounts to is that if there had been an incentive for some time to come up with the new development but no-one had thought of it before the inventor, it is hardly possible to regard it as having been an obvious thing to do.

Again, there is no difference between the Old and New Acts in respect of the concept of obviousness.

Secret prior use

Prior use which was 'secret' (i.e. the nature of which was now known to the public) is not part of the state of the art, and is nor available under the New Act as a ground of invalidity. Under the Old Act it is available as a basis for attacking the novelty of the invention, but not for alleging obviousness.

The word 'secret' is a little unfortunate, as it covers a normal works operation, provided the public are not admitted. If members of the public had access and could find out what was going on, the relevant activity is part of the state of the art and is available as such under both Acts.

The basis of the requirements of novelty and inventive step is that a patent monopoly should not be granted for technology which was already available to the public, or a mere workshop variant of it. Another basic requirement is that a patent should not be granted which could stop a person from continuing to do what he was doing before, even if he was doing it 'secretly'. Under the Old Act this was implemented by invalidating the patent. The New Act, recognising that the secret use is not part of the state of the art, provides that if a person other than the inventor was using the technology before the priority date of the patent, he shall have a free licence to continue doing so. Thus the patent remains valid and enforceable except against the individual or company who operated the invention before the priority date.

Is the technology an invention?

Patents can only be validly granted for patentable inventions. Before patentability is considered, the question must be asked: 'Is the item of technology in question an invention at all'? To enable this question to be answered, the New Act includes a definition of the sort of technology that can be patented in that section, i.e. $s1$, of the Act which defines the requirements of a patentable invention. We have given a simplifed version of this definition above. It effectively codifies the position which had been reached in the development of case law by the Patent Office and Courts to keep up with advancing technology. The same criteria can therefore be regarded as applying to both existing and new patents.

Grounds of invalidity concerned with the specification

There are two ways in which the content of the specification goes to the root of the validity of the patent:

1 The claim which defines the area of the monopoly must not be unfairly broad in scope in relation to what has actually been invented. This is a ground of revocation in the Old Act under the phrase that the claim is 'not fairly based' on the disclosure in the specification; but (as mentioned above) it is, illogically, not a ground under the New Act, although the UKPO examiner has the responsibility for enforcing it when dealing with the application for the patent. Nevertheless it is possible to conjecture that the

British Courts will find a way of maintaining this ground as part of the law by linking it with that of inadequate description – see (2) below

2 The specification must disclose the invention in a fair and intelligible manner and must not withhold significant information on its optimisation, because this information is the consideration for the grant of the patent. Failure to comply with this requirement is a ground of revocation under the Old and New Acts.

The whole of the above discussion on validity needs qualifying in view of our determination not to use the word 'invention' in a double sense. To understand the point it may be helpful to return to the analogy of a fence round an area of technology – defined with precision by the words of the patent claim – and think of the area as covering a whole range of articles or processes roughly centred on the invention. Then everything which has to be satisfied by the invention to make the patent valid must also be satisfied by the whole range of variants included in the fenced-off area. It is this which is the main factor in restraining the inventor from claiming too great an area, for the bigger the area, the more chance there is that some variant near the periphery will contravene one of the requirements for validity. In that event the whole claim is invalid – patent claims cannot be like the curate's egg, good in parts.

EMPLOYEES' INVENTIONS

In the absence of any rule of law to the contrary, an invention, including any patent rights in it at home or abroad, belongs to the inventor or joint inventors. Under common law, however, an invention made by an employee belongs to his employer if it was made 'in the course of' the employment.

The New Act (s39) has put this rule on a statutory basis. It provides that an invention made by an employee is the property of the employer if:

1 The normal duties of the employee might reasonably be expected to lead to the making of an invention, and;
2 The invention was made in the course of those duties.

The first is a legal question to be decided by the Patent Office or Courts considering a particular case. They could, however, be assisted if a job description agreed between the employer and employee included a specific statement that the job was expected to result in inventions.

Compensation to employee inventors

The New Act (s40) introduces for the first time in UK law the concept of awards or 'compensation' to employee inventors. It is important to realise that entitlement to awards arises whether or not the invention belongs to the employer (see above), although the rules are different in the two cases.

1 *Invention belongs to employee.* Compensation under the Act is payable by the employer in respect of benefit received by him from the relevant patent. The employer will, however, receive no benefit from an invention

belonging to an employee unless he (the employer) has acquired rights in it from the employee. Naturally the employee will require value for the transfer of rights, but this is the normal consideration for the contract assigning or licensing the invention to the employer. It is not the statutory compensation provided for by the New Act. That is something additional, which the employee may claim after the event if he can make out a case that the original consideration was inadequate in relation to benefit received from the patent by the employer

2 *Invention belongs to employer.* Compensation is payable in this case if and only if, the relevant *patent* has been of 'outstanding benefit' to the employer.

It should be noted that in both cases, entitlement to compensation only arises on inventions which are the subject of granted patents.

An application for compensation is made by the employee to the Patent Office, whose decision is subject to appeal to the Patents Court. It can be made at any time during the life of the patent and one year after it expires or lapses. Any number of applications can be made in respect of the patent during this period. The New Act (*s*41) sets out the considerations the tribunal must have in mind (such as relative contributions to the success of the invention by the inventor, the employer and other employees) in deciding how much compensation (if any) is payable.

Contracts on employee inventions

The New Act overrides the ordinary law of contract in certain cases. Thus, *s*42 renders unenforceable any contract between an employer and employee inventor which reduces the statutory rights of the employee, if the contract was made *before* the invention. A contract relating to an invention belonging to an employee which was entered into after the invention was made is clearly enforceable, and presumably the same applies to inventions belonging to the employer.

A collective agrement with a trade union relating to employee inventions is enforceable in respect of members of the union only. It appears that non-members retain their full statutory rights under the Act, even if they benefit from the collective agreement, but the tribunal could probably take this into account in awarding compensation.

The award of compensation is going to be a rare event because patents of outstanding benefit are themselves rare. On the other hand the singling out of inventors from other employees who help to promote innovation is potentially disruptive. It remains to be seen how significant this may be.

INFRINGEMENT OF PATENTS

A patent is infringed by anyone who makes, uses or sells an article or machine protected by the patent, or uses a process protected by the patent, or sells the direct product of such a process. To decide whether a given article is protected by the patent it is necessary to construe the definition constituted by the patent claim and determine whether the article falls within or without the definition.

British patent law is strict in holding the patentee to the words of his claim but there are two qualifications. The first is that the *de minimis* rule (that the law takes no account of trifles) applies as always. The second is the doctrine of *equivalents* or 'pith and marrow', according to which a man infringes a claim if he substitutes an element of it by an equivalent (as for instance a non-spherical float in a ball-cock claim confined to a spherical float) so as to take the pith and marrow of the claim even if it is not within its exact wording. This doctrine grew up in the days before the patentee was required to delineate the boundary of his monopoly by an accurately drafted patent claim. Today the doctrine is given lip service but is hardly ever applied. Further reference to this question is made in the section on European Patents.

Court action

If the patentee wishes to go to the limit in enforcing his patent against a supposed infringer, he must issue a writ for infringement in the Patents Court. If he cannot tell from any product sold by the alleged infringer whether what the latter is doing infringes the patent (as in the case of a chemical process, for example) he can ask the Court for an order for discovery and inspection on the basis of a reasonable suspicion.

It is routine in an infringement action for the defendant to counter-claim for revocation of the patent on the basis that it is invalid on one or more specified grounds. The question at issue at the trial is therefore whether any valid claim of the patent has been infringed.

What constitutes infringement

There are some differences in the law on infringement before and after the New Act and the new law is intended to apply only to what happens after it came into force. Curiously enough the Old Act is silent on what sort of activity constitutes infringement of a patent, the question being governed only by case law. The New Act therefore puts it in this way: that in an action for infringement under a patent existing before June 1978, in respect of an activity which is a continuation of something started before that date, infringement will be held to have taken place only if the activity would have infringed the patent under the Old (pre-1st June 1978) Law. In other words a person who was advised that he could lawfully do something under the old law will not be penalised simply because of a change in the law if he continues to do it.

This principle is easier to apply than it sounds because the changes in the law of infringement are *additions* to the basic law as stated in the first paragraph of this section. The latter applies under the Old and New Acts. The significant additions under the New Act are as follows:

1 *Contributory infringement.* (This is only a very brief summary of a section of the Act which will prove difficult to interpret.) This applies to patents where the invention essentially involves the use of some unpatented

material, substance or article. S60(2) of the New Act provides that anyone selling such unpatented material etc. knowing that the customer intends to use if for infringing the patent is guilty of infringement. S60(3) makes the additional qualification that if the material etc. is a 'staple article of commerce', the supplier must actually induce the customer to infringe before he (the supplier) can be held to infringe. A typical example would be the issue of a data sheet to customers recommending the infringing use

2   *Pharmaceutical use.* A method or process of treating the human body is not a patentable invention (s2(6)). However, the New Act provides that a patent can be obtained for a new pharmaceutical use of a substance and such patent will be infringed by a person supplying the substance for the patented use, even though the use itself, being a treatment of the human body, is not deemed to be an infringement. In other words the pharmaceutical manufacture can be sued, but not the doctor.

Threats

An important practical point in the relationship between a patentee and a person he suspects of infringing his patent is the matter of threats. Under s70 of the New Act it is actionable for the patentee to threaten with proceedings for infringement somebody such as a retailer who is re-selling a patented article or product. Such re-selling is, of course, an infringement of the patent and it would be proper to sue the retailer. However, the patentee is not likely to be interested in doing this, but wishes to get at the manufacturer by the back door, as it were. It is this that is unlawful. The threat need not be spelt out in so many words, provided what is said or written would be regarded as a threat by a reasonable business man. The patentee is free to threaten the manufacturer to his heart's content.

EUROPEAN PATENT LAW

The function of the EPO has been touched on above, and the procedural aspects will be dealt with later in this chapter. At the moment we will deal with the substantive law embodied in the EPC.

The question can be considered quite briefly because the law is mainly confined to matters relating to the criteria for granting and validity of a patent; in other words, what is a patentable invention? It is, moreover, the express intention (s130(7)) of the New Act to bring UK law into line with the EPC so far as it is practicable to equate an Act of Parliament with an international treaty. It follows that the EPC law on patentability is essentially as set out above in relation to UK law.

There is one other point which should be mentioned. The EPC includes (Article 69) a statement as to how patent claims should be interpreted. The significance of this is that in the common law countries (UK, USA and old Commonwealth countries) the scope of a patentee's monopoly (the 'area' enclosed by his 'fence') is regarded as strictly defined by the words of the claim. In most other countries, especially West Germany, the scope of the monopoly is much less certain, and is supposed to be based on a concept called the Erfindungsgedank or inventive idea. Art 69 of the EPC favours the British view, and this is reflected in s125 of the New Act, but German practitioners tend to believe otherwise (and the official German-language text of the EPC does lean slightly more in that direction than does the official English version). It remains to be seen whether these views will be reconciled in the course of time, and if so how, but in the author's view the UK Courts will hold strictly to s125 of the British New Act.

The need to harmonise UK and EPC law is increased by the CPC. Although, as mentioned above, this convention cannot yet be ratified, the New Act had to make provision for eventual ratification. Since community patents, which will be granted by the EPO under the EPC, will be effective as such in the UK after granting, it is essential that British patent law should be assimilated to the law of the EPC.

PATENTING PROCEDURE IN THE UNITED KINGDOM

Each country has its own system of patent law and administrative procedure. In broad outline the principles set out in the preceding sections, although directed primarily to the UK and EPC law, are valid for overseas countries, with a few important exceptions which will be referred to later. Administrative procedures, however, differ substantially from country to country. Those obtaining in Great Britain will be considered first.

Priority dates

The first step in obtaining a patent is to file an application at the UKPO. It has always been a special feature of the British system that the application need be accompanied only by a 'provisional' specification, which does not require the inclusion of the monopoly-defining 'claims'. This had to be followed within twelve months by a 'complete' specification, which was the one on which the grant of a patent was based. For the sake of harmony with the EPC, the New Act has formally abolished provisional specifications, but the substance of the system has been retained by an ingenious device.

Under the New Act, the applicant first files a specification, which can be informal and, in particular, need not include claims. In fact it can be just the same as a provisional specification under the Old Act. It has no official name but can conveniently be called a 'preliminary' specification. Such a document serves to establish the applicant's *priority date* for his invention. But in order to proceed to the granting of a patent, a specification which is in proper form, including the presence of claims, must be filed. We will call this the 'final' specification. If this is filed within twelve months of the preliminary specification, the priority date established by the latter remains effective. The system is thus essentially the same as the old provisional and complete specifications.

435

Publication

The final specification is published, usually just as it is filed, at 18 months from the priority date. This means that publication will normally take place about 6 months from the filing of the final specification. The specification is printed and indexed in a comprehensive classification system, and copies can be bought at the Sales Branch of the UKPO. It should be noted that this document only fulfils one part of the function of a patent specification – the provision of technical information about the invention. The other function – defining the scope of the claimed monopoly – cannot be fulfilled until the application has been accepted.

On publication of the specification, the Patent Office file of the case becomes open to public inspection, and remains so for the life of the patent and thereafter.

Search and examination

When the final specification has been filed, it is remitted to an examiner who makes a search among prior documents (in practice, existing UK patent specifications) and reports those which are relevant to the novelty of the claims. The applicant then has the opportunity of deciding whether, in the light of the search report, it is worth proceeding to the next step. The sort of considerations which usually arise can be illustrated with reference to our ball-cock invention.

Let us imagine that the applicant thinks he is entitled to claim a ball-cock with any kind of float, but that (surprisingly) an elliptical float is especially advantageous in some way. The examiner cites a specification describing a ball-cock with a spherical float. This clearly destroys the patentability of the broad claim to any kind of float but not of a claim limited to the case in which the float is elliptical. To cater for this (very common) type of situation the law provides that the applicant can make a whole series of claims directed to successively smaller fenced-off areas, each within the confines of the previous one, and that in litigation the validity and infringement of each claim is to be considered separately. In our case claim 1 would include any kind of float and claim 2 would be restricted to an elliptical float; so that on being notified of the examiner's citation, the applicant would simply strike out claim 2 and accept the grant of a patent based on claim 2.

The applicant must make up his mind whether there is enough chance of securing allowance of a claim or claims which are of worthwhile scope, to justify spending the fee of £40 for *examination* of the application.

If he decides in the affirmative, the case is sent back to the examiner, who determines on behalf of the Patent Office whether, in his view, the prior documents totally destroy the patentability of the invention, in which case he will refuse the application; or whether (as is more likely) there is something left which could be patented, in which case he reports to the applicant, who can amend his claims accordingly. If the examiner is satisfied, usually after a good deal of argument to and fro, the application is allowed and a patent is granted.

It should be emphasised that acceptance by the examiner is in no way indicative of the validity of the claims. In our illustration he could have missed the ball-cock specification in his search, so that a patent was granted containing claim 1 as well as claim 2, and this could be challenged in litigation by a defendant who managed to discover the prior specification the examiner had missed. The court would then hold claim 1 invalid but might hold claim 2 valid. If the defendant had made a ball-cock with an elliptical float, the court would order an injunction and (subject to a defined discretion) damages for infringement of claim 2, at the same time ordering the cancellation of claim 1.

The patent in its granted form is re-printed, using the same number as the previously published specification but with the letter B added. The letter A is used for the first published version.

Conflict between co-pending applications

There is one technicality that needs to be mentioned at this stage because it can cause confusion, although the position under the New Act should be clearer than under the Old.

It can happen that an Applicant B files a patent application after an application by A for closely similar subject-matter, but during the 18 months between A's priority date and publication of his (A's) final specification. This is particularly so in intensively research-based industries. We then have the paradox that A's specification was still secret at B's priority date and therefore ought not to count against B, yet patents ought not to be granted to both A and B for the same invention. In deciding how close two technological developments have to be in order to be regarded as 'the same', the Courts under the Old Act produced a lot of confusing and incomprehensible rules, collectively known as the law of 'prior claiming'. In order to cut through this undergrowth, both in the EPC and the British New Act, it was decided that A's specification in our illustration should be deemed, during the period before its publication, to be part of the 'state of the art'. However, this artificiality was a bit too much for the legislators (advised by practitioners schooled under the old law) to accept, and a compromise was arrived at whereby the prior unpublished specification is only half way to being in the state of the art: it counts against the *novelty* of the later application but cannot be used as a basis for proving *obviousness*.

It should be noted for completeness that the old law of prior claiming still applies when judging the validity of patents existing at 1 June 1978.

Adjudication of patents

The New Act has radically altered the system for judging the validity of patents. Under the Old Act the UKPO had a limited jurisdiction in proceedings known as 'opposition' to the grant of a patent. Final jurisdiction over granted patents rested with the Courts. The new system, which applies to existing as well as new patents, gives the UKPO full jurisdiction over the validity of granted patents. Opposition before grant of a patent has been abolished. Anyone interested in securing the revocation of a patent at any time in its life can apply to the UKPO for revocation under s72 of the New Act. There is a right of appeal to a new branch of the High Court called the Patents Court, but appeal from this to the Court of Appeal only lies in respect of particular grounds listed in the New Act (*s*97(3)).

The Patents Court can also adjudicate on validity at first instance, for example if a defendant in a patent infringement action puts in (as he invariably does) a counter-claim for revocation of the patent.

PATENTING PROCEDURE IN EUROPE

Since procedure under the New Act has been devised to correspond closely with that under the EPC, only a few further points need be added under this heading.

Language

The EPO is an autonomous international organization set up by a treaty (the EPC). It has no connection with the EEC. It is staffed by officials seconded from the patent offices of member countries. The UK has a full representation including posts in the higher echelons. The President is a Dutchman.

Patent Applications must be filed in one of the official languages: English, French or German. Since the system is accessible to nationals of any country, a large number of applications will originate in USA and Japan. The vast majority of all applications will therefore be filed in the English language. When a patent is granted, the *claims* will have to be translated into the other two official languages.

Application for a European patent

There are two main differences between procedures in the EPO and the UKPO. The first is that there is no counterpart in the EPO of the British provisional (now preliminary) specification system. Priority can be claimed in the EPO from a British preliminary specification, but this is part of the International Convention system (see below) rather than a specifically EPC procedure.

Secondly, as mentioned above, the applicant has to 'designate' the countries in which he wishes the European patent, if granted, to be effective, a designation fee of £60 approx being payable for each country, including of course the UK.

Opposition

Although the EPO is basically concerned only with the *granting* of patents, which then revert to the national jurisdictions of the respective designated countries, there is one exception. Within one year after grant, a European patent can be 'opposed' at the EPO. This is similar to British revocation proceedings at the UKPO. If an opposition is successful, the European patent as a whole (i.e. in respect of each designated country) is revoked.

Which route: European or national?

If a prospective applicant wants to cover his invention in more than one member country of the EPC, he has the option of applying at the EPO (the 'European route') or of filing separate national applications in each of the countries concerned (the 'national route'). The considerations which arise are as follows:

1　Financial: obviously the greater the number of countries involved, the greater the financial advantage of the European route. The calculation is complicated because it involves professional as well as official Patent Office fees, and both of these vary from country to country in the case of national applications. As a rough guide it can be said that there is a break-even point of 3 or 4 countries at which the European route becomes less expensive than the national route

2　National patents can be obtained very easily in a number of member countries (e.g. France, Belgium, Italy, Spain). If the European route is chosen, fairly strict criteria for allowing an application will be applied by the EPO, and in any case one would be putting all one's eggs in one basket

3　There is likely to be a heavy incidence of oppositions to European patents, because a single opposition can destroy the patent in all the designated countries

4　The amount of time and effort which has to be spent by the applicant and his patent agent in securing protection in more than one country should be less by the European than the national route

5　British patent agents can act directly at the EPO, whereas if the national route is used local agents have to be employed for each country.

COMMUNITY PATENT CONVENTION

We have indicated briefly the nature of the CPC, which will provide for the granting of a *single* patent for the whole Common Market. This will raise interesting questions of jurisprudence which have not yet been resolved. Procedure under the CPC should fit comfortably into that of the EPO and the UKPO. The main problem will be the cost, since the annual renewal fees to keep the patent in force will be very high.

Further discussion of the CPC in this book would be premature until ratification by all the member countries takes place, and this may be years ahead.

FOREIGN PATENTS

Nearly all the countries of the world have their own patent offices and fully autonomous patent systems. This includes the members of the EPC, whose national systems will continue to operate in parallel with the EPO. There are two treaties which operate worldwide:

1　The International Convention for the Protection of Industrial Property;
2　The Patent Co-operation Treaty (PCT).

The PCT is concerned with providing a single searching facility for all the countries which a patent applicant may wish to cover. This sounds like a simple matter, but in fact the technical and procedural complications are immense and it remains to be seen whether use of the system, which came into operation on 1 June 1978, is worthwhile.

THE INTERNATIONAL CONVENTION

This dates from 1883 and now includes all the industrial countries of the world and many more. We shall call it simply 'the Convention'.

The EPC counts as a 'Convention country', on the same footing as each individual European or other member country.

The main provisions of the Convention are:

1 That the laws of a Convention country will be applied equally to citizens of all Convention countries
2 That if a patent application for an invention is filed in one Convention country and within twelve months an application for the same invention is filed in one or more other Convention countries, then such other applications will have the priority date of the first one. Hence it is very desirable for a UK applicant to file foreign applications within twelve months of his British application. Thus if the latter was accompanied by a preliminary specification, the filing of the final in the UK normally coincides with the filing of foreign 'Convention applications'.

If an applicant (usually from abroad) files a Convention application in the UK, he files a certified copy of the original foreign application and this serves to establish his priority in much the same way as a British preliminary specification does for a British applicant in the UK. Thus there is no provision for filing a preliminary specification with a Convention application, but only a final.

Diversity of laws

It is not possible here to touch on the different procedures in different countries and only salient differences in substantive laws can be mentioned.

In the USA and Canada, the inventor's priority does not stem from the date of filing a patent application, but from the date he 'conceived' the invention.

No country except the UK and some of the old commonwealth countries has the preliminary specification system.

The examination to which a patent application is submitted before grant varies as follows:

1 Full examination of all possible grounds of invalidity – for example, the USA, Japan, Germany and other northern European countries including the UK
2 No examination at all – for example, Italy, Belgium, Spain and Latin countries generally. France has provision for an official search, although it

is left to the applicant whether to take action on the search report or not
3 Germany, Holland, Australia and Japan have adopted the system of 'deferred examination' whereby a 'provisional' patent (not to be confused with the old British provisional specification) is automatically granted for a specified period and is not examined unless the patentee or an interested party requests it within the specified period, failing which it lapses.

There is a fundamental difference in the way the UK, on the one hand, and the civil law countries and most of the rest of the world on the other (with USA somewhere in between but nearer the UK) approach the questions of definition of the monopoly area and validity. To take Germany as a typical example, there is no definition of the monopoly area in the claims or the rest of the specification or in any other document. Whether any particular manufacture is within or without the patent can only be a matter of subjective judgment after considering the specification and claims in the light of the prior art and any statements made by the patentee to the Patent Office to persuade them to grant the patent. On the other hand, the validity of a patent once issued tends to be taken for granted unless a challenger brings up fresh facts such as items of prior art which were not before the examiner. This is somewhat the reverse of the British position where the monopoly is tightly defined by the claims and the question of validity is more open.

Renewal fees

In all countries except the USA and Canada, annual renewal fees have to be paid to keep a patent in force. These vary greatly in amount and usually increase with the life of the patent. In West and, more especially, East Germany the fees are particularly onerous.

LICENSING

Instead of using his 'fence' to keep out the competition, the patentee may decide to exploit it by allowing one or more parties in for a consideration. A licence in its simplest form is a promise not to sue the licensee for infringement if he enters the forbidden territory. If at the same time the patentee agrees not to let anyone else in, and to stay out himself, the licence is 'exclusive'. An exclusive licensee has most of the rights and privileges of the patentee, including the right to sue for infringement.

If the patentee undertakes to grant no further licences, but does not exclude himself from working the invention, the licence is known as a 'sole' licence. This carries none of the statutory rights of the exclusive licence.

Territory

The effect of a licence is to give the licensee permission to do something which would otherwise be an infringement of the patent. This may be limited to a part only of the technology covered by the patent and to a part only of the UK, though the latter is probably rare in these days. If there are corresponding patents in other countries, the agreement may include a licence in one or more of these countries. A not uncommon arrangement would be to grant a British company an exclusive licence to make, use and sell in the UK and a non-exclusive licence to sell in other countries where there are patents, thus leaving it open for manufacturing licences to be granted to other companies abroad. The licensee does not need a licence to sell in countries where there are no patents, but he may (subject to legal restrictions which obtain in various countries – see below) agree collaterally *not* to sell in specified countries.

Financial arrangements

The consideration for the grant of a licence is normally monetary, and may take the form of a royalty based on use of the invention, an annual minimum payment and/or a down payment. The royalty can conveniently be expressed as a percentage of the sales value of an article, or the product of a process, covered by the patent. If, however, the article is a machine, for example for making shoes, it is difficult to get a fair return by charging a percentage of the value of the machine unless the percentage is an intimidatingly high figure. It is more realistic to charge a small percentage on the value of the shoes made by the machine. Similar considerations arise if the invention is for example a mixture of petrol and an additive present in very small quantities, in which case a royalty based on the value of the petrol has a more realistic appearance than one based on the value of the additive.

If the licence is exclusive, the patentee has a prime interest in ensuring adequate performance by the licensee. This is usually provided for by requiring the licensee to make up the royalty payment to a stated annual minimum payment. The licensee for his part is willing to do this since he is effectively buying a monopoly as well as a right of entry. The licensee may either covenant outright to pay the annual minimum or he may reserve the right not to pay it in which case he submits to a penalty such as termination of the licence or conversion to a non-exclusive one.

A down payment is appropriate if the deal includes the initial transmission of technical information such as drawings, to enable the licensee to commence manufacture.

Miscellaneous terms

If the parties so agree, the licence may permit the licensee to grant sub-licences to third parties.

It is part of the common law that a licensee cannot challenge the validity of the patent, but this is usually spelt out in the agreement.

The question of infringement usually arises during negotiations. There are two quite distinct issues: what is to happen if a third party infringes the licensed patent, and infringement of a third-party patent by the licensee. On the first issue, the licensee is justified in objecting to pay royalty if an infringer is operating for nothing. The agreement can therefore provide that the payment of royalty shall be suspended until either the infringement is stopped by the patentee or the infringer is granted a licence (assuming the original licence was non-exclusive). What is not reasonable in view of the high cost and uncertainty of patent actions is to expect the patentee to covenant to sue an infringer.

The question of infringement of a third party's patent by the licensee is not directly connected with the licence, and the licensor is justified in refusing to take any responsibility. The fact that a licensee's operation is covered by two patents, one of them being the subject of the licence and the other belonging to a third party, is in no way derogatory of the former. A patent gives no right to anyone, even the patentee, to manufacture the subject of the patent, as can be seen if we remember the fence analogy. To revert to the ball-cock example, if A gets a patent with a claim worded widely enough to cover any kind of float, but in which the specification describes only a spherical float, and later B discovers than an elliptical float has a special unexpected advantage, B may be able to get a valid patent for that particular variant and this would in no way reflect on the validity of A's patent. If B grants a licence to C there is no reason why B should be responsible for the fact that in operating under the licence C will infringe A's patent. It is up to C to make terms with A (with the sanction of a compulsory licence in the background if A's terms are so unreasonable as to frustrate exploitation of B's invention).

The duration of a licence is normally for the life of the relevant patent and it is provided in the New Act (s45) that it shall be terminable by either party when the patent expires.

Technical information and improvements

It often happens, especially if an exlusive licence is contemplated, that the parties agree to transmit know-how and improvements to each other. The point to note here is that an essential part of such an agreement is an exact definition of the technological field. If this is to be coterminous with the fenced-off area of the patent, the agreement should say so; it is not, as is often believed, an accepted meaning of the word 'improvement'. The agreement should also be clear about what rights will accrue in respect of *patentable* improvements. Possibly each party will get the benefit of these in his own territory.

Another important point is the right to use the know-how after termination of the agreement. In the absence of an explicit provision there is no such right, and this can have very serious consequences for the recipient of the know-how.

Forbidden terms

In English law the parties can negotiate a patent licence on any terms they please provided it is not in restraint of trade – a common law doctrine of fairly narrow compass – and does not contravene s44 of the New Act. This provides that the patentee shall not extend his monopoly right by making it a condition of a licence that the licensee shall buy from the patentee unpatented raw material – for example, unpatented phosphoric acid for use in a patented metal-finishing process. This is in fact frequently done, especially by implication, but the patentee is risking the enforceability of his patent if the practice ever comes to light.

In the USA and the EEC this matter comes in the province of the antitrust or competition laws, which are being applied with even more stringent effect to restrict what a licensor and licensee can lawfully agree. It is impossible here to go into any detail on this subject, but readers will be aware of the importance of not falling foul of these laws.

The practice of applying restrictions to licence agreements has been spreading in recent years, especially in developing countries, where the main motives are to foster local development and reduce the payment of royalties to other countries.

TRADE-MARKS

It has for long been part of the common law that if A has a reputation in a trade name or trade-mark and B sells his goods in association with the trade-mark in such a way as to lead the public to believe that his goods emanate from A, then A has a cause of action against B for 'passing off' his goods as A's. In such an action, A has the onus of proving both the reputation of his mark and the confusion caused by B's use of it.

By the Trade Marks Act of 1875, the owner of a trade-mark was given a new right: to enter this mark on a Register of Trade Marks, thereby gaining an entitlement to stop anyone else from using the mark – always assuming that the registration was valid.

An essential part of the system is that the registration must be in respect of a specified range of goods on which the owner uses or intends to use the mark, and that the registration is infringed only by use of the mark in connection with goods within this 'specification of goods'.

The Register

The Register of Trade Marks is kept by the Registrar, who is in fact the same person as the Comptroller of Patents. As in the case of patents, an application to register a trade-mark is examined to see if it complies with the requirements of the statute, currently the Trade Marks Act 1938. The examination extends to almost all the grounds on which a registration could be held invalid. The guiding principle is that the mark must be distinctive (in the sense that it distinguishes the owner's goods from those originating elsewhere) either inherently or because past use has in fact made it distinctive. The former is in effect a subjective judgment by the examiner or tribunal considering the matter while the latter is determined by evidence furnished by persons in the relevant trade. There are, however, two categories which are difficult to register no matter how much distinctiveness is proved, namely words of which the ordinary significance is either a geographical name or a surname (s9 of the Act). The opposite of a distinctive mark is one which is descriptive of the goods in question. This fact, coupled with the overriding requirement (s11) that the mark must not be deceptive, shows the narrow path which has to be trodden in many cases. For example, 'Silico' for polishes might be held descriptive if they contained silicones but deceptive if they did not.

All goods are divided into thirty-four classes and separate applications must be made for goods in different classes.

Conflicting marks

A further requirement of registration (s12) is that the mark must not resemble too closely a mark already on the Register for the same or similar goods, unless the applicant for registration can prove 'honest concurrent use' of the two marks for a period of some years. In borderline cases the Registrar will accept the consent of the owner of the mark already on the Register as justification for allowing the marks to coexist. Whether the consent is given and if so, subject to what conditions, is a private matter between the two parties, but in practice consent is often given gratis on the assumption that the consenting party may want the same favour from the other on some future occasion.

Opposition and rectification

There is provision for opposition to the registration (s18) and for an action to 'rectify the Register' by removing an existing registration (s26). One ground of removal which will not have been considered at the registration stage is that the owner had no bona fide intention to use the mark and has not in fact used it; or that he has not used the mark for a continuous period of five years.

Licensing

The right to use a trade-mark (whether registered or not) can be licensed by the owner but he must be careful to require the licensee to adopt his standards of quality for the goods in question, since otherwise the public may be deceived, with the result that the owner will lose his rights in the mark. It is advisable in the case of a registered trade-mark to get the official seal of approval on the terms of the licence by making the licensee a 'registered user' under s28 of the Act. This has the further advantage that use of the mark by the registered user counts as use for the purpose of s26.

International

Trade-marks are included in the International Convention for the Protection of Industrial Property, but the priority period is six months as distinct from twelve months in the case of patents. The trade-mark laws and practice of other countries differ from each other about as much as they do for patents, the main point to watch being that in some countries, notably France, there is no concept of ownership of a trade-mark until and unless the mark is registered, prior use being of no consequence. Hence a company that has failed to register a valuable mark in France can see it lost to a third party simply by registration.

Discussions have been in progress for some years under the aegis of the EEC for the setting up of an EEC trade-mark system. It will be at least a couple of years, probably more, before this is finalised and put into operation. As in the case of the EPC, national systems will continue to exist in parallel with that of the EEC.

FUNCTION OF PATENT AGENTS

Patent agents have a function in relation to patent law and practice which is analogous to that of solicitors in relation to other branches of the law. Owing to the technological subject-matter involved, a patent agent has to have achieved at least GCE *A* level standard in a science or engineering subject, and usually has a university degree, before sitting for the qualifying examinations which the Chartered Institute of Patent Agents administers on behalf of the Department of Trade.

There is a contradiction between the difficulty of the concepts underlying the patent system and the familiarity of its main visiable product – the patent specification. In many industries, patent specifications are an important if not the main source of information on recent developments and they are constantly handled by technical personnel of all grades. This means that laymen who are familiar with 'patents' (as they incorrectly term patent specifications) as items of technical information are unlikely to learn the underlying concepts of the system but substitute a rough-and-ready version which usually has little relation to reality. There are, in fact, very few matters connected with patent law or practice in which it is safe to proceed without consulting a patent agent.

It is usual for patent agents to include trade-marks in their practice, some training in trade-marks being necessary in order to pass the patent agent's qualifying examinations. Although this is elementary compared with the training in patents, a patent agent will either have acquired a full understanding by assisting an expert or will employ a fully qualified trade-mark agent in his practice. Unlike the profession of patent agency, that of trade-marks is not closed, but there is an Institute of Trade Mark Agents which administers a rigorous examination as a condition of membership. Many patent agents are members of both institutes.

The bread-and-butter work of the patent agent is the preparation of patent applications, the main part of which is the patent specification, for filing in the UK and abroad in accordance with the various local procedures; dealing with objections raised by the various examiners and with any oppositions; securing the grant of a patent; and ensuring the renewal fees are paid on it as long as the patentee requires. To do the job properly the patent agent ought to be in direct touch with the inventor in any particular case.

Analogous work arises in relation to trade-marks and here the agent should be in *direct* touch with the relevant marketing executive. Trade-marks matters sometimes seem simple, but in fact this is deceptive and the agent needs to have direct access to the principal actually involved just as much as he does in patent matters.

European patent attorneys

One of the main advantages of the EPO is that practitioners of any member country can act directly at the European office, in contradistinction to the national patent offices which require the representation to be held by a local patent practitioner. Qualification to act before the EPO will be by an examination of similar scope to that in the UK, run by the EPO. As a transitional measure, anyone qualified in his own country at 1 June 1978 can automatically go on the European Register.

Most foreign practitioners, when speaking English, call themselves 'Patent Attorneys'. Recognising that this could put British agents at a disadvantage when competing for EPO business, e.g. in USA and Japan, Parliament approved the same 'European Patent Attorney' for use by British practitioners, in s85(1) of the New Act. The Law Society put up a spirited opposition to this use of the word 'Attorney', but without success.

COSTS

The costs of obtaining and maintaining patents contain two components: government fees and professional charges. The Patent Office in each country has to carry out a number of clerical and technical operations on each patent application, the latter requiring skilled manpower, and the objective is to charge applicants and patentees enough to make the Patent Office self-supporting. The fee in the UK for an application with a preliminary specification is a nominal £5 but fees required for a final are about £50. The patent agent's charges depend on the nature of the job but they are not likely to be less than £100 for a preliminary specification and £200 for a final. Much higher charges may be made for lengthy or complex work.

The costs for foreign applications vary a good deal from country to country. A large fraction of the costs in foreign-language countries goes for translation. An idea of the order of magnitude of the costs and of their range can be given by quoting estimates of £200 for an average case in India, and of £400 in West Germany.

It is impossible to estimate the cost of prosecuting an application since it depends on the nature of the subject-matter, the procedure of the country concerned and the objections the examiner happens to turn up. The cost can vary from a few pounds in some countries to hundreds of pounds for a difficult American case.

The annual renewal fees necessary to maintain a patent in force also vary enormously from country to country and over the life of the patent, generally increasing with its age. In USA and Canada no renewal fees are payable and among the principal countries they are probably heaviest in West Germany, varying from about £25 to about £850 (including agents' charges) over the life of the patent. The UK is on the inexpensive side with a range of about £40 to £150 exclusive of agent's charges.

In addition to these main costs there are one or two smaller fees to be paid at certain stages in the life of a patent application, again depending on the country concerned, but these are generally of the order of £20 or less.

Charges for trade-mark work follow a similar pattern but on a lower scale, perhaps a quarter to a half of the charge for analogous patent work. Renewal fees are required only at relatively long periods, for example in the UK every fourteen years after an initial period of seven years.

EPO fees

A special difficulty arises in connection with fees payable to the EPO. Most fee-bearing actions need to be taken by a deadline (e.g. Convention applications during the 12 months' priority), and the EPO has laid down that the deadline will not be met if the fee is not in the hands of the office by the deadline. Since the fees must be paid in Deutschemarks and exchange control is applicable, and any remittance must be identified with the transaction concerned, this can cause difficulties if time is short, and it usually is. To ease the problem the EPO has provided two methods of payment:

1   Through an account held by the EPO in Barclay's Bank International Gracechurch Branch, 69 Old Broad Street, London EC2P 2EE
2   Through a deposit account held at the EPO in Deutschemarks. This has the disadvantage for private practitioners of tying up working capital, but can be attractive for the patent departments of industrial companies.

FURTHER READING

Baxter, J.W., *World Patent Law and Practice*, Sweet and Maxwell, London, 1968.
Bloxam, G.A., *Licensing Rights in Technology*, Gower, 1972
Cawthra, B.I., *Industrial Property Rights in the EEC*, Gower, 1973
Hearn, P., *The Business of Industrial Licensing*, Gower, 1980

PART FIVE

PURCHASING AND INVENTORY MANAGEMENT

26 Procurement policy

Peter Baily

Manufacturing organisations typically spend over half of their total sales revenue on the purchase of materials, components and services from outside organisations. Retailing organisations of course spend an even higher proportion, since what they sell is what they buy. In the case of manufacturing organisations, what they sell is what they make, and most of their purchases constitute the materials and components required for the manufacture of their products.

Although this chapter is mainly about procurement policy for manufacturers, a brief comparison between the situation for manufacturers and that for retailers will be useful to establish the policy variables. Any trading organisation needs to determine, and continually to reconsider, its *market offering*: what products it offers, what prices it charges, how its products are publicised or promoted and how they are distributed to the customer or to places convenient to the customer.

A small independent retailer selects the products offered from those available at the wholesalers, cash and carry outlets, etc. A large chain store on the other hand may develop its own products and seek suitable producers for them. It may also purchase 'own brand' goods which are sometimes nationally available products, bought at a cheaper price without the national brand label. The main trading advantage of the chain store is in fact its ability to buy in bulk and thus both to rationalise its purchases and to get cheaper prices.

A small manufacturing firm will also make much use of wholesalers, and other organisations which specialise in supplying goods and services to manufacturers; but such organisations sell standard products, and even the smaller manufacturer needs to buy special products made to its own design. A large manufacturer may devote the major part of its purchasing effort to finding and trading with suppliers of components and materials which are not nationally available but are specifically called for by the design of the products which it is offering.

Very large manufacturers, and those occupying a *de facto* monopoly position as buyers, are in a position to exert so much leverage on their supply markets that they need to consider, whenever they take a major purchasing decision, the future state of the supply market which will result from it. Such organisations as the National Coal Board, British Telecom, IBM and General Motors constantly need to bear in mind such considerations, and much research and thought may be needed to decide whether a two-supplier market would be better than a three-supplier market, for instance.

The normal purchasing situation for the larger customer is what economists call *bilateral oligopoly*: that is, a small number of powerful suppliers dominate the supply market and a small number of powerful customers dominate the sales market. No formula will determine whether supplier or customer has the whip hand. Negotiation is used to decide the arrangements for supply: the specification, the contract quantity and the delivery quantities, the price and terms of payment, the inspection or quality assurance agreement, etc.

PROCUREMENT STRATEGIES

Corey (1978) classified procurement strategies into three groups:

1 Cost-based negotiation
2 Market-price-based negotiation
3 Competitive bidding.

While these were distinguished from each other basically by pricing mode, they also differed according to Corey in the product scope of the procurement (which could be narrow or broad), in the number and kind of suppliers contacted (ranging from one or very few in the case of cost-based negotiation to many in the second group), in price-quantity determination (including risk-sharing arrangements and the form in which quotations were requested) and in negotiating strategy (which varies considerably between the three groups).

Supplier selection was not just a matter of selecting the type and number of source; it involved the construction of a sourcing system in which different suppliers had different roles, for instance, technical development, price leadership, etc. Long-term supply availability, domestic versus foreign sources, distributors versus manufacturers and the strategy of numbers were some of the factors to be considered. Single sourcing and the stability of vendor relationships were topics of considerable importance, while in certain circumstances it could be quite difficult to persuade a supplier to accept an order. If a manufacturer needs to engage in demarketing its product, the customer needs to engage in marketing its demand, a reversal of the traditional relationship which may become increasingly prominent as material shortages loom larger.

Negotiation has become the subject of an enormous literature and many training courses are available for buyers, sellers, labour union representatives, management representatives, and many others with special interests. Most of this training material stresses the importance of the groundwork which precedes negotiating sessions, in which objectives are set, the relevant facts are assembled and conclusions drawn, and tentative agenda established for the negotiations.

Corey's work is based on research carried out at six very large American corporations during the seventies. Purchasing could be carried out, and in fact in all six cases was carried out, at plant level, divisional level, and corporate level; but a strong trend was noticed to centralise procurement decision-making to corporate level, mainly perhaps because of the increasing importance of the function as perceived by corporate management. Supply shortages and long-term planning of material availability, effective response to a changing business environment, profit improvement by means of purchase cost reduction, and better selection, use and development of purchasing talent were listed as reasons for this trend.

INPUT MANAGEMENT

Similar trends have been reported by Farmer (1981), in his discussion of the management of input to the firm from its supply market. Input in the sense in which it is used here refers to the components and materials used in producing the firm's end products. It is argued that too many firms have confined their strategic planning to output managment and the marketing of their end products, regarding the input area as operational rather than strategic. This thinking may indeed have been appropriate to the supply market conditions of the recent past, but it is doubtful if it continues to be appropriate in the present and likely that it will become quite inappropriate to future supply market conditions.

Farmer argues that while input management is one of the variables in a business system, and its importance varies from company to company and from time to time, it is nevertheless hardly ever to be regarded as insignificant. And while the operational aspects of input management are certainly important to the functioning of the business, it has strategic aspects which have often been overlooked in the quest for operational efficiency. The effectiveness of the whole business is not the same thing as the efficiency of the various functions which are elements within it. Co-ordination and balance should be sought betwen the various functions, and between input and output management, at the strategic as well as at the operational levels. To focus solely on cost reduction in the input and conversion stages of a manufacturing system, and to look for profit opportunities solely at the output end, may well, according to Farmer, have been a major contributing factor in the decline and even demise of many manufacturing businesses.

Purchasing policy should thus be seen as part of business policy, purchasing strategy as part of business strategy. Long-term as well as short-term aspects need to be considered, as indeed they have been by successful Japanese manufacturers of motor cars, motor bikes, and TV sets, and by successful retailers such as Marks & Spencer.

Professor Farmer in this paper was looking particularly at the long-term and strategic aspects of supply planning; but the short-term and operational aspects are also important in the determination of procurement policy. Materials requirement planning, greatly facilitated by the more powerful computers and better systems which became available in the early 1980s, brought major improvements to supply and production operations in those companies which implemented it successfully. The insistence that management should devise and authorise a rational, feasible and appropriate master schedule, coupled with the ability to explode this into detailed schedules of what parts, components and materials to make or buy, week by week, over the whole planning horizon, came like a revelation to companies which had previously operated on a chaotic mixture of stock-controlled production and customer priorities.

Materials management was a different but related approach, also intended to improve operational efficiency, but this time by a change in departmental structures.

MATERIALS MANAGEMENT

The term 'materials management' presumably referred originally to the management of the activities within an organisation which had to do with the planning, purchasing, transport, storage and handling of the materials required by the organisation, using materials in the general sense to refer to the whole range of goods and services obtained from outside the organisation in order to provide finished products for sale. However, increasingly materials management has come to refer to the grouping together of these materials-related activities into one department under a materials manager. A typical theoretical approach is shown in Figure 26.1.

In practice, surveys have shown that adoption of some kind of materials management structure has been extremely widespread in the USA, and there has also been considerable interest in the UK; but the kind of organisation adopted has often not conformed to the theoretical approach shown in the diagram. It has been suggested that in seeking the organisation structure which is right for a particular company at a particular time, some key variables should be identified – such as:

1 Purchasing cost reduction leverage
2 Type of production: make for stock or make to customer order
3 Commonality of requirement between different divisions
4 Whether most problems occur between materials-related departments
5 Trade-offs between materials and non-materials departments.

These approaches are discussed more fully in Baily and Farmer (1982), which also quotes evidence to suggest that the adoption of efficient computer systems for materials management appears to have reduced the need to combine the materials-related departments into a single materials management department.

It is obviously not easy to discuss the organisational questions in the abstract because of the great variations in size, complexity and other dimensions which exist between companies. Several large concerns which operate a number of establishments favour some version of the materials management structure at plant level, where purchasing staff are grouped departmentally with stock control, stores, production planning and control, and transport staff, while at corporate level purchasing and contracts staff form a separate planning and negotiating group. Similar developments can be seen in

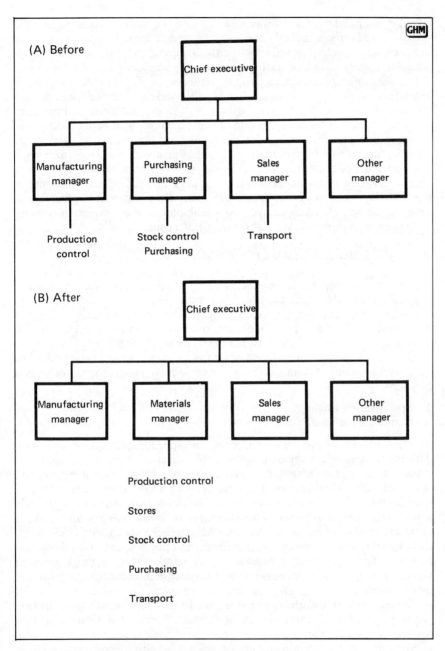

Figure 26.1   Materials management reorganisation

some retailing chains, where ordering and progessing staff are grouped organisationally with stock control, warehousing and transport, while a separate headquarters purchasing unit deals with the merchandising aspects, such as adoption of new lines and negotiation of original prices for first-time buys.

Devising appropriate organisation structures is a difficult process because so many factors affect it. One factor is the calibre and capability of the personnel affected. Purchasing staff who have the ability to contribute to long-term strategy are not necessarily the same people as those who do a sound job of ordering and progressing regular requirements from established suppliers. Another factor arises from the fact that purchasing departments exist to arrange for the supply of goods in accordance with the requirements of other departments, so that inter-departmental co-operation and communication is particularly important. Indeed many problems occur in practice in this area of inter-departmental relationships. An example is the matter of quality assurance, which forms the final topic in this chapter.

PURCHASING AND QUALITY ASSURANCE

Of fundamental importance in purchasing is to make sure that the right quality of goods, materials, etc. is bought. Both technical and commercial considerations are involved. The purchasing department operates jointly with other departments which also have important roles to play in this crucial aspect of arranging for the supply by outside organisations of what is required.

Although a number of different activities or stages occur in the process of purchasing quality assurance, it is convenient to group them under two headings:

1 Specification quality
2 Conformance quality.

The first part of the process is concerned with specifying the quality required. This may consist of a comparison of available merchandise and the selection of suitable brands or standards, or it may involve the preparation of engineering drawings and other forms of internally prepared specifications. Such a specification is a detailed statement of the features or characteristics required in a material, part or product. These features or characteristics may include chemical composition, such physical characteristics as ductility, viscosity, conductivity, weight, colour, surface finish, and physical size or dimensions – to name a few. The tolerance should also be stated: that is, the range of values within which a characteristic may vary without making the product unacceptable.

The second part of the process is concerned with arrangements to ensure that goods received conform with the specification, and that their important features or characteristics are within the allowed tolerances.

Normally in manufacturing industries a specialist department such as design, engineering, standards, etc. is entrusted with the responsibility for specifications. Such a department needs to take account of inputs from marketing (what can be sold) and from purchasing (what can be bought), as well as the production implications. It is difficult to generalise about the role of the purchasing department in this connection beyond saying that it must play some part, and that its concern will naturally be with the commercial rather than with the technical aspects of the product. Commercial aspects include the relative cost and availability of alternative materials or products, and also the feasibility of obtaining the quantity required for bulk production at an acceptable price.

A single instance may illustrate the last point. A certain company manufactures agricultural chemical products, for use mainly by farmers but also by home gardeners. New products are continually being developed by the research and development laboratories. If approved by the new products committee, which is heavily marketing orientated, they are put into a two-year field trial process intended to uncover any unwanted side-effects as well as to provide evidence that the products will in fact produce the effect claimed. During this two-year period, a purchasing research section within the purchasing department investigates the availability on world markets of all the ingredients required by the formulation of each new product under trial. Naturally at the end of the two-year trial it is not possible to change the formulation before going into bulk production. But it would be a mistake for management to authorise bulk production if some of the ingredients could not be supplied in sufficient quantities.

The second part of the process is concerned with the selection of suppliers, the approval of their quality control systems and the inspection of goods received. Inspection is an expensive process, and should not need to be carried out at all if suppliers could be relied on to supply acceptable goods. Increasingly, purchasing organisations are taking steps to ensure that this is so.

Many organisations carry out their own investigations of suppliers, but third-party investigations are also used quite widely: the British Standards Institution, the Crown Agents and a number of other organisations operate in this connection. Most systems for investigating the quality capability of suppliers classify the work into three levels, depending on the extent to which the customer relies on the supplier.

At the simplest level, all that the customer needs to know is whether the supplier has satisfactory instruments, test equipment and inspection procedures for final inspection of his products.

Many intermediate-level products require inspection at a number of successive stages of manufacture, with a reliable system for corrective action if faults occur, so that a more comprehensive system of quality control would need to be certified.

When a supplier is responsible for design as well as for manufacture, the investigation of his quality capability needs to be still more extensive and thorough.

Industries such as aerospace, motor car manufacture, atomic energy and other parts of electrical manufacturing, are already subject to strict official regulation of certain aspects of quality (mainly those which have to do with safety) and this has been one of the factors leading to the development of British Standards such as BS 5179.

At the same time as official regulation of safety and other quality standards has increased, and official guidance as to procedures for ensuring that suppliers are capable of supplying and do in fact supply goods to the standard specified has become more widespread, a parallel development has been occurring within companies. Quality is everybody's business; job security and progression for the individual depends on the organisation's ability to survive and prosper, which in turn to a large extent depends on the quality of its products.

Quality circles are a recent example of many approaches which organisations have adopted to encourage individual and small group initiative in maintaining and improving the quality of the product.

Technical inspection of incoming goods is a costly business which in principle could be dispensed with if suppliers could be relied on to supply acceptable goods. The investigation and selection process described above is intended to ensure that suppliers are in fact to be relied on, and is often used in practice to classify suppliers into three groups:

1 Accept goods on supplier's certificate
2 Accept goods after sample inspection
3 Inspect all goods received; do not order from this supplier if an alternative supplier is available.

If goods received require technical inspection before acceptance, it is often possible to obtain satisfactory results by inspecting a sample rather than every piece submitted. A large body of theory exists which can be applied in this connection to select the size of the sample and to draw conclusions from the results.

REFERENCES AND FURTHER READING

Baily, P.J.H., and Farmer, D.H., *Purchasing Principles & Management*, Pitman Publishing, London, 1981

Baily, P.J.H., and Farmer, D.H., *Materials Management Handbook*, Gower, 1982

Corey, E. Raymond, *Procurement Strategy, Organisation and Decision-Making*, CBI Publishing Company, Boston, Mass., 1978

Farmer, D.H., 'Input Management', *Purchasing & Supply Management*, Institute of Purchasing & Supply, Ascot, Berks., Aug. 1981

27 Purchasing procedures

Peter Baily

Management will naturally wish to adopt or devise purchasing procedures which suit the individual requirements of their own organisations. Retailers do not in general use quite the same systems and procedures as manufacturers, while civil engineering contractors have their own variations: procedures need to be appropriate to the type of operation.

Some of the organisations which employ purchasing staff are quite small, while others are very large and operate on a national or a worldwide scale. Procedures can be affected by the scale of operation.

Procedures are also affected by the type of office technology employed. Communications between buyer and seller can be face to face, by word of mouth, handwritten or typed and sent through the post, or some form of electronic mail can be used. Telex and facsimile have been in use for many years. Communicating word processors, teletext and direct links between customer's computer and supplier's computer are in the early stages of adoption.

The standard operating procedure for purchasing will be affected by the type and scale of operation and by the type of communications and records employed, but in addition to the standard procedure, a number of special procedures may be used. For instance many organisations adopt special procedures for routine low-value purchases, and also for non-routine high-value capital expenditure transactions. Procedures need to be appropriate to the type of purchase, and to enforce a single standard procedure for all purchases, while having the merit of simplicity, is not always the best way to do things.

This chapter outlines a standard purchasing procedure in four successive stages:

1　Initiation
2　Supplier selection
3　Contract stage
4　Completion.

Reference is made in each stage to the special or non-standard variations most commonly encountered, with examples of forms. The process is illustrated in Figure 27.1.

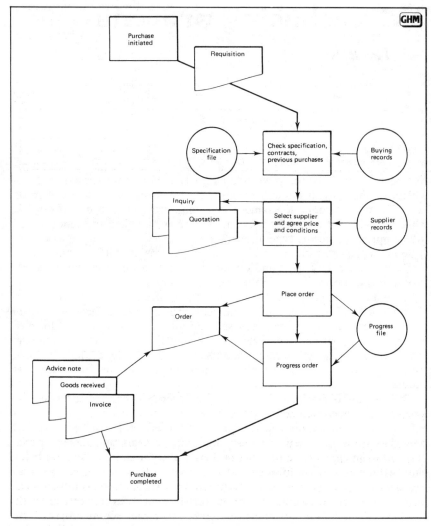

Figure 27.1   Outline of standard purchase procedure

INITIATION

Purchasing for organisations involves arranging for the supply on time and at a suitable price of the goods and materials, equipment and merchandise, services and supplies which are required to meet production programmes, sales plans or operating needs. It is normally the job of the purchase department to make the purchase on behalf of production, sales or operating departments. It is not normally the job of the purchase department to determine what needs to be purchased: most purchases are initiated by *requisitions* from other departments.

A purchase requisition is a request to the purchase department from any other department for something to be purchased. It serves to initiate the purchase, and also for audit purposes to provide evidence of authorisation and action taken. An example is shown in Figure 27.2.

Figure 27.2 Purchase requisition

Such requisitions are date-stamped on receipt by the purchasing section and allocated to an appropriate member of department for action. The buyer may need to check the requisition against specification files, buying records and contract files. Some editing may be required, since requisitioners do not always express their requirements in terms suitable for communications with suppliers. If the item requisitioned is covered by a contract, an order will be placed immediately. Otherwise, a supplier may need to be selected. After the order has been placed, the requisition is filed for a limited period in case of query: two years should be quite adequate.

Many stock items and MRO (maintenance, repair and operating) requirements are ordered several times a year, and for these a *travelling requisition* will save time. This is a card kept in the initiating department on which is entered permanent data (such as description) and variable data (such as quantity required and date). It is sent to the purchasing section to initiate a purchase. After ordering the goods, details are entered on the card which is returned to the initiating department. An example is illustrated in Figure 27.3.

Figure 27.3   Travelling requisition

Systems for production planning and control used by manufacturers, or for stock planning and control used both by manufacturers and service industries such as retailing, normally generate a large group of purchase requirements periodically. Rather than prepare separate individual requisitions for each item affected, a *blanket requisition* or schedule of requirements is produced.

Materials Requirement Planning (MRP) systems are particuarly suitable for jobbing and batch production. With suitable adaptations they have been used in mass production ever since Henry Ford devised the first assembly line for motor cars. The process starts with the regular production or revision of a master production schedule which states, period by period, what quantities of each end product need to be completed to meet sales commitment or management plans.

For each end product the quantities due in each period are exploded by means of a parts list or bill of materials to determine what parts or materials are required for its completion, and this is offset by lead times to yield a time-phased schedule of gross requirements for parts and materials. Adjustments are then made for uncommitted stock on hand and orders due in to produce a time-phased schedule of net purchase requirements, or blanket requisition.

Stock control systems fall into two main groupings: continuous, and periodic. In continuous systems, each stock item is assigned an order point and an order quantity. Whenever a stock item quantity falls to the order point, an order is triggered for the appropriate order quantity, so that the system produces orders continuously. Travelling requisitions as previously described are often used. In periodic systems, either the whole stock range or a substantial subsection of it is reviewed at regular intervals. Stock on hand is compared with target stock as previously determined, or as calculated dynamically from previously determined rules. A blanket requisition or schedule of stock replenishment requirements is produced.

SUPPLIER SELECTION

Upon receipt of a requisition, the purchasing section checks if the item in question is already covered by a contract. If it is, an order can be placed against the contract without delay. If it is not covered by a contract, the next stage is to select a supplier and agree price and terms.

There is a strong preference for continuing to deal with regular suppliers in the case of regular purchases, so long as they continue to prove satisfactory. Nevertheless it is advisable periodically to check the market, to see what other suppliers have to offer. How often this should be done is a matter for judgement, and will vary with the type and volume of requirement and the structure of the supply market. If the market is dominated by one or two major suppliers it may be greatly to the long-term advantage of purchasers to place their business in such a way as to keep competition alive. Very large purchasers which dominate a market on the customer side often devote a good deal of time and thought to the optimum supply market structure, and sometimes take direct action to support minority suppliers or to develop new suppliers.

It is good practice for purchasing staff to know their regular suppliers well, to be personally acquainted with the people who process and make decisions about their orders, to keep in touch with business plans, product developments and so forth. Suppliers are a major resource without which neither manufacturers nor traders could operate, and the management of supply markets can be a very important matter which calls for advance planning, forethought, and some difficult decisions.

When making a new purchase for which there is no regular supplier, or when checking the market for regular purchases, the usual procedure is to send a *request for quotation* to a short list of possible sources. Names of potential suppliers are obtained from trade associations, commercial directories and buyers' guides, the trade knowledge of the buyers and their colleagues, advertisements and editorial material in the trade press, salesmen and technical representatives who call on the purchaser, and catalogues and other direct mail material which is received. A number of computerised buyers' guides are also available, which can be consulted on-line or by a telephone call; their main advantage is that they can be kept up to date continually, whereas printed directories can only be updated periodically when they are reprinted. As industrialisation spreads to new parts of the world, the search area for potential suppliers continues to widen; particular care should be taken before committing sourcing arrangements for important requirements to an untried overseas source, but major competitive advantage may result.

The request for quotation form (or enquiry as it is sometimes called) is shown in Figure 27.4. The form itself is simply the usual letterhead with, to save typing, a standard preprinted text asking the addressee to quote price, terms and delivery date for supply of the undermentioned goods on the terms and conditions stated overleaf.

GHM

```
        Dear Sirs,

                PURCHASE INQUIRY

                Your quotation is invited not later than ................
        for the supply and delivery of the goods specified below, carriage
        paid, to .................

                Your tender must clearly state (a) the price which will
        remain firm, (b) the terms of payment, (c) details of appropriate
        discounts, and (d) the period required for delivery.  It must also
        incorporate all the conditions (general and special) set out overleaf.
```

```
        Dear Sirs,

                CONTRACT INQUIRY

                Your tender is invited for the supply and delivery of the
        goods specified below to any of the Board's depots listed overleaf.

                Your tender must clearly state (a) the price which will remain
        firm throughout the period of the contract, (b) the terms of payment,
        (c) details of appropriate discounts, and (d) the period required for
        delivery.  It must also incorporate all the conditions (general and special)
        set out overleaf.

                If your tender is accepted you will then supply and deliver
        the goods in accordance with draw-off orders issued by the Board's
        supplies officers and invoices should be submitted for payment in
        respect of such draw-off orders.

                I shall be pleased, therefore, to receive your tender not
        later than .................... in a plain sealed envelope marked
        "contract inquiry number .........."

                Period of contract:
                Description of goods:

                Yours faithfully,


                (Purchasing and Stores Controller)
```

Figure 27.4 Request for quotations (enquiry)

There is, however, sometimes considerable scope to structure the request for quotation in such a way as to facilitate subsequent negotiation in order to arrive at a mutually satisfactory agreement which gives better value: alternatives may be put forward as to total contract quantity, sub-quantities to be ordered against contract or delivered in particular places at particular times, terms of payment and other aspects of the deal. In some cases suppliers are asked to support their price quotation by a cost breakdown, which will be compared with a price/cost analysis prepared internally by estimating staff attached to purchasing. This latter technique is particularly favoured by mass-production manufacturers, the very scale of whose requirements limits possible suppliers to one or two in a given national economy.

In most cases the information a supplier gives on his tender or quotation needs to be supplemented by information in financial stability, quality capability, performance record, etc., which has to be obtained independently by purchasing staff. Reference was made in the previous chapter to supplier inspection visits in connection with quality assurance. All these matters are of particular importance in sourcing new requirements or considering new suppliers. When considering regular purchases or established suppliers, the track record is of particular importance – although it should not be forgotten that past history is not a sure guide to future behaviour. Management does change, new developments occur, new products are launched, new customers found: nevertheless it would not be prudent to ignore the record of how a particular supplier has behaved in the past. *Vendor rating* is an attempt to systematise this information.

Vendor rating

Vendor rating, or supplier evaluation as it is sometimes called, is the process of systematically accumulating information about a supplier's actual performance and presenting it in numerical form. The usual aspects of performance to be measured are:

1   Quality
2   On-time delivery
3   Service (although this is usually estimated rather than measured)
4   Price.

Quality is delivered or conformance quality: essentially, the proportion of goods delivered by a supplier which are accepted. In practice several rules are used to calculate a figure appropriate to the needs of a particular purchaser: one for instance is:

$$\frac{60 \text{ (number of batches accepted)}}{\text{number of batches delivered}} + \frac{40 \text{ (number of parts accepted)}}{\text{number of parts delivered}}$$

The delivery measure is again based on goods-recieved records and is essentially the proportion of goods delivered on time. Since the meaning of 'on time' may not be the same in a large-scale mass producer (within ten minutes of the due hour and date?) and a small-scale batch producer (within two weeks of

465

due date?), rules are specified to suit purchasing needs.

The price rating may be based on a comparison of the price quoted by the supplier in question with that quoted by competitors: the lowest price would score 100, and a price twice as high as the lowest would score 50 in one scheme. Often such a comparison is not feasible, and the price rating is based on a comparison of latest price with standard budget price, or last year's price, or latest target price.

It is not particularly difficult to calculate these ratings manually, since the system will be applied only to a minority of purchases from a relatively small number of suppliers, but computer salesmen have made much of the system as a further argument for extending the application of computers.

In most systems, after calculating individual numerical scores for the supplier characteristics being measured, a further calculation is made by weighting and combining the individual scores to arrive at an overall figure which is regarded as an index of the supplier's total performance – in fact a vendor rating or supplier evaluation figure which can be used in deciding how to allocate business between potential suppliers and also in persuading delinquent suppliers to improve their performance!

Such systems are considered in more detail in purchasing textbooks, and in books about industrial marketing, but it must be admitted that recent accounts in books which have a practical rather than a strictly academic bias are somewhat less than enthusiastic about their use in practice and tend to stress their limitations. See for instance Baily (1978) and Baily and Farmer (1981).

THE CONTRACT STAGE

A contract is a business agreement for the supply of goods or the performance of work in return for a price, and subject usually to a number of terms and conditions. An order on the other hand is an instruction to a trader or manufacturer to supply something.

In most cases both order and contract are incorporated in a single document, the purchase order form. Normal practice is to make it a rule that all purchases, subject to certain clearly defined exceptions, must be made by means of the official purchase order form. This if for practical rather than for legal reasons. The purpose of the rule is to prevent sharp practice, whether by some unscrupulous employee or by some shady dealer outside the organisation, and also to establish clearly what the organisation is committed to accept and pay for. Regular suppliers are made aware of the rule by printing it on the order form, or by stipulating that the order number must be quoted on advice notes and invoices. Goods-receiving personnel can then be given instructions not to accept goods which are delivered without an official order number.

Exceptions to this procedure take several forms. The contract, or agreement with the supplier, may cover the supply of aggregated requirements over a considerable period of time, or over a large geographical area as when corporate contracts are signed by headquarters staff for common requirements at a number of divisions or branches. If such a contract is placed on the standard purchase order form it might cause some confusion if the same form is also used for instructions to supply specific quantities of goods against the contract to specific locations.

Three solutions have been observed in practice. First, a special form is used for the contract document, and normal purchase orders are used to order goods against it. Second, the normal purchase order form is used for the contract, and special forms are used for the orders; these may be known as delivery schedules, delivery instructions, contract releases, or call-offs. Third, the same form is used both for order and contract, and care is taken to state on one: 'This is an order against contract', and on the other: 'This is a contract against which goods should not be delivered until orders are placed.'

Most organisations use a preprinted multipart set of forms for purchase orders. Four or five copies are usually provided, and these are distributed to supplier, goods receiving, possibly accounts, possibly originator (department which produced the requisition), to purchase order open file, and possibly to order progress file.

Some large organisations have adopted computer-output order forms, which in the recent past appear to have largely failed to live up to expectations. The clerical work was not reduced, the amount of paper was increased because each order was confined to one item from one supplier, the technology was costly, and so on. But it is likely that such developments as communicating word processors, computer-to-computer links either via telex or telephone connection or several other methods currently being developed, will alter the balance of economics and that the traditional method of typed order forms sent by letter post will gradually become less economic than the newer methods of electronic mail. (A review of the current position, rapidly changing as it is, may be found in the second edition of *Purchasing Systems and Records* mentioned at the end of the chapter under 'Further Reading'.)

Blanket orders or systems contracting methods are often used with considerable commercial advantage where it is possible to group together either numbers of different item requirements from one source, or else a sequence of requirements of one item over a substantial period of time, say, six months or a year. Instead of treating each order, or requisition, as an independent closed transaction, the idea is to look at the flow of requirements over a time and buy the flow. Instead of taking a bucket to the well every day, a waterpipe is laid on.

For example, a small or intermediate value purchase is carbon paper. Instead of placing a series of orders every months or so for the various sizes and grades required, with this technique once a year there is a review of requirements, alternative specifications and sources. Twelve months' requirements are then covered with just one or two orders which specify so many reams of A4 standard weight, so many reams of lightweight, etc., to be delivered each month. If stocks start to build up or fall short during the year, one or two adjustments may be required. Apart from that, supplies come through automatically; and the price, based on a twelve-month contract, is low.

A group one or two production purchase may not seem at first glance amenable to this approach if production programmes are not fixed twelve months in advance. There will usually be a sales forecast going at least a year ahead, and a firm production programme going only one or two months ahead.

The solution then may be to approach management to authorise purchasing to make firm commitments for 50 per cent of the sales estimate for the year, thus getting the benefit of a lower price and also the benefit of a bank stock of finished parts to handle cyclical fluctuations. In one actual case, component X was being bought in lots of 1000 approximately at a price of 26p a piece. It was built into a product with a current sales estimate of 12 000 a year. Contracting for 50 per cent of this, that is 6000 pieces, with delivery called off at 1000 a month, enabled the buyers to bring the price down to 20p, a 23 per cent reduction in invoice cost, with further reductions in administrative costs and paperwork. Both cost and availability are improved, and if sales fall short of forecast, it may well take nine or twelve months instead of six months to clear the components but they would still be used up within the year. This is a useful technique for plastic mouldings, castings, electrical and mechanical parts.

SMALL ORDER PROCEDURES

Wherever possible the small orders should be put through a special procedure. If they are repeating or regular requirements they should be bought once a year in one lot, or perhaps twice a year: it is obviously uneconomic to expend £15 worth of man-hours, cheques, stamps and paperwork in procuring an item with a usage value of only £15 a year, but it happens. Non-repeating small orders are often such things as maintenance requirements, design and development prototypes, laboratory requirements. The requisitioner knows exactly what he wants and where to get it and the price is often a listed price. One solution to this problem is the order/requisition/cheque form devised by Kaiser Aluminium in the United States, and adopted by other organisations, including one in the public service. Through clever forms design, the same document which the requisitioner prepares as a requisition serves as an order, and a blank cheque accompanying it (marked 'not valid above £X') cuts out the invoicing/purchase-ledger/payments procedure.

Other approaches to the small order problem include: local cash purchase – a man with a bag of cash goes round in a van picking up requirements and paying for them as he goes; and laundry list – the local stockholder calls once a week and delivers a wide range of sundry materials against a laundry list type of order: invoices come through once a month and prices are negotiated annually.

THE COMPLETION STAGE

Contracts (or orders) are completed when goods are delivered or work is done in accordance with the agreement and payment is made as provided.

Obtaining delivery on time can be a difficult problem: the sub-contract and component supply section of the engineering industries have got themselves a bad name for late delivery, although large numbers of purchasers throughout industry and commerce have few problems in this connection and would rightly regard late delivery as an exceptional event, to be dealt with by crisis measures when it occurs.

The fundamental step in obtaining delivery on time is to decide accurately and firmly exactly what is wanted at what time, to communicate this decision to those concerned, and to insist that delivery is made at the time specified. All too often firms which complain of late deliveries by suppliers are themselves to blame for inaccurate delivery schedules, continually amended. When both customer and supplier are struggling to operate with production planning and control systems which are defective in practice and misconceived in principle it is astonishing that anything is ever delivered on time, yet this has been the situation in certain sections of the engineering industry. Materials-requirement planning systems, if property designed and operated, have brought great improvements in this connection to manufacturers of complex products.

The next step is to ensure that suppliers know that on-time delivery is a very important element in their marketing mix: in the combination of characteristics which results in their customers doing business with them. If valid due dates are stipulated it becomes easy to measure supplier performance in meeting due dates, and delivery performance tends to improve significantly once it is measured and reported. Customers with accurate, stable and reliable schedules of delivery requirements, who insist on delivery at the time scheduled, and measure and report supplier delivery performance, are on the whole quite satisfied with the results they get. In many cases it has been shown that 99 per cent on-time delivery is normal when suppliers know and are fully aware that the schedule is accurate and that every time they fail to meet the schedule they are going to have to explain it to their customers. Nevertheless, progressing (chasing, expediting or follow-up) of orders remains necessary in many cases. This may be done:

1 At the date when tool or jig designs are to be ready
2 When the items from these designs should be available
3 When materials or components should be marshalled for production
4 When the various stages of production can be achieved
5 When final assembly and testing will be completed.

Often critical areas may be isolated in this progressing for special attention. For example, special castings with long delivery times could be delivered to suppliers and then be rejected because of their porosity. In consequence, some companies extend their progressing activities in such cases to include secondary suppliers.

Methods which can be applied to help ensure that more general orders are controlled – chased when they ought to be – include:

1 Copy orders filed in date-due order, being actioned, say, one week before that due date in general, or as necessary in the particular case.
2 Five divisions made at the top of the copy order numbered one to five (representing weeks in any month). A signal of a different colour is then allocated to each month and one is attached to the relevant square in the particular case. (Thus if January were red and the item were due in week three of that month, a red signal would be placed on square three.) The order copies are then filed in alphabetical order by supplier.
3 A diary system with the serial numbers of orders which are due being entered on the appropriate page of the diary.

It is often useful to provide space on the order form to record the date of progress action, reply, etc., as shown in Figure 27.5.

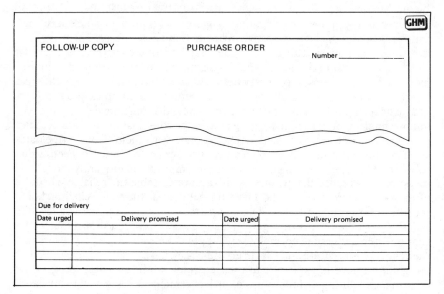

Figure 27.5   Follow-up copy of purchase order

Finally, the supplier dispatches the goods to the customer, usually including a packing note and copy advice note with the goods and also forwarding an advice note by post. The postal copy is passed to the purchasing section to note that goods are in transit and the same morning is passed on to the goods-receiving section. Each day the goods-receiving section check through their file of advice notes and if any goods appear to have been lost or delayed in transit they initiate appropriate action. When goods are actually delivered, a goods-received note is prepared, usually on a multipart form to notify purchasing, accounting, and originating sections of the delivery.

REFERENCES AND FURTHER READING

Baily, P., *Purchasing & Supply Management*, 4th edition, Chapman & Hall, London, 1978

Baily, P., and Farmer, D.H., *Purchasing Principles & Management*, Pitman London, 1981

Baily, P., *Purchasing Systems and Records*, 2nd edition, Gower, 1983

28 Controlling manufacturing stocks

Dennis Lock

The financial investment tied up in total manufacturing stocks is bound to represent a very high proportion of the capital employed in any typical manufacturing company. Total inventory comprises purchased materials and components held in stores, stocks of finished goods awaiting sales, and all the work in progress. The value of work in progress includes not only the relevant materials costs, but also the value added in terms of labour costs incurred in machining, assembly and all the other process operations throughout the factory. Stocks and work in progress away on subcontractors' premises also contribute to this total investment. Since so much capital is attributable to inventory holding, it follows that sensible and efficient control of stock levels is an essential ingredient of profitable management.

For a given level of factory output, the value of work in progress must depend largely on the average throughput time taken by work through the plant. Put very crudely, a factory with an average throughput time of three months would probably carry about twice the amount of work in progress as another factory making the same product, at the same rate, but with a throughput of six weeks. Thus efficient production control and materials movement between workstations is obviously another very important factor. Since production control and plant layout are important elements in the control of work in progress, the chapters in Part 6 are particularly relevant.

Distribution managers rightly take a wider view of total inventory costs because their responsibility extends to goods in warehouses and other premises off site, and in vehicles and vessels plying between those places. These distribution aspects are complex, and solving the problem of providing good customer service while avoiding excessive stock levels and transport costs becomes a challenging exercise in logistics. This subject is discussed in Chapter 35.

In this chapter we are concerned with the control of stocks in the factory stores. Although there may be a person in the organisation with the title 'stock controller', in reality the management of local stock levels is a team function involving the purchasing, stores, stock control and production control personnel.

STOCK RECORDS

Later in this chapter, various aspects of stock level control will be discussed. First, however, it is fairly obvious that no control over stock levels can be exercised at all unless a firm knows, with reasonable accuracy, the actual levels of stocks held at all times. All records systems cost money to operate, whether they are carried out manually or by computer. It is useful to consider the classes of stock items according to the financial value that each represents, in order that systems and management attention can be concentrated on the most significant items.

ABC stock classification

Using Pareto's rule as a basis, stock can be considered in three categories, A, B and C. This is illustrated in Figure 28.1 and demonstrates (Pareto's rule) that a high proportion of stock value is represented by a relatively small number of high-cost stock items. These can be called the A items, which demand the highest level of attention. At the other end of the scale, large numbers of small components, such as nuts, screws and washers, warrant only some simple form of recording and control: these are the C items. The remaining B items will need to be recorded in a stock level system – most probably the same system as the A items – but there will not be the same urgency to keep strict control over ordering levels and timing.

Basic stock record information

Many stock record systems depend on index cards, the information on which is entered and updated as stores inputs and issues occur. In the past such systems were duplicated in the stores and in the stock control (or purchasing) departments and where such duplicated or triplicated sets of records existed it was always a fairly safe bet that (owing to errors) no two sets of records would ever agree exactly. This is one area where a centralised computer can prove really useful, with terminals located in the stores and purchasing departments that allow information to be updated immediately stock movements take place. Whatever system is used, and whether it is clerical or computer based, the following data are usually required for each stock item:

A code number

Must be unique to the particular stock item, which allows the item to be identified without ambiguity for all purposes. This code may well be allocated to fit in with the firm's own drawing numbering system, or the costing system, or (preferably) both of these.

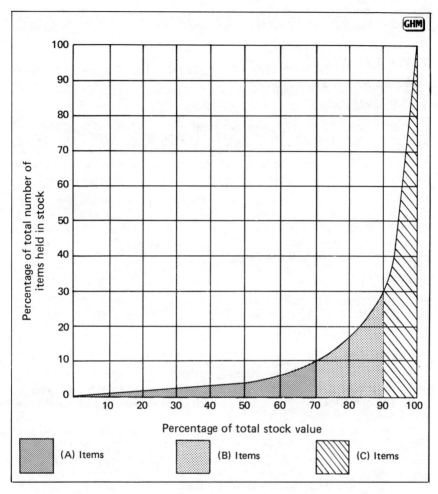

Figure 28.1 *ABC classification of stocks. By concentrating stringent control on the few most expensive A items effective inventory reduction can be achieved for least effort*

Description

Used in conjunction with the code number for identification. This may include a summary of technical data for purchased components. Descriptions are necessary as back-up identification, to avoid expensive mistakes when clerks make copying errors when writing down long code numbers. Descriptions are also obviously vital when the code number has been forgotten or is not known.

Quantity held in stock

A function of movements into and out of stock. It is usual to record these movements in addition to the actual residual stock quantity. Where issues are made, details of relevant job numbers are entered; when new stock arrives the particular batch quantity is entered together with the purchase order number.

Stores location or bin number

A coded address that positively indicates the rack, shelf, bin or other location where the item is normally stored.

Stock control information

Includes (according to the system for control in use) planned maximum and minimum stock quantities, the stock level at which re-ordering should take place, and so on.

Cost data

Shows the cost per unit of issue (for example, in pounds sterling per litre). Typically, such costs are computed and entered afresh for each new intake batch. However, in standard costing systems, such entries are used to assist the accounts department in calculating historical variances and in setting up periodically new standard cost levels.

Selling price

This is occasionally needed, especially where stock lists are generated for issue to sales staff, or where the stores is actually responsible for handling and invoicing customers' orders.

Issue restrictions

May include the reservation of certain stocks for particular jobs. Recording such information in the stores stock record system can prevent the inadvertent issue of stocks that are required against some other vital need (such restrictions are known as pre-allocations).

There is probably no such thing as a typical stock record card, because systems vary greatly from one company to another. Figure 28.2 shows an example produced by Kalamazoo which caters for a fair proportion of the requirements listed above.

Computerised stock records

Stock record systems and computers are a logical combination. Using the stock code number as the principal identifier for each item, it is a straightforward job to set up a database. Once this has been done, computer terminals in the stores and in related departments can be used to interrogate the database at any time, and fresh information on stock movements or the issue of purchase (or manufacturing) orders for replacement stocks can be fed into the system without delay.

Later in this chapter, some systems for calculating economic stock control decisions will be described: the application of such systems can become fairly automatic when a computer is used with suitable software.

Figure 28.2   Stock record card. This stock record card carries most of the data needed in a typical stock control system (Kalamazoo Limited)

Once a stock database has been set up, the computer can be made to produce reports which are edited or sequenced to suit a number of different departments in the factory. These could include a listing of all stocks, sorted according to stock numbers or by an alphabetical sorting of the first character in the description. Where, for example, retail prices are printed out alongside all items, stocklists become valuable to salesmen and others who deal directly with taking customer orders. A large 'mainframe' computer is not always required, and minicomputers can often cope. A reasonably straightforward program produced the illustration in Figure 28.3 using a minicomputer.

Stock movements

It is useful to stop at this point and list various ways and means by which stocks can be added or subtracted from stores holdings. *Inputs* can arrive in stores through three main routes. These are:

1   Receipts from outside suppliers, documented into stores by means of goods inwards inspection notes, or simply by reference to the particular purchase order number
2   Components manufactured within the factory (or by outside subcontractors) released by inspection notes or by an inspector's stamp against the final operation on the relevant batch route card
3   Goods returned to stores as surplus to factory production requirements. It

475

PRODUCT CODE	DESCRIPTION	PHYS. LEVEL	ALLOC STOCK	BACK ORDER	ON ORDER	USAGE PERIOD	USAGE TO DATE	LAST INV DATE	REORDER LEVEL	MIN. LEVEL	NO.MIN REPORT	REMARK RO MIN
A123	CLOCKS	149	2	0	140-	1	1	10.08.81	150	50	0	**
B100	BRACELET GATE 5 BAR	92	5	2	100-	8	8	10.08.81	15	5	0	
B101	BRACELET GATE 4 BAR	50	5	0	50-	0	0	00.00.00	15	10	0	
B102	BRACELET GATE 3 BAR	50	0	0	50-	0	0	00.00.00	15	10	0	
B103	BRACELET GATE 7 BAR	48	0	0	50-	2	2	10.08.81	10	5	0	
B123	EARRINGS STUDS	159	0	0	140-	1	1	10.08.81	150	100	0	
C100	CHARMS CHURCH 9C	60	0	0	60-	0	0	00.00.00	5	2	0	
C101	CHARMS CROSS 9C	48	0	0	50-	8	8	10.08.81	5	2	0	
C102	CHARM RABBIT 9C	47	0	0	50-	3	3	10.08.81	5	2	0	
C123	BRACELETS	53	0	0	3-	0	0	00.00.00	100	50	0	**
D123	GOLD BANDS	161	5	0	5-	4	4	10.08.81	50	40	0	
E123	TIARAS	15	5	0	6-	3	3	10.08.81	2	1	0	
R100	PLAIN GOLD BAND 9C	24	0	0	25-	1	1	10.08.81	20	9	0	
R101	PLAIN GOLD BAND 18C	34	0	0	35-	1	1	10.08.81	20	10	0	
R102	PLAIN GOLD BAND 22C	29	3-	0	30-	1	1	10.08.81	10	4	0	
R103	RUBY RING GOLD	27	2-	5	35-	8	8	10.08.81	10	5	0	
R104	DIAMOND SOLITAIRE GOLD	33	0	0	23-	2	2	10.08.81	6	4	0	
R105	DIAMOND SOLITAIRE 18C	32	0	0	32-	0	0	00.00.00	15	3	0	
R106	DIAMOND SOLITAIRE 22C	8	0	0	9-	2	2	10.08.81	15	5	0	**
R107	SILVER WEDDING RINGS BAND	20	0	0	17-	0	0	00.00.00	15	4	0	
R108	WHITE GOLD BANDS	24	0	0	25-	7	7	10.08.81	10	5	0	
S100	STUDS FLOWERS 9C	18	0	0	25-	7	7	10.08.81	15	5	0	
S101	STUDS CROSS 9C	40	0	3	50-	13	13	10.08.81	15	5	0	
S102	STUDS DIAMONDS 9C	24	2	1	20-	6	6	10.08.81	10	5	0	
S103	STUDS KEYS 9C	23	0	0	25-	2	2	10.08.81	10	5	0	
S104	STUDS LOOPS 9C	27	1-	0	25-	1	1	10.08.81	5	2	0	

RANGE: A123 TO T123

GHM

Figure 28.3   *Stocklisting the minicomputer. This report was specially prepared to demonstrate the type of stocklist layout and content possible from a very small computer system located in the stores area (Triumph Adler)* is usual to pass such returns through the inspection department in order that inspection dockets can be issued which clarify that the goods are fit for re-issue.

Outputs can happen through:

1 Issues to the factory, either against requisitions or against instructions contained in parts lists or raw materials lists which accompany the appropriate works order
2 Direct sales of finished goods to outside customers.
3 Management decisions to scrap or sell off redundant, surplus items.

If just one item of stock is considered over a long period, the quantity held must fluctuate in sympathy with stores receipts and issues. A rather simplified graph of such movements is shown in Figure 28.4. This leads in to some of the problems encountered in controlling stock levels.

METHODS FOR CONTROLLING STOCK LEVELS

The two-bin method

Low-cost items such as consumables (the C items if the ABC system is operated) may be suitable for stock control by the two-bin method. In the case of quantities of nuts, bolts, washers and other small parts the storekeeper has two bins for each item. One bin is used for issues and the other held in reserve. The issuing bin contains a travelling requisition. When the first bin is exhausted the travelling requisition is sent to the buyer for a suitable quantity to be reordered (possibly enough to fill two bins). The second, reserve, bin is then used for issues while the reorder quantity is awaited after which the first bin becomes the new reserve.

This method also works for stationery supplies. Consider a stock of letterhead stationery on a shelf stored in boxes of one ream (500 sheets) each. If a travelling requisition is placed to protrude at a suitable level in a stack of boxes this will ensure re-ordering when the pile has been reduced to the minimum quantity allowable. The remainder of the pile then acts as a reserve whilst new deliveries are awaited.

Economic order quantity

Stocks for continuous or batch production are liable to be over-ordered because of the lure of quantity discounts. Against any advantage in lower prices obtained through bulk ordering must be set the increased costs of storage, risk of obsolescence and the cost of capital employed. By comparing all the costs involved in carrying inventory with purchase prices in relation to quantities, it is theoretically possible to produce a set of curves similar to those shown in Figure 28.5. These curves show that there is one particular order quantity where the advantages of quanity discounts are just balanced by the increased costs of inventory carrying, this quantity being regarded as the economic order

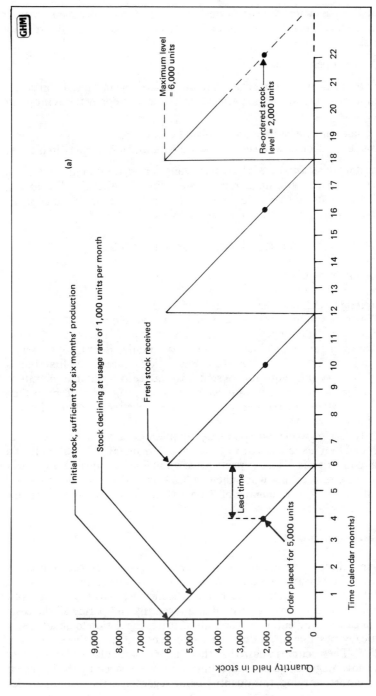

Figure 28.4 Stock movement patterns. *Figure (a) illustrates a stylised and ideal fluctuation of stock levels with the passage of time. In the lower figure (b) a more realistic and irregular pattern is shown that results from unforeseen events, demonstrating the need to hold safety stocks if production is not to be interrupted through shortages*

Figure 28.4 (continued)

Figure 28.5 *Economic order quantity. This diagram shows that the economic order quantity for each batch of purchased items will correspond to the lowest point on the curve of total costs. This curve is also of use in determining batch quantities for manufacture, in which case the set-up costs have to be considered, either instead of or in addition to the inventory-carrying costs*

quantity (EOQ) for the particular commodity under consideration.

In practice many other factors determine the actual quantity to be ordered. It may be, for example, that delivery times from suppliers are so long that high stocks must be held in order to avoid lost production time through stockouts. Also, it is generally recognised that considerable flexibility can be exercised in varying the amount ordered above or below the precise economic level. The curve representing total cost is usually shallow around its lowest point and, provided one does not stray too far from the optimum quantity, differences in the amounts ordered will not have a great effect on the total unit cost.

The formula for the economic order quantity is usually derived as follows.

The annual fixed costs of acquisition are equal to the number of orders per year multiplied by the fixed cost per order

$$= DS/Q$$

where D = annual sales volume for the demand (units)
             S = fixed cost per order (or setup costs for a manufactured batch)
             Q = order quantity (units)

The annual variable costs of possession are equal to the average stock held (monetary value) multiplied by an inventory-carrying-cost, factor. This is

$$\tfrac{1}{2} QVI$$

where V = cost per unit
             I = (cost of carrying inventory)/(value of inventory)

The annual total inventory service cost is at its lowest when the two are equal, which is when

$$DS/Q = \tfrac{1}{2}QVI$$

$$\text{whence } Q^2 = 2DS/VI$$

$$\text{and } Q = \quad (2DS/VI)$$

EOQ example

Suppose that: D = 1000 units per year
S = £10 fixed cost per order
V = £4 per unit
I = 25% inventory carrying cost

Substituting in the formula we get:

$$Q = \quad \frac{2 \times 1000 \times 10}{4 \times 0.25}$$

$$Q = \quad 20\,000/11$$

$$= 141 \text{ units}$$

This would suggest seven orders per year.

In practice there is no need for many tedious calculations. There are many EOQ tables and nomographs available. EOQ theory will certainly not cope with every type of inventory problem. Its success depends, to a large extent, on a reasonably stable usage figure. Nevertheless, its application has given many firms considerable financial benefits.

Order levels and safety stocks

Consider the artificial situation in which production is started using an initial stock of a particular item, with reordering taking place at prearranged intervals so that the stock is replenished at precisely the correct economic time. Each order is placed for the economic quantity (EOQ) and orders are spaced so that the stockholding just falls to zero as the next supply arrives. By this approach the perfect condition is presented where the average amount of inventory held is kept to a minimum. The situation is represented in Figure 28.4(a).

In practice, of course, the perfect situation can never occur. Many variables will wreck any attempt to achieve the perfect stock condition. These variables include:

1 Uneven stock usage for production
2 Unexpected wastage or losses
3 Failure by suppliers to maintain consistent delivery times
4 Goods received short or damaged from suppliers.

Some of these variations can be accommodated in planning. For example, seasonal fluctuations can often be predicted and allowed for. However, some safety factor must always be provided and this takes the form of safety stocks, sometimes called buffer stocks. A more realistic stock-level pattern is seen in Figure 28.4(b) and this illustrates the way in which buffer stocks safeguard against possible contingencies. The skill of the stock controller must be exercised in determining reorder levels and reorder quantities in order to achieve the planned maximum and minimum actual stockholdings.

The situation depicted in Figure 28.4(b) starts from the point at which production stocks have been assembled at the start of a product range. The curve shows that, for the stock item being considered, 6000 units have been provided against a predicted usage rate of 1000 units per month. In other words, sufficient stocks have been laid in to cover the first six months of production. In order to safeguard against unforeseen contingencies (a phrase familiar to most production managers) a 'safety stock' of 2000 units has been planned. With the economic order quantity having been calculated at around 6000 units, the reorder point occurs when stocks fall to 4000 units (for a supplier's lead time of two months).

In the diagram, it is apparent that all went as planned during the first 'stock cycle'. Usage took place at the predicted 1000 units per month, and an order was placed for 6000 fresh units when stocks fell to the planned reorder point of 4000. The supplier performed as promised, and stocks were replenished to the planned maximum level of 8000 units after the expected lead time of two months. The first 'unforeseen contingency' took place during the end of the second stock cycle, after the second replacement order had been placed: 1000 units were scrapped as a result of an operator's error during a guillotining process. The deficiency was immediately made good from safety stocks. During the third stock cycle, the supplier had a strike on his hands, with the result that his delivery time was extended to over three months, in place of the expected two. Again, the safety stocks were sufficient in this case to cover production requirements.

In the last stock cycle shown in Figure 28.4(b) a small disaster has occurred. The stock controller, true to his instructions, has automatically placed an order for 6000 fresh stock items as soon as stocks sank to the 4000 re-order point. What the stock controller did not know, however, was that the product range on which this stock item was solely used had been discontinued. Production ceased only one month after the new batch of stock arrived, so that the surplus stocks were in fact redundant. The same thing happened to all the other stock items used solely on this particular product range and created a serious problem of redundant stocks. With any system that generates orders automatically for fresh stocks, safeguards must be rigidly applied to prevent mistakes of this expensive nature from happening. Every order must be questioned by a production or purchasing manager who has access to forward sales and production plans.

Determination of planned maximum, minimum and re-order stock levels must obviously start from the production plans (which in turn derive from the sales forecasts). What may not be so obvious is that any change in these plans must be communicated immediately to those responsible for ordering stocks. Given a thorough and up-to-date knowledge of production requirements, the stock controller can apply a number of methods to arrive at re-order quantities, re-order points, and the theoretical safety stock levels that these quantities will produce.

Statistical determination of safety stock levels

For routine stock replacements, a commonly applied method for setting safety stock levels is to arrange that these should approximate to one month's normal production requirements, or to half the stocks used during the purchase lead time, whichever is the greater. Naturally this rule-of-thumb approach can give rise to anomalies. It is arguable that the only true way to decide safety stock requirements is to consider all the possible variables, and then to adopt a statistical approach to arrive at levels that are reasonable in the context of the probability level of stock shortages which can be tolerated. This problem can be described in terms of 'service levels' where a 100 per cent service level means that there is never any shortage of stocks when they are required. A 98 per cent service level would describe a situation where two out of every hundred applications to the stores were met with an 'out of stock' reply. It is generally recognised that 100 per cent service levels, for many reasons, are difficult to achieve and would in fact be prohibitive in terms of inventory costs. The statistical approach, therefore, attempts to reconcile a conscious policy decision on adequate service levels with the amount of stock required to achieve those levels.

Once the realms of statistics are entered, mathematical solutions beyond the understanding of most stock control clerks are encountered. The subject is complex, and the results will only be as good as the estimates of demand and the accuracy of production plans.

Figure 28.6 is a normal-distribution curve, of the type familiar to statisticians. An average (or 'mean') event has the highest probability (at the peak of the curve), while the probability falls away on both sides as the individual events differ more and more from the average. The extent to which the curve spreads out is measured by a quantity called the 'standard deviation' (sd) of the distribution: 68 per cent of cases fall in the region between mean minus 1 sd and mean plus 1 sd while 96 per cent of cases fall in the region

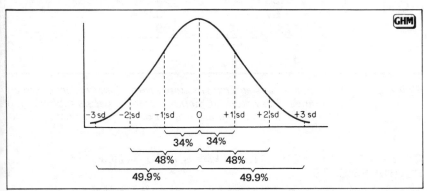

Figure 28.6   Normal distribution curve. The figure shows a normal distribution curve and illustrates the dispersion about the average, in terms of standard deviations related to percentage probabilities

between mean minus 2 sd and mean plus 2 sd.

In the field of stock control, the mean can be taken as the average monthly usage of a stock item. As the curve falls away on both sides, it can represent the probability that (production plans remaining unchanged) demand will differ from the average.

Records of stock usage can be used to find the mean and standard deviation of monthly usage for a particular item. Then, to guarantee a particular level of protection against stockout on that item it is necessary to have a safety stock of K times the standard deviation of monthly usage, where K is given by the table in Figure 28.7. It can be seen that achieving better protection against stockout requires an increasingly large investment in safety stocks.

Calculations of standard deviations demands access to detailed records of past stock usage. These records must not only be accurate, but they must also relate to present-day production requirements. If the current situation is significantly changed from that which existed when the records were taken, there is no reason to suppose that the standard deviations calculated will have any justification in future computations.

GHM

K value	Protection (%)
0	50
0.84	80
1.04	85
1.28	90
1.41	92
1.56	94
1.75	96
2.05	98
2.33	99
2.57	99.5
2.88	99.8

Figure 28.7 Table of K values against stockout protection. Amount by which the standard deviation of monthly usage must be multiplied in order to achieve particular levels of protection against stockout

CONVERTING PRODUCTION PLANS INTO STOCK REQUIREMENTS

Stock control embraces the provision of stores for all purposes from the single 'special' or project to materials used in continuous production. The basic necessity for any stock controller is the production plan for the year. This plan, derived from the marketing plan and agreeing with the annual budgets, must show the expected production rates for all products together with an estimation of the spare parts and replacement stocks to be carried.

Stock collation method for a single batch

For any particular stock item, the stock controller must know all the products or sub-assemblies on which it is used. This problem is simplest in the case of one special production batch or one product, where the provision of supplies only has to be made for one production occasion. For any stock collation exercise the buyer or stock controller must start with a complete set of parts lists or bills of materials. The procedure in the case of a single project is simple, if tedious.

Consider a main assembly (which could be a finished product) with the type number XYZ. The process of stock collation begins with the appropriate clerk checking through all the bills of materials. He must mark up the quantities on the main bill of materials to show the total number of items necessary to complete the entire batch. For example, if one main assembly needs twelve rivets type 1234, and 100 main assemblies are to be produced the clerk must enter a net requirement of 1200 rivets on the bill of materials. This procedure must be repeated for every single item, whether it is manufactured or purchased, on the bill of materials.

The bill of materials for any sub-assembly listed on the main assembly must be treated in the same way. However, a further multiplication factor will be necessary if more than one sub-assembly is used on each main assembly. Suppose that two brackets type LY are needed for each main assembly type XYZ, then every single quantity listed on the bill of materials for the bracket must be multiplied by the total production quantity for the sub-assembly (which in this example is 2 × 100).

All of these quantities are written on to stock collation cards, one of which will be required for each item. A card suitable for this simple one-batch case is illustrated in Figure 28.8. When all the bills of materials have been processed, the quantities on all stock collation cards can be added up to find the net requirements for each item.

Stock collation system for a programme of mixed products

An extension of the system just described for single-batch working is seen in the production of a mixed product range. If common parts or sub-assemblies are shared between one or more of these mixed products and if production is continued on a repeating batch basis, some method of collation must be found. Use of cards such as that shown in Figure 28.9 provides one solution.

From the annual production plan the stock controller has to transfer the number of main assemblies to be produced into the column headings of a collation card. Individual sub-assemblies or parts required on each main assembly are then listed in the left-hand column, continuing on to further cards as necessary. From the relevant bills of materials, quantities of each part required on the main assembly are calculated and these are entered in the parts

485

Figure 28.8 *Simple stock collation card. Suitable for determining total requirements for individual parts common to more than one assembly or sub-assembly, where the total production commitment is confined to one project or special batch*

of the boxes above the diagonals. When this has been done it is then possible to consider each row on the form, and for every item to multiply the quantities shown as being required for each single main assembly by the annual usage figures. The results are entered in the parts of the boxes below the diagonals. After making an allowance for spares, accessories or (in some cases) wastage, the total annual usage for each item listed can be entered in the right-hand column.

This method is simple but somewhat crude. It does not attempt to phase requirements according to a timed programme but, if the company's policy is to hold at least three months' stock in advance, the method may be adequate. Should a more sophisticated system be required for relating total usage to a detailed daily or weekly production schedule the line-of-balance technique may be considered (see Lock, 1977).

STOCKTAKING

Stocktaking is a tedious and laborious chore that has to be performed annually to the satisfaction of the company's auditors in order to evaluate the quantities of stocks of materials and work in progress. The results are used in preparing the company's financial accounts and are also important for management control. Stocktaking verifies the accuracy of stock records and discloses

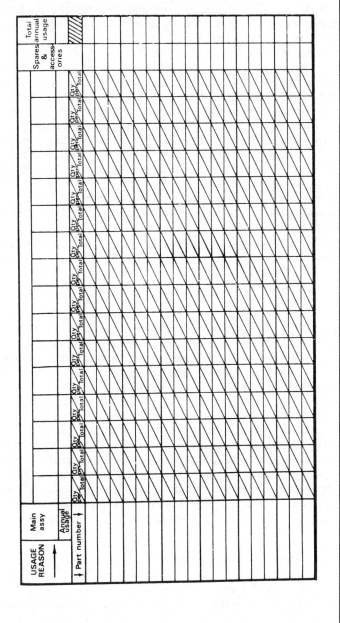

Figure 28.9 **Stock collation card for use against an annual production plan.** *This card is suitable for listing individual parts against the annual usage, as predicted from the production or sales plans. It is an extension of the method illustrated in Figure 28.8. Each column on the card can be allotted to one main assembly (or product) within a range of products which use common sub-assemblies and parts. Provision is also made for additional spares stock*

possible frauds or other losses. The Inland Revenue and the auditors (representing the shareholders) will need to be satisfied that suitable standards of accuracy are achieved. Some large organisations find it profitable to engage their own internal audit staff to undertake continuous stocktaking, but whether or not this is the case every company should practise stock checks periodically in between the major annual events.

Stocktaking needs careful planning to ensure that the whole exercise can be completed during the prescribed period. This is commonly arranged during a weekend or at some other time when production will not be interrupted. This is a necessary arrangement because stores receipts and issues have to be suspended while stocktaking is in progress. Because of the large amount of work involved all available staff have to be deployed. These will include people outside the normal stores function or people who have no connection with materials or even production during their normal working time. The role of storekeepers during stocktaking should be confined to that of guides so that the actual counting is always carried out by people who are independent of the usual stock records and stores functions. This is a safeguard against the perpetuation of errors or the concealment of possible fraud. The whole exercise can be supervised by the accountants.

Books of serially numbered tickets or, alternatively, pre-numbered list sheets have to be provided. Serial numbering means that every ticket or sheet issued can be accounted for when the accountants come to tot up all the values. The first step is for every item of stock, whether in the stores or on the factory floor, to be counted, either as a physical quantity or by weighing or measuring volume. The stores code or description is entered on a ticket together with the counted quantity. Tickets are left in prominent positions on the actual stocks. Supervisory staff or other checkers make random checks of items already counted to verify the accuracy of the 'first-line' stocktaking staff. Finally the auditors themselves may wish to carry out their own counts on selected items. Naturally, more attention will be paid to the most expensive goods.

Stocktaking provides an opportunity, which should not be missed, of identifying obsolete and redundant stocks the disposal of which can release both cash and space.

It is important to understand that the objective of stocktaking is not simply to verify the accuracy of stock records, but to assess the total value of stocks and work in progress. This means that all stocks have to be counted and valued, including materials, components and assemblies throughout the factory and its stores and stockyards. The value of these items is not represented solely by the material stocks contained in them; the investment of wages and salaries used in all work in progress has to be included.

FURTHER READING

Baily, P., *Successful Stock Control by Manual Systems*, Gower, 1971
Baily, P., and Farmer, D., *Materials Management Handbook*, Gower, 1982

Baily, P. and Tavernier, G., *Design of Stock Control Systems and Records*, Gower, 1973

Lock, D., *Factory Administration Handbook*, Gower, 1976

Thomas, A.B., *Stock Control in Manufacturing Industries*, 2nd edition, Gower, 1980

PART SIX

PRODUCTION MANAGEMENT

29 Planning for production

J Mapes and C C New

Production management is concerned with managing the physical resources necessary to create products in sufficient quantities to meet market requirements. In manufacturing organisations the majority of the workforce and a very high proportion of the total capital investment expenditure will be devoted to the production function. Efficient production management is therefore absolutely critical to the success of such organisations.

Although production management is most closely associated with the manufacturing sector, the techniques of production management are increasingly being applied in service and non-manufacturing organisations. Because of this the modern definition of a production system has been broadened to cover systems for the creation of both manufactured items and services. The problems are very similar for both manufacturing organisations and service organisations. One of the main differences is that the 'product' of service organisations is highly perishable and must be consumed immediately.

While the primary emphasis in this chapter will be on manufacturing organisations, most of the techniques discussed are equally applicable to service organisations like banks, hospitals and public utilities.

THE PRODUCTION MANAGEMENT TASK

The production management task can be divided into two main areas. First, there is the design of the production system. This will involve decisions regarding the performance requirements and desired output levels of the production system. Then decisions will need to be made about the number of production facilities which will be required and their location, the methods of production to be used and the management control procedures to be introduced.

Second, there is the task of operating the production system in order to meet the specified performance requirements. This will include production scheduling and control, inventory management and quality control.

THE PLANNING OF PRODUCTION

The planning of production in an organisation can therefore be considered at two levels, strategic and tactical. Strategic planning is concerned with the design of the production system. Tactical planning is concerned with the running of the operating system. Figure 29.1 shows the kind of planning decisions which have to be taken in production and their relative time horizons.

			GHM
Strategic	Long-term	2 years +	Introduction of new products Number and location of facilities Type of technology to be used
	Medium-term	1–2 years	Relative mix of products Changes in capacity
Tactical	Medium term	1 year	Size of workforce Subcontracting Overtime working Stockholding policy
	Short-term	3 months	Production schedule Output targets

Figure 29.1   Time-scale for planning decisions

Strategic level decisions

At the strategic level decisions will be required regarding:

The product range

While this is primarily a marketing decision the production capabilities of the organisation together with any limitations on production capacity must also be taken into account.

Product design

By taking into account production implications at the design stage substantial reductions in manufacturing costs and processing time can be achieved.

Selection of processing methods, plant and equipment

Usually there are several alternative methods of manufacturing the product, each being the most appropriate for a particular output range. The choice will depend on the trade-off between capital cost, operating costs and performance requirements.

Plant location

The number of plants, the capacity of each plant and the location of each plant must be decided. This will be influenced by the transport costs for raw materials and finished goods, availability of labour, delivery performance requirements and economics of scale.

Plant layout

Within each plant the number of departments and their relative location must be decided. Within each department the location of machines, storage areas and support facilities must be decided in order to simplify movement and handling of materials between operations.

Planning and control systems

An important part of the design of a production system is the development of procedures for planning and controlling the production process.

Decisions at the tactical level

At the tactical level decisions will need to be taken regarding:

Production control

This covers the detailed scheduling of operations, allocation of jobs to machines and monitoring of actual against planned production. The aim should be to produce a schedule which is practicable and also meets performance objectives in terms of operating costs and delivery.

Stock control

In order to ensure acceptable delivery times nearly all organisations have to carry some stocks of raw materials, sub-assemblies or finished products. For each item held in stock decisions must be made about when to replenish stocks and what the replenishment quantity should be.

Quality control

The quality specification will be set at the design stage. The operational task is to ensure that, as far as possible, all items which leave the factory meet this specification. Decisions must be taken on methods of inspection, on when a batch of items should be rejected or re-worked and on when machines should be reset.

Maintenance

The servicing, repair and replacement of equipment is an essential part of ensuring optimum operating effectiveness. Decisions must be taken regarding the frequency of equipment overhaul, the scheduling of maintenance work and the frequency of equipment replacement.

Labour control

Labour costs are an important part of total production costs. In many industries labour costs are the main component of production costs. In order to exercise effective control the work content of each task must be determined. This enables realistic work scheduling and monitoring of actual against planned performance to be carried out.

While the relative importance of these decision areas will vary for different industries and different companies every organisation will need to give some attention to each of the areas mentioned.

STRATEGIC PLANNING

Clearly strategic planning of production can only take place within the context of the overall corporate planning process. Traditionally the strategic task for the production function has been seen as the design of a production system capable of meeting the requirements of the marketing strategic plan. This is likely to lead to insufficient account being taken of the production implications of alternative strategies at the corporate planning stage. This frequently results in conflicting demands being placed on production which are impossible to resolve. Naturally the marketing department wish to provide as good a service as possible to the customer. As a consequence they may require production to manufacture special products to customer specifications using the same production facilities as standard products with no increase in production lead-times. Alternatively they may ask for immediate availability of all products while insisting that the increased stockholding costs incurred cannot be passed on to the customer.

In order to develop a strategic plan which adequately reflects both market requirements and production capabilities then the production function must play an integral part in the process of strategy formation.

An essential first step must be to gain a clear understanding of the performance measures leading to success in the market-place. Figure 29.2 lists the most common criteria for success. While most organisations would ideally like to meet all of these criteria this is not possible as many of the criteria are in conflict. In order to achieve short lead-times, then increased costs will be incurred leading to increased prices. If quality is an important criterion then it is unlikely that very short lead-times can be achieved.

Of course the key criteria may be different for different product groups provided separate production facilities are used. Problems only arise when the same production facility is required to satisfy different criteria for two product groups at the same time. Setting priorities can be almost impossible if, for example, one group of orders must be completed at minimum cost (implying high levels of machine utilisation) while another group of orders must be completed as rapidly as possible (implying low levels of machine utilisation).

Once the tasks which are vital to corporate success have been identified then a production capability analysis should be carried out. The main purpose of the analysis is to assess whether the organisation is likely to be able to meet the

1   Short lead-times

2   Lead-time reliability

3   Quality

4   Ability to alter specification at short notice

5   Ability to adjust volume at short notice

6   Price

Figure 29.2   Requirements for market success

performance requirements of the market with currently available resources.

If there is a mismatch between the capabilities of the existing production system and market requirements then either the production system must be modified or the strategy must be altered. Otherwise the consequences can be extremely serious. When the Babcock and Wilcox Corporation in the United States tried to enter the nuclear pressure vessel business they encountered very severe problems. They had considerable expertise in the manufacture of steam pressure vessels where the requirement was for a standard product with a short, reliable lead-time, sold at a competitive price. The nuclear power industry required absolute product reliability and reliable delivery but the length of the lead-time and the price were relatively unimportant. Also the large size of nuclear pressure vessels, coupled with the fact that each vessel was a special item fabricated to a very precise customer specification meant that manufacturing methods suited to steam pressure vessels were quite unsuitable for nuclear pressure vessels. Consequently, during the first three years of operation only three pressure vessels were completed instead of the twenty which were scheduled. Eventually the two main contractors transferred fourteen part-completed pressure vessels from Babcock and Wilcox to competing organisations. Between 1967 and 1969 company profits fell from $33m to £5m.

Once the production capability analysis has been completed then decisions will need to be made on the following main components of the manufacturing structure:

Plant and equipment technology

This covers the processing methods to be used, the choice of equipment and the level of automation.

Production systems

These define the procedures for detailed planning and control of production and the performance standards to be met.

Personnel policies

These specify policies on the degree of job specialisation, payment systems to be employed and the type of work group organisation to be adopted.

Product design

This is concerned with those aspects of product design which simplify manufacture and reduce production costs.

Organisation and management

This specifies the organisational structure adopted within the production function and the allocation of responsibilities between staff.

FORECASTING DEMAND

An essential requirement for the planning of production is a forecast of demand for each product. For each forecast an indication of the likely forecasting error should be provided. For forecasts with a high expected error contingency plans can then be made to cope with the occasions when actual demand is much higher or lower than the forecasts.

Forecasting techniques tend to be classified into short-term, medium-term and long-term depending on the underlying assumptions which have been made. In short-term forecasting it is assumed that the underlying trend is linear and stable with changes in external factors having little effect on demand. This enables very simple extrapolative techniques to be used. However, the assumptions are only likely to be valid when forecasting just a few months ahead. The simplest method of short-term forecasting is to use moving averages to identify the underlying trend line and then to project the trend line forward. Figure 29.3 shows the results obtained using a five-period moving average.

Increasingly, however, simple moving averages of this kind are being replaced by weighted moving averages in which the greatest weighting is given to the most recent data. The most popular technique of this kind is called exponential smoothing. This involves updating the moving average each period using the following calculation.

$$\text{new moving average} = a \times \text{sales for this period} + (1\text{-}a) \times \text{moving average for previous period}$$

a is called the smoothing constant and is normally given a value between 0.1 and

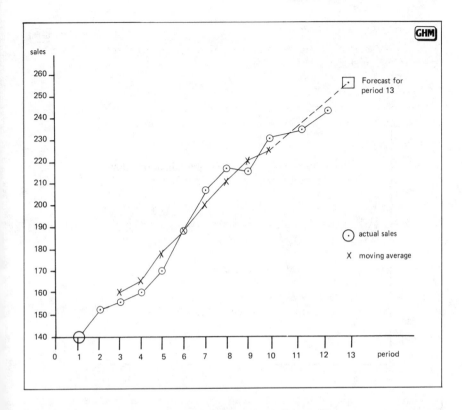

Figure 29.3   Forecast based on a 5-period moving average

0.3. Forecasts based on exponential smoothing tend to be more accurate than forecasts based on a simple moving average, particularly when there are frequent fluctuations in the trend. Figure 29.4 shows the results of using exponential smoothing for short-term forecasting when there are marked short-term fluctuations in sales.

Medium-term forecasting techniques are based on the assumption that the underlying trend follows a regular curve. The most commonly used approach is to fit a curve of the appropriate type to the data and then to project the curve forward to obtain the forecast.

In long-term forecasting it is recognised that external factors will have a considerable effect on the forecast. The emphasis is therefore placed on establishing the quantitiative relationship between demand and those factors which influence demand, using the techniques of regression analysis. This enables an equation to be developed which can then be used to forecast demand.

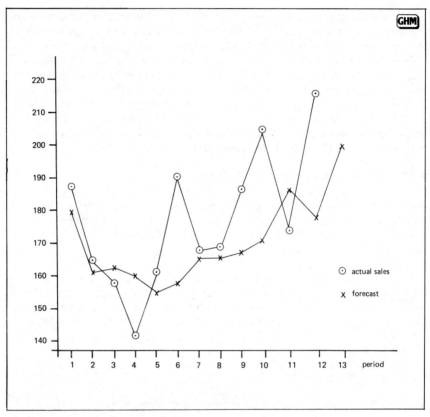

Figure 29.4   Forecast based on exponential smoothing

THE MAKE OR BUY DECISION

One very important part of the strategic planning process is the decision regarding which items are to be manufactured and which items are to be bought in. This decision will be taken primarily on financial grounds but there are other factors which should also be taken into account. Purchase of items gives greater flexibility if large fluctuations in demand occur. It also allows access to specialist skills and economies of scale which may not be available internally. On the other hand manufacture gives greater control over quality and delivery dates.

For most items a change from manufacturing to purchase or vice versa would involve such a major change to the nature of the company that it would not be acceptable on policy grounds. However, there will be a number of items which could either be manufactured or purchased depending on which involves the lowest cost.

When making cost comparisons it is important that only incremental costs are taken into account. Any costs which will be unaltered by a switch between manufacturing and purchasing should be ignored.

In practice the decision is very dependent on current utilisation of internal resources. Manufacturing will nearly always be more attractive if labour and equipment would otherwise be under-utilised. On the other hand buying-in is likely to be preferable if the decision to manufacture the item will involve substantial capital investment and the recruitment of labour. Purchasing will be particularly attractive if there is a possibility of a fall-off in the future level of requirements for the item in the long term.

PREPARING AN OPERATING PLAN

Once demand for each product has been forecast, and it has been decided which items will be manufactured and which will be purchased, then an operating plan must be devised aimed at ensuring that the company's marketing objectives are met.

In order to predict delivery periods and decide on stockholding policy a production stage chart should be constructed. This is a diagrammatic representation of all the stages in the production process including supplier delivery periods, product design and final dispatch to the customer. Estimates of the time to complete each stage are included so that the delivery time can be assessed. An outline of a production stage chart for a pigment is shown in Figure 29.5.

If the delivery time is likely to be acceptable to customers then the organisation can operate as a make-to-order company, only carrying out work on firm customer orders. Usually, however, the delivery time will be unacceptable and it will be necessary to carry out some stages in the chart in advance of customer orders. In some cases it will only be necessary to pre-order raw materials and hold stocks based on forecasts of future usage. In other cases, where customers require very short lead-times, stocks of the finished product will need to be held so that new orders can be met immediately from stock.

The next step should be to decide whether the forecast demand can be satisfied and the desired lead-times met with currently available capacity. In order to estimate capacity requirements then current capacity and forecast demand need to be expressed in the same units, for example, litres of paint or numbers of electric motors. However, with a varied range of products there will be no common physical unit of capacity and so forecast demand will need to be converted into standard hours of manufacturing time.

If average weekly demand exceeds average weekly capacity then a decision must be taken on whether capacity should be increased. This decision is likely to be influenced by the following factors.

1 Long-term forecasts of changes in market size and market share
2 The expected return on the capital investment required
3 Possible future innovations in the product or the production process.

Activity	GHM Weeks
Purchase raw materials	1
	2
Manufacture intermediates	3
	4
Manufacture base pigments	5
Standardise	6
Blend final product and test	7
Dispatch	8

Figure 29.5   Production stage chart for pigment manufacture

If it is decided that an increase in capacity cannot be justified then one or more of the following alternatives can be considered.

1 Increase the number of purchased or subcontracted items
2 Use overtime or shift working to increase effective capacity
3 Eliminate items with low profit margins from the product range releasing capacity for more profitable product lines.

Aggregate planning

The analysis described above should ensure a reasonable match between capacity and demand on an annual basis. In addition there will be the need to cope with variations in demand over the year. These may be due to seasonal variations, changing economic conditions or random fluctuations in orders from week to week. A company which has sufficient capacity to meet average demand will find that there are periods during the year when demand is appreciably above average. As a consequence either sales will be lost or delivery periods will become unacceptably long. On the other hand, if capacity is based on peak demand then the utilisation of labour and equipment will be low during periods of below average demand.

Aggregate planning is an attempt to schedule production over a six- to twelve-month period taking into account forecast variations in demand. The following methods of handling fluctuations in demand can be considered.

1 Vary the number of hours worked each week by the use of overtime or additional shifts during periods of peak demand

2 Vary the size of the workforce by recruiting casual workers during peak periods
3 Use spare capacity during periods of low demand to build up stocks of finished goods for use during periods of above average demand
4 Increase the amount of sub-contracted work during periods of high demand.

Each alternative will cause substantial additional costs to be incurred. The use of overtime or sub-contracting involves premium charges relative to the cost of manufacturing internally during normal working hours. Changes in the size of the workforce involve recruitement and lay-off costs. Stock building involves high stockholding and obsolescence costs. The optimum solution will be the combination of these alternatives which minimises total costs. A number of techniques for aggregate planning have been developed. The main approaches are outlined below.

The linear decision rule

This technique for obtaining a minimum-cost solution to the above problem was developed by Holt, Modigliani, Muth and Simon. The approach takes account of normal time and overtime labour rates, recruitment and lay-off costs, inventory holding, back ordering and machine set-up costs. These are used to derive two linear decision rules for computing the workforce levels and production rate for each period taking into account forecasts of sales for each period over a specified planning horizon.

This approach provides an optimum solution and is easy to apply once the two decision rules have been derived. However, the assumptions on cost structure may provide a poor approximation to reality. Also there are no restrictions on the size of the workforce, the hours of overtime worked or the number of units held in inventory the solution generated by this technique may be impractical.

Linear programming

The Simplex method of linear programming takes the same cost data as the linear decision rule approach and also generates a minimum cost solution giving workforce size and production rate period by period. An advantage over the linear decision rule method is that capacity constraints can be incorporated into the model. A major limitation of linear programming is that all constraints and cost functions must be linear. This will be unrealistic whenever economies of scale exist. A further limitation is that only a single objective can be optimised at a time whereas aggregate planning is usually concerned with satisfying a number of conflicting objectives simultaneously.

Goal programming is an extension of linear programming which to some extent overcomes the problem of being limited to a single objective. A set of management goals is specified and a solution is generated which is as close to this set of goals as possible.

Search decision rule

This is an iterative procedure which starts with an initial solution and determines the overall cost of this solution. The procedure then searches for an alternative solution with lower costs. This continues until a solution is reached for which further alteration would not yield significant cost reductions. Unlike the first two procedures this does not yield a mathematical optimum solution. In other words it yields a good but not necessarily minimum-cost solution. However it has the advantages of being less complicated and requiring less computation.

Management coefficients method

This is a method developed by Bowman in which management's past planning decisions are analysed statistically to determine the decision criteria which were used. A set of decision equations are then derived in which the numerical coefficients are based on this statistical analysis. These decision equations can then be used to prepare future schedules using the same criteria. This should result in an improvement in performance due to the criteria being applied more consistently.

Parametric production planning

This is a technique suggested by Jones which uses a search procedure to quantify four parameters associated with minimum cost in aggregate planning. The four parameters are then inserted into equations which are used to determine workforce size and production rate for each period. The method involves no constraints imposed by the mathematical structure of the model and the parameters and equations are specific to the company. While the method is non-optimising it is claimed to produce very good results.

A performance comparison of the alternative aggregate planning procedures

Lee and Khumawala carried out a comparative study of alternative aggregate planning procedures in a company manufacturing capital goods. The aggregate planning procedures evaluated were the linear decision rule, the search decision rule, the management coefficients method and parametric production planning. The application of these procedures was simulated and the profit performance achieved compared with the actual performance of the company. All of the planning methods yielded better profits than the company's own planning procedures. The greatest improvement (14 per cent) was achieved using the search decision rule.

Tactical planning

Once the aggregate plan has been prepared all of the key policy decisions will have been made. The next step is to prepare a detailed operating plan. This will involve a series of tactical decisions regarding;

1 the operations necessary for the manufacture of each product or order and their sequence
2 allocation of jobs to facilities
3 scheduling the start and finish times of each operation.

These tasks are more appropriately dealt with as part of production control.

FURTHER READING

Bowman, E. H., 'Consistency and Optimality in Managerial Decision Making', *Management Science* 9, January 1963. This article provides a detailed description of the management coefficients method of aggregate planning.

Buffa, E.S., *Modern Production Management*, 5th edition, Wiley, New York, 1977. An excellent and comprehensive coverage of the techniques of production management.

Constable, C. J., and New, C. C., *Operations Management*, Wiley, New York, 1976. A good general introduction to production management with particular emphasis on the strategic aspects.

Holt, C. C., Modigliani, F., and Muth, J. F., *Planning Production, Inventories and Workforce*, Prentice-Hall, Englewood Cliffs, 1960. Covers all aspects of aggregate planning with particular emphasis on the linear decision rule method.

Jones, C. H., 'Parametric Production Planning', *Management Science* 13, July 1967. This article describes the parametric production planning technique for aggregate planning.

Lee, W. B., and Khumawala, B. M., 'Simulation Testing of Aggregate Production Planning models in an Implementation Methodology', *Management Science* 20, Feb. 1974. This article describes the comparison of alternative aggregate planning techniques referred to in the text.

Skinner, W., 'Manufacturing—Missing Link in Corporate Strategy', *Harvard Business Review*, May–June 1974. This article discusses how top management can take a more active role in the formation of manufacturing strategy.

Taubert, W. H., 'Search Decision Rule for the Aggregate Scheduling Problem', *Management Science* 14, Feb. 1968. This article describes the search decision rule for aggregate planning.

Twiss, B. C., 'Developing and Implementing Strategy For Production', *Long Range Planning*, April 1974. This article provides a framework for the strategic planning of production.

Wheelwright, S. C. and Makridakis, S., *Forecasting Methods for Management*, Wiley, New York, 1973. A useful handbook for all managers involved in preparing or using forecasts.

30 Plant layout

Brian Walley

The signs of a poor plant layout can seldom be hidden. There are delays to be seen in the manufacturing process, with products and materials following no direct or obvious path. Aisles becomes cluttered with materials and components. Manual handling of materials, including machine loading and unloading, is commonplace. Service areas and stores are sited so that operatives are forced to leave their machines frequently to walk long distances for the collection of cutting tools, work instructions and materials. Production plant is under-used, and machinists are to be observed waiting, idle, for previous processes to be completed.

In a perfect world the layout of plant would allow an uninterrupted flow of work through the factory. Machines and workers would always be gainfully occupied, and they would be arranged so as to take up the least amount of space consistent with safe and efficient operation. Unfortunately, this happy state of affairs is rare. A definition of the subject, and a look at the factors and people involved in plant layout decisions will suggest why this is so.

A plant layout study is the analysis of all the factors involved in siting machinery, work stations, ancillary equipment, storage, services, manufacturing flow pattern and the functional design of buildings. The objective is to produce an arrangement which will minimise production costs.

The study must involve a wide range of specialists, either directly or as consultants. These can include architects, draughtsmen, ergonomists, design, mechanical, civil, electrical, process control, and production engineers, work study and operations research people, production planners and controllers, safety officers, materials handling experts, factory inspectors, local shop stewards and other trades union officials and (of course) line mangement. Paradoxically, the abundance of expertise, with so many diverse aims, can make the process of designing a plant layout difficult to achieve logically and simply. In all respects, plant layout design is a complex task.

BENEFITS OF A GOOD PLANT LAYOUT

Potential benefits are many, but there achievement depends largely on careful planning before production starts. It is obviously far more difficult to attempt re-laying out a plant arrangement after production has got under way. The following list of benefits is useful as a checklist against which any new layout proposals should be assessed. A perfect layout would ensure:

1 Best possible use of production warehousing and stores space.
2 Most economic investment of capital in new plant, materials handling equipment, tooling, general facilities and the building itself.
3 Efficient routing of services, so reducing installation and subsequent maintenance costs of electrical, steam, gas and air services, and of ventilation.
4 Minimum movement of materials between processes, so reducing handling costs and the volume of work in progress.
5 Through increased efficiency, a lower requirement for ancillary workers; fewer storekeepers, general labourers and internal transport drivers.
6 Easier movement of staff around the factory.
7 Reduced operator fatigue through the provision of mechanical handling aids where appropriate, and the sensible positioning of materials in relation to plant and machinery.
8 Elimination of fatigue and low morale attributable to a bad working environment (poor lighting, excessive noise, vibration, dust, fumes, heat and humidity).
9 Reduced energy consumption.
10 Production management made easier (production control and progressing, materials and stock control, work booking, costing, etc.).
11 More effective supervision and management.
12 Better housekeeping – easier to keep everything clean and tidy.
13 More easily predictable – and achievable – output and cost objectives.
14 Sensitivity to changed requirements of production volume or to product mix and new designs.
15 Promotion of good industrial relations.

Even if some of these benefits are mutually exclusive, this remains a powerful argument for taking the trouble to plan a good plant layout.

CONSTRAINTS

Anyone analysing a plant layout will quickly come up against a series of constraints having a serious effect on the search for the most efficient layout. Of necessity, a plant layout has to accommodate a number of compromises. Suppose, for example, that all potential risks to health and safety could be ignored (for instance, by operating all machinery without guards). Such an approach might allow very high levels of production. The fact that hazards do have to be considered could result in slower working, and in a more tortuous and less well-utilised production operation than would otherwise be the case.

Constraints, therefore, need to be built into the layout. These will probably raise production costs and reduce potential efficiency beyond the best theoretical limits. The most common and most important constraints are:

1 The site and the structure of the building (a single-storey building, for example), access to road and rail transport, and structural strength. It is still comparatively rare for a layout to be prepared and then a factory building put round it. A single-storey unit will make expansion easier and facilitate natural lighting, but will cost more per square metre of manufacturing or storage space. The multi-storey alternative will be cheaper per square metre but perhaps less flexible, with doubts about structural strength on upper floors.

2 Second only in importance to the structure and the site are environmental constraints:

(a) *Pollution:* the main causes of pollution are oil mists, dust and fumes and gases of various kinds. Elimination of oil mists from drillers, grinders or lathes would mean the full enclosure of a machine which may not be practical.

(b) *Dust:* there are various regulations covering such things as quarry dust and the use of asbestos. Wet manufacturing processes instead of dry ones will help to eradicate dust problems, though complete enclosure of dust-producing areas where operatives can wear masks is also a possibility.

(c) *Fumes and gases:* these are also potential pollutants. Sealing off fume-producing activities where extra ventilation is installed is perhaps the only practical way of reducing fume hazards.

(d) *Ventilation:* this is necessary even where dust hazards are minimal. Humidity control is important.

(e) *Lighting and heating:* lighting and heating installations need to conform to the Factories Act of 1961.

(f) *Noise:* noise is recognised as a prime health hazard and cause of fatigue and its supervision needs to be considered carefully.

(g) *Factory amenities:* seating, cloakrooms, rest rooms, lavatories, changing rooms, are requirements whose minimum standards are listed in the Factories Act.

(h) *Fire and safety precautions:* will determine fire escape needs, escape routes and state how the building should be used, the restrictions on its use, and the number of people to be employed in it.

(i) *The Health and Safety at Work Act:* provides the framework for good housekeeping and all this entails in plant layout.

3 Productivity requirements may sometimes impose a constraint on technical excellence. There may be occasions when a conscious decision has to be taken to sacrifice a degree of product quality or other technical objective in order to speed up a process, thus maximising production at a lower (but still acceptable) level of quality.

4   Capital available for investment may be restricted. In any case one of the recognised project appraisal techniques should be used to test the economic viability of any investment project. For short-duration projects, where results can be expected in (say) a year or so, the payback method is usually sufficient. For the more customary project durations in new plant installations, the investment appraisal will have to consider the cash flows and taxation position over several years, and in these circumstances all alternative proposals should be compared using the discounted cash flow technique, or other method acceptable to the company's accountant.

PRINCIPLES OF PLANT LAYOUT

The skills needed to ensure success in plant layout design are often complex and occasionally difficult to weld together to ensure a coherent result. While method study may, theoretically be easy to apply, its relationship with production engineering is not always an easy one. It seems important, therefore, that the plant layout team is able to refer to a set of overall principles which can guide the team's efforts and eventually provide a means of measuring whether the outcome is as satisfactory as it might appear.

The checklist which follows can be used as a fixed reference for the layout team. The principles are obviously superior to any one technique, specialist skill, or even point of view. They provide the means for answering the basic question of 'How is the layout we have proposed?'

1   The least possible space should be taken up. Any plant layout should be judged, at least in part, on the number of cubic metres and square metres needed.
2   Working conditions must be such that a safe working environment is produced, conducive to high work activity. The layout should promote good working practices which help to reduce manufacturing cost, increase flexibility and maintain or improve good industrial relations.
3   Interdependent operations, processes, activities and departments should be placed in proximity to each other, with as little product travel as possible.
4   The layout should facilitate flow process type manufacturing operations, as this tends to utilise machine and labour.
5   All product handling and re-handling should be eliminated as far as possible.
6   Material/product movement both in times and distance should be minimised.
7   Movements of products/material should be continuous as far as possible. Lead-times for manufacturing should be as low as possible.
8   Manual handling of all kinds should be eliminated and mechanised where appropriate.
9   The installation and speeds of machines should be such that few, if any, bottlenecks occur. The production process should set a uniform pace which will optimise the use of production machinery, handling equipment and associated personnel.

10 While machines should be utilised as fully as possible, in some instances production personnel may be the resource to utilise fully. Comparative costs, the need for flexibility, the imbalance in the process, may determine which resource needs to be given priority for efficient utilisiation.

11 The simplest possible materials handling equipment should be used. For example, gravity or roller conveyors are preferable to powered conveyor track. They are cheaper and often more flexible.

12 If materials or products have to be moved any distance they should do so as a 'unit load', i.e., a quantity rather than a single item, perhaps on a pallet.

13 Receiving and dispatch departments should be located near entrances and exits. Dispatch departments, obviously, should be at the end of the production line.

14 There should be centralisation of the most widely used services, such as maintenance or inspection.

15 There should be logical positioning of all stores and service areas based on least travel between service and point of use.

16 Obnoxious areas of dust, fume or noise pollution should be isolated. Dangerous sections need to be isolated, e.g. inflammable material stores and use.

17 Delicate or mentally arduous work should also be isolated (e.g. production planning). This work can be carried out at any point provided that it is isolated, for example, by sound-proofed walls. (Isolation, however, does not imply banishment to an outer corner of the building.)

18 Factory production facilities and associated clerical management activities should be interrelated. Production should be seen as a system with inputs and outputs, all of which need to be integrated within the plant layout. Management, supervision, production control, engineering and all other functions associated with the production activity should be embodied within the layout.

INFORMATION REQUIREMENTS

Information is a vital component in the analysis which the layout team will need to carry out. The team members themselves are unlikely to have all the information required and it will need to be obtained from market research people, the profit planning department, the accounting functions, engineering staff, who are not necessarily members of the team.

An opportunity to combine different objectives might occur as information is collected. For example, can finished goods stock be raised as a result of fast throughput time and reduced work in progress?

Information required is again set out in the form of a checklist in order to facilitate easy reference.

1 Range and volumes of production required based on marketing plans – types, quantities, raw materials, weights, volumes, product design, components, seasonality, delivery requirements.

2 Budgeted revenue and costs of potential operations and, once an appropriate sequence has been determined, machines, machine speeds and potential utilisation.
3 Approximate costs of new plant, buildings and associated services.
4 Site situations, building regulations, basic constraints of the site and any local environmental conditions which used to be taken into account – access to roads, railways or other means of transport.
5 Volume of work in progress, raw materials and finished goods storage likely to be required.
6 Labour and associated services required – canteens, rest rooms, lavatories etc.
7 General services required – maintenance, stores, boiler-house, toolroom, fitters' shop etc.
8 Office accommodation.
9 Materials handling equipment required.

THE TECHNOLOGY OF PLANT LAYOUT

The technology of plant layout is a fundamental precept, often based on engineering principles which have become enshrined in plant layout activities. For example, the nature of the production process will normally fit a standard pattern and these patterns have become an accepted part of the technology.

1 Typical operation and process patterns are illustrated in Figure 30.1, in the following classifications:

   (a) *Straight line* Figure 30.1(a). Raw materials are converted into one product by successive operations.
   (b) *Converging process* Figure 30.1(b). Several raw materials or components join a main line product. A motor car assembly plant is a good example.
   (c) *Diverging process* Figure 30.1(c). Materials converted into different products by separate processes or operations.
   (d) *Multiple process* Figure 30.1(d). A complex activity where cross-over between processes or operations is carried.

2 Site/floor plans – the production process will tend to prescribe the site configuration, but the site itself may be a major factor in the plant layout. Several site-production processes have become fairly commonplace over the years and these are:

   (a) *The 'I' plan* – a straight-line production process established in a simple rectangular building Figure 30.2(a)
   (b) *The 'U' plan* – the production process is often a straight line one, but because of the need to have the receipt and despatch areas adjacent to each other, a 'U' plan is adopted as shown in Figure 30.2(b).
   (c) *Modified 'U' plan* – the position of a main road and the access provided to it often promote a modified 'U' plan as in Figure 30.2(c).

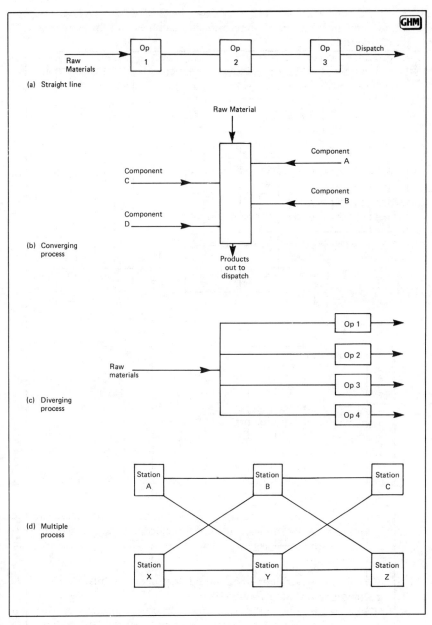

Figure 30.1   Four typical process patterns

Figure 30.2 Floor plan configurations

(d) *Multi-storey cascade* – multi-storey buildings provide the means to store raw materials on the top floor, and then allow manufacture to continue until completion on the ground floor as shown in Figure 30.2(d).

(e) *'E' plan, multiple production* – multiple product lines are normally more difficult to lay out effectively than single product manufacture. The 'E' plan Figure 30.2(e), and the multiple production line Figure 30.2(f) are two ways of tackling the problem.

3 Process versus product layouts: process and product layouts are often in contention in optimising plant layout. A process layout is one where flexibility can be obtained in the manufacturing activity (Figure 30.3). Like activities are put together. One machine may make several different products. The process, therefore, is specialised and can be subjected to efficient supervision and maintenance.

Product layouts (as shown in Figure 30.4) are typified in car assembly plants. Such layouts should reduce handling costs and production time. Work in progress should be minimised.

In many instances a combination of product and process layout is desirable.

4 Functional relationships: in any factory there will be movement of products, raw materials, tools, operatives, and services personnel of all kinds between processes, machines, stores, toolroom and fitters' shop and warehouse dispatch area. Minimising movement will be a key aspect of the plant layout.

The standard method for indicating functional relationships is a travel

L = Lathe
M = Milling machine
G = Grinder
D = Drilling

Figure 30.3 Process layout

GHM

Raw material₁ — L₁ — M₁ — G₁ → D₁ —

Raw material₂ — L₂ — M₂ — G₂ → D₂ —

Raw material₃ — L₃ — M₃ — G₃ → D₃ —

L = Lathe
M = Milling machine
G = Grinder
D = Drilling

Figure 30.4 Product layout

chart as illustrated in Figure 30.5. Each area or unit which receives or dispatches materials, components, tools or products is listed. The number of personnel who have to travel between one location and another as part of their duties should also be recorded. The number of journeys or weight of transfers should be shown against the units or areas receiving them. A numeric system can then be used to indicate the amounts and importance of items which need to travel. The higher the number (perhaps weight or quantity × distance could be used) the nearer together the parts should be.

The principle may not apply if gravity is used in the transfer process. In that case downward rather than horizontal flow can be used to move items considerable distances, provided power is not needed to raise them later. The weighted data shown in the illustration is 568. Any layout which can reduce this total but not substantially increase cost is better than the one in existence.

5 The plant layout should be designed around five major factors (illustrated in Figure 30.6).

(a) *the product, its design and markets* – this will help to determine unit load possibilities, economic batch sizes, the need for plant flexibility, speed of delivery, degree of 'change over' capacity.

(b) *the process design:* the selection of equipment, dimensions of floor area to be occupied, manufacturing operatives, operation sequences.

(c) *the operation designs:* methods study should help to set working patterns. Work measurement should help establish manning levels and equipment requirements.

(d) *the design of facilities:* materials flow, storage areas, materials handling, power, steam, heating, environmental requirements.

GHM

	A	B	C	D	E	F	G	H	TOTAL
A		31	12		11	12	10	—	76
B	11			40	12	13			76
C	21	—	61					17	99
D	13					70			83
E	41		20					16	77
F	11		20			24			55
G	21								11
H			60					21	81
TOTAL	118	31	173	40	23	119	10	54	568

Figure 30.5 Diagram of functional relationships

(e) *site design:* using the site and building to best advantage.

The design team should ensure that the interrelationships are well understood, the comparative importance of each process established and suitable priorities made and the whole project set out as a PERT diagram or network.

6 Space considerations: the allocation of space between offices and factory, productive processes and service areas, in process and finished goods storage needs to be done accordingly to predetermined rules and standards. For example, aisles are often allocated far too much space. If too much is allocated an aisle will degenerate into an inter-process storage area, holding up material flow and generally hindering the reason why aisles exist – rapid transport of materials and products, and personnel of all kinds.

Storage space too is often given an over-generous allocation of floor area. Maximum height stacking should be the rule rather than the exception, and materials handling equipment should be obtained to provide this facility.

Workplace design will often determine the space required for production machinery, rather than the machinery itself. Each workplace should be

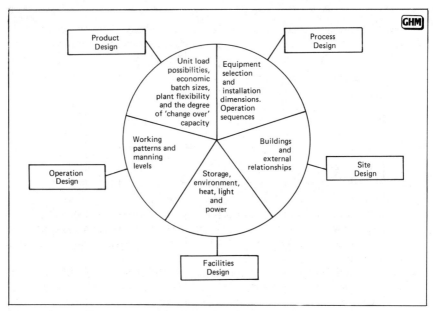

Figure 30.6   The design process

designed as a microcosm of the total plant so that it has its own receiving and dispatch areas, facilities and services and production equipment, established to maximise production efficiency. Workplace design should take account of potential scrap and finished production waiting to be moved, any inspection requirements, tools and tool storage, height of working surfaces, relationships between receipt and dispatch of materials, hazard elimination, degree of automation and mechanisation anticipated, operator comfort and conditions, floor loading constraints and general environmental considerations.

7   Line balance considerations: a plant layout analysis should promote a balance between machine/labour utilisation and use of in-progress storage space. This is often difficult where machines or operations have to be introduced which produce at a much higher or lower rate than perhaps the rest of the line.

The most common solution to this problem is to divide the work to be done into elements and thus combine them into activities which take up a similar amount of time. The related cost/performance calculations have been embodied into operations research techniques.

There are other ways of overcoming line balance problems, perhaps the easiest being the build up of partly or semi-finished stocks so as to feed in production when required at the slower operations.

Another solution is to have a reasonably peripatetic workforce which has been trained to carry out work at several operations, wherever the line has become unbalanced.

Balancing the line grows increasingly difficult as the product range becomes more complex. Variety reduction will always help this problem.

8 Equipment selection: equipment can be bought to satisfy one or more of the following criteria. To:

  (a) carry out a new activity
  (b) *replace a manual activity*
  (b) replace a manual activity
  (c) improve the environment and general working conditions
  (d) make use of new technology
  (e) improve line balance
  (f) replace a worn-out machine
  (g) reduce possibilities of accidents
  (h) improve quality of products.

9 Method study: using the simple method study symbols to describe a material flow process is often the simplest and best way of ensuring a record is made of actual or potential plant layout designs. String diagrams too can be of help.

10 The evaluation of alternative production methods and layout schemes is an essential part of any layout planning. This assumes, of course, that more than one potentially viable scheme does, in fact, exist. The merits of a proposal can be examined critically by asking how well the proposal would achieve any of the benefits listed at the beginning of this chapter, and checking that all constraint factors have been satisfied. By awarding a maximum possible number of 'score points' to each benefit factor (according to the degree of importance attached) a scale is made available against which the benefits of a scheme can be quantified. This helps to render any choice objective rather than subjective. It is obviously better still if the financial benefits of alternative schemes can be estimated and used in comparison.

MATERIALS HANDLING

The truism that 'handling adds nothing to value, only cost' suggests that materials handling should be an integral part of any consideration of a plant layout. Indeed it is difficult if not impossible to separate them. Materials handling is a term that embraces all aspects of material movement, other than when an actual production process is occurring. 'All aspects' are the physical transportation, equipment, methods, personnel and systems used in materials handling.

It must always be remembered that 'handling' is not an end in itself – the objective should be to contribute to a high performance of production, stores and despatch and to minimise the cost of production. Frequently this is synonymous with minimising the cost of handling. Handling is a service function and should never be considered as a system independent of production of warehousing.

Many of the principles which materials handling specialists apply are similar

519

to those used in plant layout. Handling and re-handling should be avoided where possible. Movement should be reduced in time and distance. Materials should be deposited as near as possible to the point of use and be prepositioned for use.

Continuous rather than intermittent movement should be a major aim. It is usually advantageous to establish definite routes for all material movement, vehicles and fork lift trucks.

Motion economy principles should apply wherever possible. Gravity should be used wherever it is feasible. Equipment and methods should be chosen to minimise in-process damage to products.

Equipment should be simple and cheap where possible. Mechanisation or automation is often unnecessary. Equipment should be used which is flexible and requires no fixed floor space.

GROUP TECHNOLOGY

Group technology is an interesting and important development, concerned with the flow of inter-process materials. It is based on the assumption that grouping manufacturing resources such as machines and making them inter-dependent in a cellular fashion has many advantages over the functional layout which has normally been found in batch or job shops. Each cell has a mix of machines sufficient to carry out all processes on a part, or family of parts.

A functional layout where, say, groups of lathes or drilling machines are brought together, produces complicated product route patterns, resulting in high work in progress, bottlenecks and more orders delivered late than early.

An analysis of batch or job shop work usually reveals that products, far from being unique, can be seen to have family likenesses in dimensions, material types, functions and general appearance. This analysis is an important element in establishing group technology. So by batching small groups of work in accordance with family features, it is possible to create large batches of basically similar work. Large batch production tends to take the place of small batch production.

A precursor of introducing group technology, therefore, is the design of a product classification system which can be used to batch material. A definitive parts numbering (drawing numbering) code system is essential.

The design of group technology flow lines can roughly be defined as 'batch flow lines' which form an integral part of the manufacturing system. Individual operations can be formed into cells by linking roller conveyors. This ensures that batches of work do not 'queue jump' and are processed in the same sequence as they are fed into the cell.

The general applications of group technology suggest that operations can be optional, and so either machine or labour resources are consequently under-utilised to create a continuous flow of work. The cost of the disadvantage is usually more than outweighed by reductions in setting up or change-over time, work in progress and finished goods stock. The improvement in customer service is also important.

The size of each cell is determined by engineering considerations and span of control, and particularly the work relationships of the primary working group. Flexibility of labour within the cell is the norm; flexibility between cells an ideal. Incentive schemes are designed to take account of breaks in rhythm needed when operatives move from one machine to another.

AUTOMATION AND ROBOTICS

Mechanisation and automation have often been confused when plant layouts are being determined. Mechanisation is the replacement of human muscle by mechanical means. Automation is the substitution of the human brain. It is the latter factor that will become more and more important in plant layout.

Industrial robots came about when it was possible to harness digital electronic circuitry in this application with sufficient reliability to stand up to the rigours of a factory environment. A robot comprises a jointed arm, a 'wrist' and a gripper or hand. These limbs are attached to a body and control unit, which is programmable. The very simplest programs were set up by means of plugging leads into an electrically connected pegboard. Modern robots can be 'taught' to carry out all the necessary operations by taking them manually through the desired sequence, comitting each action and limb position to the electronic memory, and then switching the device on to do the job repetitively, accurately and reliably.

Muscle power is such that work-pieces of 250 kilo loads can be positioned speedily with accuracy repeatable to a millimetre or so. Smaller robots have been developed which are capable of very fine assembly tasks.

Because robots are programmable, they are also *reprogrammable*. Unlike conventional automation, they do not have to be thrown away when a product is modified, redesigned or changed altogether. They are simply redeployed and 'taught' afresh.

The simplest robots are known as 'pick and place' devices, which means that they are capable of picking up a part from one given position, and placing it in another attitude and position. Such machines have a wide range of applications, but would not be suitable for work where every part of the path traced by the arm and gripper needed to be defined. In this case, a 'continuous path' robot would be required - useful for paint spraying and for seam welding for example.

One essential feature of plant layout and work planning with robots is that the part orientation must be accurately defined and controlled. A robot must be able to find the parts at the place where it has been 'taught' to find them, and in the correct attitude.

A robot can be set among a small group of machines, and sequenced to load, unload and operate them in an efficient, tireless fashion. Another application, such as in the welding of car bodies on a production line, uses stationary robots, with the work brought to them on a conveyor. A third arrangement is to mount the robots themselves on tracks or conveyors, with the work-piece stationary or on another conveyor.

Although robots contain their own controls and 'memory', they have to be sequenced and interlocked with all the surrounding plant. This needs the

521

attention of control engineers during the planning stage, as with conventional automation.

Various surveys of industrial robotics have been carried out and one considered view is that 8 per cent of manufacturing jobs will be taken over in the US by 1985. The first successful use of robots on a useful scale was in diecasting, where one robot was able to operate two diecasting machines and a trim press, producing a product of consistent high quality, unaffected by the fatigue factor which overcomes human operators working in the hostile atmosphere of a diecasting shop.

There are now many applications for robots, which include:

Diecasting
Spot welding
Arc welding
Forging
Investment casting
Plastic moulding
Machine loading
Materials handling and palletising
Paint spraying
and many, many more.

Research and development is very active, and the ambition of robot designers is to improve the intelligence of the machines, and to extend their use by giving a sense of feel or touch to the gripper, and by giving the robots some form of visual sense.

All responsible for plant layout and plant investment decisions must keep up to date with the possibilities offered by this technology if they are not to allow their companies to lose their competitive edge.

FURTHER READING

Bolz, H. A. (ed.), *Materials Handling Handbook,* Ronald Press, 1963

Chrison, G. B. (ed.), *The Production Handbook,* Ronald Press, 1962

Clay, M. J. and Walley, B. N., *Performance and Profitability,* Longmans Green, London, 1965

Engleberger, J. F., *Robotics in Practice,* Kogan Page, London, 1981

Hollinggum, J., *Mass Production With Batch Work: Group Technology Explained,* Pergamon, Oxford, 1969

Mallick, R. W. and Gaudreau, A. T., *Plant Layout Planning and Practice,* Wiley, New York, 1963

Wentworth, F., *Handbook of Physical Distribution Management,* Gower, 1976

31 Production control

Peter Jackson

Production control is concerned with producing goods in the right sequence in the least time at the lowest cost. As such it is a balancing act between contradictions. Good production control involves compromises and best fits rather than theoretical ideals. The main aspects are:

1 Loading and scheduling work
2 Provisioning material, parts and production aids
3 Monitoring and progressing work
4 Producing management information enabling the total system to be controlled.

DIFFERENCES BETWEEN SYSTEMS

Every company will have a different system depending on its products and production facilities. Some relevant factors are:

Complexity of the product

Single-operation plastic mouldings are much easier to control than components going through any combination of up to twenty operations. This is especially true if assembly of components is included.

Length of cycle time

If a job stays on a machine for a fortnight it is much easier to replan than if each operation takes only a few hours.

Repeatability of the work

Regular jobs will have predictable cycle times. The production facilities they require, such as tooling, will be known and available. One-off jobs are not so easy to control.

Forward notice available

Some companies know every job they will do for a year ahead and can plan accordingly. Others do not, or claim they do not, know a week ahead what orders will be required.

Dependence on outside suppliers and subcontractors

Where control is not completely within the company greater allowance must be made for slippage.

Seasonal nature of the workload

Where seasonal peak loads occur capacity utilisation will obviously vary.

Availability and quality of information on capacity and workload

Companies which have detailed time standards, process layouts and up-to-date capacities can load to a fuller degree and schedule to a tighter time-scale than those which have to rely on rough estimates.

Despite all these differences companies with a wide range of products and production facilities have similar problems and have developed similar solutions.

LOADING AND SCHEDULING WORK

Loading is filling available capacity with sufficient jobs in a given time period. Scheduling is determining the desired sequence of jobs. The two are inter-related and in some procedures may be indistinguishable. When work is correctly loaded and scheduled full use can be made of capacity, completion times can be predicted and met and urgent jobs can be given priority without upsetting the rest of the work.

Stages

Loading and scheduling will probably be done in several stages from the overall factory planning when a new order is received to the detailed plan for each machine in the period immediately before production. The mechanics are similar at each stage. When the order is accepted little detail may be known of the work load involved or of the machine capacity available in the proposed production period, yet some estimates mut be made to enable delivery dates to be quoted. Such forward loading is done on an overall basis using broad measures.

As the time for producing the order draws near the drawings, parts lists and process paperwork will have been extracted enabling loads on each machine to be calculated. Also, nearer the production time available capacity can be more realistically assessed. This enables detailed short-term loading to be done.

Data required

Units

The basic need is a common unit in which both capacity and load can be expressed. The most common unit is time. Load can be measured by work study or estimation or historical information can be kept. The accuracy required of these time standards depends on the degree of repetition of the work. Often good estimates are sufficient provided they are on average right. Where times for individual components are used they must be multiplied by the batch size and an allowance for setting time included.

Capacity in terms of time is easily expressed in man- or machine-hours with suitable allowances for breakdowns, re-work and other contingencies.

Where times are not available a physical count may provide a suitable unit. Foundry output is often expressed in tonnes. A shoe factory may make so many pairs a day. A warehouse may process so many orders. Here the load is already defined, capacity is found from historical data.

A third measure of capacity and load is money. Orders are often considered in terms of their financial value and this may be a convenient way of loading a factory. An output of £10 000 per week may be a good measure of a factory's production. Again capacity is measured historically. Because of the nature of material and labour costs it is unusual to use money as a unit for detailed machine loading.

Load centre capacities

A load centre is the production unit to which jobs are allocated. It could be a factory, a section, a machine group or an individual machine or operator. With several stages of loading it could be all of these in turn. When it involves more than one machine either all work loaded to it should be capable of being done on any of its sub-units or the mix of work should on average match the mix of the sub-units.

Before breaking the load down to individual machines it should be considered whether the production control department are the best people to do this. The foreman or supervisor will have detailed knowledge of the capabilities of particular men and machines and be able to react to breakdowns and other immediate problems. It may, therefore, be realistic to load to machine groups leaving the final allocation to the man on the spot.

The capacity of the load centre is calculated in the appropriate units. Some capacity may be reserved for emergency work or special customers but this must be kept to a small proportion and revised regularly.

Processes

The sequence of operations, usually called the process layout, must be known if each operation is to be loaded separately.

Parts lists

Where assemblies are manufactured the parts list of each assembly and sub-assembly will be needed. The requirements for common parts need to be batched up. For some components it may be more economical to make for stock than make on a one for one basis for final assembly.

LOADING METHODS

There are two main methods: job sequence, in which each job is loaded in strict sequence against a time-scale, and control period where a list of jobs is planned for a defined time period but can be carried out in any sequence.

Job sequence loading

To load jobs in strict sequence against a time-scale requires some visual display such as a planning board. Such boards can be purchased ready made although a home-made version can often fit particular requirements better. The load centres are usually displayed along the left-hand edge with a time-scale along the bottom. Jobs are planned to load centres either by writing on the board with an erasable medium or inserting a card in a slot (see Figure 31.1).

This method is best used close to actual production for loading individual machines. It can only be used for forward planning where contracts cannot run simultaneously. An example of this would be forward planning ships on the slipways of a shipyard.

GHM

Machine	Hour beginning							
	08 00	09 00	10 00	11 00	12 30	13 30	14 30	15 30
Capstan lathe	1053	1053	1053	1154	1154	1154	1154	1154
Herbert lathe	1186	1186	1186	1186	1186	1701	1701	1701
Holbrook lathe	1188	1188	1188	1188	1188	1188	1790	1790
Jig borer	REPAIR AND MAINTENANCE							
Universal miller	IDLE	IDLE	IDLE	IDLE	1185	1185	1185	1185
Horizontal miller	1081	1081	1081	1081	904	904	904	1225
Automatic—1	1300	1300	1300	1300	1300	1300	IDLE	IDLE
Automatic—2	IDLE	IDLE	IDLE	IDLE	IDLE	IDLE	IDLE	IDLE

Figure 31.1   A job sequence loading chart
This simple configuration is suitable for blackboard and chalk. The numbers in the squares are job numbers

Advantages of job sequence loading

1 Clear visual display of information
2 Full utilisation of capacity possible
3 Rapid throughput of jobs loaded on more than one load centre
4 Planning boards can be used for progressing.

Disadvantages of job sequence loading

1 Updating is difficult and time consuming
2 Only suitable for limited periods ahead because of the likelihood of the situation changing
3 Relies on precise measurement of load
4 Cannot cope with overall allowances for reduction of capacity. For example, 10 per cent allowance for breakdowns.

Control period loading

A list of jobs is produced for each load centre for a fixed period of time, the control period. The total load of these jobs equals the capacity of the centre. For example, a machine group of two lathes each worked 40 hours a week has a capacity of 80 hours if the chosen control period is a week. A list is produced of jobs for these machines up to a total of 80 hours. Any further work is loaded into the following week.

The list becomes the programme for that load centre for that period. Jobs can be done in any sequence on any machine in the centre, provided they are finished by the end of the control period.

Multi-operational jobs are programmed at one operation per control period resulting in all jobs going through at an equal pace. The completion time of each job can be predicted.

The choice of control period depends on the length of the jobs and the sophistication of the production control system. Setting a target of one operation per week may not be very ambitious but may compare favourably with what was achieved without a loading system. It is better to start with a long control period and shorten it when experience has been gained rather than start with an unrealistically short one.

Control period loading is used in long-term planning where the overall work load can be compared with the overall capacity; for example, accepting orders up to £10 000 value a month. It is also used for short-term planning on groups of machines. This allows supervision flexibility to allocate particular jobs to individual machines or operators.

Advantages of control period loading

1 Simple to operate
2 Not dependent on completion of every job. Late jobs can be caught up without upsetting the programme

3 Allows supervision discretion in allocating jobs to particular operators or machines
4 Enables forward load picture to be produced over a reasonable period.

Disadvantages of control period loading

1 Overall throughput time is slow compared to job sequence loading, although much quicker than if no planning is used at all
2 Work in progress is higher than for job sequence loading.

Forward and backward loading

Using either job sequence or control period loading it is usual to start at the present time and load jobs in the earliest available capacity, slowly building up a forward load picture. This is known as forward loading.

It is, however, possible to fix a completion date a number of weeks in advance and load backwards from this date thus arriving at a date when the job must start. This is called backward loading.

Assuming that delivery dates have been set realistically, backward loading ensures that jobs are not started needlessly early. If all jobs are loaded in this way capacity may well be exceeded as one of the main reasons for loading is to set achievable delivery dates. It may help to backward load a certain proportion of jobs, key ones whose delivery dates are important, and then fill in the remaining capacity by forward loading the less urgent jobs.

PROVISIONING

Provisioning is ensuring that everything required is available when production is scheduled to start. This includes drawings, tools and gauges as well as parts and material. Such aids can hold up production just as much as material shortages and lack of them is often harder to put right.

Make or buy

Preliminary decisions must be taken on whether the part is to be made in-house or bought out or part sub-contracted.

Factors affecting the decision are:

Available capacity

This may fluctuate changing the decision.

Available skills and technology

Outside firms may specialise in certain processes.

Volume required

Normally a firm would not make its own nuts and bolts but if it used millions then it would.

Available lead-times

Much tighter control can be exercised over internal manufacture.

Where external suppliers or sub-contractors are used it is vital to obtain commitment to delivery dates. Progressing is best done by personal visits. In any case it is wise to build in latitude in the lead-times of externally sourced parts. Rating of suppliers on delivery is obviously worth while but cannot guard against every contingency.

Quantities

Certain items will be made on a one-for-one basis according to sales demand with perhaps a small allowance for scrap or spares. A few items may be made continuously throughout the year. The majority of items are made in batches. The size of the batch can be determined in two ways. Economic batch sizes can be calculated as shown in the chapter on stock control. Where a batch is manufactured internally the setting cost replaces the order cost in the formula.

An alternative is to make regular batches to return the stock to a desired level. These batches will vary in size but enable the factory to be programmed on a regular repetitive basis. For example, using the Pareto stock classification, A items might be made once a month, B items once a quarter and C items once a year.

In fact the mathematics of both methods are not dissimilar. If batches are made regularly the average stockholding is slightly higher than if economic batches are made when a re-order level is breached.

Kitting and pre-allocation

Before a job is issued to the shop floor it should be established that all things needed for its production are available. It should not be the job of a skilled operator to queue for drawings, tools and gauges before he starts work. Even less should he have to spend time searching on the section for missing items. All such production aids should be collected by stores staff before a job is issued. Where a job is repeated a card can be kept recording everything required for the job.

Where assemblies are produced kitting problems are more apparent. Often a set of parts will be collected for issue and shortages found. Either the job is issued incomplete or it is held in stores where it may tie up parts which could be used elsewhere. Such parts may be removed from the kit, further complicating the problem.

In such situations a paperwork exercise can be carried out where all the components are checked for availability though not physically collected. This dummy kitting or pre-allocation means that if it is not feasible to issue Job A because of shortages it may be possible to issue Job B using some of the components from Job A.

If parts lists and stock levels are kept on computer and are up to date such pre-allocation can be done automatically and rapidly with obvious advantages.

MONITORING AND PROGRESSING

The aims of monitoring and progressing are to:

1 Highlight jobs running late
2 Assist such jobs to catch up
3 Anticipate problems further down the production cycle that late jobs would cause
4 Enable customer enquiries to be answered.

The first principle is to progress by exception. Collecting a vast amount of information about jobs which are running to time may give people a feeling of achievement but does little real good.

The second principle is that information must be up to date. Elaborate computer runs analysing where jobs were three days ago may be ignored in favour of a physical search of the section.

Monitoring

The simplest way of monitoring the position of jobs is to utilise the work booking system. At the end of each operation the completed job card is used to update a master progress record which is held in the production control office. Problems may arise where booking is not done immediately at the completion of a job.

A similar system is to have a set of tear-off tickets attached to each job. As the job passed a control point the appropriate section of the ticket is detached and sent to update the master progress record.

Increasingly the completion of jobs is being recorded on data collection devices linked to computers. These can be on the shop floor beside the machines and can given an extremely rapid update of the production situation.

Progressing

When the current state has been monitored action has to be taken. As a job running late in its initial stages can cause problems all the way down the line progress meetings are often held for all those involved. Provided such meetings are kept short and involve more than marking up lists they can be valuable.

Progress men are often used firstly to monitor the state of jobs and secondly to urge priority jobs. Again if this is largely marking lists it could be done better by a good clerical booking system. Progress men oil the wheels by putting urgent jobs at the front of the queue and arranging special transport between operations. However, sometimes their work can be self cancelling. In one engineering works there were fourteen progress men to one hundred machinists. Each of the five foremen could have up to fourteen people requesting that their job be done first.

Urgent jobs

It is common for urgent jobs to be given some distinguishing mark, a red label or a star for example. The trouble is that such labels multiply until 80 per cent of the jobs have red stars. Then someone gives the really urgent jobs two red stars and so the system escalates. Fifty urgent jobs are a contradiction in terms.

A strict upper limit, ten for example, should be placed on the number of urgent jobs. If another is required an existing one should be dropped from the list. To do this the person deciding the priorities should be senior enough to resist sectional pressures and see the overall picture. A shop floor supervisor can often be approached by many different people in the management structure each asking for different jobs to be given priority.

Long-term solutions

Although it is sensible to give a few urgent jobs an extra push, if late and rush jobs are a large and constant problem then the overall situation needs to be looked at. Are delivery dates being realistically set? Is there sufficient capacity? Could the effort spend chasing rush jobs be better spent improving the throughput time?

It may be possible to chase one job through the factory with it hardly touching the ground. What is not seen is the trail of delays and increased costs on other jobs that this action causes. Many customers will ask for jobs sooner than they need them because they know only priority jobs will be chased and the rest left to drift through.

One solution to the problem of conflicting priorities is to have each progress man responsible for all the throughput of one section. When operations are completed in this section the jobs become the responsibility of the progress man in the next section and so on. This is in contrast to the usual system where a progress man is responsible for all stages of a particular range of jobs. Sometimes there is a need for both types of progress but the balance must be held.

Where two or more divisions of a company share a common resource (for example, a machine shop), conflicts over capacity and priorities will often happen. Where possible such facilities should be split. If this cannot be done the capacity may need to be expanded over what might be theoretically required to allow for interference between the user departments.

MANAGEMENT CONTROL INFORMATION

A production control department processes vast amounts of information, levels of stock, states of orders, capacities available and so on. It should, therefore, be the source of the overview of production that higher management needs. Too often management will concentrate on solving particular problems using their authority to get things done. This may solve the particular issue but create a whole set of other problems and delays. It is management's job to look at the total picture, making decisions about capacity and load, leaving the day-to-day problems to those paid to cope with them.

531

The production control department can help by supplying regular information on relevant totals. The particular figures will vary but might include:

Order book

Forecast sales
Total orders received
Total orders dispatched
Total orders on hand

Customer service

Current average delivery times
Delivery promise achievements
Number of complaints

Factory performance

Total production
Programme achievement
Arrears
Forward load versus capacity

Stocks

Raw material
Work in progress
Finished goods

For most of these figures it would be difficult to set an ideal level though it is always good to aim for a target. The important thing is the direction in which the figures are going, improving, worsening or staying the same.

It may be necessary to break the total figures down into separate product lines. The temptation to produce lists of individual jobs for higher management should be avoided.

PAPERWORK

Production control departments produce a mass of paperwork, schedules, lists, tickets, progress records, computer printout. Over the years new systems may have been introduced partly duplicating existing ones. Records may be kept which are no longer required. Individuals produce and maintain their own systems.

It is possible to have a department called production control which produces a large amount of paper yet influences what happens on the shop floor hardly at all. It is said that when the weight of a ship being built exceeds the weight of paperwork required to build it then it is ready for launching.

Different production systems will require different paperwork but a typical outline is shown below.

Advanced warning

When an order is first received a document is raised to notify departments concerned. It will contain basic details of the order and the provisional delivery date quoted. An example is shown in Figure 31.2.

The receiving departments, typically industrial engineering, stock control and production, will confirm whether the provisional date can be accepted.

Job paperwork

Each job needs:

1 A loading/progress document which stays in the production control department and is used first to schedule the job and then to record its progress. It may well be a card which can be slotted into a planning board.
2 An identification label which goes round with the job (job ticket).
3 Instructions for the people doing each stage of the job.
4 Material or parts requisitions.
5 Paperwork for booking each stage of the job. This may be in the form of cards which are returned to the production control office showing date, time, scrap and the operator's name.

Examples of production control paperwork are given in Figures 31.3 and 31.4.

Schedules

Lists of jobs will be made of work to be done on a section in a given period. These may be in sequence or highlight jobs with a higher priority. These lists will also be used to progress the work.

Methods

Various ready made paperwork systems are available but there may be limits on their flexibility. The main proprietary systems used are:

Stockcards

Where visible edge filing can give rapid access to a large number of records.

Line selection systems

Using special spirit duplicators, information from a master can be combined in different sequences to provide sets of job cards, material requisitions, master progress cards and other required paperwork.

Computer systems

Can be used to print production paperwork. Output does not have to be on conventional computer paper but can be on cards, labels and other forms.

Whatever method is used it should be simple and functional. Periodically paperwork systems should be reviewed and improved or discarded where necessary.

GHM

WORKS ORDER

Job Number

| Customer | Send to (if different) |

| Date issued | Customer's order No. and date | Delivery date promised | Carriage by |

Items to be supplied

Quantity	Drawing number	Description	Unit price	Total price

Special instructions

£

+ VAT @   %

Total

Distribution

Catalogue items and specials			Specials only			
Stock control	Dispatch	Accounts	Chief engineer	Chief inspector	Works manager	Production control

Figure 31.2   Works order

Figure 31.3   Requisition, job ticket and stores receipt note

COMPUTERS

Computers have been applied to production control since the 1950s with varying degrees of success. With large mainframe computers at head office information was first punched on to cards and then fed into the machine when it was available from its other tasks and more importantly, when it was working. The result was that computers were good at showing what the production situation was a week last Friday.

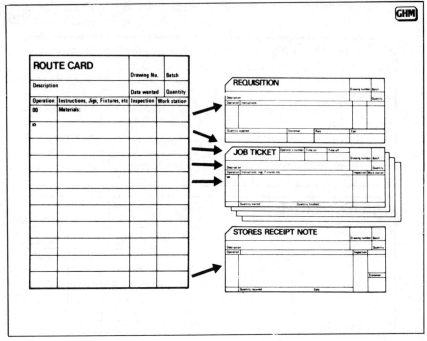

Figure 31.4   Production control and documentation package

With faster, smaller, more reliable and much cheaper computers it is possible to have one dedicated full time, at least in working hours, to production control. Remote terminals mean information can be input as it is generated on the shop floor or in the stores. Not only does this save time but it decreases copying errors. Output need no longer be thick piles of computer paper showing the current state of everything. Selective enquiries can be made via a terminal with the answer appearing at once.

Material requirements planning

The principal use of computers in production control is for material requirements planning (MRP). The forward order position is entered in terms of end products required per week. The computer checks these against finished stock and produced the net requirements. These are then broken down using the parts lists for each assembly. The requirements for each component for each week are totalled. These again are checked against existing stock and orders and the net requirements produced. These net requirements can be batched and turned into orders either manually or by computer. Lead-times can be included so that raw material is called for a number of weeks before the final assembly is due.

In complex situations assemblies may break down to sub-assemblies which break down to sub-sub-assemblies and so on. Up to as many as twelve such levels may be encountered before the basic parts or raw materials are reached. Using MRP the entire schedule of demand for each level can be produced in a few hours or less. Manually it would take weeks or months.

Conventionally the MRP file has been updated once or twice a week with all new orders, production achieved and stock delivered. It is becoming possible to feed in such changes as they happen giving a continuous updated material requirement plan.

Using MRP, orders for components and material are based on actual forward demand. Where this is not possible or feasible traditional stock control can be done on a computer. Predictions based on past usage and average lead-times are made. Reorder levels and batch sizes are calculated.

Loading and scheduling

Various packages are available for loading jobs on to machines. They are generally based on the critical path network approach.

The limitation of such packages is the sheer complexity of the task. To load even a few jobs on a limited number of machines can give several hundred possible combinations. With a realistic number of jobs and machines the possibility may be hundreds of thousands. Manually such loading can be done using a planning board. The human brain can produce a result that is adequate and takes most considerations into account. The computer can only try all possible combinations until it finds the one best solution. To shorten the process, jobs are assigned priorities and other simplifications are made. The result is still a lengthy computer run producing a result little better than a manual one. In a fast-changing production environment where machines break down, times overrun and priorities get altered the computer may not yet be the tool for sequential loading.

What the computer can do well is provide totals of loads on sections or machines so that advance warning is obtained of over or underloads.

Future development

In the future production control will be almost entirely computerised, even in small companies. The chief requirement is for comprehensive, accurate, up-to-date information. Data recorders linked to each machine and to the computer will be a large step towards this.

FURTHER READING

Burbridge, J.L., *Principles of Production Control*, Macdonald & Evans, London, 4th edition, 1978. A wide-ranging and practical book.

Lockyer, K.G., *Production Control in Practice*, 2nd edition, Pitman, London, 1975. A good introduction, particularly to the numerical side of production control.

New, C.C., *Managing Manufacturing Operations*, BIM Management Survey No. 35, 1976. A survey of practice in 186 plants giving a good basis for comparisons.

Walley, B.H., *Production Management Handbook*, Gower, 1980.

32 Industrial engineering

Dennis Whitmore

Industrial engineering is a generic term for techniques primarily aimed at increasing productivity. Many other disciplines and occupations help in the improvement of effectiveness, but this is often incidental to their main objectives. The accountant, for example, provides information for financial control, and the personnel manager must choose the most effective people for particular jobs. But the industrial engineer is *directly* charged with the task of improving productivity.

'Industrial engineering' has a transatlantic ring about it. Although the term is used in the UK *management services* is often preferred, to avoid the connotation of machine shop-floor and tool-making which the word 'engineering' implies to many people. Some organisations still cling to the rather narrow term *work study* but investigations into productivity have advanced far beyond the original techniques of the first two decades of this century.

The disciplines and techniques of industrial engineering are outlined in Figure 32.1. They can be separated into four major groups, concerned with the improvement of:

1   The organisation
2   Methods and equipment
3   Job conditions and environment
4   The product or service itself

There are no watertight compartments. Techniques may overlap and be interchanged, but essentially the first two areas above can be investigated through *work study* for most manual work, *organisation and methods* (O&M) is applicable to clerical and office work, and *operational research* (OR) is mainly concerned with corporate level operations. (Examples of such corporate level operations include distribution, product mix, planned maintenance, stock control and so on.)

The safety, well-being, and comfort of the operator are the concern of *ergonomics*, which is often known as 'fitting the job to the worker'; exactly what

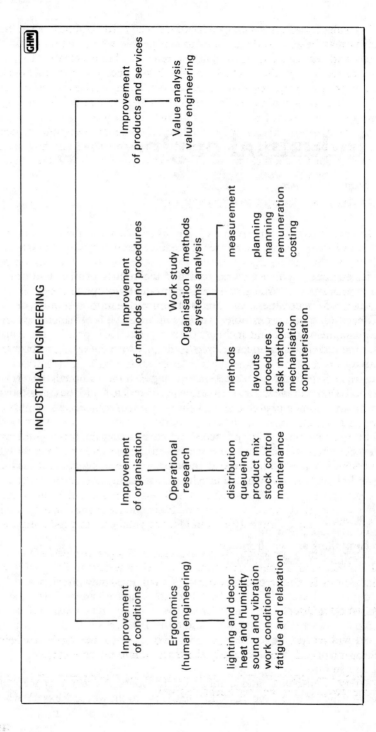

Figure 32.1 Industrial engineering techniques

it does. The subject demands a knowledge of the medical disciplines so that the ergonomists may be able to design jobs to suit people who must do them.

Products and services may be designed to remove all unnecessary parts, or simplified to retain only those which are absolutely necessary for functional, aesthetic, or prestige purposes. When these cost-reducing devices are built in at the design stage the technique is known as *value engineering*, but its sibling, *value analysis*, may be used on existing products or services.

Over all these approaches there are the two fundamental disciplines which answer the two basic questions: how should the task be done? and how long should it take? The first of these must be tackled by a *problem-solving* technique and the second by *work measurement*.

THE IMPROVEMENT OF PRODUCTIVITY

The term 'productivity improvement' has been used for many years by companies and governments as a recipe for the salvation of industry. In essence, productivity is the producing of goods and services with the minimum of resources, consistent with adequate quantity, quality, utilisation and other necessary requirements. Thus it follows that productivity can be increased by raising production for the same or lower amounts of the input resources, or by maintaining the same levels with fewer resources. These resources are materials, labour, services and money.

Productivity measurement has posed problems because it is difficult to reduce all results to a common national or international basis. This obviously makes comparisons between different industries – or even companies – extremely difficult. It is a relative consideration: productivity may be measured both before and after improvement, and the two results compared to quantify the uplift in productivity.

As a simple example, suppose 6000 printed circuit boards are being assembled by fifteen people, and when a methods improvement is introduced only ten people are needed to produce the same number of boards in the same time. Productivity was 400 boards per person, while after the improvement it becomes 600 each, giving an increase of 200 boards per head. Usually the resources are more than labour so a common basis, such as money, may be used to measure the resource input (for example, the total cost of producing the boards).

A common form of productivity measurement is operator performance, assessed by the ratio of measured time to actual time taken. This index is discussed further in the section dealing with work measurement.

PROBLEM SOLVING

People are always solving problems and making decisions both in their domestic and working lives. Basically there are four types of situation:

1   An *improvement* problem, where there is a situation which needs improving in some way, such as an inefficient method

2   A *deviation* problem is one in which the situation differs from what it ought to be, or what one desires of it
3   A *creative* problem exists where one wishes to invent or design something, given the terms of reference, or objectives to be achieved
4   In *problem avoidance* one tries to anticipate troubles or problems before they actually occur, and thinks up remedies in case they do occur.

There may be an infinite variety of problems but all can be approached using a common strategy. The general procedure applies equally to method study, organisation and methods, operational research or to any other technique.

1   *Problem definition.* Clearly, before a problem can be tackled the true problem, as opposed to the apparent problem, must be defined
2   *Data collection.* All the facts about the situation must be assembled before any solution can be attempted
3   *Examination.* The facts must be critically examined in either a logical way, or in some cases, using a completely illogical approach (*see* the following sub-section). From the results of this examination can follow:
4   *Development of a solution.* Examination will show up the deficiencies and point the way to a solution. This is now developed and tested during a 'dry run' period
5   *Installation.* When the proposed solution is as perfect as it can be, it is introduced to the situation
6   *Maintenance,* or continual monitoring and updating is necessary as the situation develops in the future.

Methods for problem solving

Problem-solving methods can be separated into logical and illogical. A chart showing how a particular technique may be selected is shown in Figure 32.2.

A logical, step-by-step method is traditional *critical examination* which asks *what* is done?, *when?*, by *whom?*, *where?*, *how* are the goals achieved? and to all of this *why?* Often tasks need not be changed or simplified, but can in fact be abandoned altogether as unnecessary.

An illogical approach is to use analogies to describe a situation, thereby making a complex one more easily understood by equating it to similar circumstances with which the observer may be more familiar, or by acting out the role of the situation.

The Kepner-Tregoe approach is to list all things about what the situation *is* and what it *is not.* From the lists, the *causes* of deviation from the desired condition are highlighted.

Another non-logical method of collecting ideas is *brainstorming.* This requires participants to throw in ideas as they occur to them in an uninhibited way, with no criticism. This method avoids stereotyped ideas, and often generates novel and 'way-out' ideas.

Trial-and-error, or heuristic methods are often used, each trial being improved upon until the optimum solution is achieved.

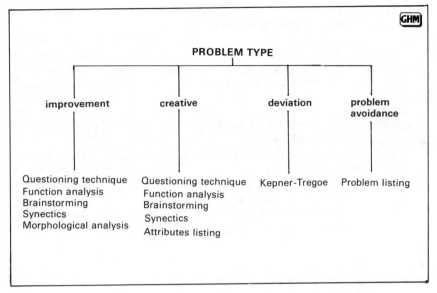

PROBLEM TYPE

improvement	creative	deviation	problem avoidance
Questioning technique	Questioning technique	Kepner-Tregoe	Problem listing
Function analysis	Function analysis		
Brainstorming	Brainstorming		
Synectics	Synectics		
Morphological analysis	Attributes listing		

Figure 32.2   Selecting the appropriate problem-solving technique

IMPROVEMENT OF WORKING METHODS

Problem solving may be applicable to all situations, but method study capitalises widely on the techniques. In the clerical field organisation and methods is the principal tool for increasing effectiveness and productivity, and includes within its orbit the technique of method study.

The first stage is to define the true problem and terms of reference. For example, a goods-inwards procedure is labour intensive and must be made more cost-effective. With such a brief must be included constraints such as costs, savings required and period of capital return.

The data collection period involves the employees through interviews about their jobs, and facts about the objectives and goals to be achieved. Information is displayed by means of flow charts, diagrams and models.

It may be necessary to investigate the document flow, goods handling and individual methods of doing the jobs (the two-handed chart). The investigator may wish to improve the layout, using a flow diagram as the basis, even using three-dimensional models, or templates which can be moved around in order to find the best configuration.

Having gathered the facts, the investigator is able to examine them and question the purpose and need for the various parts of the system. One of the problem-solving techniques outlined in the previous section of the chapter will be used. A method growing in popularity is function analysis, based on brainstorming. This technique is described later under 'value analysis', but in

543

essence a team of specialists discusses the problem, tossing ideas for improvements into the general pool of knowledge.

These suggestions are then considered and the promising ones investigated further. From the final list of recommended ideas new methods, layouts and procedures are written up as a report to management for its consideration.

The parts of the report which are approved are then implemented gradually to replace the existing ones. Full consultation with staff would be maintained, of course, and their suggestions considered too. There would be many deficiencies in the new situation needing reconsideration, but eventually an integrated system would emerge.

Quite possibly the team may consider a computer configuration to be the best solution to the manual one being used at present. This is usually the province of *systems analysis*, responsible for the examination of existing or proposed computer installations and mechanisation of procedures.

Over a period of time, situations change so it is important that the sixth phase of maintenance and updating is incorporated into any study of procedure, method or layout as a continuing process of monitoring.

THE MEASUREMENT OF WORK

Previous sections of this chapter have examined the processes of improving productivity through the medium of making work and organisations more effective. However it is of small advantage if people do a well-designed job but do not perform the task at an effective pace. The whole object of redesigning a task by method study is to reduce the time in which it can be completed, and this reduction may be entirely negated if the operative takes twice as long to do it by working so slowly.

Moreover, unless an organisation knows how long a job ought to take it cannot plan its completion and delivery dates, nor can it cost the labour content, nor even pay its employees if they are engaged on incentive payment schemes. But who is to say how long a job ought to take, and how can one determine this time?

Regardless of what some textbooks say, work can only be measured in three basic ways: by timing it with some form of chronometer, by using manuals of predetermined times, or by estimating it. Thus all work can be measured to a greater or lesser degree of precision (see Figure 32.3). One could even measure the time it would have taken Beethoven to write his Tenth Symphony by the last of the three methods! The estimate would be wild, but it *is* a time standard nevertheless.

The main objective of work measurement is to establish a time for a job which an experienced, trained, person could achieve while doing the job effectively and at a workmanlike pace. This may seem rather subjective but in practice it can be done. The techniques for setting such *basic times* are many, but they all fall under these three basic headings as shown in Figure 32.3. The most appropriate has to be selected from the toolbag of techniques. The two main guiding factors in this selection are (a) the precision desired, and (b) the speed of

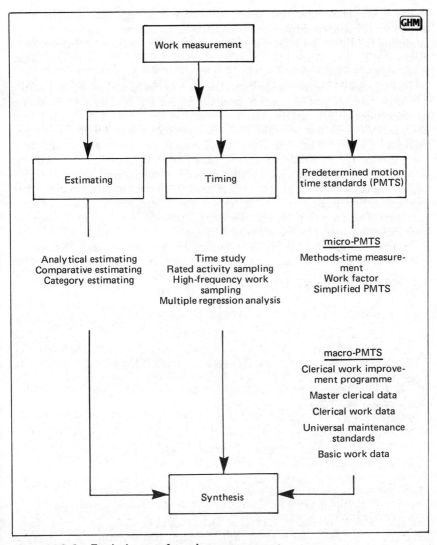

Figure 32.3 Techniques of work measurement

application or how long it takes the analyst to set the time standard compared with how long it takes to do the work.

The most precise standards are given by the generic group of predetermined motion time standards (PMTS). These exist in two main forms: micro-PMTS (with elements measured in thousandths of a minute) and macro-PMTS (with elements of the order of seconds). Many proprietary systems exist but international ones practised in USA, Europe, the Far East and Australasia are Methods-Time Measurement (MTM) and Work-Factor.

The principle of measuring work by PMTS is based upon the analysis of the work into suitable elements, looking up the tables of times for these, and then summing the times to obtain the overall time for the job. Typical elements of micro-PMTS are reach, grasp, release, move, walk, sit, stand, assemble, disassemble, etc.

The micro-PMT systems are very time consuming to use, so the originating concerns have simplified them to produce higher levels of data which are far quicker and easier to apply. The two major systems on the lowest level are Detailed Work-Factor and MTM-1. On the second level are the equivalent systems of Ready Work-Factor, and MTM-2 respectively, and on the third level Abbreviated Work-Factor and MTM-3. Higher levels of data are developed in various ways including the combination of elements, the merging of moving distances, the elimination of some elements, and the simplifying of elements. For example, in Methods-Time Measurement the first-level elements of reach, grasp, and release were combined into one new element of get, while move and position become the new element of put.

Typical elements of a mythical system are shown in Figure 32.4. The analysis of a simple operation and the derivation of the subsequent basic time for this job are illustrated in Figure 32.5. This shows how elements are identified, and times extracted for subsequent addition to obtain the time for the complete job.

In PMT systems it is appreciated that certain factors will affect the time taken to do a basic element. A reach with the hand of 45 cm will take longer to accomplish than one of only 10 cm, so distance is a factor which must be considered (see Figure 32.5). Also care must be taken if the article to be grasped is delicate or dangerous to handle; another factor. If the article is heavy, this must be taken into account. These factors and others are considered when designing a system of PMT, and due allowance of extra time must be made when any of the factors are encountered.

The basic unit of measurement in Work-Factor is called the Work-Factor Time Unit, and is equal to 0.0001 min., while the time-measurement unit (tmu) of Methods-Time Measurement is 0.00001 hr. These tiny times originally were measured using high-speed film analyses, stroboscopic photography, stop-watches, and various electrical devices. As an example, a basic 30-cm reach with the hand with no manual control or weight would take 0.0046 min.

On the macro-PMTS level are Clerical Work Data, Clerical Work Improvement Programme, Universal Office Standards, and Office Modapts, together with Basic Work Data, MTM Maintenance Standards, Universal Maintenance Standards, and others.

A typical PMTS analysis

The exact form of the analysis of jobs for PMTS varies according to the system being employed. An illustration of how a job may be analysed and the elemental times extracted from tables using a mythical system, is given in Figure 32.5. A more complete account of PMTs is found in Whitmore (1980).

Figure 32.4 Typical elements for a system of predetermined motion times (PMTS)

OBTAIN AND PLACE ASIDE TABLE
times are for OBTAIN or for PLACE ASIDE (PA)

ALL TIMES in milliminutes @ 100 rate

DISTANCE (CM)	DEGREE OF DIFFICULTY		
	SIMPLE	AVE.	DIFFICULT
Up to 5cm	2	3	6
+5 to 10cm	3	4	7
+10 to 15cm	3	5	8
+15 to 20cm	4	6	9
+20 to 25cm	5	7	10
+25 to 30cm	6	8	11
+30 to 35cm	7	9	12
+35 to 40cm	9	11	13
+above 40cm	10	12	15

MOVE TABLE (MP)

DEGREE OF DIFFICULTY			WEIGHT OR RESISTANCE
SIMPLE	AVE.	DIFFICULT	
2	5		
3	6	10	
4	7	11	
5	8	13	
6	9	13	
7	10	14	
8	11	16	
9	12	18	
10	13	20	

CRANK TABLE

DEGREES	
up to 90	4
+90 to 180	6
+180 to 270	7
+270 to 360	9

TWIST OR TURN TABLE *

WITHOUT	WITH
3	6

** For relocation (e.g. turn back screwdriver to slot) use M.PD).

SCREWDRIVER DATA
Screwing in medium and small screws 12 turns on average

Element Ref.	S 36
Sheet Ref.	20
Study Ref.	1238
Date	12 April

Description (LH)	Diffic.	Code	Time	Code	Diffic.	Description (RH)
1. Pick up screw from bin (25 cm)	Diff.	O.D25	10	O.A25	Ave.	Pick up screwdriver from bench
2. Move and position to pilot hole	Diff.	M.PD20	12	M.PA20	Ave.	Move and position driver to screw
3. Hole screw upright		H	9	M.PD5	Diff.	Locate blade to screw
4. "		H	7	T.S.	Simp	Turn screwdriver one turn
5. "		H	9	M.PD5	Diff.	Remove, twist back, relocate in head
6. "		H	77	x 11		Repeat (4) 11 more times.
7. "		H	99	x 11		Repeat (5) 11 more times.
8. "		H	12	T.S.R.	Simp	Repeat (4) for final tightening
9. Release screw	Simp	R.S.	9	M.PA25	Ave.	Place aside driver to bench (25 cm)
				Total	244	
					0.244	basic.mins.

GHM

Figure 32.5 An analysis of a job by a hypothetical system of PMT

Relaxation allowance

All techniques of work measurement produce basic times for each element of the job. However it is recognised that people must have time to recover from their exertions periodically, and so a relaxation allowance (RA) is added to the basic time to allow for this. The resulting *standard time* is the one which is used by management for their various needs. The magnitude of the RA is derived from predetermined tables (see Figure 32.6) or is sometimes just estimated.

Timing techniques

The oldest method of formal work measurement is *timing* which goes back to the early part of the century to Frederick W. Taylor, Frank B. Gilbreth and Charles Bedaux. There are three basic forms of timing: time study, rated activity sampling, and timing using multiple regression analysis.

Time study is the setting of a basic time for a job (*not* for the person doing the job). This basic time is the time for one cycle to be performed with the operative working at a standardised pace, so that different jobs may be compared, and the time is absolutely unconnected with the person doing the work. Unfortunately people do not conveniently work at this standard pace but adopt their own natural speeds. Even this may vary throughout the day as people tire.

This problem is overcome by timing (using a stop-watch) workers doing the task to be studied and then adjusting this time to what it *would* have been had the operator been working at standard pace. The process of assessing the pace is known as *rating*. Thus if a worker took 0.6 min. to do a cycle of the job and the work study practitioner rated his pace as 50 (that is, half standard pace) he would have done the cycle in half the time were he working at standard (100) rating. This gives a basic time of 50 per cent of 0.6 min. or 0.3 basic min. All cycles are rated in the same way, to extend observed times to basic times using the same formula, which is (observed time) × (observed rating ÷ 100).

A typical study is shown in Figure 32.7. It will be seen that, after the addition of RAs, the standard time is 0.939 sm.

A variation of time study, suitable for measuring long-cycle jobs is rated activity sampling. Unlike time study, jobs are not broken down into elements, but ratings are taken at regularly defined intervals such as every minute, on the minute. A study sheet for this method is shown in Figure 32.8, together with the calculation of the basic time. To this must be added suitable RA of course.

A recent addition to the range is multiple regression analysis (MRA) which is extremely useful for measuring variable work. A description of this is beyond the scope of the present book but full accounts of this and all other techniques in this section are given in Whitmore (1975).

Estimating

The most rapidly applied set of work measurement techniques is estimating. It exists in three forms: analytical, comparative and category. The first of these required the analysis of the job into elements to which *synthetic times* (see

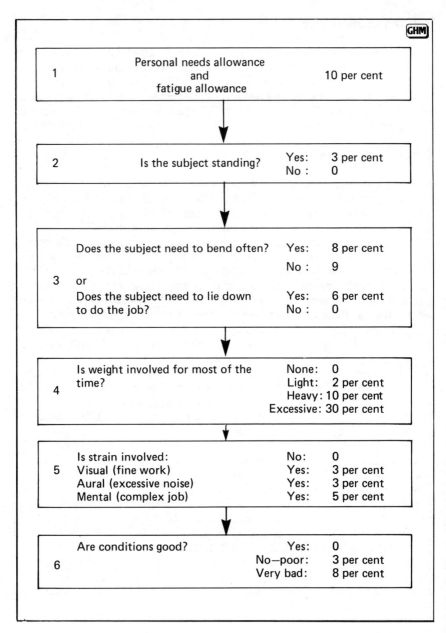

Figure 32.6   A table of relaxation allowances

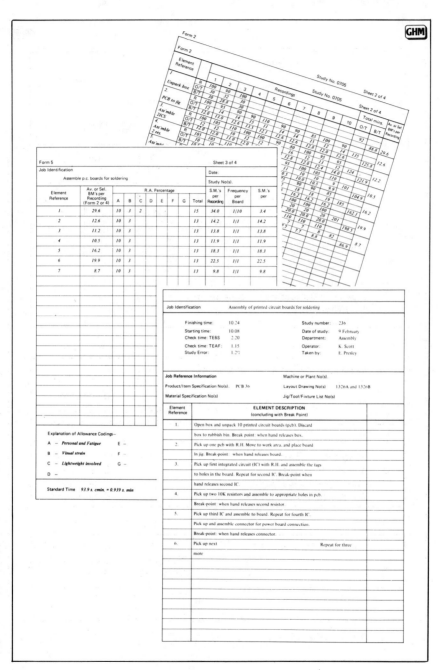

Figure 32.7 *A typical time study, showing three of the most usual forms employed*

GHM

RATED ACTIVITY SAMPLING

JOB: DIGGING TRENCH   ANALYST: A.J.B.

DURATION: 09.00 to 09.13   DATE: 10 JUNE

		DIGGING	RESTING	ABSENT
	9.00.25		X	
	50		X	
	75		X	
	1.00		X	
	25		X	
	50	95		
	75	95		
	2.00	90		
	25	90		
	50	90		
	75	90		
	3.00	100		
	25	100		
	50	100		
	75	100		
	4.00	105		
	25	105		
	50	95		
	75	95		
	5.00	95		
	25	95		
	50	100		
CALCULATION	75	100		
	6.00	95		
basic time = $\dfrac{\Sigma R \times \text{time interval}}{100 \times \text{vol. dug}}$	25	90		
	50	90		
	75	95		
time interval = 0·25 min	7.00	85		
Vol. = 0·4 cu. metre	25	85		
	50	85		
	75			X
basic time = $\dfrac{3710 \times 0.25}{100 \times 0.4}$	8.00			X
	25			X
	50			X
	75			X
= 23.19 b. min	9.00			X
per cu. metre	25			X
	50	80		
	75	80		
	10.00	85		
	25	85		
	50	90		
	75	90		
	11.00	100		
	25	110		
	50	110		
	75	110		
	12.00	90		
	25	110		
	50	110		
	75	95		
	13.00			
	25			
	Total ratings R	3710		

Figure 32.8 A rated activity sampling study with calculation of the basic
    time

below) are allocated. Those for which synthetic times are not available are estimated from experience.

Comparative estimating is a method based on work content comparison. Typical benchmark jobs are carefully measured and allocated to 'time bands' on spread sheets (Figure 32.9). Estimating is performed by the estimator comparing the job in hand with the benchmark jobs until he decides that those listed in a certain band compare in work content with the job being estimated. He then allocates the band basic time to that job. Category estimating is a variation of this but has no benchmarks, time band slotting being done purely on the experience of the estimator.

Synthetics

Much work is repetitive, so it is wasteful repeatedly to measure similar jobs over and over again. It makes more sense to create a library of study results which may be used to time future similar jobs. Such library times are *synthetic data*, which may be in the form of tables, formulae or nomographs. A typical formula may be for walking: time = $0.006S + 0.01$ where S is the number of steps taken. To walk 400 steps takes 2.41 min.

Synthetic data may be compiled from time studies, PMTS, or estimating. In complex cases formulae are derived from multiple regression analysis. An example of tabulated synthetics is given in Figure 32.10.

Applications

Work measurement standards may be used for planning, assessing completion times and durations for projects, costing of jobs, calculating operator performance or utilisation, and using these to assess bonuses.

As an example of the calculation of utilisation, suppose an operator performed three jobs; turning twenty spindles on a lathe (12 standard minutes each), drilling forty brackets (2.5 sm each), and fettling thirty components (3.0 sm), all in 450 min. Total earned minutes are $(20 \times 12) + (40 \times 2.5) + (30 \times 3)$ which equals 430 sm. Actual time taken was 450 min. so utilisation was $(430 \div 450) \times 100 = 95.6$ (or 95.6 per cent efficiency). Furthermore, if each standard minute is costed at 20 pence, the labour cost of the spindles was $240 \times 20p$ or £48, or £2.40 each. One thousand spindles would take 12 000 sm, or 27 days. If required within nine days, then three turners would be needed.

IMPROVEMENT OF PRODUCTS AND SERVICES

The subject of productivity would not be complete without consideration of the value of the product or service itself. The twin approaches of value analysis and value engineering are used to reduce the cost of an existing product, and a new design respectively. The philosophy of value analysis/engineering (VA) is to produce the same *function* in a cheaper way. Function, in this sense, has four facets. These are:

Department: Maintenance   Section: Plumbing

CATEGORY A Mean time = 9 minutes 0 to 20 minutes	CATEGORY B Mean time = 28 minutes 20 to 40 minutes	CATEGORY C Mean time = 55 minutes 40 to 80 minutes	CATEGORY D Mean time = 2 hours 80 minutes to $2\frac{3}{4}$ hours
Change tap washer Replace shower head Change short piece of burst copper pipe	Change immersion heater Replace stopcock Install bath tap and shower assembly Clean and replace waste trap on bath or wash basin	Install immersion heater Install stopcock in line Connect bath hot, cold and waste	Change cold tank in loft Install new outside tap Connect wash basin to existing supplies
etc.	etc.	etc.	etc.

Figure 32.9   A comparative estimating spread sheet

GHM

1 *Use function* – how the product or service performs
2 *Esteem function* – how it appears
3 *Exchange function* – how it will trade in
4 *Cost function* – value for money.

VA procedure follows the basic problem solving sequence:

1 Collection of data (orientation phase)
2 Examination of the situation (speculation)
3 Consideration phase
4 Recommendation phase (a report to management)
5 Implementation (when recommendations are put into operation).

VA is carried out by a team of specialists in different fields who meet at each of the phases outlined above. The orientation phase is used to collect data, costs, sales value, specifications and drawings, and specimens. The object of VA is to reduce the cost without reducing the necessary functions. This may involve removing unnecessary embellishments, combining functions, changing standards, sources of supply, designs, and simplification of the product.

Speculation uses brainstorming as its method of examination. The team suggests improvements using freethinking, with all judgements on ideas deferred until the consideration stage. Criticisms stem from prejudices against situations and methods, and generalisations which condemn certain proposals out of hand. Stereotyped thinking is another source of resistance to change.

GHM

No. of items dusted	0	2	4	6	8	10	12
Area (sq.m)							
25	6.8	8.2	9.6	11.0	12.4	13.8	15.2
30	7.6	9.0	10.3	11.7	13.1	14.5	15.9
35	8.3	9.7	11.1	12.5	13.9	15.3	16.7
40	9.0	10.4	11.8	13.2	14.6	16.0	17.4
45	9.7	11.2	12.6	14.0	15.4	16.8	18.2
50	10.5	11.9	13.3	14.7	16.1	17.5	18.9
55	11.3	12.7	14.1	15.5	16.9	18.3	19.7
60	12.0	13.4	14.8	16.2	17.6	19.0	20.4
65	12.8	14.2	15.6	17.0	18.4	19.8	21.2
70	13.5	14.9	16.3	17.7	19.1	20.5	21.9
75	14.3	15.7	17.1	18.5	19.9	21.3	22.7
80	15.0	16.4	17.8	19.2	20.6	22.0	23.4
85	15.7	17.2	18.6	20.0	21.4	22.8	24.2
90	16.5	17.9	19.3	20.7	22.1	23.5	24.0

Data include vacuum cleaning carpets, and dusting items of furniture (times in standard minutes)

Figure 32.10 A table of synthetic data (for cleaning rooms)

Brainstorming can sweep aside stereotype answers and come up with novel, original ideas.

After speculation, the team reconvenes to consider the ideas produced during that phase. Results of considering these ideas may be separated into 'rejected', 'recommended', or 'consider further'. Those eventually recommended are incorporated into a new design.

An example of a VA analysis sheet is given in Figure 32.11.

IMPROVEMENT OF CONDITIONS

The effectiveness of work can be improved, it can be measured and the product can be made less expensive. But the conditions under which the person is working must also be considered. The discipline which looks at this is *ergonomics*. The scope of ergonomics covers:

1 *The worker* – his own physical dimensions, the stresses imposed upon him and the way in which he reacts to events and conditions
2 *The workplace* – layout of work, design of equipment, furniture and seating
3 *The environment* – the effects of heat and humidity, lighting, noise, vibration and atmospheric conditions.

All of this requires some knowledge of physiology and anatomy, anthropometry and psychology.

Stresses on a worker arise from the environment, so working conditions must include suitable seating, work heights, arm rests, and footrests, correctly designed controls, good layout of controls, tools, materials and equipment, and well-designed hours of working during shifts. Attention must also be paid to relaxation periods, both length and frequency.

The workplace must be designed so that tools and controls are within easy reach of the worker. Dials which must be read should be unambiguous, and easy to understand at a glance. Similarly controls must be simple to operate, and compatible; that is, apparatus must move in the direction which one would expect, so that a lever pushed upward should move the equipment (say fork-lift truck arms) upward. Some conventions are recognised, such as a clockwise turn of a knob for increase.

The environmental factors include noise, which may be disturbing, or can sometimes be dangerous. The most important considerations are the frequency or pitch, and the intensity of the sound. Instruments measure the intensity in decibels (dB). Recommended maximum levels are published, and these depend on whether the noise is intermittent, or sustained. Ultrasonic sound, used for detecting cracks in metal, or for cleaning oily or dirty components, is particularly dangerous because one cannot judge the intensity as it is inaudible.

If the source is not bright enough, lighting can be a problem. The ergonomist is concerned with other factors such as the type of lighting, colour, glare and reflection, and the décor of the place of work. Minimum criteria are laid down for corridors, general work, fine work and other conditions. Factors which affect the amount of light needed are size of object, contrast between object and its surroundings and reflectivity of the surface. Shadows can also be a problem

VALUE ANALYSIS	GHM
SPECULATION SHEET	

SPECULATION	ANALYSIS

CONSIDER WHETHER:

FUNTION
the function can be eliminated,
the function can be achieved in a simpler way,
the function can be combined or integrated with any
other function.

NON-CONTRIBUTORY ITEMS
any of the items contributing nothing to the prestige
or use function can be eliminated.

TOLERANCES AND INSPECTION
the inspection can be eliminated,
quality control can replace 100% inspection,
tolerances are realistic,
gauging can replace measuring,
reduced quality of surface finish can be accepted,
alternative finish can be used,
alternative methods of applying finish can be used.

MATERIALS
standard items can be used to replace specially
made items,
cheaper items can be bought from external suppliers,
cheaper alternative material can be used,
amount of material used per part can be reduced,
dimensions can be reduced,
design changes can reduce material used.

PROCESSING
a cheaper process can be used for the raw materials,
a cheaper process can be used to produce any components,
a cheaper process can be used for the finish on the
article.

DESIGN
a new design will reduce the number of components
used
a re-design will combine two or more functions,
a re-design will eliminate any item or function,
excess material, scrap, or number of rejects will
be reduced by re-designing the item,
it would be cheaper to make the component in
more parts,
the part or component could be re-designed to
facilitate the use of power tools or plant.
the part or component could be re-designed to
facilitate the assembly by improved method.

Figure 32.11   Example of a value analysis speculation sheet unless they are needed for a three-dimensional effect. Colours are important in designing décor because they affect the psychological well-being of the worker. For example, grey, blue and green are cold colours, while red and orange make people feel warm. Purple is a shocking colour. Colours can also give a feeling of space, or claustrophobia.

Heat and humidity affect the effectiveness and comfort of people. Ergonomists advise on heat stress, and how it can be relieved. The ambient temperature is considered, but humidity can cause more discomfort than a relatively high temperature. Protection for the worker may be afforded in several ways, such as shielding the offending heat source. Special clothing may be worn, but often this restricts the movements of the worker.

From all this, it is evident that ergonomics is an essential part of any study into the raising of productivity.

OPERATIONAL RESEARCH (OR)

Operational research, originating between the two world wars, has been developed to assist in the solving of certain problems through mathematical and statistical theory. Extensive use is made of probability theory, of queuing and replacement theories, and of logical thought. Some applications of OR are:

1 Optimisation of stock levels with fluctuating demands
2 Optimum use of labour, plant and machinery
3 Determination of policy for maintenance and repair of plant and machinery, and replacement of parts and components
4 Product-mix problems and determination of the levels of output for each product consistent with demand and cost
5 Minimisation of transportation costs in a distribution system such as delivery of goods to wholesalers.
6 Problems where queuing or congestion occur
7 Problems of sequencing, dealt with by critical path analysis.

Applying OR

In using OR it is necessary to formulate some logical approach, so again a five-step pattern of problem solving may be used.

1 *Define the problem.* It is essential to define the problem before a start is made otherwise a great deal of time may be spent on unnecessary data collection and problem solving
2 *Record the facts.* Once defined, the plan of action must be developed and the necessary data collected and assembled in suitable form. All variables and all constraints which may limit possible solutions must be determined and specified in order that the models, equations and inequalities may be constructed. Any information omitted may invalidate the solution. Historical data are used to assess the future. These can be gathered either by collecting data until sufficient information has been obtained, or by simulating the history with the use of 'hypothetical facts'

3 *Examine the facts.* The facts are next analysed and from the data equations (or models) are formed to represent the facts in mathematical form. In certain cases actual physical models can be made as in departmental layouts. A mathematical model is an equation or inequality which may be manipulated using mathematical processes. To form the equations, statements about the job are given mathematical symbols

4 *Derive and test the solutions.* The models are processed mathematically or physically and the solutions are derived. These solutions are then tested under actual operating conditions

5 *Application and maintenance.* The solution is translated into practical and concrete terms and these are put into practice. Modifications may be necessary in the light of new knowledge or changing conditions.

Some techniques and situations are now described.

LINEAR PROGRAMMING

Linear programming may be used to solve such problems as product-mix or distribution (allocation). As the name linear suggests there are no power of the variables in the equations (that is, no x^2, x^3, etc.).

Product mix

These problems are of the type where there are several factors mixed into the problem which, if taken in the correct proportions, will produce an optimum solution for cost, time or other quantity.

For example, a tyre factory may be making its tyres from several types of rubber which are mixed together. The problem is to find the most economic mix consistent with safety, wear, durability and reliability. It would be an easy matter to mix up the cheapest materials without worrying about the *constraints* given above, but these restrictions make the problem more complicated.

In solving problems of this type it is necessary to construct mathematical models relating all the factors and constraints. For example, if a dog food contained three types of meat A, B and C, where A cost x pence per pound, B cost y pence, and C cost z pence, and the total cost must not exceed 160 pence per pound, then the model would be: $Ax + By + Cz < 160$, where A, B and C are the weights of the meats respectively. The solution to the problem would give the amount of each meat needed to make up the dog food at an economic cost, consistent with the constraints imposed.

Distribution

The use of OR in this case is to find the most economic way for the distribution of goods from dispatching points to the receiving points. For example, in distributing goods to retailers it may be possible to send one van on the round to visit all the customers over the period of one week; or alternatively to send five vans out on the same day, each serving one-fifth of the customers. In the first case it is probably cheaper but in the second case it is more convenient to the customers. These and many other facts must be considered and processed before the solution can be determined.

QUEUEING

A queue in the OR context is any line of items, people or products which are waiting for some sort of service or processing. Problems of queueing may include:

1 Queues at cash registers in a supermarket, ticket office or toll booth
2 Incoming calls at a telephone exchange
3 Aircraft stacking over a busy airport
4 Queues at a factory-stores hatch
5 Letters awaiting signature, or any documents or forms in an in-try
6 Piece-parts awaiting processing in the flow line.

Characteristics of a queue are:

1 *The queue length.* This may be self-regulating as when people get tired of waiting, or fruit goes bad while awaiting shipment
2 *The service time.* This is the time taken by the server to deal with the situation will vary according to circumstances, from constant to exponential time
3 *The arrivals* of items joining the queue may be: *regular* and cyclic, and thus may be predetermined, or *random* which are unpredictable, or *random but cyclic,* being in cycles (peak and slack periods) but the numbers are unknown.

Queueing problems may be simulated in the usual way using models.

PLANT REPLACEMENT

Under planned maintenance the scheme is often based on replacement theory. The problem is choosing between (*a*) running the system until something happens to disrupt the system (such as a breakdown due to component failure) or (*b*) replacing the components at regular intervals in order to prevent disruptions by anticipating them before they occur. The costs of these alternatives must be weight up before a choice can be made. The costs of running until failure may include:

1 The cost of the breakdown
2 Damage to other components
3 Shut down of whole line due to the breakdown of one process
4 Negligible cost if there are no breakdowns, making this policy the cheaper.

The policy of forestalling breakdowns may involve:

1 Cost of changing components which may still be perfectly good, and
2 A fixed cost, which will definitely be incurred, as against 4 above which may vary between zero and a very high value.

STOCK CONTROL

OR can be applied to problems of stock control. Again it is a choice between two different policies:

1   A large stock may be held to avoid running out of stock – expensive because of storage, insurance, depreciation, deterioration and handling cost, or
2   A minimum stock may be held with the risk of running out of stock, causing loss of production, time and customers.

The job of OR is to determine the optimum stock level to hold, and this is achieved by using statistical method, which includes probability theory.

FURTHER READING

Ackoff, R. L., *The Art of Problem Solving*, Wiley, London, 1978

De Bono, E., *P. O. Beyond Yes and No*, Penguin Books, Harmondsworth, 1977

Gordon, W. J. J., *Synectics*, Harper & Row, New York, 1968

Grandjean, E., *Fitting the Task to the Man*, Taylor & Francis, London, 1971

Karger, D. W., and Bayha, F. H., *Engineering Work Measurement*, Industrial Press, New York, 1977

Kepner, C. H., and Tregoe, B. B., *The Rational Manager*, McGraw-Hill, New York, 1964

McCormick, E. J., *Human Factors in Engineering Design*, McGraw-Hill, New York, 1976

Murrell, K. H. F., *Ergonomics*, Chapman & Hall, London, 1969

Osborne, A. F., *Applied Imagination*, Scribner's Sons, New York, 1965

Quick, J. H., Malcolm, J. H., and Duncan, J. H., *Work-Factor Time Standards*, McGraw-Hill, New York, 1962

Rivett, P., and Ackoff, R., *A Manager's Guide to Operational Research*, Wiley, London, 1963

Whitmore, D. A., *Measurement and Control of Indirect Work*, Heinemann, London, 1970

Whitmore, D. A., *Work Study and Related Management Services*, Heinemann, London, 1976

Whitmore, D. A., *Management Sciences*, Teach Yourself Books, London, 1979

Whitmore, D. A., *Work Measurement*, Heinemann, London, 1980

33 Quality control

David Desmond

There is no single definition of quality control which has universal acceptance. Certainly when Dr Walter Shewart (of Bell Telephone Laboratories) introduced the term in 1924, he was concerned with statistical methods for examining the quality of goods produced by an process for uniformity. His philosophy was that if uniformity could be established over a considerable period, then it was reasonable to infer that the quality produced was the best possible with the existing facilities.

Developments over the first thirty years were largely directed towards improving the technique through increased use of statistical methods. Later there was a reaction, and many people applied the term to any kind of procedure which had the object of supplying quality to the consumer's requirements. Much of this was merely old-fashioned inspection and the term 'quality control' became something of a gimmick. Even today it is not uncommon to hear that 'Quality control has let us down' when bad work has been produced – as if this had nothing to do with the department that actually produced the inferior goods.

PRINCIPLES

Quality control is considered here as a technique of scientific management, in the form envisaged by Dr Shewart. Thus it has the objective of making the best use of resources. It is first necessary to establish standards of quality from an analysis of existing records or by a special study. Then a suitable control has to be set up, usually based on a control chart, to ensure that the quality standard is maintained. In some cases the initial quality standard is not good enough to satisfy the technical or market requirements, in which case changed or additional operations must be introduced. These often take the form of complete inspection (sorting) but this should not reduce the need to maintain achievable quality standards. It is preferable to regard such complete inspection as a temporary expedient, and to carry out experiments to determine the optimum operating conditions so that better standards can be instituted.

Quality control is concerned with processes. It accepts variation in a process as being perfectly natural, as long as the results of the variation can be explained by statistical laws. Originally, Shewart was only concerned with manufacturing processes, but the technique can be extended to any process, such as a service (transport, dry cleaning), or performance (rate of working, absenteeism), or cost.

The method consists of making observations on a number of small samples collected from the process over a sufficient period of time so that all variation which would be expected naturally will have an opportunity to occur even if the appropriate technical control is maintained. These observations on each sample are then summarised in any convenient form and plotted in sequence on a simple chart in which the vertical axis shows the summarised measure and the horizontal axis gives the order of taking the samples. The pattern of these plotted points is scrutinised to see if it is consistent and stable and, if so, a pair of horizontal lines are drawn to contain all the plotted points.

These lines indicate the degree of scatter which will be obtained in the future if the quality remains the same. Control can be exercised by projecting the parallel lines into the future and continuing to plot the same summarised measure on the same chart. It may be confidently inferred that future quality is the same as the earlier quality if *all* the plotted points fall within the bounding lines.

There will be many occasions when the original pattern of plotted points does not satisfy the conditions of consistency and stability; this would indicate the presence of an unknown disturbing factor spoiling the uniformity of the process. Such a factor can be removed by suitable technical action but it will not be known at the time of plotting what action should have been taken. However an estimate of the achievable uniformity can be obtained by drawing the parallel lines so as to contain all the points which do produce a consistent and stable pattern. Procedures are available to examine whether any pattern is consistent and stable and, if not, provide an objective method of deciding which samples should be rejected.

A crude control will be obtained if a visual judgement is made of the plotted points and the parallel lines are drawn by eye. This will satisfy the statistical philosophy but the control will only be as good as the judgement. More objective results will be obtained by the use of mathematical procedures in deciding the acceptability of the pattern of plotted points and in computing the positions of the control lines. This will enable changes to be detected more rapidly and, more important, it will prevent unnecessary (detrimental) adjustments to the process when apparent changes are really due to the inherent variability in the process. Such mathematical procedures give rise to statistical methods and show which summary measures give the maximum information from a given amount of data. They provide an objective interpretation of the observed variation and, not only show whether a disturbing factor is present, but also provide an estimate of its effect on the quality being examined. Finally, they give a consistent method for drawing the control lines based on a known and acceptable risk.

ORGANISATION

Like every other management technique, quality control must be properly organised in a factory. It needs the active support of top management which must believe that this is in the best interests of the firm. It is a full-time job in itself and cannot be a mere appendage to another major function such as inspection or work study. It must carry sufficient status to attract the right kind of person. There will be no difficulty in arousing and maintaining interest once the programme gets under way.

The first step is the appointment of a statistical quality control (SQC) officer who can have any title which fits in with the staff structure. This is preferably an internal promotion of somebody who has an understanding of the firm's products and processes. He (or she) need not be an expert in the relevant technology but he should have an appreciation of it. Neither is it necessary for him to be highly skilled in mathematics or statistics. There are no computations which cannot be easily performed with the mini-calculators now readily available. He should gradually appreciate the statistical principles behind the procedures he has to use and ultimately he will be able to adapt them to use more efficient methods. He should be encouraged to attend one of the many short courses which deal with the simpler concepts and to get together with SQC officers from other firms (whose products may be very different but will be using the same fundamental principles to solve their quality problems).

It is important that the new section shows early successes. This can be ensured by careful selection of the processes to be subjected to SQC methods. No factory is working as well as possible all the time and in most cases nobody really knows the quality they are capable of producing! An initial analysis of recent records will indicate where substantial quality improvements can be made. If these are associated with less scrap or rectification, there will be obvious financial gains. It is easy enough to estimate what these potential savings are. The target should be to realise 50 per cent of the potential within a month and over 80 per cent permanently after three months.

It is less easy to estimate the increase in markets and consequent better utilisation of resources arising from improved quality. This is frequently much more important than the direct savings from scrap and rectification. It is the basis on which the future wellbeing of the firm is founded.

Experience shows that may SQC applications produce even greater quality improvements than can be expected from past records or from an initial study. Part of this might be due to underestimates of the initial quality standard because of the limited data available but there must be the same possibility of overestimates. Somehow, there is an evolution of better technology from the immediate feedback of information. The SQC programme should recognise this situation as soon as it occurs so that the improvement can be incorporated into the process.

A number of steps in quality management should be taken before any useful quality control application can be made. The areas that should be examined are listed in the checklist in Figure 33.1.

GHM

Workplace
  lighting
  heating
  ventilation
  space
  cleanliness
  freedom from accident
    hazards
  availability of materials
  disposal of products

Services
  power
  gas
  compressed air
  vacuum
  others

Material
  sufficient quantity
  correct specification
  required time

Plant
  capable of doing jobs
  jigs and fixtures
  maintained

Operator
  instructed how job is to be
    done
  knows what is required
  given facilities to do the job
  trained to use the facilities
    properly
  means to verify that he has
    done so
  understands he is responsible
    for quality

Product
  quality specified on a
    document
  means to measure quality
    made
  disposal of defectives
  disposal of acceptable work

Figure 33.1 Quality management checklist

REQUIREMENTS

Formal quality control requires sets of rules to:

1 Analyse data to determine whether the observed variation could occur
   without any disturbing factor
2 Estimate parameters which define the achievable quality to be taken as
   standard
3 Compute control limits within which the summarised measurements from
   future routine samples must fall if the standard quality is to be maintained.

These rules will differ according to the method of measurement, and detailed procedures are available to cope with all situations likely to arise in any factory. Full details of a simple recommended procedure are given later. This will show how to establish a preliminary quality standard for a process whose output is subject to the manufacture of random defectives. More elaborate procedures are available to provide more reliable quality standards from the same data (see Desmond, 1971).

The first group of rules applies to measurement by counting items or to occasions which do or do not possess some desirable attribute. This applies where quality is measured by the number of defectives in samples inspected visually or by Go Not-Go gauges. Exactly the same method can be used for the numbers of breakages in unit time, counts of absentees, numbers of occasions that a machine is not working during work-sampling surveys or numbers of defects per unit (such as scratches on chromium-plated lamps).

The second group applies to direct or inferred measurement on a continuous scale of some physical quantity such as diameter, length, weight, hardness, moisture, pH value, etc. Simple procedures can be very successful where the variation from unit to unit is largely associated with a single source but more complex methods will be required when several sources of variation operate simultaneously.

There are situations where either method of measurement can be used. For example, the diameter of a bolt may have a specification of 1.990–1.995 cm so any piece can be checked for compliance with a Go Not-Go gauge. But there is obviously more information in the knowledge that it has a diameter of 1.992 cm rather than merely knowing it is acceptable. One believes intuitively that the extra information obtained by direct measurement should give better control and this is found to be true. Nevertheless, the simplicity of the number defective control chart has led a majority of firms to adopt this method and the examples quoted herein are based on it.

USING CONTROL CHARTS

The *control chart* is the means by which the manufacturer is able to confirm that the quality standard is being mainted. The method consists of assessing the quality of a sample selected from the product that has just been made and comparing it with an established value – the *control limit*. The control limit is chosen so that if the process is producing standard quality then the quality of the selected sample would be outside the limit only on very rare occasions:

When the quality assessment of the sample comes within the control limit, it is accepted as verifying that standard quality is still being produced and the process is allowed to continue running without alteration. However, if the quality assessment reaches or exceeds the control limit, this is considered as sufficient evidence that standard quality is no longer being produced. Then, if normal operation of the process is known to produce standard quality, this is also evidence that technical operating conditions are no longer normal. They can be restored by appropriate technical action and it is essential that such action is taken immediately.

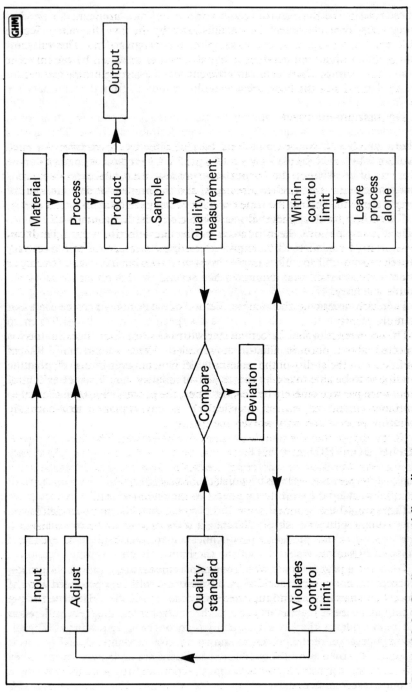

Figure 33.2 Quality control flow diagram

The way in which the control chart works is very similar to that of any other closed-cycle control system. This is illustrated by the flow diagram in Figure 33.2. The random variation due to sampling is analogous to 'noise' and any real technical deviation will produce a signal which is distorted by the inherent noise. The control chart gives an efficient way of distinguishing between a genuine signal and the background noise.

A simple control chart

The principles of control charts will be illustrated by the number defective chart, of which an example is given in Figure 33.3. At regular intervals a sample of items is taken from the output of a process, each item is examined for compliance with technical requirements, and the number of defectives in the sample is plotted against the time and date of sampling. Any technical change such as a new batch of material is marked along the horizontal scale.

This example shows the standard as having one defective per sample. It can be seen that over the twenty samples plotted, the numbers of defectives vary between zero and three. The sample size is not shown but if it is large (twenty or more) with the established average of one per sample, then about one sample in twelve will have three or more defectives just by the chance selection of the items which constitute the sample. Thus three defectives must be expected quite frequently.

The occurrence of four defectives starts to raise some doubt but this must be expected about once in fifty-three samples. There should be sufficient confidence in the ability of the technical staff in maintaining normal operating conditions to be able to accept this as just an unlucky sample which will occur about once per week merely by chance. Thus, the process should be allowed to continue without adjustment (particularly as any alteration to a correctly operating process can only worsen the quality).

Next suppose that the sample contains five defectives. The decision now is whether technical control has been maintained while a one in 273 chance sample was obtained or operating conditions had truly and unexpectedly changed. Experience will show what decision should be taken. Obviously it will be influenced by the confidence placed in the technical staff.

There would not be much doubt if the sample should contain six defectives. This would represent a one in 1700 chance if the process was truly unchanged. This must shake the confidence in technical control, no matter how strongly it was held before the inspection of the sample.

The level of probability at which one rejects the assumption that the process is operating normally is decided in advance and will depend on the kind of process being examined and the procedure used. It will also depend on finding an acceptable compromise between adjusting the process too frequently when it is working at standard quality and failing to obtain an indication of a change that has truly occurred. A limit of one in 200 is recommended for most purposes. Thus there would be a control limit at five defectives in this example.

In practice, the sample size is not very important as long as there is only a small proportion of defectives (up to 10 per cent). This limiting case will

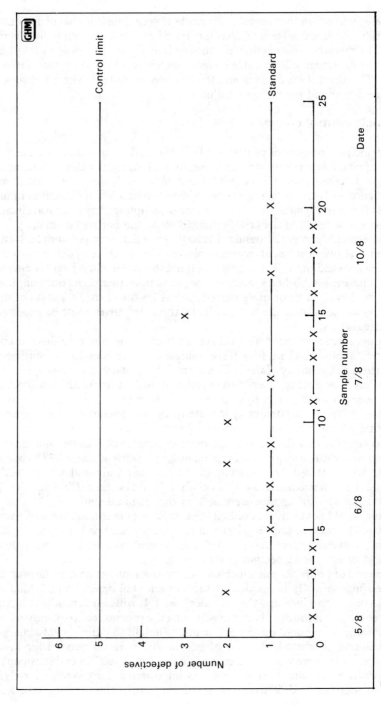

Figure 33.3 Number defective control chart

correspond to samples of ten units and then four or more defectives will be found once in seventy-eight samples (instead of fifty-three). Similarly, five or more defectives will be found once in 611 samples (instead of 273). Despite these different figures, the choice of control limit will remain at five defectives. It is safe to use Figure 33.4 to read off the control limit in terms of average number of defectives per sample for all situations where the proportion of defectives is less than 10 per cent. The control limit is the value opposite the interval containing the expected number of defectives. Use the lower value in marginal cases; for example the control limit corresponding to 2.57 defectives per sample is 8.

This table can be used for a sequence of samples. For example, if the expected number is 1.2, and the control limit is 6, two consecutive samples will expect 2.4 with the control limit at 8 while three consecutive samples will expect 3.6 with the control limit at 10.

			GHM
Expected Number of defectives per sample	Control limit 1 in 200	Expected number pf defectives per sample	Control limit 1 in 200
0.000		4.94	
	1		13
0.005		5.58	
	2		14
0.103		6.23	
	3		15
0.338		6.89	
	4		16
0.672		7.57	
	5		17
1.08		8.25	
	6		18
1.54		8.94	
	7		19
2.04		9.64	
	8		20
2.57		10.35	
	9		21
3.13		11.07	
	10		22
3.72		11.79	
	11		23
4.32		12.52	
	12		24
4.94		13.25	

Figure 33.4   Control limits for number defective charts

This method can give a tighter control, thus the sequence 4 3 3 proves an out of control situation which none of these samples can do individually.

If much smaller samples are used with a higher proportion of defectives, then different decision rules should be adopted. Thus if the samples consist of only four items giving 25 per cent defectives to maintain the average at one defective per sample, a control limit of 5 would be meaningless. Even four defectives (the whole of the sample) would be obtained by chance once in 256 samples leading to a control limit of 4 (instead of 5). Although procedures can be designed to cope with this kind of situation, it is recommended that a technical investigation should be made if the quality standard is worse than 10 per cent defectives.

THE QUALITY STANDARD

Although it is possible to set up a control chart without prior knowledge of the quality that the process is capable of producing, such a chart cannot start with a realistic control limit. After fifty or so samples have been inspected, the data can be analysed for stability and then a provisional quality standard can be established. This would enable the appropriate control limit to be incorporated on the control chart and further routine sample results examined over the course of time. These should also be analysed at more or less regular intervals to determine the latest quality standard the process is producing.

These later analyses may indicate that the quality has improved under the influence of the control chart but usually such an improvement will be small and could be due to the chance of selection of the samples rather than any technical change. On the other hand, the later samples may indicate a deterioration in quality which was not corrected by the use of the control chart. Again this could be due to sampling fluctuations.

A PROCEDURE FOR ESTIMATING THE QUALITY STANDARD

This procedure is used in an initial study of a process when quality is measured by the counting of defectives in samples selected from the output. The samples must all contain the same number of items and must be selected to cover a sufficiently long period of time so that all normal variation has an opportunity to occur.

It is also used when routine inspection data are available for analysis which relate to equal numbers of products inspected in each period.

The object of the test is to verify that standard technical operating conditions were maintained throughout the period studied and, if so, the data will directly give a valid estimate of the standard quality which the process can produce.

What the procedure does

The test method consists of comparing the sample with the largest number of defectives against the average number per sample. The data are accepted as being homogeneous if this worst sample could occur, merely by chance, more frequently than once in 200 times when technical operating conditions remain constant.

Provided that 80 per cent or more of the data are homogeneous, then the procedure gives a valid estimate of the quality standard which the process is capable of producing.

Details

1   Count the number of samples to give the quantity k.
2   Count the number of items in each sample to give the quantity n.
3   Add all the defectives in the whole k samples to give a total of $\Sigma\ c$.
4   Divide the total defectives by the number of samples. This quotient $= \Sigma\ c/k$ is represented by the symbol $\bar{c}$. Use this value of $\bar{c}$ as a first estimate of γ .
5   Read off the control limit in Figure 33.4 corresponsing to this value of γ .
6   Compare all the individual numbers of defectives in the samples against this limit and accept the set of data as being homogeneous if none is as large as the limit. If condition 6 is satisfied, accept this first estimate of γ as the average number of defectives to be expected in similar samples in future and the corresponding value of $\pi = \gamma/n$ as being the standard proportion defective for the process.
7   If condition 6 is not satisfied, remove all the sample results which reach or exceed the limit and compute the average number of defectives per sample for the remaining samples as in step 4. Use this revised value of $\bar{c}$ as a better estimate of γ and read off the corresponding limit in Figure 33.4 as was done in step 5.
8   Compare all the individual numbers of defectives in these remaining samples against this revised limit and accept them as forming a set of homogeneous data if none is as large as this limit.
9   If condition 8 is satisfied, accept this revised estimate of γ as the average number of defectives to be expected in similar samples in future and the corresponding value of $\pi\ =\ \gamma\ /n$ as being the standard proportion defective for the process.
10 Repeat steps 7 to 9 if condition 8 is not satisfied and repeat again as often as necessary for it to be satisfied.

Note: If 20 per cent of the samples have to be discarded it implies that the process is very unstable. New data should be collected and analysed after suitable technical action has been taken to stabilise the process.

Example 1.

A set of 25 samples each containing 20 items is available for analysis. The observed numbers of defectives were:

$$01100 \quad 15043 \quad 01042 \quad 10013 \quad 30000$$

Then

$$k = 25, \qquad n = 20.$$

By addition

$$\Sigma c = 30$$

and

$$\bar{c} = 30/25 = 1.2$$

Control limit = 6, corresponding to $\gamma = 1.2$ (Figure 34.4)

Largest number of defectives in any sample = 5.

Accept data as homogeneous with standard proportion defective of $\pi = 1.2/20 = 6.0$ per cent.

Example 2.

A 9-head filling machine has one head completely out of adjustment while the other heads produce 1 per cent defectives. The initial study consists of 15 samples each containing 25 packs.

Case (a)

The samples were selected at random from a box containing all the packs produced in the previous half hour. The observed numbers of defectives were:

$$35122 \quad 33370 \quad 32416$$

Then

$$k = 15, \qquad n = 25.$$

By addition

$$\Sigma c = 45$$

and

$$c = 45/15 = 3.0$$

Control limit = 9, corresponding to $\gamma = 3.0$

Accept data as homogeneous with standard proportion defective of $\pi = 3.0/25 = 12.0$ per cent.

Note that this analysis is unable to detect any real difference from sample to sample.

Case (b)

The samples consist of successive packs direct from the machine so every sample has two or three packs filled by the faulty head.

The observed numbers of defectives were:

$$23433 \quad 43323 \quad 23532$$

These give

$$n = 25 \qquad k = 15 \qquad \Sigma c = 45$$

and the interpretation is exactly the same as for case (*a*). There is a suspicion that the samples are 'abnormally uniform' but this procedure is unable to detect this.

It should be noted that one completely faulty head will produce 11.1 per cent defectives overall quite apart from any made on the other heads. As the standard worked out at 12 per cent, one completely faulty head is a plausible explanation but one should not jump to conclusions. A more advanced procedure is able to demonstrate that case (*b*) did produce abnormally uniform samples, confirming the suspicion of a faulty head.

In general one should try to collect the samples so that any item can be identified with a definite source. Although this is practical for a nine-head machine, it would not be possible from each of the 200 spindles in a frame spinning jute.

FURTHER READING

Caplen, R. H., *A Practical Approach to Quality Control*, Business Books, London, 4th edition, 1982

Desmond, D., *Quality Control Workbook*, Gower, 1971

Juran, Joseph M., *Quality Control Handbook*, McGraw-Hill, New York, 3rd edition, 1974

34 Maintenance

E N White

The demands made upon the works department concerned with the maintenance of structures, buildings, services installations, plant and machinery, vehicles, equipment or instruments, grow with the increased dependence upon these assets in today's environment. Pressures on maintenance personnel increase as high-cost assets require efficient utilisation with minimum out-of-use periods. At the same time, widening applications of new technology require added knowledge and improved techniques of servicing and repair. Clearly the role of the maintenance manager is expanded in this environment and improved systems and practices are often needed to ensure the correct degree of asset care. The manager of the maintenance function is seen as a major contributor to the "assets management' programme of the organisation and, as maintenance costs are recurring costs, he has an important part to play in controlling life cycle costs.

TEROTECHNOLOGY

The terotechnology concept grew out of a working party study on maintenance practices (see *Report by the Working Party on Maintenance Engineering*, HMSO). The scope of terotechnology is illustrated by the definition: 'A combination of management, financial, engineering and other practices applied to physical assets in pursuit of economic life cycle costs.'

This indicates the thinking behind the concept, namely, that attention to maintenance management alone would not provide the complete answer to the problems arising in the maintenance sector (or otherwise attributed to maintenance). It clearly was necessary to look at other management functions having an influence on the performance and costs of physical assets: in other words, those functions which contribute to assets management.

The broad application of the terotechnology concept is further illustrated by the note to the definition, which states:

> Its practice is concerned with the specification and design for reliability and maintainability of plant, machinery, equipment, buildings and structures; with their installation, commissioning, maintenance, modification and replacement, and with feedback of information on design, performance and costs.

Thus the terotechnology concept is applied both to buildings and plant, and to all stages of their life cycles from design to eventual replacement or disposal. Finally, terotechnology includes the feedback of data to produce management information.

The terotechnology system (Figure 34.1) is generally shown as a combination of management systems and communication channels which provide support for maintenance. Typical contributions include:

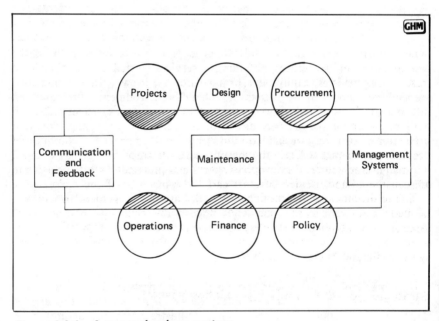

Figure 34.1 A terotechnology system

1 Design – assets designed for maintainability and reliability
2 Procurement – application of 'best buy' procurement techniques
3 Projects – provision of assets having operability and maintainability features
4 Operations – introduction of operating techniques which reduce downtime and improve care of assets
5 Finance – cost control, cost monitoring and feedback
6 Personnel – selection and training programmes for operating and maintenance personnel

Strategies for terotechnology (new assets)

Assets management is a cradle-to-grave strategy which commences with technoeconomic studies prior to an investment and proceeds through the implementation stages into the life cycle of use. During the period of use there will be operation and maintenance strategies, designed to give best use at least cost, and eventually a replacement or disposal strategy will be formulated based on technical and economic reviews.

Asset provisioning can be considered in three phases; preparation, decision and implementation. In the preparation phase it is important to consider historical data and feedback from operations and maintenance, and to attempt whole life predictions with life cycle costs. These and other data are considered during evaluation and decision, and it is important here to consider the views of operations and maintenance management. Finally, in the implementation phase the programme includes design, installation, commissioning and proving stages until the assets are handed over to the operations and maintenance personnel. Some important considerations in these phases are listed in Figure 34.2.

The utilisation phase requires the planned operation and planned maintenance of the asset with performance analyses and feedback of management information. Performance data should be recorded and used to benefit future designs and procurement decisions, and for frequent reviews of the whole life predictions. It is important also to apply controls to any modification programmes so that configuration control is maintained.

Finally there will be a review phase when all technical and economic factors are considered and the decision made to dispose of or replace the asset.

The terotechnology system demands that a number of 'trade-off' decisions be made. For example, the comparison between increased utilisation of a new asset and the attendant costs of operation and maintenance, especially if new technologies are incorporated, can be considered in a 'trade-off' against statistics for the assets to be replaced.

Strategies for terotechnology (existing assets)

Actions to implement terotechnology in the management of existing assets may be considered in two groups – actions within the maintenance function, and actions by other departments. Each of these groups further divides into actions which follow accepted practice, and actions based on analyses of feedback.

As an example, within the maintenance function, the applications of planning and control to maintenance work is probably the first reaction of many managers to a terotechnology programme. The principles are well documented, case histories exist and planned maintenance is accepted practice. However, at a later date, when the feedback inherent in a planned system is analysed, the control system may well be modified and condition-based maintenance introduced. It is the action based upon feedback which effects the most significant improvements. But it is often necessary to improve existing systems

Preparation phase
    Consideration of feedback (operations and maintenance)
    Planning (operating and maintenance policies)
    Technical forecasting
    Whole life planning
    Life cycle costing

Decision phase
    Direct participation by users (past and future)
    Preparation of procurement checklists, see Appendix 1
    Reviews of supplier profiles and quality ratings
    Specification of support systems, see Chapter 8
    Review of life plans and life cycle costs

Implementation phase
    Design (design records, design reviews, configuration control)
    Studies (maintainability, reliability, feedback from users)
    Project planning and control
    Support planning (information, training, spare parts)
    Information systems (disclosure of design data by manufacturers and suppliers)
    Preparation of documentation (manuals, specifications, training programmes)
    Maintenance planning (management systems and resources)
    Commissioning (testing, defect action, certification)
    Handover (operation, proving, final acceptance)

Utilisation phase
    Operation, maintenance, condition monitoring
    Technical and costs records
    Analysis of records
    Feedback to operations, maintenance, design, procurement
    Improvements and updating (configuration control)
    Reviews of life plans and life cycle costing

Review phase
    Technical and financial reviews
    Disposal or Replacement Decisions
    Feedback to benefit future projects

Figure 34.2 Terotechnology considerations in a life cycle as a first step, so that meaningful analyses can be made as justification for further progress.

MAINTENANCE PLANNING AND CONTROL

Total maintenance planning embraces all activities necessary to plan, control and record all work done in keeping the assets to the acceptable standard. This includes preventive maintenance and corrective maintenance, planned overhaul, planned replacement, spares provisioning, workshop functions, repairs and renewals, plant history compilation, plant modification to facilitate maintenance, spare parts manufacture, preventive maintenance on spare parts, etc. In a fully controlled situation only the time spent on emergency work is 'unplanned' and this could well be less than 10 per cent of the available man-hours in the maintenance department. The three basic requirements of a planned maintenance system are:

1 A programme of maintenance activity for the buildings, plant and equipment
2 A means of ensuring that the programme is fulfilled
3 A method of recording and assessing results.

Figure 34.3 lists the basic elements of a planned maintenance system which is represented diagrammatically in Figure 34.4.

Assets register

A comprehensive register of all plant and buildings (or of that part of the plant and buildings which are the subject of the planning) is an essential base for the planning operation. Each asset must be positively identified in terms of:

1 Name and identity code
2 Description
3 Reference numbers – manufacturers, suppliers, etc.
4 Location – with provision for changes if item is interchangeable or mobile
5 Supplier's details.

The asset code can be numerical, or alpha-numerical and it usually replaces any existing plant numbering systems. Asset codes are given to buildings, plant, services installations and mobile plant, and are attached to the asset for identification purposes. The codes can be preceded by other letters or numbers if required for corporate purposes (investment analyses, depreciation calculations, etc.).

Asset codes can identify asset type (PU = pump), accounts codes (primary and secondary) and physical locations. Additional numbers can be added to link the basic asset codes to spare parts, special tools, work specifications, or to drawings and manuals filed in the maintenance library. The asset code must be used on all work cards, defect reports, materials requisitions and other documentation as the key to effective communication, feedback, and the compilation of history records.

	Item	Description	GHM
1	Assets register	A complete inventory of the buildings and plant to be maintained	
2	Maintenance schedule	Schedules for inspection, lubrication and preventive maintenance of the items in the register. The schedules may also include planned overhaul	
3	Work specifications	Instruction cards or documents which identify exactly the tasks to be undertaken within the maintenance system	
4	Maintenance control system	A 'trigger' system which initiates the activities on the maintenance programme at predetermined intervals as listed on the maintenance schedule	
5	Resourcing schedule	A manpower allocation system to ensure that the resources are available to implement the maintenance requirements of the assets and that optimum use is made of labour	
6	Maintenance records	A record of maintenance carried out and a system for reporting to management	
7	Maintenance support organisation	The organisation of technical information, spare parts and tools, etc	
8	Liaison with production	An effective system of agreeing with the user management when maintenance work can be done	
9	Planned overhaul	Provisions for ensuring the planned overhaul of plant, either on a regular basis in accordance with the maintenance schedule or in response to condition monitoring	
10	Costing system	Costing procedures to ensure adequate cost control and apportionment of costs in the maintenance department	
11	Training	The necessary training of operatives and supervisors in the operation of the system	

Figure 34.3   Components of a planned maintenance system

Maintenance schedules

Maintenance schedules list the requirements of each asset shown on the register in so far as routine maintenance is concerned. A typical schedule card indicates:

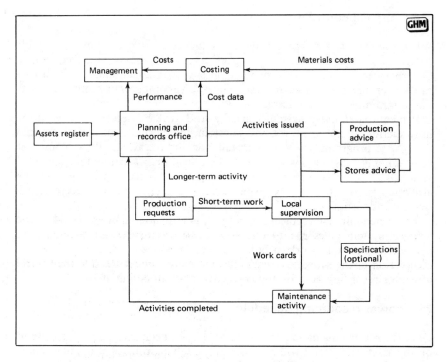

GHM

Figure 34.4 **Typical maintenance control system**

1 Grade of labour required
2 Frequency of the work to be done
3 Details of the work to be done
4 Estimated time for the execution of the work.

Where assets are identical or similar the schedules are repeated on additional cards so that a complete schedule exists for each asset. The preparation of the maintenance schedule is a skilled task. Not only must all necessary maintenance activities be identified and recorded, but the frequencies must be evaluated with availability for maintenance in mind as well as other more obvious factors including suppliers' suggestions.

Grouping work by slight adjustments of the frequencies can have a most beneficial effect on the operation of a maintenance programme.

Basic data can frequently be obtained from manufacturers' manuals but not all manuals have the necessary information, or have the information in the required form. The maintenance planning engineer must therefore use any available information as a basis but must interpret it in accordance with the local requirements and with his own knowledge and experience. (Obviously care must be taken within the guarantee period of new equipment to conform with any special instructions which form part of the supplier's guarantee.)

Maintenance controls

When the extent of the preventive maintenance activity is known, a suitable control system can be selected to 'trigger' activities at the required frequencies. Control systems range from a manually sorted card file, through automatic job-card sorter/printer devices to a system in which a computer printout represents the programme for the selected period.

If a computer-based system is used a study will be necessary, as with the introduction of any data-processing system, to determine the availability and the cost of programs, the cost of installation and the availability of computer time on any existing installation. When installing a computer-controlled system based on time from an existing computer it is necessary to safeguard the availability of that time before abandoning existing methods and accepting full computer dependence.

The functioning of a typical control system is illustrated by Figure 34.5. The 'trigger' system gives rise to the issue of the work card and materials; the detailed instructions (work specification) can be issued at the same time. At the completion of the scheduled work the documents are returned to the control office for recording and for any corrective work to be initiated.

Manpower resourcing schedule

Once the routine maintenance requirements have been determined for all items on the assets register, it will be necessary to table estimates of the man-hours needed from each grade of labour. Using these estimates, a phased schedule can be compiled by allocating the appropriate hours to the relevant dates for each planned activity. Such a chart will be made to show detailed requirements for a medium-term control period, with summaries added to extend the plan to two, three or even five years as a resource planning tool.

Manpower resourcing in the maintenance department only makes sense when full control and full support for the maintenance activity is provided. The routing of maintenance staff during work is important. Studies have shown that 15 per cent of the available working time can be devoted to obtaining instructions and making journeys to the work point in an industrial installation of average size. Full support in terms of test equipment, spare parts and technical manuals can reduce the number of journeys made to workshops or the stores.

Maintenance records

The operation of an effective maintenance records system provides the following information:

1　The percentage of planned work achieved in the period
2　The ratio of planned to unplanned work
3　Downtime for the period
4　Ratio of preventive work to corrective work

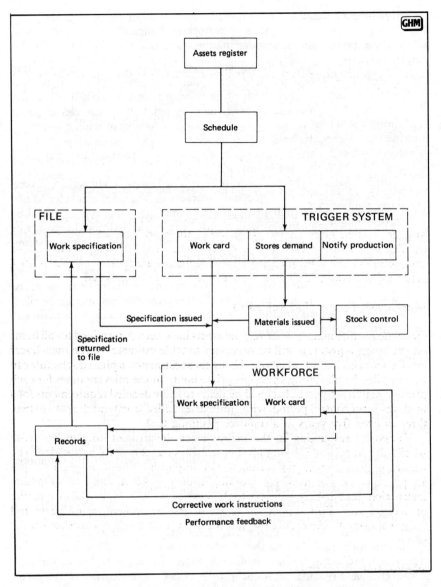

Figure 34.5   Maintenance control with trigger system

5   Maintenance requirement comparisons between individual assets, between types of asset, or between groups of assets
6   Indicators for reliability of the products of particular manufacture
7   Trends in spare parts consumption
8   Equipment failure patterns

9   Performance detail for personnel, by individual or by trade group
10 Materials used, for guidance on restocking policies
11 Indicators on possible standardisation policies.

Records are kept in many different ways, ranging from card files to computer data stores. The labour required for updating records or work done is a deterrent to many managers and can only be justified if use is made of the information. If a computer is used, lengthy printout sheets can be time consuming also. However the computer is a useful tool for providing summary information on a regular basis so that trends can be observed. Whatever system of records is used, detailed investigations have to be reserved for individual situations in which the cost is justified.

In a simple system a practical level of recording is obtained by writing on the actual work card as issued. Successive workers on the asset can refer to the working history and to their predecessors' comments. This can be useful in passing on the defect history or wear trends but can precondition the worker in his approach to the work, sometimes to bad effect. Other simple systems provide for the issue of new cards each time but for up to six or ten of the completed cards to be retained in the control office at any time to give a short history record. Thus with a two-monthly activity the continued retention of six cards would produce a one-year history. These systems do not provide detailed financial records, which would be provided on separate cards or as a function of the company accounts department.

Liaison with the user

Effective liaison between the operating managers or planners and the maintenance planners is essential to the operation of the maintenance programme. The extent of this liaison depends upon the method of operation, the worst situation occurring when continuous use is required. However, in continuous process plants the awareness of the requirement for liaison is generally such as to encourage efficient planning. The most difficult situations occure where the degree of use or the volume of production fluctuates and a peak period can coincide with an intended maintenance activity.

In an ideal working environment both long-term (annual) and short-term (monthly) plans are regularly reviewed. Short-term release of assets for maintenance purposes can substantially reduce the need for weekend working by maintenance staff. Among the disadvantages of weekend working are the supervision problems, non-availability of materials, spares, and other services at weekends, and possible personnel problems as the maintenance staff tend to become socially separated.

Another important aspect of liaison is the request for service originated by operatives. When standby maintenance staff are available, requests for assistance are frequently made verbally. Formal requests include details of the fault and of the particular item requiring attention together with a priority indication, advice as to whether operations have been halted and an indication of the maintenance trade needed. Cost code information is required for any work undertaken by the maintenance staff in response to requests by operatives. Depending upon the arrangements for cost codes this allows expenditure to be allocated to particular machines, to individual buildings or to operators stations.

Manpower allocation

In the operation of a planned maintenance system, staff of appropriate skills have to be allocated to various tasks in accordance with the requirements originated by the control office. The actual method of allocation may be a simple manual system or a computer program but this is one aspect of planning in which good local supervision often produces the best results.

A basic work programme must originate from the control system with a batch of work cards issued for the particular period. However, the issue of these cards to particular personnel is still, even in quite sophisticated systems, a matter for personnel control by the foreman/supervisor. There are many local factors which may affect the decision on sending Mr Smith or Mr Anderson on particular routes on a particular day. The system is satisfied if two men in a given labour grade are matched to a two man-day load, but with the foreman left to assign the two individuals between the jobs on the schedule.

Downtime analysis

The maintenance records must provide for an acceptable level of downtime analysis, either from the records themselves or in direct summary form from the maintenance requests (see Figure 34.6). Useful information produced in this way includes:

			GHM
Date	Item	Fault	Downtime (hours)
1	Main panel	Fuse blown	0.1
2	Spreaders	Latches snapped, main arm	1.3
6	Mixers	Gearbox shaft broken (spare gearbox fitted)	0.25
10	Main press	Burst pipe (guard to be fitted)	0.3
11	Water sprays	Valve burnt out (revert to manual – no spare)	0.1
15	Water sprays	New valve fitted	0.4
16	Dryer burner	Faulty electrode (spare fitted, jets cleared)	1.20
19	Compressor	Bearing collapsed (spare fitted – re-order)	3.00
22	Product lift	No upward drive (contacts cleaned)	0.4
24	Main press	Burst pipe (repaired – guard fitted)	0.5

Figure 34.6   Record of downtime

1   An indication of downtime per building, per machine, or if necessary per operator
2   The time taken for fault diagnosis and repair on various types of fault, or on specific machines, or by various personnel
3   Indications of the causes of breakdown.

Among the useful points made clear by analysis 1 might be:

(a)   The true ratio of downtime to use time (to answer rumours or inaccuracies being quotes against the maintenance department)
(b)   The need for further investigation, by the operations or maintenance managements, of high downtime
(c)   The relationships between operator performance and the downtime on individual assets.

Analysis 2 may help to define:

(a)   High downtime areas where permanent standby repair staff or zone workshops might be beneficial
(b)   Suppliers to be avoided on future procurements
(c)   A requirement for specific training (e.g., electronic fault-finding) for maintenance workers
(d)   The most efficient members of the maintenance staff for the various types of work (fault-diagnosis, repairs, renewals, etc.).

Analysis 3 will define:

(a)   The spare parts and materials requirements for the various assets
(b)   Any requirement for increased operator training
(c)   Problems caused by variations in the product materials used in manufacturing processes.

It will be seen that downtime analysis is complementary to any cost-analysis work. However, downtime recording in detail is relatively expensive and, if economies are sought, may be applied only in certain areas rather than generally. The areas chosen may be high-risk areas containing plant which is vital to a high production figure, or may be areas of rising maintenance cost as defined by the normal cost summary, or areas in which large consequential losses could occur.

Costing

The maintenance control system must provide for accurate costing of work and materials for all maintenance activities. Work cards, materials requisitions, work instructions, maintenance requests, defect reports and time sheets must all carry significant codes to indicate cost allocations. The level of accounting practice adopted will determine the structure of the code system which may define costs in terms of:

1   Individual factories
2   Process lines

3 Individual machines
4 Separate buildings
5 Office units
6 Administration departments
7 Canteens and other special areas.

There is a wide variety of functional and physical hierarchies which may be adopted. The cost codes can conveniently be incorporated in the asset codes, so that costs to a particular asset are cross-referenced at once to the correct accounts.

COMPUTER-CONTROLLED SYSTEMS

A variety of computer systems have been developed for the assets registers, work control, manpower resourcing, stock control, maintenance accounts and, in some systems, analyses of feedback and costs. In general these are based on mainframe computers which, in industrial and commercial applications, are also employed for a variety of other purposes. This can give rise to delays, with the works department low in priority for computer time, especially when major financial programs are being run. The ideal computer system is interactive, dynamic and dedicated. 'Dedicated' means that it is always available to the maintenance department for logging vital information or for instant retrieval of data. These requirements can be met using a minicomputer or microcomputer within the maintenance department.

Computer applications in maintenance planning and control include:

1 Recording or updating asset records or asset movements
2 Managing lubrication activities and modifying the schedules if required by feedback
3 Acting upon inspection reports from lubrication operatives
4 Managing preventive and corrective maintenance activities and incorporating emergency maintenance when necessary
5 Acting upon feedback from maintenance activities
6 Resourcing for capital works programmes
7 Acting upon feedback from emergency maintenance
8 Managing spare parts stocks.

Other uses for the computer in the maintenance department can include:

1 Management of the works department stores
2 Planning and control of capital works programmes
3 Management of production tools, dies, moulds, etc.
4 Energy conservation through monitoring and control
5 Security and fire monitoring through remote sensors
6 Monitoring of automated processes or boiler plant
7 Co-ordination of condition monitoring inputs
8 Register of technical manuals and drawings
9 Register of defects and defect actions
10 Register of tests and quality documentation.

A fuller account of computer applications in maintenance management in given in *Computerised Management in the Maintenance Department*, M and E White Consultants Ltd.

CONDITION-BASED MAINTENANCE

Condition-based maintenance is maintenance work ordered as a result of the condition of an item as discovered during routine or continuous checking. Corrective maintenance ordered after the discovery of cracks in a wall or overheating noticed in a machine during a preventive maintenance check constitutes condition-based maintenance. Condition reports arise from human observations, checks and tests, or from fixed instrumentation or alarm systems grouped under the name 'condition monitoring'.

Benefits expected from a condition monitoring programme include:

1 Reduced expenditure on preventive maintenance
2 No unnecessary dismantling of plant items
3 Less (or less serious) breakdowns
4 Avoidance of consequential damage.

Levels of monitoring

Condition monitoring can be considered at four levels:

Level 1 Inspection monitoring based on the human senses, as in preventive maintenance schedules
Level 2 Assisted monitoring, using portable equipment
Level 3 Lubricant analysis and wear debris collection
Level 4 Fixed monitoring systems connected to alarm systems or data logging equipment.

The inspections at level 1 of the monitoring programme form part of the normal preventive maintenance schedules and are generally included in the daily and weekly activities. The inspectors are expected to use sight, hearing, touch and smell and to obtain a sensory impression of the condition of the asset. The senses may be assisted by magnifiers, viewing devices, temperature sensing strips or paints, stroboscopes, fixed instruments or indicators.

At level 2 the inspector is assisted by a range of portable test equipment to make a variety of measurements. Examples of the tests to be made and the types of equipment used are:

Measurements	*Equipment*
Speed and running time	Tachometers, counters
Electrical quantities	Test meters
Fits and tolerances	Proximity testers
Temperature	Thermography
Vibration wear	Vibration analyser or shock pulse tester

| Movement | Frequency analysis |
| Deterioration of materials | Radiography; ultrasonics; dye penetration |

This type of monitoring is applied to selected assets from the asset register for which a condition history file is built up. Quantities and characteristics are recorded and variations observed and interpreted.

Level 3 monitoring is confined to lubricated items and consists of checks on component wear together with checks on contamination of the lubricant. Wear of components is usually indicated by metal particles and debris in the lubricant. Contamination of the lubricant is detected by sampling and subsequent spectrometric analysis.

Fixed monitoring systems for level 4 monitoring range from simple remote alarm systems to comprehensive data gathering systems based on minicomputers or microprocessors. A wide variety of contact points, transducers, accelerometers, counters and other sensors are employed. Data can be transmitted directly to the display or can be electronically processed on a time-shared signal transmission system.

CAPITAL PROJECT MANAGEMENT

The stages in the life cycle of a new capital project are:

1 Conception - formulation of project idea
2 Approval - preliminary discussion and agreement on study
3 Formulation - study of various implementation methods
4 Evaluation - decision on implementation
5 Procurement - selection of suppliers
6 Design - development of concept
7 Construction - manufacture of hardware
8 Installation - construction and installation (often run concurrently)
9 Commissioning - often referred to as 'start-up'
10 Hand-over - buyer accepts responsibility
11 Proving - testing under normal conditions.

The handover is sometimes partial and proving is then necessary before final acceptance by the buyer.

If time and money is to be spent in a study of a project idea, approval is sought and budgetary provisions made. This study might entail consideration of:

1 Life-cycle costs, and return on investment for the existing installation (if applicable)
2 Predictions for these after the project has been implemented
3 Predictions after implementation by the various methods available
4 The development costs, operating costs, maintenance costs and possible problems arising if new technologies are introduced
5 The possibilities for achieving similar results (technical or financial) without introducing new techniques and non-standard plant.

The operating and maintenance aspects must be fully considered and the maintenance manager consulted. The effect on maintenance investments for a separate plant or an extension of an existing plant may include increases from the sources listed in Figure 34.7.

Typical operating costs for the maintenance department will include:

1 Salaries for the additional personnel
2 Other payments for the additional personnel
3 Spares and materials costs
4 Depreciation of buildings occupied by the maintenance staff
5 Overhead charges, insurances, etc.
6 Depreciation of workshop plant, tools, spares and equipment
7 Sub-contract costs.

In the first year of a new installation additional costs may include:

1 Excessive overtime working during familiarisation period
2 Increased use of vendor service engineers
3 High spares consumption caused by start-up problems and also some wastage
4 Further training requirements for maintenance staff.

In addition, low utilisation rates and increased downtime are sometimes features of first-year working.

The maintenance budget may be 7 to 10 per cent of the total investment in an industrial installation (although actual budgets vary enormously). The approximate allocations are:

Cost item	Allowance
Materials and subcontract	25 per cent
Personnel – total costs	40 per cent
Depreciation and overheads	25 per cent
Other items	10 per cent

The maintenance manager may request a number of studies by the project engineers. Typical studies are:

1 Study of supplier's proposals for assistance.

   (a) Should the proposals for training, etc., be accepted?
   (b) Should training and product support be subcontracted to specialist firms?
   (c) Are independent commissioning engineers to be used?
   (d) Is a servicing contract desirable?

2 Study of operating and maintenance requirements.

   (a) Will required utilisation be achieved?
   (b) What numbers and grades of manpower are necessary?

Item	Separate plant	Extension
Maintenance accommodation	New maintenance building or floor space allocation in new buildings	Possibly a zone workshop. Additional floor space if existing accommodation inadequate
Workshop plant, tools and access equipment	An appropriate proportion of the project costs based on existing knowledge	Equipment for zone workshop with an evaluation of use to be made of existing main workshop. Transport between zones
Staff requirements. Installation and commissioning	Manager or assistant manager and staff. Allocation of maintenance management and staff during installation phase to achieve familiarity with new plant	Supervisors and additional staff
Product support	The capital cost and charges arising from the documentation and training aspects	
Spares provisioning	A complete range of plant spares plus standard stocks of parts and materials	The recommended range of spares, less any adjustments for rationalisation
Staff training	Requirements for special staff training, above the machine training provided by the vendor, if new techniques are introduced	
Maintenance Consultancy	Development of maintenance policy, organisation of effective product support and introduction of maintenance planning	

Figure 34.7   Effect on maintenance investments

(c) Have all services requirements been clarified?
(d) Are all aspects of maintenance support provided for?

3 Study of maintenance planning and control systems.

(a) Is planned maintenance provided for?
(b) Which control method will be used?
(c) Can this plant and others be combined to justify more sophisticated planning systems?
(d) Will a maintenance consultant be appointed?

4 Study of spare parts requirements.

(a) Are supplier's recommendations acceptable?
(b) Will drawings be supplied for local spares manufacturer?
(c) Is the spares investment at acceptable level?
(d) Are original sources of spares known?
(e) Are spares compatible with existing stocks?

5 Study of monitoring techniques.

(a) Is vibration analysis or other condition monitoring included?
(b) Is remote control or centralised surveillance desirable?
(c) Are adequate alarms provided?
(d) Are fault diagnosis methods provided for?

These and other studies set the pattern for subsequent maintenance of the plant at an acceptable utilisation factor.

The total involvement of the maintenance manager in new project work is essential if effective maintenance is to be a feature of future years. If effective maintenance planning and control methods are used in an existing maintenance department, the maintenance manager should be available for participation in new work programmes.

Figure 34.8 lists a number of factors contributing to efficiency which merit attention when a capital project is planned. Possibly the most important is item 3 – the inclusion of the support items within the penalty clauses.

It is the responsibility of the project planner, with assistance from the maintenance manager or chief engineer, to set the pattern for a controlled situation in the maintenance department. The introduction of planning methods, control systems and effective supporting organisations depends upon the disciplines imposed at procurement, first, upon the planner to know what is required and to provide for it, and second, upon the plant suppiers to meet their obligations. It is the responsibility of the project planner to discipline all concerned into a successful project. This may entail the appointment of a terotechnology consultant (see Figure 34.9). His duties would include:

1 Formulation stage – evaluation of maintenance aspects of various methods and development of monitoring and maintenance policies
2 Procurement stage – vetting of contracts for maintenance aspects
3 Design and construction – monitor maintainability aspects
4 Installation and commissioning – evaluate product support activity by

	Factor	Remedy
	GHM	
1	Insufficient attention to reliability and life maintenance predictions during research and development phase	Improved R and D management disciplines and design analysis
2	Procurement on lowest tender without regard to possible life maintenance costs	Increased technical vetting by maintenance manager during procurement
3	Procurement without specification of and enforcement of product support requirements to be met at time of installation	Includes spares, maintenance manuals, tools, training assistance, commissioning, etc.
4	Insufficient appreciation of role of maintenance by works managers, production managers, etc.	Maintenance appreciation courses for managers of associated departments
5	Failure to plan the maintenance operation and to budget accordingly	Information and training for project planners, and chief engineers
6	Ineffective communication in the maintenance hierarchy	See items 3 and 8
7	Inadequate training for maintenance staff beyond basic skills level	Maintenance training courses of wider scope (fault-finding and repair training, for example)
8	Insufficient management training for engineers required to manage maintenance departments	Training in communication, management by objectives, budgeting, control and planning, terotechnology and maintenance improvement techniques

Figure 34.8 Factors affecting maintenance efficiency adversely

vendors and enforce contract provisions. Develop planned maintenance system, plant records, and technical information system. Arrange training programmes

5 Post-commissioning – finalise technical information system, review planning system, update as necessary.

NOTE: It is unlikely that all possible benefits of the terotechnology system will be obtained without a co-ordinated approach, short-circuiting departmental interests of whole life benefits. This may best be achieved by use of a maintenance consultant to monitor all stages of a new investment.

Figure 34.9 A maintenance consultant in a project team

FURTHER READING

Report by the Working Party on Maintenance Engineering, HMSO, London
The Terotechnology Handbook, HMSO, London
Logistics, M. & E. White Consultants Ltd, Winnersh, Wokingham, Berkshire
Computerised Management in the Maintenance Department, M. & E. White Consultants Ltd, Winnersh, Wokingham, Berkshire

PART SEVEN

WAREHOUSING AND DISTRIBUTION

35 The total cost approach to distribution

J C Gentles

The more management focuses the company's efforts on cutting distribution costs, the less successful it is likely to be in reducing the real cost of distribution. This apparent paradox is no abstract play on phrases. It explains why so many companies have diligently pruned distribution costs – in the warehouse, in stocks, in order processing and shipping – only to find that these hard-earned savings have somehow been watered down or washed out altogether by increases in other costs scattered throughout the company.

These 'other cost' increments seem to have nothing to do with distribution. They appear unpredicted and inexplicable at different times and anywhere and everywhere in the business – in purchasing, in production, in paper processing. But when traced back to their root cause, these gremlin-like costs are not as haphazard as they may seem. They are in fact all interrelated, and they do have one thing in common. They all result from the way the company distribute its products.

Ten years ago the concept of a total cost of distribution (TCD) approach to evaluating distribution alternatives was introduced. The main thesis was:

1 Classicial distribution costs (transport and warehousing) do not reflect the true costs of distribution. A total view of costs from supply to delivery is more realistic
2 A total cost approach is needed to ensure that the other costs are considered and presented to management as part of a fully developed business proposal.

It is this aggregation of distribution-related costs – rather than the more commonly labelled distribution costs – that make up the *real* cost of distribution. It is these costs – rather than those usually attacked in distribution cost-cutting programmes – that represent the important and increasing drain of distribution on earnings.

The important difference between distribution costs and the real impact of distribution on the total costs and total profits of the business has now been measured and dealt with by a number of hard-headed companies. Their managements have defined this cost complex and brought it under management control by applying the total cost approach.

Since its appearance, the value of this approach has become apparent to many practitioners in the field of distribution, materials and operations management. It has grown in stature with general business management as pressures on costs and efficiency have grown in step with the increasingly difficult business environment and greater competition, especially from Japan. The feasibility of the approach has also increased with the explosion of new computer tools that have enabled managers greater access to more sophisticated techniques and large volumes of data.

Some very tangible results have been achieved:

1   A major food manufacturer, after applying effectively an assortment of belt-tightening techniques, has found that TCD is enabling him to make additional profits of $3 800 000, enough to add 1.7 per cent to his margin of sales
2   A major merchandiser, already enjoying the benefits of advanced distribution techniques, found that TCD was able to cut from its corporate costs an additional 2.8 per cent of the sales value of its products – while at the same time significantly improving service to customers
3   A large manufacturer of school supplies applied TCD techniques to his return of factories and warehouses and was able to cut his annual distribution costs by over $5 000 000 – a 20 per cent reduction

These success stories demonstrate why even companies which have tightened and tidied their distribution operations can still add substantially to their earnings by a frontal attack on the basic framework of their distribution decisions and practices. They have proved, too, that this broad and basic approach brings continuing returns. Once TCD has defined the most profitable pattern of distribution for the present operations of the business, management has a yardstick for measuring the impact on total profits of any proposed change.

The effectiveness of TCD is illustrated by the two following examples – each a different situation. The first traces the step-by-step process involved in the analysis of the factors that enter into a TCD analysis. The second shows how this information is exploited to provide management with the most profitable answers to some familiar distribution problems.

TCD APPLIED TO A CHAIN OF RETAIL OUTLETS

Consider first the problem which faced the management of a large company whose business comprised a widely dispersed chain of retail shops, plus a few factories which produced some of the goods sold in the shops. The company distributed its products from one centrally located warehouse. The question arose 'Would there be any profit advantage in changing to a system of local warehouses, distributed across the country?'

When the company looked at the combined cost of warehousing and transport that would result from introducing local warehouses it found that the lowest cost system was one with five warehouses. But this would increase its distribution costs by $12 900 000. Thus, on the basis of conventional analysis, the central warehouse method seemed best.

However, when the question of how alternative distribution networks would affect other costs in the company was investigated, the answers were quite different. In the first place, the most efficient warehouse system turned out to be a network of six, rather than one or five, field warehouses. And this six-warehouse system would cut total costs dramatically.

When all distribution cost related factors were considered for the six-warehouse system, increases in physical distribution costs amounted to $13 900 000 but there were substantial reductions in other costs amounting to $20 600 000. This total cost look at distribution demonstrated that the profits of the company could be increased by $6 700 000 a year.

What produced this increase which, incidentally, turned out to represent 22.4 per cent return on the investment required to design and install this field warehouse system? The answer is defined by tracing through the company the 'other cost' implication of this distribution change.

It was necessary first to decide which interrelationships were economically significant. These will differ from industry to industry, and even from company to company. To illustrate this point, and to demonstrate how these interrelationships worked out in this instance, Figure 35.1 presents graphically the impact of a number of cost factors on the profits of the company.

The calculations are quite complex, and these graphs serve only to represent schematically the kind of impact that the addition of field warehouses would have on each cost factor. To do this, each point on this series of curves shows how an optimally designed system including from one to thirty field warehouses would add or subtract from corporate profits.

Graphs (a) and (b) show quite clearly how a consideration of warehousing and transportation costs alone would lead to the answer this management was given when the conventional distribution cost analysis was made. It is the sum of these two graphs which leads to the conclusion that a five-warehouse system was the best alternative, although this would actually increase the costs of these two functions.

A further study of the company's operation showed that for each warehouse added there would be a different rate of inventory turnover, and therefore a change in inventory carrying costs. This is illustrated in graph (c). Including these charges in distribution evaluation is, of course, standard practice in many companies. But even the addition of this consideration would not have led management to the correct decision. A five-warehouse system would still appear to be the best alternative, even though economically unsound.

There are, however, other aspects of inventory which, in this case as in many others, prove to be more significant. These are shown in graphs (d), (e) and (f) of Figure 35.1 and they are:

1   Changes in the cost of obsolescence

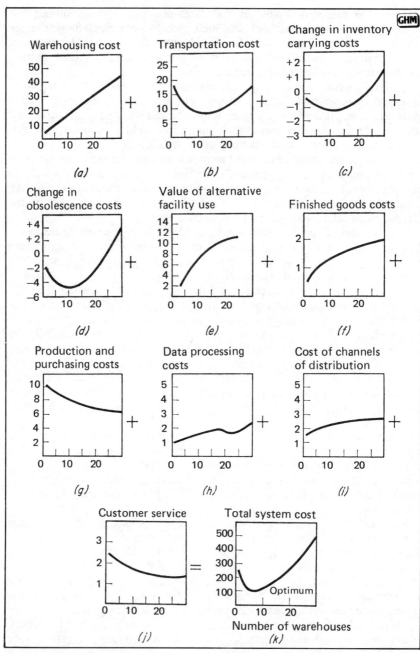

Figure 35.1 The build-up of total distribution costs
Each factor is considered in relation to the number of warehouses possible and a curve of the cost implications plotted. By adding all of these results together, a composite curve is obtained (k), which shows the total costs of distribution in relation to the possible warehouse arrangements

2   The value of alternative use of facilities
3   Changes in the cost at which the company was able to buy finished goods

When these three cost factors were taken into account, it became clear that the original calculation had been invalid. A total cost curve that included these three factors would shift the decision to a six-warehouse system and begin to show the possibility of substantial profits from such a change.

The interaction between distribution, production and purchasing is traced in the relationships described in graph (g). The number and location of the field warehouses would directly affect the loading of the company's factories, which had a definable impact on the cost of raw materials and components and on production costs per unit.

The company's data-processing costs would, of course, also be affected by decentralising its warehousing with the resulting need for the ability to exchange information between the field and headquarters. In this case, although there was substantial additional paper work, the cost was not great because it could all be put on the company's existing computer system. The projected results are shown in graph (h).

Finally, and most important, the impact of any proposed change in distribution has to be traced to its point of impact in the market-place, for ultimately that is the measure of the effectiveness of the distribution system. Here the two critical elements are the channels through which a company elects to distribute its products, and the level of customer service it decides to maintain.

In this case, because the company distributed mostly through its own retail outlets, the channels seemed not to be an important consideration. There was, nevertheless, an important reason for following out the significance of distribution channels. As this company looked ahead, it could see the possibility that at some time in the future it might want to integrate backwards, and become more heavily involved in manufacturing. In that case, the channels of distribution factor might become more important.

In this kind of analytical exercise it is essential to consider all possible directions that company growth can take. Otherwise, a new distribution system, however profitable it may be under present conditions, might freeze the company into a set of cost factors that would rule out an otherwise profitable growth opportunity.

Customer service is the other marketing decision that plays an important role in any total cost approach. In the last analysis, any distribution system is an effort to achieve at the lowest cost the level of service to customers which will afford the company the greatest opportunity for growth in the market-place. The question is: how much does it cost to improve service to customers and how much can be gained in additional sales by that improvement? Graph (j) shows how warehousing would affect sales lost at the present level of customer service.

When all these factors are added up, they produce a single total cost curve that defines the best solution to this management problem. This is shown in graph (k) of Figure 35.1, which illustrates the fact that the six-warehouse system is the best alternative and one that would return a handsome profit to the company. The actual figures from this company's experience for the six-warehouse system are shown in Figure 35.2.

The graphs and figures demonstrate better than words the management meaning of the total cost approach. Study of the cost curves one at a time makes it apparent that the most profitable distribution network is somewhat different for each of these cost factors. This is what leads to distorted decisions when companies look at one, two or six of these variables and fail to consider the others. It shows the pitfalls of considering these various factors as single and static, instead of as interrelated and dynamic. Looking again at the first two graphs, it is apparent how the consideration of distribution costs alone – the cost of warehousing plus the cost of transportation – led to the conclusion that there was no change in distribution which could add to the profitability of the business. Only the final graph summing up all the interacting factors involved, demonstrates unmitakably that a shift to the six-warehouse system would be a very profitable move for management.

These graphs show, too, why major distribution problems could not be

Item	Gain or loss ($m)		GHM
Warehousing	(14.4)		
Transport	.5		
Total distribution costs			(13.9)
Stocks			
Carrying costs	1.4		
Obsolescence costs	4.3		
Value of alternative			
Use of facilities	7.8		
		13.5	
Production and purchasing			
Production and raw			
materials costs	.2		
Reduced cost of purchased			
finished goods	6.7		
		6.9	
Data processing		(.2)	
Marketing			
Channels of distribution	.2		
Customer service	1.4		
		1.6	
Total profit impact of distribution-related items			21.8
Pretax profit increase			7.9

Figure 35.2 Profit impact of distribution
Gains or losses projected by a TCD study, based on a changeover from an existing one-warehouse system to a six-warehouse system

resolved at the operating levels of the company. In this case, a 'no-go' decision would have been valid if a traffic or transport or warehouse executive had to make that decision on the basis of the cost data available. A reduction in warehouse transport and stock costs would lead to increases in other distribution-related cost, so that total costs would be increased and this significant profit opportunity missed. Only by increasing these distribution costs could total expenses be cut and total earnings increased in this company. It is by this kind of trade-off – robbing Peter to pay Paul – that the total cost approach brings a company closer to achieving its maximum potential profit.

The total cost approach does much more than offer a one-shot solution to a perennial problem. Every time management makes a decision of any magnitude, it ought to be in a position to get an answer to the question: 'How will it affect distribution costs throughout the company?' The total cost approach enables a company to make continuing gains by applying a yardstick to any proposed corporate venture.

Every time manufacturing management designs a new plant or develops a new production process, the pattern of distribution costs will be changed throughout the business. Similar far-flung changes will take place whenever marketing management adds a new product or a promising new group of customers. The total cost approach enables boards to define how these changes will interact with distribution to affect the total costs of the company and its total profits. It tells boards what distribution decisions need to be made to avoid the loss of potential profits, or to add to them.

TCD ANALYSIS OF A LARGE MANUFACTURING ORGANISATION

How this is done can be seen quite readily in a case in which the TCD approach was used by a division of a large American manufacturing company. This division does an annual business of about $70m, with over 3000 customers located in every state in the USA. It manufactures and warehouses at five points across the country, shipping to customers via both rail and road.

Some of the profit questions this management posed have a familiar ring:

1 Without any major investment, can we increase our profits by changing our distribution system?
2 Can total cost be reduced by shifting some of our equipment from one factory to another?
3 Can we further reduce costs and increase profits by changing our marketing approach?

Then there were some longer-range questions to be resolved:

1 Is there any profit advantage in changing the capacity of one or more of our present plants, or perhaps building a new facility at another location?
2 Could we further improve profitability by changing our warehouse capacities or locations?

An analysis of this company's business showed quite readily what factors and interactions determined the total profit of the product delivered to the customer. Every distribution study has to start with a definition of where the customers are and the requirements they impose on their suppliers. In this case, it was vital to differentiate between the customers that had to be served by rail, and those that had to be served by road.

What was done, therefore, was to determine for each sales district what proportion of sales came into the district by rail, and how much was shipped in by road. And for each sales district data on f.o.b. as against delivered pricing was obtained.

The next step was to determine from which of the five plants and warehouses each sales district should be supplied. This involves an in-depth analysis of the production and warehousing costs per unit in each of the plants and warehouses. This analysis had to be carried out for various volume levels.

The total plant cost is built up by analysing the cost for varying production volume, inbound freight, direct labour and plant overhead. All of these cost elements will, of course, differ at each plant, even within the same company. These plant and warehouse cost calculations were made for each of the company's five facilities.

Figure 35.3 shows these total cost curves for all of the plants and warehouses. These costs are, of course, different for each facility at each level of volume. Not only does each curve start at a different point – reflecting different overhead costs – but the rate of increase is also different, reflecting different variable cost

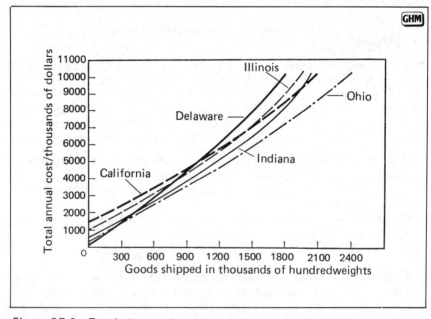

Figure 35.3 Total plant and warehousing costs at five plants
Differing fixed and variable costs of installation at five different locations for a large manufacturing organisation in the USA

factors at increasing volumes for each of these installations.

With some further analyses it became possible to determine, for every unit of product and for all individual customers the profit contribution under all possible combinations of production and distribution. The problem that remained was to put all these possibilities together into a single solution that would maximise the company's total earnings.

To introduce this data into the computer called for the use of a non-linear programming technique. The technical aspects of this are not important for its managerial implications. What is significant is that the technique does exist, that it does work, and that once the programme has been written, this kind of distribution problem can be solved in minutes. TCD was able to provide a very precise answer to each of the questions confronting the management of this company.

1　By rearranging the company's distribution pattern and making appropriate shifts in production and warehousing loads, it was possible without any change in facilities to increase this company's profits by $984 000 a year.

　　The largest ingredient in this change would come from reduced materials cost at $400 000, with warehouse savings contributing $366 000. Direct labour savings in the plants would add a further $114 000. What is particularly interesting is that transportation, so often overstressed in distribution decisions, turned out to contribute only $108 000 to this total profit improvement package.

2　Additional savings of $360 000 could be effected by shifting equipment from one plant to another. To determine this, it was necessary to develop new production cost curves for alternative arrangements of equipment and run these through the computer, comparing them with the most profitable way of using the equipment as presently located.

3　Additional savings of £894 000 a year would result if about half of the customers could be persuaded to shift from road to rail delivery. These reduced costs would be added to earnings or passed on to the customer, thus giving the company a competitively significant price advantage.

4　It was determined that there was no way to increase profitability by any change in production facilities. Although building a new plant in Michigan would result in lower production and warehousing costs amounting to $450 000, when the impact of this change on total costs was seen, this turned out to be one of those instances in which the 'other costs' which have been discussed more than offset any possible gains, so that this investment would not be a wise one.

5　On the other hand, an addition to the capacity of the warehouse at their Delaware plant would add $150 000 a year to profits and represent a sound investment. Again, this was determined by setting up new warehousing cost schedules and running them through the computer alongside the costs under existing conditions. The comparison showed that the investment in the added Delaware warehouse capacity would return almost 25 per cent a year.

The total addition to profits adds up to almost $1.5m a year.

The point that needs to be understood is that these profits could not have been generated by decisions based on the insight or the experience of even the most competent executive. Only the total cost approach could have established, for example, that the earnings of this business could be increased by supplying its customers in the Dakotas from a plant in Ohio rather than from a much nearer facility in Illinois. Yet when total profits were calculated, this turned out to be an element in the most profitable use of the existing facilities of this company.

Similarly, only a total cost calculation provided the background for estimating the return on investment that could be expected from building a new facility in Michigan. It is this ability to put precise price and profit tags on each pattern of alternatives that makes the total cost approach such an effective management tool.

WHEN THE TOTAL COST APPROACH SHOULD BE USED

1   When the company makes a significant change in its marketing strategy (for example, going direct versus selling to wholesalers).
2   When the size of the company changes significantly.
3   When new businesses or products are added to the distribution system.
4   When the company's geographic mix of shipments changes appreciably.
5   When five to ten years have passed since the last evaluation
6   When any of four symptoms appear

   (a)   Inventories that turn slowly
   (b)   Poor customer service
   (c)   Interwarehouse shipments
   (d)   Premium freight charges.

FURTHER READING

Christopher, M., Walters, D., and Gattorna, J., *Distribution Planning and Control*, Gower, 1977

36 Warehouse operation and management

Ken Firth

It cannot be said that warehousing has been a source of great inspiration to many who are in senior management positions in the UK. Too often the designing, building, running and controlling of warehousing systems have been left to individuals who have been passed over in their original speciality or those who are approaching retirement and have been given a supposedly less demanding job to do. Such lack of enthusiasm is unfortunate because standards of warehouse efficiency can have far-reaching effects upon customer relationships. A succession of missed delivery dates or failure to deliver a complete order influence a customer's thinking far more than the helpfulness of the salesman who originally obtained the order. Yet warehousing, as one of the least glamorous aspects of business systems, is often starved of resources in both physical and human terms.

Effective warehousing depends, like very other aspect of management, upon a clear understanding of what the system is expected to provide, a carefully outlined plan, and, above all, continuously supervised implementation with great attention to detail. The rewards can be considerable to small and large organisations alike, for although small systems cannot take advantage of economies of scale they often have a considerable edge in their ability to give personal service through effective managerial control.

MODERN WAREHOUSING

The seeds of modern warehousing operations were planted more than a hundred years ago with the arrival of crude but effective pallet handling equipment. Such equipment enabled human beings to move modular loads around manufacturing systems which would otherwise have been difficult to handle. It was not until the advent of a machine which could lift modular loads one above the other as well as undertaking horizontal movement – in the form of the early fork-lift truck – that the revolution in warehousing method took place. This started in the 1930s and accelerated very rapidly during the Second World

War when the United States Army recognised that such machinery could revolutionise their approach to logistics. The result was that warehouses ceased to be multi-storey affairs convenient to manhandling, and modern wide-span steel or concrete portal frame building predominated. Since that time there has been unremitting design effort to improve the lifting height capacity of fork-lift trucks and at the same time reduce operating aisle widths. The objective is to take maximum advantage of building cube in storage areas in the knowledge that building costs per cubic metre provided are substantially reduced between the heights of 6 to 15 metres for steel portal frame construction, thereby reducing the total systems cost. The term 'total systems cost' is important because in the context of the firm it is that cost which must be minimised – there are many circumstances where it is justifiable to increase warehousing operating costs *provided that greater savings are made elsewhere.*

The basis of modern warehousing is the principle of load unitisation, combined with the remaining principles of materials handling which are:

1 Utilisation of cube
2 Minimisation of movement
3 Flow effectiveness
4 Safety and security

all at lowest total systems cost.

LOAD UNITISATION

Although load unitisation is commonly associated with pallets and fork-lift trucks, there are many other forms of unit-load, large and small, which have an important place in warehousing and should not be overlooked – tote pans for small components is a typical example.

The underlying concept of load unitisation is the combining of like products together on some regularly dimensioned load board or in a container, so that they may be more easily handled by man or machine. Simple though this idea is, it is only too easy to make mistakes either through not recognising the problem involved or not being sufficiently stringent in applying the standards laid down.

Two main aspects have to be considered; on the one hand, the physical characteristics of the product including its protective packaging; and on the other, the most suitable kind of load board or container for the job in hand. When stacking products upon flat timber pallets it is preferable to have rectilinear packages or cases which are modular to the pallet dimension (to avoid loss of utilisation) and at the same time ensure that the packages will 'brick' together in layers (Figure 36.1) thereby ensuring good load stability. A package which is a perfect cube is undesirable because it cannot be bonded to its partners except by the use of strapping, stretch wrapping or other devices. Packages which overhang pallets are to be avoided because they offer scope for damage.

Figure 36.1   Cartons stacked on pallets
Here are two ways of stacking cartons on pallets. The wrong way (left-hand pallet) allows each pile of cartons to sway and topple. The right way prevents this, because the cartons are arranged in an interlocking pattern

In building up suitable pallet patterns it is usual to construct the largest feasible load because by so doing movement is reduced. The achieving of this objective is conditioned by many constraints, typical of which are the over-turning moment of the load, crush loading of packages, the height available within the warehouse, the lifting heights of the fork-lift trucks available, and by the type of vehicle on which the pallet might be transported.

Arriving at the best answer is often a matter of compromise but where over-turning or lack of stability is the problem there is a variety of devices, such as layer interleaving, strapping, stretch or shrink wrapping which help to overcome the difficulty. In cases where pallets and loads need to be stacked simply one on top of another, it is essential to perform stacking tests over a period of weeks to be certain that progressive stack collapse will not take place. Such factors as poor carton design or high humidity may well cause stacking problems which cannot immediately be detected.

Once a unit load has been properly formulated and agreed it should be recorded – if necessary the pallet stacking pattern can be printed upon the outer package so that anyone not familiar with the correct procedure can ensure uniformity.

In specifying a pallet board or other form of container it is fundamental to obtain a piece of equipment which will provide least cost over its *total life cycle*. The lowest available price is no criterion if the pallet has not been adequately designed and tested to carry its specified load, has poor resistance to damage and is difficult to repair. The attempts to achieve the ideal pallet have caused more contention than any other aspect of materials handling and a great lack of standardisation prevails. However, the International Standards Organisation (ISO) supported by the British Standards Institution (BSI) and other overseas organisations have slowly approached the problem of standardisation of through-transit pallets and dimensional and testing standards for the following sizes exist:

1200 mm × 800 mm (Europal)
1200 mm × 1000 mm (Grocery pallet)
1200 mm × 1200 mm (Oil drum pallet)
1200 mm × 1800 mm (Paper and furniture pallet)
(BS 2629 Parts I, II and III.)

The 1200 mm dimension is ideal for loading onto the side of flat vehicles in the UK, but less than convenient in box vehicles and ISO containers. A pallet size of 1100 mm × 1100 mm strongly advocated by the Japanese which fits perfectly into ISO containers has not been approved by ISO because it is not modular to 600 mm × 400 mm × 400 mm which is a specified ISO unit dimension.

Although there have been many attempts to depose timber as the most used material for the construction of pallets, no adequate substitute has emerged. In the manufacturing engineering industry and the motor car industry there has been widespread use of metal cage and box pallets because of their longevity under the arduous conditions in which they have to work and because of their ability to handle awkward shapes. Many experiments have been made with plastic pallets but their cost, which has escalated since the oil crisis, tends to restrict their use to applications where hygiene is a paramount consideration. The most used pallet in the UK is the 1200 mm × 1000 mm 4-way entry perimeter-based pallet built to BSI specification 2629. A typical life of a wooden pallet in the UK is said to be three to five years, but whether this is entirely due to fair wear and tear is a matter of some doubt. In recent years the company GKN/Chep has introduced a pallet pool exchange system which is worthy of consideration, particularly in the case of companies which have large pallet populations which have to be transported over great distances and where collection of empty pallets and their return is a costly and haphazard operation.

Loaded pallets should not normally be stacked one on top of another to a height greater than six times the minimum base dimension of the pallet and only then when the condition of the pallet and its environment have been carefully checked. For example, uneven floors can create stacking difficulties and lightly loaded pallets stacked outside can be affected by high winds. In adverse conditions the height of stack should be reduced to four times the minimum base dimension or less. There can, of course, be exception to such rules, but any change should be agreed with the appropriate safety representatives.

The care given to unit-load design must never be relaxed and what is certain is that as handling and storage sophistication increases, so must the attention to design. There are endless examples of mechanised equipment being damaged or rendered useless through permitting off-dimension or damaged pallets into the system.

Thus the establishment of the unit-load is the first step towards efficient warehouse operation and from this follows good utilisation of the cube, minimisation of movement, creating effective flow, all in keeping with high standards of safety and security at lowest total systems cost.

UTILISATION OF THE WAREHOUSE CUBE

The price of new warehousing can vary quite considerably due to a variety of factors, such as location, degree of refinement of the facilities, negotiating variations and the economic circumstances prevailing. In mid 1981 a figure between £200 and £250 per square metre would not be regarded as unusual for a warehouse building complete with a limited amount of office space and services to an acceptable standard. At such prices it is commonplace to discover that the building and building services can account for as much as 40 per cent of the operating cost of the warehouse. Support for the conservation of warehouse space has long been given by UK fork-lift truck manufacturers who have always been at the forefront in the design of narrow aisle height lift trucks. Very narrow aisle equipment which will lift 1.5 tonne loads at heights of 12 metres is readily available for use in gangways only 1.5 metres wide. Whilst reducing gangway widths is an obvious approach to the reduction of space costs, increased lift height is less so. Although increased lift height means more expensive equipment, which is also more expensive to maintain, the disadvantage is offset by the fact that as single-storey warehouses increase in height up to about 15 metres their costs per cubic metre reduce because most of the cost is in the roof and floor. This fact can produce a favourable trade-off of building cost against equipment costs.

The efficient storage of palletised loads demands a careful analysis of the stockholding profile within the warehouse. That is to say stockholding data must be collected for each product stored and the products then ranked in order of quantity of pallets held. A ranking of products in order of throughput quantities should also be prepared. Although the determination of the method of storage is primarily dependent upon the quantities by stocks held, throughput must be taken into account when considering what handling equipment is most suitable. Once the stockholding analysis has been completed it is useful to make use of the simple flow diagram (Figure 36.2) to produce a list of alternatives which require consideration. It is important to remember when using the diagram that whilst all pallet profiles can be randomly stored by individual pallet, they are not all readily block stackable. The objective of using the flow chart is to eliminate looking at unnecessary alternatives.

Pallet block storage

The concept behind palletised block storage is that of stacking pallets one above the other and in rows of suitable depth. The rows of pallet stacks (identical product within each row) are assembled side by side to form a three-dimensional matrix (see Figure 36.3).

The operation of this simple idea can become very complicated in execution due to various constraints which can be placed upon the system and the warehouse manager may find that because of such constraints, his warehouse is badly utilised so that only 60 per cent of the pallet spaces provided can actually be occupied by physical stock.

This may be brought about by one or more of the following ways:

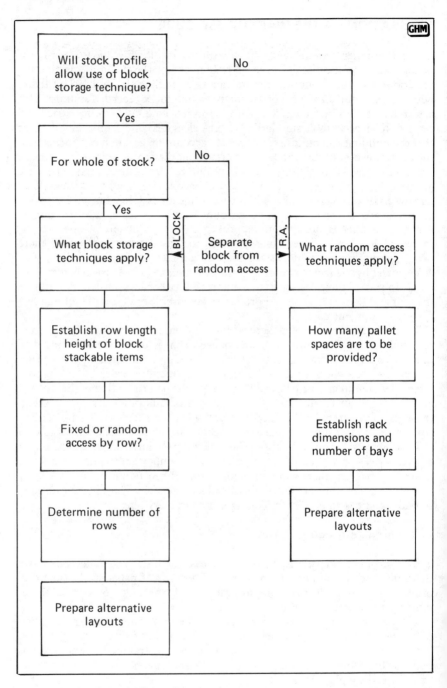

Figure 36.2 Simple flow diagram for palletised bulk storage design

Figure 36.3   Simple block stack

1   Insufficient stock per line item to form significant blocks of storage which leads to 'honeycombing' and loss of cube
2   The use of a fixed location system for products when there is a significant variation between maximum and minimum stocks. This problem may be solved by arranging rows of product randomly within the warehouse at the expense of a control system
3   Incorrect row length. At first glance the longer the row length the better the relationship between stack and gangways. Space utilisation is, however, a function of stock quantity and time of occupancy which the following simple calculation illustrates:

Twelve stacks of pallets are received into stock and the stockholding time is estimated at 24 days. The options on row length vary between 1 row of 12 stacks and 12 rows of 1 stack, but each row has the same area of gangway allocated to it.

For example, if we say that a stack occupies 2 m² and the gangway allocation per row is 3 m² the area required for a single 12 stack row will be 27 m². Moreover, the area will be unavailable for re-use until the last pallet is withdrawn after the 24th day has elapsed (unless double handling or poor stock rotation is accepted). The 'cost' incurred amounts to 24 × 27 m² = 648 m² days. A 2-row approach will mean that half the original space occupied will be free for use after 12 days and the space cost incurred will be only 540 m² days – a significant saving. The calculation for all the variants is as follows:

1 row	648 m² days
2 rows	540 m² days
3 rows	528 m² days
4 rows	540 m² days
6 rows	588 m² days
12 rows	780 m² days

In this instance a row length of 4 pallets is the most suitable choice. It is possible to conceive that this approach to row length can be considerably refined to optimise warehouse block storage layouts
4   Limitations upon stacking height. With simple block stacking i.e., pallets simply supported one on top of each other, the problem is usually that of overturning or crush-loading. This may be prevented by the use of 'drive-in' racking which has all the attributes of block storage whilst separating pallets vertically (Figure 36.4)
5   First in, first out rotation of stock can be a problem with simple and drive-in block storage systems – the best situation usually achievable is rotation by row. When stock is fast moving this does not present a significant problem, but where it is, the options of pallet live storage, or powered mobile storage offer a solution. Although in both cases the storage equipment cost is high, it usually represents a very small proportion of the total warehouse cost and there are many instances where the higher space utilisation provided by more sophisticated systems has resulted in a favourable trade-off against building costs

6　The orientation of block storage in relation to building dimension and the choice of direction of entry of forks into a four-way entry pallet can materially affect the number of pallet spaces available to the system and also the distances travelled by handling equipment. Care has to be taken that the advantage of increased storage does not interfere with flow or impede managerial control.

Figure 36.4　Drive-in racking

Palletised random access storage

Virtually every form of palletised random access storage is associated with a racking system and this means, almost by definition, some form of adjustable pallet racking. A random access system, as its name implies, enables individual access to every pallet, the disadvantage being that a record of what is held in each location has to be kept, on a first in, first out basis by product, and this can be prone to error. The other significant advantage of adjustable pallet racking is that it enables the utilisation of headroom in a building to levels beyond what is generally acceptable for simple block storage systems (provided the building headroom is available), but when used in conjunction with counterbalance or even reach fork-lift trucks can be wasteful of space due to the relatively poor aisle space to rack occupancy relationships. This disadvantage can be largely offset by the fact that the pallet space utilisation factor can be as high as 95 per cent and when this factor is coupled with a very narrow aisle system at heights above 6 metres can result in cube utilisations considerably superior to most block storage systems (see Figure 36.5). The significant exception is powered mobile storage which combines the attributes of both block and random access and can result in total cube utilisation factors in excess of 45 per cent.

The simplest way of overcoming the problem of error in placement and removal of stock is to operate a ticket system which indicates the co-ordinates of the pallet position but at the same time incorporates a random check digit which the operator has to record in placement or retrieval. If a mistake occurs this can be rapidly checked by the pallet location control clerk and the fault rectified before too much time has elapsed. The most recent development of stock location validation is the fitting of microprocessors complete with optical character readers, which enables the driver to scan the pallet ticket and pallet location to ensure a match. In the event of a mis-match, a warning signal is activated.

Damage to racking and products caused by fork-lift trucks for whatever reason is a cause of concern. The problem can be alleviated by proper training of fork-lift drivers and what is probably more important by adequate supervision once the training has been completed. It is wise to ensure that racks conform to an approved standard – that of the Storage Equipment Manufacturers Association is appropriate to the UK – and equally important that the racks are competently constructed and fixed to the floor. In the event of damage the section of the rack affected should be unloaded and remain so until the faulty component has been replaced. Efforts to straighten thin section members once distorted should be avoided.

High-bay pallet silos

The high-bay pallet silo (Figure 36.6) serviced by automatic storage and retrieval machines (stacker cranes), although by no means a new concept is arousing increased interest for storage and warehousing throughout the world, nowhere more so than in the USA and Japan at the present time. The reasons for this surge of interest are many but a common one is the economy of not having to move storage off an existing site as more and more companies become locked into urban sprawl with limited expansion potential. In addition, computing and control expertise has developed rapidly over the past ten years, both in the area of data and power transmission, which has greatly increased availability potential of such installations. It must be admitted that the cost justification in straightforward accounting terms can be difficult, but it is becoming increasingly apparent that this kind of equipment can offer

Figure 36.5   Very narrow aisle racking and truck

tremendous advantage in terms of speed and accuracy of operation, which in turn makes levels of service available previously unachievable with manually operated systems.

MINIMISING MOVEMENT

Movement, like warehouse space, is a costly resource whether it be attributable to man or machine. Whilst there are many techniques available to reduce movement time, both in a system and an equipment sense, all can be rendered virtually useless if adequate standards are not imposed. A guaranteed way of

Figure 36.6   High-bay warehouse

ensuring continuing poor performance is to overman when setting up a new warehouse – this may be due to the absence of standards or over anxiety by management in their desire to have a smooth start. Another major failing on start up is to do so without adequate commissioning of equipment or sufficient staff training. Warehouse planning should ensure that a start-up commences slowly and, for preference, at a quiet time of the year. Synthetic time study data for a variety of materials handling tasks is available which can be used until properly measured work standards can be applied.

Order selection tends to be the function of warehousing which is the most intensive user of labour per unit of throughput, although in some applications where load modularisation and quality control is extensive goods receiving comes a close second.

An order-picking system (see Figure 36.7) should be organised in such a manner that a fully representative range of stock is presented in the smallest possible area conducive with safe operation, so that orders may be selected accurately at the service level demanded, avoiding unnecessary stockouts and without excessive movement from reserve to forward location. Because many of these requirements are not complementary to one another, the process is essentially one of compromise making use of the minimisation techniques appropriate to the stock and throughput profiles of the picking systems under study. The techniques available are:

Functional separation. This is the consideration of whether to keep order picking and reserve storage in separate parts of the warehouse or physically integrate the two. In simple terms the answer depends on the ratio of stock held in reserve to that required in order picking. If the difference is large there is scope for holding the reserve in a specialised stockholding area making use of a space efficient storage system, such as high-rack stacking or drive-in storage. Where there is a closer relationship say 3 to 1 or less, it may be more sensible to hold reserve pallets in racking immediately above the order-picking pallets (see Figure 36.8). Where reserve is a very small proportion, it may be feasible to pick from multi-level locations.

Popularity

An analysis of movement within an order-picking store usually demonstrates that 80 per cent of the visits to collect product are made to only 20 per cent of locations. Knowledge relating to these products makes it theoretically possible to arrange them in a layout which minimises the movement of the order pickers. However, there are many factors which can render the concept infeasible such as congestion, seasonal changes, promotions and cataloguing difficulties, which suggest that caution should be exercised in implementing the idea. Popularity is probably of greater significance when related to a fixed-location palletised bulk loading operation or when the popularity of products can be accurately monitored by computer, provided that in the latter case the stores movement involved does not result in confusion.

Batching orders

In instances where there is a large range of products covering a wide area and the average quantity picked per order is small, it is often feasible to group orders together to be picked upon a single circuit of the order-picking area. Inevitably, some sorting must be carried out either on circuit or at the end of the pick and the justification is that the cost of sorting is less than the cost of the time saved by reduction of movement around the system. The objective should be to maximise an order-picker's carrying capacity for a given picking circuit within the limits of the capability of his handling equipment. This means that if on

Figure 36.7   Second level order-picker

Figure 36.8   Base location order-picking system

average single orders satisfy this requirement a batching system is usually unnecessary. There are occasions where a batch pick of a day's work is brought to a forward area and sorted, the advantage being that this serves as an automatic checking device provided that balancing errors in sorting have not occurred.

Zoning

Some large warehousing systems, notably mail order, find it advantageous to divide their systems departmentally according to merchandise or by size and throughput of product. The procedure is to route orders only to the departments concerned with the specific items required on an order and bypass the rest. Order pickers are allocated to each department or zone and only pick in that restricted area, passing the order and goods to the next department featured on the picking list, until the full order has been picked. This not only reduces pedestrian movement but permits specialisation.

Randomisation of order-picking locations

By far the majority of order-picking systems in the UK are based upon fixed-location systems which allow the order picker to learn, relatively quickly and easily, the location of any product. Some wide-ranging systems with constant obsolescence and introduction of lines find it impossible to cope with fixed location because when a bin has been vacated by an obsolete product, it has to be replaced by another. This automatically randomises the locations, but does keep the picking face within reasonable dimensions. A consequence is that the location is first identified by its co-ordinates and secondly by its contents. Control of such systems has to be comprehensive because a product once lost is hard to find, additionally the administrative complexity is so great that computer control is almost mandatory.

Goods-to-picker techniques

It is not unknown for an order picker to have to walk more than ten miles a day to complete his or her work, which clearly may take up more than 50 per cent of the time available. Provide a system where the goods can be brought to the picker and that time is available to carry out a lot more picking (see Figure 36.9). With a few exceptions, the endeavours to achieve such savings in a case-picking environment have met with little success – the costs, under UK conditions, have been greater than using conventional techniques. On the other hand, the potential for using goods-to-picker techniques on small components applications appears considerable because these are often associated with high range and relatively small volumes and weights per line item. The control complexity required to implement an effective system should not be under-estimated.

It is important to remember that whilst one or more of the above techniques may be used to reduce movement in an order-picking system, their applicability can only be determined through a full understanding of the system's requirements.

PAPERWORK REDUCTION

Research into the control of order-picking systems has shown that up to 30 per cent of the time spent by an operative can be in handling paperwork. This can be brought about in a wide variety of ways, for example, looking up stock location records and stock cards, documentation that is difficult to read, products listed in a sequence which does not follow the picking run, etc. It is interesting to observe that the incidence of such problems is being greatly reduced by the introduction of the small computer into warehousing which operates in real-time on either a stand alone basis or as part of a distributed system. The speed and accuracy of a well-designed warehouse computer system rapidly repays the effort and expense involved and can do much to improve customer and staff relationships. It is little wonder that more and more companies are embarking upon such projects.

Figure 36.9   Horizontal carousel order-picking machine

RECEIVING AND DISPATCH

A surprising number of relatively well-planned warehousing operations have been let down to some extent by the inadequacy of their load/unload facilities. One possible reason is that the work involved, particularly in the receiving area, is dependent upon external factors which can be difficult to control. Much more attention is being paid to how products are being delivered into the warehousing system, how well they are modularised, whether the quantities delivered relate accurately to the order quantity, whether the delivery on time, early or late, and how easy is a consignment to identify. Lack of attention to these and many other factors has caused delays, congested loading docks and made unnecessary work, but above all inadequate communication has contributed to the confusion. More and more VDU terminals are being located directly at the receiving point. Their ability to identify rapidly whether a consignment is required, to state what level of quality control should be applied and to show where the product is to be located, contributes greatly to the smooth and accurate flow of product.

The other major factors are what area should be allocated to the function, how many loading bays are required, whether the loading bays should have raised docks or be at floor level, and whether the loading and unloading areas should share common facilities or be separated. Their determination is by analysis of the products and their load unitisation, the quantities throughput per unit of time, the kinds of transport entering and leaving the systems and other criteria such as the value of the product together with safety and environmental requirements. The increasing costs of transportation are forcing some companies to consider more carefully ways of means of turning around vehicles to maximise productivity, nowhere more so than in Japan, where much attention is being paid to the mass-loading of different types of road vehicle.

Figure 36.10 is a general view of a modern loading bay.

CONCLUSION

Much remains to be done to improve standards of warehouse operation and management but evidence exists that over the past ten years the business world has become increasingly aware of the importance of the subject and how its costs need to be controlled. This may be seen by looking at the organisational and managerial changes which have been taking place in specific companies and

Figure 36.10   General view of a modern loading bay

recognition that formalised training in the skills of distribution are a necessity. Slowly universities and other educational establishments are beginning to introduce courses which will enable future warehouse managers to establish status which equates with that of more fashionable disciplines. Perhaps by the year 2000 a new professional class will be fully established.

FURTHER READING

Burton, J.A., *Effective Warehousing*, Macdonald & Evans, Plymouth, 2nd edition, 1979

Gattorna, J. (ed.), *Handbook of Physical Distribution Management*, Gower, 3rd edition, 1983

37 International trade

R C Horsley, Dennis Lock and Avison Wormald

It is obvious that any company seeking to achieve a high volume of sales will want the biggest possible market. In this context, export markets are ignored at the company's peril. The benefits of high export performance are well known: in addition to contributing to the balance of payments, higher levels of production should reduce product costs and thus improve the company's competitive position nationally and internationally, increasing profitability and creating jobs.

Unfortunately, export markets often seem remote and involve dealing in strange languages, currencies and national customs. Moreover, every new exporter is faced with a formidable barrier of unfamiliar legislation, documents and jargon. This chapter explains some of the terms associated with international trade and outlines the procedures involved.

FREIGHT FORWARDING AGENTS

The use of a good freight forwarding agent will be found invaluable to any company sending goods overseas by any mode of transport. Indeed, the agent can usually advise on the best method of transport to adopt in any individual case. One very important aspect of a forwarding agent's services is found when relatively small consignments are to be despatched. The agent is often able to 'consolidate' such small loads from a number of clients to form one bulk consignment – probably large enough to fill a container or large vehicle and so effect economy of scale.

Although they are termed 'forwarding agents' the role of such organisations is not confined to the loading of goods on to a ship, aircraft, train or road transport vehicle. There is an equally important function to be performed at the receiving port or airport and at international frontier customs posts. The agents operate international networks, either with their own offices overseas or through collaboration with other agencies. Using telex and other rapid forms of communication the progress of all consignments is monitored and necessary action taken to minimise delays at customs offices and to ensure smooth transfer from aircraft to truck, from ship to rail, and so on.

When road transport is used, agents are more likely to be able to make up bulk loads which quality for TIR treatment. This is an arrangement where the total load is sealed within a vehicle or container by customs officials before the start of a journey. A *transport international routier* (hence TIR) carnet is issued. Provided that the seals are not broken by unauthorised persons, the whole load enjoys a smoother passage through overseas customs formalities. Such loads are identified by the familiar TIR plates fitted to the backs of trucks.

Unfortunately, any operation connected with the consignment of goods seems to be weighed down with complicated documents. Some of these are outlined in the following section of this chapter. Here again the freight forwarding agent's experience will be found useful – invaluable in the case of companies new to exporting.

DOCUMENTATION

This section describes the main documents involved in international trade.

Bill of lading

A bill of lading is used when goods are transported by ship. It records the contract entered into between the shipper and the exporter and, when sent to the buyer, acts as a document of title enabling him to claim the goods. An example is shown in Figure 37.1.

The principal information given on the form includes:

1 The bill of lading serial number
2 The name of the shipping company
3 The name of the ship
4 Port of loading
5 Port of unloading
6 The final destination
7 A description of the goods
8 The number of separate cases, with their weights, dimensions and markings
9 Name and address of the exporter
10 Name and address of the consignee, or the organisation to be notified when the goods arrive (in the latter case the bill is made out to 'order')
11 A statement indicating whether or not freight charges have been prepaid, and where such charges are payable.

The document is usually prepared as an original plus one or more copies, the number of such copies (all called 'originals') being shown on each one. The exporter signs each original. The set customarily comprises two or three such originals, each of them signed by the ship's captain or his agent when the goods are loaded. The exporter is given all the originals, and these are known as the 'negotiable' copies, any one of which can prove title to the goods. One original, negotiable copy is sent to the buyer or his agent, by a route faster than the sea voyage, to enable him to clear the goods at the destination port. Other non-negotiable copies are prepared and kept for control and record purposes.

Figure 37.1   A bill of lading

Air waybill

Goods sent by airfreight are consigned under cover of an air waybill (alternatively spelled airwaybill or airway bill). An example is shown in Figure 37.2. Air waybills do not have the same commercial significance as the bills of lading used for shipping, but they are used to control and progress the passage of goods and to identify the consignment through all its stages. In this context, the air waybill number is the vital reference. When a freight forwarding agent is used, he provides his own air waybill forms (known as house air waybills) and it is one of these which is shown in the example.

Commercial invoice

The commercial invoice is an invoice prepared on the exporter's usual invoice form, for despatch to the buyer as a claim for payment. However, additional copies will have to be supplied for use by the customs authorities at the exporting and importing ends of the journey. Requirements vary from one country to another, and some require additional information to be given, such as import licence number, the commission payable to local agents, details of freight and other charges, and so on.

Special requirements

Some countries add their own demands to the weight of paper needed. Such extra forms may include a *certificate of origin*, where the exporter declares the country of origin of the goods, and a *consular invoice*, which is a form of invoice dictated by (but not provided by) the government of the importing country. Two examples of documents which combine both of these documents are shown in Figure 37.3. The exporter usually has to obtain his own stock of such forms from a printer.

Certificate of insurance

Where the exporter arranges insurance, cover should be obtained for all stages and operations of the journey. The certificate, which must not be dated *after* the date of the bill of lading, air waybill or similar evidence of despatch, is sent to the buyer with the shipping documents.

TERMS OF TRADE USED IN INTERNATIONAL BUSINESS

(with acknowledgement to the International Chamber of Commerce)

Ex works

'Ex works' means that the seller's only responsibility is to make the goods available at his premises (i.e. works or factory). In particular he is not

GHM

JARDINE
AIR CARGO

A MEMBER OF THE MATHESON GROUP OF COMPANIES
Jardine Air Cargo (UK) Ltd
Service House, Great South West Road
Feltham, Middlesex. TW14 0PL
Telephone 01-890 1355 Telex 934157
Reg. office 3 Lombard Street, London EC3
Reg. no. 445388 England
IATA International Air Cargo Consolidator VAT Reg. no. 244 2321 96

CRN	Invoice No./HAWB
Booked Flight Date	Date
Destination Airport	Master/Air Waybill No.
Departure Airport	Import Waybill No. (if transit)

Shipper — Shipper's Reference — Shipper's Account No.

Consignee

Destination A/c. No. | A/L A/c No.

Tel | Telex

Branch | Wt.

Attention of — Consignee's Order No. — Final Destination

Invoice to (if different) — Also Notify

Rotation No

Tel | Telex

Air Consignment Waybill
NOT NEGOTIABLE

Nature and Quantity of Goods, including any Special Packing Instructions	Method of Packing	Marks and Nos	Dimensions or Volume	Rate Class	Chargeable Wt lbs kgs	Rate lbs kgs £	Charge £	No. of Packages	Actual Gross Weight kgs
							Total	Total-in figs	Total-in figs

Documents Accompanying Air Waybill

Amount of Insurance - in words | Amount of Insurance - in figures

Shipper's COD - in words | Shipper's Declared Customs Value

Shipper Certifies that the particulars on the face hereof are correct and agrees to the conditions on the reverse hereto.
By Broker/Agent

Carrier Certifies above described goods were received for carriage SUBJECT TO THE CONDITIONS ON THE REVERSE OF COPIES 1 & 8 the goods being in apparent good order and condition except as noted hereon.

We hereby certify that the goods described were despatched by AIRCRAFT/SERVICE NO ' on the to the above mentioned Consignee and that a copy of this Consignment Note was forwarded to the Consignee by the Aircraft carrying the goods.

Note of any Advance Payments | Executed on

Cash Received

Date | Signature of Issuing Carrier or its Agent

Signature

At Originating Branch

All Business is undertaken subject to the Company's Conditions (on the reverse of Copies 1 & 8) which incorporates the 1981 Standard Trading Conditions of the Institute of Freight Forwarders Limited.

TATE BUSINESS FORMS LTD

	PREPAID CHARGES £	VAT Code	COLLECT CHARGES £	VAT Code
Transit Charges	2		Transit Charges 2	
FOB	3		FOB 3	
Misc.	4		Misc. 4	
Cartage	5		Cartage 5	
Sub Total Comp. Chge			Sub Agents Disb. 6	
Airline VAT 7	Air Freight 1		COD 7	
Airline Charges 8			COD Fee 8	
	Pre VAT Total 1		Air Freight	
Sub Agents Comm. 8	VAT 0			
This invoice is VAT rated at Zero 9	Total 9		Total 9	
	PAYABLE BY SHIPPER		PAYABLE BY CONSIGNEE	

Payment is due now, unless credit terms have been agreed, remit to:
HEAD OFFICE, Service House, Great South West Road
Feltham, Middlesex, TW14 0PL

1. ORIGINAL - FOR THE SHIPPER

Figure 37.2 **Air waybill**
(Jardine Air Cargo (UK) Ltd)

In accordance with Nigerian Government Notice 1989 of 1970.

FEDERATION of NIGERIA

Combined Certificate of Value and of Origin and Invoice of Goods for
Exportation to Nigeria

C.16

CERTIFICATE OF VALUE

I, ...

of . . . .

*Manufacturers/Suppliers/Exporters of the goods enumerated in this invoice amounting to . . . .

hereby declare that I have the authority to make and sign this certificate on behalf of the aforesaid *Manufacturers/
Suppliers/Exporters and that I have the means of knowing and I do hereby certify as follows:—

(1) That this invoice is in all respects correct and contains a true and full statement of the price actually paid or to
be paid for the said goods, and the actual quantity thereof.

(2) That no different invoice of the goods mentioned in the said invoice has been or will be furnished to anyone.

(3) That no arrangement or understanding affecting the purchase price of the said goods has been or will be made
or entered into between the said exporter and purchaser or by anyone on behalf of either of them either by way of
discount, rebate, compensation or in any manner whatever other than as fully shown on this invoice.

CERTIFICATE OF ORIGIN

(1) That all the goods mentioned in this invoice have been wholly produced or manufactured in. . . . .

. . . .

(2) That all the goods mentioned in this invoice have been either wholly or partially produced or manufactured in

. . . .

(3) That as regards those goods only partially produced or manufactured,

(a) the final process or processes of manufacture have been performed in . . . .

(b) the expenditure in material produced and/or labour performed in . . . . .calculated
subject to qualifications hereunder, in the case of all such goods is not less than 25 per cent of the factory or works
costs of all such goods in their finished state. *See note below.

(4) That in the calculation of such proportion of material produced and/or labour performed none of the following
items has been included or considered:—

Manufacturer's profit, or remuneration of any trader, agent, broker or other person dealing in the goods in their
finished condition; royalties; cost of outside packages, or any cost of packing the goods thereinto; any cost of conveying, insuring, or shipping the goods subsequent to their manufacture.

Dated at . . . . .this . . . . day of . . . . 19 . . . .

(Signature). . . . . (Signature of Witness) . . . .

Note: (1) The person making the declaration should be the principal or a manager, chief clerk, secretary, or responsible
employee.

(2) The place or country of origin of imports is that in which the goods were produced or manufactured and, in
the case of partly manufactured goods, the place or country in which any final operation, has altered to any
appreciable extent the character, composition and value of goods imported into that country.

(3) In the case of goods which have at some stage entered into the commerce of, or undergone a process of
manufacture in a foreign country, only that labour and material which are expected in or added to the goods
after their return to the exporting territory, shall be regarded as the produce or manufacture of the territory
in calculating the proportion of labour and material in the factory or works cost of the finished article.

(4) *Delete the inapplicable.

Enumerate the following charges and state whether each amount has been included in or excluded from the above selling price to purchaser:—	Amount in currency of exporting country	State if included in above selling price to purchaser
(1) Cartage to rail and/or docks		
(2) Inland freight (rail or canal) and other charges to the dock area, including inland insurance		
(3) Labour in packing the goods into outside packages		
(4) Value of outside packages		
(5) If the goods are subject to any charge by way of royalties		
(6) OCEAN FREIGHT		
(7) OCEAN INSURANCE		
(8) Commission, establishment and other charges of a like nature		
(9) Other costs, dues, charges and expenses incidental to the delivery of the articles		

State full particulars of Royalties below:—

Form No. 731 Published and Sold by FORMECON SERVICES LTD., Gateway, Crewe, CW1 1YN, England. Tel: 0270-587811 Telex: 36660 Eurofs G.

Figure 37.3a **Combined certificate of value, certificate of origin and consular invoice** *(in the format specified by the Nigerian Government)*

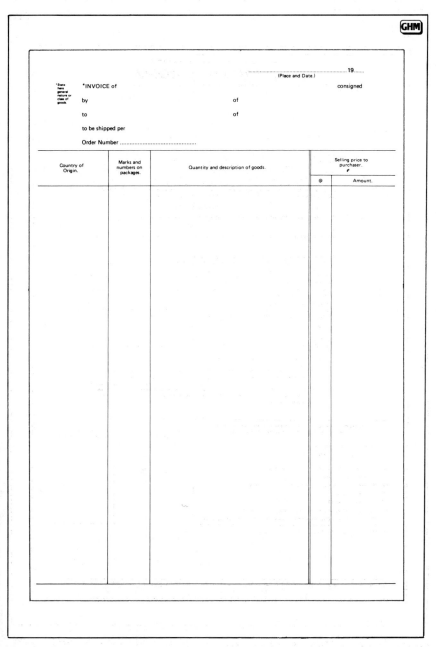

Figure 37.3a (continued)

GHM

SIERRA LEONE

Combined Form of Certificate of Value and of Origin and Invoice of Goods for Exportation to Sierra Leone

(1) Here insert Manager, Chief Clerk, or as the case may be.

(2) Here insert name of firm or company.

(3) Here insert name of city or country.

(4) These words should be omitted when the manufacturer or supplier himself signs the Certificate.

(5) Here insert particulars of any special arrangement.

(6) Seal or stamp of manufacturer or supplier.

I, _____ (1)* _____

of (2) _____ of (3) _____

$\frac{\text{manufacturer}}{\text{†supplier}}$ of the goods specified in this invoice amounting to _____

hereby declare that I [(4) have the authority to make and sign this certificate on behalf of the aforesaid $\frac{\text{manufacturer}}{\text{supplier}}$ and that I] have the means of knowing and do hereby certify as follows:—

1. That this invoice is in all respects correct and contains a true and full statement of the price actually paid or to be paid for the said goods, and the actual quantity thereof.

2. That no arrangements or understanding affecting the purchase price of the said goods have been or will be made or entered into between the exporter and purchaser, or by anyone on behalf of either of them either by way of discount, rebate, compensation or in any manner whatever other than as fully shown on this invoice, or as follows (5)

_____

_____

Dated at _____ this _____ day of _____ 19____

(Signature) _____

(Signature of Witness) _____

Enumerate the following charges and state whether each amount has been included in or excluded from the selling price to purchaser:—

	Amount in currency of exporting country	State if included in the selling price to purchaser
(1) Cartage to rail, docks or aircraft		
(2) Inland freight (rail or canal) and other charges to the dock area including Inland Insurance		
(3) Labour in packing the goods into outside packages		
(4) Cost of outside packages		
(5) Discounts		
(6) OCEAN FREIGHT		
(7) OCEAN INSURANCE		
(8) Commission, establishment and other charges of a like nature		
(9) Other costs, dues, charges and expenses incidental to the delivery of the goods at the proper port or place in Sierra Leone		

* The person making the declaration should be a principal or a manager, chief clerk, secretary, or responsible employee.
† The word "supplier" may be interpreted as including the actual exporter or consignor of the goods in Sierra Leone.

This invoice should bear the printed letter heading of the manufacturer or supplier. For casual exporters a commercial invoice with printed letter heading bearing the undermentioned certificate in support of this certified invoice must be attached:— "We hereby declare that this commercial invoice is in support of the attached certified invoice number................................ and that the particulars shown on the certified invoice are true and correct in every detail."

No. 743

Figure 37.3b Combined certificate of value, certificate of origin and consular invoice (in the format specified by the Sierra Leone Government)

GHM

INVOICE No... ....19..........
(Place and Date).

*State
here
general
nature or
class of
goods

INVOICE of*   consigned

by   of

to   of

to be shipped per

Order Number......................................   ....
Country from which consigned.

Country of Origin.	Marks and numbers on packages.	Quantity and description of goods.	Selling price to purchaser.	
			@	Amount

Figure 37.3b   (continued)

responsible for loading the goods in the vehicle provided by the buyer unless otherwise agreed. The buyer bears the full cost and risk involved in bringing the goods from there to the desired destination. This term therefore represents the minimum obligation for the seller.

Free carrier (named point)

This term has been designed to meet the requirements of modern transport, particularly such 'multimodal' transport as container or 'roll on – roll off' traffic by trailers and ferries. It is based on the same main principle as FOB except that the seller fulfills his obligations when he delivers the goods into the custody of the carrier at the named point. If no precise *point* can be mentioned at the time of the contract of sale, the parties should refer to the *place* or *range* where the carrier should take the goods into his charge. The risk of loss of or damage to the goods is transferred from seller to buyer at that time and not at the ship's rail. 'Carrier' means any person by whom or in whose name a contract of carriage by road, rail, air, sea or a combination of modes has been made. When the seller has to furnish a bill of lading, waybill or carrier's receipt, he duly fulfils this obligation by presenting such a document issued by a person so defined.

FOR/FOT

FOR and FOT mean 'free on rail' and 'free on truck'. These terms are synonymous since the word 'truck' relates to the railway wagons. They should obviously only be used when the goods are to be carried by rail.

FOB

FOB means 'free on board'. The goods are placed on board a ship by the seller at a port of shipment named in the sales contract. The risk of loss of or damage to the goods is transferred from the seller to the buyer when the goods pass the ship's rail.

FOB airport

FOB airport is based on the same main principle as the ordinary FOB term. The seller fulfils his obligations by delivering the goods to the air carrier at the airport of departure. The risk of loss of or damage to the goods is transferred from the seller to the buyer when the goods have been so delivered.

FAS

FAS means 'free alongside ship'. Under this arrangement the seller's obligations are fulfilled when the goods have been placed alongside the ship on the quay or in lighters. This means that the buyer has to bear all costs and risks of loss of or damage to the goods from that moment. It should be noted that, unlike FOB, an FAS transaction requires the buyer to clear the goods for export.

C & F

C & F means 'cost and freight'. The seller must pay the costs and freight necessary to bring the goods to the named destination, but the risk of loss of or damage to the goods, as well as of any cost increases, is transferred from the seller to the buyer when the goods pass the ship's rail in the port of shipment.

CIF

CIF means 'cost, insurance and freight'. This arrangement is the same as C & F but with the addition that the seller has to procure marine insurance against the risk of loss of or damage to the goods during the carriage. The seller contracts with the insurer and pays the insurance premium.

Freight/carriage paid to

Like C & F 'freight or carriage paid to . . .' means that the seller pays the freight for the carriage of the goods to the named destination. However, the risk of loss of or damage to the goods, as well as of any cost increases, is transferred from the seller to the buyer when the goods have been delivered into the custody of the first carrier and not at the ship's rail. It can be used for all modes of transport including multimodal operations and container or roll on – roll off traffic by trailers and ferries. When the seller has to furnish a bill of lading, waybill or carrier's receipt, he duly fulfils this obligation by presenting such a document issued by the person with whom he has contracted for carriage to the named destination.

Freight/carriage and insurance paid to

This term means the same as 'freight or carriage paid to . . .' but with the addition that the seller has to procure transport insurance against the risk of loss of or damage to the goods during the carriage. The seller contracts with the insurer and pays the insurance premium.

Ex ship

'Ex ship' means that the seller shall make the goods available to the buyer on board the ship at the destination named in the sales contract. The seller has to bear the full cost and risk involved in bringing the goods there.

Ex quay

'Ex quay' means that the seller makes the goods available to the buyer on the quay (wharf) at the destination named in the sales contract. The seller has to bear the full cost and risk involved in bringing the goods there. There are two ex quay contracts in use, namely 'ex quay (duty paid)', and 'ex quay (duties on buyer's account)' (in which the liability to clear the goods for import are to be met by the buyer instead of by the seller). Parties are recommended always to use the full descriptions of these terms, namely 'ex quay (duty paid)' or 'ex quay (duties on buyer's account)' otherwise there may be uncertainty as to who is to be responsible for the liability to clear the goods for import.

Delivered at frontier

'Delivered at frontier' means that the seller's obligations are fulfilled when the goods have arrived at the frontier – but before the 'customs border' of the country named in the sales contract. The term is primarily intended to be used when goods are to be carried by rail or road but it may be used irrespective of the mode of transport.

Delivered duty paid

While the term 'ex works' signifies the seller's minimum obligation, the term 'delivered duty paid' when followed by words naming the buyer's premises denotes the other extreme – the seller's maximum obligation. The term 'delivered duty paid' may be used irrespective of the mode of transport. If the parties wish that the seller should clear the goods for import but that some of the costs payable upon the import of the goods should be excluded – such as value added tax (VAT) and/or other similar taxes – this should be made clear by adding words to this effect (for example, 'exclusive of VAT and/or taxes').

DUTY

Duty is the money payable by a consignee to the appropriate authorities before he can take receipt of goods imported or released from bond. Types of duty as far as the UK is concerned are:

1   Customs duty
2   Excise duty

Customs duty

Customs duty is money payable by a consignee or his agent to the customs and excise when goods are imported from abroad. It includes all levies and charges due in respect of the Common Agricultural Policy of the European Economic Community (EEC) which are collected on behalf of the EEC and paid to Brussels. The amount of duty payable is shown in the customs tariff.

Customs duty ad valorem

Ad valorem duty is expressed in the customs tariff as a percentage of the CIF value of the goods (invoice value, plus freight, plus insurance and plus other dutiable charges).

Customs duty specific

In this instance the amount of duty payable is expressed in the tariff as a sum levied against the quantity of goods (for example, 1.645 European units of account per hectalitre).

Payment of customs duty

Duty can be paid immediately by one of the following methods:

1   cash
2   guaranteed cheque
3   banker's draft

Payment may be deferred.

Deferred payment of customs duty

Importers or their agents are allowed to defer payment of certain customs duty and other charges for a 30 day period subject to the lodgement of adequate security (usually a guarantee from the consignee's bank that the money will be available when called for by direct debit). Excise duty and sums payable in respect of underpayment on previous imports cannot be deferred.

Duty free goods

No customs duty is payable on the following types of goods:

1   Those shown in the customs tariff as 'free'
2   Those imported from the EEC and supported by the correct EEC documentation. (Note: To obtain release of these goods duty may have to be paid on deposit if the documentation is incorrect or incomplete).

The expression 'duty free' is used by customs to imply that customs duty has, in fact, been paid. In regulations affecting customs warehouses the expression is used constantly and care must be taken to avoid the misconception that duty was not liable at any stage of the import.

Excise duty

This is a UK tax on certain imported goods and the money collected remains with the Exchequer. The money is payable by a consignee or his agent to customs and excise when goods which attract the duty are required to be released from customs control. The amount of duty payable on such goods is shown in the tariff and the types of goods which attract such duty are:

spirits
wines
beers
tobacco
hydrocarbon oils
cigarette lighters

Excise duty payment

Excise duty cannot be deferred and must be paid before release of the goods by customs. Payment can be in cash, by guaranteed cheque or by bankers draft (as described for customs duty above), or by deposit in advance to enable customs to maintain a gross payment account.

Excise duty – gross payment accounts

Gross payment accounts are maintained for each of the differing classes of goods (separate accounts for spirits, wines, and beers and so on). The consignee or his agent pays to customs and excise a sum of money to cover anticipated needs over a trading period, adding to it as it is used so that there is always sufficient money in the accounts to cover duties payable on goods to be withdrawn from the store.

Goods subject to customs and excise duty

Goods subject to excise duty will, if imported from outside the EEC, also attract customs duty. The customs duty may be paid at the port of entry, in which case the goods are stored in bond as customs duty paid (described by customs and excise as 'duty free'). If, however, the customs duty has not been paid then the goods are stored as customs duty unpaid. Customs duty liable on goods in store may be paid in advance of or concurrently with excise duty before release of the goods. This customs duty may be 'deferred' but the excise duty cannot be so treated. Customs duty may, however, be paid through a gross payment account if such is maintained.

BONDS

A bond is a cover, negotiated by a consignee or his agent with his bank or insurance company, to ensure that all sums due in respect of duty or penalties imposed will be paid by the bonder in the event of the consignee or his agent failing to meet customs demands or to comply with the regulations.

Removal bond

A bond required to cover the movement, from one place to another, of goods on which duty, customs and/or excise duty is liable and has not been paid. Such bonds can be individual for single movements or standing.

Transhipment bond

A bond required to cover the transfer of goods from an arrival port (sea or air) when such goods are subject to customs and/or excise duty. Such bonds are usually standing.

General bond

A bond which embraces both removal and transhipment, and acts as security for the payment of duty when goods subject to customs duty are moved, removed or held pending their use in manufacture.

(Penalty) bond

This is a bond in a sum laid down by customs and excise in respect of duty (customs and/or excise) payable in respect of goods stored under control, pending payment of such duty. This is the type of bond which covers the operation of a warehouse in which goods subject to excise duty are stored.

BONDED WAREHOUSES

Bonded warehouses are premises approved by the Commissioners of Customs and Excise for storage of goods without payment of duty. An authorised bonded warehouse can only be used for the storage of those goods for which it has been approved.

Types of bonded warehouse

There are four types of bonded warehouse:

1 *Customs warehouse* – for the deposit, without payment of duty, of imported goods which are liable to customs duty but which are not liable to excise duty.
2 *Excise warehouse* – for the deposit, without payment of excise duty, of goods which are liable to excise duty. In this case the customs duty, if applicable, will have been paid.
3 *Customs and excise warehouse* – for the deposit, without payment of customs or excise duty, of goods which are liable to both customs and excise duty.
4 *Tobacco warehouse* – for the deposit, without payment of customs or excise duty, of tobacco and tobacco products liable to customs and excise duty.

Categories of bonded warehouse

There are two categories of bonded warehouse:

1 *Crown locked* – controlled by the presence of a customs officer. The building is secured with Crown locks and the warehouse keeper's own locks, so that the warehouse keeper only has access to the goods under supervision of the customs officer
2 *Open warehouse* – in which the premises are not normally Crown locked and a customs officer is not constantly present. The warehouse keeper has unrestricted access to the goods during the hours of opening.

Classes of open warehouse

Open warehouses are described as class A or class B according to the following rules:

Class A warehouses

Are those approved for beer, wines and spirits. In this class of open warehouse the goods must be kept within strictly defined and secure limits. Storage must be arranged so that consignments are easily identifiable, and to separate those goods liable only to excise duty from those which are liable to excise and customs duty. Such a warehouse will be the subject of a bond, the limits being set by HM Customs and Excise.

Class B warehouse

Are those approved for goods other than beer, wines and spirits. The goods may be stored anywhere within the warehouse, subject to their being easily identifiable by a visiting customs officer. A bond is not normally required but the company is expected to maintain a duty deferment in a sum which is at least equal to the amount of duty payable on the goods stored. Class B open warehouses subdivide into two further kinds:

1 *General warehouse* – where the space is to be available to the general public on demand.
2 *Franchise warehouse* – for the storage of a manufacturer's own goods pending operation for re-export.

FOREIGN EXCHANGE

The simplest international transaction can lead to problems in pricing and payment. The price to a foreign buyer can be in the seller's currency, in the buyer's or in a third 'international' currency such as the US dollar. For the seller, his own currency has the advantage that he knows exactly how much he is going to receive, although he (or his government) may prefer another currency if his own is depreciating rapidly, in value.*

The buyer, on the other hand, will have to purchase the necessary foreign currency, and in most cases the rate of exchange between his own currency and

---

*The text of this chapter from here on is taken directly or adapted from Avison Wormwald's chapter in *Handbook of Financial Planning and Control*, Gower, 1981

the foreign currency will not be fixed. So at least between the time of quotation and the acceptance there may be a change, favourable or unfavourable. He therefore may well prefer a quotation in his own currency or a third, such as the US dollar, which may be more familiar to him than the seller's.

The fact that the foreign exchange transaction offers both sides the opportunity for gain as well as loss is generally immaterial, since the business-man, either buyer or seller, will generally prefer not to have to bother about the speculative element. That is for the professional risk taker in currencies.

In the first place, the buyer can merely purchase the necessary foreign exchange to pay for the goods when he decides to accept the offer made. In this way he knows exactly how much the goods cost him. The foreign exchange can be deposited in a bank and will earn interest. The rate of interest, however, even on a time deposit, will frequently be below that obtainable by some alternative use of the funds. But in this way virtually all the risk has been covered, although if the exchange rate moves in favour of his own currency there will obviously have been a '*manque à gagner*' or a lost opportunity, since he would not be able to buy the currency more cheaply.

It will not always be convenient to immobilise funds in this way, a long time ahead perhaps of the payment which has to be made, or the rate of interest which can be earned may not be considered sufficient. In this case there exists the alternative of the forward exchange market. This may be of advantage to the seller also, in the contrary case where he has quoted in the buyer's currency, or in a third currency; he may wish to know at the time of concluding the trans-action how much he will receive in his own currency.

The forward exchange market, to which access may be obtained through any major commercial bank, will provide a quotation for a contract to buy or sell a wide range of currencies for delivery up to normally six months ahead. Contracts for longer periods are possible but can be very expensive.

According to the view the international money market takes of the two currencies involved, the price of the currency purchased may be higher or lower than the present price. Equally, when the contract matures and the currency is delivered it may be found that the contract price may be higher or lower than the then prevailing price. The rates for the principal currencies against the pound sterling are quoted daily in the London *Financial Times* for one month and three months.

If the forward exchange contract is made through the buyer's normal bank it may involve no down-payment at all, and therefore the funds are available for different uses. In other cases it may involve the payment of 5–10 per cent of the value, according to the credit status of the buyer and the risk involved in the particular currency. The buyer of the 'forward exchange' now knows exactly how much he will eventually have to pay, if he is the buyer of the goods, or receive if he is the seller. He will not have tied up his funds, but he will have preferred the judgement of the market to his own as regards the future relation-ship between the two currencies concerned.

These two arrangements can be combined in some cases (and dependent on exchange control regulations that may be in force) to produce a *foreign currency swap*. In this case the foreign currency is purchased in the 'spot' market and simultaneously a forward contract is arranged to sell the same amount of the currency at a future specified date. This is to cover the case when, for example, funds have to be advanced but will later be repaid in the same currency. There are also credit 'swaps' available in some countries: a bank in the foreign country makes a loan to a local borrower, for example a subsidiary of a foreign multinational, accepting the foreign exchange risk but of course charging interest on this loan. The foreign company then grants a loan to the bank outside the country, and normally this loan will be larger than the first so that the bank is compensated for the exchange risk and expenses.

All the foregoing arrangements are 'hedging' or safety devices to limit the risks implied in handling transactions involving foreign currencies. (In the strictly technical sense these measures are used to eliminate or reduce 'uncertainty', which is distinct from 'risk' in that it is possible to assign probability values to the latter.) It should be noted that normally it will be considered that the domestic currency is 'safer' than the foreign currency, since in effect the main part of the business of the buyer or seller is in any case inextricably involved in its own currency, good or bad. To take a 'bear' view of one's own currency and to hold funds in foreign currencies is normally considered to be speculative and, of course, may even be illegal.

PAYMENT AND CREDIT IN INTERNATIONAL TRADE

The question of payment arises in the simplest international transaction and it is therefore natural that there should be a wide range of methods for dealing with it and with the related problem of credit. These arrangements also cover the important aspect of 'bridging' finance: that is to say financing the exporter's outlay over the (frequently long) period between the shipment of goods and receipt of payment.

The letter of credit

The normal risks of commercial transactions are greatly increased in international trading, frequently because there is less knowledge on the part of one or both parties to a transaction about the other. Commercial practices differ greatly from country to country and there may be difficulties, imaginary as well as real, in obtaining recourse in the courts against one of the parties. The exchange risks already discussed also affect the arrangements in most cases.

The letter of credit has an important place in the list of arrangements designed to reduce risk. It consists essentially of an undertaking given by a bank, on behalf of its client, to a third party to the effect that it will honour its drafts on it provided that they comply in every respect with the requirements specified in the letter itself.

Since it constitutes an obligation to pay, the bank will require that it be backed by the necessary funds or that the bank should have control, partial or complete, over the goods involved in the transaction. Normally the credit will be irrevocable; if it is 'revocable' (in very rare instances) then the conditions under which it can be revoked will obviously have to be very precisely spelled out, otherwise the credit is valueless as a guarantee.

Letters of credit have value to both buyer and seller and the initiative to use them may come from either party to a transaction. To the seller it guarantees that the funds for payment are available; if it provides that payment may be made in his own currency it eliminates the exchange risk. If the credit is 'confirmed' through a branch or correspondent bank in the seller's country the guarantee obviously extends to payment as distinct from the availability of funds and then becomes virtually total. To the buyer also the letter of credit may have value since it immediately establishes, normally at very little cost, that his creditworthiness is unimpeachable, while it removes any risk there might have been in advance payment, if such were required by the seller.

The form of letters of credit, the legal situation, the costs and extent of discounting facilities differ from country to country so that both sides should obtain detailed information from their banks on these points. An example of an irrevocable letter of credit is shown in Figure 37.4.

The choice of payment method

Briefly the choices are between an irrevocable credit opened by the buyer in a bank in the name of the supplier and other methods mentioned above. The irrevocable letter of credit gives total security of payment, as far as both buyer and seller at least are concerned, but the seller may not obtain the funds until the goods are delivered. It is also mainly used where the seller has some doubt at least about the creditworthiness of the buyer.

Broadly speaking the choice of other methods will be between bank loans, or overdraft facilities (especially in the UK), and commercial paper which can be discounted or sold outright in the bill market. The value of commercial paper depends essentially on the credit standing of the parties concerned, and on whether it has been 'accepted' (see below) by a recognised financial institution, in the UK, a major commercial bank or an 'accepting house' or merchant banker. When the paper is graded first-class it is the cheapest available source of funds, normally being at least 0.25 per cent cheaper than bank loans, and in times of tight money this spread can be up to 2.0 per cent. This method also has the advantage that it does not affect the general debt structure of the business, since it is self-liquidating. It should be clear that it can be used independently of shipping documents; in other words the sale can be on 'open account' if the relations between buyer and seller make this preferable, while the financing arrangements are made in parallel but independently of particular shipments.

Documentary credits, in the form of bills of exchange payable for example at 30, 60 or 90 days are generally preferred since they can be discounted in the bill market through the seller's bank and enable him to obtain his money much earlier. In most countries banks themselves will advance loans on bills of exchange, where the credit of the supplier is sufficiently good. A frequently used form of bank credit is the time draft which is drawn on the bank at the same time as the bill of exchange. Whichever method is used depends on the credit standing of buyer and seller, which in turn will affect the cost of the

EXCEL BANK LTD

From:-

Excel Bank Ltd.
Registered in England
(No. 00000)

Registered Office
1074, Lombard Street,
London EC2P 2BX

Overseas Branch
P.O. Box 181760
70 St. Mary's Avenue
London EC3P 3BN
Telephone 01 000 0000 Extn:3259
Telex 000000
Telegrams Excelbank London

To:-

Camside Engineering (Cambridge) Ltd.
Chesterton,
Cambridge.

Advice of:-

Popular Bank of Africa
Mtwara
Tanzania

Irrevocable credit which bears the confirmation
of Excel Bank Ltd.

Dear Sirs,

We inform you that the above-named bank have opened with us their irrevocable credit in your favour on account of Haji Bwanamkubwa and Partners, of 24 Port Compound, Mtwara, Tanzania, to the extent of £8,000.00 (say Eight Thousand Pounds) valid at this office until 12 noon on 23rd September 19...., on or before which your drafts on us at sight may be paid if accompanied by the under-mentioned documents evidencing current shipment from Liverpool to Mtwara, Tanzania of the goods described below. The buyer's order number and reference is U.K. 1754. Part shipments prohibited. All documents to be in English. We confirm that no import licence is required for these goods on entering Tanzania.

Set of 3 clean shipped Bills of Lading issued in favour of Popular Bank of Africa, Mtwara, Tanzania, marked "FREIGHT PAID" showing the amount of freight paid.

A clean Report of Findings must be obtained from General Superintendents, Liverpool, and must accompany the other documents; also a packing list in 3 copies.

Copy of your advice note sent to Popular Bank of Africa advising details of shipment for insurance purposes, enabling them to insure in good time.

Commercial Invoice in 9 copies, showing the F.O.B. value and freight charges shown separately, giving, in all a C & F value.

Covering 8 Water Purifying units Type SD1756 at agreed price of £640 per unit
 2 aerators Type TD15 at agreed price of £540 each

We are informed that insurance will be effected by the buyers with State Insure, (Tanzania) Ltd, Mtwara, Tanzania.

Shipment must be effected in Palmate Line Vessels only. All drafts drawn under this credit to bear the clause "Drawn under Doc. Credit No 17,777,777."

We are requested to advise you of the terms of the credit, which is irrevocable on the part of our principals and also bears our confirmation. Subject to Uniform Customs and Practice for Documentary Credits (1974 Revision) International Chamber of Commerce Publication No. 290.

Figure 37.4   An irrevocable letter of credit
(Formecon Services Ltd)

transaction, and the extent to which the seller at least can finance the transaction himself.

The residual risk in these transactions is covered partially at least as far as the bank is concerned by insurance of the goods, sometimes material proof that the goods exist in the form of warehouse receipts, frequently stipulations as to the nature of the goods, e.g. that they should be readily saleable in the event of default, and finally credit insurance.

Credit insurance

This originated some sixty years ago and has increased steadily in volume and scope. It can confidently be said that the bulk of trade with the communist countries would not have been possible without it because of the lack of experience of most firms in the West in dealing with these countries, the very stringent requirements laid upon them by the buyers and the long credit terms frequently required.

The manner of operation of the British Export Credits Guarantee Department (ECGD) is typical of the many institutions, governmental and private, which now provide these services in all the principal trading countries of the west. There are 'tailor-made' policies for large capital goods, and similar transactions. The ECGD guarantees can be used as security against bank loans and thus greatly facilitate the financing of longer term projects. Normally of course a proportion of the risk, sometimes quite small, must be assumed by the seller.

These facilities, although increasingly used, are likely to be rather expensive so that other alternatives may be considered. Either the seller or the buyer, for example, can raise money through an issue of debt either in the national or the international money market, the terms being geared to the length of the repayment period, long term rates tending to be higher than short term.

HELPFUL ORGANISATIONS

British Overseas Trade Board
1 Victoria Street
London SW1H 0ET

Department of Trade
Export Services and Promotions
  Division
Export House
50 Ludgate Hill
London EC4M 7HU

Export Credits Guarantee Department
Aldermanbury House
Aldermanbury
London EC2P 2EL

H M Customs and Excise
King's Beam House
Mark Lane
London EC3R 7HE

Technical Help to Exporters
British Standards Institution
Maylands Avenue
Hemel Hempstead
Hertfordshire HP2 4SQ

FURTHER READING

Croner's Reference Book for Exporters, Croner Publications, New Malden, Surrey, UK (by subscription: updated monthly).

Croner's Reference Book for Importers, Croner Publications, New Malden, Surrey, UK.

Croner's World Directory of Freight Conferences, Croner Publications, New Malden, Surrey, UK (by subscription: updated monthly).

Export Education Packages, Formecon Services Ltd, Crewe, CW1 1YN, UK.

An Introduction to Exporting, Export Finance: Barclays and ECGD and *Documentary Letters of Credit*, all available in the *Barclays Bank Support for Exporters* Series, Barclays Bank International Limited, London, UK.

Paulden, S., *How to Deliver on Time*, Gower, 1977

Wentworth, W., and Christopher, M. (eds.), *Managing International Distribution*, Gower, 1979

38 Managing transport services

F H Woodward

There are two basic activities which are the responsibility of a transport services function:

1 Movement of goods and material necessary for the business
2 Movement of personnel.

In both of the above activities, the objective is to achieve a cost-effective operation in order to reduce the impact of the additional cost burden on product price.

The transport function is called upon to provide a service to every single function within industry. It is hard to name a function which at some time will not require goods, services or personnel to be moved. Because of this broad responsibility to give a service, those engaged in managing transport come into direct contact with all other departments within a company and will incur costs on behalf of those departments. With this licence to accept costs comes the added responsibility of ensuring that value is received for costs incurred, and of checking costs and performance of all activities within the function constantly against alternative services available.

ORGANISATION STRUCTURE

The person responsible at board level for the control of transport operations can vary from the sales director to the company secretary, from the production director to the chief executive. With increased activity in the distribution of goods, and escalation of costs in all areas of transport operations, arguments over the rightful place of the transport function in a company organisation have become more intense. Despite the strength of many proposals, it has become increasingly obvious that there is no answer which would be suitable or acceptable as a general rule for all types of industry.

A company whose activity is centred around the packaging, warehousing and distribution of goods to retail outlets would find that 'transport', a word used in the broadest sense, is responsible for anything up to 40 per cent of annual turnover and would justify direct representation on the board of directors to ensure that a full account of this expenditure is presented at the highest level in the organisation. A company whose transport requirement is only a few cars, and whose budget is a very small part of total company expenditure would not need such total executive responsibility. Unless a company 'sells' transport as a means of adding directly to the profit of the company, in other words, a company engaged in road haulage, then transport is a service function in exactly the same way as the catering activity of a company. The value of this service to the profitability of the company will determine its correct place in the organisation structure.

Line or staff. Line management is that which is responsible for achieving the main objectives of the business. Staff functions are those which assist line management to achieve those objectives. Transport is primarily a line function, especially when applied to the movement of a company product. To manufacture goods and to leave them at the end of the production line is not 'achieving the objectives of the business'. They must be placed before a customer, and to achieve this implies movement or transportation of the product.

The management organisation of a road haulage operation would be of line responsibility, in that the main objective of the business is to achieve profit by selling transport services. In the manufacturing industry, it all depends on who gives the instructions about the movements. If the manufacturing or sales function state where, when and how the goods are to be moved, then the transport function has no line responsibility and merely provides the service requested without question. On the other hand, if the transport function takes over the final stage of customer satisfaction, and is able to decide the method of movement after having been given instructions on where and when, then it is in a position of line responsibility, accountable for its own decisions. Figure 38.1 shows the distinction between line and staff functions in an industrial transport services activity.

Developing the organisation structure

Figures 38.2 to 38.4 show different types of organisation structure suitable for the transport services function of a manufacturing company. The transport services requirement is of a general nature and is not confined to a major warehousing or retailing operation. It is intended that the types of organisation illustrated will assist readers in developing their own organisation structure after taking into consideration their own special needs.

A typical organisation for the transport services function of a single factory location of a small company with only a few cars and light vans and one heavy truck used on local deliveries is shown in Figure 38.2. Dispatches are by local carrier and rail. All vehicle maintenance is carried out at local garages. A dispatch section is established which is responsible for packaging and loading goods on to vehicles.

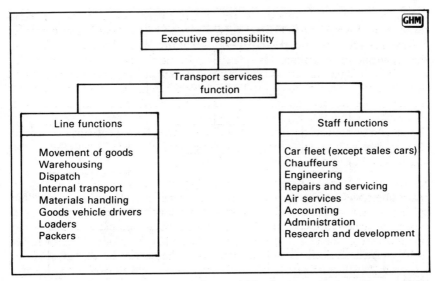

Figure 38.1   Line and staff functions within the transport services activity

Figure 38.2   A simple organisation for a small company

Organisation for the transport services function of a medium-sized company with two factory locations is shown in Figure 38.3. There are twenty cars for management and sales staff use, a number of light vans for customer after-sales service, four trucks for goods delivery to customers and a personnel carrier for personnel movements between factories. Distribution is by company transport and local carrier as well as by rail services. A company garage is available to service and repair the majority of company-owned vehicles.

Figure 38.4 shows the organisation for the transport services function of a large group of companies with many factory locations spread across the United Kingdom. A mixed vehicle fleet of over 2000 has to be controlled and

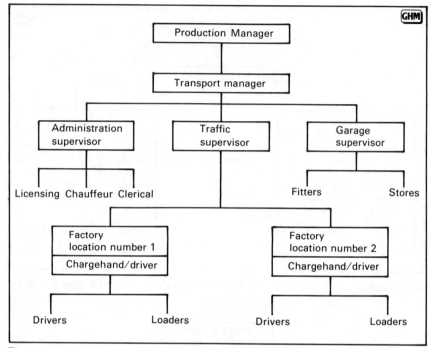

Figure 38.3   Transport services organisation for a medium sized company

administered, consisting of executive and management cars, a large sales fleet of cars and light vans, and a truck fleet exceeding 200 vehicles. A full distribution service from all factory locations to customers is carried out using company vehicles. Local carriers are used to meet peak demands. Extensive use is made of all rail facilities. Company garages are established in each transport location. The whole of the transport function is based on a regional organisation with line responsibility for the movement of company products. A corporate air service is the responsibility of the transport services function.

TRANSPORT MANAGEMENT

One of the conditions for the granting of an Operators' Licence is that the 'person' named in the application to manage that transport operation is 'professionally competent'. This means that future management within the road haulage industry will have to pass the required examination in order to obtain this standard, and a certificate will be issued stating that the person named therein is 'professionally competent'. Although this new requirement for the granting of an Operators' Licence only applies to 'hire and reward' operations, the Certificate of Professional Competence will be a good standard qualification for those 'own account' transport operators who do not offer their services for hire and reward. In recruiting or promoting managers to any

Figure 38.4   Transport services organisation for a large group of companies

transport operation, this 'Certificate' should be the minimum standard asked for.

Before starting to develop any vehicle plan, a number of questions need to be asked:

1   Does the distribution of the product, or movement of personnel need vehicles? Liquids and gases can be distributed by pipeline, personnel can communicate by telephone, closed-circuit television, or data transmission
2   If vehicles are needed, must they be road vehicles? Will railways or aircraft give a more efficient and economic service?
3   If road vehicles are needed, are the services of a haulier or hire car operator more efficient than a company operating its own fleet?
4   If road vehicles are to be operated by the company, should they be leased, on contract hire, or owned?
5   If it is finally decided to have company-owned vehicles, how should they be financed, how many are required, what types are needed, and where are they to be based?

These vital questions are 'ageless' – the answers will affect all future transport planning and must be based on sound commercial reasoning, not only taking into account basic costs, but looking at real costs, including service to the customer and the total value of the whole operation to the overall profitability of the company. The same questions can be used to test current transport policies and to change those policies should the 'answers' differ from the time those initial decisions were taken.

OPERATORS' LICENSING

The Goods Vehicles Operators (Qualifications) Regulations 1977 (as amended by SI 1980 No. 1797) implements EEC Directive 74/561 relating to admission to the occupation of road haulage operators in national and international transport operations.

There are two types of Operators' Licence:

1   *Restricted Licence.* Issued to transport operations where 'hire and reward' does not take place. It can be compared with the old 'C' Licence which was in existence before the 1968 Transport Act. The restricted licence confines the holder to 'own account' operations and *does not* require the employment of a professionally competent person as defined in the Regulations. The licence holder is free to operate both nationally and internationally provided *no* goods are carried for 'hire and reward'. There is no restriction on delivering one's own product or collecting one's own supplies on trucks operating on such a licence. The applicant for this type of licence need satisfy the Licensing Authority only that he is of good repute and has financial standing. if a restricted licence holder uses a goods vehicle to carry for hire and reward, he will be liable to a fine of up to £200. Two convictions in a period of five years will result in the licence being revoked.

2   *Standard Licence.* This licence covers goods vehicles operated for 'hire and reward' and is sub-divided to cover national and international operations or national operations only. The latter licence restricts the holder to carrying goods within the UK only – the licence will specify the type of operation allowed. Before granting a standard licence the Traffic Commissioners will require that a person must be employed to manage the operation and that person is 'professionally competent' by holding a current 'Certificate of Professional Competence' (CPC). To obtain a Standard (International) Licence, the person must hold a CPC with the international qualification. When applying for a standard licence, the applicant must also satisfy the licensing authority that he (the applicant) is of good repute and has financial standing, and the person who holds the certificate of professional competence must be *named* in the application. Where the applicant has more than one operating centre, the licensing authority may require that more than one qualified transport manager be employed. The applicant must also state whether he requires the licence to cover international operations as well as national – it is an offence to use a goods vehicle on international journeys where the licence covers only national operations.

The Certificate of Professional Competence (CPC)

A person will be considered professionally competent if holding:

1 A diploma, or other qualification issued by a body recognised by the Minister of Transport;
   (a) for national and international standard licences:
      – Fellow or Member of Chartered Institute of Transport
      – Member or Associate Member of Institute of Transport Administration
      – Member or Associate Member of Institute of Road Transport Engineers
      – Fellow or Associate of British Association of Removers
   (b) for national operations only:
      – Licentiate of Chartered Institute of Transport
      – Associate of Institute of Road Transport Engineers
      – General Certificate in Removals Management issued by the British Association of Removers
      (NB: The above memberships must be in the road haulage sectors)
2 A certificate of competence issued by the Royal Society of Arts after taking the examination for proof of professional competence. These examinations are held four times a year and are in two parts – national and international.
3 A certificate issued by the Licensing Authority conferring on the applicant 'grandfather rights'. This concession ceased on 31 December 1979, but all certificates issued remain valid for the life of the individual named.

VEHICLE MANAGEMENT AND VEHICLE STANDARDS

The object of setting vehicle operating standards is to obtain the most efficient utilisation of a fleet of vehicles. This is the key to a minimum-cost operation. Standing costs now account for more than half the total operating costs of a vehicle and it follows that the higher the utilisation, the cheaper the cost per mile. Figure 38.5 shows the standing costs and running costs of various types of vehicle.

There are four main areas of vehicle operation where an attack on utilisation can be made, and which can provide a basis for comparison of planned performance against actual performance.

Vehicle preparation

Includes checking of the vehicle before a day's work, driver administration and documentation. Work study techniques can be applied to this area of work, and standard times are easy to establish.

Vehicle loading and unloading

One way of achieving higher productivity is to keep loading and unloading time to a minimum. The use of 'swop bodies', containers and trailers are all ways of preloading vehicles while the motive unit is delivering another load. The size of

	13 tonnes GVW rigid	24 tonnes GVW articulated	32 tonnes GVW articulated	2500cc private car–chauffeur driven
Standing costs per year	£	£	£	£
Licences	421	1 071	1 227	70
Wages (55 hours)	5 200	5 980	6 580	5 720
Insurance	850	1 150	1 450	400
Depreciation	3 100	4 800	5 570	2 500
Total	9 571	13 001	15 007	8 690
Running costs per year (based on 36 000 miles)				
Fuel	3 738	5 400	6 075	3 000
Lubricants	165	180	180	100
Tyres	1 050	1 400	1 650	200
Maintenance	3 600	4 000	5 250	950
Total	8 553	10 980	13 155	4 250

Figure 38.5 Standing costs and running costs of various types of vehicle
(Tables of operating costs, Commercial Motor)

a pallet, side loading, double-deck loading are all areas where a work study investigation may be applied with advantage. The use of vehicle mounted handling aids such as tail lifts, cranes, and special tracking, can all speed up the unloading of a vehicle at customers' premises. Standard forms of labels and consignment notes, colour coding identification of depots, factories, warehouses or customer delivery areas are all ways of speeding up the loading procedure.

Vehicle running time

The running time of a vehicle between two points is governed by the speed limit of the road over which that vehicle has to travel. Figure 38.6 shows the present speed limits in the UK and the generally accepted vehicle speeds used in transport operations as a basis for calculating time taken over road routes.

The working day of a delivery vehicle can be divided into three sections:

1 Proceeding to actual delivery area
2 Delivering the goods in the delivery area
3 Returning to base.

The speed-limit factor will only affect the first and last sections as the main controlling factor in the delivery area is the number of delivery points and the number of units to be delivered at each point.

GHM

Type of road	Type of vehicle	Legal road maximum speed	Acceptable average speed for route calculations
Restricted to 30 mph (built-up areas)	All types of vehicle	30 mph	20 mph
De-restricted roads	*(a)* Goods not exceeding 30 cwt ULW not drawing a trailer	50 mph	32 mph
	(b) Goods vehicles exceeding 30 cwt ULW including articulated vehicles	40 mph	28 mph
	(c) Dual-purpose vehicles not drawing a trailer	60 mph	36 mph
	– Dual carriageway	70 mph	36 mph
	(d) Goods vehicles with draw bar trailer with four or more wheels	30 mph	20 mph
Motorways	*(a)* Goods vehicles including articulated vehicles exceeding 3 tons ULW		36 mph
	(b) All other goods vehicles not drawing a trailer	70 mph	36 mph
	(c) Goods vehicles with draw bar trailer with four or more wheels (except four wheel close coupled)	60 mph	36 mph

Figure 38.6   Speed limits for UK-registered goods vehicles

Delivering the goods

This is an area of uncertainty when trying to calculate standard times of performance and the approach to the problem will differ with each company and product. Calculations can be based on:

1 Number of delivery drops
2 A basic time allowance for each delivery point
3 Standard times for handling each parcel delivered
4 An average speed for the vehicle when delivering in towns.

The setting of vehicle and operating standards in a transport operation is called 'load assessment' and there are many ways of applying these techniques. The object in every case is to establish a standard against which the performance of a driver can be measured.

DRIVERS' HOURS AND RECORDS OF WORK

Drivers hours. The rules setting out the hours of work of drivers and other crew members of goods vehicles over 3.5 tonnes gross vehicle plated weight are contained in EEC Directive 543/69. The rules were made effective in the UK by the following Statutory Instrument: The Road Traffic (Drivers' Ages and Hours of Work) Act 1976 – (Commencement Order No. 2) 1978 – SI 1978 No. 6. Full implementation became effective from 1 January, 1981. Although the EEC rules applied only to goods vehicles over 3.5 tonnes gross vehicle weight, the existing UK restrictions for all other drivers of goods vehicles not covered by the EEC rules remained in force. From 1 January 1981, *three* sets of drivers' hours rules are now in force in the United Kingdom. These are:

1 *EEC rules*

 – for national journeys, these being within the United Kingdom
 – for international journeys, these being to countries which are members of the EEC
2 *Domestic rules*

 – for all drivers of vehicles to which the EEC rules do not apply. These are usually goods vehicles which have a plated weight below the threshold of 3.5 tonnes.

National journeys. The following summarises the drivers' hours rules for national journeys:

Continuous driving period	– maximum 4 hours
Daily driving total	– maximum 8 hours
Weekly driving total	– maximum 48 hours
Fortnightly driving total	– maximum 92 hours
Weekly rest period	– minimum 29 hours *plus* daily rest of 11 hours (total 40 hours)

Daily rest period	– minimum 11 hours
Breaks between driving periods	– *at least* ½ hour after continuous driving for four hours
Breaks between continuous working periods	– at least ½ hour after being *on duty* for 5½ hours irrespective of whether the driver has driven continuously for 4 hours.
Weekly *duty* total	– maximum 60 hours
Daily *working* period spread-over	– maximum 12½ hours

Notes: A number of exemptions to the total rules are contained in the Regulations, but generally the restrictions on maximum *driving* periods are applied without exception.

– The continuous driving limits do not apply to operations carried out within 50 kilometres of the vehicles' base.
– The maximum daily driving limit of 8 hours can be increased to 9 hours twice in any seven day period.
– A *week* is defined as any period of seven consecutive days including break and rest periods.

International journeys. The rules for international journeys are fully harmonised with the EEC Regulations and are less onerous than the national rules in that the maximum limit on duty *hours* and spreadover limits do not apply. The rules are simple and there are no exemptions:

Continuous driving	–	4 hours
Daily driving	–	8 hours
Weekly driving	–	48 hours
Fortnightly driving	–	92 hours
Weekly rest period	–	40 hours (29 plus daily rest)
Daily rest period	–	11 hours
Breaks between continuous driving periods	–	½ hour (1 hour for articulated vehicles or drawbar trailer outfits in excess of 20 tonnes G.V.W)

Again, variations are allowed on daily driving limits (2 × 9 hour periods in 7 days) and in break periods. The latter can be taken either in a full ½ hour rest, 2 × 20 minutes or 3 × 15 minutes – for the larger vehicles the 1 hour rest can be taken in 2 × ½ hour rest periods.

Domestic journeys. These are the same rules as laid down in the Transport Act 1968, and can be summarised as follows:

Daily driving	– 10 hours maximum in any working day
Duty period	– 11 hours maximum in any working day, within a spreadover period of 12½ hours

Break period	–	at least $\frac{1}{2}$ hour after each continuous $5\frac{1}{2}$ hour duty period
Rest period	–	at least 11 hours between duty days
Weekly duty	–	60 hours maximum in any working week
Rest day	–	24 hours minimum in any working week.

There are variations and exemptions for a number of special types of operations including emergencies and readers should refer to the Regulations and obtain advice from the Freight Transport Association, Tunbridge Wells, Kent.

Drivers' records of work. EEC Regulation 1463/70 requires tachographs to be used throughout the community in order to control the drivers' hours restrictions. These provisions are contained in the Passenger & Goods Vehicles (Recording Equipment) Regulations 1979 (SI 1979 No. 1746) and make use of this equipment – now well known as the tachograph – compulsory from 1 January 1982. The requirement to fit and use the tachograph applies to the same vehicles as those affected by the EEC drivers' hours rules, (goods vehicles in excess of 3.5 tonnes gross vehicle weight). Tachographs and compliance with EEC drivers' hours rules also apply to passenger vehicles constructed to carry more than 15 people including the driver if being used on national journeys, but with only 9 people if used on international journeys.

A tachograph record has to be kept by any 'crew member' of a vehicle to which the Regulation applies – this includes drivers and mates. The tachograph must be one which conforms with the EEC Regulations, and it must be able to record:

distance travelled
speed of vehicle
driving time
duty time
duty time of *all* crew members
breaks from driving and duty periods
the opening of the instrument to remove or insert a tachograph disc.

The tachograph disc must also have a facility by which the crew members can continue recording the driving and duty time in the event of the instrument becoming unserviceable during a journey.

Once a vehicle has been fitted with a tachograph, the instrument must be calibrated and sealed at an approved centre.

The tachograph record. The employer must:

– issue each crew member with sufficient 'discs' for the journey
– ensure that crew members return used charts within twenty one days of use
– retain charts for a full year and have them available for inspection on request by an authorised inspecting official.

The crew member must:

– enter on the disc his surname and first name

- enter date and place where record begins
- enter vehicle registration number (all vehicles driven if more than one);
- enter vehicle mileage 'start and finish' details
- produce discs for inspection if requested by an authorised official
- retain discs for at least the two preceding days (seven if international journeys)
- return discs to employer within twenty one days of completion.

A specimen tachograph disc is shown in Figure 38.7.

Written records. There is no requirement to keep written records for those vehicles to which Domestic Driving Rules apply and which are not of a gross plated weight in excess of 3.5 tonnes or if not plated the unladen weight does not exceed 1525 kilograms.

VEHICLE SELECTION AND DESIGN

Vehicle design is an essential part of the responsibility of transport services management. Vehicles are available in standard designs, but very few such vehicles will be as efficient as one which has been specifically designed for an intended task. As the product structure of a company changes, vehicles designed specifically to carry that product may become obsolete. Long-term planning is essential and a degree of flexibility should be built into the design features of any industrial fleet.

Once it has been decided that a custom built vehicle is needed, the following main points must be considered:

Type of chassis

Length, possible chassis extension, additional shock absorbers, extra springing, automatic lubrication points, access to chassis for servicing.

Size of body

Are pallets to be carried, if so, what size and will they be two or four-way entry? What is the maximum height of the product carried? Are there any low entrances in the factory or warehouse area? A legal maximum height of 4 metres has been proposed under EEC regulations.

Body design

Box or flat? Size of door openings, rear or side entrances. Roller shutter or hinged doors? Fixed body or demountable? Strength of floor and bulkhead. Will a tractor and semi-trailer suit the operation?

Choice of material

Wood, metal, or fibreglass panels? Steel, alloy, or wood framing? Translucent roof?

Interior fitments

Lighting requirements, handling aids, tie rails, security alarm systems, double-

KEY

1 Driver started work at 06.30
2 Driving started at 07.15
3 Driving stopped at 08.45
4 Maximum speed was 82 kph
5 Distance covered during this first spell was 90 kilometres (each peak represents 10 kilometres)
6 Driving was restarted at 09.15
7 The driver therefore had a half hour break
8 A long break occurred from 13.00 to 15.15
9 The journey ended at 17.45. Total driving time for the day was 7 hours, 45 minutes and the total distance covered was 415 kilometres.

Figure 38.7   Example of a tachograph chart
This is an actual record of a European journey

deck fitments, suspended loads.

Loading aids

Vehicle-mounted crane, tail gates, tilts, tipping gear.

Special requirements

TIR facility, sleeper cab, two-way VHF radio, cab ergonomics.

The choice of vehicles for the movement of goods varies from a small van to a 32 tonnes gross train weight drawbar trailer or articulated outfit. The design of vehicles within this range is just as varied. Today the increasing use of unit loads has seen the development of demountable bodies in almost every type of transport operation.

The development of the container concept has also affected the design of modern trucks. In selecting the body for a particular task, transport management should look to reduce the handling of the product and keep to a minimum the time a vehicle is required to stand idle for loading and unloading to take place.

ACQUIRING VEHICLES

Owning, leasing, hire-purchase or contract hire are the alternative ways of acquiring a fleet of vehicles. The first thing to understand is that an operator of a single goods vehicle receives exactly the same tax benefits and allowances per vehicle as would an operator or contract-hire company owning over a thousand vehicles. The only direct cost advantage to a large fleet operator is in the terms of purchase when bigger discounts can be negotiated. An operator who decides to obtain vehicles by lease or contract hire is only buying money, for which he has to pay interest. Once this is understood, it will be much easier to make a correct decision regarding the method of acquiring a vehicle.

Purchasing

To purchase a vehicle an operator needs cash and this can be obtained by:

1 Reducing his own cash balances;
2 Increasing his own bank overdraft;
3 Borrowing the money from a finance company, normally through hire-purchase;
4 Hire-purchase.

All the above methods cost the purchaser a price. Reducing cash balances means that interest is forgone, increasing an overdraft entails additional interest charges, and a hire-purchase agreement will include interest charges on the repayments. Buying for cash will also have an additional advantage of being able to negotiate a discount from the dealer, and the larger the fleet and purchasing power, the larger the discounts available.

Vehicles are subject to value added tax based on the *invoice* price of the vehicle. Therefore, higher discounts mean less VAT payable. The VAT on goods vehicles is an 'input' and recoverable from the Customs and Excise. On cars and estate cars VAT is not recoverable, so a reduction in invoice price is a *real* saving of VAT.

Trucks do not come under the control of hiring orders, and deposits and repayment periods vary with different finance companies. Under a hire-purchase agreement, all tax benefits and allowances may be claimed by the purchaser, these are the same as if the vehicle had been purchased.

Under a leasing or contract-hire agreement, all tax benefits and capital allowances are claimed by the finance company.

Leasing

The usual method is for the finance company to purchase a vehicle in its own name, and then the capital cost and interest charges plus usual profit margins are spread over the period of lease in either monthly or quarterly fixed amounts. The operator will be responsible for the servicing and maintenance costs during the period of the lease. At the end of the stated period, the operator has the choice of continuing the lease for a nominal monthly or quarterly payment or the leasing company will sell the vehicle to a third party crediting the operator with up to 95 per cent of the proceeds.

Contract hire

As in a leasing agreement, vehicles obtained under contract-hire arrangements remain the property of the contract-hire company during the period of the contract. The main differences are:

1 At the end of the contract, the total proceeds of the disposal are retained by the contract-hire company
2 The contract-hire company is responsible for all costs of servicing, main-tenance, licensing and, in some instances, a relief vehicle
3 A mileage charge may also be included, either by an excess charge over an agreed maximum per year, or a charge for each mile run.

Effect of taxation on purchase, leasing and contract hire

An argument used in favour of leasing and contract hire is that the payments are wholly allowable for tax purposes. This is quite true, but the fact is that tax is neutral. No matter by which method a vehicle is acquired, the payments, either revenue or capital, will qualify for tax relief in their own peculiar way. The only real difference is the *pace* at which relief is given.

Tax allowances on purchase of goods vehicles

Capital allowances given by the Finance Act 1972, and still current are:

1 A first-year allowance of up to 100 per cent of the expenditure incurred. This is called free depreciation

2   A continuing allowance in the second and subsequent years of 25 per cent calculated on any balance not claimed in the first year.

The object of granting capital allowances is to enable a company to spread the reduction in value of the asset over a period of years. Vehicles bought and sold within a period of a company's financial year need not be subject to a claim for annual capital allowance. The total loss on resale would be set against taxable profits for that year. For assets retained for more than one year, a system of 'pooling' applies.

Cars

First year 100 per cent allowances do not apply to motor cars, and this includes dual-purpose vehicles which can be adapted for the carriage of goods and people, such as estate cars. In the case of this type of vehicle a straight 25 per cent capital depreciation allowance is given each year based on a reducing balance.

Tax allowances and hire-purchase

The 1971 Finance Act now provides that if a person incurs capital expenditure (including vehicles) under a contract whereby he becomes the owner (for example, hire-purchase), then capital allowances may be taken on the total cost of the asset purchased at the time of making the contract. This makes hire-purchase of goods vehicles attractive in that, even though only part of the repayments have been made the full 100 per cent first-year allowance can be claimed. The cash flow will improve because, in some cases, the benefit will exceed the actual hire-purchase payments.

Tax allowances on contract hire and leasing

Because the ownership of the asset does not pass to the user under a contract hire or leasing agreement, no capital allowances are allowed to the user of the asset. All contract-hire and leasing rentals are treated as revenue expenditure and as such the total payments in any one year are allowed against taxable profits.

Taxation and timing the replacement

Vehicle replacement policies are generally accepted as being concerned with how frequently vehicles should be replaced, but in practice it can be of far more importance to decide when during a company financial year they should be replaced. Unlike the case of the private car or small van, seasonal fluctuations of the secondhand truck market have little influence on the timing of a replacement, but there can be big tax advantages from getting the replacement timing correct. This is so because capital allowances are set against taxable profits of the accounting period to which they relate. For example, if a vehicle was purchased on 1 January 1981 and sold on 31 December 1981, the difference between the purchase price and disposal price is allowable against tax profit for the year ending December 1981. Consequently the next tax bill payable would be reduced by 52 per cent (or whatever is the current rate of corporation tax) of the actual loss in value. With the current first-year allowance set at 100 per cent for goods registered vehicles, the cash input into a company can be brought twelve months earlier by purchasing the vehicle *one day* earlier.

Example 1

(a) Company financial year starts 1 January 1981
(b) Truck purchased 31 December 1980 for £16 000·
(c) Capital allowances claimed for year ending 31 December 1980 = £16 000
(d) Capital allowances set against taxable profits for year ending 31 December 1980 and due for payment 1 January 1981
(e) Tax bill reduced by 52 per cent (rate of corporation tax) of £16 000, that is by £8320
(f) This is equivalent to a cash flow advantage of £8320 *one year earlier* than if the vehicle had been purchased on 1 January 1981.

The same reasoning applies to selecting a date for disposal of a goods vehicle. Under the rules of 100 per cent first year capital allowance, whenever a vehicle is sold the proceeds become 'taxable' in the accounting period during which the disposal took place.

Example 2

(a) Truck purchased on 31 December 1976 for £8000; 100 per cent capital allowance claimed, and applied to the accounting period ending 31 December 1976
(b) The same truck sold for £2000 on 31 December 1980. In this case, the disposal proceeds would be *added* to the taxable profits for the year ending 31 December 1980 and a cash *outflow* of 52% × £2000 = £1040 (if corporation tax were at 52%) would result when the tax bill was due on 1 January 1982
(c) The same truck sold for £1000 on 1 January 1981. In this case the proceeds would be *added* to the taxable profits for the year ending 31 December 1981, and the £1040 cash outflow would not be due until 1 January 1983, one year later than the previous case (b) above.

Capital budget planning

From the above it is clear that attention should be given to the correct timing of purchases and disposals in a company financial year, and this part of capital budget planning is far more beneficial to a company than are the theoretical calculations as to when a vehicle is at its lowest operating cost. In the case of small vans and cars which are usually changed more often than heavy trucks, the disposal prices are usually governed by the trade values in *Glass's Guide*, a publication well known to all transport operators. Purchasing a vehicle in the last quarter of a year is seriously reflected in the price obtained when sold and any example taken from the Guide shows clearly how the value drops when it becomes 'one year' older. The following general rules can then be given in putting forward a policy of capital budget planning for vehicles:

1   *Cars and light vans*
    Avoid taking delivery of new vehicles in the last quarter of a calender year.
    Step up the purchases and taking delivery of new vehicles in the first
    quarter of the calendar year. It has been found from experience that the
    'suffix' letter change each August has little effect on residual values. A
    complete new system of registration plates will be introduced in 1985.
2   *Trucks*
    Step up the purchases and taking delivery of trucks in the last quarter of the
    company financial year in order to bring forward capital-allowance cash-
    flow benefits by one year. Defer disposals of trucks until the first quarter
    of a company financial year, in order to delay the repayment of tax due on
    the proceeds of the sale for a period of one year.

MAINTENANCE POLICIES

Good vehicle maintenance and well-planned servicing schedules are essential if
a transport operator is to be allowed to continue using a fleet of vehicles to carry
his company product. The Department of Transport has stated the following
guidelines around which operators should formulate a policy for vehicle
maintenance:

1   A positive check should be made at predetermined intervals of time or
    mileage on items which affect the safety of the vehicle; these are listed in
    the *Goods Vehicle Testers Manual* (HMSO)
2   Staff carrying out the servicing and repair of vehicles must be aware of the
    significance of defects
3   Any vehicle inspector or other staff whose duty it is to inspect vehicles must
    have the authority to have any defects rectified and to take unsafe vehicles
    off the road
4   Written records must be kept showing when and by whom inspections were
    carried out, the results of those inspections, when and by whom any
    remedial work was done and details of that work
5   Under-vehicle inspection facilities should be available, with adequate
    lighting in order that a full and detailed inspection of individual
    components can be carried out
6   A system whereby drivers can report defects must be provided, and this
    should be in writing. The clearance of a defect should be recorded on the
    same defect report
7   The mechanical condition of vehicles hired, including trailers, is the direct
    responsibility of the user. The user is defined as the employer of the driver.

Planned maintenance and inspection

A number of ready-made planned maintenance and inspection schemes are
available to operators, all of which have been designed to ensure compliance
with the legal requirements. Basically, each contains the following documents
enabling a complete history of a vehicle's maintenance and inspection to be
recorded and preserved:

1   Driver's defect report
2   Vehicle inspection check sheet
3   Servicing sheet for predetermined intervals of time or mileage;
4   Stores requisition form
5   Work order sheet or job card
6   Servicing, planning and record chart
7   Vehicle history folder.

No matter what method of planned maintenance and inspection a company adopts, whether it be in company premises by company employees, or by contracting out the entire task of maintenance, inspection and documentation, the onus of responsibility for the roadworthiness of the vehicle is always with the vehicle operator. He is still responsible in law even though an outside contractor providing the service and maintenance facilities has been neglectful.

FINANCIAL CONTROL OF THE TRANSPORT FUNCTION

The only way to ensure a cost-effective operation is to establish a system of budgetary control and accounting responsibility which ensures that any overspending is immediately highlighted at the point where the cost was incurred.

In my opinion, the best way to impose effective financial control on the transport services function is to make it an independent profit and cost centre. This principle puts an own-account transport operation on a par with the haulier.

A rate schedule for the carriage of goods within the company and to customers should be produced in exactly the same way as one would expect to see from a haulier. Similar rate schedules can also be prepared for the use of other services such as chauffeur-driven cars, pool cars, and even for the repair and maintenance of vehicles in company garages. These rate schedules should be fixed for the period of a company financial year and published to all departments to be used by the production and marketing functions as a basis for determining the transport and distribution costs borne by the product. By adopting such a system, the transport function receives regular revenue for its services against which it incurs costs.

To be effective two requirements must be met:

1   Actual expenditure should be within the budgeted expenditure
2   Recoveries should equate actual expenditure.

It is to be noted that recoveries should equate expenditure – excess recoveries only add an unnecessary price burden on the product, and an under-recovery will indicate a loss due to an insufficient charge being made for distribution costs.

To establish financial disciplines, it is necessary to keep adequate costing information for each vehicle and also to have a system of budgetary control in order that over the whole of a financial period regular checks can be made on areas of excessive expenditure and corrective action can be taken by management.

COSTING THE OPERATION

There are two main components of vehicle costs:

1 *Standing costs.*
   These generally include:
   (b) Depreciation cost of the vehicle, together with a charge equivalent to the interest which the capital invested in the vehicle can earn
   (b) Licences, including vehicle licence and operator's licence
   (c) Insurance, for both vehicles and goods in transit
   (d) Wages of the driver
2 *Running costs.*
   These are the result of operating the vehicle on the road and include:
   (a) Fuel and oil
   (b) Repair and maintenance
   (c) Tyres
   (d) Driver's expenses
   (e) Driver's overtime

The most informative costs of own-account transport operation are the running costs of a vehicle.

Monthly cost record

The vehicle monthly costings record (Figure 38.8) ignores all costs other than those directly associated with day-to-day operation. These are:

1 *Fuel.*
   Issues from company bulk installations are shown separately from the fuel picked up from garages by means of agency cards or cash. This helps to control the amount of fuel picked up from outside sources and to maximise the greater discounts available from having bulk stocks
2 *Lubricants.*
   Only issues to a vehicle during normal running are recorded. Oil changes will be recovered on maintenance job cards
3 *Tyres.*
   Expenditure on new tyres is recorded from invoices received. Sale of old casings will be entered as credits
4 *Repairs.*
   A distinction is made between repairs and maintenance carried out in company garages and repairs by outside agents
5 *Miles run.*
   This is recorded daily from driver log sheets and gives a simple but clear picture of vehicle utilisation.

This vehicle costings record also shows registration number or fleet number, make, vehicle group and operating base. Dividing a fleet into groups of similar vehicles, eg vehicles under 3.5 tonnes GVW, vehicles 3.5 tonnes GVW to 7.5 tonnes GVW, etc allows the costings to be arranged in groups and this will

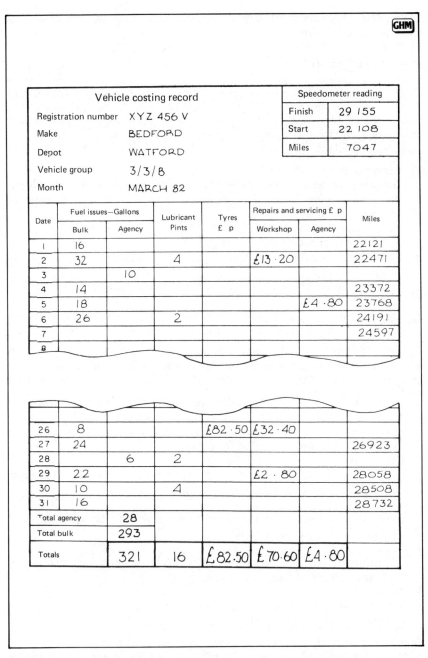

Vehicle costing record	Speedometer reading	
	Finish	29 155
Registration number XYZ 456 V	Start	22 108
Make BEDFORD	Miles	7047
Depot WATFORD		
Vehicle group 3/3/8		
Month MARCH 82		

Date	Fuel issues—Gallons		Lubricant Pints	Tyres £ p	Repairs and servicing £ p		Miles
	Bulk	Agency			Workshop	Agency	
1	16						22121
2	32		4		£13·20		22471
3		10					
4	14						23372
5	18					£4·80	23768
6	26		2				24191
7							24597
8							
26	8			£82·50	£32·40		
27	24						26923
28		6	2				
29	22				£2·80		28058
30	10		4				28508
31	16						28732
Total agency	28						
Total bulk	293						
Totals	321		16	£82·50	£70·60	£4·80	

Figure 38.8 *Layout of a simple monthly vehicle costing record (Costs shown here are to demonstrate the layout only and are not intended to be representative of current cost levels)*

highlight any variance within a group so that action can be taken to investigate the reasons for the variance.

Vehicle operating cost sheet

A layout for a vehicle operating cost sheet is shown in Figure 38.9. All costs recorded refer to the direct operation of the vehicle. Overheads, rent, rates and wages are excluded as these would tend to reduce the value of the costings as a means of comparing the costs of operating different types of vehicle. The following vehicle data is shown:

1 Registration or fleet number
2 Make, group type, gross vehicle weight, unladen weight (3/3/B indicates the HGV driving licence class, the size of the vehicle in that class and 'B' denotes a box van)
3 The invoice cost of the vehicle, reduced by the value of a set of tyres and the expected life of the vehicle in miles
4 Details of tyre size and cost of complete set. The estimated tyre life is used as a basis for costing
5 Standing costs will include interest on capital invested, licences and insurance
6 Depreciation is calculated in terms of cost per mile, based on the actual cost and the estimated life of the vehicle in miles (6473 ÷ 300 000 = £0.0216)
7 Tyre costs per mile (492 ÷ 40 000 = £0.0123).

The details of running costs are taken from the monthly vehicle costing record and over the life of the vehicle a permanent record is built up. The following points are to be noted:

Fuel

Calculating mpg is suspect unless the tanks on the vehicle are full at the start and end of a monthly accounting period.

Oil

Calculating mpg or miles per pint serves no useful purpose. Excessive oil use can be seen quite easily from total usage each month.

Tyres

Calculations are based on the tyre wear. Actual purchases are shown and if the estimated mileages are correct, then actual expenditure on tyres should balance the estimated costs over the agreed mileage.

Depreciation

Obtained by multiplying monthly mileage by estimated cost per mile.

VEHICLE OPERATING COST SHEET

VEHICLE DATA

Reg. No.	XYZ 456 V
Make	FORD D1314
Cost Group	3/3/B
Date purchased	OCT 1982
Invoice cost (less tyres)	£6473
Estimated life	300,000 MLS
Gross vehicle weight	13209 Kgs
Unladen weight	4979 Kgs

STANDING COSTS

Interest	£971
Licences	£269
Insurances	£120
Total per Annum	£1360
Total per Month	£113.33

TYRES

Size	10.00 x 20
No. per set	6
Cost per set	£492
Estimated life	40,000 MLS

ESTIMATED COST PER MILE

Tyres	£0.0123
Depreciation	£0.0216

LAST DATE COSTS UPDATED | JAN 82

Month	Mileage	Fuel gallons	Fuel Cost (1)	Fuel mpg	Oil pints	Oil Cost (2)	Tyres Estimated cost (3)	Tyres Actual	Servicing/repairs Workshop	Servicing/repairs Agents	Servicing/repairs Total (4)	Depreciation (5)	Total running costs (1-5)	Running costs per mile	Standing costs	Total operational costs	Operational costs per mile
1981 October	4284	211	139	20.3	7	1.50	52.69	/	42.40	1.60	44.00	92.53	329.72	0.077	113.33	443.05	0.103
November	4291	214	142	20.0	8	1.60	52.78	/	33.60	2.40	36.00	92.69	325.07	0.076	113.33	438.40	0.102
December	4838	236	154	20.5	6	0.80	59.50	/	42.42	5.80	48.22	104.50	367.02	0.076	113.33	480.35	0.099
1982 January	6083	297	194	20.5	14	2.30	74.82	/	82.20	11.20	93.40	131.39	495.91	0.082	113.33	609.24	0.100
February	2612	124	86	21.0	7	1.30	32.13	/	29.20	3.60	32.80	56.42	208.65	0.080	113.33	321.98	0.123
March	7047	321	211	22.0	16	2.80	86.68	82.50	70.60	4.80	75.40	152.22	529.10	0.075	113.33	641.33	0.091
April																	

GHM

Figure 38.9 *Example of a vehicle cost operating record sheet (Cost figures are intended to demonstrate the layout only and are not indicative of current levels)*

Running costs

Total cost of fuel, oil, estimated tyre wear, repairs and depreciation, divided by miles run. This figure can be compared with the performance figures of other vehicles in the fleet within the same vehicle group, with its own performance figures over previous months and with cost tables published by the transport journals.

Standing costs

These are now added to the total running costs to give the total monthly operating costs. The total operating cost per mile is of little use as this entirely depends upon the mileage recorded for the period. It will be seen from the example that total operating cost per mile varied between 9p (£0.091) per mile to cover 12p (£0.123) per mile where the performance figure of running cost was reasonably stable.

MOVEMENT OF PERSONNEL

The transport services function should be responsible for personnel movements in order to minimise the problems involved and to increase the overall efficiency of the company by reducing the fatigue associated with people moving.

Sales and service function

The responsibility for the mobility of the sales force of a company comes within the function of transport services in that the provision of small vans, cars, and estate cars and the maintenance of servicing of such a fleet is the direct responsibility of the transport department of a company. The transport services function will need to advise on the choice of vehicle allocation to personnel of the sales and service force, and will need to know the difference of law and taxation in the use of this type of vehicle.

Law on small goods vehicles

Before the Transport Act 1968, the law on the use of small goods vehicles (including goods registered estate cars) was the same as that for heavy trucks. Today different legal requirements exist both for vehicle and driver. A small goods vehicle is defined in $s60(4)$ of the Transport Act 1968 as:

> One which does not form part of a vehicle combination and has a gross plated weight not exceeding 3.5 tonnes, or if not having a plated weight, has an unladen weight not exceeding 1525 kg

The law for the small goods vehicle and its driver can be summarised as follows:

Operator's licences

Exempt.

Vehicle testing

An annual test for roadworthiness when three years old or more.

Speed limits

1   On derestricted roads, not drawing a trailer: 50 mph
2   On derestricted roads, when drawing a trailer up to 5 cwt ULW: 40 mph
3   On derestricted roads, when drawing a trailer exceeding 5 cwt ULW: 30 mph
4   Dual-purpose vehicles (estate cars goods-registered): 60 mph
5   Dual-purpose vehicles drawing a trailer: 40 mph
6   *Motorways* – not drawing a trailer: 70 mph
7   *Motorways* – when drawing a trailer: 40 mph
8   *Trailers* – subject to the weight of the vehicle not being less than the weight of the trailer being towed, the speed limit on derestricted road and motorways is 50 mph. A 50 mph disc must be displayed on the rear of the trailer, and the kerb weight of the vehicle and the maximum permitted unladen weight of the trailer must be shown on each.

Driving licences

Ordinary driving licences Group 'A' or Group 'B' if restricted to automatic transmission vehicles.

Driver's hours

Section 96 Transport Act 1968 applies to drivers of all small goods vehicles, including light vans and estate cars. There are, however, a number of exemptions which apply to drivers of small goods vehicles and these are:

1   *Part-time drivers*
    A driver who on *no* day of the working week drives for more than four hours is exempt from all the hours rules for the whole of that week
2   Drivers of small goods-registered vehicles engaged solely in certain professional activities and persons using their vehicles to assist any service of inspection, cleaning, maintenance, repair, installation or fitting, are exempt from all drivers' hours rules *except the ten-hour driving day regulation.* This exemption would cover most of the duties carried out by a sales or service engineer
3   There is a complete exemption from all drivers' hours regulations when extra hours need to be worked for the purpose of saving life or prevention of damage to property or to deal with serious interruptions to public services.

Drivers' records

Completely exempt (including tacographs).

Servicing and maintenance of sales and service vehicles

Although this class of vehicle is normally exempt from the requirements of operator licensing, it is important to understand that any convictions against a company or a vehicle user for contravention of the Construction and Use Regulations, 1978 or for instances of using, or causing to be used, vehicles which are found to be unroadworthy, may be taken into considerations when application is made for renewal of, or the initial granting of an 'O' licence. A system of reporting defects by the driver of the vehicle is recommended and a suitable form is illustrated in Figure 38.10. Drivers should also be asked to send in weekly reports stating any work done on the vehicle by outside garages.

[GHM]

DRIVER'S REPORT OF VEHICLE DEFECTS

Date _____

This form is to be used only to report defects and must be handed to the Transport Office IMMEDIATELY on your return. No verbal reports please

Depot _____

Registration number _____ Make _____

NATURE OF DEFECT. Faults must be reported at once, even if only of a minor nature

Speedometer reading _____ If anything is wrong, don't be afraid to say so

Driver's signature _____

Date rectified _____ By _____

Figure 38.10 Form for reporting vehicle defects

The company car

Mobility of personnel costs money. Just as the cost effectiveness of a goods distribution service is judged on its contribution to the total profitability of a company by giving an efficient customer service, the value of a fleet of company cars should also be assessed on its contribution to the efficient mobility of management and executives, as well as the part it plays in recruiting the right calibre of person to fulfil the needs of the company. There are many different approaches to determining a policy for the supply and allocation of cars to company employees. Each company will decide its own policy based on its own needs. For a medium-sized fleet, there are several ways of obtaining cars:

1 Outright purchase or hire purchase negotiating for the highest discount

2　Leasing, generally without maintenance but sometimes with the cost of the vehicle licence included

3　Contract hire, with maintenance cost, licences and a replacement vehicle included in the hire charges.

Each of the above methods has advantages and disadvantages and, as stated in the section dealing with the purchase of trucks, it all depends on the financial position of a company, and how it views its cash flow. There is no doubt that provided the cash-flow situation of a company will permit, outright purchase at the highest discount, followed by a direct disposal policy to trade outlets is the most cost-effective way of obtaining cars. As long as the price of new vehicles tends to increase annually, then the operator has the advantage of minimising the difference between invoice price and disposal price.

A company car issued to an individual is considered as a benefit in kind and as such the car user is liable to be taxed on the assessed benefit. The annual Finance Bill states the taxable benefit on types of car and these are subdivided into groups either by engine capacity or retail cost. Petrol supplied to car users for private use is also liable to tax and full details can be obtained from the Finance Act published after each year's annual budget presented by the Chancellor.

Replacement policies

Any replacement policies will again depend upon the cash-flow situation of a company, and any policy should be flexible in order to take advantage of changes in secondhand market values, or impending price increases of new cars. It is possible to negotiate guaranteed buy-back prices for cars when they are purchased, but this type of arrangement tends to become less flexible and arguments will arise over delays and damage when vehicles are returned to the dealers. A well-tested policy which has an in-built flexibility is as follows:

1　Outright purchase of all cars after negotiating for highest fleet discounts;
2　Replacement policy:
　　(a)　Cars 1600cc and under, replaced after 2 years
　　(b)　Other cars replaced after 60 000 miles or 3 years, whichever comes first;
3　Disposal policy. Sell to the trade (not to the dealer who sold the original vehicle) or through car auctions where special fleet terms are available.

With the above policy, the transport services function will be carrying out a responsible task and obtaining every possible cost benefit for the company. The policy is flexible in that no firm contracts are entered into and the purchase and disposal dates can be delayed or brought forward for reasons of cash flow, to avoid heavy repair bills and to take advantage of minimising the impact of balancing charges which may become due at the end of a financial year.

Chauffeur services

One of the neglected areas in transport function is that of the provision of an efficient and well-managed chauffeur operation. Even the smallest company will have a driver, whose duties will include meeting visitors at airports and stations, and driving customers between company locations. Larger companies have chauffeurs allocated to directors and executives, whose duties may include tasks other than driving a company car. A chauffeur should be trained to keep himself and his car in immacualte condition, so as to portray an image of an efficient organisation. Very often a chauffeur is the first contact a visitor will have with a company, and the initial impression can be of vital importance.

Company air services

The company aircraft, owned and operated by a company for use by company personnel is now firmly established in the United Kingdom. The need for a company air service and its justification on financial grounds are very difficult to assess, and indeed any cost exercise based solely on financial justification must fail. The task of the transport services is to operate a service based on the highest standards of safety and also to minimise the additional costs which accompany the operating of a company aircraft. Safety, comfort, punctuality and reliability are the most important features of an efficient company air service. Safety means operating to a high standard and strict compliance with the current Air Navigation Orders. Comfort of passengers means a reasonably comfortable cabin layout, quietness, facilities for reading and writing, temperature control and, above all, commonsense thinking of the crew to find a comfortable flying altitude for that particular journey. Punctuality and reliability are the two features which will test the efficiency of the service. Crews must ensure that the aircraft is always waiting for the passengers. Timings are important; not only must the passengers know the take-off time, they must also know at what time they will be at their destination.

Obtaining an aircraft

As with vehicles, there are a number of ways to obtain an aircraft:

Charter from a company which specializes in this type of operation. They will supply the aircraft and crew and carry out all maintenance, route-planning and management

Lease. This is similar to contract hire of a car. It will include all maintenance and management. The company leasing employs the crew

Purchase the aircraft and contract out all maintenance and management and also the provision of crews to an aircraft operating company

Purchase the aircraft and employ your own crews as well as providing the necessary management and maintenance controls.

Operating the aircraft

Owning your aircraft does not give you the right to operate outside the public category, and if the crew is supplied by a charter company and not employed directly by your company (that is, on the company payroll), then the operation will be subject to all the restrictions placed by the Department of Trade and Industry on a public-category operation. By employing your own crew to fly the aircraft, it is possible to operate in the private category and be free from a number of regulations which are mainly designed for the control of schedule airlines carrying fare-paying passengers.

Choosing the aircraft and costing the operation

A wide variety of aircraft are available which are suitable for company operation. They range from single engine helicopter which flies 'point to point' at speeds of up to 150 mph to the twin fan-jet aircraft capable of speeds approaching 600 mph. The costs of operating helicopters and fixed wing aircraft range from:

Helicopters	Single engine (turbine) £200 – £260 per hour
	Twin engine (turbine) £380 – £550 per hour
Fixed wing	Twin engine (piston) £150 – £200 per hour
	Twin engine (turbine) pressurized £250 – £450 per hour
	Twin engine (jet) £750 –£1000 per hour

FURTHER READING

Commercial Vehicle Buyer's Guide, Kogan Page, London, 1981

Cooke, P. N. C., *Financial Analysis of Motor Transport Operations*, Gower, 1974

Cooke, P. N. C., *The Company Car*, Gower, 1975

Duckworth, J. (Ed) *Kitchin's Road Transport Law*, 23rd edition, Butterworths, Sevenoaks, Kent, 1981

Gattorna, J. (ed.), *Handbook of Physical Distribution Management*, 3rd edition, Gower, 1983

Lowe, D., *A Study Manual of Professional Competence in Road Transport Management*, Kogan Page, London, 2nd edition, 1981

Lowe, D., *Transport Managers' Handbook 1982*, Kogan Page, London (published annually)

Pickerill, R. J., *Capital Allowances in Law and Practice*, Institute of Chartered Accountants, 2nd edition, 1981

Tables of Operating Costs (annually); *Commercial Motor*, IPC Business Press Ltd, London

Thompson, B. A., *Croner's Road Transport Operation*, Croner Publications, (by subscription, and kept up-to-date monthly)

Thompson, B. A., *Professional Driver's Guide*, Croner Publications, (revised every two years)

Toyne, C. C., *Motor Vehicle Technical Regulations*, 2nd edition, Liffon Engineering Services, London

What a Haulier Needs to Know; Commercial Motor, IPC Business Press Ltd, London

Woodward, F. H., *Managing the Transport Services Function*, 2nd edition, Gower, 1977

Yearbook, The Freight Association, Tunbridge Wells (annually)

PART EIGHT

ADMINISTRATION

39 Company law

F W Rose

It is not always appreciated that a company registered under the Companies Acts 1948 to 1981 has a legal existence and personality quite separate and distinct from that of persons holding shares in the company. Many legal formalities must be complied with before such a company comes into existence. When formed the company has rights and liabilities in law which depend upon a careful analysis of the relevant statutory rules.

It may be necessary when an individual makes an agreement with a company to determine its precise power to contract, its financial position and future prospects. If the company is experiencing difficulties in trading profitably, the rights of the shareholders to control the company may be of vital importance.

This chapter explains some of the more important legal provisions. Use of technical language which would be unfamiliar to non-lawyers has been avoided.

FORMATION OF A PUBLIC LIMITED COMPANY

A private company is often formed to carry on a family business. Frequently there are only a handful of shareholders, usually members of the same family. A private company may trade successfully for several years, but further expansion will require additional capital which cannot be supplied by existing share-holders. A public company may be formed to take over and carry on the business; members of the private company will exchange their shares for shares in the new public company. The additional capital for such items as land, new buildings and machinery will be provided by issuing shares which the general public may purchase if they wish. About 2 per cent of all UK companies are public companies.

Registration

The company must be registered. This is effected by filing the following documents with the Registrar of Companies:

1   The memorandum of association

2 The articles of association
3 A statement of nominal capital
4 A list of persons to act as directors and secretary, together with their signatures as evidence of their consent to act as such.

These formalities are usually dealt with by a solicitor, accountant or a company formation firm specialising in this type of work. This person or body also files a declaration that the company has complied with all formalities necessary for registration. The Registrar then issues a Certificate of Incorporation which is conclusive evidence that the company has been properly incorporated.

In law the company now has an existence separate and distinct from that of the individual members who hold shares in the company. The company:

1 Can own property, and members have no rights in that property: their interest is in the shares they hold
2 Can make contracts with other individuals, companies or members
3 Will continue to exist irrespective of the death of an individual member, whose shareholding is then taken over by the person who succeeds to his property
4 Must act through the medium of human agents who will control its affairs, such as directors.

Public companies existing when the Companies Act 1980 came into force are given fifteen months to decide whether to remain as public companies by complying with the requirements of the 1980 Act, or to become private companies instead. A public company is subject to stringent rules designed to protect persons investing money in the company, for example, by prohibiting loans to directors from company funds.

The memorandum of association

This is the charter of the company embodying its constitution and powers. It must state:

1 The name of the company, indicating that it is a public limited company with 'Public limited company' as the last words of the name
2 The location of the registered office of the company
3 The objects to be carried out by the company
4 A declaration that the liability of members is limited
5 The share capital and its division into shares.

The objects clause

This states the company's main business objective. It is followed by a large number of ancillary clauses giving the company power to effect other objects incidental to the main purpose. Examples would include power to buy land, borrow money and purchase shares in other companies. In practice, the objects clause will be widely drawn to include almost every conceivable business objective, coupled with a declaration that they should be construed as main objectives and not subsidiary powers.

The original purpose of the objects clause was to delimit the company's powers so that capital subscribed by investors could be used only for the company's main and, presumably commercially sound, objective; not in some other subsidiary and risky enterprise in which the investor would not have chosen to place his capital.

The concept of limited liability

An investor who purchases shares must pay to the company the purchase price agreed upon. Usually shares must be fully paid for at the time when they are allotted to a shareholder by the company. If they are only partly paid for, then the shareholder is contingently liable to pay the sum still outstanding, even if the company is in liquidation. Once the shares have been fully paid for, the shareholder's liability is complete. He cannot be required to make further contributions, even if the company fails and is unable to settle debts owed to creditors who have supplied goods and services to the company.

Limited liability is one of the most important attractions of shareholding in a public company. After fully paying for his shares the investor has fixed the amount of money that he is prepared to place at risk. However disastrous the company's financial collapse, he cannot be called upon to pay more.

Articles of association

These govern the internal management of the company, regulating the rights of the members among themselves on such matters as:

1 Appointment and power of directors
2 Issue, transfer and forfeiture of shares
3 Rules regulating meetings of a company
4 Payment of dividends
5 Preparation of accounts and auditing
6 Alterations to the capital structure of the company
7 Rights of different classes of shareholders.

It is usual for a company to register its own special set of articles which make specific provisions on matters of internal management, particularly suited to the needs of that individual business.

The prospectus

The usual object of forming a public company is to raise money from the investing public to finance the company's policies of expansion. A company may apply for a stock exchange quotation so that shares can be easily bought and sold through the medium of stockbrokers and jobbers. The company will issue a prospectus which sets out:

1 The objects it will pursue

2   Reports by experts on property owned, its financial position and trading prospects for the future
3   The names of directors; if the board of directors includes well-known experts it may be an inducement to buy the shares
4   The details of the company's capital structure.

These details will enable the investor to determine whether he wishes to purchase shares.

CAPITAL AND SHARES

The authorised (or nominal) capital is the amount of money that the company is authorised by the memorandum of association to raise from the public, for example, £5 000 000. In practice the company may not require this amount immediately, but it can issue shares up to the limit specified at any time when it wishes to do so.

The issued capital is that part of the nominal capital which has been actually issued to the public for cash or other consideration, such as land or buildings, in return for an allotment of shares, for example, an issued capital of £2 500 000 out of the nominal capital of £5 000 000. If a subscriber is required to pay only half the amount due on his share allotment, then the capital actually received by the company (that is the paid-up capital) will be only £1 250 000 in the above example. The amount not yet paid up on the shares issued is referred to as uncalled capital and it may be declared by the company to be incapable of being required from a shareholder except in a winding-up of its affairs.

Certificate of entitlement to commence business

A public company may not commence business after incorporation or borrow money unless it has received a certificate to this effect. This will not be granted until the issued capital is at least equal to the authorised minimum permitted (at present £50 000). In addition at least one-quarter of the nominal value of each share, plus any premium payable as part of the purchase price, must have been paid up.

Serious loss of capital

As a result of adverse trading or other factors, a company may have lost much of the capital that it has raised to finance its operation. Where the net assets of a public company are half or less of the company's called-up capital, then the directors on becoming so aware must convene an extraordinary general meeting of members within the next twenty-eight days. The meeting itself must be held within fifty-six days of becoming aware of the position. There are no legal provisions requiring any specific type of action that the company must take to deal with the problem. The meeting will give shareholders the chance to consider the company's financial position before insolvency supervenes to stop further trading activities.

Payment for shares

The person allotted shares in a company may pay for them in money or 'money's worth', that is granting some form of benefit instead of cash. Payment in a form other than cash may result in the company not receiving the full value of the shares given in return, thus the law has been strengthened to prevent such abuses. A public company cannot accept an undertaking by an allottee of shares to do work or perform services for the company as consideration for an issue of shares. If there is a failure to observe this requirement, the allottee still remains liable to pay the required sum in cash.

A public company is permitted to allot shares in return for an 'undertaking' to transfer a non-cash asset, such as land, within five years from the date of allotment. The non-cash asset must be valued by an independent person qualified to act as a company auditor to ensure that the company is receiving proper value in return for its shares. These provisions are inapplicable where one company takes over or merges with another company and shares in the company being taken over are exchanged for shares in the company that has made the take over.

Increasing capital and pre-emption rights

When a company has issued all of its capital and received payment in full from shareholders, it may require further cash to finance an expansion of its operations. The company will usually be authorised by its articles to alter the capital clause in its memorandum and, if the members in general meeting so decide, an ordinary resolution may be passed to increase the share capital. Shares can then be issued to raise the additional capital. Suppose that prior to the issue of the new shares for cash, an existing shareholder, Jones, holds 60 per cent of the company's total shareholding. In effect he controls the company as a majority shareholder. The issue of new shares to other persons could take this away by reducing his percentage of the total number of shares now in issue. The Companies Act 1980 now provides that a company must not allot shares for cash unless an existing shareholder has been given the opportunity to buy the new shares in proportion to his existing holding. Thus, Jones could, if he so wished, buy 60 per cent of the new shares on offer and retain the same percentage interest in the company's capital. The company's articles, or members by special resolution in general meeting, may give power to directors to exclude or modify pre-emption rights from all share allotments for a maximum period of five years. This power can be revoked at any time by ordinary resolution of members or extended for a further period up to five years maximum.

Power over unissued shares

A takeover bid occurs when one company (Company A,) offers to buy or has already acquired a majority of the voting shares in another company (Company B). The directors of Company B may wish to resist the takeover as undesirable, or because they fear that they will be removed from office once the takeover has been achieved. In the past if Company B had not yet issued all of its authorised capital, the directors could have used a power, often granted to them by the articles, to issue new shares representing hitherto unissued capital to themselves and their supporters. This manoeuvre may have given the directors and supporters control of a majority of the voting shares and so thwart the takeover to which the other shareholders were agreeable.

Under the Companies Act 1980 directors may not exercise any power of the company to allot shares, or other securities such as debentures which can be converted into shares at the holder's option, unless authorised to do so by an ordinary resolution of members in general meeting or by the articles. The power so granted may be a general authority to allot, or limited to a specified amount. When such authority is granted it must state the maximum amount of securities that may be allotted, the date of expiry of the authority and its duration, which must not exceed five years. The authority may be renewed for a further period (maximum again five years) by members in general meeting. None the less members now control the directors' actions in this area, since any authority given may be varied or revoked at any time by ordinary resolution in general meeting.

MEMBERSHIP

A shareholder is a member of the company entitled to the following rights:

1 To attend meetings and vote on issues affecting company policy, including the appointment and removal of directors. He may requisition a meeting if he wishes to discuss any matter of concern provided that he alone, or in conjunction with his supporters has at least 10 per cent of the issued share capital carrying a right to vote, or some lesser proportion as prescribed by the articles
2 To receive an annual report and accounts giving details of the company's affairs
3 To share in the profits made in the form of a dividend declared by the directors
4 To share in the assets of the company if its affairs are wound up, provided any property remains when the rights of other creditors with prior claims have been met
5 To transfer his shares when he wishes by selling or giving them to another person
6 To present a petition to wind up the company or ask for an order controlling its affairs.

Different classes of shares

A company usually issues different classes of shares, each having its attractions for the investor.

Preference shareholders are entitled to the following payments in priority to ordinary shareholders:

1   A yearly dividend out of profits, at a fixed though moderate percentage of the capital invested, for example, 7 per cent. Unless the articles of association state otherwise, arrears of dividend not paid in a previous year when there were no profits are carried forward and must be paid in future years when sufficient profits are available
2   Repayments of the capital contributed to the company when it is wound up, if, as is usual, the articles so provide.

Ordinary shareholders are entitled to:

1   The remainder of profits available for distribution, which will secure a high rate of dividend if the company is successful. However, if a loss results in any trading year a dividend may not be paid at all
2   Return of capital contributed to the company when it is wound up, if sufficient assets remain to satisfy these claims.

The market value of shares will rise if the company trades successfully and the ordinary shareholder, in particular, may make a capital profit on selling his shares.

Ordinary shareholders bear the risk of substantial loss if the company fails; consequently, they have a right to vote at meetings and control the company's affairs to the exclusion of preference shareholders who are usually entitled to vote only if:

1   Their dividend is six months in arrear
2   Their rights as a class are affected by some issue under discussion at the meeting
3   On a resolution to wind up the company.

Acquisition and transfer of shares

When shares are first issued by a company an investor may make an offer to purchase them by submitting an application form. Allotment of shares by the company creates a binding contract with the investor. Shares may be issued at a premium; for example, 50p may have to be paid for a share with a nominal or face value of only 25p. This means that existing shares already issued have a market value of 50p, thus the real worth of a share is determined by reference to the market value, not the face or par value.

A share certificate will be issued by the company stating the name of the shareholder and the extent of his shareholding. The register of members, kept by the company, will record the shareholder's name and address and the number of shares held.

The shares of public companies are quoted on the Stock Exchange and the shareholder can determine the present value of his shares by referring to the Stock Exchange list which is published in leading newspapers. One of the main advantages of shareholding is the ability to sell quickly and realise the value of the shares.

Debentures

A company needing finance for a programme of expansion may be reluctant to raise the additional capital required by issuing more shares for two reasons:

1   The money will only be needed until the new equipment purchased earns sufficient profits to repay the capital borrowed: the company may not wish to raise capital on a permanent basis for such relatively short-term needs, since regular dividends must be paid
2   Once shares have been issued a company cannot buy them back when it has sufficient cash available, with the exception of redeemable preference shares (which may be issued for the same reasons as debentures).

The company borrows money from the lender and in return issues a debenture, redeemable at a fixed or determinable time or at the company's option. The debenture holder is entitled to:

1   A fixed rate of interest which must be paid even if it is paid out of capital, not profits
2   Repayment of the principal sum when due
3   A charge on the company's property. This means that if the company fails to repay the loan and interest when due, the debenture holders may satisfy their claims by disposing of the company's assets. These claims have priority over, and must be satisfied before, claims by all types of share-holders.

MEETINGS

The company is obliged to hold various types of meetings from time to time to transact business. An annual general meeting must be held every year to deal with:

1   Declaration of dividends
2   Consideration of the accounts and balance sheet and the report of directors and auditors
3   Appointment of directors
4   Appointment and fixing of the remuneration of auditors.

Members must be given twenty-one days' notice of the meeting.

An extraordinary general meeting may be called by directors if important business needs to be transacted which cannot await the next annual general meeting. Holders of one-tenth of the paid-up share capital with voting rights may requisition such a meeting, even against the directors' wishes. Members must be given fourteen days' notice of the meeting.

DIRECTORS

Every public company must have at least two directors and a secretary. A proportion of the directors, usually about one-third, retire at each annual general meeting, and the members may re-elect them or appoint others in their place. A director may be removed by an ordinary resolution passed by members, but the director may make representations on the issue showing why he should not be removed.

The directors must manage the company's affairs by taking decisions at board meetings, otherwise they may be personally liable for their actions.

A director may be required by the articles to hold a certain number of shares in the company which are called his qualification shares, otherwise he must vacate his office. This gives him a personal interest in furthering the fortunes of the company to the best of his ability.

The articles may provide for the payment of a fixed fee to a director, but his remuneration is often stated in a service contract which he makes with the company. His remuneration must be disclosed in the annual accounts. A director is not entitled to compensation for loss of office or on retirement, unless approved by the shareholders.

The powers of the company, as determined by the memorandum and articles, are usually delegated to the directors in so far as they are not exercised by the company in general meeting. Members in general meeting cannot interfere with the manner in which the directors exercise their powers, unless they alter the articles accordingly. The directors should communicate their policy to the shareholders from time to time. If directors exceed their powers the members may ratify their actions, provided the act is within the powers of the company.

Publicity concerning directors

The company must make available the following information about a director:

1   A register of directors and secretaries must be kept at the registered office and open for public inspection, specifying a director's name, address, nationality, business occupation and other directorships held, except directorships in wholly-owned subsidiaries
2   A register of directors' interest in the company's shares and debentures must be kept at the registered office or place where the register of members is kept. It must be open for public inspection. Such holdings by a spouse and minor children must be disclosed
3   Details of a director's service contract must be kept at the registered office, or place where the register of members is kept or at the company's principal place of business. It must be open for inspection by members
4   The names of directors must appear on business letters, trade catalogues, circulars and show cards.

Shadow directors and connected persons

The various statutory provisions that impose numerous legal obligations and duties on directors, also cover any person occupying the position of director whatever name is used to describe his office. 'Shadow' directors are also treated as if they were directors for some purposes. This concept covers persons giving directions to directors, who then are accustomed to follow them irrespective of any legal or other obligation to do so. Thus directors may manage a company in accordance with the policy dictated by the controlling shareholder. That shareholder becomes a 'shadow' director. A person giving professional advice, such as an accountant, does not thereby become a 'shadow' director. Persons 'connected' with a director may also have the same restrictions placed upon their activities as the director himself. A 'connected person' includes:

1   Director's current spouse and his children up to the age of eighteen
2   Trustees of a trust which has as one of its beneficiaries the director, his children, his current spouse or an 'associated' company
3   Partner of the director or a partner of the director's spouse, his children or his trustee
4   A company with which the director is 'associated' where the director and his connected persons hold one-fifth of the nominal value of the 'associated' company's equity share capital, or where the director, his connected persons and any company he controls hold one-fifth of the voting rights at a general meeting.

Disclosure of interest in contracts

A director may have a personal interest in a contract made by the company with some other body, such as a partnership in which the director is himself a partner, or another company in which he holds shares. The company is entitled to the unbiased advice of a director, unfettered by conflict between personal interest and duties owed to the company. Every director having an interest, direct or indirect, in the contract which the company is about to enter, must disclose that fact to the board of directors when the matter is discussed. Such disclosure permits the director to make a personal profit from the contract which the company enters into, but failure to disclose enables the company to rescind the agreement so made. These principles also apply to 'shadow' directors.

Where directors have wide powers of management the risk arises that a director may sell his own property to the company at an inflated price with the connivance of fellow directors, or purchase the company's property at an undervaluation. An 'arrangement', which covers transactions not strictly enforceable at law as a contract of sale, cannot permit a director or his connected person to acquire a non-cash asset from the company or its holding company above the 'requisite value' of over £50 000, or one-tenth of the value of the company assets if over £1000, whichever sum is smaller. Further, a director or his connected person cannot sell a non-cash asset over the 'requisite value' to the company or its holding company. Arrangements exceeding the requisite value are permitted, however, if approved by members in general meeting. The holding company must consent as well as the subsidiary company directly involved. Here the shareholders have the opportunity to assess the advisability of the arrangement and will give their consent only if the company's interests have been safeguarded.

Service contract for a director

A director may be dismissed by a majority vote in favour of his removal passed by members in general meeting. To protect himself financially the director may have an express, written contract of service with the company for a fixed period of time (for example, ten years). If removed from office before expiration of the period he may claim damages for salary, less tax, that he would have earned during the unexpired portion of his service contract. The sum involved may be considerable, thus dismissal can be an expensive luxury for the company. Under the Companies Act 1980 shareholders are given the opportunity of voting at general meetings on whether directors are to be given such long-term service contracts.

A service contract for less than five years' duration, or for over five years' duration but terminable by giving reasonable notice (which means in practice about six months' notice) may still be approved by the board or the managing director, depending upon the person or body to whom the requisite power has been delegated. The consent of the members in general meeting is required for a service contract over five years' duration if not terminable by notice, or only terminable in specified circumstances. In the absence of such consent the contract itself is valid, but the term on duration is void, and the contract may be terminated by giving reasonable notice.

These new provisions are designed to prevent abuses whereby directors negotiate such contracts on terms set by themselves immediately prior to an anticipated takeover bid or removal on a vote by members, so that on loss of office they recoup substantial sums as damages for breach of contract.

Loans to directors

There are strict limitations on companies making loans to directors. Their position as managers may permit abuses at the company's, and consequently the shareholders' expense, as by making loans on terms that are commercially unsound.

A company is prohibited from making a loan to its own or a holding company's director, or providing a guarantee, indemnity or security in connection with a loan by some other person to such a director. However, a company may provide funds for a director to meet, or avoid incurring expenditure he has or will incur for company purposes, or to enable him to perform properly his duties as a company officer. Members in general meeting must give their prior approval with knowledge of the purpose and amount of the loan, or retroactive approval before or at the next annual general meeting. In the absence of such approval the loan becomes repayable, and the resultant liability must be discharged, within six months of that meeting. Not more than £10 000 must be outstanding by way of loan at any one time to a particular director or his connected person from a 'relevant' company.

Moneylending companies

There are situations where a company may make a loan 'quasi loan', or guarantee such transactions, for the benefit of its director or his connected person. Such a transaction must be part of the company's ordinary business – an important limiting factor since not many companies lend money or guarantee loans as part of its ordinary business activities. Further, the amount involved must not be greater, nor the terms more favourable then those it is reasonable to expect a company to have offered to a person unconnected with the company and having the same financial standing as the director or his connected person. A 'relevant company' must not lend over £50 000, but there is no such limit imposed on a recognised bank if the transaction is on commercial terms and disclosed to shareholders. A 'quasi loan' catches arrangements whereby the company agrees to make, or makes without so agreeing, a payment to a third party on behalf of a director of its own or its holding company or his connected person, on the understanding that the sum will be repaid by the borrower to the company. For example, the company may allow a director to use a credit card in the company's name with the director agreeing to reimburse sums spent within a year of the company settling the credit transaction.

Credit transactions

A 'relevant company' must not enter into a credit transaction or provide a guarantee, indemnity or security in respect of credit transactions for its own or a holding company's director or his connected person. Thus a company cannot lease a car for use by a director with the car being returned to its owner at the end of the hiring period. There is the usual exception for company expenses and also where the total sums involved are not over £5000. Also permitted are transactions in the ordinary course of company business, as where a company in the car hire business leases a car to its own director for his private and personal use, if the value is not above and the terms more favourable than those offered to persons unconnected with the company with the same financial standing s the director or his connected person who is party to the credit transaction.

Indirect transactions

A company cannot acquire rights and liabilities by a transaction that would have been prohibited if it had been made directly by that company. Thus, if a third party makes a loan to a director, the company cannot agree to take over the third party's rights. It would be using its resources to give a director credit with the same ultimate results as if it had made a direct loan to him. Nor may a company induce a third party to enter into a transaction, which would have been prohibited if that company and its director had been party to it, in return for a promise to benefit that third party. For example, the company cannot induce a third party to make a loan, quasi loan or credit transaction for a director's benefit by promising to place substantial orders with that third party to purchase his goods. Provisions of expenses for a director are an exception to these situations.

PROVISION FOR EMPLOYEES

A company may make provision for its own employees, or former employees, or those of a subsidiary company, when that company or one of its subsidiaries ceases business or transfers its business to a new owner. This provision permits a redundancy payment to an employee losing his job above the maximum sum authorised under the Employment Protection (Consolidation) Act 1968. The proposed payment must be sanctioned by members in general meeting approving an ordinary resolution. The articles or memorandum may state that a resolution by the directors suffices, or give a greater element of control to members by requiring a special or extraordinary resolution in general meeting.

DIVIDENDS

Dividends are trading profits divided among members in proportion to the number of shares held. The directors are responsible for fixing the rate of dividend, with the sanction of the general meeting. Shareholders cannot demand a dividend if the directors refuse to declare one, even though the annual profits seem to warrant some payment. Profits do not have to be distributed as dividends, as the directors may think it wiser to use them to offset past losses, or to transfer them to reserve to meet future liabilities. Once a dividend has been declared, however, a shareholder may sue to recover the sum he is entitled to receive if payment is not made.

The dividend is declared as a percentage of the share's nominal value; for example, a 30 per cent dividend for each 50p share held. The market value of the shares will be probably higher than the par value, say £1.50, consequently the real return on capital for a recent purchaser will be a more modest 10 per cent. A preference shareholder's dividend is usually at a fixed percentage, but ordinary shareholders will receive a dividend varying annually as the level of profits changes.

Limited companies have always been subject to rules as to what property may be used to pay dividends to its members. The basic purpose of these rules has been to prevent a reduction of capital by returning to shareholders money which the company should retain to settle debts to its outside creditors.

All companies are prohibited from paying a cash dividend to members except out of profits available for that purpose. Fixed capital may be invested in the business with the intention of retaining it more or less permanently to produce income, such as, business premises and machinery. On a sale of such items the company may make either a profit or a loss. Revenue profit or loss is the result of the company purchasing or producing property with the express intention of selling it again in the hope that a gain will accrue. Profit is made up of those accumulated and realised profits from revenue or capital from the date of incorporation which have not been used by the company for any distribution or capitalisation, minus realised losses of revenue and capital from incorporation date not previously written off. The company must also take account of losses which are anticipated but not yet realised. What constitutes a profit or a loss is left to the commercial world, to be determined in accordance with normal accounting practices. The articles may restrict the meaning of profit available for distribution, but cannot make it wider to justify a payment not authorised by statute.

It is not possible to make a distribution from a capital profit that has not yet been realised. Thus an increase in the value of land held by the company cannot support a dividend payment until the land is actually sold and the profit realised. A company's profits and losses for one accounting period cannot be treated in isolation from those of other accounting periods, but as a part of a continuing process. A company making a revenue or realised capital profit in the current accounting period cannot pay a dividend before making good previously incurred capital and revenue losses. For example a loss made in the financial year 1980–81 must be made good out of the profits for the 1981–82 financial year before a dividend can be paid for the 1981–82 period.

INSIDER DEALING

An insider dealer is someone connected with a company such as a director, company secretary, auditor, employee or other person in a business or professional relationship with the company, who has acquired in confidence specific information; that is, unpublished price-sensitive information, materially affecting the value of that company's shares and debentures or the securities of a company in the same group. The insider dealer then buys or sells such securities on the Stock Exchange without disclosing this information, which is not generally known to those persons who deal in, or would like to deal in, the securities affected. Persons who receive unpublished sensitive information are prevented from dealing in securities to which the information relates.

An individual who has price-sensitive information and/or is prohibited from dealing in a company's securities must not counsel or procure another person to so act, knowing or reasonably believing that such dealing would occur.

FURTHER READING

Northey and Leigh, *Introduction to Company Law*, 2nd edition, Butterworths, London, 1981. Good coverage in a style that is easy to follow.

Smith, K., and Keenan D. J., *Company Law*, 4th edition, Pitman, London, 1981. Some excellent background material and a useful summary of case law.

Tolley's *Companies Act 1980* (1st edition), Tolley, Croydon, 1980. A clear exposition of complex new legislation.

40 Contracts between companies

F W Rose

There are several essential elements that must be present before an agreement becomes a contract binding in law. Although the examples given concentrate on the sale of goods, the legal requirements are the same for all types of contract, whether the subject matter is a contract for the sale of goods or supply of a service by one company to another, or by a company to a private individual (or vice versa), or a contract of employment between employer and employee.

OFFER AND ACCEPTANCE

An offer is a definite indication by one party that he is willing to contract with another party on specified terms. A binding legal contract will come into existence if the terms are accepted without qualification and this fact is brought to the attention of the party making the offer. The conclusion of a contract is often preceded by lengthy discussions between the parties, but from these negotiations it must be possible to extract a firm offer followed by a firm acceptance.

Company B may ask further questions to induce better terms from Company A, but without intending to reject the original offer which will be accepted without qualification if better terms cannot be secured, for example, whether a total purchase price of £2 000 can be paid in instalments.

Any variation between the terms of the offer and the acceptance prevents the formation of a contract. For example, if Company A offers to sell Company B one hundred office desks at £120 each, the offer is not accepted if Company B agrees to buy at £110 each. Company B has rejected the original offer and made a counter-offer which is capable of acceptance by Company A. If Company A rejects the counter-offer, Company B cannot accept the original offer, unless Company A agrees. By this time Company A may have sold the goods to Company C. Company B cannot sue Company A for £2 000 damages for breach of contract if desks of the same type have to be purchased elsewhere for £140 each.

Keeping the offer open for a stipulated time

If a company offers to sell goods on stated terms, the company to whom the offer is made may be allowed a period of time to reach its decision. If an acceptance is communicated before the time allowed has elapsed, then a binding contract comes into existence. Although the company making the offer may feel morally bound to allow the company to whom the offer is made the stipulated period of time for reflection, the offer may be revoked at any time before notification of acceptance, even if the stipulated period for consideration has not ended. This right may be exercised where changed circumstances render conclusion of the contract undesirable, for example, where the market price of the goods has risen.

To safeguard its position the company to whom the offer is made may take an 'option' on the goods. This is a separate, binding contract whereby a period of time is given to reach a final decision on purchase. If during the period of the option the offer is revoked, the company making an offer commits a breach of contract for which damages are recoverable. Since the option itself is a contract, it must satsify all the essential requirements of a contract. This usually means that the company making the offer must be paid for granting the option.

Lapse and revocation of an offer

An offer lapses if it is not accepted within the stipulated time. Where a given period of time for acceptance is not prescribed in the offer, there must be acceptance within the time that is 'reasonable' in the circumstances of the case.

An offer may be revoked any time before acceptance, but revocation is effective only when actually communicated to the party to whom the offer was made. It is important to choose a reliable means of communication, so that the company to whom the offer is made cannot claim that it has not heard of the revocation. If the post is used, a revocation is effective only when it is actually received. If the communication is lost in the post the revocation is ineffective. Notification of the revocation may be made through some reliable source, such as the company's sales manager.

Need for a special method of acceptance

The company making the offer may request an acceptance in a particular form, such as telephone or telegram, a likely possibility where a speedy answer is required. Acceptance by another method, for instance a letter, would then be invalid. If the method of acceptance were quicker than the one prescribed by the offeror, such as a telegram instead of a letter, this would probably be a valid acceptance.

Where a speedy reply is not required, but a particular method of acceptance is stipulated, use of the alternative method will not invalidate the acceptance if the circumstances suggest that there was a choice. For example, pending execution of a standard written agreement containing contractual terms, an informal letter of acceptance may suffice, especially if the party making the offer expressly or by conduct waives the condition as to the special mode of acceptance.

Postal acceptance of an offer

A postal acceptance is permissible whenever the parties can be taken to have contemplated this possibility, for example, if the offer itself was made by post or where a few days have been allowed for consideration of the offer. The acceptance is complete as soon as the letter of acceptance is posted, and a legally binding contract exists even if the letter is lost in the post and is never received by the company making the offer. Before selling the goods to another buyer, the seller should, in the absence of any communication from the first intended buyer, determine whether he intends to accept the offer, for if the letter has been lost in the post the seller may finish up with two binding agreements in respect of the same goods.

Tenders

A company may invite a tender from businessmen for the supply of specified goods or services. Every tender submitted is an offer and the company can accept any tender to bring a binding contract into existence.

Where tenders are invited for the supply of goods as services as and when demanded, the company submitting the successful tender is making a standing offer. There is a separate acceptance by the company requiring the goods or services each time an order is placed with the party who has submitted the tender. A fresh contract is made each time an order is placed.

Where this type of agreement includes an estimate of the quantity required, there is no obligation to order goods of any particular quantity or indeed any goods at all. On the other hand, if the buyer undertakes to purchase all his requirements in relation to specified goods from the person whose tender is accepted, there is a breach of contract if the goods are bought elsewhere.

The standing offer may be revoked at any time by the party making it, except in relation to any goods or services that have been ordered. To prevent this happening there is usually a binding undertaking between the parties to keep the standing offer open for a stipulated period. This usually means that a sum of money must be paid to the party making the standing offer.

CONSIDERATION

The majority of contracts made are simple contracts and the presence of valuable consideration is essential to their validity. This means that each party to the contract must confer a benefit on the other party in return for the benefit received. If Company A sells goods to Company B for £1000, Company A loses the goods but receives the purchase price of £1000. Company B has to pay the £1000 but receives the benefit of the goods in return.

Consideration is a more complex doctrine than this simple illustration may suggest. It can take the form of an exchange of promises, with Company A promising to sell and deliver goods by 1 January and Company B agreeing to accept and pay £1000 for them. If Company A refuses to deliver the goods on 1 January, then Company B may sue for breach of contract or, alternatively, if Company B refuses to accept delivery, Company A may sue for breach of contract.

Consideration must be valuable. If must have an economic character and be worth something. The court will not determine how much the goods sold are worth and then determine whether the price paid is adequate. It is for business men, not courts, to make commercially sound agreements. No attempt is made to balance the respective promises or acts of the parties to determine whether the bargain is fair, provided each party has received some benefit.

FORM OF A CONTRACT

In most cases a contract does not have to be concluded in writing, but writing is useful since the precise terms agreed upon are then easily ascertainable. The following contracts must be in a written form however:

1 Bills of exchange, promissory notes and cheques
2 Contracts of marine insurance
3 Hire-purchase contracts
4 Contracts for the transfer of shares in a public company.

Although writing is not essential at the time when the contract is made, there are two cases where writing is needed for purposes of evidence, these are:

1 Contracts of guarantee whereby A promises B that he will settle C's debts to B if C cannot meet his own commitments
2 Contracts to sell or lease land.

If the writing does not exist the contract cannot be enforced in a court of law. The written document may be quite informal: a letter will suffice, provided it includes:

1 The names of the parties, or a sufficient description of them
2 A description of the subject matter
3 All material terms
4 Consideration, except in a contract of guarantee
5 The signature of the person being sued or his agent

A few contracts must be embodied in a deed, that is a written agreement, that is signed by the parties, sealed and delivered. Such contracts are:

1 A conveyance of land or interest in land, including a lease for a term exceeding three years
2 Gifts; a promise to give embodied in a deed is binding and enforceable, although consideration is not provided in return by the recipient.

Intention to create legal relations

If an agreement is supported by consideration it is assumed that the parties intended it to be legally enforceable one against the other, especially if it relates to a commercial matter. The parties are free, however, to state expressly that their agreement is not intended to be legally binding. Then it is an obligation binding in honour only and not subject to the jurisdiction of the courts. For example, collective agreements between unions and management may fall into this category if there is an express declaration to that effect.

CAPACITY TO MAKE A CONTRACT

A company does not have the contractual power to negotiate an agreement which falls outside the scope of its objects clause. The company's main business objectives are stated in the objects clause of the memorandum of association. It is followed by ancillary clauses granting power to effect other objectives incidental to the main purpose such as buying land and borrowing money. In practice the objects clause will be widely drawn to include a wide range of business objectives, with a declaration that they should be construed as main objectives. This reduces the risk of any contract negotiated by the company being held void.

The powers of the company, as set out in the memorandum and articles, are usually delegated to the directors, if not exercised by the company itself in general meeting. Members in general meeting cannot interfere with the manner in which the directors exercise their powers, unless they alter articles accordingly. The directors should communicate their policy to the shareholders from time to time.

A company does not have the contractual power to negotiate an agreement which falls outside the scope of its objects clause. Subject to the qualifications discussed below, any such agreement is void and ineffective (*ultra vires*), even though the other contracting party was unaware of this fact.

A contract is enforceable against a company if the subject matter is fairly incidental to its main objects, though not specifically authorised by the memorandum. For example, a trading company may lease premises for the purpose of carrying out its business.

The European Communities Act 1972 (Section 9) has vitally affected the law on contractual capacity of a company. Any agreement concluded by company directors, acting collectively as a board, or by a single director or other officer, for example, a company secretary acting by delegation from or with the authority of the board, will be deemed to be within the company's capacity though in fact it is *ultra vires*. The contract is enforceable by the other contracting party (or outsider) against the company, but is unenforceable by the company itself. The outsider must have acted in good faith and be unaware that the contract was *ultra vires*. He is not bound to make enquires to determine whether the company has contractual capacity to make that particular contract. The directors are liable to the company for any losses suffered as a result of negotiating the *ultra vires* contract.

Any transaction agreed upon by the directors collectively as a board, which exceeds their powers, but is within the company's powers, will be deemed to be valid. It is enforceable against the company and may be enforced by the company if ratified by the appropriate authority, usually the company in general meeting. The outsider must have acted in good faith and be unaware that the agreement was *ultra vires*. He is not bound to make enquiries to determine whether the board has contractual capacity to make that particular contract, but if he knows that it exceeds the directors' powers he cannot enforce it.

An individual director may exceed his authority when negotiating a contract. If the contract is within the company's contractual powers it is enforceable by the company and against it, if the director's actions are ratified by shareholders, or alternatively an inspection of the memorandum and articles by the outsider would not have revealed that the director was acting outside the scope of his powers. His restricted authority to contract may be a matter of internal management of which the outsider is unaware.

MISTAKES IN THE CONTRACT

A contract may have been concluded under a misapprehension as to a material fact. Where both parties mistakenly believe the subject matter of the contract to be in existence when this is not so, then the contract is void, for example, where the goods have been destroyed by fire, the buyer is not obliged to pay for the goods.

A mistake by both parties concerning the quality of the subject matter does not avoid the contract, where they have agreed on the same terms on the same subject matter, if for example, A and B mistakenly believe that land about to be sold has valuable mineral deposits. The buyer cannot claim his money back and return the land. In this situation the court may be willing on occasions to set the contract aside, thus relieving the party who suffers most because of the mistake. This would only apply on terms which are fair as between both parties, for example, allowing the seller to claim any expenses incurred.

A binding contract does not exist if the parties have negotiated completely at cross-purposes and made a mistake as to the identity of the subject matter. For example, one party intends to sell a cargo leaving New York in March on board a ship named 'Eastern Star', while the buyer intends to purchase the cargo on board a similarly named vessel leaving New York in January. The ambiguity of the circumstances make it impossible for the court to determine with reasonable certainty which cargo is subject matter of the contract. Conversely, an enforceable contract will exist on the terms as understood by one of the parties, if the mistake is basically the fault of one party only. For example, if a purchaser buys land mistakenly believing that it is more extensive in area than the plot being sold, he cannot avoid the contract simply because he failed to check the specifications of the sale which were readily available to him.

A contract is void if one party is mistaken as to a fundamental fact concerning the subject matter and the other party knows of the mistake and takes advantage of it. If Company A offers to sell goods to Company B for £1250 when

Company B's previous offer to buy at £2000 had already been refused, it is obvious that Company A really intended the price to be £2250. Company B cannot accept the offer of £1250 and enforce the agreement against Company A. On the other hand, if one party's mistake is not appreciated by the other party who accepts in ignorance of that mistake, then a binding contract exists. If Company A offers to sell goods at £350, when, because of an arithmetical error, £400 was intended, an acceptance of the offer by Company B is binding, provided the circumstances do not suggest than an obvious mistake has been made in the price charged.

Mistaken signature

A party may be induced to sign a written document embodying an agreement which is fundamentally different in nature from an obligation he intended to assume and the party inducing him to sign may be aware of the mistake. The mistaken party can escape liability in pursuance of the agreement only in the most exceptional cases, such as blindness or illiteracy. Company representatives signing contractual documents should carefully scrutinise the contents of the agreement and ensure that the agreement being signed is the agreement that they intend to sign and that all the individual terms are acceptable and have not been altered contrary to any verbal understanding that preceded the execution of a formal written document.

MISREPRESENTATION

A company may be induced to contract because of misrepresentation by the other party. A misrepresentation is defined as a false statement of a fact that is material to the agreement, made by one party to the other during negotiations leading to the agreement, which was intended to operate and did not operate as an inducement to enter the contract.

A false representation is fraudulent if it is made with knowledge of the falsity, or without belief in its truth, or recklessly not caring whether it is true or false. Honest belief in the truth of a statement negatives deceit, even though the representation is stupid, careless or negligent. A belief is not honest, however, if the representor deliberately shuts his eyes to the true facts or purposely abstains from investigating them. The aggrieved party may either avoid the contract with or without suing for damages for deceit, or affirm the contract and also seek damages.

A contract cannot be avoided (rescinded) where the aggrieved party elects to waive his rights by affirming the contract, for example, if he takes benefits provided by the contract with full knowledge of the misrepresentation, as by using goods purchased.

A contract further induced by fraudulent misrepresentation must be avoided within six years of either discovery of the fraud, or the time when it could have been discovered by using reasonable dilligence.

If the parties cannot be restored to their original positions by taking back the purchase price and goods respectively, then the contract cannot be rescinded. A buyer may have radically altered the property he purchased before discovering the misrepresentation or electing to rescind the contract; for example, there may have been substantial extractions from a mine that has been purchased. Damages may be recovered, however, to compensate the party misled where the property is now worth much less than he anticipated because of the misrepresentation.

It is too late to rescind where property has already been sold again to a third party who now has rights to the property in question.

Although a representation may be made with an honest belief in its truth, thereby negating fraud and an intention to deceive, none the less the representor may display a lack of care in either making the statement at all, or alternatively in failing to correct it before conclusion of the contract, when the true facts have been discovered or by using reasonable diligence should have discovered.

A person possessing special skills and competence who has made a negligent statement may be liable in tort at common law for the financial loss suffered as a result by the person acting in reliance upon it, if he owed the recipient of that information a duty of care to use his special knowledge when making the statement. This means that, in appropriate circumstances, a company may sue an adviser acting without payment for losses suffered as the result of his negligent misstatements which induce the company to contract with another party.

A party induced to a contract as the result of a negligent misrepresentation may sue the representor for damages as of right in respect of losses suffered. The measure of damages is probably the same as for fraudulent misrepresentation. The party misled by negligent misrepresentation may also seek rescission of the contract. The representor has an effective defence to any claim against him for damages, if he can prove that he had reasonable grounds for believing that the statement was true at the time when it was made and continued to hold this belief up until the time when the contract was concluded.

A false representation will be wholly innocent if reasonable care has been taken to check its accuracy before making it. The person misled may claim rescission of the contract. The court may award damages only, if this is fairer to the party responsible and an adequate remedy for the party misled; where, for example, the falsity is of relatively minor significance in relation to the transaction as a whole. Damages cannot be claimed in the first instance as of right; the only power in this respect is to invoke the discretion of the judge to make such an award.

Terms of a contract

The parties themselves may state expressly the detailed terms that are to govern the manner in which the contract will operate, such as delivery dates and time of payment. In addition to these express terms, others may be implied by custom or trade usage. For example, in a contract of employment the express terms may regulate many of the more important rights and duties of the employer and employee on such matters as salary, hours of work, holiday and duties to be discharged. However, an employee is also under an implied duty to obey lawful instructions, while the employer must indemnify his employee against any losses incurred while discharging his contractual duties.

In any type of contract the court may imply a term in order to fill in a gap left by the parties in the terms expressly agreed upon, which fail to regulate their respective rights and liabilities. The judge effects the presumed intention of the parties in order to give the contract business efficacy, by adding the kind of term that the parties themselves would have drafted if they had considered the matter.

In every contract for the sale of goods a number of terms are automatically implied by statute, irrespective of the intentions of the parties themselves. Exclusion of the operation of these implied terms is permissible only in specified circumstances. A number of very important terms are implied by the Sale of Goods Act 1979.

The seller of goods is bound by an implied condition that he has the right to sell the goods and can therefore transfer title to the buyer as a result of the contract sale, or will have the right to so transfer title at the time when the property is to pass, where there is a mere agreement to sell at some time in the future. A consumer sale is a sale of goods by a seller acting in the course of a business where the goods are of the type ordinarily bought for private use and consumption and are sold to a person not buying them in the course of a business. Other sales are non-consumer sales, as where the seller disposes of goods to a company which buys raw material in the course of business.

In a contract for the sale of goods by description there is an implied condition that the goods shall correspond with that description; this usually covers cases where the buyer has not seen the goods and relies on the seller's description. For example, if goods are described as 'new' it is a breach of this implied term to supply secondhand goods.

Where goods are sold in the course of business there is an implied condition that they are of merchantable quality except where the defect is specifically drawn to the buyer's attention before the contract is made, or the buyer examined the goods before contracting and the defect ought to have been revealed upon examination. Merchantable is defined as fit for the purpose(s) for which goods of that kind are commonly bought as it is reasonable to expect, having regard to any description applied to them, the price (if relevant) and all other relevant circumstances. For example, a new vehicle is not merchantable if, after purchase, it has a history of continuous breakdowns due to a number of different mechanical faults.

Where goods are sold in the course of business and the buyer, expressly or by implication, makes known to the seller the particular purpose for which the goods are being bought, there is an implied condition that the goods supplied are reasonably fit for that purpose, whether or not this is the purpose for which such goods are commonly supplied. If a buyer asks the seller to recommend a vehicle that is suitable for use by a commerical salesman covering long distances, the car sold should have those qualities of reliability and comfort that the buyer is expressly seeking in his purchase.

A specially drafted clause in the contract of sale may exclude the operation of the protections given in relation to description, merchantability or fitness. Such an exclusion clause if embodied in a consumer sale is void. In non-consumer sales exclusion or restriction of these implied terms is permitted if reasonable. Such reasonable exclusion or restriction may be imposed by express agreement, inconsistent express terms, trade usage or a course of dealings. In ascertaining reasonableness the following issues may be considered, if relevant, to the situation in question:

1   Relative bargaining strength of each party to the other, taking into account alternative means of meeting a customer's requirements
2   Whether the customer received an inducement to accept the exemption or restricting clause in relation to liability; whether when accepting it he had the chance to make a similar contract with others not imposing such a clause
3   Whether the customer knew or ought reasonably to have known of the existence and extent of the exemption or restricting clause and whether trade customs or previous dealings between the parties show that such clauses are usual
4   Where an exemption or restricting clause only operates if the customer fails to follow a prescribed procedure. For example, failing to report to the seller defects in goods purchased within a reasonable time limit, as specified. Here it is important to ascertain whether it was reasonable when contracting to expect that compliance with the procedure would be practicable
5   Whether the goods were manufactured, processed and adapted to the customer's special order.

Remedy for breach of an implied term

If goods supplied are not in accordance with the contractual description, if the seller is without title, or if the goods are not 'merchantable' or 'reasonably fit' then the seller is in breach of a contractual condition. The buyer may rescind the contract by returning the goods. He may reclaim the purchase price and additional damages, if appropriate, in respect of losses that are not too remote. Alternatively, if he wishes the buyer may claim damages only; that is monetary compensation for the difference in value between the goods delivered and the value they were supposed to have. Here the buyer retains the goods purchased. The condition is treated as a warranty, for breach of which only damages may be recovered. The buyer cannot return the goods, but may claim damages only, where 'property' in the goods has already passed to the buyer. This means that the buyer has 'accepted' the goods purchased and used them for some time before making a serious complaint. A buyer does not 'accept' goods delivered to him unless he has had a reasonable opportunity to examine them.

Unfair Contract Terms Act 1977

Liability may arise in the course of a business or from the occupation of premises used for business purposes ('business liability') for a person's death or personal injury while on the premises. If death or injury is attributable to negligence, such as failing to ensure that business premises are safe to use, then liability cannot be excluded or restricted by an exemption clause in a contract or a notice.

Business liability for loss or damage (other than death or personal injury) resulting from negligence, such as damage to clothing or personal belongings, can be excluded or restricted by the person responsible by a contractual clause or notice, provided it satisfies the reasonableness tests discussed above. A defaulting party may rely on a contract term or notice restricting liability to a specified sum, by proving that it is reasonable to do so by reference to his resources to meet liability and whether he could insure against it. For example, liability may be limited to a specified sum for loss or damage to goods left in a cloakroom where payment of a small fee cannot cover loss of expensive items of clothing. A non-contractual notice may exclude or restrict liability if fair and reasonable in the circumstances, with the burden of proof resting on the party relying on the notice. For example, a notice in a pub car-park may exclude liability for loss or damage to any car parked there or its contents. The injured party's awareness of the existence of a restricting or exemption clause is not, in itself, voluntary acceptance of any risk of loss or damage imposed by the clause, but if the injured party is unaware of the clause it cannot be operative.

DAMAGES FOR BREACH OF CONTRACT

If one party has broken the terms of a valid contract, the innocent party is entitled to recover damages for any loss suffered. He must be restored to the position he would have been in if the particular damage suffered had not occurred, in so far as money can be sufficient compensation.

Recovery may be confined to those losses that arise naturally in the usual course of events from the breach, and are thus assumed to be within the contemplation of the defaulting party. In a contract for the sale of goods, where there is a market for the goods, the measure of damages recoverable by the buyer is the difference between the contract price and the market price of goods at the time when the seller ought to have delivered them. The buyer can purchase goods similar to the contract goods in the market. On the other hand, if the buyer has refused to accept delivery, the seller recovers the sum by which the market price falls short of the contract price at the time when the goods ought to have been accepted. The seller can dispose of the contract goods in the market.

If there is no available market but the buyer has agreed to resell the goods, the resale price may be taken as representing their value. The buyer's damages will be the difference between the sale and resale prices, though the seller is unaware of the sub-sale. A loss of profit is recoverable for breach of a trading contract made between experienced parties if they can be taken to understand the ordinary practices and exigencies of one another's business.

If the seller is a dealer selling goods at a standard market price, this will be the same as the contract price, for example, the contract price and the market price of machinery may be £5000. For refusal to accept delivery the seller may recover from the buyer the profit that he would have made if the sale had been completed. Even if the item is readily sold to a new buyer, the seller has made the profit on one sale only instead of upon two sales in cases where he has plenty of stock for disposal. Conversely, if a particular item can be sold as quickly as it comes into the seller's stock, the buyer's default is a matter of indifference to the seller. In such cases only nominal damages are recoverable; for example, where a certain type of machinery is in short supply because of strikes.

Owing to special circumstances known at the time of contracting to the party ultimately committing a breach, a loss may be suffered outside the usual course of events. The defaulting party may pay damages in respect of the exceptional loss. For example, a vendor of land may know that the purchaser intends to develop the property and make a large profit. If the seller refuses to complete the sale he is accountable for this loss of profit.

The amount of damages awarded may be reduced to reflect a claimant's liability to reduce the losses suffered, if this is possible, as by selling or buying goods elsewhere.

Distinction between liquidated and unliquidated damages

Damages are unliquidated where one party to a contract sues the other to recover whatever sum the court holds to be the proper measure of damages in the circumstances. A contract may provide that, in the event of a breach, the innocent party may recover from the defaulting party a sum stated in the contract itself: this sum is called liquidated damages. This type of arrangement has the advantage of saving the time, trouble and expense of litigation should a breach of contract occur. Only the agreed sum is recoverable, even if the actual loss suffered greatly exceeds the sum fixed by the contract. If damages are to be assessed by the contract itself, it is essential to estimate with precision the monetary effect of any possible breach.

Distinction between liquidated damages and a penalty

A sum agreed as payable in the event of a breach of the contract may be liquidated damages or a penalty. The distinction is of vital importance. If the sum is liquidated damages it can be recovered from the party in default. It is regarded as a genuine pre-estimate of the damage suffered by the innocent party.

If the sum fixed by the contract is deemed to be a penalty, then essentially it is a threat held against the party likely to violate the contractual obligations. The intention of a penalty is to attempt to compel performance of the contract by severely punishing the party who refuses to implement it. The defaulting party is made liable to pay an extravagant sum, exceeding the greatest loss that could possibly result from the breach. A penalty is irrecoverable and the injured party is limited to recovering the actual loss he has suffered. If a company wishes to guard against breach of contract, a penalty clause is not the method to use.

An example will illustrate the practical operation of these rules. Company A may agree to install machinery on the premises of Company B. A term of contract may provide that if the work is not completed by 1 January, then for every extra working day taken to complete the installation Company A must pay Company B £100. If a delay of twenty working days results in lost production and lost profits of £2000, this sum is recoverable from Company A as liquidated damages if the sum is a genuine pre-estimate of the loss likely to be incurred. In the same circumstances, if the actual loss is £3000, only £2000 is recoverable. Here Company B is confined in its claim to the genuine, though incorrect, pre-estimate of the likely loss.

On the other hand, if Company B's maximum loss of profit for one day's lost production could not possibly exceed £20, the clause in the contract stipulating £100 will be recoverable is a penalty. The court will disregard the clause and only the actual loss suffered will be recovered by Company B.

Specific performance

Damages may be an inadequate remedy and the court may order the defaulting party to perform specifically the obligation undertaken in the contract. This is a discretionary remedy usually given the breach of a contract to sell or lease land, or sell chattels with unique qualities. In these cases it may be difficult for the disappointed purchaser to acquire similar property elsewhere.

FURTHER READING

Tillotson, J., *Contract Law in Perspective*, Butterworths, London, 1981. A discussion of contractual principles in their social, political and economic context.

Treitel, G. H., *An Outline of the Law of Contract*, 2nd edition, Butterworths, London, 1979. A clear, concise summary of all the important basic principles.

41 Insurance of company operations

R W Rooke

To the optimist, the establishment of a new company brings visions of steady employment, expanding wealth, increasing power and strength. To the pessimist, a new company means uncertainty, worry and possible financial disaster. Whatever the natural inclination, however, there must be somebody whose responsibility it is to face squarely the possible catastrophes to which the company is exposed, and devise economical means of preventing them or containing their cost.

RISK BEARING

Some risks are endemic to business. Even assuming that a company knows its trade, performs it well and markets its products intelligently, certain hazards of trade remain. The company may manufacture products for which there is no demand. A change in fashion may destroy an existing demand. These and similar risks, often called 'dynamic' risks, cannot be transferred to somebody else's shoulders, for they are the inevitable consequences of venturing into trade.

Other risks may arise from natural phenomena or human weakness, affecting a company's fortunes with unexpected suddenness. A fire may engulf an important building, a ship exporting its wares may sink, the carelessness of an employee may cause injury to a member of the public and cause that person to sue the company. Risks of this kind, often called 'static' or 'pure' risks, can be just as crippling in their effects. A company may decide to chance its arm, meeting such risks when or if they arise, or it may take the precaution of setting capital aside in advance. On the other hand, it would be more prudent to try to avoid both the vicissitudes of fortune and the tying-up of capital which can more profitably be used in the actual business. This can often be done by transferring the risk, that is, paying a premium to an outside party (an insurer) in return for his accepting financial responsibility for any loss. The terms of the transfer are subject to free negotiation, and defined in a legal document (the insurance policy).

A list of such insurable risks would be quite formidable, and to pay for protection against every single one (even if it were possible) would be so costly as to leave the company unable to compete against rivals. It is essential to be selective, using the concept of catastrophic loss as a criterion. Protection is mainly required against catastrophic losses which can imperil the business at one go, rather than against the small losses which occur with more frequency but even collectively could never endanger the solvency of the firm. The latter are more in the nature of overheads, and can well be costed and included as a trading expense.

Potential catastrophe is, however, relative to the size and spread of the business. Breakage of the plate-glass window could be a severe blow to a small shopkeeper, whereas a multiple store expects to have a certain number of windows broken every year and prepares for this in its budget.

In all cases, methods of preventing or avoiding losses should be fully explored first, and insurance should be reserved for those areas where the possibility of serious loss still remains. A factory may be entirely dependent upon one boiler for its production, and failure of the boiler would cause serious dislocation. Rather than seek insurance protection against such an eventuality, it might be preferable to purchase a standby boiler.

THEORY OF INSURANCE

The decision having been taken to ask an insurer to assume a certain risk of catastrophic loss, what is the theory underlying the practice of insurance? This is admirably expressed (albeit in quaint terms) in the preamble to an Act of Parliament in 1601:

> Whereas it hath been time out of mind an usage amongst merchants, both of this realm and of foreign nations when they make any great adventure (especially into remote parts), to give some consideration of money to other persons (which commonly are in no small number) to have from them assurance made of their goods, merchandises, ships and things adventured, or some part thereof, at such rates and in such sort as the parties assurers and the parties assured can agree, which course of dealing is commonly called a policy of assurance; by means of which policies of assurance it cometh to pass, upon the loss or perishing of any ship, there followeth not the undoing of any man, but the loss lighteth rather easily upon many than heavily upon few, and rather upon them that adventure not than those that do adventure, whereby all merchants, especially the younger sort, are allured to adventure more willingly and more freely.

Insurance is essentially a pooling of financial resources by a large number of individuals exposed to a certain risk, so that the unfortunate few who suffer loss may be reimbursed. Premiums collected by the guardian of the pool, the insurer, are stored against the evil day suffered by the one or two. The insurer calculates the probability and cost of expected losses and fixes the premium accordingly, with due allowance for cost of administration and profit. The insured is spared anxiety and left free to engage more fully in his chosen trade.

THE INSURANCE MARKET

A wide diversity of organisations has emerged to cater for this need for insurance, much of this diversity being accounted for by history. Moreover, a wide range of different types of insurance has also arisen. Many insurance organisations try to cater for a majority of these different forms of cover, whereas others specialise in a chosen few.

Composite offices

The 'composite' offices are prepared to underwrite all the major forms of insurance that have evolved, although it is acknowledged that an office which is a leader in certain fields may be less competitive in others. It is possible for a company to place all its insurance needs with one particular office, and for a small firm this may be convenient. Composite offices will no doubt have branches in most large towns, providing ready access and local service where required. The majority can be approached direct, without need of an intermediary. In structure, they are mainly limited companies.

Lloyd's

As an insurance market, Lloyd's evolved from the practice of underwriters in London at the end of the seventeenth century of meeting for business at a coffee-house managed by one Edward Lloyd. Today, the Lloyd's building ('the Room') houses a large number of insurance syndicates, individually open to business offered to them on behalf of clients by specially appointed Lloyd's brokers. Each syndicate is composed of individuals of a certain financial standing, pledging their capital as surety in unlimited liability. The syndicate is represented by an underwriting agent sitting at a special 'box' in the Room, transacting insurance business on its behalf.

In certain fields, mutual offices have arisen whereby those insuring (sometimes restricted by the articles of association) also share the profits accruing from the operation, usually in the form of a dividend calculated according to the total premium originally contributed. The majority may be approached direct and have a network of local branch offices.

Tariff offices

For certain types of business (mainly fire), insurers have banded together to produce minimum premium rates and standard Policy wordings, so as to impart stability and reliability into their operation. These insurers (known as 'Tariff Offices') also cooperate with each other by collating statistics of experience in those types of insurance, and discussing together any unusual requests for cover. Competition to tariff offices is, however, provided by Lloyd's underwriters and other insurers (non-Tariff Offices) who prefer their own independent line.

Other insurers

In recent years, there has been a steady extension by insurers across national boundaries, setting up overseas branch offices throughout the world or accepting business through a variety of accredited underwriting agencies. Thus, any large business centre will contain an international diversity of insurance offices with varying degrees of autonomy and underwriting methods.

Captive insurers

Many industrial or commercial companies have formed their own insurance subsidiary, into which all or selected parts of the parent's insurance portfolio is channelled.

The precise reasons for the formation of a 'captive' will in all probability be peculiar to the parent company's particular needs, but the following represent major considerations:

1   Recognition of potential profitability
2   Direct access to reinsurance companies
3   Coverage or risk which may be difficult or expensive to place with external insurers.

There may be considerable tax advantage in basing a captive overseas, and certain locations have succeeded in attracting a large insurance industry in consequence. Normally a captive will underwrite only the parent's insurance business.

Reinsurance offices have arisen from the need for ordinary direct insurers to spread the load of business, particularly where a catastrophic loss might otherwise place a severe financial strain upon the pool. Business is obtained solely from the direct insurers, and there is no official contact between the original insured and the reinsurance office.

Co-insurance

It is quite possible for an insurance (for example, a multimillion-pound factory complex) to be too big for any one insurer to assume single-handed. The normal practice in such cases is for the business to be offered first to a large insurer (the 'leading office'), to formulate the terms and conditions of the insurance and agree to bear a percentage of the total insurance. Other offices (co-insurers) are then approached with a view to their accepting other percentages on the same terms and conditions until complete cover is obtained. Each office may, of course, have its own domestic arrangements for reinsuring some of its potential liability. By such co-insurance it is possible for a large insurance to be spread over the whole market, not only at home but also abroad, and thus the risk of catastrophic loss could be shared world-wide.

It must be stressed that in co-insurance, the various insurers stand parallel to each other and are liable for meeting only their own percentage of any loss. In particular, the leading office has no responsibility for any of the insurers which follow the lead given.

PRINCIPLES OF INSURANCE CONTRACTS

For any insurance contract, whether it be with a composite office, Lloyd's or a mutual office, there are certain basic, unwritten principles which must be observed.

Insurable interest

The potential insured must, first, have an 'insurable interest', that is, he must stand to gain by the preservation of the object insured and suffer loss by its damage or destruction. Correspondingly, where he is insuring a legal liability, he must stand to gain by absence of the liability, and lose by incurring the liability.

Utmost good faith

The contract of insurance is based on the principle of *uberrimae fidei*, the 'utmost good faith'. Whereas other commerical contracts follow the common law principle of *caveat emptor*, 'let the buyer beware', and the seller is only bound not to tell lies or practise fraud, contracts of insurance greatly exceed this minimum stipulation. It is accepted that the potential insured knows all the relevant facts concerning the transaction, and is in duty bound to disclose them. These 'relevant facts' are deemed to be any features which would affect an insurer's judgment whether in the first place to offer insurance cover, and secondly on what terms. Similarly, the insurer is bound by the utmost good faith to disclose all relevant features of the cover offered before the potential insured accepts the proposition, or agrees to its renewal.

Indemnity

Most forms of insurance are, thirdly, based on the principle of indemnity. Thus, in the event of a claim upon a policy, compensation should place the insured in the same position after the loss as he was before it. The insured must not make a profit out of his misfortune, neither should he be out-of-pocket if the degree of insurance was satisfactory. The principle of indemnity does not, however, apply in the case of a person insuring his own life or limb, for it is held that he has an unlimited interest in his own well-being.

Two important corollaries apply in the field of indemnity, namely contribution and subrogation.

Contribution

If the same risk is insured twice, whether inadvertently or deliberately, it would transgress the principle of indemnity for an insured to be able to claim for the same loss twice, and in fact it would encourage 'manufactured' losses. Where double insurance has occurred, over-compensation is avoided either by each insurer contributing only a proportion of the whole loss, or by one insurer (where a clause in the Policy allows this) being excused payment.

Subrogation

Similarly, the insured may, in the event of a loss, be able to claim not only against the insurer, but against another party causing the loss. Once again, it would be invidious to allow the insured both claims, for success in both cases would provide a handsome profit out of loss. It is therefore accepted that if the insurers meet the loss, they are 'subrogated' to any rights of recovery which the insured may have elsewhere, that is the benefit of such rights passes from the insured to the insurer.

As the principle of indemnity does not operate in the insurance of life or limb, then the corollaries of contribution and subrogation do not operate either.

AVERAGE

Many policies contain a clause relating to 'average' being applied in the case of partial losses. It is the responsibility of the insured to make certain that the amount of cover is adequate if a total loss should occur. This particularly applies where values increase by virtue of inflation. Often this duty is neglected and under-insurance occurs. If a total loss should arise in such circumstances, only the sum insured under the policy would be paid and the neglectful insured would have to bear the difference between this amount and the full cost of his loss. By the principle of average, this process would apply to partial losses also and only a proportion of the cost would be borne by the insurers. This proportion would be calculated by dividing the sum insured (as per the policy) by the true value, and multiplying the amount of the loss by his fraction. Thus for an £80 000 building insured for only £60 000 but suffering £20 000 damage, the insurers would pay only

$$\frac{£60\ 000}{£80\ 000} \times £20\ 000 = £15\ 000$$

and the insured would have to find the remaining £5000 from his own resources.

In the light of competition between insurers and in recognition of the difficulty of forecasting the effect of inflation upon future replacement costs, a concession has been allowed in recent years from this strict application of average. Insurers will in general allow a margin of error of 15 per cent in valuation of assets without average being incurred. Where the margin exceeds 15 per cent, however, average would be applied in full. Thus, if it were discovered after a loss that assets had been insured for only 90 per cent of their value, no deduction through average would apply. If this were found to be 75 per cent, however, average would be imposed in full and 25 per cent of the value of the loss would be borne by the insured.

EFFECT OF INFLATION ON PROPERTY INSURANCE

The high rates of inflation in recent years have undermined the earlier confidence in sums insured remaining adequate throughout a period of insurance, and two main methods of catering for the erosive effect of inflation have been evolved by insurers:

1 An 'instantaneious reinstatement value' is calculated for the value of assets both on the first and also the last day of insurance, and in addition to the premium for this underlying value a specially-reduced premium rate is applied to this inflationery increase in value during the period
2 A similar 'instantaneous reinstatement value' is calculated and a percentage increase in value is computed to cater for inflation through the maximum rebuilding period for the assets. A set scale of premium rates applies to the inflationary increase in asset values, based upon the percentage which this increase bears to the instantaneous reinstatement value. The total premium is adjusted according to the difference in value between the first and last days of insurance.

PORTFOLIO OF INSURANCE

With all this background information in hand, how does the responsible official set about protecting his company against catastrophic loss? It is possible to regard an insurer as a supermarket and choose from the merchandise on sale what are considered to be the 'best buys'. In this, he receives advice and assistance from a representative of the insurer. Recognising the competition for business that exists between insurers, a better method might be to obtain quotations from a number of insurers to see which office offers the best terms, both in extent of cover and size of premium. Negotiation with the most competitive office could well bring even further improvement in the terms. But how can he be sure of recognising what his company's real needs are and satisfying them? May there not be some vital risk he has not spotted?

Another method is to consult an expert in the field, and after agreeing upon a programme, instruct him to obtain the necessary cover on the best terms available. In other words, the official would use the services of a reputable insurance broker.

Whichever approach is made, either directly to insurers or indirectly through a broker, the official must be well-informed upon the risks to which his business is exposed and the insurances which may be required. This may appear at first sight a formidable task, the concept of 'risk' being somewhat nebulous. It becomes manageable by dividing the subject into more tangible parts as follows:

1 Property protection
2 Loss of income
3 Legal liabilities
4 Personnel.

The extent to which these different parts apply will vary from one company to another.

Property protection

Every commercial undertaking will amass property of various kinds, whether buildings, machinery, stock, furniture or cars. Some of these it will own out-right, some it will lease but nevertheless be responsible for under the terms of the lease. The continued safety of these physical assets may well be crucial for the well-being of the company.

The first line of defence is to prevent this loss or destruction, for even if full compensation is received after a catastrophe, there has still been the disruption to the business and strain upon its executives which cannot be expressed in financial terms.

Attention should be given to defence against fire by consultation with the local fire safety officer, with companies specialising in fire detection and prevention, and with fire insurance surveyors. This should be done during the planning stage for new buildings, and also during any major transformations or extensions of a plant. Similarly, advice on burglary protection could be obtained from specialist companies and burglary insurance surveyors. In certain cases, attention might be given to possible water damage, particularly where vulnerable materials are being stored.

It is then necessary to consider the perils to which the property is exposed. Some property may be very important to the company and expensive to replace, yet prone to damage of many kinds. For this it is expedient, even if the insurers do not demand it, that all reasonable precautions be taken to prevent, or at least minimise, loss. The fullest available insurance is advisable upon this property. Such insurance is known as All Risks (rather incorrectly, seeing that there are various exclusions), and may be recommended for items such as computers. This cover is frequently provided for goods in transit, ships and their cargo, aircraft.

In other cases, it is possible to select the more likely perils and insure against these only (for example, fire, explosion, burglary or water damage), remembering that less obvious perils can be equally important. This requires an appraisal of the types of property owned and the nature of the particular perils to which they are exposed.

Yet again there may be property which it is decided should not be insured, either because there are no catastrophic perils to which it is open, or because the cost of its replacement would not impose undue financial strain.

Loss of income

If a physical asset is destroyed, there can still be other loss to the company stemming from this, namely (i) loss of net profit and continued payment of standing charges despite the reduction in sales, and/or (ii) increase in costs in order to maintain sales at the former level. If important stock is destroyed by fire or other cause (whether in the company's premises or those of a vital supplier), or an important customer loses warehousing capacity for similar reasons, or a vital piece of machinery is put out of action for a long time, there can well be loss of business and therefore profits if customers turn elsewhere for their supplies. Buying from a competitor in order to keep a customer stocked can be an expensive way of retaining his business. Moreover, certain expenses (for example local rates) continue, even if a factory is out of action for a while.

It may therefore be just as important to insure against these lost profits and increased costs as to insure against the underlying loss or destruction of the asset. This type of insurance is called Consequential Loss, or Loss of Profit, but is superimposed upon the underlying property damage (for example fire or engineering breakdown), and applies only to the consequences arising from it.

Further loss of income may arise from bad debts, or loss of rent from a tenant through fire damage to the premises. Insurance protection is available against these risks also.

Legal liabilities

The business activities of any company may cause injury to employees or outside parties, or damage to their property, arising from negligence of some kind in its activities, including the negligence of employees. There may be an unsafe method of work, or impurities in goods supplied which should have been noticed during manufacturing. An individual or corporate body taking the company to court might succeed in obtaining heavy damages from the company.

Since the passing of the Employer's Liability (Compulsory Insurance Act) 1969, all employers apart from a few exceptions are obliged to insure against their legal liability for injuries to employees arising out of and in the course of their employment. Insurance must be arranged with an insurer satisfying certain requirements, for a limit of liability not less than £2m. Certificates to this effect are supplied by the insurer and these must be displayed in suitably prominent places (for example, works or office notice-boards).

Similarly, responsibility for injury or damage may devolve upon the company as a result of committing a breach of statute. Particular attention is drawn to the Health and Safety at Work Act 1974, which provides a comprehensive and integrated system of law to deal with the health, safety and welfare of people at work.

Since the possible causes of liability are legion, there is much sense in insuring against them. The main forms of cover available are Employer's Liability, Public (or Third Party) Liability, and Products Liability.

Personnel

The most important asset which any company has is its personnel, for the entire success of the enterprise basically rests on them. While it is possible to think only of the financial effect on the company of loss of personnel and in certain respects insure against it, most companies exhibit a more humanitarian approach and provide insurance protection for the employees themselves against certain eventualities. In the long run, it is to the company's advantage that its staff shall be spared anxieties about financial hardship, whether by accident during working life or the advent of retirement.

In this respect, consideration should be given to pension schemes, group life assurance and personal accident cover.

Although the various aspects (property protection, loss of income, legal liabilities, personnel) have been differentiated for convenience, certain types of insurance to be considered in a company context stretch over two or more aspects. Thus private car and commercial vehicle insurance combine all aspects but loss of income.

Policies of insurance upon steam boilers, lifts, lifting gear and certain other types of equipment or installation will embrace inspection by a qualified person as prescribed by statute, public liability cover, and possibly also cover against material damage (both to the property insured and also to surrounding equipment).

Summary of portfolio

The exact contents of the insurance portfolio will depend on many factors, but principally the nature of the business and the extent to which the company management decide to bear risks uninsured.

The following types of insurance are suggested as a nucleus which would be appropriate for most companies:

1 *Property protection*
    (*a*) fire and explosion insurance (and selected perils if appropriate) upon buildings, machinery, contents, stock and office equipment
    (*b*) money insurance, covering losses in premises or in transit
    (*c*) all risks insurance upon expensive, vulnerable items and goods in transit by road, rail, sea or air
2 *Loss of income*
    Loss of profits insurance, to meet loss of profit and increased cost of working following loss or damage by fire
3 *Legal liabilities*
    (*a*) employer's liability insurance, to cover legal liability for injury to employees
    (*b*) public liability insurance, to cover legal liability for injury to third parties or damage to their property arising out of business activities (including products liability insurance if engaged in manufacture or distribution of goods)
4 *Personnel*
    (*a*) pension scheme, to provide adequate retirement pensions to employees;
    (*b*) personal accident insurance, for employees injured during business activities.
5 *Combined*
    (*a*) motor vehicle insurance
    (*b*) engineering insurance upon steam boilers, lifts, lifting gear, etc.
    (*c*) computer insurance.

This list is by no means exhaustive, but will serve as a guide to those forms of insurance which might prudently be obtained.

SELF-INSURANCE

Whether consciously or not, all companies practise forms of self-insurance (or sometimes, more correctly, non-insurance), that is, accept the possibility of loss arising from certain directions without financial recovery from an insurer. A non-catastrophic hazard may be so remote as not to warrant special provision for it, or so regular as to be rather an overhead cost.

In this context, can 'catastrophic loss' be assessed in financial terms, bearing in mind that this must be relative to the size and spread of the business? Where no fixed criteria are used, the process becomes entirely subjective, and the limits beyond which potential losses are insured are chosen on 'psychological' rather than financial/economic grounds. It merely 'feels right' to have a certain level of insurance for safety's sake.

If, on the other hand, a more objective approach is required, there are certain bases within the company's financial operations which can be used, namely:

1 Assets
2 Return on capital employed
3 Profits
4 Cash flow.

While there can be no hard and fast rules for calculating the degree of financial loss which would be tolerable in any one year, it is suggested that the maximum degree of self-insurance is such that the annual potential cost of uninsured losses would not:

1 Reduce the value of the total net assets attributable to the ordinary share capital by more than 2 per cent
2 Reduce the return on capital employed by more than about $\frac{1}{2}$ per cent when subtracted from the previous year's before-tax profit
3 Reduce the value of the profit by more than 5 per cent when subtracted from the previous year's before-tax profit
4 Exceed 10 per cent of the previous year's after tax profit plus depreciation less distributions.

Where application of these criteria produce different limits, it would be prudent to choose the lowest figure as the tolerable degree of self-insurance.

To assist the mechanics of self-insurance, it might be decided to set up a fund within the company in readiness for meeting any losses which may arise. This fund may be built up by regular contributions from participating sections of the business over a period, and maintained at an adequate level thereafter. This is, after all, how an insurer operates. On the other hand, it must be borne in mind that although premiums to outside insurers rank as an expense for taxation purposes, contributions to an internal fund do not, and taxation of the internal fund can have a serious effect on the economics of the operation.

Moreover, for an accurate assessment of the financial provision required against such risks, it is essential that full statistics of losses be kept and that the company's operations be large enough to give a reliable guide to the incidence of such losses.

Part insurance

A further method of insurance is to insure only part of the risk and bear the remainder internally.

Excess

Under this method, the company bears an 'excess' or 'deductible', that is, meets the cost of each claim up to an agreed amount, and the balance above this 'excess' or 'deductible' is borne by the insurers.

Co-insurance

A second form is co-insurance, where the company accepts an agreed percentage of any loss, however great or small.

First loss

A third form is known as 'first loss' insurance, applicable in situations where a complete loss is unimaginable (for example, theft of a company's entire stock of large machinery). In this case, a maximum loss is estimated and insurance for that amount arranged, but in the remote chance of a loss exceeding the estimate, the company bears the remaining cost.

Aggregate deductible

A fourth method is by means of an 'aggregate deductible', under which the company bears all losses of a particular kind until an agreed total is reached, whereupon the insurer accepts all further losses beyond that point.

Captive insurer

The company may consider that its operations are sufficiently large and well-spread that the premium otherwise payable to outside insurers would provide sufficient income for promoting an insurance company subsidiary, or 'captive insurer'. Suitable reinsurance would protect the 'captive' against an unacceptable level of potential loss.

Whether or not self-insurance in one or more of its forms is a practical proposition may depend upon the financial structure of the company, and on its costing procedures. Many giant corporations which might appear to have abundant funds for the operation are in fact split into a large number of independent profit centres, and neither central funds nor possibly even central administration are available to make the most of the overall strength.

COST OF INSURANCE

To a large extent, the total cost of insurance will vary according to the size of the company. Expansion of business will mean expansion of premium outlay. It is difficult to give guidelines upon the degree of cost that must be expected, for so much will depend upon the size and nature of the business, the prevalence of losses, and many other factors which vary from one industry to another, or between different companies in the same industry.

Furthermore, it is difficult to establish a reliable standard of comparison. Should the cost of insurance be calculated as a percentage of turnover, capital employed, assets? Whichever basis is used, there will be anomalies, but in the few cases where research has been undertaken, there has been a tendency to use turnover as the standard of comparison.

As such, premium expenditure can generally be expected to reach up to one per cent of turnover, although higher percentages are not unusual in certain occupations. Much will depend on the degree of self-insurance assumed by the company. With the steady increase in fire losses, motor accidents, and crime in recent years, the cost of most forms of insurance has tended to increase, and this may be expected to continue for the time being.

ADMINISTRATION OF INSURANCE

The number of staff required to handle insurnace will depend on the size of the company. In a small undertaking, it may only be necessary for one individual to spend an occasional hour on insurance matters. In a larger company, there will come a stage at which an insurance specialist will need to be appointed in a full-time capacity. In a giant concern, there may well be an entire insurance department.

As in many other spheres, size and overall buying power count for a great deal in obtaining insurance, and it would seem obvious that centralisation is essential for the most effective administration of insurance in the larger companies. Concentration of premium expenditure gives negotiating strength *vis-à-vis* insurers, the cost of administration is less for each party, and thus there will be scope for cutting premium rates which will benefit the entire company. Furthermore, it is more economic to recruit specialist insurance knowledge, for it will be used to the fullest advantage in a central function.

On the other hand, many giant companies favour a decentralised structure so that responsibility for profitability is more widely shared. Administration of insurance is then divided accordingly, and seeing that the fortunes of the smaller unit then have a much more direct bearing on the level of its insurance costs, it is argued that this gives greater incentive to the containment of premium expenditure.

Certain large companies have evolved a combination of these two viewpoints in their insurance administration. Wherever possible, group policies are effected so as to take fullest advantage of 'purchasing power' both as regards premium outlay and also extent of insurance cover. Within these group policies, apportionment of premium expenditure is made between separate units according to the normal underwriting factors such as claims experience, size of operation, etc. In addition, the separate units are able to effect their own particular insurance covers as dictated by their own special needs and circumstances. Thus it is possible to combine the advantages of centralisation with the greater freedom of manoeuvre provided by decentralisation.

REPORTING CHANGES IN RISK

Whichever philosophy is adopted, it is imperative that there be strong lines of communication so that all matters affecting insurance, whether new losses occurring or new risks arising, are reported for the necessary action to be taken. In this respect it is surprising how much within a company's activities can have a bearing upon insurance. New liabilities may arise from entry into different fields of industry or commerce, from new contracts and agreements or new legislation, and these must be considered in relation to the company's liability insurances. Before new buildings are erected it is advisable to notify the fire insurers so that suitable protection is incorporated against the risk of fire outbreak. Financial statistics of various kinds must be supplied to insurers, and convenient methods of collation must be evolved. These are but a sample of the ways in which communication of knowledge is vital for the most effective administration of insurance.

Liaison must be built up with a large cross-section of senior staff – works managers, accountants, transport managers, solicitors, personnel managers, sales managers, research staff – to ensure a two-way transmission of information. In this way, a clear watch may be kept to make certain that insurance provision is geared to the ever-changing face of company operations, and that specialist insurance advice is available in the right places at the right time. There will be continual need for education of all appropriate staff with regard to insurance, both formally by dissemination of written instructions and informally by social contact.

ADMINISTERING CLAIMS

Well-defined procedures are required for administration of claims. These may arise from any sector of the business, and it is vital that staff should have a judicious appreciation of what accidents or losses may be the subject of insurance claims. With some (for example, motor accidents) it is quite obvious that they must be reported, but others (for example, damage to outside property by a faulty product) may not so obviously prompt thoughts of an insurance claim.

At the very least, certain key staff such as works managers, transport and personnel officials should be trained to report incidents for insurance purposes. Agreed reporting procedures should be in force, possibly in the shape of questionnaires or insurers' report forms for submission at the earliest opportunity. Where a company's operations are scattered over a wide area, it may be appropriate for certain types of insurance claim (for example motor accidents) to be negotiated direct between the local official responsible and the district branch of the particular insurer.

In the case of major claims, consideration should be given to an early visit to the scene of operations. This will permit evidence to be taken whilst still fresh, and a detailed approach made to rectification and ultimate presentation of the claim upon the insurers. This visit may well be undertaken in company with a representative from the insurers, or with an independent assessor appointed by the insurer to handle the claim.

It is possible that in such claims, assistance or advice may be necessary from a miscellany of company officials.

Claims under certain types of insurance (for example, property damage) are essentially claims *against* the insurer, and these will require sustained attention by the company until completed. In other types of insurance (for example, liability), the insurer is handling the claim on behalf of the company and thus determines the manner in which it is handled.

INSURANCE OF OVERSEAS COMPANIES

Communication may also be of prime importance where a company has operations overseas. Even if there are no bases abroad, there may be products or services exported which must figure in insurance provision. Directors and sales representatives may travel abroad, and for them personal insurances will be necessary. It is essential that information be made available upon these overseas activities so that the implications for insurance may be considered.

Companies having only a few subsidiary offices or works abroad may control them fully from head offices and allow little autonomy. This form of administration may affect the provision of insurance, in that as far as possible, the relevant cover may be provided within the head office policies, and only where local convenience is of prime importance will insurance be arranged locally. In some cases, overseas legislation will dictate where insurance cover is to be obtained.

Overseas subsidiary companies may well have a great deal of independence from head office control, and among other freedoms, may have the right to arrange their own insurances. In such cases there will still be wisdom in participating in the major group, world-wide policies. These must, of course, have the greatest flexibility and interpretation of cover for such world-wide application. Premiums are no doubt paid by the parent company to the main offices of the insurers, but there should be arrangements for claims to be negotiated and settled locally. Where insurance is deliberately obtained locally, care should be taken in deciding whether foreign insurers or overseas offices of British-based companies are to be used.

RENEWAL DATES

Although the cost of insurance has already been seen as a relatively modest percentage of a company's turnover, modern methods of costing and budgetary control take full note of the effect which such an item can have upon profitability. The incidence of renewal dates can have a distinct bearing upon this.

The eventual premiums for certain types of insurance (for example employer's liability, third party, money) depend on certain statistics applicable to the year of insurance, which can only be known when the year is completed. Where these statistics are primarily financial (for example, salaries paid or volume of money carried), it is sensible for the year of insurance to coincide with the company's accounting year. This makes the collation of statistics easier, in that only one year's accounts are involved. The cost of the insurance is equated with the past year of accounts, and correspondingly the forecast cost of insurance for budget purposes is more reliable.

Whether all company insurances should coincide with the accounting year is a matter of opinion. This is undoubtedly very helpful in preparing annual accounts, for premiums do not have to be apportioned between different accounting years. On the other hand, negotiation of all policies in one concentrated period can mean thet there is insufficient time for judicious thought to be given to each policy. Where renewal dates are spread over a whole calendar year, deeper investigation of the cover is possible and the workload is more evenly distributed.

RECORDS

Although statistics of various kinds can be obtained from other agencies (for example, from insurers or brokers or other departments), it is advisable for certain domestic records to be kept. Renewal negotiations frequently hinge upon 'claims experience', that is, the proportion of premium expenditure swallowed up by claims payments, and it is of great benefit to have one's own facts and figures. (It is always possible for the insurers' figures to be wrong.)

Details of premiums and claims for several years of insurance are vital when considering any change from insurance to self-insurance.

These details are also useful for internal administration, such as forecast budgets. The actual method of recording is open to personal choice, but it is recommended that, at the very least, details be kept of premiums and claims paid according to insurance years.

USE OF BROKERS

For many companies, the purchase of insurance is identical with purchase of any other goods and service. Approach is made to the supplier direct and the transaction is finally effected to the satisfaction of both parties. Insurance departments of many large companies are administered in the same way. All insurance is negotiated direct with insurers (except Lloyd's), and either the commission earned pays the cost of operating the department or the net premium cost is relayed to the division which generates the cover, and their overheads are correspondingly reduced. Insurance at Lloyd's can only be placed through a specially appointed Lloyd's broker, for the syndicates do not transact business direct with the general public (including industrial and commercial clients).

Many other companies, however, employ insurance brokers as inter-mediaries in negotiations with insurers. This is particularly the case where the responsibility lies with one official in the company, often not an insurance specialist. The main services and advantages to be obtained through the use of brokers are:

1 Availability of expert knowledge of the varying strengths of differing insurers, and their representation in different parts of the world. It is hardly possible for one person to hold and keep up to date such a fund of knowledge
2 Access to Lloyd's is only possible through the agency of Lloyd's brokers
3 By constant intercourse with insurers of all kinds, brokers can be expected to have a knowledge of how a company's insurance needs can best be met at an economical cost
4 The very size of many brokers enables them to exert independent pressure upon insurers in the interest of their client
5 For large-scale policies involving many co-insurers, insurance brokers collate the various part-premiums and present one total debit note for the client, thus simplifying accounting procedure
6 Various ancillary services are provided at no additional cost; for example, discussion of contract conditions relating to insurance, surveys of premises.

The argument for use of insurance brokers is that such services can be provided at a more economic cost than is possible for a company providing a similar level of expertise.

It is possible to combine these approaches, by making direct contact with insurers wherever it is warranted but negotiating through brokers where their services are of particular value.

It should be noted that the title 'insurance broker' (or 'assurance broker', 'reinsurance broker' or 'reassurance broker') should strictly speaking only be used by persons or companies registered or enrolled under the Insurance Brokers (Registration) Act 1977. This lays down the minimum professional standards and financial backing to be held before registration can be granted.

Payment of brokers

Remuneration is made by the insurer in the form of percentage commission based on the gross premium paid. The percentage varies according to types of cover and the size of the brokers. This method has the merit of simplicity of accounting, in that the broker merely deducts the percentage when remitting to the insurers premiums paid by his client.

There are, however, various objections to this time-honoured method:

1 By being indirect, it may be difficult for a company to know exactly how much commission is earned over a year by the broker and thus to assess whether the cost of his services is economic
2 The volume of work required of a broker is not necessarily proportional to the premium. The commission earned on a large policy may greatly exceed the cost of servicing it. Conversely, many brokers are finding the cost of administering small policies out of proportion to the commission earned
3 More fundamentally, perhaps, the implied principle of 'no premium no

pay' must inevitably place a strain upon the integrity of insurance brokers, for it is in their financial interest to urge clients to have as much insurance as possible, yet the interests of the clients may be towards a greater degree of self-insurance (upon which no commission would be earned).

To a small extent, the practice of paying brokers a fee (either annually or per assignment), is gaining favour as satisfying these objections. Thus a company uses the full services of a broker in negotiations, pays premiums net to the insurer, and pays a separate fee to the broker. Negotiation of the fee is based on the cost of the work undertaken by the broker, irrespective of the amount of insurance arranged.

RISK PREVENTION

Real catastrophe apart, the cost of insurance is ultimately decided by the cost of the losses sustained. In recent years, losses by fire, theft and other insurable risks have been increasing at a steady if not an alarming rate, and the price of insurance has risen accordingly. Measures which can halt or reverse this process are of benefit to all parties and to the community at large.

Insurers have always emphasised the importance of preventing losses, on the basis that prevention is better than cure. As part of their service, they insist upon inspecting premises for fire insurance, safes and other devices for burglary insurance, accounting procedures for fidelity guarantee insurance (eg against dishonesty on the part of the insured's staff). No extra charge is made for these services, but their importance is such that insurance will not be offered unless they are undertaken and any protective recommendations put into force. It is urged, for example, that plans for a new building should be vetted by fire insurers so that measures to reduce the risk of fire may be incorporated at the outset. The offer of reduced premiums is a powerful inducement to effect such protection.

Many insurers apply similar reasoning to the reduction of accidents, and the services of qualified surveyors are made available to investigate potential causes of accident and make recommendations for reducing or eliminating them.

These specialist services do not, of course, detract from the importance of domestic attention to all potential sources of injury or loss.

UP-TO-DATE KNOWLEDGE

The whole subject of risk-bearing is one that is constantly changing, for it is moulded by so many factors that are themselves constantly changing. New legislation is continually being promulgated, not only in this country but also abroad, and some will have an influence upon insurance to greater or lesser degree. Changes taking place within the company will frequently necessitate review of the insurance portfolio, by increasing some hazards and reducing others. The insurance market itself has been subjected to radical change in recent years through mergers and takeovers, and it is likely that this pace of change will continue.

There will never be a time when the entire subject will have been completely mastered. On the contrary, there will always be a need to increase further knowledge and keep abreast of current developments in many fields.

FURTHER READING

AIRMIC (ed.), *Company Insurance Handbook*, Gower, 1973

AIRMIC, *The Status and Techniques of Insurance and Risk Managers in Industry and Commerce*, London, 1979

Baglini, N.A., *Risk Management in American Multinational and International Corporations*, Risk Studies Foundation, USA, 1976

Carter, R.L. (ed.), *Handbook of Insurance*, Kluwer Handbooks, Brentford, 1973

Carter, R. L., and Crockford, G. N., *Handbook of Risk Management*, Kluwer-Harrap, London, 1974

Catchpole, W. L., *Business Guide to Insurance*, Heinemann, London, 1974

Cockerell, H.A.L., *Insurance*, English Universities Press, Teach Yourself Books, London, 1957

Cockerell, H. A. L., *Witherby's Dictionary of Insurance*, Witherby, London, 1980

Crockford, G. N., *An Introduction to Risk Management*, Woodhead Faulkner, Cambridge, 1980

Curer-Briggs, N., Hamilton, P., and Norman, A. R. D., *Handbook of Security*, Kluwer-Harrap, London, 1974

Dickson, G. C. A., and Steele, J. T., *Elements of Insurance*, Macdonald and Evans, London, 1981

42 Administration of commercial property

John Parfitt

The administration of commercial property such as offices, showrooms, factories and warehouses, may be in the hands of an executive able to devote the whole, or only part, of his time to the subject depending upon the size of the organisation involved. If the executive concerned has no relevant specialist training, it is important that he should have ready access to professional advice.

Frequently property administration is one of the responsibilities of an office manager or personnel manager, who may find that his other duties leave him insufficient time for looking after the company's real estate, and this chapter is intended as a guide in such circumstances.

The term 'real estate' should be explained. All proprietary interests in land are at law 'real' property as distinct from other property including chattels, animals, stocks and shares, etc., which are 'personal' property. Thus, 'real estate' includes freeholds and easements, which are rights by virtue of land ownership over the land of others (for example, a right of way).

LOCATION

Modern and efficient businesses should be well located, which may involve relocation in the light of extraneous factors. The devastation of vast areas of commercial development during the last war necessitated reconstruction, and this was an opportunity for relocation to a more satisfactory area having regard to the facilities essential to efficient operation.

Certain industries, especially heavy industry, needed to be within reach of a railway, preferably to the extent of having their own railway sidings, but as even the heaviest raw materials and products are now largely transported by road it is more important to ensure access to motorways and good parking and loading facilities, with space sufficient for manoeuvring the road vehicle, ever increasing in size.

Location of industry is, therefore dependent upon easy access to raw materials, easy delivery of products to markets, docks or airports, and availability of labour force.

Commerce is affected by similar constraints; although warehousing is not so demanding on labour, distribution is even more important and the strategic placing of warehousing is influenced by the location of docks, airports and large towns which represent consumer outlets for products.

It must always be borne in mind by those responsible for commercial undertakings that relocation could be the solution to their problem of inefficiency resulting from labour problems, unavailability of space for expansion, or the need for reorganisation of production lines without interruption to output.

Selecting a site

Planning control can be very restrictive in that it will not necessarily allow a commercial organisation to develop where it wishes, but it can also be of considerable assistance. The national plan for the distribution of industry encourages relocation of long-established activities to assist the national economy. The government has set examples as demonstrated by the relocation of the Royal Mint in Llantrisant, and offices such as the Department of Transport's vehicle licencing establishment in Swansea. Various other office establishments which had traditionally been in the capital have been moved to the provinces, particularly the depressed areas where a stimulus is required to economic revival.

Accordingly with post-war redevelopment new towns were established, designed to be self-contained economic units having their own labour force, land for commercial and industrial development, communications and other facilities, making them independent of other developed communities.

Many existing towns having facilities for development, or redevelopment of blighted areas, have encouraged the migration of existing business from obsolete areas of older towns to specially developed estates, where such encouraging inducements as low initial rent for modern buildings, and relief rates are offered.

In the long term benefits from such moves also accrue to businesses as the ultimate rent and rates bills are invariably favourable compared with the cost of such outgoings in the central areas of old-established towns and cities.

Advantage is also experienced in having a more contented labour force who usually find better living conditions and fewer commuting problems. Operatives are not involved in heavy expenses in travelling to and from their work as when working in the capital or other large cities, and accordingly wages are not likely to be quite so high in new or expanding towns.

A checklist of factors to be considered in choosing a building location is given in Figure 42.1

Planning control

Planning control is exercised over the use and development of all land by the local planning authority. There is a right of appeal against a planning decision

---

1 Communications `GHM`

(a) Standard of trunk roads available
(b) Proximity of railhead
(c) Access to international airport
(d) Access to seaport
(e) Average distance from suppliers and customers as small as possible

2 Services

(a) Electric power available without restriction
(b) Mains gas supplies available
(c) Adequate water supplies

3 Climate and topography

(a) Temperate climate throughout the year
(b) Area/site well drained and free from flood danger
(c) Site sheltered from high winds and extreme weather
(d) Surrounding area pleasant; good outlook from the site

4 Government and local authority

(a) Area scheduled as development area, and eligible for investment grants
(b) Planning restrictions in the area minimal
(c) Friendly and co-operative local authority

5 Labour and labour relations

(a) Local branches of trade unions moderate and co-operative
(b) Key staff willing to move into the area
(c) Good supply of skilled or suitable workpeople already living in the area

6 Amenities

(a) Housing prices low, good supply of houses of all types (private and local authority)
(b) Good schools available, with possibilities in the area for higher education
(c) Good local transport facilities for commuters
(d) Good local health services and hospitals
(e) Adequate recreational facilities in the area
(f) Theatres, cinemas and other entertainments
(g) Police and fire services efficient
(h) Churches of all demoninations accessible

7 Specific site factors

(a) Means for disposal of waste/effluent
(b) Etc. as required by the particular industry.

Figure 42.1 Checklist of factors affecting choice of building location by an aggrieved applicant to the Secretary of State for the Environment.

Planning control, although of fairly recent origin, is most far reaching in its effect and determines the value of the land by controlling the use to which it can be put.

The use of land is categorised by the Use Classes Order 1972 made under the Town & Country Planning Act, 1971. Land use may be changed without permission to another activity within the same use class; for example, a retail shop can be changed from one trade to another so long as it is not a noxious business) but not to an office. Similarly a factory used for light industry (say, making lampshades) can change its use to another light industry (for example, making articles of clothing) without planning consent.

Changes of use class is development. All development requires planning approval, but development also includes constructing, extending or altering a building. Thus to establish a commerical enterprise on vacant land, not only will it be necessary to satisfy the planning authority that the proposal is not contrary to the approved Town Planning Scheme so far as land use is concerned, but the form of the building wil have to be acceptable as regards appearance, bulk, height, means of access, etc.

CHOOSING A BUILDING

It is indeed fortunate if an administrator faced with a move can plan his establishment *de novo* in the light of his experience of his particular business, without restraint as to the area or type of building to be employed or cost. Far more often he has to adapt the ideal production sequences of the firm's activities according to what is available by way of land, buildings, height, etc. For example, it is only rarely that in an urban site of high-land values it will be economic to construct a single-storey building. If such a form of construction is essential it should be located on a less valuable site.

Frequently a selection will have to be made from among a number of existing establishments. The first consideration is whether the firm wishes to rent or purchase the property and, if the latter, whether an existing building is being sought or specially built premises are required.

There are numerous factors affecting the first decision. The time factor is very important, since a new building may take one to two years to complete (depending upon its complexity) after all necessary consents are to hand.

The financial status and policy of the company are material. If a freehold building can be built or purchased with or without mortgage loan this represents a substantial asset and surety against rent reviews inevitable in leases.

Whenever an existing building is taken over by purchase or lease capital expenditure will be involved in adapting it to the requirements of the organisation. This could amount to complete refurbishment (which might extend to new services and perhaps the installation of air conditioning, improved insulation, and the upgrading of facilities for staff including sanitary accommodation, welfare facilities, dining accommodation, etc.).

Moreover, existing buildings are unlikely to conform to the evermore exacting legal requirements for people's workplaces; in particular, statutory requirements under the Health and Safety at Work Act 1974, and the Fire Precautions Act 1971, are the subject of constant review.

OCCUPIER'S REQUIREMENTS

In the contemplation of the occupation of alternative premises, whether newly constructed or existing, it is necessary to analyse the processes of the intended business, from arrival of post, or raw materials, to the final despatch of services or products, including the various courses through which a job of work has to pass in order that the organisation can perform its various expert functions upon it.

Working conditions

The number of personnel and amount of space allocated to each department are obviously of importance. Minimum working space is prescribed in the Offices Shops and Railway Premises Act, which also lays down minimum standards for the installation of sanitary equipment and the provision of first aid and rest rooms. (For a fuller account of working condition requirements, see Chapter 53.)

Catering facilities

Unless the location is in a city centre where external catering facilities are good and reasonably priced, the provision of dining facilities for staff is necessary. Depending upon company policy, communal or separate dining facilities must be provided for different grades of employees, usually on a self-service basis for the general grade of employee with table service for directors and higher executives. Separation is desirable where visitors have to be entertained to a meal at which business is inevitably discussed and a degree of privacy is necessary.

Usually service to all dining areas is from the same kitchen, and careful planning is required to ensure labour-saving circulation so as to keep down catering costs.

Catering facilities require a surprising amount of space which is not really capable of use for any other purpose, and represents a substantial overhead where rental values are high.

Ventilation and air conditioning

In deciding whether a building should be air conditioned a number of factors should be taken into account.

It is important that alternative ventilation facilities should be assessed; for example, if half the windows are made to open and an office is set in a quiet environment it should be possible to achieve amenable working conditions during hot summer days. If, however, there is disturbing traffic noise, as in offices facing a major traffic route, efficient work is only possible with the windows permanently closed, and air conditioning is essential. It is more usual to find that buildings in central areas are air conditioned, although there are exceptional types of buildings, with large artificially lit and densely occupied floor areas, in which air conditioning is essential.

Air-conditioned space is of considerably higher rental value (which reflects the costly installation) and it should not be overlooked that, being a sophisticated installation, maintenance costs are high. With the problems attendant upon obtaining spare parts and efficient service these days, periods of breakdown can be prolonged and troublesome to management.

Whether or not full air conditioning is to be installed, it is always necessary to consider the degree of ventilation provided, and to ensure that sufficient air changes are obtained, according to the nature of work carried out. A set of guidelines, which tabulates ventilation levels in terms of the number of air changes provided in each house, is shown in Figure 42.2.

	GHM
	Air changes/hour
General workshops	3 to 8
Paint shops	15 to 50
Spray shops	50
Foundries	8 to 20
Assembly shops	4 to 8
Offices	5 to 7
Canteens	7 to 10
WC installations	8 to 15

Figure 42.2 Ventilation levels required in various places

Computer accommodation

Computerisation of various disciplines calls for special consideration as regards the installation of computerised equipment. With larger installations the avoidance of voltage variations in electrical supply can be vital, and on occasions it is necessary to have stand-by facilities in the event of a current failure. It may therefore be necessary for the organisation to have its own generator for computer operation, and this involves careful siting and insulation of noise which might be transmitted into offices. It is usually best to install such generating equipment in an outbuilding.

Air conditioning is frequently essential in areas where computers are installed but this does not necessarily mean that the whole building must be air conditioned. It is usually desirable to separate the installation serving the computers as the period of operation of such equipment may not correspond with occupation of the building as a whole.

Distributed services

Communications are of ever-increasing importance and in order to provide the maximum adaptability trunking is required to all parts of the premises. In a new building this can probably best be provided in the thickness of the floor screed but in an existing building where no trunking exists it may be easier to install it as a skirting duct along the external walls, or as a duct at window-sill height.

Standard ducting is available with internal division which will give complete separation for post office telephone cable, private telephones, teledata, etc., and also for the normal electrical circuit for socket outlets.

Lighting

Apart from its contribution to economical operation, the ability for people to be able to see easily, without eye strain, contributes to safety and the general well-being of all staff. Illumination can be obtained from natural or artificial light, or from a combination of both. Advantages to be gained from a well-designed system of lighting include:

1 Greater accuracy
2 Improved quality
3 Less scrap
4 Increased output
5 Reduced costs
6 Better space utilisation, because there is less need to site machines or other operations alongside windows
7 Assistance to older or poor-sighted workers
8 Improved morale and reduced labour turnover
9 Fewer accidents.

Winter time, with its shorter hours of daylight, is a specially important time, when factory lighting must be adequately designed. It has been proved that a definite relationship exists between the lighting-dependent factors listed above and the onset of winter.

Two aspects of illumination are important: its quantity and its quality. The quantity of light generally means the amount of light which reaches the workplace. This is measured in terms of units of light per unit of surface area. Until fairly recently, the units were lumens per square foot, but more recently the use of lux has become more common. One lux is an illumination level of one lumen per square metre, which is approximately one-tenth as bright as one lumen per square foot. The amount of light needed in practice depends upon the class of work, but Figure 42.3 will serve as a guide.

The quality of light concerns its direction, diffusion, steadiness and colour content. Quality can be important in that even small, barely detectable differences can cause trouble. Glare will be caused if there are contrasting degrees of brightness within the field of vision (e.g., bright reflecting surfaces, or unshielded lamps). It is well known that glare, when experienced for

739

Type of work or situation	GHM Minimum illumination (lux)
Difficult seeing tasks	1200
Fine-precision work	1000
Precision grading, extra-fine finishing, etc.	1000
High-speed work, fine assembly	800
Critical tasks, bench work, machine shops, offices	600
Ordinary work, switchboards, garages	400
Casual tasks, washrooms, welding shops, stores	200
Rough tasks, corridors, passageways	100

Figure 42.3   Suggested minimum levels of illumination for various types of work (measured by intensity of illumination at table top height)

prolonged periods, results in headaches and eye fatigue. The risk of glare can be reduced by placing lights (or the machines and workplaces relative to the lights) so as to avoid direct reflection from polished work surfaces, and by the careful choise of light sources and fittings. Unsteady illumination (flicker) is a particular problem associated with fluorescent lamps, especially when the lamps become old. Even when new, such lamps flicker at mains frequency, and although this may not be annoying, it poses safety problems with moving machinery because a stroboscopic effect can be produced. Thus, for example, under certain conditions the chuck of a lathe, or the cutter on a milling machine might appear to be stationary.

There are several good reasons for consulting a reputable lighting equipment manufacturer, or an illumination consultant, before installing or renewing any lighting system. Modern luminaires are efficient in their use of energy, and power consumption costs can be significantly reduced by the correct choice and layout of lighting equipment.

Vehicle access

Vehicle access and parking varies according to location and the requirements of the organisation. Off-street loading facilities are essential to all establishments, and the inability to provide them can frustrate a planning application. Existing buildings without such facilities may therefore have to have loading bays constructed.

Limited parking for official company vehicles is also very necessary but the provision of parking spaces for the private cars of operatives will depend upon circumstances. It is obviously essential to provide such parking in an establishment located out of town with inefficient public transport services, but in urban areas it is not now regarded as necessary to provide car-parking spaces where there is adequate public transport, and it is official policy to cut down the volume of commuter traffic. This applies particularly to the central area of the metropolis, but is equally applicable to central areas of other large towns.

Other considerations

Office services are dealt with in detail in Chapter 45, but one or two aspects may be worth mentioning here. Adaptability for partitioning, for example, should be borne in mind when a new or existing building is being considered. Again, a lighting layout that conflicts with window mullions can be troublesome in planning the subdivision of space, and necessitate costly reorganisation of existing works.

Potential disturbance by noise is another troublesome question. For example, a personnel officer who has to carry out private interviews may require a higher standard of sound insulation in his office partitioning than is generally provided; this may involve reconstructing or doubling up his partitioning. Extraneous noise may permeate board or conference rooms owing to the location of plant or plumbing being inadequately insulated. It is also a fact that the reduction of external noise in a building by insulation from the street by fixed double-glazed windows, leads to the occupiers of offices being more sensitive to a typewriter in the next office.

The services of an acoustic consultant to advise on partitioning and layout of departments prior to undertaking the work can be well worth while.

FIRE PRECAUTIONS

The Fire Precautions Act 1971 now consolidates previous enactments and lays down requirements for the safety of personnel in commercial and industrial premises in the event of fire. Local authorities regard compliance with the provisions of the Act as of prior importance, and the requirements are being rigidly enforced.

Originally the Act applied to hotels only (other than of minimal size) which were described as certifiable premises, for which the owner was required to apply for a fire certificate.

By the Health and Safety at Work Act 1974 those portions of the Factories Act 1961 and the Offices Shops and Railway Premises Act 1963 which dealt with fire precautions were incorporated into the Fire Precautions Act 1971 and made certifiable.

Certain small factories and offices etc. are not certifiable premises, but there remain obligations under the Act to provide means of escape.

Other certifiable premises must be the subject of an application for a fire certificate by the owner to the Fire Authority.

The Fire Authority usually requires plans of the premises to be submitted; it then carries out an inspection, and notifies the owner of any amendments required before a certificate is issued. Requirements cover means of escape, the provision of fire-fighting equipment, fire-warning devices, etc. In addition there are requirements for limiting the occupancy of the premises, and instructing personnel on necessary action in case of fire (fire drills). Proper records must be maintained of fire drills, tests of alarms, checks of means of escape, maintenance of facilities, etc., and for this purpose a register should be kept by the person responsible to prove compliance with the regulations.

Sprinkler installations, and fire detection installations communicating with the fire stations are aids to minimising fire damage to property where there is special risk. Sprinklers are insisted upon in special circumstances, for example, in the basements of buildings of excessive size, and where part is occupied as a petrol station. Such installations are, however, advantageous in securing discounts in fire insurance premiums. This is of particular value where there is warehousing of materials of a hazardous nature which would otherwise be charged a high rate of insurance.

ALTERATIONS AND EXTENSIONS

Foresight is very valuable in development of a property so that alteration and extension can be carried out with a minimum of cost and disturbance.

The amount of additional initial trouble and expense is to some extent dependent upon the likelihood of extension in the near future, but certain items (for example, the bringing in of an electricity main cable that will adequately cope with the requirement of an extended building, welfare facilities that can be extended to serve increased staff) can be worth while precautions.

The architect or surveyor responsible for original construction should of course be informed of the possibility of further developments so that the structure can be made readily available; for example, if an additional storey is likely to be required to a new building, adequate foundations can be constructed at the initial stage.

If the area of the extension exceeds the permitted tolerance of 10 per cent of the existing development, planning approval is required for the increase. If the permitted 10 per cent extension has been built already, the tolerance is exhausted. In any event planning approval is necessary for the change in external appearance.

In the case of industrial or office development exacting questions relating to numbers employed have to be answered to the satisfaction of the planning authority.

If the property is leasehold the lessors' consent will be required, and at this stage it should be considered whether notice should be served under the Landlord and Tenant Act 1927, so as to protect the tenant's position at the end of the lease.

Assuming that the proposal has passed through these stages approval is required under the Building Regulations 1976, or the London Building Acts (Amendment) Act 1939 in the case of locations in the Inner London areas. The requirements of the Building Regulations are exacting and lay down standards relating to structural strength, daylighting, open space about buildings, spread of fire between and within buildings, thermal insulation, means of escape, etc.

The Construction Byelaws applicable to the Inner London Area, and means of escape in case of fire regulations made under the London Building Acts are based upon an older code of practice and are generally less exacting than the more recent Building Regulations.

Regulations and byelaws apply to extensions of existing buildings even though the original construction pre-dated the regulations and does not comply.

Disposal

In the initial design, alteration or extension of any building it is well to have in mind the possibility of eventual disposal. The more specialised a building in design the more difficult it is to sell, as it cannot easily be adapted for other purposes. An extreme example of this would be a steel works, although such buildings as multi-storey river-side warehouses have been converted into flats. In office buildings partitioning arrangements will almost certainly be unsuitable to a subsequent occupier, and open office floors should therefore be subdivided by demountable partitions that are easily removable or adaptable.

MAINTENANCE AND REPAIR

New buildings should require little expenditure on maintenance or repair, although after three years the external parts should be repainted where previously or usually painted. This would be the usual covenant under the lease in the case of leasehold premises, which invariably require external repainting at three-yearly intervals.

Intervals between internal redecorations are usually longer, from five to seven years, and they are not so vital to the maintenance of the fabric of the building, being usually more cosmetic than protective. Accordingly five to seven years are not strictly adhered to, and where delay in redecoration internally is not causing injury to the landlord's reversion in the case of leasehold property the internal redecorative covenant of a lease cannot be enforced by the landlord, except during the last five years of the term.

The executive responsible for a building will usually have to prepare a budget of his proposed expenditure each year on maintenance work, and it is good practice to make a systematic annual inspection of all parts, roof to basement, internally and externally so that the expenditure can be prescribed with true economy.

Accordingly it may be found that the internal redecoration of little or carefully used accommodation such as board rooms can be deferred for long intervals, but other parts such as kitchens, and lavatory accommodation may require more frequent attention – probably annually – on the grounds of hygiene.

Large organisations usually have their own building department or maintenance staff, which saves much executive time in bringing in outsiders to deal with small items of repair. Whoever is in charge of such work will probably organise a programme of redecoration to be worked through when the maintenance staff are not dealing with emergencies or urgent amendments.

It usually proves that periodic tasks such as external repainting are best placed in the hands of outside contractors, as they would tend to monopolise the time of the maintenance personnel, to the disadvantage of day-to-day items.

In the selection of maintenance staff the odd-job man, at one time invaluable, is to some extent outmoded by the sophistication of installations in a modern building requiring attention frequently. In particular a heating and ventilation engineer is necessary where there is a large air conditioning installation in order to keep the system running efficiently and to change air filters, etc. Outside maintenance contracts can be unreliable and to rely on outsiders inevitably leads to delay in dealing with emergencies.

Similarly, the numerous electrical installations in a modern building call for the employment of a skilled electrician who can cope with troubles in the electrical distribution and diagnose faults in fire alarms, fire detectors, emergency lighting, emergency generators, burglar alarms, intercom systems etc.

For major building works where outside firms are to be employed it is advisable to have a specification of works, and if necessary drawings, and bills of quantities prepared, and to send these to several contractors so as to obtain a selection of estimates. The services of an architect or surveyor should be enlisted for the preparation of tender documents unless the organisation has persons of the requisite skills on its staff.

An independent contractor should be supervised in the execution of the works. Such supervising skill may be available in the organisation or may be entrusted to the professional adviser responsible for the preparation of the contract documents.

Neglect of maintenance, particularly to old buildings, may result in deterioration at an alarming rate. In extreme cases, parts of the building may become unsafe, and there are facilities whereby local authorities may serve Dangerous Structure Notices under the London Building Acts (Amendment) Act 1939 or outside central London under the Dangerous and Neglected Structures Act, requiring owners to make such premises safe.

Similarly other defects or insanitary conditions in buildings may be required to be dealt with by the Public Health Inspector, who has a duty to inspect kitchens and places where food is prepared for staff, lavatories and sanitary arrangements periodically.

LEASEHOLD PROPERTY

A very high proportion of commerical property is leasehold, and in present times the unknown financial burden of the rent reviews is of concern to all property managers.

The period of rent review is shortening with the more recent leases, reflecting increasing inflation, and is now usually set at three-yearly intervals.

A surveyor or valuer should be consulted by an organisation receiving a notice of rent review, and it is usually possible to arrive at an acceptable compromise for the new rental period between surveyors acting for the landlord and tenant. In the event of failure to reach agreement there is provision for the matter to be settled by a third independent surveyor between the parties, which is a swift and economic procedure avoiding litigation.

Dilapidations at the end of the term of the lease are often a source of controversy as they appear to outgoing lessees as gross impositions, in that the premises, under a full repairing covenant have to be given up newly decorated and in a good state of repair. Even if in disrepair at the commencement of a lease having a full repairing covenant, a tenant must put the premises into proper repair and so hand them back at the end of the term.

Caution should therefore be exercised when entering into a lease of old and dilapidated premises, and the lessee's position can be protected by negotiating amendments to the repairing covenant, or by having a schedule of conditions at the commencement of the term and the provision that the lessee is not liable to put the premises into better condition than when he took them.

The law of dilapidations is complex and it is a subject for experts, but the principle should be borne in mind that the measure of dilapidations when they have to be valued is the amount of the injury to the landlord's revisionary interest.

If a tenant fails to hand over premises in the state of repair that the lease provides for, it is usual to negotiate a settlement, but if the landlord's intention is to pull down the premises for redevelopment, he clearly suffers no loss on account of the premises being in disrepair, and accordingly cannot succeed in a claim against the tenant.

A tenant of business premises may be entitled to a new lease on the expiration of an existing lease should he desire to continue in occupation under the terms of the Landlord and Tenant Act 1954.

The rent of the premises is subject to review under the new term, and the landlord can regain possession, thus avoiding having to grant a new lease if he proves intention to redevelop the premises or requirement for his own occupation.

Previous reference has been made to the Landlord and Tenant Act 1927 which provides for compensation for tenants making improvements, or establishing goodwill in business premises at the end of the term of the lease, or alternatively obtaining the grant of a new lease.

VALUATION

The valuation of freehold or leasehold property, is a specialised matter that should be referred to the expert.

There is a tendency for the layman to think of the value of a freehold as being the cost of the land, added to which is the cost of construction of the buildings placed upon it.

This could be true in the case of a newly constructed building, but account must be taken of fast-moving economic trends, which can almost immediately place an inflated security value or a depreciated redundancy value upon such development.

Properties sometimes need to be valued for insurance purposes, in which cases the figures required is the cost of rebuilding on the existing land. The cost of the land is not, therefore, included, but allowance has to be made for site clearance, and there will be professional and legal expenses to be considered.

There is also the necessity to consider the purpose of the valuation. It may be a valuation as a 'going concern' as would be required for accounting purposes, or a valuation of a property offered for sale with vacant possession.

Again, there may be a need to sell a freehold, and take back a lease in order to raise the capital value, and without affecting occupation of the property.

It frequently occurs that the same freehold value is carried forward in a firm's annual accounts which grossly understates the value of the asset on account of such value not having been reviewed.

Valuations of rental value are also frequently required in granting leases or negotiating rent reviews, and such valuations are the basis of rating, which represents a substantial and ever-increasing outgoing on business premises.

RATING

The present rating system has existed for many centuries and provides the basis for a tax on property which is levied locally. As a result of the Report of the Committee of Enquiry into Local Government Finance in 1976, commonly known as the Layfield Report, the Government indicated that certain amendments to the law would be implemented but the Report expressed the view that the abolition of rating was not justified when compared with other forms of taxation. The future of the rating system remains in some doubt as the Government intends to re-examine alternatives to the present system and if possible to reach a clear view within the lifetime of the present Parliament as to whether the present system should be scrapped. In the meantime, the incidence of general and water rates has become a severe burden on many businesses, reflecting increasing demands by local authorities, coupled in many areas with a falling standard of services provided.

The responsibility for valuing property for rating purposes rests with valuation officers of the Inland Revenue, and rating authorities levy rates on the assessments thus determined. Valuation lists for England and Wales contain all the rateable hereditaments for each rating area together with their assessments.

In general, liability for general rates depends on the rateable occupation of real estate and certain rights over land such as advertising rights and shooting rights. Generally it is the occupier and not the owner who is to be rated, although owners may be liable in respect of unoccupied property. For occupation to be rateable it must be exclusive and include actual possession. It must also have a degree of permanence and be of some benefit to the occupier.

The value upon which rates are levied at a rate in the £ is known as its 'rateable value' but for houses, shops, offices and warehouses, it is first necessary to ascertain the 'gross value' of the property of hereditament concerned. The gross value is then reduced to rateable value by a deduction according to a statutory scale.

Gross value is defined in section 19(6) of the General Rate Act 1967 as 'the rent at which the hereditament might reasonably be expected to let from year to year if the tenant undertook to pay all usual tenant's rates and raxes and the landlord undertook to bear the cost of repairs and insurance and the other expenses, if any, necessary to maintain the hereditament in a state to command that rent'. Rateable value, on the other hand, assumes the tenant to be responsible for repairs and other expenses referred to in the above definition. Factories and land such as sports fields, will be assessed direct to rateable value.

How the rent is to be ascertained for a property which may be owner-occupied can be a matter of some complexity. For the majority of commercial properties, however, it will be arrived at after some consideration of actual rents fixed in the two or three years prior to a revaluation. Such rental evidence as may be available will be analysed by the valuation officer and a level of assessment determined for the particular class of property, having regard to factors including size, age, quality of construction and location of each hereditament.

The basis of valuation is therefore an estimate of the rent at which the particular property might let according to the statutory definition. As the current valuation lists came into force on 1 April 1973, any subsequent alteration to those assessments or properties being assessed for the first time, should not exceed the value that would have been ascribed to the particular hereditament had it existed in the year prior to 1 April 1973. This is called 'tone of the list' and it is important to ensure that should reassessment occur, for example as a result of building alteration, the addition in assessment is not excessive and the 'tone' has been properly applied.

A ratepayer has the right to seek a reduction in assessment at any time by making a proposal although the operative date of any reduction in assessment can only be, at earliest, from the beginning of the rate year in which the proposal was served, i.e., 1 April.

Proposals in the case of commercial properties are often made by rating surveyors who specialise in such work and who over many years acquire a considerable body of evidence which will be of assistance in achieving a satisfactory outcome to an appeal.

In the period between the making of a proposal and the date of the hearing of the appeal by the local valuation court, negotiations generally take place between the ratepayer or his professional advisers and the valuation officer. The majority of appeals are determined by agreement but if agreement cannot be reached, the matter will be heard by a local valuation court. From their decision there is a right of appeal to the Lands Tribunal and on a point of law to the Court of Appeal and thence to the House of Lords.

Many tenants of commercial premises who have not lodged an appeal against the rating assessment of the premises they occupy may now decide that they should do so to ensure that a fair proportion of the present high rate burden is being borne. Also grounds frequently exist or arise where an appeal would be justified. The premises may suffer from a particular disability which the valuation officer has not taken into account in the assessment. For example, the premises may be outmoded for their present use or irregular in shape. They may have difficult access, poor natural light, low headroom etc. The effect of building works either within the hereditament or adjacent to it can give rise to a temporary reduction in assessment.

With the current pressure of rates on many businesses, the manager of commercial premises will wish to keep under constant review any opportunity which may arise to reduce the amount paid in rates and the rating surveyor can usually be of considerable assistance in this connection.

ADJOINING OWNERS

Disputes can arise very easily between adjoining owners in respect of the use and occupation of adjacent sites.

Referring first to boundaries, these in urban areas are usually defined by a fence or wall. The title to the property may define the ownership of the enclosure, but in the absence of such evidence, the convention is that the fence stands on the property of the owner, for example, the posts are on the owner's side of the boundary and the face of the fence usually represents the plane of the boundary.

Boundary walls may be built on the owner's side, or they may be party walls. It may be difficult to determine which, but the existence of piers on one side only would indicate that they were built on the owner's side.

Walls separating buildings are usually party walls, the law relating to which is well defined, requiring notice to be served by the party initiating works on the neighbours, and if the works are not agreed surveyors have to be appointed by both parties, to reach agreement, if necessary by reference to a third surveyor.

There can be rights of way across an owner's land in favour of an adjoining property, known as a private right of way as distinct from a public right of way for the benefit of the public in general.

Such rights have usually originated by grant or prescription, but it should be borne mind that if an access to be taken and used openly and as of right by a neighbour across an owner's land a prima-facie right will be acquired in twenty years, which could become a burden and possibly frustrate development.

Rights of light can be acquired by the windows of a neighbour's building enjoying light and air across an owner's property for a period of twenty years. Such rights cannot be obstructed, and can restrict an owners future development of his property.

It is therefore necessary for owners of property to be vigilant so far as neighbours' activities are concerned.

Nuisance and negligence are legal torts which may arise between adjoining owners as the result of the use of property. Nuisance can arise in the generation of smoke, fumes, noise etc. by a neighbour causing grievance to a property owner. If a dangerous substance is stored on a neighbour's land, he will be liable should it escape and cause damage. Similarly the substance need not of itself be dangerous, but could be stored in such a manner as to be potentially dangerous, for example, a reservoir of water.

Fortunately disputes between adjoining owners in occupation of land for business purposes are rare and there would seem to be a sympathetic understanding of business needs between them. When a neighbour is in residential occupation however, every consideration should be shown by the occupier of business premises as it will be seen that a business use could be very intrusive to quiet enjoyment of residential property.

FURTHER READING

The BWC Partnership, *Business Property Handbook*, Gower, 1982
Fire Precautions Register, F. P. R. Distribution, 37 Dumbarton Road, Glasgow
Guides to Fire Precautions Act 1971, HMSO, London
Taylor, N., *Property Manager's Guide to Fire Legislation in Commercial and Industrial Premises*, F. P. R. Distribution, 37 Dumbarton Road, Glasgow
Town and Country Planning (Use Classes) Order, 1972, HMSO, London
Underdown, G., *Practical Fire Precautions*, 2nd edition, Gower, 1979
West, W. A., *Law of Dilapidations*, Estates Gazette Ltd, London, 1979
Woodfall's Law of Landlord and Tenant, Sweet & Maxwell, London

43 Security

John Wilson

Managers have unpalatable facts to consider in connection with security matters, and the potential threat to profitability is difficult to predict. A progressive increase in crime shows no sign of abating; indeed it is claimed that in the United States (a good sounding-board for future developments in the UK) white collar crime will soon be the dominant source of losses. Although prepared to give advice through their crime prevention officers, the overstretched police force are not always able to follow up small thefts and the official view is that industry must put its own house in order and that responsibility for safeguarding property falls on the owner. Managers have to decide what action they can take to avoid becoming the targets of internal and external predators.

Courts and prisons suffer from the same overload. Trials can be delayed for many months, the eventual punishment often seeming inadequate as a deterrent and inconsistent with the victim's loss. The media have brought to notice successful criminal ploys (for example, in television plays) which have been copied by criminals. Inevitably the emphasis upon computer-linked frauds and their potential will produce an unwanted reaction in a field where it is often difficult to establish that any misbehaviour has taken place. There is some evidence that this process has already begun.

Fire is often regarded as part of a security responsibility remit. While this chapter will not deal with fire in any detail it should be borne in mind that many more firms are permanently put out of business by fire than by theft. Arson in the UK has recently reached an all-time peak and whether the cause is malice or intended concealment of evidence of theft is an academic question to the firm which has suffered loss of all its records or productive capacity. Since arson is rarely attributable to employees, the exclusion of intruders is an obvious security objective.

All in all, the immediate prospect is one of increasing problems, with no foreseeable solution. The impact on the business world will have to be mitigated by internal action rather than with external assistance.

ASSESSING THE RISK

It is easy to give 'security' priority at board level once a major loss has been suffered. It is far more difficult before the event, when a dispensation of immunity appears to have been granted and the only impetus to discussion is foreboding, or a knowledge of something catastrophic which has happened to another business.

There are no divine dispensations and ultimate responsibility for security of a firm's property and that of its employees cannot be disclaimed by senior management. The nature of the business may be such that the potential losses are minimal or acceptable, but without giving positive thought to what targets exist it is impossible to evaluate economically feasible defensive precautions. Such action does not necessarily involved additional manpower. Many sources of opportunity or temptation can be removed by changing procedures and documentation or by introducing checks into systems, without impeding the normal functioning of the firm.

The Police crime prevention officers relish being invited to advise before incidents happen and their training is sufficiently broadly based to enable them to comment on most aspects of activity. However, their responsibility is a public one which limits the time that can be devoted to a particular client and this may not be adequate for all problems of a medium or large firm. Even so, guidelines will be given which can be used by management as a basis for more detailed action.

The larger commercial security firms will provide consultants but it must be appreciated that use of their companies' equipment or manpower will colour their advice. Independent security advisers or consultants have no qualifying standards whereby their efficiency can be measured, other than by personal recommendation from a reliable source. They may be self-appointed in their role, lacking essential experience and expertise. Before time and money are committed to a survey from any external source an acceptable level of competence must be established.

However the assessment is carried out, departmental heads must be fully involved. Each should be the person most conversant with the risk within his own area of operations, and with the subsequent application and monitoring of agreed security measures by methods that will not detract from the efficiency of his department. But a manager is primarily concerned with his own main purpose; security may be viewed as an inconvenient and irrelevant distraction with unpopular disciplinary connotations. There is a reluctance to admit that weaknesses exist, and this can also lead to concealment of losses which might be regarded as a poor reflection on the competence of the person in charge. It may become necessary to tell individuals forcefully that, whether they like it or not, security is part and parcel of a manager's job content, to be given serious consideration, and to be discussed where appropriate with colleagues and subordinates.

AREAS OF RISK

Obviously the areas at most risk vary according to the nature of a firm's products, location, workforce, and to the susceptibility of its operations from damage through theft or pilferage, major disaster (fire, explosion, flooding), criminal damage (arson, sabotage), loss of information and disruption through problems with industrial relations. Departments deserving special scrutiny are listed in Figure 43.1.

Department	Risk exposures	GHM
1 Research and development	Information leakage to competitors regarding successful and blind-alley projects and future objectives	
2 Sales and marketing	Leakage of planning, pricing and advertising campaigns, customer lists and discounts, confidentiality of tenders	
3 Computing	Fraud, accidental or deliberate damage, industrial espionage	
4 Cashier and wages	Physical attack, frauds or thefts by employees, interference with pre-signed cheques, etc.	
5 Transport and warehousing	Collusion to defraud between employees and customers or suppliers, weights and measures frauds and credit card mal-practices by drivers, genuine and faked hijacking	
6 Purchasing and materials disposal	Corruption by suppliers or customers	
7 Stores and goods inward	Undetected staff pilferage, collusion with suppliers	
8 Production	Espionage directed at process secrets, sabotage, thefts, bonus and other employee frauds	
9 Selling areas and retail shops	Corruption of employees, employee purchase frauds and thefts, customer trespass into unauthorised areas, shoplifting	
10 Personnel and industrial relations	Confidentiality of records and negotiation data, salary structure data	
11 Company secretary's and directors' offices	Policy and planning decisions, data affecting share performance, mergers and takeovers, etc.	

Figure 43.1   Departments deserving special scrutiny

An evaluation of contributory weaknesses was included in a detailed survey of losses within the metal-using industries. This is worthy of repetition as being of wider application. Even item 4, which is peculiar to those industries, is likely to have equivalent counterparts elsewhere:

1 Management failure to fully investigate discrepancies; to instigate enquires at a sufficiently early stage; or to accept that theft is a possible causation before all other alternatives have been exhaused; neglecting to incorporate adequate checks in systems and procedures to spotlight errors and shortages.

2 Failure to note and take appropriate precautionary measures, when incidents involving substantial loss have occurred in like industries, and in circumstances which could be duplicated internally.

3 Inadequate internal liaison on matters which may give rise to risk of loss through dishonesty or other criminal action (i.e., new procedures, new products or processes, new building or structural alterations); failure to communicate information on losses that have become known.

4 Failure by management on many occasions to appreciate the potential contribution to profitability from reclaimable metal waste correctly handled, and disposed of to best advantage; allowing accumulation to a point that sheer quantity provides opportunity and temptation, or conceals loss.

5 Adhering to a belief that managerial status in itself is an endorsement of integrity in the holder – failure to accept that problems may derive from a manager rather than from other possible alternatives.

6 Allocating localised security responsibility to a disinterested manager; recruiting manpower for security purposes and failing to train, instruct and utilise adequately.

7 Inadequate care in driver recruitment and other posts where integrity is of importance; not taking up references when recruitment is that of supervisory staff status and above.

8 Accepting transit losses as primarily insurance matters and indulging in prolonged correspondence before making positive enquires. Failure to check that contract carriers have adequate insurance cover.

9 Absence of adequate inclusion of security-based requirements in conditions of contract applied to contractors working on sites to ensure adequate supervision of their employees and transport.

DOCUMENTARY LOSS

Cash and materials are often regarded as the main objectives of any intruder or thieving employee, but documents of all kinds are held by firms and their loss, or destruction, or availability to an undesirable source, could have more painful consequences in the immediate or long term.

Books, records and documents may be vandalised by thieves but are rarely their actual targets, other than during acrimonious industrial dispute, or when their contents are of industrial espionage interest. Fire is a greater threat and this is a factory which has to be borne in mind, coupled with the possibility of water damage in consequence of extinguishing an outbreak or some natural hazard of storm damage or flooding. Obsolete or obsolescent safes, which originally purported to be burglar proof, make good repositories as they contain fire-resistant ballast. Apart from the water damage potential there is an additional reason for housing the smaller varieties of these above ground-floor level; many thieves prefer to take safes away, rather than carry out a noisy break-in operation *in situ*. Anything up to a ton weight is liable to go; prevention is by sinking rag bolts into a concrete base and bolting the safe onto them. A police crime prevention officer or an insurance assessor would advise on this.

Specially constructed cabinets which offer reasonable resistance to attack and the effects of fire are increasingly expensive; alternatives should be considered before purchase. It is advisable that books, documents and records for which there is a statutory requirement of retention, should be accorded a special degree of care. These would include, minute books, registers of members and directors, certificates of incorporation, business names registrations, the common seal, title deeds and leases, material relating to property transactions and certain types of contracts. Duplication is an obvious precaution so that the originals can be lodged safely elsewhere and copies used for daily use.

Nevertheless, the risk that springs most easily to mind is that of confidential information being dishonestly or unethically obtained, posing a threat to a firm's present and future profitability or even to the company's continued existence.

THEFT OF INFORMATION

Provided a document is actually stolen, the law of theft can be applied; if, however, information is simply copied, photographed or memorised and then used to the detriment of the owner, the law is vague in the extreme. Where an employee is obtaining material for a competitor on repayment, it may be possible to prove corruption, which is criminally actionable, but the very few prosecutions under the Act (Prevention of Corruption Act 1906) have been virtually restricted to public bodies and for purposes other than business espionage. Civil actions for redress are even less promising and more likely to benefit the lawyers involved than any other participants. It should be noted that cases have failed on grounds that a firm took no steps to ensure privacy of what is subsequently claimed to be important, nor did it emphasise to employees that the operations were regarded as being in any way secret.

At least fifty companies manufacture electronic 'bugging' equipment and a similar number produce devices for detecting their use – including one leading UK manufacturer. In addition, 'marketing information research' appears among the services offered by some organisations whose previous claimed capabilities have lain mainly in the private detective spheres. It is said that at least twenty such firms have been identified as having an active interest internationally in trade spying. A US survey showed that nearly 50 per cent of the private investigation agencies contacted admitted that they would do electronic eavesdropping themselves or would recommend others that did to clients. Finally, both the French Government and the Institute of Directors in the UK have thought it necessary to produce documents dealing with counter-espionage.

A simple test for any firm in doubt about its vulnerability is to ask itself two simple questions:

1 What, if anything, do we not want our competitors or others to know about our business?
2 What information would harm our industrial relations if it became generally known?

The initial answers might indicate sufficient risk to justify a board level decision to ask more searching questions, and to conduct a complete survey to pinpoint areas where precautions are necessary. The board would also establish the amount of effort and expense that is justified.

Potential target areas

These could include departments working on:

1 Plans for production and sale of new products
2 Plans for new advertising campaigns
3 Customer lists coupled with rebate and discount particulars
4 Marketing projections
5 Evaluations of possible acquisitions or mergers
6 Sources and costings of raw materials and components
7 Policy decisions on future activites, redeployments, closures, etc.
8 Contractual or trading agreements, and customer contracts
9 Specifications and tenders
10 Research and development projects.

Of less interest to competitors but more immediately embarrassing are those matters which can cause industrial unrest. Obtaining information about these may be more a case of human curiosity than anything savouring of industrial espionage – but nevertheless can be crucially embarrassing if made general knowledge. They would include:

1 Rationalisation and redundancy plans
2 Personal files and confidential reports
3 Wage-negotiation preparatory material
4 Confidential instructions on industrial relations negotiations
5 Salary structures and job-weighting factors.

Document classification

This is a basic requirement, and a simple system, used and understood by everyone, is required; if left to individuals, all sorts of terminology will be used, and the tendency will be to classify everything, no matter how innocuous. Fixing the degree of restriction is the responsibility of the originator, and the recipients should conform to his wishes, unless they have permission to treat the material otherwise.

'Confidential' implies the senders' wish that the contents should not be general knowledge, but allows a discretion to divulge the information to those who need to act upon it or must know of it for their work. 'Secret' is much more emphatic and means not to be divulged (without the express permission of the sender) to anyone other than those upon the circulation list, which should be attached or marked upon the document.

Naturally an outer envelope which is marked 'secret' will attract attention and it is suggested that it should simply be marked 'personal' – which would convey nothing to a handler. Personal secretaries will open all mail, unless their masters decree otherwise, so that if an originator feels that the contents are such that they should be restricted purely to the named person, a second envelope may be put inside the external one and endorsed ' secret – to be opened only by. . .'

For projects vital to the profitability of the firm, an authorised circulation list should be agreed, which can be expanded as the project develops. If necessary a code word can be given to a project and it should then always be referred to in this way, either in correspondence, or in telephone conversation. The specific number of document copies needed should be printed and marked sequentially with each person on the authorised circulation list allocated an identification number. Highest priority matter is best transmitted by hand and against signature by the recipient.

Production of documents and minutes

Highly sensitive papers should by typed only by trusted personnel who are informed of the importance of secrecy and, ideally, all copying should be done by the same people. This is not a job for temporary employees from an agency who conceivably might work for a competitor, or may realise the value of what is being handled and try to capitalise accordingly. A danger lies in recipients wanting further copies for their own use for unauthorised dissemination to their subordinates or others; 'not to be copied', or some other endorsement should be overstamped on the originals and retribution follow any reproduction carried out without permission, irrespective of the offender's status.

Plastic typewriter ribbons of 'once only' use should be burnt and spare copies, carbons, shorthand notes, or other sources of information should be put into a shredder. Fortunately, most firms use only longstanding and trusted employees for the sorting and movement of mail internally, but documents of prime importance should be passed to the office of the recipient so far as possible by hand. A risk that does arise lies in the fact that mail delivered to a department is likely to be dropped in an office tray at a designated reception point where a variety of people will have access to it; if they can recognise the importance of the particular envelope, it is then at their disposal.

Safekeeping of documents

All precautions can be invalidated by a careless executive who leaves his desk littered at night with confidential papers; or the secretary who is given them to file, then leaves them in an office tray until it is convenient to do so; or locks them away, then leaves the key to the cabinet in an unlocked drawer, the top of a typewriter, or the pull out accessory tray in her desk.

Standard locks on the doors of offices likely to hold restricted information can be replaced by a master-keyed suite of locks of high security rating with restricted key-holding. Human nature being what it is, where such a system is instigated, inevitably it will be found the special lock becomes something of a status symbol which practically every manager or executive will find substantial reasons for having on the grounds of the importance of the material he handles.

Filing cabinets are rarely resistant to any forcible attack and have a major disadvantage in that the keys are usually fairly available for purchase from the number which is printed on the face of the lock. Despite the somewhat disfiguring effort, it is suggested these numbers be obliterated by drilling. An alternative is to fit a pair of brackets and a removable steel bar which can be padlocked across all drawer fronts.

Any discussions affecting documentary secrecy should include checks to ensure that important papers are not persistently left out on desks; a 'clean desk' end-of-work policy should be advocated, and practised, by all staff.

Destruction of papers

The importance of a document does not of necessity lapse when the project to which it refers is terminated. This is particularly true of industrial relations-linked matters. After being handled with every care and precaution during their lives they are than handed over for destruction to what may be the lowest paid and least skilled class of worker who is employed. It is asking too much to expect that such an individual will not be interested in any document which is stamped with 'secret', or some similar intriguing title. For immediate destruction small cheap shredders are available for departments or larger ones can be centrally sited; and in some industries the cost may be offset by the use of the shredded paper produced for packing purposes. The computer department is of special importance, although the printout material may be meaningless to most people. Heavy-duty shredders are available to destroy printouts and tapes; these should be installed, either in the department, or in a suitable room closely adjacent.

Potential forms of attack

Typical means of unethically obtaining information are:

1 Exploiting the carelessness, boastfulness, or negligence of employees
2 Corrupting employees, or forming an emotional attachment and inducing confidences
3 Inserting an agent into the workforce
4 Deliberately recruiting an employee from a position where he holds the requisite information
5 Holding a detailed interview of a knowledgeable employee for an

advertised, financially wonderful, but non-existent job
6   Electronically 'bugging' telephones and offices, or using other specialised forms of surveillance
7   Entering premises to locate information either:
     (a)   as a visitor or
     (b)   as an intruder by force.

Far and away the simplest method of operating is to walk in and see, if the target firm's procedures are so lax as to make this possible. A skilled observer, apart from possibly acquiring or having sight of the paperwork, might recognise the processes and materials in use, the general level of activity, and innumerable other factors which will supply the information wanted.

If there are areas where there must be the strictest control on personnel entering, a constantly manned reception desk could be installed, or electronic control of access may be more economic. This could be a coded lock, magnetic card-operated lock, or combination of card and code, or even a card and code linked to a minicomputer which monitors and provides a permanent record of who goes there. A further variation has a pocket transmitter which causes an electronically controlled bolt to be automatically withdrawn when the carrier approaches. Photo-identity cards can be affixed to lapels for easy recognition, and colour variations in these can clearly indicate areas to which the wearer is entitled to have access. Control of entry to a computer room has a non-security merit – it prevents distraction and interference with the work of highly paid operators.

Entry of subterfuge

This is one of the ploys of professional investigators engaged to obtain information. Latitude in asking questions and moving about premises is often given to persons carrying out safety surveys or appreciation of equipment, or posing as prospective customers etc. Impersonation of telephone engineers, gas and electricity supply employees, laundrymen, window cleaners, etc., have all been used. Preventive action is largely a matter of common sense and developing a suspicious mind. Most public utility employees will have identification cards to produce if challenged. A system of handling visitors efficiently should be devised and they should not be allowed to roam the premises unattended. Others worth bearing in mind are cleaners and temporary staff – the wastepaper basket remains one of the most prolific sources from which information can be gleaned. It may be possible to make special arrangements for the cleaning work in sensitive areas to be carried out during working hours when there is supervision on the premises. Every care should be taken to avoid the use of temporary staff on projects of importance; if this cannot reasonably be done, the supplying agency could be asked of details of the person's service with them and the firms to which he/she has previously been allocated, so that there is at least an informed option to accept or refuse. If used, there is no objection to impressing on the incumbent the confidentiality of the position.

Electronic surveillance devices

The use of 'bugs' is not yet widespread in the UK; the extent to which they have been used is a matter for some speculation, but the publicity which has been given to them may lead to temptation to try them. They are easily concealed and can be fitted into table-lighters, wall decorations, stuck under tables etc. A standard telephone bug is a transistorised oscillator which is powered by the telephone line current, using the line itself as an aerial. Variations can allow the microphone to be active even when the hand set is not in use. Offices can be checked visually, but this must be done thoroughly and patiently with a knowledge of what to look for, and where. The electronic detection equipment can be bought, but the best varieties are very expensive, and the limited number of larger private detective agencies who provide a checking service have also charges which are very substantial. Where leaks are suspected there is merit in holding vital meetings at off-site venues arranged at short notice.

Precautions – check list

1 Define key posts and areas, applying stringent selection and vetting to applicants for the former, and restricting entry to the latter
2 Establish classification, handling, copying and safe-keeping instruction procedure for documents, etc.
3 Provide means of destroying the secret material and anything connected with its production, i.e., shredders
4 Restrict copying
5 Ensure wall charts, graphs, or other visual aids are not left where they can be freely seen
6 Instigate occasional out-of-hours checks upon offices for important papers carelessly left out
7 Indoctrinate staff
8 Instigate a policy for treatment of any person with access to secret information, who is to leave the company employment for any reason.

Inadvertent disclosure

The unwordly scientist, who 'discloses all' in a learned paper for some technical journal or at some sophisticated symposium, is difficult to cater for; the best that can be hoped is that he will conform to the restrictions that may and should be contained in his contract of employment. However, ideas, inventions, and information in general may be released without thinking in the normal course of business.

It is possible to protect ideas and inventions by means of one or more patents, design registrations, registered trademarks and copyright, but it is also often the case that such protection is unobtainable or impracticable on the grounds of cost, or the idea lacking the right degree of novelty or inventiveness. At times it may be best to keep a good idea firmly under one's hat and in such instances the advice of a good patent agent is desirable and may prove invaluable.

Customers, students, prospective buyers and others may by tradition be shown around the factories and workshops with frank answers being given to their questions. Care must be taken, at the risk on occasions of causing genuine or simulated offence, to be judicious in what is shown and to decline to answer queries which would reveal too much of the firm's business. In one instance, a private detective posing as a potential (and bogus) customer's 'quality assurance expert' acquired secret process detail in all good faith. The same care may be needed in dealing with market research questionnaires, intended student thesis projects and enquiries from the media. The basic question in such circumstances is 'Will my disclosure in any way be detrimental to my company?'

SECURITY POLICIES AND DISCIPLINE

A high proportion of disciplinary matters arise from incidents with security connotations and the process of enforcing security is as productive as any for industrial discord. It is therefore advisable to have clearly defined policies and procedures in those areas where ambiguity or opportunity could create controversy or a temptation to dishonesty. Such policies and procedures could include:

1 Action to be taken in respect of a criminal offence, where the firm is the complainant, committed:
   (a) By employees – suspension, dismissal, prosecution
   (b) By contractors – prosecution, expulsion from site, other alternatives etc.
   (c) By outsiders – prosecution, or other alternatives
2 The matters to be referred to the police and at whose discretion
3 Dealing with lost and found property
4 Working of notice by person who has been dismissed, or has resigned from a position of special risk
5 Permission of sales of products to employees and the procedures to be used
6 Work permitted for company staff utilising company's labour on repayment
7 Use of firm's facilities for private purchase, i.e., discounts
8 Policies in respect of giving references
9 Communication sources for media in the event of newsworthy items, i.e., accidents, industrial action and losses, etc.
10 Policy towards losses by employees on premises – disclaimers, and permission for facilities for cash holding, i.e., collections in company safes.

These are really only sample matters and policy statements could include the use of insurance to offset risks (including the fidelity bonding of employees), bomb threats, major incidents and cash handling procedures, in addition to those already mentioned in connection with the security of documents.

Most important is that of establishing a firm line on how employee theft will be treated; since this is likely to be associated with dismissal, no grounds should be allowed whereby an appeal can arise from a legal nicety. The types of serious misconduct meriting dismissal should of course be listed by a firm amongst its rules and that of theft is generally accepted by Industrial Tribunals as a perfectly valid reason (Trust House Forte *v*. Murphy, 1977).

The following ruling is recommended in the light of changes in legislation and decided cases:

> If any act of theft, or attempted theft, or other form of dishonesty, or criminal damage, is admitted, or on reasonable grounds found to have been committed by an employee in connection with company property, or the property of another employee, then the employee responsible will be dismissed and, where company property is involved, the company will exercise its discretion in whether the matter is to be reported to the police.

Discretion

A ruling of this nature does not cover all criminally actionable offences that may be committed, either on the firm's premises, or elsewhere and contrary to its interests. The inflicting of injuries, and sexual offences, are of rare occurrence, as are those involving customers, the consequences of which would be prejudicial to the company interests. Too wide definition would prove unwieldly and the nature of the other criminal actions which can be envisaged is sufficiently serious that dismissal for their commission would be an acceptable reason to a Tribunal.

The definition as it stands leaves an ultimate discretion whether or not to prosecute and allows the taking into account of mitigating circumstances which could have bearing on the decision. The prime objective is to achieve consistency on the aspect of dismissal, rather than on that of prosecution.

Right of search

Even where a company includes a 'search clause' in its conditions of employment, there is no legal right of personal search without the consent of the individual being searched. Nevertheless, Employment Appeal Tribunal decisions have indicated that where such a condition is included, refusal can constitute reasonable grounds for dismissal; conversely, where it is not included, dismissal for refusal was found unfair, despite the fact that there were grounds for suspicion of theft. Whilst there are no publicised decision to the effect, it would seem probable that any search productive of stolen property would be considered justified – dismissal of course being for the theft, not the refusal.

Dismissed without prosecution

This is an expedient to be applied with care in the current industrial climate. No avenue should be provided for a claim of unfair dismissal, but a successful prosecution is not a prerequisite for action by the employer. This has been made clear by several judgments, one of which – British Home Stores Limited *v* Burchell (20 July 1978), an Employment Appeal Tribunal decision on dismissal for suspected involvement of theft where there was no prosecution – is worth quoting in full.

> In a case where an employee is dismissed because the employer suspects or believes that he or she has committed an act of misconduct, in determining whether that dismissal is unfair an Industrial Tribunal has to decide whether the employer who discharged the employee on the ground of the misconduct in question entertained a reasonable suspicion amounting to a belief in the guilt of the employee of that misconduct at that time. This involves three elements. First, there must be established by the employer the fact of that belief; that the employer did believe it. Second, it must be shown that the employer had in his mind reasonable grounds upon which to sustain that belief. And, third, the employer at the stage at which he formed that belief on those grounds must have carried out as much investigation into the matter as was reasonable in all the circumstances of the case. An employer who discharges the onus of demonstrating these three matters must not be examined further. It is not necessary that the Industrial Tribunal itself would have shared the same view in those circumstances.

Burchell has become a definitive industrial appeal case in that W. Weddel Ltd *v* Tepper, Court of Appeal, 1980 declared its three-stage test should be used to determine whether an employee dismissed for *any* alleged misconduct had been fairly dismissed – not simply in cases of dishonesty.

Where there is an admission of theft, and the employer does not wish court proceedings, it is highly advisable that the admission is in a form that cannot be retracted for the purposes of an appeal against dismissal. It is suggested that a signed admission be obtained or one made under circumstances which would preclude any such retraction. This could be in the presence of witnesses or of the offender's own representative.

Dismissal in the face of a denial of guilt could lead to appeals causing cost and inconvenience beyond any normal police court proceedings and a Tribunal is less restricted in the evidence that it will accept than criminal courts (Dockerty *v.* Reddy 28 September 1976); it is therefore recommended that instances where guilt is firmly denied should be referred to the police.

There are a number of points arising from other Tribunal decisions which are worthy of note in this connection:

1 An opportunity must be given for an explanation of facts by the suspect before the dismissal decision is made
2 There is no necessity of a successful prosecution to justify dismissal
3 As shown above, it is adequate that those formulating the decision to dismiss have reasonable grounds for their belief in the facts before them when making their decision
4 The decision must be based on the facts that are known at the time of the decision, not those that may arise subsequently

5 There must be as much investigation as is reasonable before the dismissal is made.

Suspension with or without pay

Suspension without pay, where such a power is not included in the contract of employment, is held to be tantamount to dismissal and therefore is subject to the normal appeal procedure.

Suspension with pay is reasonable in cases of strong suspicion pending the accumulation of all the available evidence bearing on a decision. However, if this suspension is extended to the termination of court proceedings it can be extremely expensive since the accused, by various ploys, can defer the hearing of his case interminably. In one instance five employees were suspended on average earnings for two years and six months. The evidence was such that they had to plead guilty, but the cost of their wages far exceeded the value of the theft.

No dismissal

There are cogent reasons why every instance of proven or admitted dishonesty by an employee against his firm should result in immediate dismissal. A company ruling of the type previously mentioned is invalidated if any exceptions at all to it are allowed – precedents are highly important to Industrial Courts and management could find great difficulty in explaining a variation in policy which it had naively hoped would escape notice.

Other reasons of importance exist:

1 Leniency could cause others to copy in the belief no retribution would follow
2 A repetition of the offence by the same person would invoke caustic comment from Board level on the individual who has taken the lenient view (some would say the easy way out!)
3 Retention is unfair to the offender's colleagues and the atmosphere in a department would be impossible if a fellow worker's property had been involved
4 The offender will inevitably be the focus of attention should any further offences occur, even if he is not responsible, and his continued presence be an embarrassment not least to himself.

POLICE NOTIFICATION

The reporting of a theft is not mandatory nor is, as the Criminal Law Act 1967 clearly defines, the prosecution of an individual known to have stolen from a complainant, who is also legally allowed in making a decision to press charges or not, to take into account whether the loss or injury caused by the offence is to be made good or reasonable compensation paid – a matter which could of course be made quite clear to an offender. If the police are called in, they are unlikely to be familiar with procedures, persons and places all of which might have to be explained. Their presence automatically attracts attention and workers may have to be taken from their jobs to be spoken to. The consequential loss may be out of all proportion to the effect of the offence which is being investigated. However, once they have been notified, it is highly advisable that the question of prosecuting should be left entirely in their hands – even if this causes embarrassment or inconvenience. Otherwise future co-operation might be jeopardised – and they have the power to disregard representations for the withdrawal of charges.

No prosecution

There are circumstances which can militate against a prosecution which at first sight might be justified by the nature of the offence. Amongst the considerations are:

1 Will the firm receive adverse publicity by:
    (*a*) A lax system putting temptation in the way of the employee?
    (*b*) Having put a lowly paid man in a position where he is handling property of a value out of all proportion to his salary?
    (*c*) Permitting the ventilation of a grievance in open court which would reflect adversely on the firm?
    (*d*) Compulsorily disclosing matters in court which the firm would desire should not be known?
2 Will the prosecution spotlight a weakness in the security system which could be exploited by others and which may be difficult or impractical to remove?
3 Is the end product of prosecution worth the effort and inconvenience; or considering the age, length of service, and good repute of an employee, would dismissal be a greater penalty than any the court might impose?

It must be remembered that malpractices, actual or alleged, by an employer have greater news value than routine theft by an employee.

Intruders

The same considerations do not however, apply to offences by non-employees. If these are involved in an offence of any consequence the police should be informed, particularly where identifiable property has been stolen and police assistance is the only means of recovery. Outsiders should be given no indication that they can steal from a firm with impunity, a consistent policy of prosecuting all should be followed as a deterrent to others.

Thefts from employees

Despite the fact that an offence may take place upon company premises the right to decide whether it should be referred to the police is vested in the loser and he is entitled to object if the company tries to interfere with this right. It follows that he also has the right to prosecute or not to prosecute should an offender be detected. However, this in no way affects the rule of dismissal for theft from company or employee. The employee himself may have pressure put upon him by friends of the offender not to prosecute and he may so agree, but this does not invalidate the issue of dismissal.

Prosecution

The Law of England does not (at the time of writing) preclude any person or body from instituting or carrying out criminal proceedings in which the police will assist, but, unless there are very good reasons, there is little point in acting as a private prosecutor. Once notified, the police will ensure that all necessary statements are taken, the case is prepared and witnesses warned of the time, date and place of hearing; the police solicitor will present the evidence and there can be no suggestion of bias in the conduct of the whole affair. In other words a minimum of inconvenience and cost is incurred by the firm.

Scotland has a different ruling. There is no such thing as a private prosecution in criminal matters, all of which have to be referred to the police and then presented by the Procurator Fiscal's Department who have a discretion as to whether to proceed with prosecution.

COMPANY SECURITY STAFF

Where circumstances justify the employment of security officers it is essential that they should be of good calibre, and properly trained and utilised. It is a total waste of money to follow the outdated practice of internal recruitment from redundant or ageing employees – worse, this gives an impression that security surveillance exists whereas the resultant inefficiency causes the reverse to be true.

Authority

An effective security force must be capable of earning the respect and co-operation of the whole workforce. To do this the policies adopted in security matters must be fair, clearly spelt out and applicable to all. Impartiality, good humour and a friendly attitude are all essential attributes. Smartness in dress and deportment are consistent with an image of efficiency and authority.

Duties

The duties required must be committed to writing in the form of 'Standing Orders', which in effect may be a much expanded and detailed version of their job description. The two combined, amongst other things, must specify what they are expected to do, their line of reporting and the degree of discretion allowed.

Fire-fighting and first aid are customary inclusions among responsibilities, but every firm will have others where continual presence of responsible men on premises can be utilised. The contribution that security staff can make in accident prevention is very relevant but it would be unrealistic to give special training unless there were exceptional circumstances of recurrent risk. Nevertheless, there are a number of things which may be temporarily over-looked by personnel intent on production where common sense observation by a patrolling officer may be used to advantage.

Instructions should be given to deal with these matters tactfully to avoid apparent intrusion into the disciplinary authority of line management, bearing in mind also that a procedure that appears unsafe to the uninitiated may be one which has been considered and found acceptable.

If unsafe practices are seen, security staff should draw them to the notice of the supervisor and not approach the worker himself, unless the matter is one of immediate physical risk or serious contravention of works rules.

RESPONSIBILITY FOR SECURITY

A managing director of course is ultimately answerable to shareholders for all aspects of the protection of his company's assets; obviously he will delegate a matter like security through a director down possibly to a departmental manager. In some multinationals security is deemed so essential that the administrative head may even be of director status and engaged full time in its supervision. The status of the operational head will depend on the importance attributed to the function; in larger groups, on big sites, or where special expertise is called for, he is likely to be of managerial status in his own right. In smaller units, or where the risks are limited, the usual nomenclature is that of 'Chief Security Officer' and he will report to a selected departmental manager. Be that as it may, every company should have someone designated to see that steps are taken to minimise loss from dishonesty or unethical action. This individual could be an existing manager, a purpose-recruited professional, or a part-time consultant/adviser. The danger of allocating the task to a dis-interested manager, or to one whose normal discipline has little to do with security, needs little stressing. If there is preoccupation with other commitments, or security enforcement is viewed with distaste as something of a disciplinary function, little of value to the employers will ensue; also, if there is a security staff in being, its performance and morale will rapidly deteriorate and any protection it affords become illusory.

Security staff most frequently report to personnel management; where there is an industrial relations-based nexus with its work, but alternatives such as works manager, works accountant, site engineer etc. are encountered. The personality and interest shown by the manager are most important. The responsibility should not be given to a manager simply because he is considered otherwise to be underemployed, or to prop up a sagging job description.

Staff selection

For the actual operational implementation of day-to-day security, and advising or recommending where needed, an 'in-company' appointed security manager has advantages of familiarity with persons, places, products etc., but he has to be trained to a knowledge of essential law and security expertise. Perhaps most important, he has to think in terms of security priorities as having an importance he did not perhaps previously accord them, and develop a suspicious and enquiring mind that he did not previously need for his job. This type of appointment is best for a small firm with limited problems, or for a unit within a large organisation with centralised security control and expertise which can be called upon for assistance and advice; training is, however, essential.

If the risk dictates that professional experience is called for, the main sources of supply are ex-HM Forces SIB (Special Investigation Branches), ex-police, existing senior security personnel in industry or the commercial security service-supplying firms. Alternatively, an outside consultant can be retained for services as required – which is unlikely to be financially advantageous – and care has to be taken in checking ability both personal and to carry out contractual obligations in the light of existing commitments.

Selection from 'second career incumbents' can produce know-how but a judgement must be made as to whether the job is being taken with real interest or as a means of supplementing a pension with minimum personal effort and inconvenience.

It must be expected that someone being inducted from a disciplined service into commerce and industry will have problems of adjustment and it is advisable that colleagues, with whom the prospective incumbent will have closest contact, should have an opportunity to meet and assess short-listed candidates for compatibility before the appointment is made.

Training

Security heads are apt to be drawn from the older age bracket, especially when they are 'second career' selections. One possible danger is that they become agoraphobic in attitude with their interest limited to the physical perimeter of their responsibility. If this happens, their knowledge of law and practice becomes outdated, they do not learn from the misfortunes of others, and they miss the advantages of discussion with contemporaries. Arrangements should be made for at least 'brush-up' attendance at security courses and seminars, and they should be encouraged to develop liaisons within their own industry and locally for mutual advantage.

At security guard level it is frequently forgotten that these employees need training as much as, if not more than others – their potential to hurt the firm by unwise action through ignorance is greater than that of others of considerably higher status. Apart from instruction that is available on site, it is advisable that they should have basic instruction amongst others similarly employed – if a suitable course is available. Commercially organised one- or two-day seminars are occasionally held for senior security officers and management but few, if any, at the lower level. However, the International Professional Security Association hold basic, intermediate and advanced courses throughout the country; these are essentially practical in nature, the lecturers are primarily drawn from members with specialised expertise who hold senior positions with industrial firms. Details of what is available at any given time can be obtained from the Secretary of the Association.

HIRING THE SERVICES OF A SECURITY COMPANY

Commercial firms provide a variety of services:

1 The transporting of cash to and from banks and if so required, at most branches, the making up and paying out of wage packets
2 Transporting computer tapes, data, etc.
3 Security attention to premises, with or without guard dogs
    (a) Continuously over twenty-four hours, seven days a week
    (b) For specified shorter periods
    (c) For visits at regular intervals
4 To act as key-holders of premises to reduce the inconvenience of having to attend them at all hours in consequence of some incident which requires attention
5 To protect especially valuable property on display at, for example, exhibitions and provide guards at sporting functions etc.
6 To survey premises and to recommend security measures
7 To provide a store detective service in retail premises and make check purchases
8 In some instances a facility to carry out internal investigations; in others to give a debt collection service.

In addition to these, there are of course the alarm, lock, safe, television, etc. specialist firms.

Transporting cash

When a contract is arranged for this service, it must specify the place at which the delivery is to be made. It is not sufficient to give just the address: the precise location of the transfer must be given, for example, the cashier's office on the second floor. Regrettably attacks during cash deliveries occur frequently, so the precise liability on the carriers at the time of the theft is important. The nationally known cash-in-transit companies have adequate cover spread over several insurers, but positive written confirmation of that cover should be available and the wording of contracts carefully studied. Those with current national coverage are Securicor, Group 4 and Security Express, but other internationally known – and equally reputable ones – also operate in the larger cities.

A wage packeting service is available in many areas, for which the charges made vary little from one company to another. However, the level of these charges has risen to the point where internal make-up could be more cost effective.

Very firm arrangements must be made with the carriers, and with the bank authorities, to agree procedures for cheque submission, cash collection and delivery, with adequate means of identification of both signatures and persons, to preclude any possibility of fraudulent attack.

If an unknown person purporting to be from the security company attends premises to collect cash or anything valuable, his identity documents must be inspected and his employers telephoned to confirm his instructions – his documents might have been stolen or forged.

Cash-in-transit – own personnel

If it is intended that wages or, for that matter, any large sums of money, should be carried in circumstances where they are exposed to attack, the insurers *must* be consulted. They are not enthusiastic about sums in excess of £2000 being carried without extra precautions by way of guards and vehicles which probably will outcost the expense of a professional carrier. This of course is a reasonable ploy by the insurer since it transfers the period of greatest risk to someone else's insurance.

If, however, the amounts are relatively small, or a decision is taken to accept the risk, the advice of the police crime prevention department should be sought, and their recommendations strictly followed as to how the job should best be done having regard to the special risks of the area. Special waistcoats, alarmed bags and others that deface the contents, or throw out clouds of smoke, are commercially available.

Cash-in-transit: security advice and checklist

This is too detailed to be dealt with here and reference should be made to Wilson and Oliver (1978).

SECURITY OF CASH IN OFFICES

Money in any form is just about the most attractive target for theft; it is normally non-identifiable, does not need the intervention of a receiver, and there is no delay in benefiting. Insurance against loss can be obtained either in transit or on premises; the cost is progressively rising, and premiums will be heavily loaded if claims are made – the first £100 or more will probably be excluded in any case.

The weight of claims has caused insurance companies to insist on rigorous security measures, including installation of burglar alarms, without compliance to which they will not offer cover. Even so, failure to observe elementary precautions may cause the refusal of a claim, such as has happened with an unguarded till in retail premises and failures to set alarms or to lock doors on delivery vehicles.

Cash on premises should be the minimum for needs; if it accrues to a greater than desirable amount, transfer arrangements to the bank should be made. Key holding for cash boxes and safes must be kept to an absolute minimum and locks must be changed immediately in the event of a key-loss. A spot check should be made on cashiers petty cash holding – often amounts in excess of insurance cover are kept for purely personal convenience. Excess cash (which might include unpaid wages packets) is safer on deposit at the bank, where it can also accrue interest.

Companies are apt to regard safes as continuing to fulfil their purpose long after they have become antiquated. If an insurance company insists on an examination prior to renewal of policies, many will be condemned as unfit for the storage of cash, and cover will not be extended to them. The surveyors have a classification which includes all types of safes in manufacture and equates them with the maximum amount of money the insurers are prepared to accept that they should hold. Before buying new safes, it is therefore essential to obtain confirmation that they will meet the insurers' requirements.

Petty cash and floats must not be left in locked drawers overnight but should be returned to safes and withdrawn again the following morning. Special care should be taken of cheque books, and the absolute minimum of presigned cheques be retained at any time. If possible, these should be restricted to the control of a single person. The value of presigned Giro cheques for payments to pensioners may be overlooked and a close check should be kept on these. All spoilt presigned cheques must be retained for audit purposes; the signature block and cheque machine key should have separate holders and be kept in safe places.

Cash in private possession

Employees must be told clearly that the company will not accept responsibility for any personal money kept on the premises, unless it is handed over to the cashier or other nominated person for safe keeping. This should apply also to holiday club collections, sports and social clubs funds and the like. Any discovery that this rule is not being followed should result in a verbal reprimand and, if a theft does occur, the opportunity should be taken to stress the need for everyone to comply.

Paying-out stations

Increasingly, attacks are being made on offices where money is in the process of being paid out. Shotguns and pickaxe handles are frequently used – and there should be no heroics in the face of a gun. Consideration should be given to providing personal attack alarms (button or foot operated) in cashiers' offices and at pay points. Thieves are under strain and may be 'trigger-happy', so there should be no audible alarm at the scene but an indication at a safe point from which police assistance can be sought.

Where new positions are being constructed to act as pay points, thought must be given, and if necessary professional advice obtained, as to protection from violence, including the threat of firearms, for those paying out. The point must also be so devised as to prevent casual theft of wage packets through the pay window. Complete armoured glass window and shelf units are available from specialist suppliers. It is also good practice to exhibit at each paying out point a notice that clearly indicates that the recipient is responsible for his own wage packet after collection. Where control of the pay packets and pay points changes during a wage issue, proper checking and handing over should take place between the clerks concerned. The paying out system itself should be such that the possibility of an employee being able to draw another's pay packet fraudulently is minimised. This can be done by issuing payslips twenty-four hours before the pay-out. False allegations of an unauthorised packet collection are not infrequent – all such claims should be thoroughly investigated before a repayment is authorised. Where packets of a type that allow checking of contents are used, no claims of shortage should be entertained if the packet has been opened.

BUILDINGS

Old property, though satisfactory in every respect of location, floor space and amenities, may be totally unsuitable for high-risk commodities. If this is suddenly realised after acquisition, considerable unbudgeted expenditure may be needed to rectify the condition and this will reflect on the foresight of those who conducted the negotiations.

New construction does not offer the same difficulties, provided that – from the draft-plan stage – civil engineers, architects, planners and builders have in mind what is at risk and the steps that can be taken to minimise it, without jeopardising the essential functions of the building. If no company specialist is employed, the police crime prevention officers will be delighted to give their views and advice – they regard this stage as the best time to utilise their services. Simple adjustments to plans can easily cut out avenues for walk-in theft, or such invitations to a thief as obscured windows or doors which may be forced at leisure.

A few basic essentials: endeavour to keep all parking facilities outside the premises proper; provide maximum lighting on perimeters; restrict the number of entrances to the building or site to the asbolute minimum (it is much harder to do so when employees have become accustomed to using them); ensure that persons using any entrance can be seen, either by a receptionist, or by occupants of adjoining offices; restrict keys to an absolute minimum and prohibit the making of duplicates. Leaving some interior lights on all night can deter prospective intruders, especially if they can be turned on and off at intervals by an automatic switch.

Alarm systems

The electronic alarm industry has grown to major proportions and many firms have nationwide coverage. Their equipment can be extremely sophisticated; its cost therefore should be in relation to the risk. Whole areas or selected danger points can be covered; warning can be by immediate bells, '999' connection to the police, or by direct line to the police (where this is still permitted) or to a central station operated by the alarm company. Delayed bells can be fitted so that the message can be transmitted to the police but loss restricted if for some reason their arrival is delayed. Reliance on bells alone is a dubious proposition – little attention is paid by the public. Facilities offered include ordinary door contacts, rays, pressure pads, tautened wiring, radar and sonic detectors; new conceptions are continually being developed. When costing such an installation, it is advisable to consult and seek estimates from at least three unconnected companies. Knowing that others are in competition, none will recommend an unnecessarily expensive system which might exclude their quotation. The police crime prevention officer may be willing to indicate those that have the local servicing facilities that are essential to eliminate waste of time. He cannot be expected to recommend any particular one but he might hint at which have bad false alarm performance.

A certain number of false alarms must be anticipated in the early teething stages of an installation but should clear within two or three weeks. The police will look with a jaundiced eye if false alarms continue thereafter since they implement a prearranged plan to cover the premises on each occasion as a priority to other duties; they also require key-holders to be nominated who are conversant with the contents of the building, have means of transport and preferably are available by telephone. The National Supervisory Council for Security Alarm Systems has now been established to ensure that new installations conform to British Standards and that complaints are investigated. Contracts should be carefully scrutinised before acceptance, liability restriction clauses and the precise supplier obligations under 'maintenance' merit special attention. An alarm log, showing dates and nature of work done on the system, and recording false calls and their causes should be kept. Many police forces will not respond to calls from systems which produce repeated faults, and it is advisable to consult the police before this stage is reached.

Locks and keys

A lock is just as good as its price, and a key as good as the precautions taken to restrict the holders and the opportunity to copy it. For security purposes, a five-lever lock is the minimum insurance requirement and again the insurers' advice can be obtained in cases of doubt: for privacy the 'Yale-type' lock will suffice. The locking of internal doors can frequently result in excessive damage by intruders and it is a waste of time and money putting a first-class lock on a poor door. The same is applicable to padlocks – the best are close shackled and of hardened steel, and must be used with hasps of equal calibre. Both padlocks and ordinary door locks of all kinds can be 'master-suited', which implies that the keying is such that, for example, an executive will be able to open all doors within his jurisdiction with the one key he holds, his departmental managers will have access to the offices in their departments only, and individuals will only be able to enter their own offices. The same sort of arrangement can be implemented in research departments which contain areas of different security importance.

Duplicated locks on doors are not desirable, even with cheap locks, but the main danger is that of desk locks where it is not unusual to find a single key will open almost all drawers in an office. If the desk contains matters demanding privacy, the lock itself should be unique in its environment. To obtain a desk or filing cabinet which will resist forcing, even with limited violence, is well-nigh impossible – fire-resistant cabinets are the nearest available type and even the smaller substantial ones may reach £300 in price; old safes are preferable. Keys must always be kept in personal possession.

Use of dogs

Trained dogs can be a valuable aid for patrolling or guarding premises, particularly on dispersed sites. They afford protection and given confidence to those using them and their very presence is a formidable disincentive to potential intruders.

Liability for injury caused by them is governed by the Animals Act 1971, which lays down that a keeper is not liable for damage if (a) it is wholly due to the fault of the sufferer, (b) the sufferer has voluntarily accepted the risk (an employee is not regarded as a 'volunteer'), or (c) it is caused to a trespasser by an animal kept on premises and it is proved that either it was not kept there for protective purposes or if so used, it was not unreasonable to do so.

Section 1 of the Guard Dogs Act came into force on 1 February 1976. This lays down that a guard dog shall not be used on any premises unless:

1 There is a warning notice of its presence at each entrance
2 It is in the charge of a capable handler at all times, except 'while it is so secured so that it is not at liberty to go freely about the premises'.

It seems unlikely that any other sections of the Act will now be brought into force and in any case they do not relate to the dog 'which is only used as a guard dog at premises belonging to its owner'. A Divisional Court case Hobson v. Gledhill (1977) did indicate that a handler was not always required when a dog was so tethered that a safe space was always available for the intruder to escape into, but also said that each case would be judged on its merits. There have been very few prosecutions indeed.

Closed-circuit television

Closed-circuit TV is increasingly being found of value particularly in retail concerns for observation of purchasers and employees. It is possible to create permanent records for later scrutiny by means of video-tape recording. The simple combination of fixed camera and monitor can be enhanced by special low light or infra-red lenses, pan and tilt facilities for the camera mount, all-weather protection, screen washing and wiping, heating units etc, all of which grossly increase the basic price, but make the installation much more multi-purpose adaptable.

A further use, which could result in substantial manpower economies, is that of remote control of doors and gates by coupling TV observation with microphones for 'speak through' and electronic control of the entry lock thereby allowing an under-utilised receptionist to be more gainfully employed.

It is advisable to point out reasons for installing a system to employees before doing so. To avoid opposition, it may be necessary to agree not to take any action if purely disciplinary matters are seen. Dummy cameras may be used to apparently extend a system and can be interchangeable with the genuine if necessary.

FIRE

The creation of an immediate avenue of notification to the company secretary of happenings that might result in claims or proceedings is important. A fire assessor wants to know of damage as soon as possible after it has occurred so that he can survey it to ascertain extent and causation. Any delay in checking the details of an accident can result in essentials being missed and possible failure to inform the Factory Inspectorate of one of notifiable gravity. A standardised and comprehensive system of reporting should be instituted, especially in connection with accidents.

Fire prevention officers

Full use should be made of the services of the local fire prevention officer. Under the Fire Services Act 1947, the fire authority must maintain efficient arrangements for giving, on request, advice to firms in its area on fire prevention, means of escape, and the restriction of the spread of fires. Consultation with the fire prevention officer should always take place when building alterations or new buildings are contemplated, to avoid unnecessary work and later recriminations. Advice will also be given on the provision and siting of extinguishers and other means of putting out fires. Fire drills should be carried out at regular intervals – it is too late to do so after a tragedy. Very explicit instructions should be given so that all staff know exactly what to do in emergency, and appropriate notices should be displayed. The appointment of fire wardens to be given proper training to combat fire is well worth while, and again the fire prevention officer will be glad to co-operate.

Fire: security checklists

Detailed guidance is given in Oliver and Wilson (1978).

PRECAUTIONS AGAINST TERRORIST ACTION

Regrettably, it has now become necessary for all firms to consider precautions against apparently indiscriminate and senseless acts of violence designed to achieve political ends. These are not entirely confined to the IRA or to the anti-Israeli organisations; others are being tempted to emulate, and terrorism – coupled perhaps with kidnapping – may increase before final containment.

There is also ample evidence that criminal elements are involved in some aspects for financial gain.

The threats and actual risks can take several forms, ranging from malicious telephone calls to explosive and incendiary devices, and letter bombs. The first steps that need to be taken are those of formulating and agreeing policies to deal with particular contingencies, giving due weight to the views of those who will be asked to carry out specific duties such as searching for suspect objects.

Bomb-threat calls

These may be by direct call, anonymous letter, or via a third party, i.e., the police or newspaper office; the IRA have used a code to the police to confirm the presence of a bomb but this is by no means an accurate yardstick of veracity. If sufficiently prevalent, and treated as needing automatic evacuation, these calls can disrupt a firm's activity almost as effectively as a device itself can. The decision is not easy and any individual, whatever his convictions about the validity of a message, will have at the back of his mind the consequences of ignoring a genuine call; this decision therefore must rest with the senior person available, who should be influenced by pre-considered guidelines.

Bomb-threat policy

Fundamentally, there are three basic possible alternatives:

1　To evacuate and search before re-entry
2　To search without evacuation
3　To ignore the message.

Amongst points to be considered are:

1　Nature of the call – apparent age of the caller, speech, attitude, general approach, etc.
2　Recent history of such threats, genuine or otherwise, locally and nationally
3　Prevailing conditions of industrial tension, strikes and political unrest in the neighbourhood and at the recipient's premises particularly
4　Any trading relationships between the company and countries whose opponents have used bombs
5　The implications and dangers of an evacuation.

In all instances, police and fire authorities should be informed immediately, whether an evacuation is to be ordered or not. As a neighbourly gesture, adjoining firms should be told what is happening.

It must be anticipated that the police will be reluctant to take the initiative in advising on evacuation or otherwise – unless they have positive information.

Telephone operators

As first recipients of a message, it is most important that operators have clear instructions on what to do so that there is a minimum of alarm and subsequent confusion about the content of the message. In addition to the instructions suggested below, a stereotyped form of the type shown in Figure 43.2 could be provided to the operators, and its mere availability could relieve natural tension.

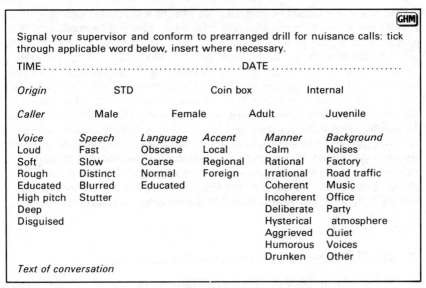

Figure 43.2 Bomb threat checklist for switchboard operator
(note that most bomb threats prove to be hoaxes)

Guidelines to telephonists

1 Let the caller finish his message without interruption
2 Get the message exactly – bearing in mind the points shown
3 If it is possible to tie the supervisor or another operator into the conversation, do so
4 Ensure that senior management or a pre-designated person are told exactly the contents of the call as soon as possible
5 If the caller is apparently prepared to carry on a conversation, encourage him to do so and try to get answers to the following:
   (a) Where has the bomb been put?
   (b) What time will it go off?
   (c) Why has it been done?
   (d) When and how was it done?

In general, if the caller is prepared to continue, try to get him to talk about possible grievances as they affect the firm, and anything which bears upon the truthfulness of the message and the identity of the caller.

It is essential that senior management should be told as soon as possible so that there is no delay in implementing policies and procedures.

Evacuation

Communications should be such that the general warning to evacuate is given simultaneously in all parts affected; otherwise there will be confusion, with people coming and going, difficulty in checking that everyone is out, and garbled messages being passed. If time permits the warning to be given verbally through a managerial chain, it should be on the lines 'At 2 p.m. instruct your staff to begin evacuation, ensure that it is complete not later than 2 15 p.m.'

Based on experience in the USA, a clear radius of 100 yards should be allowed from the threatened area, 200 yards if a car bomb is suspected. Assembly points for evacuation will not of necessity coincide with those used for fire drills. Car parks are definitely not acceptable, for obvious reasons, and there are advantages in housing evacuated staff in substantial buildings if of suitable size and outside the prescribed distance. There must be facilities for checking employees to ensure complete evacuation, the passing of messages and for expediting the return to work. A handheld loud hailer will be found invaluable to those in charge.

In case of evacuation

1   Persons who are instructed to get out must, if time permits, collect and take their personal parcels, bags and other belongings to avoid complications during searching (particularly important in cloakroom areas and office blocks generally)
2   If the time-limit given by the warning permits, there should be a quick search by supervisory staff and/or designated employees before the premises are vacated. A system should be devised to ensure that everyone is out. (Special provisions may be needed for disabled employees.)
3   After the time-limit of the threat has elapsed, a reasonable margin should be allowed before a search by security/supervisory personnel, and employees are allowed to re-enter. (Searching of course is a voluntary matter but, in general, supervisors will co-operate.)

No evacuation

A search should be made by security/supervisory personnel of likely 'planting' areas, i.e. entrances to buildings, cloakrooms and toilets, and the perimeter of buildings – with special attention to parked cars. Police and fire brigade should nevertheless be informed.

Search

1   Responsibility for search of premises lies with the occupiers. The police

cannot be expected to accept this task by themselves, since they will be unfamiliar with buildings and likely contents, but they will almost certainly
offer their assistance

2   Bearing in mind the multiplicity of forms that a bomb may take, it is the unusual object – not the normal in the particular environment – which is
suspect. Again the occupants are best qualified to identify

3   Any search made must be methodical with areas designated to individuals
to ensure that the whole is covered, and with a co-ordinator to make
certain that this is done

4   Unaccountable or suspect objects should not be interfered with. If such are
found the police should be advised and they will then instigate any
necessary action.

Recognition of explosive/incendiary devices

These can be encountered in almost any form. In retail premises, small
incendiary packets put in pockets of clothing left in cloakrooms or among
inflammable textiles may be one of the reasons why the arson rate has escalated
over the past few years. From the terrorist point of view, they have the virtue of
completely eliminating any sign of their existence.

Explosive types have been planted in parcels, suitcases, dustbins, postboxes,
biscuit tins, or where large bulk has been used, lodged in hijacked cars. On
casual inspection, they may not be recognisable for what they are and it is not
unusual for the obvious device to have been booby-trapped as a means of
attacking anti-bomb personnel. A relatively new type is clearly identifiable and
potentially very lethal to those nearby – a conventional bomb is placed with
polystyrene padding between two cans of petrol and then lowered into premises
where inflammable matter is contained, via a hole cut in the roof.

It follows that anything of a foreign nature – rough parcels, plastic shopping
bags left in odd corners or near entrances, dustbins out of place, etc. should be
regarded as suspect. In effect, there is no easy way for a layman without special
equipment to identify or otherwise a potential bomb, and at the risk of
repetition, it is the unusual thing that just should not be where it is which
should immediately arouse suspicion.

In the near vicinity of a suspect bomb, the military advise that personal or
other types of radio intercommunication be switched off as a precaution against
activating a sophisticated device.

General precautions

A general tightening of precautions in or around plant and offices can reduce
the opportunity for incidents and at the same time have the added beneft of
minimising other sources of loss. For example:

1   If not already in existence, inaugurate a registration system for immediate
identification of cars and motor cycles used by employees (helps quick
location of owner when lights left on, tyres flat etc.)

779

2 Control entrance of visitors, suppliers and contractors to the site. Visitor and vehicular passes can be used to provide a record, and to check that the person or vehicle leaves (improves privacy of firm's operation)

3 Do not allow visitors to enter on any pretext without prior confirmation that they are expected/welcome (excludes unwanted, time-wasting callers and stops a common form of impersonation to get into premises to steal). Arrange collection from reception point in cases of doubt. Always check identity of purported public officials – gas, electricity repairmen etc – who will be in possession of the necessary cards.

4 Review physical protection of buildings, i.e. adequacy of fencing, external lighting, doors, ground-floor windows, fire escapes, alarms, etc. (leads to strengthening of physical defences against intruders)

5 Ensure that the standard of housekeeping around buildings is such that unfamiliar objects will at once become noticeable

6 Restrict parking outside particularly important facilities such as computer installations, gas terminals and power substations

7 Establish a central control point which will not be evacuated unless there is a substantiated positive danger to it. This should have means of communication with outside authorities should the firm's switchboard be obliged to close down, and it should be easily accessible to incoming police and fire services

8 In the event of a bomb warning, small rough parcels and plastic-type shopping bags left in odd corners or near entrances should be at once suspect; likewise unfamiliar cars parked haphazardly, especially those with Irish registration plates.

Letter bombs

There is of course no warning given in respect of these; reasons can usually be thought of as to why a particular target has been selected but the senders are irrational, and immunity for lack of causation should not be assumed. It has been suggested in one instance of injury that the employers may be liable in that no guidance, appropriate to present circumstances, had been given to the person opening the mail.

Letters or parcel bombs mainly take the form of substantial envelopes not less than $3/16$ inches thick or of parcels containing paperbacked books delivered through normal postal channels. The weight in letter form is unlikely to exceed 4 oz.

General features

1 Letter bombs are made to withstand the handling that any normal letter or parcel would sustain during delivery; they are to all intents and purposes safe until steps are taken to open them, and can be handled normally until then

2 So far as is known, no letter/parcel bomb has been received which has borne a franking mark on the envelope or wrapping, but a franked stuck-on address label has been used on letter bombs originating on the Continent

3   Spraying with an aerosol of the Boots pain-killing type as used for sporting purposes or Holts 'Cold Start' (the first is the better) may make a manila envelope or wrapping sufficiently transparent for contents to be identified enough to alleviate suspicion if not to establish dangerous nature

4   Conventional components include detonators, connecting wire and minute batteries; no device yet used has been known to have been activated when tested with a low-power metal detector or X-ray (a wide variety of hand-held metal detectors are commercially available). The military advise that if X-ray equipment is used, it should be operated by remote control

5   The police have already dealt with innumerable suspect but innocuous letters/parcels and may be able to give immediate clearance if provided with pertinent details, i.e. town of origin, size and shape, franking or other distinctive stamping.

Points which may make unfamiliar material received suspect

1   The postmark, if foreign and unfamiliar
2   The writing, which may have an 'un-English' appearance, lack literacy, or be crudely printed
3   Name and address of sender (if shown), if address differs from area of post-mark
4   'Personal'/'Only to be opened by' or 'Private' letters addressed to senior management under the job title, e.g. Managing Director.
5   Weight, if excessive for size and apparent contents. Thickness: $3/16$ inch or more
6   Weight distribution, if uneven may indicate batteries inside
7   Grease marks showing on the exterior of the wrapping and emanating from inside may indicate 'sweating' explosive
8   Smell – some explosives smell of marzipan or almonds
9   Abnormal fastening – sealing excessive for the type of package. If such an outer contains a similar inner wrapping, this may be a form of booby trap.
10 Damaged envelopes which give sight of wire, batteries or fluid-filled plastic sachets should be left strictly alone; those that rattle or feel springy should be treated with caution; and naturally, any ticking noise should be treated as a 'red' alert. Pinholes in the outer wrapping may indicate where devices for the safety of the bomb-maker have been removed. Where conventional paperback books have been used, the resultant parcel bomb may be discernibly softer in the centre that at the edges.

If suspicions cannot be alleviated

1   Do not try to open the letter/parcel or tamper with it
2   Do not put it in water or put anything on top of it
3   Isolate it where it can do no harm with minimum handling, i.e., enclose it in a nest of sandbags but ensure that it is in a position for easy visual inspection
4   Open any windows or doors in the vicinity. Keep people away from it
5   Inform the police and seek their guidance: give them full details of the letter/parcel, its markings and peculiarities which have led to suspicion.

KIDNAPPING

In Great Britain, this has not materialised other than in infrequent instances. In the Americas, it is sufficiently widespread for the term 'executive kidnapping' to be applied to a practice which is being used for both financial gain and political advantage. Some American security firms do tender advice on the precautions that should be taken, and insurance can be obtained against it from Lloyd's. If the company secretary is called upon to arrange an itinerary for a senior director in an area where instances have occurred, there is nothing to be lost by enquiring to the appropriate government department for guidelines to be followed. This advice is now available but the essential ingredients are: maintain low profile and minimum publicity, accept that there is a risk however unattractive a target you consider yourself, and use common sense precautions in your behaviour and movements accordingly. The countries of current highest risk are the Argentine and Italy, but publicity of success elsewhere could easily create new trouble points.

WORKS CLOSURES

Regrettably, works closures have become commonplace during recent years. They bring with them security problems which are often unexpectedly serious. The risks start when the news of closure is announced, and can persist long after the intended closure date. By no means all workforces react badly, but there have been many incidents where ill will has led to theft, vandalism and fraud – to the extent that a group of senior security officers have produced guidelines for action during such periods to limit damage to disposable assets.

These guidelines, which are too detailed for inclusion here, are obtainable from The Secretary, International Professional Security Association, 292a Torquay Road, Paignton, Devon, UK.

FURTHER READING

Hughes, D. and Bowler, P., *The Security Survey*, Gower, 1982
Oliver, E. and Wilson, J., *Practical Security in Commerce and Industry*, 4th edition, Gower, 1983.
Oliver, E. and Wilson, J., *Security Manual*, 4th edition, Gower, 1983
Post, R., and Kingsbury, A., *Security Administration*, 2nd edition, Springfield, Ill., (USA) 1973
Walsh and Healey, *Protection of Assets Manual*, Merritt Co., Columbus, Ohio, (USA)
Walsh and Healey, *Industrial Security Management: A cost effective approach*, Merritt, (USA)
Wright, K. G., *Cost Effective Security*, McGraw-Hill, Maidenhead, 1973

44 Energy management

R Dick-Larkam

The industrial revolution, largely brought about by the invention of the steam engine and the exploitation of coal, was the beginning of an exponential rise in energy consumption. The energy crisis of 1973, about 150 years after man started using fossil fuels, produced a realisation that at the present rates of consumption these would not last for ever. Coal might last for several centuries, but oil and gas, the preferred fuels of the twentieth century, will probably be used up in a few decades.

Apart from the need to conserve energy for future generations and to give time for the development of more permanent sources (such as nuclear, solar, wind, wave, etc.) shortages will progressively produce much higher costs. Energy costs have already increased dramatically, so that they are no longer the insignificant costs for industry that they once were. It is thus essential that every effort is made to use energy as economically as possible. Hence the need for energy management.

It has been estimated that over half the energy used by man is wasted. There are, of course, practical difficulties, but there are very many areas where savings can easily be made and these can reduce the consumption by anything up to 20 per cent in a very short time. Once the commitment to an energy-saving programme has been made, there are four stages to go through. These are:

1 Analyse the present methods of working which use energy; with very little change or expense it is often possible to achieve the same results using less energy. An 'energy audit' is an essential part of this analysis
2 Encourage everyone in the organisation to become energy conscious, so that good energy housekeeping is established. Even turning off unwanted lights, closing windows and doors, and similar simple actions, can produce significant savings
3 Following on from the energy audit, and using ideas derived from the good housekeeping campaign, make short-term expenditure to achieve the more obvious and cost-effective energy savings

4 Make long-term plans. These may involve the commitment to invest considerable capital sums against the longer-term conservation of energy.

AUDITING AND MONITORING THE USE OF ENERGY

As with any other form of management, the first requirement is to know the present position. An audit must be conducted to find out exactly what energy is being used, where it is used and from which fuel it is derived. Energy should be accounted for in the same way as money, so that management can identify and tackle the uneconomic areas. It is surprising how many firms have no idea how the energy that they pay for is really used. No two energy users employ their energy in precisely the same way, and it is not possible to suggest an approach to auditing which is more than a general guide.

Measurement in money terms is usually comparatively easy but cost inflation can be misleading when monitoring progress from one audit to the next. Using energy units present a problem because the terms used vary from fuel to fuel, so that to find total usage or to compare one fuel with another for doing similar jobs, it is necessary to reduce them all to some common unit. Basic units in the Imperial system are British Thermal Units (Btu) and therms; in the SI metric system, megajoules (MJ). For many managers, however, these terms will have little meaning and for this reason it seems more logical to use the basic unit of one tonne of coal equivalent. This is almost the same as the old Imperial long ton (1 tonne = 0.984 ton) and is an amount that can be visualised by most people. Conversion merely entails multiplying by the factors as shown in Figure 44.1. It must be remembered that these conversions are not exact, as the calorific value of fossil fuels varies from sample to sample, but they are sufficiently close for all practical purposes.

			Equivalents	GHM
Fuel	Unit	Therms	Megajoules	Tonne of Coal
Gas	1 therm	1	105	0.004 0
Electricity	1 kWh	0.034	3.6	0.000 5
Heating oil	1 gallon	1.77	187	0.007 4
Derv	1 gallon	1.62	171	0.006 5
Petrol	1 gallon	1.48	156	0.005 8
Kerosene	1 tonne	470	49 600	1.70
Propane	1 kg	0.47	49.6	0.001 7
Coal	1 tonne	261	27 500	1.0

Figure 44.1 Approximate energy equivalents

Initially the audit need not be very sophisticated and the aim should be to obtain the results quickly. As time goes on it can be improved in the light of experience as it will undoubtedly reveal many inadequacies in metering and measurement. The first thing to be done is to find out exactly how much energy is being bought and used. This should be available in the form of invoices from the various suppliers and can be put together in common units of both energy and money. This information will be very useful in forecasting; in the past the cost of energy has tended to be neglected as it has not been very significant, but that is no longer the case.

One of the principal reasons for an audit is to try and cut consumption and costs. The audit must therefore be taken further so that each individual use can be given much closer scrutiny. The next step is to try to see how all the energy is used or wasted. Electricity, for example, is used for lighting, for driving motors and perhaps for process heating in the factory. Separate meters, installed for different areas, can be read and the different uses divided. But factories often do not have many separate meters and in these cases the amount used for lighting can be fairly closely estimated by the wattage of the lamps and the average length of time in use. By subtraction the power used for other purposes is estimated and by repeating the process the total can be broken down.

This procedure will show precisely what energy is used, how it is used and where it is used. If a few areas emerge where the use of energy is extremely high, it is obviously here that the biggest savings can be made. Each energy use must be investigated to ascertain whether there is excessive waste and if so, how it can be corrected or if there is a less wasteful way of doing the job. In most cases elimination or even reduction of losses will produce a substantial saving in the total use of energy.

By carrying out regular audits it is possible to compare, both in total and for individual areas (or fuels) how consumption of energy is rising or falling. Of course the amount of energy used will depend not only on how carefully it is used, but also on the level of activity and the weather. The first of these factors can be overcome by relating the energy consumption to the volume of production or (in the case of service industries) to turnover, due allowance being made for inflation.

To allow for weather, which has a special bearing and a considerable effect on space heating, the degree day concept is used. The degree day is defined as the daily difference in degrees of temperature between a base temperature and the 24-hour mean outside temperature when it falls below that base temperature. The base temperature taken is 15.5 °C (60 °F) and if, for example, the mean temperature on a particular day was 8 °C, that day would count as 7.5 degree days. If on another day the mean temperature was anything over 15.5 °C this would count as zero degree days. By monthly totals of degree days, which are issued by the Department of Energy each month for different regions of the UK, it is possible to compare that month with other months and with the same month in previous years.

An example of how degree-day information can be related to fuel consumption for space heating is shown in Figure 44.2 which compares oil usage in a factory over a two-year period. Between the two years, work has been

Month	Degree days °C		Fuel consumption		Gallons/degree day		GHM
	Year 1	Year 2	Year 1 Gallons	Year 2 Gallons	Year 1	Year 2	
October	172	237	2 842	3 301	16.5	13.9	
November	286	237	4 686	3 365	16.4	14.2	
December	319	218	5 318	3 065	16.7	14.1	
January	280	254	4 586	3 527	16.4	13.9	
February	274	290	4 544	4 079	16.6	14.1	
March	296	313	4 904	4 456	16.6	14.2	
April	207	212	3 469	3 056	16.8	14.4	
Totals	1 834	1 761	30 349	24 849	16.6	14.1	

Figure 44.2   Oil usage for factory space-heating analysed using degree days

carried out in an endeavour to make the boiler and the heating system more efficient. November, December and January of year 2 were noticeably warmer than in year 1 and it might have been assumed that the 5500 gallons of fuel were saved because of this. February, March and April, though colder, were not very much colder and by the time May came round, when figures were compared, the fact that October was a lot colder would have been forgotten. By comparing the amount of fuel necessary to heat the factory per degree day it will be seen that this has improved by about 2.5 gallons (the efficiency had been increased by about 15 per cent) and that only about 4 per cent of the oil was saved by better weather conditions.

GOOD HOUSEKEEPING

In any organisation the person using the facilities either wastes energy or conserves it and for this reason everyone must be involved and committed to saving energy if the campaign is to succeed. National campaigns have done much in recent years to make people in the UK aware of the need to save, but human memories are very short and it is easy to revert to old ways. Publicity is a powerful weapon but, to be effective, posters must be replaced frequently or they become part of the decorations and have no effect. Adhesive labels exhorting people to 'Turn it off' on light switches, radiators or hot-water taps are effective for a time, but again lose their impact as people become used to them.

Other ways of arousing interest and involvement are competitions and suggestion schemes. Competitions between departments on saving the most energy week by week or month by month have proved very effective and often public acknowledgement is enough reward. Results of such competitions, suggestions and other exhortations to save energy can well be made in a bulletin issued at regular intervals, copies of which should be freely available to all concerned.

Small working parties meeting for a short time regularly to discuss and suggest how energy can be saved are very useful. They should consist of people who are actually using the energy and to sustain them the membership should be changed from time to time. Yet another way of involving people is to appoint wardens of small areas of the factory or offices, whose job is to make sure that lights are switched off when not required, that radiators are turned down when the temperature is too high, that windows and ventilators are not opened unnecessarily, that outside doors are kept shut and that the many other ways of wasting energy are not practised.

SHORT-TERM EXPENDITURE

The third phase of an energy-saving campaign is often a development of good housekeeping, as many of the ideas put forward during this phase will require moderate capital expenditure. Spending a small amount of capital can often pay large dividends and it must be remembered that when the payback period has passed the savings will then become a direct contribution to profit. The most obvious savings in this area are those which can be made in buildings and services, but large savings can also very often be made in machines and equipment used in the production process.

LONG-TERM PLANS

These, of course, must be unique to any organisation; in the past, due to the low cost of energy, many processes were very energy intensive because they entailed much lower capital costs initially. Now, however, with higher energy costs they are not the most economic. Forms of lighting, heating and building construction may have been the cheapest at the time they were installed or built, but it would be more economic now to pay a higher initial cost in order to save energy afterwards. All plans for the future should be studied from the point of view of energy consumption during their life and this will often influence the original choice.

THE CONSERVATION PLAN

When putting a plan into operation it is essential that someone should be responsible; in a large company it is usual to appoint an energy manager, but with smaller concerns this may not be possible and in such circumstances a manager should be nominated to take on the task in addition to his other duties. The following are the steps that should be taken:

1 Measure what is being used and where it is being used
2 Obtain the co-operation and involvement of everyone concerned
3 Make everyone practise 'good housekeeping'

4 Monitor and publicise the results
5 Make short-term capital expenditure
6 Monitor and publicise the results
7 Prepare long-term plans, for introduction when possible.

ENERGY-SAVING METHODS

There are innumerable ways in which energy can be saved. Most of them are obvious when pointed out, but because in the past the supply of energy has been so readily available, and cheap, they are often missed. A number of practical ways in which energy can be saved, without curtailing any activities and without lowering standards, are set out below.

Lighting

Buildings cut out a considerable part of daylight, despite windows, and they therefore need artificial lighting. Also, of course, we often have to work at night. It is said that lighting consumes a negligible quantity of energy that it is not worth worrying about, but in commerce and industry this is not so. Office blocks and factories can have lighting loads of several hundred kilowatts, and a saving of only 10 or 20 per cent of this is worth while.

The best use of daylight which does enter a building is not always made. Windows and roof lights are often not very clean and the layout of workplaces often leaves a lot to be desired. For some jobs a lot of light is required while others do not need so much; the former should be situated near the windows or under the roof lights, while the latter can be away from the natural source. When artificial light is being used one of the first things that should be done, when looking for energy savings, is to measure the level of illumination at all workplaces. These measurements can be compared with the Illuminating Engineering Society's code for interior lighting which gives recommendations for various jobs and, while it is not suggested that the lighting levels should be less than they recommend, it is wasteful to exceed them. Look also at corridors, storerooms and other places where people do not usually work. These too can often be overlit.

If an office or a factory is arranged properly, for part of the day many people who are close to windows will not require artificial light. There are, however, other areas which do need lights. Yet very often the switching is such that lights near windows and lights in the dark areas are on the same circuit and this usually means that all the lights are on. At comparatively little expense this can be altered and will greatly reduce the load during daylight hours. It is not unusual to see yard lights on during daylight hours; a light-cell switch will overcome this and can also be useful for controlling lights in corridors, stairways and toilets where switching lights on and off is really no one's responsibility.

The maintenance of lights is very important to retain the lighting level and use the minimum of energy. With age all lamps give less light, and light will also be lost due to dust build-up. Figure 44.3 shows the loss in light from a fluorescent fitting in an average factory, assuming 3000 hours use per year, and it will be seen that without maintenance for two years the light given out is more than halved.

Light sources vary very much in their efficiency as is shown in Figure 44.4; the variations with each source depend on the type and size of the lamp, generally the larger lamp being the more efficient. It will be seen that tungsten lamps (still used extensively) are very inefficient, using nearly four times the energy for the same amount of light as that used by fluorescent tubes and nearly seven times the high-pressure sodium consumption. Installation and lamp cost is, of course, the cheapest for tungsten lighting, but the overall cost over a period of time, taking the cost of electricity and the shorter lamp life into account, is very much higher. To anyone using tungsten lighting the capital cost of changing to a more economical form will be repaid very quickly.

When planning new buildings or extensions it is well worth while to investigate the total cost of the more efficient lighting systems; that is not only the initial cost of installation but the cost over the period of years that the building will be in use and to compare these with the cost of lower efficiency lighting. It is also important to ensure that the building is not overlit for 'aesthetic reasons'.

Ventilation

It is necessary to ventilate any building in which people work not only because the oxygen gets used up but more especially because the concentration of carbon dioxide and humidity rise. Two changes of air per hour is all that is generally needed, but, due to air leaks round windows and doors and the passage of people to and fro, four or more are the general rule in office blocks and factory buildings. Each time the air is changed the fresh air must be heated from outside temperature to that in the building.

On the windward side of buildings leaks can often be felt as draughts. It must be remembered that where cold air can get in warm air can get out, particularly on the leeward side of the building. The elimination of draught is one of the easiest and cheapest ways of saving energy. The use of foam, rubber or metal draught excluder will usually stop the leak and still allow doors to be opened and the windows in summer. In factory buildings the eaves, roof ridges and walls must also be looked at and in these cases draughtproofing can save as much as between 20 and 25 per cent of the energy used in heating the building.

Windows offer very poor thermal material insulation and even when draught proofed it may still seem that cold air and draughts are coming from them. This is because the air near the windows is cooled and, being heavier than warm air, starts a downward circulation. Double glazing is the best way to prevent this, but is, of course, rather expensive. Tight-fitting screens covered with polythene sheet are a cheaper alternative and very often just as effective although not so attractive aesthetically.

Many modern buildings have an air-conditioning system installed. These systems can, if not carefully maintained, consume large quantities of extra fuel when they go out of adjustment. It has been found that savings can be made

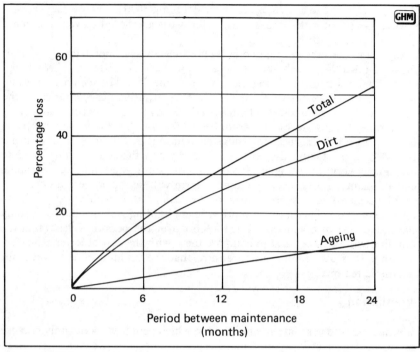

Figure 44.3 Deterioration of fluorescent light source with age and accumulated dirt

Light source	Lumens per watt
Tungsten lamp	10–22
Mercury lamp	41–59
Fluorescent tube	42–75
Mercury halide lamp	60–80
High-pressure sodium lamp	68–120
Low-pressure sodium lamp	130–175

Figure 44.4 Comparative efficiences of various light sources

without affecting anyone working in the building by turning them off about one hour before work stops.

Where air-conditioning is installed a great deal of extra energy can be used in summer by the building heating up due to solar gain; sun shining on windows produces a glasshouse effect. There are basically two ways of overcoming this problem – by suitable tinted or reflective glazing or by the use of blinds. Film is available that can be applied to ordinary glass which achieves a similar effect to tinted or reflective glass and at the same time improves the thermal efficiency of the glass. There are many types of blind, but outside blinds are far superior to those fitted inside the building as when these heat up in the sun's rays they cannot radiate this heat within the room.

Space heating

The Factory and Office Acts in the UK lay down that the temperature in any building in which people are working must attain 16 °C (60.8 °F) during the first hour of work, but regulations to promote energy conservation make a maximum of 20°C (68°F). Thus the temperature of workplaces is confined within four degrees of Celsius and generally a temperature of 18 °C is acceptable to most people not doing manual work, although for those with more strenuous occupations lower temperatures are more pleasant. It has been estimated that a 1°C increase in the temperature of a building requires an expenditure of 6 per cent more fuel, so even a small reduction in temperature will make a significant difference to the amount of energy used. Controlling the temperature is not always easy with the crude thermostatic control on most systems. Increasing the number of thermostats (or, ideally, fitting each radiator with one of its own) is one way of doing this, but careful adjustment can achieve much on any system. It is advisable to provide thermostats which cannot be reset by unauthorised persons.

Areas and offices not being used, even if only temporarily, should have their radiators or heaters turned off and should be isolated by keeping the doors closed. Doors leading to the outside, when left open, can reduce the temperature very quickly and thus require extra fuel to reheat the area. The simple remedy is to fit a spring, but this is not always convenient and it may be necessary in offices to fit either automatic or double doors. In the factory rubber doors or strip curtains can be used. Air curtains can be provided for doors which have to be open for a large percentage of the time. Hot-air curtains are expensive to run and waste a lot of energy. Cold-air curtains are effective where lorries and trucks, rather than people, pass through the door, but the most effective and economical on energy is the air curtain that takes its air from the roof space of the building (where it is hotter) and blows this across the entrance inside the building. A further way of wasting energy is to open windows in winter. Where the ventilation is adequate (about two changes per hour) radiators should be turned down instead.

Most offices and factories have some means of reducing the heating during nights and weekends when the buildings are not in use but the most economical ways are not always employed. Reliance is often placed on staff coming in early to start the boilers but little or no account is taken of the ambient temperature. There are many ways of controlling the heating cycle, some very sophisticated, but a great deal can be done using time-clocks and thermostats and very great savings can be made by installing some kind of control.

As with all plant and machinery, heating systems require maintenance. Very often they do not get the attention that they need, resulting in energy losses through inefficiency.

Undoubtedly one of the largest areas of energy waste in the UK is poor heat insulation of buildings. By observing a building it is possible to judge whether extra insulation might be economically feasible. If, for instance, snow on the roof melts quickly, the roof dries very quickly after rains, walls are of corrugated asbestos or iron, or are thin, being built of single bricks or blocks, or the building cools quickly when the heat is turned off, then the insulation is not good enough.

Every building must be considered on its merits. The internal temperature required, the external climate, the form of heating and other factors must be taken into account to arrive at an economic thickness of insulation which should be applied to the shell of the building. With many factory buildings it is possible to reduce the energy used in heating by between 60 and 70 per cent and the capital involved in carrying out insulation would be repaid in three to four years by savings in fuel.

The economies of insulation and draught-proofing can be shown most easily by means of an example. A factory building measured 30 m long, 15 m wide and 6 m in height. Walls and roof were clad with corrugated asbestos cement sheeting, except for the glazed areas which accounted for 15 per cent of the total roof and wall area. The floor was concrete. The internal temperature was maintained at 20 °C with steam unit heaters when the outside temperature was 6°C. The steam heaters consumed 192 kW under these conditions. Modifications were carried out to the building in four stages; the first consisted of fitting vertical trunking to the unit heaters to pull the heat down from the roof area, insulating all steam pipes, sealing all air leaks with plastic sealer and fitting self-closing rubber doors. This reduced the heat requirement to 149 kW, a saving of 22 per cent.

Second, the roof was insulated with insulating board, leaving an air gap between insulation and roof. The heat requirement was further reduced to 98 kW, saving another 27 per cent. The third modification was to fill the air gap between the insulation board and the roof with fibre glass and insulate the walls in the same way. This reduced the heat requirement to 60 kW (a further saving of 20 per cent) or a saving of 69 per cent in all.

The final modification was to double glaze all the windows, but this only reduced the heat requirement by 5 kW, saving less than 3 per cent. Double glazing is not usually effective as an energy saver, but it does reduce cold draughts and receipt of outside noise.

Boilers

Boiler plant is needed in most factories, office blocks and other buildings to supply space heating in winter. In factories, however, the major use is usually for the supply of hot water or steam for process work. When boilers are installed the principal factor that determines the choice is usually the initial cost. The cheapest boiler is rarely the cheapest to run. As fuel and maintenance costs for one year usually equal the initial cost of the boiler it is wise to spend more initially on an efficient boiler and save expense over its years of service.

The efficiency of any boiler falls as the load is reduced from its maximum, so that if the load is high it is often more economic to install two boilers, each of half capacity. Then, when the load decreases, one boiler can be cut out, keeping the other at its most efficient working capacity. This also gives greater safety if a boiler breaks down or has to be taken out of service for maintenance. When it is not possible to install more than one boiler attention should be paid to the boiler's part-load efficiency; some are far better than others.

With coal- and oil-fired boilers always ensure that the fuel being used is the kind for which the boiler was designed. Using the wrong fuel can seriously affect the efficiency of the boiler. Correct combustion is also important; if the fuel is not being completely burnt energy is lost up the chimney. To obtain maximum energy from fossil fuel the proportions of air and fuel must be correct. This can be checked by monitoring the carbon dioxide levels in the chimney, either with instruments provided or by portable instruments. Any fall in carbon dioxide level or a rise in flue gas temperature indicates that the firing equipment need adjustment or cleaning, or that an air leak has developed.

A boiler system should never be run at a temperature higher than that for which it was designed as this will waste considerable amounts of heat by radiation both from the boiler and the transmission lines.

In a closed system, such as used solely for space heating, the water is continuously recirculated and the amount of make-up water is small. But for boilers producing steam or hot water for process work, water must be continuously fed into the boiler to make up the losses, even if the steam is condensed and returned. It is essential that this make-up water is treated to prevent scaling up of the boiler or the efficiency will go down quickly. Energy can also be conserved by heating the make-up water using waste heat from some other process or from the waste heat that is going up the chimney. Obviously the hotter the feed water to the boiler the less heating is required from the fuel.

Equally, savings can be made by pre-heating the air required for combustion. Cold air has a cooling effect on the flame and if heat, which would otherwise be wasted, is used to bring this air nearer to flame temperature efficiency will be increased. There are several patented devices on the market which may be used for this purpose; one uses radiant heat which would otherwise be lost in the hearth. Alternatively there may be some process in the factory emitting very hot contaminated air through a chimney that could be used as a source of heat via heat exchangers.

In common with all equipment, boilers need maintenance, particularly because of the combustion process. A layer of soot on the heating surfaces or scale on the water side can cut down the rate of heat transfer quite dramatically. Burners and firing equipment need periodical cleaning and adjustment.

During the last decade the design of boilers has improved enormously and efficiencies of about 80 per cent are not uncommon. Very many boilers in use were made and installed more than thirty years ago and it is unlikely that these will have an efficiency of more than 50 per cent, even if they have been well maintained. Replacement of old boilers can very often give a return of capital cost by fuel savings in the first year.

Distribution of heat

It is generally inconvenient and inefficient to use the energy contained in a fossil fuel by burning it at the point at which it is required; thus the energy is converted at a central point to a form that can be transmitted and used where it is wanted. Unfortunately there can be severe loss in transmission. Electricity is an example of this. There are considerable losses in the grid, but even so it is more efficient to generate at large stations and have transmission losses than to generate in several small stations.

The same applies to the transmission lines that link a boiler-house with the points at which the energy is required, but much can be done to reduce losses. It is not uncommon to see a wisp of steam rising from a flange or a drop of water from a valve; leaks like these, because they are continuous, can be a large drain. A leak equivalent to a 3mm ($\frac{1}{8}$″) hole will lose 400 tonnes of steam a year at a pressure of $11\frac{1}{2}$ bars (165 psig). In a large system it would not be unusual to find a number of such leaks, amounting to a sizeable loss.

Lagging of hot-water and steam pipes is, of course, vital if losses are to be avoided, but the question arises as to the optimum thickness of insulation. Many tables are published showing the heat lost from bare pipes, and from pipes with different thicknesses of insulation, of different temperatures. If these tables are used to calculate the cost of the heat loss, this can be plotted against insulation cost with increasing thickness. By combining the two curves, as in Figure 44.5 the total cost can be found and thus the economic thickness of insulation. It will be seen that if fuel costs increase faster than insulation costs, the economic thickness gets progressively greater. Flanges and valves are often left uninsulated and can account for considerable loss; it is estimated that a flange is equal to one metre of bare pipe and a valve to about three metres.

In many factories transmission pipes are carried underground in ducts from building to building. These ducts invariably collect water and although the lagging is waterproofed initially, this covering loses its properties with time and the lagging becomes wet. Wet lagging is a little better than no lagging at all. It is useful to observe the top surface of ducts during wet weather. Quick drying is an indication of heat loss and of the need to investigate lagging.

Compressed air

It is estimated that about 10 per cent of all electrical power used in industry is employed in compressing air and as much as 30 to 40 per cent of the air compressed is wasted in losses. In almost any factory these leaks can be heard during a break when the factory is otherwise quiet but the compressor still running.

Small leaks account for quite big losses. Figure 44.6 shows the amount of air lost by leaks equivalent to 3-mm and 6-mm holes in the pipeline at various air pressures. Maintenance of the air lines is therefore of paramount importance. Leaks are not the only cause of energy waste. Excessive pressure drop, caused by inadequate pipe sizing, choked filters and wrongly sized couplings and hoses, gives high velocities and wastes energy by friction in the pipe. This can

Figure 44.5   Optimum insulation thickness

be as significant as leaks.

Compressor performance can contribute a great deal to energy usage and it is essential that they are continuously maintained and checked. The loading of the compressor is also important as it is most efficient on full load. For this reason, if there are high peak demands it is often more economical to increase the size of the receiver (which acts as a reservoir for the compressed air) than to increase the size of the compressor.

The choice of pressure in a pipeline system affects both the initial cost and the energy consumption per unit of compressed air. Figure 44.7 shows the power required to generate 30 m³/min (1060 ft³/min) of free air at different pressures and it will be seen that the same quantity of air at 7 bar (100 psig) requires 15 per cent more power than at 5 bar (70 psig). It is, therefore, essential for greatest economy that the line pressure is no higher than necessary.

In compressing air a lot of the energy used is converted to heat energy, which is removed either by air or water cooling. The energy contained in both can be used; the air by ducting for space heating and the water either via a heat exchanger or direct for washing, boiler feed or even space heating.

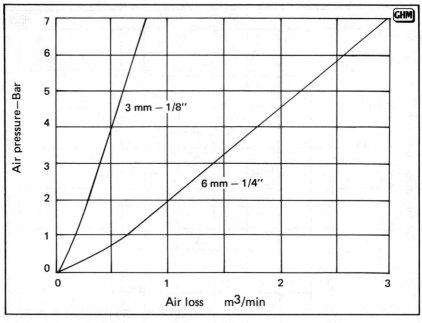

Figure 44.6   Air loss due to leaks

Ovens and furnaces

At some stage almost all manufactured articles go through a process of heating. The equipment used can broadly be termed an oven or furnace and may vary from a heated tunnel through which the products are moved on a conveyor belt to an insulated box lined with refractory material and heated almost any fuel.

Few small furnaces are now fired by solid fuel, but oil, natural gas and liquid petroleum gas are often used. The thermal efficiencies of these small furnaces can be as low as 10 per cent and they rarely exceed 50 per cent, due to the losses in combustion and waste gases which are discharged at high temperature. Electric furnaces can be much more thermally efficient as there are none of these losses, but owing to the high cost of electricity as a fuel they are not always cost effective.

The type of refactory material used in a furnace can influence the amount of fuel used. Where furnaces are used continuously the thermal capacity of the insulation is unimportant, but where they are used intermittently it is very important as high heat storage means a great loss in residual heat. Hot face refractory or ceramic fibre insulation can reduce these heat losses by up to 90 per cent over those suffered with ordinary fire brick.

To obtain optimum efficiency care should be taken to ensure that a suitable burner is used, consistent with the design of the furnace. The firing should also be regulated to give the correct fuel to air ratios as with a boiler. It is usually

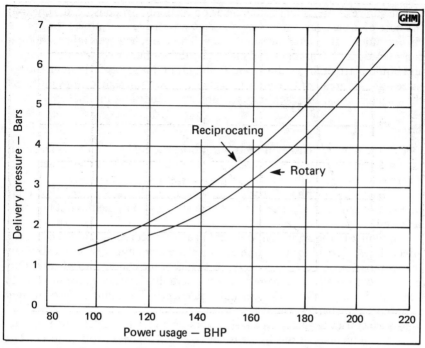

Figure 44.7   Power needed to compress 30 m³/min of air

advantageous to run a furnace at a pressure slightly above atmospheric as this ensures no leakage of cold air through doors and other openings.

Considerable fuel savings can be made by paying detailed attention to furnace loading. An empty furnace can use 75 per cent of the fuel used when it is fully loaded. It is, therefore, necessary to plan the throughput so that it is constantly fully loaded. This may mean that the furnace is running for only part of the day and this will obviously make a saving. Attention should also be paid to furnace doors to ensure they fit tightly and that the load is ready to insert with minimum of door-open time.

Where furnaces and ovens are in use there is usually plenty of opportunity to recover waste heat as they invariably have large quantities available in the exhaust gases. This can be put to use in other parts of the factory or can usefully be used to preheat the combustion air of the furnace itself.

Choosing a fuel

When a source of energy is required there is often some difficulty in deciding which type of fuel to use. With lighting and power sources for machines there is really no difficulty as electricity is almost decided for us; but for firing a boiler, or for heating an oven (for example) there is a variety of fuels that can be chosen.

The choice of fuel is most often made on economic grounds. At any one time the cost of a particular fuel may show an advantage over others, but prices change quickly and not always uniformly. There are, however, other economic considerations. Natural gas and electricity do not have to be stored. Coal, oil and liquid petroleum gas all present problems in this respect, although the last three offer far greater protection against shut-down through loss of supply. All these factors must be taken into account when choosing the fuel.

Electricity

One of the most expensive of fuels but it offers so many advantages and cost-saving features in use that, overall, it is often less expensive than other fuels. There is no storage requirement and transmission to various parts of the factory is relatively cheap with little or no maintenance on the cables. Breakdowns are rare and usually quickly corrected, so that standby equipment is not normally required.

The choice of the right tariff does not in any way conserve energy, but it can affect the price paid for the same quantity of electricity. It is often extremely rewarding to examine the various tariffs available and choose the right one. Off-peak use can usually reduce the price considerably. Electricity accounts should be studied and the total price per unit calculated. This can then be compared with what the charges would be on other tariffs.

Most factories, whatever the tariff, work on a maximum demand and great savings can be made if this figure is not exceeded or, better still, reduced. The maximum demand is usually only made for short periods over the day, and by studying the load and planning the work accordingly it can often be reduced. For example, if larger receivers are installed on the compressed-air system, the compressor could be shut down for a short time over peak loads. There are many sophisticated devices for giving warning and even shutting off load to avoid overrunning the maximum demand, but much can be done with a simple warning system.

Apart from electricity to perform work, some electrical equipment requires additional current for magnetising purposes and this lags behind the work current and is not registered on normal meters measuring kilowatts. The total current supplied can be registered on a kilovolt-ampere meter. The ratio of the current effectively used as read on a kilowatt meter and the total current supplied as read on a kilovolt-ampere meter is known as the power factor. In most factories without correction this is usually 0.6 to 0.85, but if there is a lot of arc-welding plant it can be as low as 0.35. Electricity boards penalise for low-power factor and it is usually well worth while to fit capacitors to correct it.

Natural gas

This has a calorific value about double that of the old town gas made from coal or oil. Gas is a very clean fuel with no harmful ingredients such as sulphur, and if correctly burnt will give no solid emissions, ash or sludge. Gas is a piped supply, delivered at a pressure which usually eliminates the need for any pumping or compressing before it is used on site. No storage of fuel is necessary.

Due to limited supplies of natural gas and occasional large peak demands, gas boards sell gas to industrial users on 'interruptible' tariffs. On such a tariff the user can have his supply cut off for considerable periods and to guard against interruption of production users have to store an alternative fuel, such as propane. This entails capital expenditure for the installation of pressure tanks, cash tied up in fuel stock, and space occupied by storage. These factors must be taken into account when deciding on the fuel to use.

Fuel oils

Although not so consistent as gas, these have undergone a process of refining where quality control is exercised. Basically there are two types of fuel oil: distillate fuels which have a low viscosity and require no heating in storage or at the burner, and heavy oils which (because of their high viscosity at low temperatures) require heating in order to flow along the pipelines. By volume the heavier oils have a higher calorific value and are cheaper, so that the cost per therm can be about two-thirds the cost of gas oil. But the cost of heating tanks, desludging etc. more than balances this saving except in large installations.

Storage for fuel oils initially costs far more than for any other fuel. They take up a lot of space and fire precautions are stringent. On the other hand, delivery to the point of use is easy and requires no labour. Although with heavy oil there is the cost of heating, it is clean in burning and there is no ash, but the sulphur content can cause trouble through corrosion.

Solid fuels

Coke, manufactured fuels, lignite or even wood are used as solid fuels, but in the industrial context coal is the solid fuel used most widely. It is the easiest fuel to store from the point of view of capital cost of storage equipment, but it occupies quite a large area. Handling of coal is both dirty and labour intensive and solid fuels have the additional disadvantage of producing ash when burnt, which entails removal and disposal.

Coal is usually the cheapest fuel in terms of energy content, but the handling costs often make it uneconomic in comparison with other fuels. On the other hand, coal is the one fuel which is likely to be available for some hundreds of years to come.

Liquified petroleum gases

Butane and propane are used in industry for heating and other purposes. These are clean fuels with very little sulphur content. Storage requires pressure vessels sited away from other buildings. Strict fire precautions must be taken, particularly during refuelling. Sometimes it is necessary to install evaporators in order to achieve the high take-off rates where consumption is high, and this adds to the cost because heat has to be supplied to these evaporators.

FURTHER READING

Dick-Larkam, R., *Cutting Energy Costs*, Gower, 1977. An expansion of this chapter.
Dryden, I. G. C. (ed.), *The Efficient Use of Energy*, IPC Science & Tech. Press. A comprehensive work of reference on energy utilisation.
Fuel Economy Handbook, National Industrial Fuel Efficiency Service, Graham Trotman Dudley Publications. A practical handbook on good practice to save energy.
Illuminating Engineering Society Guide, Illuminating Engineering Soc. Defines lighting standards
Payne, G. A., *The Energy Manager's Handbook*, IPC Science & Tech. Press. A useful handbook on energy management.
The Selection and Installation of Compressed Air Services, British Compressed Air Soc.
Windett, A. S., *Reducing the Cost of Electricity Supply for the Industrial and Commercial User*, 3rd edition, Gower, 1982.

A variety of publications is issued by the Department of Energy, the Department of the Environment and the Electricity Council.

45 Office services

R S Henderson

No firm can hope to operate effectively, and therefore profitably, unless it is properly supported by all the necessary services and facilities that go to make up a modern office. These range from the maintenance and cleaning of the building to the provision of stationery; from well-established security and emergency procedures to the handling and distribution of the post. The task of administering all these services is almost always a thankless one. If all goes smoothly the service is taken for granted; when it falls down, everyone looks for a scapegoat, who is invariably the unfortunate office manager.

The office manager – always underestimated, at least as far as the importance of his job is concerned – finds himself managing by complaint. He is responsible for a large number of diverse and individual systems which he probably has inherited from a predecessor, and which tend to operate much as they always have done. He hesitates to examine their workings too closely for fear of causing disruption, and indeed is probably too busy to do so thoroughly and methodically until he gets a complaint from above. He is then forced to react quickly and as a result may make ill-considered changes with potentially disastrous results and certainly unfavourable reactions from the operating staff.

ORGANISATION OF OFFICE SERVICES

In setting up an office services department, senior management should consider:

1 The person they charge with looking after the running of the building and its supporting services and facilities will probably have one of the largest budgets and workforces in their organisation. The department may not be a profit centre, but it has tremendous significance in terms of total operating cost
2 The quality of the service provided by this department impinges on all aspects of the business, including the profit centres. If that service is efficient, reliable and flexible it will be a positive aid towards profitability.

3   To maintain a high level of service the office manager must be able to predict future demands to be made upon his department. He will only be able to do so if he is kept informed and preferably forewarned of all policy changes and decisions which affect his areas of responsibility.

These three points lead to the clear conclusion that the role of office administrator should not be regarded as an inferior occupation. It should have a clearly defined place in the organisational structure with direct links to top management. Only in this way can channels of communication be maintained to ensure that the planning of office administration is based on full and accurate information.

The scope of office services

Figure 45.1 shows the potential range and scope of the services and facilities needed by a medium-sized company occupying its own office block. For smaller firms some of these items would be reduced in scope but the range of services and facilities applies to all. Even a company with only twenty or so office staff will undoubtedly need an element from each of the main headings. At this level it will probably be the company secretary or his equivalent who will be responsible, but the same principles will apply to their organisation and management as for a much larger firm.

Organisation structure

In Figure 45.1 the range of services has been grouped under ten headings. For administration and organisation purposes they could be brought together as indicated in Figure 45.2. There are obviously many variations on this theme and much will depend on the size of the company and the complexity of the administrative services needed. However, the aim should always be to avoid having every query finishing up on the office manager's desk. He should be a manager rather than a supervisor.

He should be able to plan for the future, to budget, to introduce new methods and systems, to improve existing ones; he should study trends in the development of new equipment with the aim of phasing it in as the opportunity arises; he should train and develop his staff, particularly the younger ones, to take on new responsibilities as the need occurs; and above all he should manage the administration of the office so that it runs smoothly, effectively and economically.

OFFICE LAYOUTS

This whole chapter is devoted to the provision of efficient services to the office operation and how these contribute to the smooth running of the company. An essential element of these office services and one that is often overlooked or neglected is the responsibility for the layout of the offices. All too often layouts of partitioning, and even of desks, are inherited from a previous occupier, with

GHM

Reprographics	Telecommunications	Security & Safety
Printing	Telephone exchange	Security guards
Photocopying	Internal systems	Fire precautions
Stationery issues	Paging system	Emergency procedures
Microfilming	Public address	
	Telex, telecopier terminals	Industrial and commercial espionage measures (e.g., shredding equipment and counter-surveillance measures)
		Statutory requirements

Reception	Post	Central services
Main reception	Postal service	Typing
Commissionaires	Messengers	Secretarial
Booking of meeting rooms	Document movement	Filing
Travel arrangements		Word processing
		Library

Staff welfare	Transport	Purchasing
Canteen	Company cars/vans	Stationery
Refreshments	Chauffeurs, drivers	Equipment
Social/recreation	Transport records	Furniture
First aid/medical	Car park allocations	Leasing arrangements
Rest room		Contract arrangements
Shop		

Building maintenance

Building:	Cleaning, upkeep, repairs, redecoration, rubbish and wate disposal, external upkeep (e.g., grounds and car park).
Plant & equipment:	Maintenance contracts for heating/ventilation/ air conditioning, lifts, window cleaning gear, day-to-day maintenance of plant, plumbing services, electric power and lighting, clocks etc.
Office equipment:	Typewriters, calculators, printing equipment, furniture, filing systems, etc.
Office layouts:	Planning layout revisions, alterations to lighting, partitioning, telephone and power points, furniture moves, etc.

Figure 45.1   The scope of office services

803

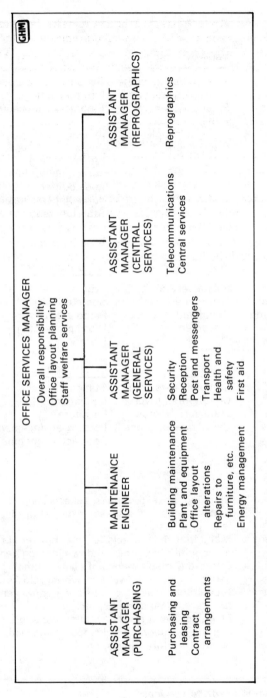

Figure 45.2   An office services departmental organisation
This is just one of a large number of possible organisations which might be found in an office services department. Obviously the organisation must depend on the size of a company and the activities which it performs; the arrangement shown here might be found in a medium to large engineering company

cost dictating a minimum of alterations, and the new users having to adapt their work routines to suit. Even when the layouts suit requirements in all respects on initial occupation, very few organisations remain static for long. Very soon, growth and/or changes in operations and structure inevitably call for modifications. If these are not responded to there begins an, at first unremarked, deterioration in the working arrangements.

Piecemeal changes in shared or open offices, even of an apparently minor nature, can have a domino effect leading to overcrowding in some areas and wasted space in others. It is a fairly straightforward matter to establish a routine whereby the office manager is consulted and controls all layout changes. It is perhaps more difficult to make sure that he has the authority to make his proposals work. In any event, a major reorganisation or relocation exercise may overstretch his resources, and it would be unwise to treat this as part of the normal office services role. If an outside specialist is called in on these occasions, it should be to work with rather than instead of the office manager. The professional planning consultancy will need his advice and guidance and his detailed knowledge of the building at all stages if their schemes are to be effective and worth while.

The subject of office planning is worthy of a book in its own right, so it is impossible to give comprehensive advice here. However, the few guidelines reproduced below may be helpful to the hard-pressed office manager.

Office planning guidelines

1   Do not underestimate the importance of planning office layouts to meet individual functional needs
2   These needs change from time to time as new working methods are developed to meet changing market forces
3   Do not assume knowledge of how people perform their day-to-day tasks and how they relate to each other in a department or organisation
4   The first step is always to study requirements by formally interviewing both the management concerned and as many of their staff as practicable
5   Base the layouts plans on your analysis of needs. For example, private rooms, only for those with a high proportion of their time spent on confidential matters; more space in the open office for those who need some measure of privacy and freedom from distraction
6   Better to arrange informal groups of desks reflecting, perhaps, a team approach, than to adopt a schoolroom regime.
7   Avoid rows of private offices along one side of the office floor with the open area on the other. This promotes the idea of 'them and us'. Try to site offices where they are needed and to create pools of related open space between them
8   Walkways and escape routes in open offices need not be straight, but should always be clearly demarked by items of furniture such as low screens and filing cabinets
9   Open planning does not necessarily save any space, but it is more adaptable to change. If properly done, it can result in pleasant working conditions for everyone.

REPROGRAPHICS

Reprographics is the business of reproducing the written word or picture. It is a vast and growing subject in itself. There is hardly an office without at least a simple photocopying machine of some kind, and sophisticated in-house printing facilities are commonplace. The reprographics function also includes the printing of plans and technical drawings and, especially in more recent years, microphotography (alternatively called microfilming or micrographics). Any but the very smallest reprographics department uses materials and bought out services at an expensive rate, takes up a lot of office space, and needs equipping with costly machinery. Effective supervision of the department is essential in order to keep operating costs down.

Photocopying

It is necessary to be aware of the abuse to which the simple photocopier can be subjected, from the illicit production of private copies to the bigger problem of wastage by taking more copies than are really needed. In the same way as the original Mr Colman is said to have made his fortune from the mustard left on the side of the plate, so must the paper and copier manufacturers be doing from the high volume of unnecessary copies.

The most effective way to control copy quantity – and quality – is to place every photocopier within a central reprographics department, staffed by one or more trained operators, and with copies only given against duly authorised requisitions. Under such supervision, the machines will prove more reliable, and print quality can be maintained at a good level.

In a large organisation, a centralised photocopying facility may not be convenient to all staff, where the ability to obtain a few copies quickly saves the time of senior people and helps to promote efficiency. The wastage inherent in allowing staff free access to unsupervised copiers can be more than offset by the time saved. One solution to cut down wastage at local copier stations is to lock the machines, and provide suitable staff with keys. Another, less cumbersome approach is to provide machines for local use capable of giving the cheapest possible copies consistent with readable quality and reliable performance. Copies for internal use do not have to be up to exhibition standard. Where high quality or large numbers are justified, then the central facility must be used.

Photocopier technology continues to develop rapidly. The basic principles come in several quite different categories, each with its own multiple variations. Plain paper copiers using xerography (an electrostatic process) produce cheap prints at the cost of high technology and, therefore, expensive machinery. Copiers using coated paper may be electrostatic, photographic or with an infrared or ultraviolet source of light. In addition to wide variations in the cost per print, each method produces different degrees of response to the colours in the original document; some copiers will not copy faint blue images and others are relatively insensitive to red.

Many factors need to be considered when choosing a copier for the first time. Will it take the size of paper needed (usually the choice is between B4, A4 or

A3)? Some machines can reduce the image if required, for example printing out an A4 copy from an A3 original. A flat bed copier is useful when books have to be copied (observe the copyright law!).

Apart from the number of copies which the machine can make in a minute (i.e., the copying speed) a more telling factor is the time needed to make the first copy. Some copiers take ten minutes or more to warm up, with the result that they are left switched on all day to consume and waste electrical power and to emit heat and noise into the office. Some form of automatic or semi-automatic document-feeding device is often justifiable as a time saver, and it may also be desirable to include a sorter than can collate multiple sets of copies into convenient stacks ready for binding or stapling. One or two copiers even do the stapling.

As with the purchase of all office equipment, it is prudent to seek out other users of similar equipment and find out whether they would recommend it. The supplier will usually be willing to give introductions to such referees, although he is unlikely to be very open about sites where major problems have occurred.

The total cost approach is essential when choosing copiers. The starting point is to determine the number of copies to be made each month at each copying station. This is bound to be a variable figure, depending on seasonal factors and the level of activity in the business generally. In addition to an estimated average usage per month (for annual budgeting) it is also necessary to estimate the maximum and minimum numbers. Knowledge of the maximum number of copies will eliminate some copiers at the outset because they would simply be too slow or too unreliable to cope with the workload predicted. Manufacturers often specify the maximum capability of their machines, although they sometimes tend to be optimistic.

The reason for estimating the minimum number of copies needed over slack periods is purely one of economics. It is important not to commit expenditure to a machine which is too big for its job, since to do so must result in the cost per copy at low levels being inflated through the high burden of machine rentals or depreciation costs.

In the total cost approach it is useful to draw a graph for every machine under consideration relating the monthly copy volume (x axis) with the total cost of those copies (y axis). This total cost should certainly include machine rentals (or depreciation), all materials such as paper, toner and consumable spares plus maintenance costs. It may also be possible to estimate operator costs, although this is not essential and may be too difficult. Where alternative tariffs are quoted for the same machine, one graph should be drawn for each option. The curves will indicate clearly penalties payable where copy volumes are low and fixed costs high, in addition to the more straightforward cost per copy at higher rates of usage. This is a practical application of marginal costing. Photocopier salesmen are persistent people, unwilling to take 'No' for an answer; they are however easily impressed and intimidated when faced with a carefully produced set of graphs that provide a good basis for negotiating discounts and reduced terms in the face of their business rivals.

Printing and duplicating

Although some large plain paper photocopiers are able to produce fairly cheap long duplicating runs, spirit duplicators or stencil machines can be considered where low cost is the only consideration, to the exclusion of high quality prints. If it is essential to maintain decent print quality, then offset litho printing commends itself.

In the offset process, an image is prepared on a printing plate by direct typing or by photography. The image is transferred to an intermediate surface in the machine (and reversed) and thence to the paper (reversed back again). Thus it is not necessary to work with a reverse print master. Copy quality is excellent, long runs are possible, and the process is cheap. A skilled operator is essential for best results.

Once an in-house printing facility has been set up it is inclined to grow. Machines for sorting, collating, punching, folding, stapling and binding may have to be acquired. Still more expense occurs when artwork and typesetting capabilities are taken on. As these facilities and their attendant staff proliferate, so may the volume of printing itself increase to take advantage of the 'cheap' service available. It becomes easy to modify forms and produce infinite variations on letterheads and other printed documents. The result can be a very expensive and unjustified operation, generating high volumes of unnecessary forms and scrap paper.

No firm should embark on an in-house printing installation without a very careful study of its requirements. When evaluating the cost performance of a proposed internal unit, it is easy to underestimate the cost of the space which the department will occupy – not only the rent and rates but also service charges, heating, lighting and a share of the upkeep costs of the building. Although a small department may be essential to some companies, it may be better to use a local printer, and ask him to stock stationery and forms for availability against call-off orders.

Plan printing

Printing of engineering drawings and plans is almost always carried out using the diazo process. Masters are drawn on translucent or transparent material, and in the printing process a coated material is exposed to ultraviolet light, passed through the original in close contact with the print, and the positive image is developed by ammonia. Such machines consume a considerable amount of electrical power – often in excess of 10 kW – and the heat and ammonia fumes produced have to be ducted off into a flue. The process is ideal for producing large-sized prints on paper, or on any other film or sensitised medium.

MICROFILMING

Any office manager responsible for providing office space is aware that document filing is usually very space consuming, and staff continually request more and more filing equipment. Indeed, it could be said that any company will eventually choke to death on its own paper files if the growth of such files is allowed to continue unchecked. Clever filing equipment, some of it mechanised, is available to minimise the space needed; this is achieved by transporting the documents within the system in such a way that waste space (e.g., roof voids) can be used. Other measures include the provision of storage space off site, in a warehouse or similar building, where files can be boxed and held available for occasional reference at (say) a day's notice.

A more drastic and usually sensible way to reduce filing bulk is to question the need to keep documents at all. Certainly, when a member of staff asks for an additional filing cabinet, he or she should be asked first to clear out unnecessary paper from the other cabinets and drawers in the office. Nevertheless, a considerable amount of information has to be stored within easy reach in most companies, and a cost-effective and convenient approach to the problem is to hold the documents on microfilm, which dramatically reduces the space needed for storage. Properly managed, access time to any required document can also be reduced, simply because the files are concentrated in a small area, and no walking is needed to retrieve items. Accurate and sensible indexing is the essential requirement for microfilm retrieval.

Microforms

There are several variations on the microfilming theme, each suitable for a particular office application.

16-mm film is used widely for the storage of complete files. The original documents can be any size up to foolscap. Longer documents can sometimes be filmed so that the image lies along the major axis of the film. By mounting the film in a cassette, and using viewing equipment with a suitable indexing device, rapid retrieval of the document required is possible. Approximately 1 500 A4 original documents can be held on a 100 ft (30 m) roll of film. The roll film method is only really suitable for files which will not be updated because the replacement of a document would entail cutting and splicing the film.

16-mm jacket fiche is a system based on the use of 16-mm roll film, but which allows editing, additions and revisions. Documents are filmed on to the roll, which is then processed and cut up into individual documents or groups of documents according to the file index. For example, one subject could be the name of an individual in a personnel records system. Using a special jig, the strips of film are inserted into transparent plastic sheets, which allow a grid of frames to be assembled. The sheets contain a series of horizontal channels to accommodate the film. Outdated information can be removed from the jacket fiche using tweezers. Additional or revised information is filmed and inserted in the appropriate place in the jacket. Retrieval is achieved with a spcial fiche viewer, using an index system that first identifies the particular jacket fiche, and then locates the frame on the sheet by a grid reference system.

Microfiche is similar in some respects to jacket fiche, but the degree of reduction is greater. Many more documents can be held on one fiche, which is a single piece of photographic film of a size suitable for filing in a card index tray.

Every frame is photographed on to the fiche sequentially to form a pattern of images in regular columns and rows. As with jacket fiche, any single frame can be identified by a grid system of co-ordinates but, since microfiche is a direct photographic image on film, it can only be updated by changing a whole fiche. Microfiche is applicable to whole books (since books do not get updated in general, and a whole book can be contained on only a very few microfiche sheets). The method is also used for catalogues and spare parts lists, the whole set of fiche being replaced when a new issue is required.

35-mm film allows larger documents, such as engineering drawings, to be microfilmed without the loss of definition which would result from any attempt to use 16mm. Drawings up to A0 size can be filmed successfully on 35 mm. *70-mm film* is used in limited applications where even greater definition is needed.

35-mm aperture cards are similar in appearance to data processing punched cards, but a rectangular aperture in the card carries a single 35-mm image frame. Usually, drawings are filmed on to a 35-mm roll, which is then cut up into individual frames for mounting into jackets cemented on the face of the aperture cards. Aperature cards can also be obtained in magazines, with the film already in place one each card. Exposure takes place in a special camera, which also develops and processes the image automatically. The advantage of aperture cards over unmounted roll film is in the ease of handling and retrieval made possible. In fact, provided care is taken not to damage the film, aperture cards can be punched and printed with the relevant drawing number and title, and mechanical sorting and automatic feeding to a printer become possible.

Quality control and techniques

With all microforms, quality control is essential at every step in the process. The exposure must be right, the original document must be well and evenly illuminated (sometimes from underneath using a glass table), the degree of reduction should be accurate in order to maintain the correct scale on reproduction, and of course the image must be in focus over the entire area. Developing, fixing and washing also require careful control to ensure that the film will keep without deterioration – especially important for archive micro-filming. Good conditions can be obtained using automatic equipment which is electronically controlled. Otherwise, a reliable bureau should be employed. An incidental, but extremely important, extension of quality control and supervision is the care given to the original documents during the process to prevent damage or loss. Obviously such originals must be protected until the microfilm has been processed and the image quality checked.

Storage and copying

Ordinary photographic film, using a silver halide emulsion, is referred to as 'silver' microfilm for short, and this is the material with the longest storage life for archival purposes – say up to fifty years or more. The diazo process can be used to make cheap contact copies from roll film or from aperture cards or fiche. Such cheap copies are usually of very high quality, with adequate storage properties for normal use. For widespread publication of books, catalogues and the like in microfilm, diazo copies are ideal. In engineering offices, 'satellite' reference files of drawing aperture cards can be arranged in a number of locations to give local access to drawing information while the silver masters are locked away for security.

Viewing and printing

A wide range of commercial viewers, viewer-printers and printers is available. There are also projectors. Many of these viewers are fitted with a retrieval device, allowing a particular frame to be found easily on a roll film cassette or fiche. Printing methods include xerography on to plain paper, an electrolytic process, and a heat-developed image using photographically sensitised paper.

Computer output on microfilm (COM) is a system in which the need for a paper document is discarded. Instead, the data output from the computer is photographed directly on microfilm from a viewing screen. More modern techniques use lasers, and video discs will replace some microfilm techniques altogether, with information stored in digital form from which an image can be printed out or projected on a viewing screen. At this point the discussion leaves the realm of office services and becomes more a question of data processing.

TELEPHONES

Telephones are often said to be the life blood of a company, although they certainly can be the death of sustained concentration for the individual! Nevertheless, a well-run telephone service is important, particularly in the way calls are handled by the operator. The first impression a potential customer receives is often from that anonymous voice. If it is helpful and obliging, and above all seems interested in being so, the impression is going to be a favourable one. It will become part of the company's image and reflect their standing in their market.

There is, of course, much more to this than making sure the operators have good telephone manners. For example, the internal telephone directory must be kept meticulously up to date, or the image will very quickly be tarnished. They should also be involved enough in the company's business to be able to direct a vague enquiry about a new product, for example, to the person dealing with it. This applies just as much to the full-time operators of large PABX systems as to the maid-of-all-work who is combined receptionist, switchboard girl and part-time invoice clerk/typist.

Another aspect of telecommunications which the office manager has to be aware of is the need to establish and foster good relations with the local British Telecom engineers and sales staff. They can be remarkably helpful over an unexpected need to move telephone extensions or to cope with some other crisis. Certainly their advice and assistance can be invaluable in planning a move of any size, a new layout, or the introduction of new equipment.

The subject of telecommunication is, of course, a complex and rapidly developing one. It is neither appropriate nor necessary to deal here with all the possible ramifications which might come under the office manager's wing. There is a wide range of equipment available to meet most normal telephonic needs. With the end of British Telecom's monopoly this choice will inevitably become even wider. Similarly, as electronic systems become cheaper and more commonplace, so will the twin technologies of data processing and tele-communications become interdependent. Such developments are discussed more fully in the chapter on the electronic office (Chapter 47).

SECURITY AND SAFETY

Not so long ago security measures were aimed at preventing pilfering and occasionally thought was given to safeguarding confidential information. Now vandalism and even bombings necessitate turning buildings into fortresses and, once again, it is the office manager who is responsible for seeing that the drawbridge is raised. It is a manifestation of a rapidly changing society that buildings planned and designed only a few years ago for ease of access for goods and staff and the general public are now considered vulnerable and therefore ill-conceived.

As usual, technology leaps to the rescue and sophisticated services abound to cope with each new problem as it arises; protective film for windows, closed circuit TV systems to monitor the thieves' progress; anti-bugging devices to confound the electronic eavesdroppers – all these and many more are readily available to cope with specific security problems. The drawback is, however, that apart from the cost, they nearly all impose constraints and discipline on the law-abiding users of the building. It is important, therefore, to strike a balance between security risk and acceptable constraints. The office manager should assess the risks, and make his recommendations so that management can decide the appropriate level of security precautions necessary.

No avoidable risks should be countenanced, however, when it comes to fire precautions. These really fall under two headings – minimising the risk of fire breaking out and spreading, and the provision of safe means of escape from the building in the event of fire. In both instances close liaison with the local fire officer and strict compliance with his recommendations, however irksome, are essential. In renovating older premises these may well include having to shorten escape distances by the provision of protected corridors, or even the construction of an additional fire escape.

Whilst under the provisions of the Health and Safety at Work Act the employer has a legal obligation to ensure as far as is reasonably practical, the health, safety and welfare of all his employees, the office manager must relate the spirit of the law to the services for which he is responsible. For example, there are a number of very real hazards which can be created by the mis-use, or irregular maintenance of electrical services. Frayed or trailing cables, the use of multi-socket adaptors, damage to electric cabling caused by inadequate protection at outlets and changes to electrical heating systems without con-sideration of current loading are all common examples of dangerous practices. Similarly, with the increasing use of furniture systems it is essential that components are put together strictly in accordance with the manufacturer's instructions to avoid, for example, accidental tipping of screens carrying storage units.

BUILDING MAINTENANCE

Chapter 42 deals with the administration of commercial property, but some aspects of building maintenance are worth touching on here in so far as they fall within the ambit of the office services manager.

There are, of course, the routine daily processes of cleaning and disposing of rubbish and waste and there is the contract maintenance of a wide range of items from typewriters to lifts. These, though, can be dealt with satisfactorily, once they have been set up, with only routine supervision and an occasional detailed check on performance. What is all too often overlooked, however, are the opportunities for preventive maintenance and planned replacement procedures.

For example, most office building leases have clauses requiring tenants to redecorate externally and, sometimes, internally on a regular basis. Apart from financial planning, or budgeting for what could be a major item of expenditure, it makes sense to plan ahead for the disruption that internal redecoration can cause. With forethought it can be done progressively, taking advantage of the inevitable changes of layout as they occur and which take place regularly in any dynamic organisation. This is far better than expensive out-of-hours working with attendant security problems, or having to shuffle people around to create working space for decorators.

Also on the preventive maintenance side, it pays to include an annual wet clean of all painted surfaces in the cleaning contracts. Here again, this can be done progressively and should show a considerable saving on the redecoration bill. The same principle applies to toilet installations, floor coverings, kitchen equipment and so on, where the work can be carried out by specialist contractors.

CENTRALISED SERVICES

Even a relatively small organisation will consider at some time or another the centralisation of typing and secretarial services. With the advent of the word processor there is now even wider scope for providing an efficient and comprehensive service. Here is yet another area which demands a proper study of the users' needs before investing in new technology. There is a wealth of information available through specialist magazines and so-called seminars, but most of it is devoted to describing what the equipment will do. Very little is said about how to analyse the need for word processing and how to match that need with an economic system. However, there are now plenty of companies with direct experience of using word-processing systems, from stand-alone machines to complex intercommunicating systems. Most of them are quite happy to pass on the benefit of this experience, not only concerning the equipment, but also their staff reactions to it, and this represents a valuable source of information.

As with all change, the new ideas and methods have to be introduced in a planned way. The operators themselves should be made to feel involved in the process and some care should be taken over the physical environment in which they will be working. The aim should be to make them feel that they are being brought together and provided with expensive computerised equipment, not with the aim of forming a typing factory, but to give them the opportunity to share the workload fairly between them and to help each other out as the need arises. It should be emphasised that there is no need for this centralised service to be restricted to typing only. With the right staff and the right telephone arrangements the group can provide a very efficient central secretarial service, handling messages, appointments, travel arrangements and so on for the whole company. The executive then should not feel deprived at the loss of his personal secretary; in fact he will get an even better service. The typists have their job horizons broadened and their working day is therefore much more varied and interesting.

Other contenders for centralisation are reprographics, stationery and filing as well, of course, as the more common services such as post and messengers, tea and coffee services, etc. In all instances centralisation should be approached with some care and a great deal of planning. It is no good setting up a photocopying service with fast, expensive equipment only to find people wanting to retain their individual machines because they need instant copies and cannot get them. Similarly, an elaborate stationery store which is only open for half an hour every fortnight will soon lead to the creation of individual mini-stores throughout the office.

A final note of warning concerns the continuing need to keep an eye on the future. In this rapidly changing world, all equipment is obsolescent virtually on the day it is installed, but awareness of this fact can help avoid costly errors.

FURTHER READING

Books
Company Administration Handbook, Gower, 5th edition, 1982
Denyer, J. C., *Office Administration,* Macdonald & Evans, Plymouth, 3rd edition, 1978

Journals

Business Equipment Digest
Business Systems and Equipment
Office Equipment News
What to Buy for Business

46 Managing information

R E Wiggins

A growing proportion of the populace is concerned with creating, processing and providing information as the developed world moves from being an industrial to an information society. Certainly the quantity of information available to individuals and organisations continues to increase. In the scientific and technical fields alone published literature has been estimated to double every ten years or so. What is more pertinent, however, is that the rate of increase far exceeds the fundamentally unchanging rate at which the information seeker can properly assimilate knowledge even in his or her area of specialisation. Since quality of information rarely increases with quantity, the problem is further compounded.

The means which should be available to organisations to minimise such problems are therefore central to the task of managing information. Particular emphasis needs to be given to exploiting sources of relevant information. Furthermore, in-house information services need to be developed where external services prove inadequate. In addition appropriate 'new technology' must be utilised, including that arising from the convergence of computing, word processing and telecommunications, and developments such as viewdata and teletext. Suitable organisational structures and staff are required to ensure, for example, that new information services and systems can be properly evaluated and implemented in the light of company requirements and broader national and international issues.

INFORMATION AND THE ORGANISATION

To be useful, information has to be communicated in the right quantity and form, and at the right time to those who have need of it. Communication processes and information flow are therefore important elements to be considered in a detailed investigation of information needs and of the ways and means of satisfying them. They are not, however, central to the present discussion.

Information types

Information can be categorised into data – facts, figures, tabular material – and text both of which may originate within or outside the organisation (see Figure 46.1). Clearly there is a spectrum of information between these extremes comprising both data and text in varying proportions.

	Internal	External	GHM
Data	Marketing Financial Engineering	Official statistics Handbooks Maths tables	
Text	Reports Memos Letters	Journals Laws Books	
Characteristics	Confidential and non-confidential Captive area Under own control	Confidential and non-confidential Amorphous mass Variable quality	

Figure 46.1   Information types (after Vander Noot, 1976)

Activities and information needs

Internal data are generally handled by management information systems (MIS) concerned with, for example, the control and monitoring of the company's production activity. It is worth remembering, however, that an MIS does not necessarily have to be computerised. Those that are designed with mechanisation in mind must be based on sound premises because the failure of an MIS can often be traced back to the use of false assumptions at the design stage.

Although the need to consider total information resource management in an organisation is important, the main emphasis is on external information and internal text with the former category together with processed internal information being particularly important for strategic planning by senior management and executives. Information for planning and change is largely subjective and qualitative. Hence it is less amenable to computerisation than that used for operational control by lower levels of management. This is summarised in Figure 46.2.

Organisational activity	Information system	GHM
Operations	Activity-oriented Mainly internal data Often computer-based	
Control	Information-oriented Mainly internal data Often computer-based	
Planning	Information-oriented Mainly external data/text (often qualitative) Difficult to computerise	
Change	Project-oriented Diverse information needs No standard approach	

Figure 46.2   Information systems for different activities
The level of management seniority increases from top to bottom

INFORMATION – ITS ACQUISITION AND VALUE

The cost of acquisition should ideally always be related to the value of the information sought and acquired.

When searching for information there has at some stage to be a limit to the time, effort and money which the enquirer is prepared to spend. Once this limit is reached, the information is in effect deemed not to exist and, if still required, the knowledge has to be created by undertaking research or market surveys, for example.

Information can play a vital role here. Initiation of research has been shown to rise roughly in proportion to the increase in the level of technical information support received by the projects.

Where the knowledge does exist, but is not discovered, there is the danger of duplicating work already undertaken or of suffering expensive consequences due to ignorance. For example, it was estimated in 1962 that avoidable and unintentional duplication of UK research was associated with 9 per cent of projects, and could be costing the country nearly 2 per cent of its research and development budget, while the collapse of some concrete buildings in the UK in the 1970s was due to the use of high alumina cement, a material banned in France in 1947 for reasons well documented in 1958. All too often it takes such disasters to awaken an organisation's information consciousness. The remedy is to be wise before the event.

SOURCES OF INFORMATION

The information seeker has two basic sources available – other people and recorded knowledge. Direct interpersonal contact is often the quickest and best method of obtaining what is required. It has the advantage that the problem can be discussed and misunderstandings resolved. However, the enquirer who is impressed by the personality, standing or experience of the person consulted, may accept too readily, and without question, the answer provided. Thus it is often wise to check the result using other sources. This practice of confirming, or otherwise, the validity of information is particularly relevant where important and expensive decisions hang on the outcome.

Aside from people, there is the vast variety of recorded knowledge which is at least theoretically available to the information seeker in published literature and internal company reports. This indirect method of transferring information between its originator and user is necessary because it ensures continuity and permanency of knowledge independent of people and time.

The broad range of sources is categorised in Figure 46.3. It incorporates the previously mentioned elemental information types of data and text which may originate from within or outside the organisation. Clearly, not every information source can be unambiguously assigned to a single category. The classification does, nevertheless, provide a structure for a more detailed consideration of particular sources of information for the end-user.

Primary, secondary and tertiary sources

The first instance of recording a piece of information in traditional documentary form – or, as is increasingly happening, in machine-readable form for access via some form of computer terminal or screen – represents the primary source for that information.

The quantity of such material produced, both within and outside the organisation, long ago rendered it impossible for the user to find, let alone read, all information which might be relevant to his query. Hence numerous services have emerged to provide various secondary sources and aids to assist the enquirer. Paramount amongst these for published material has been the abstracting and indexing services, whose origin can be traced back to the nineteenth century in the field of scientific literature. Although science and technology still represent a major proportion of this industry, it has long since broadened its subject coverage to provide summaries of and references to published material in such fields as management, social science, and the press.

As might be imagined, these services are themselves producing more products than can be effectively handled. Technology is helping to ease the problem of access to information by enabling computer-stored data bases containing indexes, abstracts and even the full text of the originals to be searched online via a computer terminal. Nevertheless, such technology takes little heed of quality. Even the emergence of the so-called tertiary services, which aim at producing quality reviews and syntheses in key subject areas, are merely adding to the information overload felt by the end-user.

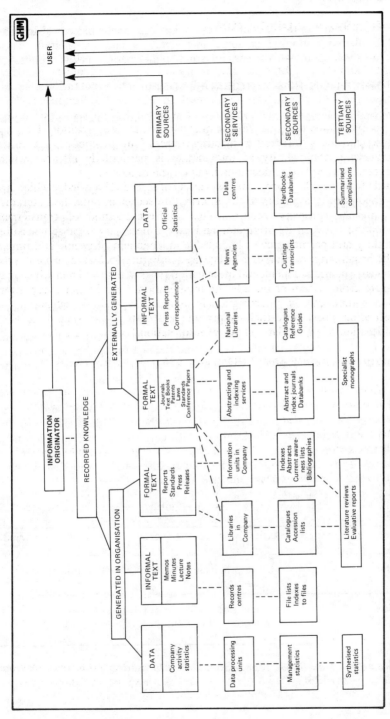

Figure 46.3   Sources of information – a general outline

A major factor in this lack of success is the occasionally piecemeal approach and blinkered outlook that some managements and information service providers assume towards the organisation of information, and its exploitation.

INFORMATION RESOURCE MANAGEMENT

In most companies the categories of information shown in Figure 46.1 are still held in different repositories, each of which is the responsibility of different parts of the organisation (see Figure 46.4). Co-ordination and co-operation between all these various units is often minimal. However, the advent of 'new technology' as exemplified by the microprocessor, and its exploitation in computing, telecommunications and office automation, has brought about a technologically possible convergence of those very parts of the company which often have responsibility for information repositories and services. As this convergence becomes a reality, the incompatabilities, overlap the gaps in information acquisition, processing and provision by libraries, data processing sections, registries and information units, for example, become all too clear. If nothing else, the microchip has made companies look long and hard at their information-handling activities.

The problem can be particularly acute for internally generated information since it is largely irreplaceable, and is rarely as well organised for retrieval as published material. This is largely due to the splits in organisational responsibility for internal information, and the fact that published material is an important, freely available resource exploited by a well-established industry which undertakes analysis, indexing, storage and dissemination for a profit (or at least not a loss).

A further complication is that much company information, and for that matter external information, does not reside in the traditional repositories. It is held by those concerned, for example, with corporate planning, investment, marketing or research and development. If a company does not take steps to organise all its captive information, and to integrate it with that which is generated externally, then no one else will.

	Internal	External	GHM
Data	Data-processing sections	Information units	
Text	Registries Record units	Libraries	

Figure 46.4 Traditional repositories for information (after Vander Noot, 1976)

Definition of an information resource system

The concept of an information resource system (IRS) needs closer definition. Such a definition does, however, depend largely on the type of environment in which the system resides and on the needs to be satisfied. Here the emphasis is on the business environment and the needs of a commercial organisation and its members, particularly management.

The information resource comprises not only internal and external data and text (recorded information), but also the expertise and knowledge of people inside and outside the organisation. The term 'system' is not to be construed simply as a computer-based facility (many effective and efficient information systems are purely manual). Rather it encompasses all the components (for example, people, recorded information, technological aids, users and originators of information) which interact and are concerned in some definable way with the creation, movement, storage, retrieval, manipulation and use of information for the benefit of the organisation and its members.

This approach makes use of systems thinking which is increasingly being used, as an effective means for tackling real-world problems that cannot be categorised into traditional subject discipline areas. In particular, it facilitates identifying the boundaries and components of the system to be examined. All too often, studies are commenced without prior thought as to the influence that changes in one part of an organisation will have on another. The systems approach may therefore be usefully applied to the analysis, design, implementation and operation of an organisation's information 'facilities'.

An information resource system exists to satisfy the needs of its users, and ultimately to further the objectives of the organisation. These objectives should be defined. If, however, they prove difficult to formulate directly, then a roundabout route using answers to such questions as what does the organisation do?, how does it do it? and why?, may suffice.

Determining the needs of users may prove equally difficult, not least because 'needs' are often confused with 'wants'. Furthermore, certain needs may never be articulated since the user often assumes that the system cannot satisfy them. Nevertheless, such needs must be established so that a specification for the IRS can be formulated.

The precise nature and content of the specification will vary from one application area to another. In general, however, an organisation's IRS should be designed to satisfy three requirements:

1 Aid the full range of management activities, from routine to planning and change
2 Match the changing pattern and structure of management at all levels
3 Produce information which meets the manager's needs and his capacity to use it.

The specification provides criteria against which the information resource system design is matched, and indicates the system components to be adopted, modified or disposed of. The need to encompass all types of relevant information in the system is likely to be a fundamental prerequisite. The mix of mechanised and manual activities has to be decided. In the design stage the aim must be to fit the IRS to the organisation and not vice versa. In this respect modern information technology is proving particularly beneficial because it enables increasingly sophisticated equipment to be decentralised and kept under local control, while still allowing any necessary centralised influence to be exercised remotely via communication networks.

Implementing the information resource system

Once the system is agreed, it has to be implemented. For complex systems involving a large number of people and the introduction of mechanisation the implementation phase requires particularly careful planning. As in the design stage, close collaboration between the system designers and users is vital. The critical interface areas between machine and human being must be identified together with the activities to be undertaken by each. Additional, superfluous and amended activities have to be identified and quantified, as do any changed levels of human effort for each discrete area of work relating to the IRS.

Following implementation, the IRS should be evaluated in terms of efficiency and effectiveness. Both these measures need to be applied if management is to be able properly to judge the worth of the venture. The ideal IRS will exhibit both high efficiency and high effectiveness; if there has to be a trade off between the two, it is effectiveness that must be given priority.

Managing the information resource system

The description of an IRS which has just been presented is, of course, generalised and idealised to a large degree. In practice, the IRS is rarely a tangible entity, but comprises a variety of discrete information systems, developed for a wide range of applications, together with other less well-defined and organised information resources. Some of these systems will be designed to satisfy specialised needs in specific departments or units of the organisation (for example, the collection and processing of data from research experiments). Others (such as a personnel records system) will have a more obvious, and direct influence across the whole of the company. The localised systems are likely to be most suitably managed, on a day-to-day basis, by relevant staff in the particular departments and units concerned. The pervasive systems will tend to be the responsibility of more senior management who have a greater company-wide role than their departmental colleagues. Given this scenario the question arises how best to manage the total IRS.

As well as the need to satisfy local requirements for information, and to delegate, as appropriate, day-to-day control of information systems, there is also the increasing need simultaneously to meet corporate-wide demands. These include the desire for ready access from any part of the organisation to information and information manipulating facilities (for example, word processing and data processing), located elsewhere, the aim being to minimise the need to replicate them locally. In addition, executives in corporate head offices wish to see consistent, reliable and timely information reaching them from all their business activities so that they can properly assess present performance, and plan for the future.

The need for a proper balance between these various demands argues for a small, central IRS management unit with emphasis on planning, policy making, co-ordinating, controlling and supervising the overall system. Although it may be involved in sponsoring projects to develop the IRS, it should not generally get involved in the provision or detailed running of specific information services and activities. Its chief responsibilities, in all likelihood, will be to monitor them so as to seek out areas for improvement such as filling information gaps and eliminating unnecessary duplication, and to lay down agreed standards, thereafter ensuring that they are adhered to. 'Standards' is an emotive word, but in this context must not be construed as being a restrictive, but rather a liberating factor. Thus it is sensible for a corporate telecommunication network design to conform to national, and international standards, otherwise remote communication may be difficult if not impossible.

Once the decision is taken to establish a central IRS management unit, a suitable person must be put in charge who will report to the executive level of the company and, if appropriate, be an actual board member. What qualifications, experience and type of person are required for this position? Certainly the previously mentioned convergence of technology in data processing, offices and communications, has been a major catalyst in causing individual managers from both inside and outside these areas to reconsider their roles. Some have felt threatened by such a development, although many have seen it as an opportunity for broadening their field of influence; examples include administrative managers, (computer) systems professionals, records managers and archivists, and librarians. A recent survey of information professionals in the USA showed that over a quarter of a million (17 per cent) were in some way managing information operations. Occupational titles included Comptroller, Database Manager, Director of Information Center, Library Director and Vice-President for Information.

What is important here, of course, is not the title which a person holds, but the experience, expertise and personality that he or she can bring to the job. As was done in the formative stages of establishing the IRS itself, a specification should be drawn up, but this time for the post of IRS manager. This being a novel venture for most organisations, there is as yet little experience on which to draw. Clearly an amalgam of the talents possessed by the managers noted aboe will form a significant element of the job specification, but there are certain dimensions to the task which are unlikely to be adequately covered in this way. A valuable contribution here arose from discussions between the Information Industry Association in the USA, and the US Federal Government concerning an occupational standard for an Information Resources Manager. The proposed standard recognises that the manager must be concerned with both technological aids and the usefulness of the information which they handle, must be the principal adviser to top and middle management on such aspects as plans, budgets, security of information, and the quality of information sources, and must above all be a resource manager. Both general and specialised experience is required, and in the latter instance it is suggested that this should ideally be drawn from at least two out of four clusters of occupations. These broadly comprise, first, library, archival, records and related areas; second, computers, telecommunications and office automation; third, statistics, operations research and finance; and, fourth, technical writing, editing and reprographics.

In the UK, the Institute for Information Scientists has developed and promulgated key criteria for information science which largely embrace these topics and include resource management as a main theme.

Staffing the information resource system

The constituent parts of the IRS, be they data processing units, record centres, libraries or information units, for example, must be adequately staffed in terms of numbers, experience and expertise. Where such staff have direct dealings with their clients, it is essential that they understand and speak 'the language' of their users' subject specialities, at least to a degree where communication and understanding do not impair the relationship. If clients do not have confidence in those there to assist them, the service will not fulfil its mission.

Unfortunately, it still happens that key collections of information or the establishment of a library service for example, are entrusted to staff ill-fitted for the role. They may have been unsuited to their present work and a position – any position – has to be found for them elsewhere, or it may be felt that a shy individual will be best employed in quiet backwaters in charge of the library. Users should not be surprised if they get the service they deserve, rather than that which they desire. Over the years, however, various professional bodies have evolved or been established to help ensure that adequately trained and educated people are available for such areas of activity. The courses include postgraduate qualifications and higher degrees which provide an information-type qualification on top of the first degree already possessed. It is therefore possible, for example, for a chemist to obtain an MSc in information science to prepare him for work as an information scientist in a research centre. Details of these professional bodies are noted at the end of this chapter.

Having given general consideration to the information resource system, attention will be directed to the particular area of information and library services.

INFORMATION AND LIBRARY SERVICES

The particular services offered, their position in the hierarchical structure and the titles they are given will vary from one organisation to another. Such decisions will mainly depend on the objectives set for the services, but should also take account of the support, both financial and moral, likely to be forth-coming from the management streams in which they may reside. It is not necessarily the case that the most appropriate management stream for a service unit will be that occupied by its main users. In order to operate effectively, the information and library service (ILS) needs the full back-up of, and preferably control over, its own administration and office services such as typing, reprographic facilities and filing.

In general, an ILS should encompass a records responsibility and be involved in acquiring, organising and exploiting external text and data (much of it published material), and internal text (records) for the benefit of the company. Internal data, as previously noted, should also be integrated in the IRS.

General ILS activities will be outlined together with an indication of the special requirements of functions such as engineering, research and development, marketing, planning and public relations. Figure 46.3 and the further reading section at the end of the chapter, provides a reference point for the matters described.

Acquisition

Relevant information, in whatever physical form, must be acquired from any suitable source, and will include:

External information:

> books, periodicals and other formally published material
> official publications of governments, etc.
> standards and specifications
> documents and reports which are not published formally and if classified
> will be available on a 'need-to-know' basis
> patents
> trade literature
> news media, papers, the press and transcripts
> audio-visual material

Internal information:

> internal reports
> laboratory notebooks
> standards and specifications
> project files
> meeting minutes
> other records containing non-ephemeral information
> expertise register
> audio-visual material

The ready availability of up-to-date standards, specifications, codes of practice and similar material is especially important for technical staff. Superseded standards should also be retained if, for example, they have been applied in the construction of existing plant.

Certain classified information will be available to a company if it has, say, a supply contract with the government. The ILS should be involved in obtaining and be responsible for safeguarding such material.

Patents are generally a sadly neglected source of knowledge. They often represent the only record outside a company of developments it has made. They are therefore an excellent way to monitor competitors' activities for the benefit of the corporate planning and research functions.

Accumulation of relevant trade literature is essential for technical and purchasing departments, and can be facilitated, although not wholly replaced, by subscription to suitable product literature agencies.

Information should be gathered from the various news media if, say, it is desired to monitor press coverage of one's company, keep an eye on competitors or acquire knowledge of political trends and government legislation to assist the public relations, marketing and planning functions.

Audio-visual material includes slides, films and video-tape, and is as worthy of acquisition as other information. It is an invaluable resource for company staff involved in meetings and exhibitions, for example.

The cost of acquiring all relevant information for retention within one's own company is clearly prohibitive. Exchange arrangements with other information providers can reduce costs, and the ILS should be a party to such agreements. In general, however, the aim should be to have on site just that primary information of high quality which needs to be at hand. Access to other external information is obtained in a more cost-effective and cost-efficient manner by buying-in selected secondary sources – published indexes, abstracting services, etc., by utilising external on-line data bases and by consulting other organisations, individuals and secondary services in response to specific enquiries, and generally as the needs arise.

The ability to select what is relevant relies heavily on the ILS staff maintainingnd regular contact with their users so that current, and future needs are known.

The mode of acquisition of internal information will depend on the type of record involved. Discrete and substantive items such as reports, laboratory notebooks, and in-house standards are probably best copied, or removed from traditional files (leaving a reference as to where they are stored) so that they can be processed as other important material. Correspondence and like records, because of their physical nature, are more difficult to handle in this way, and may be left on file but referenced, or copied, say, on to microfilm. The aim in every instance is to ensure that the existence of substantive internal information is known so that is can be suitably referenced for use at some later date.

A vital information source is an expert. There may be much to gain by maintaining within the ILS a register of staff within one's organisation who, if they agree, could usefully be contacted should an enquiry arise in their fields of expertise.

While information acquisition is a vital activity, so is disposal. There have been various estimates made as to how quickly the published literature becomes obsolete in different disciplines. However, none of these results should be rigorously applied since the information needs of people, both as individuals and groups, differ and change with time. The company and the ILS should nevertheless strive to weed out that which is no longer required to support its activities. Due consideration must be given to retention of irreplaceable material, especially internal information, and to statutory and historical requirements. The latter may most suitably be given professional attention by an archivist. The aim is to ensure a consistent policy throughout the organisation towards the retention, organisation and disposal of information.

Organisation

Once acquired, the substantive information must have its description and location catalogued, and its relevant information content analysed and recorded by classification and indexing.

Descriptive cataloguing provides a record of the discrete pieces of information held, i.e., the available source material. To aid consistency in library applications, for example, the standard cataloguing rules of the Library Association are widely employed to produce the ubiquitous catalogue card giving details of author, title, publisher, etc. The principles should be adopted for any type and form of substantive information.

Information content analysis comprises the use of index terms, keywords, identifiers, etc. which will subsequently facilitate finding the source material via the information it contains. It embraces subject classification and indexing which differ in concept from one another.

Subject classification involves the conceptual, and often physical grouping together of items dealing with the same topic. One has in effect to determine to which subject 'pigeon hole' a piece of information is assigned. Despite the availability of regularly updated, and widely accepted standard classification schemes, such as the Universal Decimal Classification (UDC), the principles are difficult to apply consistently, as anyone will know who has tried to decide on which single file a piece of correspondence dealing a variety of topics, should be placed. The classification codes are typically used to determine the filing order for the information. More than one classification code can be applied to a document to reflect different subject viewpoints. In filing terms this is similar to copying one item on to the several different files with which it is concerned.

Internal records, such as correspondence files, pose special problems because of the sheer quantity often involved and the variability in their quality and worthiness for long-term retention. If possible files should be conceptually organised to fit in with the way the users of the files work. Thus project, case and company name files are likely to satisfy the needs of those concerned with research work, litigation and suppliers respectively. If simplicity and comprehensibility are attained in this way, staff are more likely to rely on and use the filing system. Although standard classification schemes (as noted earlier) may be applied in certain circumstances to provide file titles, and hence subject 'pigeon holes' for records, it is more likely that if a subject classification is required, it will need to be tailor made.

Subject classifications, then, direct one to the part of a collection most likely to include the information that is relevant to an enquiry.

Indexes, however, will indicate specific and likely relevant items of information within that collection. Indexes exist in many forms, and may be produced manually, or with the aid of computers, or by a combination of the two. They appear in books, in card indexes and provide conceptual access to computer-stored information. More will be said of computer applications later, particularly for large quantities of information.

It is not amiss, however, to consider first smaller, personal collections of information since it is often these that will grow and merge with one another to form the larger ones. For small information collections, card indexes may prove suitable when memory alone can no longer be relied upon. The edge-punched card is an example of an 'item entry' system in which a card exists for each item indexed, and contains the bibliographic reference together with all the index terms used and possibly a summary of the item. The peripheral holes are each assigned a specific index term and are punched out according to the terms applied for a particular item. The collection is searched by inserting needles through the holes representing the selected index terms. Relevant cards will fall out as the needles lift the cards (Figure 46.5).

The 'term entry' system is an alternative and its capacity for index terms is not so rigidly limited. Here each card represents an index term, and on each card reference is made to all the documents to which that term has been assigned in indexing. The reference is usually a document accession number. This can be written on a card in a column headed by the number which terminates the accession number (Figure 46.6), or in another system is indicated by the position of a hole punched in the body of the card (Figure 46.7). The terminal digit card system is searched by seeking a common number

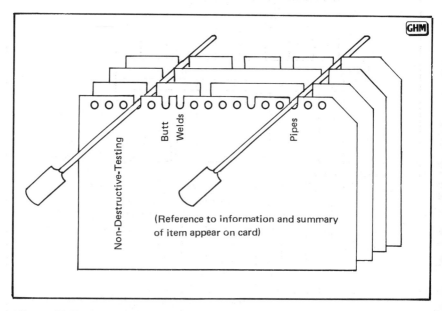

Figure 46.5   Item entry edge-punched card
Three cards relate to non-destructive-testing of pipes

on the selected terms cards, while the body punched cards are scanned by superimposing selected cards over a light source.

The concept of the 'term entry' system lies behind the way information is indexed and retrieved in most computer-based information retrieval systems as described later.

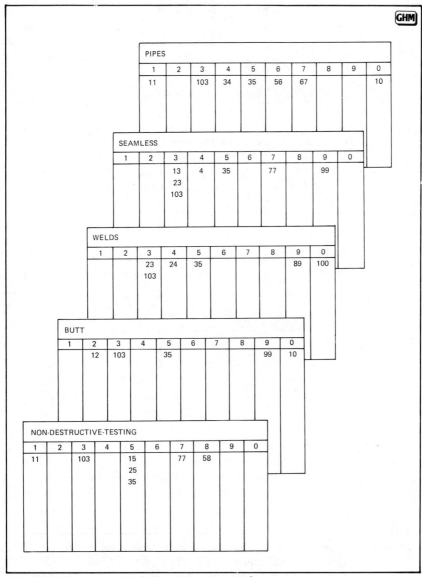

PIPES

1	2	3	4	5	6	7	8	9	0
11		103	34	35	56	67			10

SEAMLESS

1	2	3	4	5	6	7	8	9	0
		13	4	35		77		99	
		23							
		103							

WELDS

1	2	3	4	5	6	7	8	9	0
		23	24	35				89	100
		103							

BUTT

1	2	3	4	5	6	7	8	9	0
	12	103		35				99	10

NON-DESTRUCTIVE-TESTING

1	2	3	4	5	6	7	8	9	0
11		103		15		77	58		
				25					
				35					

Figure 46.6 Terminal digit term entry cards
Document numbers 35 and 103 relate to all terms shown

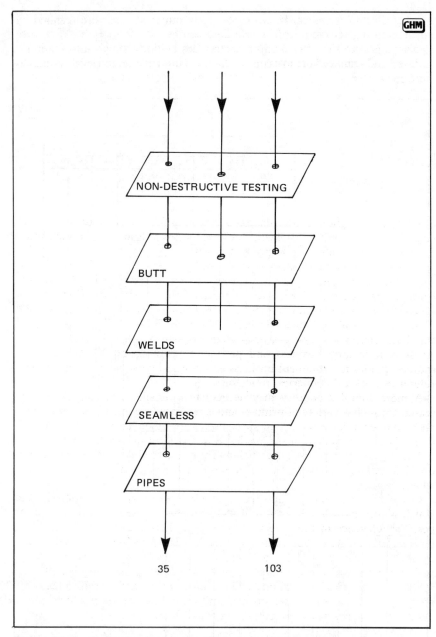

Figure 46.7 Optical coincidence (Peek-a-boo) term entry cards
Documents 35 and 103 relate to all terms shown

In choosing index terms, they may be 'natural language' terms selected, for example, from the original text, or those taken from a controlled vocabulary, or a combination of the two. The vocabulary, or so-called thesaurus, provides control, for example, over synonyms, code lists, semantic ambiguity (homographs and homonyms) and generic relationships (broader and more specific terms). As with subject classification schemes, it may be necessary to devise one's own thesaurus if the available published versions prove unacceptable. The intellectual effort and time required to create and maintain an extensive controlled vocabulary are considerable and are often underestimated. The process of information storage and retrieval as a whole should clearly be seen to benefit from such an approach before it is undertaken.

Utilisation

The ILS must exploit its information resources and know-how not only by just responding to enquiries received, but also by promulgating its services and disseminating its information products.

Enquiry answering includes dealing with requests for specific documents which may be supplied by purchase, lending from existing stock or borrowing from outside sources. The UK has a particularly well-developed public and special library network for tracing and inter-library lending of publications.

Specific information may be sought which can be answered quickly using standard reference works, a basic collection of which every ILS should have. These will include business and product directories, guides to statistical sources, guides to prominent business and political personalities, and general reference works, dictionaries, timetables, etc.

A more complex enquiry may necessitate a detailed and comprehensive search through a variety of primary and secondary sources. If such enquiries take time, or involve the use of specialised knowledge, an indexed record of them should be made to avoid having to repeat the work later.

For all enquiries, the real need behind the question should be ascertained by the ILS staff and expressed by the enquirer, since what is asked for may not be what is wanted.

Current awareness is an important dynamic aspect of an information service which will bring to the attention of its clients newly received information of possible relevance to their work. At one level there are the general blanket services such as library lists of newly accessioned material. Periodicals received by the ILS may be selected and seen on circulation by company staff. A variation is to distribute on request copies of the contents pages in place of or as well as the periodical circulation. It does, however, have the disadvantage for recipients that contents pages do not notify them of specific product information, or advertisements appearing in the publication.

A more selective service involves qualified ILS staff scanning through journals, conference proceedings, etc, to select items of relevance to the company for notification via a regularly issued bulletin. If the recipients do not have ready access to the original items, then the ILS staff may prepare abstracts of them which are included in the bulletin. If these summaries are made sufficiently informative, a reader may not need to see the original. However, the preparation of such abstracts, particularly in specialist subject fields, requires the time of skilled and experienced abstractors and is therefore expensive. An acceptable alternative may be to use abstracts which appear with the original; for example, author-prepared summaries.

Selective dissemination of information (SDI) is a personalised service which can effect still further savings in the time a recipient has to spend in scanning publications. It involves an individual, or possibly a small team working in the same field, expressing their particular interests in sufficient detail for the ILS staff to prepare an SDI profile containing the key search elements. These may be the name of a competitor, subject expert or journal coupled with subject key-words or phrases. An SDI service can be run manually by the ILS staff monitoring incoming information and comparing its content with the profiles. Notifications by phone, letter or photocopy, for example, will alert clients to the selected information. A manual service can only cater for a limited number of users, hence SDI only truly becomes a ubiquitous reality when the capacity of speed of a computer are harnessed to undertake the matching process.

Information product development goes beyond the regularly operating current awareness and SDI services. For an ILS to be truly effective it must be capable of anticipating, and not just reacting to new requirements. This will involve the production of specific and specialised products such as biblio-graphies, critical literature reviews and evaluative reports covering, for example, emerging fields of interest for corporate diversification, and competitors' activities in certain product and geographical areas. The ILS with its expertise in information storage and retrieval, and involvement with specialist users, is a likely centre for identifying and developing computerised data bases containing, say, items from its current awareness publications or the plant throughput statistics of competitors.

Examples of other areas where an information enhancement role can be exercised are:

  patents and licensing by monitoring and assessment
  press and public relations by issuing and assessing reactions to press
    releases
  standards and specifications monitoring and updating service for the
    company
  translation preparation and commissioning
  reporting procedure creation and administration
  board level services highly tuned to requirements
  extension of selected services outside the company to associated
    companies and the public.

Publicity and public relations

Publicising and marketing an ILS are just as important activites as the initial acquisition of information. All suitable means should be adopted including displays, talks by ILS staff, films and use of house journals. The ILS must be in regular contact with its existing and potential users to obtain feedback on its performance and to determine changing needs. In addition top management and line management must be kept aware of significant and regular information activities, and their support fostered in preparation for any development proposals.

TECHNOLOGICAL AIDS

Undoubtedly developments in computing, office automation and communications have greatly facilitated the storage, processing, retrieval and transmission of information. These developments have gained extensive publicity, and in some cases notoriety (viz. the microchip) and there is a danger that many are being oversold as the ultimate solution to the 'information problem'. In the end, information is created and used by people. Many of the problems inherent in the information-handling process are human ones which are not solvable technically as they relate to such factors as misinterpretation, ignorance, deficiency, overabundance, misdirection and incomprehensibility of information. So long as the human element is not forgotten, technology has much to offer.

Information retrieval

An information retrieval system is centred around a combination of hardware (the computer and associated equipment) and software (programs). The latter undertake and control the input, processing and retrieval of the stored full text or (more usually) indexed references to it. Depending on the software employed, the system will assist with the indexing by automatically selecting terms from the stored text, or from a stored controlled vocabulary (the thesaurus) or a combination of the two. During searching, the terms chosen to represent the query are entered via a terminal and matched by the computer against the stored index terms. One can typically search for number ranges (useful for dates), the beginning, end or central stem of a word (for example, all words beginning with 'plan'), combinations of words and alternative terms while at the same time exercising control over synonyms (for example, when searching for 'United Kingdom', the system can be designed to retrieve information indexed by 'UK'). In fact the presence or absence of any set of characters, including spaces, can be searched for given the appropriate software and design of data base (the machine-stored collection of information). The system displays intermediate results and the searcher can amend his strategy interactively until he is satisfied, at which time the final results are displayed or printed out. In addition to searching the data base in response to specific enquiries, the system is admirably suited to providing an SDI service as noted earlier. The interest profiles of users are stored in the computer which compares them with newly entered information. When a sufficiently close match is achieved, the client receives a suitable notification.

A variety of such software is available commercially for use within one's own company and details are maintained by Aslib (see the list of organisations given at the end of this chapter).

Increasingly the cheaper microcomputer end of the hardware market, in conjunction with developed software, is proving capable of satisfying basic demands for information handling and retrieval. In addition, developments in word processing are facilitating the creation and input of information into retrieval systems and are themselves offering increasingly improved retrieval facilities rivalling established products.

Electronic publishing and document delivery

The origins of electronic publishing lie in the publically available computer-stored bibliographic files (data bases) developed from the publishing activities of the major abstracting and indexing services in the USA. The number of such files available to Europe grew from 335 in 1975 to 654 in 1980 and contain around 150 million records (mainly references to published literature) over 80 per cent of which are accessible interactively and remotely from a suitable terminal. The number of data banks covering facts and figures has increased even more remarkably from 51 to 755 over the same period.

For bibliographic files, one generally only incurs a charge when the file is being accessed. A typical cost for access from Europe to one of the popular technical files held in the USA, is about £1 per minute, inclusive of telecommunication charges. An average search by a skilled user will take say fifteen minutes and therefore costs £15. For other services an annual charge may be made irrespective of usage.

Once relevant references are found from such a service, the documents must be acquired. Delays here can be considerable and much thought and effort is being put into electronic document delivery systems based, for example, on advanced facsimile equipment or the scanning and digitising of full text.

Many electronic publishing ventures are still based on paper products. Increasingly, though, publishers are moving some of their products wholly to electronic form or developing new ones well suited to electronic distribution. Public and syndicated electronic services linked by telecommunication or telephone networks to personal microcomputers which act as intelligent terminals are already in use.

The Prestel viewdata-type service of British Telecom and the Ceefax and Oracle teletext-type services of the two UK broadcasting authorities are examples of UK-developed electronic publishing services. Both use a modified television receiver. Prestel allows two-way communication when accessing several thousands of frames of business and leisure information placed on computers by a variety of information providers. Viewdata does not provide the highly interactive and sophisticated information retrieval facilities mentioned earlier since it is aimed more at the general and casual user. Furthermore the information is not so much indexed as classified, and the user is guided along a tree-like conceptual structure to the desired information. Unlike Prestel, the teletext services are free to use but only allow one-way communication to a more limited, but more rapidly updated, set of information frames. On

Prestel-type services, one can acquire private closed user groups with access to it open only to those nominated by the PCUG owner. The more recently developed 'gateway' facility allows a commercially acquired viewdata system, for example, to be linked to a company's computer for simple distribution of and easy access to information held on the computer. In this way viewdata technology can become an integral part of the company's computing and information services network.

Prestel technology has been marketed abroad and rival systems have since appeared overseas.

Storage

Apart from the use of electronic storage systems, information may be held on microfilm which continues to offer a highly competitive alternative to hardcopy particularly with the use of computer output microfilming (COM) techniques. Various systems exist and are being developed to mechanise the storage and retrieval of microforms, but many are limited in their capacity and require the user to have access to reading equipment and sets of the microforms which need updating. Video scanning and digitising of microform images and hard copy, for example offers the opportunity for remote access, transmission and updating of the information.

For many applications, storage systems must be able to combine text, graphics and photographic images if they are to have a major impact on the information handling activities of organisations. Video disc technology is one area of great potential and commercial applications are already being promulgated.

Putting it all together

Efficient and effective information storage and retrieval is not enough in itself. To be fully effective the system must be capable of producing a wide range of outputs such as printed products, either directly or by interfacing with other

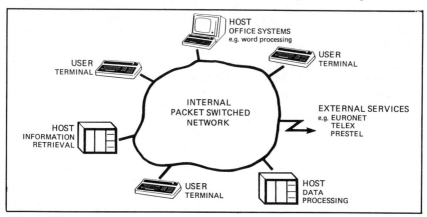

Figure 46.8   Integrated service network

systems. Word processing of the input, and computer typesetting, computer output microfilming and formatting of the output are examples of what are required to eliminate labour-intensive clerical operations and unnecessary multiple keyboarding of the same information. The system should be fully integratable with office systems, data processing and external services (Figure 46.8 on page 835). It will take some time to achieve this. Meanwhile systems introduced for specific applications should be designed as building blocks with this aim in mind.

FURTHER READING

This select list is arranged under the main headings used in the chapter itself. Titles of some journals which will enable readers to keep abreast of topics covered by this chapter are noted at the end of this list.

Information and the organisation

Allen, T.J., and Cohen, S. I., *Information Flow in Research and Development Laboratories*, Administrative Science Quarterly, vol. 14, 1969, pp. 12-20. A study of information flow including the role of technological gatekeepers as key figures in the transfer process.

Wood, C. C., *International Barriers to Information Flows*, Business Intelligence Program, SRI International, Croydon, England, March 1981. Considers transborder data flows (TBDF), the attempts to harmonise TBDF laws and the influence of these on company communications.

Information - its acquisition and value

Aguilar, F. J., *Scanning the Business Environment*, Macmillan Co., New York, 1967. A classic investigation of how top management, particularly in large chemical companies, gain relevant information about opportunities and threats. The kind of information required and methods of improving the scanning of the environment for information are covered.

Lamberton, D. M. (ed.), *Economics of Information and Knowledge*, Selected Readings, Penguin Books, Harmondsworth, 1971. A collection of eighteen previously published papers covering surveys, economic organisation, information and efficiency, information policy, international aspects and business planning.

Sources of information

It is, of course, impossible to provide a comprehensive list of sources. Those listed are only examples, and enquirers should consult their company library or information unit, or an appropriate external information source covering their field of interest. Membership of such organisations as Aslib and the British Institute of Management are well worth considering (see list of organisations at end of chapter).

Dare, G. A., and Bakewell, K. G. B., *The Manager's Guide to Getting the Answers*, Library Association, London, 1980. A basic information survival kit produced jointly by the British Institute of Management and the Library Association.

Hall, J. L., *On-line Bibliographic Data Bases*, 1979 Director, Aslib, London, 1979. A guide to computer-stored information which relates to published material and is available via a suitable computer terminal.

UNIDO Guides to Information Sources, Industrial Development Organisation, United Nations. A series of guides, primarily aimed at developing countries, which covers both published sources and organisations and can provide a useful starting point in an information search. A complete list appeared in *UNIDO Newsletter*, no. 140, Dec. 1979.

Walford, A. J., *Walford's Concise Guide to Reference Material*, Library Association, London, 1981. Over 2 500 published reference works are noted which together cover most subject fields.

Information resource management

Arnold, D. V., *The Management of the Information Department*, Institute of Information Scientists Monograph, André Deutsch, London, 1976. Aimed primarily at those concerned with the management of small or large industrial information departments, and covers communication, management, planning and design, organisation, co-ordination, control and analysis.

Anthony, L. J., 'A National Information Policy for the United Kingdom', *Aslib Proceedings*, March 1981, pp. 73–82. Recent developments and possible future policy are described and discussed.

Atherton, P., *Handbook for Information Systems and Services*, United Nations Educational, Scientific and Cultural Organisation (UNESCO), Paris, 1977. Although aimed at the emerging managers and students of information systems and services in developing countries, it provides an excellent introduction to the topic, and covers policies and plans at the national and international levels, management aspects, organisation, national and international networks, procedures and methods, standardisation, facilities and equipment, education, training, professional associations and directories.

King, D. (ed.), *Key Papers in the Design and Evaluation of Information Systems*, Knowledge Industry Publications, White Plains, N.Y., 1978. A collection of twenty-six previously published papers covering evaluation methods, evaluation applications and system design.

Smith, D., *Systems Thinking in Library and Information Management*, Clive Bingley, London, 1980. Describes and discusses the relevance and value of the systems approach to information work. Numerous references are cited to allow the interested reader to delve further.

Townley, H. M., *Systems Analysis for Information Retrieval*, Institute of Information Scientists Monograph, André Deutsch, London, 1978. Covers the application of traditional systems analysis including preliminary ideas, the initial system study, storage, search strategies, conversion to the final design and implementation.

Vajda, E., *UNISIST Guide to Standards for Information Handling*, Pt 2, United Nations Educational, Scientific and Cultural Organisation (UNESCO), Paris, 1980. An invaluable guide for all kinds of users and producers of information. It covers the intellectual preparation of documents and subject analysis, production of documents, reproduction of documents, representation of information, editing of documents, preparation of bibliographic records, interchange of machine-readable bibliographic data, management of document collections and numeric data.

Information and library services

British Standards Society, *The Operation of a Company Standards Department*, British Standards Institution, London, 1979. Provides useful guidance on the setting-up and running of a company standards department, and indicates how it may be integrated with, or make use of expertise in, other company information handling operations, for example the library.

Rowley, J. E., and Turner, C. M. D., *The Dissemination of Information*, André Deutsch, London, 1978. Although intended for library and information science students, it provides a comprehensive, well-referenced source-book for those interested and concerned with the dynamic service aspects of information and library services.

Technological aids

Advisory Council for Applied Research and Development (ACARD), *Information Technology*, HMSO, London, 1980. A report of a working group established to consider the impact of information technology in the United Kingdom, and to make recommendations arising therefrom.

British Computer Society, *A glossary of Computing Terms for Introductory Courses*, British Computer Society, 1979. A reliable concise guide.

Cook, M., *Archives and the Computer*, Butterworths, London, 1980. Describes computer systems and their application to records management and archives.

Crawford, S. (ed.), 'Perspectives on Computer and Communications Technology', *Journal of the American Society for Information Science*, March 1981. Five state-of-the-art reviews covering computer technology, transmission of information, information storage and display, technology and communication in the future, and online systems in the communication process.

Rowley, J. E., *Mechanised in-house Information Systems*, Clive Bingley, London, 1979. A description of various systems, including information retrieval systems, and case studies.

Woolfe, R., *Videotex*, Heyden, London, 1980. A description of the various videotex systems (viewdata, teletext, etc.) and their potential for business.

Selected periodical titles

Annual Review of Information Science and Technology, Knowledge Industry Publications Inc.
Aslib Proceedings, Aslib.
Electronic Publishing Review, Learned Information.
IDP Report (Information and Data Base Publishing Report), Knowledge Industry Publications Inc.
Information and Management (the International Journal of Information Systems Applications), North Holland Publishing Co.
Journal of Documentation, Aslib.
Journal of Information Science, Institute of Information Scientists, North Holland Publishing Co.
Journal of Systems Management, Association of Systems Management, Cleveland, USA.
Journal of the American Society for Information Science, John Wiley & Sons.
Online Review, Learned Information.

Selected organisations

ASLIB, 3 Belgrave Square, London SW1 8PL.
Promotes the establishment and development of special libraries and information services by means of research, publications, training, conferences, advisory and other services.

British Computer Society, 13 Mansfield St, London, W1.
The major professional and representative body of the computer profession.

British Institute of Management, Management House, Parker Street, London WC2B 5PT.
A professional institute and representational body to provide practical assistance and advice.

Business Archives Council, 37–45 Tooley St, London SE1 2PS.
Provides advice and promotion relating to business records of historical interest.

Institute of Information Scientists, Harvest House, 62 London Road, Reading RG1 5AS.
Professional body for promoting high standards in special information work and for establishing qualifications in this field.

Library Association, 7 Ridgmount St, London WC1E 7AE.
Professional body concerned with librarianship, libraries and education for the profession.

47 Managing the electronic office

Ted Bennett and Garfield Collins

Until recent times, each aspect of office equipment development could be seen as a separate, clear-cut path of progress. Thus the typewriter was the forerunner of the word processor, early mechanical calculators gave way to powerful electronic computers, plugboard telephone exchanges were the start of a communications industry which now produces fully electronic exchanges, and the handling of stored information has progressed from large paper filing systems, through microfilm techniques to data stored in digital form on videodisc. Although their origins were completely separate, each avenue of development has ended with one common feature. In every case, the handling of information is entrusted to electronic circuits using microchip circuitry, with the information coded in digital form. With this convergence has come the possibility of automatic intercommunication between office machines – and between remote offices – which were until recently regarded as separate entities.

This chapter summarises the more important recent technological developments, and discusses their role in the electronically integrated 'office of the future'.

WORD PROCESSING

The preparation of documents by word processor is, in essence, an extension of the traditional secretarial tasks of typing/retyping documents of all kinds to produce a finished product. The basic method of performing those operations is by using text composing/editing/amending software resident in a digital computer with an associated keyboard, printer and display screen. The document is entered via the keyboard, as in a normal typing operation, with the text appearing on the screen as it is typed. The format of each document may be pre-defined, leaving the operator to type as fast as he/she feels comfortable, without having to worry about tabulations or other format rules. If any errors in spelling, punctuation, etc., are seen on the screen, they can be corrected easily.

The document may be amended, edited and even rearranged by moving sections of text from one part of the document to another. The final version is printed only when it is perfect.

Word processing equipment ranges from the personal microcomputer with a television screen and simple matrix printer, through a single screen/keyboard word processor with single-element printer, to a multi-station word processing installation using a comparatively large central computer, high volumes of disk storage and several printers. It is also possible to provide word processing facilities using a large mainframe computer offering time-sharing services and specialised software to support text manipulation; in this case it is not likely that letter quality printing will be widely available unless special arrangements are made. From being a simple replacement for the electric typewriter, word processors have developed so that they now offer, amongst others, the following facilities:

> List processing, to produce, for instance, mailing lists
> Sorting of information
> Statistical/mathematical software packages
> Text communication with other word processors or equipment
> Spelling software, in various languages

Use of all the available options associated with up-to-date word processing equipment, far from deskilling the secretary's job, has produced a new job classification of word processing operator – exponents of which trade can demand, in general, higher salaries than traditional typists.

Printing facilities can be chosen to suit the exact requirements. For drafts and other documents where high print quality is not essential, a high-speed matrix printer can be used to give a legible, but inelegant typeface. For letter quality printing the options are multipass matrix printers, single element devices (golfball or daisywheel), or inkjoy or laser technology printing. These last two types use very expensive technology, and they are more likely to find use as a shared unit serving several work-stations.

The development of word processing has been rapid, and will continue. The software offered by the various suppliers will become more sophisticated including graphics and more advanced communications facilities as well as varied application programs. Eventually, as the cost of microcomputer technology decreases, the word processor of the future will perform many or all of the functions of the existing small business systems.

COMMUNICATIONS

Telephones

The most obvious basis for developing inter-office communications is the public telephone network. This is because the telephone system is already in place, serves all locations and handles large volumes of traffic. It is not necessarily the best communications medium for every office, but it should not be discarded out of hand. Of the two basic systems, analogue and digital, analogue transmission is only suitable for voice and alarm signal traffic. Thus all further discussion here refers to digital equipment.

Modern private automatic branch exchanges (PABX), controlled by a digital computer, offer a wide range of communication aids both within and between office buildings. It is possible, for example, to 'camp on' a call to an engaged number: this means that the caller can arrange for both handsets to ring when the line becomes free. Calls can be redirected automatically to follow a person around a building, simply by setting up redirection instructions from the base extension. Simultaneous connection of several extensions to give 'conference' facilities is another useful feature. The exchange can be programmed to dial external numbers which are frequently called by a shortened number – the so-called 'short code' facility. Because the exchange is controlled by a software program, changing extension numbers becomes a job which can be done by the subscriber. When office removals take place, there is no longer any need to worry about the appearance or non-appearance of engineers: a simple re-programming job allows all staff to retain their existing extension numbers.

For cost-conscious managers, call logging equipment can be attached to the PABX, providing a record of numbers dialled from each extension and the call durations – a good way of detecting abuse of the system. The level of service from every extension can be predetermined, so that at the lowest level no access to the outside servie is possible at all, at the intermediate level local public exchange calls can be made, and at the highest level of service complete access to the STD (subscriber trunk dialling) and IDD (international direct dialling) is allowed.

Further applications of digital automatic telephone exchanges will be examined later in this chapter.

Telex and facsimile

Another area of improvement is in the trasnmission of telex and facsimile documents. Telex is, of course, a very well-established method of sending information but it is also relative cumbersome and fraught with difficulty when time zone changes are involved. Telex switch equipment, using VDU consoles to prepare the message, electronic media to store the text, and digital computer techniques to control the transmission of the text, relieves many of the problems associated with the traditional telex methods. The introduction of teletex transmission standards and systems will also ease the successful trans-mission of messages across the world. Facsimile transmission of documents has its place in the office world, especially where a combination of speed and the need for an 'original' document is necessary. The development and widespread implementation of facilities to store the document images electronically and transmit them at the appropriate time will, as with the telex, improve the acceptability and use of facsimile devices, as will increases in transmission speed.

Text transmission between word processors

Combining the use of word processors and modern telephone techniques opens up another area of aid to the harassed office worker. This is the transmission of documents produced on one word processor, via the telephone system, to another word processor which could in theory be across the world although it is more likely to be a matter of metres away. This is the famed 'electronic mail' system although the term is misleading, implying as it does that every person has access to a word processing screen. This technique has great utility where it is feasible. This does mean that it is *only* possible to communicate with a compatible device; casual interchange of text will not be possible until all manufacturers comply with a single standard or set of standards for text interchange (or until the advent of a truly omni-function adaptor for word processor communications).

All-purpose communication system

The developing market in digital technology based telephone exchanges offers a potential for using these exchanges as message-switching devices for controlling a classical 'star' network for computer-type applications, allowing access to any 'extension' on the network, whether it be a telephone or a more sophisticated device. Such exchanges offer all the usual services associated with advanced telephone equipment as well as, for example, an electronic mail or 'message store and forward' service; they may also be used to provide links into the telex/teletex system.

When the exchange is used as a message-switching device, the particular mode of communication used is not material, the circuit being left open until one of the parties 'hangs up'. Other forms of local network rely on various methods of providing broadcast facilities for the propagation of messages. These may be electrical, radio link, or optical-fibre cables. Most current local area networks use transmission of addressed packets of data as their basic method. All rely on the recipient(s) recognising data which is addressed to them and processing it accordingly. There are several variants of such systems in use, all essentially incapable of communicating with each other.

With the evolution of international standards for information exchange it should become possible to communicate with any site anywhere either because the different suppliers will adopt the standard, or because there will be a series of adaptors available to interface with the standard protocols. Whichever option is chosen by a supplier, it is always wise to determine this method of complying with the standards, as there would be great loss of flexibility if there were no such compliance.

Choice of supplier will also be determined by technical factors such as line capacity which will be discussed later in the section relating to how to implement office automation projects.

DOCUMENT STORAGE AND DATA RETRIEVAL

The basic storage medium for word processing equipment is the 'floppy disk', a device allowing up to 2 million or so characters per exchangeable disk. This is not inconsiderable volume of storage when the sole requirement is the preparation and storage for reprinting of documents, some of which may be quite lengthy. The separate ('stand alone') word processor is not suitable for information retrieval, quite naturally, as this function is not normally part of the design considerations for this type of equipment.

The main requirements for storage and sensible retrieval of information are a screen/keyboard to access and display the information and a large volume of disk or other storage media together with powerful information retrieval software. The specific equipment requirements for text storage and retrieval will depend upon the environment and use to which the system is to be put and this will be discussed in detail in the section relating to project execution. Below we shall discuss in general terms what might be used for the purpose.

The major element is fixed disk storage, either in the form of the small, high-density 'Winchester' disk or the large, high-volume disks as are normally attached to mainframe/mini computers. The maximum storage volume available with these devices will depend, in real terms, upon the number of disk controllers with which the processor used can cope without any gross degradation of service. It will thus be obvious that the larger the processor used, in general, the higher the volume of disk storage which may be made available.

The software required to make effective use of the disk storage will increase in sophistication with the increase in storage volume. Access to text will, in the simplest cases, be via document name or reference. As the software becomes more complex, access will be via keywords with or without Boolean operations – this means that keywords may be specified in combination. The most sophisticated software offers 'full text' retrieval, or access on any field in any document stored, this may also include Boolean algebra facilities. At this most useful, and most complex software level, the processor used is either a large minicomputer or a dedicated computer which is often referred to as a 'database machine'. This latter device is used solely to maintain the disk files and to provide rapid access to the database.

Storage of text need not be restricted to disks. In some cases, especially for archive purposes, it is perfectly reasonable to store documents on magnetic tapes; access is slower but this need not be a problem. Other techniques for archiving may include storage on microfilm or videotape with microprocessor-controlled access via electronic cameras to give display on normal video screens.

For comparatively low-volume storage requirements, sophisticated electronic devices such as 'bubble memory' and holographic storage may be used. These give very rapid access to data, but are expensive in comparison to disks and are not really suitable, as yet, for large volume text storage and manipulation uses.

The main requirements of any document storage and retrieval system, of whatever level of complexity and sophistication are:

1 Physical reliability, especially for floppy disks, some of which are mechanically suspect
2 Consistent and reliable software operation; this need not be a function of the size of the supplier, but does tend to relate to the number of units sold.
3 Predictable response; it should be possible to know, within reason, how long it will take to retrieve a document when using a specific retrieval method
4 Coherent support for maintenance and recovery from failure. Some suppliers provide systems built from parts produced by several different manufacturers and provide their own software. This can lead to problems
5 'Suitable' software products. If it is predicted that a fairly sophisticated method of retrieval is to be used at some time, it must be possible to achieve this without major re-equipping to do it.

In general terms, the future requirement, up to say three to five years as a minimum, for storage and retrieval should be the guideline for selection of the hardware and software for the system. It may be that in the early stages of system use the system is over-sophisticated; this is preferable to major disruption when it becomes obvious that the initial system is inadequate.

A LOOK AHEAD

There are a number of developments of which a great deal is heard but of which little, so far, has been seen.

Voice response systems

Computer systems which recognise and respond to the spoken word, either with vocalised output or a more normal computer response, have been in existence for some time. As yet, the main applications of this technique have been for 'command' systems in process control and aircraft control. Here the system responds to spoken commands to initiate specific actions. The general purpose computer system which will pause and respond to normally spoken sentences in a natural language is still some way off. As and when such systems come, fully developed, to the market, a new era in office systems will begin, offering the elimination of current conventional input techniques for the small price of clear diction.

Video-disc storage

Video-disc storage devices are available now, in a prerecorded form, for reading via video screens in the same manner as the already accepted video cassettes. For office system use, a reliable and cheap method of recording the information on the discs is required. When this device is made available to the general user, the storage of massive amounts of information in small, cheap, replicable plastic discs will be possible. The availability of video discs will not alter the requirement for transient data storage devices such as magnetic disks, because the video-discs are not re-usable. Any information added to such a disc is permanent and, although it can be rendered unreadable, it cannot be erased and re-used in the same way as magnetic media.

Voice storage systems

With the advent of digital technology telephone systems has come the possibility of using digital computer techniques to store bit pattern representations of telephone messages for processing, or for onward transmission to another telephone handset. This is true message store and forward technique, giving great flexibility to a digital telephone system and allowing better communications within the office. The reproduction of such a stored message might be rather depersonalised, indeed it may not even be possible to recognise the sender of the message, but the message will be received.

Fibre optics technology

This technology is being developed rapidly and will give greatly enhanced transmission speeds to data transmission networks. This will be especially useful for local area networks in the office environment. The interface devices for fibre optics are more complex than for electronic technology, involving frequency division multiplexing techniques which are much more costly to develop and implement than the time division multiplexing techniques which are in common use.

IMPLEMENTING THE CHANGES

The introduction of any office automation, from a single word processor to a fully integrated system, can be a source of problems within an organisation. These problems will include:

1 Provision of space for the equipment, together with a suitable environment
2 Recruiting, training and establishing salary scales for staff to operate the equipment
3 Organising equipment systems, sometimes leading to quite radical changes in the office
4 Planning for the expansion of services as the equipment gains acceptance.

These and other problems will now be discussed in the context of carrying out a project to install office automation equipment of a non-specific type. The methods presented are applicable to any kind of office automation project, and to any type of equipment. Before actually starting, however, project planning is essential. Each stage of the project has to be identified and defined in terms of work to be done and the output expected in the shape of reports, plans, statistics and so forth. If possible, an estimate of the effort required for each stage should be attempted, in order to plan realistically. The separate stages will now be described.

Definition of project objectives

Objectives might include:

1 *Improvement of secretarial services:* faster document preparation, better quality of product, more efficient use of secretaries' time, increased throughput with the same staff
2 *Improved communications:* better voice, telex, facsimile and data processing communication facilities
3 *Replacement of paper files:* less storage space, easier and faster information retrieval, better security and easier transmission of documents
4 *Operational improvements:* more flexibility, more ability to cope with change, lower unit costs and wider availability of facilites.

Setting the project scope

The areas of the organisation to be studied must be determined, based upon the stated project objectives. Both the different types and levels of staff, as well as the physical areas within the organisation, must be specified and this must be communicated to those involved. If the reaction to the news is unfavourable, then attempts must be made to win over opinion, as the type of project under discussion is virtually impossible to implement successfully without active co-operation.

It is obvious that some project objectives, such as improvement of telephone facilities, will affect all areas of the organisation, whereas others may concern only specific parts. Studying a part of the organisation as an experiment, or proving ground for technology, is worth consideration as a way of gaining both experience and approval from the staff involved.

Studying the organisation

Whichever elements of the organisation are studied, the following are the actions from which a selection must be made depending upon the objectives of the project proper.

1 Produce a register of all the equipment currently installed; this must include:
   Word processors/typewriters
   Copying machines/printing facilities
   Facsimile and telex machines
   Computers – mainframe/mini/micro
   Telephones
   Microfilm equipment
   Viewdata sets/services.
   Both numbers and locations should be specified.
2 Survey secretarial staff to determine:
   Total workload, broken down by type of work – typing, filing, photo-copying, dictation, etc.

The different kinds of documents typed: letters, proformas, telexes, reports, statistical typing, originals, retyping

The need for facilities not currently available

This survey should include both secretaries and typing pool staff.

3 Carry out a mail census, of 'normal' mail, telex, facsimile and any other forms of document transfer. The volumes moving between groups within the organisation, as well as between the organisation and its environment must be measured over a representative period, excluding holiday times and any other odd periods. The disposition of the mail should be noted, whether it is filed, read and destroyed, read and redistributed, passed on, etc.

4 If it is possible, a census of telephone usage should be taken. This will indicate the numbers of calls, successful and otherwise, both within and without the organisation and any facilities such as call-blocking and redirecting which might be required.

5 Audit the computer services available, to determine the information retrieval facilities offered and their likely expansion throughout the organisation. Note that in many organisations information retrieval system use is fragmented. As part of the information retrieval audit, any library and paper-based information services should also be studied.

6 Survey the staff involved in the study to determine how the installation of office automation equipment might improve their performance. It should be made clear that the object is not to automate the functions which the staff carry out, it is rather to remove bottlnecks in the performance of the mundane and release time for more productive effort.

Collating the information

When the survey is complete, a picture of the current information system of the organisation and of its needs for the future may be drawn up. At this stage no commitment to specific equipment should be made, despite any particular items already in place. Following the digesting of the information, the next stage may be embarked upon.

Developing the strategy

A strategy for the provision of the required facilities may now be developed. The strategy will indicate the systems which must be developed, the equipment and software which must be used to support the systems, the development timetable for the installation of the systems and the staff training required for effective operation. The systems to be developed will be of several types and might include:

Advanced telephone systems based upon digital technology private exchanges.

Shared facility word processing systems, either of a proprietary nature or constructed from a variety of suppliers' equipment linked with a local communications network.

Powerful reprographics facilities based on laser technology printers; these may be linked to computer systems or word processing systems.

'Electronic mail', based either in word processing networks or digital telephone exchange equipment.

To connect a variety of word processing, computing, information retrieval and telex terminals, large volume magnetic storage and printing facilities.

The costs of all the elements of the strategy must be estimated, together with the effort involved in all stages of the strategy implementation.

Strategy implementation

The strategic plan will include a series of stages and will indicate which elements of the strategy should be implemented at each stage. Care should be taken that each stage is completed and accepted before the next stage is begun, so that the implementation proceeds in an orderly and controlled fashion.

Post-implementation review

When the implementation of the project is completed and all of the systems are operating, a review should be undertaken. Each of the systems implemented (for instance, a shared facility word processing system), should be audited and measured against the stated objectives of that system laid out at the beginning of the project. Depending upon the results of the comparison, it may be thought necessary to re-evaluate the original objectives, or to amend the implemented system to meet the original objectives.

THREE CASE STUDIES

To illustrate the practical achievement of office automation benefits in a reasonably straightforward manner, three different examples are given below.

Productivity improvement from word processing

A survey established the case for word processing in several offices within a commercial company. A common equipment range which suited the general requirement was selected. However, the system was installed first in one representative department. The work done in this department was analysed and figures for time taken for each type were obtained prior to the changeover.

After the new system was operating routinely, measurements of increase in productivity for each type of work were made.

The categories of work and productivity gains are given in Figure 47.1. Also shown are relative proportions of different types of work. Evaluation of work mixes in other departments were then made and these results applied to them. It was clear that some departments did not merit word processing as originally thought, whilst in others the productivity increase to be expected was greater.

Time saved (a)	Type of work	Proportion of total office work (b)	Weighted time saving (a) × (b)
25%	Reports	25%	6%
20%	Letters and memos	30%	6%
70%	Standardised letters	35%	25%
80%	Tabulations	10%	8%
	Totals	100%	45%

Figure 47.1 **Productivity improvements from word processing**

It all depended on the relative work mix.

The company gained benefits where they were genuinely available and avoided marginal cases. Throughout, compatible equipment was used which facilitated both staff training and the achievement of later links to mainframe computing.

Combined data processing/word processing/microform techniques

This second example illustrates the evolution of a successful real time sales ledger processing system into wider office automation techniques.

The ledger handles tens of thousands of customers and many million invoices annually. For audit reasons, copies of customer accounts need to be dumped regularly and stored for years. Also, signed copies of the invoices as proof of delivery need to be stored for many months. All this storage was in paper form, requiring a heavy print load, much storage space and significant staff time in retrieving documents.

The account records are now stored on microfiche produced from a magnetic tape at a computer bureau. The invoices are photographed internally on to microfilm. Fast access to any given record is achieved by using indexes maintained on the normal real time system and by auto searching of the microfilm. A common reader is used for both microform media.

Figure 47.2 illustrates this sytem and shows also a word processor connected on-line to the computer for production of high-quality automatically addressed debtor letters.

This company achieved major benefit from space and staff time saving by introducing this system in a single department and it affected the work of no other department. The only disadvantage could occur in the area of equipment compatibility. If different departments installed other makes of word processor and microform equipment, problems of the transferability of skill could arise.

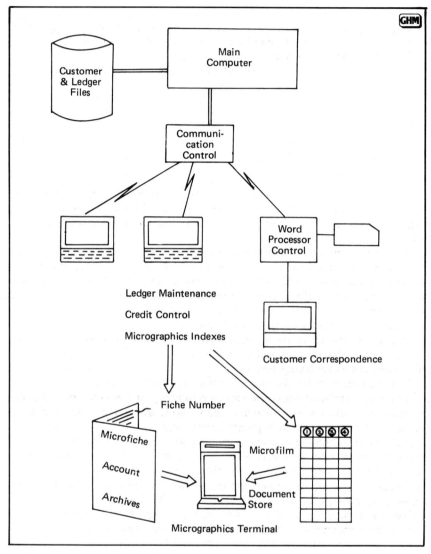

Figure 47.2 Example of an evolutionary approach to a combined word processing, data processing and microfilm system

Combined text and voice communications

The company concerned consisted of a head office with a number of major branches and had the following problems:

1   Difficulty of tracking staff within locations for telephone contact
2   High telephone line costs and frustrated calls through trunk line congestion
3   Considerable 'electronic mail' within UK and worldwide at all locations using telex with resulting:
       high cost of equipment and staff cost in establishing connection
       inconvenient input
       lack of consistent recording of messages
4   Need for timely status reports from branches to head office: for example for senior management meetings at 9.00 on Monday mornings a mixture of voice messages, dictation and telexes gave an unsatisfactory system requiring considerable activity in finalising and collating reports prior to the meetings.

A study of voice systems identified the need for linked electronic PABX systems to facilitate staff tracking and provide other benefits. Traffic analysis identified considerable savings (£200 000 a year) from use of tie lines between locations.

At the same time it was realised that simple text input terminals with limited text editing facilities could be installed in all locations. They were linked to a message switching computer which had a central telex link. Telex messages in convenient format could be input or received at any location.

This equipment was no more expensive than the telex devices it replaced. However, in addition a company-wide electronic mail system was possible. Messages were electronically pigeon-holed at the central message switch and retrieved as well. This provided the basis for a much more timely and convenient status reporting system.

Transmission costs for the electronic mail system were very cheap. Pairs of multiplexers enabled the text transmission to piggy back on the same lines as the voice network. The two systems used separate frequency channels within the line and were physically separate at each end.

The benefits to this company were major cost savings associated with a more integrated communications capability. Since they did not have to justify the electronic mail system other than on the grounds of replacing telex and an inadequate status reporting system, they could confidently install the new terminals in each location.

Growth in other uses of the electronic mail facility has threatened the capacity message switch, but this is a simple component which they foresee will be easy to enhance. The system is summarised in Figure 47.3 overleaf.

FURTHER READING

Jarrett, Dennis, *The Electronic Office: a management guide to the office of the future*, Gower, 1982
Price, S. G., *Introducing the Electronic Office*, National Computing Centre, Manchester, 1979
Saphier, Michael, *Planning the New Office*, McGraw-Hill, New York, 1978
Urwick Nexos and Francis Kinsman Associates, *The Structure and Design of Tomorrow's Office*, Urwick Nexos Ltd, 1980

Figure 47.3   Combined text and voice communications

PART NINE

HUMAN RESOURCE MANAGEMENT

48 Manpower planning

E S M Chadwick

The need for companies to take a searching look at their future manpower requirements has become more and more evident, and manpower planning is more important for management than it has ever been. There are three main arguments in favour of manpower planning at the level of the firm. Firstly, there is considerable evidence to indicate that for some time to come there will be a shortage of quality manpower, particularly technological and scientific manpower, the demand for which is steadily increasing. Secondly, changes in manpower requirements in skill terms are likely to be much more rapid in the future than they have been in the past. No longer is a man able to learn a skill in his youth which will carry him through the whole of his working life; it is probable that the young, and the not so young man will have to change his skill once, or even twice, in the course of his working life. Thirdly, the ever-increasing costs of manpower. Demands for higher standards of living and increased leisure are tending to push these up at an even faster rate.

Assuming that the *average* stay in a company of a newly recruited graduate engineer is twelve years, and that such a recruit makes normal, but not exceptional, advancements; then the cost in salary alone over the twelve-year period is likely to be (at current values) of the order of £12 000. If, however, one adds on the other costs of staff pensions, National Insurance payments, various fringe benefits, accommodation and office services, etc., then the total cost is of the order of £200 000.

No one contemplating the purchase of a piece of plant or equipment, with a similar life-span, costing that amount would do so without the most careful study of its suitability for the purpose for which it was intended, its capacity, the means by which that capacity could be utilised to the full, its place in the scheme of production, and the expected return on the investment. Few companies apply the same level of criteria or consideration to manpower. The reason for this difference in approach lies in the traditional attitude to manpower as a cost rather than as an investment. Yet while machinery depreciates and eventually becomes obsolete, properly developed manpower can continue to grow in usefulness and capacity.

The view that there is likely to be a shortage of quality staff over the longer term, or that one presently exists, is not universally shared. Some take the view that there is considerable under-use of talents and abilities, and that there is a large, as yet untapped, potential for the exercise of higher skills if only adequate training and education can be made available. This, in itself, is a very large subject. The objective of manpower planning is, and must be, to improve manpower utilisation and to ensure that there is available manpower of the right number and the right quality to meet the present and future needs of the organisation. It must, therefore, produce, *inter alia*, a realistic recruitment policy and plan and must be very much concerned with costs and productivity.

ROLE AND CONTENT OF MANPOWER PLANNING

Manpower planning has to reconcile two apparently different sets of views: those concerned with the accepted managerial yardsticks of costs, trends, projections, and so on, and those involved in the more traditional staff management approach of 'concern for individuals'. There are people, particularly in the older age groups who have long been concerned with personnel management, who see planning as a de-humanising process. In fact, the contrary is the case. These two viewpoints are not in opposition but complement each other. The really skilful manager is the man who is equipped to consider the immediate implication of an individual case in a long-term company and national context. Decisions and advice given after consideration of both short- and long-term factors are likely to be of more value both to the individual involved and to the management.

Manpower planning, in its broadest sense, covers all those activities traditionally associated with the management of personnel – records, recruitment, selection, training and development, appraisal, career planning, management succession, and so on. But it is important, both for analytical purposes and ultimately for executive purposes, to disentangle these activities and to think of them as a number of sequential phases. It has been found convenient to think of three main phases. These are illustrated in Figure 48.1. They are:

Phase 1: The development of manpower objectives. This is concerned with the development of forecasts of the manpower necessary to fulfil the company's *corporate* objectives; with looking at the totality of situations rather than at individuals. In this phase, analysis, forecasting and the setting of targets is carried out in terms of total numbers, skill groups, organisational groups, total costs, etc. It is concerned with detailed analysis in order to identify and foresee problem areas, to assess future demands and to establish how those demands may be met. It is directed towards the development of manpower *strategy* as an integral part of company strategy.

Phase 2: The management of manpower. In this phase, the question is one of managing manpower resources to meet objectives and the development, in more specific and individual terms, of recruitment plans, training and

GHM

COMPANY OBJECTIVES, POLICIES AND PLANS

Economic forecasts

Organisation objectives

Strategic plans

MANPOWER ANALYSIS
(Current situation)

— Inventory
— Employment
— Productivity
— Organisation

MANPOWER FORECASTS
(Future situation)

Overall manpower forecast → Unit manpower forecast → Budget agreement → Management manpower estimates

TOP MANAGEMENT APPROVAL

MANPOWER OBJECTIVES AND POLICIES

MANPOWER PLANS AND PROGRAMMES

— Recruitment and selection
— Redundancy
— Retirement and remuneration
— Training
— Appraisal and development
— Efficiency investigations

CONTROL AND EVALUATION

Phase one

Phase two

Phase three

Figure 48.1   A procedure for manpower planning
*Here, the three phases of manpower planning are shown in their
logical sequence, together with the information feed-back loop
which must result from the final phase of control and evaluation*

859

development plans, succession plans, appraisal systems, etc.

Phase 3: Control and evaluation. This concerns the continual evaluation and amendment of plans in the light of achievement and changing circumstances. Planning starts from a given factual position and tries to look ahead through a range of possibilities. Evaluation in this context means thoroughly checking forecasts and forecasting methods against what eventually happens, and making such revisions as may prove necessary. Any planning activity must have a system for this regular checking built into it. In other words, planning must be a continuing process.

The components of the second phase are fairly familiar in industry and are often taken to be synonymous with manpower planning. They are a part, but not the whole. Phase 1, on the other hand, while obviously supplying the general context in which phase 2 must operate, is much less familiar and it is in this area that recent developments in thinking on manpower planning have occurred.

It is the ultimate aim of any complete system of manpower planning that all three phases should be fully integrated (see Figure 48.1). It is equally clear that manpower planning must be fully integrated with the company plan. Indeed, without a company plan, there can be no realistic manpower planning.

This chapter deals primarily with phase 1. Various aspects of phase 2 are dealt with in other chapters. It is essential that this first phase of manpower planning is well understood if the vital second phase is not to take on an atmosphere of uncertainty and become an operation entirely concerned with short-term tactics, without any particular strategy in mind. The equally vital, and again less familiar, third phase will also be discussed here.

TIME SCALE

How far ahead should one attempt to plan? Obviously, as one looks forward in time, forecasts become increasingly tentative. As a generalisation, one can say that the plan period should be that which, having regard to the particular circumstances of the time and the activity, will give the lead-time necessary to deal with most manpower situations. If, for example, the time between the decision to re-equip and the installation and operation of the new equipment is two years, then one must look ahead at least that time to assess the manpower implications in terms of numbers and skills. If there is significant recruitment through apprenticeships whereby productive work is five years removed from recruitment, then for that category of employee one should look five years ahead. On the other hand, occasional operating or organisational situations can render some aspects of the future so unpredictable that, for the time being, planning in any detail has to be very short-term but even with such situations, the need for the development of a broad strategy remains.

It is also true that for some activities and for some individual career developments plans, five years can be a comparatively short period. Consequently, in some individual cases, a five-year planning period, although only possible to cover part of the plan concerning an individual, is a *practical* period for looking ahead in terms of the actual action contributing to the long-term aim.

LIMITATIONS OF MANPOWER PLANNING

It is important to bear in mind what can reasonably be expected of planning. The aim is the reduction of uncertainty, but the possibility of doing this varies inversely with time. It must be appreciated that the forecasts covering the later years of the planning period are increasingly tentative. It may be more appropriate to think of the five-year period as comprising a two-year plan (a plan implying action), followed by a three-year forecast (indicating the broad path to be followed).

Manpower does not lend itself to precise measurement and docketing; it often behaves in a quite unpredictable way. The trading and technical situation is also fluid and targets and plans have often to be radically adjusted at short notice. Consequently, the manpower planning activity shares, in a particularly acute way, the essential characteristic of all planning in an uncertain world – it is a never-ending adjustment of expectations and aims to meet changing goals within a very uncertain environment. Its language and results will, of necessity, be probablistic in nature and will *not* be inflexible commitments to some postulated single course of events.

Above all, it is not a new and revolutionary approach to problems that have only recently been identified; much of it has long been common practice in many companies. What manpower planning, as here described, sets out to do is to bring these practices together into a systematic approach that directs attention to the future and to identification of potential but avoidable manpower problems.

This chapter sets out to describe a number of possible analytical approaches which have been found to be useful. But there is no single universally applicable *system* of manpower planning, though the concepts have been found to have general applicability. It is for each company to consider the various methods which seem appropriate to its own situation. The check-list given in Figure 48.2 may be helpful in identifying particular needs.

ANALYSIS AND FORECASTING

It is axiomatic that no forecast is any better than the data upon which it is based and the judgment of the forecaster. It follows that the first essential of any planning and forecasting is data and analysis of the data in order to reveal trends, changes that have taken place in company activities and objectives and their influence upon manpower requirements. Only then can one consider future changes in company objectives and their manpower implications.

Manpower data traditionally tends to be organised with the primary aim of supplying information on individuals. For planning purposes it is vital that such information should be organised in a manner which permits information to be easily available on groups, and in such a way that it can be sorted and

	Room for improve-ment	Adequate	GHM Good – no weaknesses
1 Top management and organisational support for manpower plans and programmes			
2 An adequate information system on manpower			
3 Anticipation of future manpower requirements			
4 Integration of manpower programmes with overall company objectives			
5 Anticipation of organisational changes and preparing for their manpower implications			
6 Recruitment of necessary number of well-qualified staff at each level			
7 Effective placement of newly engaged graduate/professional staff to make them productive			
8 Filling key middle and top management posts with well-qualified staff			
9 Management of age structure to minimise wastage problems and avoid promotion blockages			
10 Reducing wastage at all levels			
11 Providing significant jobs for managers throughout their career			

Figure 48.2   Manpower planning check-list

				GHM
12	Evaluating the current performance of all staff			
13	Evaluating the potential of all staff for promotion and of managers for higher responsibilities			
14	Providing sound promotion and career opportunities for all staff with potential			
15	Motivating managers to develop their subordinates			
16	Development of managers for higher-level responsibilities			
17	Keeping the remuneration system up-to-date and effective as a motivator			
18	Investigation into the causes and solutions of serious manpower problems			
19	Measuring productivity improvements			
20	Maintenance of a system that enables the cost of manpower and its contribution to the company effort to be evaluated			
21	Maintenance of a comprehensive and systematic programme of training to enable staff to adapt to new procedures and techniques and to equip them for higher responsibilities			
22	Maintenance of a sound and flexible organisation structure			
23	Integration of the manpower management programme			

Figure 48.2 (continued)

863

arranged to illustrate not only the present position in any group or combination of groups, but also the changes that have taken place over time and to measure the trends that have become apparent. Various systems are available for this purpose from simple needle-sorting punch card systems up to computers. The decision as to which to use will depend on cost, facilities already available, the size of company, and so on.

The present position and the analysis of trends

In manpower planning there are three basic elements to be considered: the present stock of manpower; wastage; and future requirements for manpower. By a proper analysis of present manpower and wastage rates, for example, conclusions can be reached as to how much of the labour force will still be there in five or ten years time. Figure 48.3 shows such an analysis and projection by age groups. Analysis should also be done by category, department, sex, etc.

The starting point of any plan (and any control system) must be a careful analysis of the position as it exists at the beginning of the planning period. Information will be needed in a series of permutations according to the needs of the company. The following are the basic 'building blocks' that will probably be needed in most circumstances:

1 Present total manpower
2 Manpower resources by appropriate planning groups, for example, sex, grade, function/department, profession/skill, qualification, age group, and length of service
3 Total manpower costs
4 Total costs by appropriate component elements, for example, salaries, wages, pension contributions, welfare, canteen, etc.
5 Costs by functions/departments
6 Costs indices and ratios (see control and evaluation below)
7 Total numbers related to sales, production, or such other criteria as may be appropriate, in physical and financial terms
8 Attrition and retention rates by appropriate groups, that is, overall, by function/department, profession, sex, age group, etc.
9 Recruitment patterns by age, education, etc., for each function/department
10 Resources of promotable staff.

The manpower pattern revealed by this analysis will be operating in a specific context and the manpower plan will have to keep this context in mind. Obviously a large number of subtle pressures will be at work and these pressures will vary from company to company. Many of them will not normally be of immediate day-to-day concern to management but they underline how important it is to keep informed. Among the questions to be borne in mind will be: the general position of the company in relation to national policies, both economic and social; the company's market share in relation to other companies; the position of the labour market for the various categories employed.

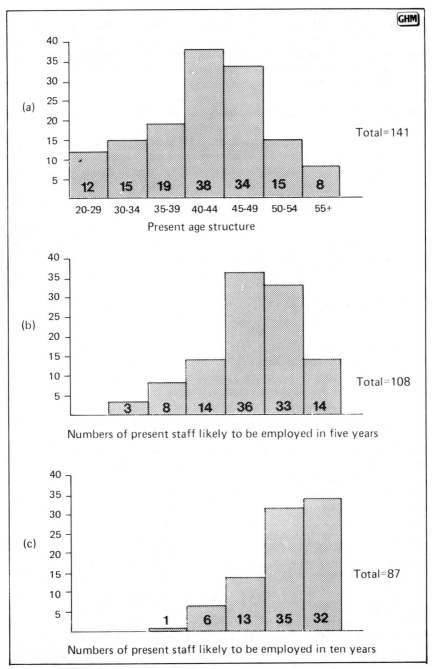

Figure 48.3 Age analysis

Forecasting future manpower movements

Future manpower requirements are self-evidently governed by the company's corporate plan and they can only be considered in that context. Indeed, without a corporate plan there can be no realistic manpower plan. It follows that no forecast for the forward demand of manpower can be more precise than the formulation of the company's overall objectives. Clearly, it is also important that a company's objectives should be so stated as to be interpretable in terms of manpower involvement. The factors affecting manpower demand fall into two main groups: trading and production patterns, and technological change. Some indication of the extent to which volume and patterns of trade, and technological change affect manpower will have been gathered from the analyses which have been described in previous paragraphs.

The method of calculating actual manpower needs against stated work targets, as indicated from the corporate plan, will depend on the type of manpower in question. On the shop floor it may be a matter of simple output volume to manpower relationships, with due allowances for technological developments. At the higher levels, ratios of manpower to volume of work are less likely to be valid, and it then becomes necessary to define the form of future management roles.

A means by which this sort of information can be gathered is given in Figure 48.4. It is emphasised that any changes from the present position have to be substantiated.

Information, estimates and forecasts so gathered need to be carefully analysed and evaluated in a variety of ways. An example of one such analysis and a method of its presentation is given in Figure 48.5. This shows the present strength by age groups, the retention rate over the next five years, expected recruitment and the forecast strength by the age groupings then applicable. For the purpose of this example, it has been assumed that there will be no expansion (or contraction) of numbers and that present recruitment and wastage patterns will continue. Should any of these three factors change, or be changed, only the arithmetic would need amendment, the principle remains.

It is not enough, however, just to build up manpower requirements in this way and to accept the present position as satisfactory. Indeed, the very act of collecting and analysing information in the way that has been described tends to raise questions. Does one really need so many laboratory technicians, or engineers, or chemists? Could one do as well with fewer highly qualified staff and more support staff? Such questions may well make the planner go back and look again at some of the estimates for parts of the organisation and review them in the light of what has been found.

Nor should one merely equate supply and demand. To do so will only perpetuate the misuse or under-use of manpower, where it exists. It is, therefore, essential that the manpower planning activity goes hand-in-hand with productivity studies and other studies of manpower utilisation. One needs also to give particular consideration to the composition of the overall manpower profile, the proportions of various levels of skills in each of the main employment categories.

			Increases and decreases in requirements and year end balances				
Categories of staff	Actual number at time of estimate	Expected number at year end 1980	Estimated			Forecast	
			1982 - + =	1983 - + =	1984 - + =	1985 - + =	1986 - + =
Totals							

Estimates of staff numbers 1982–87 [GHM]

Functional sector ....

Department ....

Brief statement of reasons for increases and/or decreases:

Signed _____ Date_____
Departmental Manager

Signed _____ Date_____
General Manager

Figure 48.4 Manpower forecast sheet

Manpower age brackets

	20-24	25-29	30-34	35-39	40-44	45-49	50-54	55-59	TOTAL
A Present strength	12	31	28	55	33	29	19	23	230
B Expected intake for 5 years	21	30	9						60
C Average retention rate (percentage)	92	94	95.5	97.5	99	99	97.5	87.5	–
D Expected retention of present employees after five years	8	23	23	50	31	27	14	–	176
E Corrected age brackets for retained employees	0	8	23	23	50	31	27	14	176
F Expected retention of intake after 5 years	11	24	16	3					54
G Forecast strength in 5 years	11	32	39	26	50	31	27	14	230
H Net change after 5 years	-1	+1	+11	-29	+17	+2	+8	-9	0

Figure 48.5   Derivation of the quantitative five-year forecast for a function

Out of these studies, and analyses, one is able to build up realistic recruit-ment targets (Figure 48.6). This shows the expected vacancies arising over the next two years by grade level from retirement, wastage and additional jobs, and how it is expected they can be filled, that is by promotion or recruitment. In the case of recruitment, a further analysis by age group, as shown in Figure 48.5, is necessary.

What has been said up to now has been concerned with the medium-term demand for manpower. The longer-term picture must also be kept in mind, even though this may have no immediate influence. The factors here include the local and national environment, the size and shape of the firm in fifteen to twenty years time, its share of the market, what the market will be, demographic projections and the rate of technological change.

Equally, one must look at the supply position. It is no good setting requirements that cannot be met. A study of the availability of the different types of manpower will be needed. The ability of the industry and the firm itself to attract recruits must also be considered. This is true of both the short and longer term.

The question of supply is not nearly so difficult as it might at first seem. All the manpower that can enter into planning studies over the time-scale is already in existence; it is simply a matter of finding out where it is and what will be done with it in terms of education. The numbers and subjects of study in the top classes of education are known and since, of all things, the education system is slowest to change, reasonable forecasts can be made. Obviously, the size of the total working population has some bearing on this. Forward projections of the working population are prepared and published by the Department of Employment.

But as important as, if not more important than, the mere numbers is the matter of quality, and the ability of the education system and industrial training in its many forms to provide the skills which will be required as a result of changing technology. The problem of manpower obsolescence at all levels is real and urgent. A high proportion, possibly as much as 50 per cent, of a company's present manpower may still be in its employment fifteen years from now (see Figure 48.3). Will they have the knowledge and skills which will then be required of them? Manpower planning has thrown up the need for some form of occupational/skill classification which can be used to indicate the changing pattern of skill requirements and the changing manpower profile.

Projections

What has been discussed up to this point is the assessment of manpower needs to meet task objectives, the supply of manpower and environmental influences and constraints. Another aspect of manpower planning is the use of mathe-matically based prediction techniques to detect trends, to assist in policy decisions to indicate the futurity in present courses of action, to assess the probable future consequences of alternative possibilities. They have been found to be particularly useful in examining wastage – a whole subject in its own right – and the development of balanced recruitment policies directed

| Grade group | Existing jobs at year-end 1982 | Vacancies arising due to | | | | | Possibilities to fill vacancies | | | Surplus of promotable staff |
		Retirement	Promotion	Wastage	New jobs by year-end 1984	Total	Promotion	Recruitment	Total	
Male										
A										
B										
C										
D										
Total										
Female										
C										
D										
Total										

GHM

Figure 48.6 Recruitment targets 1983, 1984

towards a stable age structure.

These projections are not an alternative to managerial manpower fore-casting such as has been discussed but are supplementary to it. They are generally only applicable in larger companies but the approach, if not the mathematics, can be used universally.

For the purposes of projections, the basic need is for a bank of historical data over a minimum of five years. From such a store of information, it is possible to extract such essential factors as turnover rates in whatever category is required, related to age and/or length of service, movements within or between categories, the probability of promotion between grades as related to age, length of service, and qualifications. By this means one is able to gain insights into, and an understanding of, situations and the relationships which brought them about; to isolate problem areas, present or future, and the action needed for their solution. By establishing this picture of how the system has worked, it also becomes possible to consider projections of the future to assist in policy decisions by indicating the probable future consequences in alternative courses of action. There is, of course, no method of establishing a staff position which, in five years time, will *inevitably* be achieved; decisions can, however, be made which will, in all probability, approximate to that position. The aim is to examine a variety of trends and see whether the projected position achieved by these trends is satisfactory or not. The *executive decision* lies in deciding what position is desirable, what trend produces this position, and what action, if any, is necessary in order to produce that trend.

This method of approach, which is the one that appears most to engender distrust or, perhaps, fear of manpower planning as it has developed, has the object of attempting to see a problem as it really is, not what people think it is. In order to take a decision, one must have solved a problem, and to do that one must see the problem as it really is.

It is a matter of making logical deductions in relation to a situation in which some, at least, of the elements have been measured. Logical analysis of this type of situation cannot be taken very far before running into mathematics. The choice is therefore either to use mathematics or to stop the logic short at that point. Everything depends on how much analysis is needed to solve the problem. If logic stops short, the chances are that the problem has not been solved and the decision is, therefore, likely to be wrong, and the consequences that flow from it are not those that were being aimed at.

The choice is not between something simple and good but something difficult and not to be trusted, but between something which gives the right (or best available) answer and something based on intuition and guesswork, the consequences of which cannot be foreseen.

CONTROL AND EVALUATION

Two broad and complementary approaches to the control and evaluation of the manpower plan are necessary, one in terms of numerical trends and the other in terms of costs and costs criteria.

Assuming that the planning period is five years, then the plan prepared in

1982 would go through to the end of 1987. In the autumn of 1983, the plan should have been reviewed and up-dated where necessary and extended to include 1988. The first step is, as has been stated, the review and up-dating of the corporate plan. This normally takes the form of a package of expectations and objectives, all of which are considered mutually consistent and feasible. The strategy for achieving these objectives determines the form of organisation to be used and the amount and form of resources required, including manpower.

In this review, management will want to question the degree to which the various specific goals of the manpower plan were achieved. This can be shown by the use of a number of numerical controls and gauges, such as changes in numbers by total/department/function, changes in wastage (turnover) rates and the reasons for wastage, changing age structures and their implications, all related to the original targets set.

Another approach which has been found useful in giving a comparative picture of the contribution being made by personnel to the operation of the company is the development of cost ratios.

The concept of productivity is very complex in practice and raises considerable theoretical questions of definition and data. Nevertheless, a number of simple indices can be used to illustrate the changing contribution and costs of manpower. It should be emphasised, however, that these give no more than a 'broad-brush' view and should be treated with caution, particularly in making any sort of comparison between one function and another and, more particularly, between different companies. Reliance on a single index could itself be misleading but, taken together, they can give an indication of trends and the movement of manpower costs related to company activities as a whole (see Figure 48.7).

CONCLUSION

In a world of rapidly changing technology with an ever-growing demand for more and different skills, the need to plan manpower is as great as the need to plan any other resource. The prosperity and growth of any company rests, in the end, on the quality of its manpower and the extent to which their talents are utilised to the full.

Manpower planning is concerned with safeguarding the future, with preventing the loss of opportunities through lack of appropriate human abilities and the wastefulness of 'over-braining' the organisation. It emphasises the need for rationalisation in keeping with modern needs and technological capabilities and the development of organisation structures to match.

It is not some separate, rather esoteric, activity carried on by a few people in back rooms in large companies. It is, or should be, part of the normal conduct of business which can, and has been successfully and advantageously practised in a wide range of companies in size, background and activity.

At the beginning it can appear to be a large and somewhat daunting task; it certainly needs perseverance and determination to achieve results. It is something which is best learned by doing. It is better to start simply, linking

Year	Present	1983	1984	1985	1986	1987
Sales index-units	100					
Production index	100					
Sales proceeds index	100					
Manpower costs index	100					
Staff costs per sales or production units	100					
Total staff costs/ Total operation cost	100					

Figure 48.7 Index approach for assessing trends in contributions made by manpower

planning with an existing system, such as annual budgeting, and building from there.

FURTHER READING

Bramham, J., *Practical Manpower Planning*, 2nd edition, IPM, 1978

Chadwick, E. S. M., *Integrating Manpower Planning with External Manpower Planning and Programmes*, OECD, 1970

Pettman, B. O., and Tavernier, G., *Manpower Planning Workbook*, Gower, 1976

Smith, A. R. (ed.), *Corporate Manpower Planning*, Gower, 1980

49 Recruitment and selection

P T Humphrey

No matter what has been written or said about recruitment and selection, everyone believes that he is an expert in this field. It is probably the one area of personnel management where 'the professional' is inevitably challenged by 'the layman', whatever the circumstances. Nevertheless, it is one of those situations where often a manager or supervisor has to face up to the problem of becoming totally involved in the recruitment and selection process without quite knowing how to tackle what is in reality a complicated task, in spite of the apparent simplicity of the ultimate decision to be taken – 'to hire or not to hire'.

However, before going into detail a few basic points must be established and emphasised at the outset. Almost everyone in any organisation has at some stage or other the responsibility for requesting materials or finance in order to carry out their work effectively. These requests which can lead to heated discussions between superior and subordinate, or between peers, are essentially concerned with inanimate objects – 'vegetable, mineral or abstract'. But the request for a replacement as someone is leaving the organisation, or for more staff to carry out the work, will inevitably lead to consideration of the 'animal' category. The true relevance of this is the ability, apart from the right of this 'animal' category to hold and undoubtedly voice opinion and comment, constructive or destructive, about the way in which the recruitment and selection process is handled. This 'answering back' facility is acknowledged by all professional recruiters, who only ignore it at their peril. It is probably the one point which many managers do not appreciate, for while most managers are accustomed to dealing with human problems within their own job function, they are dealing with known people within a specific and generally accepted framework. People who apply for a job with a particular organisation are not subject to, nor do they hold, the corporate values, real or imaginary, which form part of the daily working lives of those already employed.

The second point which naturally follows on from the first is that the principle of 'do unto others as you would be done by' underpins the total recruitment and selection procedure. The applicant for a job, whatever the level, expects to receive the normal human courtesies not only in the face to face situation but also at all other points of contact during the decision making process. In spite of the obvious economic nature of employment, a great deal of attention must be placed on the underlying social processes.

Thirdly it is important not only to acknowledge but also to understand that the situation is not one sided as far as the decision taking process is concerned. The conclusion of a recruitment task does not occur with the decision 'we'll offer you the job', this is merely a unilateral decision. The conclusion in reality only comes when the applicant says 'thanks, I accept your offer'.

The final basic point to be made is that in any organisation there is at the same point in time both a buyer's market and a seller's market as far as jobs are concerned. It is important to distinguish between them, for while the same basic administrative approach is both necessary and applicable, the tactics to be adopted can differ widely. This is equally true of shop floor and boardroom situations alike. Bearing these points in mind the objective now is to provide managers at all levels no matter whether they are experienced or inexperienced, with positive guidelines to tackle the job effectively, and to gain, by the end of the day, a sense of personal satisfaction from a task well done.

BASIC PLANNING AND PROCEDURE

Everyone, without exception, will realise and readily acknowledge that all organisations including one's own family must have financial resources in order to function at all, and in order to utilise these financial resources correctly some systematic methods must be devised and implemented to account for income and expenditure. But not everyone is prepared to acknowledge that the same principle has to be adopted in relation to recruiting and terminating staff, in spite of the fact that no organisation can function without staff! The total cost of recruiting an employee of average skill can be assessed at approximately three to four times the weekly wage, and very much more for senior grades. So any organisation that does not set up an effective system for handling recruitment is likely to put at risk sums of money in the immediate short term which under normal circumstances would be referred to board level for approval.

Statistical information on the numbers already employed in the organisation categorised by status, department, works or site, and sub-divided in relation to occupational skills required, levels of work involved or merely by job titles, must be available in order to provide a reference point from which the whole procedure begins.

The subsequent steps are as follows:

1 Receiving requisition and/or authorisation for replacements or additional staff
2 Gathering information about the job
3 Checking against obvious internal sources
4 Advertising the vacancy – internally and externally
5 Processing of applications

Stage 1:
Run up

6 Setting up the interview	
7 Conducting the interview	Stage 2:
8 Administering appropriate tests	Face-to-face – the
9 Making the appointment	employment interview

10 Introducing the new employee to the organisation	
11 Following up the progress of the new employee	Stage 3: Follow through
12 Reviewing and evaluating the recruitment and selection process.	

Upon examination, even the most *ad hoc* example of recruitment reveals that the above procedure has been followed and that often the tactics/approach/ mechanics vary in relation to the nature of the job to be filled. In many instances it is the level of the vacancy which is the determining factor. Therefore, where applicable, attention will be drawn to the different requirements in recruiting staff at the following levels:

1 Managerial, including supervisory
2 Clerical and technical
3 Operational.

STAGE ONE: THE RUN UP

Requisitions

The need for a sound method of producing the right statistical information, such as number employed, labour turnover and absenteeism, has already been made. However, even in cases where this information exists, many organisations are quite indifferent to the way in which requests for replacement or additional staff are made. In many respects the underlying attitudes which permitted this have been altered by the economic circumstances of the last decade. Closer scrutiny of labour costs is taking place and the requisition for staff at all levels has almost the same cachet now as the capital requisition.

What kind of information has to be included on a staff requisition form?

1 Name and location of originating department
2 Job title
3 Main job function
4 Salary or grade
5 Reason for requisition
   (*a*) Replacement
   (*b*) New appointment
   (*c*) Additional appointment
6 Required by: (date)
7 Signatures .... Department Head: Authorised Date

While it is appreciated that it does take a certain (minimal) amount of managerial time to complete such a requisition, nevertheless its value to the person responsible for recruitment is incalculable. The main advantage is that it leaves no room for doubt. No one has to rely on the recollection of what was said about the job during a lunch-time conversation which ranged from detailed shop talk through gossip to personal hair-letting down. Far too much valuable managerial time can be wasted in reference back by telephone or by personal visit to verify the position. Certainly the time of the recruiter can be spent to better effect in the next step of the process.

Job information

A great deal of confusion exists over the different terms used in this area. The term 'job description' means different things to different people, and indeed the context in which the term is used can alter its apparent meaning. Nevertheless an attempt has been made by the Department of Employment in its publication *Glossary of Training Terms* to standardise usage of such terms, e.g. 'A job description is a broad statement of the purpose, scope, duties and responsibilities of a particular job'. 'A job specification is a detailed statement of the physical and mental activities in a job'.

However, jobs must be viewed as part of a dynamic organisation, with the result (as so many management writers have said) that the job description presents at best only a point-in-time interpretation. Consequently many managers who inevitably feel 'pushed' in the everyday situation will question the necessity of having a job description at all. But there are simple operational reasons which can help in the argument to overcome such resistance. These are:

1 The job description acts as a basic means of communication between the manager and the recruiter as far as the position to be filled is concerned
2 It is an invaluable mechanism for discussing and finalising the tactical approach to the selection process
3 It can yield vital information for the candidates who have come to have a high level of expectation in terms of job information. This certainly has a useful 'plus effect' in promoting confidence about the organisation amongst the candidates
4 It ensures that there is an accepted factual basis from which information can be selected for advertising purposes
5 Finally it provides the reference point against which all decisions taken and judgements made can be evaluated.

Thus, time sensibly spent on this important preparatory work can yield significant dividends in preventing over-interviewing and indeed in ensuring that advertising and other expense is used to maximum effect.

The job description

What information, therefore, needs to be included in the job description? The following items are essential no matter what level of appointment is being considered:

1   Job title: This must be self explanatory wherever possible and certainly where either unusual technical terms or terms specific to the organisation are used, adequate explanation must be given
2   Name of department: As in (1)
3   Accountability: The job title of the person to whom the job holder is responsible
4   Main job function: A brief but lucid statement of the purpose of the job
5   Responsibilities for people and/or equipment. No need to detail every nut and bolt, but include categories and numbers of people to be supervised together with major items of equipment.

Additional items are required when considering managerial, supervisory or technical positions. These include:

6   Limits of authority – particularly in relation to spending money
7   Levels of contact – this is of special importance in a multi-divisional organisation and with working relationships outside the organisation.

Useful questions to keep in mind during this process of gathering information and writing the job description include:

1   Is the informant's statement accurate?
2   What degree of bias is contained in the statement?
3   Who can provide a second opinion?
4   Does the written description contain all the relevent facts?
5   Is it accurate?
6   Can the layman understand it? (In other words is it too simple, simple enough or too complicated?)

The job specification

The job description now has to be extended and interpreted specifically in relation to the physical and mental activities of the job, and the consequent demands to be made on the job holder.

While it might appear that there is considerable difference in requirements at the various levels of appointment, nevertheless, five basic categories of the job specification can be defined as follows:

1   Qualifications, knowledge appropriate to the job
2   Specific skills, abilities and aptitudes required
3   Experience required
4   Personal attributes
5   Physical attributes.

These categories can be qualified as appropriate for each selection by a scale of relevance – vital/desirable/of no consequence.

1   Qualifications

This category is the bane of every recruiter's life, for more heat can be generated over this than almost any other topic to do with recruitment. The stand point to take must be 'is it relevant?' Is a PhD really vital to do the job of sales manager in an electronics firm? It might be. On the other hand it is certainly not a vital qualification for the sales manager with a confectionery firm. A sense of reality must be maintained, for it is just as easy to be swayed by degrees and professional qualifications as it is by medals and decorations. Indeed the relevance of City and Guilds qualifications to the craftsman and technician, is probably more deserving of the recruiter's attention than has been the case in the past.

Instead of qualifications it is often more advisable to list areas of knowledge which are required, e.g. plastic injection moulding for a production manager, standard costing for a senior cost clerk, export procedures for a shipping clerk.

2   Specific skills, abilities and aptitudes

This category is not to be regarded as a rag-bag for glossy management 'in' phrases, which in the end result merely in directing attention away from the main purpose. Rather the intention is to define accurately (and quantify if at all possible) those factors which are regarded as necessary to achieving success in the job. For instance the skills required in negotiating with trade union officials, or the different skills required in the negotiation of commercial contracts with suppliers, must be stated in the appropriate specifications. Abilities to be considered can include the ability to sell 'an idea' or a product, or even the ability to see 'the wood for the trees'. Among the aptitudes those that readily spring to mind are verbal, numerical and mechanical, where great strides have been made in assessing and quantifying them among the population at large. All this must be geared to reality, and fanciful ideas of what might be required should be discounted. Simplicity really is the key note in this section.

3   Experience required

This is most important, and every attempt should be made to build up an accurate picture of the kind of previous experience required. In many situations accuracy in this respect can often lead to better advertisements, easier pre-selection and more searching interviews. What kind of detail then is necessary? Early 'formative years' experience – apprenticeships, studentships, exposure to more than one commercial or industrial situation, or maybe service in the Armed Forces or Merchant Navy.

First post of responsibility – chargehand, section leader – technical responsibility, e.g. in chemistry laboratory, secretary to a departmental manager, territory salesman. Subsequent responsibility requirements can then be added depending on the nature and level of the post being specified.

Indeed a relationship must be established between the foregoing and the environments in which the experience was gained. For instance with the post of foundry manager, experience of working with specified materials or in making a certain size of castings is very relevant. So also is information concerning the general standing of the companies or organisations in which the experience was gained.

The other most important aspect of the experience required is in relation to the major tasks of the job. This is just as important at operational as well as the other levels where, for example, garage fitters in general are not experienced in maintaining high-speed packing lines at peak performance. Another example can be taken from a supervisory situation which calls for experience in handling a large department of 600 employees. However, unless it is specified whether the employees are all males or all females, there is considerable scope for some fascinating misconceptions!

4 Personal attributes

More attention is being paid now to this category. The impact of the new individual on an existing work group and vice versa can be vital in many situations, particularly where incentives are based on group performance. Some attempt must be made to analyse the 'chemistry' of the situation – acceptability is probably the key word in this context.

However, on occasions it may well be absolutely necessary to specify what might appear to be unwelcome attributes. Abrasiveness is one such attribute which nevertheless can be vital in stimulating complacent teams at all levels. Preparedness to accept a challenge, to work under trying circumstances, or to subordinate one's own convictions in certain situations are other examples.

5 Physical attributes

These are probably more obvious, but it is often found that only lip service is being paid to the mental health aspects of the working situation. The question of stress and the individual's capacity to absorb stress is very important, especially at certain decision making levels; also where working hours, such as 12-hour shifts in noisy, dusty conditions, or train or aeroplane crews having to 'stop over', can have a serious effect on an individual's necessary domestic or social relationships.

These attributes must be specified accordingly and whenever possible professional advice must be obtained. The amateur doctor or psychologist can do untold harm, and such an occurrence must be avoided.

Having gone through all these steps in describing the job and obtaining the specification, a firm basis has been established. The recruiter can now proceed with great confidence to find 'Mr (or Ms) Right' for the post in question.

Internal sources

Many companies still have the tendency to overlook the bank of talent contained in their existing work forces despite the publicity of the last decade, aimed at management succession plans, or schemes for 'growing your own'. It is therefore very important to look inwards to try and identify potential internal candidates from all parts of the enterprise. In doing this the political pressures of the organisation will come into full play, and therefore it is essential to maintain a very independent stance throughout the exercise. This independence is sustained by the very nature of the factual information contained in the job description and the subsequent specification. Nevertheless if potential internal candidates are found, it is vital that they are subjected to the full selection process. This must not be regarded as an act of 'bloody mindedness' or 'bureaucracy', for its very purpose is to safeguard, for the organisation, the integrity of the process itself as well as of all those who play a part in it, especially the candidates.

Advertising

The job advertising market has developed since the 1950s from very small beginnings into a multi-million pound business, and inevitably it has given rise to various fads and fashions from time to time. Special job advertising agencies have been set up, and selection consultants, office staff bureaux and appointment registers have followed the trend by extending the range of services available. A great deal of material has been published on the subject and indeed many professional recruiters, depending on their own personal inclinations, are either disappointed or delighted if their daily postbag does not include at least one printed circular on job advertising.

The main purpose in advertising a job is to attract sufficient candidates of the right calibre to reply, thereby securing a reasonable field from which to choose the most appropriate person for that job. How does one tackle this attraction process?

1 Define the audience (i.e. the type of people to be reached)
2 Decide on the means and establish the cost of making the contact
3 Write the message
4 Monitor the results.

The audience

The level and nature of the position to be filled will largely define the audience both in terms of volume and geographical spread. At the operational level there is on most occasions a local audience which can be tapped, but from time to time instances do occur when special skills are being sought, and these are not available from the local audience. When this does happen, some preliminary investigation is called for, in order to establish the location of the required audience as well as the potential available. This also applies in the clerical and technical level, though there is a tendency for technical people to restrict their own availability by becoming too clearly identified with particular processes, even within the one organisation.

It is at managerial level that the audience becomes national in character. It is also pertinent to define the audience at this level in broad functional terms – e.g. accountants, engineers, buyers. In addition, consideration must be given to defining current salary levels from which potential candidates can be drawn.

The means

A great deal of detailed information from many sources is available to the recruiter on such matters as circulation of papers or publications of professional bodies, types of people who can be reached and the costs involved.

Decisions therefore have to be made on the worth of national coverage against local coverage, the amount of space required, and whether any apparent extraneous points, i.e. company image, or wider public relations exercise, need to be taken into account. While it seems natural to turn to press advertising, consideration mut also be given to other methods. These can include:

1 TV or cinema advertisements
2 Posters in places where the appropriate audience is likely to congregate – newsagents, public halls, schools and colleges
3 Leaflet distributions, especially on housing estates
4 Word of mouth – with the inevitable discount for mis-statements
5 Notice boards outside the place of work
6 Notice boards inside the place of work
7 Department of Employment job centres
8 'Recruitment circus' i.e. using a caravan as a travelling recruitment centre, e.g., for the armed forces
9 Use of a pre-recorded message on tape or a disc which can be distributed.

However it must be stated that most of the above means are more appropriate when considerable numbers of people are required at the same time, especially when a new site is being manned or expansion is taking place. Eventually and inevitably cost must play its part in the final decision.

The message

Above all simplicity is the key note, together with the need to use technical terms on a restricted but meaningful basis. There is certainly an art in constructing the message, for a basic emotional appeal to the audience is necessary. However not only must one present this appeal, but also sufficient hard information. These two together must make the appropriate candidates reach for their writing pads, cause them to telephone, or make them sufficiently curious to make a personal visit. However the message must be tailored to suit the means chosen. Consideration must also be given to technical detail, especially size of print, headlining, number of words that can be used, for the message includes everything within the defined physical boundaries of the medium, whether it be words, white or black space, line drawings, or company symbols. Indeed from time to time it is necessary to consider whether or not it is important to write in English or another language. But advice on many of these details is readily available from the organisation which is going to publish the message.

The results

It is extremely useful to maintain a record of the response to advertisements whatever the means used. This enables the user to evaluate in financial terms the relevance of certain media in reaching the required audience. The main statistic is 'cost per reply' which can be refined in relation to numbers interviewed, candidates short listed and appointed from that particular source. A relatively simple form can be designed and maintained at negligible cost by a clerk or a secretary. The type of information required includes:

1 Appointment title
2 Media used
3 Size of advertisement
4 Cost
5 Number of replies
6 Cost per reply
7 Numbers interviewed
8 Numbers shortlisted
9 Numbers appointed.

It is quite surprising how useful this information can be, not only in relation to developing realistic advertising budgets but also in settling arguments and destroying preconceived ideas.

A final word on advertising: a great deal of free information and help are available; a telephone call or two will soon establish a connection, for agencies who place advertisements receive their commission from the publishers, not the originators of the advertisement.

Processing of applications

The greatest sin in recruitment is not so much to lose an application (which is bad enough) but to ignore it, to leave it unacknowledged. Most applicants are prepared for the occasional 'mislaying' of letters, but not one will tolerate being ignored. This again is in the realm of extending natural courtesies to the people who have been sufficiently interested to respond to the message.

Keeping track of applications over the selection period which can extend on occasions to several months demands a good administrative system, preferably one which dovetails with the sorting process. A suggested outline appears in Figure 49.1.

Most organisations revise their application forms from time to time, but it is important to remember that the form itself can be so designed to promote effective administration by allocating space for action signals at appropriate points.

There is a strong argument for having standard letters, provided that these are individually typed and addressed. The amount of time that can be saved is considerable, apart from the important question of maintaining cordial relations with the candidates. Admittedly a certain amount of time is taken up initially in constructing standard letters, but it then avoids the necessity for dictating individual replies. This is doubly relevent when 50 to 60 replies are received and demand equal attention. The major standard letters should cover:

1 Acknowledgements of receipt of application

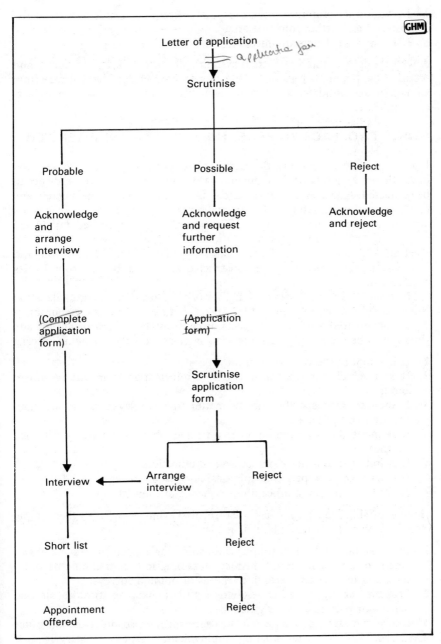

Figure 49.1   Processing of applications

2   Invitation to interview
3   Request for further information
1   It is a tool of the communication process

A well-thought out and well-tried system will not only keep candidates and recruiter happy, but will also avoid the unwelcomed letter to the chairman from an aggrieved candidate, which will inevitably lead to an embarrassing post-mortem!

STAGE TWO: FACE-TO-FACE: THE EMPLOYMENT INTERVIEW

Up to now all work on which the recruiter has been engaged has been directed inwardly on the job to be filled and outwardly only in terms of the audience to be contacted. However, the next stage – 'face to face' – is the one where many managers feel quite exposed. Confrontation is a major part of any manager's job, but it tends to be in a specific commercial or operational context where individuals are aware of the institutional constraints which surround the meeting. The employment situation cannot be classified in the same way, and therefore a framework must be constructed and a number of ground rules established.

However, before discussing the framework in more detail some explanation is necessary in order to highlight the special nature of the employment interview as compared with other aspects of confrontation. First of all, for any situation to be described as an interview it must meet the following criteria:

1   It is a tool of the communication process
2   It is a vehicle for the transmission of information from one person to another
3   It focuses upon specific subject matter that is relevant to its situation, occasion and purpose;
4   It requires the participation of two people who interact freely with one another
5   It is initiated to achieve one or several objectives
6   It takes place in a particular physical and social setting
7   It occurs as part of a procedural sequence of events.

Having established the intrinsic nature of the interview, a further simple classification test can take place. It is for:

1   Information exchange: simple acquisition or dispersion, taking down details of a person's career history, obtaining information on attitudes – sampling for market research purposes or opinion surveys
2   Problem solving: aimed at resolving conflict; changing attitudes, altering behaviour patterns; career guidance
3   Decision making: objective demands agreement on a course of action, order giving, if necessary terminating employment, engagement interview.

It will be found that most confrontation situations can be easily classified into one category or other, but such is the subtlety of the employment interview that its various stages, not necessarily in sequence, can encompass all categories within the one situation. This is of tremendous importance, for quite often it is vital for the interviewer to identify these various categories during the actual interview in order to remain in control of the situation.

Further, it is also of value to understand the various levels or planes on which the interview takes place:

1   The primary level deals mainly with facts
2   The secondary level deals with both facts and judgements
3   The tertiary (or depth) level deals with motivation and attitudes.

This basic background will help to establish a framework for the interviewer, and from this position he will then be able to develop his own pattern and style to suit the interview situation which he will have to handle.

Setting up the interview

There are three equally important aspects to be taken into account when considering this task. They are the administrative back-up, the physical setting and the social setting.

Administrative back-up

Sufficient attention is not paid to the detailed arrangements that are a necessary preliminary to the actual interview. On the pure documentation side all relevant papers for each interviewee must be to hand – original letters or copies of all correspondence, application forms, the job description and specification, plus all other documents which contain information which the candidate might want or which the interviewer wishes to pass on to the candidate. While it is quite possible to go to extremes in providing such information, too often the reverse happens to the detriment of all concerned.

It is also vital to ensure that all people to be involved in the interview process are given adequate warning and briefing. This must include internal staff such as receptionists, security officers, secretaries or personnel clerks who have the very considerable responsibility for greeting those who may ultimately become employees of the same organisation.

The question of domestic arrangements should not be neglected either. Awkward situations can arise through lack of foresight or experience, in dealing with travel arrangements, overnight accommodation where necessary, and prompt reimbursement of travelling expenses.

All these considerations are not just chores, but contribute to the interview situation by setting the tone to the meeting. This is just as important to the craftsman or operative applicant as it is to potential general managers.

The physical setting

Privacy is a prime requirement, rather than the scale or type of furnishings, for nothing can be more disturbing or distracting to both the interviewer and interviewee than being knowingly overheard. While in a certain sense the interview has a social context, it is nevertheless a business meeting. Therefore the furnishing of the room has to be functional, especially if it is a room that has been specifically designated as an interview room. Should the interview take place in an office it may well be necessary to reflect upon such things as tidiness, positioning of chairs and desks, taking the internal telephone off the hook, and turning off loudspeakers. Privacy includes avoidance of interruptions as well!

Social setting

The tone of the interview is as important to the interviewer as to the interviewee. While conditions of physical discomfort can assist in setting the appropriate tone, nevertheless every effort must be made to establish rapport with the candidate. This can be summed up in the one word 'consideration'. If this ingredient is missing, then the chances are that the objective of the meeting will not be achieved unless a deliberate stress situation has been brought about for a specific purpose. It is a good tactic to try to establish cordial relationships with candidates by setting the necessary tone during the exchange of letters. It is also important to ensure that necessary courtesies are extended to candidates during any waiting period which may have to elapse before they are seen. Feelings of being isolated or ignored can so easily be aroused in candidates through inattention or lack of foresight as to what can happen during the waiting period. Once a candidate has been placed in this position, it does take a tremendous amount of effort and time to overcome these effects and bring the situation on to an even keel.

Conducting the interview

While of necessity the discussion so far has been about the employment interview, it is nevertheless most important to define the context of the particular interview in question. For example, five different contexts can be defined:

1 Preliminary interview which may well only be concerned with meeting a person in order to exchange information and form initial judgements
2 Background information – where the purposes could be merely to record all relevant detail about a person in preparation for another situation. One such example is assisting a candidate to complete an application form
3 Discussion situation where the main objective is to elaborate on information already available and to talk around potential or real problems
4 Stress interview, where the requirement is to put pressure on a candidate in order to achieve a certain objective. In reality if a candidate is subjected to pressure and stress and reacts favourably to it, the only valid conclusion is that the candidate is capable of coping with stress and pressure in that context only. It is highly dangerous to generalise from this particular situation and claim that the candidate is capable of withstanding pressure and stress in general. The way in which the candidate has handled the situation is probably of more significance and value than anything else
5 Group situation – where a candidate is facing a number of interviewers at

the same time. This can easily develop into an uncontrolled situation, where the only person to benefit will be the candidate – for he always acts on his own behalf, and therefore will be the only consistent factor in the situation.

These then are some of the different contexts in which an interviewer can find himself. When the context has been defined the interviewer has to decide on which level he wants to operate, and also he has to determine the style which he is going to adopt. The levels have been discussed earlier, but in terms of style there are fundamentally three choices: directed, non-directed and probing.

Directed

This involves direct questions which require definite answers. There are always circumstances within employment interview situations which demand the adoption of this style, but there are also occasions when this is the style necessary for the total interview. It is especially appropriate with school leavers, with applications who have complicated job histories and when there is a suggestion that 'facts' may be in dispute.

Non-directed

This means asking open questions which allow the respondent to choose an answer. This is the best way of searching out a person's real views on a particular matter, or to allow the person to project into a situation and develop a point of view. When using this approach it is useful to develop the technique of promoting. While each interviewer will develop his own pattern, the subtle prompt – 'and so, then what happened' – places a real burden on the respondent to continue with the story, or to reveal something which was not intended.

Probing

This style of interview covers and recovers the same ground by different questions. In many situations the interviewer needs to check on work done, or claimed to have done, or to check on apparent or real inconsistencies in the job history or even on attitudes displayed which may not be in character.

It is certainly true to say that these three styles are not mutually exclusive, nevertheless it is important that the interviewer should make a positive decision to adopt a certain style. But in addition the interviewer should develop an awareness and sensitivity to the interview situation which will assist him to change styles during the course of the interview without losing control.

However, practice makes perfect, and indeed a great deal of experience is required before the interviewer can intentionally change style, and purposely lose control and still achieve his objective.

A few words about control are necessary. In the majority of cases the interviewer starts off in control of the situation and if he is to achieve his ends, he must remain in control. However there are many occasions when the interviewee will try to assert himself and assume control. These attempts can be thwarted relatively simply by a rapid change of subject, offering the interviewee a cigarette (especially if he is already smoking one), or asking an innocuous question like the date of his wedding anniversary, or even why he is married or not married. The main element here is the buying of time to re-group one's thoughts and to recommence the questioning along the lines one wants to.

Every interview has its own sequence but there are five distinct aspects of the employment interview which must now be discussed:

1 Opening
2 Giving and receiving of information
3 Recording
4 Guiding
5 Closing.

Opening

In any sales training programme a great deal of attention is paid to developing a salesman's skill both in opening and closing a sales 'interview'. The same degree of attention must also be paid to the employment interview – opening and closing.

In opening the interviewer must attempt to put the interviewee at his ease, and also at the same time to win his confidence. Normal courtesies form a base from which to operate, and it is important to get the interviewe to speak about something in order merely to loosen his vocal chords – the squeaky hesitant voice or dominant aggressive tone must be eliminated at the outset before it forms an important part of the interchange between the parties. A useful opening 'gambit' is to outline the time limits for the interview, or to clear any domestic problems over travelling, or best of all to try to establish a common link with the interviewee which assists in forming a bond between the two people. This latter gambit must be free from any social or racial overtones. In addition the interviewer must be able to conceal any prejudice, particularly in relation to ethnic origin, forms of dress, regional speech, sex or physical appearance. Conversely he must not appear to be attracted by affinities – old school ties, the shapely form of a potential secretary, or someone who smokes the same brand of tobacco, or who plays a certain sport. Apparent objectivity is the keynote to establish at the outset.

Giving and receiving of information

The why, what, where, whom and how – this is the kernel of the interview situation. It is at this point that the quality of the preparatory work is tested. If this preparation has been reasonably thorough, then the interviewer will be able to answer most questions; however it is an invariable rule of the professional recruiter not to stretch the truth too much, and to openly admit that an answer cannot be provided if that is the case. An honest approach to difficult or unanswerable questions or problems will be accepted by the interviewee on most occasions.

While one must always give the candidate every opportunity to ask pertinent questions, the interviewer must make sure that he has enough time to check all relevant details of the candidate's background and work history.

Recording

In many situations a great deal of information about the candidate will have been recorded already – either in correspondence or on an application form. However, interviewers can never hope to remember the answers to all the questions put to the candidate; therefore it is necessary to have some policy and method for making notes during the interview. Most candidates will expect this, but it must be done in the least obtrusive way possible. A common document for all interview situations is useful, particularly one which allows the interviewer to complete a preliminary assessment after the candidate has departed. One such example is shown in Figure 49.2. Quite often it is suggested that a person cannot really do more than one thing at a time, but the proficient interviewer should be capable of asking questions, listening closely to the answers and taking notes at the same time. However there are times when something is missed, and in those situations the interviewer must be strong enough to ask the candidate to repeat his answer.

Guiding

This is part of the control process, nevertheless it is important to keep the discussion within bounds both of subject and time. It is really surprising how often candidates are allowed to ramble on on unimportant points, and this then leads to pressure on time, with an inevitable dropping of standards. It must be stressed that the interviewer is in the driving seat and therefore can and must guide the candidate and the discussion along the appropriate lines.

Closing

This is possibly one of the most difficult parts of the interview to handle effectively. The interviewer must be absolutely sure of what he has to do to end the interview. A lot obviously depends on the actual place of the interview in the selection procedure, but it is very easy to mishandle the situation and promote unnecessary uncertainty and suffering in the candidate. Above all a positive approach must be taken and the candidate made aware of the position; e.g. he will be receiving a letter to let him know the outcome within 10 days; or his name will be placed on the short list; or you are sorry but you will not be able to take his application any further; or will he be good enough to wait in reception while you contact the next interviewer.

The 'silent' interview

Before going on to what might logically be described as the next step – namely the assessment – a short pause is required to think upon what may be described as the 'silent' interview. During the actual interview, while the participants have been talking, a great deal of non-verbal interaction has taken place, and this takes place on two planes – the psychological and the physical. Some of the relevant points have already been touched upon, but it is necessary to draw the attention of all interviewers to the non-verbal aspects of the situation.

First the psychological aspect; each of the participants will bring in to the interview certain expectations – to sell himself well, to gain a good under-

GHM

Date:	Time:	Ref. Number:
Name:	Age:	Job:

Education, training and qualifications

Impact

Appearance

Relevant experience

Personal

Figure 49.2 Interview notes

standing of the candidate, to show them just what a good chap he is, to demonstrate yet again that the candidate cannot put one across him.

There will also be individual prejudices and biases which will colour the situation. Irrational fears often promote feelings of inadequacy in candidates, while on the other hand interviewers are susceptible to 'halo' effects and stereotypes.

Next the physical aspect; apart from the actual interview surroundings which, depending on the colour scheme can convey a sense of lightness (pastel shades) or of depression (brown and battleship grey), the degree of comfort or austerity contributes in some measure to the quality of the interview. Physical proximity and position – chairs too near for comfort, especially with a fidgety person – can soon lead to a situation of unease without a single word being spoken. Gestures and postures provide a visual means of communication either emphasising or qualifying a verbal statement. Eye movements can also be important in establishing and maintaining contact, although most people tend to comment adversely on the person who is 'shifty-eyed'. This is very similar to the 'limp handshake' phenomenon. Voice expression conveys its own message which need not be connected with the words used. Especial care needs to be taken with the person who hesitates or stammers.

Awareness of these factors is most important for the person new to employment interviewing, for by being aware one can be on one's guard, and with experience gradually learn to cope with and interpret such phenomena.

Assessment

At the conclusion of each interview it is necessary to stop and think, and ideally to make an initial assessment of the candidate. This can be done quite quickly and effectively by using the outlines of the seven point plan as in Figure 49.3. The value of this initial assessment cannot be over-stressed, especially when there is a considerable time interval or delay between interviewing candidates and the final decision.

	GHM
Name:	**Age:**	**Job:**
Impact and appearance	very good/good/acceptable/poor
Training and qualifications	very good/good/acceptable/poor
Other abilities	very good/good/acceptable/poor
Motivation	very good/good/acceptable/poor
Adjustment	very good/good/acceptable/poor
Experience	very good/good/acceptable/poor
Assessment (all factors)	very suitable/suitable/reserve/ unsuitable

Figure 49.3 Initial assessment and interview summary
This list should be attached to the interview notes

The five-point plan developed by J. Munro Fraser from the initial seven-point plan devised by the National Institute of Industrial Psychology and A. Rodger draws the interviewer's attention to five separate points that need to be observed, discussed, and finally assessed. These points are:

First impressions (and physical make-up)
Qualifications (and expectations)
(Brains and) abilities
Motivation
Adjustment

The scale attached to each of these factors is rather crude, but nevertheless it provides a framework, and the basic simplicity of the five point plan is so attractive in this context that in these days of sophistication it does tend to be overlooked. But by this method the interviewer is able to summarise his thoughts, make an initial judgement (qualified if necessary in his notes) and then turn his attention to the next step of the selection procedure.

Administering appropriate tests

A great deal of space in management literature has been devoted to arguing the case for and against using tests of various kinds in the selection process. Although it does not generally appear under this sort of heading, the most common test applied is the medical one, whether it be a screening by a trained nurse before engaging operators for a food factory, or a full blown medical conducted at the medical centre of the Institute of Directors. The case for even this test can be argued both ways, although enacted legislation does tend to set some basic parameters. Nevertheless most companies or organisations have a reasonable defined policy and practice to follow, and therefore guidance is probably already available to the recruiter.

However, in non-medical areas questions inevitably arise over the value of using tests in the selection process. In many instances a case can be made for using appropriate tests, especially where there is already sufficient information available to establish the validity of the tests in that particular context. But a word of warning is necessary, for certain safeguards have been introduced by the National Foundation for Education Research in England and Wales, in conjunction with the British Psychological Association, into the administration of many tests in the United Kingdom. Where there are any possible problems over the use of tests in a selection or management development situation, reference to the above bodies, to a qualified person, to the test constructors or to an organisation such as Independent Assessment and Research Centre is a must.

What can tests test? Skills like manual dexterity, intelligence, aptitudes, abilities, interests, colour blindness and various aspects of the personality are some of the areas where additional and important information can be gained about candidates in order to make a full and final assessment about their suitability for the job in question.

Managerial level

This is an area where the impact of an individual personality can make a great deal of difference – both positive and negative. In terms of tests, therefore, thought must be given to the main personality characteristics which can contribute to successful performance, and to those which could be contra indicators, i.e. would detract from successful performance. Abilities, interests and aptitudes are important especially in making decisions about people who are starting out on a managerial career for the first time, and especially at this time when many people are likely to find themselves switching career paths once, twice, or even three times in their working life. Therefore in constructing a test package for a particular selection procedure leading to a managerial post, professional advice must be sought, and due weight given to professional opinions in the final assessment.

Clerical and technical

Here typing and shorthand skills are obvious, but in many routine clerical jobs tasks such as checking information against source documents are important. Tests of accuracy are available, and indeed, with the growth of mechanised accounting systems and computers, quite a number of tests of proven validity have been constructed and developed. Sometimes it is important to administer even simple arithmetic and verbal comprehension tests which can be constructed to suit the local situation, provided of course that the recruiter knows what he is trying to achieve.

Operational

Tests for would-be apprentices, dilutee craftsmen, plant operators and assemblers are available to those qualified to use them correctly and interpret the results properly. The test as to their acceptability is one which can only be resolved in each individual situation. But since a great deal of time is required in training those selected to do the job properly, the use of tests must often be justified on financial grounds.

While most tests give detailed instructions on procedure, test administration is nevertheless important, and the recruiter should make certain that he achieves as near to optimum conditions as possible for all test sessions. The correct physical conditions and the right psychological tone are essential to good test performance by the candidates, and if these conditions are not available then the test session can become a futile exercise in apparent sophistication. A guarantee as to the confidentiality of the result is highly important to candidates, and the approach to be encouraged is that of the medical profession in dealing with personal information of this nature.

Making the appointment

The moment of decision has arrived! Again it must be stressed that the decision to offer the position to one of the candidates is one-sided, and until the offer has been accepted, the recruitment task has not been completed.

At this stage the 'evidence' on all the candidates should be available for review and final assessment. In all probability, at least two people will be concerned in the final decision, and in most cases they should meet together to discuss the matter as fully as necessary. Sometimes one candidate stands out among all others, and consequently the decision comes easily. But on many occasions a 'debate' occurs with an informal cataloguing of the pros and cons, and inevitably some sort of compromise has to be made in relation to the 'ideal' job description and candidate specification prepared at the beginning of the recruitment and selection process. Indeed in filling some positions the selection decision is made, not by comparing candidate against candidate, but by assessing the only candidate in relation to the specification.

The important point here is to approach the decision making session in a systematic way, so that the reasons for the choice of one candidate and the rejection of the others become quite clear. No one should be afraid of stating and if necessary restating that a liking for a candidate has tipped the scales in his favour. As Robert Townsend says in *Up the Organization*, 'The important thing about hiring is the chemistry of the vibrations between boss and candidate; good, bad, or not there at all'. Any manager who denies this truism has already reached his level of incompetence.

Having made the decision, this must be conveyed in written form to the successful candidate. The formal offer of employment should always be qualified with the phrase 'subject to obtaining satisfactory references', unless of course references have already been obtained. No self respecting potential employee will accept and act upon a mere verbal offer, and until an acceptance letter has been received the process has not been completed. It is also useful at this stage to clear with the appointee any remaining matters relating to the conditions under which he will be employed.

STAGE THREE: THE FOLLOW-THROUGH

Introducing the new employee to the organisation

Any new employee will require a period of familiarisation before he can begin to perform his job properly. In many cases it is possible to set up a formal introductory course through which new employees learn about the policies and practices of the organisation. Sometimes it is possible to put a number of employees through the same course, while for others the introduction will have to be tailor-made. The major aim of induction, whether conducted on a formal basis or informally by the new employee's boss, is to integrate the newcomer as soon as possible. This is not an altruistic concept, but is based on sound economics, for the sooner a person is settled the sooner performance reaches standard.

Perhaps the best basis from which to start the induction process is the question: what does the newcomer want or need to know? A programme of induction must cover such matters as conditions of employment, departmental information, general health and safety. Remember also that new employees will find it difficult to assimilate a mass of information at one sitting, and a suitable time scale should therefore be devised.

For induction programmes at technical, supervisory or managerial level, a useful guide is to be found in the pamphlet *Induction – Acclimatizing People to Work* by W. R. Marks, published by the Institute of Personnel Management. However, the important principle to bear in mind is that the programme must be constructed around the requirements of the job to be done, and the time scale must also be realistic, for most newcomers just want to settle down and prove their worth.

Following up the progress of the new employee

This is of specific importance where a probationary period of employment (not more than 12 weeks) has to be served successfully before confirmation of the appointment takes place. In these cases a formal procedure has to be adopted in order to maintain adequate records and background information for the decision which has to be taken. If the review takes place on a weekly or monthly basis then the employee should be given some idea of what progress he or she is making. This need not be on a formal basis, for given good supervisors, the effect of an 'informal chat' can result in either a mending of the ways or a spurring to even better performance.

In general terms though, contact needs to be maintained with new employees until it becomes quite apparent that they have settled down and become part of the team. This contact between the recruiter, the new employee and his boss can be of considerable benefit in developing an awareness, in the recruiter, especially of the sorts of people who successfully survive the hesitation of the first week or month and become settled members of the company or organisation. In looking at labour turnover figures it is not surprising to note that in many instances most of the leavers quit within the first three months of being employed. There is therefore a real economic meaning and purpose to follow up after induction.

Reviewing and evaluating the recruitment and selection process

In basic terms most organisations check their recruitment and selection methods on the exception principle – the new recruit who doesn't fit in becomes the stick with which the recruiter is beaten about the head, no matter how many 'successes' can be listed! However it is possible to examine the actual methods by which the final decision is reached in a more objective way. Such questions must be asked: Are we advertising the vacancy properly? Are we attracting the right sort of candidates? Are we treating the candidates in the right way? Have we got the right system for obtaining the preliminary information about the job? Generally are the candidate specifications lucid enough? Are we getting the right sort of information about candidates from the tests we use? How long do new employees of various categories stay with us? Is this a result of over or under recruitment?

The answers to some of these questions will give an indication of what is going on in the selection process, and provide a reasonably sound base for further improvements.

In respect of the competence of the recruiter himself, it is to the advantage of the organisation itself to ensure that its 'gate-keepers' can discriminate (in the nicest possible sense) between those who should or should not be admitted. Apart from professional competence as an employment interviewer and a test administrator, the recruiter must be able to maintain the confidence of his peers and colleagues within the company, as well as enjoy the confidence of the candidates who come in front of him. Integrity is a vital word in this context both from a professional and personal point of view as far as the recruiter is concerned. Indeed all managers eventually build up a 'track-record' on their effectiveness in taking on the right people for the tasks in hand.

Finally it must be stated that most companies and organisations are now beginning to realise that the recruitment of the necessary human resources requires the same attention, effort, and concentration as purchasing essential raw materials, plant and supplies. In the last analysis it is people who, collectively or individually, make or break the company as a viable concern. The cost and effectiveness of the recruitment and selection process must be a major concern for top management, especially as the annual company report now contains the average numbers of people employed over the year and the amount of wages and salaries paid to them. In the last analysis, value for money is the unspoken question in the selection decision.

FURTHER READING

Higham, M., *The ABC of Interviewing*, IPM, London, 1979
Plumbley, P., *Recruitment and Selection*, 2nd edition, IPM, London, 1976
Ungerson, B. (ed.), *Recruitment Handbook*, 3rd edition, Gower, 1983

APPENDIX: THE IPM RECRUITMENT CODE *

In 1980, as a result of discussion through the columns of the *Financial Times*, the Institute of Personnel Management was prompted to publish the Recruitment Code. The Code was produced after much debate and heart searching amongst interested parties, recruiters and applicants alike. Its declared aim is 'to set down briefly and clearly guidance on those matters which most commonly cause resentment to recruiters and applicants. The faults are most often the result of inexperience or thoughtlessness, rarely the result of deliberate intent'.

The Recruitment Code sets out the obligations as follows:

Recruiters' obligations

1   Job advertisements will state clearly the form of reply desired (for example curriculum vitae, completed application form), and any preference for handwritten applications.
2   An acknowledgement or reply will be made promptly to each applicant by the employing organisation or its agent.
3   Candidates will be informed of the progress of the selection procedure, what this will be, the time likely to be involved and the policy regarding expenses.
4   Detailed personal information (for example religion, medical history, place of birth, family background, etc.), will not be called for unless and until it is relevant to the selection process.
5   Before applying for references, potential employers will secure the permission of the applicant.
6   Applications will be treated as confidential.

Applicants' obligations

1   Advertisements will be answered in the way requested (for example telephone for application form, provide brief details, send curriculum vitae, etc.).
2   Appointments and other arrangements will be kept, or the recruiter be informed promptly if the candidate discovers an agreed meeting cannot take place.
3   The recruiter will be informed as soon as a candidate decides not to proceed with the application.
4   Only accurate information will be given in applications and in reply to recruiters' questions.
5   Information given by a prospective employer will be treated as confidential, if so requested.

* Reproduced with kind permission from the Institute of Personnel Management, IPM House, Camp Road, Wimbledon, London SW19 4UW.

Sticking to the Code is a matter for personal choice, but nevertheless it is a valid and necessary statement of guidelines which deserve to be adopted by all engaged in the recruitment process. It has a particular value for those who become involved infrequently.

50 Salary management

Irene Innes

Companies employing up to fifty staff normally have an informal salary policy – and rightly so. However, when total staff exceed this number, anomalies begin to appear in the system and some form of framework is necessary. This is particularly so when rapid expansion is taking place.

Although there must be a co-ordinator, the responsibility for salary management is that of line management. What is needed therefore is a salary policy laying down administrative parameters within which discretion may be exercised and providing salary ranges based on simple job evaluation.

Involvement of line managers at this point is essential in order that they recognise the need for regularising salary management and make a positive contribution towards drawing up a salary policy.

EXAMPLE OF A SALARY POLICY STATEMENT

Introduction

The aim of this document is to set down the company's policy with regard to salary. It is the responsibility of all who apply it to explain it fully to their subordinates.

Aims

The aims of the company's policy are:

1 To recognise the value of all jobs relative to each other within the company and in comparison with similar jobs outside
2 To recognise the value of the individual to the company and to relate this to the salary range applicable to his or her job.

The foregoing is subject to government legislation, as appropriate.

901

Salary structure

The salary structure will be based on job evaluation. Each job will have a declared minimum and maximum salary range and it is the company's policy to pay at least the minimum for each job.

Job evaluation

It is the policy of the company to ensure that staff are fully involved in job evaluation, including representation on the job evaluation committee.

Job evaluation is a continuing process and once salary grades have been established, the committee will met regularly to deal with re-evaluating existing jobs as well as evaluating new jobs.

Initial salary

In determining an individual's salary on appointment, no differentiation is made on the grounds of sex. In addition, the following features are taken into account:

1 The value to the company of the relevant experience he or she brings
2 The individual's value in the outside market
3 The individual's value compared with existing staff who hold similar jobs.

Performance appraisal

An integral part of salary management is the regular appraisal of staff. This is the basis on which management counsels individuals in order that everyone has maximum opportunity to develop his or her own potential. In order that individuals utilise their abilities to the full, short and longer term objectives will be mutually agreed with management.

Salary reviews

It is the policy of the company to review quarterly the salaries of all staff under the age of eighteen years. At age eighteen years and over, all staff salaries will be reviewed annually. Performance increases, if any, will be paid effective from 1 April.

Promotion

When an individual is promoted to higher-grade work, his or her salary will be increased by 10 per cent or she will be paid the minimum for the new grade, whichever is the greater. If the individual fails to measure up to the needs of the new job, he or she will be made aware of his or her shortcomings and given an opportunity to improve and, failing this, to move to a more suitable job. If this results in moving to work of a lower grade there will be no salary decrease. Instead there will be a salary standstill until the rate for the new position equals that of the old.

Progression within salary range

Everyone will know the salary range for his or her job. Those who do their job particularly well will reach the maximum for their salary range within four years.

Long-serving staff who are already on their salary ceiling will be subject to a salary review every third year to a maximum of six years.

Grievance procedure

Anyone who feels that his or her salary indicates that an injustice has been done has the right to appeal first to his or her manager and then to the managing director whose decision will be final. The individual has a right to bring along a colleague to help support his or her appeal.

Communication

As important as the preparation of a salary policy is the need to communicate it to everyone concerned: indeed there is no reason why every staff member should not have a copy of the actual policy statement.

By far the best way of passing on information is for each departmental manager to call a briefing meeting with all his or her staff to explain what the policy covers and, more important, how it will affect each individual. Care should be taken that each employee's questions are answered sympathetically and honestly. Employees should also be fully aware of the company's intentions regarding possible salary anomalies.

JOB DESCRIPTIONS

In every company there are formal and informal arrangements about who reports to whom and how work is done. It is important, therefore, to establish and seek agreement on an organisation or accountability chart. Job titles can be very misleading and some renaming may be necessary. This in turn involves the writing of *job descriptions*.

A job description is a basic statement covering such features as:

Job title
Department
To whom responsible
Date
Tasks/areas of responsibility
Job titles of subordinates
Training and/or experience required for job.

The completed description must be agreed by both the job holder and his supervisor. (Where disagreements arise, the grievance procedure should be operated.)

A specimen job description follows.

Speciment job description

Position: Secretary to Chief Mechanical Engineer
Department: Project Engineering
Date:
Overall Aim: To provide a complete secretarial service to Chief Mechanical Engineer by organising the routine aspects of his work.

Daily tasks:

1 On receipt of mail, sort into order of priority, attach previous correspondence, if any, and type routine letters for signature
2 Take dictation from Chief Mechanical Engineer and deal also with urgent correspondence dictated by senior mechanical engineers
3 Against a tight timetable, type complicated statistical tables connected with department's project work
4 Deal with department's travel arrangements and prepare travel itineraries
5 Maintain simple time records concerning progress of experimental projects. Ensure that progress charts are kept up to date
6 Act as an assistant to Chief Mechanical Engineer by dealing with the more routine aspects of his work
7 Act as a 'shield' by dealing with callers personally and on the telephone.

Weekly tasks:

1 Prepare for accountant short summary of personal expenses incurred by department during previous week, and allocate to individual projects.

Monthly tasks:

1 Collect brief reports prepared by senior engineers on their respective projects and type draft of progress report for the Project Engineering Director.

Six-monthly tasks:

1 Transfer old files to basement and make out new files for next six months.

Annually:

1 Type statement of account showing income over expenditure on previous year's projects:

Minimum age:	Twenty-one years
Educational qualifications:	Five 'O' levels (including English Language) and secretarial college training
Experience:	Three years' practical office experience including one year in a similar firm
Induction:	Three months

Other information: The Chief Mechanical Engineer is frequently off site and the job holder is expected to deal with all routine problems arising during such absences

JOB EVALUATION

Many companies avoid installing job evaluation because they feel it is either too costly or too sophisticated. This need not be the case. Two methods should be considered as practicable:

1 Ranking
2 Job classification.

Ranking involves the study of each job description and placing it in order of importance. Note that it is the *job* which is being graded and *not* the person doing it. Here is a likely plan of attack:

1 Constitute a committee of, say, three people who have a good knowledge of all the jobs being covered
2 Select about 15–20 jobs as being a good representative sample of all the jobs being covered. These are the benchmark or key jobs and form the basis of job evaluation
3 Write job descriptions of the benchmarks
4 Separately rank those jobs in order of importance and seek agreement with other committee members
5 Design a job questionnaire (see Figure 50.1)
6 Brief all employees on how they should complete the questionnaires (see Specimen briefing notes below)
7 Ensure that all questionnaires are agreed by the respective supervisors
8 The committee finally slot in jobs according to benchmarks to reach an overall rank order.

Specimen briefing notes

Introduction

Job evaluation is a method of looking objectively at jobs and ranking them in order of importance. By comparing them one with another, each job will be placed in a salary grade relative to its worth. However, it must be stressed that it is the *job* which is being considered and *not* the individual.

A job evaluation committee has been formed under the chairmanship of Andrew Brown, the company secretary. The other members of the committee are Alan Garnett and Jill Pepperell.

The scheme

After a great deal of investigation, the committee has decided to use a classification or grading scheme, a copy of which is described later in this chapter.

```
                                                        GHM

  Job title        _____

  Department      _____

  Responsible to_____

  Agreed by       _____  Date_____


  1  What is the overall objective of the job?



  2  Draw up a family tree showing the job in perspective



  3  Give a concise description of the main areas of responsibility in the job. Take it
     area by area and stress the important features
     Daily tasks



     Weekly tasks


     Monthly tasks

     Quarterly tasks


```

Figure 50.1   Job questionnaire

1 *Overall objective.*   One sentence will normally suffice here. It should be concise and give the reason for the job's existence in order that the committee has 'something to hang its cap on' before looking at the job in depth. For example:

> Process all orders ensuring that departmental computer data codes are included and that the VAT figure is correct

2 *Family tree.*   A clearer picture of your job is given if you draw up a family tree of your department showing your job in relation to all other jobs

Figure 50.1 (continued)

3 *Job description.* It is always difficult to write one's own job description: consider therefore that you are transferring to another department in the company and that you must prepare a note for your successor covering the main elements of the job. Describe the job as it is now and not how it should be. Do not be afraid to go into detail.

Write down the area headings first, such as correspondence, planning, queries, staff; and describe the responsibility involved under each heading. For example:

> Correspondence – on receipt of mail, decide what can be delegated to subordinates and retain non-routine letters. Where necessary give instructions regarding the handling of particular letters.

4 *Supervisory responsibility.* Supervisory responsibility can only be assessed fairly by examining carefully the job descriptions of those jobs under his or her

jurisdiction. By looking at the situation as a whole, the supervisory aspect should be accorded its proper degree of responsibility.

5 *Contacts.* The strength of the company lies in the service given to customers. This does not diminish the value of internal contacts. What is important is the level at which contact is normally made and the reason for contact in the first place.

6 *Qualifications and/or experience.* Comment should be made here regarding the minimum qualifications and/or experience which must be brought to the job *before* it can be done effectively. It may be possible to state an actual qualification or the job may simply call for 'an aptitude for figures'. Experience required must be quite specific. For example: six months' practical experience in credit control.

7 *Other information.* No questionnaire can possibly cover all aspects of a job and since it is important that every member of staff has the opportunity to comment on all areas of the job which are important, space is provided for this. For example:

Large proportion of work is concerned with meeting tight time schedules

These comments should cover features which are an integral part of the job and not temporary difficulties.

Completion date for questionnaires. All questionnaires must be completed and returned to Jill Pepperell by Monday 29 January.

Completion date for job evaluation exercise. With the co-operation of everyone, the committee hopes to complete the evaluation exercise by 15 March.

Right of appeal. Any member of staff who feels his or her job has not been fairly evaluated has the right to appeal to the committee through his or her head of department. The individual can then expect to be invited, along with his or her head of department to discuss the job in detail with the members of the committee.

Paired comparisons

An extension of ranking – *paired or forced comparisons* – should be considered. Each job is compared with every other job and decision is made about which job is the more important. An example of a paired comparison is given in Figure 50.2.

A word of warning: fifty jobs is the maximum number that can be ranked manually.

Once this is done, a matrix is drawn up showing the jobs in rank order (see Figure 50.3).

Grading/classification

Grading/classification is a means whereby jobs are separated into

GHM

	Accounts clerk	Invoice typist	Receptionist/ telephonist	Wages clerk	Messenger	Costing clerk	Director's secretary	Shorthand typist	Stock clerk	Sales Clerk
Accounts clerk	X	1	0	0	2	0	0	0	1	0
Invoice typist	1	X	0	0	2	0	0	0	1	0
Receptionist/ telephonist	2	2	X	1	2	1	0	1	2	1
Wages clerk	2	2	1	X	2	1	0	1	2	1
Messenger	0	0	0	0	X	0	0	0	0	0
Costing clerk	2	2	1	1	2	X	0	1	2	1
Director's secretary	2	2	2	2	2	2	X	2	2	2
Shorthand typist	2	2	1	1	2	1	0	X	2	1
Stock clerk	1	1	0	0	2	0	0	0	X	0
Sales clerk	2	2	1	1	2	1	0	1	1	X

Figure 50.2   Ranking chart

Reading from the left, compare each job in turn with every other job shown along the top. If the job is more important, insert 2; if equally important, insert 1; if less important, insert 0. For example in this chart an accounts clerk is considered less important than a receptionist, more important than a messenger and the same as an invoice typist

natural/homogenous groups on a whole-job basis. This is achieved by:

1 Writing 15–20 benchmark job descriptions
2 Ranking them
3 Marking natural 'break points' between those jobs which have the same relative work
4 Defining in short paragraph form the common features of those jobs in each group
5 Writing job descriptions for the remaining jobs and matching them against the appropriate grade/classification definition.

	GHM								
Director's secretary	2	2	2	2	2	2	2	2	2
Receptionist/telephonist		2	2	2	2	1	1	1	1
Wages clerk		2	2	2	2	1	1	1	1
Costing clerk		2	2	2	2	1	1	1	1
Shorthand Typist		2	2	2	2	1	1	1	1
Sales clerk		2	2	2	2	1	1	1	1
Invoice typist							2	1	1
Stock clerk							2	1	1
Accounts clerk							2	1	1
Messenger									0

Figure 50.3 **Job evaluation matrix**
Derived from the ranking chart shown in Figure 50.2

Example of a grading or classification scheme

Grade 1 Tasks are simple and conform to clearly laid down procedures. No training or experience required. Continually supervised. All written work and calculations are checked. Up to a few weeks' training required.

Grade 2 Tasks are subject to laid-down procedures but can involve a limited measure of initiative. Work subject to spot checks. Up to six months' training or experience required.

Grade 3 Tasks are carried out and decisions made in accordance with standard procedures, subject to infrequent supervision. Routine contact, external – and internal – up to own level to obtain and provide information. Probably minimum of two years' experience.

Grade 3 Tasks are carried out and decisions made in accordance with standard procedures, subject to infrequent supervision. Routine contact, externally and internally, up to own level to obtain and provide information. Probably minimum of two years' experience.

Grade 4 After specific direction, plans and arranges work within main work programme with little or no supervision. Only non-routine problems referred to superior. May have supervisory responsibility. Can have contact at higher level than own, externally and internally, to obtain and give information which may be of a confidential nature. Specialised knowledge may be required. Probably four to five years' experience.

Grade 5 After general direction, plans and arranges work with little or no supervision. Tasks can involve work of a non-routine nature requiring an original approach as to planning and method. Would normally have contact at a higher level than own, externally and internally, to obtain and give information which may be of a confidential nature. Can be required to make decisions as to daily action and direct work of subordinates. More than five years' experience required.

SALARY BANDS/GRADES

Five grades ought to suffice up to and including supervisory level. To have more will mean that differentials between grades will be reduced and staff will see little financial advantage in taking on more responsibility. Alternatively, the salaries co-ordinator will be faced with an excessive number of appeals for upgrading each time there is a slight increase in responsibility.

In general, jobs will tend to fall into broad groups but there are bound to be some jobs which will cause much soul-searching. The establishing of grades completed, the jobs on either side of the break point must be scrutinised carefully to ensure they are in the right group. In the event of appeals being raised, it is likely that they will spring from this grey area.

Salary ranges

Now comes the problem of allocating actual cash to each band or grade. A number of structures is possible, but a structure like that in Figure 50.4 is recommended for its flexibility.

As will be seen, the salary ceiling is roughtly a 30–50 per cent addition on the base figure and the base for the next grade starts at approximately the midpoint of the previous grade. This means that on promotion an employee may move easily from one grade to another. It also recognises that an employee on his or her ceiling on a grade 3 job is worth more than one about to start on grade 4 work with less experience of the company's business.

Grade	1	£2 500———£3 300			GHM
	2	£2 900———£3 900			
	3	£3 400———£4 550			
	4	£4 000———£5 500			
	5	£5 000———£7 500			

*Figure 50.4 **Salary structure***
Overlapping salary structure

SALARY SURVEYS

Although salary comparison is a continuing exercise, a particular effort must be made to obtain factual information when designing a new salary structure. This can be done in four ways:

1   By consulting national or local salary surveys
2   By telephoning your opposite number in other companies in the area and exchanging information
3   By sending to selected companies a job description from each grade, and asking for a comparison. (It is wise to telephone personally to inquire if the company is willing to take part.) This must be followed up by sending to the participants details of the survey but excluding actual company names
4   By inviting four or five opposite numbers in your area to form a Salary Comparison Club with the first meeting on your premises. An agreed agenda should be drawn up stating the jobs to be discussed in order that salary information is forthcoming.

Even at this point, the salary ranges cannot be thought conclusive until a thorough internal costing is completed.

USE OF GRAPHS

The use of graphs is invaluable when creating a new salary structure. Only when the situation is presented visually do anomalies stand out. Using a bar graph to study the number of people in each grade for instance a crude distribution curve will be obtained, i.e. the bulk of the jobs will likely be in the middle grades.

As an *aid* to determining what jobs should finally be in which grade it is helpful to do a scattergram. (See Figure 50.5.) Here is how it is done:

1   On a graph plot each job holder by basic salary and grade. This will give you the scatter on your current salary structure
2   Draw a (curved) line through the centre of the scatter so that there are roughly the same number of points above as below the line. This will give you the mid-point of each new salary range. (The technical description for the line is 'line of best fit')
3   The pure approach is to fix 15–25 per cent above and below the line the minimum and maximum salary figure for each new salary range
4   The jobs falling above and below the minimum and maximum are, of course, anomalous in the new structure.

DECIDING HOW MUCH TO PAY

You now have a) an external salary survey; and b) a formal salary structure which reflects accurately the *current* company position. It is likely these two aspects require reconciliation.

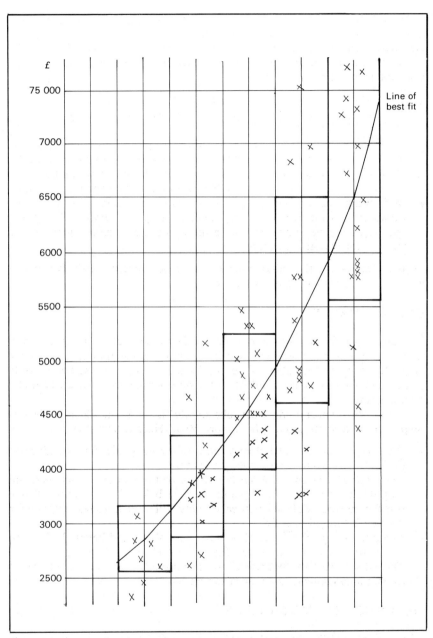

Figure 50.5   Comparison of old and new salary structures

Three terms are used to describe your own position in the marketplace – lower quartile, median and upper quartile. In simple terms, let us say that you have surveyed eight different companies' rates for, say, a wages clerk. These rates are then placed in rank order. Starting from the bottom rate, rate two is the lower quartile, rate four is the median and rate six is the upper quartile. In a bigger sample, the median figure approximates to the average rate as well.

As a *general* rule, the company which chooses to be in the lower quartile tends to have a poorer calibre of staff and consequently more of them to cope with normal business pressures. The reverse is the case with the higher quartile company. Labour turnover is a costly factor not to be viewed lightly.

RATE FOR AGE

Few companies find it useful to retain a rate-for-age scale. It is the experience of a large number of organisations that the inflexibility of such a system, even with merit rating on top, can result in a rapid turnover among staff of high potential.

If however a rate-for-age scale is maintained, care must be exercised to ensure that, on the eighteenth birthday, recognition is made of both the increase in social security contributions and rail travel (if applicable). Otherwise young adults should be paid at least the minimum of the grade applicable to their job.

SALARY ANOMALIES

Once salary grades have been established, it will be found that the majority of staff will be on a salary within the new grade boundaries. However, there will probably be a number of staff who are either over or underpaid. Those underpaid should be brought up to at least the minimum for the grade. Apart from explaining the situation to those staff who are over the maximum for their job grade, the following should be considered:

1 Promotion to higher-grade work
2 Rearrangement of job content in order that some higher-grade work is included
3 Salary standstill until the new rate catches up with the old.

EMPLOYEE BENEFITS

The subject of employee benefits is covered in Chapter 52, but it is worth while to mention that when constructing a new salary structure, consideration must at the same time be given to the adequacy and cash values of existing employee benefits. When conducting a salary survey, therefore, employee benefits must also be taken into account.

Staff accept fringe benefits as a fact of life but different social groups within the company and indeed within the area will view different benefits with varying degrees of interest. Young people are more attracted to a company by the promise of a realistic salary than by the offer of a generous sick pay or pension scheme. Assisted house purchase, membership of a hospital scheme and profit sharing is likely to appeal to management.

In designing the salary structure, therefore, it is important to consider how much influence employee benefits need have on the salary ranges.

DEPARTMENTAL BUDGETS

Every department should have a budget and within this there should be an agreed figure for salaries. This should be decided one year in advance and should take into consideration staff retirements (with recruitment on a lower salary level), promotions and increases in staff complement. It should also take into account a figure to be set aside for salary increases. This can either be an arbitrarily agreed lump sum or, more usually, something like 3-4 per cent, excluding cost-of-living increases.

PERFORMANCE

An integral part of salary management is performance appraisal. Many companies regard appraisal as a management tool for deciding staff potential but it is much more than this. Appraisal is a two way exchange of concerns and aspirations. In the past too much stress has been placed on the assessment of ethereal areas such as initiative, co-operation and judgement and ignoring the *opportunity* individuals have had to display these tendencies. Much more can be gained from a six or twelve monthly counselling session aimed not only at furthering the objects of the company but also developing each individual's potential. If a target has not been achieved, it is far easier to discuss in plain man's terms why this was not accomplished than to comment, 'He's not a born leader – yet!'. But take care . . . It is easy to set targets and not to do a follow up on the due day. Be aware, therefore, that target setting is time consuming: take it seriously or leave it alone. A drop in morale is costly.

SALARY REVIEWS

A review does not necessarily mean that all staff receive a salary increase. Staff over the age of eighteen should have their salary reviewed annually: staff under eighteen should have their salary reviewed six-monthly or even quarterly.

The timing of reviews is important. A review coinciding with Christmas should be avoided if possible. The festive spirit can overcome the managers' commonsense! October and/or April are useful periods to consider. A salary review form is shown in Figure 50.6.

MANAGEMENT SALARIES

Salary management is based on job evaluation and this is difficult when a small number of managers is involved. Furthermore, their jobs will tend to expand considerably if the company is in course of rapid growth. Individual managers are therefore paid a figure which represents their individual worth to the

Confidential

Salary review – 1 April 19XX

Department

GHM

Name	Job title	Age at 31 March	Service at 31 March	Date of last performance increase	Amount	Present salary	Grade	Maximum salary	Proposed increase	New salary	Remarks
Total											

Figure 50.6 Salary Review Form

company. It is unlikely they will have a salary ceiling unless the company's growth is fairly static.

Salary surveys are still necessary though best handled at director level.

Once a company employs fifty managers, including supervisors, then is the time to rationalise management salaries.

FURTHER READING

Bowey, Angela M. (ed.), *Handbook of Salary and Wage Systems,* 2nd edition, Gower, 1982

Lupton, T., and Bowey, Angela M., *Wages and Salaries,* 2nd edition, Gower, 1982

Vernon-Harcourt, A., *Rewarding Management,* Gower, annually.

51 Wage management

Irene Innes

The wage structure must be linked to what the company is trying to achieve. It is not unusual to find a company with a wage structure in direct conflict with the company's overall objectives. For example, a company may plan to produce a high-quality product while at the same time it may have a direct incentive geared to quantity. These questions must be asked:

Apart from profit, what are we in business for?
Where are we going during the next two to three years; in the next five to ten years?
How do we plan to get there?
What influence will these plans have on our wage structure?
How can the wage structure aid the company in meeting its objectives?

From this a business plan is built up, in simple terms, expressing the company's short- and long-term objectives and how these will affect specific areas. It may be, for example, that in two years' time a massive capital investment is planned. In terms of human resources this will probably affect the way work is organised, manning arrangements and job demands. Care must be taken, therefore, to ensure that the new wage structure will form a satisfactory springboard to cater for future developments. Consideration must also be given to the spin-off which will affect the whole company.

Management style

It is necessary to identify what the company's management style is. Is it predominantly autocratic, paternalistic, participative or *laissez-faire?* Incompatibilities arise if a wage structure is implemented in isolation of this major consideration. An autocratic management style for instance is in conflict with a Scanlon/Rucker plan. Since the pay structure expresses to employees how the company values them, a real attempt must be made to draw up a declared wage policy. A framework for a policy statement is given later in this chapter.

CHANGING A WAGE STRUCTURE

The desire to change a wage structure usually springs from an existing structure which management no longer controls. Common features are that the present structure suffers from wage drift, that it has numerous rates which are inequitable in terms of individual contribution and there has been a gradual build-up of 'special' allowances.

Most companies, when faced with the need to change their wage structure, begin by looking for alternative incentives. In reality this is prejudging the issue. The first step should be an initial investigation to ascertain the pressure points which exist in the present structure. Only by discovering the 'lumps and the bumps' in the present system will the way ahead seem clear. A discussion with the senior wages clerk will be an enlightening experience since that individual, more than anyone else, is fully aware of the inadequacies and inequities of the existing system.

Wage analysis

This should be based on a thorough examination of the gross pay earned department by department for, say, a 'typical' week at two points in the year. All special allowances should be examined and the totals expressed as a percentage of labour cost. Consideration should be given to the effectiveness of the incentive element.

Overtime

The number of hours overtime should be broken down and scrutinised to see what indicators exist. Excessive overtime working usually means an unrealistic basic hourly rate. What, for example, would be the result if overtime working were curbed? If overtime earnings were consolidated in the basic rate on the understanding that productivity was maintained, would the need for overtime working cease? And would this be socially acceptable in your locality?

Work study

One of the main reasons why a company decides to change its wage structure is because work study values have worked loose and wage drift has become a dominant feature. For example, is the pace of working closely related to that shown on the time sheets? Too often top management assumes that because performances are high on paper, all is well. If the company's present work study team cannot cope with the situation, the use of consultants should be considered. An alternative is to employ experienced work study personnel on a short-term contract.

Labour turnover

Annual figures should be produced and broken down by department. These figures are normally associated with the social aspects of employment but it is not by any means unknown for a definite correlation to be established between them and the method of payment. For example, it is possible that a very low labour turnover linked to a very high rate of absenteeism indicates that earnings may be unusually high for the area but working conditions are intolerable, leading to low morale: the employees cannot afford to leave. In other words, it is just as problematic to grossly overpay people as to underpay.

Age and sex

On a departmental basis, figures should be produced for both men and women grouping them by age, for example 16–18, 19–25, 26–40; 41–50, 51–60, 61–65, 65+. Men and women in particular age groups have different attitudes to work and how their pay packet should be made up. Additionally, they will have fairly specific ideas about what they are prepared to do to earn £x per week. It is doubtful, for example, whether a middle-aged male work force would be enthusiastic about the introduction for the first time of direct incentives.

Attitude survey

Ideally an attitude survey should be made to ascertain what needs have to be satisfied through a wage structure. What are the employees' attitudes towards the current pay structure and what are their deeper expectations? The pay structure to a large extent determines and reinforces attitudes. Two of the areas a survey ought to highlight are the reasons why employees work for a particular company and what motivates them. Every company has a reputation as an employer and if it has achieved, for example, a 'quick buck' image, it will attract a particular type of employee. Thought must therefore be given to the kind of image the company wants to have and how it plans to achieve it.

What motivates people in your geographical area? What kind of incentives are socially acceptable, for instance? The whole of the Midlands is almost incurably on direct incentives and a firm that works otherwise is viewed with suspicion. In a free bargaining situation, a company introduced a new incentive scheme which theoretically should have increased take-home pay – and the impact was nil! An investigation highlighted the fact that the social custom was for young people to lay their unopened pay packet on the kitchen table each pay day and to receive in turn a fixed amount of pocket money. A little unusual in the 1980s, perhaps, but knowledge of this factor would have saved the company much time and trouble.

The survey should be done by an outside specialist in order to gain the confidence of the work force.

Influence of production method

Insufficient consideration is normally given to the link between the technological aspects of production and how people are paid. It is obvious that this is important and yet many operatives in a machine-controlled situation are on direct incentives intended to make them work faster! Similarly, it is not unusual for a company specialising in one-offs to have a direct incentive scheme which entails on-the-spot bargaining between, say, a rate fixer and a shop steward for every unit produced: the result is a hardening industrial relation climate.

These questions should be asked:

1 Are runs short, long, one-offs?
2 How important is quality, quantity, accuracy, consistency?
3 Is the operation operator- or machine-controlled? And what happens *in practice?*
4 What are the capital investment plans for the next 3–5 years? Will these developments influence pay structure?
5 What are the market pressures? Are there seasonal fluctuations?
6 Can buffer stocks be kept or is the product perishable?
7 How much is lost through scrap? (If the material is reconstituted, cost this.)

JOB EVALUATION

Job evaluation is an essential exercise if a company is to be truly in control of its wage structure. Certainly it is the only answer to leapfrogging pay claims and escalating special allowances.

Job evaluation can be as difficult or as expensive as a company likes to make it. Ranking is quite satisfactory: the basis of job evaluation is ranking anyway and all other methods are, in simple terms, administrative systems which are in aid to maintaining the original rank order of the benchmarks. Points rating is the most commonly used system, however.

Nowadays it is normal for a joint management/union committee to introduce job evaluation though this depends to a large extent on the industrial relations climate. It is important, however, for the committee to be trained before embarking on the exercise.

At the other end of the industrial relations scale, however, is the multi-union situation, or long-established union militancy, or a combination of both. In such a situation, the unions should be consulted regarding their role but they will probably prefer to let management make all the decisions while they reserve the right to object on behalf of their respective members. In any case, such unions are probably accustomed to an autocratic management style and a large dose of participation is just as difficult for the unions to countenance as for line management. Obviously, union participation simplifies the situation but involvement does not guarantee instant success: there will still be appeals. What is important is that job evaluation is regarded as a quite separate situation from negotiating actual rates.

The Industrial Society's book *Job Evaluation* is useful.

LEGISLATION

Two Acts of Parliament are intended to safeguard, among other things, women's wage rates and how they are established:

Equal Pay Act, 1970
Sex Discrimination Act, 1975

In simple terms the legal framework provides for a right of appeal, depending on the case, to an Industrial Tribunal or to the Central Arbitration Committee, for a decision. To avoid such a situation, the following points should be observed:

1   Job evaluation should have been carried out
2   Each job grade should contain jobs carried out by either sex, e.g. there should not be a grade below 'labourer' grade comprising jobs filled entirely by women
3   The jobs in each grade should be 'the same or broadly similar' to each other.

COSTING

The basis of a carefully considered wage structure is sound costing. The company accountant, therefore, has an important role to play. Here are the major areas to be scrutinised for key indicators:

1   Budgeted labour cost for the coming year
2   Trend of total labour cost over the last five years
3   General breakdown of cost of the various wage components which contribute to the total labour cost for, say, the last two years
4   Earnings distribution for each department for 2 typical weeks
5   The unit cost of producing each selling line and the proportion of labour cost attributed
6   Cost of employee benefits. Frequently overlooked, these benefits are nonetheless part of the total labour cost
7   Cost of labour turnover. As a rule of thumb, a routine factory worker who leaves after, say, three months, has probably cost the company approximately £750. This figure includes recruitment costs, interviewing time (allowance must be made for the average number of interviews to fill each job), initial training and a scale linked to the likely contribution an individual will make as his skill and know-how increases. A new employee does not begin to function as a member of a team until one or two weeks have elapsed
8   Cost of absenteeism. (Absenteeism is being used in a wider context than simply illness.) It is a useful pulse to take: if, say, absenteeism is running at a steady 20 per cent, possible causes are overmanning, overpaying or simply low morale. The cost of morale is not a balance sheet item but it is nonetheless an important hidden cost which must not be ignored.

FINANCING THE WAGE STRUCTURE

It is inflationary to set out to design and implement a new wage structure without first agreeing with the unions concerned that the increase in the wage bill must be found from within the company's resources. The actual cost of changing a wage structure is about 5 per cent of the wage bill, excluding cost-of-living for example. At first glance this figure will appear to be high: in effect a redistribution of cash and control is taking place with a short-term gain for the operatives involved and a medium-term gain for management. In a stable economy, no matter how sophisticated a company's techniques and know-how, it is possible to find savings to cover this cost. Of prime importance at the beginning of the exercise is agreement by management and unions on how the savings are to be achieved and shared.

Running concurrently with the initial investigation should be the operation of productivity groups or quality circles bent on finding savings. These groups, under the leadership of their supervisors, should comprise *operatives* meeting on a sectional or departmental basis during working hours or at the end of a shift (on overtime). Their remit should be a broad one where they may discuss every aspect of the organisation and planning of the work in their immediate working area.

While the structure of the groups will depend on the size of the section or department, the numbers meeting at any one time should not exceed eight to ten. A simple record of decisions made should be kept by each group for the sake of continuity and an effort made to communicate this within the group. Training will be necessary to help the groups to assess each problem and to make recommendations. Many companies underestimate the wealth of untapped potential which exists at shop floor level. However, companies which have attempted a similar exercise have discovered that operatives are quite capable of using simple problem solving and costing techniques (for example). Provided the groups understand in essence the services supplied by, say, the company's work study or production engineering specialists, the groups will ask for expert advice if the need arises.

DESIGNING THE WAGE STRUCTURE

Having established the realities of the existing structure, the next step is to design one which will meet the company's needs. The trend is for a company to have a two-tier wage structure: a basic hourly/job rate tier accounting for 80–85 per cent of the wage bill; an incentive tier (if any) accounting for 15–20 per cent.

Number of grades

The trend is to have four to six grades covering all factory personnel. The more straightforward the production process, the less reason for numerous grades. Without prejudicing the situation in the early stages of the investigation, there should be at least £7.50 per week differential between each grade. To have less will act as a disincentive to internal promotion. In effect this means reducing the number of grades to a point where the differential is a significant demonstration that work in a higher grade really is more important to the company. If the pay steps are too small, management will be faced with numerous requests for regrading jobs every time a fraction of responsibility or a grain of dirt is added to the job.

The decision regarding the break point for each grade is largely arbitrary. It will probably be a negotiating point. On the whole, jobs tend to fall into homogeneous groups but no matter where the break points are made, 'grey area' jobs on either side of the line will give rise to much tooth-sucking. It is from this area that job evaluation appeals usually spring.

As an aid to deciding where the break points might be, it is useful to produce some scattergrams showing how, for example, the results of job evaluation compare in relation to job holders' basic rates as well as gross pay (see Figure 51.1). The next step is to determine the 'line of best fit': in simple terms a line is drawn through the centre of the points already plotted. It is then possible to determine roughly what the pay steps might be. In practical terms this is a quite considerable exercise and it may be that a 30 per cent sample, say, of all jobs might suffice.

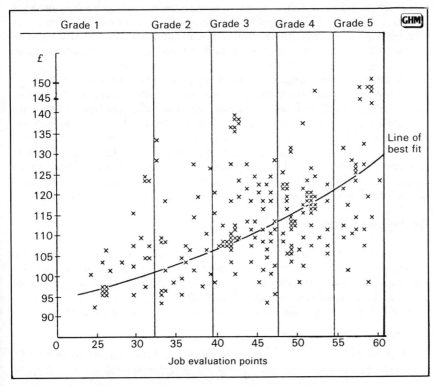

Figure 51.1 *Scattergram of earnings (excluding overtime)*
Related to job evaluation points as well as to possible break even points between grades and new pay steps

Yet another statistical aid is the use of bar graphs. In most companies the bulk of the jobs will be in the middle two grades with roughly the same number in the bottom and top grades.

Deciding the basic rate

Traditionally, manual workers have been in a position where the ratio of basic rate to incentive was 2:1. However, this ratio now tends to be nearer 4:1 largely because companies moving towards single (staff) status are rightly challenging the concept that a manual worker's earnings should fluctuate with the company's production throughput.

The case for greater security of earnings should therefore be considered as a matter of course. If nothing else, a proportion of 2:1 is a prime cause of wage drift. Theoretically, a wage survey should be conducted with other firms but since the make-up of gross pay is so variable from company to company, it is difficult to establish any meaningful form of parity. A company must examine its own costing system in terms of budgeted labour cost and the relationship this bears to unit cost. In other words, management must decide how much of the budgeted labour cost should be attributed to basic rate and how much to incentive, if any. Since this is negotiable, management should also know in advance the influence on unit costs of different break points or alternative basic rates.

One company employing about 1 000 people avoided this problem by taking the budgeted labour cost for the coming year and giving to the unions concerned three different 'mixes' of total wage cost. This was broken down into 3, 5 and 7 grades complete with incentive calculated at 80, 90 and 100 BSI. (80 BSI is a good average rate of working.) The unions were told that they could produce another option still coming to the same total if they so desired. The company in question, while unused to this level of participation, had a history of good industrial relations. Obviously some unions will question the budgeted labour cost but this does not detract from the principle proposed.

Dealing with anomalies

Once the job evaluation exercise is completed and new basic rates determined, a scattergram will pinpoint those jobs which are likely to be over or underpaid in relation to the new rates. Provided the old structure was not completely out of control, the bulk of the jobs will be just about right and roughly the same number over as underpaid. The options open to management are:

For overpaid employees

1   Retrain the individuals concerned in order that they can take on work of a more responsible or skilful nature and therefore justify the new level of payment
2   Make the difference between the old rate and the new a personal allowance which would be eroded each time a new basic rate was agreed. In time the new rate would catch up with the old
3   As for 2, but the old rate – sometimes called a Red Circle Rate – is retained for ever and ever. This is not advised. In time this becomes a thorn in the side of other employees
4   Buy out anomalies by paying a lump sum comprising the difference

multiplied by a negotiated figure. This is a strong negotiating area. What must be considered is the percentage of employees involved and whether or not most of the differences will be swallowed up within twelve to eighteen months anyway.

For underpaid employees

There are no options here: the individual's pay must be brought into line.

INCENTIVE ELEMENT

The word 'incentive' is synonymous with the word 'effort' in the minds of many. But this is not so. An incentive is some form of financial encouragement recognising a particular contribution made by the work force. It is, in effect, a sum of money additional to the basic rate which a company pays to ensure that its most important production aspects are being optimised. For example, a capital-intensive company might have an incentive linked to machine utilisation; a company making diamond-tipped tools might put particular emphasis on a low scrap value while still maintaining quality. Nonetheless many companies insist that effort is the only factor to recognise despite the fact that automation is very much with us.

Thought must be given to the *cost* of maintaining any one incentive: how many work study personnel, bonus clerks, tally clerks and inspectors are required to maintain standards? Can it be done in a more simple, effective way? Need there be an incentive? Will people only work on a carrot and stick basis? Will you, the reader, only work on this basis or are you different? What contribution does first-line supervision make to motivating people? Will the system encourage or stifle the growth of tomorrow's supervisors?

The basic decisions to be made about the incentive element are whether or not it is going to be individual, group, department or company based or a combination of these. The other important feature is whether the incentive is to be based on a straight-line formula (the more units produced the more earned *ad infinitum*) or on a curve where rather less is earned proportionately the more units produced, sometimes with a cut-off point to limit production and thereby restrict bonus. Yet another approach is to have a cut-off point beyond which any bonus earned is placed in a common pool. This in turn is used to help finance basic rates when these are renegotiated.

Direct incentives

Definition. A method of payment whereby a bonus is paid in direct relation to effort.

Advantages

1 Appropriate where a high level of physical effort is necessary and it is difficult to supervise workers effectively
2 Can generate substantial motivation as payment occurs shortly after achievement

3 Flexibility in allocating added reward for added effort
4 Introduction can mean a reduction in labour
5 Can be useful in the short term to increase the pace of working as an interim step to moving on to a more sophisticated system.

Disadvantages

1 Management is not in control of production
2 Tendency to ignore avoidance of waste
3 Supervisors in time may earn less than their subordinates, skilled less than semi-skilled
4 People learn how to achieve earnings without undue effort, for example by qualifying for special allowances, avoiding promotion to non-lucrative jobs, embarking on slow-downs during 'testing' of new rates
5 Can ruin industrial relations
6 Mobility of labour becomes virtually impossible
7 Supervisors become good progress chasers but rarely good managers.

Measured daywork

Definition. Measured daywork is a stabilised direct incentive system where the incentive element is consolidated in the basic rate, thereby achieving a high, non-fluctuating weekly wage or salary.

It is based on sound training, sophisticated work measurement techniques and sound management. It is still payment by results except that the underlying philosophy is one of trust – that an individual will work at an agreed pace provided work is available for him or her. The most common types are:

High day rate, which is suitable in an assembly-line. Each new employee is fully trained before starting work on the factory floor. He or she will be expected to produce work of a specified standard and to maintain a fixed working pace of, say, 90 BSI. The aim is to achieve a controlled work flow: those individuals who have a naturally high pace of working would normally be transferred to in-direct work. Those who have a naturally slow pace are subject to warnings and then either transferred to indirect work or dismissed, following reasonable warning.

Advantages

1 Simplified pay structure usually based on job evaluation
2 Considerable operating flexibility
3 Trust and responsibility given proper emphasis
4 Management is in control of production and uses work study standards as a condition of employment as well as for management information.

Disadvantages

1 Not always possible to elicit acceptable levels of performance without the 'pull' of a direct incentive
2 Sophisticated control techniques, such as daily computer data, are necessary

3 High calibre of supervision is essential
4 Disputes can be tougher than in direct incentive plants as employees can slow down without impairing earnings.

Philips premium pay plan is suitable where individuals can control the pace of work. The same principles as those for high day rate apply except, perhaps, the problem of disputes since PPP is based on individual effort.

The pay structure is a simple one, usually based on job evaluation, but unlike high day rate, it is graded in steps according to the pace of working (see Figure 51.2). Each individual contracts through his supervisor to work for a period of three months at a particular pace. If this pace is not maintained and the fault is not that of management, a warning is given. If the pace of working does not meet the agreed standard during the following three months, he or she is either retrained or moved back to a lower pay band. If he or she is unable to maintain an acceptable pace, he or she is liable to dismissal.

Group/departmental incentives

Definition. A method of payment whereby a bonus is paid either equally or proportionately to individuals within a group/department as a result of, say, output achieved over an agreed standard.

Advantages

1 It encourages team spirit
2 It breaks down demarcation lines
3 The group disciplines its 'slackers'
4 Job satisfaction is achieved through seeing the complete operation within the group area.

Disadvantages

1 Management is not in control of production
2 The bonus ceases in time to be an incentive and management might as well

---

SALARY AND WAGE ADMINISTRATION [GHM]

GRADE	80 BSI £	90 BSI £	100 BSI £
I	113.00	122.00	131.00
II	104.00	112.00	120.00
III	95.50	102.50	109.50
IV	87.50	93.50	99.50
V	80.00	85.00	90.00

Figure 51.2 Example of a wage structure of the Philips Premium Pay Plan type

consolidate the rate
3   Individual effort is not rewarded

Plantwide incentives

There are three main types:

Factory throughput. Linked to, say, tons leaving the factory, the bonus is distributed either equally or proportionately according to skill. Basic concept is that workers become more closely associated with the company's aims.

Advantages

1   Improved atmosphere
2   Demarcation less pronounced
3   Employees are aware of the production targets the company plans to achieve.

Disadvantages

1   Individual effort is not recognised
2   Employees find it difficult to associate themselves directly with the bonus
3   To safeguard against bad weeks/months, companies sometimes maintain a bank, so that the bonus becomes an employee benefit
4   If a bad week/month is experienced it's always the fault of 'other' departments.

Scanlon plan.   An alternative name is 'share of production plan'. The nub of the system is the formation of a joint management–union productivity committee which has *executive authority*. The bonus is based on productivity improvements and is usually calculated monthly.

Rucker plan.   An alternative name is 'cost reduction plan'. The basic theory is that there is a constant relationship between wages and production or added value. A joint management–union productivity committee is formed but it has *advisory authority* only. Savings made by reducing costs are shared either equally or proportionately and are usually distributed on a monthly basis.

In a nutshell, Scanlon is strong on industrial relations and weak on mathematics and Rucker vice versa. In practice, the best of both methods is adopted. The share-out is usually about a third of total savings. The basic concept for both is that manual workers have very much more to offer to a company than simply effort.

Advantages of Scanlon/Rucker plans

1   Can encourage better use of resources and raw materials and thereby produce substantial savings
2   Focuses attention on co-operation and teamwork to reduce costs
3   Trust and responsibility given proper emphasis
4   People accept change more readily

5 Normally covers direct and indirect workers and can include staff directly linked with production
6 Work group has a stake in how well management performs – and has freedom to criticise poor decisions: it therefore keeps management on its toes.

Disadvantages of Scanlon/Rucker plans

1 Cannot in themselves create a willingness to co-operate or a management capable of exploiting cost reduction
2 Some groups have more control over results than others and some contribute more than they receive
3 Parochialism can result: good communication is essential
4 Success largely hinges on sophisticated cost control techniques over a long period – and deciding on the 'right' calculation for distribution of savings.

Profit-sharing

Definition. On the basis of company profits, employees either receive an annual cash bonus or actual company shares. Basic concept is participation.

Advantages

1 Thrives in non-union firms
2 From management's point of view, extra rewards are allocated only when they can be afforded
3 Improved teamwork and co-operation. However, to optimise this, management must communicate the economic facts of life
4 The system is self-adjusting although the method by which profits are calculated or the form in which the money is distributed may come under attach.

Disadvantages

1 Workers have little control over final profit achieved
2 An industrious worker does not necessarily achieve extra payment
3 Tendency to withhold part of the profit to be shared against less fortunate times, thus making it a handout or employee benefit
4 Many schemes do not pay sufficient money to make an impact on motivation.

Merit-rating

Definition. A method of payment based on management decisions about an individual's personal *qualities and aptitudes*. Basic concept is that management reserves the sole right to pay people individually.

Advantages

1 Supervisors regularly consider each subordinate's contribution
2 Method of payment is flexible
3 Employees feel they are being treated as individuals.

Disadvantages

1   Because it is usually a subjective assessment, it is difficult to discuss problem areas without an element of emotionalism – always supposing they are discussed at all
2   Economic pressures often result in the system being bent with everyone ending up at the top end
3   Supervisors find it easier to pay everyone the same so that it effectively becomes an employee benefit.

ADDED VALUE

It is a well-established fact that in a *stable economy* there is an almost constant relationship between labour costs and added value. It follows, therefore, that this provides a useful formula on which to calculate savings: these in turn can be used to fund annual wage increases on a plantwide basis.

For example, assume that unions and management agree (as a result of information provided by the company's auditors) that over the last five years labour cost has been 34 per cent of added value.

	£
Sales	100 000
Less raw materials, utilities and depreciation	55 000
Added value	45 000
Labour cost	15 300
Labour cost: Added value	34%

It is agreed that any savings made in labour costs beyond this reference point of 34 per cent will be shared equally between management and unions.

Assume that sales increase 20 per cent and that with no additional increases in basic cost the cost of providing raw materials is a further £11 000, and that labour costs increase by 10 per cent. The situation would appear thus:

	£
Sales	120 000
Less raw materials, utilities and depreciation	66 000
Added value	54 000
Labour cost	16 830
34% × £54 000	18 360
Saving in labour cost	1 530
Proportion contribute to plantwide increases	765

A total of 4.5 per cent on the total wage bill

It will be obvious that companies will be required to open their books if the operation of the added-value concept is to maintain credibility. Set against this is the fact that the more information which can be produced prior to negotiation, the less conflict there will be between management and unions.

Approximately half of all disputes leading to stoppages are caused by friction over wage rates. A removal in part, even of some of the reasons behind these stoppages would give both management and unions more time to contribute to other important areas.

PRODUCTIVITY AGREEMENTS

A productivity agreement is a statement jointly agreed by management and unions on how work and people may be more effectively organised to mutual benefit. Two types of agreement are:

1 An agreement using the 'buying out' principle on the basis of *quid pro quo*. In effect, this type of agreement covers immediate wage increases in exchange for relaxation of rigid demarcation lines; elimination of tea breaks; forfeiture of mates; reduction in manning levels
2 An agreement which lays down a framework for allowing savings to be accumulated over six to twelve months. These savings are normally shared equally between management and shop floor employees.

In a nutshell, the difference between the two is 'jam today or jam tomorrow'. In selecting the right approach, a company must consider what will best match its industrial relations climate *and* its overall company objectives. It may be that its lack of operating flexibility demands a 'buying out' agreement in the short term but its longer-term objectives require phased steps towards a position where greater participation will fund wage increases as well as strengthen the company's future. But it must be *planned*.

In times of high unemployment, productivity agreements of the buying-out type are not popular with unions. In any case, it is narrow to assume that increased productivity can *only* be achieved through a reduced labour force: there are numerous options which are equally valid. For example, what would be the effect of better machine utilisation, improved work flow, reduction in scrap value, introduction of shift work? It is rather a question of selecting the right tools in order to make the best use of human resources.

Whatever form the agreement takes, it is, in effect, a *statement of intent* signed by both parties: what must not be overlooked is that it is not a once-and-for-all effort but a document calling for positive action throughout its term with regular progress reviews properly communicated. All too often companies negotiate excellent productivity agreements but fail to follow them through.

SINGLE STATUS

Employee or fringe benefits provide an element of security, a security which up until the last few years was the preserve of staff and management only. With the trend towards removing the differences in conditions between blue and white collar workers, unions are becoming increasingly aware of the value to their members of negotiating, for example, increased pensions. If the incentive element influences employee attitudes, how much more that of employee benefits? Sometimes overlooked, the Equal Pay Act requires equality in particular employee benefits as well as pay. If single status is the ultimate aim, a phasing operation must be planned in order that costs may be absorbed. The point being made is that employee benefits are part of the total labour cost and must be taken into account when looking at overall pay and conditions.

COMMUNICATION

An important area not stressed sufficiently is the need to communicate effectively. *The need to know* what is happening must be satisfied. Managers are often as starved of information as operatives! Will your present system cope? It is not the shop stewards' job to communicate management's intentions. Can your supervisors brief their subordinates face to face? What can you do to help them? Above all, every individual affected by the new pay structure must *understand* how it works. Could a simple booklet be produced? These are the main points concerning communication but since it is vital to the success of the whole project, readers are strongly advised to read the Industrial Society's booklet on 'Communication' in the *Notes for Managers* series.

SUPERVISORY STRUCTURE

Because many companies are attempting to move away from direct incentives, it is wise to comment on the need to investigate the existing supervisory structure and to consider the calibre, in effect, of first-line managers. Whatever management decides in terms of a new structure, first-line supervisors will be required to manage more effectively. Apart from training needs, the span of control must be examined. If a supervisor is to manage effectively, the most he can control and motivate is fifteen to twenty operatives. The successful implementation of a new wage structure hinges on how carefully this aspect is handled.

EXAMPLE OF A WAGE POLICY STATEMENT

It is the intention of management that this document be issued to every employee whom it concerns. It is the responsibility of first-line management to explain it fully to their subordinates. Should anyone feel that any aspect of this policy is not operating in practice, he should as a first step discuss this with his supervisor.

Aims

The aims of the policy are:

1 To recognise the value of all jobs in relation to each other within the company
2 To take account of wage rates paid by companies of similar size, product and philosophy
3 To ensure stable earnings
4 To enable individuals to reach their full earning potential as far as is reasonably practicable

---

5   To ensure employees share in the company's prosperity as a result of increasing efficiency.

Job evaluation

The basis of a sound wage structure is job evaluation. It is in the interest of both unions and management that this is carried out on a joint basis.

Job evaluation is a continuing process and therefore must be maintained if it is to retain its usefulness. To ensure that the scheme is still relevant, it will be reviewed jointly by unions and management at the end of its third operating year.

Wage structure

In designing the wage structure, the company aims to make the best use of its employees in order to achieve the company's short and longer-term business objectives. By achieving these objectives the company hopes to remain a leader in its field, thereby ensuring greater job security for all concerned.

Rate for the job

No one will be paid less than the recognised rate for the job. Equal pay is in force on the basis of 'equal pay for work of equal value'. While the company recognises the right of the unions' joint negotiating panel to negotiate on behalf of its members, management believes that first and foremost rates should be linked to the company's prosperity.

The company does not aim to pay the top rates in the area but rather to place the emphasis on good working conditions, security of employment and an atmosphere in which individuals may reach their full potential. Nonetheless the company aims to be in the top 15 per cent as far as total earnings are concerned. (Total earnings includes employee benefits.)

Number of grades

The number of grades will be as few as possible in order that differentials are of a sufficiently high level for real differences in responsibility and/or skill to be recognised.

Incentives

The company does not accept that its employees will work only on a carrot and stick basis: neither does it believe that its employees will give of their best if earnings fluctuate from week to week. This policy is reflected in the company's wage structure which is based on measured daywork.

Every employee should, wherever reasonably practicable, have the opportunity to reach maximum earnings for his grade. Provided work is available, employees are expected to work at a mutually agreed pace. Where work is not immediately available, employees will not lose financially but will be expected to move to alternative work in order to maintain production.

Where individual targets are not maintained, and management is not responsible, an employee must expect to be counselled, disciplined if necessary and, as a last resort, dismissed.

Work measurement

The basis of the wage structure is work measurement. The company aims to use the most advanced methods available. However, it does not intend to wrap these methods in a jargon not easily understood. All production managers (including first-line supervisors) and shop stewards will attend jointly sponsored appreciation courses in order that any disagreement over standards is discussed in full knowledge of how the system works.

Indirect workers

Indirect workers such as maintenance, cleaning and catering employees play an important support role in the overall production process. It is not possible to apply work measurement techniques to indirect jobs at an economic cost. An enhanced day rate will therefore be payable to employees in this category.

Minimum earnings

No employee will receive less than £80.00 for a 40-hour week. This ensures that lower-paid employees are paid a 'living wage', but employees in other grades must not expect that established differentials will necessarily be maintained.

Overtime

The wage structure is designed to ensure that excessive overtime is both unnecessary and unattractive. Overtime is a requirement which will only arise in very exceptional circumstances. Since it is management's responsibility to plan work effectively and determine manning requirements, 72 hours' notice will be given of the need for overtime working, except in very exceptional circumstances.

Promotion

The company operates a policy of internal promotion, wherever possible. When a promotion takes place, the individual will immediately take the 'rate for the job'. However, if the individual is on maximum earnings for his old grade, he will retain the old rate for three months until he has established himself in the new grade.

In exceptional cases where the individual fails to maintain a satisfactory level of performance, he will be transferred to lower-grade work. He will, however, retain the higher rate until the annual negotiation of wage rates when his personal rate will be eroded.

A similar policy operates for staff promotions.

Single status

It is company policy to remove progressively all differences in employee benefits for blue and white collar employees. To this end, the cost of such benefits will be included in overall labour costs. The ultimate aim is to move towards a 'package' concept negotiated annually.

Share of prosperity

The company believes that employees have a right to share in the company's prosperity. It also believes that increases in its labour bill should not be passed automatically to its customers. A special formula has therefore been agreed between management and unions whereby all savings made as a result of shopfloor participation will be divided on a 50/50 basis and used to finance increased wage costs.

Negotiating information

The company believes that only by providing its recognised unions with sound, factual information can a positive industrial relations climate be fostered. Agreed information will be issued quarterly to the joint negotiating panel.

CHECKLIST: CHANGING A WAGE STRUCTURE

The following checklist is intended to provide a starting point for discussion before installing a new wage structure. The list is by no means exhaustive but answering such questions should enable managers to decide the direction in which they plan to go in the short and longer term.

Company objectives

1 Apart from profit, what are you in business for?
2 Where are you going during the next two to three years; in the next five to ten years?
3 How do you plan to get there?
4 What influence will these plans have on your wage structure?
5 How can the wage structure aid the company in meeting its objectives?

Product

1 Are runs short, long, one-offs?
2 How important is quality, quantity, accuracy, consistency?
3 Is the process operator- or machine-controlled?
4 What are the capital investment plans for the next three to five years? Will these developments influence the pay policy?
5 What are the market pressures? Are there seasonal fluctuations?
6 Can buffer stocks be kept or is the product perishable?
7 How much is lost through scrap? (If the material is reconstituted, cost this.)

Work measurement

1 Are measurements loose, tight or a mixture of both?
2 Is pay related to effort? Is this what you want anyway?
3 To what extent are you subject to wage drift, that is, increasing labour costs with little or no increase in productivity?
4 Do your supervisors and shop stewards understand the principles of work measurement?
5 Have you enough industrial engineers to ensure that three separate studies are made before each standard is decided?
6 Are your existing studies sufficiently accurate to allow you to consider the introduction of synthetic ratings?
7 How about method study?
8 Will it be necessary to employ contract work-study personnel? Or experienced industrial engineers on a short-term contract?

Wage analysis

1 How many wage rates exist?
2 Where do national agreements fit in?
3 Is there a 20 per cent differential between supervisors' pay and the average gross pay (less overtime) of those they supervise?
4 What is the budgeted labour cost for the coming year? Does it include the cost of employee benefits?
5 What is the trend of *total* labour cost for the last five years?
6 How many elements make up gross pay? How many of these do you wish to consolidate? Or buy out?

7   What is the earnings distribution for each department for two, separate, typical weeks?
8   What trends are indicated from a breakdown of overtime worked?
9   What is the cost of producing each selling line and the proportion of labour cost attributed?
10 What is the cost of labour turnover?
11 What is the cost of absenteeism?

Job evaluation

1   What is the simplest possible method you could use which would satisfy the company's and the job holders' needs?
2   Should there be a joint job evaluation committee?
3   Should it be a full or part-time exercise?
4   To what extent can you involve the job holders?
5   Who should write the job description? The job holder, a job analyst or a member of the job evaluation committee?
6   How much information are you prepared to give to job holders about the scheme? Do you mean, for example, to tell each job holder the number of points allocated to his job? Could you give everyone concerned a copy of the scheme?
7   Will your existing appeals procedure match the needs of a job evaluation exercise?
8   Could you time and cost in advance the implementation of job evaluation?

Financing the wage structure

1   Can you finance from within the increased cost of the new wage structures?
2   could you negotiate initially the share-out between company and employees of any savings made?
3   How can you communicate effectively the aims of the exercise?
4   What training will have to be undertaken?
5   How can you involve your supervisors in order that they make a major contribution to the exercise?

Social aspects

1   What is the age and sex distribution by job and department?
2   What motivates your employees? What are their aspirations? Would an attitude survey be useful?
3   What kind of image does your company have? Is it what you want?
4   What kind of incentives are people used to in your geographical locality? Would your proposals cut across the expectations of your employees? What can you do to engineer the change?
5   How do you rate your industrial relations? How can this exercise improve them?
6   What is the company's predominant management style? Will the new wage structure alter this in any way? How can you involve middle and senior

management in such a way that they become party to the proposals?

7   What plans have you regarding such things as security of employment and earnings; single status?

8   How important is a stable work force to the company? Is it company policy to promote from the shop floor? Will the new pay structure influence or detract from this?

Designing the wage structure

1   From scattergrams of the existing situation, what anomalies exist? How many of these can you hope to get rid of first time around?

2   Using the scattergrams, how many grades ought you to have in the short term? What are you aiming for in the long term?

3   How can you involve your company accountant in order that the exercise is properly costed?

4   Is an alternative incentive planned? Do you need incentives anyway? If you do, will they be individual, group or company based? Or a combination of these?

5   What effect will the incentive element have on your products, the way you plan work, the way you manage people, employee attitudes?

6   Could you work out three possibilities for, say, a 3, 5 or 7 grade structure complete with differentials and incentive element, if any, each coming to the total budgeted labour cost?

7   How competitive would these rates be locally?

8   What is your policy on equal pay?

9   What will your unions be expecting at the negotiating table?

10   What kind of productivity agreement do you need? To what extent can you make it a charter for the future?

11   How far can you go in giving information to your unions in order that negotiation may be constructive?

12   How will you handle pay anomalies?

Implementing a wage structure

1   How can you improve your methods of communication in order that everyone *understands* what is happening?

2   Do senior managers understand how the new pay structure might affect them? Marketing and sales, for example?

3   What training can you give to your supervisors in order that their status and respect is strengthened and not weakened by the demands of the new pay structure?

4   Is your supervisory structure adequate in relation to the needs of the new pay structure? Can you give your supervisors more scope for decision-making without reference to the next level? Is their span of control about right in view of the demands which will be put on them?

5   What training should you give to shop stewards in order that they are aware of the implications of the new structure?

FURTHER READING

ACAS, *Advisory Booklet No. 1 – Job Evaluation*, Advisory Conciliation and Arbitration Service, London, 1979

Bowey, Angela M. (ed.), *Handbook of Salary and Wage Systems*, 2nd edition, Gower, 1982

Lupton, T., and Bowey, Angela M., *Wages and Salaries*, 2nd edition, Gower, 1983

52 Employee benefits

John Muir

Company reports invariably allude to the contribution made by the employees. This acknowledgement of the role of employees in the success of the firm itself reflects the fact that without their efforts little could be achieved. Increasingly, however, it is being recognised that the employment of a workforce is a costly business. The pressure of rising costs and greater competition is driving employers to seek ways of using that workforce more effectively. Some ways in which this can be done, like work measurement, skill flexibility and so on, are outside the scope of this chapter; but the factors which lead to a stronger sense of participation through financial means, and to a feeling that the firm's reward system is structured to meet the needs of the employee, are matters which can be examined under the heading of employee benefits.

BENEFITS IN RELATION TO OTHER EMPLOYMENT COSTS

The costs incurred in employing staff are not just the obvious items like overtime payments, allowances and direct wages. The State makes a major intervention in terms of the employer's contribution to pensions and social security benefits of all kinds including the percentage which goes to the Redundancy Fund. It has been estimated that in 1980 UK employers were paying some 30.5 per cent over and above basic wages to cover obligations like social security contributions, payment for public holidays, sick pay, holiday pay. In comparison with Western Europe there is still some way to go; a recent study showed that in West Germany such extra costs amounted to 75.2 per cent of basic wages.

Whether because the employer has to contribute by law, whether he does so on a range of additional items to keep up with his competitors or whether he does so because he feels that certain benefits are important for his workforce, the net result is a big increase over his direct labour costs. So a starting point for any employer is to determine the total amount he wishes to spend, or can afford to spend, and then to consider how this sum might be split as between direct pay and benefits. Very rarely does a company provide a single benefit; they normally come as a package which operates alongside, and very closely with, the salary structure. The best benefits package is one that combines the optimum benefits to employees with the optimum benefits to the employer. In other words, while it might at first sight seem that benefits are provided primarily for the benefit of the employee they should as a matter of equal importance provide a benefit to the employer in the form of higher motivation, more efficient working, increased co-operation and a better working atmosphere.

When establishing a complete set of benefits it is important to realise that it will be effective only so long as the salary structure is satisfactory. That structure must have integrity and be able to reward employees according to the responsibilities they carry. It does not necessarily have to be rigid in its application but any variations from established principles must have a proper basis and be capable of being explained against objective criteria. Perhaps the structure should also accommodate the notion of meritorious performance by being incremental. Whatever the detail of the scheme it should be fair in operation. The best benefits package may make a partly defective salary structure just about acceptable, but it will not turn a bad salary structure into an acceptable one. On the other hand a poorly designed benefits package can make what might otherwise be a good salary structure into a singularly unattractive feature.

What are employee benefits? Some indication has already been given in referring to pensions, social security insurance, redundancy payments and holidays. Indeed the list is a long one – house purchase, life insurance, meals and so on – and the opportunity will now be taken to examine a number of items in detail. It is important to recognise that some benefits may be more applicable to one group than another. A current feature in employment is the gradual removal of the distinction between blue collar and white collar workers. The development of personnel policies, including the benefits package, has for instance largely seen the disappearance of the holiday differentials between one and the other – indeed some would argue that the pendulum has swung the other way! Furthermore the very considerable degree of unionisation has meant (a) that the benefits package has figured in union demands and (b) that many middle managers and some senior managers are themselves in bargaining units with their conditions of employment subject to the outcome of negotiations. The employer is thus increasingly being required to consider the whole cost (salary and benefits) in his dealings with unions. To argue that for this reason there is less flexibility in dealing with benefits would be to misunderstand the nature of collective bargaining. It may be that the respective emphasis which unions and employer put on benefits will differ according to the industry, and economic indicators, but it should not stop the employer from making his offer partly in cash and partly in benefits if that is what he thinks is good for his workforce. Flexibility still has a major part to play in the managerial area where the senior executive and the company can negotiate what comes in cash and what in benefits.

The total cost concept of a benefits and salary package

The cost of an employee is made up of three components: salary, benefits and overheads. The last is difficult to quantify but the other two add up to so many pounds per year. Companies are increasingly taking the view that they should offer the senior executive a total compensation package, i.e., a ceiling is set to an employee's total compensation. For the sake of argument, assume that for a senior manager the total compensation is £20 000 p.a. Within this total certain minima and maxima are set – for example:

Salary	55–100 per cent of the ceiling
Car	£4000–£7800
House purchase	up to £7000
Insurance, medical and otherwise	up to £1000
Children's education	up to £2000

Thus an employee with a ceiling of £20 000 with two children at school, might choose £2000 for their education, £4000 for his car, £2000 for his house purchase and £12 000 for salary; whereas his rather older colleague, whose children have left school, who wants to buy a new house and who does not like driving, could choose £6000 for his house purchase, £1000 for insurance and £13 000 salary.

The obvious advantage of this system is that each employee can choose the benefits which are of most use to him. Furthermore, an employee who has no need of a particular benefit will not feel hard done by if his colleague avails himself of it because he knows that he can take other benefits or a larger salary.

The disadvantages are first that too much flexibility can create administrative difficulties and, second, an executive who chooses unwisely may feel aggrieved later in his working career. These drawbacks can be reduced to manageable proportions by limiting choice within components; for example, a particular insurance may not be reduced during its period of existence or the car may not be changed more frequently than once every three years.

CATEGORIES OF BENEFITS

In devising its remuneration policy a company will regard certain benefits as most important – like a pension or a car – and then other benefits as less so. While this approach is sound, care should be exercised in taking away or trimming back these 'other' benefits, or indeed in not adding to existing benefits on the grounds that they are trivial, lest this conflict with employees' perceptions. It is surprisingly easy to make a wrong move in this area. All benefits clearly have a monetary value which is important to the recipients, but the true value of some of them bears less relation to this than it does to the intrinsic nature of the benefit. Employees' attitudes and wishes should be taken into account – a feature which will be examined later.

Benefits can usefully be divided into three groups: status, security and work benefits.

Status	*Security*	*Work*
Cars	Pension	Office accommodation
Meals	Housing	Sabbaticals
Holidays	Share schemes	Management training
Telephone	Medical and insurance	Subscriptions
Gifts	Scholarships for children	
Entertainment facilities	Crèche	Discount, company purchase
Foreign travel	Notice period and redundancy	Sports and social clubs
		Retirement counselling

STATUS BENEFITS

Cars

The provision of company cars needs to be undertaken within a well-defined policy. Without a policy, or if a policy exists but is regularly disregarded, then the potential benefit to the company is severely reduced since recipients spend their time and energy pressing for something better and complaining in the process. Car provision can make for the extremes of satisfaction and effectiveness. Apart from office accommodation, no other benefit so easily identifies an executive's seniority in the firm. Therefore it is important for it to achieve its maximum effect.

The actual policy can have many components. Some firms stipulate that cars must be of domestic origin; others restrict the choice to EEC manufacture while a smaller number give unlimited choice of make. The cost of car will depend upon the position of the employee in the firm but here the importance of clearly defined and understood rules becomes clear. If the firm has a graded structure then the different levels of executive can be readily identified. At any particular level the employee concerned will know his entitlement. Again the policy does not have to be completely inflexible. Perhaps a group of employees undertakes representational duties where a more expensive car would be consistent with the image the company wishes to maintain. There must always be a sound reason for departing from general rules.

The type of car supplied can be determined by engine capacity, or by price, or by letting the price of one selected car determine the upper limit for that group. Some firms allow executives to add their own money, within defined limits, to car purchase but care should be exercised to avoid creating the impression that the car policy as such has been ignored.

The administration of a car scheme will inevitably entail the use of staff resources. The vehicles will have to be bought and individual requirements taken into account. It is desirable to have a policy which is as unrestrictive as possible. An entitlement to a car, however expensive, whose make is unacceptable to the individual concerned diminishes very substantially the perceived value of the benefit. The criteria in operating a car policy should be flexibility and choice within the company's administrative capability.

Meals

The provision of meals to executives is another highly sensitive area. Dining facilities do not just represent a cost saving to the individual concerned, though this can be significant. Provision of a dining room permits the company to entertain customers and clients in agreeable surroundings and it develops a corporate sense amongst executives. While it need not be a prime purpose the fact remains that informal discussions over drinks and a meal can make a material contribution to keeping executives abreast with developments and problems elsewhere in the organisation. The operation of dining facilities should be kept simple. Restricting the range of drinks for less senior staff, for example, can be very divisive indeed.

The provision of subsidised canteens for employees can be a very useful benefit both in cash terms and in convenience. In setting up a canteen or deciding to continue an arrangement a company should consider the true cost of the benefit being provided. A meal which costs the company a certain amount will not necessarily be recognised as worth that much to the employee; if left to his own devices he would almost invariably settle for something simpler.

Holidays

Differentials in holiday entitlement as between one group of staff and another have tended to disappear over the past few years. Furthermore, discussion about the length of the working week has, in some industries, been in the context of the length of the working year. In other words holiday absence and the working week have been coupled together. Both are cost items and while the calculations will vary according to the industry or job, every extra day's holiday can be expressed in money terms. While the trend is towards a common entitlement, many senior executives will still enjoy a substantial holiday allowance but claim that, due to work pressures, they are unable to take the full entitlement. If there are indeed such pressures companies should examine the reasons. It is a well-established fact that holidays, far from being a benefit in the sense of being an extra, is essential to the good health of employees in general and senior staff in particular. Companies should explore the possibility of encouraging its executives to take holidays, say, at the end of a business trip on which their wives have accompanied them, or to take a sabbatical.

Another feature of holiday absence relates to domestic and personal circumstances. Maternity leave, subject to a two-year service qualification with the employer, is an employee's right but many employers now offer more than the statutory entitlement as an employee benefit. Furthermore a substantial number of employers give paternity leave – usually about three days – so that the husband is on hand to cope at least with the first wave of changes which come with a new arrival in the family. Bereavement leave is also an established benefit and is designed to permit the immediate relative to make the necessary funeral arrangements.

Telephone

In the great majority of firms there will be key staff when it comes to out-of-hours incidents. If the refrigeration in a cold store breaks down the senior executive will need to know, even though the maintenance engineer will be the person to take action. If there is a walkout on the evening shift, the personnel director will need to know. So these, and people like them, must be contactable by telephone. There is a good case for the company paying the whole of the rental. Other senior staff may or may not be crucial in this sense but the ability to contact them by phone may be sufficient reason and justification for paying part of the rental. Companies will have to weigh the strength of the case against the cost involved but there is little doubt that support with telephone costs is a useful benefit.

Gifts

Until fairly recently most companies could boast about the number of long-service employees. Nowadays really long-service (say twenty years or more) is far less common. Nevertheless, a substantial number of companies continue to operate a long-service gift policy as a means of identifying the individual with the company and rewarding loyalty. Generally speaking the arrangements find favour with the recipients. It is, however, fair to say that many employees prefer cash, either as a lump sum or an increment to salary.

Entertainment facilities

Entertaining may be an extension of the working arrangements commented upon in the discussion on dining facilities, or it can be, for certain executives, a fundamental part of their job involving home and leisure time. In fact it is not leisure, in that the executive is entertaining the firm's clients in the interests of business. The pressure on many businessmen today has meant that entertainment for entertainment's sake is rapidly declining but that, as a means of finding extra working hours, it is extremely useful.

If entertaining at home is not possible then access to appropriate club facilities can fill the gap; and many companies in recognising this pay the club subscription. It could be argued that this is truly a business expense but on the other hand many executives see the arrangement as a benefit in that the facilities offered by the club can be used by the whole family.

Foreign travel

Like entertaining, travel is probably considered an attractive benefit initially but loses its glamour when it becomes a regular feature of the job. Indeed if this aspect of the work assumes too large a proportion it can become burdensome. However, the absence of business travel can again be counter-productive to an executive who has been used to going abroad. To executives not heavily involved in foreign travel, the occasional trip to overseas customers or overseas offices is a genuine attraction and can be used productively. There is a real gain to be made in establishing personal contact and in undertaking a representational role. It is well worth while a company considering whether wives can accompany their husbands on the occasional trip; this will not only lead to greater identification of an executive's family with his work but will also provide some compensation for the commitment he may be called upon to make to his work.

SECURITY BENEFITS

Pension

Pension schemes in the private sector are now commonplace but it would be a mistake to think that everyone is covered. Most managerial and executive staff would be, but large numbers of blue collar workers would not be in an occupational scheme. While on the one hand, therefore, many employees would regard a pension scheme as a normal feature of employment, it remains a real benefit. After all, a normal funding basis would be that for every 1 per cent of salary contributed by the employee, the employer would pay double – and indeed more if, as has generally been the case, pension schemes have run into an actuarial deficit due to inflation. A normal pension scheme has four main features:

1 A retirement pension payable at a predetermined age
2 A facility to commute a part of the pension to a lump sum free of tax
3 A death benefit
4 A widow's and dependants' pension in the event of the death of the employee in service or in retirement.

The rate at which pension accrues is often 1/60th of salary for every year of service leading to a maximum of 40/60ths but the salary determination has itself been subject to widespread improvement in the past few years. Good schemes looked at the salary of the last three years of service and took an average; nowadays the best schemes take the most advantageous definition of final salary. part of the pressure to take the final year has been a direct reflection of inflation but the net result has been that inflation by itself plus now final year salary for calculation purposes has vastly increased the cost of funding pension schemes. Much of the burden has fallen on employers.

Apart from the basic benefit element in a good pension scheme, attention has increasingly been paid to flexibility within the scheme itself. Thus better transfer value arrangements, added years for short service, payment of accrued pensions (or pensions calculated on what would have been total service) in circumstances of ill health or involuntary retirement, additional voluntary contributions, are all features which are commonly found. Voluntary retirement can be a way of making room for new managers and creating promotion opportunities.

Pension arrangements should be seen both as a major benefit and a management tool. It is certainly a vital one in the 1980s.

Housing

Banks and financial institutions have provided house purchase facilities to their employees for a long time. Many other companies have housing support schemes. They may not lend the money direct to the employees, but will offer a degree of mortgage support. The real benefit is in any case substantial. It enables the employee to buy his own property and perhaps more importantly to buy at a higher standard of housing than his salary would otherwise support. Furthermore, as house prices continue to rise and as companies expect their executives to be more mobile, it is becoming a matter of prime importance to consider the scale and extent of house purchase facilities and mortage support. Another question is whether the facility should be open to all employees or if not then to what level. In addition to the question of cost there is a danger that employees will be 'locked in' to the company by their dependence on the loan or the support. Provided care is taken to avoid these dangers, house purchase or housing support schemes can provide a very genuine attraction in recruiting and retaining appropriate staff. Such schemes are considered very important by the employees themselves.

Employee share schemes

Recent legislation in the UK has given a welcome fillip to the development of employee share schemes. Profit sharing had already been well established in the United States by 1939 but the United Kingdom had to wait until the Finance Act 1972 and 1973 provided a favourable tax basis. Then came a period of pay freezes and a reversal of legislation.

As a benefit, a share scheme must rank high and it clearly contributes to security of employment. A scheme enables the employee to have a stake in his future in the firm. Direct effort produces growth and growth will enhance the value of his holding. Thus incentive and a sense of participation are combined for the benefit of both the firm and the employee. There is no doubt that participation is a key feature for future success. By whatever means formal expression is given or might be given to participation, whether through collective bargaining, works councils, employee consultation or worker directors, the fact is that giving the employee a direct interest in the success and profitability of the firm means that more and more he will wish to turn his financial stake into one that has a strong element of active participation. This philosophy also fits in well with developments in the EEC.

To benefit from the advantageous tax arrangements, current legislation in the UK provides for a maximum shareholding on the part of any one participant in any one tax year of £1000. This will not prevent higher sums being set aside for a participant in a separate scheme, but such sums will not attract the tax concessions available to approved schemes. If the shares in the approved scheme are held for seven years or more no tax liability arises in the context of the allocation being regarded as income. Between two years (the minimum time shares must be held before sale) and seven years a sliding scale of tax liability operates. In the case of death of the participant, his ill health, retirement or redundancy, the shareholding can be sold and the proceeds do not bear a tax liability (though in all circumstances capital gains tax may have to be taken into account).

In addition to direct profit share schemes the Government introduced through the Finance Act 1980 tax concessions for participants in 'approved' savings-related schemes. The employee has to save a minimum of £10 per month with a maximum of £50 per month through a Department for National Savings fourth issue contract or a building society share-save contract. The savings period is five or seven years at the end of which period the money buys shares at the price identified when the contract started. Taking into account that the money saved will itself be increased by interest and that the shares will in all probability have increased in market value over the period the employee, at the end of five or seven years, can expect to have a holding worth very considerably more than the modest sums saved each month. All gains under such schemes are free of income tax. Again the identification with the company is clear. As the savings continue the employee has a direct interest in seeing the company do well so that the market value of its shares – and of his own holding – will be enhanced.

A number of companies launching their share schemes have included in the rules of the scheme performance targets which have to be achieved either before an option can be granted and/or can be exercised. This is particularly appropriate at times when current profit levels may be somewhat reduced but the company wishes to give its employees and the management team an opportunity for gain in the future but only if shareholders also receive the benefit from growth in profit.

Insurances

The provision of additional insurance cover for employees can be a significant benefit. The insurance cover can be provided as part of the company's pension plan or it can be additional to it. Insurance cover can be restricted to the time when the employee is working on company business or it can be operable on all occasions. It it were easy to draw a sharp line between time spent on business activity and own time the former would be an obvious choice. If, however, the employee has tasks which make it uncertain whether time is official or private who can say what insurance cover operates? If an executive is meeting a potential client out of normal hours but as part of his job, the question is: 'Is it worth risking a dispute whether insurance cover operates or not when, for a small extra cost, overall cover can be secured?' Total cover is one area where the company can get a cost-effective deal because insurance is relatively cheap to provide on a group basis.

In cases where the employee has died in service the benefits both tangible and intangible for his widow can be very large. Similarly at small extra cost provision can be made to cover permanent incapacity to work, even from month one of employment, on the simple basis that very few people indeed suffer such a misfortune. But for the individual concerned and his family the benefit accruing is very highly regarded.

In the field of medical care insurance arrangements organised by the company at no cost to employees or reduced cost are well established. This is a field hitherto almost exclusive to manager and executives, but fairly recently a major craft union negotiated such arrangements with the employer covering staff generally. Not only does this form of insurance normally provide more comfortable care in the sense that privacy is invariably a feature, but it also ensures that for treatment of a non-urgent kind specific dates can often be arranged to suit the convenience of both the employee patient and the company. Furthermore, private treatment can usually allow an executive to carry out important parts of his work from his hospital bed. This should be seen both in the context of the firm getting service out of employee and of the employee feeling that he is continuing to make a valuable contribution to the company. In this situation such insurance may be seen to be prudent from the company's point of view and (subject, naturally, to the employee's true state of health), therapeutic in so far as recovery is concerned.

While sick leave pay is common it should nevertheless be seen as a true benefit. There is no legal requirement to provide it; all the employer is legally required to do is to say whether such a scheme is in operation or not. For many blue collar workers a sick pay scheme is still an absent feature but its implementation can act as an added security benefit. Payment during sickness can be effected via insurance cover if the company does not want to bear the risk itself. Clearly the smaller the firm the greater the cost of having an employee away for a long period and insurance cover would appear to offer the better solution.

On-site medical facilities are likely to be of less importance to the average senior executive or manager – although it is as well to bear in mind the incidence of heart attack. However, where he is responsible for a plant or factory which is not close to medical facilities on-site provision can be useful.

Scholarships for children

Few companies are prepared to take the lead in providing facilities for the payment of school fees for the children of employees though some companies have set up machinery whereby an independent panel consider applications from employees and recommend awards accordingly. There is certainly a recognition on the part of senior management in companies that this is one area where executives are likely to be faced with increasing costs. One way in which the executive can be materially assisted to meet such cost is for the company to arrange for personal financial-planning consultants to advise its executives on a group basis, with the company paying the consultants' fees. Such a service, which is already fairly well established, has the advantage of giving individual freedom of choice; and it certainly indicates the company's interest in the welfare of the employee and his children.

Crèches

The increasing demand for able managers and the greater freedom being demanded by women means that a higher proportion of senior posts will be held by women in the future. The dual role of wife/mother and executive is already established but further encouragement will need to be backed up by the provision of child care facilities. Many companies have a formal equal opportunities policy. This feature, coupled with statutory provisions on rights to the job after maternity leave, has already led companies to consider the scope and extent of such support. Facilities in this area can be regarded as a benefit to both employee and employer. On the employee's side there is confidence in that care is being provided while on the employer's side there is continuing access to the employee's skills and experience. That skill and experience was probably a heavy cost to the company in terms of recruitment and training. Providing child care facilities is clearly more sensible than starting all over again with a new employee.

Notice period and redundancy pay

It may seem a contradiction to be discussing security benefits in the context of the employee leaving the firm. Nevertheless, for a variety of reasons many employees, including many executives, will find that their jobs come to an end. It may be due to merger and rationalisation, to a changing market which reduces the need for certain expertise, or to the need to insert fresh thinking into senior posts by promoting other able people. The benefit in employment terms comes with the appreciation that if the job finishes there will be reasonable compensation.

Minimum notice periods are fixed by legislation. For service with the mployer of twelve years or more, twelve weeks' notice must be given to the employee. In cases of redundancy or job loss pay in lieu of notice is often given. Notice pay can therefore a substantial sum and many employers in recognising the seniority of the employee have given via the employment contract notice periods of six and twelve months.

Since 1965 redundancy pay has been a statutory requirement but the maximum statutory entitlement is bounded by a limit of twenty years' service and an upper pay limit of £130 per week. Weighting is given for age but it means that no more than thirty weeks' worth times £130 is available. Shorter service below age forty gives a simple one week's pay for each year times pay or £130 whichever is the lesser sum. Very many employers, both private and public sector, have greatly enhanced scales of payment so that on leaving a job the employee goes with a substantial sum of money. The current tax-free limit is £25 000 so that job loss – if notice pay and severance pay are right – need not represent disaster.

WORK BENEFITS

Office accommodation

Along with the provision of the company car, the most visible sign of executive seniority is the type of office occupied. Properly planned and furnished office accommodation can reflect the general standing of the company and the importance of executive job-holders and at the same time be achieved at modest cost.

Sabbaticals

Allowing senior executives a sabbatical (a specific period of leave, for example, six months or a year's leave with pay) after they have served a number of years (typically fifteen or twenty) has been an established practice for some time in the USA. It is rare for UK companies to provide such a facility. However, as pressure on executives tends to increase, this facility is likely to become more widespread. There are two clear advantages: from the executive's point of view it enables him to 're-charge' and come back fresh to his position; and from the company's point of view, provided it has some control over the study or work undertaken during the sabbatical, it prevents senior managers from becoming too stereotyped and blinkered in their approach to the job.

Management training

This benefit comes more in the shape of skills and knowledge acquired by the employee rather than in cash terms, except that the acquisition of a formal qualification can mean an addition to salary. There has been a move away from the practice of sending executives away on general management courses unrelated to their work or potential. This reflects growing awareness of the cost and a better understanding of training needs. With more careful selection of the individual and the course or with the use of in house training (either with own resources or engaging a consultant) management training can be continued effectively within the budget.

The need for executives and senior managers fluent in another language is rapidly increasing. The company, in providing language training either direct or by way of financial support, improves the general quality and contribution of its staff. From the employee's point of view it greatly improves his own marketability. This, of course, is not an objective of the benefit but the point should not be ignored. Many companies who specifiy the need for someone to be fluent in a given language before making an appointment are unnecessarily limiting the scope of their choice. In many cases, it would make more sense to recruit somebody suitable for the post and provide the necessary language tuition afterwards.

Some companies also offer support to employees in relation to courses of study undertaken at their own violition. It would, however, be exceptional to find unqualified support irrespective of the subject. A company would normally wish to be satisifed that the course was in some way related to work.

Subscriptions

Membership of a professional body or an organisation reflecting business interests is often of concern to the employee. Such membership keeps him in touch with current trends and legal requirements and helps him to keep abreast of developments through contact with fellow members. Those leads are of considerable use to the company as well, in so far as the executive is better informed and therefore a more valuable member of staff. While subscriptions to such bodies are tax allowable many companies recognise the importance of the membership and pay the subscription in full.

Discount and company purchase plans

Many companies take advantage of their purchasing power or of their importance in the trade to provide facilities by which employees can buy goods and services at favourable prices. The company's own products can also be sold to staff at a discount. It is difficult to assess the extent to which such facilities contribute to retention and a long-term identity with the company but the value of the benefit should not be underrated.

Sports and social clubs

Like dining facilities and canteens, sports and social facilities are also a long-established benefit. They are one of the best ways by which identification with a company can be achieved by an employee and his family and such facilities are normally well accepted. Bearing in mind that from the employee's point of view a major friendship area is his place of work, the development of that circle on a family basis can be of very considerable benefit.

In the provision of facilities two problems arise. First, when setting up a club some companies make the mistake of trying to over-economise and produce facilities which are unattractive in comparison with similar facilities elsewhere. Second, in the large connurbations these facilities can be out of reach of a large percentage of the workforce. In such circumstances, it is possibly better to concentrate on providing first-class social facilites close to the place of work.

The need to keep in touch with pensioners is more readily recognised by companies than in the past. This can be regarded as a benefit in the sense that employees and pensioners themselves see the company taking positive steps to maintain contact and take a continuing interest in old employees. If there are sports and social facilities these can readily provide a focus for pensioner interests.

Retirement counselling

Clearly associated with work, but towards the end of a career, comes retirement counselling. The magnitude of the break between work and retirement is massive. Not only is there the loss of work on a regular basis but also a major financial change. More and more companies are recognising a responsibility to make employees aware of the need to adjust to the new circumstances, to find useful alternative employment (normally of a voluntary nature) and above all to plan for the next ten years and more on a sound financial basis. Pre-retirement courses can make a major contribution to a succesful transition from work to leisure; and the provision of such courses is welcomed by employees and clearly seen as a benefit.

CONCLUSION

This chapter has examines a wide range of benefits but the question may be asked 'Why provide benefits at all?'. The answer is simple. Benefits are often a much more efficient way in tax terms of providing part of a total remuneration package and their provision often directly reflects the company's real appreciation of employees' needs and the value of fostering an identity of interest between the company and its staff. Clearly, few companies can affort to provide all the benefits described (even so the list is not exhaustive) and therefore there is the question how the benefit programme should be constructed.

The two basic steps which a company should take are, first, to define precisely what it hopes to achieve by introducing the benefits or reshaping its present programme; and, second, to ascertain what level of effectiveness flows from any current programme. In defining what it wants to achieve, a company has to decide whether it wants its benefits to be linked to the performance of the company or whether it wants to give them as reward to employees so as to create, for instance, an enhanced sense of security. If a company decides that it wishes to build up a total compensation package related to the company's performance, it should be prepared to investigate and have designed either or both shares schemes and profit-sharing schemes. If, on the other hand, the emphasis is to be on non-performance-related benefits, items like pension, house purchase and retirement counselling will be of primary importance.

A company should recognise that its own assessment of what employees want in terms of benefits is not necessarily a reliable guide. For instance, generous pensions may be a desirable aim in the benefit field and socially desirable but it does not follow that all sectors of the workforce will see it in the same way.

In order to obtain the maximum effect from a benefits programme the company should be aware of the perceived effectiveness of its present arrangements. To obtain this information an audit may be carried out of the benefits currently provided and how these are received by the staff. For a company to undertake this programme by itelf is not on the face of it particularly difficult but in practice problems arise which tend to invalidate the answers. The form of questionnaire may be unsuitable, employees may think that there is a desired answer, particularly if the enquiry is conducted in house with no chance of confidentiality. The use of outside consultants could make this a more feasible operation not only in the form of the exercise but in terms of confidentiality. The results would not identify individuals in any way and employee preferences would be expressed as percentages out of the total number of employees involved.

A typical programme would involve deciding which benefits should be included in the survey and also any attitudinal points of special interest which should be covered in interviews with a cross-section of recipients and potential recipients. The recipients would then be interviewed to see if they understood precisely what benefits they were receiving and how much these were worth to them and how much they cost the company. Furthermore, they could also be asked what further benefits they would like to receive or would prefer to receive in place of benefits already in existence. This aspect touches very clearly on the notion of personal choice in electing to take some benefits in place of others or of at least scaling the size of benefits to fit in with the changing needs of the employee.

The results of this survey could be cross-referenced with the cost of a company's benefits programme and a realistic view of the cost effectiveness of the programme worked out. The company would then be in a position to decide precisely how the programme should be amended or added to or indeed how such a programme should be undertaken. It is important that, once the new programme is introduced, great care be taken to see that its effectiveness is duly checked and essential that the full impact of the new programme is communicated to the recipients and potential recipients. A regular update or audit is necessary to see if the hoped-for effect is achieved and whether failure to achieve it is due to the programme itself or to a failure to communicate it properly to employees.

It is both surprising and worrying that so many companies pay scant attention to the need to communicate. Even companies which by any standard have good benefit features in this total remuneration package, often do not take the trouble to inform staff about them. They assume that the details are understood but regrettably there is no clear understanding and in the meantime the company is getting little or no credit for its policy. Sometimes a company will content itself with an explanatory booklet or memorandum but often couched in semi-technical jargon incomprehensible to recipients. It would make better sense and certainly improve the effectiveness of the company's programme if companies took the time and trouble to make sure that their personnel department, for example, had a specialist who was responsible for communicating the programme.

A company embarking on a benefits programme or reshaping its existing policy should be prepared to take the following steps:

1 Clearly define the aims of the programme
2 Ascertain what the programme gives and what benefits are received
3 Ascertain what employees would like to receive
4 Work out what can be afforded in relation to a benefits programme
5 Draw up a new benefits programme, bearing in mind the very wide range of benefits which could be given.
6 Make sure the programme is communicated fully and effectively to all recipients

7 Check regularly to see that the benefits programme is achieving its aims and objectives
8 Be prepared to change the programme if it is not achieving its aims
9 Consider the possibility of giving flexible benefits to employees so that their personal election fits in with their changing needs
10 Be prepared to employ specialist personnel both internally and externally to ensure that a benefits programme is properly constructed.

FURTHER READING

Beacham, R., *Pay Systems: Principles and Techniques*, Heinemann, London, 1979

Company Administration Handbook, Gower, 5th edition, 1982

Di Palma, V., *Your Fringe Benefits*, David & Charles, Newton Abbot, 1977

Greenhill, Richard T., *Employee Remuneration and Profit Sharing*, Woodhead Faulkner, 1980

Kenaghan, F., and Redfearn, A., *Determining Company Pay Policy*, Institute of Personnel Management, 1979

Newman, G., *Executive Remuneration*, Guild Press, 1979

Pilch, M., and Wood, V., *Pension Schemes*, Gower, 1979

Vernon-Harcourt, A., *Rewarding Management*, Gower, annually

Wood, D., and Turton, D., *White Collar Productivity Schemes*, Oyez Publishing Ltd, 1979

53 Working conditions

Patricia George

In recent years the moral responsibility of management to provide reasonable working conditions for their employees has, more and more, been taken over by legislation. No one would deny that the objectives of such legislation are well founded, but so much has been produced (with so many changes) that a concise summary will help to ensure that readers obey the letter, as well as the intent, of the law.

HEALTH AND SAFETY AT WORK ACT 1974

One of the main purposes of this Act is to provide a comprehensive and integrated system of law to deal with the health, safety and welfare of people at work. Based on the concept of a general duty of care, the Act has been drawn up in such a way that it can be changed, expanded and adapted to cope with risks and problems in industry for many years ahead. It has been described as the most significant statutory advance in this field since Shaftesbury's Factory Act of 1833. The Act applies to all people working in any capacity: employers, employees (except domestic servants in private employment), self-employed and to certain members of the public.

The basic obligations of all employers and all employees, which the Act deliberately couches in very general terms, are given below.

Basic obligations of employers

The employer must ensure, so far as is reasonably practicable, the health, safety and welfare at work of all his employees. This duty includes the provision of (and maintenance of, as appropriate):

1 A safe, healthy working environment with adequate facilities and arrangements for welfare at work
2 A safe, healthy place of work with safe means of access and egress
3 Safe, healthy plant and systems of work

4 Means, etc., to use, handle, store or transport articles and substances without risk to health or safety
5 Information, instruction, training and supervision necessary to ensure the health and safety of his employees
6 Written statement of his general policy for the health and safety of his employees, and the organisation and arrangements for carrying out that policy.

Employers must, in specified circumstances, allow their employees to appoint their own safety representatives, consult with them and, if so requested, set up safety committees.

Directors will be required to give information in their annual reports to shareholders on what their companies are doing in this field. The Companies Act 1967 was amended accordingly by s79 of the Health and Safety at Work Act on 1 April 1975.

Additionally employers have a duty to ensure the safety of persons other than employees who enter their premises and to ensure that their activities do not endanger anybody outside their employment.

Basic obligations of employees

Every employee has a duty to take reasonable care for the health and safety of himself and of others who may be affected. He must co-operate with his employer to enable the duties and requirements of the Act to be carried out.

Many processes or activities are now, or will be, governed by regulations or approved codes of practice. In general contravention of the appropriate regulation will be an offence. A person will not however be open to criminal proceedings for failing to observe a particular code of practice but in the event of criminal proceedings any relevant code of practice is admissible in evidence.

The Health and Safety Commission, Executive and Inspectorate

In general, the Commission is responsible to the Secretary of State for Employment for making whatever arrangements are appropriate for the general purposes of the new legislation. It has an information, education and advisory role and the power to carry out investigations and inquiries within the health and safety field.

The Health and Safety Executive, responsible to the Commission, is its operational arm and has been set up to carry out the Commission's functions under the Commission's direction. In its turn, the Executive is empowered to appoint inspectors to carry out its enforcement and advisory functions. Inspectors of factories, mines and quarries, nuclear installations, alkali and clean air and explosives have been transferred to the Executive for this purpose.

An inspector can enter an employer's premises at any reasonable time (at any time in a situation which in his opinion is, or may be, dangerous) to carry out his function.

Improvement and Prohibition Notices. An inspector will be able to issue Improvement and Prohibition Notices.

Improvement Notice. Requires the employer to remedy a contravention of Act or a regulation under it within a specified period.

Prohibition Notice. Requires the employer to stop (immediately if necessary) any activity which carries risk of serious personal injury.

There is a right of appeal to an industrial tribunal against these Notices. Improvement Notices will be held in abeyance pending the appeal but Prohibition Notices will remain in force unless the employer satisfies the tribunal to the contrary, by application prior to the hearing.

Employment Medical Advisory Service

In addition to having an advisory role, the Act:

1 Authorises a medical adviser to carry out a medical examination of any employee whose health is believed to be in danger because of his work, provided the employee himself consents
2 Requires an employer to inform the local careers office when recruiting a person aged less than eighteen to work in a factory, specifying the nature of the work he will be doing.

Disclosure of information

The Commission can serve a notice on any person to reveal information affecting health and safety.

An inspector can in appropriate circumstances inform the employees at a workplace of matters affecting their safety, health and welfare.

The Safety Representatives and Safety Committees Regulations 1977 require employers to make certain information available to safety representatives.

Enforcement of the Act

The Executive is required to make adequate arrangements for enforcement except where regulations made by the Secretary of State place the duty on local authorities or other bodies.

Responsibility for fire prevention and fire precautions. S78 amends the Fire Precautions Act 1971 so that the fire authorities and the Home Office can deal with general fire precautions (means of escape in case of fire, fire-alarm systems, fire-fighting equipment and so on) under the Act. The Commission and Executive will remain responsible for control over risks of fire associated with particular processes or the use of particular substances, and for all fire precautions in certain scheduled premises (which will include major hazard factories).

Offences. S33 lists the offences and the type of penalty which may be imposed for each: fines and/or imprisonment.

Action by management. Management should:

1 Prepare and issue a written safety policy statement
2 Set up an accident prevention programme
3 Provide training in safety policy and practice
4 Designate line and functional responsibilities for health, welfare and safety.

The main provisions of the Act came into force on 1 April 1975 and largely replace most of the existing law on safety and health in industry. Among the major Acts which will eventually be replaced or mainly replaced are the Factories Act 1961, and the Offices, Shops and Railway Premises Act 1963.

THE FACTORIES ACT

The Factories Act 1961 and the regulations made under it remain in force for the time being. The Act applies to all factories as defined in *s*175 of the Act, as well as to certain other premises, such as building sites, which are not factories in the normal sense of the word. For the purpose of the Act, a factory is defined as a place to which the employer has right of access or of control and where two or more persons are employed in manual labour, by way of trade or for the purpose of gain in any of the following operations:

1 Making any article or part of an article
2 Altering, repairing, ornamenting, finishing, cleaning, washing, breaking up or demolishing any article
3 Adapting an article for sale
4 The slaughtering of cattle, sheep, swine, goats, horses, asses or mules
5 The confinement of such animals while awaiting slaughter at other premises provided those premises are not maintained primarily for agricultural purposes and do not form part of the premises used for holding of a market in respect of such animals.

Furthermore, whether or not they fall within this general definition, *s*175(2) specifically applies the Act to the following groups of premises, provided that persons are employed in manual:

1 Packing articles, washing or filling bottles or containers incidental to the purposes of the factory
2 Sorting articles prior to work in a factory
3 Printing or bookbinding carried out as a trade or incidental to a business
4 Making up or packing of yarn or cloth
5 Laundering carried on as an ancillary to a business or public institution. (Ordinary commercial laundries are factories within the general definition quoted above.)
6 Constructing, reconstructing or repairing vehicles, locomotives, or other plant used for transport purposes, when ancillary to a transport, industrial or commercial undertaking (other than running repairs to locomotives)

7 Production of films. (It would be wise to assume that the production of recordings on videotape might be treated as coming within this definition, though the point could lead to much legal argument.)

8 Making or preparing articles for the building, fishing and engineering industries, the theatre and for films

9 Dry docks in which ships are constructed, repaired or broken up

10 Gas holders of over 5000 cubic feet.

Certain sections of the Act also apply to electrical stations and substations, warehouses, docks, wharves, ships and sites where building and civil engineering are carried on.

Premises that come under the definition of a factory but are used by public authorities or charitable institutions may still be subject to the Act even though they are not actually operated 'by way of trade or for the purpose of gain'. The same applies to factory premises occupied by the Crown or a local council.

A place sited within the factory precincts is not a part of that factory if it is used solely for a purpose different to the processes carried on in the factory, for example the office buildings in the factory may not be part of the factory.

The principal matters legislated for under the Factories Act are:

1 Cleanliness, overcrowding, temperature, ventilation, lighting, sanitary conveniences, washing facilities, drinking water, seating, and accommodation for clothing. (Provision of first-aid facilities came under the Act orginally but, with effect from 1 July 1982, is covered by The Health and Safety (First Aid) Regulations, 1981.)

Cleanliness

Dirt and refuse must be removed daily from floors and benches in workrooms and from staircases and passages. Workroom floors must be washed or otherwise cleaned at least once per week. All inside walls, partitions and ceilings must be periodically washed, painted, whitewashed or otherwise treated as prescribed by the Factories (Cleanliness of Walls and Ceilings) Regulations 1960, amended by S.I. 1974 No. 427. Factories must be kept free of effluvia from drains, sanitary conveniences, etc.

Overcrowding

Workrooms must not be so overcrowded as to be dangerous to health. The employer must allow at least 400 cubic feet (11.3m³) of space for every person employed excluding any air space more than 14 feet (4.27m) from the floor.

Temperature

The temperature must be reasonable. If a substantial proportion of the work in a particular room is done sitting and does not involve serious physical effort, the temperature must be at least 15.5°C (60°F) after the first hour and at least one thermometer must be provided in every such workroom. However, Statutory Instrument 1980, No. 1013 restricts heating to a maximum temperature of 19°C (66.2°F), unless certain industrial processes require more heat.

Ventilation

Fresh air must be circulated to provide adequate ventilation, and measures taken to protect employees from inhalation of dust, fumes or impurities which may be injurious or offensive.

Lighting

Lighting, artificial or natural, must be sufficient and suitable.

Sanitary conveniences

The Statutory Rules and Orders 1938 No 611 as amended by S.I. 1974 No. 426 setting out the minimum requirements for factories can be obtained from the Stationery Office. The conveniences must be maintained, kept clean and effectively lit. The general scale is one convenience for every twenty-five men or twenty-five women but when employing more than a hundred this scale may be varied by the substitution of urinals for water or chemical closets.

Washing facilities

Must include a supply of clean, running hot and cold or warm water, soap and clean towels or other suitable means of cleaning or drying and be suitable and adequate for the number employed.

Drinking water

The employer must provide an adequate supply of drinking water, with an upward jet convenient for drinking or with suitable drinking vessels and facilities for rinsing them.

Seating

The employer must provide suitable seating where an employee (male or female) has reasonable opportunities for sitting without detriment to his/her work.

Accommodation for clothing

Adequate and suitable accommodation must be made for clothing not worn during working hours, with arrangements where practicable for drying such clothing. The risk of theft is an element which must be taken into account in deciding whether accommodation is suitable.

First aid

A box or cupboard containing first-aid requisites (one for every 150 employees or fraction of that number) must be provided in every factory. The First Aid Boxes in Factories Order 1959 stipulate the minimum contents. Such boxes must be in the charge of a responsible person. Where more than fifty persons are employed, there must be at least one person who has been trained in first aid. In addition a notice must be placed in every workroom stating the name of the person in charge of the box or cupboard provided in respect of that room.

On 1 July 1982 this section of the Factories Act was replaced by The Health and Safety (First Aid) Regulations 1981, and Code of Practice;

2 Safety: there must be:

Safe conditions of workplaces, including floors, stairs, passages and gangways, and the means of access to places where people have to work. The requirements for handrail and fencing are stipulated for means of access, for workplaces, and for openings in floors

Precautions against dangerous fumes, dust and other health and safety hazards, protection of eyes, restrictions on lifting heavy weights.

Fencing on dangerous machinery and parts of machinery which are in motion or use, restriction on cleaning machinery by persons under eighteen and women, training and supervision of young persons required to operate certain machines

Safe construction and safe operation of cranes, hoists and other plant with special hazards

3 Restrictions on the employment of women and young persons, including limitations on normal hours, overtime and holiday work

4 Statutory registers kept and statutory reports made, regarding (for example) accidents and industrial diseases, inspection of factories and other administrative matters.

In addition to the requirements of the Factories Act itself, many specific processes are subject to special regulations made by statutory instruments under the Act. These include detailed requirements for certain types of machinery, (e.g., woodworking machinery) and for certain types of industrial employment for example, building operations and works of engineering construction.

OFFICES, SHOPS AND RAILWAYS PREMISES ACT

The Offices, Shops and Railways Premises Act 1963 is in force for the time being. It extended to such premises some of the requirements formerly applied only to factories. S1 details what premises are covered but these can be briefly summarised as follows:

Office premises: A building which is used solely or principally for office purposes from filing to the preparation of material for publication. Premises used in connection with office premises, such as storerooms or canteens, are also subject to the Act even if they are not physically part of the office premises.

Shop premises: In addition to a shop of the ordinary kind, the term is defined to include any building or part of a building

> of which the sole purpose or principal use if the carrying out of retail trade, for example the sale to the public of food or drink for immediate consumption, retail sales by auction and the lending of books or

periodicals for the purpose of gain

occupied by a wholesale dealer or merchant who keeps goods there for sale

which members of the public visit to deliver goods for repair, etc, or to carry out repairs, etc, for themselves

used to sell solid fuel.

The Act does not apply to:

Offices in which the total number of man hours worked does not exceed twenty-one a week

Moveable office structures in which people work for less than six months

Permanent buildings in which persons work for less than six weeks.

The Offices, Shops and Railway Premises Act is mainly concerned with the following:

1 Physical working conditions:

Cleanliness, ventilation, lighting, drinking water, seating, accommodation for clothing.

Overcrowding: the employer must allow at least 40 square feet of floor space for each person normally employed in a room, or where the ceiling is lower than 10 feet, 400 cubic feet per person. Furniture, fittings, machinery and other such items should be ignored when measuring the size of the room.

Temperature: unless the room is used by the public and it is impracticable to do so, a reasonable temperature must be maintained. Where a substantial proportion of the work does not involve severe physical effort the temperature must not be less than 16°C (60.8°F) after the first hour but not less than 19°C (66.2°F). The employer must provide a thermometer on each floor in a conspicuous place for the use of the employees.

Sanitary conveniences and washing facilities: the Sanitary Conveniences Regulations 1964 and the Washing Facilities Regulations 1964 lay down the minimum requirements

2 Constructing, maintaining and keeping reasonably free from obstruction floors, stairs, passages and gangways

3 Restrictions on lifting heavy loads

4 Fencing dangerous machinery, restricting the cleaning of certain machines by persons under eighteen and training and supervising persons using certain prescribed machines which are registered as particularly dangerous;

5 Registration of offices and shops with the local council, obtaining a fire certificate from the fire authority, and other administrative matters

6 Eating facilities for those working in shops.

REGULATIONS

As noted earlier, many regulations have been made for special processes and industries. They are too numerous to quote here, and most apply only to a few specialised processes, but mention should be made of the regulations for safety representatives and safety committees, building operations, and canteens.

The Safety Representatives and Safety Committees Regulations 1977

These regulations provide for the appointment of safety representatives, describe their functions and give them the right to certain time off to carry out their tasks and for training. The representatives are also empowered to carry out inspections and have access to certain documents and information. The setting-up of safety committees is also prescribed if at least two safety representatives make such a request in writing.

Building operations

Regulations apply not only to the erection of new buildings but to the repair and maintenance of existing buildings, including redecorating, repointing and external cleaning of buildings. They thus affect firms, who without being engaged in the construction industry, employ their own teams of maintenance workers. The main requirements for such operations are contained in four sets of regulations:

The Construction (Working Places) Regulations 1966
The Construction (Lifting Operations) Regulations 1961
The Construction (General Provisions) Regulations 1961
The Construction (Health and Welfare) Regulations 1966
    and Amendment 1974

Building Regulations

Part III of the Act, which will be the responsibility of the Secretaries of State for the Environment and for Scotland, extends the power to make building regulations governing the structure of buildings.

Canteens

Staff and works canteens are included under Food Hygiene (General) Regulations 1970, made under the Food and Drugs Act. These regulations include provisions for cleanliness (and personal cleanliness) and other precautions against the contamination of food. A canteen within the curtilage of a factory and used by employees working on the manufacturing process is also subject to the Factories Act. A staff canteen used by office workers, whether part of the office premises or not, is subject to the Offices, Shops and Railway Premises Act.

CODES OF PRACTICE

Regulations will, where appropriate, be supplemented by Codes of Practice. These will not be statutory requirements but nevertheless may be used in criminal proceedings as evidence that statutory requirements have been contravened.

A Code of Practice covering noise was published in 1972. It applies to all persons employed in industry who are exposed to noise and sets out recommended limits to noise exposure. The Health and Safety Commission have proposed a noise law to ensure that workers are not exposed to a noise level of 90 decibels or over, averaged throughout an 8-hour day. Codes of practice have also been issued on the appointment and time off for training of safety representatives, and on the establishment of safety committees. A Code on First Aid is to be published.

EMPLOYERS' LIABILITY

The Employers' Liability (Compulsory Insurance) Act 1969 prescribes that all employers must insure against liability for personal injury and disease sustained by their employees and arising out of, or in the course of, their employment. The Social Security Act 1975 does not exempt the employer from taking out this insurance.

FIRE PRECAUTIONS ACT 1971

There must be means of escape in case of fire, adequate in regard to the circumstances and number of people employed, and suitable fire-fighting equipment and systems must be available. Application must be made to the local authority for a certificate that these requirements have been met.

CHECKLIST OF NOTICES TO BE POSTED

In the following list of statutory notices which have to be displayed, where relevant, the numerical references are to the sections of the Factories Act (FA) and the Offices, Shops and Railway Premises Act (OSRPA) in which the requirement appears. An asterisk against an item indicates that the notice displayed has to be in a prescribed form, copies of which can be obtained from the Stationery Office.

1   *Prescribed abstract of the Factories Act (FA 138). The employer is required to show on this the addresses of the employment medical adviser and the district inspector
2   *Prescribed abstract (or a copy) of any statutory regulations made under the Factories Act and applicable to the premises (FA 139)
3   *Prescribed abstract of the Offices, Shops and Railways Premises Act, unless every employee affected has been given a copy of the prescribed booklet containing the same information (OSRPA 50)
4   *Notice in each factory workroom showing the maximum numbers of persons permitted to work in that room unless the factory inspector exercises his power to exempt a factory from this requirement (FA 2)
5   Notice showing the name of the person in charge of the first-aid box for the workroom or office (FA 61 and OSRPA 24). With effect from 1 July 1982, the Health and Safety (First Aid) Regulations 1981 and Code of Practice

replaced the first-aid sections of the Factories Act and the Offices, Shops and Railway Premises Act

6   *Notice of any exemption for or granted under the Offices, Shops and Railway Premises Act (OSRPA 46)
7   Notice showing the hours of work, times of meal breaks, etc, for women and persons under eighteen (FA 88, 90, 94 and 115)
8   *Cautionary placards required to be displayed under regulations for certain special processes for example, chromium-plating and power-press regulations)
9   Placards showing the recommended treatment for electric shock, if electricity is used at voltages above 125v ac or 250v dc
10 Notice in sanitary conveniences used by persons handling food, requesting them to wash their hands (this is a requirement of the Food Hygiene Regulations 1960)
11 Notice showing the piecework rates payable for certain prescribed operations (FA 135 and orders made under the Act) unless every employee is given a written note of these rates
12 Fire regulations and drill
13 Certificate of insurance against liability to employees for injury or disease incurred whilst at work.

It is an offence for any person to deface or pull down a notice displayed under the Acts.

CHECKLIST OF NOTICES TO BE SENT TO FACTORY INSPECTOR OR OTHER AUTHORITY

The following notices must be sent to the district inspector of factories, unless otherwise stated. The numerical references are to the relevant sections of the Factories Act (FA) and the Offices, Shops and Railway Premises Act (OSRPA). An asterisk against an item shows that the notice must be sent on a prescribed form obtainable from the Stationery Office.

1   *Notice that premises are to be used as a factory (FA 137)
2   *Notice to local council that premises are to be used as offices or shops (if the offices are to be on factory premises, the notice must be sent to the factory inspector instead; if at a mine or quarry it must be sent to the inspector of mines and quarries) (OSRPA 49)
3   *Application to the fire authority for a fire certificate for a factory, office or shop (FA and OSRPA 29)
4   Notice to fire authority when material structural alterations are made to premises, or number of employees materially increased, after fire certificate has been granted (FA 41 and OSRPA 30)
5   Notice to the local careers officer of the Youth Employment Service when recruiting a person under eighteen (a requirement under the Health and Safety Act Part II) to work in a factory
6   Notice of any fatal accident or major injury to any person, whether or not an employee, and of any accident which, while not causing death or injury

is of the type specified in the Notification of Accidents and Dangerous Occurences Regulations 1980 should be notified to the Health and Safety Executive or other authority of it by the quickest possible means (usually by telephone) and confirmed by a written report within seven days

7   *Notice to factory inspector and also to employment medical adviser of any cases of industrial disease. These diseases are prescribed in s82 of the Factories Act and in various orders made under it

8   *Notice of intention to employ women or young persons on overtime (FA 90)

9   *Notice of intention to employ women or young persons at different times from those stated on routine notice posted in factory (FA 88)

10 *Notice of intention to take advantage of permitted exemptions to the legal hours for women and young persons allowed in certain industries (FA 99 to 112)

11 *Notice of intention to employ persons in an underground room, i.e. one with at least half of its height below ground level (FA 69)

12 *Biannual return to local council (in February and August) of any out-workers working on certain processes (FA 133 to 134)

13 *Intention to begin building operations or works of engineering construction expected to last for six weeks or more (FA 127).

The special regulations for certain processes also contain the requirement that the use of such processes shall be notified to the factory inspector.

CHECKLIST OF REGISTERS TO BE KEPT

All the following records and registers must be kept on the prescribed forms, published by the Stationery Office.

1   General factory register. This provides a record of young persons employed, periodical painting or limewashing of the factory, accidents and dangerous occurrences, cases of industrial disease, persons trained in first aid, testing of fire warning systems, and any exemption granted by the factory inspector concerning the hours worked by women and young persons (FA 140)

2   Certificates, etc, attached to general registers. Reports and certificates of various examinations and test of plant required by the Factories Act and regulations made under it are, in most cases, required to be entered in or attached to the general register. The fire certificate issued by the fire authority must also be attached to the general register

3   Accident book kept under the Social Security (Claims and Payments) Regulations. This book (from BI 510) must be kept by every factory and on all other premises where more than ten persons are employed. It is separate and distinct from the accident book which forms part of the general register and is provided so that an injured workman, or someone acting or him, may record details of any accident which might lead to a claim for National Insurance Benefits

4   Health registers. The regulations for certain special factory processes

require the medical examination of workers engaged in them; the results of these examinations must be recorded in the prescribed health register for the process

5 Register of overtime. This must be used to record overtime worked by women and by persons under eighteen (FA 90).

6 Record of hours worked by van boys, etc. This must be used to record the hours worked by young persons employed outside the factory on business connected with the factory, for example as van boys or messengers (FA 116).

ADVICE AND FURTHER INFORMATION

Advice on health and safety can be obtained from local offices of the Health and Safety Executive, which are represented by HM Inspectorate. A list of their addresses is given below.

Health and Safety Inspectorate addresses

Area		Address	Local authorities within each area
1	South West	Inter City House, Mitchell Lane, Bristol BS1 6AN Tel 0272 290681	Avon, Cornwall, Devon, Gloucestershire, Somerset, Isles of Scilly
2	South	Priestly House, Priestly Road, Basingstoke RG24 9NW Tel 0256 3181	Berkshire, Dorset, Hampshire, Isle of Wight, Wiltshire
3	South East	3 East Grinstead House London Road East Grinstead West Sussex RH19 1RR Tel 0342 26922	Kent, Surrey, East Sussex, West Sussex
4	London NW	Chancel House, Neasden Lane, London NW10 2UD Tel 01-459 8844	Barnet, Brent, Camden, City of London, Enfield, Hammersmith, Harrow, Hillingdon, Hounslow, Kensington & Chelsea, City of Westminster
5	London NE	Maritime House, 1 Linton Road, Barking, Essex IG11 8HF Tel 01-594 5522	Barking, Hackney, Haringey, Havering, Islington, Newham, Redbridge, Tower Hamlets, Waltham Forest
6	London S	1 Long Lane, London SE1 4PG Tel 01-407 8911	Bexley, Bromley, Croydon, Greenwich, Kingston-upon-Thames, Lambeth, Lewisham, Merton, Richmond-upon-Thames, Southwark, Sutton, Wandsworth
7	East Anglia	39 Baddow Road, Chelmsford, Essex CM2 0HL Tel 0245 84661	Essex except the London Boroughs in Essex covered by Area 5; Norfolk, Suffolk
8	Northern Home Counties	17 Cardiff Road, Luton LU1 1PP Tel 0582 34121	Bedfordshire, Buckinghamshire, Cambridgeshire, Hertfordshire

9	East Midlands	Belgrave House, 1 Greyfriars, Northampton NN1 2LQ Tel 0604 21233	Leicestershire, Northamptonshire, Oxfordshire, Warwickshire
10	West Midlands	McLaren Building, 2 Masshouse Circus, Queensway, Birmingham B4 7NP Tel 021 236 5080	West Midlands
11	Wales	Brunel House, 2 Fitzalan Road, Cardiff CF2 1SH Tel 0222 497777	Clywd, Dyfed, Gwent, Gwynedd, Mid Glamorgan, Powys, South Glamorgan, West Glamorgan
12	Marches	The Marches House, The Midway, Newcastle-under-Lyme Staffs ST5 1DT Tel 0782 610181	Hereford and Worcester, Salop, Staffordshire
13	North Midlands	Burkbeck House, Trinity Square, Nottingham NG1 4AU Tel 0602 40712	Derbyshire, Lincolnshire, Nottingham-shire
14	South Yorkshire	Sovereign House, 40 Silver Street, Sheffield S1 2ES Tel 0742 739081	Humberside, South Yorkshire
15	West & North Yorkshire	8 St Pauls Street, Leeds LS1 2LE Tel 0532 446191	North Yorkshire, West Yorkshire
16	Greater Manchester	Quay House, Quay Street, Manchester M3 3JB Tel 061-831 7111	Greater Manchester
17	Merseyside	The Triad, Stanley Road, Bootle L20 3PG Tel 051-922 7211	Cheshire, Merseyside
18	North West	Victoria House, Ormskirk Road, Preston PR1 1HH Tel 0772 59321	Cumbria, Lancashire
19	North East	Government Buildings, Kenton Bar, Newcastle-upon-Tyne NE1 2YX Tel 0632 869811	Cleveland, Durham, Northumberland, Tyne & Wear
20	Scotland East	Meadowbank House, 153 London Road, Edinburgh EH8 7AU Tel 031-661 6171	Borders, Central, Fife, Grampian, Highland, Lothian, Tayside and the island areas of Orkney & Shetland
21	Scotland West	314 Vincent Street, Glasgow G3 8XG Tel 041-204 2646	Dumfries and Galloway, Strathclyde, and the Western Isles

Employers' organisations and trade associations can also provide guidance, as do the British Safety Council and the Royal Society for the Prevention of Accidents. Detailed information about the responsibilities of employers in regard to working conditions and liability to employees will be found in the following standard works.

FURTHER READING

Fife, I., and Machin, I. A., *Redgrave's Factories Acts*, Butterworth, London 1976, and Supplement 1979. Gives the full text of the Factories Act and regulations made under it, with legal references and explanatory notes.

Fife, I., and Machin, I. A., *Redgrave's Offices and Shops (together with Agricultural and Railway Safety)*, Butterworth, London, 1973. A companion volume to the above, giving text and notes for the Offices, Shops and Railway Premises Act and the Agriculture (Safety Provisions) Act.

Goodman, M. J., (ed.), *Encyclopaedia of Health and Safety*, Sweet and Maxwell, London; and W. Green, Edinburgh. The annotated texts of the Factories Act, and the Health and Safety at Work Act, the Offices, Shops and Railway Premises Act (and other Acts), with the regulations made under them, bound in loose leaf form to accommodate periodical revised pages supplied under a follow-up service.

Munkman, J., *Employer's liability at Common Law*, Butterworth, London, 1979. A comprehensive work dealing with general common law obligations and the effect, in civil actions, of breaches of statutory duty.

The Stationery Office publishes the texts of all Acts and regulations, the prescribed forms, Codes of Practice, guidance notes and various advisory booklets. Details are given in the publications catalogue available from the Health and Safety Executive. A bi-monthly "Newsletter" is also available from the Health and Safety Executive and films can be hired or bought from the Central Film Library in London.

54 Industrial training

Derek Torrington

Those responsible for training in companies often regard their work as vulnerable. If times are hard, then training programmes are among the first to suffer cutback. It was partly to change this situation that we had the 1964 Industrial Training Act to boost the provision of training in companies. That intervention was only temporarily successful and the more rigorous circumstances of recent years have shifted governmental priorities in the UK towards provision for the unemployed, and companies are less constrained by the requirements of industrial training boards.

Company training budgets remain vulnerable because training is often regarded as an optional extra: 'without proper training we may not be here in five years, but without more productivity and cash in the bank we won't be here next week'. Sadly some training programmes are indeed expendable because they are not geared to real organisational needs and are of dubious effectiveness. The purpose of this chapter is to make a case for training and then to review some methods of putting it into practice.

THE NEED FOR TRAINING IN COMPANIES

The advantages of training range from more effective use of resources to considerations of the overall purpose of the enterprise.

Resources

The people in an organisation are its major resource. If they are not appropriately trained for the work they have to perform they will not do it as efficiently as they could and operations will not be as profitable as they might be. Some degree of investment in training can make the human resources at the disposal of the management more productive and more profitable.

Fragmentation of work

Specialisation is growing so that the work to be done within the undertaking is constantly being broken up into smaller parcels. New departments are set up to specialise in a particular aspect of the company's affairs, and each employs people to work in a specialised rather than in a general field. In the management ranks this produces the functional specialist who can do one or two things well, replacing the gifted amateur who could do many things with reasonable competence. This means that each employee needs training to undertake his duties, and this need is likely to become greater.

New skills and knowledge

One consequence of specialisation is obsolescence in skills and knowledge. Many people in the financial and administrative field, for example, have forced themselves through the traumatic experience of accepting electronic data processing in the last decade. This acceptance has made it necessary for them to take some training so that they understand the monsters that are spewing forth information at such an alarming rate. The arrival of the computer has rendered obsolete some of the established administrative skills. This effect of technological development is apparent in every part of commerical and industrial activity. Few if any people will still be practising at forty the skills they learned at twenty. The new skills have to be taught.

It is short-sighted, expensive and impractical merely to hire new people who happen to have picked up the new skills elsewhere. The challenge of retraining the adult has to be faced, both by the employer and by the individual concerned. With managerial staff especially, there is the even more demanding need constantly to develop new understanding of the environment in which the organisation is functioning. Changes in law, economic circumstances and in the community outside the organisation have great influence on affairs within the organisation, and knowledge of the environment is essential to managers.

On the job training

Some people counter this sort of argument by saying that training should take place outside the field of employment, and that the substantial proportion of the gross national product channelled into further education should take care of industrial training needs by training people in colleges and government training centres in the whole span of skills and areas of knowledge that are developing. Those who make this point would usually be surprised by the extent of what is done in this way, but still the training that is done off the job cannot be completed off the job. Just as a person learning to drive has to sit in the driving seat and drive along the street during his training, so the apprentice engineer, the trainee typist, laboratory technician, supervisor, personnel officer, sales manager and other industrial trainees all have to get their academic training in practical perspective, which is best done in the working situation.

Also much necessary training is in routines which are peculiar to one company, so that although a supervisor may learn much of great value on a supervisor's course at the local college it will be equally important for him to learn his own company's disciplinary procedures, and this can obviously come only from an agent of the employer.

Employee expectation

There is a standard of expectation which prospective employees have about what the company provides for its recruits. They will expect canteen facilities and locker rooms. Many will expect pension provision and sick pay. If these basic expectations are not met, they will not come and work for the company unless they have no choice, or unless they are likely to earn much more money than they would elsewhere. More and more employees are expecting to receive systematic training for the job when they join a new company rather than having to 'sit next to Nellie'. A well-run training scheme will be an aid to recruitment. Complete lack of training will be a disincentive to prospective recruits.

Social purpose

All administrators and managers have a view of the purpose of their enterprise that goes beyond mere survival and profitability. One of management's many objectives is that the company should be a place worth working in, and that the people working there can to some extent achieve personal fulfilment. Assuming that a company has a personnel policy which recognises its employees as people rather than simply resources, then the requirements for industrial training are the requirements of the people employed as well as the requirements of the employer.

ADMINISTERING THE TRAINING FUNCTION

The passing of the Industrial Training Act led to many companies taking the concept of specialisation too far, and training departments were set up where the managers reported directly to the managing director or to the general manager quite independently of the personnel department. The reason for this was usually the calibre of the uncumbent personnel manager, or the alarm of the managing director at the prospect of being 'fined' by his industrial training board for not meeting their requirements. In the mid 1960s many personnel managers were limited in their thinking to aspects of employee welfare such as canteen, lavatories and record-keeping rather than taking the broader view of personnel which is common today. As a result this type of personnel manager was not considered the appropriate person to be responsible for training with its new levy sanction, and most of the bright, keen training officers who started emerging were not prepared to report to that type of company executive.

This produced a split in the personnel function. Fortunately this practice is now less common except in the largest organisations with substantial training requirements, but it is important to appreciate that personnel work is an amalgam of many activities including training, employment, payment, trade union recognition, discipline, grievances, the design of jobs and consultative arrangements. Each of these interlocks with the others and they have to be co-ordinated and administered under an overall personnel policy. One cannot be isolated from the rest without risks. Effective training depends on effective selection, improved industrial relations often require new training programmes and training innovations frequently influence the industrial relations environment. In considering how the training function is administered, it is therefore of primary importance to see it as part of personnel work.

The personnel function should not usually report to a line manager. If the responsibility for any aspect of personnel comes under, say, the production manager, then managers in marketing, R & D and other areas will regard it as a specifically production function – as may the production manager. It must be seen to be available to, and necessary for, all company functions. Furthermore the responsibility of the training specialist does not interfere with the line authority of the manager. The training officer provides a specialist service to all line managers in the organisation. His particular usefulness lies in his understanding of the requirement of the training board for the relevant industry, his expertise in the skills and the knowledge needed to administer a training programme, his awareness of how people learn, his knowledge of courses and potential visiting lectures. He has a general responsibility for the quality of training provided in the organisation, but the individual line manager remains responsible for the performance and competence of his own staff. The line manager needs to appreciate what the training function can do for him in developing that competence: he cannot wash his hands of the responsibility and 'leave it to personnel'. They can only provide him with some services that he has to understand and use.

Integration with other functions

Responsibility for specialist training services needs to be integrated with the whole of the personnel function, which must in turn be integrated with the management of the enterprise. Personnel and training are actively concerned with ensuring that the organisation meets it business objectives, not some parasitical unnecessary growth imposed by an outside agency.

Objectives

Corporate objectives need to be reappraised to consider the place of training within the total personnel activity. What are its objectives? How do these fit in with the existing business objectives? What targets have to be achieved? This procedure sounds obvious, but it is perhaps the aspect of training which is most often ignored, with the consequent vulnerability of the training arrangements.

Identification of training needs

The person responsible for training has first to establish what the training needs of the organisation are. He will consider two aspects of this. First he will investigate the operational efficiency of the organisation. Later he will look at the training needs of individual people, and the need of the organisation for people to be trained. In considering operational efficiency, he will seek to identify those jobs within the organisation that appear to be holding back to the achievement of proper levels of performance and where training may help to lift this level to one that is acceptable. He will take note of the various indicators which personnel people use to 'take the temperature' of working groups.

Absenteeism, labour turnover, punctuality, sickness, changes in output level, complaints and labour troubles can all be indicators of the state of morale in a department, and low morale may be caused by inadequate training. There may be data available from work study officers who feel that the work standards in a particular department are not satisfactory. Conversations with managers and supervisors will suggest other areas requiring attention. The training officer's own experience and training will suggest others, as will the officers of the industrial training boards.

The training officer will therefore collect a mass of information about the training needs that exist within the company, and can then begin to draw up proposals about what training should be done and in what order, the priority usually being determined by the likely pay-off. He may suggest, for example, that the training of typists could be altered to enable newly recruited school-leavers to reach an acceptable level of proficiency in half the time now considered as necessary, at a saving of £x a year, followed by specially designed programmes of operator training in selected departments to reduce the level of labour turnover and to boost output. He might suggest middle managers attending courses at a business school, or supervisors having a series of discussions on the implications of recent legislation. Whatever the particular proposals, he will draw these up and require them to be endorsed by his management colleagues or superiors, so that he has a mandate to start work.

Implementation of the training programme

When the training officer has received his mandate he will also be empowered to spend some money to implement his programme. This will be based on his prediction of how much he can produce in the way of operating economies. The expenditure will come broadly under two headings. First there will be expenditure on hardware and fees, which are outgoings that would not be incurred if the training were not done. Hardware can range from boxes of chalk to overhead projectors, teaching machines and fully equipped, soundproof lecture theatres. Fees will be either the fees payable for employees to attend courses, or payable to outside experts to come and take part in internal courses. The training officer, like any other executive submitting a budget for approval, is likely to ask for more than he needs under this heading, as he expects those who have to sanction his budget to cut it. It may be sensible for a newly established training function to start off with a minimum of equipment and to invest more heavily when experience has been gained. The reason for this is that most training programmes change fundamentally after a spell of running in and the benefits of experience. Heavy initial investment can result in an accumulation of expensive equipment that is unused, and a dearth of equipment that is needed but not available because the budget has been overspent.

The second category of expenditure is salaries and wages of trainees, where the administrator perhaps needs to scrutinise proposals closely. Employees away from work on training courses are still being paid. In the case of most managers and supervisors this adds nothing to the cost of their duties being carried out. Someone else will deputise for them in their absence, they will catch up with their work when they return, and that is that. In some other cases, however, there may be expenditure of either increasing the establishment for a department so that people absent for training can be covered, or arrangements for colleagues to work expensive overtime to make up the shortfall. The training is necessary, but this type of consideration needs to be thought of before the training begins so that the cost implications are fully appreciated.

As well as hardware, the training officer will need some space to run his schemes in. Some training will be done on the job or in a training section of the normal job environment, such as the apprentice bench in an engineering shop. Some training will be carried out away from the premises altogether, as when a young manager goes to the nearby polytechnic to take a management course. But there will be a need for some of the training programme to take place away from the job but on company premises. Typists are often trained in a small school within the company, and a number of short courses may be run to give managers or others an appreciation of a subject or to give training in certain skills that are needed.

Evaluation of training effectiveness

Finally in setting up a training function, there is a need for some means of evaluating the training, and this is one of the most nebulous and unsatisfactory aspects of the training job. The starting point is to compare the results achieved with the original objectives and, where possible, to measure the degree of improvement. This can be done in such areas as labour and material utilisation, or the reduction in the number of despatch errors being made in a warehouse. It can only be guessed in the more difficult areas such as the quality of supervision by a foreman before and after a training course. This often depends on a subjective assessment that may be influenced by the reactions of the trainee.

Another possible means of evaluation is to measure the benefits that are set as objectives at the beginning of the programme. It might be a drop in labour turnover and other measures of improved efficiency and employee morale. There may be fewer accidents or reduced levels of overtime. It is also important to attempt some evaluation of the intangibles, such as atmosphere in industrial relations, customer satisfaction, self-confidence among managers and so on. To some extent this can be done by the use of an outside adviser who can come along for a day to examine the situation relating to training within the organisation and then report upon it, rather like an auditor.

It is useful from a training point of view to carry out some form of performance appraisal regularly among employees. If this is done systematically over several years, the validity of training arrangements will be confirmed – or otherwise.

TRAINING FOR DIFFERENT CATEGORIES OF EMPLOYEE

Operators

The largest single grouping in the employed population is the operator on the shop floor who has no craft skills – the general worker. His job may require such a small amount of skill and knowledge that he needs no training other than a short period of 'being shown how' by his supervisor. There are, however, very few jobs which genuinely fall into this category. Most would be done better by more satisfied employees if they were preceded by a period of training, which covered induction to the organisation and the place of the job in the manu-facturing process, as well as the mechanics of how it should be done.

As operator jobs in manufacturing are usually specific to each employer, the training needs to be set up and run within the company, as there is no outside body either with the understanding of the job or any alternative source of supply of trainees. The training officer will need to study the operations and to use a process of skills analysis to devise a programme of training to be carried out by an instructor instructing trainees. Seldom is the training load large enough to justify a full-time instructor, and it is usual for an experienced operator in each department to be trained in instruction so that he does all the instruction needed by new recruits. Another method is for the foreman to be trained so that he inducts and trains all those in his department. This may be the best method as long as the training job is not going to take up too much of his time.

Skills analysis can be learned at one of the many introductory courses for training officers run within the further education system. Alternatively there are short crash courses available. Instructors can be trained by one of the Training within Industry (TWI) courses provided by the Training Services Division of the Manpower Services Commission.

Clerical

Very little training is provided in clerical duties in most organisations, although the provision of training is spreading and companies find that it pays big dividends in cost savings and employee satisfaction. The practice of clerical training is similar to that for operator training, although there are certain more general occupational skills involved, so that the further education system is more helpful. Widely available is a course in office skills which is taken by young people on leaving school. They attend technical college for one day a week and learn simple office skills and routines to fit in with the working experience they are beginning to acquire. There are also many courses in shorthand and typing, although the demand for shorthand is declining and the school-leaver with reasonable GCE 'O' level achievement can take courses in business studies on day release.

Craft

One of the first areas to repay attention is the training of craft apprentices, as this is a long and expensive business. Some of the training boards gave the largest amount of their attention to this area in the first few years of their operation.

Apprentices are recruited at the age of sixteen on leaving school, and serve an apprenticeship of several years before being accepted as craftsmen at the end of their training, usually at the age of twenty-one or twenty-two. Most apprentices are young men, although young women do follow apprenticeships as well, but these are heavily concentrated in hairdressing. Many companies follow the customary practice of binding apprentices by indentures, under which the apprentice is obliged to stay with the employer until finishing his 'time' and the employer agrees to provide his training.

A major part of the apprentice's time is spent in further education at a local college, learning the theoretical background of his craft and some manual skills. While with the employer, he needs to practise the skills he is learning and to develop them by applying his knowledge and ability to a growing range of work. Traditionally this has been done by watching, helping and copying a craftsman at work. Gradually this method is being replaced by systematic and full-time training under an instructor in charge of a group of apprentices.

If an organisation is not big enough to warrant the services of a full-time instructor, it is often possible to join a group training scheme, in which a number of small and medium-sized companies pool resources to employ a training officer who organises the training of the apprentices in all the companies. In return, the individual company pays a relatively modest fee to the group scheme. Also, the individual apprentice has a better training as he probably moves from one firm to another in the group.

There are usually national agreements between employers and trade unions regarding the employment and training of apprentices.

Technician

A category in which the number of employees is growing is that of technician, who is one step up from a craftsman and is likely to be concerned more with design than with manufacture. In the field of engineering, the fitter is the craftsman and the draftsman is the technician, although there are many others classified as craftsmen and technicians respectively in that industry. To some extent the training needs are common, as the basic technology is the same, but the technician's training needs go further. He is likely to have better educational qualifications at the outset and his further education will go to a higher theoretical level. His practical training will tend to lie in conventional white collar rather than manual operations. It is usually carried out in close conjunction with a qualified man.

Technologist

It is difficult to distinguish between technicians and technologists and in many industries such a distinction cannot be drawn at all. A rough and ready identification would be by the word 'professional'. In engineering, for example, the technologist is the professional engineer who has achieved membership of one of the constituent bodies of the Council of Engineering Institutions. This requires a high level of academic qualification together with the appropriate working experience.

In this category will be the ex-technician who has taken the HNC/HND route through day release or evening courses, as well as the technical graduate who starts his working life in his early twenties. These are the people on whom the technical competence and progress of the organisation will depend. The HNC/D method of qualification is in the process of being replaced by the scheme of the Technical Education Council (TEC). Courses for technical graduates now have the interesting development of a small number of courses in selected universities that combine engineering and management studies, usually over four years of study.

The man who comes up through the ranks will need facilities to pursue his academic studies, either by day release or by sandwich course. His practical expertise will be acquired almost incidentally as long as he has reasonable opportunities for varied working experience, rather than being classified as a trainee who cannot be given a proper job because he has not finished his education.

The technical graduate who joins industry in his early twenties with academic qualifications of a high order but no practical experience usually needs some form of graduate apprenticeship while he spends a number of months acquiring the practical experience that is needed to go with his theoretical grounding.

Management

Training managers is a very different matter from training other categories of workers in industry. This is largely because a smaller proportion of the manager's job content can be isolated and taught. To be effective a manager needs to learn management techniques, such as various methods for the quantification of data so that decisions may be soundly based. He also needs knowledge in such areas as the behavioural sciences so that he can understand how employees may react in certain situations, and so that he may plan sensibly for the future. Beyond this, however, there is still a large area of training or development needed for the individual management trainee, so that he acquires the stature and confidence needed for the job of leadership, gains judgement and determination and develops good timing and a sensitive awareness in handling people.

Largely because of the difficulty and lack of definition in the task of managment training, most large organisations separate this particular aspect of training and give the responsibility to management development officers within the training function. The body of knowledge and some of the skills can come from the educational system. In addition to the business schools, which cater for a small fraction of the total amount of management training, there are a number of polytechnics and universities with management departments running courses with recognition from some professional body. The most widely recognised management qualification available in the field of further education is the Diploma in Management Studies, run under the auspices of the Department of Education and Science. It is operated at a limited number of centres and provides a broadly based management education for the well-qualified entrant with limited practical experience. There are also courses run under the aegis of, for instance, the Institute of Personnel Management and the Institution of Industrial Managers which provide a broad management education with particular emphasis on the specialism that the professional body represents.

In conjunction with further education, the trainee manager will need controlled working experience and career development so that he can apply his developing skills and knowledge. He may also need careful coaching to help him develop qualities such as judgement and timing. All managers need constantly to bring themselves up to date with new techniques or with new knowledge. Thus, professional bodies like the British Institute of Management and many firms of professional consultants conduct admirable short courses, running for a few days or a few weeks, to update the experienced manager. Typical of these have been the endless variety of courses and conferences to brief managers on unfair dismissal legislation, safety and health, or negotiating skills. The next chapter deals with management development in more detail.

Supervisory

Training of first-line supervisors is generally unsatisfactory in the United Kingdom, and the foreman has more than once been referred to as the forgotten man of British industry. Much of the problem lies in the uncertainty about the nature of the job. In the early years of this century the foreman was a man of considerable power and authority in a factory, with extensive discretion in decision-making, and was often a general manager in all but name. Since then we have seen the professionalisation of management and the development of shop steward authority. The professionalisation of management has spawned countless middle managers who have taken bits of the forman's job away from him, like the production engineer and the training officer. The development of shop steward authority has largely done away with the foreman's role as representative of shop-floor feeling, and he is constantly bypassed as shop stewards negotiate with middle and senior managers at meetings he is not invited to attend.

As the position of first-line supervisor is so difficult to define, training for it presents obvious problems. The most useful approach is probably the in-company course which aims to inform foremen of the changes taking place around them and give them an understanding of company procedures together with an introduction to such vague but necessary subjects as leadership and human relations. An attempt to establish a course for foremen within the further education system has not received widespread support.

Administrative

The term 'administrative' covers an amorphous group of people who are lumped together because their work is neither clerical nor managerial. They are such people as cost accounts, computer programmers and systems analysts, salesmen and O & M staff.

For the cost accountant, training will usually be on the job as a cost clerk while he makes his way through the further education courses for cost and management accountants, perhaps after starting with an Ordinary National Diploma in Business Studies while he is making up his mind about the area in which he wishes to specialise.

The training of computer personnel operates at various levels. Most courses in management include some elements of computing, even if only at the appreciation level, and there are a number of degree courses in computation. Computer operators and data input personnel are still mainly trained by computer manufacturers or specialised private agencies.

Shop stewards

The final category is shop steward. It is the joint responsibility of management and trade unions to train shop stewards. The best courses for stewards are provided by the trade unions, and an introductory course for newly elected shop stewards is run at many educational centres under the auspices of the TUC. It is difficult for many employers to provide satisfactory courses of their own, as stewards are likely to be suspicious of them, but this field of training will no doubt develop.

TRAINING METHODS

Teaching someone to *do* something requires a different approach from teaching someone to *understand* something. This broad distinction between training in skill and training in knowledge has been refined by research in the training field to produce a division of all types of learning into five basic types.

Some learning involves theoretical subject matter, knowing how, why and when certain things happen. This is *comprehension*: examples are the laws of thermodynamics, the currency structure of the EEC, or the arguments justifying the recognition of trade unions. *Reflex* learning is involved when skilled movements or perceptual capacities have to be acquired, involving practice as well as knowing what to do. Speed is usually important and the trainee needs constant repetition to develop the appropriate synchronisation and co-ordination. Typing is one of the many jobs that requires reflex learning. *Attitude* development is concerned with enabling people to alter their attitudes and social skills. *Memory* training is concerned with learning how to cope with varied situations and *procedural* learning is very similar except that the drill to be followed does not have to be memorised, but located and understood. This categorisation produces the mnemonic CRAMP.

Learning for comprehension requires the whole subject to be treated as an entity and the lecture or training manual are appropriate methods. Attitude change is typically handled by group discussion, but reflex learning is best handled by part methods, which break the task down into sections, each of which can be studied and practised separately before putting together a complete performance. Memory and procedural learning may take place either by whole or part methods, although memorisation is usually done by parts.

FURTHER READING

Annett, J., *Task Analysis*, HMSO, London, 1971

Bass, B. M., and Vaughan, J. A., *Training in Industry*, Tavistock, London, 1968

Industrial Training Research Unit, *Choose an Effective Style: A Self-instructional Approach to the Teaching of Skills*, ITRU Publications, Cambridge, 1976

Kenney, J. P. J., Donnelly, E., and Reid, M., *Manpower Training and Development*, IPM, London, 1980

Stammers, R. B., and Patrick, J., *The Psychology of Training*, Methuen, London, 1975

Winfield, I., *Learning to Teach Practical Skills*, Kogan Page, London, 1979

55 Management development

Michael Day

This chapter has a 'top-down' orientation. It takes the conventional view that ultimately the success of an organisation relies on the quality of its management since action flows from them. Since the quality of management is all important, the long-term future of an organisation is dependent on there being a continuous supply of competent, experienced and well-trained managers, alert to the changing environment.

A competent manager is the result of many differing factors; he is certainly not the product of a recognised training system like a skilled craftsman, a doctor or a pilot. Some of the factors which make for quality may be controllable, yet the effectiveness of any total system for producing managers has never been adequately measured in terms of efficiency; there have only been attempts to measure the parts (e.g., human relations training), and that with varying degrees of success. It is not possible therefore to discuss methods in terms of their cost effectiveness; indeed it is this lack of knowledge that has led management development to be an area particularly prone to fads and fashion. Yet though many of the packages which are offered are found wanting, the subject is still felt to be important because quite clearly organisations differ in their success and the only discernible reason can be the difference in quality of their management.

For this reason this chapter takes the widest view of the way an organisation may act in order to meet its manpower needs for managers. To do this it must concern itself with three areas.

1 The attributes of the individual himself
2 The effect of the opportunities and the environment as they affect the individual
3 The form of administrative assistance that may be given.

ATTRIBUTES OF THE INDIVIDUAL

In theory, senior managers have to pass through the most stringent system of selection in that to arrive at their position they must have passed a series of stages where they could be accepted or rejected. In practice most selection systems, if they are not dependent on the decision of a single individual, rely heavily on an appraisal system.

As will be mentioned, there have been some attempts to identify the essential characteristics of a good manager, but there is no general agreement on what these may be. Such attempts have been initiated, primarily, in large companies which have a greater problem is selecting people for wider 'exposure'.

On the whole, research indicates that leadership is specific to situations and perceived leaders share specific attributes with their groups but at a higher level. It follows that a manager should possess sufficient knowledge of skills to a level acceptable to the group he controls. The first point for training is that first-line managers must have sufficient technical knowledge. This will be even more important in a situation of changing technology; the danger of skill obsolescence is becoming greater and is an increasingly common reason for retiring managers prematurely.

The second point is that the skills of management are discontinuous; thus the attributes of a good lieutenant are different from those of a good general. This implies that training must be both different in content and continuous to meet the needs of an advancing career.

The third point is that organisations are formed of successive layers which interact. A good organisation is the product of mixing attributes, knowledge, skills, etc., into a complementary whole. For instance, research has indicated that a dominant creative person works best as leader of a less creative submissive group; put such a man in a group of people similar to himself and little is produced but argument. Alternate layers of good communicators and administrators and good conceptualisers are very desirable. Hence building a *team* is an important objective of management development.

There are also general personal characteristics that are likely to be important.

1 *Intelligence.* This is not only necessary because management requires the ability to deal with abstract matters, but also because learning must take place quickly and effectively in order to deal with the changing environment.
2 *A willingness to grow.* Pym's research concluded 'people who aspire to growth in their work are likely to be numbered among the more effective in mentally demanding jobs and in situations where changes increase the uncertainty of work roles'.
3 *Accuracy of self-perception.* Effective peope are conscious of their strengths and weaknesses and learn to play their strong points.
4 *Versatility.* Administrators operate very largely by labelling; however, longitudinal studies of careers show that it is increasingly common for individuals to make major switches in profession. Indeed it is commonly predicted that most of us must be prepared to have two or more careers in

our lifetime. Versatility is therefore a characteristic that must be identified; most selection puts greatest emphasis on choosing an individual for a particular job, though viewed longitudinally the individual will occupy it for a small time in his career.

Success in management therefore largely rests on factors outside the scope of training, but fortunately the growing individual is likely to have the best view of what his needs are. We should attempt to operate a system of self-appraisal and self-education.

In any case most ambitious young men are well aware that an increasing number of their contemporaries (compared with the present generation of managers) have had some form of management education. This may be a pity because the desire may merely be to attend such a course, and concern for the content, effectiveness and relevance becomes secondary.

THE OPPORTUNITIES AND THE ENVIRONMENT

A man is the product of his history; but though one can trace the effects backwards, forecasting outcomes is very dubious. Specialists usually have more limited career patterns than generalists. This is not because they lack ability but because the decision-maker will rule them out for 'lack of experience'. The pattern for specialists is therefore largely determined very early in their careers. Paradoxically many organisations can point to individuals who were thrust into positions of responsibility and are very successful – the 'Truman phenomenon'.

The rate of progression of an individual within an organisation is dependent on three factors (apart from his own abilities). These are:

1 Age structure of the organisation (or the manpower pool to which he belongs).
2 Rate of expansion or contraction of the organisation.
3 Degree of change of organisation, structure, functions, etc.

For example it is obvious that a thirty-year-old who has already had a variety of experience in an expanding organisation with elderly management has very bright prospects.

In a small organisation the problem of getting the right experience is not difficult; the rate of progression allows ample time to master new situations and yet gain a reasonable understanding of other functions. However this escalator approach is not always possible. It is a simple arithmetical exercise to compute the time a high-flying individual might stay in each level of an organisation. Thus a man spending forty years in a company which has eight layers must spend five years in each; in practice, speed through layers is usually quicker at the start of a career and gradually slows. This computation also implies that the company will be run by old men; this is commonly not a desired objective, hence the speed of movement of a future head of a large organisation must be very fast indeed. But the danger is that this makes for a narrow career, i.e., the individual has been moving up so fast he has little time for lateral movement.

The escalator also has its dangers. It can carry an individual up because of the age structure rather than because of his outstanding abilities until he appears the only possible choice for the top job. The result can be unfortunate for the organisation and eventually calamitous for the individual.

Given the right environment, individuals will grow by learning. For this to happen feedback must be effective and positive. An organisation with a good system of counselling where the individual can discuss job performance and objectives, together with his personal wishes to expand his knowledge, skills and experience, will ensure an adequate supply of potential material for promotion.

Many social scientists believe that managerial systems based on trust give the employee a better opportunity to achieve growth at work (McGregor's theory Y). Such a climate may be produced as a result of a programme of organisation development or the drive of a key individual. It can occur because an organisation is in a state of fairly rapid change when decisions are made by those possessing the key knowledge rather than a high position in the hierarchy. Jobs and responsibilities are not highly defined and opportunities are there for those with initiative. This accords with the common observation that radically new situations, e.g., in war time, cause new talents to emerge.

Lastly there is the fortunate accident of working under a first-class manager; many would say that this is the best form of management education. Some organisations try to institutionalise this by having a system of coaching but as Gellerman points out 'most people in management are rewarded for making themselves successful not for making other managers successful'.

It can be seen that becoming a successful manager is a very chancy thing. The first-class man will usually come through; the rest need some help. If the human resources of the organisation are to be used and a 'cadre' of professionally efficient individuals is to be built up, then some assistance in the form of a management development system is desirable.

FORMAL ASSISTANCE IN MANAGEMENT DEVELOPMENT

Many organisations have tried systems of management development, many of which have failed or waned. What is required is not gimmickry but a system in which the management have faith in the overall conception, and the operation of which is built into the normal working of the organisation. As Wilson says, it must become institutional in character, that is, it must operate with an agreed and acceptable set of procedures and it must have the ability to handle the inevitable conflicts which will arise (since individual managers incur short-term loss of efficiency for the organisation's long-term gain).

On the assumption that the personnel function is given the organising responsibility, it has a delicate role to play. If the total system is seen as a piece of personnel gimmickry wished on the organisation, it will fail. The chief executive is responsible for the long-term viability of the managerial team; he cannot delegate this but only the staff work and the organisation of the activities. The personnel function can assist managers to develop their subordinates; they must never seek to impose their solutions.

The overall scheme for a management development is shown in Figure 55.1. A number of elements of the scheme, manpower planning and appraisal, are discussed more fully elsewhere in this book.

There are three parts to the programme:

1 Information collection and analysis
2 Decision making
3 Action.

The scheme is elaborate but can be simplified for small organisations.

INFORMATION INPUTS

Personnel information system

This is a necessary adjunct to a manpower planning model. Apart from its obvious use as a single comprehensive source of information, it acts as a useful discipline to prevent overlooking minor parts of the organisation and particular individuals. A management development system must scan the total manpower resources and not rely on the chance knowledge of the decision-makers.

Manpower planning model

This subject was discussed in Chapter 48, but the particular aspect relevant here is the ability of a model to predict the requirement for managerial manpower some years ahead and also the pattern of the probability of promotion for different groups, e.g., departments, professional/skill groups. Some authorities see the desirable planning horizon as fifteen years; others believe that only five years is practical.

Appraisal

Again this is discussed elsewhere (Chapter 50), but to reiterate, appraisal provides an essential management information input for decisions about people and particularly for management development. It will be seen from the diagram that appraisal information underpins many parts of the management development system. Particularly important are:

1 The assessment of potential for promotion
2 The readiness for a move
3 Specific recommendations on training, movement, etc.
4 The reported views of the individual.

Draft succession plans

Succession plans must be layered, that is they encompass distant levels within the hierarchy, e.g., branch, department management, top management. A typical chart is shown in Figure 55.2 and is self-explanatory. Such a document

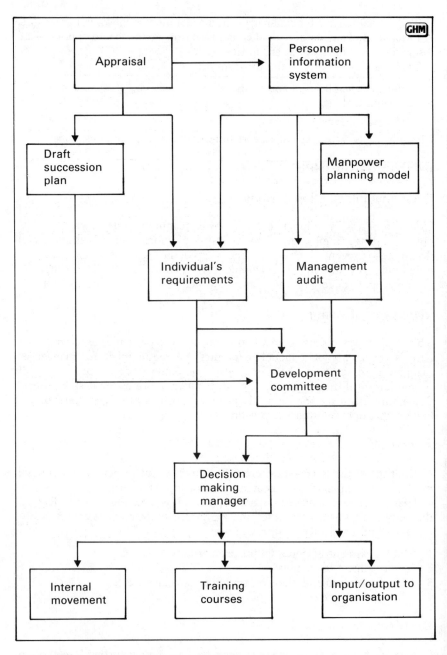

Figure 55.1   Management development system

				GHM
Job	Holder	Age	Year successor required	Possible successor
Manager, Northern Sales Div.	Evans, W. S.	55	1988 (R)	Brown, J. (44) MacPherson, A. (42)
Manager, Newcastle Branch	Brown, J.	42	1987	(E) Jameson, P. (53)
R: Retiring; E: Emergency only				

Figure 55.2   A succession plan

is completed by the senior manager in the 'layer', usually with the assistance of a specialist in manpower development or a personnel officer. It should be discussed by a management development committee to ensure that all possible candidates are considered.

The main objectives are to stimulate management into thinking about their succession problems and to identify areas where special action is called for, e.g., an adequate successor for Brown in Figure 55.2.

Management audit

The object is to collate and analyse the available information in order to arrive at an appraisal of where the organisation finds itself now and may find itself in the foreseeable future with respect to its management manpower. The audit might contain a number of elements:

1   An age distribution of manpower now
2   The same distribution in five years
3   The expected promotion prospects
4   Distribution of potential (see Figure 55.3)
5   Relationship between requirement and resources over five years (see Figure 55.4).

								GHM
Grade	Number	Immediately promotable	Foreseen potential grade					
			1	2	3	4	5	6
1	100	24	52	20	15	8	4	1
2	54	16	—	32	11	8	3	0
3	32	15	—	—	12	16	3	1
4	12	3	—	—	—	8	4	0
5	3	1	—	—	—	—	2	1
6	1	0	—	—	—	—	—	1

Figure 55.3   Distribution of potential

Organisation levels	Numbers	Core[1]	Expected Numbers[2]	Require-ment	Numbers ready now for promotion
A	10	5	10	5	—
B	30	25	32	12[3]	7
C	100	75	110	47[4]	16

1 Numbers remaining at the end of 5 years
2 Allows for change in size of organisation
3 Allows for five promotions to level A
4 Allows for 12 promotions to level B

Figure 55.4 **Relationship between requirements and resources over five years**

Individual information

Personal histories and particulars will be required but these can be included on a special card which can be used as a visual aid when discussions are taking place. The individual cards can be displayed in a format corresponding to the organisation structure. The card may contain:

Photograph of individual
Age
Grade
Performance rating
Potential rating
Present job title
Job history
Qualifications

This device is certainly useful in larger organisations where not all individuals will be directly known to the decision-makers.

Decision-making

The locus and form of decision-making will vary with the style of the organisation. It may be the head of the function or organisation alone; he may be advised by a senior group; or a committee representing different functions may be formed. No best way exists; however failure will follow if those dealing with management development have no power. To repeat, decisions about people are an important part of management responsibility, therefore the decision-making structure must be coincident with the power structure of the organisation.

It is desirable to minimise the time consumption of managers by having relatively infrequent meetings and by good staff work. One meeting a year is usually adequate.

It is clear that any manager or committee should only survey a limited number of individuals. A layered system will be required; the number of layers will depend on the organisation, but there should be basically three, all interlocking:

1 Top management
2 Department, function or geographical location
3 The working unit.

The objectives of the decision makers will be:

1 To review the manpower position. Without reviewing the overall position it is possible for organisations to run into problems of shortfall, over abundance or maldistribution of talent. Few organisations are in equilibrium
2 To ensure that sufficient numbers are available to fill foreseen management requirements. In practice more people must be available than can be promoted because at the moment of decision a number of candidates will not be available for many different reasons, e.g., recent transfer, personal circumstances, etc.
3 To ensure efficiency and equity in movement. Individuals are often penalised because they belong to a less well-favoured part of the organisation. Alternatively there is unnecessary professional exclusivity for certain jobs (e.g., accountants)
4 To encourage the utilisation of talent. Many individuals benefit from movement even if no promotion is involved; it encourages self-renewal or the use of talents for which there is little opening in the present position. Gellerman believes that such moves should always stretch a man by giving more responsibility than he is judged to be ready for; failure in practice is rare and growth is accelerated
5 To resolve conflict about the use of individuals. There will always be a limited number of outstanding individuals, and their current managers will always be tempted to try and keep them. Given the scarcity, this is unlikely to be the best strategy for the organisation as a whole, so some supra-body is required to resolve competing claims.

ACTION

Although recruitment and dismissal must be part of the scheme, in a well-run organisation these should be rare events; resorting to either points to the failure of the management development programme.

Movement

Action tends to two extremes, either 'opportunistic' or 'predetermined'. Opportunistic movement operates where the decisions are made in the light of the previous analysis and recommendation but the act is dependent on an opening occurring. Predetermined movement initiates a succession of interrelated moves. The opportunistic system is perhaps less efficient but has the advantage that it allows greater choice to the individual as the system can still operate if he refuses a move. Predetermined moves depend on the individual being willing, say, to move location; in return he can be reasonably certain of where his next job will be.

Movements (promotion) can take the following forms:

1 Transfer – in practice exchanges of individuals are administratively easier than a chain of movements if only because of the problem of handover.
2 Projects – these are valuable because they can provide an opportunity to try an individual in a new role, e.g., putting him in a managerial position without an almost irreversible commitment to keep him in his new status. It is a useful mechanism for spreading experience of a new technique throughout the managerial group by making each man serve as a project leader for a limited spell
3 'Secondments' – opportunities for these are rare but may include the civil service, education establishments and companies with close commercial relationships
4 Action learning – Revans (its progenitor) describes this as 'Learning to learn-by-doing with and from others who are also learning to learn-by-doing'. In its most usual form it involves undertaking an assignment in another company (or part of the same company) which in turn nominates an individual to form part of the learning group. The whole process is carefully guided with the group of participants meeting weekly to talk through experience and problems, with the aid of a specialist adviser.

Continuous movement is part of the way of life in some companies, but it has a cost penalty attached to it. In theory there must be a 'learning curve' for each person entering each job. This implies that for a period of time there will be a continuous but reducing deficit of efficiency.

Against this the organisation has increased the asset value of its manpower. Indeed, the R. G. Barry Corporation in the US (among others) has shown changes in the value of its human resources in its annual reports. The desirability of this can readily be seen for organisations such as architects' groups, advertising agencies and accounting practices whose strength lies primarily in the quality of the people they employ; however this form of accounting presents great technical difficulties and no agreed conventions exist.

It does indicate the need for the decision-maker to balance the cost of movement and training against the increase in asset value of the manpower.

Training

Two fundamental assumptions are made; first, training must be continuous, and second, training content must vary with the stages in the individual's career. It follows, therefore, that management training cannot be a 'one-shot' injection.

Training must be continuous because the individual changes over time, because the work environment alters, and because new knowledge and techniques are being created at an increasing rate.

Four stages in an individual's career can be identified and with each there are corresponding training needs.

Professional phase

Few start as managers; initially the individual often works as a professional – a chemist, accountant or personnel officer. This phase exploits any academic qualification. Training is predominantly a 'topping-up' process in order to keep him up to date and prevent skill obsolescence.

Gradually he is likely to acquire greater managerial responsibilities. The corresponding management training need is to introduce him to topics so that the self-educational process can start. These might include:

1   Company knowledge – this has the object of breaking down parochialism and facilitating interaction. Much of this training happens informally by virtue of mixing course members from different parts of the company.
2   Information handling and analysis – introduction to accounting and numerical analysis techniques.
3   Manpower planning, assessment, training, industrial relations. Broad management theory.

It is stressed that the treatment will be introductory; teaching in depth has no direct value unless the individual has the opportunity to practice new found skills. The exception may be social skills, e.g., lecturing, presentation of cases, interviewing and running meetings, though these are best dealt with as separate 'modules' when a need is clear.

Initial management appointment

It is common for a manager to be confronted with a requirement to undertake a number of specific administrative actions related to local procedures on taking up his appointment. These might include:

1   Budgeting method
2   Completion of assessment forms
3   Grievance procedure
4   Procedure for replacing staff
5   Authorising expenditure
6   Handling communication with subordinates.

In the first months this can be bewildering and needlessly embarrassing; costly errors can result from ignorance. So on appointment either a course or a series of individual discussions should be arranged to accelerate the learning process and the building of confidence. The actual content must be determined by a thorough analysis.

Mature management

This is one of the most difficult phases for which to cater because of the very varied experience of management matters possessed by each individual. It is a common experience that managers sent on a general management course complain that 'it was very interesting but it only partly touched on topics that are important in my job'. Such courses are not very efficient in time usage and may be positively harmful if they reinforce a latent feeling that all such training is 'useless'.

The answer would seem to be either a carefully chosen series of modules, or courses with a high degree of flexibility to meet personal needs.

The principle of selection for modules should be that the manager is certain to practise the new-found skill on return to his desk. The principle of the method is that the skill must be advanced to a level on the course where he can go through the process without outside assistance on his return; this implies a fair level of practical work on the course.

Informational topics have their place but mainly to change attitudes or to reinforce the process started in the professional phase.

Modules can be linked in time so that they run consecutively provided that a homogeneous group can be brought together, e.g., a group of marketing managers. This enables technical topics to be taken in depth.

An important module for many managers will be industrial relations. Traditional approaches have been to trace the history of trade unions or to place the emphasis on the legal aspects; such approaches are useful as an introduction but are rarely useful practically. Knowledge of local agreements and procedures is vital, and many companies use simulated disputes where course members role play the parts. Trainees can experiment with different responses, and feedback can be provided by discussion or preferably by playing back a video tape of the process. One of the advantages of role playing is that it encourages flexibility together with the realisation that no single mode of response is effective in meeting all types of situations. The process of role reversal, i.e., playing the part of the union official, fosters a deeper understanding of the powers and limitations of the full-time officer.

An approach, of which one is likely to see more, is some variety of flexible training. The theory is that all parts of the course should be tailor-made to meet the needs of every individual. For instance, if the topic is discounted cash flow, one group may be very familiar with the topic and so would be more interested in the advanced aspects, the largest group may have only a nodding acquaintance and so need their skills brought up to the working level, and one group may know nothing. The first step is to discover the groups; this can be done by self-evaluation or self-testing, though this is only a guide since the individual may choose which group he joins. The difficulty is the administration and the availability of highly flexible tutors. An alternative would be the use of self-teaching aids or guided reading. Surprisingly few managers' courses are based on reading; books appear to be for self-educators, not course-goers. There is certainly no lack of suitable material.

Higher management

The potential member of top management, if caught young enough, presents no great training problem; most large companies send such people to prestigious courses which draw their membership from all over the world. The business schools are favourites. Such a course has many advantages:

1   It will enable the 'young lion' to test himself against international standards.
2   It will expose him to some of the best minds whose jobs it is to think about business.
3   It will break down parochialism and cause him to think afresh about his own organisation.

Such courses are usually expensive and long, so organisations send only the cream. This carries the danger that unless the man is mature, with a long history of achievement, the organisation may feel it is necessary to arrange a glittering career for a man whose lustre, in fact, fades as he progresses. The comment 'we had to promote him, he'd been to . . .' is not unknown. In such instances the organisation is caught in a dilemma since young men increasingly expect to be sent on such courses, and will leave if they are not.

For the more mature manager, training is more difficult. He is unlikely to take kindly to being lectured at; nor is he very happy with the new techniques. Probably the best solution is to let these men educate each other, with stimulation from outside. This is likely to be fruitful because each will possess a depth of experience, but unless the skill of communication is present to a high degree the best format would appear to be some form of team project.

Board members rarely attend courses (unless they are that way inclined). Pressure of work is certainly one factor, but if as a pundit once said 'the mark of a great manager is the power of infinite self-delusion' then the motivation is also likely to be lacking. Perhaps this is the biggest gap in management education.

Internal v. external courses

The choice between an internal course run by the organisation and an external course, particularly those run by academic institutions, must be decided by its relevance and an assessment of cost/benefit. For the small organisation the choice does not exist because of the difficulty of mustering enough people and resources to make an internal course worth while.

Internal courses ought to be more relevant but this will depend on the skill of the training specialist. There is a good case for making practising managers or specialists give the lectures; the discipline is always beneficial. Naturally some training in lecturing is desirable beforehand. The course gains the added benefit of seeing, in action, managers of functions with which the individual does not come into contact.

There should be a freshness of ideas if the academic institution also undertakes research, and there may be an opportunity to hear the leaders in particular fields. Such courses have the use of opening up new areas and introducing ideas which do not exist in the parent organisation.

Again compromise is possible and desirable. Academic lectures can be inserted into the internal programmes; increasingly, organisations and academic institutions are collaborating to form tailor-made courses to meet special needs. There is evidence of considerable mutual gain.

A special word must be said about business schools, in particular the immediate postgraduate courses. The quality of the courses is usually high but there is a clear problem on timing. From the discussion on phasing earlier in this chapter it will be seen that such courses do not fit the desirable sequence since they occur *before* the professional phase. There is evidence from Livingston writing on the 'myth of the well-educated manager' that such courses are not producing managers but new sorts of professionals, (e.g., planners, consultants, etc.), for it is in these fields that their academic knowledge and analytic skills can most quickly be applied. Though high salaries can be commanded initially it appears that the high rate is not sustained comparatively; hence the low correlation that has been found between academic success and business achievement.

Organisation development and management training

A major problem that has been hinted at in the discussion above is that it is relatively straightforward to teach informational subjects, certain social skills and to foster an analytic approach, yet the sum of these does not turn a professional into a manager nor do they produce those subtle changes of behaviour that lead to greater efficiency. Coupled with this has been a growing body of evidence concerning the effectiveness of various management styles. Early attempts to capitalise on this were not successful because the behaviour learned on the course was not reinforced in the work situation. It is unrealistic to expect an individual to change his way of managing when his superior does not. This was particularly true when the subjects were foremen. Foremen were singled out because they formed the essential link between management and the managed; yet in many ways they were dupes. As many foremen observed 'you shouldn't be telling me but teaching my boss'. The conclusion is clear; changes in management style can only be effective if applied to a group as a whole. The ideas can be introduced into courses, but the real change can only be brought about by a process of 'organisation development' as it is now called. Usually the object of the changes is to transform an organisation's climate from the rigid and mechanistic to something more flexible or organic.

The techniques used are T-groups (or sensitivity training), Blake and Mouton's management grid or Reddin's '30' training. A number of successful applications has been reported, but they are not exempt from the usual requirements for successful innovation within an organisation. They must start with a wholehearted commitment from the top, and they must have competent practitioners or 'change agents'. However, the logistical problem of encompassing a whole organisation (to say nothing of the internal politics) has caused this to be a declining area of training.

The training situation, the trainee and the stages of training

Training courses rightly take place outside the immediate environment of work (if only to prevent interruptions). The training situation, therefore, takes place on a 'cultural island' – a special place, a particular pattern of time allocation and an institutionalised form with its own norms of behaviour.

The trainee, on the other hand, may enter with some doubts. At worst he may come from an organisation where only those that can be spared are sent on courses. The average course-goer is unlikely to have been told why he was selected, what is expected of him (except to 'have a good time') or what will happen when he returns. He may believe he was sent to have deficiencies remedied, rather than to be developed. Finally, training courses have been known to be used to get individuals out of the way while changes are made.

Because of all this, the role of the course tutor or training officer is crucial. He will set the style of behaviour of the newly formed group; he can motivate, reassure and guide. First class administration will not make a poor course good but the lack of it can make an inherently sound course into a failure. Very largely he controls the expectancy and context of the training; this is the first of the stages.

The second stage is concerned with exposure, trial and reinforcement. The training aim must be clarified and the appropriate technique selected to achieve the objective. The various methods are now familiar but it is wise to scan the possibilities before finally deciding. The range includes:

Lecture (including the use of visual aids)
Video recording and playback
Film
Discussion group
Case study
Project
Self-teaching aids (either by book or even using a computer)
Role playing
Business games
Social learning situations

But, as much educational research shows, the crucial factor is the instructor; his skill with the chosen medium, his acceptability, his knowledge and his ability to kindle the interest of his audience are all important. A cursory knowledge of the technique and a poor style are disastrous.

The next phase is the transfer of skills and knowledge to the work situation. If the situation is right this will happen automatically, but this is rare. *It is this stage where the greatest loss of value occurs.* It is uncommon for the returning individual to be debriefed adequately not only to get his evaluation but to understand what he has learnt and how it might be applied. Ideally, the man's superior should be seeking opportunities for practice and either acting as the 'apprentice-master' or arranging for someone else to play this role (this is one of the values of the change agent in the organisation development situation). In reality, life is usually too short for proper follow-up so the waste of new-found skills is immense. This is probably one of the main causes for doubt concerning the value of management training. The course notes stand on the bookshelf like a trophy from the hunt; like the stuffed antelope head, they gather dust and occasionally stimulate a memory of a past event.

Evaluation

Selection of topics for training is usually based on desirability rather than a knowledge of whether it is technically possible to achieve that objective. Yet it might be argued that it is better to teach something the result of which can be guaranteed, than a topic, however important, which has a low probability of successful outcome.

Changes in method and content will be more dependent on fashion than information, unless attempts are made to evaluate effectiveness, though the difficulties of doing such as assessment adequately are considerable.

Warr, Bird and Rackham have pointed out that there are three levels of outcome of training.

1 Immediate: new knowledge, skills and attitudes which are present immediately after training
2 Intermediate: new knowledge, skills and attitudes present in the work situation
3 Ultimate: changes in organisational effectiveness.

Immediate outcomes are the most commonly attempted in management training by means of discussion or questionnaire at the end of the course. For external courses, such a method is incorporated in the National Training Index in which a number of companies participate. The danger is that unless such an evaluation is done vigorously, one gets an 'Index of Euphoria' commonly associated with the end of courses. It is better therefore to evaluate each section of the course for:

1 Relevance
2 Content
3 Presentation
4 Enjoyment.

The evaluation is usually in the form of ratings.

Intermediate outcomes are usually based on measurement (or ratings) of the individual at periods after his return to work.

Ultimate outcomes should be based on economic criteria or, less satisfactorily questionnaire comprised of 'before' and 'after'.

Foreman and supervisor training

In principle the training (as opposed to development) of foremen does not differ from management training. In practice it is complicated by the curious role position of foremen. If he were clearly part of management then there would be no problem, but in practice this is not so. In career terms foremen tend to lie near the top of the ladder starting with the skilled or semi-skilled worker; with the increasing number of graduates and professional workers he is less and less seen as being on the way to higher management. Thus he has been variously described as 'the man in the middle' and the 'victim of double-talk'. Because much foremen training has ignored the organisational context, it has often a curiously unreal air to it. This does not mean that no training should be given, but that the dangers must be foreseen. Certainly courses will not cure any gross ineffectiveness of foremanship within an organisation; the roots of this problem are much deeper.

The phases of training for foremen correspond to the initial appointment at the mature stages of management. The same principles apply though the style and content will be different. Style is particularly important because of the length of time that usually has elapsed since they last attended a full-time educational institution; adaptation to the course environment will need special care. The emphasis should be on practicability, e.g., the discussion and role playing of case studies presented by film or film strip. Industrial relations is an essential topic since the foreman is involved with this at the grass-roots level. As the Industrial Relations Code of Practice states in section 8, 'The supervisor is in a key position to influence industrial relations. Management should ensure that he . . . is fully briefed in advance about management's policies as they affect his work group'. Communication is, therefore, another important area and includes not only content but an increase in the skills necessary for its accomplishment.

FURTHER READING

Blake, R., and Mouton, S., *The New Managerial Grid*, Gulf Publishing Co., Houston, Tex., 1978

Boydell, T., and Pedler, M., *Management Self-Development*, Gower, 1980

Gellerman, S. W., *Management by Motivation*, American Management Association, Inc., 1968

Gibb, C. A. (ed.), *Leadership*, Penguin, Harmondsworth, 1969

Kniveton, B., and Towers, B., *Training for Negotiation*, Business Books Ltd, London, 1978

Livingstone, J. S., 'Myth of the well-educated manager', *Harvard Business Review*, Jan.–Feb. 1971

Markwell, D. S., and Roberts, T. J., *Organisation of Management Development Programmes*, Gower, 1969

Revans, R. W., *Action Learning*, Blond & Briggs Ltd, London, 1980

Roethlisberger, F. J., 'The Foreman: master and victim of double talk', *Harvard Business Review*, Spring 1945

Warr, P., Bird, M., and Rackham, N., *Evaluation of Management Training*, Gower, 1970.

56 Employee relations

Derek Torrington and J L Cookson

This chapter deals with regulating the working relationship between employer and the employees collectively. It is an unrealistic and oversimplified view of management that sees managers making decisions and issuing instructions for others to obey. The conception – shaping and implementation of executive action in organising – is a complex process that depends heavily on employee consent. This consent is ceded to managers by employees individually, as they decide to accept rather than decline an offer of employment, as they work with enthusiasm rather than apathy and direct their activities towards the objectives of organisational success that managers determine.

Consent is also, however, ceded to managers by the employees collectively who give, implicitly or explicitly, a mandate to managers to make decisions and issue orders. There are many ways in which managerial action can be frustrated by collective employee resistance which would be beyond the scope of employees individually. There are not only the extremes of industrial action, but co-operative or unco-operative working within the guidelines of union agreements, the degree of enthusiasm with which changes are accepted and implemented, the care with which safety routines are followed, flexibility of manning arrangements, and many more.

Whatever the level of national unemployment and economic gloom, and no matter how tightly collective agreements are worded, managers depend on the collective consent of employees to *allow* and *support* them in their duties. That consent can perhaps be required or even forced in some situations for a short time, but sustained and productive consent has to be won: it is won by managers who earn it through paying close attention to the working relationship.

TRADE UNION RECOGNITION

When a trade union has recruited a number of members in an organisation it will seek recognition from the employer in order to represent those members. What is recognition? It involves first of all that the employer singles out that trade union from others, so that the step of recognising by an employer means that, while he will have to take seriously the representations of one union, he will not usually have to deal with others as well for the same group of employees. There are exceptions to this, especially when the number of union members is low, but it is a normal component of recognition. The second aspect is that the employer has to allow the recognition to affect his behaviour by taking seriously what the union representatives say to him. This does not necessarily mean agreeing to their claims, but it does mean taking time to talk with them to seek accommodations. It is an important, irrevocable step away from all decisions lying unilaterally with management. There are three points to consider about recognition:

1 The timing of recognition – when to recognise
2 Identifying the people, or groups of people, whom the union should represent
3 Deciding which topics should fall within the scope of recognition – for what to recognise.

Reasons for recognition

Why should an employer recognise a union at all? Is there any advantage or is it simply an unfortunate yielding to pressure? The answer to that question depends on the wishes of the employees. If they collectively want trade union representation it is unlikely that they will co-operate with the employer who refuses it. They will want recognition partly because of their general experience and beliefs about working life and partly because of their particular experience with the individual employer where a recognition claim is brought. Manual employees tend to regard trade union representation as normal and necessary, managerial employees tend to regard it as abnormal and unnecessary, and administrative and clerical employees lie between these two extremes.

A more positive reason for recognition is the benefits which can flow to the employer from having representatives with whom to discuss plans and problems. It offers at least a useful method of communication and can be a way of contriving improved working relationships, hastening necessary change and developing trust in the motives and competence of the management.

When to recognise a union

The time at which to recognise a union is a fine judgement for managers to make. If it is too soon there will not be enough support among employees, who may feel that what should be *their* decision is being made for them. A union with only 5 per cent of the employees in membership has a small and potentially clique-like constituency, recognition of which might antagonise the majority. At the other extreme, the refusal to recognise a union which has 95 per cent of the employees in membership would be antagonising the majority of the labour force in a different way, possibly with more serious results.

In the days when unions could seek recognition by legal means if an employer refused, the Advisory Conciliation and Arbitration Service (ACAS) often recommended recognition when the proportion of union members was below 40 per cent. The factors influencing the decision of when to recognise are the degree and efficiency of union organisation, the number of representatives, the size of constituency and the degree of opposition. None the less the key indicator is obviously the number of union members. It may be useful to ballot the employees to determine their wishes, although the greatest stimulus for a management to recognise union A is often the fear that union B may start recruiting members. Only recognition by management can check that move towards multi-unionism.

Identifying the groups of people to be represented by a recognised union

Another judgement to be made is to define the group of employees to be represented by the union. If the group is too large its members do not have enough interests in common for representation to be feasible. If it is too small there may be other employees, outside the group, who claim the same treatments as the union members because the terms and conditions of employment are similar. The employer either concedes the same benefits and antagonises the union members who regard the others as 'riding on their backs' or refuses and antagonises the non-union members. The normal test is to consider what different groups of employees have in common.

Some of the more common boundaries are between manual and white collar workers, where members of the two groups are seldom represented by the same union or involved in the same procedures and agreements. Another boundary is manual skill, where union membership or *grade* of membership is often jealously guarded on behalf of those who have completed a craft apprenticeship or other preparation that is acknowledged to justify special representation. In some situations the Amalgamated Union of Engineering Workers may represent employees who are skilled as well as those who are semi-skilled and unskilled, but the grade of membership would be different and arrangements with the employer would recognise that difference. The same union, through its Technical and Supervisory Section, may well represent white collar employees in the same company, but that would be through a different section of the union, with different officials and different agreements.

More difficult boundaries are those connected with status in the organisational hierarchy. Should the supervisor and those he supervises be represented by the same body? In manufacturing industry it seems that he will usually be represented separately, to cope with the problem of the union member seeking representation against the management action of his supervisor, who is a member of the same union and entitled to the assistance of the same union official. In local government it is quite common for the Chief Officers in an authority and the most humble clerical personnel all to be members of the National and Local Government Officers Association.

What to recognise

A union can seek recognition on anything that might be covered in a contract of employment, but the employer may agree to recognition for only a limited range of topics. The basis is to recognise a union to represent the grievances of members. That excludes any consultation on payment, terms and conditions, working practices and the other potential ingredients of a recognition agreement. It may be that an employer will proceed progressively with recognition, so that the range of topics grows with familiarity in the negotiating relationship. It should be noted that the potential benefits for management from a recognition arrangement come only when recognition is on a wide basis. Also, if the employees are up in arms on an issue, it may be pedantic to refuse discussion because it is not covered by the recognition agreement.

The legal position on recognition

The fragmented structure of collective bargaining in the UK is partly attributed to the traditional abstentionist policy of the State, departed from only in statutes prescribing the structures of nationalised corporations. During the 1970s, however, both major political parties were agreed upon the necessity for statutory machinery to resolve recognition disputes. The purposes embodied in the recognition provisions for the Industrial Relations Act 1971 were largely frustrated by the policy of non-cooperation on the part of the labour movement.

The Employment Protection Act 1975, sections 11–16, represented an attempt by the State to steer a course between legalism and voluntarism in this area. These sections permitted a recognition issue to be referred by an independent union to ACAS for examination, inquiry and report. If an employer failed to comply with a recommendation by ACAS for recognition and conciliation failed to resolve the dispute, the union could present a claim for specified terms and conditions to the Central Arbitration Committee (CAC) for unilaterial arbitration. Any terms and conditions awarded by the CAC would thereafter take effect as part of the contracts of the employees.

During their currency, these provisions were subjected to several criticisms:

1 The statutory processes culminating in unilaterial arbitration could only be invoked by the union side
2 Inquiry procedures were protracted
3 ACAS's functions were capable of being seriously impaired by the absence of any requirement that employees should co-operate in enquiries, and by judicial review of ACAS's exercise of its powers
4 The ultimate sanction fell short of requiring an employer to recognise a union.

The response of the Conservative Government elected in 1979 to these criticisms (in the Employment Act 1980) was to repeal sections 11–16, returning to voluntarism in union recognition.

The closed shop

In some ways the logical development of union recognition is the 'closed shop' which is an agreement whereby *all* employees in a particular category should be members of the recognised union, as a condition of employment.

Perhaps nowhere is 'the dilemma between the function of the law to protect the individual and its function to help adjust power relations in Society' (Kahn-Freund) more clearly demonstrated than in the debates which have raged since 1970 over the issue of the closed shop in British industrial relations and the extent to which the State should extend or restrict its operation. At the level of public policy, the issue is whether, given the ostensible commitment of the political parties to the system of collective bargaining, it is appropriate to provide individuals with a statutory right of disassociation and if so, in what circumstances.

The provisions of the Industrial Relations Act 1971 heavily influenced by doctrines of individual rights which paid little heed to the realities of collective labour relations, aimed to outlaw the closed shop notwithstanding a pledge of support for the principle of collective bargaining. In the event, established closed shop arrangements remained largely unaffected by the 1971 statutory measures, and it came as no surprise that the incoming Labour Government of 1974 should remove the right of disassociation from the statute book, thereby re-legalising the closed shop through providing limited statutory protection for religious objectors. Undoubtedly, statutory support for union membership agreements during the period 1974–1980 reinforced the willingness of employers (based upon administrative convenience) to conclude such agreements to the extent that, currently, approximately one-fifth of British employeers and two-fifths of trade union members are covered by some form of closed shop arrangement.

The Employment Act 1980 is calculated, if not to render closed shops unlawful, at least to limit their objectives and restrict their future development. The 1980 Act significantly narrows the circumstances in which employees may be dismissed fairly for not being a union member. It is now unfair to dismiss an employee:

1 Where the employee genuinely objects on grounds of conscience or other deeply held personal conviction to being a member of any trade union whatsoever or of a particular union

2 Where the employee was a member of the class of employees covered by the closed shop agreement before it took effect and has not subsequently been a member of a union which is party to such agreement

3 Where the closed shop was introduced on or after 15 August 1980 and has not been approved by a secret ballot of affected employees showing that at least 80 per cent of those entitled to vote supported the agreement.

Employers may also require a union or other person to be joined as a party in unfair dismissal proceedings where the employer claims that the dismissal was the result of pressure exerted by such union or person calling or threatening industrial action because of the complainant's non-membership of the union.

The 'joined' party may be ordered to contribute towards the compensation awarded if the complaint of unfair dismissal is upheld.

A further significant feature of the Employment Act 1980 is the restoration of statutory recourse to law for individuals who, in relation to employment subject to a union membership agreement, are unreasonably excluded or expelled from membership of a specified union.

Further statutory reform of the closed shop laws is embodied in the Employment (Trade Union Immunities) Act, 1982. Given the practical importance of the closed shop in British industrial relations and the doubts, based upon the experience of 1971–74, concerning the extent to which long-standing practices can be eradicated by law, the Conservative Government's intention is not to outlaw closed shops altogether but to impose further restrictions upon their operation. The Act makes the following provisions:

1 Increased compensation for unfair dismissal for refusal to join a union
2 A dismissed employee may 'join', as a party to tribunal proceedings, the union that has contributed to the dismissal by exerting pressure on the employer. An award may be against, and be recoverable directly from, that union
3 Periodic ballots at five yearly intervals to ascertain current support for continuance of existing closed shops. It is unfair to dismiss an employee refusing to join a union not receiving the support of 80 per cent of those covered or 85 per cent of those voting
4 Compensation may be payable by the Secretary of State to victims of closed shop agreements who were dismissed under legislation passed by the last Labour government and who would have been protected as existing non-union members or conscientious objectors if the EA 1980 closed shop provisions had been in force
5 It is unfair to dismiss an employee for not being a union member in a closed shop which took effect before 15 August 1980, unless in the five years preceding dismissal it had been supported in a ballot by 80 per cent of the employees covered or 85 per cent of those voting
6 The definition of a lawful trade dispute, on which the immunities from civil actions rest, is restricted to disputes between workers and their own employer if wholly or mainly related to the subjects of a 'trade dispute', as listed in TULRA s29
7 Control of the exertion of pressure on a contractor, by the person engaging his services, to employ only union labour, since this requirement can involve conscription into unions of disinterested employees. The Act stipulates that:

   (a) any clause in a contract will be void if it requires the employment only of persons who are members of a union, or persons who are not members
   (b) it is unlawful to discriminate, in inviting tenders, or making contracts, to require that those employed to perform that contract should be trade union members, or alternatively should not be members

(c) immunity is removed for industrial action which interferes with performance of a contract primarily on the grounds that those employed to do so are, or are not, union members

8 The trade union itself, as a body, is liable in tort and may be sued for both injunctions and damages in respect of:

(a) unlawful acts not committed in contemplation or furtherance of a trade dispute

(b) secondary picketing, indiscriminate secondary action and industrial action to compel union membership

(c) tortious wrongs of union officials committed on behalf of the union itself, on the principle of vicarious liability.

Further pressure for new closed shop legislation will stem from the decision by the European Commission (August 1981) that the United Kingdom was in breach of Article 11 of the European Convention of Human Rights and Fundamental Freedoms in failing to guarantee three former employees of British Rail a right to dissociate from membership of the appropriate railway union.

ARRANGEMENTS WITH TRADE UNIONS

Within the framework of a recognition agreement, which may or may not have closed shop features, there are a number of arrangements which may help to put management/union relationships on a satisfactory footing.

Collective procedures

Procedures provide a structure within which the parties can engage each other in discussion, problem solving and negotiation at the same time as exercising some degree of control over each other. Some actions are laid down to be followed and others to be avoided, so that it is commonplace for a procedure to state than an employee with a grievance about his employment must seek redress *first* from his immediate superior. It is also typical for a procedure to state that industrial action will only be resorted to when procedural steps are exhausted and that changes in payment or other major terms and conditions of employment will not be made without prior consultation.

The essence of a procedure is to predetermine how matters shall be handled, so that everyone knows what the next step is if they cannot solve a problem or reach agreement. There is a similarity to legal procedure, with its clear path from court to higher court, but it is an area of industrial relations activity that remains free from law. It is quite possible for employer and union to make legally binding agreement, but it remains most unusual.

The most common procedures cover discipline and grievance. The law relating to the contract of employment assumes that there will be a grievance procedure and the law on unfair dismissal assumes that there will be a procedure for discipline, so these are becoming almost universal, although the degree of sophistication is seldom great. The next most common are procedures for negotiation and consultation, which only exist when employer and union have reached the stage of recognition that embraces more than terms and conditions of employment. There is also a frequent link with a procedure operated by an employers' association on a regional or national basis. Procedures are likely to bring clarity, fairness and consistency to employee relations, but they have limited effectiveness in alterting the custom and practice of the workplace and they can make change difficult.

Rights of employee representatives

An inevitable consequence of recognising trade unions is the need for union representatives to have some facilities.

Conventional industrial relations wisdom holds that the conduct of collective labour relations is improved by ensuring that employee representatives are informed and enjoy those facilities which they require to perform their functions. Thus, it has been an aim of public policy in recent years to strengthen the quality of workplace representation.

Under section 27 of the Employment Protection Consolidation Act 1978 officials (including shop stewards) of independent, recognised unions have a right to take time off from work with pay to a reasonable extent and subject to reasonable conditions, in order to carry out their duties concerned with industrial relations between the employer (or associated employer) and the employees or for the purpose of undergoing training relevant to those duties. Such training must be approved either by the TUC or the official's own union. For safety representatives, an analogous right is provided by the Safety Representatives and Safety Committee's Regulations.

Disputes concerning whether these rights have been denied are ultimately determined by Industrial Tribunals, which may seek guidance from the recommendations of the ACAS Code of Practice 3, *Time Off for Trade Union Duties and Activities* (1978). This jurisdiction forced tribunals to the heart of workplace industrial relations in so far as disputes concerning time off require close consideration of both the structures of collective bargaining and of the functions which it is appropriate for shop stewards to perform.

The Code of Practice (para 13) gives examples of union officials' duties, though the list is not intended to be exhaustive:

1 Collective bargaining with the appropriate level of management
2 Informing constituents about negotiations or consultations with management
3 Meetings with other key officials or with full-time union officers on matters which are concerned with industrial relations
4 Interviews with and on behalf of constituents on grievance and discipline matters
5 Appearing on behalf of constituents before an official body such as an industrial tribunal
6 Explanations to new employees, whom he or she will represent, of the role

of the union in the workplace industrial relations structure.

The code offers no guidance, however, upon whether, in the case of multi-site organisations, time off with pay should be afforded to allow stewards from one site to consult with those from another. This has been the central issue in much of the case law to date. Tribunals have usually applied a restrictive interpretation of the statutory provisions, though more recently, the Employment Appeal Tribunal (Good v. GEC Elliott Process Automation Ltd) rejected the contention that an official's duties can only be those which fall within the area of recognition.

Disclosure of information

During the 1970s, public policy supported the view that disclosure of information by employers to employees and their representatives is conducive to sound industrial relations and improves the processes of bargaining.

The Employment Protection Act 1975 substantially re-enacts the disclosure provision of the Industrial Relations Act (never activated) by imposing a duty upon an employer to disclose (on request) to representatives of an independent, recognised union information relating to his undertaking or that of an associated employer without which the representatives would be materially impeded in their conduct of bargaining and which it would be good practice to disclose.

ACAS was required to produce a Code of Practice for the guidance of the parties. The Code on Disclosure, published in 1977, represents a disappointing gloss on the statutory provisions. Noting that the relevance of information is determined by the particular structure within which collective bargaining takes place, ACAS rejects the possibility of formulating a list of items which is universally relevant and disclosable. Instead, it provides examples of items of information which could be relevant in particular situations. These cover pay and benefits; conditions of service; manpower, performance; and finance. The central recommendation of the Code is that the parties should reach voluntary agreements on what information is to be disclosed, when and in what form. The scope of the statutory duty to disclose is restricted by the provision of certain safeguards for the employer, who is not required to disclose information communicated in confidence or which relates to an individual unless consent is given an, most importantly, which would cause substantial injury to the employer's undertaking.

Upon complaints of failure to disclose, the Central Arbitration Committee is empowered to declare what information an employer should disclose and by what date. As formerly with recognition claims, the ultimate sanction for failure to comply with such declaration is for terms and conditions to be determined by unilateral arbitration.

The Employment Protection Act provisions on disclosure are less stringent than the obligation of US employers to 'bargain in good faith' under which certain information is presumptively relevant and disclosable. Nor do they make provisions for disclosure to individual employees.

CAC hearings to date reveal little consistency in current disclosure practice as between sectors of British industry. It is, however, possible that the disclosure laws could, in the long term, contribute to more professional bargaining and alter both the structure and scope of the bargaining process.

Picketing

UK picketing laws have been the subject of public controversy. Given the variety of criticisms directed from so many different quarters, it is hard to understand how the Donovan Commission concluded that the law on picketing was satisfactory. Statutory changes were introduced in 1971 and 1974; litigation arising out of picketing received prominent coverage by the media; and the subject was a prime target of further legislative change via the Employment Act 1980. The main aims of the Act's picketing sections are to curb secondary picketing such as by miners at power stations, mass picketing as at Grunwick; and the phenomenon of the 'flying picket' used in the building industry dispute of 1972. Additionally, the Act increases the scope of legal remedies available to employers who suffer as a result of unlawful picketing.

Section 15 of the Trade Union and Labour Relations Act 1974 (as amended by section 16 of the Employment Act 1980) renders it

> lawful for one or more persons in contemplation or furtherance of a trade dispute to stand at or near *his own place of work* or if he is an official of a trade union, at or near the place of work of a member of that union who he his accompanying . . . for the purpose only of peacefully . . . persuading any person to work or abstain from working.

Special provisions apply to mobile workers and to employees who have been dismissed during a strike. Generally speaking, therefore, it is unlawful for workers to picket, albeit peacefully, at premises other than those at which they work. Picketing which is accompanied by violent, intimidating or obstructive behaviour also exceeds the lawful limits of section 15. In respect of such unlawful picketing, employers may seek legal redress via an application for an injunction. It should also be noted that lawful picketing is confined to attendance 'at or near' a worker's place of work, not inside, which constitutes trespass.

The Code of Practice (1980) makes reference to picketing with excessive numbers and suggests that, as a general rule, the purposes of peaceful communication and persuasion can reasonably be achieved by six pickets or fewer at an entrance to a workplace. Since the Code must be considered by a court during legal proceedings, this suggestion may crucially affect the outcome of an employer's injunction application. Evidence that more than six pickets were present may be construed as indicating unlawful purpose.

Hitherto, the legal remedies (injunction and/or action for damages) available to employers in respect of industrial action have been statutorily restricted via civil immunities conferred upon the organisers of such action. An extremely important feature of the Employment Act 1980 is that for the first time, such immunities (under TULR Act 1974, section 13), are linked to the legality of picketing. Where picketing exceeds the limits set by section 15, the immunity from civil liability no longer applies so far as the organisers of the action are concerned, though trade union funds remain protected. In this way, the opportunity for employers, customers and suppliers to exercise legal remedies is significantly increased.

In applying for an injunction to remove an unlawful picket, the employer must name the organisers (usually a full-time union official or shop steward) and submit evidence by affidavit that the picket was unlawful and that damage has been sustained. If granted, the injunction will ordinarily apply to both the named organisers and to others acting on their instructions or on their behalf. Employers may experience difficulty in identifying the organiser(s) of an unlawful picket. Identification, however, remains the responsibility of the employer, not that of the police, and a suggestion that the police be required to assist employers in this context appears unlikely to be implemented legislatively.

STATE AGENCIES

Several state agencies are charged with a duty to advise employers on aspects of industrial relations practice. On specific matters there is the Equal Opportunities Commission and the Commission for Racial Equality or the Race Relations Advisory Service of the Department of Employment. The main agencies are ACAS and CAC.

Advisory, Conciliation and Arbitration Service (ACAS)

ACAS is a body run by a council that has both employer and union members, and there are offices in most large UK cities. An employer can obtain from them advice on the full range of employment practice, from how to draw up a contract of employment to the administration of job evaluation. This advice is also available to unions and members of the public.

Conciliation is provided in an attempt to solve problems between employers and employees, or ex-employees by informal discussion with one or both parties. The most widespread call on this service has been in the many cases of dismissed employees seeking compensation, but it is also available to assist with collective issues, such as pay claims or other disputes.

When agreement between employer and union cannot be reached by the parties themselves, or after conciliation, ACAS can offer the services of a single arbitrator or a panel. In these situations, the arbitrator decided the matter for the parties after hearing evidence from both sides.

Central Arbitration Committee (CAC)

The statutory framework governing the processes of conciliation and arbitration was established by the Conciliation Act 1896 and extended by the

Industrial Courts Act 1919. These statutes were largely repealed by the Employment Protection Act 1975. Following the creation of ACAS and to give final effect to the aim of establishing an independent (and therefore, more acceptable), conciliation and arbitration agency, the Central Arbitration Committee replaced the Industrial Arbitration Board as a permanent, arbitral body maintained at State expense but expressly protected from ministerial direction.

Its composition is tri-partite with legal chairmen plus representatives of employers and employees, all appointed by the Secretary of State after consultation with ACAS. It may sit publicly or privately and, since its creation, it has proved to be a more regional body than its predecessor; approximately 80 per cent of its hearings have been outside London. The Committee has developed its own procedural rules having the overriding aim of achieving informality and flexibility – an aim further encouraged by the fact that there exists no direct right of appeal against its awards. In line with tradition, the Committee's awards are usually not legally enforceable. Its principal statutory functions include:

1 Adjudicating on claims under the Fair Wages Resolution 1946
2 Amending discriminatory agreements and pay structures under the Equal Pay Act 1970
3 Determining complaints from independent unions of employers' failure to disclose information under the Employment Protection Act 1975.

The Committee's philosophy is innovative and clearly expressed in its First Annual Report 1976:

> The Committee is not a court . . . its proceedings and hearings are structured so as to achieve . . . informality. The aim is to encourage the approach by way of problem-solving rather than by emphasising the aspects of conflict and verdict. Above all, there is a commitment to the principles of sound industrial relations and workable solutions.

Thus, the Committee attempts to locate both problems and solutions in an industrial relations context. The 'general considerations' section preceding the 'award' is used by the Committee to try to assist the parties in resolving industrial relations difficulties from which the issue in the terms of reference has arisen.

FURTHER READING

Advisory, Conciliation and Arbitration Service, *Industrial Relations Handbook,* HMSO, London, 1980

Brown, W. (ed.), *The Changing Contours of British Industrial Relations,* Blackwell, Oxford, 1981

Farnham, D., and Pimlott, J., *Understanding Industrial Relations,* Cassell, London, 1979

Muir, J., *Industrial Relations Procedures and Agreements,* Gower, 1981

Payne, D., *Employment Law Manual,* Gower, updated regularly

57 Redundancy and redeployment

Peter Mumford and Tom Carew

The Employment Protection (Consolidation) Act 1978 defines redundancy as occurring when an employer ceases to carry on the business for which the employee was engaged in the place where he was employed, or has insufficient work of the type which the employee was engaged to do.

When an actual redundancy situation has to be administered and decisions made about the treatment of individuals which will affect their own immediate future (and perhaps their long-term employment prospects), as well as the success and profitability of the organisation, then the many variations in interpretation and the implications of this apparently clear-cut definition becomes apparent.

Redundancy is a complex situation involving moral, social, legal, financial and operational issues such as the right of a man to his job, the needs of the organisation, the worth of one individual as opposed to another, the role of the employer and his responsibilities to his employees, the community, the owners and short-term expediency opposed to long-term needs.

To the majority of organisations, the people employed are its most valuable asset. On purely financial grounds their recruitment, training and bank of experience represent a very considerable investment per head. Like any other asset, therefore, they should not be lightly disposed of or neglected. On both moral and social grounds, they are thinking, feeling, individual human beings.

REDUNDANCY POLICY

Need for a policy

The greatest safeguard and security the employees can have is an efficient, profitable organisation, in which forward thinking and planning are of prime importance, so that the necessary action can be taken quickly to take advantage of changing circumstances, rather than have circumstances manage the organisation. A vital part of this forward thinking is the plan to regulate and control the manpower to meet the overall corporate objectives.

The most sophisticated forecasting techniques cannot, of course, cover every eventuality and there may be circumstances so outside the organisation's control that rapid reductions in the manpower requirements are inevitable. Effective planning of resources may also mean that it will be necessary to change the manpower requirements to such as extent that the redundancies are the best way of effecting these changes.

To meet these requirements, an effective plan is needed for dealing with redundancy as an integral part of the organisation's manpower policies.

The best time for formulating the redundancy provisions of the manpower plan is when the organisation is recruiting hard; when the emotional issues are least likely to obscure judgement.

Content of a policy

In drawing up redundancy policies and plans, decisions will have to be taken on:

1 The objectives of the policy
2 The different types of redundancy situations
   (a) those forced on the organisation by reductions in business or other outside factors; and (b) those designed to benefit the organisation by, for instance, taking advantage of technological change
3 Avoiding redundancy
4 Reducing the impact of redundancy
5 Transfers and retraining
6 Voluntary redundancy
7 Selection methods to be used
8 Consultation
9 Notice of redundancy
10 Compensation
11 Pension rights
12 Re-engagement.

In all these areas, both the human aspect and the legal requirements have to be taken into account in order that positive plans and procedures can be agreed.

Some general social and company considerations

If the short-term efficiency of the labour force were the only consideration, it would probably be desirable to use a redundancy as an opportunity of getting rid of the unwanted, the troublemakers, the least able, the least adaptable and the least hard-working.

If management had allowed any significant number of these categories to continue in employment until the need for redundancy occurred, it is likely that the policies and practices of the organisation would be such that getting rid of them at this late stage would have little effect.

Equally, management must consider the social implications of their actions, both upon individuals and the community in general.

So far as individuals are concerned, the chief consideration must be the degree of hardship they will suffer, which will be affected immediately by their commitments and family responsibilities and, in the longer term, their age, fitness and chances of finding alternative employment.

Sympathy for individuals must not be allowed to prevent management ensuring that the organisation has a properly trained and balanced labour force to give it the best possible chance of meeting its objectives in the future.

In a community where there is a shortage of various categories of labour, the release of suitable staff by one organisation would obviously be welcomed.

Where there is already unemployment and redundancy, where one organisation is a major or sole employer then redundancies will have far-reaching consequences on the community and individuals.

Where the redundancy is foreseeable, as part of changes which will benefit the organisation, consideration should be given to the possibility of timing, either by speeding up or delaying the dismissals to suit the circumstances in the community.

Detailed forecasting and planning starts from the corporate plan which will show the long-term growth pattern, changes in methods and products which will affect the requirements for skills of different types, the grades and perhaps the ages of staff needed in the future.

In many organisations, this plan may exist only in a most rudimentary form so that the discussion with senior executives, in order to formulate their views, will be a valuable exercise in itself. Once this process has been started, it proves far less difficult to build up an overall picture than is usually imagined. Like all other techniques, forecasting improves the more it is practised.

1 Objectives

The purpose of all personnel policy is to assist management to achieve the organisation's objectives more efficiently. Within this broad purpose, the objectives of a redundancy scheme are to reduce labour costs and protect the interests of individuals affected by it.

These objectives should be quanitifed when an actual redundancy occurs, so that precise and specific reductions can be made and the success of these plans measured. It is important not to sacrifice long-term profits for short-term savings. It would, for instance, be relatively easy to reduce costs by dismissing all the short service staff and create later difficulty as a result of shortages of certain skills and an ageing labour force.

2 Types of redundancy

Where the redundancy is forced on the organisation by outside factors, action usually has to be taken quickly and it is difficult to increase costs by over-generous compensation. The legal minimum payment may be the right amount.

In cases where the organisation will benefit from new equipment or methods, it is reasonable that all should benefit from these savings and the levels of compensation can be higher.

3 Avoiding redundancy

Adequate forecasting of future demand and changes, together with high efficiency, are the most effective ways of avoiding redundancy. If the staff requirements are known in advance, recruitment, training and retirement programmes can be used in conjunction with one another to constrain the manpower resources to the required levels.

A high level of efficiency will ensure profitability with reserves for tiding over difficult periods, together with the avoidance of surplus staff.

If, however, redundancy becomes inevitable it is still possible to reduce the effect of it.

4 Reducing the impact of redundancy

Methods which can be used include:

1 Selling surplus capacity even at marginal cost in order to retrain skilled staff
2 Bringing subcontracted work into the organisation's own workshops
3 Building up stocks against future needs to avoid losing markets to foreign competition
4 Stopping overtime so as to share out the work available: retraining of staff may be necessary
5 Restricting recruitment and filling vacancies by internal transfer and retraining wherever this is possible
6 Dismissing employees who have been allowed to work on past normal retirement age
7 Dismissing part-time workers – assuming there are full-time employees available with the required skills
8 Retraining staff to give greater flexibility and increased efficiency in future
9 Offering early retirement.

5 Transfers and retraining

The numbers to be dismissed can often be reduced, or a valuable man retained in the organisation, by transferring staff from one department to another or even to another company in a group.

Providing the work offered and the conditions are not significantly worse than the employee's present job and the work is within the employee's capacity, then he will not, in law, be considered to be redundant even if he refuses the transfer.

However, should another worker be dismissed as a result of the transfer, then he will be considered to have been made redundant and entitled to compensation.

The offer of alternative work or transfer should be made to the employee, before his notice expires, in writing, specifying the work and the conditions. Providing the transfer takes place within four weeks of the end of the original job, the employee's service will be considered to be continuous.

If the employee is offered a different type of work, he is entitled to a trial period of four weeks.

A long period to cover necessary retraining may be agreed between employer and employee. Details of such an agreement must be written.

Where they may be differences in earnings due to the operation of bonus schemes or other factors, it is usual to allow a period of make-up pay until the employee has had an opportunity to adjust to the new conditions.

It would also be reasonable to give assistance with removal expenses if the transfer would involve moving house. In the case of experienced workers, the cost of this would probably be less than the total of compensation, plus recruitment and training costs of a new employee.

Retraining to allow staff to acquire skills which are still required by the organisation can be remarkably successful if it is carried out systematically and sympathetically. The experience of many organisations has shown that most people can acquire new skills rapidly and effectively. In many cases, grants are available to reduce costs which will generally be less than the costs of compensation to long-service employees.

There will also be benefits of improved morale and greater flexibility of staff.

6 Voluntary redundancy

It is obviously advantageous in terms of morale and goodwill if people can be encouraged to leave voluntarily. There are two broad categories:

1 Those eligible for early retirement
2 Other age groups.

Both are dependent on generous compensatory packages and are therefore initially expensive, but co-operation by staff and unions, avoidance of disputes, maintenance of good relations and the meeting of social obligations to long service staff have been seen by many organisations to justify this.

In early retirement the usual approach is to offer an enhancement of the service contribution towards pension rights. Thus a male employee of 58 with 25 years service might be given 7 years enhancement, allowing him to retire with the pension he would be entitled to at age 65, i.e. $^{32}/_{60}$ of his current salary.

For staff more than 10 years away from retirement age, usually a cash sum sufficient to encourage them to leave voluntarily is required. Sums representing up to three or four years basic pay have been offered by many large organisations for this purpose. The attractiveness of the package will often depend on the possibility of obtaining other work in the locality.

Some schemes for voluntary redundancy have been too attractive, leaving the organisation short of staff, short of skills or an unbalanced age mix. Very careful planning for these factors is required before setting up a blanket scheme. A safer approach is to give selected individuals the opportunity to volunteer.

Repayment from the Redundancy Fund may be claimed only if it can be seen that the individuals leave because there is no more work for them.

7 Selection of workers to be made redundant

The most controversial and difficult aspect of any redundancy is the method for selecting those who are to be dismissed.

The simple solution is last-in first-out (LIFO), based purely on the length of service. This is favoured by many unions, is easy to operate, understandable and allows people to know fairly accurately where they stand. Because compensation is geared to length of service, it is also cheaper for the organisation.

If all employees were of equal worth and if all sections of the organisation were equally affected, then this policy could satisfy most needs. In most redundancies, and particularly in those caused by technological or product changes, it is unlikely that all departments or all grades of staff will need to be reduced by the same amount, and even in those departments whose overall numbers have to be reduced, there will be certain key jobs for which skilled workers are in short supply and whom it would be quite wrong to dismiss.

Additionally, there will be problems created by hardship cases, the registered disabled, those under training for skills required in the future and the future age structure of the company.

The effect of a number of even small-scale redundancies can be to bias the age structure significantly upwards which may create difficulties in, say, five years' time.

From the broader social point of view, there is also a danger of creating a category of worker who will always be first out and who, through no fault of their own, will never be able to build up any service to qualify them for redundancy payments.

An ideal selection method would strike the balance between the requirements of the organisation and the social needs of individuals. Both the present and future needs of the organisation in terms of skills, flexibility, potential, age range and replacement costs of individuals should be considered, together with the individual's circumstances. These include his commitments and responsibilities, likely difficulties in obtaining new work, age and length of service.

Whatever selection methods are used, they must be clarified and agreed beforehand. Dismissals which do not conform to agreed procedures or established custom will be considered unfair unless there are very good reasons for non-conformity.

It is essential to avoid the risk of charges of discrimination on grounds of union membership, sex or race being brought against the organisation because of the selection methods used.

Where LIFO is used, jobs should be categorised within departments so that selection can be made within a group of skills, rather than across the whole department which may include skills which are still required. Key personnel, whose absence could affect the output of other sections, should not be dismissed purely because of seniority considerations.

8 Consultation

Management must obviously make the decision about the need for redundancy and the scale of it but the more employees are consulted about the way in which it is to be handled and they are to be treated, the easier it will be to design a scheme which meets all needs.

The recognised trade union for the group of employees to which the affected personnel belong (whether or not they are individually trade union members), must be consulted as early as possible to allow the trade union representative to suggest alternative action, retraining, etc.

If more than 10 employees are likely to be made redundant during one month, this consultation should start at least 60 days before the dismissals take place. If more than 100 people are to be made redundant over a period of 90 days, then the consultation has to start 90 days before the dismissal date. Trade union representatives have to be given the following information:

1 The reasons for the proposed redundancies;
2 The numbers and description of jobs affected;
3 The total number employed of these descriptions at the establishment;
4 The proposed selection method;
5 The proposed methods and timing for the dismissals.

Although most unions are committed to the principle of a man having a right to his job, which means no dismissal unless there is no alternative job available, full-time union officials are realists and accept that some redundancy is inevitable. They also accept that the LIFO principle must be applied only within the grades of the jobs affected. Where it can be shown that there are substantial differences in the skill and worth of one individual over another, they will generally accept the organisation's need in preference to rigid adherence to seniority.

If there is no union representative in the organisation, staff committees or representatives can act in the same capacity as a trade union.

9 Notice of redundancy

For employees who are to be dismissed, the Act specifies minimum periods of notice according to their lengths of service (see Figure 57.1). Where necessary, payment may be given in lieu of notice.

In cases where the change can be foreseen longer in advance, it is reasonable to give longer notice of intention. However, such announcements may precipitate a rush of key workers to secure the first place in the queue for scarce jobs in other organisations.

A system of premium payments may be used to encourage staff to work out their notices. They also lose their entitlement to redundancy payments under the Act if they do not obtain their employer's permission to leave before the

Length of continuous service (years)	Minimum period of notice (weeks)	GHM
4 weeks	1	
2	2	
3	3	
4	4	
5	5	
6	6	
7	7	
8	8	
9	9	
10	10	
11	11	
12	12	

Figure 57.1   Formal notice required

expiry of their notice. Even so, a severe unemployment situation locally can make it more attractive for individuals to secure the long-term advantage of another job rather than a once-only cash payment.

It is usually best to restrict formal notice to the requirements set out above, but to give notice of intention as part of the normal consultation procedures. This will help to maintain good faith with employees and prevent the spread of rumour and loss of confidence.

10   Compensation

Lump-sum payments are made to employees dismissed through redundancy on a scale according to age and length of service as shown in Figure 57.2. These lump-sum payments to the employee are tax-free (within limits) and do not affect his entitlement to unemployment benefit or earnings-related supplements. The payments are made by the employer who then claims partial repayment from the Redundancy Fund.

Where redundancy is due to insolvency and the employer is unable to make these payments, they are made direct to the employee by the Department of Employment.

Many employers consider that these payments represent a minimum and supplement them by scales of their own, usually related to length of service. A simple way of doing this is to add a fixed percentage to the statutory payment. Only the statutory scale of payment is eligible for rebate.

It is much easier to justify more generous treatment where the redundancy is due to circumstances from which the company will benefit and there is,

GHM	

Employee's age	Payment for each complete year of service
18–22	½ week's pay
22–41	1 week's pay (max. 20 weeks at £130 per week)
41–64 (men) 41–59 (women)	1½ week's pay (max. 30 weeks)

Service under the age of 18 does not count for this purpose.

For men of 64–65 years, and women of 59–60, the entitlement is reduced by one-twelfth for every month over 64 or 59.

Full details are set out in leaflet RPL2.

Figure 57.2 Redundancy pay

therefore, merit in making additional payments in these circumstances only. Certainly in the extremes of redundancy where the organisation is insolvent, only the redundancy scheme scale can be applicable.

An alternative method of supplementing payments is to make weekly and monthly payments – again on a scale according to service – until the employee has either used his entitlement or obtains alternative employment. To avoid reducing entitlement to unemployment benefit, these payments must be limited to one-third of normal earnings.

11 Pension rights

The Social Security Act 1973 requires that occupational pensions of redundant employees, aged 26 and over who have completed at least five years' service must be preserved. The possible methods include:

1 Benefits already earned may be preserved to normal retiring age
2 Transfer of benefits to another scheme
3 Payment of reduced benefit before normal retiring age
4 Payment of increased benefit after normal retiring age
5 Repayment of members' contributions made before 6 April 1975.

A proportion of pension may be offset against redundancy payments, as outlined in leaflet RPL1.

Full details of possible pension arrangements are set out in memorandum 18 of the Occupational Pensions Board. This Board exists mainly to advise on preservation aspects of pensions.

In spite of these regulations, however, very substantial erosion of pension expectations, especially for senior executives, can take place as a result of redundancy. For an individual of 45 with 20 years of pensionable service, it has been calculated that loss of credit for service and inflation would result in a loss of value to the pension exceeding £20 000 per £10 000 of salary. Figure 57.3 shows pension damage: this table has been calculated for a pension scheme providing $\frac{1}{60}$ of final average salary for each year of service.

Pension damage arises because the new employer can rarely accept responsibility for revaluing an executive's accrued pension from earlier employment in line with salary increases in the future. Usually the rules of a pension scheme give early leavers an entitlement to deferred benefits, frozen according to salary at the time of redundancy. The loss is scarcely alleviated by a transfer payment (if this can be arranged) because these are usually sufficient to secure only a much reduced past service credit in a new employer's scheme.

To ensure adequate compensation for loss of benefits of this order, the effects on each scheme and individual need to be reviewed by pension specialists or actuaries.

12 Re-engagement

Should circumstances change more rapidly than anticipated, it may be possible to re-engage those dismissed; the fairest way being to re-engage in reverse order to dismissal.

Before re-engagement takes place, the question of service must be clarified. If payments under the redundancy payments scheme have been made, then clearly service under the re-engagement can count only from this date and similarly, if payments against pension rights have been made, then pensionable service must restart from the date of re-engagement.

Provided no payments have been made, it is usual to count service for pension purposes as continuous if the period between dismissal and re-engagement does not exceed one year. Thereafter, it is preferable to regard any re-engagement as a completely new period of service for all purposes.

Cases of hardship

Cases of special difficulty can be assisted by *ex gratia* payments or other more favourable compensations. To avoid charges of favouritism, a small committee of a senior executive, a staff or union representative, and the personnel manager or welfare officer can be formed for this purpose. The committee may be given a special budget, or terms of reference within which they make recommendations. It is essential that decisions be made rapidly.

Date of leaving

If a redundant worker finds another job he may be released before expiry of his notice (without affecting his entitlement to redundancy payments) provided he gives written notice and this is accepted by the employer. Wherever possible, arrangements should be made to release the employee in time to take up his new employment.

(1) Age of employee at withdrawal	(2) Pensionable service completed at withdrawal	(3) Value of loss of pension position per £10 000 pa salary	(4) Salary increase (as percentage of old salary to compensate for (3))
30	5	5 250	1–½
	10		
35	5	5 250	2
	10	11 500	4
40	5	5 500	2
	10	11 750	4–½
	15	17 500	7
45	5	5 500	3
	10	11 000	5–½
	15	16 500	8
	20	22 000	11
50	5	5 000	3–½
	10	10 000	6–½
	15	15 000	10
	20	20 000	13
	25	25 000	17
55	5	4 250	4
	10	8 250	8
	15	12 000	12
	20	16 500	16
	25	20 750	20
	30	25 000	24
60	5	2 750	5
	10	5 500	10
	15	8 250	16
	20	11 000	21
	25	13 750	26
	30	16 500	32
	35	19 500	37

Figure 57.3 Scale of pension damage
Source: Shucksmith & Co., Actuarial Estimates
Courtesy of Times Newspapers Limited

Time for interviews

Under the Employment Protection Act redundant full time employees with two or more years' service, or employees working between 8 and 16 hours per week with 5 years' service, are entitled to reasonable time off with pay to look for another job or to arrange for training for a new job. 'Reasonable' is not defined since individual requirements may vary so much.

The TUC in their publication 'Job Security' cite two full days as a common entitlement, but this may seem inadequate in a period of 12 weeks' notice. Excessive demands from individuals are obviously to be discouraged.

TRIBUNALS

An employee declared redundant may appeal to an industrial tribunal if he considers he has been unfairly dismissed on the following grounds:

1 The dismissal is for reasons not covered by the definition of the Employment Protection Act
2 The means of selection are unfair because:
   (a) they concern membership, or non-membership, of a trade union
   (b) the accepted or agreed selection procedures have been disregarded
   (c) the warning given was inadequate, or efforts have not been made to find alternative employment within the organisation
   (d) there has been discrimination based on the race or sex of the employee
   (e) any other reason which the employee considers unfair.

To avoid such claims, it is essential that shortage of suitable work, however caused, is the only reason for redundancy; selection procedures are agreed and followed, and that each employee is given written notice of dismissal.

This formal notice should state the reason, the period of notice and termination date, the appeals procedure. Copies of such notice may then be used in evidence at any subsequent tribunal appeal by the employee.

If they agree that dismissal is unfair, the tribunal may make an order for reinstatement in the employee's old job, re-engagement in another job or payment of compensation. Maximum compensation is currently £6250.

If an employer is considered not to have met the requirements of prior consultation, a tribunal may make an order to postpone the dismissals or make a protective award requiring payment of normal wages for a specified period. The maximum protective award may not exceed the period specified for consultation (28, 60 or 90 days as appropriate).

Approaches to an industrial tribunal are made using:

Form IT1 for employees seeking decisions on their entitlement to compensation and the amount due
Form IT17 for employers seeking a decision on their entitlement to rebate against redundancy payments
Form IT18 in all other cases

for complaints arising in England or Wales to:

The Secretary
Central Office of Industrial Tribunals
93 Ebury Bridge Road
London, SW1

or for those arising in Scotland:

> The Secretary
> Central Office of Industrial Tribunals (Scotland)
> St Andrew House
> 141 West Nile Street
> Glasgow

The proceedings of tribunals are held informally, but applicants and witnesses may be required to give evidence on oath. They may be represented by lawyers, trade union or employers' association officials.

Details of the procedures are given in leaflets:

> ITL1 for employees
> ITL2 for respondents
> ITL7 for employers appealing against failure to pay rebate

REBATES FROM THE REDUNDANCY FUND

Claims for rebates must be made to the Department of Employment within six months of the payment to the employee. Rebate may be reduced if the necessary notification is not given.

The notification is made on form RP1 which requires the following information for each employee: sex, national insurance number, income.tax reference number, date of birth, date of engagement, expected date of dismissal, amount of a week's pay.

It should be noted that the department may call for the production of records to check the claims or may ask permission for an officer to carry out the required checks on the employers' premises.

STANDARD PROCEDURES

Although every instance of redundancy is likely to be different in detail, drawing up a standard procedure will help to ensure that, if a redundancy becomes necessary, it can be dealt with rapidly and efficiently, so that administrative failures will not intensify an already emotional and critical situation.

Many of the procedures suggested have value and relevance to the organisation in general, quite apart from their value in the avoidance and administration of redundancy. They should be included in a redundancy agreement to demonstrate to staff that all possible efforts are being made to protect their interests and secure the well-being of the organisation.

Topics which should be covered in a redundancy procedure include:

1* Manpower planning as a positive part of the overall corporate plan
2* Consultation machinery
3* Categories of redundancy involving varying treatment
4* Means of avoiding redundancy, such as not subcontracting work, restric-

tion of recruitment, restriction of overtime working, voluntary retirement, retiring staff over retirement age, laying off part-time workers

5*   Transfer arrangements
6*   Training
7*   Method of categorising jobs and workers
8*   Selection procedures to be used
9*   Notification procedure – for staff and Department of Employment
10* Formal notice including arrangement for amendments
11* Compensation
12* Welfare and assistance to dismissed employees
13* Assistance in finding new jobs
14* Pension arrangements
15* Terms for re-engagement
16* Publicity
17* Calculations of payments due and notification of amounts to staff concerned
18* Formal dismissal procedures
19   Claims for rebate from Department of Employment
20   Appeals:
     (a) By the organisation
     (b) *By individuals
21   Records
22   Evaluation after redundancy has occurred in order to improve;

Once the basic procedures have been drawn up, they should be discussed with staff representatives through the normal consultation machinery.

Items marked * in this list, or extracts from them, should then be used to formulate an agreement with the staff. Details of the administrative procedures are not necessary in such an agreement. In the case of item 1, for instance, it is sufficient to give an undertaking that forward planning and forecasting of manpower requirements will be carried out in order to constrain the availability and supply of staff as near to the requirement as possible.

EMPLOYMENT SERVICES AND AGENCIES

The Manpower Services Commission is responsible for providing a wide range of services to industry and individuals including:

Advice on manpower planning and forecasting methods
Assistance and advice in documentation for redundancy
Guidance on alternative employment available for dismissed employees
Temporary employment subsidies
Guidance on assistance and service available to help those dismissed
Advice on retraining facilities
Advice on appeals and industrial tribunals.

All these services are available in a redundancy situation, the advance warning called for by the Act providing time for them to be alerted and brought into use.

Where large numbers of staff are to be dismissed, an employment office can be set up on the organisation's premises.

Initial contact with the services should be made to the local Department of Employment office. The larger offices have specialist departments for dealing with all aspects of redundancy.

The following leaflets are available:

RPL1   Offsetting pensions against redundancy payments
RPL2   Ready reckoner for payments
RPL4   Service calendar
RPL5   Calculation of a week's pay for employees on shift and rota work
RPL6   Summary of information for employees

REDEPLOYMENT

Company schemes to assist redundant employees

Whilst there is no legal requirement on organisations to assist redundant staff beyond giving time off for job hunting, the traumatic effects of large scale redundancies, high levels of unemployment and increasing recognition of social obligations have encouraged many organisations to give much greater assistance than this.

The attitude of society towards unemployed people is changing rapidly in four respects:

1   The severance payments are becoming more generous; derisory ones are becoming less frequent. The figure quoted most often for a middle manager in mid-career after about five years' service with a company is around six months' pay
2   There are moves to change the law to counteract the pension damage suffered by mobile executives. Some employers are including pension damage in the calculation of severance payments
3   Those who are out of work are not the untouchables they used to be
4   Redeployment services have emerged from the purely advisory service amateur status into a proven executive marketing service. Recognising this, employers are starting to incorporate this service into the overall severance packages.

In addition to direct benefits to the redundant employees, there is a major spin off in improving morale for the retained staff.

There are three main areas where assistance can usefully be given by an organisation:

1   Helping the employees to clarify their future needs
2   Financial arrangements
3   Assistance with finding a new job.

The priorities of each of these will vary according to the circumstances of the individual involved; thus, if early retirement has been used to effect redundancy, the order of priority would probably be 2, 1, 3, whereas for a middle level executive in his early forties 1, 3, 2 might be appropriate.

The effect of being made redundant will vary from one individual to another; for one it may be a golden opportunity to acquire sufficient capital to retire or to start his own business. For the next, it represents disaster, the scrap heap, the stigma of rejection, loss of self confidence. Therefore, the needs of each one will be different, and there is no point in offering a standard package irrespective of need.

A preliminary interview with each individual is needed to establish their specific requirements from the services which it has been decided to make available.

Individual needs

Firstly, it is essential to help the individual determine exactly what he wants to do. In many cases people may not have given any thought at all to the problem and, in most cases, their ideas will be constrained within fairly narrow limits. In fact, the range of choice open to individuals can be very wide indeed.

A skilful counselling interview may enable many people to see redundancy as an opportunity rather than a disaster, and certainly should form the first step in the build up of confidence which will enable those who have been so affected to cope with their problems.

It cannot be over-emphasised that counselling to assist people to solve their own problems, rather than the provision of a shoulder to cry on or someone who will tell them what to do, is essential if individuals are to be helped to stand on their own feet again.

Choice of objectives

The range is infinite, embracing complete retirement, partial retirement, starting up a business or joining an established business (for example by buying a directorship), emigrating, undergoing training or education, seeking a different type of work, seeking a similar job, accepting unemployment as a positive rather than a negative move.

Financial arrangements

If the employee decides on retirement, then his needs are probably to use his compensation to supplement his pension. The individual starting up a business may need a capital sum to invest, a supplement to his income or a single premium contribution to an insurance/pension package. Those taking a training or education course, would probably need a supplement to whatever grant is obtainable.

Any advice given must take into account the individual's existing financial arrangements, other income or pension, mortgage, capital, his financial needs, health, age and commitments. Additionally, the effect of the various arrangements on his tax structure must be evaluated. The range of options available is so wide, and the advantages to be gained from optimum money management so high, that expert advice should invariably be sought.

Fair severance payments

Employers, executives and staff are all subject to the unpredictable vagaries of a market economy. This must be accepted, but there needs to be a fairer system to level out the compensatory payments received by individuals which are seldom a reflection of the merit of an individual or of his needs.

If the severance payments are to be treated as compensation to pay for the period of unemployment, then some yardstick for estimating this time is required.

Figure 57.4 sets out to quantify most of the factors which affect the time taken to obtain a new job.

Other employment

For the majority, whose prime requirement is a new job, much can be done by counselling and guidance to increase firstly confidence, and then the marketing of the skills of those made redundant.

Many people constrain their search for employment by looking only for jobs similar to those they are losing. Identifying the skills which they have acquired and used as a result of their experience will invariably widen the choice of jobs available to them. They can then be assisted in marketing their skills through skilful presentation, practice in letter writing, interviewing etc. The response rate to individual applications may be as low as 1–2 per cent so that secretarial assistance will be of considerable value.

Few people realise that seeking a job is hard, demanding work, requiring a disciplined, planned approach which must in itself be tackled like a full time job. Among the benefits of any scheme providing assistance with job seeking will be the inculcation of the necessary disciplines and commitment to this task.

Training

Training may form an essential element in the search for new employment. Skills training will consist of bringing existing skills up to date, adding a complementary skill (for example a language) or, on a longer term, acquiring completely new skills or knowledge or obtaining formal qualifications to match existing skills and experience. Career counselling should ensure that skills and qualifications are those for which there is a demand, or which will improve the market value of existing assets.

Many will require training in self-marketing. A typical four-day course would cover the following:

1 Marketing – (who are you, what can you do, who wants you, how to contact them)

The average executive who is
not naturally good at
job hunting

GHM

Assumptions	The average executive	The average executive benefiting from redeployment services
That short list selection interviews will be generated at the rate of.........	1 every 2 weeks	1 every 3 weeks	2 every 3 weeks
That on average there will be 6 people on the short list making their chances of selection likely to be.........	1 every 6 interviews	1 every 9 interviews	1 every 4 interviews

From these assumptions the following
mathematical probabilities can be calculated

80% will have earned selection within.........	20 weeks	40 weeks	10 weeks
Through no fault of their own, just as a matter of chance, 5% will still be unemployed after	35 weeks	70 weeks	20 weeks

Initial delay

Add start-up time before first interviews are generated.........	5 weeks	7 weeks	3 weeks

Age Factors

Per year over 45 years	Add 1 week
Per year over 50 years	Add 2 weeks
Per year under 35 years	Deduct 1 week

Administrative factors

Delay by employers between final selection and arrival of offer	2 weeks
Delay between offer and taking up appointment	2 weeks
Delay before arrival of first pay cheque	4 weeks

Other Factors

Staying in employment during job search	Add 30%
High severance payments exceeding one year's	Add 10% per months salary
For every 100 000 over 1.5 million unemployed	Add 5%

Salary Factors

Per £1000 over £15 000 p.a.	Add 1 week
Per £1000 under £10 000 p.a.	Deduct 1 week

*Figure 57.4   Factors affecting the time taken to find a new job
(Percy Coutts & Co)*

2   Career history and letter writing, telephone skills
3   Interview training (using closed circuit television)
4   Individual counselling

Unless the organisation has the necessary expertise to provide this training, it should be left to specialists such as career counsellors or training institutions.

The 'TOPS' programmes provided by the Manpower Services Commission at colleges and other centres, are particularly appropriate for redundant staff who generally qualify for subsistence grant whilst attending.

Job search

The need is to supplement the general services provided by the Department of Employment with services geared to the requirements of particular grades, such as senior executives and specialist staff. Even in cases of large scale redundancy, where the Department of Employment will open employment offices on the organisation's premises, a great deal can be achieved by a task force approach by the organisation's own marketing staff or specialist recruitment agencies to unearth every possible employment opportunity.

This should be coupled with guidance to staff on the approach they should take and the type of job best suited to them. Individuals will frequently have to choose between waiting until the right job appears, with the risk of rejection because of a long period of unemployment, or taking any job to give continuity of employment.

A 'job shop' set up on the employer's premises and manned by sales staff can provide redundant staff with a wide range of vacancies. The key to success is the training of staff to run the job shop, their enthusiasm, and the employer's commitment to maintaining it.

Specialist agencies

Because of the expertise and resources needed to conduct a full scale redeployment operation, may organisations rely entirely on outside agencies. Such agencies should be capable of providing the following services:

Training courses to teach the skills of self-marketing
Career history writing of a similar standard to creative writers in media firms
Market researchers
Office services: mailshot facilities, word processors and secretarial support
Experienced counsellors and the availability of a professional vocational psychologist with experience in executive careers
Interview coaching with closed circuit television facilities
Promotional facilities in direct contact with the executive search and recruitment organisations.

These services should be continually available until the employee has obtained his next appointment.

Firms operating in this field who have been established for more than three years are:

Chusid
Forty Plus
Interexec
Minster
Percy Coutts & Co Ltd
Sanders & Sydney.

Financial advice can be provided by:

Douglas Deakin Young
Cockman & Copeman.

Benefits to the organisation

By involving the public relations element of the company, the negative reputation of being a company with redundancies can be turned into a positive reputation, by highlighting the image of a company which cares for its staff. Much good publicity can thereby be generated. This will help to obtain vacancies for the job shop, and will eventually attract higher quality applicants when recruiting resumes.

A company which is unprepared and has no positive redeployment policy will have managers who are reluctant to take a commercially correct decision to reduce staff because they feel they will be seriously damaging the careers of colleagues.

The adverse publicity associated with major redundancy programmes can add to the business problems of the company. A well-designed redeployment operation covering the weekly and hourly paid staff will show the employer as being forward-thinking, considerate and businesslike. This must be good publicity.

The internal morale of a company which sends off its surplus staff with positive job search support must be better than that of a company which wields the axe rapidly and ruthlessly.

FURTHER READING

Carew, T., *Get up and Go Job Search*, Percy Coutts & Co.
Daniel, W. W., *Whatever Happened to the Workers at Woolwich?* Economic Planning, London, 1972
Dobson, John, 'Planning a Voluntary Redundancy Scheme', *Works Management*, April 1975, pp 52–3
Employment Protection (Consolidation) Act 1978, chapter 44, HMSO, 1979
Gill, H. S., 'Handling Redundancy and How to Maintain Morale' *Personnel Management*, vol. 7, No. 3, March 1975, pp 34–7
Golzen, S., and Plumbley, P., *Changing Your Job*, Kogan Page, 1981
Golzen, S., *Working for Yourself*, Kogan Page, 1981

Guidelines for the Redundant Manager, 2nd edition, British Institute of Management, 1981

A Short Guide to the Preservation of Occupational Pension Benefits, Occupational Pensions Board, London

Kemp, F. et al, *Focus on Redundancy*, Kogan Page, 1980

Lubbock, Bill, *Finding Another Top Job*, Institute of Personnel Management, 1975

Mumford, P. A., *Redundancy and Security of Employment*, Gower, 1975

O'Brien, R., 'Points of Procedure', *Personnel Management*, August 1972, pp 23-5

PART TEN

THE SKILLS OF MANAGEMENT

58 Management self-development

Michael Williams

It is widely believed that management development = management training = 'send him on a course'. This view assumes that management development is 'done' by someone to someone else – applied, in other words, like an external treatment.

Management development planned in this spirit rarely involves the person who requires development in either the diagnosis of the problem or the formulation of the prescription and follow-up. Thus he tends to find himself playing a largely passive role in important activities concerned (as the case may be) with:

his growth as a person
his development for future promotion or transfer
improving his current performance or increasing his contribution as a manager
helping him make the transition from specialist to managerial role
developing his skills in specific areas.

Traditional forms of management training, moreover, are more likely to be 'off the peg' than tailor-made, and may not always be the most suitable for the individual in question.

Perhaps most serious of all is the constant failure to recognise that ultimately the company, a boss, or the management development manager is not responsible for the development of the organisation's managers. The managers themselves are. The boss's responsibility is to encourage, support and 'facilitate' the process of his subordinates' self-development and therefore is principally one of helping them to help themselves to develop and become more effective.

At its most fundamental, management development means self-development – that is, a conscious response on the part of the individual to deal with what *he* recognises as his development needs. Real development takes place when the individual sees, for himself, the need to modify his behaviour, change his attitudes, develop new skills, improve his performance, or prepare himself for a different role. The rationale that 'only the learner will learn' is recognised in some organisations and by a growing number of management development specialists, tutors and trainers.

Because many of the barriers to self-development that exist in companies and within boss-subordinate relationships are self-imposed and psychological, the process needs stimulation, guidance and sensitive managing. The next level up in the management hierarchy often serves as the best excuse for not getting things done and provides a frequent let-out for the individual who chooses to deny his responsibility for his own development:

> 'I'm employed by the company; it's up to my boss to decide what my development needs are. I don't know which way my career is going to go.'

Such self-imposed constraints are not strategies for success. They need to be recognised by managers as recipes for mediocrity. The evidence that such self-protective behaviour is prevalent at managerial and supervisory levels usually takes the form of:

- scepticism and a general 'don't want to know' attitude
- unwillingness to take ownership of problems
- reluctance to exercise initiative and authority
- opting out and buck-passing
- failure to take necessary risks leading to a record of lost opportunities
- forfeiture of influence as a 'power-source' within the organisation.

The true basis of self-development – namely that the individual takes responsibility for his own learning – may be quite alien to some managers. Traditionally much education (schools, further education and training) has put the emphasis on teaching rather than on learning. That approach tends to create inappropriately high levels of student passivity towards developing new attitudes and behaviours (It's up to *them* to teach *me*').

To some people the idea of taking responsibility for their own learning is even seen as threatening, because it involves a personal shift from a largely uncommitted or passively receptive state to one which demands the individual's commitment and action.

Others may be so disillusioned with their particular lot or with the company in general that they are demotivated and demoralised to the extent that they cease to care about self-development altogether. To people in such negative states of mind the process is likely to be seen at best as 'pie in the sky'.

More probably it will be viewed with suspicion as a management confidence trick, personnel department propaganda or (by the real cynics) as a 'do-it-yourself hangman's kit'.

Some managers may take a tougher, more calculative view and expect to see direct links between any effort on their part in self-development and the company's reward system.

Finally there will always be managers (usually senior executives) who assume inviolability. They claim, with or without coyness, that they have already 'arrived' and that 'this sort of thing is all right for other people'.

SELF-DEVELOPMENT IN THEORY AND PRACTICE

There are two aspects of the human personality which are relevant to the under-standing of self-development. These are:

1 The 'self image' (the 'me as I see myself') by which each individual identifies himself, his personal values, beliefs, knowledge, wants, needs and fears as well as his physical presence
2 The 'ego ideal' (which amounts to the individual's 'me as I would really like to be'). In essence this consists of the attainable 'plus-me' which exists in every individual in addition to the hopes, dreams and wishes which may make up the idealised or fantasy self.

Personal growth (which by definition is largely determined by self-develop-ment) is the linking route from the self-image to the ego ideal. This is illustrated in Figure 58.1.

Practical self-development in management, necessarily, is concerned with attainable realities – what have been termed the 'plus me', rather than simply with the individual's fantasy world. The 'plus me' represents the difference between what the individual currently does, how effectively he operates, what contributions he makes in his present role and what that person is realistically capable of doing and being, within *self-selected periods of time*. The concept of the 'plus me', therefore, is related to a series of progressively emerging horizons — rather than to some ultimate limit which he or others have put on his potential. The horizons become more readily discernible as the individual consciously links his current behaviour and performance to what he feels are, for him, *requisite* standards, levels or modes of behaviour and which he judges are within his identifiable capacity. In practical terms the 'plus me' can be related to and reinforced by what Hodgson and Myers refer to as the 'plus job'. This is an attainable, realistic and viable role in which there are opportunities for increased satisfaction for the individual, coupled with increased con-tribution to the organisation in which he operates.

Identifying the 'plus me' and the 'plus job' involves the individual manager working through a series of key questions, preferably with his boss and (where available) a management development specialist. From the responses are built up pictures of how the individual wants to grow as a person and how his job, or role, might be realistically developed to cater for and capitalise on that person's growth. The next stage is to evolve appropriate action plans, principally within the scope of the manager's work environment. Exercises are given later in this chapter which illustrate the processes and show how more diagnostic information can be obtained in order for the prescriptive action plans to be evolved for individual managers and for managerial teams. The crucial following activities are monitoring, review and follow-through, without which there would only be action plans – not action.

SELF-DEVELOPMENT: DISCLOSURE AND FEEDBACK

The self-diagnosis described above represents a systematic analysis of a

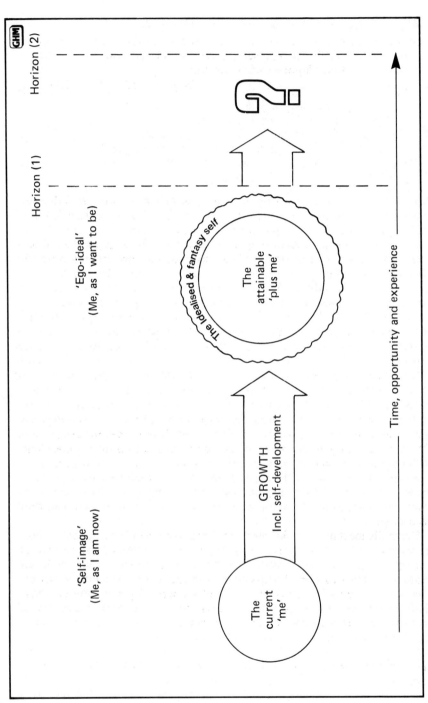

Figure 58.1 Personal growth

manager's performance, especially his behaviour in role and, therefore, his *management style*. The evidence of his immediate boss, his boss's superior, his peers and his subordinates represents crucial feedback to help him identify his real training and development needs for himself.

Informal performance reviews by his boss, periodic discussions with colleagues whose opinions and judgement he values, together with the data available to him from formal appraisal interviews all help him to place himself in relation to the demands of his job. Similarly, discussions with effective and experienced management development or training managers should provide valuable feedback and insights into how others see him and his contribution.

The process of feedback, however, is often best enhanced by *disclosure*, that is by disclosing expectations, needs or concerns which invite response and discussion. By specifically asking for information about personal effectiveness, management style, role as a colleague or boss, or contributions as a subordinate, a manager can build up a picture of both confirmatory and contradictory evidence about his perceived competence in his job. For example, he can turn what is so often the rather sterile ritual of the annual appraisal into a fruitful discussion by taking the initiative himself and encouraging his boss to ask the right questions. By using a simple self-appraisal instrument which more or less parallels the questions and areas of analysis of the company appraisal form he can prepare himself (and his reviewer) for a worthwhile and relevant diagnosis of his real performance improvement or development needs. One of the hallmarks of the really effective manager or specialist is his capacity to 'manage upwards'.

Influencing superiors is not the same as falling into the trap of self-weakening by *delegating* authority and responsibility upwards. Rather, it means letting a boss know exactly what you need from him, in order to do your own job more effectively. Equally, it means finding out from him where he needs you to change your behaviour in some way. The process is about helping a superior to act as a necessary and appropriately supportive source of organisational authority in order to open doors or give sanction to requisite innovation. Some managers may well feel vulnerable when the significance of their epaulets is drawn to their attention by a subordiante who is saying, in effect – 'Come on, you're the boss, so act like one and give me the authority to go and do what we need to get done'.

Generally most major or far-reaching changes require management at at least three levels within the organisation, as Figure 58.2 illustrates. First, there is the level at which the innovation or change is to be implemented. Immediately above that is the superior who may have to go out on a limb in order to give the necessary 'go-ahead' – hence the sense of vulnerability at this level. Then, above him is the 'umbrella' often necessary to provide senior managerial or organisational cover for the venture, even though all the evidence suggests that the change will result in necessary performance improvement.

Much of the art of the process lies in the extent to which both joint and mutually exclusive areas of accountability are identified and spelled out. In this way, mutual perceptions and expectations about obstacles to effective results and about opportunities that should or should not be exploited can be clarified.

Figure 58.2 **Hierarchial support needed for change to be implemented.**
This diagram shows the levels of support required to implement and sustain far-reaching change and improvement

Such disclosure and feedback need to be 'core' features of any boss-subordinate relationship in management, as a matter of course not just during periods of innovation and change. As an essential part of the personal (and hopefully mutual) stocktake which is what the annual performance appraisal should be, then at least the following questions need to be raised and worked through from the subordinate's point of view:

1 'These are what I see as my current priorities'
2 'This is what I believe(d) you (my boss) expect(ed) from me' or 'This is what I believe is/was expected of me in my job'
3 'These are the results I believe I have achieved'
4 'This is what I feel I have done well'
5 'This is where I see I need to improve'
6 'This is where/how I need you (my boss) to act on my behalf (or to give me support) in order for me to do my job more effectively'
7 'These are areas where I see our relationship as

   – Good
   – Less than satisfactory

8 'What do you need me to do differently in order for you to

   – act more effectively as my boss?
   – do your own job more effectively?'
9 'I see these as my main training development needs'
10 'What training or development do you feel I need'.

THE 'FLY-ON-THE-WALL'

A process which provides detailed minute-by-minute data about a manager's role and performance over several short periods of time is that of direct observation, accompanied by feedback and discussion. The purpose of the observation is to identify, record and review what a manager actually *does* in the course of several working days. Observation takes the form of a 'fly-on-the-wall' technique, which involves the observer sitting in with the manager so that the latter's every work activity can be recorded under appropriate headings and subsequently fed back to him for review and analysis. As a tool for learning, self-development and performance improvement it is invaluable, given an observer who is a credible, competent and sensitive individual in whom the manager being observed has confidence. The observer therefore may be a management development or training manager, external consultant, colleague, superior, or in some cases a subordinate.

The process can be structured to suit the situation, status and role of the manager being observed and the relationship between the observer and the observed. A case study later in this chapter illustrates a structured observation over a period of several hours. The subject in this case was a typical middle manager at work. His activities have been recorded in detail, in this format, in order to provide him with accurate data about:

1 How he spends his time in a variety of management situations, covering a range of managerial activities. In particular, where he needs to create periods of uninterrupted time for himself.
2 Where he could or should delegate and make greater use of other people – especially his secretary
3 In which situations and with which people he needs to control his 'boundaries' more effectively by developing more assertive approaches
4 How he could acquire vital information from other functions in a more timely way, with less effort
5 Where he needs to develop a more effective 'eyes and ears', or 'field intelligence' service through other people to reduce the amount of time he personally spends seeking information.

The amount of time required and frequency of observation for a 'fly-on-the-wall' exercise will vary, dependant upon –

1 The purpose and intended outcomes of the observations
2 The role and nature of the activities of the manager under observation
3 Whether or not remedial work is to begin after the first session or commence once all observation is at an end and diagnostic feedback has been completed.

Generally the process takes place in four or five phases, which are described below.

Phase 1: Initial discussion and decision to mount the exercise

This includes:

1 Agreement of the 'contract' between the observer and his client about mutual expectations and intended outcomes (N.B. the client may well not be the person to be observed; it could be his immediate superior, or other more senior executive)
2 Ice-breaking and establishment of relationship between observer and observed

3 Agreement on whether to hold observation sessions on set dates, or turn up on a random basis
4 Confirmation of what are and are not legitimate activities for observation.

Phase 2: Observation

This phase may consist of any number of sessions but, typically, four or five half-days over a period of two weeks represents the minimum necessary. During those sessions the observer is virtually 'glued' to the manager so that he may record the latter's activities and *reactions* in adequate detail. Normally the observer will use a log with appropriate headings under which he can detail what he sees happening (or not happening, since part of the observer's role during later stages will be to talk through significant omissions in the observed manager's behaviour). A typical log is illustrated in the case study later in this chapter (see Figure 58.3). Codes used are also explained in the case study. Others may be added as necessary. This is largely a matter of matching the tool to the task and evolving a relevant shorthand vocabulary which is convenient and quick to use.

Phase 3: The feedback stage

At this stage copies of the log are given to the manager. This may be done either at the end of each observation session, when his memory is fresh, or as a complete 'package' at the end of the exercise.
To stimulate review and analysis and to help the manager draw out the necessary learning points the observer usually works through a series of relevant questions, typified by the following:

1 How far do the observations match your understanding of what happened?
2 Are there any surprises in the data contained in the log?
3 Does time actually spent on some activities fit your recollections of the time you believed you spent?
4 What can you learn about the way you analyse situations, make decisions and take action?
5 When are you most effective? Which situations do you handle well?
6 When are you least effective? Which situations could you handle better?
7 What could and should you be delegating?
8 How well do you plan against contingencies and cope with events that you could not plan for?
9 How effective are you in obtaining the information you need to do your job?
10 How well do you warn others of impending difficulties, or actions likely to affect them?
11 What exactly do you need to do differently in order to be more effective at your job?

12   From all the above data what skills do you need to improve in order to be more effective and how best can you develop them?

Phase 4: The action plan stage

Both the data presented and the manager's response to that feedback provide the basis for his personal development action plans. Where appropriate the action plans may well be discussed with the manager's superior and a specialist from the personnel department or an external consultant. The plans need to be implemented and followed through to ensure that the requisite changes in operation, management style and personal development *are* taking place.

Phase 5

As a variation on a theme, a team workshop consisting of all the managers who have been through a 'fly-on-the-wall' exercise may be run to confirm development needs and action plans to meet the needs. Each manager (who is well known to the others) presents the essence of his feedback and the lessons drawn from it, together with his action plans for treatment. These are added to, modified and ratified by his colleagues or team mates on the basis of their knowledge of him. They are then implemented by the team on a mutually supportive basis which ensures a high level of monitoring, review and follow-through.

SELF-DEVELOPMENT – CASE STUDY IN ACTIVITY ANALYSIS

John Walton is a transport manager. In this exercise the procedure is described by which over three hours of his working day were recorded on an activity log in order to obtain an impression of his typical work pattern. The activity key looks fairly complicated, but it becomes relatively simple when considered under the four right-hand columns, as described below.

Format of the activity log

A proforma is used to record the activities, with the layout shown in Figure 58.3. A shorthand key is used to speed up the entry process and condense data into the limited space available on the form. In this example, the shorthand codes used were as folows:

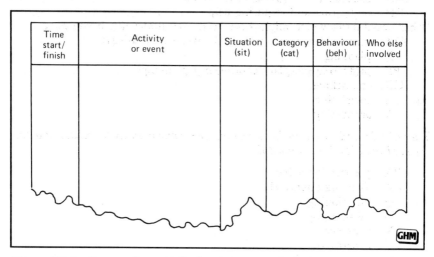

Time start/ finish	Activity or event	Situation (sit)	Category (cat)	Behaviour (beh)	Who else involved

Figure 58.3   Format for activity log

Under 'sit' (the situation in which the individual was observed)

> AW   working alone
> TI   taking an incoming telephone call
> TO   making an outgoing telephone call
> D   discussion with one other person
> MI   meeting – informal
> MF   meeting – formal
> O   outside own office

The above can be used in combination, and might have been supplemented by:
> WSP   with superior

WSB   with subordinate
WSBS   with more than one subordinate
AD   dictating to secretary
AT   working alone – thinking

Under 'cat' (the category of managerial activity observed) the codes used were:

PA   establishing causes of problems
SA   clarifying situations or problems
GD   giving data/information
BV   briefing verbally
XCA   checking data for relevance and accuracy
SDI   seeking data/information
E   evaluating or reviewing progress
O   organising
OGI   organising and giving instructions
RH   requesting and requiring help

Other possibilities which might have been used under this heading are:

DA   making decisions (choosing between alternatives)
P   planning
PP   protecting the plan (contingency planning)
CO   controlling
S   social chat
A   arbitrating

The following codes were applied under the 'beh' column, where the behaviour of the observed individual was recorded

PA   positive/assertive
LA   listening attentively
Q   questioning
D   disagreeing
X   confused
U   constructive
C   composed (when under stress)

To these codes might have been added:

UN   uncertain/indecisive
CR   critical
DI   dominant
DG   domineering
E   emotional
DF   defensive
SWO   switched off
DY   switched on (dynamo)
GA   playing psychological games
AG   aggression
H   humour
NU   nurturing/building

Codes under 'who else'

are simply the initials of others involved in the observed situation

Activity log for Mr John Walton

The activity log compiled for John Walton is shown complete in Figure 58.4. The impression gained is that the period of observation involved activities and work patterns which were typical of John Walton's normal work load and working style. Assuming this to be so, then what emerges as a representative picture is the following:

1 About 5 per cent of his time is free to work alone (thinking and planning time)
2 95 per cent of his time is spent face-to-face with someone, or on the telephone
3 50 per cent of his time is spent seeking information and clarifying situations
4 30 per cent of his time is spent giving instructions or briefing
5 The remainder is spent in arranging/organising transport, solving problems, etc.

Some questions raised by the analysis

Given that the above *is* typical of John's working day then some questions that need to be asked are:

1 How could JW create more thinking and planning time for himself?
2 How much of the time he personally spends chasing up data and information could be reduced by
   – using other information sources (production planning and control)
   – delegating to his subordinates the task of securing much of the information
   – the introduction of an up-to-the-hour information service to JW from production (or production planning and control)?
3 How much more, generally could and should he use his subordinates and push responsibility for solving problems back down to them?
4 The very nature of a transport manager's role, especially when combined with that of chief despatcher, is fraught with fire-fighting problems. Being at the 'end of the line' inevitably means collecting everyone else's rubbish, to some extent.
   BUT, there is much that JW's immediate superior could do to reduce the pressure on John by
   – sitting down with him and analysing the what, how, when and who of JW's work
   – assuming a higher profile and more assertive stance in managing the boundaries between finishing and transport/despatch.
   Ultimately, of course, many of the decision to delegate or not delegate rest with John himself.

Manager observed: John Walton
Position   :   Transport manager
Date(s) observed   :   3 August 19XX
Times observed   :   11.09am-12.30pm and 1.45pm-3.45pm

Time on/off	Subject/activity/event	sit	cat	beh	who else?
11.09		AW	PA	PA	
11.10	Arthur collects notes on transport routes	D	SA	LS	ART
11.11	Graphic statistics – analysing what, where and when	D	SA	Q	BRI
11.12	Cehcking details/facts/figures with supervisor	D	SA	Q	
			PA	PA	BRI
11.13	J. goes out to collect outwork book, disagrees on section III; agrees on sections I and II	D	SA	D	BRI
			GDI	PA	BRI
			BV	Q	BRI
	J. seeking reliable accurate information		BV	X	BRI
	(given contradictory 'facts')			Q	
11.18			SA	U	
11.19	Telephone call to Transport Haulage Company	TO	SDI	PA	
	– seeking information on lorries and drivers		SDI	Q	
11.26	– ? work completion notes to clerk	D	E	PA	CLE
11.27	Recommences work with BRI	D	BV	PA	BRI
11.28	Query work in progress	AW	O	PA	NEV
11.28	Telephone call	TI	SDI	PA	
11.28	Second telephone rings (J. also takes this one over from secretary)	TI	SA	PA	
11.29	First call finished and first 'phone rings again	TI	SDI	PA	Visitor
11.31	Organising people to do things, including	D	SA	PA/Q	Secret
11.35	gathering information	D	OGI	PA	MIK
		D	OGI	PA	DON
11.38	Given more wrong data (goes out to TER next door)	MO	SA	X	TER
	Checks paperwork with loader (loader unhelpful)	MO	SDI	PA	LOA
11.39	Wrong feedback – visitor gets data/information	D	SA	XQ	DON
	mixed up	D	SDI	Q	
11.40	Talks to driver	D	GI	PA	Driver
		D	SA	PA	
11.40	Clarifying delivery situation on goods	D	SA	PA/Q	MIK
11.42	Discussion with driver – gives more information	D	GI	PA	Driver
11.46	Reaffirms delivery date on goods	D	SA	PA	MIK
11.47	MIK returns regarding possible shortages	D	E	Q/PA	MIK
11.47	Checks numbers of 'look in'	MO	GI	Q	TER
11.52	Checks/queries tonight's deliveries	D	GI	LS	PAC
11.55	Gives routes/delivery runs and quantities	D	SA	PA	BRI
12.00	Request for transport	TO	RH	PA	
			XCA	Q	
12.05	Availability of drivers' mates for twilight shift	TO	SI	Q	RON
			DA	PA	
12.07	Call for information (no-one there)	TO	RH	Q	
12.09	Request to J. for transport and driver	TI	GDI	PA	ANON
	J. goes out to talk to driver	MO	SDI	Q	Driver
12.13	Request for situation report	TI	GDI	PA	RAY
			DA	PA	

Figure 58.4   *Activity log compiled for John Walton, Transport Manager*
Entries would, in practice, be hand-written

Time on/off	Subject/activity/event	sit	cat	beh	who else?
12.14	Checks up on transport availability	TO	SDI	Q	VIC
		D	SA	PA	TER
	Do we have a car? Do we have a driver?		SA	Q	
12.19	Spare driver?	D	SA	Q	MIK
12.19		TO	SA	Q	CLI
12.20	Situation report	D	E	PA	MIK
12.21	No driver	TO	GDI	PA	
12.22	Briefing caller	TI	BV	PA	RAY
			GDI	PA	WIL
12.23	Situation report	D	BV	PA	MIK
		TI	DA	PA	PAU
		D	SA	PA	WIL
		TO	GDI	PA	CLE
12.25					
12.28					
LUNCH					
1.49	Planning procedures	D	GDI	PA	CLE
1.51	Making up loads for tomorrow	AW	DA	PA	CLE
2.06	Phone call	TI		PA	?
2.11	Clarifying schedule	D	PA	PA	MIK
2.12	Taking message	TI	A	PA	DIC
2.14	Phone (wrong number)	TI	A	PA	?
2.15	Call TER	TO		PA	out
2.17	TER calls back	TI	XCA	Q	TER
2.22	Goods (southern deliveries)	TI	SDI	Q	PAT
2.24	Meeting	MI	SDI	Q	NOR
			GI	PA	
2.28	Goods (midlands deliveries)	TO	SA	Q	PAT
2.30	Parcel arrives – goods components				PET
2.31	Makes out rail notes	MIO	DSI	PAQ	
2.32	Clarifying/explaining procedures	TI	E/BV	PA	CLI
	+ action: sorts out detail		O/DA	QPA	JON
2.42	Parking ticket from driver	M	XCA	QPA	Driver
2.42	Clock card	D	GI	PA	PAC
2.44		D	GI	PA	Driver
2.50	Calls for notes	D	SA	X	Driver
2.57	Writing	D	SA	PA	CLE
2.57	Sorts out midlands/north deliveries	D	E/ GDI	C	ART
3.09	Delivery of two reels of cable	D	SDI	Q	Driver
3.10	Electricians call	TI	BV	QPA	RAY
3.15	Ring for transport	TO	SA	PA	PAU
3.22	Needs information for PAT for goods (southern)	D	DA	PA	Visitor
3.24	Despatch priorities: goods (southern)	D	SA	PA	DER
3.28	Phone call	TI	SA	PA	DON
	Another call holding		SA	Q	ADR
	OBSERVER REJOINS PERSONNEL DEPARTMENT				

Figure 58.4 (continued)

5   Finally, there is the question of organisation. Is the structure of work done and current reporting relationships appropriate or is there a need to rethink and reorganise the whole question or ordering and using transport both at incoming and outgoing stages? This is obviously a far wider issue but inevitably the organisation structure is a major determinant of work loads, work patterns and comparative efficiency/inefficiency of managerial time.

ACHIEVEMENT OBJECTIVES AS A MEANS FOR SELF-DEVELOPMENT

Used either as a natural consequence of discussions at the end of a 'fly-on-the-wall' exercise or as an alternative approach, specific achievement objectives can lend structure, direction and impetus to a manager's self-development. Based on a diagnosis of needs, set within the context of a manager's role and agreed with his boss, achievement objectives represent yardsticks of attainment against which the manager can measure his performance and development.

Obviously the practice of setting objectives takes various forms in business. These range from formalised management by objectives (MBO) schemes to informal (but specific) targets set between bosses and their subordinates or within a work group set up to resolve a particular problem. The very process of management is about moving from a current situation (X) to a requisite state of affairs (Y) – usually within a set time limit. Typically managers work to the basic criteria as part of their day-to-day role, namely: quantity (how many and how much); quality (how well done or in what manner); cost (how much in financial terms); deadline (by when started/completed).

At the most senior levels philosophy, policies and strategies are normally based upon certain corporate goals – even though they may be sometimes more implicit than explicit. Normally corporate objectives are then translated appropriately at different levels down the line so that, necessarily, there will be a mandatory aspect to manager's objectives as well as a discretionary one.

In setting and agreeing personal achievement objectives as a means of stimulating self-development and improving managers' effectiveness, the diagram in Figure 58.5 illustrates the basic scope open to bosses and their

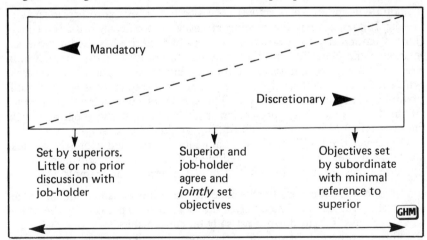

Figure 58.5 **The extent to which objective setting between superiors and subordinates may be mandatory or discretionary**
Some objectives will be mandatory themselves by their very nature (budget targets for instance) but how they are to be achieved may be largely discretionary within the boss-subordinate relationship

subordinates. That scope can be refined by a structure which enables managers to select, define and sharpen objectives in a disciplined way that more closely relates the performance of individuals to the goals of others.

First, it is helpful to determine what objectives are and what they are not. Management objectives:

are	are not
required results	activities
achievements	effort
accountabilities	duties
what is required	how it must be done
'musts'	'shoulds'

Secondly, there are different types of management objective. The principal categories are those which reflect the results to be achieved, under the following headings:

1　targets: to meet a deadline, programme of activities or product launch
2　improvements: for example, to increase profitability levels, productivity rates or quality standards
3　resolution of specific problems: examples are the removal of obstacles or constraints in order to correct deviations and restore previous conditions
4　innovation and change: this would include introducing and implementing something new which represented a departure from previous practice
5　control: aimed at ensuring or maintaining a given set conditions
6　personal or team development: principally aimed at acquiring the behavioural knowledge and levels of skill needed to operate more completely.

Undoubtedly some areas of activity are easier to measure than others in terms of results. It is usually possible to apply at least one specific, quantified objective. This is particularly the case where the type of objective has been determined ('target', 'improvement', 'problem solving', 'innovation' and so on). Even in areas of activity such as research and development or operational research, where the final outcomes might be very difficult to predict realistically, it is still possible to set quantified objectives. This can be done by making the objectives of the form 'submit and present an interim report at the progress review meeting on 13 May and show all findings to date' (for example).

Objectives need to be realistic, attainable, accurate and expressed in clear language if they are to appear credible and relevant as a self-development exercise. They must not be couched in vague terms. For example:

1　'Reduce the use of consumable materials on numbers 1 and 2 lines to budget level by the end of December, and by a further 10 per cent by the end of March' NOT 'Cut down drastically on consumables'
2　'Submit proposals by the end of the month for reducing steel procurement costs by at least 12 per cent. Method: by the use of alternative transport arrangements from the mills' NOT 'Investigate methods for reducing steel procurement costs'
3　'Revise your own and your subordinates' job descriptions by mid-January,

clarifying the principal accountabilities for each person. Progressively ensure that only agreed principal accountabilities are retained and that all other work is delegated and reallocated to section heads by 31 January' NOT 'Delegate as much work as possible to subordinates'.

In some organisations people of high potential may be deliberately moved into the 'fast line' in terms of career progression by being appointed to specially designed 'development posts'. Although they usually carry out necessary functions the real purpose of their move is to groom them for a more senior, longer term position. In most organisations this probably does not happen and only selected tasks and objectives may be available for the jobholder's development. Where this is the case the opportunities for self-development could well lie outside the mainstream of the role in the areas of:

- Short-term tasks and objectives
- Priority objectives
- Innovation and change programmes
- Trouble shooting and problem solving

Figure 58.6 represents the typical structure of many managerial jobs where objectives are divided between main-stream and short-term goals.

SOME VEHICLES FOR SELF-DEVELOPMENT

Once the task and personal objectives have been agreed, there is the question of work opportunities through which to achieve those objectives and ensure the process of development. A crucial factor in the process is the extent to which the manager's boss facilitates his subordinate's self-development by:

- providing the necessary 'trigger' and encouragement
- sustaining and restimulating it
- capitalising on it to the advantage of both the individual and the organisation
- pressing on the appropriate 'nerves' when unnecessary obstacles get in the way

Learning is fundamental to self-development and most people in managerial roles tend to learn as the result of *experience*. However, that experience needs to be analysed, discussed and worked through in order to draw the appropriate lessons from it.

Learning by experience, within a management job, is likely to involve the 'learner' in at least:

- *doing* – followed by analysis and review
- experimenting with new or different experiences and activities
- questioning and testing out existing knowledge, custom and practice, prejudices, values and beliefs
- experiencing (and reviewing) both success and failure
- examples and models (other managers) against which the learner can compare, assess and, if necessary, modify his own management style
- study and reflection, in order to put experience into perspective and context.

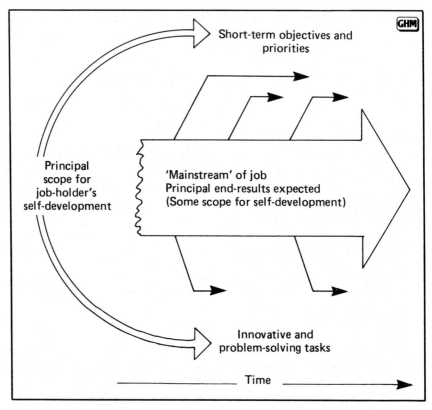

Figure 58.6 Scope for self-development within managerial jobs

Well-tried learning vehicles which provide opportunity for experiential learning and self-development include the following:

1 Keeping a work diary which is reviewed daily or, at least weekly, by the learner with his boss and/or a management development specialist
2 Setting up projects which are *relevant* and *realistic* and which have *real pay-off* for the company, the department and/or the individual. Such projects often carry far more weight when there is major representation to be made by the trainee to the chief executive or a senior panel, so that a sense of occasion is attached to the experience and it is seen to be important.
3 Cross-functional assignments involving multi-disciplinary teams of subordinates working together (for example marketing, product planning and engineering or production, industrial engineering and finance) where end results rely on co-operative, co-ordinated effort
4 Presentations on key issues – or contributions to key issues – to top management

5   Team development workshops in which members review:
   – 'our key objectives and priorities'
   – 'obstacles to achieving them'
   – 'my personal contribution to the team's goals'
   – 'our strengths and weaknesses as a team and as team members'
   – 'our action plan for the next 12 months'
6   'Bespoke' tutorials for individuals or groups using external professionals who test thinking and action plans by inputs of expertise, rigorous questioning and a wider perception
7   'Action learning', involving co-operation with managers from other companies and organisations, in the identification and resolution of each other's operational problems
8   Participation in junior 'boards', working parties, 'think tanks' or research teams, with or without senior executives involved, but where the outcomes are deemed to be important and relevant
9   Deputising for the boss:
   – by representing him at meetings, or on committees
   – visiting important external contacts, on his behalf
   – acting in his capacity for days/weeks/months at a time as appropriate.
10 Setting-up and running an entirely new product, department, function or small subsidiary company
11 Lecturing on personal accountability or a field of expertise to:
   – internal courses and seminars
   – professional courses run by universities, polytechnics or local colleges
   – educational programmes run by national, local or professional bodies
12 Planned reading, regularly reviewed and discussed with the trainee by one or more of the following acting in a mentor role:
   – his immediate superior
   – his superior's chief
   – appropriate in-company specialists, managers or supervisors
   – external professionals.

   Planned reading also involves keeping up-to-date by regularly choosing different areas of developing technology, important disciplines or relevant current events and systematically scanning the appropriate professional journals.

These, then, represent some of the learning opportunities that are available to enable a manager's self-development to take place at little or no cost to the company and with minimal interference with the day-to-day job that he is there to do.

   The term 'self-development' means exactly what it says. The real drive to make it happen must come from within the individual himself, but his superiors can do much to ensure an encouraging supportive climate in which self-development can thrive and become regenerative.

SOURCES AND RESOURCES

Some organisations and bodies concerned with self-development

Organisation	*Contacts*
Anglian Regional Management Centre High Street, Stratford, London E15 2JB 01-590 7722	I. Cunningham
Association of Teachers of Management Polytechnic of Central London, 35 Marylebone Road, London NW1 5LS 01-486 5811	M. Greatorex
Centre for the Study of Management Learning, University of Lancaster, Gillow House, Lancaster LA1 4YX Lancaster 65201	J. Burgoyne R. Boot
Hodgson Myers Assoc. 103 Walton Street, Oxford, OX2 6EB Oxford 52353	A. M. Hodgson
H.R.A. Training and Development Ltd 339/341 Grand Bldgs., Trafalgar Square, London WC2N 5HB 01-930 8931	T. Jaap H. Ware
The Open University, Walton Hill, Milton Keynes, Milton Keynes 74066	B. Lund
Polytechnic of Central London School of Management Studies 35 Marylebone Road, London NW1 5LS 01-486 5811	J. Bowden
Sheffield City Polytechnic Pond Street, Sheffield S1 1WB Sheffield 738621	M. Pedler T. Boydell
Michael Williams & Partners 27 Ferndale Park, Pedmore, Stourbridge, West Midlands DY9 0RB Hagley 884405	M. Williams

FURTHER READING

Austin, B., *Time and the Essence – A Manager's Workbook for Using Time Effectively*, British Institute of Management, 1979

Boydell, T. and Pedler M. (eds.), *Management Self-Development*, Gower, 1981

Hague, H., *Helping Managers to Help Themselves*, Context Training

Humble, J. W., *Management by Objectives*, Gower, 1975

Jaap, T., *The Steps to Self-Development*, Human Resource Associates

Mumford, A., *Real Learning – Making Experience Pay*, McGraw-Hill, 1980

Pedler, M., Burgoyne, J. and Boydell, T., *A Manager's Guide to Self-Development*, McGraw-Hill, 1978

Revans, R. W., *Action Learning*, Blond & Briggs, 1981

Toye, J., *Training for Versatility (Self Organised Learning)*, Industrial Training Unit (Cambridge)

Williams, M. R., *Coaching and Counselling*, The Leadership Trust (Symonds Yat)

59 Career planning

Michael Williams

At its simplest, career progression depends upon the interaction of two factors, or 'forces' – *personal ambition* and *organisation needs*. Figure 59.1 illustrates how these two forces act as the main determinants in the development of the individual's career path through his working life.

The more junior he is, the more will personal needs and ambition tend to be the predominant factor in the growth and direction of his career. By the time he has reached senior or top levels in the management hierarchy, the organisation's needs will usually be exerting the major influence over his career progression.

In up to thirty years in a managerial career the individual may have, typically, five or six different posts. It is unlikely that he will spend similar amounts of time in each. Generally, he may spend as little as one or two years in his earlier roles while in each of his final two posts he may spend seven, ten or more years, as Figure 59.2 shows.

The career 'plateau' apparent in this illustration may be due to many factors, both personal and organisational, but it might also be due to the onset of 'middlescence' and mid-career stagnation from which the individual never really recovers. The problem of 'died at forty, retires at sixty-five' is a common one and results in far too many career casualties, especially if there is an inadequate 'social support system' within the organisation to provide timely career counselling. Figure 59.3 shows the effects of the process on the career path of such a manager.

For many managers the mid-life period during the forties and early fifties may be something of a crucial personal 'stocktake'. It is for many a time of re-decisions, as well as decisions about career development, personal life and how the two can more satisfactorily co-exist. Fundamental reorganisation or technical change is also likely to have a significant impact upon the individual's career progression and, presupposing that the manager is prepared to respond to the organisation's needs, the picture of his career path may look like that shown in Figure 59.4. Similarly the shift from a predominantly technical role to

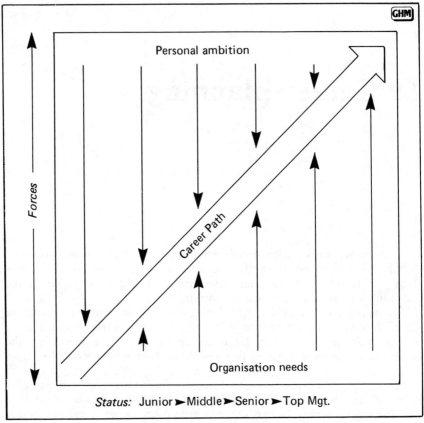

Figure 59.1 *The influence of personal ambition and organisation needs on career development*

largely managerial responsibilities which often comes with career progression to more senior levels will create learning demands upon the individual, as Figures 59.5 and 59.6 show. Whether the manager's career is largely one of transition from technical to managerial roles or a linear progression through the management hierarchy, the shift in the *type* of skills he will need to develop is depicted in Figure 59.7.

In the longer term, self-development needs to be related to the individual's career plans based upon where he or she wants to get to, within self-determined time scales.

The process begins when an individual starts by asking himself a whole series of personal questions such as:

1 What do I want from my career?
2 What don't I want from it?
3 What do I do well and what do I enjoy doing?

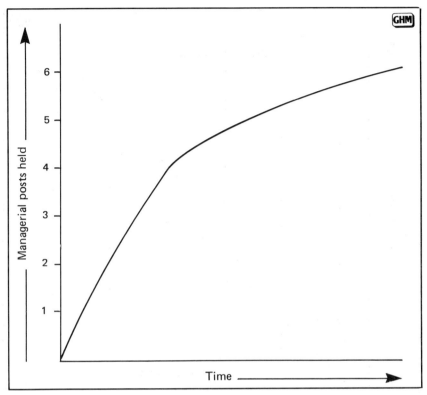

Figure 59.2   Typical managerial career progression

4   What do I want to be doing in two, five or ten years' time? Can I actually visualise the sort of job I want to be doing then?
5   What do I need to do better, or differently, to be more effective in my present job?
6   What do I need to do in order to prepare and develop myself for the jobs I believe I want to do in the future?
7   Where do I go to get the best possible help, guidance and advice about my career?

IDENTIFYING THE 'PLUS-ME' AND 'PLUS-JOB'

A first step to the process of deciding the right career path and self-development strategy might well take the form of a detailed personal 'stocktaking'. This involves identifying the 'plus-me' and 'plus-job' referred to in the previous chapter. The 'plus-me' exercise in Figure 59.8 invites you to make an assessment of you as you currently see yourself, and then to rate yourself (along the same dimensions) against the demands of effective performance in your current job. Simply use 'G' for good, 'S' to denote

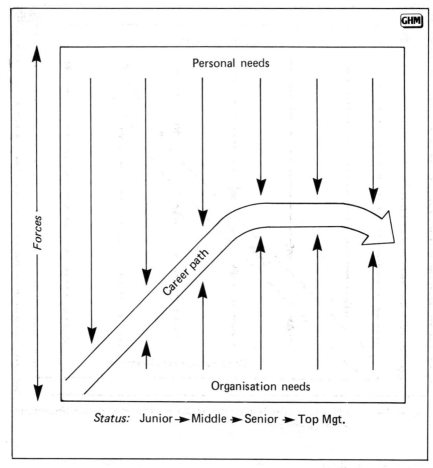

Figure 59.3 *Impact of 'middlescence' on career path*
This phenomenon appears to be complicated by a 'chicken and egg' argument about which comes first – the so-called 'mid-life crisis' or 'mid-career' crisis. The two are, however, often related.

'satisfied' with your performance or 'I' to indicate that improvement is needed.

When you have completed the 'As I am now' column, cover up your scores before filling in the right-hand column. When both columns have been completed, examine the results.

– What are your priorities for development action?
– Is there any pattern in your improvement needs – for instance, a lack of confidence – which inhibits your effectiveness?
– Are there any marked 'I' that you really cannot improve? How will you handle that?
– What about those marked 'G' – how will you build on those strengths and

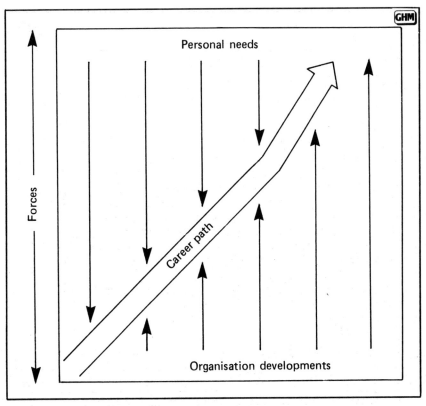

Figure 59.4 *Influence of technological or major organisation developments upon career path*

capitalise on them?
- What patterns emerge in your strengths? For instance are there any significant links between the 'G' scores? What clues do the patterns give you about your potential?
- What changes do you need to make to your job and work relationships to capitalise on the 'G' scores?
- What other key strengths do you have that make up your 'plus-me' and how do you intend to build on them?

The next part of the process is to consider your present role and the *attainable* 'plus-job' which may exist within it.

The 'plus-job' may not be your whole job, but the parts of it which match your strengths and which offer scope both for personal growth and increased contribution to your work group and your organisation. The 'plus-job' *consists of those activities that fulfil you and motivate you personally and professionally.*

Typically, the process takes the form illustrated in Figure 59.9.

Figure 59.5 **Shift in the nature of primary work**
Generally the more junior levels of management (especially in technical functions) are characterised by a considerable technical work content. This diminishes significantly with promotion, (although the manager may still cling to his original technical love)

1   Begin by listing those aspects of your work which are attainable within the overall scope of your current work which you identify as 'plus' features
2   Then against each of these features identify those strengths and positive attributes which you possess and which *strengthen* the plus aspects of your job. In other words, where do you excel, or have strengths, in the areas that motivate you?
5   Next, identify 'plus' features which you consider to be attainable in your present job, but which are not yet present
4   Against each of these potential plus features write what *action* you should take to make it feasible
5   Now, write down any personal strengths you possess, related to what you see as your 'plus-job'. Especially consider those which are not fully used at

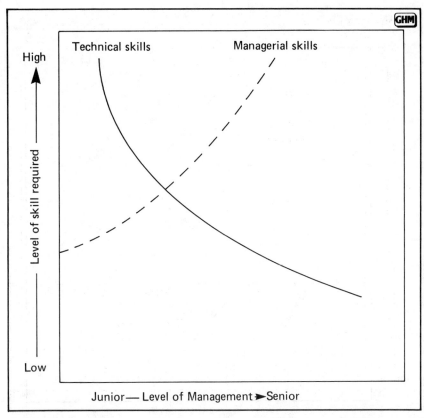

Figure 59.6 *Changing patterns of skills required to match primary work shift*

present and which you are therefore not developing as effectively as you could

6   Next, prepare an action plan for developing your attainable 'plus-job' and your strengths for discussion with your boss

7   Discuss it, implement what you can and follow through.

Particularly in the context of self-development and personal career planning, ' improvement' begins with 'I'. Other people are necessary to help the process, but only the individual himself has the ultimate responsibility for his development and growth.

CAREER TRANSITIONS

A considerable amount of research has gone into studies of the impact of major career changes upon executives and managers and most indicate that such transitions are usually accompanied by high stress and anxiety gaining the first

Figure 59.7 *Evolving needs for different skills in 'linear' career progression*
This figure shows the changing skills needed as the individual moves vertically through the hierarchy from supervisory or junior levels to the most senior executive posts

real job, obtaining significant promotion, feeling trapped in a routine 'prison', depression following redundancy, or apprehension about impending retirement are typical transition stresses.

At best, they are periods of considerable vulnerability where the individual may be unsure of

– what is expected of him in terms of skill, knowledge and performance
– whether he can cope with and come through the transition successfully
– what the ground rules, or guidelines (formal, or informal) are, which dictate how he should behave
– which are the key relationships he needs to make and use – especially who to turn to as the real source of support, help and guidance.

By definition, a crucial career transition occurs, through promotion, job stagnation, or job loss where the individual needs to *change* his

My Behaviour	As I am now	Demanded for success in my current job [GHM]
1 Securing commitment from others		
2 Managing conflict. Giving praise and appreciation to others		
4 Getting enough praise and appreciation from others		
5 Defining problems accurately and realistically		
6 Exercising judgement in technical decisions		
7 Exercising judgement in managerial decisions		
8 Being sufficiently tough when I need to be		
9 Saying what I do, or don't, want from others		
10 Being assertive (not aggresive) when feeling insecure or threatened		
11 Listening effectively		
12 Confronting others who violate my basic rights		
13 Owning my own problems – and their solutions		
14 Asking for help when I need it		
15 Allowing others to manipulate me against my will		
16 Capacity to put my role and contribution into proper organisational context		
17 Giving unpopular instructions face-to-face		
18 Expressing myself when I need to in front of a group or audience		
19 Thinking before I speak		

Figure 59.8 The 'plus-me' exercise

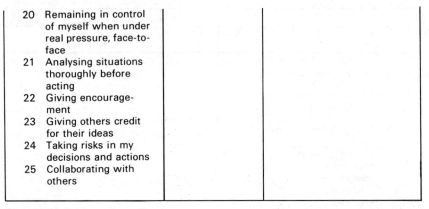

Figure 59.8 (continued)

– beliefs, assumptions and perceptions about roles, jobs and possibly work itself

– relationships with superiors, peers and/or subordinates.

Both changes usually involve breaking new ground where a cycle of stages normally follows, including

exploration

↓

testing and probation

↓

building and consolidation

↓

re-charging and maintenance

These four phases of career progression relate, to some extent, to the stages of development identified by Dalton, Thompson and Price in *Organisation Dynamics* (issue No. 19, 1977):

Apprentice ⟶ Colleague ⟶ Mentor ⟶ and Sponsor

Both concepts suggest a series of transitions which 'peak-out' at some stage which, typically, is then followed by a significant change in role, influence and relationships.

However, *before* the peak is reached, there is usually – especially in managerial and technological career progression – a crucial move, often around the age of 35, which may have far-reaching consequences for the rate of climb to the peak, the level of the peak itself and possibly subsequent stages (see Figure 59.10).

Evidence from both surveys and writings about career progression suggest that many managers did not prepare for the crucial move as they subsequently feel they should have done. Equally, many feel that they were not helped by

'Plus' Features of Job	Personal Strengths
1 Dealing with large groups face-to-face	1.1 Confidence to get up and talk to people in groups 1.2 Ability to 'sway a crowd' 1.3 Keep cool under pressure
2 Taking significant decisions	2.1 Job knowledge 2.2 Innovative thinker
etc.	etc.

Figure 59.9   The plus job

their superiors, as much as they could have been, to understand and cope with the transition surrounding the crucial move in their careers. Role conflict and identity strains are two frequently cited problems facing managers and executives at this stage. Role conflict emerges because of the pressures imposed by the promotion upon the manager's domestic life, wider interests or clash with his previous life style at work. Identity strain often manifests itself in the form of confusion about

- how to relate to key figures in the organisation
- how to preserve 'territorial' rights and boundaries
- what to do about in-company 'politics' and what roles or stances to adopt
- what image to maintain and project and who to use as a model for management style

Neither role conflict nor identity strain is confined to the most crucial career change in the early- or mid-thirties. Such crises may occur at any stage in a manager's career, but particularly may re-emerge in a 'post-plateau' period, when the individual may find himself demoted, overtaken by far younger people, or made redundant. What is more, these two phenomena are likely to be aggravated, or considerably added to, by other stresses if they occur during post-plateau 'middlescence'.

For example, general anxiety and depression – the two 'common colds' of psychology – may well be at their most severe during the middle years, or mid-career crisis and may, additionally, give rise to: over-protective (but counter-productive) behaviour; increased resistance to change; loss of incentive and motivation; low morale; loss of tendency to innovate and take risks; increased suspicion of others' motives; withdrawal, self-imposed constraints and 'self-pity' cliques; or loss of perspective and sense of reality.

Any, or all of these, are likely to lead to a reduction in personal effectiveness, at a time when the individual's impact and contribution are of prime importance.

Figure 59.10   The crucial career move

WHAT CAN THE INDIVIDUAL MANAGER DO ABOUT CAREER PROGRESSION?

A fundamental need in career planning is *information* – whether the individual is:
– at a crucial stage in shaping his career
– about to lose his job
– conscious of being 'boxed-in', or on a plateau
– taking stock and considering the next stage
– close to retirement.

Another crucial need is likely to be for support, in the form of 'sounding boards' to test out perceptions, perspectives and options. The difficulty, here, is that of finding objective and valid views – or even other people's experiences which are closely related to one's own – and, therefore, an appropriate basis for comparison. Obviously vocational guidance specialists exist – both in private practice and in many city offices of the Department of Employment. Additionally several universities have conducted surveys into career planning, though much of the research is associated with mid-career crisis, redundancy and pre-retirement planning, rather than with the crucial 32–35 transitions. There are also books on the subject, which are worth reading, *selectively*, in order to pick up ideas about career planning and the crucial importance of preparing oneself systematically for job and role changes. Some of these texts are listed at the end of this chapter but one worth mentioning at this stage as a practical guide for women in management is *Managerial Woman* by Hennig and Jardim, published by Pocket Books of New York. Men normally have a wide range of executive 'models' provided by other male managers, executives and directors whose styles they can imitate, refine or avoid, as the case may be. By contrast, women still have comparatively few female success stories in the management world to provide suitable models.

Whether there is a proliferation or scarcity of managerial models, the problem remains of what to avoid and in which fields to ensure timely action is taken.

Probably the fastest disappearing years in any executive's life are those that take place between 35 and 40. Too often, managers find themselves living out their working lives and planning – or, rather *reacting* – on a day-to-day basis with little long-term thinking about their work, jobs, skill development, or managerial *style*. Specialists, particularly, are prone to career myopia and their preoccupation with their technological specialism, their pursuit of perfection or refinement of detail tends to inhibit long-term planning *away* from technology and into general management. If these patterns are well established, the chances are that the elusive years between 35 and 40 come and go with no energy having been put into conscious long-term career planning or development. The sudden awareness of one's own mortality – the true onset of 'middlescence' – usually coincides with the realisation that it is now too late to look forward to real advancement; and many managers drift into the mid-years plateau to escape into a niche, rut or sinecure and, eventually, retirement.

The effective counter is systematic long-term career planning at the early stages of managerial life. This involves identifying the many cues that signal a manager's need to

- acquire new knowledge and skills
- develop understanding of the managerial and business world in breadth, as well as technical depth
- experience leadership and managerial roles, where there is both accountability and the exercise of *authority*
- become increasingly aware of his own behaviour and the impact other people have upon his operational effectiveness
- recognise the supreme importance in management of self-confidence, which becomes more and more put to the test as the manager moves away from technology into line roles and general management.

Part of the process of career planning is to be aware of the personal 'horizons', referred to in the last chapter, rather than to try to assess 'ultimate potential'. Horizons, based upon the time spans of two or three years, within a context of a five- or ten-year planning period, provide the manager with realistic time scales within which to work out the experience, learning, training and development necessary to make the planned moves a reality. Finally, it is vital to accept that, come the point of transition, there will inevitably be the moving out of the 'womb' of familar roles, relationships and organisation into new fields where unfamiliar issues and problems must be confronted.

The tendency at such stages is to turn inwards, inhibited by anxiety and the wish to remain with the present, familiar world. It is, in fact, by turning *outwards*, to other people, that an objective view of the transition is to be had. By seeing how other people cope, by asking questions admitting to ignorance, the manager can acquire much of the necessary knowledge about his new role, *on the job*. The important thing is to get to know how the organisation *works*, who can provide what help, support and information and to recognise, as quickly as possible, the strengths and weaknesses of different executives' management styles in critical, but constructive and analytical, terms. In career planning – especially the development of realistic and flexible management styles – the manager's most powerful asset is an enquiring mind and a refusal to accept the the present way of doing things is necessarily the best. Too often, management practices become organisational sanctities, hallowed by little more than the passage of time – and that is no guarantee of effectiveness, especially in today's rapidly changing world.

FURTHER READING

Dalton, G., Thompson, P. H. and Price, R. L., 'The Four Stages of Professional Careers – A New Look at Performance by Professionals' *Organizational Dynamics*, 19 (1977)

Robertson, John P., *You and Your Next Job*, London, British Institute of Management, 1982

Sofer, C., *Men in Mid-Career: A Study of British Managers and Technical Specialists*, The University Press, Cambridge, England, 1970

Weiss, R. S., 'Transition States and Other Stressful Situations, Their Nature and Programs for Their Management', *in* G. Caplan and M. Killilea, eds., *Support Systems and Mutual Help: Multi-disciplinary Exploration*, Grune and Stratton, New York, 1976, pp 213–232

60 Personal organisation

A N Welsh

It has been suggested that the better manager is the better organised manager, who makes the best use of his time and best use of the time of his staff. However, just as there is no such thing as a born manager, so the effectiveness of a good manager cannot really be taught. *Effectiveness has to be learned* and the suggestions in this chapter are only some pointers as to how you can look at your work, develop a personal approach, and make the best use of your time.

THE NEED FOR PERSONAL ORGANISATION

When I had my first managerial job, I naturally found it very exciting and very demanding. I would come in on or before time, and to digress, a good manager should sometimes come in before time and perhaps stay after time. All sorts of things happen outside normal working hours: some people who get their work wrong or do not complete it within the day will stay behind or come back later to finish off, others will use company facilities for private purposes. However, I would come in on or before time and work furiously throughout the day, and by the end I had never completed all that had to be done and my head was full of all that was happening. In particular, I was concerned by matters affecting the well-being of others, and also attacks on my department's activities or my own standards of performance.

When I arrived home my head was buzzing and I would wake up in the middle of the night remembering things I had forgotten to do or thinking of new ideas. I had the choice then of lying awake during the rest of the night remembering whatever it was, or going to sleep again and forgetting the matter. At least I did not decide to hold a meeting about the situation!

CREATING A LIST

I listed all the jobs which I had to do, all the work in my in-tray and the functions which I had to supervise. I kept a diary, and a brought-forward file.

The latter in my case was a concertina file with slots for the days 1–31 and for the remaining months of the year. I would pop into the brought-forward file any correspondence, assessments, buying orders and the like which I wanted to review at a future date; these items were brought into the list as they 'came up'. Having made the first rough list, I then sorted it into order of importance and urgency. At the end of each day I used to go through the list and cross off what I had done and also any items which had ceased to be relevant. I would add to the list new jobs or problems which had arisen and then I would note which jobs I planned to do the following day.

In the morning there was my list telling me what I had to do that day. Obviously unexpected matters arose – in an operational situation one can almost budget for the unexpected – but by and large I worked through the list each day.

Communications

One of the standing items on the list, apart from going through the dairy and brought forward file, was to see *all my subordinates*. I kept at hand a list of all subordinates and made a point of seeing each one even if only to say 'hello', every day. It could be, of course, that you are often away, or that you have too many staff to see. Perhaps in the first case you should consider whether you are away too much to do your job properly; in the second case either you may have too many people directly under you or should delegate some of the communication process to subordinates. Communications is the name of this game: people require *regular contact* and in particular from their boss, and they will often say things, or you will be able to sense a problem which they would be diffident about bringing to your office.

Incidentally, what does your office look like to a subordinate? Can he come and talk to you, or are you involved most of the time in meetings, discussions or telephone calls? Communications can only exist on face-to-face basis, and they are of prime importance at every level. Many managers with considerable responsibilities in large organisations do not know the names or faces of their top management and directors. An even greater proportion never see, or are seen by, their top management in any operational situation from year to year end. *No amount of personnel work can make people think you care about them if they never see you.*

Personal planning

The first list of work is much more difficult to produce than the subsequent amendments, and to help you produce it there is a checklist of questions in Figure 60.1. These are general and analytical questions to be used in any review of your responsibilities, but they would assist in preparing the first list. When, you may ask, would there ever be time to do this, and is it possible with everyone rampaging around and the telephone constantly ringing?

Well, do you intend to spend the rest of your life in a managerial pigsty, and are you seriously going to say you are too busy to do your job? Half an hour's

(GHM)

1 What are the objectives of my department or function?
2 Am I satisfied that I feel these can be achieved – that I have a plan(s) for this?
3 In what ways can my department or area be improved?
4 Is the work in my area altering in nature, quantity or quality?
5 Can the work be done in a better way?
6 Have I the right equipment and facilities?
7 Have I the right number of staff?
8 Am I happy that all my subordinates are correctly placed and loaded?
9 Are my staff doing what I want them to do?
10 Do any of my staff need further training or experience? Have I a training plan?
11 What are staffing trends?
12 Are my staff happy? Do I spend enough time with them?
13 Have I a trained deputy?
14 Am I satisfied personally? Have I defined my personal objectives?
15 Is my authority defined and adequate?
16 Is my relationship with my senior management satisfactory?
17 Where is my next promotion coming from?
18 Am I doing too much routine or administrative clerical work?
19 Have I enough time for thinking?

Figure 60.1   Checklist for reviewing your function

planning can save hours – even days – of misdirected effort; the crisis anticipated proves to be no panic, and you should find in the normal situation that if you pursue this type of personal planning for a few months, you will get right 'ahead of the game' and that you can start looking for additional responsibilities.

Decide now on a specific half hour in the coming week to go through the list. Ask someone else to take the telephone calls and say you do not want to be disturbed (unless it is the Chairman!). Some of the questions will require further investigation, but whenever you reach an unsatifactory answer, answer the question: 'What am I going to do about it?'

THE CONSTRAINT OF TIME

Managing is conducted within a large number of constraints. What is your biggest constraint? Is it capital, working finance, material resources, machinery, property or is it people? People can be a big limiting factor, but you can always train them. Are you limited by the presence of other aspects? Many factors can constrain you, but *the biggest restriction of all is your own time.* You never have enough of it. There are only twenty-four hours in a day, seven days in a week, 52 weeks in the year and so many years in your career. You cannot produce more time; it keeps slipping away. Yesterday can never come back.

We would say, therefore, that we do not have as much time as we need, but would this be equally true for everybody, or would it apply in particular to you? Time can be replaced. Certain tasks can be performed by machinery and certain office work can be done by computers. Some tasks can be delegated to other people, although this is really a transfer of time. However, *the manager cannot delegate his management work* to a machine and seldom can he share it with anyone else. There is no substitute for time as far as he is concerned. Everything he does takes time. All business, all activity, all work uses time and takes place in time.

However, we do not manage our time naturally – as a whole we take it for granted. Now we could talk for a long time about this problem, and we could say that the unhurried, unheroic manager with a clear desk, and a reliable organised office is the efficient or effective manager, but what do you do about it?

Step 1

First of all, accept that, other thing being equal, *the best and happiest manager* is the one who *makes the best use of his time*. If you do not accept this, then this chapter was not written for you, but if you feel that you can make better use of time, and that if you do so you will be a better manager, then please read on.

Step 2

The second step comprises finding out what you are doing now. A simple method of doing this is to list various activities which you perform, and record for a week or a fortnight how long you are spending on them. This can be done by using a simple daily diary sheet; the diary sheets are analysed into what is called a work distribution chart at the end of the period. The work distribution chart will show quite clearly what you are doing and what proportion of your time you are spending on your various activities.

A specimen managers' activity list, with the activites given for example only, is as follows:

1 Visiting customers
2 Visiting suppliers
3 Queries from staff over technical matters
4 Customer complaints
5 Planning and control work
6 Training
7 Supervision
8 Reading mail
9 Chasing overdue accounts
10 Checking stocks and reordering
11 Management meetings
12 Recruiting
13 Staff problems
14 Personal.

Simple form for the diary sheet and work distribution chart are shown in Figures 60.2 and 60.3.

The work of a manager is variable, particularly as regards the subject involved. Completing a work distribution chart will not give a 100 per cent accurate picture of what the manager does or should do, but it will give a representative view of the proportions of his time spent on various activities, e.g., queries; accounts queries may relate to different transactions, but they will still be accounts queries. Once the work distribution chart has been completed, one can then move on to the next step.

Step 3

The third step is the analysis of the work distribution chart. A number of questions need to be asked at this stage.

WASTED TIME

1 What would happen if I did not do this kind of activity?

Time	Activity	Inter-ruptions	Phone calls	1. Ines-sential	2. Some-body else could do	3. Wasting others' time	Notes
8.30 8.45 9.00 9.15 9.30 9.45 10.00 '' '' '' '' 5.30 5.45 6.00 Evening	Enter number against time whenever activity changes	Enter a '1' for each, e.g., 1, 11	As for interruptions. Note incidence and quantity. Analyse if too many.	Record impressions, if any, at the time	Record impressions, if any, at the time.	Record impressions, if any, at the time.	Note anything unusual or 'special'.

Date: [GHM]

Figure 60.2 Specimen manager's diary sheet

Activity no.	Activity title	Daily times										Total time	% of total	Comments and action
		1	2	3	4	5	1	2	3	4	5			(You can also do this kind of analysis with your staff.)
														These are taken to the nearest quarter hour.
											(No)	(No) (No)		If phone calls and interruptions occur which are separate from the activity being recorded – multiply by 3 minutes: if the totals exceed 15% of the day, then analyse them. Possibly something is wrong.

Figure 60.3 Manager's work distribution chart

2 Am I spending too long on it?
3 Am I doing it ineffectively – for example, am I getting it properly set up and spending enough time on it? Short periods of supervision are of limited value with persons engaged on complex work
4 Am I failing to do any task which would contribute to the business because of the lack of time?

Supervision

A manager should be able to spend time with his staff – encouraging, training, supervising and just getting to know them and keeping in touch. The time required for this varies with the staff and the complexity of the work, but a rough quick figure is an average of forty minutes per person per day. This includes normal management duties, reports and 'personnel' work. It does not include 'checking' as distinct from normal supervision and training.

Checking

Checking should be considered carefully. Twenty or thirty years ago commercial convention looked for a high degree of literal accuracy and salary costs were lower in proportion to other expenses than they are now. There is a satisfaction in getting everything 'right', but we should first consider what the customer really needs. Checking is expensive and frustrating: it is no longer a motivating factor (if it ever was) for staff to have all their work checked.

Your work distribution chart will show how much of your time is spent checking, but you should consider whether the cost of checking is justified by the errors discovered and how much these matter. If the errors do matter you may have to continue to check, but you can consider whether random checks, occasional and unexpected, will serve as well where generally quality standards and methods are the main concern.

List of jobs

In the end you will finish with a list of jobs which you want to do and which you have to do, and a subsidiary list of jobs which you feel you should not be doing but perhaps you still have to do for one reason or another. (We are, of course, well aware that you cannot get rid of all inessential tasks, but you can reduce them.) You will *rank the list of jobs in order of important* to the business, and estimate what general proportion of your time and energy should be spent on each.

You will have considered where time is being wasted on unnecessary work, and where time could be saved by better personal organisation and work methods. You should move to the next heading in your analysis of the work distribution chart.

DELEGATION

Ask yourself which of your activities could be done by somebody else to an adequate standard, or as well as you, or even better. The manager is paid to do his work, but if there are others at lower salaries who can do part of it and have the time, then is it better for the manager to be fully occupied or for the junior staff?

Another factor which comes out of this analysis is that the more senior people become, the larger becomes the proportion of their time spent on moving about and travelling, and you should think about this.

There will be certain customers who are very important, and who are accustomed to dealing with you personally; it may well be that you can introduce them to someone else who can deal with the routine parts of the account but, of course, you will remember to watch what is happening to the account from time to time subsequent to this arrangement. This would apply also to 'important jobs' and to important senior managers!

The present managing directors of several major companies in the United Kingdom were in very humble positions only a few years ago; in fact, consider where you yourself were five years ago, and now you are performing much more important work. Quite possibly within your area you have the managers or senior managers of the future, and you should keep a look out for them and give them a 'chance' as soon as you can. Not only will this be good for them, but it will also free you. Think about how to develop the business and to perform your other managerial tasks.

One thing which is very irksome to staff is to see people senior to them performing activities at greater salaries which they could perfectly well do themselves. In one major British company staff are asked the question 'What does your supervisor do that you could do yourself?' Could you ask this question of your staff, and would they know how to answer it? It is worth considering that they may have views on this subject themselves.

SUBORDINATES' TIME

A manager becomes a manager by promotion or appointment. He learns to be a manager by observing other managers, who themselves have been taught by observation, and by being shown, and from what is called the 'hard way'. There are certain training courses, but they are normally very short, and as a result most managers devise their style and system of management from their own experience. Often this is very good, but once personal inclinations creep in, funny things start to happen.

You should ask yourself the following question: 'Is there anything I do which wastes subordinates' time without contributing to their effectiveness?' You can begin to answer this question from your analysis of the work distribution chart, and you may even be able to ask it of the subordinates themselves.

Waiting around

For instance, how much time do your staff spend waiting for answers from you, items to be checked or approved, action to be taken, or for you to be available? Consider whether in your area you ever have two or more people involved in work which should be done by one person only. Normally it is more satisfying and efficient for a job which can be done by one person to be done by one person and not split between two or three. Staff learn from observing you (or colleagues), but sometimes you may be playing to an audience unnecessarily (and distracting the others).

Remember when you were a member of staff or a worker. Did your manager or foreman ever waste any of your time while you waited for him when he was late, when he had to check your work, while he had to get around to this or that but was (or allowed himself to be) interrupted by a variety of other matters? Did this frustrate you as well as waste your time? Staff are paid less than managers, but with overheads the difference is not as great as it once was. Are you working too hard; are you paying the proverbial dog then doing the barking yourself?

Crises

One thing which wastes time, particularly of subordinates, is a crisis. In many organisations crises occur regularly, and there are so many things which are unforeseen that one could almost describe crises as a routine situation. However, a recurrent crisis is a symptom of slovenliness. Certain crises such as making up the returns, the budget figures, sales figures, payroll, the peak season, are all known in advance. If the manager uses sensible planning and scheduling techniques he may well be able to provide for these, in which case they will become routine occurrences and not crises.

Panic action is expensive. People rushing off to make special deliveries, special visits to the post office, special trips out to acquire stationery, other things that are needed, people dropping things in the middle of picking up others and so on, all lead to ineffective use of time and also mistakes.

IMPROVEMENTS

The question here is, how can you use your time more effectively? The first thing to consider is your attention span. Are you a person who works best by sitting down quietly and for extended periods looking at a particular problem, or do you keep things running around in your mind? What are your best methods of working, and with whom and when?

Discretionary time

You need to have a certain amount of 'discretionary time', i.e., time at your free disposal, time available for important matters, perhaps the things you are paid for, and this must be kept in usable chunks. Not many managers feel they have much discretionary time, even after cutting out any wasted time, but they can generally set aside an hour or so each week. The question arises as to how much discretionary time is desirable. This is rather like maintenance on a car; you do not buy a car in order to service it, but if you do not carry out a certain amount of maintenance on the car it will not perform satisfactorily.

Your function

The same applies to your function. You need from time to time to review the total operation of your area and to go through the check list given previously; you need to make sure you see the staff regularly and review their situation. On a daily basis you may want to keep a list of the tasks which you have to do, and the problems with deadlines and priorities, and perhaps revise these either last thing at night or first thing in the morning. Also you may well want to use a brought-forward file or diary system so that you are automatically reminded of things that need to be done in the future. How long this should take is like the service on the car, except that it is you rather than the garage that must make the diagnosis and the decisions.

Suggestions

Simple suggestions for using your time more effectively are to concentrate on one thing at a time; deal with first things first, and one at a time. Allow enough time for what you are doing – nothing ever goes completely right and one thing you can always expect is the unexpected. Do not hurry, do not try and do several things at once. Do not assume that everything that was important yesterday is important today. Ask yourself the question 'If we had not already started on this activity would we start it now?' It is just as difficult and just as risky to do something small as something which is big, so allocate your time to the most important parts of the business.

When you have analysed your work distribution chart comparing the proportions of time spent on the various activities with their importance in terms of obtaining income, business and profit or other advantage for the company, you will most certainly find that you are spending a lot of your time on small irritating matters. Consider whether some of these can be allowed to slide without damage to the business, and whether things would be improved by concentrating on the main managerial requirements of the organisation.

FURTHER READING

Drucker, Peter F., *The Effective Executive*, Heinemann, London, 1967
Welsh, A. N., *The Skills of Management*, Gower, 1980

61 Negotiating

Bill Scott

This chapter is in three parts. The first describes a style of negotiating designed to produce the greatest area of agreement in the joint interest of both parties. This is a pattern of negotiating in which the parties work together, creatively, *Towards Agreement*. The second pattern is one in which each party is concerned more with its own advantage than with the joint advantage. Goodwill and agreement are still important, but the overriding consideration is that which is *To Independent Advantage*. Third, when goodwill is not important, negotiations can sometimes deteriorate into a pattern of *Fighting*.

NEGOTIATING TOWARDS AGREEMENT

When the parties are concerned to work together creatively Towards Agreement the key activities are exploration of one another's position, and creative recognition of what is in their joint interests.

Those phases of exploration and creativity, however, hinge on having first created a suitable climate and on having some procedure which helps the parties to work together. There is no cause for heavy use of negotiating tactics but there is a need for effective preparation.

The sequence in this section will therefore be:

Creating the climate
Opening procedure
Sequence in negotiations
Exploration
Creativity
Subsequent phases
Preparation

Creating the climate

Negotiators usually operate best when the climate is brisk and businesslike. When negotiating Towards Agreement, they need a climate which is also cordial and co-operative.

The pace of a negotiation, be it brisk or lethargic, is set very early. Within seconds of the parties coming together, during the rituals of meeting and greeting, a pace is established which is durable. It should be a brisk pace – briskness established by the pace at which the parties are moving about and by the speed at which they are communicating.

The cordial character is established in an ice-breaking phase. As the parties first meet and interact with one another, they need to adjust and to build their regard before getting into possibly controversial areas. The ice-breaking, therefore, needs to be a period in which they focus on neutral topics – the football, the weather, the journey and so on.

The ice-breaking is an essential preliminary, so important that it deserves possibly 5 per cent of the prospective negotiating time: a couple of minutes even at the outset of short negotiations; a preliminary dinner and evening out before protracted negotiations.

The brisk and cordial character is thus very soon established. The development of the businesslike and co-operative characteristics comes as the parties sit down and move towards business. Timing and the form of first remarks at the negotiating table should provide the 'business-like': timing, by an immediate statement so that there is no long gap as members get seated; and the form of the opening remarks focusing on business, Towards Agreement.

The co-operative character can be set too at this early stage. This depends on effectiveness in handling the opening procedure.

Opening procedure

There is nothing more likely to produce a co-operative atmosphere than the immediate question, on sitting down: 'Well gentlemen, can we first agree on procedure?'

Note that the word 'agree' is used at the outset. Note that the question is one which will almost certainly produce the answer 'Yes'. Note that the two parties both establish the 'agree' mood from the outset.

There are four procedural items which should be explored and agreed in this opening stage: the four Ps.

1   Pace
2   Purpose
3   Plan
4   Personalities.

The *pace* is the speed at which the parties need to move together. There needs to be harmony on this pace if parties are to work together effectively. There will not be such harmony if one believes that there is a whole afternoon available whereas the other has another engagement in half an hour.

The *purpose* is the reason why the parties are meeting. If one party thinks that the meeting is purely exploratory, while the other believes the purpose is to achieve a final settlement, then the parties are going to be working at cross-purposes.

Even when the purpose has been established in preliminary communication, it is still important at the outset to refresh the consciousness of that purpose. And to take the chance to emphasise that both parties *agree* on that purpose.

The *plan* should be in the form of a short agenda – some four main stages through which the meeting should move.

These first three Ps – Pace, Purpose and Plan – should be agreed at the outset of every negotiation.

The fourth P in the opening procedural stage is Personalities: the introduction of members who do not know one another, their backgrounds, what they can contribute to the meeting. Skilfully used, this opening procedure has great advantages:

1 The meeting can proceed with both parties recognising joint objectives and a joint means of moving forward.
2 The plan gives a framework for control of the remainder of the meeting.
3 The mood of agreement can be quickly stated and established.
4 The groundwork is set for a smooth and co-operative entry into the later stages of the negotiation.

There is a consistent sequence in these later stages of any negotiation. The sequence is:

1 Exploration
2 Creativity
3 Shaping the deal
4 Bidding
5 Bargaining
6 Settling
7 Ratifying.

These phases are – or should be – found in any negotiation, even though they may sometimes become mixed and muddled. The importance of each phase varies a lot, however.

In negotiating Towards Agreement, the key phases are those of exploration and creativity.

Exploration

When two parties come together, each has its own distinctive view of the aims and possibilities for the negotiation. If the parties want to work together to bake the biggest possible cake, it is imperative that each should

(a) recognise what both see in the same way,
(b) recognise and respect what others see in a different way, and
(c) be clear about the way in which their own interests are distinctive.

From such recognition can spring the creative spark of what is then most in their joint interests.

To achieve that recognition each party should independently make a broad statement of its own position, and give opportunity for the others to seek clarification. Then get a comparable 'broad picture' of the other party's position, and clarify that.

Each opening statement needs to cover:

Our understanding. The broad area within which we believe the negotiation will take place.

Our interests. What we would like to achieve through the negotiation.

Our priorities. What are the most important aspects for us.

Our contribution. The way in which we can help to our joint advantage.

Our attitudes. The consequence of our previous dealing with the other party; their reputation as it has come to us; any special hopes or fears which we may have for collaboration.

Characteristic of the opening statement are the following points:

1 The opening statements of each party should be independent. Each should state its own position, and not attempt at this stage to state the joint interests of the two parties
2 They should not attempt to put assumptions about the position or interests of the other party. (The giving of this assumption serves only to irritate, to confuse and to introduce disharmony.)
3 The statements should be general, not detailed, not yet quantitative
4 The statements should be brief. Each should give the other party an opportunity to come into the discussion quickly, both so that the parties can quickly interact and so that others do not get a sense of being overwhelmed by either the duration or the complexity of an opening statement. Keep it short.

As one party makes its opening statement, the other party needs to listen, clarify and summarise.

Listen

Do not waste energy by thinking up counter-arguments.

Clarify

If in any doubt, question to get clear what he is trying to say. But note: question for clarification. Do not question for justification – that forces the other negotiator on to the defensive and runs counter to the creative climate being sought.

Summarise

Feed back the key points of what you understand him to be saying, so that he can check.

Having got clear the view of one party then comes the time for the other party to offer its own opening statement, and for first party's corresponding response

– listen, clarify, summarise.

For really creative negotiations, there is a need for these opening exchanges to be carried through frankly in an environment of mutual trust and respect. For these reasons great attention has been paid to creating a positive climate and to underlining agreement and preparing minds in the opening process.

Skilled negotiators are skilled at giving and getting information.

Skilled negotiators are also conscious that some other parties will seek to exploit them. They therefore look out for danger signals which would suggest a need to change strategy.

If in the ice-breaking, the other party insists on probing about business matters ('How's trade? cash-flow? quality?') beware. Probably he is simply an unskilled negotiator, but possibly he is aggressive, seeking information that he can later use aggressively. If he is highly assertive in the phase of proposing and agreeing procedure – then again we must beware. An amber light is flashing.

If he is excessively anxious that we should be the first to make an opening statement, or in challenging that opening statement: then a further amber light is shown – indeed, this is virtually a red light.

Given a succession of amber lights, or just one red light, then the skilled negotiator will be prepared to change his strategy. He should seek a recess, even though it is still an early stage of the negotiation, reconsider the other party's behaviour and decide whether he needs to change to either of the strategies in later sections of this chapter.

But skilled negotiators practising this characteristic style of negotiating towards agreement can normally produce a positive response.

There is thus a great need for negotiators to develop the skills of creating a co-operative climate, of agreeing procedure, and of openness in the exploratory phase.

Creativity

Agreement-oriented negotiators now have a unique opportunity to achieve something to joint advantage, something bigger than either party could get when negotiating to independent advantage. This is the moment to be seeking together to bake the biggest possible cake.

To achieve that creativity they need first to be imaginative. Later they must impose the forces of reality, but the most productive of ideas may not be seen unless the parties are prepared to range as far as the borderline between reality and fantasy. Be imaginative.

Scandinavian negotiators have a special phrase to launch into this phase. Having summarised the respective positions of the parties as discussed in their opening statements, they say 'All right then – what are the creative possibilities?'

In looking for those creative possibilities there are a few guidelines:

1 The pattern of generating the ideas must be broad in its sweep, and inter-dependent.
2 It must be broad because immediately the parties focus on one suggestion

(either criticising or exploring in depth), their minds cannot revert to broad and imaginative thinking.

3 It must be interdependent, not only to sustain the co-operation between them, but also because each fresh suggestion can kindle a new spark in the imagination of the other. The parties have great potential to be creative together.

This process of recognising creative possibilities should generate a number of different ideas. There then comes the need to form a bridge between the world in which the parties have been thinking imaginatively, and the world of reality in which their performance must be measured by business criteria. They must decide which of their imaginative ideas offer realistic possibilities. They must then assess and agree on the action needed to turn possibility to mutual advantage.

Subsequent stages

The critical periods of negotiations towards agreement are the exploratory and creative phases. From them springs the recognition of mutual interest. There is, of course, need for the later realities to be foreseen, for agreement on the commercial conditions, and for the establishment of realistic plans to implement decisions. Given however the creative atmosphere, then views and possibilities for these commercial and planning discussions can be developed in a similarly open atmosphere.

The approach – 'Let us now explore together' – can be sustained through these later stages without the need to get into the tough bidding and bargaining encountered (and to be further discussed) in the context of other strategies.

However, before starting any negotiation, each party must arrive at the negotiating table well prepared.

Preparation

For any form of negotiation, the negotiator must have done his homework beforehand. He must know the facts, the figures, the arguments.

He needs also to have prepared in two other respects. First, preparing for the procedure. He should think through the Pace, Purpose and Plan which he will suggest for the meeting. And having thought them through, it is advisable to jot down the headlines of pace, purpose and plan on a postcard, to serve as a reminder during the meeting.

Second, he needs to have prepared his opening statement: his understanding of the matter for discussion, his interests, priorities, contribution, attitudes; and again, to jot the headlines on a postcard.

It is important, when negotiating Towards Agreement, not to over prepare. The negotiator who has built a detailed framework of prices, deliveries and so on in his preparations is so mentally committed to those preparations that he obscures the possibilities for being creative in any wider sense.

To summarise, when their strategy is negotiating Towards Agreement, the parties must first create a climate which is brisk, businesslike, cordial and co-operative. They must then establish and agree on a procedure helping them to work together effectively. From the opening procedural discussion they move into important exploratory and creative phases, and thereafter should be able to sustain the high co-operation already established. This must be founded on effective preparation by each party before the event.

NEGOTIATING TO INDEPENDENT ADVANTAGE

Different skills are needed when the negotiator is concerned with gaining special advantage for his party. In some ways these skills mirror those needed when negotiating Towards Agreement; in other ways, new and different skills are needed.

In particular bidding and bargaining become the crux of the negotiation. Early moves set the framework; and a different form of preparation is needed. The sequence of this section will therefore be:

1 Opening moves.
2 Bidding
3 Bargaining
4 Preparation

Opening moves

The negotiator working 'to independent advantage' must approach the negotiation with a difference of attitude. No longer is his concern to work creatively together with the other party. Rather it is to establish the best deal in the interests of his own side.

Assuming however that the deal will need the other party's co-operation to be implemented, or that there will in due course be a need to negotiate some other deal with the same party, it is important that goodwill should be sustained. Aggressive tactics and power struggles should be avoided.

The negotiator's attitude should not be that he will work towards the other party's disadvantage. His attitude must be to find the best way to divide the cake to give satisfaction to both parties. If he likes icing more than fruit, and the other party likes fruit more than icing – there is no problem. Both sides can 'win'. The skilled negotiator thus works towards influencing the other party to value the fruit more than the icing.

The opening moves will again establish the climate for the meeting. Because of the concern for sustaining goodwill it is again important that the climate should be brisk, businesslike, cordial and co-operative; and it is again important that procedure should be agreed at the outset.

Exploration now takes a different form. It becomes necessary quickly to identify the shape of the deal, rather than to look creatively for some new shape. In this process, both parties become more concerned with 'what our party wants'.

The response to the other party needs to be one of probing, to find out which issues or which ingredients are important to the others. Are they, for example, more concerned about price than delivery, quality, terms of settlement?

It is important in these exploratory stages to keep the dialogue on a broad front. If the move to discussion of a particular item (such as price) is taken too soon or too deeply, it is likely to lead to a premature conflict and also to erode some of the most effective possibilities for later bargaining.

Bidding

Negotiating to independent advantage, the guideline to bidding is to start with that which is the highest defensible. (For buyers, the corresponding phrase is of course 'lowest defensible offer'.)

The opening bid needs to be 'the highest' because:

1 The opening bid sets a limit beyond which the party cannot aspire. Having once made it, no higher bid can reasonably be put at a later stage
2 The first bid influences others in their valuation of our offer
3 A high bid gives scope for manoeuvre during the later bargaining phases. It gives something in reserve with which to trade
4 The opening bid has a real influence on the final settlement level. The higher the level of aspiration, the greater the prospective achievement.

The opening bid needs to be high. At the same time it must be defensible. Putting foward a bid which cannot be defended does positive damage to the negotiating process. It is found to be offensive by the other party; and if it cannot be defended when challenged in subsequent bargaining, there is soon a loss of face, a loss of credibility, a forced retreat.

The content of the bid of course usually needs to cover a range of issues. The components of the opening bid in a commercial negotiation will not simply be price, but a combination of price, delivery, payment terms, quality specification and a dozen other items.

The 'highest defensible bid' is not an absolute figure, it is a figure which is relevant to the particular circumstances. It is specifically a figure which relates to the way in which others are operating. If they are pressing to their independent advantage, then we must open with a high bid; but if faced with a lot of competition, the bid must be tailored to the level at which it will at least enable us to be invited to continue the negotiations. If we have established cordial relationships with others, possibly over a long period of time, then we shall know the style in which they will operate and the degree of co-operation we can expect – we know the level at which it is prudent for us to make our bid.

On each individual item the opening bid needs to be the highest defensible. We are certain, when negotiating to independent advantage, to be pushed by others to compromise on one or two issues. We cannot be sure which until the bargaining process is under way; we must aspire high on all issues and keep room to manoeuvre.

The manner in which the bid is stated is important. It should be put firmly – without reservations, without hesitations – so that it may carry the conviction of a conscientious negotiating party.

It should be put clearly so that the other party recognises precisely what is being asked. The creation of a visual aid, i.e., taking a sheet of paper and writing figures on it, within the sight of the other party, whilst one is stating the bid – this is powerful reinforcement.

It should be put without apology or comment. There is no need to apologise for anything that can be defended. There is no need to comment since the other party can be expected to raise questions on matters which concern it. And voluntary comment (before others ask for it) simply makes them aware of concern about issues which they might never have considered.

Those then are three guidelines to the way in which a bid should be presented: firmly, clearly, without comment.

In responding to bids by the other party there is a need to distinguish between clarification and justification.

The competent negotiator first ensures that he knows what the other party is bidding. Precisely. He asks any questions which are needed to ensure that he gets the picture clear. He makes sure, in the process, that the other party recognises that these are questions for clarification and not demands to justify. And once satisfied, he summarises his understanding of the other party's bid, as a check on the effectiveness of communication between them.

First party should at this stage deflect questions which demand that he justifies his position. He has put a bid, and he has a perfect right to know what other is prepared to offer in return.

Bargaining

The first two steps in the bargaining process should be:

1 Get it clear
2 Assess the situation.

It is vital to establish a clear picture of other party's requirements at the outset. We should have got a clear picture of *what* he is bidding already. Now we need to know *why*.

The need is increasingly to build an understanding of what will give him satisfaction and of how to trade to advantage whilst giving him that satisfaction.

We must discover what for him are essentials and what else is desirable but not essential, and what aspects of his bid are really of fringe interest only – where he could readily give.

To achieve this clarity, the guidelines are:

1 Check every item of his bid. Enquire why. Ask how important the item is and how much flexibility he could introduce
2 Never speculate on his opinions or on his motives. A speculation only irritates. Moreover it is often misconceived – it is out of our frame of reference, not his, and confuses the negotiations between the pair of us. Never put words into his mouth
3 Note his answers without comment. Reserve our position. Avoid deep diving or premature diving into any issue. Keep it on a broad front.

Assuming significant differences between the parties there are now three options for the negotiator;

1 He can accept
2 He can reject
3 He can carry on negotiating.

If he decides to carry on negotiating then he must be prepared for the next round. His options at this stage are:

1 To make a new offer
2 To seek a new offer from the other party
3 To change the shape of the deal (vary the quantity or the quality or the use of third parties), or
4 Embark on give-and-take bargaining.

The steps for preparing for that give-and-take are:

1 Issue identification – list the issues in the package
2 Prepare the bargaining position:
   (a) an essential conditions list – those issues on which it is impossible to concede anything.
   (b) a concessions list – those issues on which concession is conceivable. For each such issue, a progression stepped from that minimum which could be offered (against counter-concessions from the other party) in the next round of bargaining, to that ultimate limit which might be forced in successive rounds.

During the bargaining stages, each successive negotiation meeting should be opened with a new round of climate formation and with agreement on procedure. Each round should be concluded with the establishment of some means of resolving outstanding difficulties.

In between, the negotiations should be conducted laterally rather than vertically. That is to say, the aim should be to reach agreement in principle on a broad front, then to tackle more detailed negotiations, still on a broad front. A sequence of several successive moves across the broad front; not a succession of narrow penetrations.

When the time comes for compromise, neither party will readily 'lose face'. Neither party will readily concede on one issue without having some corresponding concession on another. It is thus important to solve difficulties on a broad front or, at the least, two at a time; not simply one at a time.

For example, when the parties have been exploring a difference between them in price and when they are reaching the stage of preparednes to make concessions, it is helpful to both parties if one of them interjects a comment such as 'Well, just before we finish that discussion on price, could we at the same time tie in this question about (e.g., the shipping risk) and who is to be responsible for that?'

And so sustaining goodwill and sustaining efforts to keep a co-operative climate even through tough bargaining – the negotiation should move towards settlement To Independent Advantage.

Preparation

As ever, preparation is of critical importance, and the general pattern of preparation should repeat that previously described.

With one important difference. This is the need to be more specific during preparation processes. Whereas in creative negotiations it is important to keep one's preparations general and to preserve flexibility, in more divisive negotiations the negotiator needs to be protected from exploitation. He needs to have considered his bids at an early stage. There is this constant dichotomy between the need for flexibility and the need for precise preparations. The one is the enemy of the other. The choice should reflect the strategic situation which will be referred to at the end of this chapter.

To summarise: bidding and bargaining are the key phases in negotiating to independent advantage. It is a type of negotiation needing distinctive attitudes and skills. Bidding and bargaining become more important than exploration. Climate formation and procedural development remain important. So does preparation though it takes a slightly different form.

FIGHTING

Warfare is not a commendable form of negotiation. Nevertheless, negotiators do become involved in confrontations in which the aim has to be to 'win' – or, at any rate, to ensure that they do not 'lose' at the hands of an aggressive party.

This section will review:

the use of fighting methods
the pattern of a fighting negotiation
fighting tactics
counter-measures

The use of fighting methods

The fighter's aim is to win and to make the other party the loser.

This is a dangerous attitude to negotiations. It puts goodwill at risk; it obscures the possibility of creative co-operation; it naturally provokes the other party to fight back, causing delay and putting at risk the fighter's chances of success. Even when the fighter batters an 'opponent' into submission, he is not likely to find the deal implemented energetically.

The means which the fighter uses are powerful. Both by his personal behaviour and by the negotiating tactics which he uses, he seeks to reinforce the power of his position. His methods include:

a constant search for gain at every opportunity
at each successive stage in the process of negotiating, he wants fresh advantage
any withdrawals must be deliberate, tactical withdrawals, designed only to promote greater advance
power-methods; high in terms of the pace, size and forcefulness of

demands, low in readiness to listen or to yield

task-centred. Concern for his special advantage. Not concerned with other party's pride or dignity nor with their feelings. Forcing them to 'accept or else'.

The pattern of a fighting negotiation

The central concern of the fighting negotiator is to win. This winning takes place in the fighting phase of the negotiation – a special version of the bargaining phase. A special version at which he is expert and best able to use his personal characteristics. Quickly he leads the negotiation to the point at which his form of bargaining becomes the dominant activity.

This leaves little time or interest for the early stages of negotiating; little time to get on the same wavelength as other party, or to agree on a plan; little time to explore mutual interests. Even issue identification is hastened and the negotiation quickly becomes focused on his first chosen issue.

The pattern of the negotiation is then 'vertical', deep diving on the first selected issue. He aspires high and pushes until he 'wins' on that and each successive issue.

Fighting tactics

He knows a lot of tactics and manoeuvres, and regularly uses a number. He has his own repertoire, and admires (and tries to emulate) tactics which have been used 'against' him by other negotiators. Here are some of them:

1 *Probing from the start*

The fighter enters the negotiating room, shakes hands and wishes us 'Good morning' and immediately starts probing. Probing about our business situation, probing about the product or service in which he is interested, probing even about one's personal situation.

The advantages he seeks are in getting information, in building a picture about other party and especially in recognising weaknesses and vulner-abilities. Additionally, he establishes a power position – a pattern of aggressive leadership.

2 *Get/give*

He is concerned to get something before he will give anything. To get a small concession before he will give a small concession. To get a big concession before he will give a big concession. To get information before he will give information. To get the other party's bid before he will give his own bid. To get the power of being the first to make an opening statement.

Get/give tactics used by skilled negotiators can have positive commercial advantages in the short term. They may well gain ground during the early stages of a negotiation; but in the long run, they lead to delay and deadlock (neither party being willing always to give before it gets).

3 *Showing emotion* (anger, for example)

Loud and emotional statements, possibly banging the table: the form of eye-contact, posture, gesture and voice, all displaying emotions.

4 *Good guy/bad guy*

This is a tactic for use by a team of two negotiators. One takes the role of the 'bad guy'; being aggressive, making excessive demands, dominating, un-co-operative. He holds the stage for a long time whilst his colleague remains quiet. When he has softened up the 'opposition' with his tactics, the 'good guy' takes over the lead role, constructively offering solutions, quietly trying to reach a mutual understanding.

The tactic parallels the archetypal method by which prisoners of war are cross-examined; the prisoner first ruthlessly interrogated by a tough investigator, then offered the sympathy of a different personality to whom – with luck – he would open up.

5 *Poker-faced*

Giving away nothing by expression, tone, posture or gesture. An important part of the fighting negotiator's armoury.

6 *Managing the minutes*

Taking responsibility at the end of each session for production of the record. Slanting interpretations of what has been agreed, always to his advantage. Readiness to include the odd item 'which ought to have been agreed' even if there was insufficient time to include it in the discussion – provided, of course, that the odd item is favourable.

7 *Getting upstairs*

When unable to come to an agreement with the other negotiator, taking steps to contact his boss, or boss's boss's boss.

8 *PR*

Many fights are conducted by negotiators acting on behalf of other groupings. For example, the union negotiator representing the workforce; the government negotiator representing his country. It is here important for the group which is represented to be kept informed and influenced so that they continue to give their backing to the negotiator. His ability at public relations is thus an important part of the fighter's armoury.

9 *Forcing moves*

There are, of course, yet other moves which some negotiators use. Bribery, sex, blackmail, bugging. Most negotiators would see such devices as rankly unethical; but people negotiating very important deals are at risk and need to be on their guard.

Counter-measures

Counters to those who fight are in two forms: long-term and short-term measures.

In the long term, where there is expectation of repeated rounds of negotiations, for example, in labour negotiations, there is a need for the development of attitudes, skills and relationships.

This development takes place best when the parties can come together at a place remote from their normal battlefield, and at a time during the off-season for fighting. Especially fruitful is the practice, which has been well developed in

Scandinavia, of holding joint working seminars for two or three days. The product of such seminars is not only the development of relationships but the planning of subsequent joint activities.

That is a long-term approach. In the short term, measures to counter the fighter fall into three categories:

1   Head him off
2   Control the battlefield
3   Cope with his tactics.

The most satisfying way of coping with him is of course to head off the fight before it develops. If this is to be achieved it must be done in the critical opening seconds and minutes:

> deflect his opening questions
> preserve a neutral ice-breaking period
> do not be drawn by his probing questions
> do not let him assert leadership
> do not let him dominate the early moments – what is being talked about, when to stand and when to sit, the seating arrangements

We are able to control the skirmishing if we can somehow control the battlefield. In negotiating terms, this 'control of the battlefield' is control of the procedures of negotiating. Guidelines are:

1   Seek for form and plan for the proceedings
2   Seek for opening discussion of purpose, plan and pace
3   Keep bringing him back to the agreed plan
4   Keep things fluid. Use the 'broad front' approach
5   Seek for compromise. He will be impervious either to searches for creative resolution of differences, or to sensitive attempts to influence him. His metier is that of compromise. If his position is that he is asking £120 and ours is that it is only worth £100, then settlement is likely to be at the compromise point of £110. Bargain slowly until you get him down to at most £110.

Above all, keep control of the process – keep control of what is being negotiated and in which sequence – keep to the plan. It will irritate him. He much prefers to be able to run free, but do not worry. A caged fighter cannot do as much damage as one on the loose. To cope with some of the fighter's tactics: When he is using the 'get/give' tactic, we must not give too easily, for it we give before we get, he will regard this as a sign of weakness. He will want to get yet more and will change the tactic into 'get/get/give' and soon will be aspiring even higher to 'get/get/get'.

We must not give in. We must trade scrap of information for scrap of information, scrap of readiness for scrap of readiness, scrap of concession for scrap of concession.

The only counter to displays of anger is to suspend negotiations, either temporarily or permanently. The human brain is such that emotions (such as anger) are handled in one part of it, rational thinking in another part. Once the brain becomes focused on emotive thinking, then the rational part is cut off. The angry party cannot receive rational messages and it is no use other party trying to instil them. So the counter is to suspend operations.

It does not matter if first party's anger is simply a display rather than real anger. Second party has no way of being sure about the matter. First party has behaved in ways which are not acceptable and second party should immediately suspend.

The 'good guy/bad guy' tactic is difficult to recognise and difficult to counter. But, of course, if it has been recognised in one round of negotiating then the negotiator will be alert for it during later rounds and must hope either to be able to ignore the bad guy or to separate the two 'opponents'.

The counter to 'getting upstairs' is to state strong objection to the tactic and then to arrange for our own boss to come in and make it clear that theirs was a losing tactic.

Formality is, inevitably, a device used to try to bring order to such negotiations. However, the fighting negotiator becomes expert in framing and fighting for a rule-book which is to his advantage. He is expert not only in drafting and amending rules but in interpreting and manipulating them. The effective negotiator from the other side therefore is forced to build his own corresponding expertise.

Preparation is, as ever, of critical importance for effectiveness in negotiating. When faced with a fight it is imperative to be well prepared procedurally and imperative also to have precise objectives, targets and prepared concession lists. There is special need to prepare options ('scenarios' in the current jargon), alternative approaches which could enable both parties to move forward whilst minimising loss of face.

The counter to his competence at public relations is to develop equal competence and to ensure that the relevant public is suitably influenced.

In meeting with a fighting 'opponent' then, the negotiator is operating in a world of power. He needs skill to control the battlefield and to prevent his being exploited.

But that is a short term approach. The longer term interest demands that he should work for some joint development of attitudes, skills and relationships with the other party.

SUMMARY

This chapter has been concerned with three distinct forms of negotiation. First, with negotiations in which two parties seek to move forward co-operatively to create the best possible deal in their joint interests. Second, with patterns of negotiation in which both parties aim to preserve goodwill whilst at the same time trying to maximise their independent advantage. Third and finally, with fights in which continuing goodwill is not treated as being important.

The choice amongst these approaches to negotiating will depend on a number of strategic issues:

1   The extent to which the parties will need to come together again from time
    to time
2   The respective strength of the parties in the market place
3   The character and quality of their negotiators
4   The time-scale and the importance of the prospective deal.

These strategic issues are considered at greater length in the last two books
given in the further reading list which follows.

FURTHER READING

Karrass, C. L., *Give and Take*, World Publishing Co., 1974. A good treatment
    of the tactics used by American negotiators.
Marsh, P. D. V., *Contract Negotiation Handbook*, Gower, 1971. Excellent
    treatment of negotiating strategy of general interest. Preceded by a mathe-
    matical/economic analysis of bidding – also excellent, but demanding a
    reader with mathematical talents.
Scott, Bill, *The Skills of Negotiating*, Gower, 1981. A highly readable expansion
    of his ideas by the author of this chapter of the handbook.

62 Effective communication

Gordon Bell

As a director, a manager or an aspiring manager you will be interested in facts. A survey of over 5000 men and women such as yourself revealed the following data:

1 On average, they had each received about fifteen years of formal education
2 Approximately a third of them gained degrees, diplomas or other paper qualifications
3 Only one in twenty-three felt that their subsequent achievements in life matched their abilities, qualifications or early ambitions
4 Fewer than one in twenty had taken the trouble to equip themselves with skills such as effective speaking, clear writing, handling meetings.

From the chairman of the largest industrial group to supervisors and staff, everybody uses words. Every business man and woman writes letters, reports, memoranda, orders. Reasonable people will agree that words are a vital tool in industry. The higher we go up the ladder of management the more important words become.

Many business meetings produce nothing but frustration and expense. The average executive spends a third of his working life talking at interviews, conferences and committees (to say nothing of the time and hassle involved in arranging them and getting there). How much of this talk is productive? How many business men are either confident or competent when making a presentation or delivering a speech?

The nub of effective management is communications. Time and effort that you invest in developing your own skills as a communicator must produce dividends. In this chapter we shall discuss three aspects of communications:

1 Speaking
2 Report writing
3 Meetings.

SPEAKING

Speaking is for other people. This fact about effective speaking is so obvious and so simple that many overlook it. An audience always evaluates a speaker subjectively. What did they get from the talk? The answer to this question measures the speaker.

A manager needs to command attention at conferences and other meetings: he must be able to make oral presentations to his board and to professional organisations; to brief his staff, to persuade, to convince. Particularly if he is a specialist, he must be able to clarify specialised concepts so that others, not necessarily qualified, can share his thoughts. Even the most brilliant man is useless until his ideas can be shared by others who can use them.

A successful speaker is a man who gives his audience a success.* Many managers, both male and female, suffer from the delusion that speaking in public is the same as a theatrical performance, or something suitable only for extroverts. This delusion often serves as a defence. The plain truth is that they fear exposure of their limitations as speakers. This state of affairs is deplorable. If a man has something worth saying, he should not only say it but also learn how to say it with full effect. 'Why should the devil have all the best tunes?' asked General Booth. It is also pertinent to ask, 'Why should the image-makers and the tricksters have a monopoly of effective speech?'

Let us examine the fear, sometimes amounting to terror, that afflicts otherwise intelligent men when they are asked to speak. What causes this fear? The unpopular but accurate answer is vanity – too great a concern with 'How am I going to do?' and not enough concern with 'How are they – the audience – going to do?' This truth is a hard one to face yet it applies at both ends of the scale. Vanity causes the glib, arrogant, loud-mouthed, no-nerves-at-all-I-can talk-at-the-drop-of-a-hat chap to subject his audience to a flood of waffle: it also causes the timid to worry about themselves at the expense of their hearers. If you face this fact now you can save yourself a lot of trouble.

A successful speaker is a man who gives his audience a success. The speaker's success stems from the audience reaction. If his audience reacts in the desired manner, the speaker has been effective. There is no other criterion.

Newton's third law of motion says, roughly, 'To every action there is an equal and opposite reaction'. A given stimulus creates the same response if conditions remain constant. Herein lies one of the most important points that a speaker must consider. An audience is never a constant factor. There is no such thing as a production-line human being. Everyone is unique. People in an audience vary in social levels, technical knowledge, prejudices, age, sex. Even the same people gathered together at different times or under different conditions can change an audience.

Effective speaking is a human relationship, not something that one person does alone and in isolation. A speaker wishing to get the desired reaction

---

*A note for women readers: I apologise for using words like 'man', 'his', 'him' throughout. Of course women are included in the thinking behind this chapter.

must obviously begin with a study of his audience. Unfortunately, many speakers begin with themselves and end in disaster.

So, the first point that a would-be speaker must think about is his attitude to his audience. His thinking must be positive and outward – not so much 'What subject am I going to talk about?' as 'How can I create a powerful relationship with my audience using the subject as both the generator and the cement which binds that relationship?'

Can you imagine anyone erecting Tower Bridge or building a locomotive who would begin by laying the first brick or polishing the whistle? A rational man starts with a purpose and a plan. So does a professional speaker – and you, whether you realise it or not, are a professional speaker, a professional report- and letter-writer and a professional meeting man. If you analyse your job as a manager you will find that you do little else but talk and write and discuss. Given equal knowledge of his business, a man who knows how to speak, how to write and when to listen always has the advantage over one who does not.

Preparing an effective talk

Many speakers complain that they have no time to prepare properly. If you know your subject you can prepare a talk in one hour. The method we shall discuss now is the one-hour method. There are three stages, roughly twenty minutes each. (When you have ample time, say, three weeks or six, simply extend each stage accordingly.)

Stage 1: Subject matter – gathering

Arm yourself with plenty of large sheets of paper and write down at great speed *every* idea on your subject that enters your mind. Make no attempt to think these ideas through. Get them down in rapid notes, symbols or any other shorthand form that will enable you to recognise them when you arrive at Stage 2 – the plotting stage. Work at speed. Your aim during Stage 1 is quantity; to amass hundreds of facts about your subject, various opinions, prejudices, misunderstandings, possible visual aids, thoughts about the audience, the occasion – anything which in any way may bear on your proposed talk. Note direct facts, oblique, tangential and even remotely relevant facts. Set down page after page of rough notes.

During Stage 1 it is most important that you concentrate and work non-stop at great speed. If time allows, do this several times until you have at least ten times more material than your final talk demands. Fix nothing, solidify nothing. Bear in mind that what might be old stuff, obvious to you, might well be new or in need of explanation to your hearers. So get it all down. Notes everything. A thought unnoted often disappears for ever.

Give yourself all the options. Review the whole subject. This review jogs your memory, gives you flexibility, acts as a solid background for your talk and can prove particularly helpful if you are required to answer these questions. Instead of having to excavate facts from the deep recesses of your mind, you have them near the surface, fresh and ready for use.

Quantity. Now you have raw stuff to work on, stacks of it.

Stage 2: Purpose and people

Establish your precise purpose. What reaction do you wish to induce in your hearers? What job has the talk to perform? Write down your purpose; rewrite it several times until you express, exactly, in a few cogent words, the effect you wish to achieve. Know what you are doing, explicitly. Be thorough about this. Do nothing else until you have got your objective clear.

Now that you have ample subject matter and a vividly clear purpose, you must ponder on the real material for your talk – the people who will listen to you. Examine every link they have or might have with your subject because they will be completely uninterested until what you say has something to do with them. Obvious, isn't it? What is their technical level, their social, financial level; what are their needs in connection with you and your subject? Study the people until you can see their view of your subject. You can only put your view across in relation to theirs. If you do not know anything about your audience, you would be well advised to find out at once. A discussion with the organisers, even a telephone call, can prove useful. Get to know your audience and integrate them into your presentation *now*; it will be too late when you are on your feet talking.

So, purpose and people. These two essential elements for an effective talk rarely receive enough thoughts or attention.

Stop here, please.

You must go no farther until you have checked that you have the driving force of a clear purpose working for you. You must go no farther until you have developed a real interest in your audience and their needs. These two factors should already be allies helping you to establish a partnership with your audience.

Purpose. People. Theme. Main points.

After your talk, what message will your hearers carry away with them? What big points supported your thesis? No audience will remember everything that you said. Decide at this stage in your preparation what basic theme you wish them to remember. As with your purpose, write down your theme and work on it until it becomes simple, straightforward and crystal clear. Next, separate the one, two or three really important points from the lesser points. Which are the really big points that you want them to have working in their minds? If you do not establish them clearly now, they will not stand out prominently enough in your delivered talk. Your job as a speaker is to clarify the subject for your audience. You cannot do this unless you first clarify it for yourself.

Now build your talk on the foundation of your purpose, your people, your theme and your main points.

A few reminders. A successful speaker knows his subject and is enthusiastic about it.

He makes certain that he is well prepared.

He has considered his audience and believes that the subject is important to them.

1106

Bad speakers are usually people who think about themselves too much.

Pertinent questions to be answered at the end of Stage 2:

1 What exactly is my subject?
2 Why am I speaking about it to this audience and what do I know about them?
3 What are the most important things I must tell them?
4 Have I picked out the main points which must be highlighted?
5 Have I arranged these points so that this particular audience will fully understand them and be involved in them?
6 Have I made sure that there is a glowing, dominant theme?
7 What will the audience gain from this talk?

Stage 3 – Delivering the goods

The audience must at once be made confident that the speaker knows what he is doing. They must find his first thoughts intensely interesting. This, of course, rules out the usual dreary openings, for instance, where the speaker talks about himself and his worries as a speaker.

The three-sentence technique can secure a telling impact on opening:

Sentence 1. You make any vivid, unexpected, off-beat, truly interesting remark you like (always of course bearing in mind your audience).

Sentence 2. You link, skilfully, sentence 1 to your subject and make clear exactly what your subject is.

Sentence 3. You *involve* the audience in both your opening remarks and your subject.

It is essential that you economise and discipline yourself to use only three sentences for this effect. There must be no woolly edges around these three sentences, no 'hums' and 'hahs', no interpolated oddments, no clutter. You are seeking a clean, crisp, immediate communion, a direct response. Experiment until you have got a really good beginning. Excite, Link, Involve. Do not be satisfied with the first openings you think of: try at least six ways before you decide.

Avoid the word 'I' for at least one minute. Substitute 'you', 'your', or group words describing the audience, such as engineers, Scotsmen, managers. Be as specific as you can. Talk about them and their links with the subject. Get the focus firmly on to them and away from yourself.

As soon as your impact has been achieved and the audience knows what your broad subject is, define your limits so that they will not waste their attention on parts of the subject outside the scope of your talk. Tell them where you intend to take them within your subject, sometimes even which aspects you intend to leave out. From the start concentrate their mental energy on the relevant aspects. Give them clear signposts, briefly.

Now, you have a dynamic purpose in your mind; you and your audience know where you are going. They have been intrigued by your opening remarks and are ready for the statement of your basic theme, ready for the development of your first main point supporting that theme – and they are eager to find out how and where they fit in with what you have to say.

The elements are prepared for you – the catalyst – to do your work.

There are no dull subjects. Everything under the sun teems with interest. From even such beginnings as a dirty ashtry or the Industrial Training Act a lively mind could create a fascinating talk. How are you going to tell your story, how give your facts their full value as facts plus that life which also gives them interest? The key to power in story-telling is to bind everything you say to people and things – the concrete rather than the abstract. You might well be talking about some entirely abstract technical concept. Human beings and physical, tangible things judiciously woven into your presentation will vitalise even the unlikeliest subject for a potent talk. Also, wherever you can, link your examples directly to your listeners. An earthquake killing thousands in China could leave your audience unmoved: but a gas explosion in Clay Street, Manchester will engender great interest – especially to those of your audience who live in Clay Street, Manchester.

Facts are sacred and must not be tampered with. Concrete examples emphasise facts and make facts stick in the mind. The closer the examples are to the experience and the environment of the audience the more surely your points will find their target.

Contrary to a common opinion, facts do not always speak for themselves. They need good men to speak for them. No fact of life need be colourless or less interesting than fiction. You must adroitly develop the story of each fact, giving it a good beginning, a lively motif, substance, excitement, strong, close-to-home examples and a language suitable for your hearers.

Words worry people. They say 'I have plenty of ideas but I haven't the vocabulary to express them'. This assertion is based on a fallacy. Words (or some other set of symbols such as mathematical formulae) are essential to clear thought. If you are fumbling for words, you have not clarified the thought.

Technical language and jargon incur much scorn and contempt; but they have their uses as a shorthand for the initiated. On the other hand, to use such esoteric stuff to show how clever you are or because you lack consideration for your hearers is unpardonable. Use you audience's language or explain your own. Otherwise you will waste your breath and, what is worse, waste their time.

Speaking style

A hypnotist wishing to put someone to sleep employs a subdued, monotonous voice and single soporific thought repeated and repeated and repeated until the patient gives up and slumbers. To arouse the patient he makes some sharp noise and brings his own voice to life by using a complete change of tone. The patient wakes up.

Human voices possess an immense range of volume, tone, pace, attack. Why be monotonous? Why be dull? Why mutter and bawl like a bull? Why not work out beforehand how you can give variety and the appropriate vocal clues to each part of your talk? Think in terms of main headlines and paragraphs and make sure that each new idea comes to the audience with a change in vocal approach. Particularly when introducing a fresh point, give your voice a lift. Watch sentence length; see to it that a few crisp short ones intervene between a series of protracted sentences. Watch the ends of sentences: a rising pitch holds more interest than a dying fall.

It is an odd fact of speaking technique that absolute silence for a few seconds – under control – can be the most effective part of a speech. Try to find, perhaps, two such moments when you can hold your audience to your thoughts during your calculated pauses.

The human voice is only one of the channels through which ideas can flow. Sound, sight, touch, smell, taste all provide means of conveying to other people. A good speaker gives his audience a chance to use as many of their senses as the occasion permits. With a little ingenuity you can give their ears a rest and switch channels. One obvious way of doing this is to show them the point, to demonstrate it. The term 'visual aids' does not mean only blackboard – chalk-and-talk stuff – or flipcharts or films or overhead projectors; solid-physical, three-dimensional objects have much more effect. If it is practicable show them the actual thing you are talking about. Let them handle it, smell it, taste it. Use your zest, imagination and enthusiasm to create a worthwhile experience for your audience. You can develop a reputation as a first-class speaker if you work at it and stop worrying about yourself. They will say you simply have a flair for this sort of thing, a gift. You must not mind that. A judicious use of the five senses will help you. However prosaic your subject, give it vigour, colour – life.

Please arm yourself with a pencil and a sheet of paper because we are going to create a graph. I would appreciate your comments in it and your physical co-operation. To begin with, here are the axes (Figure 62.1). Please read the notes, draw the axes exactly. Then proceed to Figure 62.2

Commentary

The shading at the foot of Figure 62.2 represents the grey sludge area at the beginning of so many talks, during what the poor speaker calls 'warming up'. The monologue here tells how unaccustomed the speaker is and what a trying ordeal he is experiencing in facing such a difficult, awesome set of people. In general, the self-centred blockhead isolates himself and destroys the goodwill of the audience by focusing in the wrong direction. No wonder he is nervous. No wonder the audience already begin to doubt whether they should have come.

Eliminate the sludge area altogether. Instead, get some vigour, elevation and impact into your beginning. Hoist the value-and-interest line clean through the sludge up to X, which marks your impact at opening.

Signposts help your hearers to concentrate on the special aspects of the subject that you intend to cover. Define your limits, briefly.

Now drive towards your first main point (*a*). You have it clear. You have already worked out how to make your facts come to life, how to link your vivid example both to the facts and to your audience. Follow your line, the theme, and support that theme with facts. Develop your message.

Summaries are a matter for your judgement. At least you must make certain that each main point holds fast in the minds of your audience before you tackle the next point.

Signposting internal to the talk, again, is a matter for you to decide. Will

[GHM]

Value
and
interest

Your comments, please.
Yes, the axes are disproportionate:
but please keep these odd ratios in
your mind. Let the horizontal axis
represent time. Let the vertical axis
represent the value and interest you
bring to your hearers in that time.
You should never take more of your
audience's time than is necessary to
do your speaking job properly. The
value and interest line should be as
high as possible in the time they give
to you.

Now, please fill in the graph for your
own planned talk, as shown in Figure
62.2.

Value
and
interest

Figure 62.1 **Axes for graph of value and interest against time**
*Use the proportions shown here to prepare the graph described in
the text*

summaries and signposting help the audience? If so, use them.

When you reach the climax of your talk, when you ram home your message
you must remind your audience of the main facts which support your theme.
Summarise crisply: remind them how the matter of your talk affects them and
do have a powerful line at the end. (Make a really sharp, hard, strong point and
sit down on it!)

Speaking for special occasions: case presentation

Persuasive speaking, getting people to say 'Yes'.

Please engrave this sentence into your mind: Nothing induces agreement

Figure 62.2   Graph of value and interest against time

faster than self-interest – the other fellow's self-interest.

Many business men have to recommend changes that will cost money. In most companies there is a procedure for this. The proposer has first to prepare a document setting out his proposal in detail. This goes through normal channels and may sometimes be agreed to or rejected as it stands. More frequently the proposer will be asked to appear before some board or committee to explain his proposal and to answer questions about it.

The written part of a proposal is a persuasive report and should be written with that in mind. The oral presentation is part speech, part meeting and part interview.

In preparing such a presentation, the proposer should ask himself these questions:

1 Do you know exactly what you want?
2 Do you really believe in your case?
3 Have you got all the facts that support your case and have you checked them?
4 What are the strongest arguments for your case?
5 What are the benefits for your listeners?
6 Why must the present situation be changed?
7 What is their problem?
8 Who else is affected? (Unions, other divisions, etc.)
9 What are the arguments against your plan?
10 What are the alternatives to your plan?
11 Do your benefits clearly outweigh these arguments and alternatives?
12 To whom are you presenting your plan? Have you done any lobbying? Do you need to?
13 Do you know who your probably allies and opponents are?
14 Have you discussed the finances with the experts?
15 Have you prepared hand-outs of any complicated figures?
16 It was a good idea when you first thought of it. Is it still – from their point of view?
17 Have you prepared a really effective presentation? (Time plus the value and interest ratio are particularly important in case presentation.)
18 How will you sum up and end?
19 Are you ready for questions?
20 Have you emphasised the benefits they (your listeners) will gain? Remember: nothing induces agreement faster than self-interest – the other fellow's self-interest.

The board is probably only interested in this question: 'Have they a problem and does your proposal solve it for them?' Ask yourself: 'Will your proposal satisfy their need, their greed, their self-esteem – or all three?'

Social speaking

Social speaking has one simple purpose: to give pleasure. What will make your audience purr? What will cause them to cry 'Hear! Hear!'? What will make them laugh? What will make them proud that they belong to this club, this company, this band of people brought together with a common cause? What sentiment will bring a lump into their throats? What will make them say afterwards 'Oh, I did enjoy that'?

Deliver the answers to these questions and they will be glad that you spoke, especially as you delivered with obvious affection for them, and warm appreciation of their values and you did so without going on and on and on. Work out a good line to end your speech and do not separate it by too long a time from your first-class opening line. Give them pleasure and enjoy the pleasure of their company.

One-to-one talking

An encounter across a desk can often make or break a manager. Failure follows almost inevitably if you present your ideas at the wrong time or if you insist on pushing a proposal from your own point of view.

By all means be relaxed but before you go in to win your point, or before the other fellow calls on you, do your homework. Get your purpose clear, have your facts ready. Know his problems in relation to your suggestion and start the discussion of the basis of his problems. Until you have established his problems and have shown that you understand them and are in sympathy with them, you must not try to sell him anything. You want him to react, to say 'Yes'. He will not react in your favour if your spend your time putting yourself across. Try it the other way round. Put him and his problems in the forefront. If what you have to sell solves his problems, he'll agree.

Some thoughts

Make contact with people. Use you eyes. Look at them. Include them in what you say. This is simply good manners. Take the trouble to prepare properly to ensure that you give them value in exchange for the time they are giving you. Develop a respect, even an affection for your audience. Remember that, however expert you may be, every man and woman there is superior to you in some way and could teach you something.

Speaking is probably the oldest form of human communication. It is certainly the most natural to modern man but, unless other minds can process and use what is said, speaking is just a useless shifting of wind.

There are few things more exhilarating than an audience reacting with interest, excitement and the sheer pleasure of enjoying a first-class speaker. Deserve such a reaction and your world will be that much better for having you around.

REPORT WRITING

John Logie Baird's discovery of the principles of television was useless. Einstein helped nobody with his thinking on relativity nor did Fleming with penicillin until they made their facts and theories known to other people.

Knowledge locked away in the recesses of a single mind has little value until other minds receive the key and gain access to it. Many specialists believe that their work stops when they have uncovered the facts. A question was asked of them. They worked on it, investigated it thoroughly and found the answer. And that, they say, is the end of their job. But is it?

Why do industrial concerns employ scientists, accountants and other specialists? The answer to that question is simple. Industrial concerns employ specialists in order to get from them information, and expert guidance towards profitable action. Yet although specialists study and sweat for 5, 10, 15, 20 years, a lifetime, to equip themselves as experts they rarely study the techniques of passing their hard-gained information to other people. And their readers do the sweating.

A report is a working document that helps the other man to do his job. A record may well form the basis for a report but it is not a report. Samuel Pepys' diary recorded his times, brilliantly, but scholars had to delve to extract the meat. Nobody expects to have to delve into a modern business report; readers expect you to present the meat ready for digestion. A long report is not necessarily better than a short one, if only because fewer people will bother to read it. On the other hand, if you are writing for qualified people who want to know not only the conclusions and recommendations but also the detailed results and the methods used to obtain them, your report must contain such facts in full.

A report is not a detective story. Agatha Christie could take a set of facts and cloak them so skilfully that few readers can get the crucial point until the final page. The facts are all there if only one has the nous to spot them. There should be no mystery about a report. The facts should be clear and the development logical so that the conclusions and recommendations follow them naturally.

There are five main considerations in thinking about reports:

1 Circulation and distribution
2 Physical layout
3 Numerical information
4 Visual aids
5 Language.

Circulation and distribution

All communications are a struggle for other people's interest and attention. The furniture in any busy man's office always includes a yawning wastepaper basket. If you have put this busy man on your circulation list for reasons of self-advertisement or because his name happened to be on a routine list, unedited for years, beware!

Before you begin to shape your report, please take the trouble to sort out the people whom it will help in their jobs. Nobody else should have it.

Many a report suffers from a false start. The managers who asked for it did not bother to discuss with the writer either the purpose of the report or the intended readership. Or the writer just said 'Yes' and ploughed on blindly into a document which did not meet the real requirements. Such a report will fail or at least have to be rewritten. Both the senior man and the writer contributed to the failure and caused the extra labour, the frustration, perhaps the anger ensuing from a job badly done.

So, before you write a syllable, establish who is going to use your report and what they have a right to expect from you. What is the purpose of the report from their point of view.

In many companies, the circulation is tacked on to the completed report as an afterthought. This deplorable custom should be opposed vigorously. Additions to the circulation list shoud be exceptional; better still, they should have been considered and meshed into the writer's reckoning from the start.

All this does not mean, however, that the facts should be coloured or slanted to affect the truth; no specialist worth his salt would wish to gain a point by distortion or trickery. His credibility would quickly disappear if he did, and rightly so.

Above all, your reader must find your report useful and the facts presented in such a way that he can absorb them easily and accurately. You cannot use suitable language, suitable layout or even select the material properly unless you know whom you are talking to and what he wants from the report. Consider your reader from the beginning. You cannot expect to do this unless you fix the circulation list at the outset. A report looks so forlorn in the wastepaper basket or even put aside – to be read 'later'. Do not plague people with reports they do not require for their own work. People have enough to do. All they want from you is help. Your useful reports will receive a welcome at the right time, at the right place and from the right man.

Physical layout

Your company has probably issued instructions on how its reports should be laid out. Such instructions were not written to while away an idle hour and it is the duty of every report writer to study them. The research department requires for its reports a different approach from the sales or public relations departments. Monsieur Ritz, the hotelier, made a fortune by following the precept 'the customer is always right'. The layout of a report depends almost entirely on how the readers like it. There are no rules, just a few principles. Your reader must be able to find his way about the report. If he is accustomed to a summary on the first page, that is where you put it. If he prefers all the graphs, tables, charts and detailed figures in appendices, put them there.

Reports should look as if they expect a welcome and want to be read. The ninety-third copy from a worn-out duplicator lacks inspiration and deserves neglect. The general appearance of a report must be appropriate to the contents and its purpose.

First appearance

The cover should immediately indicate the type of report that is inside: glossy for the chairman's annual report and other such public relations stuff; perhaps blue for research, green for personnel, or whatever the company's standard practice demands. The title and security classification must, obviously, be prominent before a page is turned.

The busy man's page

The first page must include the date of the report, the title, the author's name and that of the issuing authority and a reference/file number. Some readers also like a short circulation list on the title page – it is often useful to know who else has the report – and a very brief synopsis. This busy man's page should tell the busy man the object of the report and the reason why the work was done. It should give him a well-pruned summary of the investigation, the *main* results, the *main* conclusions and the *main* recommendations for action. He should get the guts of the report in fewer than 200 words, if possible on one page.

Any report longer than six pages should have a table of contents, clearly indicating where readers can find the special bits of the report that are all they intend to read. (Do not flatter yourself that everyone will read the whole of your tome.) Even avid readers will want to know where things are. A table of contents, reflecting a logical layout with clear, expressive headings, immediately creates an impression of order, thought and consideration.

So, you have already given your reader:

A cover that immediately tells him the style, title and security classification of the report.
A title page that tells who wrote it, when it was written, who authorised it and, sometimes, who else has the information.
A synopsis – the main elements of the report in a nutshell.
A table of contents that tells him where he can find all the details he wants.

Many of your readers, especially top management and laymen, will go no further into a report. They have all they need – a general appreciation of your work and enough information for discussion or appropriate action at their level. It is advisable to avoid technical language at this stage.

Your fellow specialists will now wish to dig into the report. They will expect an introduction which informs, or reminds, them of the circumstances which prompted your work. They will want to know how you set about your investigation, what methods, what tests, what equipment you used. They will expect a complete validation of your results and figures and to know what standards of accuracy you worked to. They will expect you to separate facts from opinions. The headlines for the main body of the work could read:

1 Introduction
2 Experimental details
3 Results
4 Discussion
5 Full summary
6 Recommendations
7 Appendices

This format cannot fit all circumstances and must be adjusted to suit the needs of your readers and the purpose of the report.

Please acknowledge the work of other people who have helped you, if only in a bibliography.

Information by numbers

Numbers form the backbone of most reports. Measurements of time, frequencies, distances, etc., are fundamental in presenting facts. Few readers need all the numbers; all readers need the significant numbers and wish them to be displayed significantly. Do not bury them or wall them up behind the background data. When you are planning your report, establish the vital numbers early on so that you can give them due prominence when writing.

Your reader will want to know your tolerances and to what degree of accuracy your figures are presented. Do not bother him with five decimal places if the approximate whole number will suffice for him. The main body of the report will flow more easily if the script is uncluttered by a mass of figures. Many thoughtful writers quote only those figures that make the point and then guide those people who may be interested in greater detail to an appendix which contains more complicated items such as mathematical formulae.

With numbers, significance is all – or nearly all.

Visual aids

If you were a sales director, how would you prefer to have the sales figures from May to October presented – as in (a), (b), (c) or (d) of Figure 62.3?

Sometimes readers would rather see the point than have it related to them. Please consider this.

Language in reports

'Tests showed that the handle gets too hot'
or:
'The results of a period of *ad hoc* experimentation supplemented by both statistical analysis and consideration of empirical factors thought to be universally viable in the context of the areas in which utilisation could be expected to approach a maximum indicated that the thermal conductivity of that portion of the equipment designed for prehensile digital contact was such as to present a surface whose temperatures would markedly exceed the generally accepted threshold of sensory discomfort.' Et cetera, et cetera, et cetera.

Why do so many technicians, trained in logic and precision, write such twaddle? Is it because they are suspicious of the arts, afraid that what they do might lose 'mystique' or is it that they cannot bother to bring logic and precision into their use of language? Many a brilliant young man, on reaching middle age, wonders what went wrong with his career. Let him re-read some of his reports. The answers could be found in them.

We have no space here to discuss grammar and the techniques of clear English, but you should learn a few basic points of control in your writing. You can then leave the rest to your genuine wish to help people to understand you. For instance, most readers will want to recognise, without much effort, two things about each of your sentences:

(*a*) The grammatical subject – whom or what you are talking of
(*b*) What happens – the action.

Let us look at (*a*) first. Concrete words such as 'polecat', 'sewing-machine', 'policeman' give your reader an exact image of what is in your mind. Abstract words and phrases leave room for doubt.

So prefer concrete words as subjects of your sentences.

Now (*b*). Your reader will readily understand the what-happens part of your sentence if you convey the action as simply as you can with power verbs, preferably active. Let us clarify this. Please examine these four sentences:

1   Oil lubricates bearings.
     The subject of the sentence, 'oil', is concrete, tangible, clear.
     The subject does the deed of the verb so the sentence is active.

[GHM]

(a)
The sales for May were 20 of type 1, 32 of type 2, 38 of type 3; for June, 28 of type 1, 30 of type 2, 36 of type 3; for July, 40 of type 1, 30 of type 2, 28 of type 3; for August, 26 of type 1, 18 of type 2, 28 of type 3; for September, 26 of type 1, 18 of type 2, 30 of type 3; and for October, 44 of type 1, 20 of type 2 and 28 of type 3

(b)
Sales figures for May to September

	Type 1	Type 2	Type 3
May	20	32	38
June	28	30	36
July	40	30	28
August	26	18	28
September	26	18	30
October	44	20	28

Figure 62.3   Four ways of displaying a set of numerical results
This shows how careful thought can result in a more effective display

Figure 62.3 (continued)

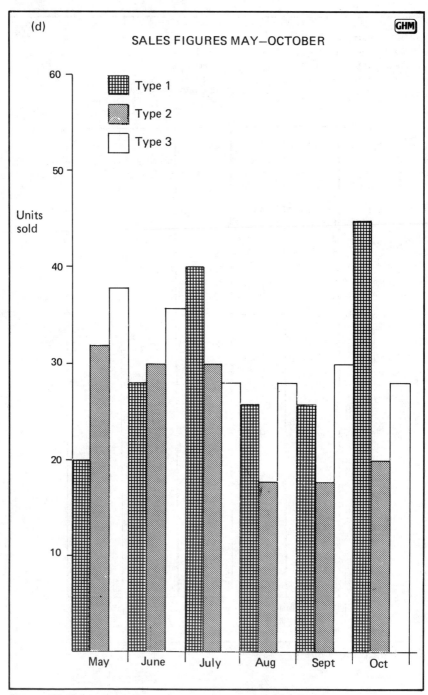

Figure 62.3 (continued)

2 Bearings are lubricated by oil.
    The subject, 'bearings', is concrete.
    The subject does not do the deed of the verb:
    it gets done to, so the sentence is passive.

3 The lubrication of bearings is carried out by the use of oil
    The subject, 'lubrication of bearings', is an abstract phrase.
    The subject does not do the deed of the verb:
    it gets done to, so the sentence is both abstract and passive.

Structure 3 often leads to:

4 In so far as the process of lubrication with respect to bearings is concerned, this is carried out by the use of an application of oil.

Exaggerated as it is, sentence 4 shows the beginnings of the decay that attacks so many specialists from about the age of twenty-eight. In any large organisation roughly one-third of the people over the age of twenty-eight are dead. They have accumulated sufficient cliché phrases and routine attitudes to lean on until their pensions turn up. There seems to be no reason for them to think any more. It is enough just to react according to the rule book and the jargon – 'We are in receipt of your favour of the 19th instant to hand, and it must be pointed out that in view of the fact that . . . ' 'The conceptual philosophy of commonality and standardisation at this point in time could be said to have, perhaps, groundings in feasibility which, with the basic assumption that . . . ' ' . . . the viability of these parameters, shiftwise . . . '. All non-think stuff, torture for the reader and highly dangerous for the writer.

Danger? What danger? We live in a sea of words. What is wrong with drifting along in the fashionable waters, swallowing the stuff and regurgitating it into the faces of our fellows? Why not? It's easier than thinking.

What happens to a muscle that gets no exercise? It becomes flabby. What happens to a machine that lies idle for years? It becomes rusty and useless. What happens to a brain that does nothing but gather verbal cobwebs? Adult thinking is impossible without a language or some other set of symbols that label the elements we develop into thoughts. If words, for instance, are the bricks and mortar with which we build the wall of thought does it not follow that the sort of words we habitually use is the sort of thinker we are? Near-enough words, that'll-do words, other people's tired old clichés provide neither keep-fit exercise nor nourishment for an active mind. A factory girl whose eight-hour day consists of fitting component A into component B and endlessly repeating the dreary process to feed some production line would go made if she thought about it very much. So she works mechanically and dreams of her boyfriend or being a duchess. But this will not do for expensively trained managers.

Technical language has the advantage of being clearly defined. Used properly, it assists constructive thought and communication among those who understand it. Abused, or flaunted because you want to imply that you are superior to people outside 'the club', it can cause trouble – for you as much as for your victims. The English language provides one of the most precise, subtle, flexible and vigorous aids to clear thought and effective reports. No manager can claim to be more than half-baked if he does not learn how to control it.

Report writing check list

Before drafting a report ask yourself:

1   Have I insisted on a thorough briefing from whoever requested the report and discussed with him in detail: *(a)* that there is a need for the report, *(b)* the exact purpose of the report, *(c)* who is going to read the report, *(d)* the exact scope of the report?
2   Have I collected all the information I may need?
3   have I selected from this the information the readers need?

When drafting a report, ask yourself:

1   Does the layout comply with any company standard and does it make things easy for the reader?
2   Is there a 'busy man's page' and does it contain the right information for him?
3   Does the report look good and can it be reproduced using the equipment available?
4   Is everybody who 'needs to know' on the circulation list?
5   Have I arranged for library copies and spare copies?
6   Is the circulation too wide?
7   Does the report need a security classification?
8   Have I used sufficient active verbs and concrete nouns?
9   Have I used short sentences and simple construction?
10   Are any technical or scientific words likely to be unknown to the readers?
11   Have I avoided padding and waffle-words?
12   Will the reader easily understand what I have written?
13   Have I avoided slant and bias?
14   Have I clearly stated conclusions and recommendations?
15   Have I used sufficient visual aids?
16   Are the visual aids in the right place, clearly labelled and cross-referenced?
17   Have I shown scales, dimensions and magnifications on my visual aids?
18   Are the tables and charts displayed in the best way?
19   Have I shown the units? Are units consistent and do they comply with British or other accepted standards?
20   Will the visual aids still be clear and easy to follow when reproduced by the available process?
21   Should I invite someone else to read the draft and discuss it with me?

A report is a working document that helps the other man to do his job. A manager who learns to write effective reports adds value to himself and his work.

MEETINGS

Believe it or not, some companies use up more cash at meetings than they spend on the raw materials with which they make their products. Much of this cash goes straight down the drain. Before you dismiss this thought as whimsical, consider the cost of meetings – air and rail fares, cars, hotel bills, salaries and expenses, conference and boardroom rents, rates, cleaning, postage of reports and other documents, typing and more money for many more items. Any large organisation spends millions of pounds each year so that people can discuss, decide and, one hopes, energise some profitable action. The waste is colossal.

Money is important – only a fool would deny that – but much more important is human life. Ineffective meetings not only waste money but they also devalue people's time and shrink the people concerned with them. Human relationships can be soured by bad meetings. A wise man takes the trouble to find meetings work and how to make them work for him and his associates.

A definition of business meetings might be 'two or more people getting together for a specific business purpose'.

The meeting itself forms only one link in a chain of events. If the other links lack strength the meeting can become merely the place where the chain breaks. Ninety per cent of an effective meeting happens before the meeting starts. Forging the before-the-meeting link requires thought, horse-sense and skill. If you intend to call a meeting, be completely clear about its intended purpose. What specific business should the meeting achieve? Is it to decide on action, to brief people, to inform, to persuade? What in specific terms – no vague abstractions – is the business purpose of the meeting? You must then face what might be a deflating question: is a meeting necessary at all? Must you deprive people of their time and put the company to expense? Can the business be done – the decision made, for instance – in some other way – a few telephone calls or half a dozen letters? Why are you proposing to call the meeting? Why?

So you decide that your meeting is a necessity; the business cannot be accomplished without a combination of other minds, interest and experience. Which people can provide you with such a combination? Nobody else should be invited. You want to get some business done. Avoid the hangers-on and the strange creatures who go to meetings just to get out of their own offices for a while. If your business is to get a decision and action, beware of the second-string man who cannot give a firm yes or no. He has to report back to his boss. Then there will have to be another meeting for his boss or even his boss's boss. Invite and accept only the people who can do the job properly. Do not forget, as so often happens, to invite the man who will have to take any action you decide upon. If your meeting decides to change the production line you cannot expect joyous co-operation from the production manager who was elsewhere when you decided how to run his department.

When and where the meeting takes place depends on the urgency of the business and the convenience of the people concerned. Be considerate about this. Merely the fact that you operate from Plymouth does not necessarily mean that your Glasgow and Ipswich colleagues will agree that your office is the perfect location. Must you start your meeting at 0900, which means an overnight trip for everyone except you? Timing, the date and the hour, can show you to be a thoughtful organiser.

If your colleagues have to examine reports, plans, figures or must equip themselves in other ways in preparation for the meeting, give them a fair chance to do so. Also make it clear to them precisely what the business of the meeting will be and that you expect them to come prepared. A meeting which has to be recalled because the relevant facts are missing reflects no credit on the convenor or the members. More meetings fail because the preparation has been neglected or skimped than for any other reason. No one should go to a meeting ill-prepared. Even if the meeting happens to be a quick get-together, and at short notice, a few minutes' thought beforehand will increase your value as a meeting-man. At least one man, you, will be able to talk sense.

The businesslike chairman will see to it that he or his secretary arranges a suitable conference room. He will indicate when the meeting is likely to finish; he will arrange breaks for the creature comforts of the conferers, and for telephone messages to be collected, outside the conference room – no interruptions will be allowed except for desperately urgent calls. He will plan an approximate timetable for the agenda so that timeworthy items get their due. Documents and, if required, suitable equipment for presentations must be available. Name cards help people to know who's who; make them bold – and do have them spelled correctly. There are of course a hundred and one other details, any of which might be important. A meeting succeeds in direct ratio to its intelligent preparation.

The formal rules for running meetings become more important when the gathering is a large one. For most business meetings, formal rules matter little. It is the spirit in which people attend the meetings that produces a good or bad meeting.

No real progress can be made without agreement. The object of meetings is to produce agreement. Even if, after disagreement, action results because of fear or force of personality, the action will only be half-hearted and possibly poorly performed. The chairman of a meeting must always be striving for agreement, not surrender.

Preparation for the meeting

The Chairman

Decide whether the meeting is really necessary. (Especially important with routine meetings which often occur even when there is nothing to be discussed or decided.)

Decide on the purpose of the meeting.

Decide on the subject or subjects.

Decide on the place and time.

Decide who is going to attend the meeting. Only those with something to contribute or who need to know exactly what was said and by whom should be present. Other people can get any necessary information from the minutes. The chairman should ensure that those attending are of sufficient standing, that they really represent their departments, and have the authority to commit them to action.

Decide on the agenda and roughly how much time to allow for each item. It is imperative that items are stated in concrete terms. Abstractions will inevitably result in rambling discussion that leads nowhere. One or two simple items first will get the meeting off to a good start. Even if the meeting is summoned hurriedly by telephone, members should be told what they are going to discuss. This is the agenda.

Study the subjects. The chairman must be sufficiently familiar with the subjects being discussed to be able to keep the discussion on the right lines.

Study the people attending. He must know the personal alignments that will help or hinder the meeting; who will not talk even though he has valuable contributions to make, and who will talk even though he has not.

The secretary

Responsible for all the mechanics of the meeting.

Must obtain for the chairman any points for the agenda and names of those attending.

Must obtain suitable accommodation, arrange for paper, etc., arrange for refreshments to be available when the chairman wants them, and arrange to disconnect the telephone.

Must circulate the agenda in good time.

Must prepare all the papers the chairman may require.

Members

Must study the subjects to be discussed and, if necessary, departmental opinions and agreements.

Must study the chairman and his idiosyncrasies.

Must study the other members.

Must work out how they are going to sell their ideas. (Refer back to Speaking for special occasions – case presentation – pages 1110, 1112.)

Conduct of the meeting

The chairman

The meeting must start on time, even if there are absentees. If the chairman is absent the next most suitable person should start it for him. If the speaker on the first point is absent, switch the agenda.

Start briskly, laying down the purpose, the time available, and any other conditions that will help to control the meeting. A chairman cannot demand respect: he can only earn it – usually by giving it to others.

The chairman must watch the time. If he sees that he is getting behind time and wants to extend the meeting he must warn the members early, so that they can make any necessary arrangements or get a move on.

The chairman must keep feeding back to the members the state of the discussion, to ensure that everyone understands the situation. This is particularly important at the end of each item. This will also enable the secretary an immediate, accurate record of the decisions reached, who is to take action and by what date, without any risk of error.

The chairman must try to be impartial and only produce his own opinions late in the discussion, if at all. Otherwise he will inhibit proper discussion.

The chairman may have to keep reminding members of the subject and aim in order to keep them to the point.

The chairman must ensure that everyone has the opportunity to express his opinion, at the same time preventing any individual from taking up an excessive amount of time. A member with very strong views that he is determined to express should be given his head, unopposed, the chairman, at least, giving all his attention to what is being said. The chairman should try to extract the relevant points from what may be a confused discourse and ensure that they are properly considered by the meeting.

The chairman must summarise, clarify and emphasise the action arising from the meeting, name specifically who is to be responsible for taking action and record who should do what in precise terms.

The meeting should finish at the stated time unless the members have agreed to go on late.

The chairman and the secretary should leave the room immediately after the meeting is over, otherwise another meeting might ensue.

The members

Disagree without being disagreeable. A member must be clear in his mind what points he wants to get across and do it with the aim of convincing the other members that he is right. At the same time, he should have a sufficiently open mind to be able to change his opinion if someone else produces better arguments or ideas.

Avoid distracting personalities.

The secretary

During the meeting the secretary must take copious notes unless he can be sure that the chairman will provide him with the minutes as the meeting goes along. It is therefore impracticable for a member to act as secretary and do both jobs adequately.

Chairmanship – reminders

Before
Ensure that there is a clear, worthwhile purpose.
Check who will be attending.
Check on the points to be discussed.
Ensure that the secretary has organised everything.
During
Introduce the meeting and purpose.
Define the limits of the subject and time available.
Control the members. Ensure that all have a fair say and none dominate.
Keep the meeting to the point. Be quick to spot when people are wandering.
Feed back. Ensure that everyone is keeping up with discussions and understands the points that are coming out of the discussions.

Summing-up. Make sure that everyone knows the conclusions reached and especially who is to take action. Be impartial. Earn respect.

After the meeting

As quickly as possible after the meeting the secretary should write up the minutes, either for rapid circulation or to go on the files. The minutes should be kept as short as is practicable.

The essential parts of the minutes are the decisions, agreed action and who is to take it and when. These must stand out.

At an appropriate time after the meeting someone, probably the secretary, should check that members are getting on with action they undertook or were instructed to take.

The chairman must have at the front of his mind all the time, and occasionally remind members, that the object of the meeting is to benefit the whole organisation and not any section or individual. He should strive to ensure that profitable action will result from the meeting.

Anybody can talk, anybody can write, anybody can hold a meeting, but only he who can also obtain the desired responses ranks as a good communicator. A computer memory and its processing unit contain great quantities of facts; but the computer is simply a speedy automaton, subject to its program. The human memory and its processing unit contain facts, experiences, feelings, prejudices, social attitudes, business needs, expediency, cussedness, warmth, love, hatred and the breath of God.

Programming a computer to obtain a useful print-out – the response – demands skill and knowledge. How much more demanding is the need for a manager to acquire the knowledge and the skills for better human relationships. At least you can make a start by speaking more effectively, writing reports that help and by making your meetings successful.

FURTHER READING

Eyre, E. C., *Effective Communication Made Simple*, W. H. Allen, London, 1979

Jay, Anthony, *Effective Presentation: the Communication of Ideas by Words and Visual Aids*, Management Publications Ltd., London, 1970

Maude, Barry, *Practical Communication for Managers*, Longman, London, 1974

Wells, Gordon, *How to Communicate*, McGraw-Hill, Maidenhead, 1978

Williams, Beryl, *Communicating Effectively: A Manager's Guide to Getting Through to People*, Thorsons, Wellingborough, 1977

Index